DRAMA

An Introductory Anthology

ALTERNATE EDITION

DRAMA

An Introductory Anthology

Edited by

OTTO REINERT

University of Washington, Seattle

BOSTON

Little, Brown and Company

TORONTO

LIBRARY OF CONGRESS CATALOG CARD NO. 64-17100

SIXTH PRINTING

Published simultaneously in Canada
by Little, Brown & Company (Canada) Limited

PRINTED IN THE UNITED STATES OF AMERICA

PREFACE

THIS ALTERNATE EDITION OF *Drama: An Introductory Anthology* includes a completely different repertory of thirteen plays but follows the plan of the companion collection. The plays are of proved literary worth and representative of major types and periods of western drama.

The general Introduction emphasizes the *literary* nature of drama. It discusses the relationship between written and performed drama and between drama and the other literary genres. It considers some of the problems peculiar to reading drama and to dramatic conventions, defines some technical terms, and analyzes a single scene in some detail. The comments on the individual plays suggest their theatrical setting and their place in the history of drama, but mainly they discuss structures of action and language. I have tried to be specific and inclusive without being exhaustive and — like the plays — to raise more questions than I answer. Although the biographies and the bibliographies in the Appendix are necessarily brief, I hope they can throw light not just on the single play included but also on the playwright's general canon.

Professor Henry H. Wasser, currently Fulbright Professor of American Literature at the University of Oslo, and Keith Brown, Lecturer in English Literature at the University of Oslo, have read parts of the editorial material in manuscript and discussed with me issues of general theory and of specific analysis. They will recognize their contributions. My wife, Dorothy, has again been a patient reader and listener and a helpful critic of both plays and commentary.

O. R.
Oslo

To

CHRIS
LARRY
ERIK
ARNE

. . . *who like plays*

CONTENTS

INTRODUCTION

A Definition of Drama

Drama, like poetry and fiction, is an art of words. In drama, the words are mainly dialogue: people talking is the basic dramatic action. The talk may be interrupted by wordless activity — sword-play, love-making, silence — but such activity will derive its significance from its context of dialogue. If not, we are dealing with pantomime and not with drama.

In general theory, however, the line between drama and the related arts is not so easy to draw. Film is even less literary than theater, and yet film scripts have been published to be read (*e.g.*, some of Ingmar Bergman's). At what point of verbal artistry do they cease being scenario and production notes and become drama? Conversely, to what extent is the concept of drama covered by Pirandello's "three boards and a passion" as a formula for theater?

Such questions are posed by the double aspect of dramatic language. As written words, drama is literature; as spoken words in a spectacle, it is theater. A novel or a poem is read (or listened to in recital). A play can be either read or performed, but performance affects its status as literature. Dialogue can be performed directly, intact, but stage directions, however skillfully written, do not survive the transfer from script to stage. Their referents in performance — speech manner, movement, costume, set, etc. — are creations of the theater rather than of literature. The significance of the look in Hedda Gabler's eyes, described by Ibsen as "expressive of cold, clear calm," must on stage be conveyed by means of acting and make-up. This is only to say that a performance of drama is much more than just an art of words. It is the joint product of many arts, of which direction, acting, and stage design are the chief.

The fact that successful playwrights make more money in the box office than in the bookstores is evidence that for most people the theatrical medium of drama takes precedence over the literary one and that they find *reading* a play a pallid substitute for *seeing* it. As stage spectacle a play is intensely *there* — a three-dimensional and audible progress of coherent, absorbing, physical action. While words are consecutive and reading is an act in the time dimension, seeing a play is an experience of both time and space. At any one moment the spectator may be simultaneously aware of weather or time of day or of rich or shabby furniture, or of one character speaking, another listening, and a third crawling noiselessly toward the speaker with a knife between his teeth. The spatial concreteness and immediacy of staged drama enlist the attention of a larger set of the spectator's sensory responses, and do so more intensely, than the purely imaginative evocations of a printed play ever can.

Still, the popular assumption that the theatrical medium of drama is primary may be challenged. Performance is no more the play than the concert is the symphony. Most plays — like symphonies — have been written to be performed, but the artistic construct exists complete in the written words, just as the melody, harmony, rhythm, tempo, and orchestration of the symphony "are" in the printed score. The only difference between a printed play and a printed musical composition in this respect is that for most of us it is easier to "see" and "hear" a play in the imagination than it is to "hear" the music in the read score. A play is a potential but never-to-be-realized performance, an "ideal" performance in the philosophical sense, inherent in the configuration of the playwright's words and independent of the artists of the theater whom it keeps challenging to produce performed drama. Items may be cut or added in the performance of a play, just as an enterprising editor may alter a text or a conductor a score, but this does not prove that the original work was not an autonomous artistic entity.

Drama is distinguished from the other forms of literature not just by performability but also by the objectivity and externality that performability implies. The statement "She is a woman without hope" is, as stage direction, undramatic. It could become a speech by one of the characters, or it could inspire an actress to perform an electrifying gesture of fluttering futility, but as *stage direction* it is novelistic. Not only does it not denote anything actable, it also violates the objectivity that is the condition for the playwright's craft: the tacit agreement between him and us that for the duration of the make-believe he does not exist at all, that the characters can be known only by what they reveal of themselves in speech and action. The play shows and tells itself; the characters speak for themselves. The theatricalist devices which certain plays (both old and new) deliberately use to distance the speaker from what happens on stage, reminding him that what he experiences is "only" theater, are themselves part of the dramatic spectacle. The god Ra's Prologue in Shaw's *Cæsar and Cleopatra,* the rehearsal frame of Pirandello's *Six Characters in Search of an Author,* and the narrative frame of Brecht's *Caucasian Chalk Circle* sophisticate the stage–audience relationship, but Shaw's god, Pirandello's Stage Manager, and Brecht's Story Teller are just as much "characters" within the playwright's imaginative artifact of drama as are Othello and Miss Julie within their formally simpler worlds. Even the play that by design expresses the playwright's inmost self or features a "playwright" (acted, it may be, by the playwright himself) as mouthpiece or commentator, who speaks directly to the audience on the significance of the "inner" play he shows us — can reach us only as objective stage reality, a dynamic spectacle of speakers of parts. Either the framing figure is simply a prologue–epilogue, in which case he is no organic part of the play, or he *is* part of the play, in which case he has exactly the same formal status as Shaw's Egyptian god, Pirandello's Manager, and Brecht's Caucasian Story Teller. As a framing device he may make it necessary for us to distinguish between the play's "outer" and its "inner" action, but not to distinguish between drama and non-drama.

Plays and movies based on novels prove that there is much that is performable in the other genres of literature as well. The art of poet and novelist, however, extends beyond dialogue and description of stageables. The lyric poet explores his own inner world of feeling and sensation, a world different in kind from the externalized world of drama. But even narrative, whether in prose or verse, is, despite an area of possible overlap, different from drama. A novelist or an epic poet can suspend action indefinitely, do without dialogue and physical setting and event altogether ("epics of the mind"), and discourse abstractly on any number of subjects in slow or quick sequence. He can judge and analyze his characters in authorial comment, by godlike ubiquity and omniscience enter at will into their hearts and souls, and just as easily exit back into straight narrative of external events. And if he never makes use of any of these novelistic freedoms, he is, in effect, a playwright, whether he calls his work a play or not.

Actually, this is a stricter definition of drama than many plays allow. Bernard Shaw, for example, often violates dramatic objectivity in stage directions that interpret his characters for us. The most flagrant example is perhaps the ending of *Candida.* When the heroine has sent her would-be lover, a young poet, "into the night" and turns to her husband, Shaw tells us, "They embrace. But they do not know the secret in the poet's heart." The former of these two sentences is stageable, a genuine stage direction. But no theatrical ingenuity can stage the latter — except as words flashed on a screen, like the subtitles of old silent movies. The point is not that Shaw's plays occasionally include bits of novels; we are concerned here with isolating a quality that all plays have in common, the quality that makes them, distinctly, *drama*. Performability is that quality. The spectator is in the theater to watch and listen. Shaw's comments do not exist for him, except insofar as they may have been translated into the language of the theater: sights and sounds the audience can perceive through the senses. A reader of *Candida* will, of course, make Shaw's last sentence part of his experience of the play, and an important part, too. But that does not make it a sentence of drama. The distinction is, if one likes, "academic," "purely theoretical." It certainly does not turn *Candida* into something other than a play. But to abandon it is to abandon an effort to make a general distinction between drama and other forms of literature. We *want* to be "theoretical" at this point; we are trying to suggest the outlines of a theory of drama.

This is not to exclude from the genre of drama works that cannot, for technical reasons, be staged (or staged in their entirety) in any existing theater or which, if staged, would overtax the patience and subtlety of an audience. Not only are such pragmatic criteria obviously relative; there is also a sense in which dramatic poems like *Samson Agonistes*, *Prometheus Unbound*, and *Peer Gynt*, though not intended for the stage and in some respects unperformable (if only by being bad box office), are completely dramatic. That is, their form is a system of speaking parts developing a coherent action. Whatever abstracts their total meaning includes are expressed in speech, and speech is performable by impersonators of the fictitious speakers.

The mode of drama is the objectivity of the performable. Movement, directness, concreteness are its characteristics. The dramatic experience, whether in the theater or over a printed page, is one of urgent immediacy, of watching and listening to human destinies in the making, here and now, which the novelist or the poet can evoke only by being, precisely, dramatic.

Drama and the Reader

From such a definition of drama it follows that in a skillful and successful reading of a play the mind is being filled with a sequence of vivid and relevant images, called up by speeches and stage directions. The reader translates everything performable into concretes that participate in the total, complex image of words, physical movement, and scene that makes up the drama being enacted in the infinitely resourceful and adaptable stage of his mind. Whatever is not performable, or whatever he cannot conceive of as being performable, he will also incorporate into his inclusive reading experience, though not, strictly speaking, as *drama.*

Basic to any kind of meaningful response to literature is understanding of the author's words in context and of the underlying conditions for action in the imagined world. "Understanding" depends on more than conscientious use of footnotes and dictionary; it entails a total response: intellectual, emotional, sensory. And though all readers cannot respond equally well, they can all make the effort to engage more than the top of their minds and the shallows of their souls. Generally, in the case of plays from ages and cultures different from our own, *some* awareness of cultural background will be imperative, and *more* desirable, but the line between some and more is hard to draw in given cases. For some readers, at least, certain plays will create their own climate of understanding.

Perhaps the ideal performance of the play, the standard by which both a theatrical production and a reading of it should be judged, will be thought of as the performance the playwright himself envisioned for his play. But this is neither a practicable nor even a really reasonable formula. There are playwrights who have left no record as to how they thought their plays should be produced, or whose ideas are too vague or incomplete to be of much help, or who refuse to answer when asked. And even if we assume that the original staging realized the playwright's ideal, for most older plays we can reconstruct it only by means of more or less inferential evidence, either within the play itself or supplied by research. Nor are the playwright's views, when available, necessarily more valid than someone else's — just as composers are not necessarily the best performers of their own works or even the best critics of the performance of their works by others. Intention is not accomplishment.

There is more force to the argument that a meaningful reading of a play requires knowledge of the kind of theater for which it was written. To read Sophocles or Shakespeare, the argument goes, we must know something about Greek and Elizabethan stagecraft, see productions that try to reproduce the contemporary performance, see models or pictures or diagrams of the playhouses, or at the very least read descriptions of them.

It is certainly true that the more knowledge the reader has of the culture — including the theatrical culture — reflected in what he reads, the more significant and enjoyable his reading will be. And the impossibility of ever knowing everything about a play and the fact that knowledge alone is insufficient for recreating the sense impressions, the beliefs, attitudes, and moods of a bygone audience cannot invalidate the efforts of historians of drama and theater to know as much as possible. Though each culture, each age, each reader, even the same reader at different times, reads a literary work differently, knowledge of what can be factually known about it and its times is a protection against an anarchic subjectivity of interpretation that could eventually destroy its continuum of identity. This is part of the justification of scholarship.

But though knowledge of theatrical conditions, past or present, can discipline and enrich one's experience of a play, and though such knowledge is valuable for its own sake, it is still not a precondition for the dramatic imagination itself. The images that arise in the mind during the reading of drama can be translated into stage actualities, but they are not images of such actualities. The reader does not ordinarily imagine a staged scene but its real life counterpart — not a stage castle, crypt, or kitchen, but the real thing — Othello, not actor A or actor B impersonating Othello. The exceptions are the director, designer, or actor who read with a projected performance in mind and — and he is the one who concerns us — the reader who comes to his reading of the play fresh from an impressive performance of it. His reading experience will no doubt be more vivid than it otherwise would have been, but it will also be more limited. His imagination will be channeled by his memory of the hundreds of big and little details of voice and mimicry, movement and set, costume and light, that together make up any particular actualization of the ideal abstract the play is. Any one performance, however brilliant, is bound to be different from — both more and less than — the literary work that occasioned it, forever detached as the latter is from the impermanent particulars of the real. A good production may help a reader imagine what he found unimaginable as he read the play, or it may cool and contain an imagination that catches fire too easily, but a reader to whom a play is nothing but a blueprint for an evening in the theater has abdicated his rights as reader. It is only because most people *can* stage a play in their imagination, alive with the sights and sounds of reality, that drama is literature at all — that is, capable of being experienced through reading. The theater is the home of drama, and drama may be the occasion for theater, but all theater is not drama, nor is the drama lost without the theater.

Dramatic Conventions

Understanding the underlying condition for action in the imagined world involves understanding dramatic conventions. These are the conditions which playwright and audience between them have implicitly (whether they are conscious of it or not) agreed to accept as reality in the play. In the sense that what is called for is a willingness to take the world of imagination as reality for the time being, acceptance of conventions enters into any kind of successful experience of figurative (representational, non-abstract) art. But because the theater makes tangible the forms of the make-believe, conventions operate with particular force in the experience of drama — most insistently in the theater, but also in reading. There is a widespread, though tacit and largely uninspected, assumption that drama is the most referential of the literary genres (*i.e.*, that it corresponds most closely to some real world of sensory phenomena) and the least purely expressive (*i.e.*, lyrical). For this the sensory immediacy of the performable must be responsible. And when an audience hesitates to accept a play that flaunts all pretense to mirror an objective world of things and facts, or which makes use of unfamiliar conventions, some form of the referential fallacy in the public concept of drama is likely to be involved. Of the social satirists represented in this collection, Jonson and Synge write plays that purport to record reality, while Molière and Albee exploit a convention by which a phase in the flux of phenomenal experience is transfixed and "seen" as pattern-with-meaning.

Chorus, soliloquy, and aside are examples of conventions, mainly of older drama. They were no more everyday realities then than they are now, but as artistic devices they were given status as reality because they satisfied needs for dramatic expression without going beyond what the contemporary public was willing to tolerate as make-believe. Some conventions may have been means to achieve certain kinds of communication under the technically limiting conditions of older theater. For example, such "facts" of the imagined world as location and time of day, which in the modern theater can be established by sets and electric lights, were on the Elizabethan stage communicated by the dialogue itself. Hence the rather remarkable number of Shakespearean characters who mention time and place in their speeches, particularly in the opening of scenes (see, for example, the conversation between Montano and the three Gentlemen in *Othello*, II, i, lines 1-29). To the extent that such information is for the benefit of the audience rather than for the listeners on stage, the device is conventional: a breach of reality for the sake of establishing, economically and often beautifully, "reality" within the play.

Conventions vary with time and place. Yesterday's conventions are today's absurdities and tomorrow's brilliant innovations. No play is without them. In the ceremonial tradition of drama (Greek, Elizabethan, neoclassical tragedy), ritualistic use of language in verse and imagery and of archetypal action of aristocratic agony raises life to a plane of greater dignity, significance, intensity, and eloquence than that of ordinary life lived on naturalistic terms (classical comedy). In the illusionistic tradition (some forms of older comedy, modern dramatic realism like Ibsen's and Chekhov's), convention ignores the theatrical situation and assumes the commonplace surface of stage life to be that of actuality. In the expressionistic tradition (allegorical and symbolic drama, some of Strindberg's and most of Pirandello's plays, aspects of the modern "theater of the absurd"), scenic abstractionism and stylization, dream sequences of realistic or distorted fragments of reality, montage techniques, and freedom of time and place are conventional means to the end of insinuating the reality of the single, subjective consciousness.

Because our popular theater of stage, film, and television is still very largely the heir of the realist tradition of the late nineteenth century, the modern reader or playgoer may at first find older drama and contemporary avant-garde experiments "odd," "unrealistic," "obscure." The distance between his own ordinary language and Elizabethan blank-verse rhetoric or the non-communication of absurdist dialogue may frustrate and alienate him, and he is not likely to be put at ease by the proposition that the spectacle has been put on not for its reality but for its art. Taking the conventions of realism for granted, he may fail to see that they *are* conventions. Or if he is sophisticated enough to recognize them for what they are, he may still feel they are the only "natural" conventions. But if he objects to the artificiality of the neoclassical convention of the three unities (which demanded that the action of the play be confined to a single plot, a single place, and a single day), he ought also to object to the convention of today's film and television that presents human beings as disembodied heads in facial close-ups and to the three-walled rooms of most post-Renaissance theater. And there is no reason to believe that playgoers of the past would have found a modern theater, with its artificially lighted box peeked into by a supposedly nonexistent audience, any less unnatural than we presume to find the choric rituals and public unburdenings of soul in soliloquy in their plays. If the naïve or stubbornly literal-minded is bothered by the hero's apparent deafness to the villain's stage whisper, by the scarcity of actors on stage during Shakespeare's battle scenes, or by the free and flexible treatment of time and place in a contemporary play like *The Caucasian Chalk Circle,* he simply fails to understand or accept dramatic convention.

Action, Plot, Conflict

Like most serious writing, drama represents man's use of words to make sense out of the myriad perplexities that befall him. The dramatist sees the world not primarily as shapes and colors and feelings, or as an object for religious or philosophical or scientific contemplation, or as a market, or as a reluctant machine that challenges his skill and ingenuity to make it run better. He sees it rather as an arena for human action manifested in speech. The arena may be expansive and crowded, as in such panoramic plays as *Othello, Cæsar and Cleopatra,* and *The Caucasian Chalk Circle,* or it may be small, close, and sparsely populated, as in such focussed plays as *Hedda Gabler, Miss Julie,* and *The American Dream.* The speech may be the heightened utterance of verse or everyday, colloquial prose. Or a single play may employ both media. In *Othello,* speech itself becomes a dramatic image as the shifts from one to the other extend the antithesis between Iago's vulgarity and rationalism ("prose") and Othello's dignity and passion ("poetry") beyond characterization and overt action.

The newcomer to the reading of drama may at first find confusing the conversations of unknowns, surprised in the embroilments with a life of which he knows nothing. He may miss preliminary explanations, the novelist's guiding hand. And if he has had experience with performed drama, he may also miss the aid to understanding provided by the presences and the voices of actors and by the physical spectacle in which they appear. That he can be guided by stage directions and ponder the dialogue at his leisure he may feel to be poor compensation for the absence of the sights and sounds of performance.

What the characters say and do begins to make sense only as we learn more about them, but we learn more about them only by what they say and do. Gradually they become more than a list of names. They reveal their antecedents and their present situations, their motives and purposes, they assume plot identity and "character." We learn to respond to the revealing remark or gesture, to listen to the eloquence of their silence, to sense their continuous pressure on the plot. Among them, they define and develop the dramatic action.

Dramatic action is neither physical activity nor simply the sum of everything that happens on stage: conversation, eating, people running up and down staircases, laughter, doors closing, lights going on. These are part of the action, but in the traditional (mainly Aristotelian) definition action itself is a more comprehensive concept. A set of definitions may be useful at this point.

A play is a patterning of language, character, event, and spectacle, each element a function of the other three. Its plot is the particular sequence of events that gives it the coherence and movement toward a given end that could not inhere in a random aggregate of happenings. Plot is the way the playwright has chosen to tell his story, the detailed arrangement of incidents for maximum meaning or beauty or suspense. The action of the play is both the summation of the plot and the abstraction of its meaning, the distillation of the play's totality, the answer, in a single phrase, to the question, "What happens?" "Mommy and Daddy finally get satisfaction from the Bye-Bye Adoption Service" defines the action of *The American Dream.* We call tragic the action that ends by exacting suffering or death from the protagonist as the price at which we (and perhaps he) are brought to new or heightened awareness of man's being and his relation to the ultimate moral or metaphysical issues in life. We call comic the action that concerns man in his mundane or social relationships, exposes vice and folly for contempt and laughter, and ends by vindicating reason, moderation, good will, love, virtue, or other sane and normal human values. Tragedy's domain is the infinite, its characteristic subject matter the mystery of evil and suffering. Comedy's domain is the finite, its characteristic subject matter man's triumphs and tribulations as gregarious animal.*

The nature and function of plot differ in different plays. It may be a strong, causal story line which we find suspenseful and convincing because of constant interaction between character and event. The nature of Iago's scheme is determined by his character and by his assessment of Othello's character, but the evolving logic of the scheme once he has set it in motion keeps revealing the characters of schemer and victim alike, until both seem defined by their entanglement in the events. Successful plot manipulation makes a character's behavior seem surprising and inevitable at the same time. Hedda Gabler's burning Eilert Lövborg's manuscript seems like an extraordinary and most unlikely event in a play that purports to be a snapshot of daily life in the upper middle class. But as an act by which a neurotic woman triumphs symbolically over her rival's superior womanliness it seems in character and not implausible at all.

In other plays plot is less a matter of dramatized narrative than of conveying a vivid sense of human presence. Molière in *The Misanthrope* and Chekhov in *The Cherry Orchard* do not base their dramas on the convenient convention that life runs in plots. They seek rather to illuminate a certain kind of human response to experience by means of juxtaposed scenes that subtly modify one another by discordant or mutually ironic styles, tones, and content. Molière takes Alceste

* "Tragedy" and "comedy" (and, on a cruder level, "melodrama" and "farce") are not inflexible absolutes and should not be taken to imply that every labeled play is all of one piece. There are elements of both melodrama and farce in serious moral fables like *Cæsar and Cleopatra* and *The Caucasian Chalk Circle.* Farce is a form of high comedy in *The Alchemist* and *Playboy*. There are clowns in the tragedies of *Antigone* (the Guard) and *Othello* (III, i, iv). Tesman in *Hedda Gabler* is a caricature of a fussy scholar in a context of serious realism. The contemporary social satire in *The American Dream* is in part expressed in terms of the gory events of Greek family tragedy. And so on.

through his paces, by turns admirable, ridiculous, and ominous, in an exposure of misanthropy in its several facets. Here plot is the display of a master passion in the round. *The Cherry Orchard* poses moments of emotional stasis against a background of moving time. The apparently arbitrary intermittence of the static moments and our simultaneous awareness of the resistless flow of time — and the contrast between them — constitute Chekhov's plot, in the sense that they give shape and point to the string of individual happenings. In *The American Dream* the vague waiting and the sudden arrivals do not so much amount to plot in the ordinary sense as they heighten our awareness of the non-human values by which life proceeds in Mommy's and Daddy's living room. As a sequence of coherent events, plot here is determined rather by sameness of moral atmosphere than by story.

In traditional anatomies of drama plot is usually divided into four parts: (1) The *exposition*, which gives essential information about the pre-play background of the characters and sets the plot in motion. (2) The *complication*, usually the bulk of the play, interweaving the characters' shifting fortunes and including the climax, a point of tension and the critical juncture at which a decision or an event irretrievably determines the outcome. (3) The *reversal*, or peripety, the point at which the complication culminates in the resolution of the plot: the protagonist's fortune changing from good to bad (tragedy) or from bad to good (comedy). (4) The *denouement*, or unraveling, which presents the consequences of the reversal, ties up loose ends, and allows the audience time to regain emotional equilibrium. Exposition and complication are likely to be the longest phases of the dramatic progress, the denouement is normally shorter, and the reversal may be marked by a single speech or event that occurs, most often, quite late in the play.

The plays in which the four parts of the plot are neatly distinct and laid end to end are few and not likely to be of the highest order. Good plots are complex, organic structures, whose parts blend into one another, overlapping and alternating. Though the exposition in *Othello* is largely confined to Iago's and Roderigo's dialogues and Iago's soliloquies in Act I, there are expository details in later scenes as well, *e.g.*, Othello's account of his courtship and of the magical properties of the handkerchief. In *The Caucasian Chalk Circle* the rebellion scenes in the beginning of the play are expository relative to the story of Grusha and the child, but so are the flashback scenes of Azdak's judgeship, which follow the completion of the story of Grusha's journey. In *Miss Julie*, Jean's account of the conditioning circumstances in his past comes early (though after the complication has begun); Julie's comes more than halfway through the play. In *Hedda Gabler* and *Six Characters*, fragments of explanation of past events responsible for the present crisis keep appearing almost throughout. As a result, both plays seem retrospective in structure. On stage we see, not the past itself, but only the consequences of the presumably buried past rushing in to overwhelm the present. They are "fifth-act plays," dramas of ripe condition, and to separate exposition from complication in such plays is not only difficult but senseless: exposition *is* complication. In fact, the traditional paradigm of formal plot analysis often seems to apply only partly, or insignificantly, or not at all, to individual plays in the heterogeneity and generic confusion of modern drama, the story of which, to a very large extent (at least, from the viewpoint of a contemporary), is the story of revolt and experimentation superseding a sense of formal tradition. Where does the complication begin and end in *The American Dream* — with Grandma's first entry and her final exit before she turns commentator? With Mrs. Barker's arrival and the arrival of the American Dream? What is the climax in *Six Characters* — the Father's visit to Madame Pace's? The Manager's decision to let the characters enact their destinies? We do not conclude that the traditional terms are useless but that to apply them mechanically is likely to end in critical disaster, particularly in analysis of modern plays. We may illustrate their use in an analysis of the plot structure of a traditional play.

The *story* of *Antigone* is the entire chronicle of the royal house of Thebes, including the fall of Oedipus and the mutual killing of his two sons during the Argive attack on the city. These events are only referred to, not shown on stage, but *because* they are referred to they bear significantly on actions and attitudes that *are* staged. The *action* is the resolution of the two related issues: to whom do the dead, and to whom do the living, belong? The *plot* is the causally connected sequence of events that follow from Antigone's defiance of her uncle's edict. The *exposition* is over and the *complication* begins when the Sentry enters in Scene I with the news that Polyneices has been surreptitiously buried. Everything preceding his entry has been in preparation of joining the Creon–Antigone issue. The complication comprises all the encounters involved in the opposition of Creon's and Antigone's wills, including the scenes with the Sentry, with Ismene, with Haimon, with Teiresias, and with the Choragos–Chorus. The *climax* is Creon's ordering Antigone's entombment, for from it follows directly, like falling dominoes, her, Haimon's, and Eurydice's suicides. The *reversal* occurs when Creon, disturbed by Teiresias' words and urged by the Choragos, decides to set Antigone free. The plot *resolution* is the three deaths, as related by the Messenger. Creon's last, humble exchanges with the Messenger and the Choragos mark the *denouement*.

Plot generates and releases suspense — the feeling in the audience that keeps it wondering what happens next. One characteristic of great drama is that suspense survives knowledge of "how things come out," because our absorbed wait for what is going to happen concerns the outcome less than it concerns the happenings themselves and the patterns we see them forming. We may know exactly what happens in *Antigone* and still attend, fascinated and moved, to every small step in the two diverging movements: Antigone's to the triumph of deliberate martyrdom, and Creon's to humiliation, loss, and recognition of guilt. In fact, superior plays have a way of seeming better in later readings. What we lose in mere thrill we gain in understanding and enjoyment through our intimacy with the characters and our knowledge of events to come. Familiarity also increases our appreciation and enjoyment of dramaturgy: the exercise of the playwright's craft, the dexterous manipulation of plot and character in the integrated structure of successful dramatic action. As the football fan goes to the game not just to learn who wins and by what score but to enjoy the game being played and the skill of coach and players, so the lover of drama seeks vicarious experience of significant action in artistic form, and not just information about a result. The ideal spectator attends both kinds of play in a mood of disinterested fascination.

Conflict is the element in plot that creates suspense. It is what the plot is about. In *Antigone* the conflict may be variously defined. Most simply and obviously it is one between Antigone's commitment to supernatural values and Creon's to political ones. In a larger sense, we may define it as god against man. Or we may chiefly be aware of dramatic irony: the discrepancy between, on the one hand, Creon's assumption that his fatherly concern for law and order represents the will of the gods and that Antigone's refusal to distinguish between the loyal and the disloyal dead represents rebellious impiety, and, on the other, the truth of the bitter lesson he learns at the end.

Conflict may be multiple, a collection of variants of a many-sided subject, each presenting it in a new view, and all covered by a wider definition of the play's conflict. In Shakespeare's *King Lear* the main plot about Lear and his daughters and the subplot of Gloucester and his sons allow Shakespeare a fuller treatment of the theme of filial ingratitude than either plot alone would have allowed him, and the doubleness of the plot suggests the pervasiveness of the evil. In *Cæsar and Cleopatra* there is no subplot in this sense (nor is there in *Othello*), but the conflicts of Rome against Egypt and of Cæsar against Pothinus are in the end seen to be, respectively, military and political variants of the moral conflict between Cæsar and Cleopatra and of the still more comprehensive conflict between saint and sinner, god and man, promoter and frustrater of the Life Force. In Chekhov, the situations of the several characters who fail in different ways to fulfil themselves, to achieve happiness, to establish human contact, to take decisive action, cohere in a single image of frustration, the clash of hope with reality. Plot unity is obviously not the same kind of thing in all plays. Contrasting the rambling diffuseness of events in *The Cherry Orchard* with the concentrated complexity of the major intrigue scenes in *The Rivals* suggests the range in kinds and patterns of conflict.

Conflict is opposition of forces, one of which is likely to be a human will — heroically uncompromising and therefore doomed in tragedy, abortive or reformable in comedy. Man against god, man against nature (a mountain, the sea, hunger), man against society, man against man, and man against himself, represent (in rough terms) the five main kinds of conflict. Conflict may be as simple as it is in a fairy tale (bad queen against good princess, bad guy against good sheriff). It may be morally unequivocal as in *Othello* and *The Caucasian Chalk Circle*, delicately ambiguous as in *The Misanthrope* and *The Playboy of the Western World*, elemental as the sex battle in *Miss Julie* or as the cunning exploitation of greed by greed in *The Alchemist*, religious as in *Antigone*, philosophical as in *Six Characters in Search of an Author*, psychological as in *Hedda Gabler*, historical as in *Cæsar and Cleopatra*, farcically contrived as in *The Rivals*, banal as in *The Cherry Orchard*, preposterous as in *The American Dream*. Drama without conflict is unthinkable. For the essence of the dramatic experience is the fascination with the progress of clashing forces toward resolution: the hero's death or enlightenment, the villain's defeat; the re-integration of a threatened social order in a wedding, a settlement of a quarrel, an eviction, a verdict; the revelation of the transcendent nature that shapes our lives as order and meaning or as silence and darkness.

The spoken word is the medium of drama, the objectivity of the performable its mode or manner of being, the surrender of our imaginations to that of the playwright the condition for its existence for us, but the drama itself is the action of man in conflict. This action we witness partly as safe and superior deities, enjoying the pleasure of dramatic irony at the expense of people who do not know what is happening to them; partly as sympathetic observers, commiserating with the good, relishing the downfall of the bad; and partly as fellow fools and sufferers: there, but for the grace of God, *we* strut and fret.

Anatomy of a Scene

The climactic scene in Sheridan's *The Rivals* may be studied as an example of successful plotting. Manipulated intrigue, which is the kind of plot the scene represents, is not the only significant mode of drama, hardly even the most important one, but it is a mode that turns up in plays as far apart in time and dramatic convention as *Othello, Hedda Gabler,* and *The Caucasian Chalk Circle.* The intricacy, daring, and luck of Iago's scheming in Shakespeare; the story of Lövborg's manuscript and Judge Brack's discreetly sinister moves behind the scenes in Ibsen; and the moment at the end of Section 3 of Brecht's play when the Ironshirts ask Grusha if little Michael is her child and she realizes that an affirmative answer will cost her Simon's love and a negative one most likely Michael's life, all share the quality of self-generating and unbearable tension drawing near inevitable release that Sheridan's scene illustrates in a comical vein. Intrigue has no part in the drama of interweaving strands of Shakespearean imagery, or in a Shavian play of ideas, or in the separate moments of poignant realism in Chekhov. But because superior intrigue is a piece of fine literary machinery, it lends itself more readily, perhaps, than other modes of drama to an illustration of drama as technique.

The climax in *The Rivals* comes in the early part of the second scene of Act IV, when the complex of mistaken assumptions surrounding Captain Absolute's pose as "Ensign Beverley" is resolved as he confronts Lydia Languish in his true identity. As in all plays of well-built intrigue, relishing the scene and realizing its climactic function is a matter of having previous plot developments clearly in mind. The reader or spectator who does not thrill with anticipation of fun to come when Lydia announces that she "won't even speak to, or look at" Captain Absolute is a lost soul as far as the comedy of the climax of *The Rivals* is concerned.

Lydia Languish is a romantic girl who prefers elopement to a conventional wedding and is ready to forfeit her fortune by marrying against the worldly wishes of her aunt and guardian, Mrs. Malaprop. Knowing her whim, Captain Absolute wins her heart in the character of the penniless "Ensign Beverley." Mrs. Malaprop intercepts a letter from the "Ensign" to Lydia, in which he ridicules the older woman and boasts to his love that he is going to make her aunt their go-between. Without consulting his son, Sir Anthony Absolute, the Captain's father, makes arrangements with Mrs. Malaprop for the Captain's marriage to Lydia. When the Captain learns the identity of the girl his father has picked for him, he decides that Sir Anthony's "too summary . . . method of proceeding in these matters" may lose him Lydia's favor, and he conceals his connection with her by feigning tepid compliance with his father's plans. His indifference to marrying "blooming, love-breathing seventeen" is a great disappointment to Sir Anthony. When the Captain calls on Mrs. Malaprop and Lydia, the former receives him warmly, both because she finds his manners charming and because she thinks he will be her means for triumphing over both the insolent "Ensign" and her stubborn ward. She forces his presence on Lydia, whose reluctance changes to delight when she discovers her "Ensign" in the role (as she thinks) of Captain Absolute. When later that same day Sir Anthony and his son together visit Mrs. Malaprop and her niece, the climactic scene begins.*

What makes it effective drama is not theme (there is none) or psychology (which is schematic) or sentiment (which is obvious), but a plot situation that builds a crescendo of expectation of hilarious resolution. The bubble inflates; we know it soon will burst and that it won't really matter that it does, and it is fun to watch it grow and to wonder how much longer the burst can be delayed. The art of the drama here is the controlled elegance with which a charged situation moves toward explosion.

The explosion is a recognition scene: one in which one or several of the characters make a sudden discovery of unsuspected identity. Creon discovering that the "criminal" who has given burial to Polyneices' body is his own niece, Othello that it is "honest Iago" who has told the lies that have destroyed him, Face and Subtle (in *The Alchemist*) that the Spanish don is Surly in disguise, Captain Absolute that his father "wants to *force* me to marry the very girl I am plotting to run away with," are all examples of recognition scenes. In this case, the discovery that "Ensign Beverley" and Captain Absolute are one and the same person is made simultaneously by Lydia and her aunt, while Sir Anthony discovers the reason for his son's strangely flaccid indifference to Lydia's charms.

More important than these discoveries themselves, however, are their implications for our view of the character of the discoverers. Sir Anthony is so delighted that his son is not the "dull, insensible varlet" he had pretended to be that he does not mind having been fooled. In fact, he is rather proud of the Captain's ruse: he has proved himself a chip off the old block. Mrs. Malaprop is so mortified when she realizes that she *has*, in fact, been Lydia's and the "Ensign's" go-between and that she has pledged her obstreperous niece to marry the very man she loves and who had called her (Mrs. Malaprop) "an old, weather-beaten dragon," that only Sir Anthony's appeal to her incurable coquetry can overcome her resentment. Lydia alone refuses to forgive the Captain his double identity. She resents having been humored like a child, but she resents even more having to give up the romantic elopement she had dreamed of and to settle for a regular church wedding with lawyers and license. Her resentment, still implacable at the end of the scene,

* At this point, the reader should turn to Act IV, scene 2, in *The Rivals*, and read from the beginning of the scene to Sir Anthony's speech, "Come, we must leave them together; . . ." (pp. 356-360).

shows the strength of her romantic caprice and provides matter for further intrigue. It is also an amusing variant of the hackneyed romantic motif of the heroine who discovers that the ragged youth she has fallen in love with is a splendid prince in disguise. As for the Captain himself, his efforts to be alone with Lydia present the ironic spectacle of a man trying to get out of a tight situation he has got himself into and failing because of the very success of his deceit. Our enjoyment of his plight is balanced by our admiration for the frank manliness and eloquence of his confession when he sees that his game is up. Deviousness has only been a lover's stratagem; it is not his real character.

What we enjoy, in other words, are the antics of people who are too much in the thick of the plot to grasp its total compass. As god-like surveyors of the whole pattern of their interlocking confusions, we are their superiors. We know more about them than they know themselves: much of the drama of the scene is in our awareness of their unawareness.

Characters in literature are aware of themselves only as people in real life are aware of *them*selves. Even when we look at ourselves from the outside and try to see ourselves as others see us (as Othello does in his last, magnificent moment of self-punishing histrionics), we can never, by the very nature of things, see ourselves in the detached view-in-the-round available to others. We are disqualified as objective and all-informed observers by our own identity: we are that which we are trying to observe. But relative to characters in literature we enjoy — or *can* enjoy — absolute omniscience. We know all there is to be known about them, because they have no existence outside the work in which they appear. Captain Absolute's profession as officer denotes no battles or drills, but only an occupation fit for the dashing hero of romantic comedy, a public pretext for his presence in Bath, and an occasion for the demotion motif which expresses both Lydia's singular whim and the strength of the Captain's love for her.

Literary characters, after all, are only constituent moving parts in shaped patterns of action. And because they are, what happens to them can seem more meaningful than the random events that befall ourselves, living as we are among the uncontrollable recalcitrance of real things. Only if we see characters in this double aspect, as men and as artifacts mimicking men, can we experience their world as literature, as art, rather than as life substitute or daydream. To seek a "yes" or a "no" to the question whether Emilia has been unfaithful to Iago is to seek something Shakespeare did not choose to offer. We may speculate, more or less plausibly, but speculation presupposes that Shakespeare was dramatizing real lives and arbitrarily withheld information we would like to have. As sole maker and master of the world of *Othello* he would presumably have settled the issue if it had seemed important to him to do so. Since he did not, it seems reasonable to suppose that he wanted it left unsettled. "Othello either has or has not slept with Emilia" would be a logical proposition if Othello were a real person, but it is an invalid statement about the play. The possibility of Emilia's adultery is the whole extent of its reality. It exists only within the play and has no other function than to rankle in Iago's proud and cynical mind, to help explain his hatred of Othello and Cassio, and to determine the nature of his revenge.

The very transparency of Sheridan's contrivances is a precondition for our vicarious participation in the act of dramatic creation. He places himself under rigid and elaborate rules in a game in which characters are pawns whose moves are limited by the requirements that they seem plausible in context and obedient to the dynamics of the developing comical intrigue. When Lydia turns her back on the unwelcome suitor before he enters, we appreciate the rightness of the playwright's move. Plausibility is observed, because, as far as Lydia knows, Captain Absolute is a threat to her romance with "Beverley." Comic decorum is observed, because her act allows Sheridan to exploit farcical confusion to the limit: Lydia wondering why her aunt fails to see that Captain Absolute and "Beverley" are not identical, Sir Anthony bullying his son for his feeble wooing, Mrs. Malaprop chiding Lydia for her surliness, and the Captain losing his voice in an effort to get a chance to speak to Lydia alone. These four together, three of them wrong about their relationship to the fourth, and he trying to keep them from finding it out, fill with scenic life the pattern of the climax which the main intrigue has been building up to from the beginning of the play. Having Lydia discover her lover's double identity as soon as he enters would be to kill an appetite whetted by apéritifs and a look at the menu with a dish of oatmeal. We would, rightly, have felt cheated of a treat. We are not satisfied till our anticipations of comedy are enacted, our expectations of laughter dissolve in laughter, and our enjoyment proves our understanding.

s, a double death
t the Argive army
is, nothing.
is why I wanted you
ere is something we must do.
angely?

ocles
m a soldier's funeral,
ld; but Polyneices,
lied as miserably, —
rn
ne mourn for him,
fields, a sweet treasure
they search for food.
our good Creon is coming here
nd the penalty —
ublic square!
There it is,
hat you are:
to your family.
mad! What could I possibly do?
de whether you will help me or not.
nd you. Help you in what?
going to bury him. Will you come?
have just said the new law forbids it.
her. And he is your brother, too.
e danger! Think what Creon will do!
strong enough to stand in my way.

ne hating him
rch brought to light, his eyes
wn hand; and Iocaste died,
e at once: she twisted the cords
life; and our two brothers died,
other's sword. And we are left:

more terrible than these
ould be if we should go against Creon
as forbidden! We are only women,
with men, Antigone!
, we must give in to the law
d in worse. I beg the Dead

DRAMA

An Introductory Anthology

A

Perso

ANTI
ISMEN
EURYD
CREON

SCENE: *Befo*
door, and
façade, and
"orchestra,"
TIME: *Dawn of*
assault on The

PROLOGUE

(ANTIGONE *and* IS

ANTIGONE: Ismene, de
You would think tha
For the curse on Oed
I cannot imagine any
That you and I have n
Have they told you of t
ISMENE: I have heard noth

The Antigone of Sophocles
Robert Fitzgerald, copyright
reprinted with their permissio

That two sisters lost two brothe
In a single hour; and I know tha
Fled in the night; but beyond t
ANTIGONE: I thought so. And tha
To come out here with me. Th
ISMENE: Why do you speak so st
ANTIGONE: Listen, Ismene:
Creon buried our brother Ete
With military honors, gave h
And it was right that he shou
Who fought as bravely and
They say that Creon has sw
No one shall bury him, no
But his body must lie in th
For carrion birds to find as
That is what they say, and
To announce it publicly; a
Stoning to death in the p

And now you can prove
A true sister, or a traitor
ISMENE: Antigone, you are
ANTIGONE: You must dec
ISMENE: I do not underst
ANTIGONE: Ismene, I am
ISMENE: Bury him! You
ANTIGONE: He is my bro
ISMENE: But think of th
ANTIGONE: Creon is not
ISMENE: Ah sister!
Oedipus died, every
For what his own se
Ripped out by his o
His mother and wi
That strangled her
Each killed by the
But oh, Antigone,
Think how much
Our own death w
And do what he
We cannot fight
The law is stron
In this thing, a

To forgive me, but I am helpless: I must yield
To those in authority. And I think it is dangerous business
To be always meddling.

ANTIGONE: If that is what you think,
I should not want you, even if you asked to come.
You have made your choice, you can be what you want to be.
But I will bury him; and if I must die,
I say that this crime is holy: I shall lie down
With him in death, and I shall be as dear
To him as he is to me.
It is the dead,
Not the living, who make the longest demands:
We die for ever . . .
You may do as you like,
Since apparently the laws of the gods mean nothing to you.

ISMENE: They mean a great deal to me; but I have no strength
To break laws that were made for the public good.

ANTIGONE: That must be your excuse, I suppose. But as for me,
I will bury the brother I love.

ISMENE: Antigone,
I am so afraid for you!

ANTIGONE: You need not be:
You have yourself to consider, after all.

ISMENE: But no one must hear of this, you must tell no one!
I will keep it a secret, I promise!

ANTIGONE: Oh tell it! Tell everyone!
Think how they'll hate you when it all comes out
If they learn that you knew about it all the time!

ISMENE: So fiery! You should be cold with fear.

ANTIGONE: Perhaps. But I am doing only what I must.

ISMENE: But can you do it? I say that you cannot.

ANTIGONE: Very well: when my strength gives out, I shall do no more.

ISMENE: Impossible things should not be tried at all.

ANTIGONE: Go away, Ismene:
I shall be hating you soon, and the dead will too,
For your words are hateful. Leave me my foolish plan:
I am not afraid of the danger; if it means death,
It will not be the worst of deaths — death without honor.

ISMENE: Go then, if you feel that you must.
You are unwise,
But a loyal friend indeed to those who love you.

(*Exit into the Palace.* ANTIGONE *goes off, L.* *Enter the* CHORUS.)

PARODOS

CHORUS: Now the long blade of the sun, lying [STROPHE 1
Level east to west, touches with glory
Thebes of the Seven Gates. Open, unlidded
Eye of golden day! O marching light
Across the eddy and rush of Dirce's stream,
Striking the white shields of the enemy
Thrown headlong backward from the blaze of morning!
CHORAGOS: Polyneices their commander
Roused them with windy phrases,
He the wild eagle screaming
Insults above our land,
His wings their shields of snow,
His crest their marshalled helms.

CHORUS: Against our seven gates in a yawning ring [ANTISTROPHE 1
The famished spears came onward in the night;
But before his jaws were sated with our blood,
Or pinefire took the garland of our towers,
He was thrown back; and as he turned, great Thebes —
No tender victim for his noisy power —
Rose like a dragon behind him, shouting war.
CHORAGOS: For God hates utterly
The bray of bragging tongues;
And when he beheld their smiling,
Their swagger of golden helms,
The frown of his thunder blasted
Their first man from our walls.

CHORUS: We heard his shout of triumph high in the air [STROPHE 2
Turn to a scream; far out in a flaming arc
He fell with his windy torch, and the earth struck him.
And others storming in fury no less than his
Found shock of death in the dusty joy of battle.
CHORAGOS: Seven captains at seven gates
Yielded their clanging arms to the god
That bends the battle-line and breaks it.
These two only, brothers in blood,
Face to face in matchless rage,
Mirroring each the other's death,
Clashed in long combat.

CHORUS: But now in the beautiful morning of victory [ANTISTROPHE 2
Let Thebes of the many chariots sing for joy!
With hearts for dancing we'll take leave of war:
Our temples shall be sweet with hymns of praise,
And the long night shall echo with our chorus.

SCENE I

CHORAGOS: But now at last our new King is coming:
Creon of Thebes, Menoikeus' son.
In this auspicious dawn of his reign
What are the new complexities
That shifting Fate has woven for him?
What is his counsel? Why has he summoned
The old men to hear him?

(*Enter* CREON *from the Palace, C. He addresses the* CHORUS *from the top step.*)

CREON: Gentlemen: I have the honor to inform you that our Ship of State, which recent storms have threatened to destroy, has come safely to harbor at last, guided by the merciful wisdom of Heaven. I have summoned you here this morning because I know that I can depend upon you: your devotion to King Laïos was absolute; you never hesitated in your duty to our late ruler Oedipus; and when Oedipus died, your loyalty was transferred to his children. Unfortunately, as you know, his two sons, the princes Eteocles and Polyneices, have killed each other in battle; and I, as the next in blood, have succeeded to the full power of the throne.

I am aware, of course, that no Ruler can expect complete loyalty from his subjects until he has been tested in office. Nevertheless, I say to you at the very outset that I have nothing but contempt for the kind of Governor who is afraid, for whatever reason, to follow the course that he knows is best for the State; and as for the man who sets private friendship above the public welfare, — I have no use for him, either. I call God to witness that if I saw my country headed for ruin, I should not be afraid to speak out plainly; and I need hardly remind you that I would never have any dealings with an enemy of the people. No one values friendship more highly than I; but we must remember that friends made at the risk of wrecking our Ship are not real friends at all.

These are my principles, at any rate, and that is why I have made the following decision concerning the sons of Oedipus: Eteocles, who died as a man should die, fighting for his country, is to be buried with full military honors, with all the ceremony that is usual when the greatest heroes die; but his brother Polyneices, who broke his exile to come back with fire and sword against his native city and the shrines of his fathers' gods, whose one idea was to spill the blood of his blood and sell his own people into slavery — Polyneices, I say, is to have no burial: no man is to touch him or say the least prayer for him; he shall lie on the plain, unburied; and the birds and the scavenging dogs can do with him whatever they like.

This is my command, and you can see the wisdom behind it. As long as I am King, no traitor is going to be honored with the loyal man. But whoever shows by word and deed that he is on the side of the State, — he shall have my respect while he is living, and my reverence when he is dead.

CHORAGOS: If that is your will, Creon son of Menoikeus,
You have the right to enforce it: we are yours.

CREON: That is my will. Take care that you do your part.

CHORAGOS: We are old men: let the younger ones carry it out.

CREON: I do not mean that: the sentries have been appointed.

CHORAGOS: Then what is it that you would have us do?

CREON: You will give no support to whoever breaks this law.

CHORAGOS: Only a crazy man is in love with death!

CREON: And death it is; yet money talks, and the wisest
Have sometimes been known to count a few coins too many.

(*Enter* SENTRY *from L.*)

SENTRY: I'll not say that I'm out of breath from running, King, because every time I stopped to think about what I have to tell you, I felt like going back. And all the time a voice kept saying, "You fool, don't you know you're walking straight into trouble?"; and then another voice: "Yes, but if you let somebody else get the news to Creon first, it will be even worse than that for you!" But good sense won out, at least I hope it was good sense, and here I am with a story that makes no sense at all; but I'll tell it anyhow, because, as they say, what's going to happen's going to happen, and —

CREON: Come to the point. What have you to say?

SENTRY: I did not do it. I did not see who did it. You must not punish me for what someone else has done.

CREON: A comprehensive defense! More effective, perhaps,
If I knew its purpose. Come: what is it?

SENTRY: A dreadful thing . . . I don't know how to put it —

CREON: Out with it!

SENTRY: Well, then;

The dead man —
Polyneices —

(*Pause. The* SENTRY *is overcome, fumbles for words.* CREON *waits impassively.*)

out there —
someone, —
New dust on the slimy flesh!

(*Pause. No sign from* CREON.)

Someone has given it burial that way, and
Gone . . .

(*Long pause.* CREON *finally speaks with deadly control.*)

CREON: And the man who dared do this?
SENTRY: I swear I
Do not know! You must believe me!
Listen:
The ground was dry, not a sign of digging, no,
Not a wheeltrack in the dust, no trace of anyone.
It was when they relieved us this morning: and one of them,
The corporal, pointed to it.
There it was,
The strangest —
Look:
The body, just mounded over with light dust: you see?
Not buried really, but as if they'd covered it
Just enough for the ghost's peace. And no sign
Of dogs or any wild animal that had been there.

And then what a scene there was! Every man of us
Accusing the other: we all proved the other man did it,
We all had proof that we could not have done it.
We were ready to take hot iron in our hands,
Walk through fire, swear by all the gods,
It was not I!
I do not know who it was, but it was not I!

(CREON'S *rage has been mounting steadily, but the* SENTRY *is too intent upon his story to notice it.*)

And then, when this came to nothing, someone said
A thing that silenced us and made us stare
Down at the ground: you had to be told the news,

And one of us had to do it! We threw the dice,
And the bad luck fell to me. So here I am,
No happier to be here than you are to have me:
Nobody likes the man who brings bad news.

CHORAGOS: I have been wondering, King: can it be that the gods have done this?

CREON (*furiously*): Stop!
Must you doddering wrecks
Go out of your heads entirely? "The gods!"
Intolerable!
The gods favor this corpse? Why? How had he served them?
Tried to loot their temples, burn their images,
Yes, and the whole State, and its laws with it!
Is it your senile opinion that the gods love to honor bad men?
A pious thought! —
No, from the very beginning
There have been those who have whispered together,
Stiff-necked anarchists, putting their heads together,
Scheming against me in alleys. These are the men,
And they have bribed my own guard to do this thing.

(*Sententiously.*)

Money!
There's nothing in the world so demoralizing as money.
Down go your cities,
Homes gone, men gone, honest hearts corrupted,
Crookedness of all kinds, and all for money!
(*To* SENTRY.) But you — !
I swear by God and by the throne of God,
The man who has done this thing shall pay for it!
Find that man, bring him here to me, or your death
Will be the least of your problems: I'll string you up
Alive, and there will be certain ways to make you
Discover your employer before you die;
And the process may teach you a lesson you seem to have missed:
The dearest profit is sometimes all too dear:
That depends on the source. Do you understand me?
A fortune won is often misfortune.

SENTRY: King, may I speak?

CREON: Your very voice distresses me.

SENTRY: Are you sure that it is my voice, and not your conscience?

CREON: By God, he wants to analyze me now!

SENTRY: It is not what I say, but what has been done, that hurts you.

CREON: You talk too much.
SENTRY: Maybe; but I've done nothing.
CREON: Sold your soul for some silver: that's all you've done.
SENTRY: How dreadful it is when the right judge judges wrong!
CREON: Your figures of speech
May entertain you now; but unless you bring me the man,
You will get little profit from them in the end.

(*Exit* CREON *into the Palace.*)

SENTRY: "Bring me the man" — !
I'd like nothing better than bringing him the man!
But bring him or not, you have seen the last of me here.
At any rate, I am safe!

(*Exit* SENTRY.)

ODE I

CHORUS: Numberless are the world's wonders, but none [STROPHE 1
More wonderful than man; the stormgray sea
Yields to his prows, the huge crests bear him high;
Earth, holy and inexhaustible, is graven
With shining furrows where his plows have gone
Year after year, the timeless labor of stallions.

The lightboned birds and beasts that cling to cover, [ANTISTROPHE 1
The lithe fish lighting their reaches of dim water,
All are taken, tamed in the net of his mind;
The lion on the hill, the wild horse windy-maned,
Resign to him; and his blunt yoke has broken
The sultry shoulders of the mountain bull.

Words also, and thought as rapid as air, [STROPHE 2
He fashions to his good use; statecraft is his,
And his the skill that deflects the arrows of snow,
The spears of winter rain: from every wind
He has made himself secure — from all but one:
In the late wind of death he cannot stand.

O clear intelligence, force beyond all measure! [ANTISTROPHE 2
O fate of man, working both good and evil!
When the laws are kept, how proudly his city stands!

When the laws are broken, what of his city then?
Never may the anárchic man find rest at my hearth,
Never be it said that my thoughts are his thoughts.

SCENE II

(*Re-enter* SENTRY *leading* ANTIGONE.)

CHORAGOS: What does this mean? Surely this captive woman
Is the Princess, Antigone. Why should she be taken?
SENTRY: Here is the one who did it! We caught her
In the very act of burying him. — Where is Creon?
CHORAGOS: Just coming from the house.

(*Enter* CREON, C.)

CREON: What has happened?
Why have you come back so soon?
SENTRY (*expansively*): O King,
A man should never be too sure of anything: I would have sworn
That you'd not see me here again: your anger
Frightened me so, and the things you threatened me with;
But how could I tell then
That I'd be able to solve the case so soon?

No dice-throwing this time: I was only too glad to come!

Here is this woman. She is the guilty one:
We found her trying to bury him.
Take her, then; question her; judge her as you will.
I am through with the whole thing now, and glád óf it.
CREON: But this is Antigone! Why have you brought her here?
SENTRY: She was burying him, I tell you!
CREON (*severely*): Is this the truth?
SENTRY: I saw her with my own eyes. Can I say more?
CREON: The details: come, tell me quickly!
SENTRY: It was like this:
After those terrible threats of yours, King,
We went back and brushed the dust away from the body.
The flesh was soft by now, and stinking,
So we sat on a hill to windward and kept guard.
No napping this time! We kept each other awake.

But nothing happened until the white round sun
Whirled in the center of the round sky over us:
Then, suddenly,
A storm of dust roared up from the earth, and the sky
Went out, the plain vanished with all its trees
In the stinging dark. We closed our eyes and endured it.
The whirlwind lasted a long time, but it passed;
And then we looked, and there was Antigone!
I have seen
A mother bird come back to a stripped nest, heard
Her crying bitterly a broken note or two
For the young ones stolen. Just so, when this girl
Found the bare corpse, and all her love's work wasted,
She wept, and cried on heaven to damn the hands
That had done this thing.
And then she brought more dust
And sprinkled wine three times for her brother's ghost.

We ran and took her at once. She was not afraid,
Not even when we charged her with what she had done.
She denied nothing.
And this was a comfort to me,
And some uneasiness: for it is a good thing
To escape from death, but it is no great pleasure
To bring death to a friend.
Yet I always say
There is nothing so comfortable as your own safe skin!

CREON (*slowly, dangerously*): And you, Antigone,
You with your head hanging, — do you confess this thing?

ANTIGONE: I do. I deny nothing.

CREON (*to* SENTRY): You may go. (*Exit* SENTRY.)
(*To* ANTIGONE) Tell me, tell me briefly:
Had you heard my proclamation touching this matter?

ANTIGONE: It was public. Could I help hearing it?

CREON: And yet you dared defy the law.

ANTIGONE: I dared.
It was not God's proclamation. That final Justice
That rules the world below makes no such laws.
Your edict, King, was strong,
But all your strength is weakness itself against
The immortal unrecorded laws of God.
They are not merely now: they were, and shall be,
Operative for ever, beyond man utterly.

I knew I must die, even without your decree:
I am only mortal. And if I must die
Now, before it is my time to die,
Surely this is no hardship: can anyone
Living, as I live, with evil all about me,
Think Death less than a friend? This death of mine
Is of no importance; but if I had left my brother
Lying in death unburied, I should have suffered.
Now I do not.
You smile at me. Ah Creon,
Think me a fool, if you like; but it may well be
That a fool convicts me of folly.

CHORAGOS: Like father, like daughter: both headstrong, deaf to reason!
She has never learned to yield.

CREON: She has much to learn.
The inflexible heart breaks first, the toughest iron
Cracks first, and the wildest horses bend their necks
At the pull of the smallest curb.
Pride? In a slave?
This girl is guilty of a double insolence,
Breaking the given laws and boasting of it.
Who is the man here,
She or I, if this crime goes unpunished?
Sister's child, or more than sister's child,
Or closer yet in blood — she and her sister
Win bitter death for this!
(*To* SERVANTS.) Go, some of you,
Arrest Ismene. I accuse her equally.
Bring her: you will find her sniffling in the house there.

Her mind's a traitor: crimes kept in the dark
Cry for light, and the guardian brain shudders;
But how much worse than this
Is brazen boasting of barefaced anarchy!

ANTIGONE: Creon, what more do you want than my death?

CREON: Nothing.
That gives me everything.

ANTIGONE: Then I beg you: kill me.
This talking is a great weariness: your words
Are distasteful to me, and I am sure that mine
Seem so to you. And yet they should not seem so:
I should have praise and honor for what I have done.

All these men here would praise me
Were their lips not frozen shut with fear of you.

(*Bitterly.*)

Ah the good fortune of kings,
Licensed to say and do whatever they please!

CREON: You are alone here in that opinion.
ANTIGONE: No, they are with me. But they keep their tongues in leash.
CREON: Maybe. But you are guilty, and they are not.
ANTIGONE: There is no guilt in reverence for the dead.
CREON: But Eteocles — was he not your brother too?
ANTIGONE: My brother too.
CREON: And you insult his memory?
ANTIGONE (*softly*): The dead man would not say that I insult it.
CREON: He would: for you honor a traitor as much as him.
ANTIGONE: His own brother, traitor or not, and equal in blood.
CREON: He made war on his country. Eteocles defended it.
ANTIGONE: Nevertheless, there are honors due all the dead.
CREON: But not the same for the wicked as for the just.
ANTIGONE: Ah Creon, Creon,
Which of us can say what the gods hold wicked?
CREON: An enemy is an enemy, even dead.
ANTIGONE: It is my nature to join in love, not hate.
CREON (*finally losing patience*): Go join them, then; if you must have your love,
Find it in hell!
CHORAGOS: But see, Ismene comes:

(*Enter* ISMENE, *guarded.*)

Those tears are sisterly, the cloud
That shadows her eyes rains down gentle sorrow.
CREON: You too, Ismene,
Snake in my ordered house, sucking my blood
Stealthily — and all the time I never knew
That these two sisters were aiming at my throne!
Ismene,
Do you confess your share in this crime, or deny it?
Answer me.
ISMENE: Yes, if she will let me say so. I am guilty.
ANTIGONE (*coldly*): No, Ismene. You have no right to say so.
You would not help me, and I will not have you help me.
ISMENE: But now I know what you meant; and I am here

To join you, to take my share of punishment.
ANTIGONE: The dead man and the gods who rule the dead
Know whose act this was. Words are not friends.
ISMENE: Do you refuse me, Antigone? I want to die with you:
I too have a duty that I must discharge to the dead.
ANTIGONE: You shall not lessen my death by sharing it.
ISMENE: What do I care for life when you are dead?
ANTIGONE: Ask Creon. You're always hanging on his opinions.
ISMENE: You are laughing at me. Why, Antigone?
ANTIGONE: It's a joyless laughter, Ismene.
ISMENE: But can I do nothing?
ANTIGONE: Yes. Save yourself. I shall not envy you.
There are those who will praise you; I shall have honor, too.
ISMENE: But we are equally guilty!
ANTIGONE: No more, Ismene.
You are alive, but I belong to Death.
CREON (*to the* CHORUS): Gentlemen, I beg you to observe these girls:
One has just now lost her mind; the other,
It seems, has never had a mind at all.
ISMENE: Grief teaches the steadiest minds to waver, King.
CREON: Yours certainly did, when you assumed guilt with the guilty!
ISMENE: But how could I go on living without her?
CREON: You are.
She is already dead.
ISMENE: But your own son's bride!
CREON: There are places enough for him to push his plow.
I want no wicked women for my sons!
ISMENE: O dearest Haimon, how your father wrongs you!
CREON: I've had enough of your childish talk of marriage!
CHORAGOS: Do you really intend to steal this girl from your son?
CREON: No; Death will do that for me.
CHORAGOS: Then she must die?
CREON (*ironically*): You dazzle me.
— But enough of this talk!

(*To* GUARDS.)

You, there, take them away and guard them well:
For they are but women, and even brave men run
When they see Death coming.

(*Exeunt* ISMENE, ANTIGONE, *and* GUARDS.)

ODE II

[STROPHE 1

CHORUS: Fortunate is the man who has never tasted God's vengeance!
Where once the anger of heaven has struck, that house is shaken
For ever: damnation rises behind each child
Like a wave cresting out of the black northeast,
When the long darkness under sea roars up
And bursts drumming death upon the windwhipped sand.

I have seen this gathering sorrow from time long past [ANTISTROPHE 1
Loom upon Oedipus' children: generation from generation
Takes the compulsive rage of the enemy god.
So lately this last flower of Oedipus' line
Drank the sunlight! but now a passionate word
And a handful of dust have closed up all its beauty.

What mortal arrogance [STROPHE 2
Transcends the wrath of Zeus?
Sleep cannot lull him, nor the effortless long months
Of the timeless gods: but he is young for ever,
And his house is the shining day of high Olympos.
All that is and shall be,
And all the past, is his.
No pride on earth is free of the curse of heaven.

The straying dreams of men [ANTISTROPHE 2
May bring them ghosts of joy:
But as they drowse, the waking embers burn them;
Or they walk with fixed éyes, as blind men walk.
But the ancient wisdom speaks for our own time:
Fate works most for woe
With Folly's fairest show.
Man's little pleasure is the spring of sorrow.

SCENE III

CHORAGOS: But here is Haimon, King, the last of all your sons.
Is it grief for Antigone that brings him here,
And bitterness at being robbed of his bride?

(*Enter* HAIMON.)

CREON: We shall soon see, and no need of diviners.
— Son,
You have heard my final judgment on that girl:
Have you come here hating me, or have you come
With deference and with love, whatever I do?
HAIMON: I am your son, father. You are my guide.
You make things clear for me, and I obey you.
No marriage means more to me than your continuing wisdom.
CREON: Good. That is the way to behave: subordinate
Everything else, my son, to your father's will.
This is what a man prays for, that he may get
Sons attentive and dutiful in his house,
Each one hating his father's enemies,
Honoring his father's friends. But if his sons
Fail him, if they turn out unprofitably,
What has he fathered but trouble for himself
And amusement for the malicious?
So you are right
Not to lose your head over this woman.
Your pleasure with her would soon grow cold, Haimon,
And then you'd have a hellcat in bed and elsewhere.
Let her find her husband in Hell!
Of all the people in this city, only she
Has had contempt for my law and broken it.
Do you want me to show myself weak before the people?
Or to break my sworn word? No, and I will not.
The woman dies.
I suppose she'll plead "family ties." Well, let her.
If I permit my own family to rebel,
How shall I earn the world's obedience?
Show me the man who keeps his house in hand,
He's fit for public authority.
I'll have no dealings
With law-breakers, critics of the government:
Whoever is chosen to govern should be obeyed —
Must be obeyed, in all things, great and small,
Just and unjust! O Haimon,
The man who knows how to obey, and that man only,
Knows how to give commands when the time comes.
You can depend on him, no matter how fast
The spears come: he's a good soldier, he'll stick it out.

Anarchy, anarchy! Show me a greater evil!
This is why cities tumble and the great houses rain down,
This is what scatters armies!

No, no: good lives are made so by discipline.
We keep the laws then, and the lawmakers,
And no woman shall seduce us. If we must lose,
Let's lose to a man, at least! Is a woman stronger than we?

CHORAGOS: Unless time has rusted my wits,
What you say, King, is said with point and dignity.

HAIMON (*boyishly earnest*): Father:
Reason is God's crowning gift to man, and you are right
To warn me against losing mine. I cannot say —
I hope that I shall never want to say! — that you
Have reasoned badly. Yet there are other men
Who can reason, too; and their opinions might be helpful.
You are not in a position to know everything
That people say or do, or what they feel:
Your temper terrifies them — everyone
Will tell you only what you like to hear.
But I, at any rate, can listen; and I have heard them
Muttering and whispering in the dark about this girl.
They say no woman has ever, so unreasonably,
Died so shameful a death for a generous act:
"She covered her brother's body. Is this indecent?
She kept him from dogs and vultures. Is this a crime?
Death? — She should have all the honor that we can give her!"

This is the way they talk out there in the city.

You must believe me:
Nothing is closer to me than your happiness.
What could be closer? Must not any son
Value his father's fortune as his father does his?
I beg you, do not be unchangeable:
Do not believe that you alone can be right.
The man who thinks that,
The man who maintains that only he has the power
To reason correctly, the gift to speak, the soul —
A man like that, when you know him, turns out empty.

It is not reason never to yield to reason!

In flood time you can see how some trees bend,
And because they bend, even their twigs are safe,
While stubborn trees are torn up, roots and all.
And the same thing happens in sailing:
Make your sheet fast, never slacken, — and over you go,
Head over heels and under: and there's your voyage.
Forget you are angry! Let yourself be moved!
I know I am young; but please let me say this:
The ideal condition
Would be, I admit, that men should be right by instinct;
But since we are all too likely to go astray,
The reasonable thing is to learn from those who can teach.

CHORAGOS: You will do well to listen to him, King,
If what he says is sensible. And you, Haimon,
Must listen to your father. — Both speak well.

CREON: You consider it right for a man of my years and experience
To go to school to a boy?

HAIMON: It is not right
If I am wrong. But if I am young, and right,
What does my age matter?

CREON: You think it right to stand up for an anarchist?

HAIMON: Not at all. I pay no respect to criminals.

CREON: Then she is not a criminal?

HAIMON: The City would deny it, to a man.

CREON: And the City proposes to teach me how to rule?

HAIMON: Ah. Who is it that's talking like a boy now?

CREON: My voice is the one voice giving orders in this City!

HAIMON: It is no City if it takes orders from one voice.

CREON: The State is the King!

HAIMON: Yes, if the State is a desert.

(*Pause.*)

CREON: This boy, it seems, has sold out to a woman.

HAIMON: If you are a woman: my concern is only for you.

CREON: So? Your "concern"! In a public brawl with your father!

HAIMON: How about you, in a public brawl with justice?

CREON: With justice, when all that I do is within my rights?

HAIMON: You have no right to trample on God's right.

CREON (*completely out of control*): Fool, adolescent fool! Taken in by a woman!

HAIMON: You'll never see me taken in by anything vile.

CREON: Every word you say is for her!

HAIMON (*quietly, darkly*): And for you.

And for me. And for the gods under the earth.
CREON: You'll never marry her while she lives.
HAIMON: Then she must die. — But her death will cause another.
CREON: Another?
Have you lost your senses? Is this an open threat?
HAIMON: There is no threat in speaking to emptiness.
CREON: I swear you'll regret this superior tone of yours!
You are the empty one!
HAIMON: If you were not my father,
I'd say you were perverse.
CREON: You girlstruck fool, don't play at words with me!
HAIMON: I am sorry. You prefer silence.
CREON: Now, by God — !
I swear, by all the gods in heaven above us,
You'll watch it, I swear you shall!
(*To the* SERVANTS.) Bring her out!
Bring the woman out! Let her die before his eyes!
Here, this instant, with her bridegroom beside her!
HAIMON: Not here, no; she will not die here, King.
And you will never see my face again.
Go on raving as long as you've a friend to endure you.

(*Exit* HAIMON.)

CHORAGOS: Gone, gone.
Creon, a young man in a rage is dangerous!
CREON: Let him do, or dream to do, more than a man can.
He shall not save these girls from death.
CHORAGOS: These girls?
You have sentenced them both?
CREON: No, you are right.
I will not kill the one whose hands are clean.
CHORAGOS: But Antigone?
CREON (*somberly*): I will carry her far away
Out there in the wilderness, and lock her
Living in a vault of stone. She shall have food,
As the custom is, to absolve the State of her death.
And there let her pray to the gods of hell:
They are her only gods:
Perhaps they will show her an escape from death,
Or she may learn,
though late,
That piety shown the dead is pity in vain.

(*Exit* CREON.)

ODE III

CHORUS: Love, unconquerable [STROPHE
Waster of rich men, keeper
Of warm lights and all-night vigil
In the soft face of a girl:
Sea-wanderer, forest-visitor!
Even the pure Immortals cannot escape you,
And mortal man, in his one day's dusk,
Trembles before your glory.

Surely you swerve upon ruin [ANTISTROPHE
The just man's consenting heart,
As here you have made bright anger
Strike between father and son —
And none has conquered but Love!
A girl's glánce wórking the will of heaven:
Pleasure to her alone who mocks us,
Merciless Aphrodite.

SCENE IV

(*As* ANTIGONE *enters guarded.*)

CHORAGOS: But I can no longer stand in awe of this,
Nor, seeing what I see, keep back my tears.
Here is Antigone, passing to that chamber
Where all find sleep at last.

ANTIGONE: Look upon me, friends, and pity me [STROPHE 1
Turning back at the night's edge to say
Good-by to the sun that shines for me no longer;
Now sleepy Death
Summons me down to Acheron, that cold shore:
There is no bridesong there, nor any music.
CHORUS: Yet not unpraised, not without a kind of honor,
You walk at last into the underworld;
Untouched by sickness, broken by no sword.
What woman has ever found your way to death?

ANTIGONE: How often I have heard the story of Niobe, [ANTISTROPHE 1

Tantalos' wretched daughter, how the stone
Clung fast about her, ivy-close: and they say
The rain falls endlessly
And sifting soft snow; her tears are never done.
I feel the loneliness of her death in mine.
CHORUS: But she was born of heaven, and you
Are woman, woman-born. If her death is yours,
A mortal woman's, is this not for you
Glory in our world and in the world beyond?

ANTIGONE: You laugh at me. Ah, friends, friends, [STROPHE 2
Can you not wait until I am dead? O Thebes,
O men many-charioted, in love with Fortune,
Dear springs of Dirce, sacred Theban grove,
Be witnesses for me, denied all pity,
Unjustly judged! and think a word of love
For her whose path turns
Under dark earth, where there are no more tears.
CHORUS: You have passed beyond human daring and come at last
Into a place of stone where Justice sits.
I cannot tell
What shape of your father's guilt appears in this.

ANTIGONE: You have touched it at last: that bridal bed [ANTISTROPHE 2
Unspeakable, horror of son and mother mingling:
Their crime, infection of all our family!
O Oedipus, father and brother!
Your marriage strikes from the grave to murder mine.
I have been a stranger here in my own land:
All my life
The blasphemy of my birth has followed me.
CHORUS: Reverence is a virtue, but strength
Lives in established law: that must prevail.
You have made your choice,
Your death is the doing of your conscious hand.

ANTIGONE: Then let me go, since all your words are bitter, [EPODE
And the very light of the sun is cold to me.
Lead me to my vigil, where I must have
Neither love nor lamentation; no song, but silence.

(CREON *interrupts impatiently.*)

CREON: If dirges and planned lamentations could put off death,
Men would be singing for ever.
(*To the* SERVANTS.) Take her, go!
You know your orders: take her to the vault
And leave her alone there. And if she lives or dies,
That's her affair, not ours: our hands are clean.
ANTIGONE: O tomb, vaulted bride-bed in eternal rock,
Soon I shall be with my own again
Where Persephone welcomes the thin ghosts underground:
And I shall see my father again, and you, mother,
And dearest Polyneices —
dearest indeed
To me, since it was my hand
That washed him clean and poured the ritual wine:
And my reward is death before my time!

And yet, as men's hearts know, I have done no wrong,
I have not sinned before God. Or if I have,
I shall know the truth in death. But if the guilt
Lies upon Creon who judged me, then, I pray,
May his punishment equal my own.
CHORAGOS: O passionate heart,
Unyielding, tormented still by the same winds!
CREON: Her guards shall have good cause to regret their delaying.
ANTIGONE: Ah! That voice is like the voice of death!
CREON: I can give you no reason to think you are mistaken.
ANTIGONE: Thebes, and you my fathers' gods,
And rulers of Thebes, you see me now, the last
Unhappy daughter of a line of kings,
Your kings, led away to death. You will remember
What things I suffer, and at what men's hands,
Because I would not transgress the laws of heaven.

(*To the* GUARDS, *simply.*)

Come: let us wait no longer.

(*Exit* ANTIGONE, *L., guarded.*)

ODE IV

CHORUS: All Danae's beauty was locked away [STROPHE 1
In a brazen cell where the sunlight could not come:

A small room, still as any grave, enclosed her.
Yet she was a princess too,
And Zeus in a rain of gold poured love upon her.
O child, child,
No power in wealth or war
Or tough sea-blackened ships
Can prevail against untiring Destiny!

And Dryas' son also, that furious king, [ANTISTROPHE 1
Bore the god's prisoning anger for his pride:
Sealed up by Dionysos in deaf stone,
His madness died among echoes.
So at the last he learned what dreadful powei
His tongue had mocked:
For he had profaned the revels,
And fired the wrath of the nine
Implacable Sisters that love the sound of the flute.

And old men tell a half-remembered tale [STROPHE 2
Of horror done where a dark ledge splits the sea
And a double surf beats on the gráy shóres:
How a king's new woman, sick
With hatred for the queen he had imprisoned,
Ripped out his two sons' eyes with her bloody hands
While grinning Ares watched the shuttle plunge
Four times: four blind wounds crying for revenge,

Crying, tears and blood mingled. — Piteously born, [ANTISTROPHE 2
Those sons whose mother was of heavenly birth!
Her father was the god of the North Wind
And she was cradled by gales,
She raced with young colts on the glittering hills
And walked untrammeled in the open light:
But in her marriage deathless Fate found means
To build a tomb like yours for all her joy.

SCENE V

(*Enter blind* TEIRESIAS, *led by a* BOY. *The opening speeches of* TEIRESIAS *should be in singsong contrast to the realistic lines of* CREON.)

TEIRESIAS: This is the way the blind man comes, Princes, Princes,
Lock-step, two heads lit by the eyes of one.
CREON: What new thing have you to tell us, old Teiresias?
TEIRESIAS: I have much to tell you: listen to the prophet, Creon.
CREON: I am not aware that I have ever failed to listen.
TEIRESIAS: Then you have done wisely, King, and ruled well.
CREON: I admit my debt to you. But what have you to say?
TEIRESIAS: This, Creon: you stand once more on the edge of fate.
CREON: What do you mean? Your words are a kind of dread.
TEIRESIAS: Listen, Creon:
I was sitting in my chair of augury, at the place
Where the birds gather about me. They were all a-chatter,
As is their habit, when suddenly I heard
A strange note in their jangling, a scream, a
Whirring fury; I knew that they were fighting,
Tearing each other, dying
In a whirlwind of wings clashing. And I was afraid.
I began the rites of burnt-offering at the altar,
But Hephaistos failed me: instead of bright flame,
There was only the sputtering slime of the fat thigh-flesh
Melting: the entrails dissolved in gray smoke,
The bare bone burst from the welter. And no blaze!

This was a sign from heaven. My boy described it,
Seeing for me as I see for others.

I tell you, Creon, you yourself have brought
This new calamity upon us. Our hearths and altars
Are stained with the corruption of dogs and carrion birds
That glut themselves on the corpse of Oedipus' son.
The gods are deaf when we pray to them, their fire
Recoils from our offering, their birds of omen
Have no cry of comfort, for they are gorged
With the thick blood of the dead.
O my son,
These are no trifles! Think: all men make mistakes,

But a good man yields when he knows his course is wrong,
And repairs the evil. The only crime is pride.

Give in to the dead man, then: do not fight with a corpse —
What glory is it to kill a man who is dead?
Think, I beg you:
It is for your own good that I speak as I do.
You should be able to yield for your own good.

CREON: It seems that prophets have made me their especial province.
All my life long
I have been a kind of butt for the dull arrows
Of doddering fortune-tellers!
No, Teiresias:
If your birds — if the great eagles of God himself
Should carry him stinking bit by bit to heaven,
I would not yield. I am not afraid of pollution:
No man can defile the gods.
Do what you will,
Go into business, make money, speculate
In India gold or that synthetic gold from Sardis,
Get rich otherwise than by my consent to bury him.
Teiresias, it is a sorry thing when a wise man
Sells his wisdom, lets out his words for hire!
TEIRESIAS: Ah Creon! Is there no man left in the world —
CREON: To do what? — come, let's have the aphorism!
TEIRESIAS: No man who knows that wisdom outweighs any wealth?
CREON: As surely as bribes are baser than any baseness.
TEIRESIAS: You are sick, Creon! You are deathly sick!
CREON: As you say: it is not my place to challenge a prophet.
TEIRESIAS: Yet you have said my prophecy is for sale.
CREON: The generation of prophets has always loved gold.
TEIRESIAS: The generation of kings has always loved brass.
CREON: You forget yourself! You are speaking to your King.
TEIRESIAS: I know it. You are a king because of me.
CREON: You have a certain skill; but you have sold out.
TEIRESIAS: King, you will drive me to words that —
CREON: Say them, say them!
Only remember: I will not pay you for them.
TEIRESIAS: No, you will find them too costly.
CREON: No doubt. Speak:
Whatever you say, you will not change my will.
TEIRESIAS: Then take this, and take it to heart!

The time is not far off when you shall pay back
Corpse for corpse, flesh of your own flesh.
You have thrust the child of this world into living night,
You have kept from the gods below the child that is theirs:
The one in a grave before her death, the other,
Dead, denied the grave. This is your crime:
And the Furies and the dark gods of Hell
Are swift with terrible punishment for you.

Do you want to buy me now, Creon?
Not many days,
And your house will be full of men and women weeping,
And curses will be hurled at you from far
Cities grieving for sons unburied, left to rot
Before the walls of Thebes.

These are my arrows, Creon: they are all for you.

(*To* BOY.)

But come, child: lead me home.
Let him waste his fine anger upon younger men.
Maybe he will learn at last
To control a wiser tongue in a better head.

(*Exit* TEIRESIAS.)

CHORAGOS: The old man has gone, King, but his words
Remain to plague us. I am old, too,
But I cannot remember that he was ever false.
CREON: That is true. . . . It troubles me.
Oh it is hard to give in! but it is worse
To risk everything for stubborn pride.
CHORAGOS: Creon: take my advice.
CREON: What shall I do?
CHORAGOS: Go quickly: free Antigone from her vault
And build a tomb for the body of Polyneices.
CREON: You would have me do this?
CHORAGOS: Creon, yes!
And it must be done at once: God moves
Swiftly to cancel the folly of stubborn men.
CREON: It is hard to deny the heart! But I
Will do it: I will not fight with destiny.
CHORAGOS: You must go yourself, you cannot leave it to others.

CREON: I will go.
— Bring axes, servants:
Come with me to the tomb. I buried her, I
Will set her free.
Oh quickly!
My mind misgives —
The laws of the gods are mighty, and a man must serve them
To the last day of his life!

(*Exit* CREON.)

PAEAN

CHORAGOS: God of many names [STROPHE 1
CHORUS: O Iacchos
son
of Kadmeian Sémele
O born of the Thunder!
Guardian of the West
Regent
of Eleusis' plain
O Prince of maenad Thebes
and the Dragon Field by rippling Ismenos:

CHORAGOS: God of many names [ANTISTROPHE 1
CHORUS: the flame of torches
flares on our hills
the nymphs of Iacchos
dance at the spring of Castalia:

from the vine-close mountain
come ah come in ivy:
Evohé evohé! sings through the streets of Thebes

CHORAGOS: God of many names [STROPHE 2
CHORUS: Iacchos of Thebes
heavenly Child
of Sémele bride of the Thunderer!
The shadow of plague is upon us:
come
with clement feet
oh come from Parnasos

down the long slopes
                across the lamenting water

CHORAGOS: Io Fire! Chorister of the throbbing stars! [ANTISTROPHE 2
O purest among the voices of the night!
Thou son of God, blaze for us!
CHORUS: Come with choric rapture of circling Maenads
Who cry *Io Iacche!*
                God of many names!

EXODOS

(*Enter* MESSENGER, *L.*)

MESSENGER: Men of the line of Kadmos, you who live
Near Amphion's citadel:
                I cannot say
Of any condition of human life "This is fixed,
This is clearly good, or bad." Fate raises up,
And Fate casts down the happy and unhappy alike:
No man can foretell his Fate.
                Take the case of Creon:
Creon was happy once, as I count happiness:
Victorious in battle, sole governor of the land,
Fortunate father of children nobly born.
And now it has all gone from him! Who can say
That a man is still alive when his life's joy fails?
He is a walking dead man. Grant him rich,
Let him live like a king in his great house:
If his pleasure is gone, I would not give
So much as the shadow of smoke for all he owns.
CHORAGOS: Your words hint at sorrow: what is your news for us?
MESSENGER: They are dead. The living are guilty of their death.
CHORAGOS: Who is guilty? Who is dead? Speak!
MESSENGER: Haimon.
Haimon is dead; and the hand that killed him
Is his own hand.
CHORAGOS: His father's? or his own?
MESSENGER: His own, driven mad by the murder his father had done.
CHORAGOS: Teiresias, Teiresias, how clearly you saw it all!
MESSENGER: This is my news: you must draw what conclusions you can from it.

CHORAGOS: But look: Eurydice, our Queen:
Has she overheard us?

(*Enter* EURYDICE *from the Palace, C.*)

EURYDICE: I have heard something, friends:
As I was unlocking the gate of Pallas' shrine,
For I needed her help today, I heard a voice
Telling of some new sorrow. And I fainted
There at the temple with all my maidens about me.
But speak again: whatever it is, I can bear it:
Grief and I are no strangers.
MESSENGER: Dearest Lady,
I will tell you plainly all that I have seen.
I shall not try to comfort you: what is the use,
Since comfort could lie only in what is not true?
The truth is always best.
I went with Creon
To the outer plain where Polyneices was lying,
No friend to pity him, his body shredded by dogs.
We made our prayers in that place to Hecate
And Pluto, that they would be merciful. And we bathed
The corpse with holy water, and we brought
Fresh-broken branches to burn what was left of it,
And upon the urn we heaped up a towering barrow
Of the earth of his own land.
When we were done, we ran
To the vault where Antigone lay on her couch of stone.
One of the servants had gone ahead,
And while he was yet far off he heard a voice
Grieving within the chamber, and he came back
And told Creon. And as the King went closer,
The air was full of wailing, the words lost,
And he begged us to make all haste. "Am I a prophet?"
He said, weeping, "And must I walk this road,
The saddest of all that I have gone before?
My son's voice calls me on. Oh quickly, quickly!
Look through the crevice there, and tell me
If it is Haimon, or some deception of the gods!"
We obeyed; and in the cavern's farthest corner
We saw her lying:
She had made a noose of her fine linen veil
And hanged herself. Haimon lay beside her,
His arms about her waist, lamenting her,

His love lost under ground, crying out
That his father had stolen her away from him.
When Creon saw him the tears rushed to his eyes
And he called to him: "What have you done, child? Speak to me.
What are you thinking that makes your eyes so strange?
O my son, my son, I come to you on my knees!"
But Haimon spat in his face. He said not a word,
Staring —
And suddenly drew his sword
And lunged. Creon shrank back, the blade missed; and the boy,
Desperate against himself, drove it half its length
Into his own side, and fell. And as he died
He gathered Antigone close in his arms again,
Choking, his blood bright red on her white cheek.
And now he lies dead with the dead, and she is his
At last, his bride in the houses of the dead.

(*Exit* EURYDICE *into the Palace.*)

CHORAGOS: She has left us without a word. What can this mean?
MESSENGER: It troubles me, too; yet she knows what is best,
Her grief is too great for public lamentation,
And doubtless she has gone to her chamber to weep
For her dead son, leading her maidens in his dirge.
CHORAGOS: It may be so: but I fear this deep silence.

(*Pause.*)

MESSENGER: I will see what she is doing. I will go in.

(*Exit* MESSENGER *into the Palace. Enter* CREON *with attendants, bearing* HAIMON's *body.*)

CHORAGOS: But here is the King himself: oh look at him,
Bearing his own damnation in his arms.
CREON: Nothing you say can touch me any more.
My own blind heart has brought me
From darkness to final darkness. Here you see
The father murdering, the murdered son —
And all my civic wisdom!

Haimon my son, so young, so young to die,
I was the fool, not you; and you died for me.
CHORAGOS: That is the truth; but you were late in learning it.
CREON: This truth is hard to bear. Surely a god
Has crushed me beneath the hugest weight of heaven.

And driven me headlong a barbaric way
To trample out the thing I held most dear.

The pains that men will take to come to pain!

(*Enter* MESSENGER *from the Palace.*)

MESSENGER: The burden you carry in your hands is heavy,
But it is not all: you will find more in your house.
CREON: What burden worse than this shall I find there?
MESSENGER: The Queen is dead.
CREON: O port of death, deaf world,
Is there no pity for me? And you, Angel of evil,
I was dead, and your words are death again.
Is it true, boy? Can it be true?
Is my wife dead? Has death bred death?
MESSENGER: You can see for yourself.

(*The doors are opened, and the body of* EURYDICE *is disclosed within.*)

CREON: Oh pity!
All true, all true, and more than I can bear!
O my wife, my son!
MESSENGER: She stood before the altar, and her heart
Welcomed the knife her own hand guided,
And a great cry burst from her lips for Megareus dead,
And for Haimon dead, her sons; and her last breath
Was a curse for their father, the murderer of her sons.
And she fell, and the dark flowed in through her closing eyes.
CREON: O God, I am sick with fear.
Are there no swords here? Has no one a blow for me?
MESSENGER: Her curse is upon you for the deaths of both.
CREON: It is right that it should be. I alone am guilty.
I know it, and I say it. Lead me in,
Quickly, friends.
I have neither life nor substance. Lead me in.
CHORAGOS: You are right, if there can be right in so much wrong.
The briefest way is best in a world of sorrow.
CREON: Let it come,
Let death come quickly, and be kind to me.
I would not ever see the sun again.
CHORAGOS: All that will come when it will; but we, meanwhile,
Have much to do. Leave the future to itself.
CREON: All my heart was in that prayer!

CHORAGOS: Then do not pray any more: the sky is deaf.
CREON: Lead me away. I have been rash and foolish.
I have killed my son and my wife.
I look for comfort; my comfort lies here dead.
Whatever my hands have touched has come to nothing.
Fate has brought all my pride to a thought of dust.

(*As* CREON *is being led into the house, the* CHORAGOS *advances and speaks directly to the audience.*)

CHORAGOS: There is no happiness where there is no wisdom;
No wisdom but in submission to the gods.
Big words are always punished,
And proud men in old age learn to be wise.

IACCHOS OF THEBES . . .

The shadow of plague is upon us:
come
with clement feet
oh come from Parnassos
down the long slopes
across the lamenting water

So chants the Chorus in dark apprehension of further doom as the shaken Creon goes off to save his victim Antigone. The invocation of Dionysos, the many-named god of fertility and rebirth, is only incidental to the plot proper, but it is very much to the purpose of the tragic feeling in the play, and it is everything to an understanding of the position of tragedy in the communal life of fifth-century Athens.* In the spring of every year three tetralogies (three tragedies and a satyr play, all acted in one day) were selected for performance in a competition that was part of the larger rites of the Greater (or Urban) Dionysia. Although we do not know the origin of tragedy, nothing in the plays themselves nor in what we know of the manner of their performance prevents our believing that tragic drama arose from the desire in the celebrants of nature's seasonal revival to express, in music, movement, chant, and spectacle, their sense of divine power over human

* By tragic drama in this connection is meant serious drama on metaphysically important themes but not necessarily of catastrophic outcome. The word "tragedy" means literally "goat-song," perhaps with reference to the early satyr plays in which the choric performers of the dithyrambic dance-song were dressed in goat skins.

life. Staging and acting in Dionysiac plays was a religious and civic obligation on free citizens and victory in the contest one of the supreme communal honors. For us drama is primarily entertainment, or, at most, stimulus to reflection and debate. To a fifth-century Athenian it was a ceremony that was meaningful in more than one area of his being. Only with this in mind will we understand the partly extra-dramatic function of the chorus as a kind of audience representative on the periphery of the action, worried and ignorant, affected by what happens but not participant in it.

Our knowledge of the specific physical features of the Dionysiac theater of Athens is uncertain. The audience — perhaps as many as 15,000 — was seated on benches in rising concentric tiers on the southeastern slope of the Acropolis. The plays were enacted before a long, low, wooden building (*skene*), that served both as dressing room and as the palace front of conventional dramatic setting. The main action took place immediately before it. Nearer the audience and probably on a somewhat lower level was a circular area (*orchestra*), with an altar for Dionysos in the center. Here the chorus — in Sophoclean tragedy a group of fifteen men — led by the Choragos and accompanied by flute playing, moved in slow and stately measures while chanting lyrical odes dealing with the inscrutable ways of gods with men and usually having some particular reference to the immediate dramatic situation. Thus, when Haimon, desperate and angry, leaves at the end of Scene III after pleading in vain with his father for Antigone's life, the Chorus praises the power of Aphrodite, the goddess of love. The odes were divided into stanzas, called *strophes* and *antistrophes*, delivered, respectively, as the chorus moved first in one and then in the opposite direction. In the absence of a curtain one function of the odes was to mark the divisions between the different episodes (the first of which was the *prologos*, the last the *exodos*). Both actors and chorus wore masks, partly for reasons of acoustics (the masks served as sound chambers) and partly in order to create an impression of de-personalized and universal myth. They were dressed in colored robes and (probably) wore elevated shoes (*kothurnoi*). Women's parts were played by men. Performance of a tetralogy took most of the daylight hours.

Antigone was written about 440 B.C., when Sophocles was already in his mid-fifties. It is among his earliest plays. We do not know its fortune in the annual competition, but together with *Oedipus Rex* (not part of the same tetralogy; we don't have *Antigone*'s companion pieces), *Antigone* is traditionally considered one of the purest specimens of Greek tragedy.

The two plays have more in common than a high reputation. In both Sophocles imparts a tragic lesson about man's powerlessness before the gods, and in both he does so by means of the old legend of the divine curse on the Theban royal family, the house of Labdacus.* Dramatic irony is important in both, as it almost inevitably must be in any literary expression of man's tragic–absurd awareness of the perils of his position. Dramatic irony is what we are aware of when, in something said or in some circumstance of the plot, we sense a meaning beyond or at odds with the overt meaning. Below the surface truth there is a larger truth, usually inimical to the speaker and unsuspected by him. When Oedipus in *Oedipus Rex* swears to revenge the murdered King Laios "as if he were my own father," it is by dramatic irony that we sense the nature of his approaching doom. We are dealing here not just with an artistic device or a trick of playmaking but with a mode of language by which parts of a complex truth are perceived and held in suspension. The irony points up the discrepancy between what the speaker is and what he thinks he is — between what is and what appears to be. It gives expression, situational or verbal, to the inadequacy of man's defenses and the folly of his feeling of safety and power (*hubris*) in an existence he can actually neither comprehend nor control. It is the literary equivalent of the paradox that we both master and are mastered by our circumstances, that our entrapment in time gives to each of our free acts a terrible and final significance. It is existential tension encapsuled and made available for disinterested contemplation. Creon's telling the Chorus that the defiant Antigone "has much to learn" and his words to the girl herself that "your death will give me everything" convey, in context, a sense that pride and complacency are forms of ignorance.

The tragic place is bare and bleak and its climate violent. Tragic life runs to extremes, stripped of the softening and sheltering loose ends and compromises, half-tones and compensations, of ordinary

* Labdacus' son was Laios. Despite Laios' and his wife Jocasta's efforts to circumvent the prophecy of the Delphic oracle, he was killed by his son Oedipus, who next, in further unwitting fulfilment of his destiny, married Jocasta. Their children were Eteocles, Polyneices, Ismene, and Antigone. Later Oedipus discovered his true parentage and realized that his terrible fate had come to pass.

There is nothing extraordinary in the fact that the story of *Oedipus Rex* is referred to in *Antigone*, though the latter is the earlier of the two plays. The history of the royal house of Thebes was part of traditional legend and as well known to Sophocles' audience as to Sophocles himself. For a playwright there is limitation in this but also strength. He is tied to the known facts, but by the same token he can dispense with the laborious exposition that clutters many an "original" play of more modern times. With the tragic myth given, he can proceed at once to essentials: not the telling of a story but dramatizing its meaning.

life. In Aeschylean and Sophoclean tragedy dramatic movement is so spare and single and so momentous that the busy fuss of illusionism would be an impertinence. Larger issues are involved than making the world look and sound like everyday reality. Tragic realism confronts man with the supernatural dimension. When Aristotle said (in the *Poetics*) that the end of tragedy is imitation of action, he did not lay down a law. He was being inductive; he stated what seemed to him a fact about existing plays. They were imitations of action not by being faithful copies of appearances (as is representational art), but by dramatizing archetypes.

The function of tragedy, Aristotle says, is to effect *katharsis, i.e.,* the purgation of the emotions of pity and fear in the audience. The exact meaning of the concept has been debated, but the medical denotation suggests that Aristotle had in mind some kind of soul therapy: witnessing the tragic action the spectator harmlessly expends his subrational passions on vicarious suffering. Because the effect presupposes a degree of audience identification, the protagonist can be neither vicious nor perfect. Suffering vice commands no sympathy, and suffering perfection would seem merely preposterous.

Art is moral to the extent that it furthers the percipient's grasp of reality, principally the reality of himself. But the nature of that for which a moral function is predicated is, precisely, artistic, and all criticism is in a sense criticism of form. First, because form and moral content are inseparable (though not indistinguishable), just as the "meaning" of any work of art inheres in the configuration our senses perceive rather than, abstractly, in any detachable dictum. Thus, in the middle part of *Antigone* the changes in Creon's emotions from the sententiousness of his opening address to the Chorus, through his anger and contempt and impatience in the scenes with the two sisters and with Haimon, to his fear of Teiresias constitute a scenic image of instability that defines a condition in which and by which man suffers. Second, the achievement of meaningful form is itself meaningful. In tragedy the containment of metaphysics in coherent speech-action is a demiurgic gesture shaping order out of debris, beauty out of pain. In the imagined world his art makes, man, the maker, triumphs over agony and anger by transfixing them in art's frozen moment. Form illumines his fate and allows him to see that it matters. This is why elation and dignity, not depression, attend the tragic vision and *katharsis* becomes one with enlightenment.

The action of both *Oedipus Rex* and *Antigone* illustrates the tragic formula of "the evil that good men do." Creon is unaware, till it is too late, of what he is doing to his life. But if good intentions exculpate, does he deserve his punishment? "The sky is deaf." Tragedy cannot answer; it only shows punishment taking place. If the spectacle offends our sense of justice, so be it. Existence is not answerable before our puny tribunals. What the play *does* do is describe a dramatic movement that exactly covers its larger "truth." When the play begins, Antigone is alone against all the others: Ismene, Creon, the Chorus, the Guard. At the end it is Creon who is isolated. First Ismene, then Haimon, take Antigone's side. Then Teiresias appears with his warning, the Chorus wavers in fear and uncertainty, Creon himself goes off to submit to his enemy, and finally the eloquent Messenger takes the boorish Guard's place as spokesman for the common soldier's judgment on the issue between king and girl. The shift in public support from one to the other is as simple and striking as theater as it is subtle in meaning. Take the Guard. Too often dismissed as mere "comic relief," actually his two appearances (apart from their obvious plot function) foreshadow in a lower key Creon's equally sudden and unexpected change of attitude near the end. First timid and trembling, then all smug swagger, the Guard undergoes a psychological movement that is reversely analogous to Creon's from imperious bluster to broken pathos. He serves to make Sophocles' religious point that clown and king alike are pawns in the hands of higher powers that mock man's firmest resolutions.

That Creon rather than Antigone might be the tragic protagonist may seem contradicted by the title, and the issue of whose play *Antigone* is is less simple than the discussion above has suggested. Without Antigone, no challenge, no conflict, no play. The tragedy is double: first hers, then Creon's. But the title does not imply her tragic precedence — if it did the play would be imbalanced, as she disappears about two thirds of the way through — and her almost perfect integrity of character and singleness of purpose suggest a saint rather than an erring and embattled hero. The tragic status of the sainted martyr is problematic, for eschatology annuls the tragic premise that human existence is finite. The saint's tragedy is less the saint's own than the world's, which in ignorance deprives itself of its savior. Of the two tragic destinies in the play, only Creon's completes the tragic arc into self-recognition: "I have been rash and foolish." By the time the play ends, Antigone's and Ismene's opening scene appears as the first phase in Creon's tragedy, a prologue introducing the issue on which he is going to be wrecked.

Antigone is simple where Creon is complex, strong where he is weak. Her mind is made up from the beginning, and hardly anything happens to her that she has not foreseen. Her strength marks her "right" against her uncle's "wrong," but it also comes close to making her a character without inner conflict. She is dramatically the less interesting of the two. Her humanity is first evident in the scene (II) in which Ismene appears a second time and pleads with her sister to let her share her punishment. Its point is not the superfluous one of strengthening the justice of Antigone's cause but the rescue of Creon's antagonist from the thin, chill air of homiletic parable. In her cruelty to Ismene the professional martyr vanishes and the anguished young woman takes her place, jealous of the lonely glory of her death.*

For Antigone's character is compact with uncompromising religious idealism, which the play consistently presents as an absolute right (in both senses of the word), and her martyrdom is victory and not defeat. But for Creon both the inner and the outer universe go to pieces. When Antigone departs for her cave death at the end of Scene IV, the conflict is no longer that of two equally stubborn convictions. It, too, turns inward, as Creon's *hubris* begins to disintegrate under the successive blows of religious fear and family deaths. Perhaps the grimmest irony of all in the play is the fact that he who would force his sister's child and his son's bride to repudiate a family bond pays for his tyranny with the loss of niece, son, and wife. Eurydice's late entry into the action only to die is therefore not gratuitous melodrama. It illustrates the rationale of tragic nemesis, the power of retribution.

To Creon, newly called to power and as yet untried in authority, anarchy is the greatest evil. In the light of the immediate Theban past he can hardly be held to be wrong. And his fierce stubbornness in upholding his edict does not so much bespeak a tyrant's temper as the defense mechanism of a troubled and conscientious man in a responsible position in which he has yet to prove himself. He cannot afford to see more than one side of the issue. Political circumstance joins his own character in limiting his vision to the immediate business of governing a war-torn state. A more fatal limitation in his psyche, one of imagination, is suggested by his repeated assertion that money must be the motive behind the unlawful burial of Polyneices.

Up to a point Creon's attitude is of course right. Within the sphere of good government and social order anarchy is indeed a very great evil. But there is a sphere, the play says, beyond law and order which Creon, the anxious king, has lost sight of. On one level the conflict between Antigone and him is a conflict between individual liberty—

* Read in this light, the scene serves to support Professor Kitto's contention (in *Greek Tragedy*) that there is added tragic feeling and psychological penetration in Antigone's pitifully sophistical defense of her action on the grounds that only a brother is worthy of the sacrifice she makes, because, both her parents being dead, a brother, unlike a husband and a son, is irreplaceable. Fitts and Fitzgerald omit the passage from their translation as "dismal stuff," which "the best critics" have thought spurious. It consists of sixteen lines at the very end of Scene IV, just before Antigone asks to be led away.

freedom of faith, if one likes — and a totalitarian tyranny that presumes to dictate to the individual conscience in all areas of life. It was as exponent of this topical theme that the play was performed on several of Europe's liberated stages right after World War II. But on another level the dramatic allegory is not political at all or even ethical, but religious, and the conflict is one between eternal and temporal schemes of value, or, more exactly, between a sacramental and a civic–pragmatic view of life. Not that Creon's tragic flaw (*hamartia*) is that he is irreligious. He, too, is sure that he executes the will of the gods. But it does not occur to him that the gods rule by higher considerations than those of police-state expediency. As the purely symbolic nature of Antigone's burial of Polyneices suggests, disposal of a body is not the issue but which of two allegiances is to have priority, that to the state or that to the gods. By pursuing punishment of the traitor (and note that Antigone never denies the justice of Creon's label for her brother) beyond the limits of life Creon seeks to extend his rule into eschatological regions. In retaliation, the angry gods strike the trespasser down. Again truth is communicated in dramatic irony: Theban events prove that he who is nothing but a good citizen fails to be even that, for Antigone's course of action would have saved the city from further supernatural visitation. By the laws of a larger realm than the city state it is Creon himself, the usurper of divine power, who stands convicted of anarchy. And the difference in the nature of the two realms is pointed up in the paradox — from the world's point of view — that a young girl, a subject, triumphs over a mature man, a king.

The Messenger who reports Creon's punishment expresses a wisdom of humble resignation to the fact of human finitude that keeps man from challenging fate.

> I cannot say
> Of any condition of human life, "This is fixed,
> This is clearly good or bad." Fate raises up,
> And Fate casts down the happy and unhappy alike:
> No man can foretell his Fate.
> Take the case of Creon:
> . . .
> I would not give
> So much as the shadow of smoke for all he owns.

The Messenger is the individual spokesman for this view — the classical view — of human existence. The Chorus is the communal voice. With Sophocles the chorus is not, as with Aeschylos, one of the two main actors in the tragic dialogue, but neither is it the merely traditional and rather cumbersome appendage that it tended to be with Euripides. At times, its comments here are amusingly naive, as when it remains anxiously neutral in the quarrel between father and son:

> You will do well to listen to him, King,
> If what he says is sensible. And you, Haimon,
> Must listen to your father. — Both speak well.

The choric odes are above such comical inanity. Often they extend the relevance of the archetypal action by mythical allusion (as in Ode IV), or they contribute to the pervasive ironic pattern by expressing the fears and ignorance of the common man. A particularly striking example is the first ode, which praises ingenious man's many achievements. Its second strophe ends in what we later perceive to have been an ominous warning:

> . . . from every wind
> He [man] has made himself secure — from all but one:
> In the late wind of death he cannot stand.

This is what the play is about: the fact that with death the survivor's control must cease, lest he transcend the limits set to mortality, and the fact of death itself — here Antigone's, Haimon's, and Eurydice's — which smashes all Creon's arrogance.

Literally, the Chorus is a group of old Thebans — councillors, according to traditional interpretation. As such, they speak in character when they chant the triumphant end of the war with Argos and when the Choragos sums up the meaning of Creon's fate:

> There is no happiness where there is no wisdom;
> No wisdom but in submission to the gods.

The Chorus's continuous stage presence relates Creon's tragedy to the weal of the community he meant to govern so well. Creon's tragic dilemma of reconciling allegiance to the world with allegiance to the world's supernatural rulers is everyman's dilemma.

But his royal position implies that his failure to resolve the dilemma matters more than everyman's. The calamity that follows upon his sacrilegious refusal to bury the dead Polyneices is, as Teiresias knows, not just Creon's but all Thebes'. Creon's suffering is public expiation for an act of suprapersonal consequence, for in the traditional view the king incarnates his people. His fall from fortune followed from his kingly rank, and his redemptive suffering is therefore properly witnessed by representatives of the people whose scapegoat the stricken king of the myth, innocent of intent if not of act, in the end becomes. In the tragic spectacle of the "rash and foolish" Creon the Athenian spectator sensed his own ambiguous position in the cosmic drama and his own dark destiny — both as man and as citizen.

William Shakespeare

OTHELLO

Characters

DUKE OF VENICE
BRABANTIO, *a Senator*
SENATORS
GRATIANO, *Brother to Brabantio*
LODOVICO, *Kinsman to Brabantio*
OTHELLO, *a noble Moor; in the service of the Venetian State*
CASSIO, *his Lieutenant*
IAGO, *his Ancient*
RODERIGO, *a Venetian Gentleman*
MONTANO, *Othello's predecessor in the Government of Cyprus*
CLOWN, *Servant to Othello*
DESDEMONA, *Daughter to Brabantio, and Wife to Othello*
EMILIA, *Wife to Iago*
BIANCA, *Mistress to Cassio*
SAILOR, OFFICERS, GENTLEMEN, MESSENGERS, MUSICIANS, HERALDS, ATTENDANTS

SCENE: *For the first Act, in Venice; during the rest of the Play, at a Sea-port in Cyprus*

ACT I

Scene 1 [Venice. A street.]

(*Enter* RODERIGO *and* IAGO.)

RODERIGO: Tush! Never tell me; I take it much unkindly
That thou, Iago, who hast had my purse

As if the strings were thine, shouldst know of this.[1]
IAGO: 'Sblood,[2] but you will not hear me:
If ever I did dream of such a matter,
Abhor me.
RODERIGO: Thou told'st me thou didst hold him[3] in thy hate.
IAGO: Despise me if I do not. Three great ones of the city,
In personal suit to make me his lieutenant,
Off-capp'd[4] to him; and, by the faith of man,
I know my price, I am worth no worse a place;
But he, as loving his own pride and purposes,
Evades them, with a bombast circumstance[5]
Horribly stuff'd with epithets of war;
And, in conclusion,
Nonsuits[6] my mediators;[7] for, 'Certes,'[8] says he,
'I have already chose my officer.'
And what was he?
Forsooth, a great arithmetician,
One Michael Cassio, a Florentine,
A fellow almost damn'd in a fair wife;[9]
That never set a squadron in the field,
Nor the division of a battle knows
More than a spinster; unless[10] the bookish theoric,[11]
Wherein the toged consuls can propose
As masterly as he: mere prattle, without practice,
Is all his soldiership. But he, sir, had the election;
And I — of whom his eyes had seen the proof
At Rhodes, at Cyprus, and on other grounds
Christian and heathen — must be be-lee'd[12] and calm'd
By debitor and creditor; this counter-caster,[13]
He, in good time, must his lieutenant be,
And I — God bless the mark! — his Moorship's ancient.[14]
RODERIGO: By heaven, I rather would have been his hangman.
IAGO: Why, there's no remedy: 'tis the curse of the service,
Preferment goes by letter and affection,

[1] *i.e.*, Othello's successful courtship of Desdemona [2] by God's blood [3] *i.e.*, Othello [4] took off their caps [5] pompous wordiness, circumlocution [6] turns down [7] spokesmen [8] in truth [9] A much debated phrase. In the Italian source the Captain (*i.e.*, Cassio) was married, and it may be that Shakespeare originally intended Bianca to be Cassio's wife but later changed his mind and failed to alter the phrase here accordingly. Or perhaps Iago simply sneers at Cassio as a notorious ladies' man. [10] except [11] theory [12] left without wind for my sails [13] bookkeeper (*cf.* "arithmetician" above) [14] ensign (but Iago's position in the play seems to be that of Othello's aide-de-camp)

Not by the old gradation,[15] where each second
Stood heir to the first. Now, sir, be judge yourself,
Whe'r[16] I in any just term am affin'd[17]
To love the Moor.

RODERIGO: I would not follow him then.

IAGO: O! sir, content you;
I follow him to serve my turn upon him;
We cannot all be masters, nor all masters
Cannot be truly follow'd. You shall mark
Many a duteous and knee-crooking knave,
That, doting on his own obsequious bondage,
Wears out his time, much like his master's ass,
For nought but provender, and when he 's old, cashier'd;
Whip me such honest knaves. Others there are
Who, trimm'd in forms and visages of duty,
Keep yet their hearts attending on themselves,
And, throwing but shows of service on their lords,
Do well thrive by them, and when they have lin'd their coats
Do themselves homage: these fellows have some soul;
And such a one do I profess myself. For, sir,
It is as sure as you are Roderigo,
Were I the Moor, I would not be Iago:
In following him, I follow but myself;
Heaven is my judge, not I for love and duty,
But seeming so, for my peculiar end:
For when my outward action doth demonstrate
The native act and figure of my heart
In compliment extern,[18] 'tis not long after
But I will wear my heart upon my sleeve
For daws to peck at: I am not what I am.

RODERIGO: What a full fortune does the thick-lips owe,[19]
If he can carry 't thus!

IAGO: Call up her father;
Rouse him, make after him, poison his delight,
Proclaim him in the streets, incense her kinsmen,
And, though he in a fertile climate dwell,[20]
Plague him with flies; though that his joy be joy,
Yet throw such changes of vexation on 't
As it may lose some colour.

RODERIGO: Here is her father's house; I'll call aloud.

IAGO: Do; with like timorous[21] accent and dire yell

[15] seniority [16] whether [17] obliged [18] external show [19] own
[20] *i.e.*, is fortunate [21] frightening

As when, by night and negligence, the fire
Is spied in populous cities.

RODERIGO: What, ho! Brabantio! Signior Brabantio, ho!

IAGO: Awake! what, ho! Brabantio! thieves! thieves! thieves!
Look to your house, your daughter, and your bags!
Thieves! thieves!

(*Enter* BRABANTIO, *above, at a window.*)

BRABANTIO: What is the reason of this terrible summons?
What is the matter there?

RODERIGO: Signior, is all your family within?

IAGO: Are your doors lock'd?

BRABANTIO: Why? wherefore ask you this?

IAGO: 'Zounds! [22] sir, you're robb'd; for shame, put on your gown;
Your heart is burst, you have lost half your soul;
Even now, now, very now, an old black ram
Is tupping[23] your white ewe. Arise, arise!
Awake the snorting[24] citizens with the bell,
Or else the devil will make a grandsire of you.
Arise, I say.

BRABANTIO: What! have you lost your wits?

RODERIGO: Most reverend signior, do you know my voice?

BRABANTIO: Not I, what are you?

RODERIGO: My name is Roderigo.

BRABANTIO: The worser welcome:
I have charg'd thee not to haunt about my doors:
In honest plainness thou hast heard me say
My daughter is not for thee; and now, in madness,
Being full of supper and distempering draughts,
Upon malicious knavery dost thou come
To start my quiet.

RODERIGO: Sir, sir, sir!

BRABANTIO: But thou must needs be sure
My spirit and my place[25] have in them power
To make this bitter to thee.

RODERIGO: Patience, good sir.

BRABANTIO: What tell'st thou me of robbing? this is Venice;
My house is not a grange.[26]

RODERIGO: Most grave Brabantio,
In simple and pure soul I come to you.

IAGO: 'Zounds! sir, you are one of those that will not serve God if the

[22] by God's wounds [23] copulating [24] snoring [25] position
[26] isolated farm house

devil bid you. Because we come to do you service and you think we are ruffians, you'll have your daughter covered with a Barbary horse; you 'll have your nephews neigh to you; you 'll have coursers for cousins and gennets[27] for germans.[28]

BRABANTIO: What profane wretch art thou?

IAGO: I am one, sir, that comes to tell you, your daughter and the Moor are now making the beast with two backs.

BRABANTIO: Thou art a villain.

IAGO: You are — a senator.

BRABANTIO: This thou shalt answer; I know thee, Roderigo.

RODERIGO: Sir, I will answer any thing. But, I beseech you,
If 't be your pleasure and most wise consent, —
As partly, I find, it is, — that your fair daughter,
At this odd-even[29] and dull watch o' the night,
Transported with no worse nor better guard
But with a knave of common hire, a gondolier,
To the gross clasps of a lascivious Moor, —
If this be known to you, and your allowance,[30]
We then have done you bold and saucy wrongs;
But if you know not this, my manners tell me
We have your wrong rebuke. Do not believe
That, from[31] the sense of all civility,
I thus would play and trifle with your reverence:
Your daughter, if you have not given her leave,
I say again, hath made a gross revolt;
Tying her duty, beauty, wit and fortunes
In[32] an extravagant[33] and wheeling stranger
Of here and every where. Straight satisfy yourself:
If she be in her chamber or your house,
Let loose on me the justice of the state
For thus deluding you.

BRABANTIO: Strike on the tinder, ho!
Give me a taper! call up all my people!
This accident[34] is not unlike my dream;
Belief of it oppresses me already.
Light, I say! light! *(Exit, from above.)*

IAGO: Farewell, for I must leave you:
It seems not meet nor wholesome to my place
To be produc'd,[35] as, if I stay, I shall,
Against the Moor; for I do know the state,

[27] Spanish horses [28] blood relations [29] between night and morning
[30] by your approval [31] away from [32] to [33] expatriate [34] happening
[35] *i.e.*, as a witness

However this may gall him with some check,[36]
Cannot with safety cast him; for he 's embark'd
With such loud reason to the Cyprus wars, —
Which even now stand in act, — that, for their souls,
Another of his fathom[37] they have none,
To lead their business; in which regard,
Though I do hate him as I do hell-pains,
Yet, for necessity of present life,
I must show out a flag and sign of love,
Which is indeed but sign. That you shall surely find him,
Lead to the Sagittary[38] the raised search;
And there will I be with him. So, farewell. (*Exit.*)

(*Enter below,* BRABANTIO, *and* SERVANTS *with torches.*)

BRABANTIO: It is too true an evil: gone she is,
And what 's to come of my despised time
Is nought but bitterness. Now, Roderigo,
Where didst thou see her? O, unhappy girl!
With the Moor, sayst thou? Who would be a father!
How didst thou know 'twas she? O, she deceives me
Past thought. What said she to you? Get more tapers!
Raise all my kindred! Are they married, think you?

RODERIGO: Truly, I think they are.

BRABANTIO: O heaven! How got she out? O treason of the blood:
Fathers, from hence trust not your daughters' minds
By what you see them act. Are there not charms
By which the property of youth and maidhood
May be abus'd? Have you not read, Roderigo,
Of some such thing?

RODERIGO: Yes, sir, I have indeed.

BRABANTIO: Call up my brother. O! that you had had her.
Some one way, some another! Do you know
Where we may apprehend her and the Moor?

RODERIGO: I think I can discover him, if you please
To get good guard and go along with me.

BRABANTIO: Pray you, lead on. At every house I 'll call;
I may command at most. Get weapons, ho!
And raise some special officers of night.
On, good Roderigo; I 'll deserve[39] your pains. (*Exeunt.*)

36 restraining adversity 37 caliber, ability 38 the name of an inn(?)
39 *i.e.*, reward

Scene 2 [Another street.]

(*Enter* OTHELLO, IAGO, *and* ATTENDANTS, *with torches.*)

IAGO: Though in the trade of war I have slain men,
Yet do I hold it very stuff o' the conscience
To do no contriv'd murder: I lack iniquity
Sometimes to do me service. Nine or ten times
I had thought to have yerk'd [40] him here under the ribs.
OTHELLO: 'Tis better as it is.
IAGO: Nay, but he prated,
And spoke such scurvy and provoking terms
Against your honour
That, with the little godliness I have,
I did full hard forbear him. But, I pray, sir,
Are you fast married? Be assur'd of this,
That the magnifico[41] is much belov'd,
And hath in his effect a voice potential
As double[42] as the duke's; he will divorce you,
Or put upon you what restraint and grievance
The law — with all his might to enforce it on —
Will give him cable.[43]
OTHELLO: Let him do his spite:
My services which I have done the signiory[44]
Shall out-tongue his complaints. 'Tis yet to know,[45]
Which when I know that boasting is an honour
I shall promulgate, I fetch my life and being
From men of royal siege, and my demerits[46]
May speak unbonneted[47] to as proud a fortune
As this[48] that I have reach'd; for know, Iago,
But that I love the gentle Desdemona,
I would not my unhoused[49] free condition
Put into circumscription and confine
For the sea's worth. But, look! what lights come yond?
IAGO: Those are the raised[50] father and his friends:
You were best[51] go in.
OTHELLO: Not I; I must be found:

[40] stabbed [41] one of the grandees, or rulers, of Venice; here, Brabantio [42] Iago means that Brabantio's influence equals that of the Doge's, with his double vote. [43] *i.e.*, scope [44] the Venetian government [45] *i.e.*, the signiory does not as yet know [46] merits [47] *i.e.*, as equals [48] *i.e.*, that of Desdemona's family [49] unconfined [50] aroused [51] had better

My parts, my title, and my perfect[52] soul
Shall manifest me rightly. Is it they?
IAGO: By Janus,[53] I think no.

(*Enter* CASSIO *and certain* OFFICERS, *with torches.*)

OTHELLO: The servants of the duke, and my lieutenant.
The goodness of the night upon you, friends!
What is the news?
CASSIO: The duke does greet you, general,
And he requires your haste-post-haste appearance,
Even on the instant.
OTHELLO: What is the matter, think you?
CASSIO: Something from Cyprus, as I may divine.
It is a business of some heat;[54] the galleys
Have sent a dozen sequent[55] messengers
This very night at one another's heels,
And many of the consuls,[56] rais'd and met,
Are at the duke's already. You have been hotly call'd for;
When, being not at your lodging to be found,
The senate hath sent about three several [57] quests
To search you out.
OTHELLO: 'Tis well I am found by you.
I will but spend a word here in the house,
And go with you. (*Exit.*)
CASSIO: Ancient, what makes he here?
IAGO: Faith, he to-night hath boarded a land carrack;[58]
If it prove lawful prize, he 's made for ever.
CASSIO: I do not understand.
IAGO: He 's married.
CASSIO: To who?

(*Re-enter* OTHELLO.)

IAGO: Marry,[59] to — Come, captain, will you go?
OTHELLO: Have with you.
CASSIO: Here comes another troop to seek for you.
IAGO: It is Brabantio. General, be advis'd;
He comes to bad intent.

(*Enter* BRABANTIO, RODERIGO, *and* OFFICERS, *with torches and weapons.*)

[52] untroubled by a bad conscience [53] the two-faced Roman god of portals and doors and (hence) of beginnings and ends [54] urgency [55] following one another [56] *i.e.*, senators [57] separate [58] treasure ship [59] by the Virgin Mary

OTHELLO: Holla! stand there!
RODERIGO: Signior, it is the Moor.
BRABANTIO: Down with him, thief!

(*They draw on both sides.*)

IAGO: You, Roderigo! come, sir, I am for you.[60]
OTHELLO: Keep up your bright swords, for the dew will rust them.
Good signior, you shall more command with years
Than with your weapons.
BRABANTIO: O thou foul thief! where hast thou stow'd my daughter?
Damn'd as thou art, thou hast enchanted her;
For I 'll refer me to all things of sense,
If she in chains of magic were not bound,
Whether a maid so tender, fair, and happy,
So opposite to marriage that she shunn'd
The wealthy curled darlings of our nation,
Would ever have, to incur a general mock,
Run from her guardage to the sooty bosom
Of such a thing as thou; to fear, not to delight.
Judge me the world, if 'tis not gross in sense[61]
That thou hast practis'd on her with foul charms,
Abus'd her delicate youth with drugs or minerals
That weaken motion:[62] I 'll have 't disputed on;
'Tis probable, and palpable to thinking.
I therefore apprehend and do attach[63] thee
For an abuser of the world, a practiser
Of arts inhibited and out of warrant.[64]
Lay hold upon him: if he do resist,
Subdue him at his peril.
OTHELLO: Hold your hands,
Both you of my inclining,[65] and the rest:
Were it my cue to fight, I should have known it
Without a prompter. Where will you that I go
To answer this your charge?
BRABANTIO: To prison; till fit time
Of law and course of direct session[66]
Call thee to answer.
OTHELLO: What if I do obey?
How may the duke be therewith satisfied,
Whose messengers are here about my side,

[60] let you and me fight [61] obvious [62] normal reactions [63] arrest
[64] prohibited and illegal [65] party [66] normal process of law

Upon some present[67] business of the state
To bring me to him?

OFFICER: 'Tis true, most worthy signior;
The duke 's in council, and your noble self,
I am sure, is sent for.

BRABANTIO: How! the duke in council!
In this time of the night! Bring him away.
Mine 's not an idle cause: the duke himself,
Or any of my brothers of the state,[68]
Cannot but feel this wrong as 'twere their own;
For if such actions may have passage free,
Bond-slaves and pagans shall our statesmen be. (*Exeunt.*)

Scene 3 [A Council Chamber.]

(*The* DUKE *and* SENATORS *sitting at a table.* OFFICERS *attending.*)

DUKE: There is no composition[69] in these news
That gives them credit.

FIRST SENATOR: Indeed, they are disproportion'd;
My letters say a hundred and seven galleys.

DUKE: And mine, a hundred and forty.

SECOND SENATOR: And mine, two hundred:
But though they jump[70] not on a just[71] account, —
As in these cases, where the aim[72] reports,
'Tis oft with difference, — yet do they all confirm
A Turkish fleet, and bearing up to Cyprus.

DUKE: Nay, it is possible enough to judgment:
I do not so secure me in[73] the error,
But the main article[74] I do approve[75]
In fearful sense.

SAILOR (*within*): What, ho! what, ho! what, ho!

OFFICER: A messenger from the galleys.

(*Enter a* SAILOR.)

DUKE: Now, what 's the business?

SAILOR: The Turkish preparation makes for Rhodes;
So was I bid report here to the state
By Signior Angelo.

[67] immediate, pressing [68] fellow senators [69] consistency, agreement
[70] coincide [71] exact [72] conjecture [73] draw comfort from [74] substance
[75] believe

DUKE: How say you by this change?

FIRST SENATOR: This cannot be
By no[76] assay[77] of reason; 'tis a pageant[78]
To keep us in false gaze.[79] When we consider
The importancy of Cyprus to the Turk,
And let ourselves again but understand,
That as it more concerns the Turk than Rhodes,
So may he with more facile question bear[80] it,
For that it stands not in such warlike brace,[81]
But altogether lacks the abilities
That Rhodes is dress'd in: if we make thought of this,
We must not think the Turk is so unskilful
To leave that latest which concerns him first,
Neglecting an attempt of ease and gain,
To wake and wage a danger profitless.

DUKE: Nay, in all confidence, he 's not for Rhodes.

OFFICER: Here is more news.

(*Enter a* MESSENGER.)

MESSENGER: The Ottomites,[82] reverend and gracious,
Steering with due course toward the isle of Rhodes,
Have there injointed [83] them with an after fleet.[84]

FIRST SENATOR: Ay, so I thought. How many, as you guess?

MESSENGER: Of thirty sail; and now they do re-stem[85]
Their backward course, bearing with frank appearance
Their purposes toward Cyprus. Signior Montano,
Your trusty and most valiant servitor,
With his free duty[86] recommends[87] you thus,
And prays you to believe him.

DUKE: 'Tis certain then, for Cyprus.
Marcus Luccicos, is not he in town?

FIRST SENATOR: He 's now in Florence.

DUKE: Write from us to him; post-post-haste dispatch.

FIRST SENATOR: Here comes Brabantio and the valiant Moor.

(*Enter* BRABANTIO, OTHELLO, IAGO, RODERIGO, *and* OFFICERS.)

DUKE: Valiant Othello, we must straight employ you
Against the general enemy Ottoman.
(*To* BRABANTIO) I did not see you; welcome, gentle signior;

[76] any [77] test [78] (deceptive) show [79] looking in the wrong direction [80] more easily capture [81] state of defense [82] Turks [83] joined [84] fleet that followed after [85] steer again [86] unqualified expressions of respect [87] informs

We lack'd your counsel and your help to-night.
BRABANTIO: So did I yours. Good your Grace, pardon me;
Neither my place nor aught I heard of business
Hath rais'd me from my bed, nor doth the general care
Take hold of me, for my particular grief
Is of so flood-gate[88] and o'erbearing nature
That it engluts and swallows other sorrows
And it is still itself.
DUKE: Why, what 's the matter?
BRABANTIO: My daughter! O! my daughter.
DUKE: / SENATORS: Dead?
BRABANTIO: Ay, to me;
She is abus'd, stol'n from me, and corrupted
By spells and medicines bought of mountebanks;
For nature so preposterously to err,
Being not deficient, blind, or lame of sense,
Sans[89] witchcraft could not.
DUKE: Whoe'er he be that in this foul proceeding
Hath thus beguil'd your daughter of herself
And you of her, the bloody book of law
You shall yourself read in the bitter letter
After your own sense; yea, though our proper[90] son
Stood[91] in your action.[92]
BRABANTIO: Humbly I thank your Grace.
Here is the man, this Moor; whom now, it seems,
Your special mandate for the state affairs
Hath hither brought.
DUKE: / SENATORS: We are very sorry for it.
DUKE (*to* OTHELLO): What, in your own part, can you say to this?
BRABANTIO: Nothing, but this is so.
OTHELLO: Most potent, grave, and reverend signiors,
My very noble and approv'd[93] good masters,
That I have ta'en away this old man's daughter,
It is most true; true, I have married her:
The very head and front of my offending
Hath this extent, no more. Rude am I in my speech,
And little bless'd with the soft phrase of peace;
For since these arms of mine had seven years' pith,[94]
Till now some nine moons wasted,[95] they have us'd

88 torrential 89 without 90 own 91 were accused 92 suit
93 tested (by past experience) 94 strength 95 past

Their dearest action in the tented field;
And little of this great world can I speak,
More than pertains to feats of broil and battle;
And therefore little shall I grace my cause
In speaking for myself. Yet, by your gracious patience,
I will a round[96] unvarnish'd tale deliver
Of my whole course of love; what drugs, what charms,
What conjuration, and what mighty magic,
For such proceeding I am charg'd withal,
I won his daughter.

BRABANTIO: A maiden never bold;
Of spirit so still and quiet, that her motion
Blush'd at herself;[97] and she, in spite of nature,
Of years, of country, credit, every thing,
To fall in love with what she fear'd to look on!
It is a judgment maim'd and most imperfect
That will confess[98] perfection so could err
Against all rules of nature, and must be driven
To find out practices of cunning hell,
Why this should be. I therefore vouch again
That with some mixtures powerful o'er the blood,
Or with some dram conjur'd to this effect,
He wrought upon her.

DUKE: To vouch this, is no proof,
Without more certain and more overt test
Than these thin habits[99] and poor likelihoods
Of modern[100] seeming do prefer against him.

FIRST SENATOR: But, Othello, speak:
Did you by indirect and forced courses
Subdue and poison this young maid's affections;
Or came it by request and such fair question[101]
As soul to soul affordeth?

OTHELLO: I do beseech you;
Send for the lady to the Sagittary,
And let her speak of me before her father:
If you do find me foul in her report,
The trust, the office I do hold of you,
Not only take away, but let your sentence
Even fall upon my life.

DUKE: Fetch Desdemona hither.

[96] blunt [97] *i.e.*, (her modesty was such that) she blushed at her own emotions; or: could not move without blushing [98] assert [99] weak appearances [100] commonplace [101] conversation

OTHELLO: Ancient, conduct them; you best know the place.
(*Exeunt* IAGO *and* ATTENDANTS.)
And, till she come, as truly as to heaven
I do confess the vices of my blood,
So justly to your grave ears I 'll present
How I did thrive in this fair lady's love,
And she in mine.
DUKE: Say it, Othello.
OTHELLO: Her father lov'd me; oft invited me;
Still [102] question'd me the story of my life
From year to year, the battles, sieges, fortunes
That I have pass'd.
I ran it through, even from my boyish days
To the very moment that he bade me tell it;
Wherein I spake of most disastrous chances,
Of moving accidents by flood and field,
Of hair-breadth 'scapes i' the imminent deadly breach,
Of being taken by the insolent foe
And sold to slavery, of my redemption thence
And portance[103] in my travel's history;
Wherein of antres[104] vast and deserts idle,[105]
Rough quarries, rocks, and hills whose heads touch heaven,
It was my hint[106] to speak, such was the process;
And of the Cannibals that each other eat,
The Anthropophagi,[107] and men whose heads
Do grow beneath their shoulders. This to hear
Would Desdemona seriously incline;
But still the house-affairs would draw her thence;
Which ever as she could with haste dispatch,
She'd come again, and with a greedy ear
Devour up my discourse. Which I observing,
Took once a pliant [108] hour, and found good means
To draw from her a prayer of earnest heart
That I would all my pilgrimage dilate,[109]
Whereof by parcels[110] she had something heard,
But not intentively:[111] I did consent;
And often did beguile her of her tears,
When I did speak of some distressful stroke
That my youth suffer'd. My story being done,
She gave me for my pains a world of sighs:

[102] always, regularly [103] behavior [104] caves [105] empty, sterile
[106] opportunity [107] man-eaters [108] suitable [109] relate in full
[110] piecemeal [111] in sequence

She swore, in faith, 'twas strange, 'twas passing[112] strange;
'Twas pitiful, 'twas wondrous pitiful:
She wish'd she had not heard it, yet she wish'd
That heaven had made her[113] such a man; she thank'd me,
And bade me, if I had a friend that lov'd her,
I should but teach him how to tell my story,
And that would woo her. Upon this hint I spake.
She lov'd me for the dangers I had pass'd,
And I lov'd her that she did pity them.
This only is the witchcraft I have us'd:
Here comes the lady; let her witness it.

(*Enter* DESDEMONA, IAGO, *and* ATTENDANTS.)

DUKE: I think this tale would win my daughter too.
Good Brabantio,
Take up this mangled matter at the best;
Men do their broken weapons rather use
Than their bare hands.

BRABANTIO: I pray you, hear her speak:
If she confess that she was half the wooer,
Destruction on my head, if my bad blame
Light on the man! Come hither, gentle mistress:
Do you perceive in all this noble company
Where most you owe obedience?

DESDEMONA: My noble father,
I do perceive here a divided duty:
To you I am bound for life and education;
My life and education both do learn[114] me
How to respect you; you are the lord of duty,
I am hitherto your daughter: but here 's my husband;
And so much duty as my mother show'd
To you, preferring you before her father,
So much I challenge[115] that I may profess
Due to the Moor my lord.

BRABANTIO: God be with you! I have done.
Please it your Grace, on to the state affairs:
I had rather to adopt a child than get it.
Come hither, Moor:
I here do give thee that with all my heart
Which, but thou hast[116] already, with all my heart
I would keep from thee. For your sake,[117] jewel,

[112] surpassing [113] direct object; not "for her" [114] teach [115] claim as right
[116] didn't you have it [117] because of you

I am glad at soul I have no other child;
For thy escape would teach me tyranny,
To hang clogs on them. I have done, my lord.

DUKE: Let me speak like yourself and lay a sentence,[118]
Which as a grize[119] or step, may help these lovers
Into your favour.
When remedies are past, the griefs are ended
By seeing the worst, which[120] late on hopes depended.
To mourn a mischief that is past and gone
Is the next way to draw new mischief on.
What cannot be preserv'd when Fortune takes,
Patience her injury a mockery makes.[121]
The robb'd that smiles steals something from the thief;
He robs himself that spends a bootless grief.

BRABANTIO: So let the Turk of Cyprus us beguile;
We lose it not so long as we can smile.
He bears the sentence[122] well that nothing bears
But the free comfort which from thence he hears;
But he bears both the sentence and the sorrow
That, to pay grief, must of poor patience borrow.
These sentences, to sugar, or to gall,
Being strong on both sides, are equivocal:[123]
But words are words; I never yet did hear
That the bruis'd heart was pierced[124] through the ear.
I humbly beseech you, proceed to the affairs of state.

DUKE: The Turk with a most mighty preparation makes for Cyprus. Othello, the fortitude[125] of the place is best known to you; and though we have there a substitute of most allowed sufficiency,[126] yet opinion, a sovereign mistress of effects, throws a more safer voice on you:[127] you must therefore be content to slubber[128] the gloss of your new fortunes with this more stubborn[129] and boisterous expedition.

OTHELLO: The tyrant custom, most grave senators,
Hath made the flinty and steel couch of war
My thrice-driven[130] bed of down: I do agnize[131]
A natural and prompt alacrity

[118] provide a maxim [119] step [120] the antecedent is "griefs" [121] to suffer an irreparable loss patiently is to make light of injury (*i.e.*, to triumph over adversity) [122] (1) verdict, (2) maxim [123] sententious comfort (like the Duke's trite maxims) can hurt as well as soothe [124] (1) lanced (*i.e.*, cured), (2) wounded [125] strength [126] admitted competence [127] general opinion, which mainly determines action, thinks Cyprus safer with you in command [128] besmear [129] rough [130] made as soft as possible [131] recognize

I find in hardness, and do undertake
These present wars against the Ottomites.
Most humbly therefore bending to your state,[132]
I crave fit disposition[133] for my wife,
Due reference of place and exhibition,[134]
With such accommodation and besort[135]
As levels with[136] her breeding.

DUKE: If you please,
Be 't at her father's.

BRABANTIO: I 'll not have it so.

OTHELLO: Nor I.

DESDEMONA: Nor I; I would not there reside,
To put my father in impatient thoughts
By being in his eye. Most gracious duke,
To my unfolding[137] lend your gracious ear;
And let me find a charter[138] in your voice
To assist my simpleness.

DUKE: What would you, Desdemona?

DESDEMONA: That I did love the Moor to live with him,
My downright violence and storm of fortunes
May trumpet to the world; my heart 's subdu'd
Even to the very quality of my lord;[139]
I saw Othello's visage in his mind,
And to his honours and his valiant parts
Did I my soul and fortunes consecrate.
So that, dear lords, if I be left behind,
A moth of peace, and he go to the war,
The rites[140] for which I love him are bereft me,
And I a heavy interim shall support[141]
By his dear[142] absence. Let me go with him.

OTHELLO: Let her have your voices.
Vouch with me, heaven, I therefore beg it not
To please the palate of my appetite,
Nor to comply with heat, — the young affects[143]
In me defunct, — and proper satisfaction,
But to be free and bounteous to her mind;
And heaven defend [144] your good souls that you think
I will your serious and great business scant

[132] submitting to your authority [133] disposal [134] provision [135] fitness [136] is proper to [137] explanation [138] permission [139] *i.e.*, I have become a soldier, like Othello [140] *i.e.*, of marriage, or of war, or of both [141] endure [142] closely concerning (*i.e.*, Desdemona) [143] the passions of youth (hence, here, *immoderate* sexual passion) [144] forbid

For[145] she is with me. No, when light-wing'd toys
Of feather'd Cupid seel [146] with wanton dulness
My speculative and offic'd instruments,[147]
That[148] my disports corrupt and taint my business,
Let housewives make a skillet of my helm,
And all indign[149] and base adversities
Make head against my estimation! [150]

DUKE: Be it as you shall privately determine,
Either for her stay or going. The affair cries haste,
And speed must answer it.

FIRST SENATOR: You must away to-night.

OTHELLO: With all my heart.

DUKE: At nine i' the morning here we'll meet again.
Othello, leave some officer behind,
And he shall our commission bring to you;
With such things else of quality and respect
As doth import you.[151]

OTHELLO: So please your Grace, my ancient;
A man he is of honesty and trust:
To his conveyance I assign my wife,
With what else needful your good grace shall think
To be sent after me.

DUKE: Let it be so.
Good-night to every one. (*To* BRABANTIO) And, noble signior,
If virtue no delighted [152] beauty lack,
Your son-in-law is far more fair than black.

FIRST SENATOR: Adieu, brave Moor! use Desdemona well.

BRABANTIO: Look to her, Moor, if thou hast eyes to see:
She has deceiv'd her father, and may thee.

(*Exeunt* DUKE, SENATORS, OFFICERS, *&c.*)

OTHELLO: My life upon her faith! Honest Iago,
My Desdemona must I leave to thee:
I prithee, let thy wife attend on her;
And bring them after in the best advantage.[153]
Come, Desdemona; I have but an hour
Of love, of worldly matters and direction,
To spend with thee: we must obey the time.

(*Exeunt* OTHELLO *and* DESDEMONA.)

RODERIGO: Iago!

IAGO: What sayst thou, noble heart?

[145] because [146] blind (v.) by sewing up the eyelids (a term from falconry)
[147] reflective and executive faculties and organs [148] so that [149] shameful
[150] reputation [151] concern [152] delightful [153] opportunity

RODERIGO: What will I do, think'st thou?

IAGO: Why, go to bed, and sleep.

RODERIGO: I will incontinently[154] drown myself.

IAGO: Well, if thou dost, I shall never love thee after.
Why, thou silly gentleman!

RODERIGO: It is silliness to live when to live is torment; and then have we a prescription to die when death is our physician.

IAGO: O! villanous; I have looked upon the world for four times seven years, and since I could distinguish betwixt a benefit and an injury, I never found man that knew how to love himself. Ere I would say, I would drown myself for the love of a guinea-hen, I would change my humanity with a baboon.

RODERIGO: What should I do? I confess it is my shame to be so fond;[155] but it is not in my virtue[156] to amend it.

IAGO: Virtue! a fig! 'tis in ourselves that we are thus, or thus. Our bodies are our gardens, to the which our wills are gardeners; so that if we will plant nettles or sow lettuce, set hyssop and weed up thyme, supply it with one gender[157] of herbs or distract it with many, either to have it sterile with idleness or manured with industry, why, the power and corrigible[158] authority of this lies in our wills. If the balance of our lives had not one scale of reason to poise another of sensuality, the blood and baseness of our natures would conduct us to most preposterous conclusions; but we have reason to cool our raging motions, our carnal stings, our unbitted[159] lusts, whereof I take this that you call love to be a sect or scion.[160]

RODERIGO: It cannot be.

IAGO: It is merely a lust of the blood and a permission of the will. Come, be a man. Drown thyself! drown cats and blind puppies. I have professed me thy friend, and I confess me knit to thy deserving with cables of perdurable toughness; I could never better stead thee than now. Put money in thy purse; follow these wars; defeat thy favour[161] with a usurped[162] beard; I say, put money in thy purse. It cannot be that Desdemona should long continue her love to the Moor, — put money in thy purse, — nor he his to her. It was a violent commencement in her, and thou shalt see an answerable sequestration;[163] put but money in thy purse. These Moors are changeable in their wills; — fill thy purse with money: — the food that to him now is as luscious as locusts,[164] shall be to him shortly as bitter as

[154] forthwith [155] infatuated [156] strength [157] kind [158] corrective
[159] *i.e.*, uncontrolled [160] offshoot [161] change thy appearance (for the worse?)
[162] assumed [163] estrangement [164] sweet-tasting fruits (perhaps the carob, the edible seed-pod of an evergreen tree in the Mediterranean area)

coloquintida.[165] She must change for youth: when she is sated with his body, she will find the error of her choice. She must have change, she must: therefore put money in thy purse. If thou wilt needs damn thyself, do it a more delicate way than drowning. Make all the money thou canst. If sanctimony and a frail vow betwixt an erring[166] barbarian and a super-subtle[167] Venetian be not too hard for my wits and all the tribe of hell, thou shalt enjoy her; therefore make money. A pox of drowning thyself! it is clean out of the way: seek thou rather to be hanged in compassing thy joy than to be drowned and go without her.

RODERIGO: Wilt thou be fast to my hopes, if I depend on the issue?[168]

IAGO: Thou art sure of me: go, make money. I have told thee often, and I re-tell thee again and again, I hate the Moor; my cause is hearted; thine hath no less reason. Let us be conjunctive[169] in our revenge against him; if thou canst cuckold him, thou dost thyself a pleasure, me a sport. There are many events in the womb of time which will be delivered. Traverse;[170] go: provide thy money. We will have more of this to-morrow. Adieu.

RODERIGO: Where shall we meet i' the morning?

IAGO: At my lodging.

RODERIGO: I 'll be with thee betimes.

IAGO: Go to: farewell. Do you hear, Roderigo?

RODERIGO: What say you?

IAGO: No more of drowning, do you hear?

RODERIGO: I am changed. I 'll sell all my land.

IAGO: Go to; farewell! put money enough in your purse.

(*Exit* RODERIGO.)

Thus do I ever make my fool my purse;
For I mine own gain'd knowledge should profane,
If I would time expend with such a snipe[171]
But for my sport and profit. I hate the Moor,
And it is thought abroad [172] that 'twixt my sheets
He has done my office: I know not if 't be true,
But I, for mere suspicion in that kind,
Will do as if for surety.[173] He holds me well;[174]
The better shall my purpose work on him.
Cassio's a proper[175] man; let me see now:
To get his place; and to plume up[176] my will
In double knavery; how, how? Let's see:
After some time to abuse Othello's ear

165 purgative derived from a bitter apple 166 vagabond 167 exceedingly refined
168 rely on the outcome 169 allied 170 march 171 dupe 172 people think
173 as if it were certain 174 in high regard 175 handsome 176 make ready

That he[177] is too familiar with his wife:
He hath a person and a smooth dispose[178]
To be suspected; framed [179] to make women false,
The Moor is of a free and open nature,
That thinks men honest that but seem to be so,
And will as tenderly be led by the nose
As asses are.
I have 't; it is engender'd: hell and night
Must bring this monstrous birth to the world's light. (*Exit.*)

ACT II

Scene 1 [A Sea-port Town in Cyprus. An open place near the Quay.]

(*Enter* MONTANO *and two* GENTLEMEN.)

MONTANO: What from the cape can you discern at sea?
FIRST GENTLEMAN: Nothing at all: it is a high-wrought flood;
I cannot 'twixt the heaven and the main[180]
Descry a sail.
MONTANO: Methinks the wind hath spoke aloud at land;
A fuller blast ne'er shook our battlements;
If it hath ruffian'd so upon the sea,
What ribs of oak, when mountains melt on them,
Can hold the mortise?[181] what shall we hear of this?
SECOND GENTLEMAN: A segregation[182] of the Turkish fleet;
For do but stand upon the foaming shore,
The chidden billow seems to pelt the clouds;
The wind-shak'd surge, with high and monstrous mane,
Seems to cast water on the burning bear[183]
And quench the guards of the ever-fixed pole:[184]
I never did like[185] molestation view
On the enchafed [186] flood.
MONTANO: If that[187] the Turkish fleet
Be not enshelter'd and embay'd, they are drown'd;
It is impossible they bear it out.

(*Enter a* THIRD GENTLEMAN.)

[177] *i.e.*, Cassio [178] bearing [179] designed, apt [180] ocean [181] hold the joints together [182] scattering [183] Ursa Minor (the Little Dipper) [184] Polaris, the North Star, almost directly above the Earth's axis, is part of the constellation of the Little Bear, or Dipper. [185] similar [186] agitated [187] if

THIRD GENTLEMAN: News, lad! our wars are done.
The desperate tempest hath so bang'd the Turks
That their designment halts;[188] a noble ship of Venice
Hath seen a grievous wrack and suffrance[189]
On most part of their fleet.
MONTANO: How! is this true?
THIRD GENTLEMAN: The ship is here put in,
A Veronesa;[190] Michael Cassio,
Lieutenant to the warlike Moor Othello,
Is come on shore: the Moor himself 's at sea,
And is in full commission here for Cyprus.
MONTANO: I am glad on 't; 'tis a worthy governor.
THIRD GENTLEMAN: But this same Cassio, though he speak of comfort
Touching the Turkish loss, yet he looks sadly
And prays the Moor be safe; for they were parted
With foul and violent tempest.
MONTANO: Pray heaven he be;
For I have serv'd him, and the man commands
Like a full soldier. Let's to the sea-side, ho!
As well to see the vessel that 's come in
As to throw out our eyes for brave Othello,
Even till we make the main and the aerial blue
An indistinct regard.[191]
THIRD GENTLEMAN: Come, let's do so;
For every minute is expectancy
Of more arrivance.

(*Enter* CASSIO.)

CASSIO: Thanks, you the valiant of this warlike isle,
That so approve the Moor. O! let the heavens
Give him defence against the elements,
For I have lost him on a dangerous sea.
MONTANO: Is he well shipp'd?
CASSIO: His bark is stoutly timber'd, and his pilot
Of very expert and approv'd allowance;[192]
Therefore my hopes, not surfeited to death,[193]
Stand in bold cure.[194]

(*Within,* 'A sail! — a sail! — a sail!' *Enter a* MESSENGER.)

[188] plan is stopped [189] damage [190] probably a *type* of ship, rather than a ship from Verona — not only because Verona is an inland city but also because of "a noble ship of Venice" above [191] till our (straining) eyes can no longer distinguish sea and sky [192] admitted and proven to be expert [193] over-indulged [194] with good chance of being fulfilled

CASSIO: What noise?
MESSENGER: The town is empty; on the brow o' the sea
Stand ranks of people, and they cry 'A sail!'
CASSIO: My hopes do shape him for the governor.

(*Guns heard.*)

SECOND GENTLEMAN: They do discharge their shot of courtesy;
Our friends at least.
CASSIO: I pray you, sir, go forth.
And give us truth who 'tis that is arriv'd.
SECOND GENTLEMAN: I shall. (*Exit.*)
MONTANO: But, good lieutenant, is your general wiv'd?
CASSIO: Most fortunately: he hath achiev'd a maid
That paragons[195] description and wild fame;
One that excels the quirks[196] of blazoning pens,
And in th' essential vesture of creation[197]
Does tire the ingener.[198]

(*Re-enter* SECOND GENTLEMAN.)

How now! who has put in?
SECOND GENTLEMAN: 'Tis one Iago, ancient to the general.
CASSIO: He has had most favourable and happy speed:
Tempests themselves, high seas, and howling winds,
The gutter'd[199] rocks, and congregated sands,
Traitors ensteep'd[200] to clog the guiltless keel,
As having sense of beauty, do omit
Their mortal[201] natures, letting go safely by
The divine Desdemona.
MONTANO: What is she?
CASSIO: She that I spake of, our great captain's captain,
Left in the conduct of the bold Iago,
Whose footing[202] here anticipates our thoughts
A se'nnight's[203] speed. Great Jove, Othello guard,
And swell his sail with thine own powerful breath,
That he may bless this bay with his tall [204] ship,
Make love's quick pants in Desdemona's arms,
Give renew'd fire to our extincted spirits,
And bring all Cyprus comfort!

(*Enter* DESDEMONA, EMILIA, IAGO, RODERIGO, *and* ATTENDANTS.)

195 exceeds, surpasses 196 ingenuities 197 *i.e.*, just as God made her; or: (even in) the (mere) essence of human nature 198 inventor (*i.e.*, of her praises?) 199 jagged; or: submerged 200 submerged 201 deadly 202 landing 203 week's 204 brave

O! behold,
The riches of the ship is come on shore.
Ye men of Cyprus, let her have your knees.
Hail to thee, lady! and the grace of heaven,
Before, behind thee, and on every hand,
Enwheel thee round!

DESDEMONA: I thank you, valiant Cassio.
What tidings can you tell me of my lord?

CASSIO: He is not yet arriv'd; nor know I aught
But that he's well, and will be shortly here.

DESDEMONA: O! but I fear — How lost you company?

CASSIO: The great contention of the sea and skies
Parted our fellowship. But hark! a sail.

(*Cry within*, 'A sail — a sail!' *Guns heard.*)

SECOND GENTLEMAN: They give their greeting to the citadel:
This likewise is a friend.

CASSIO: See for the news! (*Exit* GENTLEMAN.)
Good ancient, you are welcome: — (*To* EMILIA) welcome, mistress.
Let it not gall your patience, good Iago,
That I extend my manners; 'tis my breeding
That gives me this bold show of courtesy. (*Kissing her.*)

IAGO: Sir, would she give you so much of her lips
As of her tongue she oft bestows on me,
You'd have enough.

DESDEMONA: Alas! she has no speech.

IAGO: In faith, too much;
I find it still when I have list[205] to sleep:
Marry, before your ladyship, I grant,
She puts her tongue a little in her heart,
And chides with thinking.[206]

EMILIA: You have little cause to say so.

IAGO: Come on, come on; you are pictures[207] out of doors,
Bells[208] in your parlours, wild cats in your kitchens,
Saints in your injuries, devils being offended,
Players[209] in your housewifery,[210] and housewives[211] in your beds.

DESDEMONA: O! fie upon thee, slanderer.

IAGO: Nay, it is true, or else I am a Turk:
You rise to play and go to bed to work.

EMILIA: You shall not write my praise.

[205] wish [206] *i.e.*, without words [207] *i.e.*, made up, "painted" [208] *i.e.*, jangly [209] triflers, wastrels [210] housekeeping [211] (1) hussies, (2) (unduly) frugal with their sexual favors, (3) businesslike, serious

IAGO: No, let me not.

DESDEMONA: What wouldst thou write of me, if thou shouldst praise me?

IAGO: O gentle lady, do not put me to 't,
For I am nothing if not critical.

DESDEMONA: Come on; assay. There 's one gone to the harbour?

IAGO: Ay, madam.

DESDEMONA: I am not merry, but I do beguile
The thing I am by seeming otherwise.
Come, how wouldst thou praise me?

IAGO: I am about it; but indeed my invention
Comes from my pate[212] as birdlime does from frize;[213]
It plucks out brains and all: but my muse labours
And thus she is deliver'd.
If she be fair and wise, fairness and wit,
The one 's for use, the other useth it.

DESDEMONA: Well prais'd! How if she be black and witty?

IAGO: If she be black,[214] and thereto have a wit,
She 'll find a white that shall her blackness fit.

DESDEMONA: Worse and worse.

EMILIA: How if fair and foolish?

IAGO: She never yet was foolish that was fair,
For even her folly[215] help'd to an heir.

DESDEMONA: These are old fond[216] paradoxes to make fools laugh i' the alehouse. What miserable praise hast thou for her that 's foul and foolish?

IAGO: There 's none so foul and foolish thereunto,
But does foul pranks which fair and wise ones do.

DESDEMONA: O heavy ignorance! thou praisest the worst best. But what praise couldst thou bestow on a deserving woman indeed, one that, in the authority of her merit, did justly put on the vouch[217] of very malice itself?

IAGO: She that was ever fair and never proud,
Had tongue at will and yet was never loud,
Never lack'd gold and yet went never gay,
Fled from her wish and yet said 'Now I may,'
She that being anger'd, her revenge being nigh,
Bade her wrong stay and her displeasure fly,
She that in wisdom never was so frail
To change the cod's head for the salmon's tail,[218]

[212] head [213] coarse cloth [214] brunette, dark-haired [215] here also, wantonness [216] foolish [217] compel the approval [218] to make a foolish exchange (a bawdy secondary meaning is probable)

She that could think and ne'er disclose her mind,
See suitors following and not look behind,
She was a wight, if ever such wight were, —

DESDEMONA: To do what?

IAGO: To suckle fools and chronicle small beer.[219]

DESDEMONA: O most lame and impotent conclusion! Do not learn of him, Emilia, though he be thy husband. How say you, Cassio? Is he not a most profane and liberal [220] counsellor?

CASSIO: He speaks home,[221] madam; you may relish him more in the soldier than in[222] the scholar.

IAGO (*aside*): He takes her by the palm: ay, well said, whisper; with as little a web as this will I ensnare as great a fly as Cassio. Ay, smile upon her, do; I will gyve[223] thee in thine own courtship. You say true, 'tis so, indeed. If such tricks as these strip you out of your lieutenantry, it had been better you had not kissed your three fingers so oft, which now again you are most apt to play the sir[224] in. Very good; well kissed! an excellent courtesy! 'tis so, indeed. Yet again your fingers to your lips? would they were clyster-pipes[225] for your sake! (*A trumpet heard.*) The Moor! I know his trumpet.[226]

CASSIO: 'Tis truly so.

DESDEMONA: Let 's meet him and receive him.

CASSIO: Lo! where he comes.

(*Enter* OTHELLO *and* ATTENDANTS.)

OTHELLO: O my fair warrior!

DESDEMONA: My dear Othello!

OTHELLO: It gives me wonder great as my content
To see you here before me. O my soul's joy!
If after every tempest come such calms,
May the winds blow till they have waken'd death!
And let the labouring bark climb hills of seas
Olympus-high, and duck again as low
As hell 's from heaven! If it were now to die,
'Twere now to be most happy, for I fear
My soul hath her content so absolute
That not another comfort like to this
Succeeds in unknown fate.

DESDEMONA: The heavens forbid
But that our loves and comforts should increase
Even as our days do grow!

[219] *i.e.*, keep petty household accounts [220] free-spoken, licentious [221] to the mark, aptly [222] as . . . as [223] entangle [224] gentleman [225] syringes, enema pipes [226] *i.e.*, Othello's distinctive trumpet call

OTHELLO: Amen to that, sweet powers!
I cannot speak enough of this content;
It stops me here; it is too much of joy:
And this, and this, the greatest discords be (*Kissing her.*)
That e'er our hearts shall make!

IAGO (*aside*): O! you are well tun'd now,
But I 'll set down[227] the pegs that make this music,
As honest as I am.

OTHELLO: Come, let us to the castle.
News, friends; our wars are done, the Turks are drown'd.
How does my old acquaintance of this isle?
Honey, you shall be well desir'd[228] in Cyprus;
I have found great love amongst them. O my sweet,
I prattle out of fashion, and I dote
In mine own comforts. I prithee, good Iago,
Go to the bay and disembark my coffers.
Bring thou the master to the citadel;
He is a good one, and his worthiness
Does challenge much respect. Come, Desdemona,
Once more well met at Cyprus.

(*Exeunt all except* IAGO *and* RODERIGO.)

IAGO: Do thou meet me presently at the harbour. Come hither. If thou be'st valiant, as they say base men being in love have then a nobility in their natures more than is native to them, list[229] me. The lieutenant to-night watches on the court of guard:[230] first, I must tell thee this, Desdemona is directly in love with him.

RODERIGO: With him! Why, 'tis not possible.

IAGO: Lay thy finger thus, and let thy soul be instructed. Mark me with what violence she first loved the Moor but for bragging and telling her fantastical lies; and will she love him still for prating? let not thy discreet heart think it. Her eye must be fed; and what delight shall she have to look on the devil? When the blood is made dull with the act of sport, there should be, again to inflame it, and to give satiety a fresh appetite, loveliness in favour, sympathy in years, manners, and beauties; all which the Moor is defective in. Now, for want of these required conveniences, her delicate tenderness will find itself abused, begin to heave the gorge,[231] disrelish and abhor the Moor; very nature will instruct her in it, and compel her to some second choice. Now, sir, this granted, as it is a most pregnant[232] and unforced position, who stands so eminently in the degree of this fortune as Cassio does? a knave very voluble, no further conscionable[233]

[227] loosen [228] welcomed [229] listen to [230] guardhouse [231] vomit
[232] obvious [233] conscientious

than in putting on the mere form of civil and humane seeming, for the better compassing of his salt[234] and most hidden loose affection? why, none; why, none: a slipper[235] and subtle knave, a finder-out of occasions, that has an eye can stamp and counterfeit advantages, though true advantage never present itself; a devilish knave! Besides, the knave is handsome, young, and hath all those requisites in him that folly and green minds look after; a pestilent complete knave! and the woman hath found him already.

RODERIGO: I cannot believe that in her; she is full of most blessed condition.

IAGO: Blessed fig's end! the wine she drinks is made of grapes;[236] if she had been blessed she would never have loved the Moor; blessed pudding! Didst thou not see her paddle with the palm of his hand? didst not mark that?

RODERIGO: Yes, that I did; but that was but courtesy.

IAGO: Lechery, by this hand! an index[237] and obscure prologue to the history of lust and foul thoughts. They met so near with their lips, that their breaths embraced together. Villanous thoughts, Roderigo! when these mutualities so marshal the way, hard at hand comes the master and main exercise, the incorporate[238] conclusion. Pish![239] But, sir, be you ruled by me: I have brought you from Venice. Watch you to-night; for the command, I 'll lay 't upon you: Cassio knows you not. I 'll not be far from you: do you find some occasion to anger Cassio, either by speaking too loud, or tainting[240] his discipline; or from what other course you please, which the time shall more favourably minister.

RODERIGO: Well.

IAGO: Sir, he is rash and very sudden in choler, and haply may strike at you: provoke him, that he may; for even out of that will I cause these of Cyprus to mutiny, whose qualification[241] shall come into no true taste again but by the displanting of Cassio. So shall you have a shorter journey to your desires by the means I shall then have to prefer[242] them; and the impediment most profitably removed, without the which there were no expectation of our prosperity.

RODERIGO: I will do this, if I can bring it to any opportunity.

IAGO: I warrant thee. Meet me by and by at the citadel: I must fetch his necessaries ashore. Farewell.

RODERIGO: Adieu. (*Exit.*)

IAGO: That Cassio loves her, I do well believe it;
That she loves him, 'tis apt,[243] and of great credit:[244]

[234] lecherous [235] slippery [236] *i.e.*, she is only flesh and blood [237] pointer
[238] carnal [239] exclamation of disgust [240] disparaging [241] appeasement
[242] advance [243] natural, probable [244] easily believable

The Moor, howbeit that I endure him not,
Is of a constant, loving, noble nature;
And I dare think he 'll prove to Desdemona
A most dear[245] husband. Now, I do love her too;
Not out of absolute lust, — though peradventure[246]
I stand accountant[247] for as great a sin, —
But partly led to diet my revenge,
For that I do suspect the lusty Moor
Hath leap'd into my seat; the thought whereof
Doth like a poisonous mineral gnaw my inwards;
And nothing can or shall content my soul
Till I am even'd with him, wife for wife;
Or failing so, yet that I put the Moor
At least into a jealousy so strong
That judgment cannot cure. Which thing to do,
If this poor trash[248] of Venice, whom I trash[249]
For his quick hunting, stand the putting-on,[250]
I 'll have our Michael Cassio on the hip;
Abuse him to the Moor in the rank garb,[251]
For I fear Cassio with my night-cap too,
Make the Moor thank me, love me, and reward me
For making him egregiously an ass
And practising upon his peace and quiet
Even to madness. 'Tis here, but yet confus'd:
Knavery's plain face is never seen till us'd. *(Exit.)*

Scene 2 [A Street.]

(Enter a HERALD *with a proclamation; people following.)*

HERALD: It is Othello's pleasure, our noble and valiant general, that, upon certain tidings now arrived, importing the mere[252] perdition of the Turkish fleet, every man put himself into triumph; some to dance, some to make bonfires, each man to what sport and revels his addiction leads him; for, besides these beneficial news, it is the celebration of his nuptial. So much was his pleasure should be proclaimed. All offices[253] are open, and there is full liberty of feasting from this present hour of five till the bell have told eleven. Heaven bless the isle of Cyprus and our noble general Othello! *(Exeunt.)*

[245] a pun on the word in the sense of: expensive [246] perchance, perhaps
[247] accountable [248] *i.e.*, Roderigo [249] check, control [250] inciting
[251] gross manner [252] utter [253] kitchens and storehouses

Scene 3 [A Hall in the Castle.]

(*Enter* OTHELLO, DESDEMONA, CASSIO, *and* ATTENDANTS.)

OTHELLO: Good Michael, look you to the guard to-night:
Let 's teach ourselves that honourable stop,[254]
Not to outsport discretion.

CASSIO: Iago hath direction what to do:
But, notwithstanding, with my personal[255] eye
Will I look to 't.

OTHELLO: Iago is most honest.
Michael, good-night; to-morrow with your earliest
Let me have speech with you. (*To* DESDEMONA.) Come, my dear love,
The purchase made, the fruits are to ensue;
That profit 's yet to come 'twixt me and you.
Good-night.

(*Exeunt* OTHELLO, DESDEMONA, *and* ATTENDANTS.)

(*Enter* IAGO.)

CASSIO: Welcome, Iago; we must to the watch.

IAGO: Not this hour, lieutenant; 'tis not yet ten o' the clock. Our general casts us thus early for the love of his Desdemona, who let us not therefore blame; he hath not yet made wanton the night with her, and she is sport for Jove.

CASSIO: She's a most exquisite lady.

IAGO: And, I 'll warrant her, full of game.

CASSIO: Indeed, she is a most fresh and delicate creature.

IAGO: What an eye she has! methinks it sounds a parley[256] of provocation.

CASSIO: An inviting eye: and yet methinks right modest.

IAGO: And when she speaks, is it not an alarum[257] to love?

CASSIO: She is indeed perfection.

IAGO: Well, happiness to their sheets! Come, lieutenant, I have a stoup of wine, and here without are a brace[258] of Cyprus gallants that would fain have a measure to the health of black Othello.

CASSIO: Not to-night, good Iago: I have very poor and unhappy brains for drinking: I could well wish courtesy would invent some other custom of entertainment.

IAGO: O! they are our friends; but one cup: I 'll drink for you.

CASSIO: I have drunk but one cup to-night, and that was craftily quali-

[254] discipline [255] own [256] conference [257] call-to-arms [258] pair

fied[259] too, and, behold, what innovation[260] it makes here: I am unfortunate in the infirmity, and dare not task my weakness with any more.

IAGO: What, man! 'tis a night of revels; the gallants desire it.

CASSIO: Where are they?

IAGO: Here at the door; I pray you, call them in.

CASSIO: I 'll do 't; but it dislikes me. (*Exit.*)

IAGO: If I can fasten but one cup upon him,
With that which he hath drunk to-night already,
He 'll be as full of quarrel and offence
As my young mistress' dog. Now, my sick fool Roderigo,
Whom love has turn'd almost the wrong side out,
To Desdemona hath to-night carous'd
Potations pottle-deep;[261] and he 's to watch.
Three lads of Cyprus, noble swelling spirits,
That hold their honours in a wary distance,[262]
The very elements[263] of this warlike isle,
Have I to-night fluster'd with flowing cups,
And they watch too. Now, 'mongst this flock of drunkards,
Am I to put our Cassio in some action
That may offend the isle. But here they come.
If consequence[264] do but approve my dream,
My boat sails freely, both with wind and stream.

(*Re-enter* CASSIO, *with him* MONTANO, *and* GENTLEMEN. SERVANT *following with wine.*)

CASSIO: 'Fore God, they have given me a rouse[265] already.

MONTANO: Good faith, a little one; not past a pint, as I am a soldier.

IAGO: Some wine, ho!
(*Sings*) And let me the canakin[266] clink, clink;
And let me the canakin clink:
A soldier 's a man;
A life 's but a span;
Why then let a soldier drink.
Some wine, boys!

CASSIO: 'Fore God, an excellent song.

IAGO: I learned it in England, where indeed they are most potent in potting; your Dane, your German, and your swag-bellied[267] Hollander, — drink, ho! — are nothing to your English.

CASSIO: Is your Englishman so expert in his drinking?

259 diluted 260 change, revolution 261 bottoms-up 262 take offense easily 263 types 264 succeeding events 265 drink 266 small cup 267 with a pendulous belly

IAGO: Why, he drinks you[268] with facility your Dane dead drunk; he sweats not to overthrow your Almain;[269] he gives your Hollander a vomit ere the next pottle can be filled.

CASSIO: To the health of our general!

MONTANO: I am for it, lieutenant; and I 'll do you justice.

IAGO: O sweet England!

(*Sings*) King Stephen was a worthy peer,
His breeches cost him but a crown;
He held them sixpence all too dear,
With that he call'd the tailor lown.[270]
He was a wight of high renown,
And thou art but of low degree:
'Tis pride that pulls the country down,
Then take thine auld cloak about thee.

Some wine, ho!

CASSIO: Why, this is a more exquisite song than the other.

IAGO: Will you hear 't again?

CASSIO: No; for I hold him to be unworthy of his place that does those things. Well, God 's above all; and there be souls must be saved, and there be souls must not be saved.

IAGO: It 's true, good lieutenant.

CASSIO: For mine own part, — no offence to the general, nor any man of quality, — I hope to be saved.

IAGO: And so do I too, lieutenant.

CASSIO: Ay; but, by your leave, not before me; the lieutenant is to be saved before the ancient. Let 's have no more of this; let 's to our affairs. God forgive us our sins! Gentlemen, let 's look to our business. Do not think, gentlemen, I am drunk: this is my ancient; this is my right hand, and this is my left hand. I am not drunk now; I can stand well enough, and speak well enough.

ALL: Excellent well.

CASSIO: Why, very well, then; you must not think then that I am drunk. (*Exit.*)

MONTANO: To the platform, masters; come, let 's set the watch.

IAGO: You see this fellow that is gone before;
He is a soldier fit to stand by Caesar
And give direction; and do but see his vice;
'Tis to his virtue a just equinox,[271]
The one as long as the other; 'tis pity of him.
I fear the trust Othello puts him in,
On some odd time of his infirmity,

268 the "ethical" dative, *i.e.*, you'll see that he drinks 269 German
270 lout, rascal 271 equivalent

Will shake this island.

MONTANO: But is he often thus?

IAGO: 'Tis evermore the prologue to his sleep;
He 'll watch the horologe a double set,[272]
If drink rock not his cradle.

MONTANO: It were well
The general were put in mind of it.
Perhaps he sees it not; or his good nature
Prizes the virtue that appears in Cassio,
And looks not on his evils. Is not this true?

(*Enter* RODERIGO.)

IAGO (*aside to him*): How now, Roderigo!
I pray you, after the lieutenant; go. (*Exit* RODERIGO.)

MONTANO: And 'tis great pity that the noble Moor
Should hazard such a place as his own second
With one of an ingraft[273] infirmity;
It were an honest action to say
So to the Moor.

IAGO: Not I, for this fair island:
I do love Cassio well, and would do much
To cure him of this evil. But hark! what noise?

(*Cry within,* 'Help! Help!' *Re-enter* CASSIO, *driving in* RODERIGO.)

CASSIO: You rogue! you rascal!

MONTANO: What 's the matter, lieutenant?

CASSIO: A knave teach me my duty!
I 'll beat the knave into a twiggen[274] bottle.

RODERIGO: Beat me!

CASSIO: Dost thou prate, rogue?

(*Striking* RODERIGO.)

MONTANO (*staying him*): Nay, good lieutenant;
I pray you, sir, hold your hand.

CASSIO: Let me go, sir,
Or I 'll knock you o'er the mazzard.[275]

MONTANO: Come, come; you're drunk.

CASSIO: Drunk!

(*They fight.*)

IAGO (*aside to* RODERIGO): Away, I say! go out, and cry a mutiny.
(*Exit* RODERIGO.)

272 stand watch twice twelve hours 273 ingrained 274 wicker 275 head

Nay, good lieutenant! God's will, gentlemen!
Help, ho! Lieutenant! sir! Montano! sir!
Help, masters! Here 's a goodly watch indeed!

(*Bell rings.*)

Who 's that that rings the bell? Diablo, ho!
The town will rise: God's will! lieutenant, hold!
You will be sham'd for ever.

(*Re-enter* OTHELLO *and* ATTENDANTS.)

OTHELLO: What is the matter here?
MONTANO: 'Zounds! I bleed still; I am hurt to the death.

(*He faints.*)

OTHELLO: Hold, for your lives!
IAGO: Hold, ho, lieutenant! Sir! Montano! gentlemen!
Have you forgot all sense of place and duty?
Hold! the general speaks to you; hold for shame!
OTHELLO: Why, how now, ho! from whence ariseth this?
Are we turn'd Turks, and to ourselves do that
Which heaven hath forbid the Ottomites?
For Christian shame put by this barbarous brawl;
He that stirs next to carve for his own rage
Holds his soul light; he dies upon his motion.
Silence that dreadful bell! it frights the isle
From her propriety. What is the matter, masters?
Honest Iago, that look'st dead with grieving,
Speak, who began this? on thy love, I charge thee.
IAGO: I do not know; friends all but now, even now,
In quarter[276] and in terms like bride and groom
Devesting[277] them for bed; and then, but now, —
As if some planet had unwitted men, —
Swords out, and tilting one at other's breast,
In opposition bloody. I cannot speak
Any beginning to this peevish odds,[278]
And would in action glorious I had lost
Those legs that brought me to a part of it!
OTHELLO: How comes it, Michael, you are thus forgot?
CASSIO: I pray you, pardon me; I cannot speak.
OTHELLO: Worthy Montano, you were wont be civil;
The gravity and stillness of your youth

[276] on duty [277] undressing [278] silly quarrel

The world hath noted, and your name is great
In mouths of wisest censure:[279] what 's the matter,
That you unlace[280] your reputation thus
And spend your rich opinion[281] for the name
Of a night-brawler? give me answer to it.

MONTANO: Worthy Othello, I am hurt to danger;
Your officer, Iago, can inform you,
While I spare speech, which something now offends[282] me,
Of all that I do know; nor know I aught
By me that 's said or done amiss this night,
Unless self-charity be sometimes a vice,
And to defend ourselves it be a sin
When violence assails us.

OTHELLO: Now, by heaven,
My blood begins my safer guides to rule,
And passion, having my best judgment collied,[283]
Assays to lead the way. If I once stir,
Or do but lift this arm, the best of you
Shall sink in my rebuke. Give me to know
How this foul rout began, who set it on;
And he that is approv'd [284] in this offence,
Though he had twinn'd with me — both at a birth —
Shall lose me. What! in a town of war,
Yet wild, the people's hearts brimful of fear,
To manage private and domestic quarrel,
In night, and on the court and guard of safety!
'Tis monstrous. Iago, who began 't?

MONTANO: If partially affin'd, [285] or leagu'd in office,
Thou dost deliver more or less than truth,
Thou art no soldier.

IAGO: Touch me not so near;
I had rather[286] have this tongue cut from my mouth
Than it should do offence to Michael Cassio;
Yet, I persuade myself, to speak the truth
Shall nothing wrong him. Thus it is, general.
Montano and myself being in speech,
There comes a fellow crying out for help,
And Cassio following with determin'd sword
To execute upon him. Sir, this gentleman
Steps in to Cassio, and entreats his pause;

[279] judgment [280] undo [281] high reputation [282] pains, harms [283] clouded [284] proved (*i.e.*, guilty) [285] favorably biased (by ties of friendship, or as Cassio's fellow officer) [286] more quickly

Myself the crying fellow did pursue,
Lest by his clamour, as it so fell out,
The town might fall in fright; he, swift of foot,
Outran my purpose, and I return'd the rather
For that I heard the clink and fall of swords,
And Cassio high in oath, which till to-night
I ne'er might say before. When I came back, —
For this was brief, — I found them close together,
At blow and thrust, even as again they were
When you yourself did part them.
More of this matter can I not report:
But men are men; the best sometimes forget:
Though Cassio did some little wrong to him,
As men in rage strike those that wish them best,
Yet, surely Cassio, I believe, receiv'd
From him that fled some strange indignity,
Which patience could not pass.

OTHELLO: I know, Iago,
Thy honesty and love doth mince[287] this matter,
Making it light to Cassio. Cassio, I love thee;
But never more be officer of mine.

(*Enter* DESDEMONA, *attended.*)

Look! if my gentle love be not rais'd up;
(*To* CASSIO.) I'll make thee an example.

DESDEMONA: What's the matter?

OTHELLO: All 's well now, sweeting; come away to bed.
Sir, for your hurts, myself will be your surgeon.
Lead him off. (MONTANO *is led off.*)
Iago, look with care about the town,
And silence those whom this vile brawl distracted.
Come, Desdemona; 'tis the soldier's life,
To have their balmy slumbers wak'd with strife.

(*Exeunt all but* IAGO *and* CASSIO.)

IAGO: What! are you hurt, lieutenant?

CASSIO: Ay; past all surgery.

IAGO: Marry, heaven forbid!

CASSIO: Reputation, reputation, reputation! O! I have lost my reputation. I have lost the immortal part of myself, and what remains is bestial. My reputation, Iago, my reputation!

IAGO: As I am an honest man, I thought you had received some bodily

[287] tone down

wound; there is more offence in that than in reputation. Reputation is an idle and most false imposition;[288] oft got without merit, and lost without deserving: you have lost no reputation at all, unless you repute yourself such a loser. What! man; there are ways to recover the general again; you are but now cast in his mood,[289] a punishment more in policy[290] than in malice; even so as one would beat his offenceless dog to affright an imperious lion. Sue to him again, and he is yours.

CASSIO: I will rather sue to be despised than to deceive so good a commander with so slight, so drunken and so indiscreet an officer. Drunk! and speak parrot![291] and squabble, swagger, swear, and discourse fustian[292] with one's own shadow! O thou invisible spirit of wine! if thou hast no name to be known by, let us call thee devil!

IAGO: What was he that you followed with your sword? What hath he done to you?

CASSIO: I know not.

IAGO: Is 't possible?

CASSIO: I remember a mass of things, but nothing distinctly; a quarrel, but nothing wherefore. O God! that men should put an enemy in their mouths to steal away their brains; that we should, with joy, pleasance,[293] revel, and applause, transform ourselves into beasts.

IAGO: Why, but you are now well enough; how came you thus recovered?

CASSIO: It hath pleased the devil drunkenness to give place to the devil wrath; one unperfectness shows me another, to make me frankly despise myself.

IAGO: Come, you are too severe a moraler. As the time, the place, and the condition of this country stands, I could heartily wish this had not befallen, but since it is as it is, mend it for your own good.

CASSIO: I will ask him for my place again; he shall tell me I am a drunkard! Had I as many mouths as Hydra,[294] such an answer would stop them all. To be now a sensible man, by and by a fool, and presently a beast! O strange! Every inordinate cup is unblessed and the ingredient[295] is a devil.

IAGO: Come, come; good wine is a good familiar creature if it be well used; exclaim no more against it. And, good lieutenant, I think you think I love you.

CASSIO: I have well approved it, sir. I drunk!

IAGO: You or any man living may be drunk at some time, man. I 'll tell

288 something external 289 dismissed because he is angry 290 *i.e.*, more for the sake of the example, or to show his fairness 291 *i.e.*, without thinking 292 *i.e.*, nonsense 293 pleasure 294 many-headed snake in Greek mythology 295 contents

you what you shall do. Our general's wife is now the general: I may say so in this respect, for that he hath devoted and given up himself to the contemplation, mark, and denotement of her parts and graces: confess yourself freely to her; importune her; she 'll help to put you in your place again. She is of so free, so kind, so apt, so blessed a disposition, that she holds it a vice in her goodness not to do more than she is requested. This broken joint between you and her husband entreat her to splinter;[296] and, my fortunes against any lay[297] worth naming, this crack of your love shall grow stronger than it was before.

CASSIO: You advise me well.

IAGO: I protest, in the sincerity of love and honest kindness.

CASSIO: I think it freely; and betimes in the morning I will beseech the virtuous Desdemona to undertake for me. I am desperate of my fortunes if they check me here.

IAGO: You are in the right. Good-night, lieutenant; I must to the watch.

CASSIO: Good-night, honest Iago! *(Exit.)*

IAGO: And what's he then that says I play the villain?
When this advice is free I give and honest,
Probal [298] to thinking and indeed the course
To win the Moor again? For 'tis most easy
The inclining Desdemona to subdue
In any honest suit; she 's fram'd as fruitful [299]
As the free elements. And then for her
To win the Moor, were 't to renounce his baptism,
All seals and symbols of redeemed sin,
His soul is so enfetter'd to her love,
That she may make, unmake, do what she list,
Even as her appetite shall play the god
With his weak function.[300] How am I then a villain
To counsel Cassio to this parallel [301] course,
Directly to his good? Divinity of hell!
When devils will the blackest sins put on,
They do suggest at first with heavenly shows,
As I do now; for while this honest fool
Plies Desdemona to repair his fortunes,
And she for him pleads strongly to the Moor,
I 'll pour this pestilence into his ear
That she repeals[302] him for her body's lust;
And, by how much she strives to do him good,
She shall undo her credit with the Moor.

[296] bind up with splints [297] wager [298] provable [299] generous
[300] faculties [301] purposeful [302] *i.e.*, seeks to recall

So will I turn her virtue into pitch,
And out of her own goodness make the net
That shall enmesh them all.

(*Re-enter* RODERIGO.)

How now, Roderigo!

RODERIGO: I do follow here in the chase, not like a hound that hunts, but one that fills up the cry.[303] My money is almost spent; I have been to-night exceedingly well cudgelled; and I think the issue will be, I shall have so much experience for my pains; and so, with no money at all and a little more wit, return again to Venice.

IAGO: How poor are they that have not patience!
What wound did ever heal but by degrees?
Thou know'st we work by wit and not by witchcraft,
And wit depends on dilatory time.
Does 't not go well? Cassio hath beaten thee,
And thou by that small hurt hast cashiered Cassio.
Though other things grow fair against the sun,
Yet fruits that blossom first will first be ripe:
Content thyself awhile. By the mass, 'tis morning;
Pleasure and action make the hours seem short.
Retire thee; go where thou art billeted:
Away, I say; thou shalt know more hereafter:
Nay, get thee gone. (*Exit* RODERIGO.) Two things are to be done,
My wife must move for Cassio to her mistress;
I 'll set her on;
Myself the while to draw the Moor apart,
And bring him jump[304] when he may Cassio find
Soliciting his wife: ay, that 's the way:
Dull not device by coldness and delay. (*Exit.*)

ACT III

Scene 1 [Cyprus. Before the Castle.]

(*Enter* CASSIO, *and some* MUSICIANS.)

CASSIO: Masters, play here, I will content your pains;[305]
Something that 's brief; and bid 'Good-morrow, general.' (*Music.*)

(*Enter* CLOWN.)

303 pack (hunting term) 304 at the exact moment 305 reward your efforts

CLOWN: Why, masters, have your instruments been in Naples, that they speak i' the nose[306] thus?

FIRST MUSICIAN: How, sir, how?

CLOWN: Are these, I pray you, wind-instruments?

FIRST MUSICIAN: Ay, marry, are they, sir.

CLOWN: O! thereby hangs a tail.

FIRST MUSICIAN: Whereby hangs a tale, sir?

CLOWN: Marry, sir, by many a wind-instrument that I know. But, masters, here 's money for you; and the general so likes your music, that he desires you, for love's sake, to make no more noise with it.

FIRST MUSICIAN: Well, sir, we will not.

CLOWN: If you have any music that may not be heard, to 't again; but, as they say, to hear music the general does not greatly care.

FIRST MUSICIAN: We have none such, sir.

CLOWN: Then put up your pipes in your bag, for I 'll away.
Go; vanish into air; away! (*Exeunt* MUSICIANS.)

CASSIO: Dost thou hear, mine honest friend?

CLOWN: No, I hear not your honest friend; I hear you.

CASSIO: Prithee, keep up thy quillets.[307] There 's a poor piece of gold for thee. If the gentlewoman that attends the general's wife be stirring, tell her there 's one Cassio entreats her a little favour of speech: wilt thou do this?

CLOWN: She is stirring, sir: if she will stir hither, I shall seem to notify unto her.

CASSIO: Do, good my friend. (*Exit* CLOWN.)

(*Enter* IAGO.)

In happy time, Iago.

IAGO: You have not been a-bed, then?

CASSIO: Why, no; the day had broke
Before we parted. I have made bold, Iago,
To send in to your wife; my suit to her
Is, that she will to virtuous Desdemona
Procure me some access.

IAGO: I 'll send her to you presently;
And I 'll devise a mean to draw the Moor
Out of the way, that your converse and business
May be more free.

CASSIO: I humbly thank you for 't. (*Exit* IAGO.)
I never knew

[306] Naples was notorious for venereal disease, and syphilis was believed to affect the nose. [307] quibbles

A Florentine more kind and honest.[308]

(*Enter* EMILIA.)

EMILIA: Good-morrow, good lieutenant: I am sorry
For your displeasure;[309] but all will soon be well.
The general and his wife are talking of it,
And she speaks for you stoutly: the Moor replies
That he you hurt is of great fame in Cyprus
And great affinity,[310] and that in wholesome wisdom
He might not but refuse you; but he protests he loves you,
And needs no other suitor but his likings
To take the safest occasion by the front[311]
To bring you in again.[312]

CASSIO: Yet, I beseech you,
If you think fit, or that it may be done,
Give me advantage of some brief discourse
With Desdemona alone.

EMILIA: Pray you, come in:
I will bestow you where you shall have time
To speak your bosom[313] freely.

CASSIO: I am much bound to you.

(*Exeunt.*)

Scene 2 [A Room in the Castle.]

(*Enter* OTHELLO, IAGO, *and* GENTLEMEN.)

OTHELLO: These letters give, Iago, to the pilot,
And by him do my duties to the senate;
That done, I will be walking on the works;
Repair there to me.

IAGO: Well, my good lord, I 'll do 't.

OTHELLO: This fortification, gentlemen, shall we see 't?

GENTLEMEN: We 'll wait upon your lordship. (*Exeunt.*)

Scene 3 [Before the Castle.]

(*Enter* DESDEMONA, CASSIO, *and* EMILIA.)

DESDEMONA: Be thou assur'd, good Cassio, I will do
All my abilities in thy behalf.

308 Cassio means that not even a fellow Florentine could behave to him in a friendlier fashion than does Iago. 309 disgrace 310 family connection 311 forelock 312 restore you (to Othello's favor) 313 heart, inmost thoughts

EMILIA: Good madam, do: I warrant it grieves my husband,
As if the case were his.
DESDEMONA: O! that's an honest fellow. Do not doubt, Cassio,
But I will have my lord and you again
As friendly as you were.
CASSIO: Bounteous madam,
Whatever shall become of Michael Cassio,
He 's never any thing but your true servant.
DESDEMONA: I know 't; I thank you. You do love my lord;
You have known him long; and be you well assur'd
He shall in strangeness[314] stand no further off
Than in a politic[315] distance.
CASSIO: Ay, but, lady,
That policy may either last so long,
Or feed upon such nice[316] and waterish diet,
Or breed itself so out of circumstance,
That, I being absent and my place supplied,
My general will forget my love and service.
DESDEMONA: Do not doubt[317] that; before Emilia here
I give thee warrant of thy place. Assure thee,
If I do vow a friendship, I 'll perform it
To the last article; my lord shall never rest;
I 'll watch him tame,[318] and talk him out of patience;
His bed shall seem a school, his board a shrift;[319]
I 'll intermingle every thing he does
With Cassio's suit. Therefore be merry, Cassio;
For thy solicitor shall rather die
Than give thy cause away.[320]

(*Enter* OTHELLO, *and* IAGO *at a distance.*)

EMILIA: Madam, here comes my lord.
CASSIO: Madam, I 'll take my leave.
DESDEMONA: Why, stay, and hear me speak.
CASSIO: Madam, not now; I am very ill at ease,
Unfit for mine own purposes.
DESDEMONA: Well, do your discretion. (*Exit* CASSIO.)
IAGO: Ha! I like not that.
OTHELLO: What dost thou say?
IAGO: Nothing, my lord: or if — I know not what.
OTHELLO: Was not that Cassio parted from my wife?

[314] aloofness [315] *i.e.*, dictated by policy [316] slight, trivial [317] fear
[318] outwatch him (*i.e.*, keep him awake) till he submits [319] confessional
[320] abandon your cause

IAGO: Cassio, my lord? No, sure, I cannot think it,
That he would steal away so guilty-like,
Seeing you coming.
OTHELLO: I do believe 'twas he.
DESDEMONA: How now, my lord!
I have been talking with a suitor here,
A man that languishes in your displeasure.
OTHELLO: Who is 't you mean?
DESDEMONA: Why, your lieutenant, Cassio. Good my lord,
If I have any grace or power to move you,
His present[321] reconciliation take;
For if he be not one that truly loves you,
That errs in ignorance and not in cunning,
I have no judgment in an honest face.
I prithee[322] call him back.
OTHELLO: Went he hence now?
DESDEMONA: Ay, sooth; so humbled,
That he hath left part of his grief with me,
To suffer with him. Good love, call him back.
OTHELLO: Not now, sweet Desdemona; some other time.
DESDEMONA: But shall 't be shortly?
OTHELLO: The sooner, sweet, for you.
DESDEMONA: Shall 't be to-night at supper?
OTHELLO: No, not to-night.
DESDEMONA: To-morrow dinner, then?
OTHELLO: I shall not dine at home;
I meet the captains at the citadel.
DESDEMONA: Why, then, to-morrow night; or Tuesday morn;
Or Tuesday noon, or night; or Wednesday morn:
I prithee name the time, but let it not
Exceed three days: in faith, he 's penitent;
And yet his trespass, in our common reason, —
Save that they say, the wars must make examples
Out of their best, — is not almost[323] a fault
To incur a private check.[324] When shall he come?
Tell me, Othello: I wonder in my soul,
What you could ask me, that I should deny,
Or stand so mammering[325] on. What! Michael Cassio,
That came a wooing with you, and so many a time,
When I have spoke of you dispraisingly,
Hath ta'en your part; to have so much to do

321 immediate 322 pray thee 323 hardly 324 (even) a private reprimand
325 shilly-shallying

To bring him in! Trust me, I could do much, —
OTHELLO: Prithee, no more; let him come when he will;
I will deny thee nothing.
DESDEMONA: Why, this is not a boon;
'Tis as I should entreat you wear your gloves,
Or feed on nourishing dishes, or keep you warm,
Or sue to you to do a peculiar profit
To your own person: nay, when I have a suit
Wherein I mean to touch your love indeed,
It shall be full of poise[326] and difficult weight,
And fearful to be granted.
OTHELLO: I will deny thee nothing:
Whereon, I do beseech thee, grant me this,
To leave me but a little to myself.
DESDEMONA: Shall I deny you? no: farewell, my lord.
OTHELLO: Farewell, my Desdemona: I'll come to thee straight.
DESDEMONA: Emilia, come. Be as your fancies teach you;
Whate'er you be, I am obedient. (*Exit, with* EMILIA.)
OTHELLO: Excellent wretch![327] Perdition catch my soul,
But I do love thee! and when I love thee not,
Chaos is[328] come again.
IAGO: My noble lord, —
OTHELLO: What dost thou say, Iago?
IAGO: Did Michael Cassio, when you woo'd my lady,
Know of your love?
OTHELLO: He did, from first to last: why dost thou ask?
IAGO: But for a satisfaction of my thought;
No further harm.
OTHELLO: Why of thy thought, Iago?
IAGO: I did not think he had been acquainted with her.
OTHELLO: O! yes; and went between us very oft.
IAGO: Indeed!
OTHELLO: Indeed! ay, indeed; discern'st thou aught in that?
Is he not honest?
IAGO: Honest, my lord?
OTHELLO: Honest! ay, honest.
IAGO: My lord, for aught I know.
OTHELLO: What dost thou think?
IAGO: Think, my lord!
OTHELLO: Think, my lord!
By heaven, he echoes me,

[326] weight [327] here, a term of endearment [328] will have

As if there were some monster in his thought
Too hideous to be shown. Thou dost mean something:
I heard thee say but now, thou lik'dst not that,
When Cassio left my wife; what didst not like?
And when I told thee he was of my counsel
In my whole course of wooing, thou criedst, 'Indeed!'
And didst contract and purse thy brow together,
As if thou then hadst shut up in thy brain
Some horrible conceit.[329] If thou dost love me,
Show me thy thought.

IAGO: My lord, you know I love you.

OTHELLO: I think thou dost;
And, for[330] I know thou art full of love and honesty,
And weigh'st thy words before thou givest them breath,
Therefore these stops[331] of thine fright me the more;
For such things in a false disloyal knave
Are tricks of custom, but in a man that 's just
They are close delations,[332] working from the heart
That passion cannot rule.

IAGO: For Michael Cassio,
I dare be sworn I think that he is honest.

OTHELLO: I think so too.

IAGO: Men should be what they seem;
Or those that be not, would they might seem none!

OTHELLO: Certain, men should be what they seem.

IAGO: Why then, I think Cassio 's an honest man.

OTHELLO: Nay, yet there's more in this.
I pray thee, speak to me as to thy thinkings,
As thou dost ruminate, and give thy worst of thoughts
The worst of words.

IAGO: Good my lord, pardon me;
Though I am bound to every act of duty,
I am not bound to[333] that all slaves are free to.
Utter my thoughts? Why, say they are vile and false;
As where 's that palace whereinto foul things
Sometimes intrude not? who has a breast so pure
But some uncleanly apprehensions[334]
Keep leets and law-days,[335] and in session sit
With meditations lawful?

OTHELLO: Thou dost conspire against thy friend, Iago,

329 fancy 330 because 331 interruptions, hesitations 332 secret (*i.e.*, involuntary, unconscious) revelations 333 bound with regard to 334 conceptions 335 sittings of the local courts

If thou but think'st him wrong'd, and mak'st his ear
A stranger to thy thoughts.

IAGO: I do beseech you,
Though I perchance am vicious in my guess, —
As, I confess, it is my nature's plague
To spy into abuses, and oft my jealousy[336]
Shapes faults that are not, — that your wisdom yet,
From one that so imperfectly conceits,
Would take no notice, nor build yourself a trouble
Out of his scattering and unsure observance.
It were not for your quiet nor your good,
Nor for my manhood, honesty, or wisdom,
To let you know my thoughts.

OTHELLO: What dost thou mean?

IAGO: Good name in man and woman, dear my lord,
Is the immediate jewel of [337] their souls:
Who steals my purse steals trash; 'tis something, nothing;
'Twas mine, 'tis his, and has been slave to thousands;
But he that filches from me my good name
Robs me of that which not enriches him,
And makes me poor indeed.

OTHELLO: By heaven, I 'll know thy thoughts.

IAGO: You cannot, if my heart were in your hand;
Nor shall not, whilst 'tis in my custody.

OTHELLO: Ha!

IAGO: O! beware, my lord, of jealousy;
It is the green-ey'd monster which doth mock
The meat it feeds on; that cuckold [338] lives in bliss
Who, certain of his fate, loves not his wronger;
But, O! what damned minutes tells[339] he o'er
Who dotes, yet doubts; suspects, yet soundly loves!

OTHELLO: O misery!

IAGO: Poor and content is rich, and rich enough,
But riches fineless[340] is as poor as winter
To him that ever fears he shall be poor.
Good heaven, the souls of all my tribe defend
From jealousy!

OTHELLO: Why, why is this?
Think'st thou I'd make a life of jealousy,
To follow still the changes of the moon
With fresh suspicions? No; to be once in doubt

[336] suspicion [337] jewel closest to [338] husband of an adulterous woman
[339] counts [340] boundless

Is once to be resolved. Exchange me for a goat
When I shall turn the business of my soul
To such exsufflicate[341] and blown[342] surmises,
Matching thy inference. 'Tis not to make me jealous
To say my wife is fair, feeds well, loves company,
Is free of speech, sings, plays, and dances well;
Where virtue is, these are more virtuous:
Nor from mine own weak merits will I draw
The smallest fear, or doubt of her revolt;
For she had eyes, and chose me. No, Iago;
I 'll see before I doubt; when I doubt, prove;
And, on the proof, there is no more but this,
Away at once with love or jealousy!

IAGO: I am glad of it; for now I shall have reason
To show the love and duty that I bear you
With franker spirit; therefore, as I am bound,
Receive it from me; I speak not yet of proof.
Look to your wife; observe her well with Cassio;
Wear your eye thus, not jealous nor secure:
I would not have your free and noble nature
Out of self-bounty[343] be abus'd; look to 't:
I know our country disposition[344] well;
In Venice they do let heaven see the pranks
They dare not show their husbands; their best conscience
Is not to leave 't undone, but keep 't unknown.

OTHELLO: Dost thou say so?

IAGO: She did deceive her father, marrying you;
And when she seem'd to shake and fear your looks,
She lov'd them most.

OTHELLO: And so she did.

IAGO: Why, go to,[345] then;
She that so young could give out such a seeming,
To seel her father's eyes up close as oak,
He thought 'twas witchcraft; but I am much to blame;
I humbly do beseech you of your pardon
For too much loving you.

OTHELLO: I am bound to thee for ever.

IAGO: I see, this hath a little dash'd your spirits.

OTHELLO: Not a jot, not a jot.

IAGO: I' faith, I fear it has.
I hope you will consider what is spoke

[341] spat out (?) [342] fly-blown [343] innate generosity [344] *i.e.*, that of Venice [345] colloquialism; here, something like "all right"

Comes from my love. But I do see you're mov'd;
I am to pray you not to strain my speech
To grosser issues nor to larger reach
Than to suspicion.

OTHELLO: I will not.

IAGO: Should you do so, my lord,
My speech should fall into such vile success
As my thoughts aim not at. Cassio 's my worthy friend —
My lord, I see you're mov'd.

OTHELLO: No, not much mov'd:
I do not think but Desdemona's honest.[346]

IAGO: Long live she so! and long live you to think so!

OTHELLO: And yet, how nature erring from itself, —

IAGO: Ay, there's the point: as, to be bold with you,
Not to affect many proposed matches
Of her own clime,[347] complexion, and degree,[348]
Whereto, we see, in all things nature tends;
Foh! one may smell in such, a will most rank,
Foul disproportion, thoughts unnatural.
But pardon me; I do not in position[349]
Distinctly[350] speak of her, though I may fear
Her will, recoiling[351] to her better judgment,
May fall to match you with her country forms
And happily[352] repent.

OTHELLO: Farewell, farewell:
If more thou dost perceive, let me know more;
Set on thy wife to observe. Leave me, Iago.

IAGO: My lord, I take my leave. *(Going.)*

OTHELLO: Why did I marry? This honest creature, doubtless,
Sees and knows more, much more, than he unfolds.

IAGO (*returning*): My lord, I would I might entreat your honour
To scan this thing no further; leave it to time.
Although 'tis fit that Cassio have his place,
For, sure he fills it up with great ability,
Yet, if you please to hold him off awhile,
You shall by that perceive him and his means:
Note if your lady strain his entertainment[353]
With any strong or vehement importunity;
Much will be seen in that. In the mean time,
Let me be thought too busy[354] in my fears,

[346] chaste [347] country [348] social rank [349] in definite assertion
[350] specifically [351] reverting (*i.e.*, to Othello's trust and favor) [352] perhaps [353] urge his re-welcome
[354] meddlesome

As worthy cause I have to fear I am,
And hold her free, I do beseech your honour.

OTHELLO: Fear not my government.

IAGO: I once more take my leave. (*Exit.*)

OTHELLO: This fellow 's of exceeding honesty,
And knows all qualities, with a learned spirit,
Of human dealings; if I do prove her haggard,[355]
Though that her jesses[356] were my dear heart-strings,
I 'd whistle her off and let her down the wind,[357]
To prey at fortune. Haply, for I am black,
And have not those soft parts of conversation
That chamberers[358] have, or, for I am declin'd
Into the vale of years — yet that 's not much —
She 's gone, I am abus'd;[359] and my relief
Must be to loathe her. O curse of marriage!
That we can call these delicate creatures ours,
And not their appetites. I had rather be a toad,
And live upon the vapour of a dungeon,
Than keep a corner in the thing I love
For others' uses. Yet, 'tis the plague of great ones;
Prerogativ'd [360] are they less than the base;
'Tis destiny unshunnable, like death:
Even then this forked plague[361] is fated to us
When we do quicken.[362]
Look! where she comes.
If she be false, O! then heaven mocks itself.
I 'll not believe it.

(*Re-enter* DESDEMONA *and* EMILIA.)

DESDEMONA: How now, my dear Othello!
Your dinner and the generous[363] islanders
By you invited, do attend your presence.

OTHELLO: I am to blame.

DESDEMONA: Why do you speak so faintly?
Are you not well?

OTHELLO: I have a pain upon my forehead here.[364]

DESDEMONA: Faith, that 's with watching; 'twill away again:
Let me but bind it hard, within this hour

[355] wild hawk [356] leather thongs by which the hawk's legs were strapped to the trainer's wrist [357] I'd let her go and take care of herself [358] courtiers; or (more specifically): gallants, frequenters of bed chambers [359] deceived [360] privileged [361] *i.e.*, the cuckold's proverbial horns [362] are conceived, come alive [363] noble [364] Othello again refers to his cuckoldom.

It will be well.

OTHELLO: Your napkin[365] is too little:

(*She drops her handkerchief.*)

Let it alone. Come, I 'll go in with you.

DESDEMONA: I am very sorry that you are not well.

(*Exeunt* OTHELLO *and* DESDEMONA.)

EMILIA: I am glad I have found this napkin;
This was her first remembrance from the Moor;
My wayward husband hath a hundred times
Woo'd me to steal it, but she so loves the token,
For he conjur'd her she should ever keep it,
That she reserves it evermore about her
To kiss and talk to. I 'll have the work ta'en out,[366]
And give 't Iago:
What he will do with it heaven knows, not I;
I nothing but[367] to please his fantasy.[368]

(*Enter* IAGO.)

IAGO: How now! what do you here alone?

EMILIA: Do not you chide; I have a thing for you.

IAGO: A thing for me? It is a common thing —

EMILIA: Ha!

IAGO: To have a foolish wife.

EMILIA: O! is that all? What will you give me now
For that same handkerchief?

IAGO: What handkerchief?

EMILIA: What handkerchief!
Why, that the Moor first gave to Desdemona:
That which so often you did bid me steal.

IAGO: Hath stol'n it from her?

EMILIA: No, faith; she let it drop by negligence,
And, to the advantage, I, being there, took 't up.
Look, here it is.

IAGO: A good wench; give it me.

EMILIA: What will you do with 't, that you have been so earnest
To have me filch it?

IAGO: Why, what 's that to you? (*Snatches it.*)

EMILIA: If it be not for some purpose of import
Give 't me again; poor lady! she 'll run mad
When she shall lack it.

[365] handkerchief [366] pattern copied [367] *i.e.*, only want [368] whim

IAGO: Be not acknown on 't;[369] I have use for it.
Go, leave me. (*Exit* EMILIA.)
I will in Cassio's lodging lose this napkin,
And let him find it; trifles light as air
Are to the jealous confirmations strong
As proofs of holy writ; this may do something.
The Moor already changes with my poison:
Dangerous conceits are in their natures poisons,
Which at the first are scarce found to distaste,[370]
But with a little act upon the blood,
Burn like the mines of sulphur. I did say so:
Look! where he comes!

(*Enter* OTHELLO.)

Not poppy,[371] nor mandragora,[372]
Nor all the drowsy syrups[373] of the world,
Shall ever medicine thee to that sweet sleep
Which thou owedst yesterday.

OTHELLO: Ha! ha! false to me?

IAGO: Why, how now, general! no more of that.

OTHELLO: Avaunt! be gone! thou hast set me on the rack;
I swear 'tis better to be much abus'd
Than but to know 't a little.

IAGO: How now, my lord!

OTHELLO: What sense had I of her stol'n hours of lust?
I saw 't not, thought it not, it harm'd not me;
I slept the next night well, was free and merry;
I found not Cassio's kisses on her lips;
He that is robb'd, not wanting what is stol'n,
Let him not know 't, and he 's not robb'd at all.

IAGO: I am sorry to hear this.

OTHELLO: I had been happy, if the general camp,[374]
Pioners[375] and all, had tasted her sweet body,
So[376] I had nothing known. O! now, for ever
Farewell the tranquil mind; farewell content!
Farewell the plumed troop and the big wars
That make ambition virtue! O, farewell!
Farewell the neighing steed, and the shrill trump,
The spirit-stirring drum, the ear-piercing fife,
The royal banner, and all quality,

[369] you know nothing about it [370] scarce can be tasted [371] opium [372] a soporific [373] *i.e.*, soporifics [374] whole army [375] lowest rank of manual laborers in the army [376] as long as

Pride, pomp, and circumstance[377] of glorious war!
And, O you mortal engines,[378] whose rude throats
The immortal Jove's dread clamours counterfeit,
Farewell! Othello's occupation 's gone!

IAGO: Is it possible, my lord?

OTHELLO: Villain, be sure thou prove my love a whore,
Be sure of it; give me the ocular proof;
Or, by the worth of mine eternal soul,
Thou hadst been better have been born a dog
Than answer my wak'd wrath.

IAGO: Is 't come to this?

OTHELLO: Make me to see 't; or, at the least, so prove it,
That the probation[379] bear no hinge nor loop
To hang a doubt on; or woe upon thy life!

IAGO: My noble lord, —

OTHELLO: If thou dost slander her and torture me,
Never pray more; abandon all remorse;
On horror's head horrors accumulate;
Do deeds to make heaven weep, all earth amaz'd;
For nothing canst thou to damnation add
Greater than that.

IAGO: O grace! O heaven forgive me!
Are you a man! have you a soul or sense?
God be wi' you; take mine office. O wretched fool!
That liv'st to make thine honesty a vice.
O monstrous world! Take note, take note, O world!
To be direct and honest is not safe.
I thank you for this profit,[380] and, from hence
I 'll love no friend, sith[381] love breeds such offence.

OTHELLO: Nay, stay; thou shouldst be honest.

IAGO: I should be wise; for honesty 's a fool,
And loses that it works for.

OTHELLO: By the world,
I think my wife be honest and think she is not;
I think that thou art just and think thou art not.
I 'll have some proof. Her name, that was as fresh
As Dian's[382] visage, is now begrim'd and black
As mine own face. If there be cords or knives,
Poison or fire or suffocating streams,
I 'll not endure it. Would I were satisfied!

IAGO: I see, sir, you are eaten up with passion.

377 pageantry 378 deadly artillery 379 proof 380 lesson 381 since
382 Diana's, the goddess of the moon

I do repent me that I put it to you.
You would be satisfied?

OTHELLO: Would! nay, I will.

IAGO: And may; but how? how satisfied, my lord?
Would you, the supervisor,[383] grossly gape on;
Behold her tupp'd?

OTHELLO: Death and damnation! O!

IAGO: It were a tedious[384] difficulty, I think,
To bring them to that prospect; damn them then,
If ever mortal eyes do see them bolster[385]
More[386] than their own! What then? how then?
What shall I say? Where 's satisfaction?
It is impossible you should see this,
Were they as prime[387] as goats, as hot as monkeys,
As salt as wolves in pride,[388] and fools as gross
As ignorance made drunk; but yet, I say,
If imputation, and strong circumstances,
Which lead directly to the door of truth,
Will give you satisfaction, you may have it.

OTHELLO: Give me a living reason she 's disloyal.

IAGO: I do not like the office;
But, sith I am enter'd in this cause so far,
Prick'd to 't by foolish honesty and love,
I will go on. I lay with Cassio lately;
And, being troubled with a raging tooth,
I could not sleep.
There are a kind of men so loose of soul
That in their sleeps will mutter their affairs;
One of this kind is Cassio.
In sleep I heard him say, 'Sweet Desdemona,
Let us be wary, let us hide our loves!'
And then, sir, would he gripe[389] and wring my hand,
Cry, 'O, sweet creature!' and then kiss me hard,
As if he pluck'd up kisses by the roots,
That grew upon my lips; then laid his leg
Over my thigh, and sigh'd, and kiss'd; and then
Cried, 'Cursed fate, that gave thee to the Moor!'

OTHELLO: O monstrous! monstrous!

IAGO: Nay, this was but his dream.

OTHELLO: But this denoted a foregone conclusion:[390]

[383] observer [384] laborious [385] lie together [386] other [387] lustful
[388] heat [389] seize [390] previous consummation

'Tis a shrewd doubt,[391] though it be but a dream.
IAGO: And this may help to thicken other proofs
That do demonstrate thinly.
OTHELLO: I 'll tear her all to pieces.
IAGO: Nay, but be wise; yet we see nothing done;
She may be honest yet. Tell me but this:
Have you not sometimes seen a handkerchief
Spotted with strawberries in your wife's hand?
OTHELLO: I gave her such a one; 'twas my first gift.
IAGO: I know not that; but such a handkerchief —
I am sure it was your wife's — did I to-day
See Cassio wipe his beard with.
OTHELLO: If it be that, —
IAGO: If it be that, or any that was hers,
It speaks against her with the other proofs.
OTHELLO: O! that the slave had forty thousand lives;
One is too poor, too weak for my revenge.
Now do I see 'tis true. Look here, Iago;
All my fond love thus do I blow to heaven:
'Tis gone.
Arise, black vengeance, from the hollow hell!
Yield up, O love! thy crown and hearted throne
To tyrannous hate. Swell, bosom, with thy fraught,[392]
For 'tis of aspics' [393] tongues!
IAGO: Yet be content.[394]
OTHELLO: O! blood, blood, blood!
IAGO: Patience, I say; your mind, perhaps, may change.
OTHELLO: Never, Iago. Like to the Pontic sea,[395]
Whose icy current and compulsive course
Ne'er feels retiring ebb, but keeps due on
To the Propontic and the Hellespont,[396]
Even so my bloody thoughts, with violent pace,
Shall ne'er look back, ne'er ebb to humble love,
Till that a capable[397] and wide revenge
Swallow them up. (*Kneels.*)
Now, by yond marble heaven,
In the due reverence of a sacred vow
I here engage my words.
IAGO: Do not rise yet. (*Kneels.*)
Witness, you ever-burning lights above!

391 (1) cursed, (2) acute, suspicion 392 burden 393 poisonous snakes
394 patient 395 the Black Sea 396 the Sea of Marmara, the Dardanelles
397 comprehensive

You elements that clip[398] us round about!
Witness, that here Iago doth give up
The execution of his wit, hands, heart,
To wrong'd Othello's service! Let him command,
And to obey shall be in me remorse,[399]
What bloody business ever.[400] (*They rise.*)

OTHELLO: I greet thy love,
Not with vain thanks, but with acceptance bounteous,
And will upon the instant put thee to 't:
Within these three days let me hear thee say
That Cassio 's not alive.

IAGO: My friend is dead; 'tis done at your request:
But let her live.

OTHELLO: Damn her, lewd minx! O, damn her!
Come, go with me apart; I will withdraw.
To furnish me with some swift means of death
For the fair devil. Now art thou my lieutenant.

IAGO: I am your own for ever. (*Exeunt.*)

Scene 4 [Before the Castle.]

(*Enter* DESDEMONA, EMILIA, *and* CLOWN.)

DESDEMONA: Do you know, sirrah,[401] where Lieutenant Cassio lies?[402]

CLOWN: I dare not say he lies any where.

DESDEMONA: Why, man?

CLOWN: He is a soldier; and for one to say a soldier lies, is stabbing.[403]

DESDEMONA: Go to;[404] where lodges he?

CLOWN: To tell you where he lodges is to tell you where I lie.

DESDEMONA: Can anything be made of this?

CLOWN: I know not where he lodges, and for me to devise[405] a lodging, and say he lies here or he lies there, were to lie in mine own throat.

DESDEMONA: Can you inquire him out, and be edified by report?

CLOWN: I will catechize the world for him; that is, make questions, and by them answer.

DESDEMONA: Seek him, bid him come hither; tell him I have moved my lord in his behalf, and hope all will be well.

CLOWN: To do this is within the compass of man's wit, and therefore I will attempt the doing it. (*Exit.*)

[398] encompass [399] probably a corrupt line; the meaning appears to be: "to obey shall be my solemn obligation" [400] soever [401] common form of address to inferiors [402] lives [403] *i.e.*, is cause for stabbing [404] here apparently: "Come on!" [405] invent

DESDEMONA: Where should I lose that handkerchief, Emilia?
EMILIA: I know not, madam.
DESDEMONA: Believe me, I had rather have lost my purse
Full of cruzadoes;[406] and, but my noble Moor
Is true of mind, and made of no such baseness
As jealous creatures are, it were enough
To put him to ill thinking.
EMILIA: Is he not jealous?
DESDEMONA: Who! he? I think the sun where he was born
Drew all such humours from him.
EMILIA: Look! where he comes.
DESDEMONA: I will not leave him now till Cassio
Be call'd to him.

(*Enter* OTHELLO.)

How is 't with you, my lord?
OTHELLO: Well, my good lady. (*Aside*) O! hardness to dissemble.
How do you, Desdemona?
DESDEMONA: Well, my good lord.
OTHELLO: Give me your hand. This hand is moist,[407] my lady.
DESDEMONA: It yet has felt no age nor known no sorrow.
OTHELLO: This argues fruitfulness and liberal [408] heart;
Hot, hot, and moist; this hand of yours requires
A sequester[409] from liberty, fasting and prayer,
Much castigation, exercise devout;
For here 's a young and sweating devil here,
That commonly rebels. 'Tis a good hand,
A frank one.
DESDEMONA: You may, indeed, say so;
For 'twas that hand that gave away my heart.
OTHELLO: A liberal hand; the hearts of old gave hands,
But our new heraldry[410] is hands not hearts.
DESDEMONA: I cannot speak of this. Come now, your promise.
OTHELLO: What promise, chuck? [411]
DESDEMONA: I have sent to bid Cassio come speak with you.
OTHELLO: I have a salt and sorry rheum offends me.
Lend me thy handkerchief.
DESDEMONA: Here, my lord.
OTHELLO: That which I gave you.

[406] Portuguese gold coins [407] a supposed symptom of a lustful nature [408] with overtones of: too free, loose [409] separation [410] *i.e.*, new heraldic symbolism (Othello means that the new way is not to give the heart together with the hand.) [411] common term of endearment

DESDEMONA: I have it not about me.
OTHELLO: Not?
DESDEMONA: No, indeed, my lord.
OTHELLO: That is a fault.
That handkerchief
Did an Egyptian[412] to my mother give;
She was a charmer,[413] and could almost read
The thoughts of people; she told her, while she kept it,
'Twould make her amiable[414] and subdue my father
Entirely to her love, but if she lost it
Or made a gift of it, my father's eye
Should hold her loathed, and his spirits should hunt
After new fancies.[415] She dying gave it me;
And bid me, when my fate would have me wive,
To give it her. I did so: and take heed on 't;
Make it a darling like your precious eye;
To lose 't or give 't away, were such perdition
As nothing else could match.
DESDEMONA: Is 't possible?
OTHELLO: 'Tis true; there 's magic in the web of it;
A sibyl,[416] that had number'd in the world
The sun to course two hundred compasses,
In her prophetic fury sew'd the work;
The worms were hallow'd that did breed the silk,
And it was dy'd in mummy[417] which the skilful
Conserv'd of maidens' hearts.
DESDEMONA: Indeed! is 't true?
OTHELLO: Most veritable; therefore look to 't well.
DESDEMONA: Then would to heaven that I had never seen it!
OTHELLO: Ha! wherefore?
DESDEMONA: Why do you speak so startingly and rash?
OTHELLO: Is 't lost? is 't gone? speak, is it out o' the way?
DESDEMONA: Heaven bless us!
OTHELLO: Say you?
DESDEMONA: It is not lost: but what an if [418] it were?
OTHELLO: How!
DESDEMONA: I say, it is not lost.
OTHELLO: Fetch 't, let me see 't!
DESDEMONA: Why, so I can, sir, but I will not now.
This is a trick to put me from my suit:
Pray you let Cassio be receiv'd again.

[412] Gypsy [413] sorceress [414] lovable, desirable [415] loves [416] prophetess
[417] drug (medicinal or magic) derived from embalmed bodies [418] if

OTHELLO: Fetch me the handkerchief; my mind misgives.
DESDEMONA: Come, come;
You'll never meet a more sufficient[419] man.
OTHELLO: The handkerchief!
DESDEMONA: I pray, talk[420] me of Cassio.
OTHELLO: The handkerchief!
DESDEMONA: A man that all his time
Hath founded his good fortunes on your love,
Shar'd dangers with you, —
OTHELLO: The handkerchief!
DESDEMONA: In sooth, you are to blame.
OTHELLO: Away! (*Exit.*)
EMILIA: Is not this man jealous?
DESDEMONA: I ne'er saw this before.
Sure, there 's some wonder in this handkerchief;
I am most unhappy in the loss of it.
EMILIA: 'Tis not a year or two shows us a man;
They are all but[421] stomachs, and we all but[421] food;
They eat us hungerly, and when they are full
They belch us. Look you! Cassio and my husband.

(*Enter* IAGO *and* CASSIO.)

IAGO: There is no other way; 'tis she must do 't:
And, lo! the happiness:[422] go and importune her.
DESDEMONA: How now, good Cassio! what 's the news with you?
CASSIO: Madam, my former suit: I do beseech you
That by your virtuous means I may again
Exist, and be a member of his love
Whom I with all the office[423] of my heart
Entirely honour; I would not be delay'd.
If my offence be of such mortal kind
That nor my service past, nor present sorrows,
Nor purpos'd merit in futurity,
Can ransom me into his love again,
But to know so must be my benefit;
So shall I clothe me in a forc'd content,
And shut myself up in some other course
To fortune's alms.
DESDEMONA: Alas! thrice-gentle Cassio!
My advocation is not now in tune;
My lord is not my lord; nor should I know him,

[419] adequate [420] talk to [421] only . . . only [422] "what luck!"
[423] duty

Were he in favour[424] as in humour alter'd.
So help me every spirit sanctified,
As I have spoken for you all my best
And stood within the blank of [425] his displeasure
For my free speech. You must awhile be patient;
What I can do I will, and more I will
Than for myself I dare: let that suffice you.

IAGO: Is my lord angry?

EMILIA: He went hence but now,
And certainly in strange unquietness.

IAGO: Can he be angry? I have seen the cannon,
When it hath blown his ranks[426] into the air,
And, like the devil, from his very arm
Puff'd his own brother; and can he be angry?
Something of moment[427] then; I will go meet him;
There 's matter in 't indeed, if he be angry.

DESDEMONA: I prithee, do so. (*Exit* IAGO.) Something, sure, of state,[428]
Either from Venice, or some unhatch'd[429] practice
Made demonstrable here in Cyprus to him,
Hath puddled[430] his clear spirit; and, in such cases
Men's natures wrangle with inferior things,
Though great ones are their object. 'Tis even so;
For let our finger ache, and it indues[431]
Our other healthful members even to that sense
Of pain. Nay, we must think men are not gods,
Nor of them look for such observancy[432]
As fits the bridal.[433] Beshrew me much, Emilia,
I was — unhandsome warrior as I am —
Arraigning his unkindness with[434] my soul;
But now I find I had suborn'd the witness,[435]
And he 's indicted falsely.

EMILIA: Pray heaven it be state matters, as you think,
And no conception,[436] nor no jealous toy[437]
Concerning you.

DESDEMONA: Alas the day! I never gave him cause.

EMILIA: But jealous souls will not be answer'd so;
They are not ever jealous for the cause,
But jealous for they are jealous; 'tis a monster
Begot upon itself, born on itself.

[424] appearance [425] as the target for [426] *i.e.*, his soldiers [427] important [428] public affairs [429] abortive or budding plot [430] muddied [431] brings, leads [432] attention [433] wedding [434] to [435] *i.e.*, caused my soul to bring in wrong charges [436] fancy, supposition [437] fancy

DESDEMONA: Heaven keep that monster from Othello's mind!
EMILIA: Lady, amen.
DESDEMONA: I will go seek him. Cassio, walk hereabout;
If I do find him fit, I 'll move your suit
And seek to effect it to my uttermost.
CASSIO: I humbly thank your ladyship.
(*Exeunt* DESDEMONA *and* EMILIA.)

(*Enter* BIANCA.)

BIANCA: Save you, friend Cassio!
CASSIO: What make you from home?
How is it with you, my most fair Bianca?
I' faith, sweet love, I was coming to your house.
BIANCA: And I was going to your lodging, Cassio.
What! keep a week away? seven days and nights?
Eight score eight hours? and lovers' absent hours.
More tedious than the dial eight score times?
O weary reckoning!
CASSIO: Pardon me, Bianca,
I have this while with leaden thoughts been press'd;
But I shall, in a more continuate[438] time,
Strike off [439] this score of absence. Sweet Bianca,

(*Giving her* DESDEMONA'S *handkerchief*.)

Take me this work out.
BIANCA: O Cassio! whence came this?
This is some token from a newer friend;
To the felt absence now I feel a cause;
Is 't come to this? Well, well.
CASSIO: Go to, woman!
Throw your vile guesses in the devil's teeth,
From whence you have them. You are jealous now
That this is from some mistress, some remembrance:
No, in good troth, Bianca.
BIANCA: Why, whose is it?
CASSIO: I know not, sweet; I found it in my chamber.
I like the work well; ere it be demanded, — [440]
As like enough it will, — I'd have it copied;
Take it and do 't; and leave me for this time.
BIANCA: Leave you! wherefore?
CASSIO: I do attend here on[441] the general,

[438] uninterrupted [439] cancel (*i.e.*, make up for) [440] asked for [441] wait for

And think it no addition,[442] nor my wish,
To have him see me woman'd.

BIANCA: Why, I pray you?

CASSIO: Not that I love you not.

BIANCA: But that you do not love me.
I pray you, bring me on the way a little
And say if I shall see you soon at night.

CASSIO: 'Tis but a little way that I can bring you,
For I attend here; but I 'll see you soon.

BIANCA: 'Tis very good; I must be circumstanc'd.[443] (*Exeunt.*)

ACT IV

Scene 1 [Cyprus. Before the Castle.]

(*Enter* OTHELLO *and* IAGO.)

IAGO: Will you think so?

OTHELLO: Think so, Iago!

IAGO: What!
To kiss in private?

OTHELLO: An unauthoriz'd kiss.

IAGO: Or to be naked with her friend a-bed
An hour or more, not meaning any harm?

OTHELLO: Naked a-bed, Iago, and not mean harm?
It is hypocrisy against the devil:[444]
They that mean virtuously, and yet do so,
The devil their virtue tempts, and they tempt heaven.

IAGO: If they do nothing, 'tis a venial slip;
But if I give my wife a handkerchief, —

OTHELLO: What then?

IAGO: Why, then, 'tis hers, my lord; and, being hers,
She may, I think, bestow 't on any man.

OTHELLO: She is protectress of her honour too;
May she give that?

IAGO: Her honour is an essence that 's not seen;
They have it very oft that have it not:[445]
But for the handkerchief, —

OTHELLO: By heaven, I would most gladly have forgot it: —

442 advantage, credit 443 governed by circumstances 444 *i.e.*, by not committing the sin which the situation invites 445 *i.e.*, some unchaste women are thought chaste

Thou said'st, — O! it comes o'er my memory,
As doth the raven[446] o'er the infected house,
Boding to all, — he had my handkerchief.

IAGO: Ay, what of that?

OTHELLO: That 's not so good now.

IAGO: What,
If I had said I had seen him do you wrong?
Or heard him say, as knaves be such abroad,[447]
Who having, by their own importunate suit,
Or voluntary dotage[448] of some mistress,
Convinced or supplied them,[449] cannot choose
But they must blab.

OTHELLO: Hath he said any thing?

IAGO: He hath, my lord; but be you well assur'd,
No more than he 'll unswear.

OTHELLO: What hath he said?

IAGO: Faith, that he did — I know not what he did.

OTHELLO: What? what?

IAGO: Lie —

OTHELLO: With her?

IAGO: With her, on her; what you will.

OTHELLO: Lie with her; lie on her! We say, lie on her, when they belie her. Lie with her! that's fulsome. Handkerchief, — confessions, — handkerchief! To confess, and be hanged for his labour. First, to be hanged, and then to confess: I tremble at it. Nature would not invest herself in such shadowing passion without some instruction.[450] It is not words that shake me thus. Pish! Noses, ears, and lips. Is it possible? — Confess! — Handkerchief! — O devil!

(*Falls in a trance.*)

IAGO: Work on,
My medicine, work! Thus credulous fools are caught;
And many worthy and chaste dames even thus,
All guiltless, meet reproach. What, ho! my lord!
My lord, I say! Othello!

(*Enter* CASSIO.)

How now, Cassio!

CASSIO: What's the matter?

[446] (1) a bad omen, (2) a carrier of the plague [447] as there are some such in the world [448] foolish affection [449] overcome (their reluctance) or satisfied (their desires) [450] I would not fall into such passion unless there were some real grounds for it.

IAGO: My lord is fallen into an epilepsy;[451]
This is his second fit; he had one yesterday.
CASSIO: Rub him about the temples.
IAGO: No, forbear;
The lethargy[452] must have his quiet course,
If not, he foams at mouth, and by and by
Breaks out to savage madness. Look! he stirs;
Do you withdraw yourself a little while,
He will recover straight; when he is gone,
I would on great occasion[453] speak with you. (*Exit* CASSIO.)
How is it, general? have you not hurt your head?
OTHELLO: Dost thou mock me?[454]
IAGO: I mock you! no, by heaven.
Would you would bear your fortune like a man!
OTHELLO: A horned man's a monster and a beast.
IAGO: There 's many a beast then, in a populous city,
And many a civil [455] monster.
OTHELLO: Did he confess it?
IAGO: Good sir, be a man;
Think every bearded fellow that 's but yok'd
May draw[456] with you; there 's millions now alive
That nightly lie in those unproper[457] beds
Which they dare swear peculiar;[458] your case is better.
O! 'tis the spite of hell, the fiend's arch-mock,
To lip[459] a wanton in a secure[460] couch,
And to suppose her chaste. No, let me know;
And knowing what I am, I know what she shall be.
OTHELLO: O! thou art wise; 'tis certain.
IAGO: Stand you awhile apart;
Confine yourself but in a patient list.[461]
Whilst you were here o'erwhelmed with your grief, —
A passion most unsuiting such a man, —
Cassio came hither; I shifted him away,
And laid good 'scuse upon your ecstasy;[462]
Bade him anon return and here speak with me;
The which he promis'd. Do but encave yourself,
And mark the fleers, the gibes, and notable scorns,
That dwell in every region of his face;

[451] seizure, fit [452] coma [453] important matter [454] another allusion to the cuckold's horns [455] citizen [456] *i.e.*, pull the burden of cuckolddom [457] not exclusively their own [458] exclusively their own [459] kiss [460] *i.e.*, without suspicion of having a rival [461] bounds of patience [462] derangement, trance

For I will make him tell the tale anew,
Where, how, how oft, how long ago, and when
He hath, and is again to cope[463] your wife:
I say, but mark his gesture. Marry, patience;
Or I shall say you are all in all in spleen,[464]
And nothing of a man.

OTHELLO: Dost thou hear, Iago?
I will be found most cunning in my patience;
But — dost thou hear? — most bloody.

IAGO: That's not amiss;
But yet keep time[465] in all. Will you withdraw?
(OTHELLO *goes apart.*)
Now will I question Cassio of Bianca,
A housewife[466] that by selling her desires
Buys herself bread and clothes; it is a creature
That dotes on Cassio; as 'tis the strumpet's plague
To beguile many and be beguil'd by one.
He, when he hears of her, cannot refrain
From the excess of laughter. Here he comes:

(*Re-enter* CASSIO.)

As he shall smile, Othello shall go mad;
And his unbookish[467] jealousy must construe
Poor Cassio's smiles, gestures, and light behaviour
Quite in the wrong. How do you now, lieutenant?

CASSIO: The worser that you give me the addition[468]
Whose want [469] even kills me.

IAGO: Ply Desdemona well, and you are sure on 't.
(*Speaking lower*) Now, if this suit lay in Bianca's power,
How quickly should you speed!

CASSIO: Alas! poor caitiff![470]

OTHELLO: Look! how he laughs already!

IAGO: I never knew woman love man so.

CASSIO: Alas! poor rogue, I think, i' faith, she loves me.

OTHELLO: Now he denies it faintly, and laughs it out.

IAGO: Do you hear, Cassio?

OTHELLO: Now he importunes him
To tell it o'er: go to; well said, well said.

IAGO: She gives it out that you shall marry her;

463 close with 464 completely overcome by passion 465 maintain control
466 hussy 467 unpracticed, naïve 468 title 469 the want of which
470 wretch

Do you intend it?

CASSIO: Ha, ha, ha!

OTHELLO: Do you triumph, Roman?[471] do you triumph?

CASSIO: I marry her! what? a customer?[472] I prithee, bear some charity to my wit;[473] do not think it so unwholesome. Ha, ha, ha!

OTHELLO: So, so, so, so. They laugh that win.[474]

IAGO: Faith, the cry goes that you shall marry her.

CASSIO: Prithee, say true.

IAGO: I am a very villain else.

OTHELLO: Have you scored me?[475] Well.

CASSIO: This is the monkey's own giving out: she is persuaded I will marry her, out of her own love and flattery, not out of my promise.

OTHELLO: Iago beckons me;[476] now he begins the story.

CASSIO: She was here even now; she haunts me in every place. I was the other day talking on the sea-bank with certain Venetians, and thither comes this bauble,[477] and, by this hand, she falls me thus about my neck; —

OTHELLO: Crying, 'O dear Cassio!' as it were; his gesture imports it.

CASSIO: So hangs and lolls and weeps upon me; so hales[478] and pulls me; ha, ha, ha!

OTHELLO: Now he tells how she plucked him to my chamber. O! I see that nose of yours, but not the dog I shall throw it to.

CASSIO: Well, I must leave her company.

IAGO: Before me![479] look, where she comes.

CASSIO: 'Tis such another fitchew![480] marry, a perfumed one.

(*Enter* BIANCA.)

What do you mean by this haunting of me?

BIANCA: Let the devil and his dam haunt you! What did you mean by that same handkerchief you gave me even now? I was a fine fool to take it. I must take out the work! A likely piece of work, that you should find it in your chamber, and not know who left it there! This is some minx's token, and I must take out the work! There, give it your hobby-horse;[481] wheresoever you had it I'll take out no work on 't.

CASSIO: How now, my sweet Bianca! how now, how now!

OTHELLO: By heaven, that should be[482] my handkerchief!

BIANCA: An you 'll come to supper to-night, you may; an you will not,

[471] *i.e.*, one who triumphs (?) [472] courtesan, prostitute [473] give me credit for some sense [474] "he who laughs last laughs longest" (?) [475] wounded, defaced (?); or: settled my account (?) [476] signals [477] plaything [478] hauls [479] an exclamation of surprise [480] polecat, noted both for its strong smell and for its lechery [481] harlot [482] *i.e.*, I think that is

come when you are next prepared[483] for. (*Exit.*)

IAGO: After her, after her.

CASSIO: Faith, I must; she 'll rail in the street else.

IAGO: Will you sup there?

CASSIO: Faith, I intend so.

IAGO: Well, I may chance to see you, for I would very fain[484] speak with you.

CASSIO: Prithee come; will you?

IAGO: Go to; say no more. (*Exit* CASSIO.)

OTHELLO (*advancing*): How shall I murder him, Iago?

IAGO: Did you perceive how he laughed at his vice?

OTHELLO: O! Iago!

IAGO: And did you see the handkerchief?

OTHELLO: Was that mine?

IAGO: Yours, by this hand; and to see how he prizes the foolish woman your wife! she gave it him, and he hath given it his whore.

OTHELLO: I would have him nine years a-killing. A fine woman! a fair woman! a sweet woman!

IAGO: Nay, you must forget that.

OTHELLO: Ay, let her rot, and perish, and be damned to-night; for she shall not live. No, my heart is turned to stone; I strike it, and it hurts my hand. O! the world hath not a sweeter creature; she might lie by an emperor's side and command him tasks.

IAGO: Nay, that's not your way.[485]

OTHELLO: Hang her! I do but say what she is. So delicate with her needle! An admirable musician! O, she will sing the savageness out of a bear. Of so high and plenteous wit and invention!

IAGO: She 's the worse for all this.

OTHELLO: O! a thousand, a thousand times. And then, of so gentle a condition![486]

IAGO: Ay, too gentle.[487]

OTHELLO: Nay, that 's certain; — but yet the pity of it, Iago!
O! Iago, the pity of it, Iago!

IAGO: If you are so fond over her iniquity, give her patent to offend; for, if it touch not you, it comes near nobody.

OTHELLO: I will chop her into messes.[488] Cuckold me!

IAGO: O! 'tis foul in her.

OTHELLO: With mine officer!

IAGO: That 's fouler.

OTHELLO: Get me some poison, Iago; this night: I 'll not expostulate

[483] expected (Bianca means that if he does not come that night, she will never want to see him again.) [484] gladly [485] proper course [486] so much the high-born lady [487] *i.e.*, yielding [488] bits

with her, lest her body and beauty unprovide my mind again.[489] This night, Iago.

IAGO: Do it not with poison, strangle her in her bed, even the bed she hath contaminated.

OTHELLO: Good, good; the justice of it pleases; very good.

IAGO: And for Cassio, let me be his undertaker;[490] you shall hear more by midnight.

OTHELLO: Excellent good. (A *trumpet within.*) What trumpet is that same?

IAGO: Something from Venice, sure. 'Tis Lodovico,
Come from the duke; and see, your wife is with him.

(*Enter* LODOVICO, DESDEMONA, *and* ATTENDANTS.)

LODOVICO: God save you, worthy general!
OTHELLO: With all my heart, sir.
LODOVICO: The duke and senators of Venice greet you.

(*Gives him a packet.*)

OTHELLO: I kiss the instrument of their pleasures.

(*Opens the packet, and reads.*)

DESDEMONA: And what's the news, good cousin Lodovico?
IAGO: I am very glad to see you, signior;
Welcome to Cyprus.
LODOVICO: I thank you. How does Lieutenant Cassio?
IAGO: Lives, sir.
DESDEMONA: Cousin, there 's fall'n between him and my lord
An unkind [491] breach; but you shall make all well.
OTHELLO: Are you sure of that?
DESDEMONA: My lord?
OTHELLO (*reads*): 'This fail you not to do, as you will' —
LODOVICO: He did not call; he 's busy in the paper.
Is there division[492] 'twixt my lord and Cassio?
DESDEMONA: A most unhappy one; I would do much
To atone[493] them, for the love I bear to Cassio.
OTHELLO: Fire and brimstone!
DESDEMONA: My lord?
OTHELLO: Are you wise?
DESDEMONA: What! is he angry?
LODOVICO: May be the letter mov'd him;
For, as I think, they do command him home,

[489] unsettle my intention [490] dispatcher [491] unnatural [492] estrangement
[493] reconcile

Deputing Cassio in his government.
DESDEMONA: Trust me, I am glad on 't.
OTHELLO: Indeed!
DESDEMONA: My lord?
OTHELLO: I am glad to see you mad.
DESDEMONA: Why, sweet Othello?
OTHELLO: Devil! (*Strikes her.*)
DESDEMONA: I have not deserved this.
LODOVICO: My lord, this would not be believ'd in Venice,
Though I should swear I saw 't: 'tis very much;
Make her amends, she weeps.
OTHELLO: O devil, devil!
If that the earth could teem with woman's tears,
Each drop she falls[494] would prove a crocodile.[495]
Out of my sight!
DESDEMONA: I will not stay to offend you. (*Going.*)
LODOVICO: Truly, an obedient lady;
I do beseech your lordship, call her back.
OTHELLO: Mistress!
DESDEMONA: My lord?
OTHELLO: What would you with her, sir?
LODOVICO: Who, I, my lord?
OTHELLO: Ay; you did wish that I would make her turn:
Sir, she can turn, and turn, and yet go on,
And turn again; and she can weep, sir, weep;
And she 's obedient, as you say, obedient,
Very obedient. Proceed you in your tears.
Concerning this, sir, — O well-painted passion! —
I am commanded home. Get you away;
I 'll send for you anon. Sir, I obey the mandate,
And will return to Venice. Hence! avaunt![496] (*Exit* DESDEMONA.)
Cassio shall have my place. And, sir, to-night,
I do entreat that we may sup together;
You are welcome, sir, to Cyprus. Goats and monkeys! (*Exit.*)
LODOVICO: Is this the noble Moor whom our full senate
Call all-in-all sufficient? is this the noble nature
Whom passion could not shake? whose solid virtue
The shot of accident nor dart of chance
Could neither graze nor pierce?
IAGO: He is much chang'd.
LODOVICO: Are his wits safe? is he not light of brain?

494 lets fall
495 the crocodile's tears were supposed to be hypocritical
496 begone!

IAGO: He 's that he is; I may not breathe my censure.
What he might be, if, what he might, he is not,
I would to heaven he were![497]
LODOVICO: What! strike his wife!
IAGO: Faith, that was not so well; yet would I knew
That stroke would prove the worst!
LODOVICO: Is it his use?
Or did the letters work upon his blood,
And new-create this fault?
IAGO: Alas, alas!
It is not honesty in me to speak
What I have seen and known. You shall observe him,
And his own courses[498] will denote him so
That I may save my speech. Do but go after
And mark how he continues.
LODOVICO: I am sorry that I am deceiv'd in him. (*Exeunt.*)

Scene 2 [A Room in the Castle.]

(*Enter* OTHELLO *and* EMILIA.)

OTHELLO: You have seen nothing, then?
EMILIA: Nor ever heard, nor ever did suspect.
OTHELLO: Yes, you have seen Cassio and her together.
EMILIA: But then I saw no harm, and then I heard
Each syllable that breath made up between them.
OTHELLO: What! did they never whisper?
EMILIA: Never, my lord.
OTHELLO: Nor send you out o' the way?
EMILIA: Never.
OTHELLO: To fetch her fan, her gloves, her mask, nor nothing? [499]
EMILIA: Never, my lord.
OTHELLO: That 's strange.
EMILIA: I durst, my lord, to wager she is honest,
Lay down my soul at stake: if you think other,
Remove your thought; it doth abuse your bosom.
If any wretch have put this in your head,
Let heaven requite it with the serpent's curse!
For, if she be not honest, chaste, and true,
There 's no man happy; the purest of their wives
Is foul as slander.

[497] another of Iago's gnomic speeches; perhaps approximately: "If now he is not himself, I wish he would be what he could be!" [498] actions [499] anything

OTHELLO: Bid her come hither; go. *(Exit* EMILIA.)
She says enough; yet she 's a simple[500] bawd
That cannot say as much. This is a subtle whore,
A closet lock and key of villanous secrets;
And yet she 'll kneel and pray; I have seen her do 't.

(Re-enter EMILIA *with* DESDEMONA.)

DESDEMONA: My lord, what is your will?
OTHELLO: Pray, chuck, come hither.
DESDEMONA: What is your pleasure?
OTHELLO: Let me see your eyes;
Look in my face.
DESDEMONA: What horrible fancy 's this?
OTHELLO (*to* EMILIA): Some of your function,[501] mistress;
Leave procreants alone and shut the door;
Cough or cry 'hem' if any body come;
Your mystery,[502] your mystery; nay, dispatch. *(Exit* EMILIA.)
DESDEMONA: Upon my knees, what doth your speech import?
I understand a fury in your words.
But not the words.
OTHELLO: Why, what art thou?
DESDEMONA: Your wife, my lord; your true
And loyal wife.
OTHELLO: Come, swear it, damn thyself;
Lest, being like one of heaven, the devils themselves
Should fear to seize thee; therefore be double-damn'd;
Swear thou art honest.
DESDEMONA: Heaven doth truly know it.
OTHELLO: Heaven truly knows that thou art false as hell.
DESDEMONA: To whom, my lord? with whom? how am I false?
OTHELLO: Ah! Desdemona; away, away, away!
DESDEMONA: Alas, the heavy day! — Why do you weep?
Am I the motive of these tears, my lord?
If haply you my father do suspect
An instrument of this your calling back,
Lay not your blame on me; if you have lost him,
Why, I have lost him too.
OTHELLO: Had it pleas'd heaven
To try me with affliction, had he rain'd
All kinds of sores and shames on my bare head,
Steep'd me in poverty to the very lips,

[500] simpleminded [501] duty, business [502] trade

Given to captivity me and my utmost hopes,
I should have found in some part of my soul
A drop of patience; but, alas! to make me
The fixed figure for the time of scorn[503]
To point his slow and moving finger at;
Yet could I bear that too; well, very well:
But there, where I have garner'd [504] up my heart,
Where either I must live or bear no life,
The fountain from the which my current runs
Or else dries up; to be discarded thence!
Or keep it as a cistern for foul toads
To knot and gender in![505] Turn thy complexion there,[506]
Patience, thou young and rose-lipp'd cherubin;
Ay, there, look grim as hell!

DESDEMONA: I hope my noble lord esteems me honest.

OTHELLO: O! ay; as summer flies are in the shambles,[507]
That quicken even with blowing. O thou weed!
Who art so lovely fair and smell'st so sweet
That the sense aches at thee, would thou hadst ne'er been born.

DESDEMONA: Alas! what ignorant sin have I committed?

OTHELLO: Was this fair paper, this most goodly book,
Made to write 'whore' upon? What committed!
Committed! O thou public commoner![508]
I should make very forges of my cheeks,
That would to cinders burn up modesty,
Did I but speak thy deeds. What committed!
Heaven stops the nose at it and the moon winks,[509]
The bawdy wind that kisses all it meets
Is hush'd within the hollow mine of earth,
And will not hear it. What committed!
Impudent strumpet!

DESDEMONA: By heaven, you do me wrong.

OTHELLO: Are not you a strumpet?

DESDEMONA: No, as I am a Christian.
If to preserve this vessel for my lord
From any other foul unlawful touch
Be not to be a strumpet, I am none.

OTHELLO: What! not a whore?

DESDEMONA: No, as I shall be sav'd.

OTHELLO: Is it possible?

[503] *i.e.*, the scornful world [504] stored [505] bunch up and procreate [506] *i.e.*, change your color to suit the "cistern for foul toads" [507] slaughterhouse [508] harlot [509] closes her eyes

DESDEMONA: O! heaven forgive us.
OTHELLO: I cry you mercy,[510] then;
I took you for that cunning whore of Venice
That married with Othello. You, mistress,
That have the office opposite to Saint Peter,
And keep the gate of hell!

(*Re-enter* EMILIA.)

You, you, ay, you!
We have done our course; there 's money for your pains.
I pray you, turn the key and keep our counsel. (*Exit.*)
EMILIA: Alas! what does this gentleman conceive? [511]
How do you, madam? how do you, my good lady?
DESDEMONA: Faith, half asleep.
EMILIA: Good madam, what 's the matter with my lord?
DESDEMONA: With who?
EMILIA: Why, with my lord, madam.
DESDEMONA: Who is thy lord?
EMILIA: He that is yours, sweet lady.
DESDEMONA: I have none; do not talk to me, Emilia;
I cannot weep, nor answer have I none,
But what should go by water.[512] Prithee, to-night
Lay on my bed my wedding sheets: remember:
And call thy husband hither.
EMILIA: Here is a change indeed! (*Exit.*)
DESDEMONA: 'Tis meet I should be us'd so, very meet.
How have I been behav'd, that he might stick
The small'st opinion on my least misuse? [513]

(*Re-enter* EMILIA, *with* IAGO.)

IAGO: What is your pleasure, madam? How is it with you?
DESDEMONA: I cannot tell. Those that do teach young babes
Do it with gentle means and easy tasks;
He might have chid me so; for, in good faith,
I am a child to chiding.
IAGO: What 's the matter, lady?
EMILIA: Alas; Iago, my lord hath so bewhor'd her,
Thrown such despite[514] and heavy terms upon her,
As true hearts cannot bear.
DESDEMONA: Am I that name, Iago?

[510] beg your pardon [511] imagine [512] be conveyed by means of tears
[513] the least suspicion on my slightest misconduct [514] abuse

IAGO: What name, fair lady?
DESDEMONA: Such as she says my lord did say I was.
EMILIA: He call'd her whore; a beggar in his drink
Could not have laid such terms upon his callat.[515]
IAGO: Why did he so?
DESDEMONA: I do not know; I am sure I am none such.
IAGO: Do not weep, do not weep. Alas the day!
EMILIA: Has she forsook so many noble matches,
Her father and her country and her friends,
To be call'd whore? would it not make one weep?
DESDEMONA: It is my wretched fortune.
IAGO: Beshrew[516] him for it!
How comes this trick upon him?
DESDEMONA: Nay, heaven doth know.
EMILIA: I will be hang'd, if some eternal villain,
Some busy and insinuating rogue,
Some cogging[517] cozening slave, to get some office,
Have not devis'd this slander; I 'll be hang'd else.
IAGO: Fie! there is no such man; it is impossible.
DESDEMONA: If any such there be, heaven pardon him!
EMILIA: A halter pardon him, and hell gnaw his bones!
Why should he call her whore? who keeps her company?
What place? what time? what form? what likelihood?
The Moor 's abus'd by some most villanous knave,
Some base notorious knave, some scurvy fellow.
O heaven! that such companions[518] thou'dst unfold,
And put in every honest hand a whip
To lash the rascals naked through the world,
Even from the east to the west!
IAGO: Speak within door.
EMILIA: O! fie upon them. Some such squire he was
That turn'd your wit the seamy side without,[519]
And made you to suspect me with the Moor.
IAGO: You are a fool; go to.
DESDEMONA: O good Iago,
What shall I do to win my lord again?
Good friend, go to him; for, by this light of heaven,
I know not how I lost him. Here I kneel:
If e'er my will did trespass 'gainst his love,
Either in discourse of thought or actual deed,
Or that mine eyes, mine ears, or any sense,

[515] slut [516] curse [517] cheating [518] fellows (derogatory) [519] outward

Delighted them[520] in any other form;
Or that I do not yet,[521] and ever did,
And ever will, though he do shake me off
To beggarly divorcement, love him dearly,
Comfort forswear me! Unkindness may do much;
And his unkindness may defeat[522] my life,
But never taint my love. I cannot say 'whore':
It does abhor me now I speak the word;
To do the act that might the addition earn
Not the world's mass of vanity could make me.

IAGO: I pray you be content, 'tis but his humour;
The business of the state does him offence,
And he does chide with you.

DESDEMONA: If 'twere no other, —

IAGO: 'Tis but so, I warrant. (*Trumpets.*)
Hark! how these instruments summon to supper;
The messengers of Venice stay the meat:
Go in, and weep not; all things shall be well.

(*Exeunt* DESDEMONA *and* EMILIA.)

(*Enter* RODERIGO.)

How now, Roderigo!

RODERIGO: I do not find that thou dealest justly with me.

IAGO: What in the contrary? [523]

RODERIGO: Every day thou daffest me[524] with some device, Iago; and rather, as it seems to me now, keepest from me all conveniency,[525] than suppliest me with the least advantage of hope. I will indeed no longer endure it, nor am I yet persuaded to put up[526] in peace what already I have foolishly suffered.

IAGO: Will you hear me, Roderigo?

RODERIGO: Faith, I have heard too much, for your words and performances are no kin together.

IAGO: You charge me most unjustly.

RODERIGO: With nought but truth. I have wasted myself out of my means. The jewels you have had from me to deliver to Desdemona would half have corrupted a votarist;[527] you have told me she has received them, and returned me expectations and comforts of sudden respect[528] and acquaintance, but I find none.

IAGO: Well; go to; very well.

[520] found delight [521] still [522] destroy [523] *i.e.*, what reason do you have for saying that [524] you put me off [525] favorable circumstances [526] put up with [527] nun [528] immediate consideration

RODERIGO: Very well! go to! I cannot go to, man; nor 'tis not very well: by this hand, I say, it is very scurvy, and begin to find myself fobbed[529] in it.

IAGO: Very well.

RODERIGO: I tell you 'tis not very well. I will make myself known to Desdemona; if she will return me my jewels, I will give over my suit and repent my unlawful solicitation; if not, assure yourself I will seek satisfaction of you.

IAGO: You have said now.[530]

RODERIGO: Ay, and said nothing, but what I protest intendment of doing.

IAGO: Why, now I see there's mettle in thee, and even from this instant do build on thee a better opinion than ever before. Give me thy hand, Roderigo; thou hast taken against me a most just exception; but yet, I protest, I have dealt most directly in thy affair.

RODERIGO: It hath not appeared.

IAGO: I grant indeed it hath not appeared, and your suspicion is not without wit and judgment. But, Roderigo, if thou hast that in thee indeed, which I have greater reason to believe now than ever, I mean purpose, courage, and valour, this night show it: if thou the next night following enjoy not Desdemona, take me from this world with treachery and devise engines for[531] my life.

RODERIGO: Well, what is it? is it within reason and compass?

IAGO: Sir, there is especial commission come from Venice to depute Cassio in Othello's place.

RODERIGO: Is that true? why, then Othello and Desdemona return again to Venice.

IAGO: O, no! he goes into Mauritania, and takes away with him the fair Desdemona, unless his abode be lingered here by some accident; wherein none can be so determinate[532] as the removing of Cassio.

RODERIGO: How do you mean, removing of him?

IAGO: Why, by making him uncapable of Othello's place; knocking out his brains.

RODERIGO: And that you would have me do?

IAGO: Ay; if you dare do yourself a profit and a right. He sups to-night with a harlotry,[533] and thither will I go to him; he knows not yet of his honourable fortune. If you will watch his going thence, — which I will fashion to fall out between twelve and one, — you may take him at your pleasure; I will be near to second your attempt, and he shall fall between us. Come, stand not amazed at it, but go along with me; I will show you such a necessity in his death that

529 cheated 530 *i.e.*, "I suppose you're through?" (?); or: "Now you're talking" (?) 531 devices against 532 effective 533 harlot

you shall think yourself bound to put it on him. It is now high supper-time, and the night grows to waste; about it.

RODERIGO: I will hear further reason for this.

IAGO: And you shall be satisfied. *(Exeunt.)*

Scene 3 [Another Room in the Castle.]

(*Enter* OTHELLO, LODOVICO, DESDEMONA, EMILIA, *and* ATTENDANTS.)

LODOVICO: I do beseech you, sir, trouble yourself no further.

OTHELLO: O! pardon me; 'twill do me good to walk.

LODOVICO: Madam, good-night; I humbly thank your ladyship.

DESDEMONA: Your honour is most welcome.

OTHELLO: Will you walk, sir?
O! Desdemona, —

DESDEMONA: My lord?

OTHELLO: Get you to bed on the instant; I will be returned forthwith; dismiss your attendant there; look it be done.

DESDEMONA: I will, my lord.

(*Exeunt* OTHELLO, LODOVICO, *and* ATTENDANTS.)

EMILIA: How goes it now? He looks gentler than he did.

DESDEMONA: He says he will return incontinent;[534]
He hath commanded me to go to bed,
And bade me to dismiss you.

EMILIA: Dismiss me!

DESDEMONA: It was his bidding; therefore, good Emilia,
Give me my nightly wearing, and adieu:
We must not now displease him.

EMILIA: I would you had never seen him.

DESDEMONA: So would not I; my love doth so approve him,
That even his stubbornness,[535] his checks[536] and frowns, —
Prithee, unpin me, — have grace and favour in them.

EMILIA: I have laid those sheets you bade me on the bed.

DESDEMONA: All 's one.[537] Good faith! how foolish are our minds!
If I do die before thee, prithee, shroud me
In one of those same sheets.

EMILIA: Come, come, you talk.

DESDEMONA: My mother had a maid call'd Barbara;
She was in love, and he she lov'd prov'd mad[538]
And did forsake her; she had a song of 'willow';
An old thing 'twas, but it express'd her fortune,

[534] at once [535] roughness [536] rebukes [537] *i.e.*, it doesn't matter
[538] wild

And she died singing it; that song to-night
Will not go from my mind; I have much to do
But to go hang my head all at one side,
And sing it like poor Barbara. Prithee, dispatch.

EMILIA: Shall I go fetch your night-gown?

DESDEMONA: No, unpin me here.
This Lodovico is a proper man.

EMILIA: A very handsome man.

DESDEMONA: He speaks well.

EMILIA: I know a lady in Venice would have walked barefoot to Palestine for a touch of his nether lip.

DESDEMONA (*sings*):

The poor soul sat sighing by a sycamore tree,
Sing all a green willow;
Her hand on her bosom, her head on her knee,
Sing willow, willow, willow:
The fresh streams ran by her, and murmur'd her moans;
Sing willow, willow, willow:
Her salt tears fell from her, and soften'd the stones; —

Lay by these: —
Sing willow, willow, willow:

Prithee, hie thee;[539] he 'll come anon. —

Sing all a green willow must be my garland.
Let nobody blame him, his scorn I approve, —

Nay, that 's not next. Hark! who is it that knocks?

EMILIA: It is the wind.

DESDEMONA:

I call'd my love false love; but what said he then?
Sing willow, willow, willow:
If I court moe[540] women, you 'll couch with moe men.

So, get thee gone; good-night. Mine eyes do itch;
Doth that bode weeping?

EMILIA: 'Tis neither here nor there.

DESDEMONA: I have heard it said so. O! these men, these men!
Dost thou in conscience think, tell me, Emilia,
That there be women do abuse their husbands
In such gross kind?

EMILIA: There be some such, no question.

[539] hurry [540] more

DESDEMONA: Wouldst thou do such a deed for all the world?
EMILIA: Why, would not you?
DESDEMONA: No, by this heavenly light!
EMILIA: Nor I neither by this heavenly light;
I might do 't as well i' the dark.
DESDEMONA: Wouldst thou do such a deed for all the world?
EMILIA: The world is a huge thing; 'tis a great price
For a small vice.
DESDEMONA: In troth, I think thou wouldst not.
EMILIA: In troth, I think I should, and undo 't when I had done. Marry, I would not do such a thing for a joint-ring,[541] nor measures of lawn,[542] nor for gowns, petticoats, nor caps, nor any petty exhibition;[543] but for the whole world, who would not make her husband a cuckold to make him a monarch? I should venture purgatory for 't.
DESDEMONA: Beshrew me, if I would do such a wrong
For the whole world.
EMILIA: Why, the wrong is but a wrong i' the world; and having the world for your labour, 'tis a wrong in your own world, and you might quickly make it right.
DESDEMONA: I do not think there is any such woman.
EMILIA: Yes, a dozen; and as many to the vantage,[544] as
Would store[545] the world they played for.
But I do think it is their husbands' faults
If wives do fall. Say that they slack their duties,
And pour our treasures into foreign laps,
Or else break out in peevish jealousies,
Throwing restraint upon us; or say they strike us,
Or scant[546] our former having[547] in despite;
Why, we have galls,[548] and though we have some grace,
Yet have we some revenge. Let husbands know
Their wives have sense like them; they see and smell,
And have their palates both for sweet and sour,
As husbands have. What is it that they do
When they change us for others? Is it sport?[549]
I think it is; and doth affection breed it?
I think it doth; is 't frailty that thus errs?
It is so too; and have not we affections,
Desires for sport, and frailty, as men have?
Then, let them use us well; else let them know,
The ills we do, their ills instruct us so.

541 ring made in separable halves 542 fine linen 543 offer, gift 544 over and above 545 populate 546 reduce 547 allowance 548 spirits, temper 549 lust, sexual enjoyment

DESDEMONA: Good-night, good-night; heaven me such usage[550] send,
Not to pick bad from bad, but by bad mend! (*Exeunt.*)

ACT V

Scene 1 [Cyprus. A Street.]

(*Enter* IAGO *and* RODERIGO.)

IAGO: Here, stand behind this bulk;[551] straight will he come:
Wear thy good rapier bare, and put it home.
Quick, quick; fear nothing; I 'll be at thy elbow.
It makes us, or it mars us; think on that,
And fix most firm thy resolution.
RODERIGO: Be near at hand; I may miscarry in 't.
IAGO: Here, at thy hand: be bold, and take thy stand. (*Retires.*)
RODERIGO: I have no great devotion to the deed;
And yet he has given me satisfying reasons:
'Tis but a man gone: forth, my sword; he dies.
IAGO: I have rubb'd this young quat[552] almost to the sense,[553]
And he grows angry. Now, whether he kill Cassio,
Or Cassio him, or each do kill the other,
Every way makes my gain: live Roderigo,
He calls me to a restitution large
Of gold and jewels that I bobb'd[554] from him,
As gifts to Desdemona;
It must not be: if Cassio do remain,
He hath a daily beauty in his life
That makes me ugly: and, besides, the Moor
May unfold me to him; there stand I in much peril.
No, he must die. But so;[555] I hear him coming.

(*Enter* CASSIO.)

RODERIGO: I know his gait; 'tis he. Villain, thou diest!

(*Makes a pass at* CASSIO.)

CASSIO: That thrust had been mine enemy indeed
But that my coat is better than thou know'st;
I will make proof of thine.

(*Draws, and wounds* RODERIGO.)

[550] habits (?), treatment (?) [551] jutting part of a wall [552] pimple
[553] to the quick [554] swindled [555] *i.e.*, that's the only way

RODERIGO: O! I am slain.

(IAGO *from behind wounds* CASSIO *in the leg, and exit.*)

CASSIO: I am maim'd for ever. Help, ho! murder! murder! (*Falls.*)

(*Enter* OTHELLO, *at a distance.*)

OTHELLO: The voice of Cassio: Iago keeps his word.
RODERIGO: O! villain that I am!
OTHELLO: It is e'en so.
CASSIO: O, help, ho! light! a surgeon!
OTHELLO: 'Tis he: O brave Iago, honest and just!
That hast such noble sense of thy friend's wrong;
Thou teachest me. Minion,[556] your dear lies dead,
And your unblest fate hies; strumpet, I come!
Forth of my heart those charms, thine eyes, are blotted;
Thy bed lust-stain'd shall with lust's blood be spotted. (*Exit.*)

(*Enter* LODOVICO *and* GRATIANO, *at a distance.*)

CASSIO: What ho! no watch? no passage?[557] murder! murder!
GRATIANO: 'Tis some mischance; the cry is very direful.
CASSIO: O, help!
LODOVICO: Hark!
RODERIGO: O wretched villain!
LODOVICO: Two or three groans: it is a heavy[558] night;
These may be counterfeits; let 's think 't unsafe
To come in to the cry[559] without more help.
RODERIGO: Nobody come? then shall I bleed to death.
LODOVICO: Hark!

(*Re-enter* IAGO, *with a light.*)

GRATIANO: Here 's one comes in his shirt, with light and weapons.
IAGO: Who 's there? whose noise is this that cries on murder?
LODOVICO: We do not know.
IAGO: Did not you hear a cry?
CASSIO: Here, here! for heaven's sake, help me.
IAGO: What 's the matter?
GRATIANO: This is Othello's ancient, as I take it.
LODOVICO: The same indeed; a very valiant fellow.
IAGO: What are you here that cry so grievously?
CASSIO: Iago? O! I am spoil'd, undone by villains!
Give me some help.

556 (Cassio's) darling, *i.e.*, Desdemona 557 passer-by 558 dark
559 where the cry comes from

IAGO: O me, lieutenant! what villains have done this?
CASSIO: I think that one of them is hereabout,
And cannot make away.
IAGO: O treacherous villains!
(*To* LODOVICO *and* GRATIANO.) What are you there? come in, and give some help.
RODERIGO: O! help me here.
CASSIO: That 's one of them.
IAGO: O murderous slave! O villain!

(*Stabs* RODERIGO.)

RODERIGO: O damn'd Iago! O inhuman dog!
IAGO: Kill men i' the dark! Where be these bloody thieves?
How silent is this town! Ho! murder! murder!
What may you be? are you of good or evil?
LODOVICO: As you shall prove us, praise us.
IAGO: Signior Lodovico?
LODOVICO: He, sir.
IAGO: I cry you mercy. Here 's Cassio hurt by villains.
GRATIANO: Cassio!
IAGO: How is it, brother?
CASSIO: My leg is cut in two.
IAGO: Marry, heaven forbid.
Light, gentlemen; I 'll bind it with my shirt.

(*Enter* BIANCA.)

BIANCA: What is the matter, ho? who is 't that cried?
IAGO: Who is 't that cried!
BIANCA: O my dear Cassio! my sweet Cassio!
O Cassio, Cassio, Cassio!
IAGO: O notable strumpet! Cassio, may you suspect
Who they should be that have thus mangled you?
CASSIO: No.
GRATIANO: I am sorry to find you thus; I have been to seek you.
IAGO: Lend me a garter. So. O! for a chair,
To bear him easily hence!
BIANCA: Alas; he faints! O Cassio, Cassio, Cassio!
IAGO: Gentlemen all, I do suspect this trash [560]
To be a party in this injury.
Patience awhile, good Cassio. Come, come.
Lend me a light. Know we this face, or no?

[560] *i.e.*, Bianca

Alas! my friend and my dear countryman,
Roderigo? no: yes, sure, O heaven! Roderigo.
GRATIANO: What! of Venice?
IAGO: Even he, sir: did you know him?
GRATIANO: Know him! ay.
IAGO: Signior Gratiano? I cry you gentle pardon;
These bloody accidents must excuse my manners,
That so neglected you.
GRATIANO: I am glad to see you.
IAGO: How do you, Cassio? O! a chair, a chair!
GRATIANO: Roderigo!

(*A chair brought in.*)

IAGO: He, he, 'tis he, — O! that 's well said; the chair:
Some good men bear him carefully from hence;
I 'll fetch the general's surgeon. (*To* BIANCA.) For you, mistress,
Save you your labour. He that lies slain here, Cassio,
Was my dear friend. What malice was between you?
CASSIO: None in the world; nor do I know that man.
IAGO (*to* BIANCA): What! look you pale? O! bear him out o' the air —

(CASSIO *and* RODERIGO *are borne off.*)

Stay you, good gentlemen. Look you pale, mistress? —
Do you perceive the gastness[561] of her eye?
Nay, if you stare, we shall hear more anon.
Behold her well; I pray you, look upon her.
Do you see, gentlemen? nay, guiltiness will speak
Though tongues were out of use.

(*Enter* EMILIA.)

EMILIA: 'Las! what 's the matter? what 's the matter, husband?
IAGO: Cassio hath here been set on in the dark
By Roderigo and fellows that are 'scaped:
He 's almost slain, and Roderigo dead.
EMILIA: Alas! good gentleman; alas! good Cassio!
IAGO: This is the fruit of whoring. Prithee, Emilia,
Go know of Cassio where he supp'd to-night.
(*To* BIANCA.) What! do you shake at that?
BIANCA: He supp'd at my house; but I therefore shake not.
IAGO: O! did he so? I charge you, go with me.
EMILIA: Fie, fie upon thee, strumpet!

[561] terror

BIANCA: I am no strumpet, but of life as honest
  As you that thus abuse me.
EMILIA: As I! foh! fie upon thee!
IAGO: Kind gentlemen, let 's go see poor Cassio dress'd.[562]
  Come, mistress, you must tell 's another tale.
  Emilia, run you to the citadel,
  And tell my lord and lady what hath happ'd.
  Will you go on afore? (*Aside.*) This is the night
  That either makes me or fordoes[563] me quite. (*Exeunt.*)

Scene 2 [A Bedchamber in the Castle. DESDEMONA in bed asleep. A light burning.]

(*Enter* OTHELLO.)

OTHELLO: It is the cause,[564] it is the cause, my soul;
  Let me not name it to you, you chaste stars!
  It is the cause. Yet I 'll not shed her blood,
  Nor scar that whiter skin of hers than snow,
  And smooth as monumental alabaster.
  Yet she must die, else she 'll betray more men.
  Put out the light, and then put out the light:
  If I quench thee, thou flaming minister,[565]
  I can again thy former light restore,
  Should I repent me; but once put out thy light,
  Thou cunning'st[566] pattern of excelling nature,
  I know not where is that Promethean[567] heat
  That can thy light relume.[568] When I have pluck'd the rose,
  I cannot give it vital growth again,
  It needs must wither: I 'll smell it on the tree. (*Kisses her.*)
  O balmy breath, that dost almost persuade
  Justice to break her sword! One more, one more.
  Be thus when thou art dead, and I will kill thee,
  And love thee after. One more, and this the last:
  So sweet was ne'er so fatal. I must weep,
  But they are cruel tears; this sorrow 's heavenly,
  It strikes where it doth love. She wakes.
DESDEMONA: Who 's there? Othello?

[562] bandaged [563] ruins [564] *i.e.*, Desdemona's unchastity (Othello means that the severity of the punishment is required by the nature of her sin.) [565] *i.e.*, the candle [566] most intricately wrought [567] in Greek mythology the demi-god Prometheus stole fire from the gods and gave it to man [568] relight

OTHELLO: Ay, Desdemona.
DESDEMONA: Will you come to bed, my lord?
OTHELLO: Have you pray'd to-night, Desdemona?
DESDEMONA: Ay, my lord.
OTHELLO: If you bethink yourself of any crime
Unreconcil'd as yet to heaven and grace,
Solicit for it straight.
DESDEMONA: Alas! my lord, what may you mean by that?
OTHELLO: Well, do it, and be brief; I will walk by:[569]
I would not kill thy unprepared spirit;
No; heaven forfend! [570] I would not kill thy soul.
DESDEMONA: Talk you of killing?
OTHELLO: Ay, I do.
DESDEMONA: Then heaven
Have mercy on me!
OTHELLO: Amen! with all my heart.
DESDEMONA: If you say so, I hope you will not kill me.
OTHELLO: Hum!
DESDEMONA: And yet I fear you; for you are fatal then
When your eyes roll so. Why I should fear I know not,
Since guiltiness I know not; but yet I feel I fear.
OTHELLO: Think on thy sins.
DESDEMONA: They are loves I bear to you.
OTHELLO: Ay, and for that thou diest.
DESDEMONA: That death 's unnatural that kills for loving.
Alas! why gnaw you so your nether lip?
Some bloody passion shakes your very frame;
These are portents,[571] but yet, I hope, I hope
They do not point on me.
OTHELLO: Peace, and be still!
DESDEMONA: I will so. What 's the matter?
OTHELLO: That handkerchief which I so lov'd and gave thee
Thou gav'st to Cassio.
DESDEMONA: No, by my life and soul!
Send for the man and ask him.
OTHELLO: Sweet soul, take heed,
Take heed of perjury; thou 'rt on thy death-bed.
DESDEMONA: Ay, but not yet to die.
OTHELLO: Yes, presently;[572]
Therefore confess thee freely of thy sin;
For to deny each article with oath

[569] nearby [570] forbid [571] omens [572] at once

Cannot remove nor choke the strong conception[573]
That I do groan withal. Thou art to die.
DESDEMONA: Then Lord have mercy on me!
OTHELLO: I say, amen.
DESDEMONA: And have you mercy too! I never did
Offend you in my life; never lov'd Cassio
But with such general warranty[574] of heaven
As I might love; I never gave him token.
OTHELLO: By heaven, I saw my handkerchief in 's hand.
O perjur'd woman! thou dost stone[575] my heart,
And mak'st me call what I intend to do
A murder, which I thought a sacrifice:
I saw the handkerchief.
DESDEMONA: He found it then;
I never gave it him. Send for him hither;
Let him confess a truth.
OTHELLO: He hath confessed.
DESDEMONA: What, my lord?
OTHELLO: That he hath us'd thee.
DESDEMONA: How? Unlawfully?
OTHELLO: Ay.
DESDEMONA: He will not say so.
OTHELLO: No; his mouth is stopp'd:
Honest Iago hath ta'en order for 't.[576]
DESDEMONA: O! my fear interprets. What! is he dead?
OTHELLO: Had all his hairs been lives, my great revenge
Had stomach[577] for them all.
DESDEMONA: Alas! he is betray'd and I undone.
OTHELLO: Out, strumpet! Weep'st thou for him to my face?
DESDEMONA: O! banish me, my lord, but kill me not!
OTHELLO: Down, strumpet!
DESDEMONA: Kill me to-morrow; let me live to-night!
OTHELLO: Nay, if you strive, —
DESDEMONA: But half an hour!
OTHELLO: Being done, there is no pause.
DESDEMONA: But while I say one prayer!
OTHELLO: It is too late.
(*He smothers her.*)

EMILIA (*within*): My lord, my lord! what, ho! my lord, my lord!
OTHELLO: What noise is this? Not dead? not yet quite dead?
I that am cruel am yet merciful;

573 belief 574 permission 575 turn to stone 576 taken steps
577 appetite

I would not have thee linger in thy pain.
So, so.
EMILIA (*within*): What, ho! my lord, my lord!
OTHELLO: Who's there?
EMILIA (*within*): O! good my lord, I would speak a word with you!
OTHELLO: Yes; 'tis Emilia: by and by.[578] She 's dead.
'Tis like[579] she comes to speak of Cassio's death;
The noise was high. Ha! no more moving?
Still as the grave. Shall she come in? Were 't good? [580]
I think she stirs again: no. What 's best to do?
If she come in she 'll sure speak to my wife:
My wife! my wife! what wife? I have no wife:
O, insupportable! O heavy hour!
Methinks it should be now a huge eclipse
Of sun and moon, and that the affrighted globe
Should yawn[581] at alteration.
EMILIA (*within*): I do beseech you
That I may speak with you, O! good my lord.
OTHELLO: I had forgot thee: O! come in, Emilia:
Soft, by and by: let me the curtains draw.
Where art thou? (*Unlocks the door.*)

(*Enter* EMILIA.)

What 's the matter with thee now?
EMILIA: O! my good lord, yonder 's foul murder done.
OTHELLO: What! now?
EMILIA: But now, my lord.
OTHELLO: It is the very error[582] of the moon;
She comes more near the earth than she was wont,
And makes men mad.
EMILIA: Cassio, my lord, has kill'd a young Venetian
Call'd Roderigo.
OTHELLO: Roderigo kill'd!
And Cassio kill'd?
EMILIA: No, Cassio is not kill'd.
OTHELLO: Not Cassio kill'd! then murder 's out of tune,
And sweet revenge grows harsh.
DESDEMONA: O! falsely, falsely murder'd.
EMILIA: Alas! what cry is that?
OTHELLO: That! what?
EMILIA: Out, and alas! that was my lady's voice:

[578] *i.e.*, "just a moment" [579] likely [580] would that be wise [581] open up (as in an earthquake) [582] straying

Help! Help, ho! help! O lady, speak again!
Sweet Desdemona! O! sweet mistress, speak.
DESDEMONA: A guiltless death I die.
EMILIA: O! who hath done this deed?
DESDEMONA: Nobody; I myself; farewell:
Commend me to my kind lord. O! farewell! (*Dies.*)
OTHELLO: Why, how should she be murder'd?
EMILIA: Alas! who knows?
OTHELLO: You heard her say herself it was not I.
EMILIA: She said so; I must needs report the truth.
OTHELLO: She 's like a liar gone to burning hell;
'Twas I that kill'd her.
EMILIA: O! the more angel she,
And you the blacker devil.
OTHELLO: She turn'd to folly, and she was a whore.
EMILIA: Thou dost belie her, and thou art a devil.
OTHELLO: She was false as water.
EMILIA: Thou art rash as fire to say
That she was false: O! she was heavenly true.
OTHELLO: Cassio did tup her; ask thy husband else.
O! I were damn'd beneath all depth in hell
But that I did proceed[583] upon just grounds
To this extremity. Thy husband knew it all.
EMILIA: My husband!
OTHELLO: Thy husband.
EMILIA: That she was false to wedlock?
OTHELLO: Ay, with Cassio. Nay, had she been true,
If heaven would make me such another world
Of one entire and perfect chrysolite,[584]
I 'd not have sold her for it.
EMILIA: My husband!
OTHELLO: Ay, 'twas he that told me first:
An honest man he is, and hates the slime
That sticks on filthy deeds.
EMILIA: My husband!
OTHELLO: What needs this iterance,[585] woman? I say thy husband.
EMILIA: O mistress! villany hath made mocks with love.
My husband say that she was false!
OTHELLO: He, woman;
I say, thy husband: dost understand the word?
My friend, thy husband, honest, honest Iago.

[583] had I not proceeded [584] topaz [585] repetition

EMILIA: If he say so, may his pernicious soul
Rot half a grain a day! he lies to the heart:
She was too fond of her most filthy bargain.[586]
OTHELLO: Ha!
EMILIA: Do thy worst:
This deed of thine is no more worthy heaven
Than thou wast worthy her.
OTHELLO: Peace! you were best.[587]
EMILIA: Thou hast not half the power to do me harm
As I have to be hurt. O gull! O dolt!
As ignorant as dirt! thou hast done a deed, —
I care not for thy sword; I 'll make thee known,
Though I lost twenty lives. Help! help, ho! help!
The Moor has kill'd my mistress! murder! murder!

(*Enter* MONTANO, GRATIANO, IAGO, *and others.*)

MONTANO: What is the matter? How now, general!
EMILIA: O! are you come, Iago? you have done well,
That men must lay their murders on your neck.
GRATIANO: What is the matter?
EMILIA: Disprove this villain if thou be'st a man:
He says thou told'st him that his wife was false.
I know thou didst not, thou 'rt not such a villain.
Speak, for my heart is full.
IAGO: I told him what I thought, and told no more
Than what he found himself was apt and true.
EMILIA: But did you ever tell him she was false?
IAGO: I did.
EMILIA: You told a lie, an odious damned lie;
Upon my soul, a lie, a wicked lie;
She false with Cassio! Did you say with Cassio?
IAGO: With Cassio, mistress. Go to, charm[588] your tongue.
EMILIA: I will not charm my tongue; I am bound to speak.
My mistress here lies murder'd in her bed.
ALL: O heavens forfend!
EMILIA: And your reports have set the murder on.
OTHELLO: Nay, stare not, masters; it is true, indeed.
GRATIANO: 'Tis a strange truth.
MONTANO: O monstrous act!
EMILIA: Villany! villany! villany!
I think upon 't, I think, I smell 't; O villany!

[586] *i.e.*, Othello [587] you'd better be quiet [588] *i.e.*, into silence

I thought so then;[589] I 'll kill myself for grief.
O! villany, villany!

IAGO: What! are you mad? I charge you, get you home.

EMILIA: Good gentlemen, let me have leave to speak:
'Tis proper I obey him, but not now.
Perchance, Iago, I will ne'er go home.

OTHELLO: O! O! O! (*Falls on the bed.*)

EMILIA: Nay, lay thee down and roar,
For thou hast kill'd the sweetest innocent
That e'er did lift up eye.

OTHELLO: O! she was foul. (*Rises.*)
I scarce did know you, uncle. There lies your niece,
Whose breath, indeed, these hands have newly stopp'd:
I know this act shows terrible and grim.

GRATIANO: Poor Desdemona! I am glad thy father 's dead.
Thy match was mortal to him, and pure grief
Shore[590] his old thread in twain: did he live now,
This sight would make him do a desperate turn,
Yea, curse his better angel from his side,
And fall to reprobation.[591]

OTHELLO: 'Tis pitiful; but yet Iago knows
That she with Cassio hath the act of shame
A thousand times committed; Cassio confess'd it:
And she did gratify[592] his amorous works
With that recognizance and pledge of love
Which I first gave her. I saw it in his hand:
It was a handkerchief, an antique token
My father gave my mother.

EMILIA: O heaven! O heavenly powers!

IAGO: Come, hold your peace.

EMILIA: 'Twill out, 'twill out; I hold my peace, sir? no;
No, I will speak as liberal as the north;[593]
Let heaven and men and devils, let them all,
All, all, cry shame against me, yet I 'll speak.

IAGO: Be wise, and get you home.

EMILIA: I will not.

(IAGO *threatens to stab* EMILIA.)

[589] *cf.* "I will be hang'd, if some eternal villain, / Some busy and insinuating rogue, / Some cogging cozening slave, to get some office, / Have not devis'd this slander; . . ." (IV, ii, p. 113). Emilia means, not that she guessed Iago's guilt, but that she rightly guessed the slanderer's motive. [590] cut [591] damnation [592] reward [593] *i.e.*, the north wind (?), the supposedly free-spoken people of north England (?)

GRATIANO: Fie!
Your sword upon a woman!
EMILIA: O thou dull Moor! that handkerchief thou speak'st of
I found by fortune and did give my husband;
For often, with a solemn earnestness,
More than, indeed, belong'd to such a trifle,
He begg'd of me to steal it.
IAGO: Villainous whore!
EMILIA: She give it Cassio! no, alas! I found it,
And I did give 't my husband.
IAGO: Filth, thou liest!
EMILIA: By heaven, I do not, I do not, gentlemen.
O murderous coxcomb! [594] what should such a fool
Do with so good a wife?
OTHELLO: Are there no stones[595] in heaven
But what serve for the thunder? Precious villain!

(*He runs at* IAGO. IAGO *stabs* EMILIA.)

GRATIANO: The woman falls: sure, he has kill'd his wife. (*Exit* IAGO.)
EMILIA: Ay, ay; O! lay me by my mistress' side.
GRATIANO: He 's gone; but his wife 's kill'd.
MONTANO: 'Tis a notorious[596] villain. Take you this weapon,
Which I have here recover'd from the Moor.
Come, guard the door without; let him not pass,
But kill him rather. I 'll after that same villain,
For 'tis a damned slave. (*Exeunt* MONTANO *and* GRATIANO.)
OTHELLO: I am not valiant neither,
But every puny whipster[597] gets my sword.
But why should honour outlive honesty?
Let it go all.
EMILIA: What did thy song bode, lady?
Hark, canst thou hear me? I will play the swan,
And die in music: —
(*Sings.*) Willow, willow, willow.
Moor, she was chaste; she lov'd thee, cruel Moor;
So come my soul to bliss as I speak true;
So speaking as I think, I die, I die. (*Dies.*)
OTHELLO: I have another weapon in this chamber;
It is a sword of Spain, the ice-brook's temper.[598]

[594] idiot [595] *i.e.*, thunderbolts (to strike Iago down) [596] notable
[597] *i.e.*, a small boy whipping a top [598] tempered in icy water (or the reference may be to Innsbruck, famed for the quality of its steel, but this hardly fits "a sword of Spain")

O! here it is. Uncle, I must come forth.
GRATIANO (*within*): If thou attempt it, it will cost thee dear:
Thou hast no weapon, and perforce must suffer.
OTHELLO: Look in upon me then, and speak with me,
Or, naked[599] as I am, I will assault thee.

(*Re-enter* GRATIANO.)

GRATIANO: What is the matter?
OTHELLO: Behold! I have a weapon;
A better never did itself sustain
Upon a soldier's thigh: I have seen the day,
That with this little arm, and this good sword,
I have made my way through more impediments
Than twenty times your stop: but, O vain boast!
Who can control his fate? 'tis not so now.
Be not afraid, though you do see me weapon'd;
Here is my journey's end, here is my butt,[600]
And very sea-mark of my utmost sail.[601]
Do you go back dismay'd? 'tis a lost fear;
Man but a rush[602] against Othello's breast,
And he retires. Where should Othello go?
Now how dost thou look now? O ill-starr'd wench!
Pale as thy smock! when we shall meet at compt,[603]
This look of thine will hurl my soul from heaven,
And fiends will snatch at it. Cold, cold, my girl!
Even like thy chastity.
O! cursed, cursed slave. Whip me, ye devils,
From the possession of this heavenly sight!
Blow me about in winds! roast me in sulphur!
Wash me in steep-down gulfs of liquid fire!
O Desdemona! Desdemona! dead!
Oh! Oh! Oh!

(*Enter* LODOVICO, MONTANO, CASSIO *carried in a chair, and* OFFICERS *with* IAGO, *prisoner*.)

LODOVICO: Where is this rash and most unfortunate man?
OTHELLO: That 's he that was Othello; here I am.
LODOVICO: Where is that viper? bring the villain forth.
OTHELLO: I look down towards his feet;[604] but that 's a fable.
If that thou be'st a devil, I cannot kill thee. (*Wounds* IAGO.)

599 unarmed 600 goal, end, limit 601 destination of my farthest journey
602 wield but a reed 603 on the day of judgment 604 *i.e.*, for the Devil's cloven hoof

LODOVICO: Wrench his sword from him. (OTHELLO *is disarmed.*)
IAGO: I bleed, sir; but not kill'd.
OTHELLO: I am not sorry neither; I 'd have thee live;
For, in my sense,[605] 'tis happiness to die.
LODOVICO: O thou Othello! that wert once so good,
Fall'n in the practice[606] of a damned slave,[607]
What shall be said to thee?
OTHELLO: Why, any thing:
An honourable murderer, if you will;
For nought did I in hate, but all in honour.
LODOVICO: This wretch hath part confess'd his villany:
Did you and he consent in Cassio's death?
OTHELLO: Ay.
CASSIO: Dear general, I never gave you cause.
OTHELLO: I do believe it, and I ask your pardon.
Will you, I pray, demand that demi-devil
Why he hath thus ensnar'd my soul and body?
IAGO: Demand me nothing: what you know, you know:
From this time forth I never will speak word.
LODOVICO: What! not to pray?
GRATIANO: Torments will ope[608] your lips.
OTHELLO: Well, thou dost best.
LODOVICO: Sir, you shall understand what hath befall'n,
Which, as I think, you know not. Here is a letter
Found in the pocket of the slain Roderigo,
And here another; the one of them imports
The death of Cassio to be undertook
By Roderigo.
OTHELLO: O villain!
CASSIO: Most heathenish and most gross!
LODOVICO: Now here's another discontented paper,
Found in his pocket too; and this, it seems,
Roderigo meant to have sent this damned villain,
But that, belike,[609] Iago in the interim[610]
Came in and satisfied him.
OTHELLO: O the pernicious caitiff!
How came you, Cassio, by that handkerchief
That was my wife's?
CASSIO: I found it in my chamber;
And he himself confess'd but even now
That there he dropp'd it for a special purpose

605 the way I feel 606 plot, machination 607 *i.e.*, Iago 608 open
609 most likely 610 in the meantime

Which wrought to his desire.

OTHELLO: O fool! fool! fool!

CASSIO: There is besides in Roderigo's letter
How he upbraids Iago that he made him
Brave me upon the watch; whereon it came
That I was cast:[611] and even but now he spake,
After long seeming dead, Iago hurt him,
Iago set him on.

LODOVICO: You must forsake this room and go with us;
Your power and your command is taken off,
And Cassio rules in Cyprus. For this slave,
If there be any cunning cruelty
That can torment him much and hold him long,
It shall be his. You shall close prisoner rest,
Till that the nature of your fault be known
To the Venetian state. Come, bring him away.

OTHELLO: Soft you; a word or two before you go.
I have done the state some service, and they know 't;
No more of that. I pray you, in your letters,
When you shall these unlucky deeds relate,
Speak of me as I am; nothing extenuate,
Nor set down aught[612] in malice: then, must you speak
Of one that lov'd not wisely but too well;
Of one not easily jealous, but, being wrought,
Perplex'd[613] in the extreme; of one whose hand
Like the base Indian,[614] threw a pearl away
Richer than all his tribe; of one whose subdu'd[615] eyes
Albeit unused to the melting mood,
Drop tears as fast as the Arabian trees
Their med'cinable gum. Set you down this;
And say besides, that in Aleppo once,
Where a malignant and a turban'd Turk
Beat a Venetian and traduc'd the state,
I took by the throat the circumcised dog,
And smote him, thus. (*Stabs himself.*)

LODOVICO: O bloody period! [616]

GRATIANO: All that's spoke is marr'd.

OTHELLO: I kiss'd thee ere I killed thee; no way but this,

(*Falling upon* DESDEMONA.)

[611] dismissed [612] anything [613] distracted [614] The Folio reads "Iudean." Both readings denote the foolish infidel who fails to appreciate the treasure he possesses. [615] overcome (by grief) [616] ending

Killing myself to die upon a kiss. *(Dies.)*

CASSIO: This did I fear, but thought he had no weapon;
For he was great of heart.

LODOVICO (*to* IAGO): O Spartan dog!
More fell[617] than anguish, hunger, or the sea.
Look on the tragic loading of this bed;
This is thy work; the object poisons sight;
Let it be hid. Gratiano, keep the house,
And seize upon the fortunes of the Moor,
For they succeed on you. To you, lord governor,
Remains the censure of this hellish villain,
The time, the place, the torture; O! enforce it.
Myself will straight aboard, and to the state
This heavy act with heavy heart relate. *(Exeunt.)*

[617] grim, cruel

COURT RECORDS show that *Othello* was performed before King James I on November 1, 1604. We do not know the date of composition; most likely it did not much precede the performance. There is a probable allusion to Desdemona's death in Thomas Dekker's play *The Honest Whore* from 1604. The metre and the dramatic rather than merely decorative use of imagery are internal evidence that *Othello* belongs to Shakespeare's maturity as playwright, and the theme of nobility corrupted and innocence destroyed suggests that it belongs to the period of the other great tragedies of evil rampant and of the "dark" comedies of cynical disgust. It was a time when the Elizabethan exuberance of the 1590's was turning into the restless ennui and tortured introspection of the Jacobean age.

Othello was included in the first collected edition of Shakespeare's plays, the famous First Folio* of 1623, compiled by John Heminges and Henry Condell, two of Shakespeare's actor friends and partners in the King's Men company. The year before, *Othello* had appeared in a quarto* edition, whose text at some points differs from that of the Folio. Most modern editions, including the present, give a compromise reading, with the Folio as base.

Although first given at court, subsequent performances of *Othello* took place at the Globe Theater on the south side of the Thames, in

* "Folio" and "quarto" are printer's terms and refer to page format. Folio is the size of a printer's sheet folded once. Thus folded, a sheet makes two leaves (four pages). Quarto is the size of a sheet folded twice (four leaves, eight pages).

the suburb of Bankside. The Globe had been built by the King's Men in 1599. It was an octagonal building of three levels of galleries surrounding a center space, 55 by 55 feet, almost half of which was occupied by the stage, "the apron," that jutted out from the dressing room, or tiring-house, in the building itself. Two doors, one on each side, led from the tiring-house to the stage. Between them was a recess that could be curtained off. In *Othello* this inner stage would conceal the eavesdropping Othello in IV, 1, and contain Desdemona's bed in V, 2. The apron itself was a low, wooden platform, partly covered by a roof, or "shadow," supported by posts and with a trap door in the floor for ghosts and devils. Above the recess was a balcony for physically high action. Here Brabantio would appear in I, 1, and the gentleman lookout for the Venetian ships in II, 1. Behind the balcony there may have been an upper recess. The open area surrounding the apron on three sides was called the "pit." Here stood the poorer spectators, or "groundlings." Their social betters were seated in the galleries. Fully occupied, the theater may have held upward of 2,000 spectators. Costumes were elaborate but historically unauthentic. Props were used (lanterns, swords, a chair of state, a bed), but hardly any effort was made to create stage verisimilitude. Performance took place in the daytime. It was an intimate theater, a theater of convention rather than of illusion, and one in which actor and audience were both physically and psychologically closer than in a modern, picture-frame theater of artificial lighting. And the absence of elaborate sets or stage machinery invited an imaginative, fluid, and fast-paced dramatic form.

Shakespeare's source for *Othello* was a tale in a collection entitled *Hecatommithi* by Giraldi Cinthio, which appeared in Venice in 1566. There is no record of an English translation, but Shakespeare may have read the story in French or even in the original Italian (we do not know what foreign languages, if any, Shakespeare knew). He altered Cinthio's tale on several points. Lust for Desdemona rather than resentment at a failed promotion is Iago's motive for revenge in the original. There is no Roderigo and instead of Brabantio only a brief reference to Desdemona's parents opposing the marriage. Bianca is Cassio's wife, not his mistress as in Shakespeare, and neither she nor Emilia is connected with the handkerchief plot. The Turkish wars, Othello's and Desdemona's separate sea voyages, the tempest, and Cassio's drunkenness are all original with Shakespeare. In Cinthio, Desdemona is beaten to death with a stocking filled with sand, the Moor goes mad after the murder, is tortured, and long afterward killed by his wife's relatives. In Cinthio only Desdemona is given a proper name.

What Shakespeare saw in Cinthio's sprawling tale was the story of the monstrous conception, growth, and murderous issue of sexual jealousy. Unlike Lear, Othello does not arraign the very order of the universe at the bar of human justice. Compared with Hamlet's exquisitely labyrinthine mind his seems like a child's. And his fall does not, like Macbeth's, shake the whole structure of society. It is a domestic tragedy. But the smaller scope makes for a swiftness of compacted drama and a degree of poignancy lacking in the larger tragedies. *Othello* is the most tidily constructed of all Shakespeare's plays, in effect if not in literal fact faithful to "the rules." Every character, every incident, every speech, contributes to the single, accelerating assault on our emotions.

The formative pressure of imaginative intelligence is exerted in every area of the drama. In consequence, the shaped substance of the whole play is not caught in plot synopsis. Images of scene and speech register psychological movement and moral values, fleshing the narrative skeleton with interlocking meanings of symbolic hyperbole and contrast and with enriched immediacy of scene, figure, gesture, and voice. The result is the kind of realism that gives an audience not a replica of its own reality, but an overwhelming sense of tragic life. The double time scheme in Othello is an example of the freedom and economy of means Shakespeare employed to achieve a certain end.* The foreground of swift and the background of slow events reconcile the conflicting demands for a rush of tragic fate and for gradual psychological change in the protagonist. The inconsistency also suggests the irrationality of the jealous mind that fails to arrest the manifest untruth of Iago's lies with the obvious question which it remains for Emilia to ask in IV, 2:

> Who keeps her company?
> What place? What time? What form? What likelihood?

* The action begins on the night of Othello's and Desdemona's wedding. That same night Othello, Cassio, and Iago all set sail for Cyprus, aboard different ships. Desdemona travels with Iago. The day of the landing is declared a public holiday. During the celebration that night Cassio forfeits his lieutenancy. The next morning Desdemona promises to plead for his reinstatement, and Iago is able to set his plot in motion.

Clearly, this time scheme allows no opportunity for an affair between Cassio and Desdemona. To conceal the absurdity Shakespeare introduces passages that imply a background of events of longer duration than the thirty-some hours that actually pass between the arrival in Cyprus and the murder of Desdemona (that is, if the action is assumed to be continuous between Acts III and IV, as dramatic "feeling" certainly suggests that it is). Examples of such passages are Emilia's finding the handkerchief which Iago "a hundred times" had asked her to steal (III, 3), Iago's "I lay with Cassio lately" (III, 3), Bianca's complaint of Cassio's long neglect (III, 4), Lodovico's arrival with the senate's new directives after the destruction of the Turkish fleet (IV, 1), and Othello's questioning Emilia about his wife (IV, 2). See M. R. Ridley's Introduction to his edition of *Othello* in the New Arden Shakespeare (London, 1958), pp. lxvii-lxx.

And in the gathering fear and suspense we cease to be aware of any discrepancy between chronological and psychological time, feeling instead the action to take place in some timeless void in which the hero-victim is suspended with his agony between absolute evil and absolute innocence.

The device of the double time scheme is characteristic of Shakespeare's dramatic method. Facts and circumstance assume symbolic power without losing their primary status. In *Othello* they build a world, mysterious, capricious, dangerous, in which an Iago is allowed to exercise his evil intelligence on corruptible and incorruptible innocence alike, and in which the question of *why* he is allowed to is as irrepressible as it is unanswerable. "Demand me nothing," says Iago at the end. "What you know you know." But what the tragic hero knows is only the fact of suffering and his own responsibility for it, not its ultimate reason.

The move from Venice to Cyprus between Acts I and II is both a plausible narrative event and a structural device that separates the prologue from the main phase of the action: Iago's unsuccessful from his successful raid on Othello's happiness. But it also represents a move from an ordered polity to

> a town of war
> Yet wild, the people's hearts brimful of fear,

less a fortified island in the Mediterranean than a place for the exhibition of tragic passion. In Act I Iago's obscene cries in the night are silenced by Othello's calm and beautiful rhetoric and by the fair and disciplined deliberations of the Venetian senate, including Brabantio's submission to its judgment in favor of Othello. In contrast, Cyprus is a place of drunken revelry and riot, of assassination in the dark, governed by a general who can rule neither himself nor his men, who cashiers his most devoted officer, trusts his worst enemy, and murders his innocent wife.

Whether Shakespeare and his audience thought of Othello as a Negro or as an Arab or whether they made the distinction at all is less important than the fact that he is the one dark-skinned person in the play. Not that race in the modern sense is at issue, but the contrast keeps attention fastened on the hero and emphasizes his position as an alien. Almost literally, he is seen to represent an ethos darker, more inscrutable, perhaps wilder and more barbaric, than that of his plausible Venetian environment. His blackness suggests the magic and witchcraft which Brabantio charges him with having used to win Desdemona and gives insinuating power to Iago's hint that Desdemona's feelings have only been a young girl's short-lived infatuation with an exotic stranger.

As Othello's blackness bears upon theme and feeling so does his speech. Iago's poison disintegrates his eloquence. In Act I Othello vindicates his courtship of Desdemona in dignified narrative of rich and sonorous imagery. In Acts III and IV he talks in spasmodic ejaculations of broken syntax and images of animal sexuality. There is no more striking evidence of Iago's skill than his success in befouling Othello's imagination. It accounts for the peculiar power of the scene (IV, 2) in which Othello treats Desdemona as an inmate of a brothel of which Emilia is the madam. But while such images in Othello come out in half-crazed expletives, hideous symptoms of beclouding passion, in Iago they are a facile, casual jargon, as in his conversations with Roderigo. And from V, 2, till the end Othello is again in full possession of his eloquence. Desdemona's killer is not a raging cuckold but an impartial judge–executor.

> It is the cause, it is the cause, my soul.
> Let me not name it to you, you chaste stars.
> It is the cause. Yet I'll not shed her blood,
> Nor scar that whiter skin of hers than snow,
> And smooth as monumental alabaster.
> Yet she must die, else she'll betray more men.

Power of discourse is proof of man's grasp of his experience, and when in his final soliloquy Othello sees himself as the "malignant Turk" who "Beat a Venetian and traduced the state," he recognizes the nature of his destiny. The catastrophe is past and unalterable, but his language makes of the sufferer's suicide a ceremony in which suffering is absorbed and which restores him to his prelapsarian state. Iago ends by deserting the language that for a while served him so well: "From this time forth I never will speak word." Language in the end does not desert Othello.

Part of the heartbreaking quality of *Othello* is the disparity between the injury Iago thinks he has received and the nature of the revenge he seeks. ". . . when I love thee not, Chaos is come again," says Othello as his eyes follow the departing Desdemona in III, 3. The cosmos that Iago immediately proceeds to undermine is built of Othello's pride of profession and his trust in Desdemona's virtue and love. Iago's revenge may be defined as cynicism assaulting faith. He abnegates all values but the rational exercise of the selfish will. Even the perfection of womanhood, he says in a moment of almost pleasant banter (II, 1), is good for nothing but

> To suckle fools and chronicle small beer.

His evil spreads like a contamination. He violates civic peace, military order, property, justice, friendship, marriage, life itself. "If thou be'st a devil, I cannot kill thee," says Othello, lunging at his tormentor. "I bleed, sir, but not killed," is Iago's terrifying reply. Recurrent imagery of devils, monsters, conjurers, thieves, and animals establish the Satanic nature of Iago's world. It is a world of impish irony. Othello escapes the storm at sea only to be ravaged by jealousy ashore. He denies having won Desdemona's heart by witchcraft but relies on the handkerchief of the magic web as sole proof of her fidelity. It is, like *Hamlet*'s, a world of seeming. Othello seems proof against jealousy but is, if not easily, then terribly, jealous. His character and behavior belie his savage looks — until passion reduces him to Desdemona's "most filthy bargain." In deceptiveness there is actually little to choose between him and honest Iago. Cassio seems a reliable officer but isn't, Desdemona seems bewitched but isn't, does not seem chaste but is, and, for all her innocence, *does* deceive her father, *does* "beguile The thing I am by seeming otherwise," and *does* lie about the handkerchief (saying it is not lost when she knows it is). Emilia speaks coarsely but acts nobly, seems a most loyal wife but isn't. Even external events participate: Rhodes seems threatened but isn't, the rescue from the tempest seems a blessing but isn't. That *Othello* is the only one of Shakespeare's tragedies that could have turned to comedy (in the sense of having a happy outcome) as late as the middle of the fifth act is further evidence that its setting is a world ruled by whim.

Whim ultimately controls even Iago. His success, certainly, is to an extent the triumph of reason over instinct and passion. He skillfully acts the part of the bluff soldier, the rough diamond, whose integrity compels him to speak the truth even when it hurts his friends. He knows how to exploit Othello's "free and open nature That thinks men honest that but seem to be so." He plays upon his victim's half-suppressed awareness that his race, his age, and his profession all argue against the depth and durability of Desdemona's love and that he is ignorant of the silken ways of Venetian ladies. He knows how to make use of Desdemona's passivity in suffering, a defect inherent in the very virtue of her love, obedience, and forgivingness.

But at any time after Act III any one of a number of chance meetings and chance remarks would have exposed Iago's plot. That no such meeting or remark occurs is a matter of luck, and so is the fact that, instead, the handkerchief comes to his hand just when Othello demands proof and that first Cassio and then Bianca arrive at the scene at exactly the right moment to further his scheme (IV, 1). All along he brilliantly improvises each new step in his plot, but in Act V his improvisations suddenly stop working, and events begin to get away from him. He is pressed for time. He realizes that murder breeds murder. Roderigo, blundering gull to the last, does *not* kill Cassio. Dead himself, his letters incriminate Iago. And Emilia will not obey her husband's command to be silent. The master manipulator manipulates himself into shackles and torture and sees all his machinations end in as bitter an irony for himself as any he ever ensnared Othello in: the promotion of Cassio to the governorship.

Coleridge found in Iago a "motiveless malignity," but his character may rather be thought a critical problem because his revenge is too amply motivated: by professional frustration and jealousy, suspicion of an affair between Othello and Emilia, hatred of Cassio's winning ways, and lust for Desdemona. As his own soliloquies are the authority for all these motives and as soliloquies are always, by dramatic convention, sincere, this cool and cynical egotist, this penetrating judge of others, comes to seem confused as to the reasons for his own actions. There is a paradox that diminishes his stature as a force of evil in the fact that he is driven to destroy virtues he professes not to believe exist. That the combination of Othello's soldierliness and Desdemona's innocence should amount to a tragic flaw seems due to such a special and unlikely set of circumstances that Iago's strategy appears gratuitous. At the end he looms in our mind less as a consummate deceiver-intriguer than as a horrible accident in Othello's life. Here again, as in so many other of his plays, Shakespeare has used and transcended a convention of Elizabethan drama. Machiavellian stage villainy, a commonplace by 1604, has been made subservient to a tragic metaphysic. In 1692 the neoclassical critic Thomas Rymer dismissed *Othello* with a sneer as a "bloody farce," good only for teaching housewives to "look well to their linen." * But in responding to the trivial and accidental nature of the pivotal plot event Rymer responded to something crucial to the tragic effect. The world of *Othello* is one in which a dropped handkerchief *will* lead to catastrophe. Its controlling force remains a dark riddle, but the final events of the play make it clear that the riddler, whoever he is, is not Iago. Scheming malice does not conquer. And not his cynicism and silence but the dying Desdemona's words of love and Othello's self-recognition and dying kiss mark the human gesture.

* *A Short View of Tragedy* (dated 1693).

Ben Jonson

THE ALCHEMIST

TO THE

Lady Most Deserving Her Name and Blood,

LADY MARY WROTH

MADAM, —

In the age of sacrifices, the truth of religion was not in the greatness and fat of the offerings, but in the devotion and zeal of the sacrificers: else what could a handful of gums have done in the sight of a hecatomb? or how might I appear at this altar, except with those affections that no less love the light and witness, than they have the conscience of your virtue? If what I offer bear an acceptable odour, and hold the first strength, it is your value of it, which remembers where, when, and to whom it was kindled. Otherwise, as the times are, there comes rarely forth that thing so full of authority or example, but by assiduity and custom grows less and loses. This yet, safe in your judgment (which is a SIDNEY'S) is forbidden to speak more, lest it talk or look like one of the ambitious faces of the time, who the more they paint are the less themselves.

Your Ladyship's true Honourer,

BEN JONSON

TO THE READER

If thou beest more, thou art an understander, and then I trust thee. If thou art one that takest up, and but a Pretender, beware of what hands thou receivest thy commodity; for thou wert never more fair in the way to be cozened, than in this age, in Poetry, especially in Plays: wherein now the concupiscence of dances and of antics so reigneth, as to run away from nature, and be afraid of her, is the only point of art that tickles the spectators. But how out of purpose, and place, do I name art? When the professors are grown so obstinate contemners of it, and presumers on their own naturals, as they are deriders of all diligence that way, and, by simple mocking at the terms, when they understand not the things, think to get off wittily with their ignorance. Nay, they are esteemed the more learned, and sufficient for this, by the many, through their excellent vice of judgment. For they commend writers as they do fencers or wrestlers; who if they come in robustuously, and put for it with a great deal of violence, are received for the braver fellows: when many times their own rudeness is the cause of their disgrace, and a little touch of their adversary gives all that boisterous force the foil. I deny not but that these men, who always seek to do more than enough, may some time happen on some thing that is good and great; but very seldom: and when it comes it doth not recompense the rest of their ill. It sticks out perhaps, and is more eminent, because all is sordid and vile about it: as lights are more discerned in a thick darkness than a faint shadow. I speak not this out of a hope to do good to any man against his will; for I know if it were put to the question of theirs and mine, the worst would find more suffrages: because the most favour common errors. But I give thee this warning that there is a great difference between those that, to gain the opinion of copy, utter all they can, however unfitly; and those that use election and a mean. For it is only the disease of the unskilful to think rude things greater than polished: or scattered more numerous than composed.

PROLOGUE

Fortune, that favours fools, these two short hours
  We wish away, both for your sakes and ours,
Judging spectators; and desire, in place,
  To th' author justice, to ourselves but grace.
Our scene is London, 'cause we would make known,
  No country's mirth is better than our own:
No clime breeds better matter for your whore,
  Bawd, squire, impostor, many persons more,
Whose manners, now called humours, feed the stage;
  And which have still been subject for the rage
Or spleen of comic writers. Though this pen
  Did never aim to grieve, but better men;
Howe'er the age he lives in doth endure
  The vices that she breeds, above their cure.
But when the wholesome remedies are sweet,
  And in their working gain and profit meet,
He hopes to find no spirit so much diseased,
  But will with such fair correctives be pleased:
For here he doth not fear who can apply.
  If there be any that will sit so nigh
Unto the stream, to look what it doth run,
  They shall find things, they'd think or wish were done;
They are so natural follies, but so shown,
  As even the doers may see, and yet not own.

Dramatis Personæ

SUBTLE, *the Alchemist*
FACE, *the House-keeper*
DOL COMMON, *their colleague*
DAPPER, *a Lawyer's clerk*
DRUGGER, *a Tobacco-man*
LOVEWIT, *Master of the House*
SIR EPICURE MAMMON, *a Knight*
PERTINAX SURLY, *a Gamester*
TRIBULATION WHOLESOME, *a Pastor of Amsterdam*
ANANIAS, *a Deacon there*
KASTRIL, *the angry boy*
DAME PLIANT, *his sister, a Widow*
NEIGHBOURS, OFFICERS, ATTENDANTS, &C.

SCENE: *London*

ARGUMENT

T he sickness hot,[1] a master quit, for fear,
H is house in town, and left one servant there;
E ase him corrupted, and gave means to know

A Cheater and his punk; who now brought low,
L eaving their narrow practice, were become
C ozeners at large; and only wanting some
H ouse to set up, with him they here contract,
E ach for a share, and all begin to act.
M uch company they draw, and much abuse,
I n casting figures, telling fortunes, news,
S elling of flies,[2] flat bawdry with the stone,[3]
T ill it, and they, and all in fume are gone.

[1] the plague raging [2] familiar spirits [3] the philosopher's stone

ACT THE FIRST

Scene I [*A Room in* LOVEWIT'S *House.*]

(*Enter* FACE, *in a captain's uniform, with his sword drawn, and* SUBTLE *with a vial, quarrelling, and followed by* DOL COMMON.)

FACE: Belive 't, I will.
SUBTLE: Thy worst. I fart at thee.
DOL: Have you your wits? why, gentlemen! for love ——
FACE: Sirrah, I'll strip you ——
SUBTLE: What to do? lick figs[4]
Out at my ——
FACE: Rogue, rogue! — out of all your sleights.
DOL: Nay, look ye, sovereign, general, are you madmen?
SUBTLE: O, let the wild sheep loose. I'll gum[5] your silks
With good strong water, an[6] you come.
DOL: Will you have
The neighbours hear you? will you betray all?
Hark! I hear somebody.
FACE: Sirrah ——
SUBTLE: I shall mar
All that the tailor has made if you approach.
FACE: You most notorious whelp, you insolent slave,
Dare you do this?
SUBTLE: Yes, faith; yes, faith.
FACE: Why, who
Am I, my mungrel,[7] who am I?
SUBTLE: I'll tell you,
Since you know not yourself.
FACE: Speak lower, rogue.
SUBTLE: Yes, you were once (time's not long past) the good,
Honest, plain, livery-three-pound-thrum,[8] that kept
Your master's worship's house here in the Friers,
For the vacations ——
FACE: Will you be so loud?
SUBTLE: Since, by my means, translated [9] suburb-captain.[10]
FACE: By your means, doctor dog!
SUBTLE: Within man's memory,

[4] See Rabelais, *Pantagruel*, IV, ch. xlv. The allusion is to an obscene kiss signifying debasement and submission. [5] smear [6] if [7] mongrel [8] an inferior servant dressed in cast-off livery [9] transformed into [10] *i.e.*, pimp (brothels were located in the suburbs)

All this I speak of.
FACE: Why, I pray you, have I
Been countenanced by you, or you by me?
Do but collect,[11] sir, where I met you first.
SUBTLE: I do not hear well.
FACE: Not of this, I think it.
But I shall put you in mind, sir; — at Pie-corner,
Taking your meal of steam in, from cooks' stalls
Where, like the father of hunger, you did walk
Piteously costive, with your pinched-horn-nose,
And your complexion of the Roman wash,[12]
Stuck full of black and melancholic worms,
Like powder-corns[13] shot at the artillery-yard.
SUBTLE: I wish you could advance your voice a little.
FACE: When you went pinned up in the several rags
You had raked and picked from dunghills, before day;
Your feet in mouldy slippers, for your kibes;
A felt of rug, and a thin threaden cloak,
That scarce would cover your no buttocks ——
SUBTLE: So, sir!
FACE: When all your alchemy, and your algebra,
Your minerals, vegetals, and animals,[14]
Your conjuring, cozening, and your dozen of trades,
Could not relieve your corpse with so much linen
Would make you tinder, but to see a fire;[15]
I gave you countenance, credit for your coals,
Your stills, your glasses, your materials;
Built you a furnace, drew you customers,
Advanced all your black arts; lent you, beside,
A house to practise in ——
SUBTLE: Your master's house!
FACE: Where you have studied the more thriving skill
Of bawdry since.
SUBTLE: Yes, in your master's house,
You and the rats here kept possession.
Make it not strange.[16] I know you were one could keep
The buttery-hatch still locked, and save the chippings,[17]
Sell the dole beer[18] to aqua-vitæ men,[19]

[11] recollect [12] facial lotion used to cure skin disease caused by disreputable habits (?) [13] grains of powder [14] alchemist's terms for the three "kingdoms" of created things [15] that would enable you to spark a fire that could even be seen [16] don't deny it [17] scraps of bread [18] free beer for the poor [19] liquor dealers

The which, together with your Christmas vails[20]
At post-and-pair,[21] your letting out of counters,[22]
Made you a pretty stock, some twenty marks,
And gave you credit to converse with cobwebs,
Here, since your mistress' death hath broke up house.

FACE: You might talk softlier, rascal.

SUBTLE: No, you scarab,
I'll thunder you in pieces: I will teach you
How to beware to tempt a Fury again
That carries tempest in his hand and voice.

FACE: The place has made you valiant.

SUBTLE: No, your clothes. —
Thou vermin, have I ta'en thee out of dung,
So poor, so wretched, when no living thing
Would keep thee company, but a spider, or worse?
Raised thee from brooms, and dust, and watering-pots,
Sublimed thee, and exalted thee, and fixed thee
In the third region, called our state of grace?
Wrought thee to spirit, to quintessence, with pains
Would twice have won me the philosopher's work? [23]
Put thee in words and fashion, made thee fit
For more than ordinary fellowships?
Given thee thy oaths, thy quarrelling dimensions,
Thy rules to cheat at horse-race, cock-pit, cards,
Dice, or whatever gallant tincture else?
Made thee a second in mine own great art?
And have I this for thanks! Do you rebel,
Do you fly out in the projection? [24]
Would you be gone now?

DOL: Gentlemen, what mean you?
Will you mar all?

SUBTLE: Slave, thou hadst had no name ——

DOL: Will you undo yourselves with civil war?

SUBTLE: Never been known, past *equi clibanum,*
The heat of horse-dung, under ground, in cellars,
Or an ale-house darker than deaf John's; been lost
To all mankind, but laundresses and tapsters,
Had not I been.

DOL: Do you know who hears you, sovereign?

FACE: Sirrah ——

[20] tips [21] a card game [22] supplying (gamblers) with chips [23] alchemist's jargon, ordinarily not glossed in these notes [24] the successful completion of the alchemic process

DOL: Nay, general, I thought you were civil.
FACE: I shall turn desperate, if you grow thus loud.
SUBTLE: And hang thyself, I care not.
FACE: Hang thee, collier.
And all thy pots and pans, in pictures, I will,
Since thou hast moved me ——
DOL: O, this will o'erthrow all.
FACE: Write thee up bawd in Paul's, have all thy tricks
Of cozening with a hollow cole, dust, scrapings,
Searching for things lost, with a sieve and sheers,
Erecting figures[25] in your rows of houses,[26]
And taking in of shadows with a glass,
Told in red letters; and a face cut for thee,
Worse than Gamaliel Ratsey's.[27]
DOL: Are you sound?
Have you your senses, masters?
FACE: I will have
A book, but barely reckoning thy impostures,
Shall prove a true philosopher's stone to printers.
SUBTLE: Away, you trencher-rascal!
FACE: Out, you dog-leech!
The vomit of all prisons ——
DOL: Will you be
Your own destructions, gentlemen?
FACE: Still spewed out
For lying too heavy on the basket.[28]
SUBTLE: Cheater!
FACE: Bawd!
SUBTLE: Cow-herd!
FACE: Conjurer!
SUBTLE: Cutpurse!
FACE: Witch!
DOL: O me!
We are ruined, lost! have you no more regard
To your reputations? where's your judgment? 'slight,
Have yet some care of me, of your republic ——[29]
FACE: Away, this brach![30] I'll bring thee, rogue, within
The statute of sorcery, tricesimo tertio[31]

25 determining the position of planets for the purpose of casting a horoscope 26 signs of the zodiac 27 highwayman hanged in 1605, notorious for the hideous masks in which he committed his robberies 28 eating more than his share (of the prisoners' scraps) 29 *i.e.*, "commonwealth" or guild of cheats 30 bitch 31 thirty-third (*i.e.*, the thirty-third year of the reign of Henry VIII, 1541)

Of Harry the Eighth: ay, and perhaps thy neck
Within a noose, for laundring[32] gold and barbing[33] it.

DOL (*snatches* FACE'S *sword*): You'll bring your head within a cockscomb, will you?
And you, sir, with your menstrue[34] (*Dashes* SUBTLE'S *vial out of his hand.*) — gather it up.
'Sdeath, you abominable pair of stinkards,
Leave off your barking, and grow one again,
Or, by the light that shines, I'll cut your throats.
I'll not be made a prey unto the marshal
For ne'er a snarling dog-bolt[35] of you both.
Have you together cozened all this while,
And all the world, and shall it now be said,
You've made most courteous shift to cozen yourselves?
You will accuse him! you will "bring him in (*To* FACE.)
Within the statute!" Who shall take your word?
A whoreson, upstart, apocryphal captain,
Whom not a Puritan in Blackfriers will trust
So much as for a feather: and you, too, (*To* SUBTLE.)
Will give the cause, forsooth! you will insult,
And claim a primacy in the divisions![36]
You must be chief! as if you only had
The powder to project with, and the work
Were not begun out of equality?
The venture tripartite? all things in common?
Without priority? 'Sdeath! you perpetual curs,
Fall to your couples again, and cozen kindly,
And heartily, and lovingly, as you should
And lose not the beginning of a term,
Or, by this hand, I shall grow factious too,
And take my part, and quit you.

FACE: 'Tis his fault;
He ever murmurs, and objects his pains,
And says, the weight of all lies upon him.

SUBTLE: Why, so it does.

DOL: How does it? do not we
Sustain our parts?

SUBTLE: Yes, but they are not equal.

DOL: Why, if your part exceed to-day, I hope
Ours may to-morrow match it.

SUBTLE: Ay, they *may*.

[32] washing off the surface (in acid) [33] clipping [34] solvent [35] useless arrow [36] *i.e.*, of the loot

DOL: May, murmuring mastiff! ay, and do. Death on me!
Help me to throttle him. (*Seizes* SUBTLE *by the throat.*)
SUBTLE: Dorothy! Mistress Dorothy!
'Ods precious,[37] I'll do anything. What do you mean?
DOL: Because o' your fermentation and cibation?
SUBTLE: Not I, by heaven ——
DOL: Your Sol and Luna — help me.[38] (*To* FACE.)
SUBTLE: Would I were hanged then! I'll conform myself.
DOL: Will you, sir? do so then, and quickly: swear.
SUBTLE: What should I swear?
DOL: To leave your faction,[39] sir,
And labour kindly in the common work.
SUBTLE: Let me not breathe if I meant aught beside.
I only used those speeches as a spur
To him.
DOL: I hope we need no spurs, sir. Do we?
FACE: 'Slid,[40] prove to-day who shall shark[41] best.
SUBTLE: Agreed.
DOL: Yes, and work close and friendly.
SUBTLE: 'Slight,[42] the knot
Shall grow the stronger for this breach, with me. (*They shake hands.*)
DOL: Why, so, my good baboons! Shall we go make
A sort of sober, scurvy, precise[43] neighbours,
That scarce have smiled twice since the king came in,[44]
A feast of laughter at our follies? Rascals,
Would run themselves from breath, to see me ride,[45]
Or you t' have but a hole to thrust your heads in,
For which you should pay ear-rent? [46] No, agree,
And may Don Provost[47] ride a feasting[48] long,
In his old velvet jerkin and stained scarfs,
My noble sovereign, and worthy general,
Ere we contribute a new crewel[49] garter
To his most worsted [50] worship.
SUBTLE: Royal Dol!
Spoken like Claridiana,[51] and thyself.
FACE: For which at supper, thou shalt sit in triumph,

[37] God's precious (blood) [38] *i.e.*, to throttle Subtle [39] *i.e.*, quarrelsomeness [40] God's eyelid [41] cheat [42] God's light [43] scrupulous (*i.e.*, Puritanical) [44] *i.e.*, 1603 [45] be carted as a whore [46] *i.e.*, have your ears cropped in the pillory [47] the hangman, who received the clothes of the criminal as part of his perquisite [48] thriving [49] (1) worsted, (2) cruel [50] here with a pun on "defeated," "tricked" [51] the heroine of *The Mirror of Princely Deeds and Knighthood*, a Spanish romance

And not be styled Dol Common, but Dol Proper,
Dol Singular: the longest cut at night,
Shall draw thee for his Dol Particular. (*Bell rings without.*)

SUBTLE: Who's that? one rings. To the window, Dol: (*Exit* DOL.) — pray heaven,
The master do not trouble us this quarter.

FACE: O, fear not him. While there dies one a week
O' the plague, he's safe, from thinking toward London:
Beside, he's busy at his hop-yards now;
I had a letter from him. If he do,
He'll send such word, for airing of the house,
As you shall have sufficient time to quit it:
Though we break up a fortnight, 'tis no matter.

(*Re-enter* DOL.)

SUBTLE: Who is it, Dol?

DOL: A fine young quodling.[52]

FACE: O,
My lawyer's clerk, I lighted on last night,
In Holborn, at the Dagger. He would have
(I told you of him) a familiar,
To rifle[53] with at horses, and win cups.

DOL: O, let him in.

SUBTLE: Stay. Who shall do't?

FACE: Get you
Your robes on: I will meet him, as going out.

DOL: And what shall I do?

FACE: Not be seen; away! (*Exit* DOL.)
Seem you very reserved.

SUBTLE: Enough. (*Exit.*)

FACE (*aloud and retiring*): God be wi' you, sir,
I pray you let him know that I was here:
His name is Dapper. I would gladly have staid but ——

DAPPER (*within*): Captain, I am here.

FACE: Who's that? — He's come, I think, doctor.

(*Enter* DAPPER.)

Good faith, sir, I was going away.

DAPPER: In truth,
I am very sorry, captain.

FACE: But I thought

[52] raw youth [53] play at dice

Sure I should meet you.
DAPPER: Ay, I am very glad.
I had a scurvy writ or two to make
And I had lent my watch last night to one
That dines to-day at the sheriff's, and so was robbed
Of my pass-time.

(*Re-enter* SUBTLE *in his velvet cap and gown.*)

Is this the cunning-man? [54]
FACE: This is his worship.
DAPPER: Is he a doctor?
FACE: Yes.
DAPPER: And have you broke with him,[55] captain?
FACE: Ay.
DAPPER: And how?
FACE: Faith, he does make the matter, sir, so dainty, I know not what to say.
DAPPER: Not so, good captain.
FACE: Would I were fairly rid of it, believe me.
DAPPER: Nay, now you grieve me, sir. Why should you wish so?
I dare assure you, I'll not be ungrateful.
FACE: I cannot think you will, sir. But the law
Is such a thing —— and then he says, Read's matter[56]
Falling so lately.
DAPPER: Read! he was an ass,
And dealt, sir, with a fool.
FACE: It was a clerk, sir.
DAPPER: A clerk!
FACE: Nay, hear me, sir, you know the law
Better, I think ——
DAPPER: I should, sir, and the danger:
You know, I showed the statute to you.
FACE: You did so.
DAPPER: And will I tell then! By this hand of flesh,
Would it might never write good courthand more,
If I discover. What do you think of me,
That I am a chiaus? [57]
FACE: What's that?
DAPPER: The Turk was here.
As one would say, do you think I am a Turk?

[54] learned man, (here) magician [55] *i.e.*, told him my business [56] In 1608 Dr. Simon Read had been granted a pardon for having invoked spirits to find stolen goods. [57] messenger, herald (Turk)

FACE: I'll tell the doctor so.
DAPPER: Do, good sweet captain.
FACE: Come, noble doctor, pray thee let's prevail,
This is the gentleman, and he is no chiaus.
SUBTLE: Captain, I have returned you all my answer.
I would do much, sir, for your love —— But this
I neither may, nor can.
FACE: Tut, do not say so.
You deal now with a noble fellow, doctor,
One that will thank you richly; and he is no chiaus:
Let that, sir, move you.
SUBTLE: Pray you, forbear ——
FACE: He has
Four angels[58] here.
SUBTLE: You do me wrong, good sir.
FACE: Doctor, wherein? To tempt you with these spirits?
SUBTLE: To tempt my art and love, sir, to my peril.
Fore heaven, I scarce can think you are my friend,
That so would draw me to apparent danger.
FACE: I draw you! a horse draw you, and a halter,
You, and your flies together ——
DAPPER: Nay, good captain.
FACE: That knows no difference of men.
SUBTLE: Good words, sir.
FACE: Good deeds, sir, doctor dog's-meat.[59] 'Slight, I bring you
No cheating Clim o' the Cloughs,[60] or Claribels,[61]
That look as big as five-and-fifty, and flush;[62]
And spit out secrets like hot custard ——
DAPPER: Captain!
FACE: Nor any melancholic underscribe,
Shall tell [63] the vicar; but a special gentle,
That is the heir to forty marks a year,
Consorts with the small poets of the time,
Is the sole hope of his old grandmother;
That knows the law, and writes you six fair hands,
Is a fine clerk, and has his cyphering perfect,
Will take his oath o' the Greek Testament,
If need be, in his pocket; and can court
His mistress out of Ovid.

[58] gold coins, each worth c. 10 shillings [59] offal [60] one of three northern outlaws in an old ballad [61] a lewd knight in Spenser's *Faerie Queene*, IV, ix [62] a complete sequence of cards in the same suit, the winning hand in the game of primero [63] *i.e.*, who'll tell

DAPPER: Nay, dear captain ——
FACE: Did you not tell me so?
DAPPER: Yes; but I'd have you
Use master doctor with some more respect.
FACE: Hang him, proud stag, with his broad velvet head! —
But for your sake, I'd choke ere I would change
An article of breath with such a puck-fist![64]
Come, let's be gone. (*Going.*)
SUBTLE: Pray you let me speak with you.
DAPPER: His worship calls you, captain.
FACE: I am sorry
I e'er embarked myself in such a business.
DAPPER: Nay, good sir; he did call you.
FACE: Will he take then?
SUBTLE: First, hear me ——
FACE: Not a syllable, 'less you take.
SUBTLE: Pray you, sir ——
FACE: Upon no terms but an *assumpsit*.[65]
SUBTLE: Your humour must be law. (*He takes the four angels.*)
FACE: Why now, sir, talk.
Now I dare hear you with mine honour. Speak.
So may this gentleman too.
SUBTLE: Why, sir —— (*Offering to whisper.*)
FACE: No whispering.
SUBTLE: 'Fore heaven, you do not apprehend the loss
You do yourself in this.
FACE: Wherein? for what?
SUBTLE: Marry, to be so importunate for one
That, when he has it, will undo you all:
He'll win up all the money in the town.
FACE: How?
SUBTLE: Yes, and blow up gamester after gamester,
As they do crackers in a puppet-play.
If I do give him a familiar,
Give you him all you play for; never set him:[66]
For he will have it.
FACE: You are mistaken, doctor.
Why, he does ask one but for cups and horses,
A rifling fly; none of your great familiars.
DAPPER: Yes, captain, I would have it for all games.
SUBTLE: I told you so.

[64] puff-ball, empty braggart [65] a verbal pledge to pay or to perform a certain service [66] set a stake against, challenge

FACE (*taking* DAPPER *aside*): 'Slight, that is a new business!
I understood you, a tame bird, to fly
Twice in a term, or so, on Friday nights,
When you had left the office, for a nag
Of forty or fifty shillings.
DAPPER: Ay, 'tis true, sir;
But I do think now I shall leave the law,
And therefore ——
FACE: Why, this changes quite the case.
Do you think that I dare move him?
DAPPER: If you please, sir;
All's one to him, I see.
FACE: What! for that money?
I cannot with my conscience; nor should you
Make the request, methinks.
DAPPER: No, sir, I mean
To add consideration.
FACE: Why then, sir,
I'll try. (*Goes to* SUBTLE.) Say that it were for all games, doctor?
SUBTLE: I say then, not a mouth shall eat for him
At any ordinary,[67] but on the score,
That is a gaming mouth, conceive me.
FACE: Indeed!
SUBTLE: He'll draw you all the treasure of the realm,
If it be set him.
FACE: Speak you this from art?
SUBTLE: Ay, sir, and reason too, the ground of art.
He is of the only best complexion,
The queen of Fairy loves.
FACE: What! is he?
SUBTLE: Peace.
He'll overhear you. Sir, should she but see him ——
FACE: What?
SUBTLE: Do not you tell him.
FACE: Will he win at cards too?
SUBTLE: The spirits of dead Holland, living Isaac,[68]
You'd swear, were in him; such a vigorous luck
As cannot be resisted. 'Slight, he'll put
Six of your gallants to a cloak,[69] indeed.
FACE: A strange success, that some man shall be born to!
SUBTLE: He hears you, man ——

[67] tavern [68] John and John Isaac Holland, 15th century Dutch alchemists
[69] *i.e.*, strip to the cloak, the last garment a gambling gallant would part with

DAPPER: Sir, I'll not be ingrateful.
FACE: Faith, I have confidence in his good nature:
You hear, he says he will not be ingrateful.
SUBTLE: Why, as you please; my venture follows yours.
FACE: Troth, do it, doctor; think him trusty, and make him.
He may make us both happy[70] in an hour;
Win some five thousand pound, and send us two on't.
DAPPER: Believe it, and I will, sir.
FACE: And you shall, sir. (*Takes him aside.*)
You have heard all?
DAPPER: No, what was't? Nothing, I, sir.
FACE: Nothing!
DAPPER: A little, sir.
FACE: Well, a rare star
Reigned at your birth.
DAPPER: At mine, sir! No.
FACE: The doctor
Swears that you are ——
SUBTLE: Nay, captain, you'll tell all now.
FACE: Allied to the queen of Fairy.
DAPPER: Who? that I am?
Believe it, no such matter ——
FACE: Yes, and that
You were born with a cawl [71] on your head.
DAPPER: Who says so?
FACE: Come,
You know it well enough, though you dissemble it.
DAPPER: I' fac, I do not; you are mistaken.
FACE: How!
Swear by your fac, and in a thing so known
Unto the doctor? how shall we, sir, trust you
In the other matter; can we ever think,
When you have won five or six thousand pound,
You'll send us shares in't by this rate?
DAPPER: By Jove, sir,
I'll win ten thousand pound, and send you half.
I' fac's no oath.
SUBTLE: No, no, he did but jest.
FACE: Go to. Go thank the doctor: he's your friend,
To take it so.
DAPPER: I thank his worship.

[70] rich [71] a sign of luck

FACE: So!
Another angel.
DAPPER: Must I?
FACE: Must you! 'slight,
What else is thanks? will you be trivial? — Doctor,
(DAPPER *gives him the money.*)
When must he come for his familiar?
DAPPER: Shall I not have it with me?
SUBTLE: O, good sir!
There must be a world of ceremonies pass;
You must be bathed and fumigated first:
Besides, the queen of Fairy does not rise
Till it be noon.
FACE: Not, if she danced, to-night,[72]
SUBTLE: And she must bless it.
FACE: Did you never see
Her royal grace yet?
DAPPER: Whom?
FACE: Your aunt of Fairy?
SUBTLE: Not since she kist him in the cradle, captain;
I can resolve[73] you that.
FACE: Well, see her grace,
Whate'er it cost you, for a thing that I know.
It will be somewhat hard to compass; but
However, see her. You are made, believe it,
If you can see her. Her grace is a lone woman,
And very rich; and if she takes a fancy,
She will do strange things. See her, at any hand.
'Slid, she may hap to leave you all she has:
It is the doctor's fear.
DAPPER: How will't be done, then?
FACE: Let me alone, take you no thought. Do you
But say to me, captain, I'll see her grace.
DAPPER: "Captain, I'll see her grace."
FACE: Enough. (*Knocking within.*)
SUBTLE: Who's there?
Anon. — Conduct him forth by the back way. (*Aside to* FACE.)
Sir, against[74] one o'clock prepare yourself;
Till when you must be fasting; only take
Three drops of vinegar in at your nose,
Two at your mouth, and one at either ear;

[72] last night [73] assure [74] for

Then bathe your fingers' ends and wash your eyes,
To sharpen your five senses, and cry *hum*
Thrice, and then *buz* as often; and then come. (*Exit.*)

FACE: Can you remember this?

DAPPER: I warrant you.

FACE: Well then, away. It is but your bestowing
Some twenty nobles 'mong her grace's servants,
And put on a clean shirt: you do not know
What grace her grace may do you in clean linen.

(*Exeunt* FACE *and* DAPPER.)

SUBTLE (*within*): Come in? Good wives, I pray you forbear me now;
Troth, I can do you no good till afternoon —

(*Re-enters, followed by* DRUGGER.)

What is your name, say you Abel Drugger?

DRUGGER: Yes, sir.

SUBTLE: A seller of tobacco?

DRUGGER: Yes, sir.

SUBTLE: Umph!
Free of the grocers? [75]

DRUGGER: Ay, an't please you.

SUBTLE: Well ——
Your business, Abel?

DRUGGER: This, an't please your worship;
I am a young beginner, and am building
Of a new shop, an't like your worship, just
At corner of a street: — Here is the plot on't ——
And I would know by art, sir, of your worship,
Which way I should make my door, by necromancy,
And where my shelves; and which should be for boxes,
And which for pots. I would be glad to thrive, sir:
And I was wished to your worship by a gentleman,
One Captain Face, that says you know men's planets,
And their good angels, and their bad.

SUBTLE: I do,
If I do see them ——

(*Re-enter* FACE.)

FACE: What! my honest Abel?
Thou art well met here.

[75] of the Grocers' Company

DRUGGER: Troth, sir, I was speaking,
Just as your worship came here, of your worship:
I pray you speak for me to master doctor.
FACE: He shall do anything. Doctor, do you hear?
This is my friend, Abel, an honest fellow;
He lets me have good tobacco, and he does not
Sophisticate[76] it with sack-lees[77] or oil,
Nor washes it in muscadel and grains,
Nor buries it in gravel, under ground,
Wrapped up in greasy leather, or pissed clouts:
But keeps it in fine lily pots, that, opened,
Smell like conserve of roses, or French beans.
He has his maple block, his silver tongs,
Winchester pipes, and fire of juniper:
A neat, spruce, honest fellow, and no goldsmith.[78]
SUBTLE: He is a fortunate fellow, that I am sure on.
FACE: Already, sir, have you found it? Lo thee, Abel!
SUBTLE: And in right way toward riches ——
FACE: Sir!
SUBTLE: This summer
He will be of the clothing[79] of his company,
And next spring called to the scarlet;[80] spend what he can.
FACE: What, and so little beard?
SUBTLE: Sir, you must think,
He may have a receipt to make hair come:
But he'll be wise, preserve his youth, and fine for 't;[81]
His fortune looks for him another way.
FACE: 'Slid, doctor, how canst thou know this so soon?
I am amused [82] at that.
SUBTLE: By a rule, captain,
In metoposcopy,[83] which I do work by;
A certain star in the forehead, which you see not.
Your chestnut or your olive-coloured face
Does never fail: and your long ear doth promise.
I knew't, by certain spots, too, in his teeth,
And on the nail of his mercurial finger.
FACE: Which finger's that?
SUBTLE: His little finger. Look.
You were born upon a Wednesday?
DRUGGER: Yes, indeed, sir.

[76] adulterate [77] dregs of a dry white wine [78] *i.e.*, usurer [79] wear the livery
[80] be made sheriff [81] pay the fine for refusing the office [82] puzzled
[83] study of the forehead, for the purpose of reading a person's character

SUBTLE: The thumb, in chiromancy,[84] we give Venus;
The forefinger to Jove; the midst to Saturn;
The ring to Sol; the least to Mercury,
Who was the lord, sir, of his horoscope,
His house of life being Libra; which foreshowed
He should be a merchant, and should trade with balance.
FACE: Why, this is strange! Is it not, honest Nab?
SUBTLE: There is a ship now coming from Ormus,
That shall yield him such a commodity
Of drugs —— This is the west, and this the south?
(*Pointing to the plan.*)
DRUGGER: Yes, sir.
SUBTLE: And those are your two sides?
DRUGGER: Ay, sir.
SUBTLE: Make me[85] your door then, south; your broad side, west:
And on the east side of your shop, aloft,
Write Mathlai, Tarmiel, and Baraborat;
Upon the north part, Rael, Velel, Thiel.
They are the names of those Mercurial spirits
That do fright flies from boxes.
DRUGGER: Yes, sir.
SUBTLE: And
Beneath your threshold, bury me a loadstone
To draw in gallants that wear spurs: the rest,
They'll seem[86] to follow.
FACE: That's a secret, Nab!
SUBTLE: And, on your stall, a puppet, with a vice[87]
And a court-fucus,[88] to call city-dames:
You shall deal much with minerals.
DRUGGER: Sir, I have
At home, already ——
SUBTLE: Ay, I know you have arsenic,
Vitriol, sal-tartar, argaile, alkali,
Cinoper: I know all. — This fellow, captain,
Will come, in time, to be a great distiller,
And give a say[89] — I will not say directly,
But very fair — at the philosopher's stone.
FACE: Why, how now, Abel! is this true?
DRUGGER: Good captain,
What must I give? (*Aside to* FACE.)

[84] palmistry [85] "me" here is the "ethical dative"; the expression is the equivalent of "I want you to make . . ." [86] be seen [87] vise [88] cosmetic used at court [89] an assay, an attempt

FACE: Nay, I'll not counsel thee.
Thou hear'st what wealth (he says, spend what thou canst),
Thou'rt like to come to.
DRUGGER: I would gi' him a crown.
FACE: A crown! and toward such a fortune? heart,
Thou shalt rather gi' him thy shop. No gold about thee?
DRUGGER: Yes, I have a portague,[90] I have kept this half year.
FACE: Out on thee, Nab! 'Slight, there was such an offer —
Shalt keep't no longer, I'll give't him for thee. Doctor,
Nab prays your worship to drink this,[91] and swears
He will appear more grateful, as your skill
Does raise him in the world.
DRUGGER: I would entreat
Another favour of his worship.
FACE: What is't, Nab?
DRUGGER: But to look over, sir, my almanack,
And cross out my ill-days, that I may neither
Bargain, nor trust upon them.
FACE: That he shall, Nab:
Leave it, it shall be done, 'gainst afternoon.
SUBTLE: And a direction for his shelves.
FACE: Now, Nab,
Art thou well pleased, Nab?
DRUGGER: 'Thank, sir, both your worships.
FACE: Away. (*Exit* DRUGGER.)
Why, now, you smoaky persecutor of nature!
Now do you see, that something's to be done,
Beside your beech-coal, and your corsive[92] waters,
Your crosslets,[93] crucibles, and cucurbites? [94]
You must have stuff, brought home to you, to work on:
And yet you think, I am at no expense
In searching out these veins, then following them,
Then trying them out. 'Fore God, my intelligence
Costs me more money than my share oft comes to,
In these rare works.
SUBTLE: You are pleasant, sir.

(*Re-enter* DOL.)

How now!
What says my dainty Dolkin?
DOL: Yonder fish-wife

[90] gold coin worth c. 3½ pounds [91] *i.e.*, buy yourself a drink [92] corrosive
[93] melting pots [94] retorts

Will not away. And there's your giantess,
The bawd of Lambeth.
SUBTLE: Heart, I cannot speak with them.
DOL: Not afore night, I have told them in a voice,
Thorough the trunk,[95] like one of your familiars.
But I have spied Sir Epicure Mammon ——
SUBTLE: Where?
DOL: Coming along, at far end of the lane,
Slow of his feet, but earnest of his tongue
To one that's with him.
SUBTLE: Face, go you and shift.[96] (*Exit* FACE.)
Dol, you must presently[97] make ready too.
DOL: Why, what's the matter?
SUBTLE: O, I did look for him
With the sun's rising: marvel he could sleep.
This is the day I am to perfect for him
The magisterium, our great work, the stone;
And yield it, made, into his hands: of which
He has, this month, talked as he were possessed.
And now he's dealing pieces on't away.
Methinks I see him entering ordinaries,
Dispensing for the pox, and plaguy houses,
Reaching[98] his dose, walking Moorfields for lepers,
And offering citizens' wives pomander-bracelets,
As his preservative, made of the elixir;
Searching the spittle, to make old bawds young;
And the highways, for beggars, to make rich:
I see no end of his labours. He will make
Nature ashamed of her long sleep: when art,
Who's but a step-dame, shall do more then[99] she,
In her best love to mankind, ever could:
If his dream last, he'll turn the age to gold. (*Exeunt.*)

ACT THE SECOND

Scene I [*An outer Room in* LOVEWIT'*s House.*]

(*Enter* SIR EPICURE MAMMON *and* SURLY.)

MAMMON: Come on, sir. Now you set your foot on shore
In *Novo Orbe*;[100] here's the rich Peru:

[95] tube [96] change your clothes [97] at once [98] offering [99] than
[100] the new world

And there within, sir, are the golden mines,
Great Solomon's Ophir! he was sailing to't,
Three years, but we have reached it in ten months.
This is the day wherein, to all my friends,
I will pronounce the happy word, BE RICH;
THIS DAY YOU SHALL BE SPECTATISSIMI.[101]
You shall no more deal with the hollow dye,[102]
Or the frail card. No more be at charge of keeping
The livery-punk [103] for the young heir, that must
Seal, at all hours, in his shirt: no more,
If he deny, have him beaten to't, as he is
That brings him the commodity. No more
Shall thirst of satin, or the covetous hunger
Of velvet entrails[104] for a rude-spun cloak,
To be displayed at Madam Augusta's,[105] make
The sons of Sword and Hazard [106] fall before
The golden calf, and on their knees, whole nights,
Commit idolatry with wine and trumpets:
Or go a feasting after drum and ensign.
No more of this. You shall start up young viceroys,
And have your punks and punketees,[107] my Surly.
And unto thee I speak it first, BE RICH.
Where is my Subtle, there? Within, ho!
FACE (*within*): Sir, he'll come to you by and by.
MAMMON: This is his fire-drake,
His Lungs,[108] his Zephyrus, he that puffs his coals,
Till he firk[109] nature up, in her own centre.
You are not faithful,[110] sir. This night I'll change
All that is metal in my house to gold:
And, early in the morning, will I send
To all the plumbers and the pewterers,
And buy their tin and lead up; and to Lothbury
For all the copper.
SURLY: What, and turn that, too?
MAMMON: Yes, and I'll purchase Devonshire and Cornwall,
And make them perfect Indies! you admire[111] now?
SURLY: No, faith.
MAMMON: But when you see th' effects of the Great Medicine,

[101] pre-eminent, most highly esteemed [102] loaded dice [103] prostitute accomplice in swindling a young heir [104] lining [105] name of a brothel (?) [106] *i.e.*, highwaymen and gamblers [107] young prostitutes [108] *i.e.*, Mammon thinks that Face blows the coals for Subtle [109] stir [110] skeptical [111] wonder

Of which one part projected on a hundred
Of Mercury, or Venus, or the moon,
Shall turn it to as many of the sun;[112]
Nay, to a thousand, so *ad infinitum:*
You will believe me.

SURLY: Yes, when I see't, I will.
But if my eyes do cozen me so, and I
Giving them no occasion, sure I'll have
A whore shall piss them out next day.

MAMMON: Ha! why?
Do you think I fable with you? I assure you,
He that has once the flower of the sun,
The perfect ruby, which we call elixir,
Not only can do that, but by its virtue,
Can confer honour, love, respect, long life;
Give safety, valour, yea, and victory,
To whom he will. In eight and twenty days,
I'll make an old man of fourscore, a child.

SURLY: No doubt; he's that already.

MAMMON: Nay, I mean,
Restore his years, renew him, like an eagle,
To the fifth age;[113] make him get sons and daughters,
Young giants; as our philosophers[114] have done,
The ancient patriarchs, afore the flood,
But taking, once a week, on a knife's point,
The quantity of a grain of mustard of it;
Become stout Marses, and beget young Cupids.

SURLY: The decayed vestals[115] of Pict-hatch[116] would thank you,
That keep the fire alive there.

MAMMON: 'Tis the secret
Of nature naturized 'gainst all infections,
Cures all diseases coming of all causes;
A month's grief in a day, a year's in twelve;
And, of what age soever, in a month:
Past all the doses of your drugging doctors,
I'll undertake, withal, to fight the plague
Out of the kingdom in three months.

SURLY: And I'll
Be bound, the players shall sing your praises then,[117]
Without their poets.

[112] *i.e.*, quicksilver, copper, silver, gold [113] *i.e.*, of man's seven [114] *i.e.*, alchemists [115] *i.e.*, old whores [116] a London red-light district [117] because the theaters would never have to close

MAMMON: Sir, I'll do't. Meantime,
I'll give away so much unto my man,
Shall serve the whole city with preservative
Weekly; each house his dose, and at the rate ——
SURLY: As he that built the Water-work does with water?
MAMMON: You are incredulous.
SURLY: Faith, I have a humour,
I would not willingly be gulled. Your stone
Cannot transmute me.
MAMMON: Pertinax [my] Surly,
Will you believe antiquity? records?
I'll show you a book where Moses and his sister,
And Solomon have written of the art;
Ay, and a treatise penned by Adam ——
SURLY: How!
MAMMON: Of the philosopher's stone, and in High Dutch.
SURLY: Did Adam write, sir, in High Dutch?
MAMMON: He did;
Which proves it was the primitive tongue.
SURLY: What paper?
MAMMON: On cedar board.
SURLY: O that, indeed, they say,
Will last 'gainst worms.
MAMMON: 'Tis like your Irish wood,
'Gainst cobwebs. I have a piece of Jason's fleece too,
Which was no other than a book of alchemy,
Writ in large sheepskin, a good fat ram-vellum.
Such was Pythagoras' thigh, Pandora's tub,
And all that fable of Medea's charms,
The manner of our work; the bulls, our furnace,
Still breathing fire; our argent-vive,[118] the dragon:
The dragon's teeth, mercury sublimate,
That keeps the whiteness, hardness, and the biting;
And they are gathered into Jason's helm,
The alembic,[119] and then sowed in Mars his field,
And thence sublimed so often, till they're fixed,
Both this, the Hesperian garden, Cadmus' story,
Jove's shower, the boon of Midas, Argus' eyes,
Boccace his Demogorgon, thousands more,
All abstract riddles of our stone. —

(*Enter* FACE, *as a* SERVANT.)

[118] quicksilver [119] top of the retort, to which the fumes rise during distillation

How now!
Do we succeed? Is our day come? and holds it?
FACE: The evening will set red upon you, sir;
You have colour for it, crimson: the red ferment
Has done his office; three hours hence prepare you
To see projection.
MAMMON: Pertinax, my Surly.
Again I say to thee, aloud, Be rich.
This day thou shalt have ingots; and to-morrow
Give lords th' affront.[120] — Is it, my Zephyrus, right?
Blushes the bolt's-head? [121]
FACE: Like a wench with child, sir,
That were but now discovered to her master.
MAMMON: Excellent witty Lungs! — my only care is
Where to get stuff enough now, to project on;
This town will not half serve me.
FACE: No, sir! buy
The covering off o' churches.
MAMMON: That's true.
FACE: Yes.
Let them stand bare, as do their auditory;[122]
Or cap them new with shingles.
MAMMON: No, good thatch:
Thatch will lie light upon the rafters, Lungs. —
Lungs, I will manumit thee from the furnace;
I will restore thee thy complexion, Puffe,
Lost in the embers; and repair this brain,
Hurt with the fume o' the metals.
FACE: I have blown, sir,
Hard, for your worship; thrown by many a coal,
When 'twas not beech; weighed those I put in, just
To keep your heat still even; these bleared eyes
Have waked to read your several colours, sir,
Of the pale citron, the green lion, the crow,
The peacock's tail, the plumed swan.[123]
MAMMON: And lastly,
Thou hast descried the flower, the sanguis agni.
FACE: Yes, sir.
MAMMON: Where's master?
FACE: At his prayers, sir, he;
Good man, he's doing his devotions

[120] act the equal of lords [121] globular flask with a long neck [122] audience
[123] alchemist's jargon for different colors of fire

For the success.
MAMMON: Lungs, I will set a period
To all thy labours; thou shalt be the master
Of my seraglio.[124]
FACE: Good, sir.
MAMMON: But do you hear?
I'll geld you, Lungs.
FACE: Yes, sir.
MAMMON: For I do mean
To have a list of wives and concubines
Equal with Solomon, who had the stone
Alike with me; and I will make me a back
With the elixir, that shall be as tough
As Hercules, to encounter fifty a night.—
Thou art sure thou saw'st it blood?
FACE: Both blood and spirit, sir.
MAMMON: I will have all my beds blown up, not stuft:
Down is too hard: and then, mine oval room
Filled with such pictures as Tiberius took
From Elephantis, and dull Aretine
But coldly imitated. Then, my glasses
Cut in more subtle angles, to disperse
And multiply the figures, as I walk
Naked between my succubæ.[125] My mists
I'll have of perfume, vapoured 'bout the room,
To lose our selves in; and my baths, like pits
To fall into; from whence we will come forth,
And roll us dry in gossamer and roses.—
Is it arrived at ruby? —— Where I spy
A wealthy citizen, or [a] rich lawyer,
Have a sublimed pure wife, unto that fellow
I'll send a thousand pound to be my cuckold.
FACE: And I shall carry it?
MAMMON: No. I'll have no bawds[126]
But fathers and mothers: they will do it best,
Best of all others. And my flatterers
Shall be the pure and gravest of divines,
That I can get for money. My mere fools,
Eloquent burgesses, and then my poets
The same that writ so subtly of the fart,
Whom I will entertain still for that subject.

[124] harem [125] concubines [126] pimps

The few that would give out themselves to be
Court and town-stallions, and, each-where, bely[127]
Ladies who are known most innocent, for them;
Those will I beg, to make me eunuchs of:
And they shall fan me with ten estrich[128] tails
A-piece, made in a plume to gather wind.
We will be brave, Puffe, now we have the med'cine.
My meat shall all come in, in Indian shells,
Dishes of agat set in gold, and studded
With emeralds, sapphires, hyacinths, and rubies.
The tongues of carps, dormice, and camels' heels,
Boiled in the spirit of sol, and dissolved pearl,
Apicius' diet, 'gainst the epilepsy:
And I will eat these broths with spoons of amber,
Headed with diamond and carbuncle.
My foot-boy shall eat pheasants, calvered salmons,
Knots,[129] godwits,[130] lampreys: I myself will have
The beards of barbel[131] served, instead of salads;
Oiled mushrooms; and the swelling unctuous paps
Of a fat pregnant sow, newly cut off,
Drest with an exquisite and poignant sauce;
For which, I'll say unto my cook, *There's gold,*
Go forth, and be a knight.

FACE: Sir, I'll go look
A little, how it heightens. (*Exit.*)

MAMMON: Do. — My shirts
I'll have of taffeta-sarsnet,[132] soft and light
As cobwebs; and for all my other raiment,
It shall be such as might provoke the Persian,
Were he to teach the world riot anew.
My gloves of fishes and birds' skins, perfumed
With gums of paradise, and Eastern air ——

SURLY: And do you think to have the stone with this?

MAMMON: No, I do think t' have all this with the stone.

SURLY: Why, I have heard he must be *homo frugi,*[133]
A pious, holy, and religious man,
One free from mortal sin, a very virgin.

MAMMON: That makes it, sir; he is so: but I buy it;[134]
My venture brings it me. He, honest wretch,

127 (1) lie with, (2) slander 128 ostrich 129 a kind of sandpiper 130 wading-birds of the snipe family 131 a fresh-water fish of the carp tribe 132 fine silk 133 a sober, abstentious man 134 Mammon contrasts the person who *makes* the stone (Subtle) with the person who *buys* it (himself).

A notable, superstitious, good soul,
Has worn his knees bare, and his slippers bald,
With prayer and fasting for it; and, sir, let him
Do it alone, for me, still. Here he comes.
Not a profane word afore him; 'tis poison. —

(*Enter* SUBTLE.)

Good morrow, father.
SUBTLE: Gentle son, good morrow,
And to your friend there. What is he, is with you?
MAMMON: An heretic, that I did bring along,
In hope, sir, to convert him.
SUBTLE: Son, I doubt[135]
You are covetous, that thus you meet your time
In the just point; prevent your day[136] at morning.
This argues something worthy of a fear
Of importune and carnal appetite.
Take heed you do not cause the blessing leave you,
With your ungoverned haste. I should be sorry
To see my labours, now even at perfection,
Got by long watching and large patience,
Not prosper where my love and zeal hath placed them.
Which[137] (heaven I call to witness, with your self,
To whom I have poured my thoughts) in all my ends,
Have looked no way, but unto public good,
To pious uses, and dear charity
Now grown a prodigy with men. Wherein
If you, my son, should now prevaricate,
And to your own particular lusts employ
So great and catholic a bliss, be sure
A curse will follow, yea, and overtake
Your subtle and most secret ways.
MAMMON: I know, sir;
You shall not need to fear me; I but come
To have you confute this gentleman.
SURLY: Who is,
Indeed, sir, somewhat costive of belief
Toward your stone; would not be gulled.
SUBTLE: Well, son,
All that I can convince him in, is this,
The WORK IS DONE, bright Sol is in his robe.

[135] fear, suspect [136] come before your appointed time [137] *i.e.*, I, who

We have a medicine of the trible[138] soul,
The glorified spirit. Thanks be to heaven,
And make us worthy of it! — Ulen Spiegel![139]

FACE (*within*): Anon, sir.

SUBTLE: Look well to the register.[140]
And let your heat still lessen by degrees,
To the aludels.[141]

FACE (*within*): Yes, sir.

SUBTLE: Did you look
O' the bolt's head yet?

FACE (*within*): Which? on D, sir?

SUBTLE: Ay;
What's the complexion?

FACE (*within*): Whitish.

SUBTLE: Infuse vinegar,
To draw his volatile substance and his tincture:
And let the water in glass E be filtered,
And put into the gripe's egg. Lute[142] him well;
And leave him closed in balneo.[143]

FACE (*within*): I will, sir.

SURLY: What a brave language here is! next to canting.[144]

SUBTLE: I have another work you never saw, son,
That three days since past the philosopher's wheel,
In the lent[145] heat of Athanor;[146] and's become
Sulphur of Nature.

MAMMON: But 'tis for me?

SUBTLE: What need you?
You have enough in that is perfect.

MAMMON: O, but ——

SUBTLE: Why, this is covetise!

MAMMON: No, I assure you,
I shall employ it all in pious uses,
Founding of colleges and grammar schools,
Marrying young virgins, building hospitals,
And now and then a church.

(*Re-enter* FACE.)

SUBTLE: How now!

FACE: Sir, please you,

[138] triple [139] Till Eulenspiegel ("Owl-mirror"), the knave-hero of a popular German jest book [140] a device regulating the air draught in a furnace [141] alchemical vessels [142] seal with clay [143] in a pan of warm water [144] thieves' slang [145] mild [146] *i.e.*, furnace

Shall I not change the filter?
SUBTLE: Marry, yes;
And bring me the complexion of glass B. (*Exit* FACE.)
MAMMON: Have you another?
SUBTLE: Yes, son; were I assured
Your piety were firm, we would not want
The means to glorify it: but I hope the best.
I mean to tinct C in sand-heat to-morrow,
And give him imbibition.[147]
MAMMON: Of white oil?
SUBTLE: No, sir, of red. F is come over the helm too,
I thank my maker, in S. Mary's bath,
And shows *lac virginis*. Blessed be heaven!
I sent you of his fæces there calcined;
Out of that calx,[148] I have won the salt of mercury.
MAMMON: By pouring on your rectified water?
SUBTLE: Yes, and reverberating in Athanor.

(*Re-enter* FACE.)

How now! what colour says it?
FACE: The ground black, sir.
MAMMON: That's your crow's head.
SURLY: Your cock's-comb's, is it not?
SUBTLE: No, 'tis not perfect. Would it were the crow!
That work wants something.
SURLY: O, I looked for this.
The hay's[149] a pitching. (*Aside.*)
SUBTLE: Are you sure you loosed them
In their own menstrue?
FACE: Yes, sir, and then married them.
And put them in a bolt's-head nipped to digestion,
According as you bade me, when I set
The liquor of Mars[150] to circulation
In the same heat.
SUBTLE: The process then was right.
FACE: Yes, by the token, sir, the retort brake,
And what was saved was put into the pelican,
And signed with Hermes' seal.
SUBTLE: I think 'twas so.
We should have a new amalgama.[151]
SURLY: O, this ferret

[147] steeping in liquid [148] ashy powder of metals and minerals produced by calcination [149] net for catching rabbits [150] molten iron [151] mercury alloy

Is rank as any polecat. (*Aside.*)
SUBTLE: But I care not;
Let him e'en die; we have enough beside,
In embrion. H has his white shirt on?
FACE: Yes, sir,
He's ripe for inceration, he stands warm,
In his ash-fire. I would not you should let
Any die now, if I might counsel, sir,
For luck's sake to the rest: it is not good.
MAMMON: He says right.
SURLY: Ah, are you bolted? [152] (*Aside.*)
FACE: Nay, I know't, sir,
I have seen the ill fortune. What is some three ounces
Of fresh materials?
MAMMON: Is't no more?
FACE: No more, sir,
Of gold, t' amalgame with some six of mercury.
MAMMON: Away, here's money. What will serve?
FACE: Ask him, sir.
MAMMON: How much?
SUBTLE: Give him nine pound; you may give him ten.
SURLY: Yes, twenty, and be cozened, do.
MAMMON: There 'tis. (*Gives* FACE *the money.*)
SUBTLE: This needs not; but that you will have it so.
To see conclusions of all: for two
Of our inferior works are at fixation,
A third is in ascension. Go your ways.
Have you set the oil of luna in kemia?
FACE: Yes, sir.
SUBTLE: And the philosopher's vinegar?
FACE: Ay. (*Exit.*)
SURLY: We shall have a sallad!
MAMMON: When do you make projection?
SUBTLE: Son, be not hasty, I exalt our med'cine,
By hanging him in *balneo vaporoso*.
And giving him solution; then congeal him;
And then dissolve him; then again congeal him;
For look, how oft I iterate the work,
So many times I add unto his virtue.
As if at first one ounce convert a hundred,
After his second loose,[153] he'll turn a thousand;

[152] *i.e.*, moved [153] solution

His third solution, ten; his fourth, a hundred;
After his fifth, a thousand thousand ounces
Of any imperfect metal, into pure
Silver or gold, in all examinations,
As good as any of the natural mine.
Get you your stuff here against afternoon,
Your brass, your pewter, and your andirons.
MAMMON: Not those of iron?
SUBTLE: Yes, you may bring them too;
We'll change all metals.
SURLY: I believe you in that.
MAMMON: Then I may send my spits?
SUBTLE: Yes, and your racks.
SURLY: And dripping-pans, and pot-hangers, and hooks?
Shall he not?
SUBTLE: If he please.
SURLY: — To be an ass.
SUBTLE: How, sir!
MAMMON: This gentleman you must bear withal:
I told you he had no faith.
SURLY: And little hope, sir;
But much less charity, should I gull myself.
SUBTLE: Why, what have you observed, sir, in our art,
Seems so impossible?
SURLY: But your whole work, no more.
That you should hatch gold in a furnace, sir,
As they do eggs in Egypt!
SUBTLE: Sir, do you
Believe that eggs are hatched so?
SURLY: If I should?
SUBTLE: Why, I think that the greater miracle.
No egg but differs from a chicken more
Than metals in themselves.
SURLY: That cannot be.
The egg's ordained by nature to that end,
And is a chicken *in potentia*.[154]
SUBTLE: The same we say of lead and other metals,
Which would be gold if they had time.
MAMMON: And that
Our art doth further.
SUBTLE: Ay, for 'twere absurd

[154] potential

To think that nature in the earth bred gold
Perfect in the instant: something went before.
There must be remote matter.

SURLY: Ay, what is that?

SUBTLE: Marry, we say ——

MAMMON: Ay, now it heats: stand, father,
Pound him to dust.

SUBTLE: It is, of the one part,
A humid exhalation, which we call
Materia liquida, or the unctuous water;
On the one part, a certain crass and viscous
Portion of earth; both which, concorporate,
Do make the elementary matter of gold;
Which is not yet *propria materia*,
But common to all metals and all stones;
For, where it is forsaken of that moisture,
And hath more dryness, it becomes a stone:
Where it retains more of the humid fatness,
It turns to sulphur, or to quicksilver,
Who are the parents of all other metals.
Nor can this remote matter suddenly
Progress so from extreme unto extreme,
As to grow gold, and leap o'er all the means.
Nature doth first beget the imperfect, then
Proceeds she to the perfect. Of that airy
And oily water, mercury is engendered;
Sulphur of the fat and earthy part; the one,
Which is the last, supplying the place of male,
The other, of the female, in all metals.
Some do believe hermaphrodeity,
That both do act and suffer.[155] But these two
Make the rest ductile, malleable, extensive.
And even in gold they are; for we do find
Seeds of them by our fire, and gold in them;
And can produce the species of each metal
More perfect thence, than nature doth in earth.
Beside, who doth not see in daily practice
Art can beget bees, hornets, beetles, wasps,
Out of the carcases and dung of creatures;
Yea, scorpions of an herb, being rightly placed?
And these are living creatures, far more perfect

155 *i.e.*, perform both the male and the female sexual functions

And excellent than metals.
MAMMON: Well said, father!
Nay, if he take you in hand, sir, with an argument,
He'll bray[156] you in a mortar.
SURLY: Pray you, sir, stay.
Rather than I'll be brayed, sir, I'll believe
That Alchemy is a pretty kind of game,
Somewhat like tricks o' the cards, to cheat a man
With charming.
SUBTLE: Sir?
SURLY: What else are all your terms.
Whereon no one of your writers 'grees with other?
Of your elixir, your *lac virginis*,
Your stone, your med'cine, and your chrysosperme,
Your sal, your sulphur, and your mercury,
Your oil of height, your tree of life, your blood,
Your marchesite, your tutie, your magnesia,
Your toad, your crow, your dragon, and your panther;
Your sun, your moon, your firmament, your adrop,
Your lato, azoch, zernich, chibrit, heautarit,
And then your red man, and your white woman,
With all your broths, your menstrues, and materials
Of piss and egg-shells, women's terms, man's blood,
Hair o' the head, burnt clouts, chalk, merds, and clay,
Powder of bones, scalings of iron, glass,
And worlds of other strange ingredients,
Would burst a man to name?
SUBTLE: And all these named,
Intending but one thing; which art our writers
Used to obscure their art.
MAMMON: Sir, so I told him —
Because[157] the simple idiot should not learn it,
And make it vulgar.
SUBTLE: Was not all the knowledge
Of the Ægyptians writ in mystic symbols?
Speak not the scriptures oft in parables?
Are not the choicest fables of the poets,
That were the fountains and first springs of wisdom,
Wrapped in perplexed allegories?
MAMMON: I urged that,
And cleared to him, that Sisyphus was damned

[156] pulverize [157] in order that

To roll the ceaseless stone, only because
He would have made OURS common. (DOL *appears at the door.*) —
Who is this?
SUBTLE: 'Sprecious! — What do you mean? go in, good lady,
Let me entreat you. (DOL *retires.*) — Where's this varlet?

(*Re-enter* FACE.)

FACE: Sir.
SUBTLE: You very knave! do you use me thus?
FACE: Wherein, sir?
SUBTLE: Go in and see, you traitor. Go! (*Exit* FACE.)
MAMMON: Who it is, sir?
SUBTLE: Nothing, sir; nothing.
MAMMON: What's the matter, good sir?
I have not seen you thus distempered: who is't?
SUBTLE: All arts have still had, sir, their adversaries;
But ours the most ignorant. —

(*Re-enter* FACE.)

What now?
FACE: 'Twas not my fault, sir; she would speak with you.
SUBTLE: Would she, sir! Follow me. (*Exit.*)
MAMMON (*stopping him*): Stay, Lungs.
FACE: I dare not, sir.
MAMMON: Stay, man; what is she?
FACE: A lord's sister, sir.
MAMMON: How! pray thee, stay.
FACE: She's mad, sir, and sent hither —
He'll be mad too. —
MAMMON: I warrant[158] thee. —
Why sent hither?
FACE: Sir, to be cured.
SUBTLE (*within*): Why, rascal!
FACE: Lo you — Here, sir! (*Exit.*)
MAMMON: 'Fore God, a Bradamante,[159] a brave piece.
SURLY: Heart, this is a bawdy house! I will be burnt else.
MAMMON: O, by this light, no: do not wrong him. He's
Too scrupulous that way: it is his vice.
No, he's a rare physician, do him right,
An excellent Paracelsian,[160] and has done
Strange cures with mineral physic. He deals all

[158] *i.e.*, protect [159] heroine of Ariosto's *Orlando Furioso* [160] Paracelsus, 1493-1541, Swiss chemist and physician, of legendary fame as alchemist

With spirits, he; he will not hear a word
Of Galen;[161] or his tedious recipes. —

(*Re-enter* FACE.)

How now, Lungs!
FACE: Softly, sir; speak softly. I meant
To have told your worship all. This[162] must not hear.
MAMMON: No, he will not be "gulled"; let him alone.
FACE: You are very right, sir; she is a most rare scholar,
And is gone mad with studying Broughton's[163] works.
If you but name a word touching the Hebrew,
She falls into her fit, and will discourse
So learnedly of genealogies,
As you would run mad too, to hear her, sir.
MAMMON: How might one do t' have conference with her, Lungs?
FACE: O, divers have run mad upon the conference:
I do not know, sir. I am sent in haste
To fetch a vial.
SURLY: Be not gulled, Sir Mammon.
MAMMON: Wherein? pray ye, be patient.
SURLY: Yes, as you are.
And trust confederate knaves and bawds and whores.
MAMMON: You are too foul, believe it. — Come here, Ulen,
One word.
FACE: I dare not, in good faith. (*Going.*)
MAMMON: Stay, knave.
FACE: He is extreme angry that you saw her, sir.
MAMMON: Drink that. (*Gives him money.*) What is she when she's out of her fit?
FACE: O, the most affablest creature, sir! so merry!
So pleasant! she'll mount you up, like quicksilver,
Over the helm; and circulate like oil,
A very vegetal: discourse of state,
Of mathematics, bawdry, anything ——
MAMMON: Is she no way accessible? no means,
No trick to give a man a taste of her —— wit ——
Or so?
SUBTLE (*within*): Ulen!
FACE: I'll come to you again, sir. (*Exit.*)
MAMMON: Surly, I did not think one of your breeding

161 Claudius Galenus, A.D. 130-201, Greek physician 162 *i.e.*, Surly 163 Hugh Broughton, 1549-1612, rabbinical scholar, author of *A Concert of Scripture* (1588), an attempt to establish scriptural chronology

Would traduce personages of worth.
SURLY: Sir Epicure,
Your friend to use; yet still loth to be gulled:
I do not like your philosophical bawds.
Their stone is lechery enough to pay for,
Without this bait.
MAMMON: 'Heart, you abuse yourself.
I know the lady, and her friends, and means,
The original of this disaster. Her brother
Has told me all.
SURLY: And yet you never saw her
Till now!
MAMMON: O yes, but I forgot. I have, believe it,
One of the treacherousest memories, I do think,
Of all mankind.
SURLY: What call you her brother?
MAMMON: My lord ——
He will not have his name known, now I think on't.
SURLY: A very treacherous memory!
MAMMON: On my faith ——
SURLY: Tut, if you have it not about you, pass it,
Till we meet next.
MAMMON: Nay, by this hand, 'tis true.
He's one I honour, and my noble friend;
And I respect his house.
SURLY: Heart! can it be
That a grave sir, a rich, that has no need,
A wise sir, too, at other times, should thus,
With his own oaths, and arguments, make hard means
To gull himself? And this be your elixir,
Your *lapis mineralis*, and your lunary,
Give me your honest trick yet at primero,[164]
Or gleek;[164] and take your *lutum sapientis*,
Your *menstruum simplex!* I'll have gold before you,
And with less danger of the quicksilver,
Or the hot sulphur.

(*Re-enter* FACE.)

FACE: Here's one from Captain Face, sir. (*To* SURLY.)
Desires you meet him in the Temple-church,
Some half-hour hence, and upon earnest business.

[164] card games

Sir (*whispers* MAMMON), if you please to quit us now; and come
Again within two hours, you shall have
My master busy examining o' the works;
And I will steal you in, unto the party,
That you may see her converse. — Sir, shall I say
You'll meet the captain's worship?

SURLY: Sir, I will. — (*Walks aside.*)
But, by attorney, and to a second purpose.
Now, I am sure it is a bawdy-house;
I'll swear it, were the marshal here to thank me:
The naming this commander doth confirm it.
Don Face! why, he's the most authentic dealer
In these commodities, the superintendent
To all the quainter[165] traffickers in town!
He is the visitor, and does appoint
Who lies with whom, and at what hour; what price;
Which gown, and in what smock; what fall;[166] what tire.[167]
Him will I prove, by a third person, to find
The subtleties of this dark labyrinth:
Which if I do discover, dear Sir Mammon,
You'll give your poor friend leave, though no philosopher,
To laugh: for you that are, 'tis thought, shall weep.

FACE: Sir, he does pray you'll not forget.

SURLY: I will not, sir.
Sir Epicure, I shall leave you. (*Exit.*)

MAMMON: I follow you straight.

FACE: But do so, good sir, to avoid suspicion.
This gentleman has a parlous[168] head.

MAMMON: But wilt thou, Ulen,
Be constant to thy promise?

FACE: As my life, sir.

MAMMON: And wilt thou insinuate what I am, and praise me,
And say I am a noble fellow?

FACE: O, what else, sir.
And that you'll make her royal with the stone,
An empress; and yourself King of Bantam.[169]

MAMMON: Wilt thou do this?

FACE: Will I, sir.

MAMMON: Lungs, my Lungs!
I love thee.

FACE: Send your stuff, sir, that my master

[165] craftier [166] collar, ruff [167] attire [168] perilous [169] capital of a rich Javanese kingdom

May busy himself about projection.
MAMMON: Thou hast witched me, rogue: take, go. (*Gives him money.*)
FACE: Your jack, and all, sir.
MAMMON: Thou art a villain — I will send my jack,[170]
And the weights too. Slave, I could bite thine ear,
Away, thou dost not care for me.
FACE: Not I, sir!
MAMMON: Come, I was born to make thee, my good weasel,
Set thee on a bench, and have thee twirl a chain
With the best lord's vermin of 'em all.
FACE: Away, sir.
MAMMON: A count, nay, a count palatine ——
FACE: Good sir, go.
MAMMON: Shall not advance thee better: no, nor faster. (*Exit.*)

(*Re-enter* SUBTLE *and* DOL.)

SUBTLE: Has he bit? has he bit?
FACE: And swallowed, too, my Subtle.
I have given him line, and now he plays, i' faith.
SUBTLE: And shall we twitch him?
FACE: Through both the gills.
A wench is a rare bait, with which a man
No sooner's taken, but he straight firks mad.
SUBTLE: Dol, my Lord What'ts'hum's sister, you must now
Bear yourself *statelich*.[171]
DOL: O, let me alone.
I'll not forget my race, I warrant you.
I'll keep my distance, laugh and talk aloud;
Have all the tricks of a proud scurvy lady,
And be as rude as her woman.
FACE: Well said, sanguine!
SUBTLE: But will he send his andirons?
FACE: His jack too.
And 's iron shoeing-horn; I have spoke to him. Well,
I must not lose my wary gamester yonder.
SUBTLE: O, Monsieur Caution, that *will not be gulled.*
FACE: Ay,
If I can strike a fine hook into him, now! —
The Temple-church, there I have cast mine angle.
Well, pray for me. I'll about it. (*Knocking without.*)
SUBTLE: What, more gudgeons![172]

170 turnspit moved by weights 171 in a stately manner (Ger.) 172 small carps, easily caught

Dol, scout, scout! (DOL *goes to the window.*) Stay, Face, you must go to the door,
'Pray God it be my anabaptist — Who is't, Dol?
DOL: I know him not: he looks like a gold-end-man.[173]
SUBTLE: 'Ods so! 'tis he, he said he would send what call you him?
The sanctified elder, that should deal
For Mammon's jack and andirons. Let him in.
Stay, help me off, first, with my gown. (*Exit* FACE *with the gown.*) Away,
Madam, to your withdrawing chamber. (*Exit* DOL.) Now,
In a new tune, new gesture, but old language. —
This fellow is sent from one negotiates with me
About the stone too; for the holy brethren
Of Amsterdam, the exiled saints; that hope
To raise their discipline[174] by it. I must use him
In some strange fashion now, to make him admire me.

(*Enter* ANANIAS.)

Where is my drudge? (*Aloud.*)

(*Re-enter* FACE.)

FACE: Sir!
SUBTLE: Take away the recipient,
And rectify your menstrue from the phlegma.
Then pour it on the Sol, in the cucurbite,
And let them macerate together.
FACE: Yes, sir.
And save the ground?
SUBTLE: No: *terra damnata*
Must not have entrance in the work. — Who are you?
ANANIAS: A faithful brother,[175] if it please you.
SUBTLE: What's that?
A Lullianist? a Ripley? [176] Filius artis? [177]
Can you sublime and dulcify? calcine?
Know you the sapor pontic? sapor stiptic?
Or what is homogene, or heterogene?
ANANIAS: I understand no heathen language, truly.
SUBTLE: Heathen! you Knipper-doling? [178] is Ars sacra,

[173] one who buys odds and ends of gold [174] *i.e.*, church government [175] *i.e.*, Puritan [176] followers of Raymond Lully (1232-1315) and Sir George Ripley d. 1490), two earlier alchemists [177] a son of the art (*i.e.*, of alchemy) [178] Bernt Knipperdollinck, a leader of the Anabaptist rising in Munster, 1534-1536

Or chrysopœia, or spagyrica,
Or the pamphysic, or panarchic knowledge,
A heathen language?

ANANIAS: Heathen Greek, I take it.

SUBTLE: How! heathen Greek?

ANANIAS: All's heathen but the Hebrew.

SUBTLE: Sirrah my varlet, stand you forth and speak to him,
Like a philosopher: answer, in the language.
Name the vexations, and the martyrizations
Of metals in the work.

FACE: Sir, putrefaction,
Solution, ablution, sublimation,
Cohobation, calcination, ceration, and
Fixation.

SUBTLE: This is heathen Greek, to you, now! —
And when comes vivification?

FACE: After mortification.

SUBTLE: What's cohobation?

FACE: 'Tis the pouring on
Your aqua regis, and then drawing him off,
To the trine circle of the seven spheres.

SUBTLE: What's the proper passion of metals?

FACE: Malleation.

SUBTLE: What's your *ultimum supplicium auri?*

FACE: Antimonium.

SUBTLE: This is heathen Greek to you! — And what's your mercury?

FACE: A very fugitive, he will be gone, sir.

SUBTLE: How know you him?

FACE: By his viscosity,
His oleosity,[179] and his suscitability.[180]

SUBTLE: How do you sublime him?

FACE: With the calce of egg-shells,
White marble, talc.

SUBTLE: Your magisterium now,
What's that?

FACE: Shifting, sir, your elements,
Dry into cold, cold into moist, moist into hot,
Hot into dry.

SUBTLE: This is heathen Greek to you still!
Your *lapis philosophicus?*

FACE: 'Tis a stone,

[179] oiliness [180] excitability

And not a stone; a spirit, a soul, and a body:
Which if you do dissolve, it is dissolved.
If you coagulate, it is coagulated;
If you make it to fly, it flieth.
SUBTLE: Enough. (*Exit* FACE.)
This is heathen Greek to you! What are you, sir?
ANANIAS: Please you, a servant of the exiled brethren,
That deal with widows' and with orphans' goods,
And make a just account unto the saints:
A deacon.
SUBTLE: O, you are sent from Master Wholsome,
Your teacher?
ANANIAS: From Tribulation Wholsome,
Our very zealous pastor.
SUBTLE: Good! I have
Some orphans' goods to come here.
ANANIAS: Of what kind, sir?
SUBTLE: Pewter and brass, andirons and kitchen-ware
Metals, that we must use our medicine on:
Wherein the brethren may have a penny-worth
For ready money.
ANANIAS: Were the orphans' parents
Sincere professors?[181]
SUBTLE: Why do you ask?
ANANIAS: Because
We then are to deal justly, and give, in truth,
Their utmost value.
SUBTLE: 'Slid, you'd cozen else,
And if their parents were not of the faithful! —
I will not trust you, now I think on it,
Till I have talked with your pastor. Have you brought money
To buy more coals?
ANANIAS: No, surely.
SUBTLE: No! how so?
ANANIAS: The brethren bid me say unto you, sir,
Surely, they will not venture any more
Till they may see projection.
SUBTLE: How!
ANANIAS: You have had,
For the instruments, as bricks, and lome, and glasses,
Already thirty pound; and for materials,

[181] believers (*i.e.*, Puritans)

They say, some ninety more: and they have heard since,
That one, at Heidelberg, made it of an egg,
And a small paper of pin-dust.

SUBTLE: What's your name?

ANANIAS: My name is Ananias.

SUBTLE: Out, the varlet
That cozened the apostles! [182] Hence, away!
Flee, mischief! had your holy consistory
No name to send me, of another sound,
Than wicked Ananias? send your elders
Hither, to make atonement for you, quickly,
And give me satisfaction; or out goes
The fire; and down th' alembecs, and the furnace,
Piger Henricus, or what not. Thou wretch!
Both sericon and bufo shall be lost,
Tell them. All hope of rooting out the bishops,
Or the anti-Christian hierarchy shall perish,
If they stay threescore minutes: the aqueity,
Terreity, and sulphureity
Shall run together again, and all be annulled,
Thou wicked Ananias! (*Exit* ANANIAS.) This will fetch 'em,
And make them haste toward their gulling more.
A man must deal like a rough nurse, and fright
Those that are froward, to an appetite.

(*Re-enter* FACE *in his uniform, followed by* DRUGGER.)

FACE: He is busy with his spirits, but we'll upon him.

SUBTLE: How now! what mates,[183] what Baiards[184] have we here?

FACE: I told you he would be furious. — Sir, here's Nab
Has brought you another piece of gold to look on:
— We must appease him. Give it me, — and prays you,
You would devise — what is it, Nab?

DRUGGER: A sign, sir.

FACE: Ay, a good lucky one, a thriving sign, doctor.

SUBTLE: I was devising now.

FACE: 'Slight, do not say so,
He will repent he gave you any more —
What say you to his constellation, doctor,
The Balance?

SUBTLE: No, that way is stale and common.
A townsman born in Taurus, gives the bull,

[182] see *Acts* 5:1-11 [183] *i.e.*, wretches [184] *i.e.*, blind fools (after Baiard, Charlemagne's blind horse)

Or the bull's head: in Aries, the ram,
A poor-device! No, I will have his name
Formed in some mystic character; whose radii,
Striking the senses of the passers-by,
Shall, by a virtual influence, breed affections,
That may result upon the party owns it:
And thus ——

FACE: Nab!

SUBTLE: He shall have *a bel,* that's *Abel;*
And by it standing one whose name is *Dee,*[185]
In a *rug* gown, there's D, and *Rug,*[186] that's *drug:*
And right anenst[187] him a dog snarling *er;*
There's Drugger, Abel Drugger. That's his sign.
And here's now mystery and hieroglyphic!

FACE: Abel, thou art made.

DRUGGER: Sir, I do thank his worship.

FACE: Six o' thy legs[188] more will not do it, Nab.
He has brought you a pipe of tobacco, doctor.

DRUGGER: Yes, sir;
I have another thing I would impart ——

FACE: Out with it, Nab.

DRUGGER: Sir, there is lodged, hard by me,
A rich young widow —

FACE: Good! a bona roba? [189]

DRUGGER: But nineteen at the most.

FACE: Very good, Abel.

DRUGGER: Marry, she's not in the fashion yet; she wears
A hood, but it stands a cop.[190]

FACE: No matter, Abel.

DRUGGER: And I do now and then give her a fucus ——

FACE: What! dost thou deal, Nab?

SUBTLE: I did tell you, captain.

DRUGGER: And physic too, sometime, sir; for which she trusts me
With all her mind. She's come up here of purpose
To learn the fashion.

FACE: Good (his match too!) — On, Nab.

DRUGGER: And she does strangely long to know her fortune.

FACE: 'Ods lid, Nab, sent her to the doctor, hither.

DRUGGER: Yes, I have spoke to her of his worship already;
But she's afraid it will be blown abroad,

[185] John Dee, 1527-1608, mathematician and astrologer, popularly thought to be a magician [186] coarse cloth [187] opposite [188] bows [189] fine wench [190] conically, "on high"

And hurt her marriage.
FACE: Hurt it! 'tis the way
To heal it, if 'twere hurt; to make it more
Followed and sought. Nab, thou shalt tell her this.
She'll be more known, more talked of; and your widows
Are ne'er of any price till they be famous;
Their honour is their multitude of suitors:
Send her, it may be thy good fortune. What!
Thou dost not know?
DRUGGER: No, sir, she'll never marry
Under a knight: her brother has made a vow.
FACE: What! and dost thou despair, my little Nab,
Knowing what the doctor has set down for thee,
And seeing so many of the city dubbed? [191]
One glass o' thy water, with a madam I know,
Will have it done, Nab: what's her brother, a knight?
DRUGGER: No, sir, a gentleman newly warm in his land, sir,
Scarce cold in his one and twenty, that does govern
His sister here; and is a man himself
Of some three thousand a year, and is come up
To learn to quarrel, and to live by his wits,
And will go down again, and die in the country.
FACE: How, to quarrel?
DRUGGER: Yes, sir, to carry quarrels,
As gallants do; to manage them by line.[192]
FACE: 'Slid, Nab, the doctor is the only man
In Christendom for him. He has made a table,
With mathematical demonstrations,
Touching the art of quarrels: he will give him
An instrument to quarrel by. Go, bring them both,
Him and his sister. And, for thee, with her
The doctor happ'ly may persuade. Go to:
'Shalt give his worship a new damask suit
Upon the premises.
SUBTLE: O, good captain!
FACE: He shall;
He is the honestest fellow, doctor. Stay not,
No offers; bring the damask, and the parties.
DRUGGER: I'll try my power, sir.
FACE: And thy will too, Nab.
SUBTLE: 'Tis good tobacco, this! what is't an ounce?

[191] so many citizens knighted [192] by rule, accurately

FACE: He'll send you a pound, doctor.
SUBTLE: O no.
FACE: He will do't.
It is the goodest soul! — Abel, about it.
Thou shalt know more anon. Away, be gone. (*Exit* ABEL.)
A miserable rogue, and lives with cheese,
And has the worms. That was the cause, indeed,
Why he came now: he dealt with me in private,
To get a med'cine for them.
SUBTLE: And shall, sir. This works.
FACE: A wife, a wife for one of us, my dear Subtle!
We'll e'en draw lots, and he that fails, shall have
The more in goods, the other has in tail.
SUBTLE: Rather the less: for she may be so light
She may want grains.[193]
FACE: Ay, or be such a burden,
A man would scarce endure her for the whole.
SUBTLE: Faith, best let's see her first, and then determine.
FACE: Content: but Dol must have no breath on't.
SUBTLE: Mum.
Away you, to your Surly yonder, catch him.
FACE: Pray God I have not staid too long.
SUBTLE: I fear it. (*Exeunt.*)

ACT THE THIRD

Scene I [*The Lane before* LOVEWIT'S *House.*]

(*Enter* TRIBULATION WHOLSOME *and* ANANIAS.)

TRIBULATION: These chastisements are common to the saints,
And such rebukes we of the separation[194]
Must bear with willing shoulders, as the trials
Sent forth to tempt our frailties.
ANANIAS: In pure zeal,
I do not like the man, he is a heathen,
And speaks the language of Canaan, truly.
TRIBULATION: I think him a profane person indeed.
ANANIAS: He bears
The visible mark of the beast[195] in his forehead.
And for his stone, it is a work of darkness,

[193] (1) unit of weight, (2) groins [194] dissent [195] see *Revelation* 16:2, 19:20

And with philosophy blinds the eyes of man.
TRIBULATION: Good brother, we must bend unto all means,
That may give furtherance to the holy cause.
ANANIAS: Which his cannot: the sanctified cause
Should have a sanctified course.
TRIBULATION: Not always necessary:
The children of perdition are ofttimes
Made instruments even of the greatest works:
Beside, we should give[196] somewhat to man's nature,
The place he lives in, still about the fire,
And fume of metals, that intoxicate
The brain of man, and make him prone to passion.
Where have you greater atheists than your cooks?
Or more profane, or choleric, than your glass-men?
More anti-Christian than your bell-founders?
What makes the devil so devilish, I would ask you,
Sathan, our common enemy, but his being
Perpetually about the fire, and boiling
Brimstone and arsenic? We must give, I say,
Unto the motives, and the stirrers up
Of humours in the blood. It may be so,
When as[197] the work is done, the stone is made,
This heat of his may turn into a zeal,
And stand up for the beauteous discipline,
Against the menstruous cloth and rag of Rome.
We must await his calling, and the coming
Of the good spirit. You did fault, t' upbraid him
With the brethren's blessing of Heidelberg, weighing
What need we have to hasten on the work,
For the restoring of the silenced saints,[198]
Which ne'er will be but by the philosopher's stone.
And so a learned elder, one of Scotland,
Assured me; *aurum potabile*[199] being
The only med'cine, for the civil magistrate,
T' incline him to a feeling of the cause;
And must be daily used in the disease.
ANANIAS: I have not edified more, truly, by man;
Not since the beautiful light first shone on me;
And I am sad my zeal hath so offended.
TRIBULATION: Let us call on him then.
ANANIAS: The motion's good,

[196] concede [197] when [198] *i.e.*, Puritan preachers forbidden to preach
[199] literally, "drinkable gold," hence, a bribe

And of the spirit; I will knock first. (*Knocks.*) Peace be within!
(*The door is opened, and they enter.*)

Scene II [*A Room in* LOVEWIT'S *House.*]

(*Enter* SUBTLE, *followed by* TRIBULATION *and* ANANIAS.)

SUBTLE: O, are you come? 'twas time. Your three-score minutes
Were at last thread, you see; and down had gone
Furnus acediæ, turris circulatorius:
Lembec, bolt's-head, retort, and pelican
Had all been cinders. Wicked Ananias!
Art thou returned? nay, then it goes down yet.
TRIBULATION: Sir, be appeased; he is come to humble
Himself in spirit, and to ask your patience,
If too much zeal hath carried him aside
From the due path.
SUBTLE: Why, this doth qualify![200]
TRIBULATION: The brethren had no purpose, verily,
To give you the least grievance: but are ready
To lend their willing hands to any project
The spirit and you direct.
SUBTLE: This qualifies more!
TRIBULATION: And for the orphans' goods, let them be valued.
Or what is needful else to the holy work,
It shall be numbered; here, by me, the saints
Throw down their purse before you.
SUBTLE: This qualifies most!
Why, thus it should be, now you understand.
Have I discoursed so unto you of our stone,
And of the good that it shall bring your cause?
Showed you (beside the main[201] of hiring forces
Abroad, drawing the Hollanders, your friends,
From the Indies, to serve you, with all their fleet)
That even the med'cinal use shall make you a faction,
And party in the realm? As, put the case,
That some great man in state, he have the gout,
Why, you but send three drops of your elixir,
You help him straight: there you have made a friend.
Another has the palsy or the dropsy,
He takes of your incombustible stuff,

200 modify (*i.e.*, my anger) 201 important matter

He's young again: there you have made a friend.
A lady that is past the feat of body,
Though not of mind, and hath her face decayed
Beyond all cure of paintings, you restore,
With the oil of talc: there you have made a friend
And all her friends. A lord that is a leper,
A knight that has the bone-ache, or a squire
That hath both these, you make them smooth and sound,
With a bare fricace[202] of your med'cine: still
You increase your friends.

TRIBULATION: Ay, it is very pregnant.

SUBTLE: And then the turning of this lawyer's pewter
To plate at Christmas ——

ANANIAS: Christ-tide, I pray you.

SUBTLE: Yet,[203] Ananias!

ANANIAS: I have done.

SUBTLE: Or changing
His parcel [204] gilt to massy gold. You cannot
But raise your friends. Withal, to be of power
To pay an army in the field, to buy
The King of France out of his realms, or Spain
Out of his Indies. What can you not do
Against lords spiritual or temporal,
That shall oppone[205] you?

TRIBULATION: Verily, 'tis true.
We may be temporal lords ourselves, I take it.

SUBTLE: You may be anything, and leave off to make
Long-winded exercises; or suck up
Your *ha!* and *hum!* in a tune. I not deny,
But such as are not graced in a state,
May, for their ends, be adverse in religion,
And get a tune to call the flock together:
For, to say sooth, a tune does much with women
And other phlegmatic people; it is your bell.

ANANIAS: Bells are profane; a tune may be religious.

SUBTLE: No warning with you! then farewell my patience.
'Slight, it shall down; I will not be thus tortured.

TRIBULATION: I pray you, sir.

SUBTLE: All shall perish. I have spoke it.

TRIBULATION: Let me find grace, sir, in your eyes; the man
He stands corrected: neither did his zeal,

202 rubbing 203 an exclamation of impatience: "still at it?" 204 part (adj.)
205 oppose

But as your self, allow a tune somewhere.
Which now, being tow'rd [206] the stone, we shall not need.

SUBTLE: No, nor your holy vizard,[207] to win widows
To give you legacies; or make zealous wives
To rob their husbands for the common cause:
Nor take the start of bonds broke but one day,[208]
And say they were forfeited by providence.
Nor shall you need o'er night to eat huge meals,
To celebrate your next day's fast the better;
The whilst the brethren and the sisters humbled,
Abate the stiffness of the flesh. Nor cast
Before your hungry hearers scrupulous bones;
As whether a Christian may hawk or hunt,
Or whether matrons of the holy assembly
May lay their hair out, or wear doublets,
Or have that idol starch about their linen.

ANANIAS: It is indeed an idol.

TRIBULATION: Mind him not, sir.
I do command thee, spirit of zeal, but trouble,
To peace within him! Pray you, sir, go on.

SUBTLE: Nor shall you need to libel 'gainst the prelates,
And shorten so your ears[209] against the hearing
Of the next wire-drawn grace. Nor of necessity
Rail against plays, to please the alderman
Whose daily custard you devour: nor lie
With zealous rage till you are hoarse. Not one
Of these so singular arts. Nor call yourselves
By names of Tribulation, Persecution,
Restraint, Long-patience, and such like, affected
By the whole family or wood [210] of you,
Only for glory, and to catch the ear
Of the disciple.

TRIBULATION: Truly, sir, they are
Ways that the godly brethren have invented,
For propagation of the glorious cause,
As very notable means, and whereby also
Themselves grow soon, and profitably famous.

SUBTLE: O, but the stone, all's idle to it! nothing!
The art of angels, nature's miracle,
The divine secret that doth fly in clouds
From east to west: and whose tradition

[206] *i.e.*, nearly in possession of [207] mask [208] foreclose obligations no more than one day overdue [209] thus cause your ears to be cropped [210] crowd

Is not from men, but spirits.
ANANIAS: I hate traditions;
I do not trust them ——
TRIBULATION: Peace!
ANANIAS: They are popish all.
I will not peace: I will not ——
TRIBULATION: Ananias!
ANANIAS: Please the profane, to grieve the godly; I may not.
SUBTLE: Well, Ananias, thou shalt overcome.
TRIBULATION: It is an ignorant zeal that haunts him, sir:
But truly else a very faithful brother,
A botcher,[211] and a man by revelation,
That hath a competent knowledge of the truth.
SUBTLE: Has he a competent sum there in the bag
To buy the goods within? I am made guardian,
And must, for charity and conscience' sake,
Now see the most be made for my poor orphan;
Though I desire the brethren too good gainers:
There they are within. When you have viewed and bought 'em,
And ta'en the inventory of what they are,
They are ready for projection; there's no more
To do: cast on the med'cine, so much silver
As there is tin there, so much gold as brass,
I'll give't you in by weight.
TRIBULATION: But how long time,
Sir, must the saints expect yet?
SUBTLE: Let me see,
How's the moon now? Eight, nine, ten days hence,
He will be silver potate; then three days
Before he citronise. Some fifteen days,
The magisterium will be perfected.
ANANIAS: About the second day of the third week,
In the ninth month?
SUBTLE: Yes, my good Ananias.
TRIBULATION: What will the orphans' goods arise to, think you?
SUBTLE: Some hundred marks, as much as filled three cars,[212]
Unladed now: you'll make six millions of them ——
But I must have more coals laid in.
TRIBULATION: How?
SUBTLE: Another load,
And then we have finished. We must now increase

[211] tailor (slang term for a Puritan) [212] carts

Our fire to *ignis ardens*, we are past
Fimus equinus, balnei, cineris,
And all those lenter heats. If the holy purse
Should with this draught fall low, and that the saints
Do need a present sum, I have a trick
To melt the pewter, you shall buy now instantly,
And with a tincture make you as good Dutch dollars
As any are in Holland.

TRIBULATION: Can you so?

SUBTLE: Ay, and shall bide the third examination.

ANANIAS: It will be joyful tidings to the brethren.

SUBTLE: But you must carry it secret.

TRIBULATION: Ay; but stay,
This act of coining, is it lawful?

ANANIAS: Lawful!
We know[213] no magistrate: or, if we did,
This is foreign coin.

SUBTLE: It is no coining, sir.
It is but casting.

TRIBULATION: Ha! you distinguish well:
Casting of money may be lawful.

ANANIAS: 'Tis, sir.

TRIBULATION: Truly, I take it so.

SUBTLE: There is no scruple,
Sir, to be made of it; believe Ananias:
This case of conscience he is studied in.

TRIBULATION: I'll make a question of it to the brethren.

ANANIAS: The brethren shall approve it lawful, doubt not.
Where shall it be done? (*Knocking without.*)

SUBTLE: For that we'll talk anon.
There's some to speak with me. Go in, I pray you,
And view the parcels. That's the inventory.
I'll come to you straight. (*Exeunt* TRIBULATION *and* ANANIAS.) Who is it? — Face! appear.

(*Enter* FACE *in his uniform.*)

How now! good prize?

FACE: Good pox![214] yond' costive cheater
Never came on.

SUBTLE: How then?

FACE: I have walked the round

[213] acknowledge [214] syphilis

Till now, and no such thing.
SUBTLE: And have you quit him?
FACE: Quit him! an hell would quit him too, he were happy.
'Slight! would you have me stalk like a mill-jade,
All day, for one that will not yield us grains?
I know him of old.
SUBTLE: O, but to have gulled him,
Had been a mastery.
FACE: Let him go, black boy!
And turn thee, that some fresh news may possess thee.
A noble count, a don of Spain, my dear
Delicious compeer, and my party-bawd,[215]
Who is come hither private for his conscience,
And brought munition with him, six great slops,[216]
Bigger than three Dutch hoys,[217] beside round trunks,[218]
Furnished with pistolets,[219] and pieces of eight,
Will straight be here, my rogue, to have thy bath,
(That is the colour,[220]) and to make his battery
Upon our Dol, our castle, our cinqueport,[221]
Our Dover pier, our what thou wilt. Where is she?
She must prepare perfumes, delicate linen,
The bath in chief, a banquet, and her wit,
For she must milk his epididymis.[222]
Where is the doxy?
SUBTLE: I'll send her to thee:
And but despatch my brace of little John Leydens,[223]
And come again myself.
FACE: Are they within then?
SUBTLE: Numbering the sum.
FACE: How much?
SUBTLE: A hundred marks, boy. (*Exit.*)
FACE: Why, this is a lucky day. Ten pounds of Mammon!
Three of my clerk! a portague of my grocer!
This of the brethren! beside reversions,
And states to come in the window, and my count!
My share to-day will not be bought for forty ——

(*Enter* DOL.)

[215] partner in bawdy [216] loose breeches [217] ships [218] trunk hose [219] gold coins [220] pretext [221] one of the five strategic channel ports [222] bring him to sexual climax [223] Jan Bockelson of Leyden was the leader of the "kingdom of the saints" in Munster, 1534-1536. Their rule was marked by despotism and debauchery. (See note 178 above.)

DOL: What?
FACE: Pounds, dainty Dorothy! art thou so near?
DOL: Yes; say, lord general, how fares our camp?
FACE: As with the few that had entrenched themselves
Safe, by their discipline, against a world, Dol,
And laughed within those trenches, and grew fat
With thinking on the booties, Dol, brought in
Daily by their small parties. This dear hour,
A doughty don is taken with my Dol;
And thou mayst make his ransom what thou wilt
My Dousabel;[224] he shall be brought here fettered
With thy fair looks, before he sees thee; and thrown
In a down-bed, as dark as any dungeon;
Where thou shalt keep him waking with thy drum;
Thy drum, my Dol, thy drum; till he be tame
As the poor blackbirds were in the great frost,[225]
Or bees are with a bason;[226] and so hive him
In the swan-skin coverlid and cambric sheets,
Till he work honey and wax, my little God's-gift.[227]
DOL: What is he, general?
FACE: An adalantado,[228]
A grandee, girl. Was not my Dapper here yet?
DOL: No.
FACE: Nor my Drugger?
DOL: Neither.
FACE: A pox on 'em,
They are so long a furnishing! such stinkards
Would [229] not be seen upon these festive days.—

(*Re-enter* SUBTLE.)

How now! have you done?
SUBTLE: Done. They are gone: the sum
Is here in bank, my Face. I would we knew
Another chapman[230] who would buy 'em outright.
FACE: 'Slid, Nab shall do't against he have[231] the widow,
To furnish household.
SUBTLE: Excellent, well thought on:
Pray God he come.
FACE: I pray he keep away
Till our new business be o'erpast.

[224] *i.e.*, sweet-and-pretty (*douce et belle*) [225] from Dec. 1607 till Feb. 1608 [226] basin [227] "Dorothea" means "God's gift" [228] Adelantado, a Spanish governor [229] *i.e.*, should [230] dealer [231] for having

SUBTLE: But, Face,
  How camst thou by this secret don?
FACE: A spirit
  Brought me th' intelligence in a paper here,
  As I was conjuring yonder in my circle
  For Surly; I have my flies abroad. Your bath
  Is famous, Subtle, by my means. Sweet Dol,
  You must go tune your virginal, no losing
  O' the least time: and, do you hear? good action.
  Firk, like a flounder; kiss, like a scallop, close;
  And tickle him with thy mother tongue. His great
  Verdugoship[232] has not a jot of language;[233]
  So much the easier to be cozened, my Dolly.
  He will come here in a hired coach, obscure,
  And our own coachman, whom I have sent as guide,
  No creature else. (*Knocking without.*) Who's that?
SUBTLE: It is not he? (*Exit* DOL.)
FACE: O no, not yet this hour.

(*Re-enter* DOL.)

SUBTLE: Who is't?
DOL: Dapper,
  Your clerk.
FACE: God's will then, Queen of Fairy,
  On with your tire; (*Exit* DOL.) and, doctor, with your robes.
  Let's despatch him for God's sake.
SUBTLE: 'Twill be long.
FACE: I warrant you, take but the cues I give you,
  It shall be brief enough. (*Goes to the window.*) 'Slight, here are more!
  Abel, and I think the angry boy,[234] the heir,
  That fain would quarrel.
SUBTLE: And the widow?
FACE: No,
  Not that I see. Away! (*Exit* SUBTLE.)

(*Enter* DAPPER.)

O, sir, you are welcome.
  The doctor is within a moving for you;
  I have had the most ado to win him to it! —
  He swears you'll be the darling of the dice:

232 lit., "hangmanship," but the meaning here is obscure
233 *i.e.*, English
234 roisterer, bully

He never heard her highness dote till now.
Your aunt has given you the most gracious words
That can be thought on.

DAPPER: Shall I see her grace?

FACE: See her, and kiss her too.—

(*Enter* ABEL, *followed by* KASTRIL.)

What, honest Nab!
Hast brought the damask?

NAB: No, sir; here's tobacco.

FACE: 'Tis well done, Nab: thou'lt bring the damask too?

DRUGGER: Yes: here's the gentleman, captain, Master Kastril,
I have brought to see the doctor.

FACE: Where's the widow?

DRUGGER: Sir, as he likes, his sister, he says, shall come.

FACE: O, is it so? good time. Is your name Kastril, sir?

KASTRIL: Ay, and the best of the Kastrils, I'd be sorry else,
By fifteen hundred a year. Where is the doctor?
My mad tobacco-boy here tells me of one
That can do things: has he any skill?

FACE: Wherein, sir?

KASTRIL: To carry a business, manage a quarrel fairly,
Upon fit terms.

FACE: It seems, sir, you are but young
About the town, that can make that question.

KASTRIL: Sir, not so young but I have heard some speech
Of the angry boys, and seen them take tobacco;
And in his shop; and I can take it too.
And I would fain be one of 'em, and go down
And practise in the country.

FACE: Sir, for the duello,
The doctor, I assure you, shall inform you,
To the least shadow of a hair; and show you
An instrument he has of his own making,
Wherewith no sooner shall you make report
Of any quarrel, but he will take the height on't
Most instantly, and tell in what degree
Of safety it lies in, or mortality.[235]
And how it may be borne, whether in a right line,
Or a half circle; or may else be cast
Into an angle blunt, if not acute:

235 deadliness

And this he will demonstrate. And then, rules
To give and take the lie by.

KASTRIL: How! to take it?

FACE: Yes, in oblique[236] he'll show you, or in circle;
But never in diameter.[237] The whole town
Study his theorems, and dispute them ordinarily[238]
At the eating academies.

KASTRIL: But does he teach
Living by the wits too?

FACE: Anything whatever.
You cannot think that subtlety but he reads it.[239]
He made me a captain. I was a stark pimp,
Just of your standing, 'fore I met with him;
It is not two months since. I'll tell you his method:
First, he will enter you at some ordinary.

KASTRIL: No, I'll not come there: you shall pardon me.

FACE: For why, sir?

KASTRIL: There's gaming there, and tricks.

FACE: Why, would you be
A gallant, and not game?

KASTRIL: Ay, 'twill spend a man.

FACE: Spend you! it will repair you when you are spent,
How do they live by their wits there, that have vented [240]
Six times your fortunes?

KASTRIL: What, three thousand a year!

FACE: Ay, forty thousand.

KASTRIL: Are there such?

FACE: Ay, sir,
And gallants yet. Here's a gentleman
Is born to nothing — (*Points to* DAPPER.) forty marks a year
Which I count nothing: — he is to be initiated,
And have a fly of the doctor. He will win you
By unresistible luck, within this fortnight,
Enough to buy a barony. They will set him
Upmost, at the groom porters,[241] all the Christmas:
And for the whole year through at every place
Where there is play, present him with the chair;
The best attendance, the best drink, sometimes
Two glasses of Canary, and pay nothing;
The purest linen and the sharpest knife,

236 *i.e.*, the circumstantial or indirect lie 237 *i.e.*, the direct lie 238 with a pun on "ordinary": tavern, "eating academy" 239 which he does not grasp 240 spent 241 officers of the court superintending gambling

The partridge next his trencher: and somewhere
The dainty bed, in private, with the dainty.
You shall have your ordinaries bid for him,
As playhouses for a poet; and the master
Pray him aloud to name what dish he affects,
Which must be buttered shrimps: and those that drink
To no mouth else, will drink to his, as being
The goodly president mouth of all the board.

KASTRIL: Do you not gull one?

FACE: 'Ods my life! do you think it?
You shall have a cast[242] commander, (can[243] but get
In credit with a glover, or a spurrier,[244]
For some two pair of either's ware aforehand,)
Will, by most swift posts,[245] dealing [but] with him,
Arrive at competent means to keep himself,
His punk, and naked boy, in excellent fashion,
And be admired for't.

KASTRIL: Will the doctor teach this?

FACE: He will do more, sir: when your land is gone,
As men of spirit hate to keep earth long
In a vacation, when small money is stirring,
And ordinaries suspended till the term,
He'll show a perspective,[246] where on one side
You shall behold the faces and the persons
Of all sufficient young heirs in town,
Whose bonds are current for commodity;[247]
On th' other side, the merchants' forms,[248] and others,
That without help of any second broker,
Who would expect a share, will trust[249] such parcels:
In the third square, the very street and sign
Where the commodity dwells, and does but wait
To be delivered, be it pepper, soap,
Hops, or tobacco, oatmeal, wood, or cheeses.
All which you may so handle, to enjoy
To your own use, and never stand obliged.

KASTRIL: I' faith! is he such a fellow?

FACE: Why, Nab here knows him.
And then for making matches for rich widows,
Young gentlewomen, heirs, the fortunat'st man!

242 cashiered, fired 243 *i.e.*, who can 244 maker of spurs 245 post horses
246 picture the appearance of which changes with the angle of vision 247 *i.e.*, who are willing to sign over interests for worthless goods, gulls 248 appearance
249 take on trust

He's sent to, far and near, all over England,
To have his counsel, and to know their fortunes.
KASTRIL: God's will, my suster[250] shall see him.
FACE: I'll tell you, sir,
What he did tell me of Nab. It's a strange thing
By the way, you must eat no cheese, Nab, it breeds melancholy,
And that same melancholy breeds worms; but pass it:[251] —
He told me, honest Nab here was ne'er at tavern
But once in's life.
DRUGGER: Truth, and no more I was not.
FACE: And then he was so sick ——
DRUGGER: Could he tell you that too?
FACE: How should I know it?
DRUGGER: In troth, we had been a shooting,
And had a piece of fat ram-mutton to supper,
That lay so heavy o' my stomach ——
FACE: And he has no head
To bear any wine; for what with the noise of the fiddlers,
And care of his shop, for he dares keep no servants ——
DRUGGER: My head did so ache ——
FACE: And he was fain to be brought home,
The doctor told me: and then a good old woman ——
DRUGGER: Yes, faith, she dwells in Seacoal-lane, — did cure me,
With sodden[252] ale, and pellitory[253] of the wall
Cost me but twopence. I had another sickness
Was worse than that.
FACE: Ay, that was with the grief
Thou took'st for being cessed at[254] eighteenpence,
For the waterwork.
DRUGGER: In truth, and it was like
T' have cost me almost my life.
FACE: Thy hair went off?
DRUGGER: Yes, sir; 'twas done for spite.
FACE: Nay, so says the doctor.
KASTRIL: Pray thee, tobacco-boy, go fetch my suster;
I'll see this learned boy before I go;
And so shall she.
FACE: Sir, he is busy now
But if you have a sister to fetch hither,
Perhaps your own pains may command her sooner:
And he by that time will be free.

[250] sister [251] *i.e.*, never mind that now (a colloquialism by which the speaker dismisses his own digression) [252] heated [253] an herb [254] assessed

KASTRIL: I go. *(Exit.)*

FACE: Drugger, she's thine: the damask! — *(Exit* ABEL.*)* Subtle and I
Must wrestle for her. *(Aside.)* Come on, Master Dapper,
You see how I turn clients here away,
To give your cause dispatch; have you performed
The ceremonies were enjoined you?

DAPPER: Yes, of the vinegar,
And the clean shirt.

FACE: 'Tis well: that shirt may do you
More worship than you think. Your aunt's a-fire,
But that she will not show it, t' have a sight of you.
Have you provided for her grace's servants?

DAPPER: Yes, here are six score Edward shillings.

FACE: Good!

DAPPER: And an old Harry's sovereign.

FACE: Very good!

DAPPER: And three James shillings, and an Elizabeth groat,[255]
Just twenty nobles.[256]

FACE: O, you are too just.
I would you had had the other noble in Maries.

DAPPER: I have some Philip and Maries.

FACE: Ay, those same
Are best of all: where are they? Hark, the doctor.

(Enter SUBTLE, *disguised like a priest of Fairy, with a stripe of cloth.)*

SUBTLE *(in a feigned voice)*: Is yet her grace's cousin come?

FACE: He is come.

SUBTLE: And is he fasting?

FACE: Yes.

SUBTLE: And hath cried hum?

FACE: Thrice you must answer.

DAPPER: Thrice.

SUBTLE: And as oft buz?

FACE: If you have, say.

DAPPER: I have.

SUBTLE: Then, to her cuz,
Hoping that he hath vinegared his senses,
As he was bid, the Fairy queen dispenses,
By me, this robe, the petticoat of fortune;
Which that he straight put on, she doth importune.

[255] a small coin, worth c. 4 pence [256] gold coins, each worth c. 7 shillings

And though to fortune near be her petticoat,
Yet nearer is her smock, the queen doth note:
And therefore, even of that a piece she has sent,
Which, being a child, to wrap him in was rent;
And prays him for a scarf he now will wear it,
With as much love as then her grace did tear it,
About his eye, (*They blind him with the rag.*) to show he is fortunate.
And, trusting unto her to make his state,[257]
He'll throw away all wordly pelf [258] about him;
Which that he will perform, she doth not doubt him.

FACE: She need not doubt him, sir. Alas, he has nothing
But what he will part withal as willingly,
Upon her grace's word — throw away your purse —
As she would ask it: — handkerchiefs and all —
(*He throws away, as they bid him.*)
She cannot bid that thing but he'll obey. —
If you have a ring about you, cast it off,
Or a silver seal at your wrist; her grace will send
Her fairies here to search you, therefore deal
Directly[259] with her highness: if they find
That you conceal a mite, you are undone.

DAPPER: Truly, there's all.

FACE: All what?

DAPPER: My money; truly.

FACE: Keep nothing that is transitory about you.
Bid Dol play music. (*Aside to* SUBTLE.) — Look, the elves are come
(DOL *plays on the cittern within.*)
To pinch you, if you tell not truth. Advise you. (*They pinch him.*)

DAPPER: O! I have a paper with a spur-ryal [260] in't.

FACE: *Ti, ti.*
They knew't, they say.

SUBTLE: *Ti, ti, ti, ti.* He has more yet.

FACE: *Ti, ti-ti-ti.* In the other pocket? (*Aside to* SUBTLE.)

SUBTLE: *Titi, titi, titi, titi, titi.*
They must pinch him or he will never confess, they say.
(*They pinch him again.*)

DAPPER: O, O!

FACE: Nay, pray you hold: he is her grace's nephew,
Ti, ti, ti? What care you? good faith, you shall care. —
Deal plainly, sir, and shame the fairies. Show

[257] estate [258] property (derogatory) [259] *i.e.*, honestly, in a straightforward manner [260] spur-royal, gold coin, worth c. 15 shillings

You are innocent.
DAPPER: By this good light, I have nothing.
SUBTLE: *Ti, ti, ti, ti, to, ta.* He does equivocate she says:
Ti, ti, do ti, ti ti do, ti da; and swears by the *light* when he is blinded.
DAPPER: By this good *dark,*[261] I have nothing but a half-crown
Of gold about my wrist, that my love gave me;
And a leaden heart I wore since she forsook me.
FACE: I thought 'twas something. And would you incur
Your aunt's displeasure for these trifles? Come,
I had rather you had thrown away twenty half-crowns. (*Takes it off.*)
You may wear your leaden heart still. —

(*Enter* DOL, *hastily.*)

How now!
SUBTLE: What news, Dol?
DOL: Yonder's your knight, Sir Mammon.
FACE: 'Ods lid, we never thought of him till now!
Where is he?
DOL: Here hard by: he is at the door.
SUBTLE: And you are not ready now! Dol, get his suit.[262] (*Exit* DOL.)
He must not be sent back.
FACE: O, by no means.
What shall we do with this same puffin[263] here,
Now he's on the spit?
SUBTLE: Why, lay him back awhile,
With some device.

(*Re-enter* DOL COMMON *with* FACE'S *clothes.*)

— *Ti, ti, ti, ti, ti, ti,* Would her grace speak with me?
I come. — Help, Dol! (*Knocking without.*)
FACE (*speaks through the keyhole*): — Who's there? Sir Epicure,
My master's in the way. Please you to walk
Three or four turns, but till his back be turned,
And I am for you. — Quickly, Dol!
SUBTLE: Her grace
Commends her kindly to you, Master Dapper.
DAPPER: I long to see her grace.
SUBTLE: She now is set
At dinner in her bed, and she has sent you
From her own private trencher, a dead mouse,
And a piece of gingerbread, to be merry withal,

261 *i.e.,* because he is blindfolded 262 *i.e.,* Face's servant suit 263 here: a puffed-up person

And stay your stomach, lest you faint with fasting:
Yet if you could hold out till she saw you, she says,
It would be better for you.

FACE: Sir, he shall
Hold out, an 'twere this two hours, for her highness;
I can assure you that. We will not lose
All we have done. ——

SUBTLE: He must not see, nor speak
To anybody, till then.

FACE: For that we'll put, sir,
A stay in's mouth.

SUBTLE: Of what?

FACE: Of gingerbread.
Make you it fit. He that hath pleased her grace
Thus far, shall not now crincle[264] for a little. ——
Gape, sir, and let him fit you.

(*They thrust a gag of gingerbread in his mouth.*)

SUBTLE: Where shall we now bestow him?

DOL: In the privy.

SUBTLE: Come along, sir,
I must now show you Fortune's privy lodgings.

FACE: Are they perfumed, and his bath ready?

SUBTLE: All:
Only the fumigation's somewhat strong.

FACE (*speaking through the keyhole*): Sir Epicure, I am yours, sir, by and by.[265] (*Exeunt with* DAPPER.)

ACT THE FOURTH

Scene I [*A Room in* LOVEWIT'S *House.*]

(*Enter* FACE *and* MAMMON.)

FACE: O, sir, you are come in the only finest time. ——

MAMMON: Where's master?

FACE: Now preparing for projection, sir.
Your stuff will be all changed shortly.

MAMMON: Into gold?

FACE: To gold and silver, sir.

MAMMON: Silver I care not for.

264 shrink, recoil 265 in a moment

FACE: Yes, sir, a little to give beggars.
MAMMON: Where's the lady?
FACE: At hand here. I have told her such brave things of you,
Touching your bounty and your noble spirit ——
MAMMON: Hast thou?
FACE: As she is almost in her fit to see you.
But, good sir, no divinity in your conference,
For fear of putting her in a rage. ——
MAMMON: I warrant thee.
FACE: Six men [sir] will not hold her down: and then,
If the old man should hear or see you ——
MAMMON: Fear not.
FACE: The very house, sir, would run mad. You know it,
How scrupulous he is, and violent,
'Gainst the least act of sin. Physic or mathematics,
Poetry, state, or bawdry, as I told you,
She will endure, and never startle; but
No word of controversy.
MAMMON: I am schooled, good Ulen.
FACE: And you must praise her house, remember that,
And her nobility.
MAMMON: Let me alone:
No herald, no, nor antiquary, Lungs,
Shall do it better. Go.
FACE: Why, this is yet
A kind of modern[266] happiness,[267] to have
Dol Common for a great lady. (*Aside, and exit.*)
MAMMON: Now, Epicure,
Heighten thyself, talk to her all in gold;
Rain her as many showers as Jove did drops
Unto his Danäe; show the god a miser,
Compared with Mammon. What! the stone will do't.
She shall feel gold, taste gold, hear gold, sleep gold;
Nay, we will *concumbere*[268] gold: I will be puissant,
And mighty in my talk to her. —

(*Re-enter* FACE *with* DOL *richly dressed.*)

Here she comes.
FACE: To him, Dol, suckle him. This is the noble knight I told your ladyship ——
MAMMON: Madam, with your pardon,

[266] commonplace [267] fitness [268] lie with

I kiss your vesture.
DOL: Sir, I were uncivil
If I would suffer that: my lip to you, sir.
MAMMON: I hope my lord your brother be in health, lady.
DOL: My lord my brother is, though I no lady, sir.
FACE: Well said, my Guinea bird.[269] (*Aside.*)
MAMMON: Right noble madam ——
FACE: O, we shall have most fierce idolatry. (*Aside.*)
MAMMON: 'Tis your prerogative.
DOL: Rather your courtesy.
MAMMON: Were there nought else t'enlarge your virtues to me,
These answers speak your breeding and your blood.
DOL: Blood we boast none, sir, a poor baron's daughter.
MAMMON: Poor! and gat you? profane not. Had your father
Slept all the happy remnant of his life
After that act, lien[270] but there still, and panted,
He had done enough to make himself, his issue,
And his posterity noble.
DOL: Sir, although
We may be said to want the gilt and trappings,
The dress of honour, yet we strive to keep
The seeds and the materials.
MAMMON: I do see
The old ingredient, virtue, was not lost,
Nor the drug money used to make your compound.
There is a strange nobility in your eye,
This lip, that chin! methinks you do resemble
One of the Austriac[271] princes.
FACE: Very like!
Her father was an Irish costarmonger.[272] (*Aside.*)
MAMMON: The house of Valois just had such a nose,
And such a forehead yet the Medici
Of Florence boast.
DOL: Troth, and I have been likened
To all these princes.
FACE: I'll be sworn, I heard it.
MAMMON: I know not how! it is not any one,
But e'en the very choice of all their features.
FACE: I'll in, and laugh. (*Aside, and exit.*)
MAMMON: A certain touch, or air,
That sparkles a divinity beyond

269 *i.e.*, prostitute 270 lain 271 Austrian 272 apple-seller

An earthly beauty!
DOL: O, you play the courtier.
MAMMON: Good lady, give me leave ——
DOL: In faith, I may not,
To mock me, sir.
MAMMON: To burn in this sweet flame;
The phœnix never knew a nobler death.
DOL: Nay, now you court the courtier, and destroy
What you would build: this art, sir, in your words,
Calls your whole faith in question.
MAMMON: By my soul ——
DOL: Nay, oaths are made of the same air, sir.
MAMMON: Nature
Never bestowed upon mortality
A more unblamed,[273] a more harmonious feature;
She played the step-dame in all faces else:
Sweet madam, let me be particular[274] ——
DOL: Particular, sir! I pray you know your distance.
MAMMON: In no ill sense, sweet lady; but to ask
How your fair graces pass the hours? I see
You are lodged here, in the house of a rare man,
An excellent artist; but what's that to you?
DOL: Yes, sir; I study here the mathematics,
And distillation.
MAMMON: O, I cry your pardon.
He's a divine instructor! can extract
The souls of all things by his art; call all
The virtues, and the miracles of the sun,
Into a temperate furnace; teach dull nature
What her own forces are. A man, the emperor
Has courted above Kelly;[275] sent his medals
And chains, to invite him.
DOL: Ay, and for his physic, sir —
MAMMON: Above the art of Æsculapius,
That drew the envy of the thunderer![276]
I know all this, and more.
DOL: Troth, I am taken, sir,
Whole with these studies, that contemplate nature.
MAMMON: It is a noble humour; but this form
Was not intended to so dark a use.
Had you been crooked, foul, of some course[277] mould,

[273] unblemished [274] personal [275] Edward Kelly, 1555-1595, Dee's partner, employed by Emperor Rudolph II [276] Zeus [277] coarse

A cloister had done well; but such a feature
That might stand up the glory of a kingdom,
To live recluse! is a mere solœcism,
Though in a nunnery. It must not be.
I muse,[278] my lord your brother will permit it:
You should spend half my land first, were I he.
Does not this diamond better on my finger
Than in the quarry?

DOL: Yes.

MAMMON: Why, you are like it.
You were created, lady, for the light.
Here, you shall wear it; take it, the first pledge
Of what I speak, to bind you to believe me.

DOL: In chains of adamant?

MAMMON: Yes, the strongest bands.
And take a secret too — here, by your side,
Doth stand this hour the happiest man in Europe.

DOL: You are contented, sir?

MAMMON: Nay, in true being,
The envy of princes and the fear of states.

DOL: Say you so, Sir Epicure?

MAMMON: Yes, and thou shalt prove it,
Daughter of honour. I have cast mine eye
Upon thy form, and I will rear this beauty
Above all styles.

DOL: You mean no treason, sir?

MAMMON: No, I will take away that jealousy.[279]
I am the lord of the philosopher's stone,
And thou the lady.

DOL: How, sir! have you that?

MAMMON: I am the master of the mastery.
This day the good old wretch here o' the house
Has made it for us: now he's at projection.
Think therefore thy first wish now, let me hear it;
And it shall rain into thy lap, no shower,
But floods of gold, whole cataracts, a deluge,
To get a nation on thee.

DOL: You are pleased, sir,
To work on the ambition of our sex.

MAMMON: I am pleased the glory of her sex should know,
This nook here of the Friers[280] is no climate

[278] am amazed [279] suspicion [280] friars

For her to live obscurely in, to learn
Physic and surgery, for the constable's wife
Of some odd hundred [281] in Essex; but come forth,
And taste the air of palaces; eat, drink
The toils of empirics,[282] and their boasted practice;
Tincture of pearl, and coral, gold, and amber;
Be seen at feasts and triumphs; have it asked
What miracle she is? set all the eyes
Of court a-fire, like a burning glass,
And work them into cinders, when the jewels
Of twenty states adorn thee, and the light
Strikes out the stars! that, when thy name is mentioned,
Queens may look pale; and we but showing our love,
Nero's Poppæa may be lost in story!
Thus will we have it.

DOL: I could well consent, sir.
But in a monarchy, how will this be?
The prince will soon take notice, and both seize
You and your stone, it being a wealth unfit
For any private subject.

MAMMON: If he knew it.

DOL: Yourself do boast it, sir.

MAMMON: To thee, my life.

DOL: O, but beware, sir! you may come to end
The remnant of your days in a lothed prison,
By speaking of it.

MAMMON: 'Tis no idle fear:
We'll therefore go withal,[283] my girl, and live
In a free state, where we will eat our mullets,
Soused in high-country wines, sup pheasants' eggs
And have our cockles boiled in silver shells;
Our shrimps to swim again, as when they lived,
In a rare butter made of dolphins' milk,
Whose cream does look like opals; and with these
Delicate meats set ourselves high for pleasure,
And take us down again, and then renew
Our youth and strength with drinking the elixir,
And so enjoy a perpetuity
Of life and lust! And thou shalt have thy wardrobe
Richer than nature's, still to change thyself,
And vary oftener, for thy pride, than she,

281 division of a county
282 products of the labors of experiments
283 with all

Or art, her wise and almost-equal servant.

(*Re-enter* FACE.)

FACE: Sir, you are too loud. I hear you every word
Into[284] the laboratory. Some fitter place;
The garden, or great chamber above. How like you her?
MAMMON: Excellent! Lungs. There's for thee. (*Gives him money.*)
FACE: But do you hear?
Good sir, beware, no mention of the rabins.
MAMMON: We think not on 'em. (*Exeunt* MAMMON *and* DOL.)
FACE: O, it is well, sir. — Subtle!

(*Enter* SUBTLE.)

Dost thou not laugh?
SUBTLE: Yes; are they gone?
FACE: All's clear.
SUBTLE: The widow is come.
FACE: And your quarrelling disciple?
SUBTLE: Ay.
FACE: I must to my captainship again then.
SUBTLE: Stay, bring them in first.
FACE: So I meant. What is she?
A bonnibel? [285]
SUBTLE: I know not.
FACE: We'll draw lots:
You'll stand to that?
SUBTLE: What else?
FACE: O, for a suit,[286]
To fall now like a curtain, flap!
SUBTLE: To the door, man.
FACE: You'll have the first kiss, 'cause I am not ready. (*Exit.*)
SUBTLE: Yes, and perhaps hit you through both the nostrils.[287]
FACE (*within*): Who would you speak with?
KASTRIL (*within*): Where's the captain?
FACE (*within*): Gone, sir.
About some business.
KASTRIL (*within*): Gone!
FACE (*within*): He'll return straight.
But, master doctor, his lieutenant, is here.

(*Enter* KASTRIL, *followed by* DAME PLIANT.)

[284] in [285] *i.e.*, bonnie belle (fair beauty) [286] *i.e.*, his captain's suit
[287] put your nose out of joint

SUBTLE: Come near, my worshipful boy, my *terræ fili,*
That is, my boy of land; makes thy approaches:
Welcome; I know thy lusts, and thy desires,
And I will serve and satisfy them. Begin,
Charge me from thence, or thence, or in this line;
Here is my centre: ground thy quarrel.
KASTRIL: You lie.
SUBTLE: How, child of wrath and anger! the loud lie?
For what, my sudden boy?
KASTRIL: Nay, that look you to,
I am aforehand.[288]
SUBTLE: O, this is no true grammar,
And as ill logic! You must render causes, child,
Your first and second intentions, know your canons
And your divisions, moods, degrees, and differences,
Your predicaments, substance, and accident,
Series extern and intern, with their causes,
Efficient, material, formal, final,
And have your elements perfect? [289]
KASTRIL: What is this!
The angry tongue he talks in? (*Aside.*)
SUBTLE: That false precept,
Of being aforehand, has deceived a number,
And made them enter quarrels oftentimes
Before they were aware; and afterward,
Against their wills.
KASTRIL: How must I do then, sir?
SUBTLE: I cry this lady mercy: she should first
Have been saluted. (*Kisses her.*) I do call you lady,
Because you are to be one ere 't be long,
My soft and buxom widow.
KASTRIL: Is she, i' faith?
SUBTLE: Yes, or my art is an egregious liar.
KASTRIL: How know you?
SUBTLE: By inspection on her forehead,
And subtlety of her lip, which must be tasted
Often to make a judgment. (*Kisses her again.*) 'Slight, she melts
Like a myrobolane:[290] here is yet a line,
In *rivo frontis,*[291] tells me he is no knight.
DAME PLIANT: What is he then, sir?
SUBTLE: Let me see your hand.

[288] *i.e., I* challenged *you* [289] a passage of terms from scholastic logic
[290] a kind of dried plum [291] the frontal vein

O, your *linea fortunæ*[292] makes it plain;
And stella here *in monte Veneris*.[293]
But, most of all, *junctura annularis*.[294]
He is a soldier, or a man of art, lady,
But shall have some great honour shortly.

DAME PLIANT: Brother,
He's a rare man, believe me!

(*Re-enter* FACE, *in his uniform.*)

KASTRIL: Hold your peace.
Here comes the t' other rare man. — 'Save you, captain.

FACE: Good Master Kastril! Is this your sister?

KASTRIL: Ay, sir.
Please you to kiss her, and be proud to know her.

FACE: I shall be proud to know you, lady. (*Kisses her.*)

DAME PLIANT: Brother,
He calls me lady too.

KASTRIL: Ay, peace: I heard it. (*Takes her aside.*)

FACE: The count is come.

SUBTLE: Where is he?

FACE: At the door.

SUBTLE: Why, you must entertain him.

FACE: What will you do
With these the while?

SUBTLE: Why, have them up, and show them
Some fustian[295] book, or the dark glass.[296]

FACE: 'Fore God,
She is a delicate dabchick![297] I must have her. (*Exit.*)

SUBTLE: Must you! ay, if your fortune will, you must. —
Come, sir, the captain will come to us presently:
I'll have you to my chamber of demonstrations,
Where I will show you both the grammar and logic,
And rhetoric of quarrelling: my whole method
Drawn out in tables; and my instrument,
That hath the several scales upon't, shall make you
Able to quarrel at a straw's-breadth by moonlight.
And, lady, I'll have you look in a glass,
Some half an hour, but to clear your eyesight,
Against you see your fortune; which is greater

[292] line of fortune (term of palmistry) [293] the mount of Venus at the root of the thumb [294] joint of the ring finger [295] high-sounding nonsense [296] *i.e.*, the fortune teller's crystal ball [297] water hen (here with the connotation of feminine daintiness)

Than I may judge upon the sudden, trust me.
(*Exit, followed by* KASTRIL *and* DAME PLIANT.)

(*Re-enter* FACE.)

FACE: Where are you, doctor?
SUBTLE (*within*): I'll come to you presently.
FACE: I will have this same widow, now I have seen her,
On any composition.

(*Re-enter* SUBTLE.)

SUBTLE: What do you say?
FACE: Have you disposed of them?
SUBTLE: I have sent them up.
FACE: Subtle, in troth, I needs must have this widow.
SUBTLE: Is that the matter?
FACE: Nay, but hear me.
SUBTLE: Go to.
If you rebel once, Dol shall know it all:
Therefore be quiet, and obey your chance.
FACE: Nay, thou art so violent now. Do but conceive,
Thou art old, and canst not serve ——
SUBTLE: Who cannot? I?
'Slight, I will serve her with thee, for a ——
FACE: Nay,
But understand: I'll give you composition.[298]
SUBTLE: I will not treat with thee; what! sell my fortune?
'Tis better than my birthright. Do not murmur:
Win her, and carry her. If you grumble, Dol
Knows it directly.
FACE: Well, sir, I am silent.
Will you go help to fetch in Don in state? (*Exit.*)
SUBTLE: I follow you, sir: we must keep Face in awe,
Or he will overlook[299] us like a tyrant.

(*Re-enter* FACE, *introducing* SURLY *disguised as a Spaniard.*)

Brain of a tailor! who comes here? Don John!
SURLY: *Senores, beso las manos a vuestras mercedes.*[300]
SUBTLE: Would you had stooped a little, and kist our anos!
FACE: Peace, Subtle.
SUBTLE: Stab me; I shall never hold, man,

[298] equal compensation [299] lord it over [300] gentlemen, I kiss your worships' hands

He looks in that deep ruff like a head in a platter,
Served in by a short cloak upon two trestles.[301]
FACE: Or what do you say to a collar of brawn,[302] cut down
Beneath the souse,[303] and wriggled [304] with a knife?
SUBTLE: 'Slud,[305] he does look too fat to be a Spaniard.
FACE: Perhaps some Fleming or some Hollander got him
In d'Alva's[306] time; Count Egmont's[307] bastard.
SUBTLE: Don,
Your scurvy, yellow, Madrid face is welcome.
SURLY: *Gratia.*[308]
SUBTLE: He speaks out of a fortification.
Pray God he have no squibs[309] in those deep sets.[310]
SURLY: *Por dios, senores, muy linda casa!*[311]
SUBTLE: What says he?
FACE: Praises the house I think;
I know no more but's action.
SUBTLE: Yes, the *casa,*
My precious Diego will prove fair enough
To cozen you in. Do you mark? you shall
Be cozened, Diego.
FACE: Cozened, do you see,
My worthy Donzel,[312] cozened.
SURLY: *Entiendo.*[313]
SUBTLE: Do you intend it? so do we, dear Don.
Have you brought pistolets, or portagues,
My solemn Don? Dost thou feel any?
FACE (*feels his pockets*): Full.
SUBTLE: You shall be emptied, Don, pumped and drawn
Dry, as they say.
FACE: Milked, in troth, sweet Don.
SUBTLE: See all the monsters;[314] the great lion of all, Don.
SURLY: *Con licencia, se puede ver a esta senora?* [315]
SUBTLE: What talks he now?
FACE: Of the sennora.
SUBTLE: O, Don,
This is the lioness, which you shall see
Also, my Don.

301 stilts, *i.e.*, legs 302 roll of boar's flesh 303 ear 304 slashed 305 God's blood 306 Duke of Alva, 1508-1582, Spanish governor of the Netherlands 307 1522-1568, Flemish patriot, executed on the Duke of Alva's order 308 thanks 309 firecrackers 310 plaits of the ruff 311 by God, gentlemen, a very fine house 312 little don 313 I understand 314 *i.e.*, see the sights 315 with your permission, may I see the lady

FACE: 'Slid, Subtle, how shall we do?
SUBTLE: For what?
FACE: Why, Dol's employed, you know.
SUBTLE: That's true.
'Fore heaven I know not: he must stay, that's all.
FACE: Stay! that he must not by no means.
SUBTLE: No! why?
FACE: Unless you'll mar all. 'Slight, he will suspect it:
And then he will not pay not half so well.
This is a travelled punk-master, and does know
All the delays; a notable hot rascal.
And looks already rampant.
SUBTLE: 'Sdeath, and Mammon
Must not be troubled.
FACE: Mammon! In no case.
SUBTLE: What shall we do then?
FACE: Think: you must be sudden.
SURLY: *Entiendo que la senora es tan hermosa, que codicio tan verla, como la bien aventuranza de mi vida.*[316]
FACE: *Mi vida!* 'Slid, Subtle, he puts me in mind o' the widow.
What dost thou say to draw her to it, ha!
And tell her 'tis her fortune? all our venture
Now lies upon't. It is but one man more,
Which of us chance to have her: and beside,
There is no maidenhead to be feared or lost.
What dost thou think on't, Subtle?
SUBTLE: Who, I? why ——
FACE: The credit of our house too is engaged.
SUBTLE: You make me an offer for my share erewhile.
What wilt thou give me, 'i faith?
FACE: O, by that light
I'll not buy now. You know your doom[317] to me.
E'en take your lot, obey your chance, sir; win her,
And wear her out for me.
SUBTLE: 'Slight, I'll not work her then.
FACE: It is the common cause; therefore bethink you.
Dol else must know it, as you said.
SUBTLE: I care not.
SURLY: *Senores, porque se tarda tanto?*[318]
SUBTLE: Faith, I am not fit, I am old.
FACE: That's now no reason, sir.

[316] I understand that the lady is so beautiful that I wish to see her as much the greatest fortune of my life [317] sentence [318] gentlemen, why this delay

SURLY: *Puede ser de hazer burla de mi amor?* [319]
FACE: You hear the Don too? by this air I call,
And loose the hinges, Dol!
SUBTLE: A plague of hell ——
FACE: Will you then do?
SUBTLE: You are a terrible rogue!
I'll think of this: will you, sir, call the widow?
FACE: Yes, and I'll take her too with all her faults,
Now I do think on't better.
SUBTLE: With all my heart, sir;
Am I discharged o' the lot?
FACE: As you please.
SUBTLE: Hands. (*They take hands.*)
FACE: Remember now, that upon any change,
You never claim her.
SUBTLE: Much good joy and health to you, sir,
Marry a whore! fate, let me wed a witch first.
SURLY: *Por estas honradas barbas* —— [320]
SUBTLE: He swears by his beard.
Dispatch, and call the brother too. (*Exit* FACE.)
SURLY: *Tengo duda, senores, que no me hagan alguna traycion.*[321]
SUBTLE: How, issue on? yes, præsto,[322] sennor. Please you
Enthratha the *chambratha*, worthy don:
Where if you please the fates, in your *bathada*,
You shall be soaked, and stroked, and tubbed, and rubbed,
And scrubbed, and fubbed,[323] dear don, before you go,
You shall in faith, my scurvy baboon don,
Be curried, clawed, and flawed,[324] and tawed,[325] indeed,
I will the heartlier go about it now,
And make the widow a punk so much the sooner,
To be revenged on this impetuous Face:
The quickly doing of it is the grace.
(*Exeunt* SUBTLE *and* SURLY.)

Scene II [*Another Room in the same.*]

(*Enter* FACE, KASTRIL, *and* DAME PLIANT.)

FACE: Come, lady: I knew the doctor would not leave
Till he had found the very nick[326] of her fortune.

[319] could it be that you are making fun of my love [320] by this honored beard [321] I am afraid, gentlemen, that you are playing some trick on me [322] right away [323] cheated [324] flayed [325] soaked for tanning [326] turning point

KASTRIL: To be a countess, say you, a Spanish countess, sir?
DAME PLIANT: Why, is that better than an English countess?
FACE: Better! 'Slight, make you that a question, lady?
KASTRIL: Nay, she is a fool, captain, you must pardon her.
FACE: Ask from your courtier, to your inns-of-court-man,
To your mere milliner; they well tell you all,
Your Spanish jennet is the best horse; your Spanish
Stoup[327] is the best garb;[328] your Spanish beard
Is the best cut; your Spanish ruffs are the best
Wear; your Spanish pavin[329] the best dance;
Your Spanish titillation[330] in a glove
The best perfume: and for your Spanish pike,
And Spanish blade, let your poor captain speak —
Here comes the doctor.

(*Enter* SUBTLE *with a paper.*)

SUBTLE: My most honoured lady,
For so I am now to style you, having found
By this my scheme, you are to undergo
An honourable fortune very shortly.
What will you say now, if some ——
FACE: I have told her all, sir;
And her right worshipful brother here, that she shall be
A countess; do not delay them, sir: a Spanish countess.
SUBTLE: Still,[331] my scarce-worshipful captain, you can keep
No secret! Well, since he has told you, madam,
Do you forgive him, and I do.
KASTRIL: She shall do that, sir;
I'll look to it, 'tis my charge.
SUBTLE: Well then: nought rests
But that she fit her love now to her fortune.
DAME PLIANT: Truly I shall never brook a Spaniard.
SUBTLE: No!
DAME PLIANT: Never since eighty-eight,[332] could I abide them,
And that was some three years afore I was born, in truth.
SUBTLE: Come, you must love him, or be miserable;
Choose which you will.
FACE: By this good rush,[333] persuade her,
She will cry strawberries[334] else within this twelve month.

[327] stoop, bow [328] fashion [329] pavan, a stately Spanish dance [330] perfuming [331] *i.e.*, as always [332] 1588, the year of the Armada [333] switch, rod [334] *i.e.*, be a street vendor

SUBTLE: Nay, shads and mackerel,[335] which is worse.
FACE: Indeed, sir!
KASTRIL: 'Ods lid, you shall love him, or I'll kick you.
DAME PLIANT: Why,
I'll do as you will have me, brother.
KASTRIL: Do,
Or by this hand I'll maul you.
FACE: Nay, good sir,
Be not so fierce.
SUBTLE: No, my enraged child;
She will be ruled. What, when she comes to taste
The pleasures of a countess! to be courted ——
FACE: And kissed, and ruffled![336]
SUBTLE: Ay, behind the hangings.
FACE: And then come forth in pomp!
SUBTLE: And know her state!
FACE: Of keeping all the idolaters of the chamber
Barer to her, than at their prayers!
SUBTLE: Is served
Upon the knee!
FACE: And has her pages, ushers,
Footmen, and coaches ——
SUBTLE: Her six mares ——
FACE: Nay, eight!
SUBTLE: To hurry her through London, to the Exchange,[337]
Bethlem,[338] the china-houses ——
FACE: Yes, and have
The citizens gape at her, and praise her tires,
And my lord's goose-turd [339] bands, that ride with her!
KASTRIL: Most brave![340] By this hand, you are not my suster
If you refuse.
DAME PLIANT: I will not refuse, brother.

(*Enter* SURLY.)

SURLY: *Que es esto, senores, que no venga? Esta tardanza me mata!*[341]
FACE: It is the count come:
The doctor knew he would be here, by his art.
SUBTLE: *En gallanta madama, Don! gallantissima!*

[335] *i.e.*, rather than selling strawberries she'll be a fish-wife [336] tousled [337] where the shops were located [338] watching the insane at Bethlehem hospital was a popular form of amusement [339] *i.e.*, yellowish green [340] fine [341] how is it, gentlemen, that she does not come? This delay is killing me.

SURLY: *Por todos los dioses, la mas acabada hermosura, que he visto en mi vida!* [342]

FACE: Is't not a gallant language that they speak?

KASTRIL: An admirable language? Is't not French?

FACE: No, Spanish, sir.

KASTRIL: It goes like law French,
And that, they say, is the courtliest language.

FACE: List, sir.

SURLY: *El sol ha perdido su lumbre, con el esplandor que trae esta dama! Valgame dios!*[343]

FACE: He admires your sister.

KASTRIL: Must not she make curt'sy?

SUBTLE: 'Ods will, she must go to him, man, and kiss him!
It is the Spanish fashion, for the women
To make first court.

FACE: 'Tis true he tells you, sir:
His art knows all.

SURLY: *Porque no se acude?* [344]

KASTRIL: He speaks to her, I think.

FACE: That he does, sir.

SURLY: *Por el amor de dios, que es esto que se tarda?* [345]

KASTRIL: Nay, see: she will not understand him! gull,
Noddy.

DAME PLIANT: What say you, brother?

KASTRIL: Ass, my suster,
Go kuss him, as the cunning man would have you;
I'll thrust a pin in your buttocks else.

FACE: O no, sir.

SURLY: *Senora mia, mi persona esta muy indigna de allegar a tanta hermosura.*[346]

FACE: Does he not use her bravely?

KASTRIL: Bravely, i' faith!

FACE: Nay, he will use her better.

KASTRIL: Do you think so?

SURLY: *Senora, si sera servida, entremonos.*[347]

(*Exit with* DAME PLIANT.)

KASTRIL: Where does he carry her?

FACE: Into the garden, sir;

[342] by all the gods, the most perfect beauty I have ever seen. [343] the sun has lost his light with the splendor that this lady brings. God bless me [344] why doesn't she come to me [345] for the love of God, why does she delay [346] my lady, my person is quite unworthy to approach such a beauty [347] lady, if it is convenient to you, let us enter

Take you no thought: I must interpret for her.
SUBTLE: Give Dol the word. (*Aside to* FACE, *who goes out.*) — Come, my fierce child, advance,
We'll to our quarrelling lesson again.
KASTRIL: Agreed.
I love a Spanish boy with all my heart.
SUBTLE: Nay, and by this means, sir, you shall be brother
To a great count.
KASTRIL: Ay, I knew that at first,
This match will advance the house of the Kastrils.
SUBTLE: 'Pray God your sister prove but pliant!
KASTRIL: Why,
Her name is so, by her other husband.
SUBTLE: How!
KASTRIL: The Widow Pliant. Knew you not that?
SUBTLE: No, faith, sir;
Yet, by erection of her figure,[348] I guess it.
Come, let's go practise.
KASTRIL: Yes, but do you think, doctor,
I e'er shall quarrel well?
SUBTLE: I warrant you. (*Exeunt.*)

Scene III [*Another Room in the same.*]

(*Enter* DOL COMMON *in her fit of raving, followed by* MAMMON.)

DOL: *For after Alexander's death* ——[349]
MAMMON: Good lady ——
DOL: *That Perdiccas and Antigonus were slain,*
The two that stood, Seleuc and Ptolomee ——
MAMMON: Madam ——
DOL: *Make up the two legs, and the fourth beast,*
That was Gog-north and Egypt-south: which after
Was called Grog-iron-leg and South-iron-leg.
MAMMON: Lady ——
DOL: *And then Gog-horned. So was Egypt, too.*
Then Egypt-clay-leg, and Gog-clay-leg ——
MAMMON: Sweet madam ——
DOL: *And last Gog-dust, and Egypt-dust, which fall*

[348] the primary meaning "the casting of her horoscope," is attended by an obvious bawdy pun [349] The italics mark Dol's quotation of jumbled passages from Hugh Broughton's *Concent of Scripture*. Cf. note 163.

In the last link of the fourth chain. And these
Be stars in story, which none see, or look at ——

MAMMON: What shall I do?

DOL: *For,* as he says, *except*
We call the rabbins, and the heathen Greeks ——

MAMMON: Dear lady ——

DOL: *To come from Salem, and from Athens,*
And teach the people of Great Britain ——

(*Enter* FACE *hastily, in his servant's dress.*)

FACE: What's the matter, sir?

DOL: *To speak the tongue of Eber and Favan* ——

MAMMON: O,
She's in her fit.

DOL: *We shall know nothing* ——

FACE: Death, sir,
We are undone!

DOL: *Where then a learned linguist*
Shall see the ancient used communion
Of vowels and consonants ——

FACE: My master will hear!

DOL: A *wisdom, which Pythagoras held most high* ——

MAMMON: Sweet honourable lady!

DOL: *To comprise*
All sounds of voices, in few marks of letters.

FACE: Nay, you must never hope to lay her now.

(*They all speak together.*)

DOL: *And so we may arrive by Talmud skill,*
And profane Greek, to raise the building up
Of Helen's house against the Ismaelite,
King of Thogarma, and his habergions
Brimstony, blue, and fiery; and the force
Of king Abaddon, and the beast of Cittim,
Which rabbi David Kimchi, Onkelos,
And Aben Ezra do interpret Rome.

FACE: How did you put her into't?

MAMMON: Alas, I talked
Of a fifth monarchy I would erect,
With the philosophers' stone, by chance, and she
Falls on the other four straight.

FACE: Out of Broughton!
I told you so. 'Slid, stop her mouth.

MAMMON: Is't best?

FACE: She'll never leave else. If the old man hear her,
We are but fæces, ashes.
SUBTLE (*within*): What's to do there?
FACE: O, we are lost! Now she hears him, she is quiet.

(*Enter* SUBTLE: *they run different ways.*)

MAMMON: Where shall I hide me!
SUBTLE: How! what sight is here?
Close[350] deeds of darkness, and that shun the light!
Bring him again. Who is he? What, my son!
O, I have lived too long.
MAMMON: Nay, good, dear father,
There was no unchaste purpose.
SUBTLE: Not! and flee me,
When I come in?
MAMMON: That was my error.
SUBTLE: Error!
Guilt, guilt, my son: give it the right name. No marvel,
If I found check in your great work within,
When such affairs as these were managing!
MAMMON: Why, have you so?
SUBTLE: It has stood still this half hour:
And all the rest of our less works gone back.
Where is the instrument of wickedness,
My lewd false drudge?
MAMMON: Nay, good sir, blame not him;
Believe me, 'twas against his will or knowledge:
I saw her by chance.
SUBTLE: Will you commit more sin,
To excuse a varlet?
MAMMON: By my hope, 'tis true, sir.
SUBTLE: Nay, then I wonder less, if you, for whom
The blessing was prepared, would so tempt heaven,
And lose your fortunes.
MAMMON: Why, sir?
SUBTLE: This will retard
The work a month at least.
MAMMON: Why, if it do,
What remedy? But think it not, good father:
Our purposes were honest.[351]
SUBTLE: As they were,

[350] secret [351] chaste

So the reward will prove. (*A loud explosion within.*) — How now! ah me!
God and all saints be good to us. ——

(*Re-enter* FACE.)

What's that?

FACE: O, sir, we are defeated! all the works
Are flown *in fumo*, every glass is burst:
Furnace, and all rent down! as if a bolt
Of thunder had been driven through the house.
Retorts, receivers, pelicans, bolt-heads,
All struck in shivers! (SUBTLE *falls down as in a swoon.*)
Help, good sir! alas,
Coldness and death invades him. Nay, Sir Mammon,
Do the fair offices of a man! you stand,
As you were readier to depart than he. (*Knocking within.*)
Who's there? my lord her brother is come.
MAMMON: Ha, Lungs!
FACE: His coach is at the door. Avoid his sight,
For he's as furious as his sister's mad.
MAMMON: Alas!
FACE: My brain is quite undone with the fume, sir,
I ne'er must hope to be mine own man again.
MAMMON: Is all lost, Lungs? will nothing be preserved
Of all our cost?
FACE: Faith, very little, sir;
A peck of coals or so, which is cold comfort, sir.
MAMMON: O, my voluptuous mind! I am justly punished.
FACE: And so am I, sir.
MAMMON: Cast from all hopes ——
FACE: Nay, certainties, sir.
MAMMON: By mine own base affections.
SUBTLE (*seeming to come to himself*): O, the curst fruits of vice and lust!
MAMMON: Good father,
It was my sin. Forgive it.
SUBTLE: Hangs my roof
Over us still, and will not fall, O justice,
Upon us, for this wicked man!
FACE: Nay, look, sir,
You grieve him now with staying in his sight:
Good sir, the nobleman will come too, and take you,

And that may breed a tragedy.
MAMMON: I'll go.
FACE: Ay, and repent at home, sir. It may be,
For some good penance you may have it yet;
A hundred pound to the box at Bethlem ——
MAMMON: Yes.
FACE: For the restoring such as — have their wits.
MAMMON: I'll do't.
FACE: I'll send one to you to receive it.
MAMMON: Do.
Is no projection left?
FACE: All flown, or stinks, sir.
MAMMON: Will nought be saved that's good for med'cine, think'st thou?
FACE: I cannot tell, sir. There will be perhaps
Something about the scraping of the shards,
Will cure the itch, — though not your itch of mind, sir. (*Aside.*)
It shall be saved for you, and sent home. Good sir,
This way for fear the lord should meet you. (*Exit* MAMMON.)
SUBTLE (*raising his head*): Face!
FACE: Ay.
SUBTLE: Is he gone?
FACE: Yes, and as heavily
As all the gold he hoped for were in's blood.
Let us be light though.
SUBTLE (*leaping up*): Ay, as balls, and bound
And hit our heads against the roof for joy:
There's so much of our care now cast away.
FACE: Now to our don.
SUBTLE: Yes, your young widow by this time
Is made a countess, Face; she has been in travail
Of a young heir for you.
FACE: Good, sir.
SUBTLE: Off with your case,[352]
And greet her kindly, as a bridegroom should,
After these common hazards.
FACE: Very well, sir.
Will you go fetch Don Diego off the while?
SUBTLE: And fetch him over too,[353] if you'll be pleased, sir:
Would Dol were in her place, to pick his pockets now!
FACE: Why, you can do't as well, if you would set to't.

[352] clothes [353] get the better of him

I pray you prove your virtue.
SUBTLE: For your sake, sir. *(Exeunt.)*

Scene IV [*Another Room in the same.*]

(*Enter* SURLY *and* DAME PLIANT.)

SURLY: Lady, you see into what hands you are fallen;
'Mongst what a nest of villains! and how near
Your honour was t'have catched a certain clap,
Through your credulity, had I but been
So punctually forward,[354] as place, time,
And other circumstances would have made a man;
For you're a handsome woman; would you were wise too!
I am a gentleman come here disguised,
Only to find the knaveries of this citadel;
And where I might have wronged your honour, and have not,
I claim some interest in your love. You are,
They say, a widow, rich; and I'm a bachelor,
Worth nought: your fortunes may make me a man,
As mine have preserved you a woman. Think upon it,
And whether I have deserved you or no.
DAME PLIANT: I will, sir.
SURLY: And for these household-rogues, let me alone
To treat with them.

(*Enter* SUBTLE.)

SUBTLE: How doth my noble Diego,
And my dear madam countess? hath the count
Been courteous, lady? liberal and open?
Donzel, methinks you look melancholic,
After your coitum, and scurvy: truly,
I do not like the dulness of your eye;
It hath a heavy cast, 'tis upsee Dutch,[355]
And says you are a lumpish whore-master.
Be lighter, I will make your pockets so. (*Attempts to pick them.*)
SURLY (*throws open his cloak*): Will you, don bawd and pick-purse?
(*Strikes him down.*) How now! reel you?
Stand up, sir, you shall find, since I am so heavy,
I'll give you equal weight.
SUBTLE: Help! murder!

[354] presumptuously bold [355] in the Dutch fashion

SURLY: No, sir,
There's no such thing intended: a good cart
And a clean whip shall ease you of that fear.
I am the Spanish don *that should be cozened,*
Do you see, cozened! Where's your Captain Face,
That parcel-broker,[356] and whole-bawd, all rascal?

(*Enter* FACE *in his uniform.*)

FACE: How, Surly!
SURLY: O, make your approach, good captain.
I have found from whence your copper rings and spoons
Come now, wherewith you cheat abroad in taverns.
'Twas here you learned t'anoint your boot with brimstone,
Then rub men's gold on't for a kind of touch,
And say 'twas naught, when you had changed the colour,
That you might have't for nothing. And this doctor,
Your sooty, smoky-bearded compeer,[357] he
Will close you so much gold, in a bolt's-head,
And, on a turn, convey in the stead another
With sublimed mercury, that shall burst in the heat,
And fly out all *in fumo!* Then weeps Mammon;
Then swoons his worship. (FACE *slips out.*) Or, he is the Faustus,
That casteth figures and can conjure, cures
Plagues, piles, and pox, by the ephemerides,[358]
And holds intelligence with all the bawds
And midwives of three shires: while you send in ——
Captain! — what! is he gone? — damsels with child,
Wives that are barren, or the waiting-maid
With the green sickness. (*Seizes* SUBTLE *as he is retiring.*) — Nay, sir, you must tarry,
Though he be scaped; and answer by the ears, sir.

(*Re-enter* FACE *with* KASTRIL.)

FACE: Why, now's the time, if ever you will quarrel
Well, as they say, and be a true-born child:
The doctor and your sister both are abused.
KASTRIL: Where is he? which is he? he is a slave,
Whate'er he is, and the son of a whore. — Are you
The man, sir, I would know?
SURLY: I should be loth, sir,
To confess so much.

[356] part broker [357] *i.e.*, accomplice [358] astronomical almanacs

KASTRIL: Then you lie in your throat.
SURLY: How!
FACE (*to* KASTRIL): A very errant rogue, sir, and a cheater,
Employed here by another conjurer
That does not love the doctor, and would cross him
If he knew how.
SURLY: Sir, you are abused.
KASTRIL: You lie:
And 'tis no matter.
FACE: Well said, sir! He is
The impudent'st rascal ——
SURLY: You are indeed. Will you hear me, sir?
FACE: By no means: bid him be gone.
KASTRIL: Begone, sir, quickly.
SURLY: This is strange! — Lady, do you inform your brother.
FACE: There is not such a foist[359] in all the town,
The doctor had him presently; and finds yet
The Spanish count will come here. — Bear up, Subtle. (*Aside.*)
SUBTLE: Yes, sir, he must appear within this hour.
FACE: And yet this rogue would come in a disguise,
By the temptation of another spirit,
To trouble our art, though he could not hurt it!
KASTRIL: Ay,
I know — Away, (*To his sister.*) you talk like a foolish mauther.[360]
SURLY: Sir, all is truth she says.
FACE: Do not believe him, sir.
He is the lying'st swabber! Come your ways, sir.
SURLY: You are valiant out of company!
KASTRIL: Yes, how then, sir?

(*Enter* DRUGGER *with a piece of damask.*)

FACE: Nay, here's an honest fellow too that knows him,
And all his tricks. Make good what I say, Abel,
This cheater would have cozened thee o' the widow.
(*Aside to* DRUGGER.)
He owes this honest Drugger here seven pound,
He has had on him in[361] twopenny'orths of tobacco.
DRUGGER: Yes, sir.
And he has damned himself three terms to pay me.
FACE: And what does he owe for lotium? [362]
DRUGGER: Thirty shillings, sir;

[359] rogue [360] silly wench [361] charged with him [362] lotion

And for six syringes.
SURLY: Hydra[363] of villainy!
FACE: Nay, sir, you must quarrel him out o' the house.
KASTRIL: I will:
— Sir, if you get not out o' doors, you lie;
And you are a pimp.
SURLY: Why, this is madness, sir,
Not valour in you; I must laugh at this.
KASTRIL: It is my humour; you are a pimp and a trig.[364]
And an *Amadis de Gaul*,[365] or a Don Quixote.
DRUGGER: Or a knight o' the curious coxcomb, do you see?

(*Enter* ANANIAS.)

ANANIAS: Peace to the household!
KASTRIL: I'll keep peace for no man.
ANANIAS: Casting of dollars is concluded lawful.
KASTRIL: Is he the constable?
SUBTLE: Peace, Ananias.
FACE: No, sir.
KASTRIL: Then you are an otter, and a shad, a whit,
A very tim.[366]
SURLY: You'll hear me, sir?
KASTRIL: I will not.
ANANIAS: What is the motive?
SUBTLE: Zeal in the young gentleman,
Against his Spanish slops.
ANANIAS: They are profane,
Lewd, superstitious, and idolatrous breeches.
SURLY: New rascals!
KASTRIL: Will you be gone, sir?
ANANIAS: Avoid, Sathan!
Thou art not of the light! [367] That ruff of pride
About thy neck, betrays thee; and is the same
With that which the unclean birds, in seventy-seven,[368]
Were seen to prank it with on divers coasts:
Thou look'st like antichrist, in that lewd hat.
SURLY: I must give way.
KASTRIL: Be gone, sir.
SURLY: But I'll take

363 many-headed water-snake in Greek mythology
364 fool, coxcomb
365 title and hero of early Renaissance Spanish romance of knightly chivalry
366 meaning obscure
367 *i.e.*, the "inner light" of the Puritans
368 1577 (but the historical allusion is obscure)

A course with you ——
ANANIAS: Depart, proud Spanish fiend!
SURLY: Captain and doctor.
ANANIAS: Child of perdition!
KASTRIL: Hence, sir! — (*Exit* SURLY.)
Did I not quarrel bravely?
FACE: Yes, indeed, sir.
KASTRIL: Nay, an I give my mind to't, I shall do't.
FACE: O, you must follow, sir, and threaten him tame:
He'll turn again else.
KASTRIL: I'll re-turn him then. (*Exit.*)

(SUBTLE *takes* ANANIAS *aside.*)

FACE: Drugger, this rogue prevented[369] us, for thee:
We had determined that thou should'st have come
In a Spanish suit, and have carried her so; and he
A brokerly[370] slave! goes, puts it on himself.
Hast brought the damask?
DRUGGER: Yes, sir.
FACE: Thou must borrow
A Spanish suit: hast thou no credit with the players?
DRUGGER: Yes, sir; did you never see me play the Fool?
FACE: I know not, Nab: thou shalt, if I can help[371] it. — (*Aside.*)
Hieronimo's[372] old cloak, ruff, and hat will serve;
I'll tell thee more when thou bring'st 'em. (*Exit* DRUGGER.)
ANANIAS: Sir, I know
The Spaniard hates the brethren, and hath spies
Upon their actions: and that this was one
I make no scruple. — But the holy synod
Have been in prayer and meditation for it;
And 'tis revealed no less to them than me,
That casting of money is most lawful.
SUBTLE: True.
But here I cannot do it: if the house
Shou'd chance to be suspected, all would out,
And we be locked up in the Tower for ever,
To make gold there for the state, never come out;
And then are you defeated.
ANANIAS: I will tell
This to the elders and the weaker brethren,
That the whole company of the separation

369 forestalled 370 pettifogging 371 do something about 372 the chief character in Thomas Kyd's *The Spanish Tragedy* (c. 1589)

May join in humble prayer again.
SUBTLE: And fasting.
ANANIAS: Yea, for some fitter place. The peace of mind
Rest with these walls! (*Exit.*)
SUBTLE: Thanks, courteous Ananias.
FACE: What did he come for?
SUBTLE: About casting dollars,
Presently out of hand. And so I told him,
A Spanish minister came here to spy,
Against the faithful ——
FACE: I conceive. Come, Subtle,
Thou art so down upon the least disaster!
How wouldst thou ha' done, if I had not help't thee out?
SUBTLE: I thank thee, Face, for the angry boy, i' faith.
FACE: Who would have looked [373] it should have been that rascal
Surly? He has dyed his beard and all. Well, sir,
Here's damask come to make you a suit.
SUBTLE: Where's Drugger?
FACE: He is gone to borrow me a Spanish habit;
I'll be the count now.
SUBTLE: But where's the widow?
FACE: Within, with my lord's sister; Madam Dol
Is entertaining her.
SUBTLE: By your favour, Face.
Now she is honest, I will stand again.
FACE: You will not offer it? [374]
SUBTLE: Why?
FACE: Stand to your word,
Or — here comes Dol, she knows ——
SUBTLE: You are tyrannous still.

(*Enter* DOL *hastily.*)

FACE: — Strict for my right. — How now, Dol! Hast [thou] told her,
The Spanish count will come?
DOL: Yes; but another is come,
You little looked for!
FACE: Who is that?
DOL: Your master;
The master of the house.
SUBTLE: How, Dol!
FACE: She lies,

[373] expected [374] surely, you don't mean that

This is some trick. Come, leave your quiblins,[375] Dorothy.
DOL: Look out and see. (FACE *goes to the window.*)
SUBTLE: Art thou in earnest?
DOL: 'Slight,
Forty o' the neighbours are about him, talking.
FACE: 'Tis he, by this good day.
DOL: 'Twill prove ill day
For some on us.
FACE: We are undone, and taken.
DOL: Lost, I'm afraid.
SUBTLE: You said he would not come,
While there died one a week within the liberties.[376]
FACE: No: 'twas within the walls.
SUBTLE: Was't so! cry you mercy.[377]
I thought the liberties. What shall we do now, Face?
FACE: Be silent: not a word, if he call or knock.
I'll into mine old shape again and meet him,
Of Jeremy, the butler. In the meantime,
Do you two pack up all the goods and purchase.[378]
That we can carry in the two trunks. I'll keep him
Off for to-day, if I cannot longer: and then
At night, I'll ship you both away to Ratcliff,
Where we will meet to-morrow, and there we'll share.
Let Mammon's brass and pewter keep the cellar;
We'll have another time for that. But, Dol,
Prithee go heat a little water quickly;
Subtle must shave me: all my captain's beard
Must off, to make me appear smooth Jeremy.
You'll do it?
SUBTLE: Yes, I'll shave you as well as I can.
FACE: And not cut my throat, but trim me?
SUBTLE: You shall see, sir. (*Exeunt.*)

ACT THE FIFTH

Scene I [*Before* LOVEWIT'S *door.*]

(*Enter* LOVEWIT, *with several of the* NEIGHBOURS.)

LOVEWIT: Has there been such resort,[379] say you?
1ST NEIGHBOUR: Daily, sir.

[375] quibbles [376] district outside the London city walls [377] beg your pardon
[378] loot [379] *i.e.*, traffic

2ND NEIGHBOUR: And nightly, too.
3RD NEIGHBOUR: Ay, some as brave as lords.
4TH NEIGHBOUR: Ladies and gentlewomen.
5TH NEIGHBOUR: Citizens' wives.
1ST NEIGHBOUR: And knights.
6TH NEIGHBOUR: In coaches.
2ND NEIGHBOUR: Yes, and oyster-women.
1ST NEIGHBOUR: Beside other gallants.
3RD NEIGHBOUR: Sailors' wives.
4TH NEIGHBOUR: Tobacco-men.
5TH NEIGHBOUR: Another Pimlico! [380]
LOVEWIT: What should my knave advance,
To draw this company? he hung out no banners
Of a strange calf with five legs to be seen,
Or a huge lobster with six claws?
6TH NEIGHBOUR: No, sir.
3RD NEIGHBOUR: We had gone in then, sir.
LOVEWIT: He has no gift
Of teaching in the nose[381] that e'er I knew of.
You saw no bills set up that promised cure
Of agues, or the tooth-ache?
2ND NEIGHBOUR: No such thing, sir!
LOVEWIT: Nor heard a drum struck for baboons or puppets?
5TH NEIGHBOUR: Neither, sir.
LOVEWIT: What device should he bring forth now?
I love a teeming wit as I love my nourishment:
'Pray God he have not kept such open house,
That he hath sold my hangings, and my bedding!
I left him nothing else. If he have eat them,
A plague o' the moth, say I! Sure he has got
Some bawdy pictures to call all this ging;[382]
The friar and the nun; or the new motion[383]
Of the knight's courser covering the parson's mare;
The boy of six year old with the great thing;
Or't may be, he has the fleas that run a tilt
Upon a table, or some dog to dance.
When saw you him?
1ST NEIGHBOUR: Who, sir, Jeremy?
2ND NEIGHBOUR: Jeremy butler?
We saw him not this month.

[380] popular summer resort in Hoxton, a suburb north of early 17th-century London [381] *i.e.*, preaching in the Puritan manner [382] gang [383] puppet-show

LOVEWIT: How!
4TH NEIGHBOUR: Not these five weeks, sir.
6TH NEIGHBOUR: These six weeks at the least.
LOVEWIT: You amaze me, neighbours!
5TH NEIGHBOUR: Sure, if your worship know not where he is,
He's slipt away.
6TH NEIGHBOUR: Pray God he be not made away.
LOVEWIT: Ha! it's no time to question, then. (*Knocks at the door.*)
6TH NEIGHBOUR: About
Some three weeks since I heard a doleful cry,
As I sat up a mending my wife's stockings.
LOVEWIT: 'Tis strange that none will answer! Did'st thou hear
A cry, sayst thou?
6TH NEIGHBOUR: Yes, sir, like unto a man
That had been strangled an hour, and could not speak.
2ND NEIGHBOUR: I heard it too, just this day three weeks, at two o'clock
Next morning.
LOVEWIT: These be miracles, or you make them so!
A man an hour strangled, and could not speak,
And both you heard him cry?
3RD NEIGHBOUR: Yes, downward, sir.
LOVEWIT: Thou art a wise fellow. Give me thy hand, I pray thee,
What trade art thou on?
3RD NEIGHBOUR: A smith, an't please your worship.
LOVEWIT: A smith! then lend me thy help to get this door open.
3RD NEIGHBOUR: That I will presently, sir, but fetch my tools — (*Exit.*)
1ST NEIGHBOUR: Sir, best to knock again afore you break it.
LOVEWIT (*knocks again*): I will.

(*Enter* FACE *in his butler's livery.*)

FACE: What mean you, sir?
1ST, 2ND, 4TH NEIGHBOUR: Oh, here's Jeremy!
FACE: Good sir, come from the door.
LOVEWIT: Why, what's the matter?
FACE: Yet farther, you are too near yet.
LOVEWIT: In the name of wonder,
What means the fellow!
FACE: The house, sir, has been visited.
LOVEWIT: What, with the plague? stand thou then farther.
FACE: No, sir,
I had it not.
LOVEWIT: Who had it then? I left
None else but thee in the house.

FACE: Yes, sir, my fellow,
The cat that kept the buttery, had it on her
A week before I spied it; but I got her
Conveyed away in the night: and so I shut
The house up for a month ——
LOVEWIT: How!
FACE: Purposing then, sir,
To have burnt rose-vinegar, treacle, and tar,
And have made it sweet, that you should ne'er have known it;
Because I knew the news would but afflict you, sir.
LOVEWIT: Breathe less, and farther off! Why this is stranger:
The neighbours tell me all here that the doors
Have still been open ——
FACE: How, sir!
LOVEWIT: Gallants, men and women,
And of all sorts tag-rag, been seen to flock here
In threaves,[384] these ten weeks, as to a second Hoksden,[385]
In days of Pimlico and Eye-bright.[386]
FACE: Sir,
Their wisdoms will not say so.
LOVEWIT: To-day they speak
Of coaches and gallants; one in a French hood [387]
Went in, they tell me; and another was seen
In a velvet gown at the window: divers more
Pass in and out.
FACE: They did pass through the doors then,
Or walls, I assure their eye-sights, and their spectacles;
For here, sir, are the keys, and here have been,
In this my pocket, now above twenty days:
And for before, I kept the fort alone there.
But that 'tis yet not deep in the afternoon,
I should believe my neighbours had seen double
Through the black pot, and made these apparitions!
For, on my faith to your worship, for these three weeks
And upwards, the door has not been opened.
LOVEWIT: Strange!
1ST NEIGHBOUR: Good faith, I think I saw a coach.
2ND NEIGHBOUR: And I too,
I'd have been sworn.
LOVEWIT: Do you but think it now?
And but one coach?

[384] droves [385] (now) Hoxton [386] an inn in Hoxton [387] *i.e.*, Dame Pliant

4TH NEIGHBOUR: We cannot tell, sir: Jeremy
Is a very honest fellow.
FACE: Did you see me at all?
1ST NEIGHBOUR: No; that we are sure on.
2ND NEIGHBOUR: I'll be sworn o' that.
LOVEWIT: Fine rogues to have your testimonies built on!

(*Re-enter third* NEIGHBOUR, *with his tools.*)

3RD NEIGHBOUR: Is Jeremy come!
1ST NEIGHBOUR: O yes; you may leave your tools;
We were deceived, he says.
2ND NEIGHBOUR: He has had the keys;
And the door has been shut these three weeks.
3RD NEIGHBOUR: Like enough.
LOVEWIT: Peace, and get hence, you changelings.

(*Enter* SURLY *and* MAMMON.)

FACE: Surly come!
And Mammon made acquainted! they'll tell all.
How shall I beat them off? what shall I do?
Nothing's more wretched than a guilty conscience. (*Aside.*)
SURLY: No, sir, he was a great physician. This,
It was no bawdy-house, but a mere[388] chancel!
You knew the lord and his sister.
MAMMON: Nay, good Surly. ——
SURLY: The happy word, BE RICH ——
MAMMON: Play not the tyrant. —
SURLY: *Should be to-day pronounced to all your friends.*
And where be your andirons now? and your brass pots,
That should have been golden flaggons, and great wedges?
MAMMON: Let me but breathe. What, they have shut their doors,
Methinks!
SURLY: Ay, now 'tis holiday with them.
MAMMON: Rogues, (*He and* SURLY *knock.*)
Cozeners, impostors, bawds!
FACE: What mean you, sir?
MAMMON: To enter if we can.
FACE: Another man's house!
Here is the owner, sir; turn you to him,
And speak your business.
MAMMON: Are you, sir, the owner?

[388] absolute

LOVEWIT: Yes, sir.
MAMMON: And are those knaves within your cheaters!
LOVEWIT: What knaves, what cheaters?
MAMMON: Subtle and his Lungs.
FACE: The gentleman is distracted, sir! No lungs,
Nor lights have been seen here these three weeks, sir,
Within these doors, upon my word.
SURLY: Your word,
Groom arrogant!
FACE: Yes, sir, I am the housekeeper,
And know the keys have not been out of my hands.
SURLY: This is a new Face.
FACE: You do mistake the house, sir:
What sign was't at?
SURLY: You rascal! this is one
Of the confederacy. Come, let's get officers,
And force the door.
LOVEWIT: Pray you stay, gentlemen.
SURLY: No, sir, we'll come with warrant.
MAMMON: Ay, and then
We shall have your doors open. (*Exeunt* MAMMON *and* SURLY.)
LOVEWIT: What means this?
FACE: I cannot tell, sir.
1ST NEIGHBOUR: These are two of the gallants
That we do think we saw.
FACE: Two of the fools!
You talk as idly as they. Good faith, sir,
I think the moon has crased 'em all. — O me,

(*Enter* KASTRIL.)

The angry boy come too! He'll make a noise,
And ne'er away till he have betrayed us all. (*Aside.*)
KASTRIL (*knocking*): What rogues, bawds, slaves, you'll open the door, anon!
Punk, cockatrice,[389] my suster! By this light
I'll fetch the marshal to you. You are a whore
To keep your castle ——
FACE: Who would you speak with, sir?
KASTRIL: The bawdy doctor, and the cozening captain,
And puss my suster.
LOVEWIT: This is something, sure.

[389] *i.e.*, prostitute

FACE: Upon my trust, the doors were never open, sir.
KASTRIL: I have heard all their tricks told me twice over,
By the fat knight and the lean gentleman.
LOVEWIT: Here comes another.

(*Enter* ANANIAS *and* TRIBULATION.)

FACE: Ananias too!
And his pastor!
TRIBULATION (*beating at the door*): The doors are shut against us.
ANANIAS: Come forth, you seed of sulphur, sons of fire!
Your stench it is broke forth; abomination
Is in the house.
KASTRIL: Ay, my suster's there.
ANANIAS: The place,
It is become a cage of unclean birds.
KASTRIL: Yes, I will fetch the scavenger, and the constable.
TRIBULATION: You shall do well.
ANANIAS: We'll join to weed them out.
KASTRIL: You will not come then, punk devise,[390] my suster!
ANANIAS: Call her not sister; she's a harlot verily.
KASTRIL: I'll raise the street.
LOVEWIT: Good gentlemen, a word.
ANANIAS: Sathan avoid, and hinder not our zeal!
(*Exeunt* ANANIAS, TRIBULATION, *and* KASTRIL.)
LOVEWIT: The world's turned Bethlem.
FACE: These are all broke loose,
Out of St. Katherine's,[391] where they use to keep
The better sort of mad-folks.
1ST NEIGHBOUR: All these persons
We saw go in and out here.
2ND NEIGHBOUR: Yes, indeed, sir.
3RD NEIGHBOUR: These were the parties.
FACE: Peace, you drunkards! Sir,
I wonder at it: please you to give me leave
To touch the door, I'll try an the lock be changed.
LOVEWIT: It amazes me!
FACE (*goes to the door*): Good faith, sir, I believe
There's no such thing: 'tis all *deceptio visus*.[392] —
Would I could get him away. (*Aside*.)
DAPPER (*within*): Master captain! master doctor!

[390] arrant whore [391] an older insane asylum than Bethlehem [392] optical illusion

LOVEWIT: Who's that?
FACE: Our clerk within, that I forgot! (*Aside.*) I know not, sir.
DAPPER (*within*): For God's sake, when will her grace be at leisure?
FACE: Ha!
Illusions, some spirit 'o the air! — His gag is melted,
And now he sets out the throat.[393] (*Aside.*)
DAPPER (*within*): I am almost stifled ——
FACE: Would you were together.[394] (*Aside.*)
LOVEWIT: 'Tis in the house.
Ha! list.
FACE: Believe it, sir, in the air.
LOVEWIT: Peace, you.
DAPPER (*within*): Mine aunt's grace does not use me well.
SUBTLE: (*within*): You fool,
Peace, you'll mar all.
FACE (*speaks through the keyhole, while* LOVEWIT *advances to the door unobserved*): Or you will else, you rogue.
LOVEWIT: O, is it so? then you converse with spirits! —
Come, sir. No more of your tricks, good Jeremy.
The truth, the shortest way.
FACE: Dismiss this rabble, sir. —
What shall I do? I am catched. (*Aside.*)
LOVEWIT: Good neighbours,
I thank you all. You may depart. (*Exeunt* NEIGHBOURS.) — Come, sir,
You know that I am an indulgent master;
And therefore conceal nothing. What's your medicine,
To draw so many several sorts of wild fowl?
FACE: Sir, you were wont to affect mirth and wit —
But here's no place to talk on't in the street.
Give me but leave to make the best of my fortune,
And only pardon me the abuse of your house:
It's all I beg. I'll help you to a widow,
In recompense, that you shall give me thanks for,
Will make you seven years younger, and a rich one.
'Tis but your putting on a Spanish cloak:
I have her within. You need not fear the house:
It was not visited.
LOVEWIT: But by me, who came
Sooner than you expected.
FACE: It is true, sir.

393 shoots off his mouth 394 altogether

'Pray you forgive me.
LOVEWIT: Well: let's see your widow. *(Exeunt.)*

Scene II [*A Room in the same.*]

(Enter SUBTLE, *leading in* DAPPER, *with his eyes bound as before.)*

SUBTLE: How! have you eaten your gag?
DAPPER: Yes, faith, it crumbled
Away in my mouth.
SUBTLE: You have spoiled all then.
DAPPER: No!
I hope my aunt of Fairy will forgive me.
SUBTLE: Your aunt's a gracious lady; but in troth
You were to blame.
DAPPER: The fume did overcome me,
And I did do't to stay my stomach. Pray you
So satisfy her grace.

(Enter FACE *in his uniform.)*

Here comes the captain.
FACE: How how! is his mouth down?
SUBTLE: Ay, he has spoken!
FACE: A pox, I heard him, and you too. He's undone then.—
I have been fain to say, the house is haunted
With spirits, to keep churl [395] back.
SUBTLE: And hast thou done it?
FACE: Sure, for this night.
SUBTLE: Why, then triumph and sing
Of Face so famous, the precious king
Of present wits.
FACE: Did you not hear the coil [396]
About the door?
SUBTLE: Yes, and I dwindled [397] with it.
FACE: Show him his aunt, and let him be dispatched:
I'll send her to you. *(Exit* FACE.*)*
SUBTLE: Well, sir, your aunt her grace
Will give you audience presently, on my suit,
And the captain's word that you did not eat your gag
In any contempt of her highness. *(Unbinds his eyes.)*
DAPPER: Not I, in troth, sir.

[395] countryman, *i.e.*, Lovewit [396] disturbance [397] shrank

(*Enter* DOL COMMON *like the Queen of Fairy.*)

SUBTLE: Here she is come. Down o' your knees and wriggle:
  She has a stately presence. (DAPPER *kneels and shuffles toward her.*)
      Good! Yet nearer,
  And bid, God save you!
DAPPER: Madam!
SUBTLE: And your aunt.
DAPPER: And my most gracious aunt, God save your grace.
DOL: Nephew, we thought to have been angry with you;
  But that sweet face of yours hath turned the tide,
  And made it flow with joy, that ebbed of love.
  Arise, and touch our velvet gown.
SUBTLE: The skirts,
  And kiss 'em. So!
DOL: Let me now stroke that head.
  Much, nephew, shalt thou win, much shalt thou spend;
  Much shalt thou give away, much shalt thou lend.
SUBTLE: Ay, much! indeed. (*Aside.*) Why do you not thank her grace?
DAPPER: I cannot speak for joy.
SUBTLE: See, the kind wretch!
  Your grace's kinsman's right.
DOL: Give me the bird.
  Here is your fly in a purse, about your neck, cousin;
  Wear it, and feed it about this day sev'n-night
  On your right wrist——
SUBTLE: Open a vein with a pin.
  And let it suck but once a week; till then,
  You must not look on't.
DOL: No: and, kinsman,
  Bear yourself worthy of the blood you come on.
SUBTLE: Her grace would have you eat no more Woolsack [398] pies,
  No Dagger[398] frumenty.[399]
DOL: Nor break his fast
  In Heaven and Hell.[398]
SUBTLE: She's with you everywhere!
  Nor play with costarmongers, at mumchance, tray-trip,
  God make you rich;[400] (when as your aunt has done it;)
  But keep
  The gallant'st company, and the best games——
DAPPER: Yes, sir.

[398] names of taverns [399] frumenty, wheat boiled in milk [400] games of chance

SUBTLE: Gleek and primero: and what you get, be true to us.
DAPPER: By this hand, I will.
SUBTLE: You may bring's a thousand pound
Before to-morrow night, if but three thousand
Be stirring, an you will.
DAPPER: I swear I will then.
SUBTLE: Your fly will learn[401] you all games.
FACE (*within*): Have you done there?
SUBTLE: Your grace will command him no more duties?
DOL: No:
But come, and see me often. I may chance
To leave him three or four hundred chests of treasure,
And some twelve thousand acres of fairy land,
If he game well and comely with good gamesters.
SUBTLE: There's a kind aunt: kiss her departing part.—
But you must sell your forty mark a year now.
DAPPER: Ay, sir, I mean.
SUBTLE: Or, give 't away; pox on't!
DAPPER: I'll give 't mine aunt: I'll go and fetch the writings. (*Exit.*)
SUBTLE: 'Tis well, away.

(*Re-enter* FACE.)

FACE: Where's Subtle?
SUBTLE: Here: what news?
FACE: Drugger is at the door, go take his suit,
And bid him fetch a parson presently:
Say he shall marry the widow. Thou shalt spend
A hundred pound by the service! (*Exit* SUBTLE.)
Now, Queen Dol,
Have you packed up all?
DOL: Yes.
FACE: And how do you like
The Lady Pliant?
DOL: A good dull innocent.

(*Re-enter* SUBTLE.)

SUBTLE: Here's your Hieronimo's cloak and hat.
FACE: Give me them.
SUBTLE: And the ruff too?
FACE: Yes; I'll come to you presently. (*Exit.*)
SUBTLE: Now he is gone about his project, Dol,

401 teach

I told you of, for the widow.
DOL: 'Tis direct
Against our articles.[402]
SUBTLE: Well, we will fit him, wench.
Hast thou gulled her of her jewels or her bracelets?
DOL: No; but I will do 't.
SUBTLE: Soon at night, my Dolly,
When we are shipped, and all our goods aboard,
Eastward for Ratcliff; we will turn our course
To Brainford, westward, if thou sayst the word,
And take our leaves of this o'erweening rascal,
This peremptory Face.
DOL: Content, I'm weary of him.
SUBTLE: Thou'st cause, when the slave will run a wiving, Dol,
Against the instrument that was drawn between us.
DOL: I'll pluck his bird as bare as I can.
SUBTLE: Yes, tell her
She must by any means address some present
To the cunning man, make him amend for wronging
His art with her suspicion; send a ring,
Or chain of pearl; she will be tortured else
Extremely in her sleep, say, and have strange things
Come to her. Wilt thou?
DOL: Yes.
SUBTLE: My fine flitter-mouse,[403]
My bird o' the night! we'll tickle it at the Pigeons,[404]
When we have all, and may unlock the trunks,
And say, this's mine, and thine; and thine, and mine. (*They kiss.*)

(*Re-enter* FACE.)

FACE: What now! a billing?
SUBTLE: Yes, a little exalted
In the good passage of our stock-affairs.
FACE: Drugger has brought his parson; take him in, Subtle,
And send Nab back again to wash his face.
SUBTLE: I will: and shave himself? (*Exit.*)
FACE: If you can get him.
DOL: You are hot upon it, Face, whate'er it is!
FACE: A trick that Dol shall spend ten pound a month by.

(*Re-enter* SUBTLE.)

Is he gone?

[402] *i.e.*, of agreement [403] bat [404] tavern at Brentford

SUBTLE: The chaplain waits you in the hall, sir.
FACE: I'll go bestow him. (*Exit.*)
DOL: He'll now marry her instantly.
SUBTLE: He cannot yet, he is not ready. Dear Dol,
Cozen her of all thou canst. To deceive him
Is no deceit, but justice, that would break
Such an inextricable tie as ours was.
DOL: Let me alone to fit him.

(*Re-enter* FACE.)

FACE: Come, my venturers,
You have packed up all? where be the trunks? bring forth.
SUBTLE: Here.
FACE: Let us see them. Where's the money?
SUBTLE: Here.
In this.
FACE: Mammon's ten pound; eight score before:
The brethren's money this. Drugger's and Dapper's.
What paper's that?
DOL: The jewel of the waiting maid's,
That stole it from her lady, to know certain ——
FACE: If she should have precedence of her mistress.
DOL: Yes.
FACE: What box is that?
SUBTLE: The fish-wives' rings, I think,
And the ale-wives' single money.[405] Is't not, Dol?
DOL: Yes; and the whistle that the sailor's wife
Brought you to know an her husband were with Ward.[406]
FACE: We'll wet it to-morrow; and our silver beakers
And tavern cups. Where be the French petticoats
And girdles and hangers?[407]
SUBTLE: Here, in the trunk,
And the bolts of lawn.[408]
FACE: Is Drugger's damask there,
And the tobacco?
SUBTLE: Yes.
FACE: Give me the keys.
DOL: Why you the keys?
SUBTLE: No matter, Dol; because
We shall not open them before he comes.
FACE: 'Tis true, you shall not open them, indeed;

[405] small change [406] John Ward (fl. 1603-1615), a notorious pirate
[407] loops by which swords were hung [408] rolls

Nor have them forth, do you see? not forth, Dol.

DOL: No!

FACE: No, my smock-rampant. The right is, my master
Knows all, has pardoned me, and he will keep them;
Doctor, 'tis true — you look — for all your figures:
I send for him, indeed. Wherefore, good partners,
Both he and she be satisfied; for here
Determines[409] the indenture[410] tripartite
'Twixt Subtle, Dol, and Face. All I can do
Is to help you over the wall, o' the back-side,
Or lend you a sheet to save your velvet gown, Dol.
Here will be officers presently, bethink you
Of some course suddenly to 'scape the dock;
For thither you will come else. (*Loud knocking.*) Hark you, thunder.

SUBTLE: You are a precious fiend!

OFFICER (*without*): Open the door.

FACE: Dol, I am sorry for thee i' faith; but hearst thou?
It shall go hard but I will place thee somewhere:
Thou shalt have my letter to Mistress Amo ——

DOL: Hang you!

FACE: Or Madam Cæsarean.

DOL: Pox upon you, rogue,
Would I had but time to beat thee!

FACE: Subtle,
Let's know where you set up next; I will send you
A customer now and then, for old acquaintance:
What new course have you?

SUBTLE: Rogue, I'll hang myself;
That I may walk a greater devil than thou,
And haunt thee in the flock-bed [411] and the buttery. (*Exeunt.*)

Scene III [*An outer Room in the same.*]

(*Enter* LOVEWIT *in the Spanish dress, with the* PARSON.)

(*Loud knocking at the door.*)

LOVEWIT: What do you mean, my masters?

MAMMON (*without*): Open your door,
Cheaters, bawds, conjurers.

OFFICER (*without*): Or we will break it open.

LOVEWIT: What warrant have you?

[409] terminates [410] contract [411] a bed stuffed with pieces of wool or cloth

OFFICER (*without*): Warrant enough, sir, doubt not,
If you'll not open it.
LOVEWIT: Is there an officer there?
OFFICER (*without*): Yes, two or three for failing.[412]
LOVEWIT: Have but patience,
And I will open it straight.

(*Enter* FACE, *as butler.*)

FACE: Sir, have you done?
Is it a marriage? perfect?
LOVEWIT: Yes, my brain.
FACE: Off with your ruff and cloak then: be yourself, sir.
SURLY (*without*): Down with the door.
KASTRIL (*without*): 'Slight, ding[413] it open.
LOVEWIT (*opening the door*): Hold,
Hold, gentlemen, what means this violence?

(MAMMON, SURLY, KASTRIL, ANANIAS, TRIBULATION, *and* OFFICERS *rush in.*)

MAMMON: Where is this collier?
SURLY: And my Captain Face?
MAMMON: These day owls.[414]
SURLY: That are birding in men's purses.
MAMMON: Madam suppository.
KASTRIL: Doxy, my suster.
ANANIAS: Locusts
Of the foul pit.
TRIBULATION: Profane as Bel and the Dragon.
ANANIAS: Worse than the grasshoppers, or the lice of Egypt.
LOVEWIT: Good gentlemen, hear me. Are you officers,
And cannot stay this violence?
1ST OFFICER: Keep the peace.
LOVEWIT: Gentlemen, what is the matter? whom do you seek?
MAMMON: The chemical cozener.
SURLY: And the captain pander.
KASTRIL: The nun[415] my suster.
MAMMON: Madam Rabbi.
ANANIAS: Scorpions.
And caterpillars.
LOVEWIT: Fewer at once, I pray you.

412 *i.e.*, for fear of failing 413 break 414 because they have done dark deeds in the daytime? 415 *i.e.*, whore

1ST OFFICER: One after another, gentlemen, I charge you,
By virtue of my staff.
ANANIAS: They are the vessels
Of pride, lust, and the cart.
LOVEWIT: Good zeal, lie still
A little while.
TRIBULATION: Peace, Deacon Ananias.
LOVEWIT: The house is mine here, and the doors are open;
If there be any such persons as you seek for,
Use your authority, search on o' God's name.
I am but newly come to town, and finding
This tumult 'bout my door, to tell you true,
It somewhat mazed me; till my man here, fearing
My more[416] displeasure, told me he had done
Somewhat an insolent part, let out my house
(Belike presuming on my known aversion
From any air o' the town while there was sickness),
To a doctor and a captain: who, what they are
Or where they be, he knows not.
MAMMON: Are they gone?
LOVEWIT: You may go in and search, sir. (MAMMON, ANANIAS *and* TRIBULATION *go in.*) Here, I find
The empty walls worse than I left them, smoked,
A few cracked pots, and glasses, and a furnace;
The ceiling filled with poesies of the candle,
And madam with a dildo[417] writ o' the walls:
Only one gentlewoman I met here
That is within, that said she was a widow ——
KASTRIL: Ay, that's my suster; I'll go thump her. Where is she?
(*Goes in.*)
LOVEWIT: And should have married a Spanish count, but he,
When he came to't, neglected her so grossly,
That I, a widower, am gone through with her.
SURLY: How! have I lost her then?
LOVEWIT: Were you the don, sir?
Good faith, now she does blame you extremely, and says
You swore, and told her you had taken the pains
To dye your beard, and umbre[418] o'er your face,
Borrowed a suit, and ruff, all for her love:
And then did nothing. What an oversight,
And want of putting forward, sir, was this!

416 greater 417 artificial phallus (The whole phrase may be the title of an obscene ballad.) 418 shadow (v.)

Well fare an old harquebusier[419] yet,
Could prime his powder, and give fire, and hit,
All in a twinkling!

(*Re-enter* MAMMON.)

MAMMON: The whole nest are fled!
LOVEWIT: What sort of birds were they?
MAMMON: A kind of choughs,[420]
Or thievish daws, sir, that have picked my purse
Of eight score and ten pound within these five weeks,
Beside my first materials; and my goods,
That lie in the cellar, which I am glad they have left,
I may have home yet.
LOVEWIT: Think you so, sir?
MAMMON: Ay.
LOVEWIT: By order of law, sir, but not otherwise.
MAMMON: Not mine own stuff!
LOVEWIT: Sir, I can take no knowledge
That they are yours, but by public means.
If you can bring certificate that you were gulled of them,
Or any formal writ out of a court,
That you did cozen yourself, I will not hold them.
MAMMON: I'll rather lose them.
LOVEWIT: That you shall not, sir,
By me, in troth: upon these terms, they are yours.
What, should they have been, sir, turned into gold, all?
MAMMON: No.
I cannot tell — it may be they should — What then?
LOVEWIT: What a great loss in hope have you sustained!
MAMMON: Not I, the commonwealth has.
FACE: Ay, he would have built
The city new; and made a ditch about it
Of silver, should have run with cream from Hogsden;
That every Sunday in Moorfields the younkers,[421]
And tits and tom-boys[422] should have fed on, gratis.
MAMMON: I will go mount a turnip-cart, and preach
The end of the world within these two months. Surly,
What! in a dream?
SURLY: Must I needs cheat myself,
With that same foolish vice of honesty!
Come, let us go and hearken[423] out the rogues:

419 musketeer 420 crows 421 youths 422 young wenches 423 search

That Face I'll mark for mine, if e'er I meet him.

FACE: If I can hear of him, sir, I'll bring you word
Unto your lodging; for in troth, they were strangers
To me, I thought them honest as myself, sir.

(*Exeunt* MAMMON *and* SURLY.)

(*Re-enter* ANANIAS *and* TRIBULATION.)

TRIBULATION: 'Tis well, the saints shall not lose all yet. Go
And get some carts ——

LOVEWIT: For what, my zealous friends?

ANANIAS: To bear away the portion of the righteous
Out of this den of thieves.

LOVEWIT: What is that portion?

ANANIAS: The goods sometimes the orphans', that the brethren
Bought with their silver pence.

LOVEWIT: What, those in the cellar,
The knight Sir Mammon claims?

ANANIAS: I do defy
The wicked Mammon, so do all the brethren,
Thou profane man! I ask thee with what conscience
Thou canst advance that idol against us,
That have the seal? [424] were not the shillings numbered
That made the pounds; were not the pounds told out
Upon the second day of the fourth week,
In the eighth month, upon the table dormant,[425]
The year of the last patience of the saints,
Six hundred and ten?

LOVEWIT: Mine earnest vehement botcher,
And deacon also, I cannot dispute with you:
But if you get you not away the sooner,
I shall confute you with a cudgel.

ANANIAS: Sir!

TRIBULATION: Be patient, Ananias.

ANANIAS: I am strong,
And will stand up, well girt, against a host
That threaten Gad in exile.

LOVEWIT: I shall send you
To Amsterdam, to your cellar.

ANANIAS: I will pray there,
Against thy house: may dogs defile thy walls,
And wasps and hornets breed beneath thy roof,

[424] *i.e.*, the elect [425] permanent side table

This seat of falsehood, and this cave of cozenage!
(*Exeunt* ANANIAS *and* TRIBULATION.)

(*Enter* DRUGGER.)

LOVEWIT: Another too?
DRUGGER: Not I, sir, I am no brother.
LOVEWIT (*beats him*): Away, you Harry Nicholas! [426] do you talk?
(*Exit* DRUGGER.)

FACE: No, this was Abel Drugger. Good sir, go, (*To the* PARSON.)
And satisfy him; tell him all is done:
He staid too long a washing of his face.
The doctor, he shall hear of him at Westchester;
And of the captain, tell him, at Yarmouth, or
Some good port-town else, lying for a wind. (*Exit* PARSON.)
If you can get off the angry child now, sir ——

(*Enter* KASTRIL, *dragging in his sister.*)

KASTRIL: Come on, you ewe, you have matched most sweetly, have you not?
Did not I say, I would never have you tupped [427]
But by a dubbed boy,[428] to make you a lady-tom?
'Slight, you are a mammet! [429] O, I could touse[430] you now.
Death, mun' [431] you marry with a pox!
LOVEWIT: You lie, boy!
As sound as you; and I'm aforehand with you.
KASTRIL: Anon!
LOVEWIT: Come, will you quarrel? I will feize[432] you, sirrah;
Why do you not buckle to your tools?
KASTRIL: Od's light,
This is a fine old boy as e'er I saw!
LOVEWIT: What, do you change your copy[433] now? proceed,
Here stands my dove: stoop[434] at her if you dare.
KASTRIL: 'Slight, I must love him! I cannot choose, i' faith,
An I should be hanged for't! Suster, I protest,
I honour thee for this match.
LOVEWIT: Oh, do you so, sir?
KASTRIL: Yes, and thou canst take tobacco and drink, old boy,
I'll give her five hundred pound more to her marriage,
Than her own state.

[426] 1502-1580?, Anabaptist mystic, founder of the sect "the Family of Love"
[427] "tupping" is the mating of ram and ewe. (Cf. *Othello*, note 23.) [428] *i.e.*, knight [429] puppet [430] handle roughly [431] must [432] frighten away
[433] "tune" [434] swoop ("Kastril" means "young hawk")

LOVEWIT: Fill a pipe full, Jeremy.
FACE: Yes; but go in and take it, sir.
LOVEWIT: We will —
I will be ruled by thee in anything, Jeremy.
KASTRIL: 'Slight, thou art not hide-bound, thou art a jovy[435] boy!
Come, let us in, I pray thee, and take our whiffs.
LOVEWIT: Whiff in with your sister, brother boy. (*Exeunt* KASTRIL *and* DAME PLIANT.) That master
That had received such happiness by a servant,
In such a widow, and with so much wealth,
Were very ungrateful, if he would not be
A little indulgent to that servant's wit,
And help his fortune, though with some small strain
Of his own candour.[436] (*Advancing.*) "Therefore, gentlemen,
And kind spectators, if I have outstript
An old man's gravity, or strict canon, think
What a young wife and a good brain may do;
Stretch age's truth sometimes, and crack it too.
Speak for thyself, knave."
FACE: So I will, sir. (*Advancing to the front of the stage.*) "Gentlemen,
My part a little fell in this last scene,
Yet 'twas decorum.[437] And though I am clean
Got off from Subtle, Surly, Mammon, Dol,
Hot Ananias, Dapper, Drugger, all
With whom I traded; yet I put myself
On you, that are my country:[438] and this pelf,
Which I have got, if you do quit[439] me, rests
To feast you often, and invite new guests." (*Exeunt.*)

The Alchemist is quite literally a contemporary report on Ben Jonson's home town. It was written in 1610 and produced at the Globe theater by the King's Men that same year, presumably soon after the theaters had reopened in the fall, after the plague season. As the references to Dame Pliant's age (II, 1, and IV, 2) and to the date of the brethren's hoped-for "projection" of Mammon's iron goods (III, 2) establish the time of the action as that very same fall of 1610, Lovewit, just back in town with the arrival of cool and safe weather, may be thought to have seen himself on the Globe stage.

It was suggested earlier that the Globe's freedom from stage illu-

[435] jovial [436] integrity, honesty [437] *i.e.*, dramatic propriety [438] *i.e.*, jury
[439] acquit

sion invited the spectator's imaginative participation in the action. In *The Alchemist,* its inner stage could with equal ease represent the interior of Lovewit's house in the street scenes and Subtle's study or Dol Common's boudoir in the indoor scenes. Yet, it is probably true that the structure and the staging conventions of the Elizabethan theater influenced Shakespeare's playwriting practice to a greater extent than they did Jonson's. This, at any rate, is what the different nature of their respective plays suggests: Shakespeare's are fluid and panoramic, Jonson's classically focussed.

It is Jonson's distinction among Elizabethan playwrights that he combines classical erudition and temperament with a realistic bent. In *The Alchemist* the classicism is evident in the generalized concepts of ethics and psychology, in the wryly dispassionate quality of the whole exhibit of vice and folly, and in the tightness of the dramatic structure.* The realism is evident in the robust relish and the fullness of detail with which Jonson evokes the seamy fringes of the London underworld and its gallery of crooks and dupes. Whether the cynical outcome of the plot is an aspect of classicism or of realism is a moot point, but the use of type characters motivated by an overriding bias or eccentricity ("humor") † as comedic agents reflects both classical and medieval theories of human psychology that still were potent in the Renaissance, if mainly as literary convention. The querulous Kastril and the sensualist Sir Epicure Mammon are examples. And classicism and realism together account for the continuing value of the play as dramatic art — a value best expressed, perhaps, in the formula of "the concrete universal." Not *in spite* of but partly *because* of its powerful local color of time and place *The Alchemist* will seem dated only when confidence games are a thing of the past, that is, when people no longer rise to the chance of getting something for nothing. Timeless cupidities converge on Subtle's shop: Drugger's prudence seeking necromantic aid to ensure business profits, Sir Epicure's lust seeking the philosopher's stone to realize its gorgeous dreams. Greed begets gulls. But the fate of the grasping visionary who is the prototype of all the gulls in the play would seem less relevant as enduring moral *exemplum* were he less plausibly real in each of his various versions and less solidly placed in his social contexts.

* The more specific formal requirement that plays observe the three unities was a rule established by Renaissance neoclassicists who over-interpreted Aristotle and was not a standard convention of classical drama itself.

† In pre-modern physiology, "humor" referred to one of the four main bodily fluids, blood, phlegm, black and yellow bile. Imbalance among them was supposed to result in some prevailing disposition of mind or temper ("humor" in a looser sense), like melancholy or avarice or the misanthrope Alceste's hatred of social man's common foibles.

The timelessness of the play's montage of foolish greed goes far to remove the need for complete understanding of the topical allusions, rogue's slang, and alchemist's jargon which are so much a part of the contemporary setting. If much inevitably is lost for a modern reader and if footnotes at best can furnish only explanation and not the rich fullness of connotation which the terms held for the contemporary Londoner, enough remains for the characters to establish themselves in our imaginations with the authority of scenic life and to produce in us that salutary twinge of self-recognition without which serious comedy fails to serve its purpose. In the particular case of the terms of alchemy it may even be held that a degree of strangeness and incomprehension is functional. The jargon anesthetizes skepticism with a sense of vast and awesome occultism — exactly as Subtle intends it to do. But even references to taverns and brothels, foods and public events, alchemists and religious fanatics, are sufficiently well understood when footnotes have helped to make them part of the teeming image of life in early seventeenth-century London.

The descriptive and symbolical or allusive names break with strict realism, but they justify themselves as short cuts to characterization — conventional in humor comedy — somewhat in the manner of the allegorical personifications of vices and virtues in medieval morality plays. Dame Pliant's entire nature is summed up in her name; that of Face (Jeremy, Lungs, Ulenspiegel) represents the elaborate mask of Subtle's establishment, the beguilement motif of the whole play; with Tribulation Wholesome the audience knows it is in for some good fun at the expense of long-faced Puritans; and no one is likely to lose his moral bearings with names like Dol Common and Sir Epicure Mammon. If the convention of descriptive naming precludes psychological complexity in the vein of modern realism, there is compensating gain: quietly and effectively the expectation of seeing the names enacted becomes part of the dramatic suspense. Modern readers are not always sufficiently aware of the fact that older drama did not so much seek to surprise its audiences as to gratify the expectations aroused by their knowledge of literary genre and convention.

Most of the characters fall into one or the other of the two groups of knaves and fools (cheats and gulls, cozeners and cozened). Subtle, Face, and Dol Common make up the former group. That the victims either arrive in or tend to group themselves in pairs — Dapper and Drugger, Mammon and Surly, Ananias and Tribulation Wholesome, Kastril and Dame Pliant — somehow slyly impugns their individuality and independence of judgment. Only Lovewit remains outside of either group, a *deus ex machina* figure both in a metaphorical and in a dramaturgical sense. In the former he is the master reasserting his authority. In the latter he is the outsider whose unexpected return unties the dramatic knot.

Surly, too, resists the neatness of classification to which the other victims of the alchemist gang submit. *The Alchemist* is essentially a farce, because it is first of all a comedy of situation and of human type and only secondarily and by implication one of theme or of psychological or philosophical complexity. But Surly is not really a farcical figure. He is a profound skeptic and not a naive dupe like his friend Mammon. As Dame Pliant's overreached suitor he ends up among the victims of cheat, after all, but that is due to bad luck and to Lovewit's sharp dealings and not to his own greed and gullibility. In fact, both Surly and Lovewit are something like problem characters, denizens of a realm of acid irony rather than one of simple and boisterous farce. Without breaking the decorum of farce they give the play its astringent tone, without which the farce would have failed to be — also — great comedy.

For Surly's personality and Lovewit's morality are both ambiguous. As his name indicates Surly is not an attractive character, but he *does* represent virtue, resourcefully (and even with a kind of grim humor) taking action against villainy. And yet, Jonson allows him to be silenced in the debate with Subtle on the "naturalness" of alchemy in II, 1. And though we probably find Dame Pliant less of a prize catch than do Face, Subtle, Drugger, Surly, and Lovewit, the facts are that she is rich and eminently nubile, that Surly rescues her from what is (among other things) a bawdy house, that he wants to marry her, and that his intentions are gratuitously defeated by Face acting on behalf of his master in order to gain his forgiveness for his own knavery. Lovewit has good nature and a boyish, easygoing charm in his favor, but his crucially self-defining speech, "I love a teeming wit as I love my nourishment," marks him, too, as a kind of humor character with all the humor character's susceptibility to moral aberration. His bias condones the crimes in which his servant has been an accomplice, of which his own house has been the scene, and from which he profits. His retention of Mammon's property is morally if not judicially dubious, and he wins his wife by a trick. Reading the play as symbolic action, Lovewit's escape from the pest-ridden town represents a citizen's selfish surrender of responsibility that allows the body politic (the house) to be usurped by moral disorder (the misrule of Face and his fellow cheats). The pestilence is a metaphor for contagious greed and lust. And so far from bringing about the purgation of the infected house by the hands of its just and vengeful master, Lovewit's return simply substitutes the master's indulgent and mercenary amorality, which ownership makes respectable, for the servant's more flagrant but hardly more vicious criminality. The festering disease has only been plastered over, not cured. The play ends, not in the triumph of poetic justice but in a complacent shrug and a crooked grin at the wicked ways of the world. It is Face, the consummate double-crosser and escape artist, who has the last word.

In a larger context the conclusion may be regarded as part of an exposé of some of the more unsavory forms of the individual economic enterprise that was one of the most vital and viable aspects of the Renaissance. Both master and servant represent the new economic man: the bright, agile, jovial, enterprising, and unprincipled opportunist. The almost innocent acquisitiveness of the pious Puritan is part of the same general cultural complex that the play so deftly probes. "Peace to the household! — Casting of dollars is concluded lawful," Ananias intones as he returns to Subtle and Face in IV, 4.

In such a view of the play, Subtle, the alchemist, is hardly the most prominent or memorable character. But the structural importance of his profession is rightly recognized in the title. It is alchemy, as a plausible pretext for the unity of time and place, that unifies the action. This, too, reflects a fact of the time. Condemned by religion, yet clandestinely condoned and even pursued by Catholic and Protestant clergy alike, part science, part vision, part mystical rite, part foolishness, part humbug, food for men's dreams, an object for their ridicule and vilification, believed in, feared, exploited, indicted, laughed at — alchemy was a wonderfully centripetal device by which to cast wide the satirist's net within the limits of a single action. Jonson never grants alchemy the least bit of credence, but his play does not obscure the appeal it actually held for some quite powerful contemporary minds. Subtle, too, is appropriately named. His dialectic victory over Surly in II, 1, is not just a matter of confidence man glibness but of cogent reasoning which even today has a certain impressiveness.

But the unity of action goes beyond the circumstance that the alchemist–necromancer–astrologer is sought by a crowd of diverse but equally gullible clients. Their fortunes don't just converge; they make a mesh. Dame Pliant is a magnetic lady whose attractions cause a complex of rivalries. Drugger's ambition to marry her brings about the defeat not only of his own but also of Surly's suit. Mammon's session with Dol forces Subtle and Face to use Dame Pliant as a bawd to hold the rich Spanish don. The nature of Surly's disguise plays into Lovewit's hands and turns Kastril and Drugger into his and Face's pawns in the game for the wealthy widow. Mammon's hardware is bought by the brethren. Face enlists the aid of Ananias and Kastril to force Surly to withdraw in IV, 4. Dapper, finally, frames the entire sequence of cozening transactions by being both the first and the last customer.

The action is continuous; that is, imaginative (or "ideal") time coincides with theater (or acting) time. The result is compression of action and heightening of realistic immediacy. In the last two acts the pace accelerates to a crescendo of sudden turns and counterturns, of intricately timed exits and entrances, schemes upset and escapes improvised, which at a first reading (but not in performance) is likely to leave the reader numb with a sense of swift, kaleidoscopic chaos. Actually, the crisis and the denouement represent a piece of brilliant dramatic construction, best perceived, perhaps, if one reads the play a second time with an eye on a single strand of action and its function in the whole — say, the fortunes of the Spanish costume which Drugger brings to marry the widow in, or the transactions involving the iron goods in the cellar, or the combination of lust, greed, and the middle-class male's sexual bigotry in Subtle's and Face's deals concerning Dame Pliant. As keen a critic as Coleridge thought the plot of *The Alchemist* one of the "three most perfect . . . ever planned" (the other two being those of *Oedipus Rex* and Fielding's *Tom Jones*).

Only in *Volpone* and *The Alchemist* did Jonson transcend the limitations of human stereotypes and of diffuse action characteristic of such pure humor comedies as *Every Man In* and *Out of His Humour,* of the ineradicable triviality of even a superior farce like *The Silent Woman,* and of the panoramic shapelessness of the social realism of *Bartholomew Fair.* But unlike *Volpone, The Alchemist* does not provide shuddering vistas into the depths of human depravity. Subtle and Face are engaging rascals — partly because their machinations have no really serious consequences. The fools of greed get only what they deserve, and the suddenness of the innocent Dame Pliant's marriage need not disturb us since she is too true to her name ever to be unhappy and too null really to matter. There are no tragic overtones in *The Alchemist,* as there are in *Volpone* and in Molière's *Misanthrope.* But there are compensations: in comparison with *Volpone* comic zest and plausibility, in comparison with *The Misanthrope* suspense and sheer fun.

And like these other comedies *The Alchemist* is an achievement of a kind of poetry that does not simply convey but generates moral meanings and dramatic structures, by means of variations in dialogue content and modulations of dialogue tones. One example will have to suffice. Act I begins with the stark, uglily abrupt vulgarities of Face and Subtle, Act II with the almost hypnotic magnificence of image and rhythm in Mammon's visions of sensual delights — a poetic indulgence of Marlovian dimensions in "the fury of men's gullets and their groins," as Jonson was to put it in *The Staple of News*. The juxtaposition amounts to satiric hits against both sets of values and both modes of discourse, and the range in tone measures not just Jonson's versatility as a mimic of the languages of proletarian vituperation and aristocratic daydream, but also the mature inclusiveness of the neoclassical realist's vision of greed and folly.

Molière

THE MISANTHROPE

English Version by Richard Wilbur

Characters

ALCESTE, *in love with Célimène*
PHILINTE, *Alceste's friend*
ORONTE, *in love with Célimène*
CÉLIMÈNE, *Alceste's beloved*
ÉLIANTE, *Célimène's cousin*
ARSINOÉ, *a friend of Célimène's*
ACASTE, CLITANDRE } *Marquesses*
BASQUE, *Célimène's servant*
A GUARD *of the Marshalsea*
DUBOIS, *Alceste's valet*

The Scene throughout is in Célimène's house at Paris.

ACT I

Scene 1 [PHILINTE, ALCESTE]

PHILINTE: Now, what's got into you?
ALCESTE (*seated*): Kindly leave me alone.
PHILINTE: Come, come, what is it? This lugubrious tone . . .
ALCESTE: Leave me, I said; you spoil my solitude.

PHILINTE: Oh, listen to me, now, and don't be rude.
ALCESTE: I choose to be rude, Sir, and to be hard of hearing.
PHILINTE: These ugly moods of yours are not endearing;
Friends though we are, I really must insist . . .
ALCESTE (*abruptly rising*): Friends? Friends, you say? Well, cross me off your list.
I've been your friend till now, as you well know;
But after what I saw a moment ago
I tell you flatly that our ways must part.
I wish no place in a dishonest heart.
PHILINTE: Why, what have I done, Alceste? Is this quite just?
ALCESTE: My God, you ought to die of self-disgust.
I call your conduct inexcusable, Sir,
And every man of honor will concur.
I see you almost hug a man to death,
Exclaim for joy until you're out of breath,
And supplement these loving demonstrations
With endless offers, vows, and protestations;
Then when I ask you "Who was that?" I find
That you can barely bring his name to mind!
Once the man's back is turned, you cease to love him,
And speak with absolute indifference of him!
By God, I say it's base and scandalous
To falsify the heart's affections thus;
If I caught myself behaving in such a way,
I'd hang myself for shame, without delay.
PHILINTE: It hardly seems a hanging matter to me;
I hope that you will take it graciously
If I extend myself a slight reprieve,
And live a little longer, by your leave.
ALCESTE: How dare you joke about a crime so grave?
PHILINTE: What crime? How else are people to behave?
ALCESTE: I'd have them be sincere, and never part
With any word that isn't from the heart.
PHILINTE: When someone greets us with a show of pleasure,
It's but polite to give him equal measure,
Return his love the best that we know how,
And trade him offer for offer, vow for vow.
ALCESTE: No, no, this formula you'd have me follow,
However fashionable, is false and hollow,
And I despise the frenzied operations
Of all these barterers of protestations,
These lavishers of meaningless embraces,

These utterers of obliging commonplaces,
Who court and flatter everyone on earth
And praise the fool no less than the man of worth.
Should you rejoice that someone fondles you,
Offers his love and service, swears to be true,
And fills your ears with praises of your name,
When to the first damned fop he'll say the same?
No, no: no self-respecting heart would dream
Of prizing so promiscuous an esteem;
However high the praise, there's nothing worse
Than sharing honors with the universe.
Esteem is founded on comparison:
To honor all men is to honor none.
Since you embrace this indiscriminate vice,
Your friendship comes at far too cheap a price;
I spurn the easy tribute of a heart
Which will not set the worthy man apart:
I choose, Sir, to be chosen; and in fine,
The friend of mankind is no friend of mine.
PHILINTE: But in polite society, custom decrees
That we show certain outward courtesies. . . .
ALCESTE: Ah, no! we should condemn with all our force
Such false and artificial intercourse.
Let men behave like men; let them display
Their inmost hearts in everything they say;
Let the heart speak, and let our sentiments
Not mask themselves in silly compliments.
PHILINTE: In certain cases it would be uncouth
And most absurd to speak the naked truth;
With all respect for your exalted notions,
It's often best to veil one's true emotions.
Wouldn't the social fabric come undone
If we were wholly frank with everyone?
Suppose you met with someone you couldn't bear;
Would you inform him of it then and there?
ALCESTE: Yes.
PHILINTE: Then you'd tell old Emilie it's pathetic
The way she daubs her features with cosmetic
And plays the gay coquette at sixty-four?
ALCESTE: I would.
PHILINTE: And you'd call Dorilas a bore,
And tell him every ear at court is lame
From hearing him brag about his noble name?

ALCESTE: Precisely.
PHILINTE: Ah, you're joking.
ALCESTE: *Au contraire:*
In this regard there's none I'd choose to spare.
All are corrupt; there's nothing to be seen
In court or town but aggravates my spleen.
I fall into deep gloom and melancholy
When I survey the scene of human folly,
Finding on every hand base flattery,
Injustice, fraud, self-interest, treachery. . . .
Ah, it's too much; mankind has grown so base,
I mean to break with the whole human race.
PHILINTE: This philosophic rage is a bit extreme;
You've no idea how comical you seem;
Indeed, we're like those brothers in the play
Called *School for Husbands,* one of whom was prey . . .
ALCESTE: Enough, now! None of your stupid similes.
PHILINTE: Then let's have no more tirades, if you please.
The world won't change, whatever you say or do;
And since plain speaking means so much to you,
I'll tell you plainly that by being frank
You've earned the reputation of a crank,
And that you're thought ridiculous when you rage
And rant against the manners of the age.
ALCESTE: So much the better; just what I wish to hear.
No news could be more grateful to my ear.
All men are so detestable in my eyes,
I should be sorry if they thought me wise.
PHILINTE: Your hatred's very sweeping, is it not?
ALCESTE: Quite right: I hate the whole degraded lot.
PHILINTE: Must all poor human creatures be embraced,
Without distinction, by your vast distaste?
Even in these bad times, there are surely a few . . .
ALCESTE: No, I include all men in one dim view:
Some men I hate for being rogues; the others
I hate because they treat the rogues like brothers,
And, lacking a virtuous scorn for what is vile,
Receive the villain with a complaisant smile.
Notice how tolerant people choose to be
Toward that bold rascal who's at law with me.
His social polish can't conceal his nature;
One sees at once that he's a treacherous creature;
No one could possibly be taken in

By those soft speeches and that sugary grin.
The whole world knows the shady means by which
The low-brow's grown so powerful and rich,
And risen to a rank so bright and high
That virtue can but blush, and merit sigh.
Whenever his name comes up in conversation,
None will defend his wretched reputation;
Call him knave, liar, scoundrel, and all the rest,
Each head will nod, and no one will protest.
And yet his smirk is seen in every house,
He's greeted everywhere with smiles and bows,
And when there's any honor that can be got
By pulling strings, he'll get it, like as not.
My God! It chills my heart to see the ways
Men come to terms with evil nowadays;
Sometimes, I swear, I'm moved to flee and find
Some desert land unfouled by humankind.

PHILINTE: Come, let's forget the follies of the times
And pardon mankind for its petty crimes;
Let's have an end of rantings and of railings,
And show some leniency toward human failings.
This world requires a pliant rectitude;
Too stern a virtue makes one stiff and rude;
Good sense views all extremes with detestation,
And bids us to be noble in moderation.
The rigid virtues of the ancient days
Are not for us; they jar with all our ways
And ask of us too lofty a perfection.
Wise men accept their times without objection,
And there's no greater folly, if you ask me,
Than trying to reform society.
Like you, I see each day a hundred and one
Unhandsome deeds that might be better done,
But still, for all the faults that meet my view,
I'm never known to storm and rave like you.
I take men as they are, or let them be,
And teach my soul to bear their frailty;
And whether in court or town, whatever the scene,
My phlegm's as philosophic as your spleen.

ALCESTE: This phlegm which you so eloquently commend,
Does nothing ever rile it up, my friend?
Suppose some man you trust should treacherously
Conspire to rob you of your property,

And do his best to wreck your reputation?
Wouldn't you feel a certain indignation?
PHILINTE: Why, no. These faults of which you so complain
Are part of human nature, I maintain,
And it's no more a matter for disgust
That men are knavish, selfish and unjust,
Than that the vulture dines upon the dead,
And wolves are furious, and apes ill-bred.
ALCESTE: Shall I see myself betrayed, robbed, torn to bits,
And not . . . Oh, let's be still and rest our wits.
Enough of reasoning, now. I've had my fill.
PHILINTE: Indeed, you would do well, Sir, to be still.
Rage less at your opponent, and give some thought
To how you'll win this lawsuit that he's brought.
ALCESTE: I assure you I'll do nothing of the sort.
PHILINTE: Then who will plead your case before the court?
ALCESTE: Reason and right and justice will plead for me.
PHILINTE: Oh, Lord. What judges do you plan to see?
ALCESTE: Why, none. The justice of my cause is clear.
PHILINTE: Of course, man; but there's politics to fear. . . .
ALCESTE: No, I refuse to lift a hand. That's flat.
I'm either right, or wrong.
PHILINTE: Don't count on that.
ALCESTE: No, I'll do nothing.
PHILINTE: Your enemy's influence
Is great, you know . . .
ALCESTE: That makes no difference.
PHILINTE: It will; you'll see.
ALCESTE: Must honor bow to guile?
If so, I shall be proud to lose the trial.
PHILINTE: Oh, really . . .
ALCESTE: I'll discover by this case
Whether or not men are sufficiently base
And impudent and villainous and perverse
To do me wrong before the universe.
PHILINTE: What a man!
ALCESTE: Oh, I could wish, whatever the cost,
Just for the beauty of it, that my trial were lost.
PHILINTE: If people heard you talking so, Alceste,
They'd split their sides. Your name would be a jest.
ALCESTE: So much the worse for jesters.
PHILINTE: May I enquire
Whether this rectitude you so admire,

And these hard virtues you're enamored of
Are qualities of the lady whom you love?
It much surprises me that you, who seem
To view mankind with furious disesteem,
Have yet found something to enchant your eyes
Amidst a species which you so despise.
And what is more amazing, I'm afraid,
Is the most curious choice your heart has made.
The honest Éliante is fond of you,
Arsinoé, the prude, admires you too;
And yet your spirit's been perversely led
To choose the flighty Célimène instead,
Whose brittle malice and coquettish ways
So typify the manners of our days.
How is it that the traits you most abhor
Are bearable in this lady you adore?
Are you so blind with love that you can't find them?
Or do you contrive, in her case, not to mind them?

ALCESTE: My love for that young widow's not the kind
That can't perceive defects; no, I'm not blind.
I see her faults, despite my ardent love,
And all I see I fervently reprove.
And yet I'm weak; for all her falsity,
That woman knows the art of pleasing me,
And though I never cease complaining of her,
I swear I cannot manage not to love her.
Her charm outweighs her faults; I can but aim
To cleanse her spirit in my love's pure flame.

PHILINTE: That's no small task; I wish you all success.
You think then that she loves you?

ALCESTE: Heavens, yes!
I wouldn't love her did she not love me.

PHILINTE: Well, if her taste for you is plain to see,
Why do these rivals cause you such despair?

ALCESTE: True love, Sir, is possessive, and cannot bear
To share with all the world. I'm here today
To tell her she must send that mob away.

PHILINTE: If I were you, and had your choice to make,
Éliante, her cousin, would be the one I'd take;
That honest heart, which cares for you alone,
Would harmonize far better with your own.

ALCESTE: True, true: each day my reason tells me so;
But reason doesn't rule in love, you know.

PHILINTE: I fear some bitter sorrow is in store;
This love . . .

Scene 2 [ORONTE, ALCESTE, PHILINTE]

ORONTE (*to* ALCESTE): The servants told me at the door
That Éliante and Célimène were out,
But when I heard, dear Sir, that you were about,
I came to say, without exaggeration,
That I hold you in the vastest admiration,
And that it's always been my dearest desire
To be the friend of one I so admire.
I hope to see my love of merit requited,
And you and I in friendship's bond united.
I'm sure you won't refuse — if I may be frank —
A friend of my devotedness — and rank.

(*During this speech of* ORONTE'S, ALCESTE *is abstracted, and seems unaware that he is being spoken to. He only breaks off his reverie when* ORONTE *says:*)

It was for you, if you please, that my words were intended.
ALCESTE: For me, Sir?
ORONTE: Yes, for you. You're not offended?
ALCESTE: By no means. But this much surprises me. . . .
The honor comes most unexpectedly. . . .
ORONTE: My high regard should not astonish you;
The whole world feels the same. It is your due.
ALCESTE: Sir . . .
ORONTE: Why, in all the State there isn't one
Can match your merits; they shine, Sir, like the sun.
ALCESTE: Sir . . .
ORONTE: You are higher in my estimation
Than all that's most illustrious in the nation.
ALCESTE: Sir . . .
ORONTE: If I lie, may heaven strike me dead!
To show you that I mean what I have said,
Permit me, Sir, to embrace you most sincerely,
And swear that I will prize our friendship dearly.
Give me your hand. And now, Sir, if you choose,
We'll make our vows.
ALCESTE: Sir . . .
ORONTE: What! You refuse?
ALCESTE: Sir, it's a very great honor you extend:

But friendship is a sacred thing, my friend;
It would be profanation to bestow
The name of friend on one you hardly know.
All parts are better played when well-rehearsed;
Let's put off friendship, and get acquainted first.
We may discover it would be unwise
To try to make our natures harmonize.

ORONTE: By heaven! You're sagacious to the core;
This speech has made me admire you even more.
Let time, then, bring us closer day by day;
Meanwhile, I shall be yours in every way.
If, for example, there should be anything
You wish at court, I'll mention it to the King.
I have his ear, of course; it's quite well known
That I am much in favor with the throne.
In short, I am your servant. And now, dear friend,
Since you have such fine judgment, I intend
To please you, if I can, with a small sonnet
I wrote not long ago. Please comment on it,
And tell me whether I ought to publish it.

ALCESTE: You must excuse me, Sir; I'm hardly fit
To judge such matters.

ORONTE: Why not?

ALCESTE: I am, I fear,
Inclined to be unfashionably sincere.

ORONTE: Just what I ask; I'd take no satisfaction
In anything but your sincere reaction.
I beg you not to dream of being kind.

ALCESTE: Since you desire it, Sir, I'll speak my mind.

ORONTE: *Sonnet*. It's a sonnet. . . . *Hope* . . . The poem's addressed
To a lady who wakened hopes within my breast.
Hope . . . this is not the pompous sort of thing,
Just modest little verses, with a tender ring.

ALCESTE: Well, we shall see.

ORONTE: *Hope* . . . I'm anxious to hear
Whether the style seems properly smooth and clear,
And whether the choice of words is good or bad.

ALCESTE: We'll see, we'll see.

ORONTE: Perhaps I ought to add
That it took me only a quarter-hour to write it.

ALCESTE: The time's irrelevant, Sir: kindly recite it.

ORONTE (*reading*):

Hope comforts us awhile, 'tis true,

Lulling our cares with careless laughter,
And yet such joy is full of rue,
My Phyllis, if nothing follows after.

PHILINTE: I'm charmed by this already; the style's delightful.

ALCESTE (*sotto voce, to* PHILINTE): How can you say that? Why, the thing is frightful.

ORONTE:
Your fair face smiled on me awhile,
But was it kindness so to enchant me?
'Twould have been fairer not to smile,
If hope was all you meant to grant me.

PHILINTE: What a clever thought! How handsomely you phrase it!

ALCESTE (*sotto voce, to* PHILINTE): You know the thing is trash. How dare you praise it?

ORONTE:
If it's to be my passion's fate
Thus everlastingly to wait,
Then death will come to set me free:
For death is fairer than the fair;
Phyllis, to hope is to despair
When one must hope eternally.

PHILINTE: The close is exquisite — full of feeling and grace.

ALCESTE (*sotto voce, aside*): Oh, blast the close; you'd better close your face
Before you send your lying soul to hell.

PHILINTE: I can't remember a poem I've liked so well.

ALCESTE (*sotto voce, aside*): Good Lord!

ORONTE (*to* PHILINTE): I fear you're flattering me a bit.

PHILINTE: Oh, no!

ALCESTE (*sotto voce, aside*): What else d'you call it, you hypocrite?

ORONTE (*to* ALCESTE): But you, Sir, keep your promise now: don't shrink
From telling me sincerely what you think.

ALCESTE: Sir, these are delicate matters; we all desire
To be told that we've the true poetic fire.
But once, to one whose name I shall not mention,
I said, regarding some verse of his invention,
That gentlemen should rigorously control
That itch to write which often afflicts the soul;
That one should curb the heady inclination
To publicize one's little avocation;
And that in showing off one's works of art
One often plays a very clownish part.

ORONTE: Are you suggesting in a devious way
That I ought not . . .

ALCESTE: Oh, that I do not say.
Further, I told him that no fault is worse
Than that of writing frigid, lifeless verse,
And that the merest whisper of such a shame
Suffices to destroy a man's good name.
ORONTE: D'you mean to say my sonnet's dull and trite?
ALCESTE: I don't say that. But I went on to cite
Numerous cases of once-respected men
Who came to grief by taking up the pen.
ORONTE: And am I like them? Do I write so poorly?
ALCESTE: I don't say that. But I told this person, "Surely
You're under no necessity to compose;
Why you should wish to publish, heaven knows.
There's no excuse for printing tedious rot
Unless one writes for bread, as you do not.
Resist temptation, then, I beg of you;
Conceal your pastimes from the public view;
And don't give up, on any provocation,
Your present high and courtly reputation,
To purchase at a greedy printer's shop
The name of silly author and scribbling fop."
These were the points I tried to make him see.
ORONTE: I sense that they are also aimed at me;
But now — about my sonnet — I'd like to be told . . .
ALCESTE: Frankly, that sonnet should be pigeonholed.
You've chosen the worst models to imitate.
The style's unnatural. Let me illustrate:
For example, *Your fair face smiled on me awhile,*
Followed by, *'Twould have been fairer not to smile!*
Or this: *such joy is full of rue;*
Or this: *For death is fairer than the fair;*
Or, *Phyllis, to hope is to despair*
When one must hope eternally!
This artificial style, that's all the fashion,
Has neither taste, nor honesty, nor passion;
It's nothing but a sort of wordy play,
And nature never spoke in such a way.
What, in this shallow age, is not debased?
Our fathers, though less refined, had better taste;
I'd barter all that men admire today
For one old love song I shall try to say:
If the King had given me for my own
Paris, his citadel,

And I for that must leave alone
Her whom I love so well,
I'd say then to the Crown,
Take back your glittering town;
My darling is more fair, I swear,
My darling is more fair.

The rhyme's not rich, the style is rough and old,
But don't you see that it's the purest gold
Beside the tinsel nonsense now preferred,
And that there's passion in its every word?

If the King had given me for my own
Paris, his citadel,
And I for that must leave alone
Her whom I love so well,
I'd say then to the Crown,
Take back your glittering town;
My darling is more fair, I swear,
My darling is more fair.

There speaks a loving heart. (*To* PHILINTE.) You're laughing,eh?
Laugh on, my precious wit. Whatever you say,
I hold that song's worth all the bibelots
That people hail today with ah's and oh's.

ORONTE: And I maintain my sonnet's very good.

ALCESTE: It's not at all suprising that you should.
You have your reasons; permit me to have mine
For thinking that you cannot write a line.

ORONTE: Others have praised my sonnet to the skies.

ALCESTE: I lack their art of telling pleasant lies.

ORONTE: You seem to think you've got no end of wit.

ALCESTE: To praise your verse, I'd need still more of it.

ORONTE: I'm not in need of your approval, Sir.

ALCESTE: That's good; you couldn't have it if you were.

ORONTE: Come now, I'll lend you the subject of my sonnet;
I'd like to see you try to improve upon it.

ALCESTE: I might, by chance, write something just as shoddy;
But then I wouldn't show it to everybody.

ORONTE: You're most opinionated and conceited.

ALCESTE: Go find your flatterers, and be better treated.

ORONTE: Look here, my little fellow, pray watch your tone.

ALCESTE: My great big fellow, you'd better watch your own.

PHILINTE (*stepping between them*): Oh, please, please, gentlemen! This will never do.

ORONTE: The fault is mine, and I leave the field to you.

I am your servant, Sir, in every way.
ALCESTE: And I, Sir, am your most abject valet.

Scene 3 [PHILINTE, ALCESTE]

PHILINTE: Well, as you see, sincerity in excess
Can get you into a very pretty mess;
Oronte was hungry for appreciation. . . .
ALCESTE: Don't speak to me.
PHILINTE: What?
ALCESTE: No more conversation.
PHILINTE: Really, now . . .
ALCESTE: Leave me alone.
PHILINTE: If I . . .
ALCESTE: Out of my sight!
PHILINTE: But what . . .
ALCESTE: I won't listen.
PHILINTE: But . . .
ALCESTE: Silence!
PHILINTE: Now, is it polite . . .
ALCESTE: By heaven, I've had enough. Don't follow me.
PHILINTE: Ah, you're just joking. I'll keep you company.

ACT II

Scene 1 [ALCESTE, CÉLIMÈNE]

ALCESTE: Shall I speak plainly, Madam? I confess
Your conduct gives me infinite distress,
And my resentment's grown too hot to smother.
Soon, I foresee, we'll break with one another.
If I said otherwise, I should deceive you;
Sooner or later, I shall be forced to leave you,
And if I swore that we shall never part,
I should misread the omens of my heart.
CÉLIMÈNE: You kindly saw me home, it would appear,
So as to pour invectives in my ear.
ALCESTE: I've no desire to quarrel. But I deplore
Your inability to shut the door
On all these suitors who beset you so.
There's what annoys me, if you care to know.
CÉLIMÈNE: Is it my fault that all these men pursue me?

Am I to blame if they're attracted to me?
And when they gently beg an audience,
Ought I to take a stick and drive them hence?

ALCESTE: Madam, there's no necessity for a stick;
A less responsive heart would do the trick.
Of your attractiveness I don't complain;
But those your charms attract, you then detain
By a most melting and receptive manner,
And so enlist their hearts beneath your banner.
It's the agreeable hopes which you excite
That keep these lovers round you day and night;
Were they less liberally smiled upon,
That sighing troop would very soon be gone.
But tell me, Madam, why it is that lately
This man Clitandre interests you so greatly?
Because of what high merits do you deem
Him worthy of the honor of your esteem?
Is it that your admiring glances linger
On the splendidly long nail of his little finger?
Or do you share the general deep respect
For the blond wig he chooses to affect?
Are you in love with his embroidered hose?
Do you adore his ribbons and his bows?
Or is it that this paragon bewitches
Your tasteful eye with his vast German breeches?
Perhaps his giggle, or his falsetto voice,
Makes him the latest gallant of your choice?

CÉLIMÈNE: You're much mistaken to resent him so.
Why I put up with him you surely know:
My lawsuit's very shortly to be tried,
And I must have his influence on my side.

ALCESTE: Then lose your lawsuit, Madam, or let it drop;
Don't torture me by humoring such a fop.

CÉLIMÈNE: You're jealous of the whole world, Sir.

ALCESTE: That's true,
Since the whole world is well-received by you.

CÉLIMÈNE: That my good nature is so unconfined
Should serve to pacify your jealous mind;
Were I to smile on one, and scorn the rest,
Then you might have some cause to be distressed.

ALCESTE: Well, if I musn't be jealous, tell me, then,
Just how I'm better treated than other men.

CÉLIMÈNE: You know you have my love. Will that not do?

ALCESTE: What proof have I that what you say is true?
CÉLIMÈNE: I would expect, Sir, that my having said it
Might give the statement a sufficient credit.
ALCESTE: But how can I be sure that you don't tell
The selfsame thing to other men as well?
CÉLIMÈNE: What a gallant speech! How flattering to me!
What a sweet creature you make me out to be!
Well then, to save you from the pangs of doubt,
All that I've said I hereby cancel out;
Now, none but yourself shall make a monkey of you:
Are you content?
ALCESTE: Why, why am I doomed to love you?
I swear that I shall bless the blissful hour
When this poor heart's no longer in your power!
I make no secret of it: I've done my best
To exorcise this passion from my breast;
But thus far all in vain; it will not go;
It's for my sins that I must love you so.
CÉLIMÈNE: Your love for me is matchless, Sir; that's clear.
ALCESTE: Indeed, in all the world it has no peer;
Words can't describe the nature of my passion,
And no man ever loved in such a fashion.
CÉLIMÈNE: Yes, it's a brand-new fashion, I agree:
You show your love by castigating me,
And all your speeches are enraged and rude.
I've never been so furiously wooed.
ALCESTE: Yet you could calm that fury, if you chose.
Come, shall we bring our quarrels to a close?
Let's speak with open hearts, then, and begin . . .

Scene 2 [CÉLIMÈNE, ALCESTE, BASQUE]

CÉLIMÈNE: What is it?
BASQUE: Acaste is here.
CÉLIMÈNE: Well, send him in.

Scene 3 [CÉLIMÈNE, ALCESTE]

ALCESTE: What! Shall we never be alone at all?
You're always ready to receive a call,
And you can't bear, for ten ticks of the clock,
Not to keep open house for all who knock.
CÉLIMÈNE: I couldn't refuse him: he'd be most put out.

ALCESTE: Surely that's not worth worrying about.
CÉLIMÈNE: Acaste would never forgive me if he guessed
That I consider him a dreadful pest.
ALCESTE: If he's a pest, why bother with him then?
CÉLIMÈNE: Heavens! One can't antagonize such men;
Why, they're the chartered gossips of the court,
And have a say in things of every sort.
One must receive them, and be full of charm;
They're no great help, but they can do you harm,
And though your influence be ever so great,
They're hardly the best people to alienate.
ALCESTE: I see, dear lady, that you could make a case
For putting up with the whole human race;
These friendships that you calculate so nicely . . .

Scene 4 [ALCESTE, CÉLIMÈNE, BASQUE]

BASQUE: Madam, Clitandre is here as well.
ALCESTE: Precisely.
CÉLIMÈNE: Where are you going?
ALCESTE: Elsewhere.
CÉLIMÈNE: Stay.
ALCESTE: No, no.
CÉLIMÈNE: Stay, Sir.
ALCESTE: I can't.
CÉLIMÈNE: I wish it.
ALCESTE: No, I must go.
I beg you, Madam, not to press the matter;
You know I have no taste for idle chatter.
CÉLIMÈNE: Stay: I command you.
ALCESTE: No, I cannot stay.
CÉLIMÈNE: Very well; you have my leave to go away.

Scene 5 [ÉLIANTE, PHILINTE, ACASTE, CLITANDRE, ALCESTE, CÉLIMÈNE, BASQUE]

ÉLIANTE (*to* CÉLIMÈNE): The Marquesses have kindly come to call.
Were they announced?
CÉLIMÈNE: Yes. Basque, bring chairs for all.

(BASQUE *provides the chairs, and exits.*)

(*To* ALCESTE.) You haven't gone?
ALCESTE: No; and I shan't depart

Till you decide who's foremost in your heart.
CÉLIMÈNE: Oh, hush.
ALCESTE: It's time to choose; take them, or me.
CÉLIMÈNE: You're mad.
ALCESTE: I'm not, as you shall shortly see.
CÉLIMÈNE: Oh?
ALCESTE: You'll decide.
CÉLIMÈNE: You're joking now, dear friend.
ALCESTE: No, no; you'll choose; my patience is at an end.
CLITANDRE: Madam, I come from court, where poor Cléonte
Behaved like a perfect fool, as is his wont.
Has he no friend to counsel him, I wonder,
And teach him less unerringly to blunder?
CÉLIMÈNE: It's true, the man's a most accomplished dunce;
His gauche behavior charms the eye at once;
And every time one sees him, on my word,
His manner's grown a trifle more absurd.
ACASTE: Speaking of dunces, I've just now conversed
With old Damon, who's one of the very worst;
I stood a lifetime in the broiling sun
Before his dreary monologue was done.
CÉLIMÈNE: Oh, he's a wondrous talker, and has the power
To tell you nothing hour after hour:
If, by mistake, he ever came to the point,
The shock would put his jawbone out of joint.
ÉLIANTE (*to* PHILINTE): The conversation takes its usual turn,
And all our dear friends' ears will shortly burn.
CLITANDRE: Timante's a character, Madam.
CÉLIMÈNE: Isn't he, though?
A man of mystery from top to toe,
Who moves about in a romantic mist
On secret missions which do not exist.
His talk is full of eyebrows and grimaces;
How tired one gets of his momentous faces;
He's always whispering something confidential
Which turns out to be quite inconsequential;
Nothing's too slight for him to mystify;
He even whispers when he says "good-by."
ACASTE: Tell us about Géralde.
CÉLIMÈNE: That tiresome ass.
He mixes only with the titled class,
And fawns on dukes and princes, and is bored
With anyone who's not at least a lord.

The man's obsessed with rank, and his discourses
Are all of hounds and carriages and horses;
He uses Christian names with all the great,
And the word Milord, with him, is out of date.
CLITANDRE: He's very taken with Bélise, I hear.
CÉLIMÈNE: She is the dreariest company, poor dear.
Whenever she comes to call, I grope about
To find some topic which will draw her out,
But, owing to her dry and faint replies,
The conversation wilts, and droops, and dies.
In vain one hopes to animate her face
By mentioning the ultimate commonplace;
But sun or shower, even hail or frost
Are matters she can instantly exhaust.
Meanwhile her visit, painful though it is,
Drags on and on through mute eternities,
And though you ask the time, and yawn, and yawn,
She sits there like a stone and won't be gone.
ACASTE: Now for Adraste.
CÉLIMÈNE: Oh, that conceited elf
Has a gigantic passion for himself;
He rails against the court, and cannot bear it
That none will recognize his hidden merit;
All honors given to others give offense
To his imaginary excellence.
CLITANDRE: What about young Cléon? His house, they say,
Is full of the best society, night and day.
CÉLIMÈNE: His cook has made him popular, not he:
It's Cléon's table that people come to see.
ÉLIANTE: He gives a splendid dinner, you must admit.
CÉLIMÈNE: But must he serve himself along with it?
For my taste, he's a most insipid dish
Whose presence sours the wine and spoils the fish.
PHILINTE: Damis, his uncle, is admired no end.
What's your opinion, Madam?
CÉLIMÈNE: Why, he's my friend.
PHILINTE: He seems a decent fellow, and rather clever.
CÉLIMÈNE: He works too hard at cleverness, however.
I hate to see him sweat and struggle so
To fill his conversation with bons mots.
Since he's decided to become a wit
His taste's so pure that nothing pleases it;
He scolds at all the latest books and plays,

Thinking that wit must never stoop to praise,
That finding fault's a sign of intellect,
That all appreciation is abject,
And that by damning everything in sight
One shows oneself in a distinguished light.
He's scornful even of our conversations:
Their trivial nature sorely tries his patience;
He folds his arms, and stands above the battle,
And listens sadly to our childish prattle.

ACASTE: Wonderful, Madam! You've hit him off precisely.

CLITANDRE: No one can sketch a character so nicely.

ALCESTE: How bravely, Sirs, you cut and thrust at all
These absent fools, till one by one they fall:
But let one come in sight, and you'll at once
Embrace the man you lately called a dunce,
Telling him in a tone sincere and fervent
How proud you are to be his humble servant.

CLITANDRE: Why pick on us? *Madame's* been speaking, Sir,
And you should quarrel, if you must, with her.

ALCESTE: No, no, by God, the fault is yours, because
You lead her on with laughter and applause,
And make her think that she's the more delightful
The more her talk is scandalous and spiteful.
Oh, she would stoop to malice far, far less
If no such claque approved her cleverness.
It's flatterers like you whose foolish praise
Nourishes all the vices of these days.

PHILINTE: But why protest when someone ridicules
Those you'd condemn, yourself, as knaves or fools?

CÉLIMÈNE: Why, Sir? Because he loves to make a fuss.
You don't expect him to agree with us,
When there's an opportunity to express
His heaven-sent spirit of contrariness?
What other people think, he can't abide;
Whatever they say, he's on the other side;
He lives in deadly terror of agreeing;
'Twould make him seem an ordinary being.
Indeed, he's so in love with contradiction,
He'll turn against his most profound conviction
And with a furious eloquence deplore it,
If only someone else is speaking for it.

ALCESTE: Go on, dear lady, mock me as you please;
You have your audience in ecstasies.

PHILINTE: But what she says is true: you have a way
Of bridling at whatever people say;
Whether they praise or blame, your angry spirit
Is equally unsatisfied to hear it.
ALCESTE: Men, Sir, are always wrong, and that's the reason
That righteous anger's never out of season;
All that I hear in all their conversation
Is flattering praise or reckless condemnation.
CÉLIMÈNE: But . . .
ALCESTE: No, no, Madam, I am forced to state
That you have pleasures which I deprecate,
And that these others, here, are much to blame
For nourishing the faults which are your shame.
CLITANDRE: I shan't defend myself, Sir; but I vow
I'd thought this lady faultless until now.
ACASTE: I see her charms and graces, which are many;
But as for faults, I've never noticed any.
ALCESTE: I see them, Sir; and rather than ignore them,
I strenuously criticize her for them.
The more one loves, the more one should object
To every blemish, every least defect.
Were I this lady, I would soon get rid
Of lovers who approved of all I did,
And by their slack indulgence and applause
Endorsed my follies and excused my flaws.
CÉLIMÈNE: If all hearts beat according to your measure,
The dawn of love would be the end of pleasure;
And love would find its perfect consummation
In ecstasies of rage and reprobation.
ÉLIANTE: Love, as a rule, affects men otherwise,
And lovers rarely love to criticize.
They see their lady as a charming blur,
And find all things commendable in her.
If she has any blemish, fault, or shame,
They will redeem it by a pleasing name.
The pale-faced lady's lily-white, perforce;
The swarthy one's a sweet brunette, of course;
The spindly lady has a slender grace;
The fat one has a most majestic pace;
The plain one, with her dress in disarray,
They classify as *beauté négligée;*
The hulking one's a goddess in their eyes,
The dwarf, a concentrate of Paradise;

The haughty lady has a noble mind;
The mean one's witty, and the dull one's kind;
The chatterbox has liveliness and verve,
The mute one has a virtuous reserve.
So lovers manage, in their passion's cause,
To love their ladies even for their flaws.

ALCESTE: But I still say . . .

CÉLIMÈNE: I think it would be nice
To stroll around the gallery once or twice.
What! You're not going, Sirs?

CLITANDRE AND ACASTE: No, Madam, no.

ALCESTE: You seem to be in terror lest they go.
Do what you will, Sirs; leave, or linger on,
But I shan't go till after you are gone.

ACASTE: I'm free to linger, unless I should perceive
Madame is tired, and wishes me to leave.

CLITANDRE: And as for me, I needn't go today
Until the hour of the King's *coucher*.

CÉLIMÈNE (*to* ALCESTE): You're joking, surely?

ALCESTE: Not in the least; we'll see
Whether you'd rather part with them, or me.

Scene 6 [ALCESTE, CÉLIMÈNE, ÉLIANTE, ACASTE, PHILINTE, CLITANDRE, BASQUE]

BASQUE (*to* ALCESTE): Sir, there's a fellow here who bids me state
That he must see you, and that it can't wait.

ALCESTE: Tell him that I have no such pressing affairs.

BASQUE: It's a long tailcoat that this fellow wears,
With gold all over.

CÉLIMÈNE (*to* ALCESTE): You'd best go down and see.
Or — have him enter.

Scene 7 [ALCESTE, CÉLIMÈNE, ÉLIANTE, ACASTE, PHILINTE, CLITANDRE, GUARD]

ALCESTE (*confronting the* GUARD): Well, what do you want with me?
Come in, Sir.

GUARD: I've a word, Sir, for your ear.

ALCESTE: Speak it aloud, Sir; I shall strive to hear.

GUARD: The Marshals have instructed me to say
You must report to them without delay.

ALCESTE: Who? Me, Sir?

GUARD: Yes, Sir; you.
ALCESTE: But what do they want?
PHILINTE (*to* ALCESTE): To scotch your silly quarrel with Oronte.
CÉLIMÈNE (*to* PHILINTE): What quarrel?
PHILINTE: Oronte and he have fallen out
Over some verse he spoke his mind about;
The Marshalls wish to arbitrate the matter.
ALCESTE: Never shall I equivocate or flatter!
PHILINTE: You'd best obey their summons; come, let's go.
ALCESTE: How can they mend our quarrel, I'd like to know?
Am I to make a cowardly retraction,
And praise those jingles to his satisfaction?
I'll not recant; I've judged that sonnet rightly.
It's bad.
PHILINTE: But you might say so more politely. . . .
ALCESTE: I'll not back down; his verses make me sick.
PHILINTE: If only you could be more politic!
But come, let's go.
ALCESTE: I'll go, but I won't unsay
A single word.
PHILINTE: Well, let's be on our way.
ALCESTE: Till I am ordered by my lord the King
To praise that poem, I shall say the thing
Is scandalous, by God, and that the poet
Ought to be hanged for having the nerve to show it.

(*To* CLITANDRE *and* ACASTE, *who are laughing.*)

By heaven, Sirs, I really didn't know
That I was being humorous.
CÉLIMÈNE: Go, Sir, go;
Settle your business.
ALCESTE: I shall, and when I'm through,
I shall return to settle things with you.

ACT III

Scene 1 [CLITANDRE, ACASTE]

CLITANDRE: Dear Marquess, how contented you appear;
All things delight you, nothing mars your cheer.
Can you, in perfect honesty, declare
That you've a right to be so debonair?

ACASTE: By Jove, when I survey myself, I find
No cause whatever for distress of mind.
I'm young and rich; I can in modesty
Lay claim to an exalted pedigree;
And owing to my name and my condition
I shall not want for honors and position.
Then as to courage, that most precious trait,
I seem to have it, as was proved of late
Upon the field of honor, where my bearing,
They say, was very cool and rather daring.
I've wit, of course; and taste in such perfection
That I can judge without the least reflection,
And at the theater, which is my delight,
Can make or break a play on opening night,
And lead the crowd in hisses or bravos,
And generally be known as one who knows.
I'm clever, handsome, gracefully polite;
My waist is small, my teeth are strong and white;
As for my dress, the world's astonished eyes
Assure me that I bear away the prize.
I find myself in favor everywhere,
Honored by men, and worshiped by the fair;
And since these things are so, it seems to me
I'm justified in my complacency.
CLITANDRE: Well, if so many ladies hold you dear,
Why do you press a hopeless courtship here?
ACASTE: Hopeless, you say? I'm not the sort of fool
That likes his ladies difficult and cool.
Men who are awkward, shy, and peasantish
May pine for heartless beauties, if they wish,
Grovel before them, bear their cruelties,
Woo them with tears and sighs and bended knees,
And hope by dogged faithfulness to gain
What their poor merits never could obtain.
For men like me, however, it makes no sense
To love on trust, and foot the whole expense.
Whatever any lady's merits be,
I think, thank God, that I'm as choice as she;
That if my heart is kind enough to burn
For her, she owes me something in return;
And that in any proper love affair
The partners must invest an equal share.
CLITANDRE: You think, then, that our hostess favors you?

ACASTE: I've reason to believe that that is true.
CLITANDRE: How did you come to such a mad conclusion?
You're blind, dear fellow. This is sheer delusion.
ACASTE: All right, then: I'm deluded and I'm blind.
CLITANDRE: Whatever put the notion in your mind?
ACASTE: Delusion.
CLITANDRE: What persuades you that you're right?
ACASTE: I'm blind.
CLITANDRE: But have you any proofs to cite?
ACASTE: I tell you I'm deluded.
CLITANDRE: Have you, then,
Received some secret pledge from Célimène?
ACASTE: Oh, no: she scorns me.
CLITANDRE: Tell me the truth, I beg.
ACASTE: She just can't bear me.
CLITANDRE: Ah, don't pull my leg.
Tell me what hope she's given you, I pray.
ACASTE: I'm hopeless, and it's you who win the day.
She hates me thoroughly, and I'm so vexed
I mean to hang myself on Tuesday next.
CLITANDRE: Dear Marquess, let us have an armistice
And make a treaty. What do you say to this?
If ever one of us can plainly prove
That Célimène encourages his love,
The other must abandon hope, and yield,
And leave him in possession of the field.
ACASTE: Now, there's a bargain that appeals to me;
With all my heart, dear Marquess, I agree.
But hush.

Scene 2 [CÉLIMÈNE, ACASTE, CLITANDRE]

CÉLIMÈNE: Still here?
CLITANDRE: 'Twas love that stayed our feet.
CÉLIMÈNE: I think I heard a carriage in the street.
Whose is it? D'you know?

Scene 3 [CÉLIMÈNE, ACASTE, CLITANDRE, BASQUE]

BASQUE: Arsinoé is here,
Madame.
CÉLIMÈNE: Arsinoé, you say? Oh, dear.
BASQUE: Éliante is entertaining her below.

CÉLIMÈNE: What brings the creature here, I'd like to know?
ACASTE: They say she's dreadfully prudish, but in fact
I think her piety . . .
CÉLIMÈNE: It's all an act.
At heart she's worldly, and her poor success
In snaring men explains her prudishness.
It breaks her heart to see the beaux and gallants
Engrossed by other women's charms and talents,
And so she's always in a jealous rage
Against the faulty standards of the age.
She lets the world believe that she's a prude
To justify her loveless solitude,
And strives to put a brand of moral shame
On all the graces that she cannot claim.
But still she'd love a lover; and Alceste
Appears to be the one she'd love the best.
His visits here are poison to her pride;
She seems to think I've lured him from her side;
And everywhere, at court or in the town,
The spiteful, envious woman runs me down.
In short, she's just as stupid as can be,
Vicious and arrogant in the last degree,
And . . .

Scene 4 [ARSINOÉ, CÉLIMÈNE, CLITANDRE, ACASTE]

CÉLIMÈNE: Ah! What happy chance has brought you here?
I've thought about you ever so much, my dear.
ARSINOÉ: I've come to tell you something you should know.
CÉLIMÈNE: How good of you to think of doing so!

(CLITANDRE *and* ACASTE *go out, laughing.*)

Scene 5 [ARSINOÉ, CÉLIMÈNE]

ARSINOÉ: It's just as well those gentlemen didn't tarry.
CÉLIMÈNE: Shall we sit down?
ARSINOÉ: That won't be necessary.
Madam, the flame of friendship ought to burn
Brightest in matters of the most concern,
And as there's nothing which concerns us more
Than honor, I have hastened to your door
To bring you, as your friend, some information

About the status of your reputation.
I visited, last night, some virtuous folk,
And, quite by chance, it was of you they spoke;
There was, I fear, no tendency to praise
Your light behavior and your dashing ways.
The quantity of gentlemen you see
And your by now notorious coquetry
Were both so vehemently criticized
By everyone, that I was much surprised.
Of course, I needn't tell you where I stood;
I came to your defense as best I could,
Assured them you were harmless, and declared
Your soul was absolutely unimpaired.
But there are some things, you must realize,
One can't excuse, however hard one tries,
And I was forced at last into conceding
That your behavior, Madam, is misleading,
That it makes a bad impression, giving rise
To ugly gossip and obscene surmise,
And that if you were more *overtly* good,
You wouldn't be so much misunderstood.
Not that I think you've been unchaste — no! no!
The saints preserve me from a thought so low!
But mere good conscience never did suffice:
One must avoid the outward show of vice.
Madam, you're too intelligent, I'm sure,
To think my motives anything but pure
In offering you this counsel — which I do
Out of a zealous interest in you.

CÉLIMÈNE: Madam, I haven't taken you amiss;
I'm very much obliged to you for this;
And I'll at once discharge the obligation
By telling you about *your* reputation.
You've been so friendly as to let me know
What certain people say of me, and so
I mean to follow your benign example
By offering you a somewhat similar sample.
The other day, I went to an affair
And found some most distinguished people there
Discussing piety, both false and true.
The conversation soon came round to you.
Alas! Your prudery and bustling zeal
Appeared to have a very slight appeal.

Your affectation of a grave demeanor,
Your endless talk of virtue and of honor,
The aptitude of your suspicious mind
For finding sin where there is none to find,
Your towering self-esteem, that pitying face
With which you contemplate the human race,
Your sermonizings and your sharp aspersions
On people's pure and innocent diversions —
All these were mentioned, Madam, and, in fact,
Were roundly and concertedly attacked.
"What good," they said, "are all these outward shows,
When everything belies her pious pose?
She prays incessantly; but then, they say,
She beats her maids and cheats them of their pay;
She shows her zeal in every holy place,
But still she's vain enough to paint her face;
She holds that naked statues are immoral,
But with a naked *man* she'd have no quarrel."
Of course, I said to everybody there
That they were being viciously unfair;
But still they were disposed to criticize you,
And all agreed that someone should advise you
To leave the morals of the world alone,
And worry rather more about your own.
They felt that one's self-knowledge should be great
Before one thinks of setting others straight;
That one should learn the art of living well
Before one threatens other men with hell,
And that the Church is best equipped, no doubt,
To guide our souls and root our vices out.
Madam, you're too intelligent, I'm sure,
To think my motives anything but pure
In offering you this counsel — which I do
Out of a zealous interest in you.

ARSINOÉ: I dared not hope for gratitude, but I
Did not expect so acid a reply;
I judge, since you've been so extremely tart,
That my good counsel pierced you to the heart.

CÉLIMÈNE: Far from it, Madam. Indeed, it seems to me
We ought to trade advice more frequently.
One's vision of oneself is so defective
That it would be an excellent corrective.
If you are willing, Madam, let's arrange

Shortly to have another frank exchange
In which we'll tell each other, *entre nous*,
What you've heard tell of me, and I of you.

ARSINOÉ: Oh, people never censure you, my dear;
It's me they criticize. Or so I hear.

CÉLIMÈNE: Madam, I think we either blame or praise
According to our taste and length of days.
There is a time of life for coquetry,
And there's a season, too, for prudery.
When all one's charms are gone, it is, I'm sure,
Good strategy to be devout and pure:
It makes one seem a little less forsaken.
Some day, perhaps, I'll take the road you've taken:
Time brings all things. But I have time aplenty,
And see no cause to be a prude at twenty.

ARSINOÉ: You give your age in such a gloating tone
That one would think I was an ancient crone;
We're not so far apart, in sober truth,
That you can mock me with a boast of youth!
Madam, you baffle me. I wish I knew
What moves you to provoke me as you do.

CÉLIMÈNE: For my part, Madam, I should like to know
Why you abuse me everywhere you go.
Is it my fault, dear lady, that your hand
Is not, alas, in very great demand?
If men admire me, if they pay me court
And daily make me offers of the sort
You'd dearly love to have them make to you,
How can I help it? What would you have me do?
If what you want is lovers, please feel free
To take as many as you can from me.

ARSINOÉ: Oh, come. D'you think the world is losing sleep
Over that flock of lovers which you keep,
Or that we find it difficult to guess
What price you pay for their devotedness?
Surely you don't expect us to suppose
Mere merit could attract so many beaux?
It's not your virtue that they're dazzled by;
Nor is it virtuous love for which they sigh.
You're fooling no one, Madam; the world's not blind;
There's many a lady heaven has designed
To call men's noblest, tenderest feelings out,
Who has no lovers dogging her about;

From which it's plain that lovers nowadays
Must be acquired in bold and shameless ways,
And only pay one court for such reward
As modesty and virtue can't afford.
Then don't be quite so puffed up, if you please,
About your tawdry little victories;
Try, if you can, to be a shade less vain,
And treat the world with somewhat less disdain.
If one were envious of your amours,
One soon could have a following like yours;
Lovers are no great trouble to collect
If one prefers them to one's self-respect.

CÉLIMÈNE: Collect them then, my dear; I'd love to see
You demonstrate that charming theory;
Who knows, you might . . .

ARSINOÉ: Now, Madam, that will do;
It's time to end this trying interview.
My coach is late in coming to your door,
Or I'd have taken leave of you before.

CÉLIMÈNE: Oh, please don't feel that you must rush away;
I'd be delighted, Madam, if you'd stay.
However, lest my conversation bore you,
Let me provide some better company for you;
This gentleman, who comes most apropos,
Will please you more than I could do, I know.

Scene 6 [ALCESTE, CÉLIMÈNE, ARSINOÉ]

CÉLIMÈNE: Alceste, I have a little note to write
Which simply must go out before tonight;
Please entertain *Madame;* I'm sure that she
Will overlook my incivility.

Scene 7 [ALCESTE, ARSINOÉ]

ARSINOÉ: Well, Sir, our hostess graciously contrives
For us to chat until my coach arrives;
And I shall be forever in her debt
For granting me this little tête-à-tête.
We women very rightly give our hearts
To men of noble character and parts,
And your especial merits, dear Alceste,
Have roused the deepest sympathy in my breast.

Oh, how I wish they had sufficient sense
At court, to recognize your excellence!
They wrong you greatly, Sir. How it must hurt you
Never to be rewarded for your virtue!

ALCESTE: Why, Madam, what cause have I to feel aggrieved?
What great and brilliant thing have I achieved?
What service have I rendered to the King
That I should look to him for anything?

ARSINOÉ: Not everyone who's honored by the State
Has done great services. A man must wait
Till time and fortune offer him the chance.
Your merit, Sir, is obvious at a glance,
And . . .

ALCESTE: Ah, forget my merit; I am not neglected.
The court, I think, can hardly be expected
To mine men's souls for merit, and unearth
Our hidden virtues and our secret worth.

ARSINOÉ: *Some* virtues, though, are far too bright to hide;
Yours are acknowledged, Sir, on every side.
Indeed, I've heard you warmly praised of late
By persons of considerable weight.

ALCESTE: This fawning age has praise for everyone,
And all distinctions, Madam, are undone.
All things have equal honor nowadays,
And no one should be gratified by praise.
To be admired, one only need exist,
And every lackey's on the honors list.

ARSINOÉ: I only wish, Sir, that you had your eye
On some position at court, however high;
You'd only have to hint at such a notion
For me to set the proper wheels in motion;
I've certain friendships I'd be glad to use
To get you any office you might choose.

ALCESTE: Madam, I fear that any such ambition
Is wholly foreign to my disposition.
The soul God gave me isn't of the sort
That prospers in the weather of a court.
It's all too obvious that I don't possess
The virtues necessary for success.
My one great talent is for speaking plain;
I've never learned to flatter or to feign;
And anyone so stupidly sincere
Had best not seek a courtier's career.

Outside the court, I know, one must dispense
With honors, privilege, and influence;
But still one gains the right, foregoing these,
Not to be tortured by the wish to please.
One needn't live in dread of snubs and slights,
Nor praise the verse that every idiot writes,
Nor humor silly Marquesses, nor bestow
Politic sighs on Madam So-and-So.

ARSINOÉ: Forget the court, then; let the matter rest.
But I've another cause to be distressed
About your present situation, Sir.
It's to your love affair that I refer.
She whom you love, and who pretends to love you,
Is, I regret to say, unworthy of you.

ALCESTE: Why, Madam? Can you seriously intend
To make so grave a charge against your friend?

ARSINOÉ: Alas, I must. I've stood aside too long
And let that lady do you grievous wrong;
But now my debt to conscience shall be paid:
I tell you that your love has been betrayed.

ALCESTE: I thank you, Madam; you're extremely kind.
Such words are soothing to a lover's mind.

ARSINOÉ: Yes, though she *is* my friend, I say again
You're very much too good for Célimène.
She's wantonly misled you from the start.

ALCESTE: You may be right; who knows another's heart?
But ask yourself if it's the part of charity
To shake my soul with doubts of her sincerity.

ARSINOÉ: Well, if you'd rather be a dupe than doubt her,
That's your affair. I'll say no more about her.

ALCESTE: Madam, you know that doubt and vague suspicion
Are painful to a man in my position;
It's most unkind to worry me this way
Unless you've some real proof of what you say.

ARSINOÉ: Sir, say no more: all doubts shall be removed,
And all that I've been saying shall be proved.
You've only to escort me home, and there
We'll look into the heart of this affair.
I've ocular evidence which will persuade you
Beyond a doubt, that Célimène's betrayed you.
Then, if you're saddened by that revelation,
Perhaps I can provide some consolation.

ACT IV

Scene 1 [ÉLIANTE, PHILINTE]

PHILINTE: Madam, he acted like a stubborn child;
I thought they never would be reconciled;
In vain we reasoned, threatened, and appealed;
He stood his ground and simply would not yield.
The Marshals, I feel sure, have never heard
An argument so splendidly absurd.
"No, gentlemen," said he, "I'll not retract.
His verse is bad: extremely bad, in fact.
Surely it does the man no harm to know it.
Does it disgrace him, not to be a poet?
A gentleman may be respected still,
Whether he writes a sonnet well or ill.
That I dislike his verse should not offend him;
In all that touches honor, I commend him;
He's noble, brave, and virtuous — but I fear
He can't in truth be called a sonneteer.
I'll gladly praise his wardrobe; I'll endorse
His dancing, or the way he sits a horse;
But, gentlemen, I cannot praise his rhyme.
In fact, it ought to be a capital crime
For anyone so sadly unendowed
To write a sonnet, and read the thing aloud."
At length he fell into a gentler mood
And, striking a concessive attitude,
He paid Oronte the following courtesies:
"Sir, I regret that I'm so hard to please,
And I'm profoundly sorry that your lyric
Failed to provoke me to a panegyric."
After these curious words, the two embraced,
And then the hearing was adjourned — in haste.
ÉLIANTE: His conduct has been very singular lately;
Still, I confess that I respect him greatly.
The honesty in which he takes such pride
Has — to my mind — its noble, heroic side.
In this false age, such candor seems outrageous;
But I could wish that it were more contagious.
PHILINTE: What most intrigues me in our friend Alceste
Is the grand passion that rages in his breast.

The sullen humors he's compounded of
Should not, I think, dispose his heart to love;
But since they do, it puzzles me still more
That he should choose your cousin to adore.
ÉLIANTE: It does, indeed, belie the theory
That love is born of gentle sympathy,
And that the tender passion must be based
On sweet accords of temper and of taste.
PHILINTE: Does she return his love, do you suppose?
ÉLIANTE: Ah, that's a difficult question, Sir. Who knows?
How can we judge the truth of her devotion?
Her heart's a stranger to its own emotion.
Sometimes it thinks it loves, when no love's there;
At other times it loves quite unaware.
PHILINTE: I rather think Alceste is in for more
Distress and sorrow than he's bargained for;
Were he of my mind, Madam, his affection
Would turn in quite a different direction,
And we would see him more responsive to
The kind regard which he receives from you.
ÉLIANTE: Sir, I believe in frankness, and I'm inclined,
In matters of the heart, to speak my mind.
I don't oppose his love for her; indeed,
I hope with all my heart that he'll succeed,
And were it in my power, I'd rejoice
In giving him the lady of his choice.
But if, as happens frequently enough
In love affairs, he meets with a rebuff —
If Célimène should grant some rival's suit —
I'd gladly play the role of substitute;
Nor would his tender speeches please me less
Because they'd once been made without success.
PHILINTE: Well, Madam, as for me, I don't oppose
Your hopes in this affair; and heaven knows
That in my conversations with the man
I plead your cause as often as I can.
But if those two should marry, and so remove
All chance that he will offer you his love,
Then I'll declare my own, and hope to see
Your gracious favor pass from him to me.
In short, should you be cheated of Alceste,
I'd be most happy to be second best.
ÉLIANTE: Philinte, you're teasing.

PHILINTE: Ah, Madam, never fear;
No words of mine were ever so sincere,
And I shall live in fretful expectation
Till I can make a fuller declaration.

Scene 2 [ALCESTE, ÉLIANTE, PHILINTE]

ALCESTE: Avenge me, Madam! I must have satisfaction,
Or this great wrong will drive me to distraction!
ÉLIANTE: Why, what's the matter? What's upset you so?
ALCESTE: Madam, I've had a mortal, mortal blow.
If Chaos repossessed the universe,
I swear I'd not be shaken any worse.
I'm ruined. . . . I can say no more. . . . My soul . . .
ÉLIANTE: Do try, Sir, to regain your self-control.
ALCESTE: Just heaven! Why were so much beauty and grace
Bestowed on one so vicious and so base?
ÉLIANTE: Once more, Sir, tell us. . . .
ALCESTE: My world has gone to wrack;
I'm — I'm betrayed; she's stabbed me in the back:
Yes, Célimène (who would have thought it of her?)
Is false to me, and has another lover.
ÉLIANTE: Are you quite certain? Can you prove these things?
PHILINTE: Lovers are prey to wild imaginings
And jealous fancies. No doubt there's some mistake. . . .
ALCESTE: Mind your own business, Sir, for heaven's sake.

(*To* ÉLIANTE.)

Madam, I have the proof that you demand
Here in my pocket, penned by her own hand.
Yes, all the shameful evidence one could want
Lies in this letter writen to Oronte —
Oronte! whom I felt sure she couldn't love,
And hardly bothered to be jealous of.
PHILINTE: Still, in a letter, appearances may deceive;
This may not be so bad as you believe.
ALCESTE: Once more I beg you, Sir, to let me be;
Tend to your own affairs; leave mine to me.
ÉLIANTE: Compose yourself; this anguish that you feel . . .
ALCESTE: Is something, Madam, you alone can heal.
My outraged heart, beside itself with grief,
Appeals to you for comfort and relief.
Avenge me on your cousin, whose unjust

And faithless nature has deceived my trust;
Avenge a crime your pure soul must detest.

ÉLIANTE: But how, Sir?

ALCESTE: Madam, this heart within my breast
Is yours; pray take it; redeem my heart from her,
And so avenge me on my torturer.
Let her be punished by the fond emotion,
The ardent love, the bottomless devotion,
The faithful worship which this heart of mine
Will offer up to yours as to a shrine.

ÉLIANTE: You have my sympathy, Sir, in all you suffer;
Nor do I scorn the noble heart you offer;
But I suspect you'll soon be mollified,
And this desire for vengeance will subside.
When some belovèd hand has done us wrong
We thirst for retribution — but not for long;
However dark the deed that she's committed,
A lovely culprit's very soon acquitted.
Nothing's so stormy as an injured lover,
And yet no storm so quickly passes over.

ALCESTE: No, Madam, no — this is no lovers' spat;
I'll not forgive her; it's gone too far for that;
My mind's made up; I'll kill myself before
I waste my hopes upon her any more.
Ah, here she is. My wrath intensifies.
I shall confront her with her tricks and lies,
And crush her utterly, and bring you then
A heart no longer slave to Célimène.

Scene 3 [CÉLIMÈNE, ALCESTE]

ALCESTE (*aside*): Sweet heaven, help me to control my passion.

CÉLIMÈNE (*aside*): Oh, Lord.

(*To* ALCESTE.)

Why stand there staring in that fashion?
And what d'you mean by those dramatic sighs,
And that malignant glitter in your eyes?

ALCESTE: I mean that sins which cause the blood to freeze
Look innocent beside your treacheries;
That nothing Hell's or Heaven's wrath could do
Ever produced so bad a thing as you.

CÉLIMÈNE: Your compliments were always sweet and pretty.

ALCESTE: Madam, it's not the moment to be witty.
No, blush and hang your head; you've ample reason,
Since I've the fullest evidence of your treason.
Ah, this is what my sad heart prophesied;
Now all my anxious fears are verified;
My dark suspicion and my gloomy doubt
Divined the truth, and now the truth is out.
For all your trickery, I was not deceived;
It was my bitter stars that I believed.
But don't imagine that you'll go scot-free;
You shan't misuse me with impunity.
I know that love's irrational and blind;
I know the heart's not subject to the mind,
And can't be reasoned into beating faster;
I know each soul is free to choose its master;
Therefore had you but spoken from the heart,
Rejecting my attentions from the start,
I'd have no grievance, or at any rate
I could complain of nothing but my fate.
Ah, but so falsely to encourage me —
That was a treason and a treachery
For which you cannot suffer too severely,
And you shall pay for that behavior dearly.
Yes, now I have no pity, not a shred;
My temper's out of hand; I've lost my head;
Shocked by the knowledge of your double-dealings,
My reason can't restrain my savage feelings;
A righteous wrath deprives me of my senses,
And I won't answer for the consequences.
CÉLIMÈNE: What does this outburst mean? Will you please explain?
Have you, by any chance, gone quite insane?
ALCESTE: Yes, yes, I went insane the day I fell
A victim to your black and fatal spell,
Thinking to meet with some sincerity
Among the treacherous charms that beckoned me.
CÉLIMÈNE: Pooh. Of what treachery can you complain?
ALCESTE: How sly you are, how cleverly you feign!
But you'll not victimize me any more.
Look: here's a document you've seen before.
This evidence, which I acquired today,
Leaves you, I think, without a thing to say.
CÉLIMÈNE: Is this what sent you into such a fit?
ALCESTE: You should be blushing at the sight of it.

CÉLIMÈNE: Ought I to blush? I truly don't see why.
ALCESTE: Ah, now you're being bold as well as sly;
Since there's no signature, perhaps you'll claim . . .
CÉLIMÈNE: I wrote it, whether or not it bears my name.
ALCESTE: And you can view with equanimity
This proof of your disloyalty to me!
CÉLIMÈNE: Oh, don't be so outrageous and extreme.
ALCESTE: You take this matter lightly, it would seem.
Was it no wrong to me, no shame to you,
That you should send Oronte this billet-doux?
CÉLIMÈNE: Oronte! Who said it was for him?
ALCESTE: Why, those
Who brought me this example of your prose.
But what's the difference? If you wrote the letter
To someone else, it pleases me no better.
My grievance and your guilt remain the same.
CÉLIMÈNE: But need you rage, and need I blush for shame,
If this was written to a *woman* friend?
ALCESTE: Ah! Most ingenious. I'm impressed no end;
And after that incredible evasion
Your guilt is clear. I need no more persuasion.
How dare you try so clumsy a deception?
D'you think I'm wholly wanting in perception?
Come, come, let's see how brazenly you'll try
To bolster up so palpable a lie:
Kindly construe this ardent closing section
As nothing more than sisterly affection!
Here, let me read it. Tell me, if you dare to,
That this is for a woman . . .
CÉLIMÈNE: I don't care to.
What right have you to badger and berate me,
And so highhandedly interrogate me?
ALCESTE: Now, don't be angry; all I ask of you
Is that you justify a phrase or two . . .
CÉLIMÈNE: No, I shall not. I utterly refuse,
And you may take those phrases as you choose.
ALCESTE: Just show me how this letter could be meant
For a woman's eyes, and I shall be content.
CÉLIMÈNE: No, no, it's for Oronte; you're perfectly right.
I welcome his attentions with delight,
I prize his character and his intellect,
And everything is just as you suspect.
Come, do your worst now; give your rage free rein;

But kindly cease to bicker and complain.
ALCESTE (*aside*): Good God! Could anything be more inhuman?
Was ever a heart so mangled by a woman?
When I complain of how she has betrayed me,
She bridles, and commences to upbraid me!
She tries my tortured patience to the limit;
She won't deny her guilt; she glories in it!
And yet my heart's too faint and cowardly
To break these chains of passion, and be free,
To scorn her as it should, and rise above
This unrewarded, mad, and bitter love.

(*To* CÉLIMÈNE.)

Ah, traitress, in how confident a fashion
You take advantage of my helpless passion,
And use my weakness for your faithless charms
To make me once again throw down my arms!
But do at least deny this black transgression;
Take back that mocking and perverse confession;
Defend this letter and your innocence,
And I, poor fool, will aid in your defense.
Pretend, pretend, that you are just and true,
And I shall make myself believe in you.
CÉLIMÈNE: Oh, stop it. Don't be such a jealous dunce,
Or I shall leave off loving you at once.
Just why should I *pretend?* What could impel me
To stoop so low as that? And kindly tell me
Why, if I loved another, I shouldn't merely
Inform you of it, simply and sincerely!
I've told you where you stand, and that admission
Should altogether clear me of suspicion;
After so generous a guarantee,
What right have you to harbor doubts of me?
Since women are (from natural reticence)
Reluctant to declare their sentiments,
And since the honor of our sex requires
That we conceal our amorous desires,
Ought any man for whom such laws are broken
To question what the oracle has spoken?
Should he not rather feel an obligation
To trust that most obliging declaration?
Enough, now. Your suspicions quite disgust me;
Why should I love a man who doesn't trust me?

I cannot understand why I continue,
Fool that I am, to take an interest in you.
I ought to choose a man less prone to doubt,
And give you something to be vexed about.
ALCESTE: Ah, what a poor enchanted fool I am;
These gentle words, no doubt, were all a sham;
But destiny requires me to entrust
My happiness to you, and so I must.
I'll love you to the bitter end, and see
How false and treacherous you dare to be.
CÉLIMÈNE: No, you don't really love me as you ought.
ALCESTE: I love you more than can be said or thought;
Indeed, I wish you were in such distress
That I might show my deep devotedness.
Yes, I could wish that you were wretchedly poor,
Unloved, uncherished, utterly obscure;
That fate had set you down upon the earth
Without possessions, rank, or gentle birth;
Then, by the offer of my heart, I might
Repair the great injustice of your plight;
I'd raise you from the dust, and proudly prove
The purity and vastness of my love.
CÉLIMÈNE: This is a strange benevolence indeed!
God grant that I may never be in need. . . .
Ah, here's Monsieur Dubois, in quaint disguise.

Scene 4 [CÉLIMÈNE, ALCESTE, DUBOIS]

ALCESTE: Well, why this costume? Why those frightened eyes?
What ails you?
DUBOIS: Well, Sir, things are most mysterious.
ALCESTE: What do you mean?
DUBOIS: I fear they're very serious.
ALCESTE: What?
DUBOIS: Shall I speak more loudly?
ALCESTE: Yes; speak out.
DUBOIS: Isn't there someone here, Sir?
ALCESTE: Speak, you lout!
Stop wasting time.
DUBOIS: Sir, we must slip away.
ALCESTE: How's that?
DUBOIS: We must decamp without delay.
ALCESTE: Explain yourself.

DUBOIS: I tell you we must fly.
ALCESTE: What for?
DUBOIS: We mustn't pause to say good-by.
ALCESTE: Now what d'you mean by all of this, you clown?
DUBOIS: I mean, Sir, that we've got to leave this town.
ALCESTE: I'll tear you limb from limb and joint from joint
If you don't come more quickly to the point.
DUBOIS: Well, Sir, today a man in a black suit,
Who wore a black and ugly scowl to boot,
Left us a document scrawled in such a hand
As even Satan couldn't understand.
It bears upon your lawsuit, I don't doubt;
But all hell's devils couldn't make it out.
ALCESTE: Well, well, go on. What then? I fail to see
How this event obliges us to flee.
DUBOIS: Well, Sir: an hour later, hardly more,
A gentleman who's often called before
Came looking for you in an anxious way.
Not finding you, he asked me to convey
(Knowing I could be trusted with the same)
The following message. . . . Now, what *was* his name?
ALCESTE: Forget his name, you idiot. What did he say?
DUBOIS: Well, it was one of your friends, Sir, anyway.
He warned you to begone, and he suggested
That if you stay, you may well be arrested.
ALCESTE: What? Nothing more specific? Think, man, think!
DUBOIS: No, Sir. He had me bring him pen and ink,
And dashed you off a letter which, I'm sure,
Will render things distinctly less obscure.
ALCESTE: Well — let me have it!
CÉLIMÈNE: What *is* this all about?
ALCESTE: God knows; but I have hopes of finding out.
How long am I to wait, you blitherer?
DUBOIS (*after a protracted search for the letter*): I must have left it on your table, Sir.
ALCESTE: I ought to . . .
CÉLIMÈNE: No, no, keep your self-control;
Go find out what's behind his rigmarole.
ALCESTE: It seems that fate, no matter what I do,
Has sworn that I may not converse with you;
But, Madam, pray permit your faithful lover
To try once more before the day is over.

ACT V

Scene 1 [ALCESTE, PHILINTE]

ALCESTE: No, it's too much. My mind's made up, I tell you.
PHILINTE: Why should this blow, however hard, compel you . . .
ALCESTE: No, no, don't waste your breath in argument;
Nothing you say will alter my intent;
This age is vile, and I've made up my mind
To have no further commerce with mankind.
Did not truth, honor, decency, and the laws
Oppose my enemy and approve my cause?
My claims were justified in all men's sight;
I put my trust in equity and right;
Yet, to my horror and the world's disgrace,
Justice is mocked, and I have lost my case!
A scoundrel whose dishonesty is notorious
Emerges from another lie victorious!
Honor and right condone his brazen fraud,
While rectitude and decency applaud!
Before his smirking face, the truth stands charmed,
And virtue conquered, and the law disarmed!
His crime is sanctioned by a court decree!
And not content with what he's done to me,
The dog now seeks to ruin me by stating
That I composed a book now circulating,
A book so wholly criminal and vicious
That even to speak its title is seditious!
Meanwhile Oronte, my rival, lends his credit
To the same libelous tale, and helps to spread it!
Oronte! a man of honor and of rank,
With whom I've been entirely fair and frank;
Who sought me out and forced me, willy-nilly,
To judge some verse I found extremely silly;
And who, because I properly refused
To flatter him, or see the truth abused,
Abets my enemy in a rotten slander!
There's the reward of honesty and candor!
The man will hate me to the end of time
For failing to commend his wretched rhyme!
And not this man alone, but all humanity
Do what they do from interest and vanity;

They prate of honor, truth, and righteousness,
But lie, betray, and swindle nonetheless.
Come then: man's villainy is too much to bear;
Let's leave this jungle and this jackal's lair.
Yes! treacherous and savage race of men,
You shall not look upon my face again.

PHILINTE: Oh, don't rush into exile prematurely;
Things aren't as dreadful as you make them, surely.
It's rather obvious, since you're still at large,
That people don't believe your enemy's charge.
Indeed, his tale's so patently untrue
That it may do more harm to him than you.

ALCESTE: Nothing could do that scoundrel any harm:
His frank corruption is his greatest charm,
And, far from hurting him, a further shame
Would only serve to magnify his name.

PHILINTE: In any case, his bald prevarication
Has done no injury to your reputation,
And you may feel secure in that regard.
As for your lawsuit, it should not be hard
To have the case reopened, and contest
This judgment . . .

ALCESTE: No, no, let the verdict rest.
Whatever cruel penalty it may bring,
I wouldn't have it changed for anything.
It shows the times' injustice with such clarity
That I shall pass it down to our posterity
As a great proof and signal demonstration
Of the black wickedness of this generation.
It may cost twenty thousand francs; but I
Shall pay their twenty thousand, and gain thereby
The right to storm and rage at human evil,
And send the race of mankind to the devil.

PHILINTE: Listen to me. . . .

ALCESTE: Why? What can you possibly say?
Don't argue, Sir; your labor's thrown away.
Do you propose to offer lame excuses
For men's behavior and the times' abuses?

PHILINTE: No, all you say I'll readily concede:
This is a low, conniving age indeed;
Nothing but trickery prospers nowadays,
And people ought to mend their shabby ways.
Yes, man's a beastly creature; but must we then

Abandon the society of men?
Here in the world, each human frailty
Provides occasion for philosophy,
And that is virtue's noblest exercise;
If honesty shone forth from all men's eyes,
If every heart were frank and kind and just,
What could our virtues do but gather dust
(Since their employment is to help us bear
The villainies of men without despair)?
A heart well-armed with virtue can endure. . . .
ALCESTE: Sir, you're a matchless reasoner, to be sure;
Your words are fine and full of cogency;
But don't waste time and eloquence on me.
My reason bids me go, for my own good.
My tongue won't lie and flatter as it should;
God knows what frankness it might next commit,
And what I'd suffer on account of it.
Pray let me wait for Célimène's return
In peace and quiet. I shall shortly learn,
By her response to what I have in view,
Whether her love for me is feigned or true.
PHILINTE: Till then, let's visit Éliante upstairs.
ALCESTE: No, I am too weighed down with somber cares.
Go to her, do; and leave me with my gloom
Here in the darkened corner of this room.
PHILINTE: Why, that's no sort of company, my friend;
I'll see if Éliante will not descend.

Scene 2 [CÉLIMÈNE, ORONTE, ALCESTE]

ORONTE: Yes, Madam, if you wish me to remain
Your true and ardent lover, you must deign
To give me some more positive assurance.
All this suspense is quite beyond endurance.
If your heart shares the sweet desires of mine,
Show me as much by some convincing sign;
And here's the sign I urgently suggest:
That you no longer tolerate Alceste,
But sacrifice him to my love, and sever
All your relations with the man forever.
CÉLIMÈNE: Why do you suddenly dislike him so?
You praised him to the skies not long ago.
ORONTE: Madam, that's not the point. I'm here to find

Which way your tender feelings are inclined.
Choose, if you please, between Alceste and me,
And I shall stay or go accordingly.

ALCESTE (*emerging from the corner*): Yes, Madam, choose; this gentleman's demand
Is wholly just, and I support his stand.
I too am true and ardent; I too am here
To ask you that you make your feelings clear.
No more delays, now; no equivocation;
The time has come to make your declaration.

ORONTE: Sir, I've no wish in any way to be
An obstacle to your felicity.

ALCESTE: Sir, I've no wish to share her heart with you;
That may sound jealous, but at least it's true.

ORONTE: If, weighing us, she leans in your direction . . .

ALCESTE: If she regards you with the least affection . . .

ORONTE: I swear I'll yield her to you there and then.

ALCESTE: I swear I'll never see her face again.

ORONTE: Now, Madam, tell us what we've come to hear.

ALCESTE: Madam, speak openly and have no fear.

ORONTE: Just say which one is to remain your lover.

ALCESTE: Just name one name, and it will all be over.

ORONTE: What! Is it possible that you're undecided?

ALCESTE: What! Can your feelings possibly be divided?

CÉLIMÈNE: Enough: this inquisition's gone too far:
How utterly unreasonable you are!
Not that I couldn't make the choice with ease;
My heart has no conflicting sympathies;
I know full well which one of you I favor,
And you'd not see me hesitate or waver.
But how can you expect me to reveal
So cruelly and bluntly what I feel?
I think it altogether too unpleasant
To choose between two men when both are present;
One's heart has means more subtle and more kind
Of letting its affections be divined,
Nor need one be uncharitably plain
To let a lover know he loves in vain.

ORONTE: No, no, speak plainly; I for one can stand it.
I beg you to be frank.

ALCESTE: And I demand it.
The simple truth is what I wish to know,
And there's no need for softening the blow.

You've made an art of pleasing everyone,
But now your days of coquetry are done:
You have no choice now, Madam, but to choose,
For I'll know what to think if you refuse;
I'll take your silence for a clear admission
That I'm entitled to my worst suspicion.

ORONTE: I thank you for this ultimatum, Sir,
And I may say I heartily concur.

CÉLIMÈNE: Really, this foolishness is very wearing:
Must you be so unjust and overbearing?
Haven't I told you why I must demur?
Ah, here's Éliante; I'll put the case to her.

Scene 3 [ÉLIANTE, PHILINTE, CÉLIMÈNE, ORONTE, ALCESTE]

CÉLIMÈNE: Cousin, I'm being persecuted here
By these two persons, who, it would appear,
Will not be satisfied till I confess
Which one I love the more, and which the less,
And tell the latter to his face that he
Is henceforth banished from my company.
Tell me, has ever such a thing been done?

ÉLIANTE: You'd best not turn to me; I'm not the one
To back you in a matter of this kind:
I'm all for those who frankly speak their mind.

ORONTE: Madam, you'll search in vain for a defender.

ALCESTE: You're beaten, Madam, and may as well surrender.

ORONTE: Speak, speak, you must; and end this awful strain.

ALCESTE: Or don't, and your position will be plain.

ORONTE: A single word will close this painful scene.

ALCESTE: But if you're silent, I'll know what you mean.

Scene 4 [ARSINOÉ, CÉLIMÈNE, ÉLIANTE, ALCESTE, PHILINTE, ACASTE, CLITANDRE, ORONTE]

ACASTE (*to* CÉLIMÈNE): Madam, with all due deference, we two
Have come to pick a little bone with you.

CLITANDRE (*to* ORONTE *and* ALCESTE): I'm glad you're present, Sirs; as you'll soon learn,
Our business here is also your concern.

ARSINOÉ (*to* CÉLIMÈNE): Madam, I visit you so soon again
Only because of these two gentlemen,
Who came to me indignant and aggrieved

About a crime too base to be believed.
Knowing your virtue, having such confidence in it,
I couldn't think you guilty for a minute,
In spite of all their telling evidence;
And, rising above our little difference,
I've hastened here in friendship's name to see
You clear yourself of this great calumny.

ACASTE: Yes, Madam, let us see with what composure
You'll manage to respond to this disclosure.
You lately sent Clitandre this tender note.

CLITANDRE: And this one, for Acaste, you also wrote.

ACASTE (*to* ORONTE *and* ALCESTE): You'll recognize this writing, Sirs, I think;
The lady is so free with pen and ink
That you must know it all too well, I fear.
But listen: this is something you should hear.

"How absurd you are to condemn my lightheartedness in society, and to accuse me of being happiest in the company of others. Nothing could be more unjust; and if you do not come to me instantly and beg pardon for saying such a thing, I shall never forgive you as long as I live. Our big bumbling friend the Viscount . . ."

What a shame that he's not here.

"Our big bumbling friend the Viscount, whose name stands first in your complaint, is hardly a man to my taste; and ever since the day I watched him spend three-quarters of an hour spitting into a well, so as to make circles in the water, I have been unable to think highly of him. As for the little Marquess . . ."

In all modesty, gentlemen, that is I.

"As for the little Marquess, who sat squeezing my hand for such a long while yesterday, I find him in all respects the most trifling creature alive; and the only things of value about him are his cape and his sword. As for the man with the green ribbons . . ."

(*To* ALCESTE.) It's your turn now, Sir.

"As for the man with the green ribbons, he amuses me now and then with his bluntness and his bearish ill-humor; but there are many times indeed when I think him the greatest bore in the world. And as for the sonneteer . . ."

(*To* ORONTE.) Here's your helping.

"And as for the sonneteer, who has taken it into his head to be witty, and insists on being an author in the teeth of opinion, I simply cannot be bothered to listen to him, and his prose wearies me quite as much as his poetry. Be assured that I am not always so well-entertained as you suppose; that I long for your company, more than I dare to say, at all these entertainments to which people drag me; and that the presence of those one loves is the true and perfect seasoning to all one's pleasures."

CLITANDRE: And now for me.

"Clitandre, whom you mention, and who so pesters me with his saccharine speeches, is the last man on earth for whom I could feel any affection. He is quite mad to suppose that I love him, and so are you, to doubt that you are loved. Do come to your senses; exchange your suppositions for his; and visit me as often as possible, to help me bear the annoyance of his unwelcome attentions."

It's a sweet character that these letters show,
And what to call it, Madam, you well know.
Enough. We're off to make the world acquainted
With this sublime self-portrait that you've painted.
ACASTE: Madam, I'll make you no farewell oration;
No, you're not worthy of my indignation.
Far choicer hearts than yours, as you'll discover,
Would like this little Marquess for a lover.

Scene 5 [CÉLIMÈNE, ÉLIANTE, ARSINOÉ, ALCESTE, ORONTE, PHILINTE]

ORONTE: So! After all those loving letters you wrote,
You turn on me like this, and cut my throat!
And your dissembling, faithless heart, I find,
Has pledged itself by turns to all mankind!
How blind I've been! But now I clearly see;
I thank you, Madam, for enlightening me.
My heart is mine once more, and I'm content;
The loss of it shall be your punishment.

(*To* ALCESTE.)

Sir, she is yours; I'll seek no more to stand
Between your wishes and this lady's hand.

Scene 6 [CÉLIMÈNE, ÉLIANTE, ARSINOÉ, ALCESTE, PHILINTE]

ARSINOÉ (*to* CÉLIMÈNE): Madam, I'm forced to speak. I'm far too stirred
To keep my counsel, after what I've heard.
I'm shocked and staggered by your want of morals.
It's not my way to mix in others' quarrels;
But really, when this fine and noble spirit,
This man of honor and surpassing merit,
Laid down the offering of his heart before you,
How *could* you . . .
ALCESTE: Madam, permit me, I implore you,
To represent myself in this debate.
Don't bother, please, to be my advocate.
My heart, in any case, could not afford
To give your services their due reward;
And if I chose, for consolation's sake,
Some other lady, 'twould not be you I'd take.
ARSINOÉ: What makes you think you could, Sir? And how dare you
Imply that I've been trying to ensnare you?
If you can for a moment entertain
Such flattering fancies, you're extremely vain.
I'm not so interested as you suppose
In Célimène's discarded gigolos.
Get rid of that absurd illusion, do.
Women like me are not for such as you.
Stay with this creature, to whom you're so attached;
I've never seen two people better matched.

Scene 7 [CÉLIMÈNE, ÉLIANTE, ALCESTE, PHILINTE]

ALCESTE (*to* CÉLIMÈNE): Well, I've been still throughout this exposé,
Till everyone but me has said his say.
Come, have I shown sufficient self-restraint?
And may I now . . .
CÉLIMÈNE: Yes, make your just complaint.
Reproach me freely, call me what you will;
You've every right to say I've used you ill.
I've wronged you, I confess it; and in my shame
I'll make no effort to escape the blame.
The anger of those others I could despise;
My guilt toward you I sadly recognize.

Your wrath is wholly justified, I fear;
I know how culpable I must appear,
I know all things bespeak my treachery,
And that, in short, you've grounds for hating me.
Do so; I give you leave.

ALCESTE: Ah, traitress — how,
How should I cease to love you, even now?
Though mind and will were passionately bent
On hating you, my heart would not consent.

(*To* ÉLIANTE *and* PHILINTE.)

Be witness to my madness, both of you;
See what infatuation drives one to;
But wait; my folly's only just begun,
And I shall prove to you before I'm done
How strange the human heart is, and how far
From rational we sorry creatures are.

(*To* CÉLIMÈNE.)

Woman, I'm willing to forget your shame,
And clothe your treacheries in a sweeter name;
I'll call them youthful errors, instead of crimes,
And lay the blame on these corrupting times.
My one condition is that you agree
To share my chosen fate, and fly with me
To that wild, trackless, solitary place
In which I shall forget the human race.
Only by such a course can you atone
For those atrocious letters; by that alone
Can you remove my present horror of you,
And make it possible for me to love you.

CÉLIMÈNE: What! *I* renounce the world at my young age,
And die of boredom in some hermitage?

ALCESTE: Ah, if you really loved me as you ought,
You wouldn't give the world a moment's thought;
Must you have me, and all the world beside?

CÉLIMÈNE: Alas, at twenty one is terrified
Of solitude. I fear I lack the force
And depth of soul to take so stern a course.
But if my hand in marriage will content you,
Why, there's a plan which I might well consent to,
And . . .

ALCESTE: No, I detest you now. I could excuse
Everything else, but since you thus refuse
To love me wholly, as a wife should do,
And see the world in me, as I in you,
Go! I reject your hand, and disenthrall
My heart from your enchantments, once for all.

Scene 8 [ÉLIANTE, ALCESTE, PHILINTE]

ALCESTE (*to* ÉLIANTE): Madam, your virtuous beauty has no peer;
Of all this world, you only are sincere;
I've long esteemed you highly, as you know;
Permit me ever to esteem you so,
And if I do not now request your hand,
Forgive me, Madam, and try to understand.
I feel unworthy of it; I sense that fate
Does not intend me for the married state,
That I should do you wrong by offering you
My shattered heart's unhappy residue,
And that in short . . .
ÉLIANTE: Your argument's well taken:
Nor need you fear that I shall feel forsaken.
Were I to offer him this hand of mine,
Your friend Philinte, I think, would not decline.
PHILINTE: Ah, Madam, that's my heart's most cherished goal,
For which I'd gladly give my life and soul.
ALCESTE (*to* ÉLIANTE *and* PHILINTE): May you be true to all you now profess,
And so deserve unending happiness.
Meanwhile, betrayed and wronged in everything,
I'll flee this bitter world where vice is king,
And seek some spot unpeopled and apart
Where I'll be free to have an honest heart.
PHILINTE: Come, Madam, let's do everything we can
To change the mind of this unhappy man.

WHEN Molière's company first performed *The Misanthrope* in 1666 the success of the play was greater with the sophisticated literati at court than with the general audience. The same split response has attended most subsequent productions. Audiences and readers have felt that to understand the play is to be made uncomfortable rather than to be pleased and that Alceste is an interesting rather than an attractive character. Neither characteristic is dimmed by the likelihood that Alceste's fierce disgust with the polite shams of society was in part Molière's own at the time when he wrote the play.

The Palais Royal in Paris, Molière's theater, was a typical playhouse of French neoclassicism. From Italian stagecraft of the late Renaissance the theater of King Louis XIV took over and developed most of the features of the conventional modern theater: box stage within a proscenium arch, curtain, wings for movable sets, painted backdrop, artificial lighting, and women in women parts.

The play itself, however, observes the crucial neoclassical unities only in a somewhat casual manner. It is a comprehensive anatomy of social attitudes, an exposé of an entire milieu, and its action, accordingly, is static rather than dynamic, analytical and expository rather than narrative. Molière's singleness of intent has not left him much room for suspense or ordinary plot causality. He achieves his tart meanings less by means of events, singly or in structure, than by juxtapositions of characters, situations, and tones (almost the whole of Act II is an example). The gain in concentration on social manners is considerable: the whole series of episodes and confrontations of rivalries and animosities that substitutes for a coherent, climaxing plot exhibits the conflict between Alceste and society. This is true even of the only major scene in which Alceste himself is not on stage: the verbal duel between Célimène and Arsinoé, which, at the exact midpoint of the play, demonstrates what social intercourse would be like if Alceste's code of absolute frankness were to prevail.

The place throughout is a salon in Célimène's house, and the time appears to be limited to a single day, but neither place nor time is an active ingredient in the action, except insofar as a short time span strengthens psychological plausibility in a comedy that is based on a static concept of character. The setting is a neutral locale for visits and conversation. The time span is arbitrarily cut off at the beginning and the end (the opening conversation between Philinte and Alceste is a running start, and the ending is inconclusive) and could be any day in the usual routine of Célimène's idle and fashionable set. The absence of particulars about Alceste's and Célimène's lawsuits is another instance of indefiniteness. The cumulative effect of such nonparticularity is that the action seems "typical," a randomly selected illustration of a general pattern. Alceste becomes something like the Good Man Indignant.

The Misanthrope differs from several of Molière's other comedies in showing little influence from the *commedia dell' arte*, the vigorous, popular theater of contemporary Italy, in which professional companies performed semi-farces of stock plot, situation, and character, but of improvised dialogue. In Célimène there may be traces of the conventional stage courtesan, and Alceste's valet Dubois suggests the impertinent and stupid servant of standard farce. But Alceste himself belongs rather to the tradition of humor comedy, though here, too, Molière has modified convention. Society is under examination almost as much as the title character. Much of the action originates not in Alceste's eccentricity but in the foibles of his human environment: Oronte's literary vanity, Arsinoé's jealousy, and the Marquesses' foppish suit of Célimène.

The Misanthrope is the maturest of comedies of manners; that is, plays in which comedy results from the clash between a group code of upper-class social behavior and an individual deviating from the code. In simple specimens of the genre one or the other is felt to represent a sane norm and the antagonist a corresponding aberration which is exposed to laughter. In subtler kinds, right and wrong, approval and ridicule, are more evenly distributed. In *The Misanthrope* the ambivalence is carried to the point of paradox. The norm of the foolish and corrupt group code is opposed by the life-negating idiosyncrasy of the virtuous individual. The main audience problem becomes that of choosing sides between Alceste and society.

In the ambivalence resides the play's "darkness" as comedy, and it explains why, of all Molière's great comedies, it is the least gay and least popular and the most widely discussed. It has been called Molière's *Hamlet*, a label particularly fitting in the light of recent views of the Prince of Denmark as a homicidal neurotic. The "problem," in a narrow, technical sense, is that Alceste's character resists any effort to fit the play into the mold of Molière's other plays of comically deviant eccentrics. The jealous Arnolphe, the pious fraud Tartuffe, the miser Harpagon, and the would-be gentleman M. Jourdain are not fit company for the noble-minded Alceste. The Restoration playwright William Wycherley called his English adaptation *The Plain Dealer* and his hero Manly, and both title and name reflect a degree of unease with Alceste and his fate which Wycherley has not been alone in feeling.

Jean Jacques Rousseau, the French *philosophe* who godfathered Romantic individualism and "naturalness," may be taken to represent the opposition to Molière's treatment of Alceste. The real misanthrope, Rousseau argued, is not a man but a monster, "an enemy of the human race," an example of "natural depravity." But Alceste is very much a man — a good and honest man, unhappily in love with a charming but heartless coquette and opposed to her meretricious world. To affix the label of "misanthrope" to such a man and to show him behaving in a silly fashion is a betrayal of militant virtue.

The basis for Rousseau's attack is the theory that the function of literature is to teach good morals (if only implicitly, by showing models of exemplary behavior and attitude for the reader's emulation). Molière would have accepted the theory but differed on the degree of subtlety and indirection allowed the playwright in putting it to practice. The function of comedy has been defined as the eliciting of thoughtful laughter. By this definition *The Misanthrope* must be accounted at least a partial failure, for the spectacle of honest integrity in the role of furious and futile zeal may have provoked thought but hardly the liberating laughter of pure comedy — at most a wry and painful smile. And yet, the play's distinction as comedy rests on the impossibility of dismissing altogether the tragic alternative to the comic interpretation.

There is, on the one hand, the vital point of the comparison with *Hamlet*. Both plays give off a sense of life's dark ambiguities, of the disparity between social appearance and social reality. Both title characters are brooding and somber outsiders in a glittering company. In *Hamlet* the tragic irony is that in the rotten realm of Denmark the infection spreads to the noble Prince himself as he seeks to purify his heritage, paralyzing his will and poisoning his conscience with acts of rash injustice. In *The Misanthrope* there is the parallel irony that in an elegantly corrupt and superficially amiable society the blunt and virtuous hero necessarily appears absurd. The social evil of deception, murderous in the tragedy, frivolous in the comedy, not only opposes the uncompromising, heroic stance, but undermines it as well. And about Philinte, Alceste's friend and foil and the character who comes as close as any in the play to being Molière's spokesman (*raisonneur*), there hangs a curious air of tepid prig. If his reasonableness sets off Alceste's fanaticism, so does Alceste's idealism set off his compromise with the tainted world. And after his quaint love scene with Éliante in Act IV, in which both smother romance in good manners and selflessness, Philinte's common sense about social life appears less as wise conviction than as absence of strong feeling. The tone of the lovers' engagement scene at the end approaches that of parody:

> ÉLIANTE [*to* ALCESTE]: Your argument's well taken:
> Nor need you fear that I shall feel forsaken.
> Were I to offer him this hand of mine,
> Your friend Philinte, I think, would not decline.

PHILINTE: Ah Madam, that's my heart's most cherished goal,
For which I'd gladly give my life and soul.

The contrast with the spirited exchanges between Alceste and Célimène is obvious. With Éliante and Philinte ceremony is all. The quality of the peculiar sociality which the misanthrope rejects and which his friend wants him to accept is suggested by the fact that it does not involve a single family relationship. In the absence of ties of blood and marriage all social intimacy somehow seems precarious, transient, and shallow.

This is the play's (not Alceste's) case against society. But the play makes a case also against Alceste, and it is part of its subtle balance of values that this case is only partly also society's case. Alceste *is* impossible, and not just by the norms of a society that thrives on the pretense and the compromise entailed by good manners. He is also ridiculous. Act I serves to establish Alceste's position and the values he represents, but it also insinuates the vulnerability of both. We see him in double exposure vis à vis each of his three antagonists: the polite but insincere conventions of friends and acquaintances, the law that represents the contentious reality behind the affable surface of social life, and, finally, Célimène. There is the hint of temporizing in his repeated "I don't say that" in his comments on Oronte's sonnet — a hint all the more incongruous after his defense of frankness a few minutes earlier. (There is also the dubiousness of the critical judgment itself that prefers the artless "old love song" to Oronte's artificial but deft manipulation of a formally exacting set of paradoxes on love.) There is his cranky perverseness in welcoming the loss of his lawsuit for the sake of having his distrust of the court vindicated. Justice clearly means less to him than to be proved right in his cynicism. And there is, above all, the admitted unreason of his love for Célimène.

Throughout the play Alceste's naïveté, exposing him to furious and sometimes inarticulate disillusionment with each new instance of the world's hypocrisy, malice, fickleness, and affectation, is incongruous in a confirmed and self-confessed misanthrope. He never learns to expect the world to be as wicked as he says it is. And the cynicism which in theory is his armor against the slings and arrows of the world is never more easily penetrable than in his encounters with Célimène: he, tense with reluctant tenderness; she, thrilled with the risk of teasing her boorish lover. Against his better judgment and announced intentions he stoops again and again to vie with contemptible drones for her attention. Our sympathy is tempered by the spectacle of the self-declared hater of mankind in love with a flirtatious woman who aims to please indiscriminately. There is irony, both hilarious and touching, in the moment when his love wrings from him — from *him!* — this plea:

> Pretend, pretend, that you are just and true,

There is pathos in Alceste's fate, but his rigid pose in a pliable society is a comical rather than a tragical kind of *hubris*. It suggests petulant pride, childish self-indulgence, narcissistic love of an impressive attitude. We laugh, not at his virtue, or at his bluntness, or even at his lack of a sense of humor and self-irony, but at his monomania. The comic vision is committed to uphold even a flawed sociality in the face of however virtuous an isolating eccentricity, if only because it *is* eccentricity.

> . . . all you say I'll readily concede [says PHILINTE]
> This is a low, conniving age indeed;
> Nothing but trickery prospers nowadays,
> And people ought to mend their shabby ways.
> Yes, man's a beastly creature; but must we then
> Abandon the society of men?

The voice that answers "no" is the voice of wisdom. Not the highest wisdom, not tragic wisdom, but the wisdom of the world in which it takes prudence and virtue to remain both uncorrupted and unbeguiled by corruption, and both tolerance and good nature to be able to see a gathering of gossiping prudes and coquettes, fops and witlings, as the regrettable but inevitable and rather amusing excrescence on a sophisticated court culture.

The comic spirit is the spirit that has learned to live with the fact of man's limitations. To this spirit Alceste represents a threat. No man's integrity or idealism is worth the disintegration of the social fabric, the bonds that tie man to man. Alceste's demand for instant and radical reform is the utopian dream of a ridiculous crank. The fanatic of virtue is just as much an enemy of the social system as any other kind of fanatic. The smallness, the stiffness, the frozen constriction, of his attitude qualify him for the wilderness he sets out for at the end. In Act I he had called it a "desert land, unfouled by humankind." The monstrosity of the phrase proves the justice of the title of the play, even on Rousseau's strict terms. Philinte's final reference to Alceste as an "unhappy man" is a piece of ironic charity, for the almost-tragic victim of virtue has, by resigning from the human family, made himself less than man.

The dramatized image of virtue as a potential destroyer, in an imperfect world, of man's humanity deepens and darkens the comical incongruity between what Alceste stands for and what his behavior actually makes him. Molière's control of tone and situation is largely a matter of his control of Alceste. He is given tirades to speak, not soliloquies; we always see him through the eyes of the group among whom he stalks. As a result, the latent tragedy of Alceste, the virtuous hero, never takes the play away from the overt comedy of the social misfit. Even our final glimpse of the solitude he seeks is comically tempered by the possibility that Philinte and Éliante may succeed in changing his mind. And Célimène in the wilderness is a less pleasing figure than Célimène elegantly at home. In the counterpoint effect, both witty and serious, rests the play's greatness as drama celebrating tact and tolerance, sanity, laughter, moderation, and breadth of spirit — in short, and pre-eminently, *civilization.*

Richard Brinsley Sheridan

THE RIVALS

Characters

CAPTAIN ABSOLUTE
LYDIA LANGUISH
SIR ANTHONY ABSOLUTE, *father of Captain Absolute*
MRS. MALAPROP, *aunt of Lydia Languish*
FAULKLAND
JULIA MELVILLE, *cousin of Lydia Languish*
BOB ACRES
SIR LUCIUS O'TRIGGER
FAG, *valet of Captain Absolute*
LUCY, *lady's maid of Lydia Languish*
DAVID, *valet of Bob Acres*
COACHMAN
MAID
BOY
SERVANTS

SCENE: *Bath.*
TIME OF ACTION: *Within one day.*

PROLOGUE

To the Revised Production, Presented on the Tenth Night

JULIA: Granted our cause, our suit and trial o'er,
The worthy serjeant[1] need appear no more:
In pleasing I a different client choose,
He served the Poet — I would serve the Muse:

[1] a reference to a character in the original Prologue

Like him, I'll try to merit your applause,
A female counsel in a female's cause.
Look on this form — (*pointing to* COMEDY[2])
where humor, quaint and sly,
Dimples the cheek, and points the beaming eye;
Where gay invention seems to boast its wiles
In amorous hint, and half-triumphant smiles;
While her light mask or[3] covers satire's strokes,
Or hides the conscious blush her wit provokes.
— Look on her well — does she seem formed to teach?
Should you expect to hear this lady — preach?
Is grey experience suited to her youth?
Do solemn sentiments become that mouth?
Bid her be grave, those lips should rebel prove
To every theme that slanders mirth or love.
Yet thus adorned with every graceful art
To charm the fancy and yet reach the heart —
Must we displace her? And instead advance
The goddess of the woful countenance —
The sentimental Muse! — Her emblems view,
The Pilgrim's Progress, and a sprig of rue!
View her — too chaste to look like flesh and blood —
Primly portray'd on emblematic wood!
There fixed in usurpation should she stand,
She'll snatch the dagger from her sister's hand:
And having made her votaries weep a flood,
Good heaven! she'll end her comedies in blood —
Bid Harry Woodward break poor Dunstall's crown!
Imprison Quick — and knock Ned Shuter down;
While sad Barsanti — weeping o'er the scene —
Shall stab himself — or poison Mrs. Green.[4]
Such dire encroachments to prevent in time,
Demands the critic's voice — the poet's rhyme.
Can our light scenes add strength to holy laws?
Such puny patronage but hurts the cause:
Fair virtue scorns our feeble aid to ask;
And moral truth disdains the trickster's mask.
For here their favorite stands, (*pointing to* TRAGEDY)
whose brow, severe
And sad — claims youth's respect, and pity's tear;

[2] carved wooden images of the muses of comedy and tragedy appeared on either side of the proscenium arch [3] either [4] passage contains names of actors in the play

Who — when oppressed by foes her worth creates —
Can point a poniard at the guilt she hates.

ACT I

Scene 1 [A street in Bath.]

(COACHMAN *crosses the stage. Enter* FAG, *looking after him.*)

FAG: What! — Thomas! — Sure, 'tis he? — What! — Thomas! — Thomas!

COACHMAN: Hey! — Odd's life![5] — Mr. Fag! — give us your hand, my old fellow-servant.

FAG: Excuse my glove, Thomas: — I'm dev'lish glad to see you, my lad: why, my prince of charioteers, you look as hearty! — but who the deuce thought of seeing you in Bath!

COACHMAN: Sure, Master, Madam Julia, Harry, Mrs. Kate, and the postilion be all come!

FAG: Indeed!

COACHMAN: Aye! Master thought another fit of the gout was coming to make him a visit: so he'd a mind to gi't the slip, and whip! we were all off at an hour's warning.

FAG: Aye, aye! hasty in everything, or it would not be Sir Anthony Absolute!

COACHMAN: But tell us, Mr. Fag, how does young master? Odd! Sir Anthony will stare to see the Captain here!

FAG: I do not serve Captain Absolute now.

COACHMAN: Why sure!

FAG: At present I am employed by Ensign Beverley.

COACHMAN: I doubt,[6] Mr. Fag, you ha'n't changed for the better.

FAG: I have not changed, Thomas.

COACHMAN: No! why, didn't you say you had left young master?

FAG: No. —— Well, honest Thomas, I must puzzle you no farther: briefly then — Captain Absolute and Ensign Beverley are one and the same person.

COACHMAN: The devil they are!

FAG: So it is indeed, Thomas; and the *Ensign*-half of my master being on guard at present — the *Captain* has nothing to do with me.

COACHMAN: So, so! — What, this is some freak, I warrant! —— Do

[5] God's life (a blasphemy euphemistically altered, like most of the oaths in the play) [6] fear

tell us, Mr. Fag, the meaning o't—you know I ha' trusted you.

FAG: You'll be secret, Thomas?

COACHMAN: As a coach-horse.

FAG: Why then the cause of all this is—LOVE—Love, Thomas, who (as you may get read to you) has been a masquerader ever since the days of Jupiter.

COACHMAN: Aye, aye;—I guessed there was a lady in the case: but pray, why does your master pass only for *Ensign?* Now if he had shammed *General*, indeed——

FAG: Ah! Thomas, there lies the mystery o' the matter. Hark'ee,[7] Thomas, my master is in love with a lady of a very singular taste: a lady who likes him better as a *half-pay Ensign* than if she knew he was son and heir to Sir Anthony Absolute, a baronet of three thousand a year!

COACHMAN: That is an odd taste indeed!—but has she got the stuff, Mr. Fag? is she rich, hey?

FAG: Rich!—why, I believe she owns half the stocks—Z——ds![8] Thomas, she could pay the national debt as easily as I could my washerwoman! She has a lap-dog that eats out of gold—she feeds her parrot with small pearls—and all her thread-papers[9] are made of bank-notes!

COACHMAN: Bravo!—Faith!—Odd! I warrant she has a set of thousands[10] at least. But does she draw kindly with the Captain?

FAG: As fond as pigeons.

COACHMAN: May one hear her name?

FAG: Miss Lydia Languish. But there is an old tough aunt in the way; though, by the bye, she has never seen my master, for he got acquainted with Miss while on a visit in Gloucestershire.

COACHMAN: Well—I wish they were once harnessed together in matrimony.——But pray, Mr. Fag, what kind of a place is this Bath? I ha' heard a deal of it—here's a mort[11] o' merry-making, hey?

FAG: Pretty well, Thomas, pretty well—'tis a good lounge.[12] In the morning we go to the Pump-room (though neither my master nor I drink the waters); after breakfast we saunter on the Parades, or play a game at billiards; at night we dance: but d——n the place, I'm tired of it: their regular hours stupefy me—not a fiddle nor a card after eleven! However, Mr. Faulkland's gentleman and I keep it up a little in private parties—I'll introduce you there, Thomas: you'll like him much.

[7] listen [8] *i.e.*, Zounds, God's wounds [9] papers folded so as to hold and keep separate different skeins of thread [10] team of horses worth thousands of pounds [11] great amount [12] place for leisure

COACHMAN: Sure I know Mr. Du-Peigne — you know his master is to marry Madam Julia.

FAG: I had forgot. —— But Thomas, you must polish a little — indeed you must. Here now — this wig! what the devil do you do with a *wig*, Thomas? — none of the London whips[13] of any degree of *ton*[14] wear *wigs* now.

COACHMAN: More's the pity! more's the pity, I say — Odd's life! when I heard how the lawyers and doctors had took to their own hair, I thought how 'twould go next: — Odd rabbit it! when the fashion had got foot on the Bar,[15] I guessed 'twould mount to the Box![16] But 'tis all out of character, believe me, Mr. Fag: and look'ee, I'll never gi' up mine — the lawyers and doctors may do as they will.

FAG: Well, Thomas, we'll not quarrel about that.

COACHMAN: Why, bless you, the gentlemen of they[17] professions ben't all of a mind — for in our village now, tho'ff[18] *Jack Gauge*, the *exciseman*, has ta'en to his carrots,[19] there's little Dick, the farrier, swears he'll never forsake his *bob*,[20] tho' all the college should appear with their own heads!

FAG: Indeed! well said, Dick! But hold — mark! mark! Thomas.

COACHMAN: Zooks![21] 'tis the Captain! — Is that the lady with him?

FAG: No! no! that is Madam Lucy — my master's mistress's maid. They lodge at that house — but I must after him to tell him the news.

COACHMAN: Odd! he's giving her money! —— Well, Mr. Fag ——

FAG: Good-bye, Thomas. — I have an appointment in Gyde's Porch this evening at eight; meet me there, and we'll make a little party.

(*Exeunt severally.*)

Scene 2

[*A dressing-room in* MRS. MALAPROP'S *lodgings.*]

(LYDIA *sitting on a sofa, with a book in her hand.* LUCY, *as just returned from a message.*)

LUCY: Indeed, Ma'am, I traversed half the town in search of it: I don't believe there's a circulating library in Bath I ha'n't been at.

LYDIA: And could not you get *The Reward of Constancy?*

LUCY: No, indeed, Ma'am.

[13] coachmen [14] fashion, style, class [15] *i.e.*, foothold in the legal profession [16] the coachman's seat [17] *i.e.*, those [18] though [19] red hair (*i.e.*, his own) [20] here, wig [21] God's hooks (*i.e.*, the nails of the cross)

LYDIA: Nor *The Fatal Connection?*

LUCY: No, indeed, Ma'am.

LYDIA: Nor *The Mistakes of the Heart?*

LUCY: Ma'am, as ill-luck would have it, Mr. Bull said Miss Sukey Saunter had just fetched it away.

LYDIA: Heigh-ho! Did you inquire for *The Delicate Distress?*

LUCY: Or *The Memoirs of Lady Woodford?* Yes, indeed, Ma'am. I asked everywhere for it; and I might have brought it from Mr. Frederick's, but Lady Slattern Lounger, who had just sent it home, had so soiled and dog's-eared it, it wa'n't fit for a Christian to read.

LYDIA: Heigh-ho! — Yes, I always know when Lady Slattern has been before me. She has a most observing thumb; and I believe cherishes her nails for the convenience of making marginal notes. —— Well, child, what *have* you brought me?

LUCY: Oh! here, Ma'am (*taking books from under her cloak, and from her pockets*). This is *The Gordian Knot,* and this *Peregrine Pickle.* Here are *The Tears of Sensibility* and *Humphry Clinker.* This is *The Memoirs of a Lady of Quality, written by herself,* and here the second volume of *The Sentimental Journey.*

LYDIA: Heigh-ho! — What are those books by the glass?

LUCY: The great one is only *The Whole Duty of Man* — where I press a few blonds,[22] Ma'am.

LYDIA: Very well — give me the *sal volatile.*

LUCY: Is it in a blue cover, Ma'am?

LYDIA: My smelling bottle, you simpleton!

LUCY: Oh, the drops! — Here, Ma'am.

LYDIA: Hold! — here's some one coming —— quick! see who it is.

(*Exit* LUCY.)

Surely I heard my cousin Julia's voice!

(*Re-enter* LUCY.)

LUCY: Lud! Ma'am, here is Miss Melville.

LYDIA: It is possible! —— (*Enter* JULIA.) My dearest Julia, how delighted am I! — (*Embrace.*) How unexpected was this happiness!

JULIA: True, Lydia — and our pleasure is the greater; but what has been the matter? — you were denied to me[23] at first!

LYDIA: Ah! Julia, I have a thousand things to tell you! But first inform me what has conjured you to Bath? Is Sir Anthony here?

JULIA: He is — we are arrived within this hour, and I suppose he will

[22] silk laces [23] I was not allowed to see you

be here to wait on Mrs. Malaprop as soon as he is dressed.

LYDIA: Then, before we are interrupted, let me impart to you some of my distress! I know your gentle nature will sympathize with me, though your prudence may condemn me! My letters have informed you of my whole connexion with Beverley — but I have lost him, Julia! My aunt has discovered our intercourse by a note she intercepted, and has confined me ever since! Yet, would you believe it? she has fallen absolutely in love with a tall Irish baronet she met one night since we have been here, at Lady Macshuffle's rout.[24]

JULIA: You jest, Lydia!

LYDIA: No, upon my word. She really carries on a kind of correspondence with him, under a feigned name though, till she chooses to be known to him; but it is a *Delia* or a *Celia*, I assure you.

JULIA: Then surely she is now more indulgent to her niece.

LYDIA: Quite the contrary. Since she has discovered her own frailty she is become more suspicious of mine. Then I must inform you of another plague! That odious Acres is to be in Bath to-day; so that I protest I shall be teased out of all spirits!

JULIA: Come, come, Lydia, hope the best. Sir Anthony shall use his interest with Mrs. Malaprop.

LYDIA: But you have not heard the worst. Unfortunately I had quarreled with my poor Beverley just before my aunt made the discovery, and I have not seen him since to make it up.

JULIA: What was his offence?

LYDIA: Nothing at all! But, I don't know how it was, as often as we had been together we had never had a quarrel! And, somehow, I was afraid he would never give me an opportunity. So last Thursday I wrote a letter to myself to inform myself that Beverley was at that time paying his addresses to another woman. I signed it *your friend unknown*, showed it to Beverley, charged him with his falsehood, put myself in a violent passion, and vowed I'd never see him more.

JULIA: And you let him depart so, and have not seen him since?

LYDIA: 'Twas the next day my aunt found the matter out. I intended only to have teased him three days and a half, and now I've lost him forever!

JULIA: If he is as deserving and sincere as you have represented him to me, he will never give you up so. Yet consider, Lydia, you tell me he is but an ensign, and you have thirty thousand pounds!

LYDIA: But you know I lose most of my fortune if I marry without my aunt's consent, till of age; and that is what I have determined

24 fashionable evening party or reception

to do ever since I knew the penalty. Nor could I love the man who would wish to wait a day for the alternative.

JULIA: Nay, this is caprice!

LYDIA: What, does Julia tax me with caprice? I thought her lover Faulkland had enured her to it.

JULIA: I do not love even *his* faults.

LYDIA: But a-propos — you have sent to him, I suppose?

JULIA: Not yet, upon my word, nor has he the least idea of my being in Bath. Sir Anthony's resolution was so sudden I could not inform him of it.

LYDIA: Well, Julia, you are your own mistress (though under the protection of Sir Anthony), yet have you for this long year been a slave to the caprice, the whim, the jealousy of this ungrateful Faulkland, who will ever delay assuming the right of a husband, while you suffer him to be equally imperious as a lover.

JULIA: Nay, you are wrong entirely. We were contracted before my father's death. That, and some consequent embarrassments, have delayed what I know to be my Faulkland's most ardent wish. He is too generous to trifle on such a point. And for his character, you wrong him there too. No, Lydia, he is too proud, too noble to be jealous: if he is captious, 'tis without dissembling; if fretful, without rudeness. Unused to the fopperies of love, he is negligent of the little duties expected from a lover — but being unhackneyd in the passion, his affection is ardent and sincere; and as it engrosses his whole soul, he expects every thought and emotion of his mistress to move in unison with his. Yet, though his pride calls for this full return, his humility makes him undervalue those qualities in him which would entitle him to it; and not feeling why he should be loved to the degree he wishes, he still suspects that he is not loved enough. This temper, I must own, has cost me many unhappy hours; but I have learned to think myself his debtor for those imperfections which arise from the ardour of his attachment.

LYDIA: Well, I cannot blame you for defending him. But tell me candidly, Julia, had he never saved your life, do you think you should have been attached to him as you are? Believe me, the rude blast that overset your boat was a prosperous gale of love to him.

JULIA: Gratitude may have strengthened my attachment to Mr. Faulkland, but I loved him before he had preserved me; yet surely that alone were an obligation sufficient ——

LYDIA: Obligation! Why, a water-spaniel would have done as much! Well, I should never think of giving my heart to a man because he could swim!

JULIA: Come, Lydia, you are too inconsiderate.

LYDIA: Nay, I do but jest. —— What's here?

(*Enter* LUCY *in a hurry.*)

LUCY: O Ma'am, here is Sir Anthony Absolute just come home with your aunt.

LYDIA: They'll not come here. —— Lucy, do you watch.

(*Exit* LUCY.)

JULIA: Yet I must go. Sir Anthony does not know I am here, and if we meet, he'll detain me, to show me the town. I'll take another opportunity of paying my respects to Mrs. Malaprop, when she shall treat me, as long as she chooses, with her select words so ingeniously *misapplied,* without being *mispronounced.*

(*Re-enter* LUCY.)

LUCY: O lud! Ma'am, they are both coming upstairs.

LYDIA: Well, I'll not detain you, coz. Adieu, my dear Julia. I'm sure you are in haste to send to Faulkland. There — through my room you'll find another stair-case.

JULIA: Adieu. —— (*Embrace. Exit* JULIA.)

LYDIA: Here, my dear Lucy, hide these books. Quick, quick! Fling *Peregrine Pickle* under the toilet — throw *Roderick Random* into the closet — put *The Innocent Adultery* into *The Whole Duty of Man* — thrust *Lord Aimworth* under the sofa — cram *Ovid* behind the bolster — there — put *The Man of Feeling* into your pocket — so, so, — now lay *Mrs. Chapone* in sight, and leave *Fordyce's Sermons* open on the table.

LUCY: Oh burn it, Ma'am! the hair-dresser has torn away as far as *Proper Pride.*

LYDIA: Never mind — open at *Sobriety.* — Fling me *Lord Chesterfield's Letters.* — Now for 'em.

(*Enter* MRS. MALAPROP, *and* SIR ANTHONY ABSOLUTE.)

MRS. MALAPROP: There, Sir Anthony, there sits the deliberate simpleton who wants to disgrace her family, and lavish herself on a fellow not worth a shilling!

LYDIA: Madam, I thought you once ——

MRS. MALAPROP: You thought, Miss! I don't know any business you have to think at all. Thought does not become a young woman. But the point we would request of you is, that you will promise to forget this fellow — to illiterate[25] him, I say, quite from your memory.

LYDIA: Ah! Madam! our memories are independent of our wills. It is not so easy to forget.

MRS. MALAPROP: But I say it is, Miss; there is nothing on earth so easy as to *forget*, if a person chooses to set about it. I'm sure I have as much forgot your poor dear uncle as if he had never existed — and I thought it my duty so to do; and let me tell you, Lydia, these violent memories don't become a young woman.

SIR ANTHONY: Why sure she won't pretend to remember what she's ordered not! — aye, this comes of her reading!

LYDIA: What crime, Madam, have I committed to be treated thus?

MRS. MALAPROP: Now don't attempt to extirpate yourself from the matter; you know I have proof controvertible of it. But tell me, will you promise to do as you're bid? Will you take a husband of your friend's choosing?

LYDIA: Madam, I must tell you plainly, that had I no preference for anyone else, the choice you have made would be my aversion.

MRS. MALAPROP: What business have you, Miss, with *preference* and *aversion?* They don't become a young woman; and you ought to know, that as both always wear off, 'tis safest in matrimony to begin with a little *aversion*. I am sure I hated your poor dear uncle before marriage as if he'd been a blackamoor — and yet, Miss, you are sensible what a wife I made! — and when it pleased heaven to release me from him, 'tis unknown what tears I shed! But suppose we were going to give you another choice, will you promise us to give up this Beverley?

LYDIA: Could I belie my thoughts so far as to give that promise, my actions would certainly as far belie my words.

MRS. MALAPROP: Take yourself to your room. You are fit company for nothing but your own ill-humours.

LYDIA: Willingly, Ma'am — I cannot change for the worse. (*Exit.*)

MRS. MALAPROP: There's a little intricate hussy for you!

SIR ANTHONY: It is not to be wondered at, Ma'am — all this is the natural consequence of teaching girls to read. Had I a thousand daughters, by heaven! I'd as soon have them taught the black art as their alphabet!

[25] *i.e.*, obliterate (This will suggest the nature of malapropisms. In the rest of the play these notes leave it to the reader's own enjoyment to find the word Mrs. Malaprop *should* have used for the word she *does* use. Her mistakes vary in their degree of transparency, and some of them admit of more than a single "translation.")

MRS. MALAPROP: Nay, nay, Sir Anthony, you are an absolute misanthropy.

SIR ANTHONY: In my way hither, Mrs. Malaprop, I observed your niece's maid coming forth from a circulating library! She had a book in each hand — they were half-bound volumes, with marble covers! From that moment I guessed how full of duty I should see her mistress!

MRS. MALAPROP: Those are vile places, indeed!

SIR ANTHONY: Madam, a circulating library in a town is as an evergreen tree of diabolical knowledge! It blossoms through the year! And depend on it, Mrs. Malaprop, that they who are so fond of handling the leaves, will long for the fruit at last.

MRS. MALAPROP: Fie, fie, Sir Anthony, you surely speak laconically!

SIR ANTHONY: Why, Mrs. Malaprop, in moderation, now, what would you have a woman know?

MRS. MALAPROP: Observe me, Sir Anthony. I would by no means wish a daughter of mine to be a progeny of learning; I don't think so much learning becomes a young woman; for instance — I would never let her meddle with Greek, or Hebrew, or Algebra, or Simony, or Fluxions, or Paradoxes, or such inflammatory branches of learning — neither would it be necessary for her to handle any of your mathematical, astronomical, diabolical instruments; — but, Sir Anthony, I would send her, at nine years old, to a boarding-school, in order to learn a little ingenuity and artifice. Then, Sir, she should have a supercilious knowledge in accounts — and as she grew up, I would have her instructed in geometry, that she might know something of the contagious countries — but above all, Sir Anthony, she should be mistress of orthodoxy, that she might not misspell, and mispronounce words so shamefully as girls usually do; and likewise that she might reprehend the true meaning of what she is saying. This, Sir Anthony, is what I would have a woman know — and I don't think there is a superstitious article in it.

SIR ANTHONY: Well, well, Mrs. Malaprop, I will dispute the point no further with you; though I must confess that you are a truly moderate and polite arguer, for almost every third word you say is on my side of the question. But, Mrs. Malaprop, to the more important point in debate — you say you have no objection to my proposal.

MRS. MALAPROP: None, I assure you. I am under no positive engagement with Mr. Acres, and as Lydia is so obstinate against him, perhaps your son may have better success.

SIR ANTHONY: Well, Madam, I will write for the boy directly. He knows not a syllable of this yet, though I have for some time had the proposal in my head. He is at present with his regiment.

MRS. MALAPROP: We have never seen your son, Sir Anthony; but I hope no objection on his side.

SIR ANTHONY: Objection! — let him object if he dare! No, no, Mrs. Malaprop, Jack knows that the least demur puts me in a frenzy directly. My process was always very simple — in their young days, 'twas "Jack do this"; — if he demurred — I knocked him down — and if he grumbled at that — I always sent him out of the room.

MRS. MALAPROP: Aye, and the properest way, o' my conscience! — nothing is so conciliating to young people as severity. Well, Sir Anthony, I shall give Mr. Acres his discharge, and prepare Lydia to receive your son's invocations; and I hope you will represent *her* to the Captain as an object not altogether illegible.

SIR ANTHONY: Madam, I will handle the subject prudently. Well, I must leave you — and let me beg you, Mrs. Malaprop, to enforce this matter roundly to the girl; take my advice — keep a tight hand; if she rejects this proposal — clap her under lock and key — and if you were just to let the servants forget to bring her dinner for three or four days, you can't conceive how she'd come about! (*Exit.*)

MRS. MALAPROP: Well, at any rate I shall be glad to get her from under my intuition. She has somehow discovered my partiality for Sir Lucius O'Trigger — sure, Lucy can't have betrayed me! No, the girl is such a simpleton, I should have made her confess it. —— (*Calls*) Lucy! — Lucy — Had she been one of your artificial ones, I should never have trusted her.

(*Enter* LUCY.)

LUCY: Did you call, Ma'am?

MRS. MALAPROP: Yes, girl. Did you see Sir Lucius while you was out?

LUCY: No, indeed, Ma'am, not a glimpse of him.

MRS. MALAPROP: You are sure, Lucy, that you never mentioned ——

LUCY: O Gemini! I'd sooner cut my tongue out.

MRS. MALAPROP: Well, don't let your simplicity be imposed on.

LUCY: No, Ma'am.

MRS. MALAPROP: So, come to me presently, and I'll give you another letter to Sir Lucius; but mind, Lucy — if ever you betray what you are intrusted with (unless it be other people's secrets to me) you forfeit my malevolence forever, and your being a simpleton shall be no excuse for your locality. (*Exit.*)

LUCY: Ha! ha! ha! — So, my dear *simplicity*, let me give you a little respite — (*altering her manner*) — let girls in my station be as fond as they please of appearing expert, and knowing in their trusts — commend me to a mask of *silliness*, and a pair of sharp eyes for my own interest under it! Let me see to what account have I turned my *simplicity* lately — (*Looks at a paper.*) For *abetting Miss Lydia Languish in a design of running away with an Ensign! — in money — sundry times — twelve pound twelve — gowns, five — hats, ruffles, caps, &c., &c. — numberless! From the said Ensign, within this last month, six guineas and a half.* — About a quarter's pay! — Item, *from Mrs. Malaprop, for betraying the young people to her* — when I found matters were likely to be discovered — *two guineas, and a black paduasoy.*[26] — Item, *from Mr. Acres, for carrying divers letters* — which I never delivered — *two guineas, and a pair of buckles.* — Item, *from Sir Lucius O'Trigger — three crowns — two gold pocket-pieces — and a silver snuff-box!* — Well done, *simplicity!* — Yet I was forced to make my Hibernian believe that he was corresponding, not with the *aunt*, but with the *niece*: for, though not overrich, I found he had too much pride and delicacy to sacrifice the feelings of a gentleman to the necessities of his fortune. (*Exit.*)

ACT II

Scene 1 [CAPTAIN ABSOLUTE's *lodgings.*]

(CAPTAIN ABSOLUTE *and* FAG.)

FAG: Sir, while I was there Sir Anthony came in: I told him you had sent me to inquire after his health, and to know if he was at leisure to see you.

ABSOLUTE: And what did he say on hearing I was at Bath?

FAG: Sir, in my life I never saw an elderly gentleman more astonished! He started back two or three paces, rapped out a dozen interjectoral oaths, and asked what the devil had brought you here!

ABSOLUTE: Well, Sir, and what did you say?

FAG: Oh, I lied, Sir — I forget the precise lie; but you may depend on't, he got no truth from me. Yet, with submission, for fear of blunders in future, I should be glad to fix what *has* brought us to Bath, in order that we may lie a little consistently. Sir Anthony's servants were curious, Sir, very curious indeed.

ABSOLUTE: You have said nothing to them?

FAG: Oh, not a word, Sir — not a word. Mr. Thomas, indeed, the coachman (whom I take to be the discreetest of whips) ——

ABSOLUTE: 'Sdeath! — you rascal! you have not trusted him!

FAG: Oh, *no*, Sir! — no — no — not a syllable, upon my veracity! He

[26] garment made of Padua silk

was, indeed, a little inquisitive; but I was sly, Sir — devilish sly! — My master (said I), honest Thomas (you know, Sir, one says *honest* to one's inferiors), is come to Bath to *recruit* — yes, Sir — I said, *to recruit* — and whether for men, money, or constitution, you know, Sir, is nothing to him, nor anyone else.

ABSOLUTE: Well — *recruit* will do — let it be so ——

FAG: Oh, Sir, recruit will do surprisingly — indeed, to give the thing an air. I told Thomas that your Honour had already enlisted five disbanded chairmen,[27] seven minority[28] waiters, and thirteen billiard markers.

ABSOLUTE: You blockhead, never say more than is necessary.

FAG: I beg pardon, Sir — I beg pardon —— But with submission, a lie is nothing unless one supports it. Sir, whenever I draw on my invention for a good current lie, I always forge indorsements, as well as the bill.

ABSOLUTE: Well, take care you don't hurt your credit by offering too much security. Is Mr. Faulkland returned?

FAG: He is above, Sir, changing his dress.

ABSOLUTE: Can you tell whether he has been informed of Sir Anthony's and Miss Melville's arrival?

FAG: I fancy not, Sir; he has seen no one since he came in but his gentleman, who was with him at Bristol. —— I think, Sir, I hear Mr. Faulkland coming down ——

ABSOLUTE: Go tell him I am here.

FAG: Yes, Sir (*going*). I beg pardon, Sir, but should Sir Anthony call, you will do me the favour to remember that we are *recruiting*, if you please.

ABSOLUTE: Well, well.

FAG: And in tenderness to my character, if your Honour could bring in the chairmen and waiters, I shall esteem it as an obligation; for though I never scruple a lie to serve my master, yet it hurts one's conscience to be found out. (*Exit.*)

ABSOLUTE: Now for my whimsical friend — if he does not know that his mistress is here, I'll tease him a little before I tell him —— (*Enter* FAULKLAND.) Faulkland, you're welcome to Bath again; you are punctual in your return.

FAULKLAND: Yes; I had nothing to detain me when I had finished the business I went on. Well, what news since I left you? How stand matters between you and Lydia?

ABSOLUTE: Faith, much as they were; I have not seen her since our quarrel; however, I expect to be recalled every hour.

[27] porters of sedan chairs [28] meaning obscure, but perhaps "unemployed" or "not regularly employed"

FAULKLAND: Why don't you persuade her to go off with you at once?

ABSOLUTE: What, and lose two-thirds of her fortune? You forget that, my friend. No, no, I could have brought her to that long ago.

FAULKLAND: Nay then, you trifle too long — if you are sure of *her*, propose to the aunt *in your own character*, and write to Sir Anthony for his consent.

ABSOLUTE: Softly, softly, for though I am convinced my little Lydia would elope with me as Ensign Beverley, yet am I by no means certain that she would take me with the impediment of our friend's consent, a regular humdrum wedding, and the reversion of [29] a good fortune on my side; no, no, I must prepare her gradually for the discovery, and make myself necessary to her, before I risk it. —— Well, but Faulkland, you'll dine with us to-day at the hotel?

FAULKLAND: Indeed, I cannot: I am not in spirits to be of such a party.

ABSOLUTE: By heavens! I shall foreswear your company. You are the most teasing, captious, incorrigible lover! Do love like a man!

FAULKLAND: I own I am unfit for company.

ABSOLUTE: Am not *I* a lover; aye, and a romantic one too? Yet do I carry everywhere with me such a confounded farrago of doubts, fears, hopes, wishes, and all the flimsy furniture of a country miss's brain!

FAULKLAND: Ah! Jack, your heart and soul are not, like mine, fixed immutably on one only object. You throw for a large stake, but losing — you could stake, and throw again. But I have set my sum of happiness on this cast, and not to succeeed were to be stripped of all.

ABSOLUTE: But, for heaven's sake! what grounds for apprehension can your whimsical brain conjure up at present?

FAULKLAND: What grounds for apprehension did you say? Heavens! are there not a thousand! I fear for her spirits — her health — her life. My absence may fret her; her anxiety for my return, her fears for me, may oppress her gentle temper. And for her health — does not every hour bring me cause to be alarmed? If it rains, some shower may even then have chilled her delicate frame! If the wind be keen, some rude blast may have affected her! The heat of noon, the dews of the evening, may endanger the life of her, for whom only I value mine. O! Jack, when delicate and feeling souls are separated, there is not a feature in the sky, not a movement of the elements, not an aspiration of the breeze, but hints some cause for a lover's apprehension!

ABSOLUTE: Aye, but we may choose whether we will take the hint or

[29] prospect of inheriting

not. So then, Faulkland, if you were convinced that Julia were well and in spirits, you would be entirely content?

FAULKLAND: I should be happy beyond measure — I am anxious only for that.

ABSOLUTE: Then to cure your anxiety at once — Miss Melville is in perfect health, and is at this moment in Bath!

FAULKLAND: Nay, Jack — don't trifle with me.

ABSOLUTE: She is arrived here with my father within this hour.

FAULKLAND: Can you be serious?

ABSOLUTE: I thought you knew Sir Anthony better than to be surprised at a sudden whim of this kind. Seriously then, it is as I tell you — upon my honour.

FAULKLAND: My dear friend! — Hollo, Du-Peigne! my hat — my dear Jack — now nothing on earth can give me a moment's uneasiness.

(*Enter* FAG.)

FAG: Sir, Mr. Acres just arrived is below.

ABSOLUTE: Stay, Faulkland, this Acres lives within a mile of Sir Anthony, and he shall tell you how your mistress has been ever since you left her. —— Fag, show the gentleman up. (*Exit* FAG.)

FAULKLAND: What, is he much acquainted in the family?

ABSOLUTE: Oh, very intimate. I insist on your not going: besides, his character will divert you.

FAULKLAND: Well, I should like to ask him a few questions.

ABSOLUTE: He is likewise a rival of mine — that is of my *other self's*, for he does not think his friend Captain Absolute ever saw the lady in question; and it is ridiculous enough to hear him complain to me of *one Beverley*, a concealed skulking rival, who ——

FAULKLAND: Hush! He's here.

(*Enter* ACRES.)

ACRES: Hah! my dear friend, noble captain, and honest Jack, how dost thou? Just arrived, faith, as you see. Sir, your humble servant. Warm work on the roads, Jack! — Odds whips and wheels! I've travelled like a comet, with a tail of dust all the way as long as the Mall.[30]

ABSOLUTE: Ah! Bob, you are indeed an eccentric planet, but we know your attraction hither. Give me leave to introduce Mr. Faulkland to you; Mr. Faulkland, Mr. Acres.

ACRES: Sir, I am most heartily glad to see you: Sir, I solicit your connexions. —— Hey, Jack — what — this is Mr. Faulkland, who ——?

ABSOLUTE: Aye, Bob, Miss Melville's Mr. Faulkland.

ACRES: Odd so! she and your father can be but just arrived before me

30 fashionable promenade in St. James's Park in London

— I suppose you have seen them. Ah! Mr. Faulkland, you are indeed a happy man.

FAULKLAND: I have not seen Miss Melville yet, Sir. I hope she enjoyed full health and spirits in Devonshire?

ACRES: Never knew her better in my life, Sir — never better. Odds blushes and blooms! she has been as healthy as the German Spa.[31]

FAULKLAND: Indeed! I did hear that she had been a little indisposed.

ACRES: False, false, Sir — only said to vex you: quite the reverse, I assure you.

FAULKLAND: There, Jack, you see she has the advantage of me; I had almost fretted myself ill.

ABSOLUTE: Now are you angry with your mistress for not having been sick.

FAULKLAND: No, no, you misunderstand me: yet surely a little trifling indisposition is not an unnatural consequence of absence from those we love. Now confess — isn't there something unkind in this violent, robust, unfeeling health?

ABSOLUTE: Oh, it was very unkind of her to be well in your absence, to be sure!

ACRES: Good apartments, Jack.

FAULKLAND: Well, Sir, but you were saying that Miss Melville has been so *exceedingly* well — what, then she has been merry and gay, I suppose? Always in spirits — hey?

ACRES: Merry! Odds crickets! she has been the belle and spirit of the company wherever she has been — so lively and entertaining! so full of wit and humour!

FAULKLAND: There, Jack, there! Oh, by my soul! there is an innate levity in woman, that nothing can overcome. What! happy, and I away!

ABSOLUTE: Have done — how foolish this is! Just now you were only apprehensive for your mistress's *spirits*.

FAULKLAND: Why, Jack, have I been the joy and spirit of the company?

ABSOLUTE: No, indeed, you have not.

FAULKLAND: Have I been lively and entertaining?

ABSOLUTE: Oh, upon my word, I acquit you.

FAULKLAND: Have I been full of wit and humour?

ABSOLUTE: No, faith; to do you justice, you have been confoundedly stupid[32] indeed.

ACRES: What's the matter with the gentleman?

ABSOLUTE: He is only expressing his great satisfaction at hearing that Julia has been so well and happy — that's all — hey, Faulkland?

[31] the original watering place, in Belgium [32] *i.e.*, dull company

FAULKLAND: Oh! I am rejoiced to hear it — yes, yes, she has a *happy* disposition!

ACRES: That she has indeed. Then she is so accomplished — so sweet a voice — so expert at her harpsichord — such a mistress of flat and sharp, squallante, rumblante, and quiverante![33] There was this time month — Odds minims and crotchets![34] how she did chirrup at Mrs. Piano's concert!

FAULKLAND: There again, what say you to this? You see she has been all mirth and song — not a thought of me!

ABSOLUTE: Pho! man, is not music the food of love?

FAULKLAND: Well, well, it may be so. —— Pray, Mr. —— what's his d——d name? Do you remember what songs Miss Melville sung?

ACRES: Not I, indeed.

ABSOLUTE: Stay now, they were some pretty, melancholy, purling-stream airs, I warrant; perhaps you may recollect; did she sing "*When absent from my soul's delight*"?

ACRES: No, that wa'n't it.

ABSOLUTE: Or "*Go, gentle gales*"? — "*Go, gentle gales!*" (*Sings.*)

ACRES: Oh no! nothing like it. Odds! now I recollect one of them — "*My heart's my own, my will is free.*" (*Sings.*)

FAULKLAND: Fool! fool that I am! to fix all my happiness on such a trifler! 'Sdeath! to make herself the pipe and ballad-monger of a circle! to soothe her light heart with catches and glees![35] What can you say to this, Sir?

ABSOLUTE: Why, that I should be glad to hear my mistress had been so merry, *Sir*.

FAULKLAND: Nay, nay, nay — I am not sorry that she has been happy — no, no, I am glad of that — I would not have had her sad or sick — yet surely a sympathetic heart would have shown itself even in the choice of a song: she might have been temperately healthy, and, somehow, plaintively gay; but she has been dancing too, I doubt not!

ACRES: What does the gentleman say about dancing?

ABSOLUTE: He says the lady we speak of dances as well as she sings.

ACRES: Aye, truly, does she — there was at our last race-ball ——

FAULKLAND: Hell and the devil! There! there! — I told you so! I told you so! Oh! she thrives in my absence! Dancing! But her whole feelings have been in opposition with mine! I have been anxious, silent, pensive, sedentary — my days have been hours of care, my nights of watchfulness. She has been all Health! Spirit! Laugh! Song! Dance! Oh! d——n'd d——n'd levity!

[33] made-up musical terms [34] half-notes and quarter-notes [35] rounds and other songs for several voices

ABSOLUTE: For heaven's sake! Faulkland, don't expose yourself so. Suppose she has danced, what then? Does not the ceremony of society often oblige ——

FAULKLAND: Well, well, I'll contain myself. Perhaps, as you say, for form sake. What, Mr. Acres, you were praising Miss Melville's manner of dancing a *minuet* — hey?

ACRES: Oh I dare insure her for that — but what I was going to speak of was her *country dancing*. Odds swimmings! she has such an air with her!

FAULKLAND: Now disappointment on her! Defend this, Absolute, why don't you defend this? Country-dances! jigs, and reels! Am I to blame now? A minuet I could have forgiven — I should not have minded that — I say I should not have regarded a minuet — but *country-dances!* Z——ds! had she made one in a cotillion — I believe I could have forgiven even that — but to be monkey-led for a night! to run the gauntlet through a string of amorous palming puppies! to show paces like a managed filly! O Jack, there never can be but *one* man in the world whom a truly modest and delicate woman ought to pair with in a *country-dance;* and even then, the rest of the couples should be her great uncles and aunts!

ABSOLUTE: Aye, to be sure! — grandfathers and grandmothers!

FAULKLAND: If there be but one vicious mind in the Set, 'twill spread like a contagion — the action of their pulse beats to the lascivious movement of the jig — their quivering, warm-breathed sighs impregnate the very air — the atmosphere becomes electrical to love, and each amorous spark darts through every link of the chain; I must leave you — I own I am somewhat flurried — and that confounded looby[36] has perceived it (*going*).

ABSOLUTE: Nay, but stay, Faulkland, and thank Mr. Acres for his good news.

FAULKLAND: D——n his news! (*Exit.*)

ABSOLUTE: Ha! ha! ha! Poor Faulkland! Five minutes since — "nothing on earth could give him a moment's uneasiness!"

ACRES: The gentleman wa'n't angry at my praising his mistress, was he?

ABSOLUTE: A little jealous, I believe, Bob.

ACRES: You don't say so? Ha! ha! jealous of me? — that's a good joke.

ABSOLUTE: There's nothing strange in that, Bob: let me tell you, that sprightly grace and insinuating manner of yours will do some mischief among the girls here.

ACRES: Ah! you joke — ha! ha! — mischief — ha! ha! But you know I am not my own property; my dear Lydia has forestalled me. She

[36] oaf

could never abide me in the country, because I used to dress so badly — but odds frogs and tambours![37] I shan't take matters so here — now ancient madam has no voice in it. I'll make my old clothes know who's master. I shall straightway cashier the hunting-frock, and render my leather breeches incapable. My hair has been in training some time.

ABSOLUTE: Indeed!

ACRES: Aye — and tho'ff the side-curls are a little restive, my hind-part takes to it very kindly.

ABSOLUTE: O, you'll polish, I doubt not.

ACRES: Absolutely I propose so. Then if I can find out this Ensign Beverley, odds triggers and flints! I'll make him know the difference o't.

ABSOLUTE: Spoke like a man — but pray, Bob, I observe you have got an odd kind of a new method of swearing ——

ACRES: Ha! ha! you've taken notice of it? 'Tis genteel, isn't it? I didn't invent it myself, though; but a commander in our militia — a great scholar, I assure you — says that there is no meaning in the common oaths, and that nothing but their antiquity makes them respectable, because, he says, the ancients would never stick to an oath or two, but would say, by Jove! or by Bacchus! or by Mars! or by Venus! or by Pallas! according to the sentiment; so that to swear with propriety, says my little major, the "oath should be an echo to the sense";[38] and this we call the *oath referential,* or *sentimental swearing* — ha! ha! ha! 'tis genteel, isn't it?

ABSOLUTE: Very genteel, and very new, indeed — and I dare say will supplant all other figures of imprecation.

ACRES: Aye, aye, the best terms will grow obsolete. Damns have had their day.

(*Enter* FAG.)

FAG: Sir, there is a gentleman below desires to see you. Shall I show him into the parlour?

ABSOLUTE: Aye — you may.

ACRES: Well, I must be gone ——

ABSOLUTE: Stay; who is it, Fag?

FAG: Your father, Sir.

ABSOLUTE: You puppy, why didn't you show him up directly?

(*Exit* FAG.)

[37] embroidered loop fastenings [38] cf. Pope, "The sound must seem an echo to the sense," *Essay on Criticism*, 365

ACRES: You have business with Sir Anthony. I expect a message from Mrs. Malaprop at my lodgings. I have sent also to my dear friend, Sir Lucius O'Trigger. Adieu, Jack! We must meet at night, when you shall give me a dozen bumpers to little Lydia.

ABSOLUTE: That I will, with all my heart. (*Exit* ACRES.) Now for a parental lecture. I hope he has heard nothing of the business that has brought me here. I wish the gout had held him fast in Devonshire, with all my soul! (*Enter* SIR ANTHONY.) Sir, I am delighted to see you here; and looking so well! Your sudden arrival at Bath made me apprehensive for your health.

SIR ANTHONY: Very apprehensive, I dare say, Jack. What, you are recruiting here, hey?

ABSOLUTE: Yes, Sir, I am on duty.

SIR ANTHONY: Well, Jack, I am glad to see you, though I did not expect it, for I was going to write to you on a little matter of business. Jack, I have been considering that I grow old and infirm, and shall probably not trouble you long.

ABSOLUTE: Pardon me, Sir, I never saw you look more strong and hearty; and I pray frequently that you may continue so.

SIR ANTHONY: I hope your prayers may be heard with all my heart. Well then, Jack, I have been considering that I am so strong and hearty, I may continue to plague you a long time. Now, Jack, I am sensible that the income of your commission, and what I have hitherto allowed you, is but a small pittance for a lad of your spirit.

ABSOLUTE: Sir, you are very good.

SIR ANTHONY: And it is my wish, while yet I live, to have my boy make some figure in the world. I have resolved, therefore, to fix you at once in a noble independence.

ABSOLUTE: Sir, your kindness overpowers me — such generosity makes the gratitude of reason more lively than the sensations even of filial affection.

SIR ANTHONY: I am glad you are so sensible of my attention — and you shall be master of a large estate in a few weeks.

ABSOLUTE: Let my future life, Sir, speak my gratitude: I cannot express the sense I have of your munificence. Yet, Sir, I presume you would not wish me to quit the army?

SIR ANTHONY: Oh, that shall be as your wife chooses.

ABSOLUTE: My wife, Sir!

SIR ANTHONY: Aye, aye — settle that between you — settle that between you.

ABSOLUTE: A *wife*, Sir, did you say?

SIR ANTHONY: Aye, a wife — why; did not I mention her before?

ABSOLUTE: Not a word of her, Sir.

SIR ANTHONY: Odd so! — I mus'n't forget *her*, though. Yes, Jack, the independence I was talking of is by a marriage — the fortune is saddled with a wife — but I suppose that makes no difference.

ABSOLUTE: Sir! Sir! — you amaze me!

SIR ANTHONY: Why, what the devil's the matter with the fool? Just now you were all gratitude and duty.

ABSOLUTE: I was, Sir — you talked to me of independence and a fortune, but not a word of a wife.

SIR ANTHONY: Why — what difference does that make? Odd's life, Sir! if you have the estate, you must take it with the live stock on it, as it stands.

ABSOLUTE: If my happiness is to be the price, I must beg leave to decline the purchase. Pray, Sir, who is the lady?

SIR ANTHONY: What's that to you, Sir? Come, give me your promise to love, and to marry her directly.

ABSOLUTE: Sure, Sir, this is not very reasonable, to summon my affections for a lady I know nothing of!

SIR ANTHONY: I am sure, Sir, 'tis more unreasonable in you to *object* to a lady you know nothing of.

ABSOLUTE: Then, Sir, I must tell you plainly that my inclinations are fixed on another — my heart is engaged to an angel.

SIR ANTHONY: Then pray let it send an excuse. It is very sorry — but *business* prevents its waiting on her.

ABSOLUTE: But my vows are pledged to her.

SIR ANTHONY: Let her foreclose, Jack; let her foreclose, they are not worth redeeming: besides, you have the angel's vows in exchange, I suppose; so there can be no loss there.

ABSOLUTE: You must excuse me, Sir, if I tell you, once for all, that in this point I cannot obey you.

SIR ANTHONY: Hark'ee, Jack: I have heard you for some time with patience — I have been cool — quite cool; but take care — you know I am compliance itself when I am not thwarted — no one more easily led when I have my own way; but don't put me in a frenzy.

ABSOLUTE: Sir, I must repeat it — in this I cannot obey you.

SIR ANTHONY: Now, d——n me! if ever I call you *Jack* again while I live!

ABSOLUTE: Nay, Sir, but hear me.

SIR ANTHONY: Sir, I won't hear a word — not a word! not one word! so give me your promise by a nod — and I'll tell you what, Jack — I mean, you dog — if you don't, by ——

ABSOLUTE: What, Sir, promise to link myself to some mass of ugliness! to——

SIR ANTHONY. Z——ds! Sirrah! the lady shall be as ugly as I choose: she shall have a hump on each shoulder; she shall be as crooked as the Crescent;[39] her one eye shall roll like the Bull's in Cox's Museum[40]— she shall have a skin like a mummy, and the beard of a Jew — she shall be all this, Sirrah! — yet I'll make you ogle her all day, and sit up all night to write sonnets on her beauty.

ABSOLUTE: This is reason and moderation indeed!

SIR ANTHONY: None of your sneering, puppy! no grinning, jackanapes![41]

ABSOLUTE: Indeed, Sir, I never was in a worse humour for mirth in my life.

SIR ANTHONY: 'Tis false, Sir! I know you are laughing in your sleeve; I know you'll grin when I am gone, Sirrah!

ABSOLUTE: Sir, I hope I know my duty better.

SIR ANTHONY: None of your passion, Sir! none of your violence! if you please. It won't do with me, I promise you.

ABSOLUTE: Indeed, Sir, I never was cooler in my life.

SIR ANTHONY: 'Tis a confounded lie! — I know you are in a passion in your heart; I know you are, you hypocritical young dog! But it won't do.

ABSOLUTE: Nay, Sir, upon my word.

SIR ANTHONY: So you will fly out! Can't you be cool, like me? What the devil good can *passion* do! *Passion* is of no service, you impudent, insolent, overbearing reprobate! — There you sneer again! don't provoke me! But you rely upon the mildness of my temper — you do, you dog! you play upon the meekness of my disposition! Yet take care — the patience of a saint may be overcome at last! — but mark! I give you six hours and a half to consider of this: if you then agree, without any condition, to do everything on earth that I choose, why — confound you! I may in time forgive you. If not, z——ds! don't enter the same hemisphere with me! don't dare to breathe the same air, or use the same light with me; but get an atmosphere and a sun of your own! I'll strip you of your commission; I'll lodge[42] a five-and-threepence in the hands of trustees, and you shall live on the interest. I'll disown you, I'll disinherit you, I'll unget you! and — d——n me, if ever I call you Jack again! (*Exit.*)

ABSOLUTE: Mild, gentle, considerate Father — I kiss your hands. What a tender method of giving his opinion in these matters Sir Anthony has! I dare not trust him with the truth. I wonder what old wealthy hag it is that he wants to bestow on me! Yet he married himself for love! and was in his youth a bold intriguer, and a gay companion!

[39] the Royal Crescent, a semi-ellipse of fashionable houses in Bath [40] a mechanical bull, a popular show-piece at the time [41] pert, insolent fellow [42] deposit

(*Enter* FAG.)

FAG: Assuredly, Sir, our father is wrath to a degree; he comes down-stairs eight or ten steps at a time — muttering, growling, and thumping the bannisters all the way: I, and the cook's dog, stand bowing at the door — rap! he gives me a stroke on the head with his cane; bids me carry that to my master; then kicking the poor turnspit[43] into the area,[44] d——ns us all for a puppy triumvirate! Upon my credit, Sir, were I in your place, and found my father such very bad company, I should certainly drop his acquaintance.

ABSOLUTE: Cease your impertinence, Sir, at present. Did you come in for nothing more? Stand out of the way! (*Pushes him aside, and exit.*)

FAG: Soh! Sir Anthony trims[45] my master. He is afraid to reply to his father — then vents his spleen on poor Fag! When one is vexed by one person, to revenge one's self on another who happens to come in the way is the vilest injustice. Ah! it shows the worst temper — the basest ——

(*Enter* ERRAND-BOY.)

BOY: Mr. Fag! Mr. Fag! your master calls you.

FAG: Well, you little dirty puppy, you need not bawl so! —— The meanest disposition! the ——

BOY: Quick, quick, Mr. Fag!

FAG: *Quick, quick,* you impudent jackanapes! am I to be commanded by you too? you little, impertinent, insolent, kitchen-bred —— (*Exit, kicking and beating him.*)

Scene 2 [The North Parade]

(*Enter* LUCY.)

LUCY: So — I shall have another rival to add to my mistress's list — Captain Absolute. However, I shall not enter his name till my purse has received notice in form. Poor Acres is dismissed! Well, I have done him a last friendly office in letting him know that Beverley was here before him. Sir Lucius is generally more punctual when he expects to hear from his *dear Delia,* as he calls her: I wonder he's not here! I have a little scruple of conscience from this deceit; though I should not be paid so well, if my hero knew that *Delia* was near fifty, and her own mistress.

[43] *i.e.,* kitchen drudge; or: a little dog trained to turn the spit by means of a treadmill [44] areaway [45] *i.e.,* scolds

(*Enter* SIR LUCIUS O'TRIGGER.)

SIR LUCIUS: Hah! my little embassadress — upon my conscience, I have been looking for you; I have been on the South Parade this half-hour.

LUCY (*speaking simply*): O Gemini! and I have been waiting for your worship here on the North.

SIR LUCIUS: Faith! — maybe that was the reason we did not meet; and it is very comical, too, how you could go out and I not see you — for I was only taking a nap at the Parade Coffee-house, and I chose the *window* on purpose that I might not miss you.

LUCY: My stars! Now I'd wager a sixpence I went by while you were asleep.

SIR LUCIUS: Sure enough it must have been so — and I never dreamt it was so late, till I waked. Well, but my little girl, have you got nothing for me?

LUCY: Yes, but I have: I've got a letter for you in my pocket.

SIR LUCIUS: Oh faith! I guessed you weren't come empty-handed — well — let me see what the dear creature says.

LUCY: There, Sir Lucius. (*Gives him a letter.*)

SIR LUCIUS (*reads*): *Sir — there is often a sudden incentive impulse in love, that has a greater induction than years of domestic combination: such was the commotion I felt at the first superfluous view of Sir Lucius O'Trigger.* — Very pretty, upon my word. — *Female punctuation forbids me to say more; yet let me add, that it will give me joy infallible to find Sir Lucius worthy the last criterion of my affections.* DELIA. Upon my conscience! Lucy, your lady is a great mistress of language. Faith, she's quite the queen of the dictionary! — for the devil a word dare refuse coming at her call — though one would think it was quite out of hearing.

LUCY: Aye, Sir, a lady of her experience ——

SIR LUCIUS: Experience! what, at seventeen?

LUCY: O true, Sir — but then she reads so — my stars! how she will read off-hand!

SIR LUCIUS: Faith, she must be very deep read to write this way — though she is rather an arbitrary writer too — for here are a great many poor words pressed into the service of this note, that would get their *habeas corpus* from any court in Christendom.

LUCY: Ah! Sir Lucius, if you were to hear how she talks of you!

SIR LUCIUS: Oh tell her I'll make her the best husband in the world, and Lady O'Trigger into the bargain! But we must get the old gentlewoman's consent — and do everything fairly.

LUCY: Nay, Sir Lucius, I thought you wa'n't rich enough to be so nice!

SIR LUCIUS: Upon my word, young woman, you have hit it: I am so poor that I can't afford to do a dirty action. If I did not want money I'd steal your mistress and her fortune with a great deal of pleasure. However, my pretty girl (*gives her money*), here's a little something to buy you a ribband; and meet me in the evening, and I'll give you an answer to this. So, hussy, take a kiss beforehand to put you in mind. (*Kisses her.*)

LUCY: O lud! Sir Lucius — I never seed such a gemman![46] My lady won't like you if you're so impudent.

SIR LUCIUS: Faith she will, Lucy — That same — pho! what's the name of it? — *Modesty!* — is a quality in a lover more praised by the women than liked; so, if your mistress asks you whether Sir Lucius ever gave you a kiss, tell her *fifty* — my dear.

LUCY: What, would you have me tell her a lie?

SIR LUCIUS: Ah, then, you baggage! I'll make it a truth presently.

LUCY: For shame now; here is someone coming.

SIR LUCIUS: Oh faith, I'll quiet your conscience. (*Sees* FAG. — *Exit, humming a tune. Enter* FAG.)

FAG: So, so, Ma'am. I humbly beg pardon.

LUCY: O lud! — now, Mr. Fag, you flurry one so.

FAG: Come, come, Lucy, here's no one by — so a little less simplicity, with a grain or two more sincerity, if you please. You play false with us, Madam. I saw you give the baronet a letter. My master shall know this, and if he don't call him out — I will.

LUCY: Ha! ha! ha! you gentlemen's gentlemen are so hasty. That letter was from Mrs. Malaprop, simpleton. She is taken with Sir Lucius's address.

FAG: How! what tastes some people have! Why, I suppose I have walked by her window an hundred times. But what says our young lady? Any message to my master?

LUCY: Sad news, Mr. Fag! A worse rival than Acres! Sir Anthony Absolute has proposed his son.

FAG: What, Captain Absolute?

LUCY: Even so. I overheard it all.

FAG: Ha! ha! ha! — very good, faith. Good-bye, Lucy, I must away with this news.

LUCY: Well — you may laugh, but it is true, I assure you (*going*). But — Mr. Fag — tell your master not to be cast down by this.

FAG: Oh, he'll be so disconsolate!

LUCY: And charge him not to think of quarrelling with young Absolute.

[46] gentleman

FAG: Never fear! — never fear!

LUCY: Be sure — bid him keep up his spirits.

FAG: We will — we will. (*Exeunt severally.*)

ACT III

Scene 1 [The North Parade]

(*Enter* ABSOLUTE.)

ABSOLUTE: 'Tis just as Fag told me, indeed. Whimsical enough, faith! My father wants to *force* me to marry the very girl I am plotting to run away with! He must not know of my connexion with her yet awhile. He has too summary a method of proceeding in these matters. However, I'll read my recantation instantly. My conversion is something sudden, indeed, but I can assure him it is very *sincere.* —— So, so — here he comes. He looks plaguy gruff. (*Steps aside.*)

(*Enter* SIR ANTHONY.)

SIR ANTHONY: No — I'll die sooner than forgive him. *Die,* did I say? I'll live these fifty years to plague him. At our last meeting, his impudence had almost put me out of temper. An obstinate, passionate, self-willed boy! Who can he take after? This is my return for getting him before all his brothers and sisters! — for putting him, at twelve years old, into a marching regiment, and allowing him fifty pounds a year, beside his pay ever since! But I have done with him; he's anybody's son for me. I never will see him more — never — never — never!

ABSOLUTE: Now for a penitential face.

SIR ANTHONY: Fellow, get out of my way.

ABSOLUTE: Sir, you see a penitent before you.

SIR ANTHONY: I see an impudent scoundrel before me.

ABSOLUTE: A sincere penitent. I am come, Sir, to acknowledge my error, and to submit entirely to your will.

SIR ANTHONY: What's that?

ABSOLUTE: I have been revolving, and reflecting, and considering on your past goodness, and kindness, and condescension to me.

SIR ANTHONY: Well, Sir?

ABSOLUTE: I have been likewise weighing and balancing what you were pleased to mention concerning duty, and obedience, and authority.

SIR ANTHONY: Well, puppy?

ABSOLUTE: Why, then, Sir, the result of my reflections is — a resolution to sacrifice every inclination of my own to your satisfaction.

SIR ANTHONY: Why, now you talk sense — absolute sense — I never heard anything more sensible in my life. Confound you, you shall be *Jack* again!

ABSOLUTE: I am happy in the appellation.

SIR ANTHONY: Why then, Jack, my dear Jack, I will now inform you who the lady really is. Nothing but your passion and violence, you silly fellow, prevented my telling you at first. Prepare, Jack, for wonder and rapture! prepare! —— What think you of Miss Lydia Languish?

ABSOLUTE: Languish! What, the Languishes of Worcestershire?

SIR ANTHONY: Worcestershire! No. Did you never meet Mrs. Malaprop and her niece, Miss Languish, who came into our country just before you were last ordered to your regiment?

ABSOLUTE: Malaprop! Languish! I don't remember ever to have heard the names before. Yet, stay — I think I do recollect something. —— *Languish! Languish!* She squints, don't she? A little, red-haired girl?

SIR ANTHONY: Squints? A red-haired girl! Z——ds, no!

ABSOLUTE: Then I must have forgot; it can't be the same person.

SIR ANTHONY: Jack! Jack! what think you of blooming, love-breathing seventeen?

ABSOLUTE: As to that, Sir, I am quite indifferent. If I can please you in the matter, 'tis all I desire.

SIR ANTHONY: Nay, but Jack, such eyes! such eyes! so innocently wild! so bashfully irresolute! Not a glance but speaks and kindles some thought of love! Then, Jack, her cheeks! her cheeks, Jack! so deeply blushing at the insinuations of her tell-tale eyes! Then, Jack, her lips! — O Jack, lips smiling at their own discretion; and if not smiling, more sweetly pouting, more lovely in sullenness!

ABSOLUTE (*aside*): That's she, indeed. Well done, old gentleman!

SIR ANTHONY: Then, Jack, her neck! — O Jack! Jack!

ABSOLUTE: And which is to be mine, Sir, the niece or the aunt?

SIR ANTHONY: Why, you unfeeling, insensible puppy, I despise you! When I was of your age, such a description would have made me fly like a rocket! The *aunt*, indeed! Odd's life! when I ran away with your mother, I would not have touched anything old or ugly to gain an empire.

ABSOLUTE: Not to please your father, Sir?

SIR ANTHONY: To please my father! Z——ds! not to please —— Oh, my father! — Odd so! — yes — yes! — if my father, indeed, had desired — that's quite another matter. Though he wa'n't the indulgent father that I am, Jack.

ABSOLUTE: I dare say not, Sir.

SIR ANTHONY: But, Jack, you are not sorry to find your mistress is so beautiful?

ABSOLUTE: Sir, I repeat it; if I please you in this affair, 'tis all I desire. Not that I think a woman the worse for being handsome; but, Sir, if you please to recollect, you before hinted something about a hump or two, one eye, and a few more graces of that kind. Now, without being very nice, I own I should rather choose a wife of mine to have the usual number of limbs, and a limited quantity of back: and though *one* eye may be very agreeable, yet as the prejudice has always run in favour of *two*, I would not wish to affect a singularity in that article.

SIR ANTHONY: What a phlegmatic sot it is! Why, Sirrah, you're an anchorite! a vile, insensible stock. You a soldier! you're a walking block, fit only to dust the company's regimentals[47] on! Odd's life! I've a great mind to marry the girl myself!

ABSOLUTE: I am entirely at your disposal, Sir; if you should think of addressing Miss Languish yourself, I suppose you would have me marry the *aunt*; or if you should change your mind, and take the old lady — 'tis the same to me — I'll marry the *niece*.

SIR ANTHONY: Upon my word, Jack, thou'rt either a very great hypocrite, or——But come, I know your indifference on such a subject must be all a lie — I'm sure it must — come, now — damn your demure face! — come, confess, Jack — you have been lying — ha'n't you? you have been playing the hypocrite, hey? — I'll never forgive you if you ha'n't been lying and playing the hypocrite.

ABSOLUTE: I'm sorry, Sir, that the respect and duty which I bear to you should be so mistaken.

SIR ANTHONY: Hang your respect and duty! But come along with me, I'll write a note to Mrs. Malaprop, and you shall visit the lady directly. Her eyes shall be the Promethean torch to you[48] — come along. I'll never forgive you if you don't come back stark mad with rapture and impatience. If you don't, egad, I'll marry the girl myself! (*Exeunt.*)

Scene 2 [Julia's dressing-room]

(FAULKLAND, *alone*.)

FAULKLAND: They told me Julia would return directly; I wonder she is not yet come! How mean does this captious, unsatisfied temper

[47] uniform characteristic of a particular regiment [48] *i.e.*, they will kindle love's first flame in you (The titan Prometheus stole fire from the gods and gave it to man.)

of mine appear to my cooler judgment! Yet I know not that I indulge it in any other point: but on this one subject, and to this one subject, whom I think I love beyond my life, I am ever ungenerously fretful, and madly capricious! I am conscious of it — yet I cannot correct myself! What tender, honest joy sparkled in her eyes when we met! How delicate was the warmth of her expressions! I was ashamed to appear less happy, though I had come resolved to wear a face of coolness and upbraiding. Sir Anthony's presence prevented my proposed expostulations, yet I must be satisfied that she has not been so *very* happy in my absence. She is coming! Yes! I know the nimbleness of her tread when she thinks her impatient Faulkland counts the moments of her stay.

(*Enter* JULIA.)

JULIA: I had not hoped to see you again so soon.

FAULKLAND: Could I, Julia, be contented with my first welcome — restrained as we were by the presence of a third person?

JULIA: O Faulkland, when your kindness can make me thus happy, let me not think that I discovered something of coldness in your first salutation.

FAULKLAND: 'Twas but your fancy, Julia. I *was* rejoiced to see you — to see you in such health. Sure I had no cause for coldness?

JULIA: Nay then, I see you have taken something ill. You must not conceal from me what it is.

FAULKLAND: Well then — shall I own to you — that my joy at hearing of your health and arrival here, by your neighbour Acres, was somewhat damped by his dwelling much on the high spirits you had enjoyed in Devonshire — on your mirth, your singing, dancing, and I know not what! For such is my temper, Julia, that I should regard every mirthful moment in your absence as a treason to constancy. The mutual tear that steals down the cheek of parting lovers is a compact that no smile shall live there till they meet again.

JULIA: Must I never cease to tax my Faulkland with this teasing minute[49] caprice? Can the idle reports of a silly boor weigh in your breast against my tried affection?

FAULKLAND: They have no weight with me, Julia: no, no — I am happy if you have been so — yet only say that you did not sing with *mirth* — say that you *thought* of Faulkland in the dance.

JULIA: I never can be happy in your absence. If I wear a countenance of content, it is to show that my mind holds no doubt of my Faulkland's truth. If I seemed sad, it were to make malice triumph,

[49] over-scrupulous, fussy

and say that I had fixed my heart on one who left me to lament his roving, and my own credulity. Believe me, Faulkland, I mean not to upbraid you when I say that I have often dressed sorrow in smiles, lest my friends should guess whose unkindness had caused my tears.

FAULKLAND: You were ever all goodness to me. Oh, I am a brute when I but admit a doubt of your true constancy!

JULIA: If ever, without such cause from you, as I will not suppose possible, you find my affections veering but a point, may I become a proverbial scoff for levity and base ingratitude.

FAULKLAND: Ah! Julia, that last word is grating to me. I would I had no title to your *gratitude!* Search your heart, Julia; perhaps what you have mistaken for love, is but the warm effusion of a too thankful heart!

JULIA: For what quality must I love you?

FAULKLAND: For no quality! To regard me for any quality of mind or understanding were only to *esteem* me. And for person — I have often wished myself deformed, to be convinced that I owed no obligation *there* for any part of your affection.

JULIA: Where Nature has bestowed a show of nice attention in the features of a man,[50] he should laugh at it as misplaced. I have seen men who in *this* vain article perhaps might rank above you; but my heart has never asked my eyes if it were so or not.

FAULKLAND: Now this is not well from *you,* Julia. I despise person in a man. Yet if you loved me as I wish, though I were an Æthiop, you'd think none so fair.

JULIA: I see you are determined to be unkind. The *contract* which my poor father bound us in gives you more than a lover's privilege.

FAULKLAND: Again, Julia, you raise ideas that feed and justify my doubts. I would not have been more free — no — I am proud of my restraint. Yet — yet — perhaps your high respect alone for this solemn compact has fettered your inclinations, which else had made a worthier choice. How shall I be sure, had you remained unbound in thought and promise, that I should still have been the object of your persevering love?

JULIA: Then try me now. Let us be free as strangers as to what is past: *my* heart will not feel more liberty!

FAULKLAND: There now! so hasty, Julia! so anxious to be free! If your love for me were fixed and ardent, you would not loose your hold, even though I wished it!

JULIA: Oh, you torture me to the heart! I cannot bear it.

FAULKLAND: I do not mean to distress you. If I loved you less I should

50 *i.e.*, made a man good-looking

never give you an uneasy moment. But hear me. All my fretful doubts arise from this: women are not used to weigh, and separate the motives of their affections; the cold dictates of prudence, gratitude, or filial duty, may sometimes be mistaken for the pleadings of the heart. I would not boast — yet let me say that I have neither age, person, or character to found dislike on; my fortune such as few ladies could be charged with *indiscretion* in the match. O Julia! when *Love* receives such countenance from *Prudence*, nice minds will be suspicious of its birth.

JULIA: I know not whither your insinuations would tend, but as they seem pressing to insult me, I will spare you the regret of having done so. I have given you no cause for this! (*Exit in tears.*)

FAULKLAND: In tears! Stay, Julia: stay but for a moment. —— The door is fastened! Julia! — my soul — but for one moment. I hear her sobbing! 'Sdeath! what a brute am I to use her thus! Yet stay! —— Aye — she is coming now. How little resolution there is in woman! How a few soft words can turn them! —— No, faith! — she is *not* coming either! Why, Julia — my love — say but that you forgive me — come but to tell me that. Now, this is being *too* resentful. —— Stay! she *is* coming too — I thought she would — no *steadiness* in anything! her going away must have been a mere trick then. She sha'n't see that I was hurt by it. I'll affect indifference. (*Hums a tune: then listens.*) —— No — Z——ds! she's *not* coming! — nor don't intend it, I suppose. This is not *steadiness*, but *obstinacy!* Yet I deserve it. What, after so long an absence to quarrel with her tenderness! — 'twas barbarous and unmanly! I should be ashamed to see her now. I'll wait till her just resentment is abated — and when I distress her so again, may I lose her forever, and be linked instead to some antique virago,[51] whose gnawing passions, and long-hoarded spleen shall make me curse my folly half the day, and all the night! (*Exit.*)

Scene 3 [MRS. MALAPROP'S *lodgings*]

(MRS. MALAPROP, *with a letter in her hand, and* CAPTAIN ABSOLUTE.)

MRS. MALAPROP: Your being Sir Anthony's son, Captain, would itself be a sufficient accommodation; but from the ingenuity of your appearance, I am convinced you deserve the character here given of you.

ABSOLUTE: Permit me to say, Madam, that as I never yet have had the pleasure of seeing Miss Languish, my principal inducement in

[51] fierce, quarrelsome woman, shrew

this affair at present is the honour of being allied to Mrs. Malaprop; of whose intellectual accomplishments, elegant manners, and unaffected learning, no tongue is silent.

MRS. MALAPROP: Sir, you do me infinite honour! I beg, Captain, you'll be seated. (*Sit.*) Ah! few gentlemen now-a-days know how to value the ineffectual qualities in a woman! few think how a little knowledge becomes a gentlewoman! Men have no sense now but for the worthless flower of beauty!

ABSOLUTE: It is but too true, indeed, Ma'am. Yet I fear our ladies should share the blame — they think our admiration of *beauty* so great, that *knowledge* in *them* would be superfluous. Thus, like garden-trees, they seldom show fruit till time has robbed them of the more specious blossom. Few, like Mrs. Malaprop and the orange-tree, are rich in both at once!

MRS. MALAPROP: Sir — you overpower me with good-breeding. (*Aside.*) He is the very pineapple of politeness!—— You are not ignorant, Captain, that this giddy girl has somehow contrived to fix her affections on a beggarly, strolling, eaves-dropping Ensign, whom none of us have seen, and nobody knows anything of.

ABSOLUTE: Oh, I have heard the silly affair before. I'm not at all prejudiced against her on *that* account.

MRS. MALAPROP: You are very good, and very considerate, Captain. I am sure I have done everything in my power since I exploded the affair! Long ago I laid my positive conjunctions on her never to think on the fellow again; I have since laid Sir Anthony's preposition before her; but, I'm sorry to say, she seems resolved to decline every particle that I enjoin her.

ABSOLUTE: It must be very distressing, indeed, Ma'am.

MRS. MALAPROP: Oh! it gives me the hydrostatics to such a degree! I thought she had persisted from corresponding with him; but behold this very day I have interceded another letter from the fellow! I believe I have it in my pocket.

ABSOLUTE (*aside*): Oh the devil! my last note.

MRS. MALAPROP: Aye, here it is.

ABSOLUTE (*aside*): Aye, my note, indeed! Oh the little traitress Lucy!

MRS. MALAPROP: There; perhaps you may know the writing. (*Gives him the letter.*)

ABSOLUTE: I think I have seen the hand before — yes, I certainly must have seen this hand before ——

MRS. MALAPROP: Nay, but read it, Captain.

ABSOLUTE (*reads*): "*My soul's idol, my adored Lydia!*"——Very tender, indeed!

MRS. MALAPROP: Tender! aye, and profane, too, o' my conscience!

ABSOLUTE: *"I am excessively alarmed at the intelligence you send me, the more so as my new rival"*——

MRS. MALAPROP: That's *you*, Sir.

ABSOLUTE: *"Has universally the character of being an accomplished gentleman, and a man of honour."*—— Well, that's handsome enough.

MRS. MALAPROP: Oh, the fellow had some design in writing so.

ABSOLUTE: That he had, I'll answer for him, Ma'am.

MRS. MALAPROP: But go on, Sir — you'll see presently.

ABSOLUTE: *"As for the old weather-beaten she-dragon who guards you"* ——Who can he mean by that?

MRS. MALAPROP: Me! Sir — *me!* — he means *me!* There — what do you think now? But go on a little further.

ABSOLUTE: Impudent scoundrel! — *"it shall go hard but I will elude her vigilance, as I am told that the same ridiculous vanity which makes her dress up her coarse features, and deck her dull chat with hard words which she don't understand"*——

MRS. MALAPROP: There, Sir! an attack upon my language! What do you think of that? — an aspersion upon my parts of speech! Was ever such a brute! Sure if I reprehend anything in this world, it is the use of my oracular tongue, and a nice derangement of epitaphs!

ABSOLUTE: He deserves to be hanged and quartered! Let me see — *"same ridiculous vanity"*——

MRS. MALAPROP: You need not read it again, Sir.

ABSOLUTE: I beg pardon, Ma'am — *"does also lay her open to the grossest deceptions from flattery and pretended admiration"* — an impudent coxcomb! — *"so that I have a scheme to see you shortly with the old harridan's consent, and even to make her a go-between in our interviews."* — Was ever such assurance!

MRS. MALAPROP: Did you ever hear anything like it? He'll elude my vigilance, will he? Yes, yes! ha! ha! He's very likely to enter these doors! We'll try who can plot best!

ABSOLUTE: So we will, Ma'am — so we will. Ha! ha! ha! A conceited puppy, ha! ha! ha! Well, but Mrs. Malaprop, as the girl seems so infatuated by this fellow, suppose you were to wink at her corresponding with him for a little time — let her even plot an elopement with him — then do you connive at her escape — while *I*, just in the nick, will have the fellow laid by the heels, and fairly contrive to carry her off in his stead.

MRS. MALAPROP: I am delighted with the scheme; never was anything better perpetrated!

ABSOLUTE: But, pray, could not I see the lady for a few minutes now? I should like to try her temper a little.

MRS. MALAPROP: Why, I don't know — I doubt she is not prepared for a visit of this kind. There is a decorum in these matters.

ABSOLUTE: O Lord! she won't mind *me* — only tell her Beverley——

MRS. MALAPROP: Sir!——

ABSOLUTE (*aside*): Gently, good tongue.

MRS. MALAPROP: What did you say of Beverley?

ABSOLUTE: Oh, I was going to propose that you should tell her, by way of jest, that it was Beverley who was below — she'd come down fast enough then — ha! ha! ha!

MRS. MALAPROP: 'Twould be a trick she well deserves. Besides, you know the fellow tells her he'll get my consent to see her — ha! ha! Let him if he can, I say again. (*Calling.*) Lydia, come down here! —— He'll make me a *go-between in their interviews!* — ha! ha! ha! — Come down, I say, Lydia! — I don't wonder at your laughing, ha! ha! ha! — his impudence is truly ridiculous.

ABSOLUTE: 'Tis very ridiculous, upon my soul, Ma'am, ha! ha! ha!

MRS. MALAPROP: The little hussy won't hear. Well, I'll go and tell her at once who it is. She shall know that Captain Absolute is come to wait on her. And I'll make her behave as becomes a young woman.

ABSOLUTE: As you please, Ma'am.

MRS. MALAPROP: For the present, Captain, your servant. Ah! you've not done laughing yet, I see — *elude my vigilance!* — yes, yes, ha! ha! ha! (*Exit.*)

ABSOLUTE: Ha! ha! ha! one would think now that I might throw off all disguise at once, and seize my prize with security — but such is Lydia's caprice that to undeceive were probably to lose her. I'll see whether she knows me. (*Walks aside, and seems engaged in looking at the pictures. Enter* LYDIA.)

LYDIA: What a scene am I now to go through! Surely nothing can be more dreadful than to be obliged to listen to the loathsome addresses of a stranger to one's heart. I have heard of girls persecuted as I am, who have appealed in behalf of their favoured lover to the generosity of his rival: suppose I were to try it. There stands the hated rival — an officer, too! — but oh, how unlike my Beverley! I wonder he don't begin. Truly he seems a very negligent wooer! Quite at his ease, upon my word! I'll speak first. (*Aloud.*) Mr. Absolute.

ABSOLUTE: Madam. (*Turns around.*)

LYDIA: O heavens! Beverley!

ABSOLUTE: Hush! — hush, my life! Softly! Be not surprised.

LYDIA: I am so astonished! and so terrified! and so overjoyed! For heaven's sake! how came you here?

ABSOLUTE: Briefly — I have deceived your aunt. I was informed that my new rival was to visit here this evening, and contriving to have him kept away, have passed myself on *her* for Captain Absolute.

LYDIA: Oh, charming! And she really takes you for young Absolute?

ABSOLUTE: Oh, she's convinced of it.

LYDIA: Ha! ha! ha! I can't forbear laughing to think how her sagacity is overreached!

ABSOLUTE: But we trifle with our precious moments. Such another opportunity may not occur. Then let me now conjure my kind, my condescending angel, to fix the time when I may rescue her from undeserved persecution, and with a licensed warmth plead for my reward.

LYDIA: Will you then, Beverley, consent to forfeit that portion of my paltry wealth? that burden on the wings of love?

ABSOLUTE: Oh, come to me — rich only thus — in loveliness. Bring no portion to me but thy love — 'twill be generous in you, Lydia — for well you know, it is the only dower your poor Beverley can repay.

LYDIA: How persuasive are his words! How charming will poverty be with him!

ABSOLUTE: Ah! my soul, what a life will we then live! Love shall be our idol and support! We will worship him with a monastic strictness; abjuring all worldly toys, to center every thought and action there. Proud of calamity, we will enjoy the wreck of wealth; while the surrounding gloom of adversity shall make the flame of our pure love show doubly bright. By heavens! I would fling all goods of fortune from me with a prodigal hand to enjoy the scene where I might clasp my Lydia to my bosom, and say, the world affords no smile to me — but here (*embracing her*). —— (*Aside.*) If she holds out now the devil is in it!

LYDIA (*aside*): Now could I fly with him to the Antipodes! but my persecution is not yet come to a crisis.

(*Enter* MRS. MALAPROP, *listening.*)

MRS. MALAPROP (*aside*): I am impatient to know how the little hussy deports herself.

ABSOLUTE: So pensive, Lydia! — is then your warmth abated?

MRS. MALAPROP (*aside*): *Warmth abated!* So! she has been in a passion, I suppose.

LYDIA: No — nor ever can while I have life.

MRS. MALAPROP (*aside*): An ill-tempered little devil! She'll be *in a passion all her life* — will she?

LYDIA: Think not the idle threats of my ridiculous aunt can ever have any weight with me.

MRS. MALAPROP (*aside*): Very dutiful, upon my word!

LYDIA: Let her choice be Captain Absolute, but Beverley is mine.

MRS. MALAPROP (*aside*): I am astonished at her assurance! — to his face — this is to his face!

ABSOLUTE: Thus then let me enforce my suit (*kneeling*).

MRS. MALAPROP (*aside*): Aye — poor young man! down on his knees entreating for pity! I can contain no longer. — (*Aloud.*) Why, thou vixen! I have overheard you.

ABSOLUTE (*aside*): Oh, confound her vigilance!

MRS. MALAPROP: Captain Absolute — I know not how to apologize for her shocking rudeness.

ABSOLUTE (*aside*): So — all's safe, I find. — (*Aloud.*) I have hopes, Madam, that time will bring the young lady ——

MRS. MALAPROP: Oh, there's nothing to be hoped for from her! She's as headstrong as an allegory on the banks of Nile.

LYDIA: Nay, Madam, what do you charge me with now?

MRS. MALAPROP: Why, thou unblushing rebel — didn't you tell this gentleman to his face that you loved another better? — didn't you say you never would be his?

LYDIA: No, Madam — I did not.

MRS. MALAPROP: Good heavens! what assurance! Lydia, Lydia, you ought to know that lying don't become a young woman! Didn't you boast that Beverley — that stroller Beverley — possessed your heart? Tell me that, I say.

LYDIA: 'Tis true, Ma'am, and none but Beverley ——

MRS. MALAPROP: Hold — hold, Assurance! you shall not be so rude.

ABSOLUTE: Nay, pray Mrs. Malaprop, don't stop the young lady's speech: she's very welcome to talk thus — it does not hurt *me* in the least, I assure you.

MRS. MALAPROP: You are *too* good, Captain — *too* amiably patient — but come with me, Miss. Let us see you again soon, Captain. Remember what we have fixed.

ABSOLUTE: I shall, Ma'am.

MRS. MALAPROP: Come, take a graceful leave of the gentleman.

LYDIA: May every blessing wait on my Beverley, my loved Bev ——

MRS. MALAPROP: Hussy! I'll choke the word in your throat! — come along — come along.

(*Exeunt severally,* ABSOLUTE *kissing his hand to* LYDIA — MRS. MALAPROP *stopping her from speaking.*)

Scene 4 [ACRES's *lodgings*]

(ACRES *and* DAVID, ACRES *as just dressed.*)

ACRES: Indeed, David — do you think I become it so?

DAVID: You are quite another creature, believe me, master, by the Mass! an'[52] we've any luck we shall see the Devon monkeyrony[53] in all the print-shops in Bath!

ACRES: Dress *does* make a difference, David.

DAVID: 'Tis all in all,[54] I think. Difference! why, an' you were to go now to Clod-Hall, I am certain the old lady[55] wouldn't know you: Master Butler wouldn't believe his own eyes, and Mrs. Pickle would cry, "Lard presarve[56] me!" — our dairy-maid would come giggling to the door, and I warrant Dolly Tester, your Honour's favorite, would blush like my waistcoat. Oons! I'll hold a gallon, there a'n't a dog in the house but would bark, and I question whether *Phillis* would wag a hair of her tail!

ACRES: Aye, David, there's nothing like polishing.

DAVID: So I says of your Honour's boots; but the boy never heeds me!

ACRES: But, David, has Mr. De-la-Grace been here? I must rub up my balancing, and chasing, and boring.[57]

DAVID: I'll call again, Sir.

ACRES: Do — and see if there are any letters for me at the post office.

DAVID: I will. By the Mass, I can't help looking at your head! If I hadn't been by at the cooking, I wish I may die if I should have known the dish again myself! (*Exit.*)

(ACRES *comes forward, practising a dancing step.*)

ACRES: Sink, slide — coupee! Confound the first inventors of cotillions! say I — they are as bad as algebra to us country gentlemen. I can walk a minuet easy enough when I'm forced! and I have been accounted a good stick in a country-dance. Odds jigs and tabours! I never valued your cross-over to couple — figure in — right and left — and I'd foot it with e'er a[58] captain in the county! But these outlandish heathen allemandes and cotillions are quite beyond me! I shall never prosper at 'em, that's sure. Mine are true-born English legs — they don't understand their curst French lingo! their *pas* this, and *pas* that, and *pas* t'other! D——n me! my feet don't like

52 if 53 corruption, by association with "monkey," of "macaroni," contemporary slang for fops and dandies affecting Continental ways 54 everything 55 *i.e.*, Acres's mother 56 Lord preserve 57 anglicized French dancing terms 58 any

to be called paws! No, 'tis certain I have most anti-Gallican toes!

(*Enter* SERVANT.)

SERVANT: Here is Sir Lucius O'Trigger to wait on you, Sir.
ACRES: Show him in.

(*Enter* SIR LUCIUS.)

SIR LUCIUS: Mr. Acres, I am delighted to embrace you.
ACRES: My dear Sir Lucius, I kiss your hands.
SIR LUCIUS: Pray, my friend, what has brought you so suddenly to Bath?
ACRES: Faith! I have followed Cupid's Jack-a-Lantern, and find myself in a quagmire at last. In short, I have been very ill-used, Sir Lucius. I don't choose to mention names, but look on me as on a very ill-used gentleman.
SIR LUCIUS: Pray, what is the case? I ask no names.
ACRES: Mark me, Sir Lucius, I fall as deep as need be in love with a young lady — her friends take my part — I follow her to Bath — send word of my arrival, and receive answer that the lady is to be otherwise disposed of. This, Sir Lucius, I call being ill-used.
SIR LUCIUS: Very ill, upon my conscience. Pray, can you divine the cause of it?
ACRES: Why, there's the matter: she has another lover, one Beverley, who, I am told, is now in Bath. Odds slanders and lies! he must be at the bottom of it.
SIR LUCIUS: A rival in the case, is there? And you think he has supplanted you unfairly?
ACRES: Unfairly! — to be sure he has. He never could have done it fairly.
SIR LUCIUS: Then sure you know what is to be done!
ACRES: Not I, upon my soul!
SIR LUCIUS: We wear no swords here, but you understand me.
ACRES: What! fight him?
SIR LUCIUS: Aye, to be sure: what can I mean else?
ACRES: But he has given me no provocation.
SIR LUCIUS: Now, I think he has given you the greatest provocation in the world. Can a man commit a more heinous offense against another than to fall in love with the same woman? Oh, by my soul, it is the most unpardonable breach of friendship!
ACRES: Breach of friendship! Aye, aye; but I have no acquaintance with this man. I never saw him in my life.
SIR LUCIUS: That's no argument at all — he has the less right then to take such a liberty.

ACRES: 'Gad, that's true. I grow full of anger, Sir Lucius! I fire apace! Odds hilts and blades! I find a man may have a deal of valour in him and not know it! But couldn't I contrive to have a little right of my side?

SIR LUCIUS: What the devil signifies *right* when your *honour* is concerned? Do you think Achilles, or my little Alexander the Great ever inquired where the right lay? No, by my soul, they drew their broadswords, and left the lazy sons of peace to settle the justice of it.

ACRES: Your words are a grenadier's march to my heart! I believe courage must be catching! I certainly do feel a kind of valour rising, as it were — a kind of courage, as I may say. Odds flints, pans,[59] and triggers! I'll challenge him directly.

SIR LUCIUS: Ah, my little friend! if we had Blunderbuss-Hall here — I could show you a range of ancestry, in the O'Trigger line, that would furnish the New Room, every one of whom had killed his man! For though the mansion-house and dirty acres have slipped through my fingers, I thank heaven our honour, and the family-pictures, are as fresh as ever.

ACRES: O Sir Lucius! I have had ancestors too! every man of 'em colonel or captain in the militia! Odds balls and barrels! say no more — I'm braced for it. The thunder of your words has soured the milk of human kindness[60] in my breast! Z——ds! as the man in the play[61] says, "I could do such deeds!"

SIR LUCIUS: Come, come, there must be no passion at all in the case — these things should always be done civilly.

ACRES: I must be in a passion, Sir Lucius — I must be in a rage. Dear Sir Lucius, let me be in a rage, if you love me. Come, here's pen and paper. (*Sits down to write.*) I would the ink were red! Indite, I say, indite! How shall I begin? Odds bullets and blades! I'll write a good bold hand, however.

SIR LUCIUS: Pray compose yourself.

ACRES: Come now, shall I begin with an oath? Do, Sir Lucius, let me begin with a damme.

SIR LUCIUS: Pho! pho! do the thing decently and like a Christian. Begin now — "*Sir*" ——

ACRES: That's too civil by half.

SIR LUCIUS: "*To prevent the confusion that might arise*" ——

[59] in old guns, the hollow part of the gunlock in which the powder was placed
[60] cf. Lady Macbeth's "Yet do I fear thy nature. / It is too full o' th' milk of human kindness / To catch the nearest way." (I, v, 14-16)
[61] probably Hamlet: "Now could I drink hot blood / And do such bitter business as the day / Would quake to look on." (III, ii, 375-377) and "O, such a deed / As from the body of contraction plucks / The very soul, . . ." (III, iv, 46-48)

ACRES: Well ——

SIR LUCIUS: "*From our both addressing the same lady*" ——

ACRES: Aye — there's the reason — "*same lady*" — Well ——

SIR LUCIUS: "*I shall expect the honour of your company*" ——

ACRES: Z——ds! I'm not asking him to dinner.

SIR LUCIUS: Pray be easy.

ACRES: Well then — "*honour of your company*" ——

SIR LUCIUS: "*To settle our pretensions*" ——

ACRES: Well ——

SIR LUCIUS: Let me see — aye, King's-Mead-Fields will do —"*In King's-Mead-Fields.*"

ACRES: So that's done. —— Well, I'll fold it up presently; my own crest — a hand and dagger shall be the seal.

SIR LUCIUS: You see now, this little explanation will put a stop at once to all confusion or misunderstanding that might arise between you.

ACRES: Aye, we fight to prevent any misunderstanding.

SIR LUCIUS: Now, I'll leave you to fix your own time. Take my advice, and you'll decide it this evening if you can; then let the worst come of it, 'twill be off your mind to-morrow.

ACRES: Very true.

SIR LUCIUS: So I shall see nothing more of you, unless it be by letter, till the evening. I would do myself the honour to carry your message; but, to tell you a secret, I believe I shall have just such another affair on my own hands. There is a gay captain here who put a jest on me lately at the expense of my country, and I only want to fall in with the gentleman to call him out.

ACRES: By my valour, I should like to see you fight first! Odd's life! I should like to see you kill him, if it was only to get a little lesson.

SIR LUCIUS: I shall be very proud of instructing you. Well for the present — but remember now, when you meet your antagonist, do everything in a mild and agreeable manner. Let your courage be as keen, but at the same time as polished, as your sword.

(*Exeunt severally.*)

ACT IV

Scene 1 [ACRES's *lodgings*]

(ACRES *and* DAVID.)

DAVID: Then, by the Mass, Sir! I would do no such thing — ne'er a Sir Lucius O'Trigger in the kingdom should make me fight, when I wa'n't so minded. Oons! what will the old lady say when she hears o't!

ACRES: Ah! David, if you had heard Sir Lucius! Odds sparks and flames! he would have roused your valour.

DAVID: Not he, indeed. I hates such bloodthirsty cormorants. Look'ee, master, if you'd wanted a bout at boxing, quarterstaff, or shortstaff, I should never be the man to bid you cry off: but for your curst sharps and snaps,[62] I never knew any good come of 'em.

ACRES: But my honour, David, my honour! I must be very careful of my honour.

DAVID: Aye, by the Mass! and I would be very careful of it; and I think in return my *honour* couldn't do less than to be very careful of *me*.

ACRES: Odds blades! David, no gentleman will ever risk the loss of his honour!

DAVID: I say then, it would be but civil in *honour* never to risk the loss of a *gentleman*. Look'ee, master, this *honour* seems to me to be a marvellous false friend; aye, truly, a very courtier-like servant. Put the case, I was a gentleman (which, thank God, no one can say of me); well — my honour makes me quarrel with another gentleman of my acquaintance. So — we fight. (Pleasant enough that.) Boh! — I kill him (the more's my luck). Now, pray who gets the profit of it? Why, my *honour*. But put the case that he kills me! — by the Mass! I go to the worms, and my honour whips over to my enemy!

ACRES: No, David — in that case — odds crowns and laurels! — your honour follows you to the grave.

DAVID: Now, that's just the place where I could make a shift to do without it.

ACRES: Z——ds, David, you're a coward! It doesn't become any valour to listen to you. What, shall I disgrace my ancestors? Think of that, David — think what it would be to disgrace my ancestors!

DAVID: Under favour, the surest way of not disgracing them is to keep as long as you can out of their company. Look'ee now, master, to

62 swords and guns

go to them in such haste — with an ounce of lead in your brains — I should think might as well be let alone. Our ancestors are very good kind of folks; but they are the last people I should choose to have a visiting acquaintance with.

ACRES: But David, now, you don't think there is such very, very, *very* great danger, hey? Odd's life! people often fight without any mischief done!

DAVID: By the Mass, I think 'tis ten to one against you! Oons! here to meet some lion-headed fellow, I warrant, with his d——n'd double-barrelled swords, and cut-and-thrust pistols! Lord bless us! it makes me tremble to think o't. Those be such desperate bloody-minded weapons! Well, I never could abide 'em! from a child I never could fancy 'em! I suppose there a'n't so merciless a beast in the world as your loaded pistol!

ACRES: Z——ds! I *won't* be afraid! Odds fire and fury! you sha'n't make me afraid! Here is the challenge, and I have sent for my dear friend Jack Absolute to carry it for me.

DAVID: Aye, i' the name of mischief, let *him* be the messenger. For my part, I wouldn't lend a hand to it for the best horse in your stable. By the Mass! it don't look like another letter! It is, as I may say, a designing and malicious-looking letter! and I warrant smells of gunpowder, like a soldier's pouch! Oons! I wouldn't swear it mayn't go off!

ACRES: Out, you poltroon! You ha'n't the valour of a grasshopper.

DAVID: Well, I say no more — 'twill be sad news, to be sure, at Clod-Hall! — but I ha' done. How Phillis will howl when she hears of it! Aye, poor bitch, she little thinks what shooting her master's going after! And I warrant old Crop, who has carried your Honour, field and road, these ten years, will curse the hour he was born (*whimpering*).

ACRES: It won't do, David — I am determined to fight — so get along, you coward, while I'm in the mind.

(*Enter* SERVANT.)

SERVANT: Captain Absolute, Sir.

ACRES: Oh! show him up. (*Exit* SERVANT.)

DAVID: Well, heaven send we be all alive this time to-morrow.

ACRES: What's that! Don't provoke me, David!

DAVID: Good-bye, master (*whimpering*).

ACRES: Get along, you cowardly, dastardly, croaking raven.

(*Exit* DAVID.)

(*Enter* ABSOLUTE.)

ABSOLUTE: What's the matter, Bob?

ACRES: A vile, sheep-hearted blockhead! If I hadn't the valour of St. George and the dragon to boot ——

ABSOLUTE: But what did you want with me, Bob?

ACRES: Oh! There —— (*Gives him the challenge.*)

ABSOLUTE: "*To Ensign Beverley.*" (*Aside.*) So — what's going on now? (*Aloud.*) Well, what's this?

ACRES: A challenge!

ABSOLUTE: Indeed! Why, you won't fight him, will you, Bob?

ACRES: 'Egad, but I will, Jack. Sir Lucius has wrought me to it. He has left me full of rage, and I'll fight this evening, that so much good passion mayn't be wasted.

ABSOLUTE: But what have I to do with this?

ACRES: Why, as I think you know something of this fellow, I want you to find him out for me, and give him this mortal defiance.

ABSOLUTE: Well, give it to me, and trust me he gets it.

ACRES: Thank you, my dear friend, my dear Jack; but it is giving you a great deal of trouble.

ABSOLUTE: Not in the least — I beg you won't mention it. No trouble in the world, I assure you.

ACRES: You are very kind. What it is to have a friend! You couldn't be my second — could you, Jack?

ABSOLUTE: Why no, Bob — not in *this* affair. It would not be quite so proper.

ACRES: Well then, I must get my friend Sir Lucius. I shall have your good wishes, however, Jack.

ABSOLUTE: Whenever he meets you, believe me.

(*Enter* SERVANT.)

SERVANT: Sir Anthony Absolute is below, inquiring for the Captain.

ABSOLUTE: I'll come instantly. Well, my little hero, success attend you (*going*).

ACRES: Stay — stay, Jack. If Beverley should ask you what kind of a man your friend Acres is, do tell him I am a devil of a fellow — will you, Jack?

ABSOLUTE: To be sure I shall. I'll say you are a determined dog — hey, Bob?

ACRES: Aye, do, do — and if that frightens him, 'egad, perhaps he mayn't come. So tell him I generally kill a man a week — will you, Jack?

ABSOLUTE: I will, I will; I'll say you are called in the country "*Fighting Bob!*"

ACRES: Right, right — 'tis all to prevent mischief; for I don't want to take his life if I clear my honour.

ABSOLUTE: No! — that's very kind of you.

ACRES: Why, you don't wish me to kill him — do you, Jack?

ABSOLUTE: No, upon my soul, I do not. But a devil of a fellow, hey? (*Going.*)

ACRES: True, true — but stay — stay, Jack. You may add that you never saw me in such a rage before — a most devouring rage!

ABSOLUTE: I will, I will.

ACRES: Remember, Jack — a determined dog!

ABSOLUTE: Aye, aye, "*Fighting Bob!*" (*Exeunt severally.*)

Scene 2 [MRS. MALAPROP's lodgings.]

(MRS. MALAPROP *and* LYDIA.)

MRS. MALAPROP: Why, thou perverse one! tell me what you can object to him? Isn't he a handsome man? tell me that. A genteel man? a pretty figure of a man?

LYDIA (*aside*): She little thinks whom she is praising! — (*Aloud.*) So is Beverley, Ma'am.

MRS. MALAPROP: No caparisons, Miss, if you please! Caparisons don't become a young woman. No! Captain Absolute is indeed a fine gentleman!

LYDIA (*aside*): Aye, the Captain Absolute *you* have seen.

MRS. MALAPROP: Then he's *so* well bred; so full of alacrity, and adulation! and has *so much* to say for himself — in such good language, too! His physiognomy so grammatical! Then his presence is so noble! I protest, when I saw him, I thought of what Hamlet says[63] in the play: "Hesperian curls! — the front of *Job* himself! An eye, like *March*, to threaten at command — a station, like Harry Mercury, new" — something about kissing on a hill — however, the similitude struck me directly.

LYDIA (*aside*): How enraged she'll be presently when she discovers her mistake!

(*Enter* SERVANT.)

[63] Mrs. Malaprop continues to misquote from the bedroom scene in *Hamlet*. Cf. III, iv, 57-60: "Hyperion's curls, the front of Jove himself, / An eye like Mars, to threaten and command, / A station like the herald Mercury / New lighted on a heaven-kissing hill —" The allusion to Hamlet's comparison of the ideal man represented by the portrait of his father and the despicable reality represented by Claudius anticipates Captain Absolute's comparison later in the same scene of Lydia's loving looks in her portrait and the sulk of her actual face.

SERVANT: Sir Anthony and Captain Absolute are below, Ma'am.

MRS. MALAPROP: Show them up here. (*Exit* SERVANT.) Now, Lydia, I insist on your behaving as becomes a young woman. Show your good breeding at least, though you have forgot your duty.

LYDIA: Madam, I have told you my resolution; I shall not only give him no encouragement, but I won't even speak to, or look at him.

(*Flings herself into a chair with her face from the door. Enter* SIR ANTHONY *and* ABSOLUTE.)

SIR ANTHONY: Here we are, Mrs. Malaprop, come to mitigate the frowns of unrelenting beauty — and difficulty enough I had to bring this fellow. I don't know what's the matter; but if I hadn't held him by force, he'd have given me the slip.

MRS. MALAPROP: You have infinite trouble, Sir Anthony, in the affair. I am ashamed for the cause! — (*Aside to her.*) Lydia, Lydia, rise, I beseech you! — pay your respects!

SIR ANTHONY: I hope, Madam, that Miss Languish has reflected on the worth of this gentleman, and the regard due to her aunt's choice, and *my* alliance. — (*Aside to him.*) Now, Jack, speak to her!

ABSOLUTE (*aside*): What the devil shall I do! — (*Aloud.*) You see, Sir, she won't even look at me whilst you are here. I knew she wouldn't! I told you so. Let me entreat you, Sir, to leave us together! (ABSOLUTE *seems to expostulate with his father.*)

LYDIA (*aside*): I wonder I ha'n't heard my aunt exclaim yet! Sure she can't have looked at him! Perhaps their regimentals are alike, and she is something[64] blind.

SIR ANTHONY: I say, Sir, I won't stir a foot yet!

MRS. MALAPROP: I am sorry to say, Sir Anthony, that my affluence over my niece is very small. — (*Aside to her.*) Turn round, Lydia; I blush for you!

SIR ANTHONY: May I not flatter myself that Miss Languish will assign what cause of dislike she can have to my son! Why don't you begin, Jack? — (*Aside to him.*) Speak, you puppy — speak!

MRS. MALAPROP: It is impossible, Sir Anthony, she can have any. She will not *say* she has. — (*Aside to her.*) Answer, hussy! why don't you answer?

SIR ANTHONY: Then, Madam, I trust that a childish and hasty predilection will be no bar to Jack's happiness. — (*Aside to him.*) Z——ds! Sirrah! why don't you speak?

LYDIA (*aside*): I think my lover seems as little inclined to conversation as myself. How strangely blind my aunt must be!

64 somewhat

ABSOLUTE: Hem! hem! — Madam — hem! — (ABSOLUTE *attempts to speak, then returns to* SIR ANTHONY.) — Faith! Sir, I am so confounded! and so — so — confused! I told you I should be so, Sir, I knew it. The — the — tremor of my passion entirely takes away my presence of mind.

SIR ANTHONY: But it don't take away your voice, fool, does it? Go up, and speak to her directly!

(ABSOLUTE *makes signs to* MRS. MALAPROP *to leave them together.*)

MRS. MALAPROP: Sir Anthony, shall we leave them together? — (*Aside to her.*) Ah! you stubborn little vixen!

SIR ANTHONY: Not yet, Ma'am, not yet! — (*Aside to him.*) What the devil are you at? Unlock your jaws, Sirrah, or ——

(ABSOLUTE *draws near* LYDIA.)

ABSOLUTE (*aside*): Now heaven send she may be too sullen to look round! I must disguise my voice. — (*Speaks in a low hoarse tone.*) Will not Miss Languish lend an ear to the mild accents of true love? Will not ——

SIR ANTHONY: What the devil ails the fellow? Why don't you speak out? — not stand croaking like a frog in a quinsy!

ABSOLUTE: The — the — excess of my awe, and my — my — my modesty quite choke me!

SIR ANTHONY: Ah! your *modesty* again! I'll tell you what, Jack, if you don't speak out directly, and glibly, too, I shall be in such a rage! Mrs. Malaprop, I wish the lady would favour us with something more than a side-front!

(MRS. MALAPROP *seems to chide* LYDIA.)

ABSOLUTE: So! All will out I see! (*Goes up to* LYDIA, *speaks softly.*) Be not surprised, my Lydia; suppress all surprise at present.

LYDIA (*aside*): Heavens! 'tis Beverley's voice! Sure he can't have imposed on Sir Anthony, too! — (*Looks round by degrees, then starts up.*) Is this possible — my Beverley! — how can this be? — my Beverley?

ABSOLUTE (*aside*): Ah! 'tis all over.

SIR ANTHONY: Beverley! — the devil! — Beverley! What can the girl mean? This is my son, Jack Absolute!

MRS. MALAPROP: For shame, hussy! for shame! your head runs so on that fellow that you have him always in your eyes! Beg Captain Absolute's pardon directly.

LYDIA: I see no Captain Absolute, but my loved Beverley!

SIR ANTHONY: Z——ds! the girl's mad! — her brain's turned by reading!

MRS. MALAPROP: O' my conscience, I believe so! What do you mean by Beverley, hussy? You saw Captain Absolute before to-day; there he is — your husband that shall be.

LYDIA: With all my soul, Ma'am. When I refuse my Beverley ——

SIR ANTHONY: Oh! she's as mad as Bedlam! Or has this fellow been playing us a rogue's trick! Come here, Sirrah! — who the devil are you?

ABSOLUTE: Faith, Sir, I am not quite clear myself, but I'll endeavour to recollect.

SIR ANTHONY: Are you my son, or not? Answer for your mother, you dog, if you won't for me.

MRS. MALAPROP: Aye, Sir, who are you? Oh mercy! I begin to suspect! ——

ABSOLUTE (*aside*): Ye Powers of Impudence befriend me! — (*Aloud.*) Sir Anthony, most assuredly I am your wife's son; and that I sincerely believe myself to be *yours* also, I hope my duty has always shown. —— Mrs. Malaprop, I am your most respectful admirer — and shall be proud to add *affectionate nephew.* —— I need not tell my Lydia, that she sees her faithful Beverley, who, knowing the singular generosity of her temper, assumed that name, and a station which has proved a test of the most disinterested love, which he now hopes to enjoy in a more elevated character.

LYDIA (*sullenly*): So! — there will be no elopement after all!

SIR ANTHONY: Upon my soul, Jack, thou art a very impudent fellow! to do you justice, I think I never saw a piece of more consummate assurance!

ABSOLUTE: Oh you flatter me, Sir — you compliment — 'tis my *modesty* you know, Sir — my *modesty* that has stood in my way.

SIR ANTHONY: Well, I am glad you are not the dull, insensible varlet[65] you pretended to be, however! I'm glad you have made a fool of your father, you dog — I am. So this was your *penitence,* your *duty,* and *obedience!* I thought it was d——d sudden! You *never heard their names before,* not you! *What!* The *Languishes of Worcestershire,* hey? — *if you could please me in the affair, 'twas all you desired!* — Ah! you dissembling villain! What! — (*pointing to* LYDIA) *she squints, don't she? — a little red-haired girl!* — hey? Why, you hypocritical young rascal! I wonder you a'n't ashamed to hold up your head!

65 scoundrel

ABSOLUTE: 'Tis with difficulty, Sir. I *am* confused — very much confused, as you must perceive.

MRS. MALAPROP: O lud! Sir Anthony! — a new light breaks in upon me! Hey! how! what! Captain, did *you* write the letters then? What! — am I to thank you for the elegant compilation of "*an old weather-beaten she-dragon*" — hey? O mercy! was it *you* that reflected on my parts of speech?

ABSOLUTE: Dear Sir! my modesty will be overpowered at last, if you don't assist me. I shall certainly not be able to stand it!

SIR ANTHONY: Come, come, Mrs. Malaprop, we must forget and forgive. Odd's life! matters have taken so clever a turn all of a sudden, that I could find in my heart to be so good-humoured! and so gallant! — hey! Mrs. Malaprop!

MRS. MALAPROP: Well, Sir Anthony, since *you* desire it, we will not anticipate the past; so mind, young people: our retrospection will now be all to the future.

SIR ANTHONY: Come, we must leave them together; Mrs. Malaprop, they long to fly into each other's arms. I warrant! — (*Aside.*) Jack — isn't the cheek as I said, hey? — and the eye, you rogue! — and the lip — hey? Come, Mrs. Malaprop, we'll not disturb their tenderness — theirs is the time of life for happiness! — (*Sings.*) "*Youth's the season made for joy*" — hey! Odd's life! I'm in such spirits, I don't know what I couldn't do! Permit me, Ma'am — (*Gives his hand to* MRS. MALAPROP. *Sings.*) Tol-de-rol! — 'gad, I should like a little fooling myself. Tol-de-rol! de-rol! (*Exit singing, and handing* MRS. MALAPROP. LYDIA *sits sullenly in her chair.*)

ABSOLUTE (*aside*): So much thought bodes me no good. —— (*Aloud.*) So grave, Lydia!

LYDIA: Sir!

ABSOLUTE (*aside*): So! — egad! I thought as much! That d——d monosyllable has froze me! —— (*Aloud.*) What, Lydia, now that we are as happy in our friends' consent, as in our mutual vows ——

LYDIA (*peevishly*): *Friends' consent,* indeed!

ABSOLUTE: Come, come, we must lay aside some of our romance — a little *wealth* and *comfort* may be endured after all. And for your fortune, the lawyers shall make such settlements as ——

LYDIA: *Lawyers!* I *hate* lawyers!

ABSOLUTE: Nay then, we will not wait for their lingering forms but instantly procure the license, and ——

LYDIA: The *license!* I *hate* license!

ABSOLUTE: O my love! be not so unkind! Thus let me intreat —— (*kneeling*).

LYDIA: Pshaw! what signifies kneeling when you know I *must* have you?

ABSOLUTE (*rising*): Nay, Madam, there shall be no constraint upon your inclinations, I promise you. If I have lost your heart, I resign the rest. — (*Aside.*) 'Gad, I must try what a little *spirit*[66] will do.

LYDIA (*rising*): Then, Sir, let me tell you, the interest you had there was acquired by a mean, unmanly imposition, and deserves the punishment of fraud. What, you have been treating *me* like a child! — humouring my romance! and laughing, I suppose, at your success!

ABSOLUTE: You wrong me, Lydia, you wrong me. Only hear ——

LYDIA: So, while *I* fondly imagined we were deceiving my relations, and flattered myself that I should outwit and incense them all — behold! my hopes are to be crushed at once, by my aunt's consent and approbation! — and *I* am myself the only dupe at last! (*Walking about in heat.*) But here, Sir, here is the picture — Beverley's picture! (*taking a miniature from her bosom*) — which I have worn, night and day, in spite of threats and entreaties! There, Sir (*flings it to him*) — and be assured I throw the original from my heart as easily.

ABSOLUTE: Nay, nay, Ma'am, we will not differ as to that. Here (*taking out a picture*), here is Miss Lydia Languish. What a difference! Aye, *there* is the heavenly assenting smile that first gave soul and spirit to my hopes! — those are the lips which sealed a vow, as yet scarce dry in Cupid's calendar! — and *there*, the half resentful blush that *would* have checked the ardour of my thanks. Well, all that's past — all over indeed! There, Madam, in beauty, that copy is not equal to you, but in my mind its merit over the original, in being still the same, in such — that — I cannot find in my heart to part with it. (*Puts it up again.*)

LYDIA (*softening*): 'Tis *your own* doing, Sir. I — I — I suppose you are perfectly satisfied.

ABSOLUTE: Ah, most certainly. Sure now this is much better than being in love! Ha! ha! ha! — there's some spirit in *this!* What signifies breaking some scores of solemn promises, half an hundred vows, under one's hand, with the marks of a dozen or two angels to witness! — all that's of no consequence, you know. To be sure, people will say that Miss didn't know her own mind — but never mind that: or perhaps they may be ill-natured enough to hint that the gentleman grew tired of the lady and forsook her — but don't let that fret you.

66 *i.e.*, temper, pride

LYDIA: There's no bearing his insolence. (*Bursts into tears.*)

(*Enter* MRS. MALAPROP *and* SIR ANTHONY.)

MRS. MALAPROP (*entering*): Come, we must interrupt your billing and cooing a while.

LYDIA: This is worse than your treachery and deceit, you base ingrate! (*Sobbing.*)

SIR ANTHONY: What the devil's the matter now! Z——ds! Mrs. Malaprop, this is the *oddest billing* and *cooing* I ever heard! But what the deuce is the meaning of it? I'm quite astonished!

ABSOLUTE: Ask the lady, Sir.

MRS. MALAPROP: Oh mercy! I'm quite analysed, for my part! Why, Lydia, what is the reason of this?

LYDIA: Ask the *gentleman*, Ma'am.

SIR ANTHONY: Z——ds! I shall be in a frenzy! —— Why, Jack, you are not come out to be anyone else, are you?

MRS. MALAPROP: Aye, Sir, there's no more *trick*, is there? You are not like Cerberus, *three* gentlemen at once, are you?

ABSOLUTE: You'll not let me speak. I say the lady can account for this much better than I can.

LYDIA: Ma'am, you once commanded me never to think of Beverley again. There is the man — I now obey you: — for, from this moment, I renounce him forever. (*Exit.*)

MRS. MALAPROP: Oh mercy! and miracles! what a turn here is! Why, sure, Captain, you haven't behaved disrespectfully to my niece?

SIR ANTHONY: Ha! ha! ha! — ha! ha! ha! — now I see it — ha! ha! ha! — now I see it — you have been too lively, Jack.

ABSOLUTE: Nay, Sir, upon my word ——

SIR ANTHONY: Come, no lying, Jack — I'm sure '*twas* so.

MRS. MALAPROP: O lud! Sir Anthony! Oh fie, Captain!

ABSOLUTE: Upon my soul, Ma'am ——

SIR ANTHONY: Come, no excuses, Jack; why, your father, you rogue, was so before you: the blood of the Absolutes was always impatient. Ha! ha! ha! poor little Lydia! — why, you've frightened her, you dog, you have.

ABSOLUTE: By all that's good, Sir ——

SIR ANTHONY: Z——ds! say no more, I tell you. Mrs. Malaprop shall make your peace. —— You must make his peace, Mrs. Malaprop; you must tell her 'tis Jack's way — tell her 'tis all our ways — it runs in the blood of our family! Come, away, Jack — ha! ha! ha! Mrs. Malaprop — a young villain! (*Pushes him out.*)

MRS. MALAPROP: Oh, Sir Anthony! Oh fie, Captain!

(*Exeunt severally.*)

Scene 3 [The North Parade.]

(*Enter* SIR LUCIUS O'TRIGGER.)

SIR LUCIUS: I wonder where this Captain Absolute hides himself. Upon my conscience! these officers are always in one's way in love-affairs. I remember I might have married Lady Dorothy Carmine, if it had not been for a little rogue of a major, who ran away with her before she could get a sight of me! And I wonder too what it is the ladies can see in them to be so fond of them — unless it be a touch of the old serpent in 'em, that makes the little creatures be caught, like vipers, with a bit of red cloth. —— Hah! — isn't this the Captain coming? — faith it is! There is a probability of succeeding about that fellow that is mighty provoking! Who the devil is he talking to? (*Steps aside. Enter* CAPTAIN ABSOLUTE.)

ABSOLUTE: To what fine purpose I have been plotting! A noble reward for all my schemes, upon my soul! A little gypsy! I did not think her romance could have made her so d——d absurd either. 'Sdeath, I never was in a worse humour in my life! I could cut my own throat, or any other person's, with the greatest pleasure in the world!

SIR LUCIUS: Oh, faith! I'm in the luck of it — I never could have found him in a sweeter temper for my purpose — to be sure I'm just come in the nick![67] Now to enter into conversation with him, and so quarrel genteelly. (SIR LUCIUS *goes up to* ABSOLUTE.) — With regard to that matter, Captain, I must beg leave to differ in opinion with you.

ABSOLUTE: Upon my word then, you must be a very subtle disputant, because, Sir, I happened just then to be giving no opinion at all.

SIR LUCIUS: That's no reason. For give me leave to tell you, a man may *think* an untruth as well as *speak* one.

ABSOLUTE: Very true, Sir, but if a man never utters his thoughts I should think they might stand a chance of escaping controversy.

SIR LUCIUS: Then, Sir, you differ in opinion with me, which amounts to the same thing.

ABSOLUTE: Hark'ee, Sir Lucius — if I had not before known you to be a gentleman, upon my soul, I should not have discovered it at this interview, for what you can drive at, unless you mean to quarrel with me, I cannot conceive!

SIR LUCIUS: I humbly thank you, Sir, for the quickness of your appre-

[67] at the critical moment

hension. (*Bowing.*) You have named the very thing I would be at.

ABSOLUTE: Very well, Sir — I shall certainly not balk your inclinations but I should be glad you would please to explain your motives.

SIR LUCIUS: Pray, Sir, be easy: the quarrel is a very pretty quarrel as it stands — we should only spoil it by trying to explain it. However, your memory is very short or you could not have forgot an affront you passed on me within this week. So no more, but name your time and place.

ABSOLUTE: Well, Sir, since you are so bent on it, the sooner the better; let it be this evening — here, by the Spring-Gardens. We shall scarcely be interrupted.

SIR LUCIUS: Faith! that same interruption in affairs of this nature shows very great ill-breeding. I don't know what's the reason, but in England, if a thing of this kind gets wind, people make such a pother that a gentleman can never fight in peace and quietness. However, if it's the same to you, Captain, I should take it as a particular kindness if you'd let us meet in King's-Mead-Fields, as a little business will call me there about six o'clock, and I may dispatch both matters at once.

ABSOLUTE: 'Tis the same to me exactly. A little after six, then, we will discuss this matter more seriously.

SIR LUCIUS: If you please, Sir, there will be very pretty small-sword light, though it won't do for a long shot. So that matter's settled! and my mind's at ease! (*Exit.*)

(*Enter* FAULKLAND, *meeting* ABSOLUTE.)

ABSOLUTE: Well met. I was going to look for you. O Faulkland! all the dæmons of spite and disappointment have conspired against me! I'm so vexed that if I had not the prospect of a resource in being knocked o' the head by and by, I should scarce have spirits to tell you the cause.

FAULKLAND: What can you mean? Has Lydia changed her mind? I should have thought her duty and inclination would now have pointed to the same object.

ABSOLUTE: Aye, just as the eyes do of a person who squints: when her love-eye was fixed on me — t'other — her eye of duty, was finely obliqued: — but when duty bid her point that the same way — off t'other turned on a swivel, and secured its retreat with a frown!

FAULKLAND: But what's the resource you ——

ABSOLUTE: Oh, to wind up the whole, a good-natured Irishman here has (*mimicking* SIR LUCIUS) begged leave to have the pleasure of cutting my throat, and I mean to indulge him — that's all.

FAULKLAND: Prithee, be serious.

ABSOLUTE: 'Tis fact, upon my soul. Sir Lucius O'Trigger — you know him by sight — for some affront, which I am sure I never intended, has obliged me to meet him this evening at six o'clock: 'tis on that account I wished to see you — you must go with me.

FAULKLAND: Nay, there must be some mistake, sure. Sir Lucius shall explain himself — and I dare say matters may be accommodated. But this evening, did you say? I wish it had been any other time.

ABSOLUTE: Why? there will be light enough. There will (as Sir Lucius says) "be very pretty small-sword light, though it won't do for a long shot." Confound his long shots!

FAULKLAND: But I am myself a good deal ruffled by a difference I have had with Julia. My vile tormenting temper has made me treat her so cruelly that I shall not be myself till we are reconciled.

ABSOLUTE: By heavens, Faulkland, you don't deserve her.

(*Enter* SERVANT, *gives* FAULKLAND *a letter.*)

FAULKLAND: O Jack! this is from Julia. I dread to open it. I fear it may be to take a last leave — perhaps to bid me return her letters and restore —— Oh! how I suffer for my folly!

ABSOLUTE: Here — let me see. (*Takes the letter and opens it.*) Aye, a final sentence indeed! — 'tis all over with you, faith!

FAULKLAND: Nay, Jack — don't keep me in suspense.

ABSOLUTE: Hear then. — "*As I am convinced that my dear* FAULKLAND'S *own reflections have already upbraided him for his last unkindness to me, I will not add a word on the subject. I wish to speak with you as soon as possible. — Yours ever and truly,* JULIA." — There's stubbornness and resentment for you! (*Gives him the letter.*) Why, man, you don't seem one whit happier at this.

FAULKLAND: Oh, yes, I am — but — but ——

ABSOLUTE: Confound your *buts*. You never hear anything that would make another man bless himself, but you immediately d——n it with a *but*.

FAULKLAND: Now, Jack, as you are my friend, own honestly — don't you think there is something forward, something indelicate, in this haste to forgive? Women should never sue for reconciliation: that should always come from us. They should retain their coldness till *wooed* to kindness — and their *pardon*, like their *love*, should "not unsought be won."

ABSOLUTE: I have not patience to listen to you — thou'rt incorrigible! — so say no more on the subject. I must go to settle a few matters. Let me see you before six — remember — at my lodgings. A poor industrious devil like me, who have toiled, and drudged, and plotted to gain my ends, and am at last disappointed by other people's folly, may in pity be allowed to swear and grumble a little; but a captious sceptic in love, a slave to fretfulness and whim, who has no difficulties but of his own creating, is a subject more fit for ridicule than compassion! (*Exit.*)

FAULKLAND: I feel his reproaches, yet I would not change this too exquisite nicety for the gross content with which *he* tramples on the thorns of love. His engaging me in this duel has started an idea in my head, which I will instantly pursue. I'll use it as the touchstone of Julia's sincerity and disinterestedness. If her love prove pure and sterling ore, my name will rest on it with honour! — and once I've stamped it there, I lay aside my doubts forever — ; but if the dross of selfishness, the alloy of pride predominate, 'twill be best to leave her as a toy for some less cautious fool to sigh for. (*Exit.*)

ACT V

Scene 1 [JULIA's dressing-room.]

(JULIA *alone.*)

JULIA: How his message has alarmed me! What dreadful accident can he mean? why such charge to be alone? O Faulkland! how many unhappy moments, how many tears, have you cost me!

(*Enter* FAULKLAND.)

JULIA: What means this? — why this caution, Faulkland?

FAULKLAND: Alas! Julia, I am come to take a long farewell.

JULIA: Heavens! what do you mean?

FAULKLAND: You see before you a wretch whose life is forfeited. Nay, start not! the infirmity of my temper has drawn all this misery on me. I left you fretful and passionate[68] — an untoward accident drew me into a quarrel — the event[69] is that I must fly this kingdom instantly. O Julia, had I been so fortunate as to have called you mine entirely before this mischance had fallen on me, I should not so deeply dread my banishment!

JULIA: My soul is oppressed with sorrow at the nature of your misfortune: had these adverse circumstances arisen from a less fatal cause, I should have felt strong comfort in the thought that I could now chase from your bosom every doubt of the warm sincerity of my love. My heart has long known no other guardian. I now entrust my

[68] I was fretful and passionate when I left you [69] outcome

person to your honour — we will fly together. When safe from pursuit, my father's will may be fulfilled, and I receive a legal claim to be the partner of your sorrows, and tenderest comforter. Then on the bosom of your wedded Julia, you may lull your keen regret to slumbering; while virtuous love, with a cherub's hand, shall smooth the brow of upbraiding thought, and pluck the thorn from compunction.

FAULKLAND: O Julia! I am bankrupt in gratitude! But the time is so pressing, it calls on you for so hasty a resolution — would you not wish some hours to weigh the advantages you forego, and what little compensation poor Faulkland can make you beside his solitary love?

JULIA: I ask not a moment. No, Faulkland, I have loved you for yourself: and if I now, more than ever, prize the solemn engagement which so long has pledged us to each other, it is because it leaves no room for hard aspersions on my fame, and puts the seal of duty to an act of love. —— But let us not linger. Perhaps this delay ——

FAULKLAND: 'Twill be better I should not venture out again till dark. Yet am I grieved to think what numberless distresses will press heavy on your gentle disposition!

JULIA: Perhaps your fortune may be forfeited by this unhappy act. I know not whether 'tis so, but sure that alone can never make us unhappy. The little I have will be sufficient to support us; and exile never should be splendid.

FAULKLAND: Aye, but in such an abject state of life, my wounded pride perhaps may increase the natural fretfulness of my temper, till I become a rude, morose companion, beyond your patience to endure. Perhaps the recollection of a deed my conscience cannot justify may haunt me in such gloomy and unsocial fits that I shall hate the tenderness that would relieve me, break from your arms, and quarrel with your fondness!

JULIA: If your thoughts should assume so unhappy a bent, you will the more want some mild and affectionate spirit to watch over and console you, one who, by bearing *your* infirmities with gentleness and resignation, may teach you *so* to bear the evils of your fortune.

FAULKLAND: Julia, I have proved you to the quick! and with this useless device I throw away all my doubts. How shall I plead to be forgiven this last unworthy effect of my restless, unsatisfied disposition?

JULIA: Has no such disaster happened as you related?

FAULKLAND: I am ashamed to own that it was all pretended; yet in pity, Julia, do not kill me with resenting a fault which never can be repeated, but sealing, this once, my pardon, let me to-morrow, in the face of heaven, receive my future guide and monitress, and expiate my past folly by years of tender adoration.

JULIA: Hold, Faulkland! That you are free from a crime which I before feared to name, heaven knows how sincerely I rejoice! These are tears of thankfulness for that! But that your cruel doubts should have urged you to an imposition that has wrung my heart, gives me now a pang more keen than I can express!

FAULKLAND: By heavens! Julia ——

JULIA: Yet hear me. My father loved you, Faulkland! and you preserved the life that tender parent gave me; in his presence I pledged my hand — joyfully pledged it — where before I had given my heart. When, soon after, I lost that parent, it seemed to me that Providence had, in Faulkland, shown me whither to transfer without a pause my grateful duty, as well as my affection: hence I have been content to bear from you what pride and delicacy would have forbid me from another. I will not upbraid you by repeating how you have trifled with my sincerity.

FAULKLAND: I confess it all! yet hear ——

JULIA: After such a year of trial, I might have flattered myself that I should not have been insulted with a new probation of my sincerity, as cruel as unnecessary! I now see it is not in your nature to be content or confident in love. With this conviction, I never will be yours. While I had hopes that my persevering attention and unreproaching kindness might in time reform your temper, I should have been happy to have gained a dearer influence over you; but I will not furnish you with a licensed power to keep alive an incorrigible fault, at the expense of one who never would contend with you.

FAULKLAND: Nay, but Julia, by my soul and honour, if after this ——

JULIA: But one word more. As my faith has once been given to you, I never will barter it with another. I shall pray for your happiness with the truest sincerity; and the dearest blessing I can ask of heaven to send you will be to charm you from that unhappy temper which alone has prevented the performance of our solemn engagement. All I request of *you* is that you will yourself reflect upon this infirmity, and when you number up the many true delights it has deprived you of, let it not be your *least* regret that it lost you the love of one, who would have followed you in beggary through the world! (*Exit.*)

FAULKLAND: She's gone! — forever! There was an awful resolution in her manner, that riveted me to my place. O fool! — dolt! — barbarian! Curst as I am with more imperfections than my fellow-wretches, kind Fortune sent a heaven-gifted cherub to my aid, and, like a ruffian, I have driven her from my side! I must now haste to my appointment. Well, my mind is tuned for such a scene. I shall wish only to become a principal in it, and reverse the tale my cursed folly put me upon forging here. O love! — tormentor! — fiend! whose influence, like the moon's, acting on men of dull souls, makes idiots of them, but meeting subtler spirits, betrays their course, and urges sensibility to madness! (*Exit.*)

(*Enter* MAID *and* LYDIA.)

MAID: My mistress, Ma'am, I know, was here just now — perhaps she is only in the next room. (*Exit.*)

LYDIA: Heigh-ho! Though he has used me so, this fellow runs strangely in my head. I believe one lecture from my grave cousin will make me recall him.

(*Enter* JULIA.)

LYDIA: O Julia, I am come to you with such an appetite for consolation. — Lud! child, what's the matter with you? You have been crying! I'll be hanged if that Faulkland has not been tormenting you!

JULIA: You mistake the cause of my uneasiness. Something *has* flurried me a little. Nothing that you can guess at. — (*Aside.*) I would not accuse Faulkland to a sister!

LYDIA: Ah! whatever vexations you may have, I can assure you mine surpass them. —— You know who Beverley proves to be?

JULIA: I will now own to you, Lydia, that Mr. Faulkland had before informed me of the whole affair. Had young Absolute been the person you took him for, I should not have accepted your confidence on the subject without a serious endeavour to counteract your caprice.

LYDIA: So, then, I see I have been deceived by everyone! But I don't care — I'll never have him.

JULIA: Nay, Lydia ——

LYDIA: Why, is it not provoking? when I thought we were coming to the prettiest distress imaginable, to find myself made a mere Smithfield bargain[70] of at last! There had I projected one of the most sentimental elopements! so becoming a disguise! so amiable a ladder of ropes! Conscious moon — four horses — Scotch parson — with such surprise to Mrs. Malaprop, and such paragraphs in the newspapers! Oh, I shall die with disappointment!

JULIA: I don't wonder at it!

LYDIA: Now — sad reverse! — what have I to expect, but, after a deal of flimsy preparation, with a bishop's license, and my aunt's blessing, to go simpering up to the altar; or perhaps be cried three times in a country-church, and have an unmannerly fat clerk ask the con-

70 *i.e.*, an object of a mercenary marriage (Smithfield, a suburb northwest of London, was the site of a popular market notorious for its sharp bargaining.)

sent of every butcher in the parish to join John Absolute and Lydia Languish, Spinster! Oh, that I should live to hear myself called Spinster!

JULIA: Melancholy, indeed!

LYDIA: How mortifying to remember the dear delicious shifts I used to be put to, to gain half a minute's conversation with this fellow! How often have I stole forth in the coldest night in January, and found him in the garden, stuck like a dripping statue! There would he kneel to me in the snow, and sneeze and cough so pathetically! he shivering with cold, and I with apprehension! and while the freezing blast numbed our joints, how warmly would he press me to pity his flame, and glow with mutual ardour! Ah, Julia, that was something like being in love!

JULIA: If I were in spirits, Lydia, I should chide you only by laughing heartily at you: but it suits more the situation of my mind, at present, earnestly to entreat you not to let a man, who loves you with sincerity, suffer that unhappiness from your caprice, which I know too well caprice can inflict.

LYDIA: O lud! what has brought my aunt here?

(*Enter* MRS. MALAPROP, FAG, *and* DAVID.)

MRS. MALAPROP: So! so! here's fine work! — here's fine suicide, parricide, and simulation going on in the fields! and Sir Anthony not to be found to prevent the antistrophe!

JULIA: For heaven's sake, Madam, what's the meaning of this?

MRS. MALAPROP: That gentleman can tell you — 'twas he enveloped the affair to me.

LYDIA (*to* FAG): Do, Sir, will you, inform us.

FAG: Ma'am, I should hold myself very deficient in every requisite that forms the man of breeding if I delayed a moment to give all the information in my power to a lady so deeply interested in the affair as you are.

LYDIA: But quick! quick, Sir!

FAG: True, Ma'am, as you say, one should be quick in divulging matters of this nature; for should we be tedious, perhaps while we are flourishing on the subject, two or three lives may be lost!

LYDIA: O patience! Do, Ma'am, for heaven's sake! tell us what is the matter!

MRS. MALAPROP: Why, murder's the matter! slaughter's the matter! killing's the matter! But he can tell you the perpendiculars.

LYDIA: Then, prithee, Sir, be brief.

FAG: Why then, Ma'am — as to murder, I cannot take upon me to say — and as to slaughter, or manslaughter, that will be as the jury finds it.

LYDIA: But who, Sir — who are engaged in this?

FAG: Faith, Ma'am, one is a young gentleman whom I should be very sorry anything was to happen to — a very pretty behaved gentleman! We have lived much together, and always on terms.

LYDIA: But who is this? who! who! who!

FAG: My master, Ma'am, my master — I speak of my master.

LYDIA: Heavens! What, Captain Absolute!

MRS. MALAPROP: Oh, to be sure, you are frightened now!

JULIA: But who are with him, Sir?

FAG: As to the rest, Ma'am, this gentleman can inform you better than I.

JULIA (*to* DAVID): Do speak, friend.

DAVID: Look'ee, my lady — by the Mass! there's mischief going on. Folks don't use to meet for amusement with fire-arms, fire-locks, fire-engines, fire-screens, fire-office, and the devil knows what other crackers beside! This, my lady, I say, has an angry favour.[71]

JULIA: But who is there beside Captain Absolute, friend?

DAVID: My poor master — under favour, for mentioning him first. You know me, my lady — I am David, and my master, of course, is, or *was,* Squire Acres. Then comes Squire Faulkland.

JULIA: Do, Ma'am, let us instantly endeavour to prevent mischief.

MRS. MALAPROP: Oh fie — it would be very inelegant in us: we should only participate things.

DAVID: Ah! do, Mrs. Aunt, save a few lives. They are desperately given, believe me. Above all, there is that bloodthirsty Philistine, Sir Lucius O'Trigger.

MRS. MALAPROP: Sir Lucius O'Trigger! O mercy! have they drawn poor little dear Sir Lucius into the scrape? Why, how you stand, girl! you have no more feeling than one of the Derbyshire putrefactions![72]

LYDIA: What are we to do, Madam?

MRS. MALAPROP: Why, fly with the utmost felicity, to be sure, to prevent mischief. Here, friend — you can show us the place?

FAG: If you please, Ma'am, I will conduct you. —— David, do you look for Sir Anthony. (*Exit* DAVID.)

MRS. MALAPROP: Come, girls! — this gentleman will exhort us, —— Come, Sir, you're our envoy — lead the way, and we'll precede.

FAG: Not a step before the ladies for the world!

MRS. MALAPROP: You're sure you know the spot?

[71] attraction [72] *i.e.* famous rock formations

FAG: I think I can find it, Ma'am; and one good thing is we shall hear the report of the pistols as we draw near, so we can't well miss them; never fear, Ma'am, never fear. (*Exeunt, he talking.*)

Scene 2 [South parade]

(*Enter* ABSOLUTE, *putting his sword under his greatcoat.*)

ABSOLUTE: A sword seen in the streets of Bath would raise as great an alarm as a mad dog. How provoking this is in Faulkland! never punctual! I shall be obliged to go without him at last. Oh, the devil! here's Sir Anthony! How shall I escape him? (*Muffles up his face, and takes a circle to go off. Enter* SIR ANTHONY.)

SIR ANTHONY: How one may be deceived at a little distance! Only that I see he don't know me, I could have sworn that was Jack!—— Hey! 'Gad's life! it is. Why, Jack! — what are you afraid of, hey! — Sure I'm right. — Why, Jack! — Jack Absolute! (*Goes up to him.*)

ABSOLUTE: Really, Sir, you have the advantage of me: I don't remember ever to have had the honour. My name is Saunderson, at your service.

SIR ANTHONY: Sir, I beg your pardon — I took you — hey! — why, z——ds! it is — stay — (*Looks up to his face.*) So, so — your humble servant, Mr. Saunderson! Why, you scoundrel, what tricks are you after now?

ABSOLUTE: Oh! a joke, Sir, a joke! I came here on purpose to look for you, Sir.

SIR ANTHONY: You did! Well, I am glad you were so lucky. But what are you muffled up so for? What's this for? — hey?

ABSOLUTE: 'Tis cool, Sir; isn't it? — rather chilly, somehow. But I shall be late — I have a particular engagement.

SIR ANTHONY: Stay. Why, I thought you were looking for me? Pray, Jack, where is't you are going?

ABSOLUTE: Going, Sir!

SIR ANTHONY: Aye — where are you going?

ABSOLUTE: Where am I going?

SIR ANTHONY: You unmannerly puppy!

ABSOLUTE: I was going, Sir, to — to — to — to Lydia — Sir, to Lydia, to make matters up if I could; and I was looking for you, Sir, to — to ——

SIR ANTHONY: To go with you, I suppose. Well, come along.

ABSOLUTE: Oh! z——ds! no, Sir, not for the world! I wished to meet with you, Sir — to — to — to —— You find it cool, I'm sure, Sir — you'd better not stay out.

SIR ANTHONY: Cool! — not at all. Well Jack — and what will you say to Lydia?

ABSOLUTE: O, Sir, beg her pardon, humour her, promise and vow. But I detain you, Sir — consider the cold air on your gout.

SIR ANTHONY: Oh, not at all! — not at all! I'm in no hurry. Ah! Jack, you youngsters, when once you are wounded here — (*putting his hand to* ABSOLUTE'*s breast*) Hey! what the deuce have you got here?

ABSOLUTE: Nothing, Sir — nothing.

SIR ANTHONY: What's this? here's something d——d hard!

ABSOLUTE: Oh, trinkets, Sir! trinkets — a bauble for Lydia!

SIR ANTHONY: Nay, let me see your taste. (*Pulls his coat open, the sword falls.*) Trinkets! — a bauble for Lydia! Z——ds! Sirrah, you are not going to cut her throat, are you?

ABSOLUTE: Ha! ha! ha! I thought it would divert you, Sir; though I didn't mean to tell you till afterwards.

SIR ANTHONY: You didn't? Yes, this is a very diverting trinket, truly!

ABSOLUTE: Sir, I'll explain to you. You know, Sir, Lydia is romantic, dev'lish romantic, and very absurd of course. Now, Sir, I intend, if she refuses to forgive me, to unsheathe this sword and swear I'll fall upon its point, and expire at her feet!

SIR ANTHONY: Fall upon a fiddle-stick's end! Why, I suppose it is the very thing that would please her. Get along, you fool.

ABSOLUTE: Well, Sir, you shall hear of my success — you shall hear. "O Lydia! — forgive me, or this pointed steel" — says I.

SIR ANTHONY: "O, booby! stab away and welcome" — says she. Get along! — and d——n your trinkets! (*Exit* ABSOLUTE.)

(*Enter* DAVID, *running.*)

DAVID: Stop him! Stop him! Murder! Thief! Fire! Stop fire! Stop fire! O! Sir Anthony — call! call! bid 'em stop! Murder! Fire!

SIR ANTHONY: Fire! Murder! Where?

DAVID: Oons![73] he's out of sight! and I'm out of breath, for my part! O, Sir Anthony, why didn't you stop him? why didn't you stop him?

SIR ANTHONY: Z——ds! the fellow's mad. Stop whom? Stop Jack?

DAVID: Aye, the Captain, Sir! there's murder and slaughter ——

SIR ANTHONY: Murder!

DAVID: Aye, please you, Sir Anthony, there's all kinds of murder, all sorts of slaughter to be seen in the fields: there's fighting going on, Sir — bloody sword-and-gun fighting!

[73] a variant of "Zounds"

SIR ANTHONY: Who are going to fight, dunce?

DAVID: Everybody that I know of, Sir Anthony — everybody is going to fight; my poor master, Sir Lucius O'Trigger, your son, the Captain ——

SIR ANTHONY: Oh, the dog! I see his tricks. —— Do you know the place?

DAVID: King's-Mead-Fields.

SIR ANTHONY: You know the way?

DAVID: Not an inch; but I'll call the mayor — aldermen — constables — church-wardens — and beadles — we can't be too many to part them.

SIR ANTHONY: Come along — give me your shoulder! we'll get assistance as we go. The lying villain! Well, I shall be in such a frenzy! So — this was the history of his trinkets! I'll bauble him! (*Exeunt.*)

Scene 3 [King's-Mead-Fields]

(SIR LUCIUS *and* ACRES, *with pistols.*)

ACRES: By my valour! then, Sir Lucius, forty yards is a good distance. Odds levels and aims! I say it is a good distance.

SIR LUCIUS: Is it for muskets or small field-pieces?[74] Upon my conscience, Mr. Acres, you must leave those things to me. Stay now — I'll show you. (*Measures paces along the stage.*) There now, that is a very pretty distance — a pretty gentleman's distance.

ACRES: Z——ds! we might as well fight in a sentry-box! I tell you, Sir Lucius, the farther he is off, the cooler I shall take my aim.

SIR LUCIUS: Faith! then I suppose you would aim at him best of all if he was out of sight!

ACRES: No, Sir Lucius, but I should think forty, or eight and thirty yards ——

SIR LUCIUS: Pho! pho! nonsense! Three or four feet between the mouths of your pistols is as good as a mile.

ACRES: Odds bullets, no! By my valour! there is no merit in killing him so near: do, my dear Sir Lucius, let me bring him down at a long shot — a long shot, Sir Lucius, if you love me!

SIR LUCIUS: Well — the gentleman's friend and I must settle that. But tell me now, Mr. Acres, in case of an accident, is there any little will or commission I could execute for you?

ACRES: I am much obliged to you, Sir Lucius, but I don't understand ——

[74] artillery

SIR LUCIUS: Why, you may think there's no being shot at without a little risk, and if an unlucky bullet should carry a *quietus* with it — I say it will be no time then to be bothering you about family matters.

ACRES: A *quietus!*

SIR LUCIUS: For instance, now — if that should be the case — would you choose to be pickled and sent home? or would it be the same to you to lie here in the Abbey? I'm told there is very snug lying in the Abbey.

ACRES: Pickled! Snug lying in the Abbey! Odds tremors! Sir Lucius, don't talk so!

SIR LUCIUS: I suppose, Mr. Acres, you never were engaged in an affair of this kind before?

ACRES: No, Sir Lucius, never before.

SIR LUCIUS: Ah! that's a pity! there's nothing like being used to a thing. Pray now, how would you receive the gentleman's shot?

ACRES: Odds files! I've practised that. There, Sir Lucius — there (*Puts himself in an attitude.*) — a side-front, hey? Odd! I'll make myself small enough: I'll stand edge-ways.

SIR LUCIUS: Now — you're quite out, for if you stand so when I take my aim —— (*levelling at him.*)

ACRES: Z——ds! Sir Lucius — are you sure it is not cocked?

SIR LUCIUS: Never fear.

ACRES: But — but — you don't know — it may go off of its own head!

SIR LUCIUS: Pho! be easy. Well, now if I hit you in the body, my bullet has a double chance, for if it misses a vital part on your right side, 'twill be very hard if it don't succeed on the left!

ACRES: A vital part!

SIR LUCIUS: But, there — fix yourself so. (*Placing him.*) Let him see the broad side of your full front — there — now a ball or two may pass clean through your body, and never do any harm at all.

ACRES: Clean through me! a ball or two clean through me!

SIR LUCIUS: Aye, may they; and it is much the genteelest attitude into the bargain.

ACRES: Look'ee! Sir Lucius — I'd just as lieve be shot in an awkward posture as a genteel one — so, by my valour! I will stand edge-ways.

SIR LUCIUS (*looking at his watch*): Sure they don't mean to disappoint us. Hah? No, faith — I think I see them coming.

ACRES: Hey! what! — coming! ——

SIR LUCIUS: Aye. Who are those yonder getting over the stile?

ACRES: There are two of them indeed! Well — let them come — hey, Sir Lucius? We — we — we — we — won't run.

SIR LUCIUS: Run!

ACRES: No — I say — we *won't* run, by my valour!

SIR LUCIUS: What the devil's the matter with you?

ACRES: Nothing — nothing — my dear friend — my dear Sir Lucius — but — I — I — I don't feel quite so bold, somehow — as I did.

SIR LUCIUS: Oh fie! consider your honour.

ACRES: Aye — true — my honour. Do, Sir Lucius, edge in a word or two every now and then about my honour.

SIR LUCIUS (*looking*): Well, here they're coming.

ACRES: Sir Lucius — if I wa'n't[75] with you, I should almost think I was afraid. If my valour should leave me! Valour will come and go.

SIR LUCIUS: Then, pray, keep it fast while you have it.

ACRES: Sir Lucius — I doubt it is going — yes — my valour is certainly going! it is sneaking off! I feel it oozing out as it were at the palms of my hands!

SIR LUCIUS: Your honour — your honour. Here they are.

ACRES: Oh mercy! now that I were safe at Clod-Hall! or could be shot before I was aware!

(*Enter* FAULKLAND *and* ABSOLUTE.)

SIR LUCIUS: Gentlemen, your most obedient — hah! — what — Captain Absolute! So, I suppose, Sir, you are come here, just like myself — to do a kind office, first for your friend — then to proceed to business on your own account.

ACRES: What, Jack! my dear Jack! my dear friend!

ABSOLUTE: Hark'ee, Bob, Beverley's at hand.

SIR LUCIUS: Well, Mr. Acres, I don't blame your saluting the gentleman civilly. So, Mr. Beverley (*to* FAULKLAND), if you'll choose your weapons, the Captain and I will measure the ground.

FAULKLAND: *My* weapons, Sir!

ACRES: Odd's life! Sir Lucius, I'm not going to fight Mr. Faulkland; these are my particular friends.

SIR LUCIUS: What, Sir, did not you come here to fight Mr. Acres?

FAULKLAND: Not I, upon my word, Sir.

SIR LUCIUS: Well, now, that's mighty provoking! But I hope, Mr. Faulkland, as there are three of us come on purpose for the game, you won't be so cantankerous as to spoil the party by sitting out.

ABSOLUTE: Oh pray, Faulkland, fight to oblige Sir Lucius.

FAULKLAND: Nay, if Mr. Acres is so bent on the matter ——

ACRES: No, no, Mr. Faulkland — I'll bear my disappointment like a Christian. Look'ee, Sir Lucius, there's no occasion at all for me to fight; and if it is the same to you, I'd as lieve let it alone.

[75] weren't

SIR LUCIUS: Observe me, Mr. Acres — I must not be trifled with. You have certainly challenged somebody, and you came here to fight him. Now, if that gentleman is willing to represent him, I can't see, for my soul, why it isn't just the same thing.

ACRES: Why no, Sir Lucius — I tell you, 'tis one Beverley I've challenged — a fellow you see, that dare not show his face! If *he* were here, I'd make him give up his pretensions directly!

ABSOLUTE: Hold, Bob — let me set you right. There is no such man as Beverley in the case. The person who assumed that name is before you; and as his pretensions are the same in both characters, he is ready to support them in whatever way you please.

SIR LUCIUS: Well, this is lucky! Now you have an opportunity ——

ACRES: What, quarrel with my dear friend Jack Absolute? Not if he were fifty Beverleys! Z——ds! Sir Lucius, you would not have me be so unnatural.

SIR LUCIUS: Upon my conscience, Mr. Acres, your valour has *oozed* away with a vengeance!

ACRES: Not in the least! Odds backs and abettors! I'll be your second with all my heart, and if you should get a *quietus,* you may command me entirely. I'll get you *snug lying* in the *Abbey here;* or *pickle* you, and send you over to Blunderbuss-Hall, or anything of the kind, with the greatest pleasure.

SIR LUCIUS: Pho! pho! you are little better than a coward.

ACRES: Mind, gentlemen, he calls me a *coward;* coward was the word, by my valour!

SIR LUCIUS: Well, Sir?

ACRES: Look'ee, Sir Lucius, 'tisn't that I mind the word coward — *coward* may be said in joke. But if you had called me a *poltroon,* odds daggers and balls! ——

SIR LUCIUS: Well, Sir?

ACRES: —— I should have thought you a very ill-bred man.

SIR LUCIUS: Pho! you are beneath my notice.

ABSOLUTE: Nay, Sir Lucius, you can't have a better second than my friend Acres. He is a most *determined dog,* called in the country, *Fighting Bob.* He generally *kills a man a week;* don't you, Bob?

ACRES: Aye — at home!

SIR LUCIUS: Well then, Captain, 'tis we must begin. So come out, my little counsellor (*draws his sword*), and ask the gentleman whether he will resign the lady without forcing you to proceed against him.

ABSOLUTE: Come on then, Sir (*draws*); since you won't let it be an amicable suit, here's my reply.

(*Enter* SIR ANTHONY, DAVID, *and the Women.*)

DAVID: Knock 'em all down, sweet Sir Anthony; knock down my master in particular, and bind his hands over to their good behaviour!

SIR ANTHONY: Put up, Jack, put up, or I shall be in a frenzy. How came you in a duel, Sir?

ABSOLUTE: Faith, Sir, that gentleman can tell you better than I; 'twas he called on me, and you know, Sir, I serve his Majesty.

SIR ANTHONY: Here's a pretty fellow! I catch him going to cut a man's throat, and he tells me he serves his Majesty! Z——ds! Sirrah, then how durst you draw the King's sword against one of his subjects?

ABSOLUTE: Sir, I tell you! That gentleman called me out, without explaining his reasons.

SIR ANTHONY: Gad! Sir, how came you to call my son out, without explaining your reasons?

SIR LUCIUS: Your son, Sir, insulted me in a manner which my honour could not brook.

SIR ANTHONY: Z——ds! Jack, how durst you insult the gentleman in a manner which his honour could not brook?

MRS. MALAPROP: Come, come, let's have no honour before ladies. Captain Absolute, come here. How could you intimidate us so? Here's Lydia has been terrified to death for you.

ABSOLUTE: For fear I should be killed, or escape, Ma'am?

MRS. MALAPROP: Nay, no delusions to the past. Lydia is convinced; speak, child.

SIR LUCIUS: With your leave, Ma'am, I must put in a word here. I believe I could interpret the young lady's silence. Now mark——

LYDIA: What is it you mean, Sir?

SIR LUCIUS: Come, come, Delia, we must be serious now — this is no time for trifling.

LYDIA: 'Tis true, Sir; and your reproof bids me offer this gentleman my hand, and solicit the return of his affections.

ABSOLUTE: O! my little angel, say you so? Sir Lucius, I perceive there must be some mistake here. With regard to the affront which you affirm I have given you, I can only say that it could not have been intentional. And as you must be convinced that I should not fear to support a real injury, you shall now see that I am not ashamed to atone for an inadvertency. I ask your pardon. But for this lady, while honoured with her approbation, I will support my claim 'gainst any man whatever.

NTHONY: Well said, Jack! and I'll stand by you, my boy.

Mind, I give up all my claim — I make no pretensions to any- in the world — and if I can't get a wife without fighting for my valour! I'll live a bachelor.

Captain, give me your hand — an affront handsomely

acknowledged becomes an obligation — and as for the lady, if she chooses to deny her own handwriting here —— (*Takes out letters.*)

MRS. MALAPROP: Oh, he will dissolve my mystery! Sir Lucius, perhaps there's some mistake — perhaps, I can illuminate ——

SIR LUCIUS: Pray, old gentlewoman, don't interfere where you have no business. Miss Languish, are you my Delia, or not?

LYDIA: Indeed, Sir Lucius, I am not. (LYDIA *and* ABSOLUTE *walk aside.*)

MRS. MALAPROP: Sir Lucius O'Trigger, ungrateful as you are, I own the soft impeachment — pardon my blushes, I am Delia.

SIR LUCIUS: You Delia! — pho! pho! be easy.

MRS. MALAPROP: Why, thou barbarous Vandyke! — those letters are mine. When you are more sensible of my benignity, perhaps I may be brought to encourage your addresses.

SIR LUCIUS: Mrs. Malaprop, I am extremely sensible of your condescension; and whether you or Lucy have put this trick upon me, I am equally beholden to you. And to show you I'm not ungrateful —— Captain Absolute! since you have taken that lady from me, I'll give you my Delia into the bargain.

ABSOLUTE: I am much obliged to you, Sir Lucius; but here's our friend, Fighting Bob, unprovided for.

SIR LUCIUS: Hah! little Valour — here, will you make your fortune?

ACRES: Odds wrinkles! No. But give me your hand, Sir Lucius; forget and forgive; but if ever I give you a chance of *pickling* me again, say Bob Acres is a dunce, that's all.

SIR ANTHONY: Come, Mrs. Malaprop, don't be cast down — you are in your bloom yet.

MRS. MALAPROP: O Sir Anthony! — men are all barbarians ——

(*All retire but* JULIA *and* FAULKLAND.)

JULIA (*aside*): He seems dejected and unhappy — not sullen. There was some foundation, however, for the tale he told me. O woman! how true should be your judgment, when your resolution is so weak!

FAULKLAND: Julia! how can I sue for what I so little deserve? I dare not presume — yet Hope is the child of Penitence.

JULIA: Oh! Faulkland, you have not been more faulty in your unkind treatment of me than I am now in wanting inclination to resent it. As my heart honestly bids me place my weakness to the account of love, I should be ungenerous not to admit the same plea for yours.

FAULKLAND: Now I shall be blest indeed!

(SIR ANTHONY *comes forward.*)

SIR ANTHONY: What's going on here? So you have been quarrelling too, I warrant. Come, Julia, I never interfered before; but let me have a hand in the matter at last. All the faults I have ever seen in my friend Faulkland seemed to proceed from what he calls the *delicacy* and *warmth* of his affection for you. There, marry him directly, Julia; you'll find he'll mend surprisingly!

(*The rest come forward.*)

SIR LUCIUS: Come now, I hope there is no dissatisfied person but what is content; for as I have been disappointed myself, it will be very hard if I have not the satisfaction of seeing other people succeed better ——

ACRES: You are right, Sir Lucius. So, Jack, I wish you joy — Mr. Faulkland the same. —— Ladies, — come now, to show you I'm neither vexed nor angry, odds tabours and pipes! I'll order the fiddles in half an hour to the New Rooms, and I insist on your all meeting me there.

SIR ANTHONY: Gad! Sir, I like your spirit; and at night we single lads will drink a health to the young couples, and a husband to Mrs. Malaprop.

FAULKLAND: Our partners are stolen from us, Jack — I hope to be congratulated by each other — *yours* for having checked in time the errors of an ill-directed imagination, which might have betrayed an innocent heart; and *mine*, for having, by her gentleness and candour, reformed the unhappy temper of one who by it made wretched whom he loved most, and tortured the heart he ought to have adored.

ABSOLUTE: Well, Faulkland, we have both tasted the bitters, as well as the sweets, of love — with this difference only, that *you* always prepared the bitter cup for yourself, while *I* ——

LYDIA: Was always obliged to *me* for it, hey! Mr. Modesty? —— But come, no more of that: our happiness is now as unalloyed as general.

JULIA: Then let us study to preserve it so; and while Hope pictures to us a flattering scene of future Bliss, let us deny its pencil those colours which are too bright to be lasting. When Hearts deserving Happiness would unite their fortunes, Virtue would crown them with an unfading garland of modest, hurtless flowers; but ill-judging Passion will force the gaudier Rose into the wreath, whose thorn offends them, when its leaves are dropt! (*Exeunt.*)

EPILOGUE

JULIA: Ladies, for you — I heard our poet say —
He'd try to coax some moral from his play:

"One moral's plain," cried I, "without more fuss;
Man's social happiness all rests on us:
Through all the drama — whether damned or not —
Love gilds the scene, and women guide the plot.
From every rank obedience is our due —
D'ye doubt? — The world's great stage shall prove it true."
The CIT,[76] well skilled to shun domestic strife
Will sup abroad; but first he'll ask his wife:
John Trot,[77] his friend, for once will do the same,
But then — he'll just step home to tell his dame.
The surly SQUIRE at noon resolves to rule,
And half the day — Zounds! madam is a fool!
Convinced at night, the vanquished victor says,
"Ah, Kate! you women have such coaxing ways!"
The jolly TOPER chides each tardy blade,[78]
Till reeling Bacchus calls on Love for aid:
Then with each toast he sees fair bumpers swim,
And kisses Chloe on the sparkling brim!
Nay, I have heard that STATESMEN — great and wise —
Will sometimes counsel with a lady's eyes!
The servile suitors watch her various face,
She smiles preferment, or she frowns disgrace,
Curtsies a pension here — there nods a place.
Nor with less awe, in scenes of humbler life,
Is viewed the mistress, or is heard the wife.
The poorest peasant of the poorest soil,
The child of poverty, and heir to toil,
Early from radiant Love's impartial light
Steals one small spark to cheer this world of night:
Dear spark! that oft through winter's chilling woes
Is all the warmth his little cottage knows!
The wandering TAR, who not for years has pressed
The widowed partner of his day of rest,
On the cold deck, far from her arms removed,
Still hums the ditty which his Susan loved;
And while around the cadence rude is blown,
The boatswain whistles in a softer tone.
The SOLDIER, fairly proud of wounds and toil,
Pants for the triumph of his Nancy's smile;
But ere the battle should he list[79] her cries,
The lover trembles — and the hero dies!

76 the citizen
77 proverbial name for a boorish, silly, awkward fellow
78 dashing young man-about-town
79 listen to

That heart, by war and honor steeled to fear,
Droops on a sigh, and sickens at a tear!
  But ye more cautious, ye nice-judging few,
Who give to beauty only beauty's due,
Though friends to love — ye view with deep regret
Our conquests marred, our triumphs incomplete,
Till polished wit more lasting charms disclose,
And judgment fix the darts which beauty throws!
In female breasts did sense and merit rule,
The lover's mind would ask no other school;
Shamed into sense, the scholars of our eyes,
Our beaux from gallantry would soon be wise;
Would gladly light, their homage to improve,
The lamp of knowledge at the torch of love!

The Rivals was the first product of Sheridan's brief and brilliant dramatic career (1775-1779). For all the young playwright's confidence in its stage merits it very nearly failed on its first night at the Covent Garden theater on January 17, 1775. People thought it was too long, the actor who played Sir Anthony did not know his lines, and Sir Lucius O'Trigger was a failure both as character and as performed part. But after Sheridan had revised the play, Sir Anthony had become letter perfect, and the part of Sir Lucius had been recast with a less mannered actor, the second showing eleven days later was a huge success. The success was repeated outside of London — most brilliantly in Bath, the fashionable resort town in Somersetshire which is the scene of its action.

The idea of building a romantic farce on a plot of mistaken identity goes back to classical Greek and Roman comedy. But even in the English theater of the 1770's Sheridan's choice of subject was not original. Less than two years earlier a Covent Garden audience had applauded another such play into success: Oliver Goldsmith's *She Stoops to Conquer*. Its hero mistakes the heroine for a barmaid and her home for an inn, and she, for reasons of romance, does not undeceive him till near the end. There are also in Goldsmith's play a country oaf something like Bob Acres in Sheridan's and a she-dragon parent whose position (though not her vocabulary) is similar to Mrs. Malaprop's, but Sheridan's main borrowing from Goldsmith is Captain Absolute's "stooping to conquer" by demoting himself to ensign in order to please the whim of his mistress.

For the reader who does not think that *The Rivals* is, before anything else, *fun,* criticism is pointless, and for him who does it is in a sense superfluous. But only in a sense. Criticism of comedy, like all criticism, justifies itself as a rational rather than an emotional discipline on the premise that informed and intelligent enjoyment is the highest kind.

Part of the fun of *The Rivals* lies in responding in turn to a range of comic strategies and appreciating how effortlessly they have been co-ordinated. A plot of misunderstandings is a time-tested comic device. Here it accounts for most of the suspense and for the farcical dialogues in which one of the speakers is mistaken about the identity or the real attitude of the other. The challenge to the reader to keep in mind which of the characters knows who is who at any given time is part of the intellectual zest that characterizes the entire play and is one of its chief assets. "The cause" of all the misunderstandings, Fag tells a fellow servant early in Act I, "is — Love, — Love, Thomas, who . . . has been a masquerader ever since the days of Jupiter." There is an excellent reason for the emphatic position of the speech: it defines the main action as a lovers' masquerade. Captain Absolute poses as "Ensign Beverley," Lydia manufactures a romantically interesting tiff with her ensign by acting the role of malicious and anonymous letter-writer, the beauteous "Delia" conceals the amorous Mrs. Malaprop, the maid Lucy profitably puts on a "mask of silliness" in her several roles as carrier of love letters and protector–betrayer of Lydia's romance, and it is because Faulkland perversely fails to see Julia's genuine love for him behind her mask of conventional public manners that he "tests" her love by pretending to be in mortal danger.

Of all these masquerades Captain Absolute's is clearly the most important. Every scene of high farce follows from it. Lydia fails to realize that "Beverley" is *not* an impostor when he parades as Jack Absolute. Mrs. Malaprop is tricked into giving a cordial welcome to the very man whose romantic suit she thinks her welcome frustrates and whose letters have made fun of her. In the recognition scene in IV, 2, the title of the play assumes its subtlest meaning as the Captain realizes that he is his own most dangerous rival. The scene qualifies as the comical equivalent of true Aristotelian *anagnorisis,* or recognition, in being more than just an important and funny turn of the plot. It objectifies the central theme of love's folly in the paradox that the girl who was his when he could not have her turns him down now that he can. The Beverley pose accounts also for another paradox on the delightful nonsense of young love — one "whimsical enough, faith!" as the Captain puts it: "my father wants to *force* me to marry the very girl I propose to run away with!" Less crucial, but still amusing, is Bob Acres' use of his good friend Jack to carry his challenge to Beverley, and less directly dependent on the Captain's double identity are the wonderful scenes of cross-purpose conversation between the Captain and his father. For all the disparity in age and intelligence between the two, Sir Anthony's gallant memories and his and his son's shared delight in a fine woman render their relationship both touching and plausible and give Sir Anthony distinction among the stock of heavy, apoplectic fathers in contemporary drama and fiction. Only the Delia plot, involving Sir Lucius, Lucy, Mrs. Malaprop, and — in the last scene — Lydia, does not evolve from Jack Absolute's masquerade.

Satire is another comic ingredient in *The Rivals*. There is, first, the social or psychological satire in the two romantic plots. The reason for the Captain's assumption of a new identity is Lydia's romantic longing for

> . . . one of the most sentimental elopements! — so becoming a disguise! — so amiable a ladder of ropes! — conscious moon — four horses — Scotch parson . . .

In the complementary Julia–Faulkland plot it is the man who is sentimentally capricious, and we get the scenes of parallelism–with–variety in which the two men and the two women separately discuss their romantic troubles. Sheridan divides good sense equally between the sexes: as sensible lover–confidantes Jack and Julia are Lydia's and Faulkland's foils. But though Lydia's "caprice" is a pretty young girl's prettily romantic notion of true love, held with a touch of disarming self-irony, Faulkland's is made of matter less readily accommodated by comedy.

> . . . his affection is ardent and sincere; and as it engrosses his whole soul, he expects every thought and emotion of his mistress to move in unison with his. Yet, though his pride calls for this full return, his humility makes him undervalue those qualities in him which would entitle him to it; and not feeling why he should be loved to the degree he wishes, he still suspects he is not loved enough.

Julia's balanced antitheses do not represent realistic speech, but they are acute psychology. Faulkland's is the non-comical humor of the neurotic who dissipates happiness in a restless shuttle between self-pride and self-doubt. The plot requires Julia to believe in his cure at the end, but we might reflect that in his torment of himself and his love a later literary fashion would have found the seeds of marital tragedy.

Nor is the anti-duel propaganda in the play altogether in a comic vein. The satire is obvious enough when David, Acres' servant, exposes the intrinsic absurdity of the duelling code in terms that echo Falstaff's in *1 Henry IV*. But there are serious overtones in the portrait of Sir Lucius O'Trigger, the cool and suave killer whom the code encouraged. They are not made less serious by the fact that Sir Lucius with all his combativeness is not an unlikeable character.

But the greatest satiric triumph in *The Rivals* is both less explicit and more general. With excellent comic tact Sheridan has transposed some of the grimmer facts of eighteenth-century family life into a comic key: parental tyranny in the choice of marriage partner and the sinister matrimonial role played both by "fortune" and by "birth" in an age when capital was less fluid than today and the socio-economic hierarchy, still semi-feudal, was more rigid. The plots of the century's two greatest novels, Richardson's *Clarissa* and Fielding's *Tom Jones*, both bear witness to the paramount importance of these facts to social and individual life. When Sheridan contrasts Lydia's sentimental–romantic humor with the Captain's determination to marry his lovely heiress *with* her money rather than *without* it, he is tempering both comedy and romance with the prudent worldliness of the mature lover who knows that passion is likely to fare all the better for being fortified by wealth. The implications ballast but do not burden the farcical intrigue and achieve both social realism and moral commentary.

The literary satire is less successful. It is directed against the contemporary vogue of sentimental comedy, a genre of drama that had become popular about the turn of the century, in self-conscious reaction against the coarse and cynical libertinism of the Restoration stage. Sentimental comedies appealed primarily to middle-class audiences, more particularly still to women, who enjoyed seeing patient and long-suffering heroines reclaim errant lovers and husbands from their rakish ways in last-act conversion–reconciliations showered with delicate tears and tirades of lofty platitudes on the innate goodness of human nature. In *The Rivals* the pure ideality of Lydia's love for Beverley is guaranteed by her imprudently democratic–romantic whim of preferring elopement with a penniless commoner ensign to a prosperous match and sanctioned wedding to a titled captain. Her caprice, an early scene suggests, is the result of reading volumes with titles like *The Reward of Constancy* and *The Delicate Distress*. There is satiric sting in the circumstance that Lucy does not use these but Jeremy Taylor's religious tome on *The Whole Duty of Man* to press Lydia's lace in. But in view of Sheridan's Prologue and his not altogether indulgent smile at Lydia's languishing in schoolgirl sentimentality, it comes as a bit of a shock to discover him apparently taking quite seriously Julia's and Faulkland's romance of psychological distress, a situation almost insufferably sentimental, if not in concept, then in event and tone. Julia's concluding set piece of edifying rhetoric, with Hope and Virtue, Roses and Hearts, properly capitalized, must have come straight from the lending library's *Tears of Sensibility*— the sequel (no doubt) of *The Mistakes of the Heart* and *The Fatal Connexion*. When Sheridan came to write *The School for Scandal* in 1777, one way in which he manifested his growth in maturity since the period of *The Rivals* was by putting Julia's estimable "sentiments" into the mouth of the smooth hypocrite Joseph Surface. It is only charitable to Sheridan — and not implausible — to suggest that in the Julia–Faulkland plot he cold-bloodedly catered to the current taste for stage sentimentality. But whether he was sincere or mercenary, the fact is that for a modern reader and spectator the delightful satire of sentimentalism and sensibility in the Lydia–Absolute plot is all but cancelled by the nearly disastrous pomposity of the Julia–Faulkland plot. Today the latter seems salvageable only by being acted as straight parody.

Skill and variety of literary style join farce and satire (both successful and unsuccessful) in accounting for the play's versatile charm. When Bob Acres awkwardly moves his "anti-Gallican toes," when Sir Lucius pleads that "the quarrel is a very pretty quarrel as it stands — we should only spoil it by trying to explain it," and when Mrs. Malaprop envisions an "allegory on the banks of the Nile" and Absolute as "the very pineapple of politeness," one feels that delight in manipulating words for their own sake must have been at the heart of Sheridan's creative impulse. The play is a masterpiece if for no other reason than that it is a feat — or feast — of language. Its range of voices is impressive. There is the heightening of normal speech in Fag's pert quips and in his master's precise and elegant cadences. There are Lydia's girlish hyperboles. There are the verbal antics of the grotesques: Mrs. Malaprop's "nice derangement of epitaphs," Sir Anthony's explosive bluster, Acres' "oaths referential," Faulkland's tortuous oxymorons in II, 1 ("she might have been *temperately* healthy, and somehow *plaintively* gay"). Some of the malapropisms are fiendishly accurate in meaning: "my oracular tongue," "I'm quite analyzed," and (on the advisability of trying to prevent the duels) "we should only participate things." Others are innocently sarcastic: "Fie, fie, Sir Anthony, you speak laconically." A few approach a kind of surrealist profundity à la Lewis Carroll: "we will not anticipate the past; . . . our retrospection will be all to the future."

But it must be admitted that the variety of comic modes in *The Rivals* has exacted a price in significant unity. Mrs. Malaprop is a comic achievement of high order, but the fact that she has become the play's most memorable item does not bespeak a finely compact and integrated dramatic structure. The duelling scene in Act V neatly brings all the principals together, clarifies confusions, and resolves lovers' quarrels. But rather than a compendious dramatic image it is a mechanical plot device, of the linking order of Bob Acres' being both Lydia's suitor and Julia's country neighbor. That Sir Lucius' quarrel with the Captain is motivated by Irish patriotism and not by romance — and that we do not see its origin — is a seam that shows. Because the play is less an anatomy of love than a romantic farce, even the image of Love's masquerade, though it does symbolize the main action, is more in the nature of plot premise than an encompassing dramatic metaphor. There is nothing in *The Rivals* to equal in focusing function the trek of greedy gulls toward Subtle's shop in *The Alchemist* or the lonely figure of Alceste in Célimène's salon in *The Misanthrope*. Structural analysis of Sheridan's play immediately turns up a main plot of comical romance, a secondary plot in serio-romantic counterpoint, and two subsidiary plotlets (Sir Lucius' romance with "Delia" and the duel intrigues). To analyze Jonson's and Molière's comedies in such terms is scarcely meaningful. In *The Alchemist* all the several gulls' actions are analogous variants of the same single moral exhibit, and Alceste is surrounded by secondary characters who all serve to illumine the misanthropy which is the play's central object. A degree of concentration and, hence, depth of meaning remains beyond the reach of Sheridan's play as it pursues its merry and casual way of wit of speech and situation. It is the sunny work of a very bright and very young man, happy and confident in his evident abilities, himself recently and romantically married. But it is unlike its predecessors in the comic genre in this volume in only intermittently achieving significant moral comment or genuine comedy of manners. There are the makings of the former in the characters of Lydia and Faulkland and of the latter in the Malaprop scenes, but neither dimension is explored much beyond dramatic symmetry, sententious satire, and lexical equilibristics. And so, *The Rivals* amounts in the end only to a fine specimen of eighteenth-century artificial farce of character and situation. The laughter it evokes is more hearty than reflective. In a way it is a happier play than its sophisticated successor, *The School for Scandal*, but (by the same token) further removed from the greatest kind of comedy. But it is something perhaps equally rare and almost as precious: intelligent and graceful farce, scintillating with fun and wit, and radiant with romantic joy.

Henrik Ibsen

HEDDA GABLER

Translated by Otto Reinert

Characters

JØRGEN TESMAN, *University Research Fellow in the History of Civilization*

HEDDA, *his wife*

MISS JULIANE TESMAN, *his aunt*

MRS. ELVSTED

JUDGE BRACK

EILERT LØVBORG

BERTE, *the Tesmans' maid*

SCENE: *The Tesmans' villa in a fashionable residential section of the town.*

A note on pronunciation

The approximate Norwegian pronunciation of names likely to be difficult to a speaker of English is suggested below (the syllable in capitals is accented; the unaccented *e* is close to English *e* in *quiet*).

JØRGEN YUR-gen (*g* as in *bargain*)
JULLE YOOL-le (short *oo*)

EILERT LØVBORG AY-lert LUV-borg*
BERTE BAIR-te

ACT ONE

(*A spacious, handsome, tastefully furnished room. Dark décor. In the rear, a wide doorway with open portieres. Beyond is a smaller room, furnished in the same style as the front room. A door, right, leads to the front hall. Left, French doors, with portieres drawn aside, through which can be seen a part of a roofed verandah and trees with autumn foliage. Front center, an oval table covered with a cloth. Chairs around it. Front right, a wide, dark, porcelain stove, a high-backed easy chair, a footstool with a pillow, and two ottomans. In the corner far right, a sofa and a small, round table. Front left, a sofa, set out from the wall. Far left, beyond the French doors, an upright piano. On both sides of the doorway, rear center, whatnots with knickknacks. Against the rear wall of the inner room, a sofa, and in front of it a table and two chairs. Above the sofa, a portrait of a handsome, elderly man in general's uniform. Over the table hangs a lamp with milky, white glass. There are several bouquets of flowers, in vases and glasses, in various places in the front room. Others are lying on the tables. Thick carpets on the floors of both rooms. The morning sun is shining through the French doors.*

MISS JULIANE TESMAN, *with hat and parasol, enters right, followed by* BERTE, *who carries a bouquet of flowers wrapped in paper.* MISS TESMAN *is a nice-looking woman of 65, of pleasant mien, neatly but not expensively dressed in a gray suit.* BERTE *is a middle-aged servant girl, of rather plain and countrified appearance.*)

MISS TESMAN (*stops inside the door, listens, says in a low voice*): On my word — I don't think they are even up yet!

BERTE (*also softly*): That's what I told you, miss. When you think how late the steamer got in last night. And afterwards — ! Goodness! — all the stuff she wanted unpacked before she turned in.

MISS TESMAN: Well — just let them sleep. But fresh morning air — *that* we can give them when they come in here. (*Goes and opens the French doors wide.*)

* *Løvborg* means, literally, "leaf-castle" — a fact of possible bearing on the play's symbolism.

BERTE (*by the table, lost, still holding the flowers*): Please, miss — I just don't see a bit of space anywhere! I think I'd better put these over here. (*Puts the flowers down on the piano.*)

MISS TESMAN: Well, well, my dear Berte. So you've got yourself a new mistress now. The good Lord knows it was hard for me to let you go.

BERTE (*near tears*): What about me, then, miss! What shall *I* say? I who have served you and Miss Rina all these blessed years.

MISS TESMAN: We shall just have to make the best of it, Berte. That's all. Jørgen can't do without you, you know. He just can't. You've looked after him ever since he was a little boy.

BERTE: Yes, but miss — I'm ever so worried about leaving Miss Rina. The poor dear lying there all helpless. With that new girl and all! She'll never learn how to make things nice and comfortable for an invalid.

MISS TESMAN: Oh yes, you'll see. I'll teach her. And of course, you know, I'll do most of it myself. So don't you worry yourself about my poor sister, Berte.

BERTE: Yes, but there's another thing, too, miss. I'm scared I won't be able to suit young Mrs. Tesman.

MISS TESMAN: Oh, well. Good heavens. So there is a thing or two — Right at first —

BERTE: For I believe she's ever so particular.

MISS TESMAN: Can you wonder? General Gabler's daughter? Just think of the kind of life she was used to when the General was alive. Do you remember when she rode by with her father? That long black riding habit she wore? And the feather in her hat?

BERTE: Oh, I remember, all right. But I'll be blessed if I ever thought she and the young master would make a pair of it.

MISS TESMAN: Nor did I. By the way, while I think of it, Berte. Jørgen has a new title now. From now on you should call him "the Doctor."

BERTE: Yes, the young mistress said something about that, too, last night. Soon as they were inside the door. Then it's really so, miss?

MISS TESMAN: It certainly is. Just think, Berte — they have made him a doctor abroad. During the trip, you know. I hadn't heard a thing about it till last night on the pier.

BERTE: Well, I daresay he could be anything he put his mind to, *he* could — smart as *he* is. But I must say I'd never thought he'd turn to doctoring people, too.

MISS TESMAN: Oh, that's not the kind of doctor he is. (*Nods significantly.*) And as far as that is concerned, there is no telling but pretty soon you may have to call him something grander yet.

BERTE: You don't say! What might that be, miss?

MISS TESMAN (*smiles*): Wouldn't you like to know! (*Moved.*) Ah yes, indeed — ! If only dear Jochum could see from his grave what has become of his little boy! (*Looking around.*) But look, Berte — what's this for? Why have you taken off all the slip covers?

BERTE: She told me to. Said she can't stand slip covers on chairs.

MISS TESMAN: Do you think they mean to make this their everyday living room, then?

BERTE: It sure sounded that way. Mrs. Tesman did, I mean. For he — the doctor — he didn't say anything.

(JØRGEN TESMAN *enters from the right side of the inner room. He is humming to himself. He carries an open, empty suitcase. He is of medium height, youthful-looking, thirty-three years old; somewhat stoutish. Round, open, cheerful face. Blond hair and beard. He wears glasses and is dressed in a comfortable, rather casual suit.*)

MISS TESMAN: Good morning, good morning, Jørgen!

TESMAN (*in the doorway*): Auntie! Dearest Aunt Julle! (*Comes forward and shakes her hand.*) All the way out here — as early as this! Hm?

MISS TESMAN: Well — I just had to drop in for a moment. To see how you are getting along, you know.

TESMAN: Even though you haven't had a good night's sleep.

MISS TESMAN: Oh, that doesn't matter at all.

TESMAN: But you did get home from the pier all right, I hope. Hm?

MISS TESMAN: Oh yes, I certainly did, thank you. The Judge was kind enough to see me all the way to my door.

TESMAN: We were so sorry we couldn't give you a ride in our carriage. But you saw for yourself — all the boxes Hedda had.

MISS TESMAN: Yes, she certainly brought quite a collection.

BERTE (*to* TESMAN): Should I go and ask Mrs. Tesman if there's anything I can help her with?

TESMAN: No, thank you, Berte — you'd better not. She said she'll ring if she wants you.

BERTE (*going right*): Well, all right.

TESMAN: But, look — you might take this suitcase with you.

BERTE (*takes it*): I'll put it in the attic. (*Exits right.*)

TESMAN: Just think, Auntie — that whole suitcase was brimful of copies of old documents. You wouldn't believe me if I told you all the things I have collected from libraries and archives all over. Quaint old items nobody has known anything about.

MISS TESMAN: Well, no, Jørgen. I'm sure you haven't wasted your time on your honeymoon.

TESMAN: No, I think I may say I have not. But take your hat off,

Auntie — for goodness' sake. Here! Let me untie the ribbon for you. Hm?

MISS TESMAN (*while he does so*): Ah, God forgive me, if this isn't just as if you were still at home with us!

TESMAN (*inspecting the hat*): My, what a fine-looking hat you've got yourself!

MISS TESMAN: I bought it for Hedda's sake.

TESMAN: For Hedda's sake? Hm?

MISS TESMAN: So she won't need to feel ashamed of me if we ever go out together.

TESMAN (*patting her cheek*): If you don't think of everything, Auntie! (*Puts the hat down on a chair by the table.*) And now — over here to the sofa — we'll just sit and chat for a while till Hedda comes.

(*They seat themselves. She places her parasol in the corner by the sofa.*)

MISS TESMAN (*takes both his hands in hers and gazes at him*): What a blessing it is to have you back again, Jørgen, big as life! You — Jochum's little boy!

TESMAN: For me, too, Aunt Julle. Seeing you again. For you have been both father and mother to me.

MISS TESMAN: Ah, yes — don't you think I know you'll always keep a spot in your heart for these two old aunts of yours!

TESMAN: So Aunt Rina isn't any better, hm?

MISS TESMAN: Oh no. We mustn't look for improvement in her case, poor dear. She is lying there just as she has been all these years. Just the same, may the good Lord keep her for me a long time yet! For else I just wouldn't know what to do with myself, Jørgen. Especially now, when I don't have you to look after any more.

TESMAN (*pats her back*): There, there, now!

MISS TESMAN (*changing tone*): And to think that you are a married man, Jørgen! And that you were the one to walk off with Hedda Gabler. The lovely Hedda Gabler. Just think! As many admirers as she had!

TESMAN (*hums a little, smiles complacently*): Yes, I daresay I have quite a few good friends here in town who'd gladly be in my shoes, hm?

MISS TESMAN: And such a long and lovely honeymoon you had! More than five — almost six months!

TESMAN: Well, you know — for me it has been a kind of study tour as well. All the collections I had to go through. And the books I had to read!

MISS TESMAN: Yes, I suppose. (*More confidentially, her voice lowered a little.*) But listen, Jørgen — haven't you got something — something special to tell me?

TESMAN: About the trip?

MISS TESMAN: Yes.

TESMAN: No — I don't know of anything besides what I wrote in my letters. They gave me a doctor's degree down there — but I told you that last night; I'm sure I did.

MISS TESMAN: Well, yes, that sort of thing — What I mean is — don't you have certain — certain — expectations?

TESMAN: Expectations?

MISS TESMAN: Ah for goodness' sake, Jørgen! I am your old Auntie, after all!

TESMAN: Certainly I have expectations.

MISS TESMAN: Well!!

TESMAN: I fully expect to be made a professor one of these days.

MISS TESMAN: Professor — oh yes —

TESMAN: I may even say I am quite certain of it. But dear Aunt Julle — you know this just as well as I do!

MISS TESMAN (*laughing a little*): Of course I do. You're quite right. (*Changing topic.*) But about the trip. It must have cost a great deal of money — hm, Jørgen?

TESMAN: Well, now; you know that large stipend went quite a long way.

MISS TESMAN: I just don't see how you made it do for both of you, though.

TESMAN: No, I suppose that's not so easy to understand, hm?

MISS TESMAN: Particularly with a lady along. For I have always heard that is ever so much more expensive.

TESMAN: Well, yes, naturally. That *is* rather more expensive. But Hedda had to have this trip, Auntie! She really had to. Nothing less would do.

MISS TESMAN: No, I daresay. For a wedding journey is quite the thing these days. But now tell me — have you had a chance to look around here yet?

TESMAN: I certainly have. I have been up and about ever since dawn.

MISS TESMAN: And what do you think of it all?

TESMAN: Delightful! Perfectly delightful! The only thing is I don't see what we are going to do with the two empty rooms between the second sitting room in there and Hedda's bedroom.

MISS TESMAN (*with a chuckle*): Oh my dear Jørgen — you may find them useful enough — when the time comes!

TESMAN: Of course, you're right, Auntie! As my library expands, hm?

MISS TESMAN: Quite so, my dear boy. It was your library I was thinking of.

TESMAN: But I'm really most happy on Hedda's behalf. For you know, before we were engaged she used to say she wouldn't care to live anywhere but in Secretary Falk's house.

MISS TESMAN: Yes, just think — wasn't that a lucky coincidence, that it was up for sale right after you had left?

TESMAN: Yes, Aunt Julle. We've certainly been lucky. Hm?

MISS TESMAN: But it will be expensive, my dear Jørgen. Terribly expensive — all this.

TESMAN (*looks at her, a bit crestfallen*): Yes, I daresay it will, Auntie.

MISS TESMAN: Heavens, yes!

TESMAN: How much, do you think? Roughly. Hm?

MISS TESMAN: No, I couldn't possibly say till all the bills arrive.

TESMAN: Well, anyway, Judge Brack managed to get very reasonable terms for us. He said so himself in a letter to Hedda.

MISS TESMAN: Yes, and I won't have you uneasy on that account, Jørgen. Besides, I have given security for the furniture and the carpets.

TESMAN: Security? You? But dear Aunt Julle — what kind of security could you give?

MISS TESMAN: The annuity.

TESMAN (*jumps up*): What! Your and Aunt Rina's annuity?

MISS TESMAN: Yes. I didn't know what else to do, you see.

TESMAN (*standing before her*): But are you clear out of your mind, Auntie! That annuity — that's all the two of you have to live on!

MISS TESMAN: Oh well, there's nothing to get so excited about, I'm sure. It's all just a matter of form, you know. That's what the Judge said, too. For he was kind enough to arrange the whole thing for me. Just a matter of form — those were his words.

TESMAN: That's all very well. Still —

MISS TESMAN: For now you'll have your own salary, you know. And, goodness — what if we do have a few expenses — Help out a bit right at first — ? That would only be a joy for us —

TESMAN: Oh, Auntie! When will you ever stop making sacrifices for my sake!

MISS TESMAN (*gets up, puts her hands on his shoulders*): But what other happiness do I have in this world than being able to smooth your way a little, my own dear boy? Orphan as you were, with no one to lean on but us? And now the goal is in sight, Jørgen. Things may have looked black at times. But heaven be praised; now you've arrived!

TESMAN: Yes, it's really quite remarkable the way things have worked out.

MISS TESMAN: Yes — and those who were against you — who tried to block your way — now they are tasting defeat. They are down, Jørgen! He, the most dangerous of them all, his fall was the greatest! He made his bed, and now he is lying in it — poor, lost wretch that he is!

TESMAN: Have you had any news about Eilert? Since I went away, I mean?

MISS TESMAN: Just that he is supposed to have published a new book.

TESMAN: What? Eilert Løvborg? Recently? Hm?

MISS TESMAN: That's what they say. But I wonder if there can be much to it. What do you think? Ah — but when *your* new book comes, that will be something quite different, Jørgen! What is it going to be about?

TESMAN: It deals with the domestic industries of Brabant during the Middle Ages.

MISS TESMAN: Just think — being able to write about something like that!

TESMAN: But as far as that is concerned, it may be quite some time before it is ready. I have all these collections to put in order first, you see.

MISS TESMAN: Yes, collecting and putting things in order — you certainly know how to do that. In that you are your father's own son.

TESMAN: Well, I must say I am looking forward to getting started. Particularly now, that I've got my own delightful home to work in.

MISS TESMAN: And most of all now that you have the one your heart desired, dear Jørgen.

TESMAN (*embracing her*): Oh yes, yes, Aunt Julle! Hedda — she is the most wonderful part of it all! (*Looks toward the doorway.*) There — I think she is coming now, hm?

(HEDDA *enters from the left side of the inner room. She is twenty-nine years old. Both features and figure are noble and elegant. Pale, ivory complexion. Steel-gray eyes, expressive of cold, clear calm. Beautiful brown hair, though not particularly ample. She is dressed in a tasteful, rather loose-fitting morning costume.*)

MISS TESMAN (*going toward her*): Good morning, my dear Hedda! A very happy morning to you!

HEDDA (*giving her hand*): Good morning, dear Miss Tesman! So early a call? That is most kind.

MISS TESMAN (*seems slightly embarrassed*): And — has the little lady of the house slept well the first night in her new home?

HEDDA: Passably, thank you.

TESMAN (*laughs*): Passably! You are a good one, Hedda! You were sleeping like a log when I got up.

HEDDA: Fortunately. And then, of course, Miss Tesman, it always takes time to get used to new surroundings. That has to come gradually. (*Looks left.*) Oh dear. The maid has left the verandah doors wide open. There's a veritable flood of sunlight in here.

MISS TESMAN (*toward the doors*): Well, then, we'll just close them.

HEDDA: No, no, not that. Tesman, dear, please pull the curtains. That will give a softer light.

TESMAN (*over by the French doors*): Yes, dear. There, now! Now you have both shade and fresh air, Hedda.

HEDDA: We certainly can use some air in here. Such loads of flowers — But, Miss Tesman, please — won't you be seated?

MISS TESMAN: No thanks. I just wanted to see if everything was all right — and so it is, thank goodness. I had better get back to Rina. I know she is waiting for me, poor thing.

TESMAN: Be sure to give her my love, Auntie. And tell her I'll be around to see her later today.

MISS TESMAN: I'll certainly do that! — Oh my! I almost forgot! (*Searches the pocket of her dress.*) I have something for you, Jørgen. Here.

TESMAN: What's that, Auntie? Hm?

MISS TESMAN (*pulls out a flat parcel wrapped in newspaper and gives it to him*): Here you are, dear.

TESMAN (*opens the parcel*): Well, well, well! So you took care of them for me, Aunt Julle! Hedda! Now, isn't that sweet, hm?

HEDDA (*by the whatnot, right*): If you'd tell me what it is —

TESMAN: My old slippers! *You* know!

HEDDA: Oh really? I remember you often talked about them on the trip.

TESMAN: Yes, for I missed them so. (*Walks over to her.*) Here — now you can see what they're like, Hedda.

HEDDA (*crosses toward stove*): Thanks. I don't know that I really care.

TESMAN (*following*): Just think — Aunt Rina embroidered these slippers for me. Ill as she was. You can't imagine how many memories they hold for me!

HEDDA (*by the table*): Hardly for me.

MISS TESMAN: That's true, you know, Jørgen.

TESMAN: Yes, but — I just thought that now that she's one of the family —

HEDDA (*interrupting*): I don't think we'll get on with that maid, Tesman.

MISS TESMAN: Not get on with Berte?

TESMAN: Whatever makes you say that, dear? Hm?

HEDDA (*points*): Look — she has left her old hat on the chair over there.

TESMAN (*appalled, drops the slippers*): But Hedda — !

HEDDA: What if somebody were to come and see it!

TESMAN: No, no, Hedda — that's Aunt Julle's hat!

HEDDA: Oh?

MISS TESMAN (*picking up the hat*): Yes, indeed it is. And it isn't old either, my dear young lady.

HEDDA: I really didn't look that closely —

MISS TESMAN (*tying the ribbons*): I want you to know that this is the first time I have had it on my head. On my word it is!

TESMAN: And very handsome it is, too. Really a splendid-looking hat!

MISS TESMAN: Oh, I don't know that it is anything so special, Jørgen. (*Looks around.*) My parasol — ? Ah, here it is. (*Picks it up.*) For that is mine, too. (*Mutters.*) Not Berte's.

TESMAN: New hat and new parasol! What do you think of that, Hedda!

HEDDA: Very nice indeed.

TESMAN: Yes, don't you think so? Hm? But, Auntie, take a good look at Hedda before you leave. She how pretty and blooming she looks.

MISS TESMAN: Dear me, Jørgen; that's nothing new. Hedda has been lovely all her days. (*She nods and walks right.*)

TESMAN (*following*): Yes, but have you noticed how full-figured and healthy she looks after the trip? How she has filled out?

HEDDA (*crossing*): Oh — stop it!

MISS TESMAN (*halts, turns around*): Filled out?

TESMAN: Yes, Aunt Julle. You can't see it so well now when she wears that dress. But I, who have the opportunity —

HEDDA (*by the French doors, impatiently*): Oh, you haven't any opportunities at all!

TESMAN: It must be the mountain air in Tyrol.

HEDDA (*curtly interrupting*): I am just as I was when I left.

TESMAN: Yes, so you say. I just don't think you're right. What do you think, Auntie?

MISS TESMAN (*has folded her hands, gazes at* HEDDA): Lovely — lovely — lovely; that is what Hedda is. (*Goes over to her, inclines her head forward with both her hands, and kisses her hair.*) God bless and keep Hedda Tesman. For Jørgen's sake.

HEDDA (*gently freeing herself*): There, there. Now let me go.

MISS TESMAN (*in quiet emotion*): Every single day I'll be over and see you two.

TESMAN: Yes, please do, Auntie. Hm?

MISS TESMAN: Goodbye, goodbye!

(She leaves through door, right. TESMAN *sees her out. The door remains ajar.* TESMAN *is heard repeating his greetings for* AUNT RINA *and his thanks for the slippers. In the meantime,* HEDDA *paces up and down, raises her arms, clenching her fists, as in quiet rage. Opens the curtains by the French doors and stands looking out. In a few moments,* TESMAN *re-enters and closes the door behind him.)*

TESMAN *(picking up the slippers)*: What are you looking at, Hedda?

HEDDA *(once again calm and controlled)*: Just the leaves. They are so yellow. And withered.

TESMAN *(wrapping the slippers in their paper, putting the parcel down on the table)*: Well, you know — we're in September now.

HEDDA *(again restless)*: Yes — just think. It's already — September.

TESMAN: Don't you think Aunt Julle acted strange, Hedda? Almost solemn. I wonder why. Hm?

HEDDA: I hardly know her, you see. Isn't she often like that?

TESMAN: Not the way she was today.

HEDDA *(turning away from the French doors)*: Do you think she minded that business with the hat?

TESMAN: Oh, I don't think so. Not much. Perhaps a little bit right at the moment —

HEDDA: Well, I'm sorry, but I must say it strikes me as very odd — putting her hat down here in the living room. One just doesn't do that.

TESMAN: Well, you may be sure Aunt Julle won't ever do it again.

HEDDA: Anyway, I'll make it up to her, somehow.

TESMAN: Oh yes, Hedda; if only you would!

HEDDA: When you go over there today, why don't you ask her over for tonight?

TESMAN: I'll certainly do that. And then there is one other thing you could do that she'd appreciate ever so much.

HEDDA: What?

TESMAN: If you could just bring yourself to call her Auntie. For my sake, Hedda, hm?

HEDDA: No, Tesman, no. You really mustn't ask me to do that. I have already told you I can't. I'll try to call her Aunt Juliane. That will have to do.

TESMAN: All right, if you say so. I just thought that now that you're in the family —

HEDDA: Hmmm — I don't know about that — *(She walks toward the doorway.)*

TESMAN (*after a brief pause*): Anything the matter, Hedda? Hm?

HEDDA: I'm just looking at my old piano. It doesn't quite go with the other furniture in here.

TESMAN: As soon as I get my first pay check we'll have it traded in.

HEDDA: No — I don't want to do that. I want to keep it. But let's put it in this inner room and get another one for out here. Whenever it's convenient, I mean.

TESMAN (*a little taken back*): Well — yes — we could do that —

HEDDA (*picks up the bouquet from the piano*): These flowers weren't here last night.

TESMAN: I suppose Aunt Julle brought them for you.

HEDDA (*looking at the flowers*): There's a card here. (*Takes it out and reads.*) "Will be back later." Can you guess who it's from?

TESMAN: No. Who? Hm?

HEDDA: Thea Elvsted.

TESMAN: No, really? Mrs. Elvsted! Miss Rysing that was.

HEDDA: That's right. The one with that irritating head of hair she used to show off with. An old flame of yours, I understand.

TESMAN (*laughs*): Well, now — that didn't last long! Anyway, that was before I knew you, Hedda. Just think — her being in town.

HEDDA: Strange, that she'd call on us. I have hardly seen her since we went to school together.

TESMAN: As far as that goes, I haven't seen her either for — God knows how long. I don't see how she can stand living in that out-of-the-way place. Hm?

HEDDA (*suddenly struck by a thought*): Listen, Tesman — isn't it some place near there that he lives — what's his name — Eilert Løvborg?

TESMAN: Yes, that's right. He is up there, too.

(BERTE *enters right.*)

BERTE: Ma'am, she's here again, that lady who brought those flowers a while back. (*Pointing.*) The flowers you're holding in your hand, ma'am.

HEDDA: Ah, she is? Well, show her in, please.

(BERTE *opens the door for* MRS. ELVSTED *and exits.* MRS. ELVSTED *is of slight build, with a pretty, soft face. Her eyes are light blue, large, round, rather prominent, of a timid and querying expression. Her hair is strikingly light in color, almost whitish, and unusually rich and wavy. She is a couple of years younger than* HEDDA. *She is dressed in a dark visiting dress, tasteful, but not quite in the most recent fashion.*)

HEDDA (*walks toward her. Friendly*): Good morning, my dear Mrs. Elvsted. How very nice to see you again.

MRS. ELVSTED (*nervous, trying not to show it*): Well, yes, it is quite some time since we met.

TESMAN (*shaking hands*): And we, too. Hm?

HEDDA: Thank you for your lovely flowers —

MRS. ELVSTED: Please, don't — I would have come here yesterday afternoon. But I was told you were still traveling —

TESMAN: You've just arrived in town, hm?

MRS. ELVSTED: I got here yesterday, at noon. Oh, I was quite desperate when I learned you weren't home.

HEDDA: Desperate? But why?

TESMAN: But my dear Mrs. Rysing — I mean Mrs. Elvsted —

HEDDA: There is nothing wrong, I hope?

MRS. ELVSTED: Yes there IS. And I don't know a single soul other than you that I can turn to here.

HEDDA (*putting the flowers down on the table*): Come — let's sit down here on the sofa.

MRS. ELVSTED: Oh, I'm in no mood to sit!

HEDDA: Of course you are. Come on. (*She pulls* MRS. ELVSTED *over to the sofa and sits down next to her.*)

TESMAN: Well, now, Mrs. — ? Exactly what — ?

HEDDA: Has something — special happened at home?

MRS. ELVSTED: Well, yes — and no. Oh, but I am so afraid you won't understand!

HEDDA: In that case, it seems to me you ought to tell us exactly what has happened, Mrs. Elvsted.

TESMAN: After all, that's why you are here. Hm?

MRS. ELVSTED: Yes, yes, of course. Well, then, maybe you already know — Eilert Løvborg is in town.

HEDDA: Is Løvborg — !

TESMAN: No! You don't say! Just think, Hedda — Løvborg's back!

HEDDA: All right. I can hear.

MRS. ELVSTED: He has been here a week already. Imagine — a whole week! In this dangerous place. Alone! With all that bad company around.

HEDDA: But my dear Mrs. Elvsted — why is he a concern of yours?

MRS. ELVSTED (*with an apprehensive look at her, says quickly*): He tutored the children.

HEDDA: Your children?

MRS. ELVSTED: My husband's. I don't have any.

HEDDA: In other words, your stepchildren.

MRS. ELVSTED: Yes.

TESMAN (*with some hesitation*): But was he — I don't quite know how to put this — was he sufficiently — regular — in his way of life to be thus employed? Hm?

MRS. ELVSTED: For the last two years, there hasn't been a thing to object to in his conduct.

TESMAN: No, really? Just think, Hedda!

HEDDA: I hear.

MRS. ELVSTED: Not the least little bit, I assure you! Not in any respect. And yet — knowing he's here — in the big city — And with all that money, too! I'm scared to death!

TESMAN: But in that case, why didn't he remain with you and your husband? Hm?

MRS. ELVSTED: After his book came out, he was too restless to stay.

TESMAN: Ah yes, that's right. Aunt Julle said he has published a new book.

MRS. ELVSTED: Yes, a big new book, about the course of civilization in general. It came out about two weeks ago. And since it has had such big sales and been discussed so much and made such a big splash —

TESMAN: It has, has it? I suppose this is something he has had lying around from better days?

MRS. ELVSTED: You mean from earlier?

TESMAN: Yes.

MRS. ELVSTED: No; it's all been written since he came to stay with us. During this last year.

TESMAN: Well, now! That's very good news, Hedda! Just think!

MRS. ELVSTED: Yes, if it only would last!

HEDDA: Have you seen him since you came to town?

MRS. ELVSTED: No, not yet. I had a great deal of trouble finding his address. But this morning I finally tracked him down.

HEDDA (*looks searchingly at her*): Isn't it rather odd that your husband — hm —

MRS. ELVSTED (*with a nervous start*): My husband! What about him?

HEDDA: That he sends you to town on such an errand? That he doesn't go and look after his friend himself?

MRS. ELVSTED: Oh, no, no — my husband doesn't have time for things like that. Besides, I have some — some shopping to do, anyway.

HEDDA (*with a slight smile*): Well, in that case, of course —

MRS. ELVSTED (*getting up, restlessly*): And now I beg of you, Mr. Tesman — won't you please receive Eilert Løvborg nicely if he calls on you? And I am sure he will. After all — Such good friends as you two used to be. And then you both do the same kind of work — the same field of study, as far as I know.

TESMAN: We used to, at any rate.

MRS. ELVSTED: Yes. And that's why I implore you to please, please, try to keep an eye on him — you too. You'll do that, Mr. Tesman, won't you? Promise?

TESMAN: With the greatest pleasure, Mrs. Rysing.

HEDDA: Elvsted.

TESMAN: I'll gladly do as much for Eilert as I possibly can. You may certainly count on that.

MRS. ELVSTED: Oh, how good and kind you are! (*Clasps his hands.*) Thank you, thank you, thank you! (*Nervously.*) You see, my husband is so very fond of him.

HEDDA (*getting up*): You ought to write him a note, Tesman. Maybe he won't come without an invitation.

TESMAN: Yes, I suppose that would be the right thing to do, Hedda. Hm?

HEDDA: The sooner the better. Right away, *I* think.

MRS. ELVSTED (*pleadingly*): If only you would!

TESMAN: I'll write this minute. Do you have his address, Mrs. — Mrs. Elvsted?

MRS. ELVSTED: Yes. (*Pulls a slip of paper from her bag and gives it to him.*) Here it is.

TESMAN: Very good. Well, then, if you'll excuse me — (*Looks around.*) By the way — the slippers? Ah, here we are. (*Leaving with the parcel.*)

HEDDA: Be sure you write a nice, warm, friendly letter, Tesman. And a long one, too.

TESMAN: Certainly, certainly.

MRS. ELVSTED: But not a word that it is I who — !

TESMAN: No, that goes without saying, I should think. Hm? (*Goes out right through inner room.*)

HEDDA (*goes over to* MRS. ELVSTED, *smiles, says in a low voice*): There! We just killed two birds with one stone.

MRS. ELVSTED: What do you mean?

HEDDA: Didn't you see I wanted him out of the room?

MRS. ELVSTED: Yes, to write that letter —

HEDDA: And to speak to you alone.

MRS. ELVSTED (*flustered*): About this same thing?

HEDDA: Exactly.

MRS. ELVSTED (*anxious*): But there *is* nothing more, Mrs. Tesman! Really, there isn't!

HEDDA: Oh yes, there is. There is considerably more. I can see that much. Over here — We are going to have a real, nice, confidential talk, you and I. (*She forces* MRS. ELVSTED *down in the easy chair and seats herself on one of the ottomans.*)

MRS. ELVSTED (*worried, looks at her watch*): But my dear Mrs. Tesman — I had really thought I would be on my way now.

HEDDA: Oh I am sure there is no rush. Now, then. Tell me about yourself. How are things at home?

MRS. ELVSTED: That is just what I don't want to talk about.

HEDDA: But to me — ! After all, we are old schoolmates.

MRS. ELVSTED: But you were a year ahead of me. And I used to be so scared of you!

HEDDA: Scared of me?

MRS. ELVSTED: Terribly. For when we met on the stairs, you always ruffled my hair.

HEDDA: Did I really?

MRS. ELVSTED: Yes. And once you said you were going to burn it off.

HEDDA: Oh, but you know — I wasn't serious!

MRS. ELVSTED: No, but I was such a silly, then. Anyway, afterwards we drifted far apart. Our circles are so very different, you know.

HEDDA: All the more reason for getting close again. Listen. In school we called each other by our first names.

MRS. ELVSTED: Oh I'm sure you're wrong —

HEDDA: I'm sure I'm not! I remember it quite clearly. And now we want to be open with one another, just the way we used to. (*Moves the ottoman closer.*) There, now! (*Kisses her cheek.*) You call me Hedda.

MRS. ELVSTED (*seizes her hands*): Oh, you are so good and kind! I'm not used to that.

HEDDA: There, there! And I'll call you my dear Thora, just as in the old days.

MRS. ELVSTED: My name is Thea.

HEDDA: So it is. Of course. I meant Thea. (*Looks at her with compassion.*) So you're not much used to goodness and kindness, Thea? Not in your own home?

MRS. ELVSTED: If I even had a home! But I don't. I never have had one.

HEDDA (*looks at her for a moment*): I thought there might be something like this.

MRS. ELVSTED (*helplessly, looking straight ahead*): Yes — yes — yes —

HEDDA: I am not sure if I quite remember — Didn't you first come to your husband as his housekeeper?

MRS. ELVSTED: I was really hired as governess. But his wife — his first wife — was ailing already then and practically bedridden. So I had to take charge of the household as well.

HEDDA: But in the end you became his wife.

MRS. ELVSTED (*dully*): So I did.

HEDDA: Let's see. How long ago is that?

MRS. ELVSTED: Since my marriage?

HEDDA: Yes.

MRS. ELVSTED: About five years.

HEDDA: Right. It must be that long.

MRS. ELVSTED: Oh, those five years! Or mostly the last two or three! Oh, Mrs. Tesman — if you could just imagine!

HEDDA (*slaps her hand lightly*): Mrs. Tesman? Shame on you!

MRS. ELVSTED: Oh yes; all right, I'll try. Yes — if you could just — conceive — understand —

HEDDA (*casually*): And Eilert Løvborg has been living near you for some three years or so, hasn't he?

MRS. ELVSTED (*looks at her uncertainly*): Eilert Løvborg? Yes — he has.

HEDDA: Did you know him before? Here in town?

MRS. ELVSTED: Hardly at all. That is, of course I did in a way. I mean, I knew *of* him.

HEDDA: But up there — You saw a good deal of him; did you?

MRS. ELVSTED: Yes, he came over to us every day. He was supposed to tutor the children, you see. For I just couldn't do it all by myself.

HEDDA: Of course not. And your husband — ? I suppose he travels quite a bit.

MRS. ELVSTED: Well, yes, Mrs. Tes — Hedda — as a public magistrate, you know, he very often has to travel all over his district.

HEDDA (*leaning against the armrest on the easy chair*): Thea — poor, sweet Thea — now you have to tell me everything — just as it is.

MRS. ELVSTED: You'd better ask me, then.

HEDDA: How *is* your husband, Thea? I mean — you know — *really?* To be with. What kind of person is he? Is he good to you?

MRS. ELVSTED (*evasively*): I believe he thinks he does everything for the best.

HEDDA: But isn't he altogether too old for you? He is more than twenty years older, isn't he?

MRS. ELVSTED (*with irritation*): Yes, there is that, too. But there isn't just one thing. Every single little thing about him repels me! We don't have a thought in common, he and I. Not a thing in the world!

HEDDA: But isn't he fond of you all the same? I mean in his own way?

MRS. ELVSTED: I don't know. I think I am just useful to him. And I don't use much money. I am inexpensive.

HEDDA: That is foolish of you.

MRS. ELVSTED (*shakes her head*): Can't be changed. Not with him.

I don't think he cares for anybody much except himself. Perhaps the children a little.

HEDDA: And Eilert Løvborg, Thea.

MRS. ELVSTED (*looks at her*): Eilert Løvborg? What makes you think that?

HEDDA: Well, it seems to me that when he sends you all the way to town to look after him — (*With an almost imperceptible smile.*) Besides, you said so yourself. To Tesman.

MRS. ELVSTED (*with a nervous twitch*): Did I? I suppose I did. (*With a muted outburst.*) No! I might as well tell you now as later. For it's bound to come out, anyway.

HEDDA: But my dear Thea — ?

MRS. ELVSTED: All right. My husband doesn't know I've gone!

HEDDA: What! He doesn't know?

MRS. ELVSTED: He wasn't even home. He's away again. Oh, I just couldn't take it any longer, Hedda! It had become utterly impossible. All alone as I was.

HEDDA: So what did you do?

MRS. ELVSTED: I packed some of my things. Just the most necessary. Without telling anybody. And left.

HEDDA: Just like that?

MRS. ELVSTED: Yes. And took the next train to town.

HEDDA: But dearest Thea — how did you dare to do a thing like that!

MRS. ELVSTED (*rises, walks*): What else could I do?

HEDDA: But what do you think your husband will say when you go back?

MRS. ELVSTED (*by the table; looks at her*): Go back to him?

HEDDA: Yes!

MRS. ELVSTED: I'll never go back.

HEDDA (*rises, approaches her slowly*): So you have really, seriously — left everything?

MRS. ELVSTED: Yes. It seemed to me there was nothing else I could do.

HEDDA: And quite openly, too.

MRS. ELVSTED: You can't keep a thing like that secret, anyway.

HEDDA: But what do you think people will say, Thea?

MRS. ELVSTED: In God's name, let them say whatever they like. (*Sits down on the sofa, dully, tired.*) For I have only done what I had to do.

HEDDA (*after a brief silence*): And what do you plan to do with yourself? What sort of work will you do?

MRS. ELVSTED: I don't know yet. I only know I have to live where Eilert Løvborg is. If I am to live at all.

HEDDA (*moves a chair from the table closer to* MRS. ELVSTED, *sits down, strokes her hands*): Thea — tell me. How did this — this friendship between you and Eilert Løvborg — how did it begin?

MRS. ELVSTED: Oh, it grew little by little. I got some sort of power over him.

HEDDA: Oh?

MRS. ELVSTED: He dropped his old ways. Not because I asked him to. I never dared to do that. But I think he must have noticed how I felt about that kind of life. So he changed.

HEDDA (*quickly suppresses a cynical smile*): So you have — rehabilitated him, as they say. Haven't you, Thea?

MRS. ELVSTED: At least, that's what *he* says. On the other hand, he has turned me into a real human being. Taught me to think — and understand — all sorts of things.

HEDDA: Maybe he tutored you, too?

MRS. ELVSTED: No, not tutored exactly. But he talked to me. About so many, many things. And then came that lovely, lovely time when I could share his work with him. He let me help him!

HEDDA: He did?

MRS. ELVSTED: Yes! Whatever he wrote, he wanted us to be together about it.

HEDDA: Just like two good comrades.

MRS. ELVSTED (*with animation*): Comrades! — that's it! Imagine, Hedda — that's just what he called it, too. Oh, I really ought to feel so happy. But I can't. For you see, I don't know if it will last.

HEDDA: You don't trust him any more than that?

MRS. ELVSTED (*heavily*): The shadow of a woman stands between Eilert Løvborg and me.

HEDDA (*tensely, looks at her*): Who?

MRS. ELVSTED: I don't know. Somebody or other from — his past. I don't think he has ever really forgotten her.

HEDDA: What has he told you about it?

MRS. ELVSTED: He has mentioned it only once — just casually.

HEDDA: And what did he say?

MRS. ELVSTED: He said that when they parted she was going to kill him with a gun.

HEDDA (*cold, controlled*): Oh, nonsense. People don't do that sort of thing here.

MRS. ELVSTED: No, I know. And that is why I think it must be that red-headed singer he used to —

HEDDA: Yes, I suppose so.

MRS. ELVSTED: For I remember people said she carried a loaded gun.

HEDDA: Well, then I'm sure it's she.

MRS. ELVSTED (*wringing her hands*): Yes, but just think, Hedda — now I hear that she — that singer — that she's here in town again, too! Oh, I'm just desperate — !

HEDDA (*with a glance toward the inner room*): Shhh! Here's Tesman. (*Rises and whispers.*) Not a word about all this to anybody, Thea!

MRS. ELVSTED (*jumps up*): No, no. For God's sake — !

(TESMAN, *carrying a letter, enters from the right side of the inner room.*)

TESMAN: There, now — here's the missive, all ready to go!

HEDDA: Good. But I believe Mrs. Elvsted wants to be on her way. Wait a moment. I'll see you to the garden gate.

TESMAN: Say, Hedda — do you think Berte could take care of this?

HEDDA (*takes the letter*): I'll tell her.

(BERTE *enters right.*)

BERTE: Judge Brack is here and wants to know if you're receiving.

HEDDA: Yes, ask the Judge please to come in. And — here — drop this in a mailbox, will you?

BERTE (*takes the letter*): Yes, ma'am.

(*She opens the door for* JUDGE BRACK *and exits. The* JUDGE *is forty-five years of age. Rather thickset, but well-built and with brisk, athletic movements. Roundish face, aristocratic profile. His hair is short, still almost completely black, very neatly dressed. Lively, sparkling eyes. Thick eyebrows and mustache with cut-off points. He is dressed in an elegant suit, a trifle youthful for his age. He wears pince-nez glasses, attached to a string, and lets them drop from time to time.*)

JUDGE BRACK (*hat in hand, salutes*): May one pay one's respects as early as this?

HEDDA: One certainly may.

TESMAN (*shaking his hand*): You are always welcome. (*Introducing.*) Judge Brack — Miss Rysing —

(HEDDA *groans.*)

BRACK (*bowing*): Delighted!

HEDDA (*looks at him, laughs*): How nice it is to see you in daylight, Judge!

BRACK: You find me changed, perhaps?

HEDDA: A bit younger, I think.

BRACK: Much obliged.

TESMAN: But what do you think of Hedda? Hm? Did you ever see her in such bloom? She positively —

HEDDA: Will you please leave me out of this? You had better thank the Judge for all the trouble he has taken.

BRACK: Oh, nonsense. It's been a pleasure.

HEDDA: Yes, you are indeed a faithful soul. But my friend here is dying to be off. Don't leave, Judge. I'll be back in a minute.

(*Mutual goodbyes.* MRS. ELVSTED *and* HEDDA *exit, right.*)

BRACK: Well, now — your wife — is she tolerably satisfied?

TESMAN: Yes, indeed, and we really can't thank you enough. That is, I understand there will have to be some slight changes made here and there. And there are still a few things — just a few trifles — we'll have to get.

BRACK: Oh? Really?

TESMAN: But we certainly don't want to bother you with that. Hedda said she's going to take care of it herself. But do sit down, hm?

BRACK: Thanks. Maybe just for a moment — (*Sits down by the table.*) There's one thing I'd like to talk to you about, my dear Tesman.

TESMAN: Oh? Ah, I see! (*Sits down.*) I suppose it's the serious part of the festivities that's beginning now. Hm?

BRACK: Oh — there's no great rush as far as the money is concerned. Though I must say I wish we could have established ourselves a trifle more economically.

TESMAN: Out of the question, my dear fellow! Remember, it's all for Hedda! You, who know her so well — ! After all, I couldn't put her up like any little middle-class housewife —

BRACK: No, I suppose — That's just it.

TESMAN: Besides — fortunately — it can't be long now before I receive my appointment.

BRACK: Well, you know — things like that have a way of hanging fire.

TESMAN: Perhaps you have heard something? Something definite? Hm?

BRACK: No, nothing certain — (*Interrupting himself.*) But that reminds me. I have some news for you.

TESMAN: Oh?

BRACK: Your old friend Eilert Løvborg is back in town.

TESMAN: I know that already.

BRACK: So? Who told you?

TESMAN: The lady who just left.

BRACK: I see. What did you say her name was again? I didn't quite catch —

TESMAN: Mrs. Elvsted.

BRACK: Ah yes — the Commissioner's wife. Yes, it's up in her part of the country that Løvborg has been staying, too.

TESMAN: And just think. I am so glad to hear it. He is quite respectable again.

BRACK: Yes, so they say.

TESMAN: And he has published a new book, hm?

BRACK: Oh yes.

TESMAN: Which is making quite a stir.

BRACK: Quite an unusual stir.

TESMAN: Just think! Isn't that just wonderful! He — with his remarkable gifts. And I was so sure he'd gone under for good.

BRACK: That seems to have been the general opinion.

TESMAN: What I don't understand, though, is what he is going to do with himself. What sort of living can he make? Hm?

(*During the last remark* HEDDA *re-enters, right.*)

HEDDA (*to* BRACK, *with a scornful little laugh*): Tesman is forever worrying about how people are going to make a living.

TESMAN: Well, you see, we are talking about poor Eilert Løvborg, Hedda.

HEDDA (*with a quick look at him*): You are? (*Sits down in the easy chair by the stove and asks casually.*) What is the matter with him?

TESMAN: Well, you see, I believe he's run through his inheritance a long time ago. And I don't suppose he can write a new book every year. Hm? So I really must ask how he is going to make out.

BRACK: Maybe I could help you answer that.

TESMAN: Yes?

BRACK: Remember, he has relatives with considerable influence.

TESMAN: Ah — unfortunately, those relatives have washed their hands of him long ago.

BRACK: Just the same, they used to call him the hope of the family.

TESMAN: Yes, before! But he has ruined all that.

HEDDA: Who knows? (*With a little smile.*) I hear the Elvsteds have rehabilitated him.

BRACK: And then this book —

TESMAN: Well, I certainly hope they will help him to find something or other. I just wrote him a letter. Hedda, dear, I asked him to come out here tonight.

BRACK: Oh dear, I am sorry. Don't you remember — you're supposed to come to my little stag dinner tonight? You accepted last night on the pier, you know.

HEDDA: Had you forgotten, Tesman?

TESMAN: So I had.

BRACK: Oh well. I'm sure he won't come, so it doesn't really make any difference.

TESMAN: Why is that? Hm?

BRACK (*gets up somewhat hesitantly, rests his hands on the back of the chair*): Dear Tesman — and you, too, Mrs. Tesman — I cannot in good conscience let you remain in ignorance of something, which — which —

TESMAN: Something to do with Eilert?

BRACK: With both you and him.

TESMAN: But my dear Judge, do speak!

BRACK: You must be prepared to find that your appointment will not come through as soon as you hope and expect.

TESMAN (*jumps up, nervously*): Something's happened? Hm?

BRACK: It may conceivably be made contingent upon the result of a competition.

TESMAN: Competition! Just think, Hedda!

HEDDA (*leaning farther back in her chair*): Ah — I see, I see — !

TESMAN: But with whom? Don't tell me with — ?

BRACK: Precisely. With Eilert Løvborg.

TESMAN (*claps his hands together*): No, no! This can't be! It is unthinkable! Quite impossible! Hm?

BRACK: All the same, that's the way it may turn out.

TESMAN: No, but Judge, this would amount to the most incredible callousness toward me! (*Waving his arms.*) For just think — I'm a married man! We married on the strength of these prospects, Hedda and I. Got ourselves deep in debt. Borrowed money from Aunt Julle, too. After all, I had practically been promised the post, you know. Hm?

BRACK: Well, well. I daresay you'll get it in the end. If only after a competition.

HEDDA (*motionless in her chair*): Just think, Tesman. It will be like a kind of contest.

TESMAN: But dearest Hedda, how can you be so unconcerned!

HEDDA (*still without moving*): I'm not at all unconcerned. I'm dying to see who wins.

BRACK: In any case, Mrs. Tesman, I'm glad you know the situation as it is. I mean — before you proceed to make the little additional purchases I understand you threaten us with.

HEDDA: This makes no difference as far as that is concerned.

BRACK: Really? Well, in that case, of course — Goodbye! (*To* TESMAN.) I'll pick you up on my afternoon walk.

TESMAN: What? Oh yes, yes, of course. I'm sorry; I'm just all flustered.

HEDDA (*without getting up, gives her hand*): Goodbye, Judge. Come back soon.

BRACK: Thanks. Goodbye, goodbye.

TESMAN (*sees him to the door*): Goodbye, my dear Judge. You really must excuse me —

(JUDGE BRACK *exits, right.*)

TESMAN (*pacing the floor*): Oh, Hedda, Hedda! One should never venture into fairyland. Hm?

HEDDA (*looks at him, smiles*): Do *you* do that?

TESMAN: Well, yes — it can't be denied — it was most venturesome of me to rush into marriage and set up a home on the strength of mere prospects.

HEDDA: Well, maybe you're right.

TESMAN: Anyway — we do have our own nice, comfortable home, now. Just think, Hedda — the very home both of us dreamed about. Set our hearts on, I may almost say. Hm?

HEDDA (*rises, slowly, tired*): The agreement was that we were to maintain a certain position — entertain —

TESMAN: Don't I know it! Dearest Hedda — I have been so looking forward to seeing you as hostess in a select circle! Hm? Well, well, well! In the meantime, we'll just have to be content with one another. See Aunt Julle once in a while. Nothing more. And you were meant for such a different kind of life, altogether!

HEDDA: I suppose a footman is competely out of the question.

TESMAN: I'm afraid so. Under the circumstances, you see — we couldn't possibly —

HEDDA: And as for getting my own riding horse —

TESMAN (*aghast*): Riding horse!

HEDDA: I suppose I mustn't even think of that.

TESMAN: Good heavens, no! That goes without saying, I hope!

HEDDA (*walking*): Well — at least I have one thing to amuse myself with in the meantime.

TESMAN (*overjoyed*): Oh thank goodness for that! And what *is* that, Hedda, hm?

HEDDA (*in the doorway, looks at him with suppressed scorn*): My guns — Jørgen!

TESMAN (*in fear*): Your guns!

HEDDA (*with cold eyes*): General Gabler's guns. (*She exits left, through the inner room.*)

TESMAN (*runs up to the doorway, calls after her*): But Hedda! Good gracious! Hedda, dear! Please don't touch those dangerous things! For my sake, Hedda! Hm?

ACT TWO

(*The same room at the* TESMANS'. *The piano has been moved out and replaced by an elegant little writing desk. A small table has been placed near the sofa, left. Most of the flowers have been removed.* MRS. ELVSTED'S *bouquet is on the big table front center. Afternoon.*

HEDDA, *dressed to receive callers, is alone. She is standing near the open French doors, loading a revolver. Its mate is lying in an open case on the desk.*)

HEDDA (*looking down into the garden, calls*): Hello there, Judge! Welcome back!

JUDGE BRACK (*off stage*): Thanks, Mrs. Tesman!

HEDDA (*raises the gun, sights*): I am going to shoot you, Judge Brack!

BRACK (*calls off stage*): No — no — no! Don't point the gun at me like that!

HEDDA: That's what you get for sneaking in the back door! (*Fires.*)

BRACK (*closer*): Are you out of your mind — !

HEDDA: Oh dear — did I hit you?

BRACK (*still off stage*): Stop that nonsense!

HEDDA: Come on in, then.

(JUDGE BRACK, *dressed for dinner, enters, left. He carries a light overcoat over his arm.*)

BRACK: Dammit! Do you still fool around with that thing? What are you shooting at, anyway?

HEDDA: Oh — just firing off into blue air.

BRACK (*gently but firmly taking the gun away from her*): With your permission, Mrs. Tesman. (*Looks at it.*) Ah yes, I remember this gun very well. (*Looks around.*) Where is the case? Ah, here we are. (*Puts the gun in the case and closes it.*) That's enough of that silliness for today.

HEDDA: But in the name of heaven, what do you expect me to do with myself?

BRACK: No callers?

HEDDA (*closing the French doors*): Not a soul. All my close friends are still out of town, it seems.

BRACK: And Tesman is out, too, perhaps?

HEDDA (*by the desk, puts the gun case in a drawer*): Yes. He took off for the aunts' right after lunch. He didn't expect you so early.

BRACK: I should have thought of that. That was stupid of me.

HEDDA (*turns her head, looks at him*): Why stupid?

BRACK: I would have come a little — sooner.

HEDDA (*crossing*): If you had, you wouldn't have found anybody home. For I have been in my room ever since lunch, changing my clothes.

BRACK: And isn't there the tiniest little opening in the door for negotiations?

HEDDA: You forgot to provide one.

BRACK: Another stupidity.

HEDDA: So we'll have to stay in here. And wait. For I don't think Tesman will be back for some time.

BRACK: By all means. I'll be very patient.

(HEDDA *sits on the sofa in the corner.* BRACK *puts his overcoat over the back of the nearest chair and sits down, keeping his hat in his hand. Brief silence. They look at one another.*)

HEDDA: Well?

BRACK (*in the same tone*): Well?

HEDDA: I said it first.

BRACK (*leans forward a little*): All right. Let's have a nice little chat, Mrs. Tesman.

HEDDA (*leans back*): Don't you think it's an eternity since last time we talked! I don't count last night and this morning. That was nothing.

BRACK: You mean — just the two of us?

HEDDA: Mmm. If you like.

BRACK: There hasn't been a day I haven't wished you were back again.

HEDDA: My feelings, exactly.

BRACK: Yours? Really, Mrs. Tesman? And I have been assuming you were having such a wonderful time.

HEDDA: I'd say!

BRACK: All Tesman's letters said so.

HEDDA: Oh yes, he! He's happy just poking through old collections of books. And copying old parchments — or whatever they are.

BRACK (*with a touch of malice*): Well, that's his calling, you know. Partly, anyway.

HEDDA: Yes, so it is. And in that case I suppose — But I! Oh, Judge! You've no idea how bored I've been.

BRACK (*with sympathy*): Really? You're serious?

HEDDA: Surely you can understand that? For a whole half year never to see anyone who knows even a little bit about our circle? And talks our language?

BRACK: Yes, I think I would find that trying, too.

HEDDA: And then the most unbearable thing of all —

BRACK: Well?

HEDDA: — everlastingly to be in the company of the same person —

BRACK (*nods in agreement*): Both early and late — yes. I can imagine — at all possible times —

HEDDA: I said everlastingly.

BRACK: All right. Still, it seems to me that with as excellent a person as our Tesman, it ought to be possible —

HEDDA: My dear Judge — Tesman is a specialist.

BRACK: Granted.

HEDDA: And specialists are not at all entertaining travel companions. Not in the long run, at any rate.

BRACK: Not even — the specialist — one happens to love?

HEDDA: Bah! That nauseating word!

BRACK (*puzzled*): Really, now, Mrs. Tesman — ?

HEDDA (*half laughing, half annoyed*): *You* ought to try it some time! Listening to talk about the history of civilization, early and late —

BRACK: Everlastingly —

HEDDA: All right. And then this business about the domestic industry in the Middle Ages — ! That's the ghastliest part of it all!

BRACK (*looking searchingly at her*): But in that case — tell me — how am I to explain — ?

HEDDA: That Jørgen Tesman and I made a pair of it, you mean?

BRACK: If you want to put it that way — yes.

HEDDA: Come now. Do you really find that so strange?

BRACK: Both yes and no — Mrs. Tesman.

HEDDA: I had danced myself tired, my dear Judge. My season was over — (*Gives a slight start.*) No, no — I don't really mean that. Won't think it, either!

BRACK: Nor do you have the slightest reason to, I am sure.

HEDDA: Oh — as far as reasons are concerned — (*Looks at him as if trying to read his mind.*) And, after all, Jørgen Tesman must be said to be a most proper young man in all respects.

BRACK: Both proper and substantial. Most certainly.

HEDDA: And one can't say there is anything exactly comical about him. Do you think there is?

BRACK: Comical? No — o. I wouldn't say that —

HEDDA: All right, then. And he is a most assiduous collector. Nobody can deny that. I think it is perfectly possible he may go quite far, after all.

BRACK (*looks at her rather uncertainly*): I assumed that you, like everybody else, thought he'll in time become an exceptionally eminent man?

HEDDA (*with a weary expression*): Yes, I did. And then, you see —

there he was, wanting so desperately to be allowed to provide for me — I don't know why I shouldn't have accepted?

BRACK: No, certainly. From that point of view —

HEDDA: For you know, Judge, that was considerably more than my other admirers were willing to do.

BRACK (*laughs*): Well! Of course I can't answer for all the others. But as far as I am concerned, I have always had a certain degree of — respect for the bonds of matrimony. You know — as a general proposition, Mrs. Tesman.

HEDDA (*lightly*): Well, I never really counted very heavily on *you* —

BRACK: All I want is a nice, confidential circle, in which I can be of service, both in deed and in counsel. Be allowed to come and go like a true and trusted friend —

HEDDA: You mean, of the master of the house — ?

BRACK (*with a slight bow*): To be perfectly frank — rather of the mistress. But by all means — the master, too, of course. Do you know, that kind of — shall I say, triangular? — relationship can really be a great comfort to all parties involved.

HEDDA: Yes, many were the times I missed a second travel companion. To be twosome in the compartment — brrr!

BRACK: Fortunately, the wedding trip is over.

HEDDA (*shakes her head*): There's a long journey ahead. I've just arrived at a station on the way.

BRACK: Well, at the station one gets out and moves around a bit, Mrs. Tesman.

HEDDA: I never get out.

BRACK: Really?

HEDDA: No. For there's always someone around, who —

BRACK (*laughs*): — looks at one's legs; is that it?

HEDDA: Exactly.

BRACK: Oh well, really, now —

HEDDA (*with a silencing gesture*): I won't have it! Rather stay in my seat — once I'm seated. Twosome and all.

BRACK: I see. But what if a third party were to join the couple?

HEDDA: Well, now — *that* would be something altogether different!

BRACK: A proven, understanding friend —

HEDDA: — entertaining in all sorts of lively ways —

BRACK: — and not at all a specialist!

HEDDA (*with audible breath*): Yes, that would indeed be a comfort.

BRACK (*hearing the front door open, looking at her*): The triangle is complete.

HEDDA (*half aloud*): And the train goes on.

(TESMAN, *in gray walking suit and soft hat, enters, right. He carries a pile of paperbound books under his arm. Others are stuffed in his pockets.*)

TESMAN (*as he walks up to the table in front of the corner sofa*): Puuhh — ! Quite some load to carry, all this — and in this heat, too. (*Puts the books down.*) I am positively perspiring, Hedda. Well, well. So you're here already, my dear Judge. Hm? And Berte didn't tell me.

BRACK (*rises*): I came through the garden.

HEDDA: What are all those books?

TESMAN (*leafing through some of them*): Just some new publications in my special field.

HEDDA: Special field, hm?

BRACK: Ah yes — professional publications, Mrs. Tesman.

(BRACK *and* HEDDA *exchange knowing smiles.*)

HEDDA: Do you still need more books?

TESMAN: Yes, my dear. There is no such thing as having too many books in one's special field. One has to keep up with what is being written and published, you know.

HEDDA: I suppose.

TESMAN (*searching among the books*): And look. Here is Eilert Løvborg's new book, too. (*Offers it to her.*) Want to take a look at it, Hedda? Hm?

HEDDA: No — thanks just the same. Or perhaps later.

TESMAN: I glanced at it on my way home.

BRACK: And what do you think of it? As a specialist yourself?

TESMAN: It is remarkable for its sobriety. He never wrote like that before. (*Gathers up all the books.*) I just want to take these into my study. I am so much looking forward to cutting them open! And then I'll change. (*To* BRACK.) I assume there's no rush to be off, is there?

BRACK: Not at all. We have plenty of time.

TESMAN: In that case, I think I'll indulge myself a little. (*On his way out with the books he halts in the doorway and turns.*) By the way, Hedda — Aunt Julle won't be out to see you tonight, after all.

HEDDA: No? Is it that business with the hat, do you think?

TESMAN: Oh, no — not at all. How can you believe a thing like that about Aunt Julle! Just think! No, it's Aunt Rina. She's feeling very poorly.

HEDDA: Isn't she always?

TESMAN: Yes, but it's especially bad today, poor thing.

HEDDA: Well, in that case I suppose she ought to stay home. I shall have to put up with it; that's all.

TESMAN: And you have no idea how perfectly delighted Aunt Julle was, even so. Because of how splendid you look after the trip, Hedda!

HEDDA (*half aloud, rising*): Oh, these everlasting aunts!

TESMAN: Hm?

HEDDA (*walks over to the French doors*): Nothing.

TESMAN: No? All right. Well, excuse me. (*Exits right, through inner room.*)

BRACK: What is this about a hat?

HEDDA: Oh, something with Miss Tesman this morning. She had put her hat down on the chair over there. (*Looks at him, smiles.*) So I pretended to think it was the maid's.

BRACK (*shakes his head*): But my dear Mrs. Tesman — how could you do a thing like that! And to that excellent old lady, too!

HEDDA (*nervously pacing the floor*): Well, you see — something just takes hold of me at times. And then I can't help myself — (*Throws herself down in the easy chair near the stove.*) Oh I can't explain it even to myself.

BRACK (*behind her chair*): You aren't really happy — that's the trouble.

HEDDA (*staring into space*): I don't know any reason why I should be. Do you?

BRACK: Well, yes — partly because you've got the home you've always wanted.

HEDDA (*looks up at him and laughs*): So you too believe that story about my great wish?

BRACK: You mean, there is nothing to it?

HEDDA: Well, yes; there is *something* to it.

BRACK: Well?

HEDDA: There is this much to it, that last summer I used Tesman to see me home from evening parties.

BRACK: Unfortunately — my route was in quite a different direction.

HEDDA: True. You walked on other roads last summer.

BRACK (*laughs*): Shame on you, Mrs. Tesman! So, all right — you and Tesman — ?

HEDDA: One evening we passed by here. And Tesman, poor thing, was practically turning himself into knots trying to find something to talk about. So I felt sorry for all that erudition —

BRACK (*with a doubting smile*): You did? Hm —

HEDDA: I really did. So, just to help him out of his misery, I happened to say that I'd like to live in this house.

BRACK: Just that?

HEDDA: That was all — *that* evening.

BRACK: But afterwards — ?

HEDDA: Yes, my frivolity had consequences, Judge.

BRACK: Unfortunately — that's often the way with frivolities. It happens to all of us, Mrs. Tesman.

HEDDA: Thanks! So in our common enthusiasm for Mr. Secretary Falk's villa Tesman and I found each other, you see! The result was engagement and wedding and honeymoon abroad and all the rest of it. Well, yes, my dear Judge — I've made my bed — I almost said.

BRACK: But this is priceless! And you didn't really care for the house at all?

HEDDA: Certainly not.

BRACK: Not even now? After all, we've set up quite a comfortable home for you here, haven't we?

HEDDA: Oh — it seems to me I smell lavender and rose sachets in all the rooms. But maybe that's a smell Aunt Julle brought with her.

BRACK (*laughs*): My guess is rather the late lamented Secretary's wife.

HEDDA: It smells of mortality, whoever it is. Like corsages — the next day. (*Clasps her hands behind her neck, leans back, looks at him.*) Judge, you have no idea how dreadfully bored I'll be — out here.

BRACK: But don't you think life may hold some task for you, too, Mrs. Tesman?

HEDDA: A task? With any kind of appeal?

BRACK: Preferably that, of course.

HEDDA: Heaven knows what kind of task that might be. There are times when I wonder if — (*Interrupts herself.*) No; I'm sure that wouldn't work, either.

BRACK: Who knows? Tell me.

HEDDA: It has occurred to me that maybe I could get Tesman to enter politics.

BRACK (*laughs*): Tesman! No, really — I must confess that — politics doesn't strike me as being exactly Tesman's line.

HEDDA: I agree. But suppose I were to prevail on him, all the same?

BRACK: What satisfaction could you possibly find in that? If he can't succeed — why do you want him even to try?

HEDDA: Because I am bored, I tell you! (*After a brief pause.*) So you think it's quite out of the question that Tesman could ever become prime minister?

BRACK: Well, you see, Mrs. Tesman — to do that he'd first of all have to be a fairly wealthy man.

HEDDA (*getting up, impatiently*): Yes! There we are! These shabby circumstances I've married into! (*Crosses the floor.*) That's what makes life so mean. So — so — ridiculous! For that's what it is, you know.

BRACK: Personally I believe something else is to blame.

HEDDA: What?

BRACK: You've never been through anything that's really stirred you.

HEDDA: Something serious, you mean?

BRACK: If you like. But maybe it's coming now.

HEDDA (*with a toss of her head*): You are thinking of that silly old professorship! That's Tesman's business. I refuse to give it a thought.

BRACK: As you wish. But now — to put it in the grand style — now when a solemn challenge of responsibility is being posed? Demands made on you? (*Smiles.*) New demands, Mrs. Tesman.

HEDDA (*angry*): Quiet! You'll never see anything of the kind.

BRACK (*cautiously*): We'll talk about this a year from now — on the outside.

HEDDA (*curtly*): I'm not made for that sort of thing, Judge! No demands for me!

BRACK: But surely you, like most women, are made for a duty, which —

HEDDA (*over by the French doors*): Oh, do be quiet! Often it seems to me there's only one thing in the world that I am made for.

BRACK (*coming close*): And may I ask what that is?

HEDDA (*looking out*): To be bored to death. Now you know. (*Turns, looks toward the inner room, laughs.*) Just as I thought. Here comes the professor.

BRACK (*warningly, in a low voice*): Steady, now, Mrs. Tesman!

(TESMAN, *dressed for a party, carrying his hat and gloves, enters from the right side of the inner room.*)

TESMAN: Hedda, any word yet from Eilert Løvborg that he isn't coming, hm?

HEDDA: No.

TESMAN: In that case, I wouldn't be a bit surprised if we have him here in a few minutes.

BRACK: You really think he'll come?

TESMAN: I am almost certain he will. For I'm sure it's only idle gossip that you told me this morning.

BRACK: Oh?

TESMAN: Anyway, that's what Aunt Julle said. She doesn't for a moment believe he'll stand in my way. Just think!

BRACK: I'm very glad to hear that.

TESMAN (*puts his hat and his gloves down on a chair, right*): But you must let me wait for him as long as possible.

BRACK: By all means. We have plenty of time. Nobody will arrive at my place before seven — seven-thirty, or so.

TESMAN: And in the meantime we can keep Hedda company. Take our time. Hm?

HEDDA (*carrying* BRACK'S *hat and coat over to the sofa in the corner*): And if worst comes to worst, Mr. Løvborg can stay here with me.

BRACK (*trying to take the things away from her*): Let me, Mrs. Tesman — What do you mean — "if worst comes to worst?"

HEDDA: If he doesn't want to go with you and Tesman.

TESMAN (*looks dubiously at her*): But, dearest Hedda — do you think that will quite do? He staying here with you? Hm? Remember, Aunt Julle won't be here.

HEDDA: No, but Mrs. Elvsted will. The three of us will have a cup of tea together.

TESMAN: Oh yes; *that* will be perfectly all right!

BRACK (*with a smile*): And perhaps the wiser course of action for him.

HEDDA: What do you mean?

BRACK: Begging your pardon, Mrs. Tesman — you've often enough looked askance at my little stag dinners. It's been your opinion that only men of the firmest principles ought to attend.

HEDDA: I should think Mr. Løvborg is firm-principled enough now. A reformed sinner —

(BERTE *appears in door, right.*)

BERTE: Ma'am — there's a gentleman here who asks if —

HEDDA: Show him in, please.

TESMAN (*softly*): I'm sure it's he! Just think!

(EILERT LØVBORG *enters, right. He is slim, gaunt. Of* TESMAN'S *age, but he looks older and somewhat dissipated. Brown hair and beard. Pale, longish face, reddish spots on the cheekbones. Dressed for visiting in elegant, black, brand-new suit. He carries a silk hat and dark gloves in his hand. He remains near the door, makes a quick bow. He appears a little embarrassed.*)

TESMAN (*goes over to him, shakes his hand*): My dear Eilert — at last we meet again!

EILERT LØVBORG (*subdued voice*): Thanks for your note, Jørgen! (*Approaching* HEDDA.) Am I allowed to shake your hand, too, Mrs. Tesman?

HEDDA (*accepting his proffered hand*): I am very glad to see you, Mr. Løvborg. (*With a gesture.*) I don't know if you two gentlemen —

LØVBORG (*with a slight bow*): Judge Brack, I believe.

BRACK (*also bowing lightly*): Certainly. Some years ago —

TESMAN (*to* LØVBORG, *both hands on his shoulders*): And now I want you to feel quite at home here, Eilert! Isn't that right, Hedda? For you plan to stay here in town, I understand. Hm?

LØVBORG: Yes, I do.

TESMAN: Perfectly reasonable. Listen — I just got hold of your new book, but I haven't had a chance to read it yet.

LØVBORG: You may save yourself the trouble.

TESMAN: Why do you say that?

LØVBORG: There's not much to it.

TESMAN: Just think — you saying that!

BRACK: Nevertheless, people seem to have very good things to say about it.

LØVBORG: That's exactly why I wrote it — so everybody would like it.

BRACK: Very wise of you.

TESMAN: Yes, but Eilert — !

LØVBORG: For I am trying to rebuild my position. Start all over again.

TESMAN (*with some embarrassment*): Yes, I suppose you are, aren't you? Hm?

LØVBORG (*smiles, puts his hat down, pulls a parcel out of his pocket*): When *this* appears — Jørgen Tesman — this you must read. For this is the real thing. This is me.

TESMAN: Oh really? And what is it?

LØVBORG: The continuation.

TESMAN: Continuation? Of what?

LØVBORG: Of the book.

TESMAN: Of the new book?

LØVBORG: Of course.

TESMAN: But Eilert — you've carried the story all the way up to the present!

LØVBORG: So I have. And this is about the future.

TESMAN: The future! But, heavens — we don't know a thing about the future!

LØVBORG: No, we don't. But there are a couple of things to be said about it all the same. (*Unwraps the parcel.*) Here, let me show you —

TESMAN: But that's not your handwriting.

LØVBORG: I have dictated it. (*Leafs through portions of the manuscript.*) It's in two parts. The first is about the forces that will shape the civilization of the future. And the second (*riffling through more pages*) — about the course which that future civilization will take.

TESMAN: How remarkable! It would never occur to me to write anything like that.

HEDDA (*over by the French doors, her fingers drumming the pane*): Hmm — I dare say —

LØVBORG (*replacing the manuscript in its wrappings and putting it down on the table*): I brought it along, for I thought maybe I'd read parts of it aloud to you this evening.

TESMAN: That's very good of you, Eilert. But this evening — ? (*Looks at* BRACK.) I'm not quite sure how to arrange that —

LØVBORG: Some other time, then. There's no hurry.

BRACK: You see, Mr. Løvborg, there's a little get-together over at my house tonight. Mainly for Tesman, you know —

LØVBORG (*looking for his hat*): In that case, I certainly won't —

BRACK: No, listen. Won't you do me the pleasure to join us?

LØVBORG (*firmly*): No, I won't. But thanks all the same.

BRACK: Oh come on! Why don't you do that? We'll be a small, select circle. And I think I can promise you a fairly lively evening, as Hed — as Mrs. Tesman would say.

LØVBORG: I don't doubt that. Nevertheless —

BRACK: And you may bring your manuscript along and read aloud to Tesman over at my house. I have plenty of room.

TESMAN: Just think, Eilert! Wouldn't that be nice, hm?

HEDDA (*intervening*): But can't you see that Mr. Løvborg doesn't want to? I'm sure he would rather stay here and have supper with me.

LØVBORG (*looks at her*): With you, Mrs. Tesman?

HEDDA: And with Mrs. Elvsted.

LØVBORG: Ah — ! (*Casually.*) I ran into her at noon today.

HEDDA: Oh? Well, she'll be here tonight. So you see your presence is really required, Mr. Løvborg. Otherwise she won't have anybody to see her home.

LØVBORG: True. All right, then, Mrs. Tesman — I'll stay, thank you.

HEDDA: Good. I'll just tell the maid. (*She rings for* BERTE *over by the door, right.*)

(BERTE *appears just off stage.* HEDDA *talks with her in a low voice, points toward the inner room.* BERTE *nods and exits.*)

TESMAN (*while* HEDDA *and* BERTE *are talking, to* LØVBORG): Tell me, Eilert — is it this new subject — about the future — is that what you plan to lecture on?

LØVBORG: Yes.

TESMAN: For the bookseller told me you have announced a lecture series for this fall.

LØVBORG: Yes, I have. I hope you won't mind too much.

TESMAN: Of course not! But —

LØVBORG: For of course I realize it is rather awkward for you.

TESMAN (*unhappily*): Oh well — I certainly can't expect — that just for my sake —

LØVBORG: But I will wait till you receive your appointment.

TESMAN: Wait? But — but — but — you mean you aren't going to compete with me? Hm?

LØVBORG: No. Just triumph over you. In people's opinion.

TESMAN: Oh, for goodness' sake! Then Aunt Julle was right, after all! I knew it all the time. Hedda! Do you hear that! Just think — Eilert Løvborg isn't going to stand in our way after all.

HEDDA (*tersely*): *Our?* I have nothing to do with this.

(HEDDA *walks into the inner room, where* BERTE *is bringing in a tray with decanters and glasses.* HEDDA *nods her approval and comes forward again.*)

TESMAN (*during the foregoing business*): How about that, Judge? What do you say to this? Hm?

BRACK: I say that moral victory and all that — hm — may be glorious enough and beautiful enough —

TESMAN: Oh, I agree. All the same —

HEDDA (*looks at* TESMAN *with a cold smile*): You look thunderstruck.

TESMAN: Well, I am — pretty much — I really believe —

BRACK: After all, Mrs. Tesman, that was quite a thunderstorm that just passed over.

HEDDA (*points to the inner room*): How about a glass of cold punch, gentlemen?

BRACK (*looks at his watch*): A stirrup cup. Not a bad idea.

TESMAN: Splendid, Hedda. Perfectly splendid. In such a lighthearted mood as I am now —

HEDDA: Please. You, too, Mr. Løvborg.

LØVBORG (*with a gesture of refusal*): No, thanks. Really. Nothing for me.

BRACK: Good heavens, man! Cold punch isn't poison, you know!

LØVBORG: Perhaps not for everybody.

HEDDA: I'll keep Mr. Løvborg company in the meantime.

TESMAN: All right, Hedda. You do that.

(*He and* BRACK *go into the inner room, sit down, drink punch, smoke cigarettes, and engage in lively conversation during the next scene.* EILERT LØVBORG *remains standing near the stove.* HEDDA *walks over to the desk.*)

HEDDA (*her voice a little louder than usual*): I'll show you some pictures, if you like. You see — Tesman and I, we took a trip through Tyrol on our way back.

(*She brings an album over to the table by the sofa. She sits down in the far corner of the sofa.* LØVBORG *approaches, stops, looks at her. He takes a chair and sits down at her left, his back toward the inner room.*)

HEDDA (*opens the album*): Do you see these mountains, Mr. Løvborg? They are the Ortler group. Tesman has written their name below. Here it is: "The Ortler group near Meran."

LØVBORG (*has looked steadily at her all this time. Says slowly*): Hedda — Gabler!

HEDDA (*with a quick glance sideways*): Not that! Shhh!

LØVBORG (*again*): Hedda Gabler!

HEDDA (*looking at the album*): Yes, that used to be my name. When — when we two knew each other.

LØVBORG: And so from now on — for the whole rest of my life — I must get used to never again saying Hedda Gabler.

HEDDA (*still occupied with the album*): Yes, you must. And you might as well start right now. The sooner the better, I think.

LØVBORG (*with indignation*): Hedda Gabler married? And married to — Jørgen Tesman!

HEDDA: Yes — that's the way it goes.

LØVBORG: Oh, Hedda, Hedda — how could you throw yourself away like that!

HEDDA (*with a fierce glance at him*): What's this? I won't have any of that!

LØVBORG: What do you mean?

(TESMAN *enters from the inner room.*)

HEDDA (*hears him coming and remarks casually*): And this here, Mr. Løvborg, this is from somewhere in the Ampezzo valley. Just look at those peaks over there. (*With a kindly look at* TESMAN.) What did you say those peaks were called, dear?

TESMAN: Let me see. Oh, they — they are the Dolomites.

HEDDA: Right. Those are the Dolomites, Mr. Løvborg.

TESMAN: Hedda, I thought I'd just ask you if you don't want me to bring you some punch, after all? For you, anyway? Hm?

HEDDA: Well, yes; thanks. And a couple of cookies, maybe.

TESMAN: No cigarettes?

HEDDA: No.

TESMAN: All right.

(He returns to the inner room, then turns right. BRACK *is in there, keeping an eye on* HEDDA *and* LØVBORG *from time to time.)*

LØVBORG *(still in a low voice)*: Answer me, Hedda. How could you do a thing like that?

HEDDA *(apparently engrossed in the album)*: If you keep on using my first name I won't talk to you.

LØVBORG: Not even when we're alone?

HEDDA: No. You may think it, but you must not say it.

LØVBORG: I see. It offends your love for — Jørgen Tesman.

HEDDA *(glances at him, smiles)*: Love? That's a good one!

LØVBORG: Not love, then.

HEDDA: But no infidelities, either! I won't have it.

LØVBORG: Hedda — answer me just this one thing —

HEDDA: Shhh!

*(*TESMAN *enters with a tray from the inner room.)*

TESMAN: Here! Here are the goodies. *(Puts the tray down.)*

HEDDA: Why don't you get Berte to do it?

TESMAN *(pouring punch)*: Because I think it's so much fun waiting on you, Hedda.

HEDDA: But you've filled both glasses. And Mr. Løvborg didn't want any —

TESMAN: I know, but Mrs. Elvsted will soon be here, won't she?

HEDDA: That's right. So she will.

TESMAN: Had you forgotten about her? Hm?

HEDDA: We've been so busy looking at this. *(Shows him a picture.)* Remember that little village?

TESMAN: That's the one just below the Brenner Pass, isn't it? We spent the night there —

HEDDA: — and ran into that lively crowd of summer guests.

TESMAN: Right! Just think — if we only could have had you with us, Eilert! Oh well.

(Returns to the inner room, sits down, and resumes his conversation with BRACK.*)*

LØVBORG: Just tell me this, Hedda —

HEDDA: What?

LØVBORG: Wasn't there love in your feelings for me, either? Not a touch — not a shimmer of love? Wasn't there?

HEDDA: I wonder. To me, we seemed to be simply two good comrades. Two close friends. *(Smiles.)* You, particularly, were very frank.

LØVBORG: You wanted it that way.

HEDDA: And yet — when I look back upon it now, there was something beautiful, something thrilling, something brave, I think, about the secret frankness — that comradeship that not a single soul so much as suspected.

LØVBORG: Yes, wasn't there, Hedda? Wasn't there? When I called on your father in the afternoons — And the General sat by the window with his newspapers — his back turned —

HEDDA: And we two in the sofa in the corner —

LØVBORG: — always with the same illustrated magazine —

HEDDA: — for want of an album, yes —

LØVBORG: Yes, Hedda — and then when I confessed to you — ! Told you all about myself, things the others didn't know. Sat and told you about my orgies by day and night. Dissipation day in and day out! Oh, Hedda — what sort of power in you was it that forced me to tell you things like that?

HEDDA: You think there was some power in me?

LØVBORG: How else can I explain it? And all those veiled questions you asked —

HEDDA: — which you understood so perfectly well —

LØVBORG: That you could ask such questions! With such complete frankness!

HEDDA: *Veiled*, if you please.

LØVBORG: But frankly all the same. All about — that!

HEDDA: And to think that you answered, Mr. Løvborg!

LØVBORG: Yes, that's just what I can't understand — now, afterwards. But tell me, Hedda; wasn't love at the bottom of our whole relationship? Didn't you feel some kind of urge to — purify me — when I came to you in confession? Wasn't that it?

HEDDA: No, not quite.

LØVBORG: Then what made you do it?

HEDDA: Do you find it so very strange that a young girl — when she can do so, without anyone knowing —

LØVBORG: Yes — ?

HEDDA: — that she wants to take a peek into a world which —

LØVBORG: — which — ?

HEDDA: — she is not supposed to know anything about?

LØVBORG: So that was it!

HEDDA: That, too. That, too — I think —

LØVBORG: Companionship in the lust for life. But why couldn't *that* at least have continued?

HEDDA: That was your own fault.

LØVBORG: You were the one who broke off.

HEDDA: Yes, when reality threatened to enter our relationship. Shame on you, Eilert Løvborg! How could you want to do a thing like that to your frank and trusting comrade!

LØVBORG (*clenching his hands*): Oh, why didn't you do it! Why didn't you shoot me down, as you said you would!

HEDDA: Because I'm scared of scandal.

LØVBORG: Yes, Hedda. You are really a coward.

HEDDA: A terrible coward. (*Changing her tone.*) But that was your good luck, wasn't it? And now the Elvsteds have healed your broken heart very nicely.

LØVBORG: I know what Thea has told you.

HEDDA: Perhaps you have told her about us?

LØVBORG: Not a word. She is too stupid to understand.

HEDDA: Stupid?

LØVBORG: In things like that.

HEDDA: And I'm a coward. (*Leans forward, without looking in his eyes, whispers.*) But now *I* am going to confess something to *you.*

LØVBORG (*tense*): What?

HEDDA: That I didn't dare to shoot —

LØVBORG: Yes — ?

HEDDA: — that was not the worst of my cowardice that night.

LØVBORG (*looks at her a moment, understands, whispers passionately*): Oh, Hedda! Hedda Gabler! Now I begin to see what was behind the companionship! You and I! So it *was* your lust for life — !

HEDDA (*in a low voice, with an angry glance*): Take care! Don't you believe it!

(*Darkness is falling. The door, right, is opened, and* BERTE *enters.*)

HEDDA (*closing the album, calls out, smiling*): At last! So there you are, dearest Thea! Come in!

(MRS. ELVSTED *enters. She is dressed for a party.* BERTE *exits, closing the door behind her.*)

HEDDA (*on the sofa, reaching out for* MRS. ELVSTED): Sweetest Thea, you have no idea how I've waited for you.

(*In passing,* MRS. ELVSTED *exchanges quick greetings with* TESMAN *and* BRACK *in the inner room. She walks up to the table and shakes* HEDDA'S *hand.* EILERT LØVBORG *rises. He and* MRS. ELVSTED *greet one another with a silent nod.*)

MRS. ELVSTED: Shouldn't I go in and say hello to your husband?

HEDDA: No, never mind that. Leave them alone. They're soon leaving, anyway.

MRS. ELVSTED: Leaving?

HEDDA: They're going out to drink.

MRS. ELVSTED (*quickly, to* LØVBORG): Not you?

LØVBORG: No.

HEDDA: Mr. Løvborg stays here with us.

MRS. ELVSTED (*pulls up a chair, is about to sit down next to* LØVBORG): Oh, how wonderful it is to be here!

HEDDA: Oh no, little Thea. Not that. Not there. Over here by me, please. *I* want to be in the middle.

MRS. ELVSTED: Just as you like. (*She walks in front of the table and seats herself on the sofa, on* HEDDA'S *right.* LØVBORG *sits down again on his chair.*)

LØVBORG (*after a brief pause, to* HEDDA): Isn't she lovely to look at?

HEDDA (*gently stroking her hair*): Just to look at?

LØVBORG: Yes. For you see — she and I — we are real comrades. We have absolute faith in one another. And we can talk together in full freedom.

HEDDA: Unveiled, Mr. Løvborg?

LØVBORG: Well —

MRS. ELVSTED (*in a low voice, clinging to* HEDDA): Oh, I am so happy, Hedda! For just think — he also says I have inspired him!

HEDDA (*looks at her with a smile*): No, really! He says that?

LØVBORG: And she has such courage, Mrs. Tesman! Such courage of action.

MRS. ELVSTED: Oh, my God — courage — ! I!

LØVBORG: Infinite courage — when it concerns the comrade.

HEDDA: Yes, courage — if one only had that.

LØVBORG: What then?

HEDDA: Then maybe life would be tolerable, after all. (*Changing her tone.*) But now, dearest Thea, you want a glass of nice, cold punch.

MRS. ELVSTED: No, thanks. I never drink things like that.

HEDDA: Then what about you, Mr. Løvborg?

LØVBORG: Thanks. Nothing for me, either.

MRS. ELVSTED: No, nothing for him, either.

HEDDA (*looks firmly at him*): If I say so?

LØVBORG: Makes no difference.

HEDDA (*laughs*): Oh dear! So I have no power over you at all. Is that it?

LØVBORG: Not in that respect.

HEDDA: Seriously, though; I really think you should. For your own sake.

MRS. ELVSTED: No, but Hedda — !

LØVBORG: Why so?

HEDDA: Or rather for people's sake.

LØVBORG: Oh?

HEDDA: For else they might think you don't really trust yourself — That you lack self-confidence —

MRS. ELVSTED (*softly*): Don't, Hedda!

LØVBORG: People may think whatever they like for all I care — for the time being.

MRS. ELVSTED (*happy*): Exactly!

HEDDA: I could easily tell from watching Judge Brack just now.

LØVBORG: Tell what?

HEDDA: He smiled so contemptuously when you didn't dare to join them in there.

LØVBORG: Didn't I dare to! It's just that I'd much rather stay here and talk with you!

MRS. ELVSTED: But that's only natural, Hedda.

HEDDA: The Judge had no way of knowing that. And I also noticed he smiled and looked at Tesman when you didn't dare to go to his silly old party.

LØVBORG: Didn't dare! Are you saying I didn't dare?

HEDDA: *I* am not. But that's how Judge Brack understood it.

LØVBORG: Let him.

HEDDA: So you're not going?

LØVBORG: I'm staying here with you and Thea.

MRS. ELVSTED: Of course, he is, Hedda!

HEDDA (*smiles, nods approvingly*): That's what I call firm foundations. Principled forever; that's the way a man ought to be! (*Turning to* MRS. ELVSTED, *stroking her cheek.*) What did I tell you this morning — when you came here, quite beside yourself — ?

LØVBORG (*puzzled*): Beside herself?

MRS. ELVSTED (*in terror*): Hedda — Hedda — don't!

HEDDA: Now do you see? There was no need at all for that mortal fear of yours — (*Interrupting herself.*) There, now! Now we can all three relax and enjoy ourselves.

LØVBORG (*startled*): What's all this, Mrs. Tesman?

MRS. ELVSTED: Oh, God, Hedda — what are you saying? What are you doing?

HEDDA: Please be quiet. That horrible Judge is looking at you.

LØVBORG: In mortal fear? So that's it. For my sake.

MRS. ELVSTED (*softly, wailing*): Oh, Hedda — if you only knew how utterly miserable you have made me!

LØVBORG (*stares at her for a moment. His face is distorted.*): So that was the comrade's happy confidence in me!

MRS. ELVSTED: Oh, my dearest friend — listen to me first — !

LØVBORG (*picks up one of the glasses of punch, raises it, says hoarsely*): Here's to you, Thea! (*Empties the glass, puts it down, picks up the other one.*)

MRS. ELVSTED (*softly*): Hedda, Hedda — why did you want to do this?

HEDDA: Want to! I! Are you mad?

LØVBORG: And here's to you, too, Mrs. Tesman! Thanks for telling me the truth. Long live the truth! (*He drains the glass and is about to fill it again.*)

HEDDA (*restrains him*): That's enough for now. Remember you are going to a party.

MRS. ELVSTED: No, no, no!

HEDDA: Shhh! They are looking at you.

LØVBORG (*puts his glass down*): Listen, Thea — tell me the truth —

MRS. ELVSTED: I will, I will!

LØVBORG: Did your husband know you were coming after me?

MRS. ELVSTED (*wringing her hands*): Oh, Hedda — do you hear what he's asking?

LØVBORG: Did the two of you agree that you were to come here and look after me? Maybe it was his idea, even? Did he send you? Ah, I know what it was — he missed me in the office, didn't he? Or was it at the card table?

MRS. ELVSTED (*softly, in agony*): Oh, Løvborg, Løvborg!

LØVBORG (*grabs a glass and is about to fill it*): Here's to the old Commissioner, too!

HEDDA (*stops him*): No more now. You're supposed to read aloud for Tesman tonight — remember?

LØVBORG (*calm again, puts the glass down*): This was silly of me, Thea. I'm sorry. Taking it this way. Please, don't be angry with me. You'll see — both you and all those others — that even if I have been down — ! With your help, Thea — dear comrade.

MRS. ELVSTED (*beaming*): Oh, thank God — !

(*In the meantime,* BRACK *has looked at his watch. He and* TESMAN *get up and come forward.*)

BRACK (*picking up his coat and hat*): Well, Mrs. Tesman; our time is up.

HEDDA: I suppose it is.

LØVBORG (*rising*): Mine, too, Judge.

MRS. ELVSTED (*softly, pleadingly*): Oh, Løvborg — don't do it!

HEDDA (*pinches her arm*): They can hear you!

MRS. ELVSTED (*with a soft exclamation*): Ouch!

LØVBORG (*to* BRACK): You were good enough to ask me —

BRACK: So you're coming, after all?

LØVBORG: If I may.

BRACK: I'm delighted.

LØVBORG (*picks up his manuscript and says to* TESMAN): For there are a couple of things here I'd like to show you before I send it off.

TESMAN: Just think! Isn't that nice! But — dearest Hedda — ? In that case, how are you going to get Mrs. Elvsted home? Hm?

HEDDA: We'll manage somehow.

LØVBORG (*looking at the two women*): Mrs. Elvsted? I'll be back to pick her up, of course. (*Coming closer.*) About ten o'clock, Mrs. Tesman? Is that convenient?

HEDDA: Certainly. That will be fine.

TESMAN: Then everything is nice and settled. But don't expect me that early, Hedda.

HEDDA: You just stay as long as — as long as you want to, dear.

MRS. ELVSTED (*in secret fear*): I'll be waiting for you here, then, Mr. Løvborg.

LØVBORG (*hat in hand*): Of course, Mrs. Elvsted.

BRACK: All aboard the pleasure train, gentlemen! I hope we'll have a lively evening — as a certain fair lady would say.

HEDDA: Ah — if only the fair lady could be present. Invisibly.

BRACK: Why invisibly?

HEDDA: To listen to some of your unadulterated liveliness, Judge.

BRACK (*laughs*): I shouldn't advise the fair lady to do that!

TESMAN (*also laughing*): You're a good one, Hedda! Just think!

BRACK: Well — good night, ladies!

LØVBORG (*with a bow*): Till about ten, then.

(BRACK, LØVBORG, *and* TESMAN *go out, right. At the same time* BERTE *enters from the inner room with a lighted lamp, which she places on the table, front center. She goes out the same way.*)

MRS. ELVSTED (*has risen and paces restlessly up and down*): Hedda, Hedda — how do you think all this will end?

HEDDA: At ten o'clock he'll be here. I see him already. With vine leaves in his hair. Flushed and confident.

MRS. ELVSTED: I only hope you're right.

HEDDA: For then, you see, he'll have mastered himself. And be a free man for all the days of his life.

MRS. ELVSTED: Dear God — how I hope you are right! That he'll come back like that.

HEDDA: That is the way he will come. No other way. (*She rises and goes closer to* MRS. ELVSTED.) *You* may doubt as long as you like. I believe in him. And now we'll see —

MRS. ELVSTED: There is something behind all this, Hedda. Some hidden purpose.

HEDDA: Yes, there is! For once in my life I want to have power over a human destiny.

MRS. ELVSTED: But don't you already?

HEDDA: I don't and I never have.

MRS. ELVSTED: But your husband — ?

HEDDA: You think that's worth the trouble? Oh, if you knew how poor I am! And you got to be so rich! (*Embraces her passionately.*) I think I'll have to burn your hair off, after all!

MRS. ELVSTED: Let me go! Let me go! You scare me, Hedda!

BERTE (*in the doorway*): Supper is served, ma'am.

HEDDA: Good. We're coming.

MRS. ELVSTED: No, no, no! I'd rather go home by myself! Right now!

HEDDA: Nonsense! You'll have your cup of tea first, you little silly. And then — at ten o'clock — Eilert Løvborg comes — with vine leaves in his hair! (*She almost pulls* MRS. ELVSTED *toward the doorway.*)

ACT THREE

(*The same room at the* TESMANS'. *The doorway and the French windows both have their portieres closed. The lamp, turned half down, is still on the table. The stove is open. Some dying embers can be seen.*

MRS. ELVSTED, *wrapped in a big shawl, is in the easy chair near the stove, her feet on a footstool.* HEDDA, *also dressed, is lying on the sofa, covered by a blanket.*)

MRS. ELVSTED (*after a while suddenly sits up, listens anxiously; then she wearily sinks back in her chair, whimpers softly*): Oh my God, my God — not yet!

(BERTE *enters cautiously, right, carrying a letter.*)

MRS. ELVSTED (*turns and whispers tensely*): Well — has anybody been here?

BERTE (*in a low voice*): Yes. Just now there was a girl with this letter.

MRS. ELVSTED (*quickly, reaches for it*): A letter! Give it to me.

BERTE: No, ma'am. It's for the Doctor.

MRS. ELVSTED: I see.

BERTE: Miss Tesman's maid brought it. I'll leave it here on the table.

MRS. ELVSTED: All right.

BERTE (*puts the letter down*): I'd better put out the lamp. It just reeks.

MRS. ELVSTED: Yes, do that. It must be daylight soon, anyway.

BERTE (*putting out the lamp*): It's light already, ma'am.

MRS. ELVSTED: Light already! And still not back!

BERTE: No, so help us. Not that I didn't expect as much —

MRS. ELVSTED: You did?

BERTE: Yes, when I saw a certain character was back in town. Taking them off with him. We sure heard enough about him in the old days!

MRS. ELVSTED: Not so loud. You are waking up Mrs. Tesman.

BERTE (*looks toward the sofa, sighs*): God forbid — ! Let her sleep, poor thing. Do you want me to get the fire going again?

MRS. ELVSTED: Not on my account, thank you.

BERTE: All right. (*Exits quietly, right.*)

HEDDA (*awakened by the closing door*): What's that?

MRS. ELVSTED: Just the maid.

HEDDA (*looks around*): Why in here — ? Oh, I remember! (*Sits up, rubs her eyes, stretches.*) What time is it, Thea?

MRS. ELVSTED (*looks at her watch*): Past seven.

HEDDA: When did Tesman get home?

MRS. ELVSTED: He didn't.

HEDDA: Not home yet!

MRS. ELVSTED (*getting up*): Nobody's come.

HEDDA: And we waited till four!

MRS. ELVSTED (*wringing her hands*): And *how* we waited!

HEDDA (*her hand covering a yawn*): We — ll. We could have saved ourselves that trouble.

MRS. ELVSTED: Did you get any sleep at all?

HEDDA: Yes, I slept pretty well, I think. Didn't you?

MRS. ELVSTED: Not a wink. I just couldn't, Hedda! It was just impossible.

HEDDA (*rises, walks over to her*): Well, now! There's nothing to worry about, for heaven's sake. I know exactly what's happened.

MRS. ELVSTED: Then tell me please. Where do you think they are?

HEDDA: Well, first of all, I'm sure they were terribly late leaving the Judge's —

MRS. ELVSTED: Dear, yes. I'm sure you're right. Still —

HEDDA: — and so Tesman didn't want to wake us up in the middle of the night. (*Laughs.*) Maybe he didn't want us to see him, either — after a party like that.

MRS. ELVSTED: But where do you think he has gone?

HEDDA: To the aunts', of course. His old room is still there, all ready for him.

MRS. ELVSTED: No, he can't be there. Just a few minutes ago there came a letter for him from Miss Tesman. It's over there.

HEDDA: Oh? (*looks at the envelope.*) So it is — Auntie Julle herself. In that case, I suppose he's still at Brack's. And there's Eilert Løvborg, too — reading aloud, with vine leaves in his hair.

MRS. ELVSTED: Oh Hedda — you're only saying things you don't believe yourself.

HEDDA: My, what a little imbecile you really are, Thea!

MRS. ELVSTED: Yes, I suppose I am.

HEDDA: And you look dead tired, too.

MRS. ELVSTED: I *am* dead tired.

HEDDA: Why don't you do as I say. Go into my room and lie down.

MRS. ELVSTED: No, no — I wouldn't be able to go to sleep, anyway.

HEDDA: Of course, you would.

MRS. ELVSTED: And your husband is bound to be home any minute now. And I have to know right away.

HEDDA: I'll let you know as soon as he gets here.

MRS. ELVSTED: You promise me that, Hedda?

HEDDA: I do. You just go to sleep.

MRS. ELVSTED: Thanks. At least I'll try. (*Exits through inner room.*)

(HEDDA *goes to the French doors, opens the portieres. The room is now in full daylight. She picks up a little hand mirror from the desk, looks at herself, smooths her hair. Walks over to door, right, rings the bell for the maid.* BERTE *presently appears.*)

BERTE: You want something, ma'am?

HEDDA: Yes. You'll have to start the fire again. I'm cold.

BERTE: Yes, ma'am! I'll get it warm in no time. (*Rakes the embers together and puts in another piece of wood. Then she suddenly listens.*) There's the doorbell, ma'am.

HEDDA: All right. See who it is. I'll take care of the stove myself.

BERTE: You'll have a nice blaze going in a minute. (*Exits right.*)

(HEDDA *kneels on the footstool and puts in more pieces of wood. Presently* TESMAN *enters, right. He looks tired and somber. He tiptoes toward the doorway and is about to disappear between the portieres.*)

HEDDA (*by the stove, without looking up*): Good morning.

TESMAN (*turning*): Hedda! (*Comes closer.*) For heaven's sake — you up already! Hm?

HEDDA: Yes, I got up very early this morning.

TESMAN: And I was sure you'd still be sound asleep! Just think!

HEDDA: Not so loud. Mrs. Elvsted is asleep in my room.

TESMAN: Mrs. Elvsted stayed here all night?

HEDDA: Yes. Nobody came for her, you know.

TESMAN: No, I suppose —

HEDDA (*closes the stove, rises*): Well, did you have a good time at the Judge's?

TESMAN: Were you worried about me? Hm?

HEDDA: I'd never dream of worrying about you. I asked if you had a good time.

TESMAN: Yes, indeed. Nice for a change, anyway. But I think I liked it best early in the evening. For then Eilert read to me. Just think — we were more than an hour early! And Brack, of course, had things to see to. So Eilert read.

HEDDA (*sits down at the right side of the table*): So? Tell me all about it.

TESMAN (*sits down on an ottoman near the stove*): Oh Hedda, you'll never believe what a book that will be! It must be just the most remarkable thing ever written! Just think!

HEDDA: Yes, but I don't really care about that —

TESMAN: I must tell you, Hedda — I have a confession to make. As he was reading — something ugly came over me —

HEDDA: Ugly?

TESMAN: I sat there envying Eilert for being able to write like that! Just think, Hedda!

HEDDA: All right. I'm thinking!

TESMAN: And yet, with all his gifts — he's incorrigible, after all.

HEDDA: I suppose you mean he has more courage for life than the rest of you?

TESMAN: No, no — I don't mean that. I mean that he's incapable of exercising moderation in his pleasures.

HEDDA: What happened — in the end?

TESMAN: Well — *I* would call it a bacchanal, Hedda.

HEDDA: Did he have vine leaves in his hair?

TESMAN: Vine leaves? No, I didn't notice any vine leaves. But he gave a long, muddled speech in honor of the woman who had inspired him in his work. Those were his words.

HEDDA: Did he mention her name?

TESMAN: No, he didn't. But I'm sure it must be Mrs. Elvsted. You just wait and see if I'm not right!

HEDDA: And where did you and he part company?

TESMAN: On the way back to town. We left — the last of us did —

at the same time. And Brack came along, too, to get some fresh air. Then we decided we'd better see Eilert home. You see, he had had altogether too much to drink!

HEDDA: I can imagine.

TESMAN: But then the strangest thing of all happened, Hedda! Or maybe I should say the saddest. I'm almost ashamed — on Eilert's behalf — even talking about it.

HEDDA: Well — ?

TESMAN: You see, on the way back I happened to be behind the others a little. Just for a minute or two — you know —

HEDDA: All right, all right — !

TESMAN: And when I hurried to catch up with them, can you guess what I found by the roadside? Hm?

HEDDA: How can I possibly — ?

TESMAN: You mustn't tell this to a living soul, Hedda! Do you hear! Promise me that, for Eilert's sake. (*Pulls a parcel out of his coat pocket.*) Just think — I found this!

HEDDA: Isn't that what he had with him here yesterday?

TESMAN: Yes! It's his whole, precious, irreplaceable manuscript! And he had dropped it — just like that! Without even noticing! Just think, Hedda! Isn't that awfully sad?

HEDDA: But why didn't you give it back to him?

TESMAN: In the condition he was in! Dear — I just didn't dare to.

HEDDA: And you didn't tell any of the others that you had found it, either?

TESMAN: Of course not. I didn't want to, for Eilert's sake — don't you see?

HEDDA: So nobody knows that you have Eilert Løvborg's papers?

TESMAN: Nobody. And nobody must know, either.

HEDDA: And what did you and he talk about afterwards?

TESMAN: I didn't have a chance to talk to him at all after that. For when we came into town, he and a couple of the others simply vanished. Just think!

HEDDA: Oh? I expect they took him home.

TESMAN: I suppose that must be it. And Brack took off on his own, too.

HEDDA: And what have you been doing with yourself since then?

TESMAN: Well, you see, I and some of the others went home with one of the younger fellows and had a cup of early morning coffee. Or night coffee maybe, rather. Hm? And now, after I've rested a bit and poor Eilert's had some sleep, I'll take this back to him.

HEDDA (*reaches for the parcel*): No — don't do that! Not right away, I mean. Let me look at it first.

TESMAN: Dearest Hedda — honestly, I just don't dare to.

HEDDA: Don't you dare to?

TESMAN: No, for I'm sure you realize how utterly desperate he'll be when he wakes up and finds that the manuscript is gone. For he hasn't a copy, you know. He said so himself.

HEDDA (*looks searchingly at him*): But can't a thing like that be written over again?

TESMAN: Hardly. I really don't think so. For, you see — the inspiration —

HEDDA: Yes, I daresay that's the main thing. (*Casually.*) By the way, here's a letter for you.

TESMAN: Imagine!

HEDDA (*gives it to him*): It came early this morning.

TESMAN: It's from Aunt Julle, Hedda! I wonder what it can be. (*Puts the manuscript down on the other ottoman, opens the letter, skims the content, jumps up.*) Oh Hedda! She says here that poor Aunt Rina is dying!

HEDDA: You know we had to expect that.

TESMAN: And if I want to see her again I had better hurry. I'll rush over right away.

HEDDA (*suppressing a smile*): You'll rush?

TESMAN: Dearest Hedda of mine — if only you could bring yourself to come along! Hm?

HEDDA (*rises, weary, with an air of refusal*): No, no. You mustn't ask me that. I don't want to look at death and disease. I don't want anything to do with ugliness.

TESMAN: Well, all right — (*Rushing around.*) My hat? My coat? Oh — out here in the hall. I just hope I won't be too late, Hedda. Hm?

HEDDA: Oh I'm sure that if you rush —

(BERTE *appears in the door, right.*)

BERTE: Judge Brack is here and wants to know if he may see you.

TESMAN: At this hour! No, no. I can't possibly see him now!

HEDDA: But *I* can. (*To* BERTE.) Tell the Judge please to come in.

(BERTE *exits.*)

HEDDA (*with a quick whisper*): Tesman! The package! (*She grabs it from the ottoman.*)

TESMAN: Yes! Give it to me!

HEDDA: No, no. I'll hide it for you till later.

(*She walks over to the desk and sticks the parcel in among the books on the shelf. In his hurry* TESMAN *is having difficulties getting his gloves on.* JUDGE BRACK *enters, right.*)

HEDDA (*nods to him*): If *you* aren't an early bird —

BRACK: Yes, don't you think so? (*To* TESMAN.) You're going out, too?

TESMAN: Yes, I must go and see the aunts. Just think, the invalid — she's dying!

BRACK: Oh, I'm terribly sorry! In that case, don't let me keep you. At such a moment —

TESMAN: Yes, I really must run. Goodbye, goodbye! (*Hurries out, right.*)

HEDDA (*approaching* BRACK): It appears that things were quite lively last night over at your house.

BRACK: Indeed, Mrs. Tesman — I didn't get to bed at all.

HEDDA: You didn't either?

BRACK: As you see. But tell me — what has Tesman told you about the night's adventures?

HEDDA: Just some tiresome story about having coffee with somebody someplace —

BRACK: I believe I know all about that coffee. Eilert Løvborg wasn't one of them, was he?

HEDDA: No, they had taken him home first.

BRACK: Tesman, too?

HEDDA: No. Some of the others, he said.

BRACK (*smiles*): Jørgen Tesman is really an ingenuous soul, you know.

HEDDA: He certainly is. But why do you say that? Is there something more to all this?

BRACK: Yes, there is.

HEDDA: Well! In that case, why don't we make ourselves comfortable, Judge. You'll tell your story better, too.

(*She sits down at the left side of the table,* BRACK *near her at the adjacent side.*)

HEDDA: All right?

BRACK: For reasons of my own I wanted to keep track of my guests' movements last night. Or, rather — some of my guests.

HEDDA: Eilert Løvborg was one of them, perhaps?

BRACK: As a matter of fact — he was.

HEDDA: Now you are really making me curious.

BRACK: Do you know where he and a couple of the others spent the rest of the night, Mrs. Tesman?

HEDDA: No — tell me. If it can be told.

BRACK: Oh, certainly. They turned up at an exceptionally gay early morning gathering.

HEDDA: Of the lively kind?

BRACK: Of the liveliest.

HEDDA: A little more about this, Judge.

BRACK: Løvborg had been invited beforehand. I knew about that. But he had declined. He is a reformed character, you know.

HEDDA: As of his stay with the Elvsteds — yes. But he went after all?

BRACK: Well, yes, you see, Mrs. Tesman — unfortunately, the spirit moved him over at my house last evening.

HEDDA: Yes, I understand he became inspired.

BRACK: Quite violently inspired. And that, I gather, must have changed his mind. You know, we men don't always have as much integrity as we ought to have.

HEDDA: Oh, I'm sure you're an exception, Judge Brack. But about Løvborg — ?

BRACK: To make a long story short — he ended up at Miss Diana's establishment.

HEDDA: Miss Diana's?

BRACK: She was the hostess at this gathering — a select circle of intimate friends, male and female.

HEDDA: Is she a redhead, by any chance?

BRACK: That's correct.

HEDDA: And a singer — of sorts?

BRACK: Yes — that, too. And a mighty huntress — of men, Mrs. Tesman. You seem to have heard of her. Eilert Løvborg used to be one of her most devoted protectors in his more affluent days.

HEDDA: And how did it all end?

BRACK: Not in a very friendly fashion, apparently. It seems that after the tenderest reception Miss Diana resorted to brute force —

HEDDA: Against Løvborg?

BRACK: Yes. He accused her or her women friends of having stolen something of his. Said his wallet was gone. And other things, too. In brief, he's supposed to have started a pretty wicked row.

HEDDA: And — ?

BRACK: Well — there was a general free-for-all — men and women both. Fortunately, the police stepped in —

HEDDA: The police —!

BRACK: Yes. But I'm afraid this will be an expensive escapade for Eilert Løvborg, crazy fool that he is.

HEDDA: Well!

BRACK: It appears that he made quite violent objection — struck an officer in the ear and tore his coat. So they had to take him along.

HEDDA: How do you know all this?

BRACK: From the police.

HEDDA (*staring straight ahead*): So that's how it was. No vine leaves in his hair.

BRACK: Vine leaves, Mrs. Tesman?

HEDDA (*changing her tone*): But tell me, Judge Brack — why did you keep such a close watch on Eilert Løvborg?

BRACK: Well — for one thing, it is obviously of some concern to me if he testifies that he came straight from my party.

HEDDA: So you think there will be an investigation?

BRACK: Naturally. But I suppose that doesn't really matter too much. However, as a friend of the house I considered it my duty to give you and Tesman a full account of his night-time exploits.

HEDDA: Yes, but why?

BRACK: Because I very strongly suspect that he intends to use you as a kind of screen.

HEDDA: Really! Why do you think that?

BRACK: Oh, come now, Mrs. Tesman! We can use our eyes, can't we? This Mrs. Elvsted — she isn't leaving town right away, you know.

HEDDA: Well, even if there should be something going on between those two, I'd think there would be plenty of other places they could meet.

BRACK: But no home. After last night, every respectable house will once again be closed to Eilert Løvborg.

HEDDA: And so should mine, you mean?

BRACK: Yes. I admit I would find it more than embarrassing if the gentleman were to become a daily guest here, Mrs. Tesman. If he, as an outsider — a highly dispensable outsider — if he were to intrude himself —

HEDDA: — into the triangle?

BRACK: Precisely. It would amount to homelessness for me.

HEDDA (*smiling*): Sole cock-o'-the-walk — so, that's your goal, is it, Judge?

BRACK (*nods slowly, lowers his voice*): Yes. That is my goal. And for that I will fight with every means at my disposal.

HEDDA (*her smile fading*): You're really a dangerous person, you know — when you come right down to it.

BRACK: You think so?

HEDDA: Yes. I am beginning to think so now. And I must say I am exceedingly glad you don't have any kind of hold on me.

BRACK (*with a noncommittal laugh*): Well, well, Mrs. Tesman! Maybe there is something to what you are saying, at that. Who knows what I might do if I did.

HEDDA: Really, now, Judge Brack! Are you threatening me?

BRACK (*rising*): — Nonsense! For the triangle, you see — is best maintained on a voluntary basis.

HEDDA: My sentiments, exactly.

BRACK: Well, I have said what I came to say. And now I should get back to town. Goodbye, Mrs. Tesman! (*Walks toward the French doors.*)

HEDDA (*rises*): You're going through the garden?

BRACK: Yes. For me that's a short cut.

HEDDA: Yes, and then it's a back way.

BRACK: Quite true. I have nothing against back ways. There are times when they are most intriguing.

HEDDA: You mean when real ammunition is used?

BRACK (*in the doorway, laughs back at her*): Oh good heavens! I don't suppose one shoots one's tame roosters!

HEDDA (*laughs also*): No — not if one has only one — !

(*They nod to each other, both still laughing. He leaves. She closes the door behind him. For a few moments she remains by the door, quite serious now, looking into the garden. Then she walks over to the doorway and opens the portieres wide enough to look into the inner room. Goes to the desk, pulls* LØVBORG'S *manuscript from the bookshelf and is about to read in it when* BERTE'S *voice, very loud, is heard from the hall, right.* HEDDA *turns around, listens. She hurriedly puts the manuscript into the drawer of the desk and puts the key down on its top.* EILERT LØVBORG, *wearing his coat and with his hat in his hand, flings open the door, right. He looks somewhat confused and excited.*)

LØVBORG (*turned toward the invisible* BERTE *in the hall*): — And I say I must! You can't stop me! (*He closes the door, turns, sees* HEDDA, *immediately controls himself, greets her.*)

HEDDA (*by the desk*): Well, well, Mr. Løvborg — aren't you a trifle late coming for Thea?

LØVBORG: Or a trifle early for calling on you. I apologize.

HEDDA: How do you know she is still here?

LØVBORG: The people she is staying with told me she's been gone all night.

HEDDA (*walks over to the table*): Did they seem — strange — when they said it?

LØVBORG (*puzzled*): Strange?

HEDDA: I mean, did they seem to find it a little — unusual?

LØVBORG (*suddenly understands*): Ah, I see what you mean! Of course! I'm dragging her down with me. No, as a matter of fact, I didn't notice anything. I suppose Tesman isn't up yet?

HEDDA: I — I don't think so —

LØVBORG: When did he get home?

HEDDA: Very late.

LØVBORG: Did he tell you anything?
HEDDA: Yes, he said you'd all had quite a time over at Brack's.
LØVBORG: Just that?
HEDDA: I think so. But I was so awfully sleepy —

(MRS. ELVSTED *enters through portieres in the rear.*)

MRS. ELVSTED (*toward him*): Oh, Løvborg! At last!
LØVBORG: Yes, at last. And too late.
MRS. ELVSTED (*in fear*): What is too late?
LØVBORG: Everything is too late now. It's all over with me.
MRS. ELVSTED: Oh no, no! Don't say things like that!
LØVBORG: You'll say the same yourself when you hear —
MRS. ELVSTED: I don't want to hear — !
HEDDA: Maybe you'd rather talk with her alone? I'll leave.
LØVBORG: No, stay — you, too. I beg you to.
MRS. ELVSTED: But I don't want to listen, do you hear?
LØVBORG: It isn't last night I want to talk about.
MRS. ELVSTED: What about, then?
LØVBORG: We'll have to part, Thea.
MRS. ELVSTED: Part!
HEDDA (*involuntarily*): I knew it!
LØVBORG: For I don't need you any more.
MRS. ELVSTED: And you can stand there and tell me a thing like that! Don't need me! Why can't I help you the way I did before? Aren't we going to keep on working together?
LØVBORG: I don't intend to work any more.
MRS. ELVSTED (*desperately*): What am I going to do with my life, then?
LØVBORG: You'll have to try to live your life as if you'd never known me.
MRS. ELVSTED: But I can't do that!
LØVBORG: Try, Thea. Go back home.
MRS. ELVSTED (*agitated*): Never again! Where you are I want to be! And you can't chase me away just like that. I want to stay right here! Be with you when the book appears.
HEDDA (*in a tense whisper*): Ah — yes — the book!
LØVBORG (*looks at her*): My book — and Thea's. For that's what it is.
MRS. ELVSTED: That's what I feel, too. And that's why I have the right to be with you when it comes out. I want to see all the honor and all the fame you'll get. And the joy — I want to share the joy, too.
LØVBORG: Thea, our book is never going to come out.
HEDDA: Ah!

MRS. ELVSTED: It won't!

LØVBORG: *Can't* ever appear.

MRS. ELVSTED (*with fearful suspicion*): Løvborg, what have you done with the manuscript?

HEDDA (*watching him tensely*): Yes — what about the manuscript?

MRS. ELVSTED: Where is it?

LØVBORG: Oh Thea — please, don't ask me about that!

MRS. ELVSTED: Yes, yes — I want to be told! I have the right to know — right now!

LØVBORG: All right. I've torn it to pieces.

MRS. ELVSTED (*screams*): Oh, no! No!

HEDDA (*involuntarily*): But that's not — !

LØVBORG (*looks at her*): Not true, you think?

HEDDA (*composing herself*): Well, of course, if you say so. You should know. It just sounds so — so unbelievable.

LØVBORG: All the same, it's true.

MRS. ELVSTED (*hands clenched*): Oh God — oh God, Hedda. He has torn his own work to pieces!

LØVBORG: I have torn my whole life to pieces, so why not my life's work as well?

MRS. ELVSTED: And that's what you did last night?

LØVBORG: Yes, I tell you! In a thousand pieces. And scattered them in the fjord. Far out — where the water is clean and salty. Let them drift there, with wind and current. Then they'll sink. Deep, deep down. Like me, Thea.

MRS. ELVSTED: Do you know, Løvborg — this thing you've done to the book — all the rest of my life I'll think of it as killing a little child.

LØVBORG: You are right. It is like murdering a child.

MRS. ELVSTED: But then, how could you? For the child was mine, too!

HEDDA (*almost soundlessly*): The child —

MRS. ELVSTED (*with a deep sigh*): So it's all over. I'll go now, Hedda.

HEDDA: But you aren't leaving town?

MRS. ELVSTED: Oh, I don't know myself what I'll do. There's only darkness before me. (*Exits, right.*)

HEDDA (*waits for a moment*): Aren't you going to see her home, Mr. Løvborg?

LØVBORG: I? Through the streets? Letting people see her with me?

HEDDA: Of course, I don't know what else may have happened last night. But is it really so absolutely irreparable — ?

LØVBORG: Last night is not the end of it. That I know. And yet, I don't really care for that kind of life any more. Not again. She has broken all the courage for life and all the defiance that was in me.

HEDDA (*staring ahead*): So that sweet little goose has had her hand in a human destiny. (*Looks at him.*) But that you could be so heartless, even so!

LØVBORG: Don't tell me I was heartless!

HEDDA: To ruin everything that's filled her soul for a such a long time! You don't call that heartless!

LØVBORG: Hedda — to you I can tell the truth.

HEDDA: The truth?

LØVBORG: But first promise me — give me your word you'll never let Thea know what I'm going to tell you now.

HEDDA: You have it.

LØVBORG: All right. It isn't true, what I just told her.

HEDDA: About the manuscript?

LØVBORG: Yes. I have not torn it up. Not thrown it in the sea, either.

HEDDA: But then — where is it?

LØVBORG: I've destroyed it just the same. Really, I have, Hedda!

HEDDA: I don't understand.

LØVBORG: Thea said that what I had done seemed to her like murdering a child.

HEDDA: Yes — she did.

LØVBORG: But killing a child, that's not the worst thing a father can do to it.

HEDDA: No?

LØVBORG: No. And the worst is what I don't want Thea to know.

HEDDA: What *is* the worst?

LØVBORG: Hedda — suppose a man, say, early in the morning, after a stupid, drunken night — suppose he comes home to his child's mother and says: Listen, I've been in such and such a place. I've been here — and I've been there. And I had our child with me. In all those places. And the child is lost. Gone. Vanished. I'll be damned if I know where it is. Who's got hold of it —

HEDDA: Yes — but when all is said and done — it is only a book, you know.

LØVBORG: Thea's pure soul was in that book.

HEDDA: I realize that.

LØVBORG: Then you surely also realize that she and I can have no future together.

HEDDA: Where do you go from here?

LØVBORG: Nowhere. Just finish everything off. The sooner the better.

HEDDA (*a step closer*): Listen — Eilert Løvborg — Couldn't you make sure it's done beautifully?

LØVBORG: Beautifully? (*Smiles.*) With vine leaves in the hair, as you used to say.

HEDDA: Oh no. I don't believe in vine leaves any more. But still beautifully! For once. Goodbye. Go now. And don't come back.

LØVBORG: Goodbye, Mrs. Tesman. Give my regards to Jørgen Tesman. (*He is about to leave.*)

HEDDA: Wait! I want to give you something — a remembrance. (*Goes to the desk, opens the drawer, takes out the gun case. Returns to* LØVBORG *with one of the revolvers.*)

LØVBORG: The gun? That's the remembrance?

HEDDA (*nods slowly*): Do you recognize it? It was pointed at you once.

LØVBORG: You should have used it then.

HEDDA: Take it! *You* use it.

LØVBORG (*pockets the gun*): Thanks!

HEDDA: And beautifully, Eilert Løvborg! That's all I ask!

LØVBORG: Goodbye, Hedda Gabler. (*Exits, right.*)

(HEDDA *listens by the door for a moment. Then she crosses to the desk, takes out the manuscript, glances inside the cover, pulls some of the pages halfway out and looks at them. Carries the whole manuscript over to the chair by the stove. She sits down with the parcel in her lap. After a moment she opens the stove and then the manuscript.*)

HEDDA (*throws a bundle of sheets into the fire, whispers*): Now I'm burning your child, Thea. You — curlyhead! (*Throws more sheets in.*) Your and Eilert Løvborg's child. (*Throws all the rest of the manuscript into the stove.*) I am burning — I am burning your child.

ACT FOUR

(*The same rooms at the* TESMANS'. *Evening. The front room is dark. The inner room is lighted by the ceiling lamp over the table. Portieres cover the French doors.*

HEDDA, *in black, is walking up and down in the dark of the front room. She goes into the inner room, turning left in the doorway. She is heard playing a few bars on the piano. She reappears and comes forward again.* BERTE *enters from the right side of the inner room. She carries a lighted lamp, which she puts down on the table in front of the corner sofa. Her eyes show signs of weeping; she wears black ribbons on her uniform. She exits quietly, right.* HEDDA *goes over to the French windows, looks between the portieres into the dark. Presently* MISS TESMAN, *in mourning, with hat and veil, enters, right.* HEDDA *walks over to meet her, gives her her hand.*)

MISS TESMAN: Yes, my dearest Hedda — here you see me in my garb of grief. For now at last my poor sister has fought her fight to the end.

HEDDA: I already know — as you see. Tesman sent word.

MISS TESMAN: Yes, he promised he'd do that. But I thought that to you, Hedda — here in the house of life — I really ought to bring you the tidings of death myself.

HEDDA: That is very kind of you.

MISS TESMAN: Ah, but Rina shouldn't have died just now. There should be no mourning in Hedda's house at this time.

HEDDA (*changing the topic*): I understand she had a very quiet end.

MISS TESMAN: Oh so beautiful, so peaceful! She left us so quietly! And then the unspeakable happiness of seeing Jørgen one more time! To say goodbye to him to her heart's content! Isn't he back yet?

HEDDA: No. He wrote I mustn't expect him back very soon. But do sit down.

MISS TESMAN: No — no, thanks, my dear, blessed Hedda. Not that I wouldn't like to. But I don't have much time. I must go back and prepare her as best I can. I want her to look right pretty when she goes into her grave.

HEDDA: Is there anything I can help you with?

MISS TESMAN: I won't have you as much as think of it! That's not for Hedda Tesman to lend a hand to. Or lend thoughts to, either. Not now, of all times!

HEDDA: Oh — thoughts! We can't always control our thoughts —

MISS TESMAN (*still preoccupied*): Ah yes — such is life. At home we're making a shroud for Rina. And here, too, there'll be sewing to do soon, I expect. But of quite a different kind, thank God!

(TESMAN *enters, right.*)

HEDDA: Finally!

TESMAN: You here, Aunt Julle? With Hedda? Just think!

MISS TESMAN: I am just about to leave, Jørgen dear. Well — did you do all the things you promised me you'd do?

TESMAN: No, I'm afraid I forgot half of them, Auntie. I'd better run in again tomorrow. I'm all confused today. I can't seem to keep my thoughts together.

MISS TESMAN: But dearest Jørgen — you mustn't take it this way!

TESMAN: Oh, I mustn't? How do you mean?

MISS TESMAN: You ought to be joyful in the midst of your sorrow. Glad for what's happened. The way I am.

TESMAN: Oh yes, of course. You're thinking of Aunt Rina.

HEDDA: You're going to feel lonely now, Miss Tesman.

MISS TESMAN: The first few days, yes. But I hope that won't last long. Dear Rina's little parlor won't be empty for long, if I can help it!

TESMAN: Oh? And who do you want to move in there. Hm?

MISS TESMAN: Ah — it's not very hard to find some poor soul who needs nursing and comfort.

HEDDA: And you really want to take on such a burden all over again?

MISS TESMAN: Heavens! God forgive you, child — burden? It has not been a burden to me.

HEDDA: Still — a stranger, who —

MISS TESMAN: Oh, it's easy to make friends with sick people. And I need somebody to live for, too. Well, the Lord be praised, maybe soon there'll be a thing or two an old aunt can turn her hand to here.

HEDDA: Oh, never mind us —

TESMAN: Yes, just think — how lovely it would be for the three of us, if only —

HEDDA: If only — ?

TESMAN (*uneasy*): Oh, nothing. I daresay it will all work out. Let's hope it will, hm?

MISS TESMAN: Well, well. I can see that you two have something to talk about. (*With a smile.*) And perhaps Hedda has something to tell *you*, Jørgen! Goodbye! I'm going home to Rina, now. (*Turns around in the door.*) Dear, dear — how strange to think — Now Rina is both with me and with Jochum!

TESMAN: Yes, just think, Aunt Julle! Hm?

(MISS TESMAN *exits, right.*)

HEDDA (*coldly scrutinizing* TESMAN): I wouldn't be at all surprised if you aren't more affected by this death than she is.

TESMAN: Oh, it isn't just Aunt Rina's death, Hedda. It's Eilert I worry about.

HEDDA (*quickly*): Any news about him?

TESMAN: I went over to his room this afternoon to tell him the manuscript is safe.

HEDDA: Well? And didn't you see him?

TESMAN: No. He wasn't home. But I ran into Mrs. Elvsted and she told me he'd been here early this morning.

HEDDA: Yes, right after you'd left.

TESMAN: And he said he'd torn up the manuscript? Did he really say that?

HEDDA: Yes. So he claimed.

TESMAN: But dear God — in that case he really must have been out of his mind! So I assume you didn't give it to him either, hm, Hedda?

HEDDA: No. He didn't get it.

TESMAN: But you told him we had it, of course?

HEDDA: No. (*Quickly.*) Did you tell Mrs. Elvsted?

TESMAN: No, I didn't want to. But you ought to have told him, Hedda. Just think — what if he does something rash — something to hurt himself! Give me the manuscript, Hedda! I want to rush down to him with it right this minute. Where is it?

HEDDA (*cold, motionless, one arm resting on the chair*): I haven't got it any more.

TESMAN: You haven't got it! What do you mean by that?

HEDDA: I burned it — the whole thing.

TESMAN (*jumps up*): Burned it! Burned Eilert's book!

HEDDA: Don't shout. The maid might hear you.

TESMAN: Burned it? But good God — no, no, no — ! This can't be — !

HEDDA: It is, all the same.

TESMAN: But do you realize what you've done, Hedda? It's illegal! Willful destruction of lost property! You just ask Judge Brack! He'll tell you!

HEDDA: You'd better not talk about this to anyone — the Judge or anybody else.

TESMAN: But how could you do a thing like that! I never heard anything like it! What came over you? What can possibly have been going on in your head? Answer me! Hm?

HEDDA (*suppresses an almost imperceptible smile*): I did it for your sake, Jørgen.

TESMAN: For my sake!

HEDDA: When you came back this morning and told me he had read aloud to you —

TESMAN: Yes, yes! What then?

HEDDA: You admitted you were jealous of him for having written such a book.

TESMAN: But good gracious — ! I didn't mean it as seriously as all that!

HEDDA: All the same. I couldn't stand the thought that somebody else was to overshadow you.

TESMAN (*in an outburst of mingled doubt and joy*): Hedda — oh Hedda! Is it true what you're saying! But — but — but — I never knew you loved me like that! Just think!

HEDDA: In that case, I might as well tell you — that — just at this time — (*Breaks off, vehemently.*) No, no! You can ask Aunt Julle. She'll tell you.

TESMAN: I almost think I know what you mean, Hedda! (*Claps his hands.*) For goodness sake! Can that really be so! Hm?

HEDDA: Don't shout so! The maid can hear you.

TESMAN (*laughing with exuberant joy*): The maid! Well, if you don't take the prize, Hedda! The maid — but that's Berte! I'm going to tell Berte myself this very minute!

HEDDA (*her hands clenched in despair*): Oh I'll die — I'll die, in all this!

TESMAN: In what, Hedda? Hm?

HEDDA (*cold and composed*): In all this — ludicrousness, Jørgen.

TESMAN: Ludicrous? That I'm so happy? Still — maybe I oughtn't to tell Berte, after all.

HEDDA: Oh, go ahead. What difference does it make?

TESMAN: No, not yet. But on my word — Aunt Julle must be told. And that you've started to call me "Jørgen," too! Just think! She'll be ever so happy — Aunt Julle will!

HEDDA: Even when you tell her that I have burned Eilert Løvborg's papers?

TESMAN: No, oh no! That's true! That about the manuscript — nobody must know about that. But to think that you'd burn for me, Hedda — I certainly want to tell *that* to Aunt Julle! I wonder now — is that sort of thing usual with young wives, hm?

HEDDA: Why don't you ask Aunt Julle about that, too?

TESMAN: I shall — I certainly shall, when I get the chance. (*Looks uneasy and disturbed again.*) But the manuscript! Good God — I don't dare to think what this is going to do to poor Eilert!

(MRS. ELVSTED, *dressed as on her first visit, wearing hat and coat, enters, right.*)

MRS. ELVSTED (*gives a hurried greeting, is obviously upset*): Oh Hedda, you must forgive me for coming here again!

HEDDA: What has happened, Thea?

TESMAN: Something to do with Eilert Løvborg again? Hm?

MRS. ELVSTED: Yes, yes — I'm so terribly afraid something's happened to him.

HEDDA (*seizing her arm*): Ah — you think so?

TESMAN: Oh dear — why do you think that, Mrs. Elvsted?

MRS. ELVSTED: I heard them talking about him in the boarding house, just as I came in. And people are saying the most incredible things about him today.

TESMAN: Yes, imagine! I heard that, too! And I can testify that he went straight home to bed! Just think!

HEDDA: And what did they say in the boarding house?

MRS. ELVSTED: Oh, I didn't find out anything. Either they didn't know any details or — They all became silent when they saw me. And I didn't dare to ask.

TESMAN (*pacing the floor uneasily*): We'll just have to hope — to hope that you heard wrong, Mrs. Elvsted!

MRS. ELVSTED: No, no. I'm sure it was he they were talking about. And somebody said something about the hospital or —

TESMAN: The hospital — !

HEDDA: Surely, that can't be so!

MRS. ELVSTED: I got so terribly frightened! So I went up to his room and asked for him there.

HEDDA: Could you bring yourself to do that, Thea?

MRS. ELVSTED: What else could I do? For I felt I just couldn't stand the uncertainty any longer.

TESMAN: But I suppose you didn't find him in, either, did you? Hm?

MRS. ELVSTED: No. And the people there didn't know anything about him. He hadn't been home since yesterday afternoon, they said.

TESMAN: Yesterday! Just think! How could they say that!

MRS. ELVSTED: I don't know what else *to* think — something bad must have happened to him!

TESMAN: Hedda, dear — ? What if I were to walk downtown and ask around for him — ?

HEDDA: No, no — don't you go and get mixed up in all this.

(JUDGE BRACK, *hat in hand, enters through the door, right, which* BERTE *opens and closes for him. He looks serious and greets the others in silence.*)

TESMAN: So here you are, Judge, hm?

BRACK: Yes. I had to see you this evening.

TESMAN: I can see you have got Aunt Julle's message.

BRACK: That, too — yes.

TESMAN: Isn't it sad, though?

BRACK: Well, my dear Tesman — that depends on how you look at it.

TESMAN (*looks at him uncertainly*): Has something else happened?

BRACK: Yes.

HEDDA (*tense*): Something sad, Judge Brack?

BRACK: That, too, depends on how you look at it, Mrs. Tesman.

MRS. ELVSTED (*bursting out*): Oh, I'm sure it has something to do with Eilert Løvborg!

BRACK (*looks at her for a moment*): Why do you think that, Mrs. Elvsted? Maybe you already know something — ?

MRS. ELVSTED (*confused*): No, no; not at all. It's just —

TESMAN: For heaven's sake, Brack, out with it!

BRACK (*shrugging his shoulders*): Well — unfortunately, Eilert Løvborg's in the hospital. Dying.

MRS. ELVSTED (*screams*): Oh God, oh God!

TESMAN: In the hospital! And dying!

HEDDA (*without thinking*): So soon — !

MRS. ELVSTED (*wailing*): And we didn't even part as friends, Hedda!

HEDDA (*whispers*): Thea, Thea — for heaven's sake — !

MRS. ELVSTED (*paying no attention to her*): I want to see him! I want to see him alive!

BRACK: Won't do you any good, Mrs. Elvsted. Nobody can see him.

MRS. ELVSTED: Then tell me what's happened to him! What?

TESMAN: For, surely, he hasn't himself — !

HEDDA: I'm sure he has.

TESMAN: Hedda! How can you — !

BRACK (*observing her all this time*): I am sorry to say that your guess is absolutely correct, Mrs. Tesman.

MRS. ELVSTED: Oh, how awful!

TESMAN: Did it himself! Just think!

HEDDA: Shot himself!

BRACK: Right again, Mrs. Tesman.

MRS. ELVSTED (*trying to pull herself together*): When did this happen, Judge?

BRACK: This afternoon. Between three and four.

TESMAN: But dear me — where can he have done a thing like that? Hm?

BRACK (*a little uncertain*): Where? Well — I suppose in his room. I don't really know —

MRS. ELVSTED: No, it can't have been there. For I was up there sometime between six and seven.

BRACK: Well, then, some other place. I really can't say. All I know is that he was found. He had shot himself — in the chest.

MRS. ELVSTED: Oh, how horrible to think! That he was to end like that!

HEDDA (*to* BRACK): In the chest?

BRACK: Yes — as I just told you.

HEDDA: Not the temple?

BRACK: In the chest, Mrs. Tesman.

HEDDA: Well, well — the chest is a good place, too.

BRACK: How is that, Mrs. Tesman?

HEDDA (*turning him aside*): Oh — nothing.

TESMAN: And you say the wound is fatal? Hm?

BRACK: No doubt about it — absolutely fatal. He's probably dead already.

MRS. ELVSTED: Yes, yes! I feel you're right! It's over! It's all over! Oh, Hedda!

TESMAN: But tell me — how do *you* know all this?

BRACK (*tersely*): A man on the force told me. One I had some business with.

HEDDA (*loudly*): At last a deed!

TESMAN (*appalled*): Oh dear — what are you saying, Hedda!

HEDDA: I am saying there is beauty in this.

BRACK: Well, now — Mrs. Tesman —

TESMAN: Beauty — ! Just think!

MRS. ELVSTED: Oh, Hedda — how can you talk about beauty in a thing like this!

HEDDA: Eilert Løvborg has settled his account with himself. He has had the courage to do — what had to be done.

MRS. ELVSTED: But you mustn't believe it happened that way! He did it when he was not himself!

TESMAN: In despair! That's how!

HEDDA: He did not. I am certain of that.

MRS. ELVSTED: Yes he did! He was not himself! That's the way he tore up the book, too!

BRACK (*puzzled*): The book? You mean the manuscript? Has he torn it up?

MRS. ELVSTED: Yes, last night.

TESMAN (*whispers*): Oh, Hedda — we'll never get clear of all this!

BRACK: That is strange.

TESMAN (*walking the floor*): To think that this was to be the end of Eilert! Not to leave behind him anything that would have preserved his name —

MRS. ELVSTED: Oh, if only it could be put together again!

TESMAN: Yes, if only it could. I don't know what I wouldn't give —

MRS. ELVSTED: Maybe it can, Mr. Tesman.

TESMAN: What do you mean?

MRS. ELVSTED (*searching her dress pocket*): Look. I have kept these little slips he dictated from.

HEDDA (*a step closer*): Ah — !

TESMAN: You've kept them, Mrs. Elvsted? Hm?

MRS. ELVSTED: Yes. Here they are. I took them with me when I left. And I've had them in my pocket ever since —

TESMAN: Please, let me see —

MRS. ELVSTED (*gives him a pile of small paper slips*): But it's such a mess. Without any kind of system or order — !

TESMAN: But just think if we could make sense out of them, all the same! Perhaps if we helped each other —

MRS. ELVSTED: Oh yes! Let's try, anyway!

TESMAN: It will work! It *has* to work! I'll stake my whole life on this!

HEDDA: You, Jørgen? Your life?

TESMAN: Yes, or at any rate all the time I can set aside. My own collections can wait. Hedda, you understand — don't you? Hm? This is something I owe Eilert's memory.

HEDDA: Maybe so.

TESMAN: And now, my dear Mrs. Elvsted, we want to get to work. Good heavens, there's no point brooding over what's happened. Hm? We'll just have to acquire sufficient peace of mind to —

MRS. ELVSTED: All right, Mr. Tesman. I'll try to do my best.

TESMAN: Very well, then. Come over here. Let's look at these slips right away. Where can we sit? Here? No, it's better in the other room. If you'll excuse us, Judge! Come along, Mrs. Elvsted.

MRS. ELVSTED: Oh dear God — if only it were possible — !

(TESMAN *and* MRS. ELVSTED *go into the inner room. She takes off her hat and coat. Both sit down at the table under the hanging lamp and absorb themselves in the slips.* HEDDA *walks over toward the stove and sits down in the easy chair. After a while,* BRACK *walks over to her.*)

HEDDA (*in a low voice*): Ah, Judge — what a liberation there is in this thing with Eilert Løvborg!

BRACK: Liberation, Mrs. Tesman? Well, yes, for him perhaps one may say there was liberation of a kind —

HEDDA: I mean for me. There is liberation in knowing that there is such a thing in the world as an act of free courage. Something which becomes beautiful by its very nature.

BRACK (*smiles*): Well — dear Mrs. Tesman —

HEDDA: Oh I know what you're going to say! For you see — you really are a kind of specialist, too!

BRACK (*looks at her fixedly*): Eilert Løvborg has meant more to you than perhaps you're willing to admit, even to yourself. Or am I wrong?

HEDDA: I won't answer such questions. All I know is that Eilert Løvborg had the courage to live his own life. And then now — this — magnificence! The beauty of it! Having the strength and the will to get up and leave life's feast — so early —

BRACK: Believe me, Mrs. Tesman, this pains me, but I see it is necessary that I destroy a pretty illusion —

HEDDA: An illusion?

BRACK: Which could not have been maintained for very long, anyway.

HEDDA: And what is that?

BRACK: He didn't shoot himself — of his own free will.

HEDDA: Not of his own — !

BRACK: No. To tell the truth, the circumstances of Eilert Løvborg's death aren't exactly what I said they were.

HEDDA (*tense*): You've held something back? What?

BRACK: For the sake of poor Mrs. Elvsted I used a few euphemisms.

HEDDA: What?

BRACK: First — he is already dead.

HEDDA: In the hospital.

BRACK: Yes. And without regaining consciousness.

HEDDA: What else haven't you told?

BRACK: That fact that it didn't happen in his room.

HEDDA: Well, does that really make much difference?

BRACK: Some. You see — Eilert Løvborg was found shot in Miss Diana's bedroom.

HEDDA (*is about to jump up, but sinks back*): That's impossible, Judge Brack! He can't have been there again today!

BRACK: He was there this afternoon. He came to claim something he said they had taken from him. Spoke some gibberish about a lost child —

HEDDA: So that's why — !

BRACK: I thought maybe he meant his manuscript. But now I hear he has destroyed that himself. So I suppose it must have been something else.

HEDDA: I suppose. So it was there — so they found him there?

BRACK: Yes. With a fired gun in his pocket. Mortally wounded.

HEDDA: Yes — in the chest.

BRACK: No — in the guts.

HEDDA (*looks at him with an expression of disgust*): That, too! What is this curse that turns everything I touch into something ludicrous and low!

BRACK: There is something else, Mrs. Tesman. Something I'd call — nasty.

HEDDA: And what is that?

BRACK: The gun they found —

HEDDA (*breathless*): What about it?

BRACK: He must have stolen it.

HEDDA (*jumps up*): Stolen! That's not true! He didn't!

BRACK: Anything else is impossible. He *must* have stolen it. — Shhh!

(TESMAN *and* MRS. ELVSTED *have risen from the table and come forward into the front room.*)

TESMAN (*with papers in both hands*): D'you know, Hedda — you can hardly see in there with that lamp! Just think!

HEDDA: I am thinking.

TESMAN: I wonder if you'd let us use your desk, hm?

HEDDA: Certainly, if you like. (*Adds quickly.*) Wait a minute, though! Let me clear it off a bit first.

TESMAN: Ah, there's no need for that, Hedda. There's plenty of room.

HEDDA: No, no. I want to straighten it up. I'll carry all this in here. I'll put it on top of the piano for the time being.

(*She has pulled an object, covered by note paper, out of the bookcase. She puts several other sheets of paper on top of it and carries the whole pile into the left part of the inner room.* TESMAN *puts the papers down on the desk and moves the lamp from the corner table over to the desk. He and* MRS. ELVSTED *sit down and resume their work.* HEDDA *returns.*)

HEDDA (*behind* MRS. ELVSTED'S *chair, softly ruffling her hair*): Well, little Thea — how is Eilert Løvborg's memorial coming along?

MRS. ELVSTED (*looks up at her, discouraged*): Oh God — I'm sure it's going to be terribly hard to make anything out of all this.

TESMAN: But we have to. We just don't have a choice. And putting other people's papers in order — that's just the thing for me.

(HEDDA *walks over to the stove and sits down on one of the ottomans.* BRACK *stands over her, leaning on the easy chair.*)

HEDDA (*whispers*): What were you saying about the gun?

BRACK (*also softly*): That he must have stolen it.

HEDDA: Why, necessarily?

BRACK: Because any other explanation ought to be out of the question, Mrs. Tesman.

HEDDA: Oh?

BRACK (*looks at her for a moment*): Eilert Løvborg was here this morning, of course. Isn't that so?

HEDDA: Yes.

BRACK: Were you alone with him?

HEDDA: Yes, for a while.

BRACK: You didn't leave the room while he was here?

HEDDA: No.

BRACK: Think. Not at all? Not even for a moment?

HEDDA: Well — maybe just for a moment — out in the hall.

BRACK: And where was the gun case?

HEDDA: In the —

BRACK: Mrs. Tesman?

HEDDA: On the desk.

BRACK: Have you looked to see if both guns are still there?

HEDDA: No.

BRACK: You needn't bother. I saw the gun they found on Løvborg, and I knew it immediately. From yesterday — and from earlier occasions, too.

HEDDA: Perhaps you have it?

BRACK: No, the police do.

HEDDA: What are the police going to do with it?

BRACK: Try to find the owner.

HEDDA: Do you think they will?

BRACK (*leans over her, whispers*): No, Hedda Gabler — not as long as I keep quiet.

HEDDA (*with a hunted look*): And if you don't?

BRACK (*shrugs his shoulders*): Of course, there's always the chance that the gun was stolen.

HEDDA (*firmly*): Rather die!

BRACK (*smiles*): People *say* things like that. They don't *do* them.

HEDDA (*without answering*): And if the gun was not stolen — and if they find the owner — then what happens?

BRACK: Well, Hedda — then comes the scandal!

HEDDA: The scandal!

BRACK: Yes — the scandal. That you are so afraid of. You will of course be required to testify. Both you and Miss Diana. Obviously, she'll have to explain how the whole thing happened. Whether it was accident or homicide. Did he try to pull the gun out of his pocket to threaten her? And did it fire accidentally? Or did she grab the gun away from him, shoot him, and put it back in his pocket? She might just possibly have done that. She's a pretty tough girl — Miss Diana.

HEDDA: But this whole disgusting mess has nothing to do with me.

BRACK: Quite so. But you'll have to answer the question: Why did you give Eilert Løvborg the gun? And what inferences will be drawn from the fact that you did?

HEDDA (*lowers her head*): That's true. I hadn't thought of that.

BRACK: Well — luckily, there's nothing to worry about as long as I don't say anything.

HEDDA (*looks up at him*): So then I'm in your power, Judge. From now on you can do anything you like with me.

BRACK (*in an even softer whisper*): Dearest Hedda — believe me, I'll not misuse my position.

HEDDA: In your power, all the same. Dependent on your will. Servant to your demands. Not free. Not free! (*Rises suddenly.*) No — I can't stand that thought! Never!

BRACK (*looks at her, half mockingly*): Most people submit to the inevitable.

HEDDA (*returning his glance*): Perhaps. (*Walks over to the desk. Sup-*

presses a smile and mimics TESMAN'S *way of speaking.*) Well? Do you think you can do it, Jørgen? Hm?

TESMAN: Lord knows, Hedda. Anyway, I can already see it will take months.

HEDDA (*still mimicking*): Just think! (*Runs her hands lightly through* MRS. ELVSTED'S *hair.*) Doesn't this seem strange to you, Thea? Sitting here with Tesman — just the way you used to with Eilert Løvborg?

MRS. ELVSTED: Oh dear — if only I could inspire your husband, too!

HEDDA: Oh, I'm sure that will come — in time.

TESMAN: Well, yes — do you know, Hedda? I really think I begin to feel something of the kind. But why don't you go and talk to the Judge again.

HEDDA: Isn't there anything you two can use me for?

TESMAN: No, not a thing, dear. (*Turns around.*) From now on, you must be good enough to keep Hedda company, my dear Judge!

BRACK (*glancing at* HEDDA): I'll be only too delighted.

HEDDA: Thank you. But I'm tired tonight. I think I'll go and lie down for a while.

TESMAN: Yes, you do that, dear; why don't you? Hm?

(HEDDA *goes into the inner room, closes the portieres behind her. Brief pause. Suddenly, she is heard playing a frenzied dance tune on the piano.*)

MRS. ELVSTED (*jumps up*): Oh God! What's that!

TESMAN (*running to the doorway*): But dearest Hedda — you mustn't play dance music tonight, for goodness' sake! Think of Aunt Rina! And Eilert, too!

HEDDA (*peeks in from between the portieres*): And Aunt Julle. And everybody. I'll be quiet. (*She pulls the portieres shut again.*)

TESMAN (*back at the desk*): I don't think it's good for her to see us at such a melancholy task. I'll tell you what, Mrs. Elvsted. You move in with Aunt Julle, and then I'll come over in the evenings. Then we can sit and work over there. Hm?

MRS. ELVSTED: Maybe that would be better —

HEDDA (*from the inner room*): I hear every word you're saying, Tesman. And how am I going to spend my evenings?

TESMAN (*busy with the papers*): Oh, I'm sure Judge Brack will be good enough to come out and see you, anyway.

BRACK (*in the easy chair, calls out gaily*): Every single night, as far as I'm concerned, Mrs. Tesman! I'm sure we're going to have a lovely time, you and I!

HEDDA (*loud and clear*): Yes, don't you think that would be nice, Judge Brack? You — sole cock-o'-the walk —

(*A shot is heard from the inner room.* TESMAN, MRS. ELVSTED, *and* JUDGE BRACK *all jump up.*)

TESMAN: There she is, fooling with those guns again.

(*He pulls the portieres apart and runs inside.* MRS. ELVSTED *also.* HEDDA, *lifeless, is lying on the sofa. Cries and confusion.* BERTE, *flustered, enters, right.*)

TESMAN (*shouts to* BRACK): She's shot herself! In the temple! Just think!

BRACK (*half stunned in the easy chair*): But, merciful God — ! One just doesn't *do* that!

DURING THE second half of his playwriting career Ibsen produced plays almost exactly on a two-year schedule and by the daily work habits of a punctilious clerk. The genius that revolutionized the nineteenth-century theater apparently worked best by the discipline of both clock and calendar.

After the completion of one play his mind lay fallow for a year, slowly generating new motifs. Actual work on a new play began with note-taking and sketching of character descriptions and fragments of dialogue. The writing itself took only a few months of summer and fall. The last month or so Ibsen revised his first draft, rarely altering basics in theme or plot but often adding telling details of imagery and characterization. In *Hedda Gabler* Tesman's fussy "just think"s and "hm?"s, the slipper episode in Act I, Hedda's phrase "vine leaves in the hair," and the many references to her and Thea Elvsted's hair, were all added during revision. The second draft, executed in a meticulous hand, was sent off to the printer in Copenhagen, to be published in time for the Christmas trade. In addition to being a bit of a philistine and pedant Ibsen was also an excellent businessman.

The genesis of *Hedda Gabler* followed this general scheme. The play was written between July–August and November, 1890, published on December 16, and first performed (in Munich) on January 31, 1891.

It was not an unqualified success. By 1890, both critical and popular consensus had decided that Ibsen was a problem playwright of implicit social and moral reform. One walked away from his plays disturbed or even possibly irritated and scandalized, but salutarily provoked to serious thought about oneself and one's society, one's moral sensitivity alerted and refined. With this preconception it was a little difficult to know exactly what one was supposed to make of this story of "a pointless suicide ending a useless life," as one critic summed it up. Here was no obvious problem — beyond, possibly, that of what the bourgeois housewife is to do with her time — no moral, not even a provocative slogan like *Rosmersholm*'s "joyous guiltlessness" and *The Lady of the Sea*'s "freedom with responsibility." There was only a Bacchic image, mystifying and a little lost in the contemporary drawing room. To observe that Brack's final speech was Ibsen's retort to critics who had presumed to find certain of his earlier plays implausible — "One just doesn't *do* that!" — was clever, but it clearly did not account for the *play*. Interpretation would have to come to grips with Hedda herself.

Is she a sardonic sequel to Nora in *A Doll's House*, a twisted product of wifely emancipation, the caged pet turned beast of the jungle? Does she, like Oswald in *Ghosts*, belong to Ibsen's "huge family of victims of bourgeois morality," her *joie de vivre* perverted by conventional hypocrisy to cowardly spite, her passions to prurient curiosity? Is she the eternal female incarnate, "splendidly immoral"? Is the play an allegory on woman's nature, with Hedda, Thea, Aunt Julle, and Miss Diana representing, respectively, woman's Will, Soul, Heart, and Body? Is it "pure psychological drama," a study in frigidity and irrational obsession, a portrait of an abnormal lady? And as such, is it, as Chekhov suggested, shallow melodrama, because the much deeper real-life tragedy is that a Hedda Gabler does *not* shoot herself? And does Hedda herself, whatever her larger significance, come across the footlights as a believable human being? Gerhard Gran, a contemporary Norwegian critic, did not think so:

> My imagination cannot grasp her as . . . one, single, integrated person. She falls apart in contradictions, and I don't find the common denominator. . . . When I think of her now, a few weeks after reading the play, I think of a rather odd woman, who astonished me with her strange behavior, who excited my curiosity without capturing my interest.

The critical difficulty is not to separate valid from invalid in this welter of views, but to apprehend their several truths as something other than an amorphous aggregate of opinion. The difficulty is compounded by our tendency to make the play coextensive with the title character. This probably underlies Gran's bewilderment. It has made of the play a wonderful, if sometimes rather showy, vehicle for great actresses, and it has helped to conceal such glaring dramatic flaws as the pretentiously demoniac doom of the Byronic Løvborg, unconvincing alike as genius of sociology and as conqueror of women, and the air of strain and contrivance that surrounds the checkered fortune of his manuscript (including Ibsen's amusing concept of scholarship as a pocket full of notes). But it has also isolated Hedda from her dramatic context. She has become a case history. Critics ask how she became what she has become and ignore what happens in the play.

This is not to deny that Hedda is both a fascinating and a consummate psychological portrait or that she represents a type of general validity, and of validity perhaps more urgent today than in the 1890's. But it is to insist that Hedda, as individual and type, emerges from the traffic on the stage and is not a preconceived postulate of psychology, exhibited, for greater vividness, in her natural habitat. In her, Ibsen prefigured a psyche felt to be peculiarly modern: the atomized self, the alienated identity. He anticipated a major theme — *the* major theme? — of contemporary drama. But whereas the expressionists and the semi-surrealistic absurdists put the fragments of the broken personality on stage as separate characters, scenically objectifying the soul's war with itself, somewhat in the manner of the medieval morality play, Ibsen achieved the same end within the limiting realist conventions of stage illusion and plot coherence — given the theme, a far more difficult achievement. Hedda's case is that of the modern existentialist anti-hero who witnesses his own dereliction and disintegration in a meaningless world made boring by overstimulation and violent with inarticulateness. As relativist skeptics of absolutes and formulas we are less likely than some of the positivist critics of the '90's or the Freudians and the social conscience school of the 1920's and '30's to consider *Hedda Gabler* a failure because Hedda herself is a riddle the solution to which Ibsen failed to embody in his play. We respond to the play to the extent to which we can sense Hedda as a stage presence, a kind of modern Medea, but the force of that presence is a function of the pervasive patterns of ironies, of images of words and actions, of juxtapositions of moral values and of moments of farce, melodrama, and tragedy, in which it exists.

Hedda's fatal crisis plays itself out in a sequence of calls. Visiting as recurrent stage event not only establishes the upper-class milieu that has shaped her personality and causes the middle-class manners of Tesman and Aunt Julle to set her teeth on edge. It also serves as plausible pretext for keeping several people coming and going within a single setting and ironically emphasizes Hedda's position as hostess "at home." The other characters come and go, active beyond the September smell of mortality in the late Mrs. Falk's rooms. They are rooms that never turn into a home for Hedda. She is trapped in the drawing room she seems to dominate. Early in Act I Aunt Julle and Berte evoke for us a picture of Hedda on horseback. The contrast between the aristocratic girl rider's free and graceful movements and her present situation as bored and restless passenger on a train endlessly journeying through middle-class domesticity lends pathos to the somewhat obvious point of the title: that she is her father's daughter rather than her husband's wife.

Three kinds of people move in and out of her enclosed existence, each associated with a different realm of values. There is Brack's world of elegant sophistication, a world of wit, grace, social form, and ruthless libertinism. There is the decent and cozy world of the aunts, its virtues genuine though tame, its narrow horizons stable, its kindly concerns trivial. Tesman, bookful blockhead, well-meaning and slippered, is its characteristic product. And there is the triply oriented world of Løvborg, part brilliant intellectual vistas (though Ibsen never lets us share them), part manly rehabilitation under the influence of a good woman, part debauch with demimondaines. Hedda is in the middle of the triangle, homeless in her new home, dislocated, in search of an identity fragmentized by the pressures — for propriety, for marriage — which imparted attitudes have exerted on her Dionysiac personality. Identityless, she is in the grip of impulses she neither comprehends nor controls. Seeking to live vicariously through Løvborg, she succeeds only in killing both him and herself. Her mania for manipulating men's lives — and Tesman in politics is even more grotesque than Løvborg with vine leaves in his hair — is a symptom of her inner emptiness. By birth and background she belongs to Brack, by temperament and her own half-understood ideology to Løvborg, by matrimony to Tesman. The split corrupts her. In tense boredom she can only define herself by fierce devotion to manners and prudence. She substitutes convention for morality. She refuses to have her legs looked at but calmly contemplates a discreet affair. She excites passionate men and ends up married to an old maid. Life's primary realities, sex, pregnancy, birth, and death, are all hateful to her. Her two decisive actions in the play both entail infanticide, one symbolic, the other real. Her erotic frustration precedes her marriage. Two of the three or four glimpses we get of her past show her in destructive poses: the schoolgirl on a staircase threatening to burn off her friend's beautiful hair, the affronted young lady threatening her overeager lover with a gun. It is one of the play's many ironic paradoxes that Thea, a life force of pure femininity (the contrasting symbolic values that attach to her and Hedda's hair are relevant in this connection), whose emblem is a little child, is literally childless, whereas Hedda, deadly as her pistols, is pregnant. That "lively" is Hedda's favorite adjective is another.

As in just about every one of Ibsen's plays of social realism the action is set in motion by an arrival/return, here the newlywed Tesmans' and Mrs. Elvsted's and Løvborg's. The past returning explosively in the present is the core action in Ibsen's dramas, evidence, perhaps, both that he shared the century's sense of causality and continuum in human affairs and that he rejected its prevailing belief in progress. Acts I and II take place in the morning and evening, respectively, of one day; Acts III and IV repeat the same pattern for the following day. But although the morning of Act III is earlier than that of Act I and the evening of Act IV later than that of Act II, the last two acts taken together are shorter than the first two. It is as if the tempo of Hedda's life accelerates after the sunny hush of the opening through scenes of more and more hectic social activity to the final gunshot. She is adrift on a river rushing toward its deadly rapids.

Consider another example of Ibsen's use of patterned action as vehicle for crucial meanings. In the beginning of Act IV Aunt Julle reports the death of the invalid Aunt Rina to Hedda. The occasion, as she says, represents a visit from the house of death to the house of life. But at the end of the act the contrast has been reversed. Thea will move into Aunt Rina's room, and there she and Tesman will resurrect her "child," whereas Hedda's suicide means that the empty rooms in the Tesman villa will not become nurseries. With their larger ramifications Aunt Rina's and Hedda's deaths, flanking Act IV, not only juxtapose two kinds of paralysis, one physical and one emotional, they also suggest the central moral polarity in the play: between the virtuous and unselfish world of the aunts, to which Berte already belongs, Thea naturally moves, and the erring Tesman at the end returns, and the negative world of the selfish hedonists, Hedda, Brack, and Løvborg.

If the play is thought of as dramatic pattern rather than as a polemic against the prudish upbringing of young Victorian ladies or a study in psychopathology, we see Hedda also as the main participant in a sequence of interlocking rivalries that maintains tension throughout the play and is an action–image of the flux and disharmony that characterize its social climate. Hedda and Thea are rivals for Løvborg already in Act I. Brack considers Løvborg a threat to his own hoped-for liaison with Hedda. There is talk of a competition for a professorship between Tesman and Løvborg. Although Tesman does not know it both his friends threaten his domestic felicity. At the end Thea and Hedda are once again rivals for the same man — Tesman, this time.

Their rivalry frames the entire action and is its ironic center. Hedda takes Løvborg away from Thea, but the sordid manner of his death nullifies her triumph. Upon this flawed success follows unmitigated defeat, as Hedda's husband, by virtue of the very quality she finds most ludicrous in him, his indefatigable scholarship, is about to become the second father of Thea's book-child with Løvborg. That Hedda does not love Tesman and therefore hardly takes his and Thea's intimacy much to heart is immaterial in this connection; it is the pattern that counts, the pattern manifest in Hedda's question, "Isn't there anything you two can use me for?" and Tesman's answer, "No, not a thing, dear." It spells Thea's double triumph: as "mother" and as inspiring soul mate. Cleverer than her rival, Hedda yet loses to her on all fronts. The would-be liberator is herself caught. Realizing her defeat she disappears into the back room where the General's portrait hangs like an altarpiece over the sofa on which she is about to perform, in self-immolation, the deed of beauty and courage of which Løvborg has cheated her. She veils the sanctum from the sight of the others, plays out her frustrated love of life and freedom in one, last, wild burst of dance music, promises to be quiet — and fires her gun. If she is not allowed to break the decorous quiet by playing she can do so by dying.

In another way, also, the suicide scene gathers up the entire play in its imagery. Hedda escapes both Brack and scandal by doing exactly what Brack, with his "specialist's" assurance, had assumed "people don't do." The phrase haunts the play. Hedda herself uses it twice: once, apropos of Aunt Julle's hapless hat on the drawing-room chair, a second time apropos of the girl-with-the-gun from Løvborg's past. Thus, verbal echoes associate Hedda's death with two other, mutually contrasting, kinds of unconventionality: Aunt Julle's (actually Tesman's) gaucheries, and Miss Diana's (actually Hedda's own) erotic flamboyance. The curtain drops on a comical–grisly tableau, on the death of a neurotic woman, but also on the defeat of the social expertise, the moral evil, and the unscrupulous use of a constrictive convention, which Hedda, her impossible dream intact, frustrates by dying.

Miss Diana never appears on stage. Is it — also — because she represents the suppressed part of Hedda's psyche, the vital component in the complete and fulfilled woman she might have become in another kind of society? Their plot connection, at any rate, takes on mythological resonance. Hedda shares with Miss Diana the role of Løvborg's *femme fatale*. She, too, once leveled one of General Gabler's guns at him, and in his death society lady and "tough girl," frigid wife and bohemian mistress, merge in the figure of the changeable goddess of the moon, fiercely and fatally asserting her virginally inviolate nature.

August Strindberg

MISS JULIE

Translated by Elizabeth Sprigge

Characters

MISS JULIE, *aged 25*
JEAN, *the valet, aged 30*
KRISTIN, *the cook, aged 35*

SCENE: *The large kitchen of a Swedish manor house in a country district in the eighties. Midsummer Eve. The kitchen has three doors, two small ones into* JEAN'S *and* KRISTIN'S *bedrooms, and a large, glass-fronted double one, opening on to a courtyard. This is the only way to the rest of the house. Through these glass doors can be seen part of a fountain with a cupid, lilac bushes in flower and the tops of some Lombardy poplars. On one wall are shelves edged with scalloped paper on which are kitchen utensils of copper, iron and tin. To the left is the corner of a large tiled range and part of its chimney-hood, to the right the end of the servants' dinner table with chairs beside it. The stove is decorated with birch boughs, the floor strewn with twigs of juniper. On the end of the table is a large Japanese spice jar full of lilac. There are also an ice-box, a scullery table and a sink. Above the double door hangs a big old-fashioned bell; near it is a speaking-tube.*

A fiddle can be heard from the dance in the barn near-by.

KRISTIN *is standing at the stove, frying something in a pan. She wears a light-coloured cotton dress and a big apron.*

JEAN *enters, wearing livery and carrying a pair of large riding-boots with spurs, which he puts in a conspicuous place.*

JEAN: Miss Julie's crazy again to-night, absolutely crazy.

KRISTIN: Oh, so you're back, are you?

JEAN: When I'd taken the Count to the station, I came back and dropped in at the Barn for a dance. And who did I see there but our young lady leading off with the gamekeeper. But the moment she sets eyes on me, up she rushes and invites me to waltz with her. And how she waltzed — I've never seen anything like it! She's crazy.

KRISTIN: Always has been, but never so bad as this last fortnight since the engagement was broken off.

JEAN: Yes, that was a pretty business, to be sure. He's a decent enough chap, too, even if he isn't rich. Oh, but they're choosy! (*Sits down at the end of the table.*) In any case, it's a bit odd that our young — er — lady would rather stay at home with the yokels than go with her father to visit her relations.

KRISTIN: Perhaps she feels a bit awkward, after that bust-up with her fiancé.

JEAN: Maybe. That chap had some guts, though. Do you know the sort of thing that was going on, Kristin? I saw it with my own eyes, though I didn't let on I had.

KRISTIN: You saw them . . . ?

JEAN: Didn't I just! Came across the pair of them one evening in the stable-yard. Miss Julie was doing what she called "training" him. Know what that was? Making him jump over her riding-whip — the way you teach a dog. He did it twice and got a cut each time for his pains, but when it came to the third go, he snatched the whip out of her hand and broke it into smithereens. And then he cleared off.

KRISTIN: What goings on! I never did!

JEAN: Well, that's how it was with that little affair . . . Now, what have you got for me, Kristin? Something tasty?

KRISTIN (*serving from the pan to his plate*): Well, it's just a little bit of kidney I cut off their joint.

JEAN (*smelling it*): Fine! That's my special delice. (*Feels the plate.*) But you might have warmed the plate.

KRISTIN: When you choose to be finicky you're worse than the Count himself. (*Pulls his hair affectionately.*)

JEAN (*crossly*): Stop pulling my hair. You know how sensitive I am.

KRISTIN: There, there! It's only love, you know.

(JEAN *eats.* KRISTIN *brings a bottle of beer.*)

JEAN: Beer on Midsummer Eve? No thanks! I've got something better than that. (*From a drawer in the table brings out a bottle of red wine with a yellow seal.*) Yellow seal, see! Now get me a glass. You use a glass with a stem of course when you're drinking it straight.

KRISTIN (*giving him a wine-glass*): Lord help the woman who gets you for a husband, you old fusser! (*She puts the beer in the ice-box and sets a small saucepan on the stove.*)

JEAN: Nonsense! You'll be glad enough to get a fellow as smart as me. And I don't think it's done you any harm people calling me your fiancé. (*Tastes the wine.*) Good. Very good indeed. But not quite warmed enough. (*Warms the glass in his hand.*) We bought this in Dijon. Four francs the litre without the bottle, and duty on top of that. What are you cooking now? It stinks.

KRISTIN: Some bloody muck Miss Julie wants for Diana.

JEAN: You should be more refined in your speech, Kristin. But why should you spend a holiday cooking for that bitch? Is she sick or what?

KRISTIN: Yes, she's sick. She sneaked out with the pug at the lodge and got in the usual mess. And that, you know, Miss Julie won't have.

JEAN: Miss Julie's too high-and-mighty in some respects, and not enough in others, just like her mother before her. The Countess was more at home in the kitchen and cowsheds than anywhere else, but would she ever go driving with only one horse? She went round with her cuffs filthy, but she had to have the coronet on the cuff-links. Our young lady — to come back to her — hasn't any proper respect for herself or her position. I mean she isn't refined. In the Barn just now she dragged the gamekeeper away from Anna and made him dance with her — no waiting to be asked. We wouldn't do a thing like that. But that's what happens when the gentry try to behave like the common people — they become common . . . Still she's a fine girl. Smashing! What shoulders! And what — er — etcetera!

KRISTIN: Oh come off it! I know what Clara says, and she dresses her.

JEAN: Clara? Pooh, you're all jealous! But I've been out riding with her . . . and as for her dancing!

KRISTIN: Listen, Jean. You will dance with me, won't you, as soon as I'm through?

JEAN: Of course I will.

KRISTIN: Promise?

JEAN: Promise? When I say I'll do a thing I do it. Well, thanks for the supper. It was a real treat. (*Corks the bottle.* JULIE *appears in the doorway, speaking to someone outside.*)

JULIE: I'll be back in a moment. Don't wait. (JEAN *slips the bottle into the drawer and rises respectfully.* JULIE *enters and joins* KRISTIN *at the stove.*) Well, have you made it? (KRISTIN *signs that* JEAN *is near them.*)

JEAN (*gallantly*): Have you ladies got some secret?

JULIE (*flipping his face with her handkerchief*): You're very inquisitive.

JEAN: What a delicious smell! Violets.

JULIE (*coquettishly*): Impertinence! Are you an expert of scent too? I must say you know how to dance. Now don't look. Go away. (*The music of a schottische begins.*)

JEAN (*with impudent politeness*): Is it some witches' brew you're cooking on Midsummer Eve? Something to tell your stars by, so you can see your future?

JULIE (*sharply*): If you could see that you'd have good eyes. (*To* KRISTIN.) Put it in a bottle and cork it tight. Come and dance this schottische with me, Jean.

JEAN (*hesitating*): I don't want to be rude, but I've promised to dance this one with Kristin.

JULIE: Well, she can have another, can't you, Kristin? You'll lend me Jean, won't you?

KRISTIN (*bottling*): It's nothing to do with me. When you're so condescending, Miss, it's not his place to say no. Go on, Jean, and thank Miss Julie for the honour.

JEAN: Frankly speaking, Miss, and no offence meant, I wonder if it's wise for you to dance twice running with the same partner, specially as those people are so ready to jump to conclusions.

JULIE (*flaring up*): What did you say? What sort of conclusions? What do you mean?

JEAN (*meekly*): As you choose not to understand, Miss Julie, I'll have to speak more plainly. It looks bad to show a preference for one of your retainers when they're all hoping for the same unusual favour.

JULIE: Show a preference! The very idea! I'm surprised at you. I'm doing the people an honour by attending their ball when I'm mistress of the house, but if I'm really going to dance, I mean to have a partner who can lead and doesn't make me look ridiculous.

JEAN: If those are your orders, Miss, I'm at your service.

JULIE (*gently*): Don't take it as an order. To-night we're all just people enjoying a party. There's no question of class. So now give me your arm. Don't worry, Kristin. I shan't steal your sweetheart.

(JEAN *gives* JULIE *his arm and leads her out. Left alone,* KRISTIN *plays her scene in an unhurried, natural way, humming to the tune of the schottische, played on a distant violin. She clears* JEAN'S *place, washes up and puts things away, then takes off her apron, brings out a small mirror from a drawer, props it against the jar of lilac, lights a candle, warms a small pair of tongs and curls her fringe. She goes to the door and listens, then turning back to the table finds* MISS JULIE's *forgotten handkerchief. She smells it, then meditatively smooths it out and folds it. Enter* JEAN.)

JEAN: She really *is* crazy. What a way to dance! With people standing grinning at her too from behind the doors. What's got into her, Kristin?

KRISTIN: Oh, it's just her time coming on. She's always queer then. Are you going to dance with me now?

JEAN: Then you're not wild with me for cutting that one.

KRISTIN: You know I'm not — for a little thing like that. Besides, I know my place.

JEAN (*putting his arm round her waist*): You're a sensible girl, Kristin, and you'll make a very good wife . . .

(*Enter* JULIE, *unpleasantly surprised.*)

JULIE (*with forced gaiety*): You're a fine beau — running away from your partner.

JEAN: Not away, Miss Julie, but as you see back to the one I deserted.

JULIE (*changing her tone*): You really can dance, you know. But why are you wearing your livery on a holiday. Take it off at once.

JEAN: Then I must ask you to go away for a moment, Miss. My black coat's here. (*Indicates it hanging on the door to his room.*)

JULIE: Are you so shy of me — just over changing a coat? Go into your room then — or stay here and I'll turn my back.

JEAN: Excuse me then, Miss. (*He goes to his room and is partly visible as he changes his coat.*)

JULIE: Tell me, Kristin, is Jean your fiancé? You seem very intimate.

KRISTIN: My fiancé? Yes, if you like. We call it that.

JULIE: Call it?

KRISTIN: Well, you've had a fiancé yourself, Miss, and . . .

JULIE: But we really were engaged.

KRISTIN: All the same it didn't come to anything.

(JEAN *returns in his black coat.*)

JULIE: Très gentil, Monsieur Jean. Très gentil.

JEAN: Vous voulez plaisanter, Madame.

JULIE: Et vous voulez parler français. Where did you learn it?

JEAN: In Switzerland, when I was sommelier at one of the biggest hotels in Lucerne.

JULIE: You look quite the gentleman in that get-up. Charming. (*Sits at the table.*)

JEAN: Oh, you're just flattering me!

JULIE (*annoyed*): Flattering you?

JEAN: I'm too modest to believe you would pay real compliments to a man like me, so I must take it you are exaggerating — that this is what's known as flattery.

JULIE: Where on earth did you learn to make speeches like that? Perhaps you've been to the theatre a lot.

JEAN: That's right. And travelled a lot too.

JULIE: But you come from this neighbourhood, don't you?

JEAN: Yes, my father was a labourer on the next estate — the District Attorney's place. I often used to see you, Miss Julie, when you were little, though you never noticed me.

JULIE: Did you really?

JEAN: Yes. One time specially I remember . . . but I can't tell you about that.

JULIE: Oh do! Why not? This is just the time.

JEAN: No, I really can't now. Another time perhaps.

JULIE: Another time means never. What harm in now?

JEAN: No harm, but I'd rather not. (*Points to* KRISTIN, *now fast asleep.*) Look at her.

JULIE: She'll make a charming wife, won't she? I wonder if she snores.

JEAN: No, she doesn't, but she talks in her sleep.

JULIE (*cynically*): How do you know she talks in her sleep?

JEAN (*brazenly*): I've heard her. (*Pause. They look at one another.*)

JULIE: Why don't you sit down?

JEAN: I can't take such a liberty in your presence.

JULIE: Supposing I order you to.

JEAN: I'll obey.

JULIE: Then sit down. No, wait a minute. Will you get me a drink first?

JEAN: I don't know what's in the ice-box. Only beer, I expect.

JULIE: There's no only about it. My taste is so simple I prefer it to wine.

(JEAN *takes a bottle from the ice-box, fetches a glass and plate and serves the beer.*)

JEAN: At your service.

JULIE: Thank you. Won't you have some yourself?

JEAN: I'm not really a beer-drinker, but if it's an order . . .

JULIE: Order? I should have thought it was ordinary manners to keep your partner company.

JEAN: That's a good way of putting it. (*He opens another bottle and fetches a glass.*)

JULIE: Now drink my health. (*He hesitates.*) I believe the man really is shy.

(JEAN *kneels and raises his glass with mock ceremony.*)

JEAN: To the health of my lady!

JULIE: Bravo! Now kiss my shoe and everything will be perfect. (*He hesitates, then boldly takes hold of her foot and lightly kisses it.*) Splendid. You ought to have been an actor.

JEAN (*rising*): We can't go on like this, Miss Julie. Someone might come in and see us.

JULIE: Why would that matter?

JEAN: For the simple reason that they'd talk. And if you knew the way their tongues were wagging out there just now, you . . .

JULIE: What were they saying? Tell me. Sit down.

JEAN (*sitting*): No offence meant, Miss, but . . . well, their language wasn't nice, and they were hinting . . . oh, you know quite well what. You're not a child, and if a lady's seen drinking alone at night with a man — and a servant at that — then . . .

JULIE: Then what? Besides, we're not alone. Kristin's here.

JEAN: Yes, asleep.

JULIE: I'll wake her up. (*Rises.*) Kristin, are you asleep? (KRISTIN *mumbles in her sleep.*) Kristin! Goodness, how she sleeps!

KRISTIN (*in her sleep*): The Count's boots are cleaned — put the coffee on — yes, yes, at once . . . (*Mumbles incoherently.*)

JULIE (*tweaking her nose*): Wake up, can't you!

JEAN (*sharply*): Let her sleep.

JULIE: What?

JEAN: When you've been standing at the stove all day you're likely to be tired at night. And sleep should be respected.

JULIE (*changing her tone*): What a nice idea. It does you credit. Thank you for it. (*Holds out her hand to him.*) Now come out and pick some lilac for me.

(*During the following* KRISTIN *goes sleepily in to her bedroom.*)

JEAN: Out with you, Miss Julie?

JULIE: Yes.

JEAN: It wouldn't do. It really wouldn't.

JULIE: I don't know what you mean. You can't possibly imagine that . . .

JEAN: I don't, but others do.

JULIE: What? That I'm in love with the valet?

JEAN: I'm not a conceited man, but such a thing's been known to happen, and to these rustics nothing's sacred.

JULIE: You, I take it, are an aristocrat.

JEAN: Yes, I am.

JULIE: And I am coming down in the world.

JEAN: Don't come down, Miss Julie. Take my advice. No one will believe you came down of your own accord. They'll all say you fell.

JULIE: I have a higher opinion of our people than you. Come and put it to the test. Come on. (*Gazes into his eyes.*)

JEAN: You're very strange, you know.

JULIE: Perhaps I am, but so are you. For that matter everything is strange. Life, human beings, everything, just scum drifting about on the water until it sinks — down and down. That reminds me of a dream I sometimes have, in which I'm on top of a pillar and can't see any way of getting down. When I look down I'm dizzy; I have to get down but I haven't the courage to jump. I can't stay there and I long to fall, but I don't fall. There's no respite. There can't be any peace at all for me until I'm down, right down on the ground. And if I did get to the ground I'd want to be under the ground . . . Have you ever felt like that?

JEAN: No. In my dream I'm lying under a great tree in a dark wood. I want to get up, up to the top of it, and look out over the bright landscape where the sun is shining and rob that high nest of its golden eggs. And I climb and climb, but the trunk is so thick and smooth and it's so far to the first branch. But I know if I can once reach that first branch I'll go to the top just as if I'm on a ladder. I haven't reached it yet, but I shall get there, even if only in my dreams.

JULIE: Here I am chattering about dreams with you. Come on. Only into the park. (*She takes his arm and they go towards the door.*)

JEAN: We must sleep on nine midsummer flowers tonight; then our dreams will come true, Miss Julie. (*They turn at the door. He has a hand to his eye.*)

JULIE: Have you got something in your eye? Let me see.

JEAN: Oh, it's nothing. Just a speck of dust. It'll be gone in a minute.

JULIE: My sleeve must have rubbed against you. Sit down and let me see to it. (*Takes him by the arm and makes him sit down, bends his head back and tries to get the speck out with the corner of her handkerchief.*) Keep still now, quite still. (*Slaps his hand.*) Do as I tell you. Why, I believe you're trembling, big, strong man though you are! (*Feels his biceps.*) What muscles!

JEAN (*warning*): Miss Julie!

JULIE: Yes, Monsieur Jean?

JEAN: Attention. Je ne suis qu'un homme.

JULIE: Will you stay still! There now. It's out. Kiss my hand and say thank you.

JEAN (*rising*): Miss Julie, listen. Kristin's gone to bed now. Will you listen?

JULIE: Kiss my hand first.

JEAN: Very well, but you'll have only yourself to blame.

JULIE: For what?

JEAN: For what! Are you still a child at twenty-five? Don't you know it's dangerous to play with fire?

JULIE: Not for me. I'm insured.

JEAN (*bluntly*): No, you're not. And even if you are, there's still stuff here to kindle a flame.

JULIE: Meaning yourself?

JEAN: Yes. Not because I'm me, but because I'm a man and young and . . .

JULIE: And good-looking? What incredible conceit! A Don Juan perhaps? Or a Joseph? Good Lord, I do believe you are a Joseph!

JEAN: Do you?

JULIE: I'm rather afraid so.

(JEAN *goes boldly up and tries to put his arms round her and kiss her. She boxes his ears.*)

How dare you!

JEAN: Was that in earnest or a joke?

JULIE: In earnest.

JEAN: Then what went before was in earnest too. You take your games too seriously and that's dangerous. Anyhow I'm tired of playing now and beg leave to return to my work. The Count will want his boots first thing and it's past midnight now.

JULIE: Put those boots down.

JEAN: No. This is my work, which it's my duty to do. But I never undertook to be your playfellow and I never will be. I consider myself too good for that.

JULIE: You're proud.

JEAN: In some ways — not all.

JULIE: Have you ever been in love?

JEAN: We don't put it that way, but I've been gone on quite a few girls. And once I went sick because I couldn't have the one I wanted. Sick, I mean, like those princes in the Arabian Nights who couldn't eat or drink for love.

JULIE: Who was she? (*No answer.*) Who was she?

JEAN: You can't force me to tell you that.

JULIE: If I ask as an equal, ask as a — friend? Who was she?

JEAN: You.

JULIE (*sitting*): How absurd!

JEAN: Yes, ludicrous if you like. That's the story I wouldn't tell you before, see, but now I will . . . Do you know what the world looks like from below? No, you don't. No more than the hawks and falcons do whose backs one hardly ever sees because they're always soaring up aloft. I lived in a labourer's hovel with seven other children and a pig, out in the grey fields where there isn't a single tree. But from the window I could see the wall round the Count's park with apple-trees above it. That was the Garden of Eden, guarded by many terrible angels with flaming swords. All the same I and the other boys managed to get to the tree of life. Does all this make you despise me?

JULIE: Goodness, all boys steal apples!

JEAN: You say that now, but all the same you do despise me. However, one time I went into the Garden of Eden with my mother to weed the onion beds. Close to the kitchen garden there was a Turkish pavilion hung all over with jasmine and honeysuckle. I hadn't any idea what it was used for, but I'd never seen such a beautiful building. People used to go in and then come out again, and one day the door was left open. I crept up and saw the walls covered with pictures of kings and emperors, and the windows had red curtains with fringes — you know now what the place was, don't you? I . . . (*Breaks off a piece of lilac and holds it for* JULIE *to smell. As he talks, she takes it from him.*) I had never been inside the manor, never seen anything but the church, and this was more beautiful. No matter where my thoughts went, they always came back — to that place. The longing went on growing in me to enjoy it fully, just once. Enfin, I sneaked in, gazed and admired. Then I heard someone coming. There was only one way out for the gentry, but for me there was another and I had no choice but to take it. (JULIE *drops the lilac on the table.*) Then I took to my heels, plunged through the raspberry canes, dashed across the strawberry beds and found myself on the rose terrace. There I saw a pink dress and a pair of white stockings — it was you. I crawled into a weed pile and lay there right under it among prickly thistles and damp rank earth. I watched you walking among the roses and said to myself: "If it's true that a thief can get to heaven and be with the angels, it's pretty strange that a labourer's child here on God's earth mayn't come in the park and play with the Count's daughter."

JULIE (*sentimentally*): Do you think all poor children feel the way you did?

JEAN (*taken aback, then rallying*): *All* poor children? . . . Yes, of course they do. Of course.

JULIE: It must be terrible to be poor.

JEAN (*with exaggerated distress*): Oh yes, Miss Julie, yes. A dog may lie on the Countess's sofa, a horse may have his nose stroked by a young lady, but a servant . . . (*change of tone*) well, yes, now and then you meet one with guts enough to rise in the world, but how often? Anyhow, do you know what I did? Jumped in the millstream with my clothes on, was pulled out and got a hiding. But the next Sunday, when Father and all the rest went to Granny's, I managed to get left behind. Then I washed with soap and hot water, put my best clothes on and went to church so as to see you. I did see you and went home determined to die. But I wanted to die beautifully and peacefully, without any pain. Then I remembered it was dangerous to sleep under an elder bush. We had a big one in full bloom, so I stripped it and climbed into the oats-bin with the flowers. Have you ever noticed how smooth oats are? Soft to touch as human skin . . . Well, I closed the lid and shut my eyes, fell asleep, and when they woke me I was very ill. But I didn't die, as you see. What I meant by all that I don't know. There was no hope of winning you — you were simply a symbol of the hopelessness of ever getting out of the class I was born in.

JULIE: You put things very well, you know. Did you go to school?

JEAN: For a while. But I've read a lot of novels and been to the theatre. Besides, I've heard educated folk talking — that's what's taught me most.

JULIE: Do you stand round listening to what we're saying?

JEAN: Yes, of course. And I've heard quite a bit too! On the carriage box or rowing the boat. Once I heard you, Miss Julie, and one of your young lady friends . . .

JULIE: Oh! Whatever did you hear?

JEAN: Well, it wouldn't be nice to repeat it. And I must say I was pretty startled. I couldn't think where you had learnt such words. Perhaps, at bottom, there isn't as much difference between people as one's led to believe.

JULIE: How dare you! We don't behave as you do when we're engaged.

JEAN (*looking hard at her*): Are you sure? It's no use making out so innocent to me.

JULIE: The man I gave my love to was a rotter.

JEAN: That's what you always say — afterwards.

JULIE: Always?

JEAN: I think it must be always. I've heard the expression several times in similar circumstances.

JULIE: What circumstances?

JEAN: Like those in question. The last time . . .

JULIE (*rising*): Stop. I don't want to hear any more.

JEAN: Nor did *she* — curiously enough. May I go to bed now please?

JULIE (*gently*): Go to bed on Midsummer Eve?

JEAN: Yes. Dancing with that crowd doesn't really amuse me.

JULIE: Get the key of the boathouse and row me out on the lake. I want to see the sun rise.

JEAN: Would that be wise?

JULIE: You sound as though you're frightened for your reputation.

JEAN: Why not? I don't want to be made a fool of, nor to be sent packing without a character when I'm trying to better myself. Besides, I have Kristin to consider.

JULIE: So now it's Kristin.

JEAN: Yes, but it's you I'm thinking about too. Take my advice and go to bed.

JULIE: Am I to take orders from you?

JEAN: Just this once, for your own sake. Please. It's very late and sleepiness goes to one's head and makes one rash. Go to bed. What's more, if my ears don't deceive me, I hear people coming this way. They'll be looking for me, and if they find us here, you're done for.

(*The* CHORUS *approaches, singing. During the following dialogue the song is heard in snatches, and in full when the peasants enter.*)

Out of the wood two women came,
Tridiri-ralla, tridiri-ra.
The feet of one were bare and cold
Tridiri-ralla-la.

The other talked of bags of gold,
Tridiri-ralla, tridiri-ra.
But neither had a sou to her name,
Tridiri-ralla-la.

The bridal wreath I give to you,
Tridiri-ralla, tridiri-ra.
But to another I'll be true,
Tridiri-ralla-la.

JULIE: I know our people and I love them, just as they do me. Let them come. You'll see.

JEAN: No, Miss Julie, they don't love you. They take your food, then spit at it. You must believe me. Listen to them, just listen to what they're singing . . . No, don't listen.

JULIE (*listening*): What are they singing?

JEAN: They're mocking — you and me.

JULIE: Oh no! How horrible! What cowards!

JEAN: A pack like that's always cowardly. But against such odds there's nothing we can do but run away.

JULIE: Run away? Where to? We can't get out and we can't go into Kristin's room.

JEAN: Into mine then. Necessity knows no rules. And you can trust me. I really am your true and devoted friend.

JULIE: But supposing . . . supposing they were to look for you in there?

JEAN: I'll bolt the door, and if they try to break in I'll shoot. Come on. (*Pleading.*) Please come.

JULIE (*tensely*): Do you promise . . . ?

JEAN: I swear!

(JULIE *goes quickly into his room and he excitedly follows her. Led by the fiddler, the peasants enter in festive attire with flowers in their hats. They put a barrel of beer and a keg of spirits, garlanded with leaves, on the table, fetch glasses and begin to carouse. The scene becomes a ballet. They form a ring and dance and sing and mime:* "Out of the wood two women came." *Finally they go out, still singing.* JULIE *comes in alone. She looks at the havoc in the kitchen, wrings her hands, then takes out her powder puff and powders her face.* JEAN *enters in high spirits.*)

JEAN: Now you see! And you heard, didn't you? Do you still think it's possible for us to stay here?

JULIE: No, I don't. But what can we do?

JEAN: Run away. Far away. Take a journey.

JULIE: Journey? But where to?

JEAN: Switzerland. The Italian lakes. Ever been there?

JULIE: No. Is it nice?

JEAN: Ah! Eternal summer, oranges, evergreens . . . ah!

JULIE: But what would we do there?

JEAN: I'll start a hotel. First-class accommodation and first-class customers.

JULIE: Hotel?

JEAN: There's life for you. New faces all the time, new languages — no time for nerves or worries, no need to look for something to do — work rolling up of its own accord. Bells ringing night and day, trains whistling, buses coming and going, and all the time gold pieces rolling on to the counter. There's life for you!

JULIE: For *you.* And I?

JEAN: Mistress of the house, ornament of the firm. With your looks, and your style . . . oh, it's bound to be a success! Terrific! You'll sit like a queen in the office and set your slaves in motion by pressing an electric button. The guests will file past your throne and nervously lay their treasure on your table. You've no idea the way people tremble when they get their bills. I'll salt the bills and you'll sugar them with your sweetest smiles. Ah, let's get away from here! (*Produces a time-table.*) At once, by the next train. We shall be at Malmö at six-thirty, Hamburg eight-forty next morning, Frankfurt-Basle the following day, and Como by the St. Gothard pass in — let's see — three days. Three days!

JULIE: That's all very well. But Jean, you must give me courage. Tell me you love me. Come and take me in your arms.

JEAN (*reluctantly*): I'd like to, but I daren't. Not again in this house. I love you — that goes without saying. You can't doubt that, Miss Julie, can you?

JULIE (*shyly, very feminine*): Miss? Call me Julie. There aren't any barriers between us now. Call me Julie.

JEAN (*uneasily*): I can't. As long as we're in this house, there *are* barriers between us. There's the past and there's the Count. I've never been so servile to anyone as I am to him. I've only got to see his gloves on a chair to feel small. I've only to hear his bell and I shy like a horse. Even now, when I look at his boots, standing there so proud and stiff, I feel my back beginning to bend. (*Kicks the boots.*) It's those old, narrow-minded notions drummed into us as children . . . but they can soon be forgotten. You've only got to get to another country, a republic, and people will bend themselves double before my porter's livery. Yes, double they'll bend themselves, but I shan't. I wasn't born to bend. I've got guts, I've got character, and once I reach that first branch, you'll watch me climb. Today I'm valet, next year I'll be proprietor, in ten years I'll have made a fortune, and then I'll go to Roumania, get myself decorated and I may, I only say *may,* mind you, end up as a Count.

JULIE (*sadly*): That would be very nice.

JEAN: You see in Roumania one can buy a title, and then you'll be a Countess after all. My Countess.

JULIE: What do I care about all that? I'm putting those things behind me. Tell me you love me, because if you don't . . . if you don't, what am I?

JEAN: I'll tell you a thousand times over — later. But not here. No sentimentality now or everything will be lost. We must consider this thing calmly like reasonable people. (*Takes a cigar, cuts and lights it.*) You sit down there and I'll sit here and we'll talk as if nothing has happened.

JULIE: My God, have you no feelings at all?

JEAN: Nobody has more. But I know how to control them.

JULIE: A short time ago you were kissing my shoe. And now . . .

JEAN (*harshly*): Yes, that was then. Now we have something else to think about.

JULIE: Don't speak to me so brutally.

JEAN: I'm not. Just sensibly. One folly's been committed, don't let's have more. The Count will be back at any moment and we've got to settle our future before that. Now, what do you think of my plans? Do you approve?

JULIE: It seems a very good idea — but just one thing. Such a big undertaking would need a lot of capital. Have you got any?

JEAN (*chewing his cigar*): I certainly have. I've got my professional skill, my wide experience and my knowledge of foreign languages. That's capital worth having, it seems to me.

JULIE: But it won't buy even one railway ticket.

JEAN: Quite true. That's why I need a backer to advance some ready cash.

JULIE: How could you get that at a moment's notice?

JEAN: You must get it, if you want to be my partner.

JULIE: I can't. I haven't any money of my own. (*Pause.*)

JEAN: Then the whole thing's off.

JULIE: And . . . ?

JEAN: We go on as we are.

JULIE: Do you think I'm going to stay under this roof as your mistress? With everyone pointing at me. Do you think I can face my father after this? No. Take me away from here, away from this shame, this humiliation. Oh my God, what have I done? My God, my God! (*Weeps.*)

JEAN: So that's the tune now, is it? What have you done? Same as many before you.

JULIE (*hysterically*): And now you despise me. I'm falling, I'm falling.

JEAN: Fall as far as me and I'll lift you up again.

JULIE: Why was I so terribly attracted to you? The weak to the strong, the falling to the rising? Or was it love? Is that love? Do you know what love is?

JEAN: Do I? You bet I do. Do you think I never had a girl before?

JULIE: The things you say, the things you think!

JEAN: That's what life's taught me, and that's what I am. It's no good getting hysterical or giving yourself airs. We're both in the same boat now. Here, my dear girl, let me give you a glass of something special. (*Opens the drawer, takes out the bottle of wine and fills two used glasses.*)

JULIE: Where did you get that wine?

JEAN: From the cellar.

JULIE: My father's burgundy.

JEAN: Why not, for his son-in-law?

JULIE: And I drink beer.

JEAN: That only shows your taste's not so good as mine.

JULIE: Thief!

JEAN: Are you going to tell on me?

JULIE: Oh God! The accomplice of a petty thief! Was I blind drunk? Have I dreamt this whole night? Midsummer Eve, the night for innocent merrymaking.

JEAN: Innocent, eh?

JULIE: Is anyone on earth as wretched as I am now?

JEAN: Why should *you* be? After such a conquest. What about Kristin in there? Don't you think she has any feelings?

JULIE: I did think so, but I don't any longer. No. A menial is a menial . . .

JEAN: And a whore is a whore.

JULIE (*falling to her knees, her hands clasped*): O God in heaven, put an end to my miserable life! Lift me out of this filth in which I'm sinking. Save me! Save me!

JEAN: I must admit I'm sorry for you. When I was in the onion bed and saw you up there among the roses, I . . . yes, I'll tell you now . . . I had the same dirty thoughts as all boys.

JULIE: You, who wanted to die because of me?

JEAN: In the oats-bin? That was just talk.

JULIE: Lies, you mean.

JEAN (*getting sleepy*): More or less. I think I read a story in some paper about a chimney-sweep who shut himself up in a chest full of lilac because he'd been summonsed for not supporting some brat . . .

JULIE: So this is what you're like.

JEAN: I had to think up something. It's always the fancy stuff that catches the women.

JULIE: Beast!

JEAN: Merde!

JULIE: Now you have seen the falcon's back.

JEAN: Not exactly its *back*.

JULIE: I was to be the first branch.

JEAN: But the branch was rotten.

JULIE: I was to be a hotel sign.

JEAN: And I the hotel.

JULIE: Sit at your counter, attract your clients and cook their accounts.

JEAN: I'd have done that myself.

JULIE: That any human being can be so steeped in filth!

JEAN: Clean it up then.

JULIE: Menial! Lackey! Stand up when I speak to you.

JEAN: Menial's whore, lackey's harlot, shut your mouth and get out of here! Are you the one to lecture me for being coarse? Nobody of my kind would ever be as coarse as you were tonight. Do you think any servant girl would throw herself at a man that way? Have you ever seen a girl of my class asking for it like that? I haven't. Only animals and prostitutes.

JULIE (*broken*): Go on. Hit me, trample on me — it's all I deserve. I'm rotten. But help me! If there's any way out at all, help me.

JEAN (*more gently*): I'm not denying myself a share in the honour of seducing you, but do you think anybody in my place would have dared look in your direction if you yourself hadn't asked for it? I'm still amazed . . .

JULIE: And proud.

JEAN: Why not? Though I must admit the victory was too easy to make me lose my head.

JULIE: Go on hitting me.

JEAN (*rising*): No. On the contrary I apologise for what I've said. I don't hit a person who's down — least of all a woman. I can't deny there's a certain satisfaction in finding that what dazzled one below was just moonshine, that that falcon's back is grey after all, that there's powder on the lovely cheek, that polished nails can have black tips, that the handkerchief is dirty although it smells of scent. On the other hand it hurts to find that what I was struggling to reach wasn't high and isn't real. It hurts to see you fallen so low you're far lower than your own cook. Hurts like when you see the last flowers of summer lashed to pieces by rain and turned to mud.

JULIE: You're talking as if you're already my superior.

JEAN: I am. I might make you a Countess, but you could never make me a Count, you know.

JULIE: But I am the child of a Count, and you could never be that.

JEAN: True, but I might be the father of Counts if . . .

JULIE: You're a thief. I'm not.

JEAN: There are worse things than being a thief — much lower. Besides, when I'm in a place I regard myself as a member of the family to some extent, as one of the children. You don't call it stealing when children pinch a berry from overladen bushes. (*His passion is roused again.*) Miss Julie, you're a glorious woman, far too good for a man like me. You were carried away by some kind of madness, and now you're trying to cover up your mistake by persuading yourself you're in love with me. You're not, although you may find me physically attractive, which means your love's no better than mine. But I wouldn't be satisfied with being nothing but an animal for you, and I could never make you love me.

JULIE: Are you sure?

JEAN: You think there's a chance? Of my loving you, yes, of course. You're beautiful, refined — (*takes her hand*) — educated, and you can be nice when you want to be. The fire you kindle in a man isn't likely to go out. (*Puts his arm round her.*) You're like mulled wine, full of spices, and your kisses . . . (*He tries to pull her to him, but she breaks away.*)

JULIE: Let go of me! You won't win me that way.

JEAN: Not that way, how then? Not by kisses and fine speeches, not by planning the future and saving you from shame? How then?

JULIE: How? How? I don't know. There isn't any way. I loathe you — loathe you as I loathe rats, but I can't escape from you.

JEAN: Escape with me.

JULIE (*pulling herself together*): Escape? Yes, we must escape. But I'm so tired. Give me a glass of wine. (*He pours it out. She looks at her watch.*) First we must talk. We still have a little time. (*Empties the glass and holds it out for more.*)

JEAN: Don't drink like that. You'll get tipsy.

JULIE: What's that matter?

JEAN: What's it matter? It's vulgar to get drunk. Well, what have you got to say?

JULIE: We've got to run away, but we must talk first — or rather, I must, for so far you've done all the talking. You've told me about your life, now I want to tell you about mine, so that we really know each other before we begin this journey together.

JEAN: Wait. Excuse my saying so, but don't you think you may be sorry afterwards if you give away your secrets to me?

JULIE: Aren't you my friend?

JEAN: On the whole. But don't rely on me.

JULIE: You can't mean that. But anyway everyone knows my secrets. Listen. My mother wasn't well-born; she came of quite humble people, and was brought up with all those new ideas of sex-equality and women's rights and so on. She thought marriage was quite wrong. So when my father proposed to her, she said she would never become his *wife* . . . but in the end she did. I came into the world, as far as I can make out, against my mother's will, and I was left to run wild, but I had to do all the things a boy does — to prove women are as good as men. I had to wear boys' clothes; I was taught to handle horses — and I wasn't allowed in the dairy. She made me groom and harness and go out hunting; I even had to try to plough. All the men on the estate were given the women's jobs, and the women the men's, until the whole place went to rack and ruin and we were the laughing-stock of the neighbourhood. At last my father seems to have come to his senses and rebelled. He changed everything and ran the place his own way. My mother got ill — I don't know what was the matter with her, but she used to have strange attacks and hide herself in the attic or the garden. Sometimes she stayed out all night. Then came the great fire which you have heard people talking about. The house and the stables and the barns — the whole place burnt to the ground. In very suspicious circumstances. Because the accident happened the very day the insurance had to be renewed, and my father had sent the new premium, but through some carelessness of the messenger it arrived too late. (*Refills her glass and drinks.*)

JEAN: Don't drink any more.

JULIE: Oh, what does it matter? We were destitute and had to sleep in the carriages. My father didn't know how to get money to rebuild, and then my mother suggested he should borrow from an old friend of hers, a local brick manufacturer. My father got the loan and, to his surprise, without having to pay interest. So the place was rebuilt. (*Drinks.*) Do you know who set fire to it?

JEAN: Your lady mother.

JULIE: Do you know who the brick manufacturer was?

JEAN: Your mother's lover?

JULIE: Do you know whose the money was?

JEAN: Wait . . . no, I don't know that.

JULIE: It was my mother's.

JEAN: In other words the Count's, unless there was a settlement.

JULIE: There wasn't any settlement. My mother had a little money of her own which she didn't want my father to control, so she invested it with her — friend.

JEAN: Who grabbed it.

JULIE: Exactly. He appropriated it. My father came to know all this. He couldn't bring an action, couldn't pay his wife's lover, nor prove it was his wife's money. That was my mother's revenge because he made himself master in his own house. He nearly shot himself then — at least there's a rumour he tried and didn't bring it off. So he went on living, and my mother had to pay dearly for what she'd done. Imagine what those five years were like for me. My natural sympathies were with my father, yet I took my mother's side, because I didn't know the facts. I'd learnt from her to hate and distrust men — you know how she loathed the whole male sex. And I swore to her I'd never become the slave of any man.

JEAN: And so you got engaged to that attorney.

JULIE: So that he should be my slave.

JEAN: But he wouldn't be.

JULIE: Oh yes, he wanted to be, but he didn't have the chance. I got bored with him.

JEAN: Is that what I saw — in the stable-yard?

JULIE: What did you see?

JEAN: What I saw was him breaking off the engagement.

JULIE: That's a lie. It was I who broke it off. Did he say it was him? The cad.

JEAN: He's not a cad. Do you hate men, Miss Julie?

JULIE: Yes . . . most of the time. But when that weakness comes, oh . . . the shame!

JEAN: Then do you hate me?

JULIE: Beyond words. I'd gladly have you killed like an animal.

JEAN: Quick as you'd shoot a mad dog, eh?

JULIE: Yes.

JEAN: But there's nothing here to shoot with — and there isn't a dog. So what do we do now?

JULIE: Go abroad.

JEAN: To make each other miserable for the rest of our lives?

JULIE: No, to enjoy ourselves for a day or two, for a week, for as long as enjoyment lasts, and then — to die . . .

JEAN: Die? How silly! I think it would be far better to start a hotel.

JULIE (*without listening*): . . . die on the shores of Lake Como, where the sun always shines and at Christmas time there are green trees and glowing oranges.

JEAN: Lake Como's a rainy hole and I didn't see any oranges outside the shops. But it's a good place for tourists. Plenty of villas to be rented by — er — honeymoon couples. Profitable business that. Know why? Because they all sign a lease for six months and all leave after three weeks.

JULIE (*naïvely*): After three weeks? Why?

JEAN: They quarrel, of course. But the rent has to be paid just the same. And then it's let again. So it goes on and on, for there's plenty of love although it doesn't last long.

JULIE: You don't want to die with me?

JEAN: I don't want to die at all. For one thing I like living and for another I consider suicide's a sin against the Creator who gave us life.

JULIE: You believe in God — *you?*

JEAN: Yes, of course. And I go to church every Sunday. Look here, I'm tired of all this. I'm going to bed.

JULIE: Indeed! And do you think I'm going to leave things like this? Don't you know what you owe the woman you've ruined?

JEAN (*taking out his purse and throwing a silver coin on the table*): There you are. I don't want to be in anybody's debt.

JULIE (*pretending not to notice the insult*): Don't you know what the law is?

JEAN: There's no law unfortunately that punishes a woman for seducing a man.

JULIE: But can you see anything for it but to go abroad, get married and then divorce?

JEAN: What if I refuse this mésalliance?

JULIE: Mésalliance?

JEAN: Yes, for me. I'm better bred than you, see! Nobody in my family committed arson.

JULIE: How do you know?

JEAN: Well, you can't prove otherwise, because we haven't any family records outside the Registrar's office. But I've seen your family tree in that book on the drawing-room table. Do you know who the founder of your family was? A miller who let his wife sleep with the King one night during the Danish war. I haven't any ancestors like that. I haven't any ancestors at all, but I might become one.

JULIE: This is what I get for confiding in someone so low, for sacrificing my family honour . . .

JEAN: Dishonour! Well, I told you so. One shouldn't drink, because then one talks. And one shouldn't talk.

JULIE: Oh, how ashamed I am, how bitterly ashamed! If at least you loved me!

JEAN: Look here — for the last time — what do you want? Am I to burst into tears? Am I to jump over your riding whip? Shall I kiss you and carry you off to Lake Como for three weeks, after which . . . What am I to do? What do you want? This is getting unbearable, but that's what comes of playing around with women. Miss Julie, I can see how miserable you are; I know you're going through hell, but I don't understand you. We don't have scenes like this; we don't go in for hating each other. We make love for fun in our spare time, but we haven't all day and all night for it like you. I think you must be ill. I'm sure you're ill.

JULIE: Then you must be kind to me. You sound almost human now.

JEAN: Well, be human yourself. You spit at me, then won't let me wipe it off — on you.

JULIE: Help me, help me! Tell me what to do, where to go.

JEAN: Jesus, as if I knew!

JULIE: I've been mad, raving mad, but there must be a way out.

JEAN: Stay here and keep quiet. Nobody knows anything.

JULIE: I can't. People do know. Kristin knows.

JEAN: They don't know and they wouldn't believe such a thing.

JULIE (*hesitating*): But — it might happen again.

JEAN: That's true.

JULIE: And there might be — consequences.

JEAN (*in panic*): Consequences! Fool that I am I never thought of that. Yes, there's nothing for it but to go. At once. I can't come with you. That would be a complete giveaway. You must go alone — abroad — anywhere.

JULIE: Alone? Where to? I can't.

JEAN: You must. And before the Count gets back. If you stay, we know what will happen. Once you've sinned you feel you might as well go on, as the harm's done. Then you get more and more reckless and in the end you're found out. No. You must go abroad. Then write to the Count and tell him everything, except that it was me. He'll never guess that — and I don't think he'll want to.

JULIE: I'll go if you come with me.

JEAN: Are you crazy, woman? "Miss Julie elopes with valet." Next day it would be in the headlines, and the Count would never live it down.

JULIE: I can't go. I can't stay. I'm so tired, so completely worn out. Give me orders. Set me going. I can't think any more, can't act . . .

JEAN: You see what weaklings you are. Why do you give yourselves airs and turn up your noses as if you're the lords of creation? Very well, I'll give you your orders. Go upstairs and dress. Get money for the journey and come down here again.

JULIE (*softly*): Come up with me.

JEAN: To your room? Now you've gone crazy again. (*Hesitates a moment.*) No! Go along at once. (*Takes her hand and pulls her to the door.*)

JULIE (*as she goes*): Speak kindly to me, Jean.

JEAN: Orders always sound unkind. Now you know. Now you know.

(*Left alone,* JEAN *sighs with relief, sits down at the table, takes out a note-book and pencil and adds up figures, now and then aloud. Dawn begins to break.* KRISTIN *enters dressed for church, carrying his white dickey and tie.*)

KRISTIN: Lord Jesus, look at the state the place is in! What have you been up to? (*Turns out the lamp.*)

JEAN: Oh, Miss Julie invited the crowd in. Did you sleep through it? Didn't you hear anything?

KRISTIN: I slept like a log.

JEAN: And dressed for church already.

KRISTIN: Yes, you promised to come to Communion with me today.

JEAN: Why, so I did. And you've got my bib and tucker, I see. Come on then. (*Sits.* KRISTIN *begins to put his things on. Pause. Sleepily.*) What's the lesson today?

KRISTIN: It's about the beheading of John the Baptist, I think.

JEAN: That's sure to be horribly long. Hi, you're choking me! Oh Lord, I'm so sleepy, so sleepy!

KRISTIN: Yes, what have you been doing up all night? You look absolutely green.

JEAN: Just sitting here talking with Miss Julie.

KRISTIN: She doesn't know what's proper, that one. (*Pause.*)

JEAN: I say, Kristin.

KRISTIN: What?

JEAN: It's queer really, isn't it, when you come to think of it? Her.

KRISTIN: What's queer?

JEAN: The whole thing. (*Pause.*)

KRISTIN (*looking at the half-filled glasses on the table*): Have you been drinking together too?

JEAN: Yes.

KRISTIN: More shame you. Look me straight in the face.

JEAN: Yes.

KRISTIN: Is it possible? Is it possible?

JEAN (*after a moment*): Yes, it is.

KRISTIN: Oh! This I would never have believed. How low!

JEAN: You're not jealous of her, surely?

KRISTIN: No, I'm not. If it had been Clara or Sophie I'd have scratched your eyes out. But not of her. I don't know why; that's how it is though. But it's disgusting.

JEAN: You're angry with her then.

KRISTIN: No. With you. It was wicked of you, very very wicked. Poor girl. And, mark my words, I won't stay here any longer now — in a place where one can't respect one's employers.

JEAN: Why should one respect them?

KRISTIN: You should know since you're so smart. But you don't want to stay in the service of people who aren't respectable, do you? I wouldn't demean myself.

JEAN: But it's rather a comfort to find out they're no better than us.

KRISTIN: I don't think so. If they're no better there's nothing for us to live up to. Oh and think of the Count! Think of him. He's been through so much already. No, I won't stay in the place any longer. A fellow like you too! If it had been that attorney now or somebody of her own class . . .

JEAN: Why, what's wrong with . . .

KRISTIN: Oh, you're all right in your own way, but when all's said and done there is a difference between one class and another. No, this is something I'll never be able to stomach. That our young lady who was so proud and so down on men you'd never believe she'd let one come near her should go and give herself to one like you. She who wanted to have poor Diana shot for running after the lodge-keeper's pug. No, I must say . . . ! Well, I won't stay here any longer. On the twenty-fourth of October I quit.

JEAN: And then?

KRISTIN: Well, since you mention it, it's about time you began to look around, if we're ever going to get married.

JEAN: But what am I to look for? I shan't get a place like this when I'm married.

KRISTIN: I know you won't. But you might get a job as porter or caretaker in some public institution. Government rations are small but sure, and there's a pension for the widow and children.

JEAN: That's all very fine, but it's not in my line to start thinking at once about dying for my wife and children. I must say I had rather bigger ideas.

KRISTIN: You and your ideas! You've got obligations too, and you'd better start thinking about them.

JEAN: Don't *you* start pestering me about obligations. I've had enough of that. (*Listens to a sound upstairs.*) Anyway we've plenty of time to work things out. Go and get ready now and we'll be off to church.

KRISTIN: Who's that walking about upstairs?

JEAN: Don't know — unless it's Clara.

KRISTIN (*going*): You don't think the Count could have come back without our hearing him?

JEAN (*scared*): The Count? No, he can't have. He'd have rung for me.

KRISTIN: God help us! I've never known such goings-on. (*Exit.*)

(*The sun has now risen and is shining on the treetops. The light gradually changes until it slants in through the windows.* JEAN *goes to the door and beckons.* JULIE *enters in travelling clothes, carrying a small bird-cage covered with a cloth which she puts on a chair.*)

JULIE: I'm ready.

JEAN: Hush! Kristin's up.

JULIE (*in a very nervous state*): Does she suspect anything?

JEAN: Not a thing. But, my God, what a sight you are!

JULIE: Sight? What do you mean?

JEAN: You're white as a corpse and — pardon me — your face is dirty.

JULIE: Let me wash then. (*Goes to the sink and washes her face and hands.*) There. Give me a towel. Oh! The sun is rising!

JEAN: And that breaks the spell.

JULIE: Yes. The spell of Midsummer Eve . . . But listen, Jean. Come with me. I've got the money.

JEAN (*sceptically*): Enough?

JULIE: Enough to start with. Come with me. I can't travel alone today. It's Midsummer Day, remember. I'd be packed into a suffocating train among crowds of people who'd all stare at me. And it would stop at every station while I yearned for wings. No, I can't do that, I simply can't. There will be memories too; memories of Midsummer Days when I was little. The leafy church — birch and lilac — the gaily spread dinner table, relatives, friends — evening in the park — dancing and music and flowers and fun. Oh, however far you run away — there'll always be memories in the baggage car — and remorse and guilt.

JEAN: I will come with you, but quickly now then, before it's too late. At once.

JULIE: Put on your things. (*Picks up the cage.*)

JEAN: No luggage mind. That would give us away.

JULIE: No, only what we can take with us in the carriage.

JEAN (*fetching his hat*): What on earth have you got there? What is it?

JULIE: Only my greenfinch. I don't want to leave it behind.

JEAN: Well, I'll be damned! We're to take a bird-cage along, are we? You're crazy. Put that cage down.

JULIE: It's the only thing I'm taking from my home. The only living creature who cares for me since Diana went off like that. Don't be cruel. Let me take it.

JEAN: Put that cage down, I tell you — and don't talk so loud. Kristin will hear.

JULIE: No, I won't leave it in strange hands. I'd rather you killed it.

JEAN: Give the little beast here then and I'll wring its neck.

JULIE: But don't hurt it, don't . . . no, I can't.

JEAN: Give it here. I *can.*

JULIE (*taking the bird out of the cage and kissing it*): Dear little Serena, must you die and leave your mistress?

JEAN: Please don't make a scene. It's *your* life and future we're worrying about. Come on, quick now! (*He snatches the bird from her, puts it on a board and picks up a chopper.* JULIE *turns away.*) You should have learnt how to kill chickens instead of target-shooting. Then you wouldn't faint at a drop of blood.

JULIE (*screaming*): Kill me too! Kill me! You who can butcher an innocent creature without a quiver. Oh, how I hate you, how I loathe you! There is blood between us now. I curse the hour I first saw you. I curse the hour I was conceived in my mother's womb.

JEAN: What's the use of cursing? Let's go.

JULIE (*going to the chopping-block as if drawn against her will*): No, I won't go yet. I can't . . . I must look. Listen! There's a carriage. (*Listens without taking her eyes off the board and chopper.*) You don't think I can bear the sight of blood. You think I'm so weak. Oh, how I should like to see your blood and your brains on a chopping-block! I'd like to see the whole of your sex swimming like that in a sea of blood. I think I could drink out of your skull, bathe my feet in your broken breast and eat your heart roasted whole. You think I'm weak. You think I love you, that my womb yearned for your seed and I want to carry your offspring under my heart and nourish it with my blood. You think I want to bear your child and take your name. By the way, what is your name? I've never heard your surname. I don't suppose you've got one. I should be "Mrs. Hovel" or "Madam Dunghill." You dog wearing my collar, you lackey with my crest on your buttons! I share you with my cook; I'm my own servant's rival! Oh! Oh! Oh! . . . You think I'm a coward and will run away. No, now I'm going to stay — and let the storm break. My father will come back . . . find his desk broken open . . . his money gone. Then he'll ring that bell — twice for the valet — and then he'll send for the police . . . and I shall tell everything. Everything. Oh how wonderful to make an end of it all — a real end! He has a stroke and dies and that's the end of all of us. Just peace and quietness . . . eternal rest. The coat of arms broken on the coffin and the Count's line extinct . . . But the valet's line goes on in an orphanage, wins laurels in the gutter and ends in jail.

JEAN: There speaks the noble blood! Bravo, Miss Julie. But now, don't let the cat out of the bag.

(KRISTIN *enters dressed for church, carrying a prayer-book.* JULIE *rushes to her and flings herself into her arms for protection.*)

JULIE: Help me, Kristin! Protect me from this man!

KRISTIN (*unmoved and cold*): What goings-on for a feast day morning! (*Sees the board.*) And what a filthy mess. What's it all about? Why are you screaming and carrying on so?

JULIE: Kristin, you're a woman and my friend. Beware of that scoundrel!

JEAN (*embarrassed*): While you ladies are talking things over, I'll go and shave. (*Slips into his room.*)

JULIE: You must understand. You must listen to me.

KRISTIN: I certainly don't understand such loose ways. Where are you off to in those travelling clothes? And he had his hat on, didn't he, eh?

JULIE: Listen, Kristin. Listen, I'll tell you everything.

KRISTIN: I don't want to know anything.

JULIE: You must listen.

KRISTIN: What to? Your nonsense with Jean? I don't care a rap about that; it's nothing to do with me. But if you're thinking of getting him to run off with you, we'll soon put a stop to that.

JULIE (*very nervously*): Please try to be calm, Kristin, and listen. I can't stay here, nor can Jean — so we must go abroad.

KRISTIN: Hm, hm!

JULIE (*brightening*): But you see, I've had an idea. Supposing we all three go — abroad — to Switzerland and start a hotel together . . . I've got some money, you see . . . and Jean and I could run the whole thing — and I thought you would take charge of the kitchen. Wouldn't that be splendid? Say yes, do. If you come with us everything will be fine. Oh do say yes! (*Puts her arms round* KRISTIN.)

KRISTIN (*coolly thinking*): Hm, hm.

JULIE (*presto tempo*): You've never travelled, Kristin. You should go abroad and see the world. You've no idea how nice it is travelling by train — new faces all the time and new countries. On our way through Hamburg we'll go to the zoo — you'll love that — and we'll go to the theatre and the opera too . . . and when we get to Munich there'll be the museums, dear, and pictures by Rubens and Raphael — the great painters, you know . . . You've heard of Munich, haven't you? Where King Ludwig lived — you know, the king who went mad. . . . We'll see his castles — some of his castles are still just like in fairy-tales . . . and from there it's not far to Switzerland — and the Alps. Think of the Alps, Kristin dear, covered with snow in the middle of summer . . . and there are oranges there and trees that are green the whole year round . . .

(JEAN *is seen in the door of his room, sharpening his razor on a strop which he holds with his teeth and his left hand. He listens to the talk with satisfaction and now and then nods approval.* JULIE *continues, tempo prestissimo.*)

And then we'll get a hotel . . . and I'll sit at the desk, while Jean receives the guests and goes out marketing and writes letters . . . There's life for you! Trains whistling, buses driving up, bells ringing upstairs and downstairs . . . and I shall make out the bills — and I shall cook them too . . . you've no idea how nervous travellers are when it comes to paying their bills. And you — you'll sit like a queen in the kitchen . . . of course there won't be any standing at the stove for you. You'll always have to be nicely dressed and ready to be seen, and with your looks — no, I'm not flattering you — one fine day you'll catch yourself a husband . . . some rich Englishman, I shouldn't wonder — they're the ones who are easy — (*slowing down*) — to catch . . . and then we'll get rich and build ourselves a villa on Lake Como . . . of course it rains there a little now and then — but — (*dully*) — the sun must shine there too sometimes — even though it seems gloomy — and if not — then we can come home again — come back — (*pause*) — here — or somewhere else . . .

KRISTIN: Look here, Miss Julie, do you believe all that yourself?

JULIE (*exhausted*): Do I believe it?

KRISTIN: Yes.

JULIE (*wearily*): I don't know. I don't believe anything any more. (*Sinks down on the bench; her head in her arms on the table.*) Nothing. Nothing at all.

KRISTIN (*turning to* JEAN): So you meant to beat it, did you?

JEAN (*disconcerted, putting the razor on the table*): Beat it? What are you talking about? You've heard Miss Julie's plan, and though she's tired now with being up all night, it's a perfectly sound plan.

KRISTIN: Oh, is it? If you thought I'd work for that . . .

JEAN (*interrupting*): Kindly use decent language in front of your mistress. Do you hear?

KRISTIN: Mistress?

JEAN: Yes.

KRISTIN: Well, well, just listen to that!

JEAN: Yes, it would be a good thing if you did listen and talked less. Miss Julie is your mistress and what's made you lose your respect for her now ought to make you feel the same about yourself.

KRISTIN: I've always had enough self-respect —

JEAN: To despise other people.

KRISTIN: — not to go below my own station. Has the Count's cook ever gone with the groom or the swineherd? Tell me that.

JEAN: No, you were lucky enough to have a high-class chap for your beau.

KRISTIN: High-class all right — selling the oats out of the Count's stable.

JEAN: You're a fine one to talk — taking a commission on the groceries and bribes from the butcher.

KRISTIN: What the devil . . . ?

JEAN: And now you can't feel any respect for your employers. You, you!

KRISTIN: Are you coming to church with me? I should think you need a good sermon after your fine deeds.

JEAN: No, I'm not going to church today. You can go alone and confess your own sins.

KRISTIN: Yes, I'll do that and bring back enough forgiveness to cover yours too. The Saviour suffered and died on the cross for all our sins, and if we go to Him with faith and a penitent heart, He takes all our sins upon Himself.

JEAN: Even grocery thefts?

JULIE: Do you believe that, Kristin?

KRISTIN: That is my living faith, as sure as I stand here. The faith I learnt as a child and have kept ever since, Miss Julie. "But where sin abounded, grace did much more abound."

JULIE: Oh, if I had your faith! Oh, if . . .

KRISTIN: But you see you can't have it without God's special grace, and it's not given to all to have that.

JULIE: Who is it given to then?

KRISTIN: That's the great secret of the workings of grace, Miss Julie. God is no respecter of persons, and with Him the last shall be first . . .

JULIE: Then I suppose He does respect the last.

KRISTIN (*continuing*): . . . and it is easier for a camel to go through the eye of a needle than for a rich man to enter into the kingdom of God. That's how it is, Miss Julie. Now I'm going — alone, and on my way I shall tell the groom not to let any of the horses out, in case anyone should want to leave before the Count gets back. Goodbye.

(*Exit.*)

JEAN: What a devil! And all on account of a greenfinch.

JULIE (*wearily*): Never mind the greenfinch. Do you see any way out of this, any end to it?

JEAN (*pondering*): No.

JULIE: If you were in my place, what would you do?

JEAN: In your place? Wait a bit. If I was a woman — a lady of rank who had — fallen. I don't know. Yes, I do know now.

JULIE (*picking up the razor and making a gesture*): This?

JEAN: Yes. But *I* wouldn't do it, you know. There's a difference between us.

JULIE: Because you're a man and I'm a woman? What is the difference?

JEAN: The usual difference — between man and woman.

JULIE (*holding the razor*): I'd like to. But I can't. My father couldn't either, that time he wanted to.

JEAN: No, he didn't want to. He had to be revenged first.

JULIE: And now my mother is revenged again, through me.

JEAN: Didn't you ever love your father, Miss Julie?

JULIE: Deeply, but I must have hated him too — unconsciously. And he let me be brought up to despise my own sex, to be half woman, half man. Whose fault is what's happened? My father's, my mother's or my own? My own? I haven't anything that's my own. I haven't one single thought that I didn't get from my father, one emotion that didn't come from my mother, and as for this last idea — about all people being equal — I got that from him, my fiancé — that's why I call him a cad. How can it be my fault? Push the responsibility on to Jesus, like Kristin does? No, I'm too proud and — thanks to my father's teaching — too intelligent. As for all that about a rich person not being able to get into heaven, it's just a lie, but Kristin, who has money in the savings-bank, will certainly not get in. Whose fault is it? What does it matter whose fault it is? In any case I must take the blame and bear the consequences.

JEAN: Yes, but . . . (*There are two sharp rings on the bell.* JULIE *jumps to her feet.* JEAN *changes into his livery.*) The Count is back. Supposing Kristin . . . (*Goes to the speaking-tube, presses it and listens.*)

JULIE: Has he been to his desk yet?

JEAN: This is Jean, sir. (*Listens.*) Yes, sir. (*Listens.*) Yes, sir, very good, sir. (*Listens.*) At once, sir? (*Listens.*) Very good, sir. In half an hour.

JULIE (*in panic*): What did he say? My God, what did he say?

JEAN: He ordered his boots and his coffee in half an hour.

JULIE: Then there's half an hour . . . Oh, I'm so tired! I can't do anything. Can't be sorry, can't run away, can't stay, can't live — can't die. Help me. Order me, and I'll obey like a dog. Do me this last service — save my honour, save his name. You know what I ought to do, but haven't the strength to do. Use your strength and order me to do it.

JEAN: I don't know why — I can't now — I don't understand . . . It's just as if this coat made me — I can't give you orders — and now that the Count has spoken to me — I can't quite explain, but . . . well, that devil of a lackey is bending my back again. I believe if the Count came down now and ordered me to cut my throat, I'd do it on the spot.

JULIE: Then pretend you're him and I'm you. You did some fine acting before, when you knelt to me and played the aristocrat. Or . . . Have you ever seen a hypnotist at the theatre? (*He nods.*) He says to the person "Take the broom," and he takes it. He says "Sweep," and he sweeps . . .

JEAN: But the person has to be asleep.

JULIE (*as if in a trance*): I am asleep already . . . the whole room has turned to smoke — and you look like a stove — a stove like a man in black with a tall hat — your eyes are glowing like coals when the fire is low — and your face is a white patch like ashes. (*The sunlight has now reached the floor and lights up* JEAN.) How nice and warm it is! (*She holds out her hands as though warming them at a fire.*) And so light — and so peaceful.

JEAN (*putting the razor in her hand*): Here is the broom. Go now while it's light — out to the barn — and . . . (*Whispers in her ear.*)

JULIE (*waking*): Thank you. I am going now — to rest. But just tell me that even the first can receive the gift of grace.

JEAN: The first? No, I can't tell you that. But wait . . . Miss Julie, I've got it! You aren't one of the first any longer. You're one of the last.

JULIE: That's true. I'm one of the very last. I *am* the last. Oh! . . . But now I can't go. Tell me again to go.

JEAN: No, I can't now either. I can't.

JULIE: And the first shall be last.

JEAN: Don't think, don't think. You're taking my strength away too and making me a coward. What's that? I thought I saw the bell move . . . To be so frightened of a bell! Yes, but it's not just a bell. There's somebody behind it — a hand moving it — and something else moving the hand — and if you stop your ears — if you stop your ears — yes, then it rings louder than ever. Rings and rings until you answer — and then it's too late. Then the police come and . . . and . . . (*The bell rings twice loudly.* JEAN *flinches, then straightens himself up.*) It's horrible. But there's no other way to end it . . . Go!

(JULIE *walks firmly out through the door.*)

In the eyes of the world Scandinavian drama begins and ends with Ibsen and Strindberg. The view is ruthlessly simple (mainly in leaving out Holberg's eighteenth-century comedies) but sound as far as the history of drama is concerned. And historically Ibsen and Strindberg are large items. It could be argued that all subsequent drama derives, directly or indirectly, either from Ibsen's retrospective realism or from Strindberg's expressionism. There is no accounting for literary genius and hardly for revolutions in taste and form, but it is surely significant that the two playwrights who took Europe's stages away from blank-verse closet plays, Gothic melodramas, and well-plotted boulevard frivolities both came from small countries on the fringe of the entrenched literary and theatrical conventions. Also, in Norway and Sweden the emergent bourgeois culture could make its way without much resistance from surviving courtly and feudal institutions or much burdened with puritanical prejudice against plays. Whatever the reasons, about 1880 the center of western drama suddenly shifted north for some twenty years.

In the most characteristic form of nineteenth-century stage realism the stage is the middle-class living room with one wall removed without the family noticing. The less plot such a play has the closer it is to slice-of-life realism, which seeks to give an illusion of realism-in-the-raw, untampered with by art. The art is the concealment of the art. Chekhov's carefully juxtaposed, semi-autonomous episodes in discordant sequence are closer to the slice-of-life manner than are Ibsen's tightly plotted disclosures of past iniquities in the complacent present. Formally, Ibenism is a continuous balancing act between a too-conspicuous form and the formlessness of the lifelike surface. In his naturalist phase Strindberg's method is somewhere between Ibsen's and Chekhov's. In *Miss Julie* (1888) the unbroken continuity of action, the tiny cast, the singleness of the situation, and the glimpses of the conditioning past make for a degree of concentration that exceeds that of any of Ibsen's own plays, with the possible exception of *Ghosts*. But Strindberg depends less on intrigue than Ibsen does. In the post-climactic part of *Miss Julie* much of the dialogue gives the impression of going around in more and more tired circles. The effect is possible because the slightness of plot allows Strindberg space and freedom to practice a kind of Chekhovian diffuseness and stasis — before Chekhov. But artistically the combination is hazardous. The texture of *Miss Julie* is less stringent than Ibsen's, less delicately consistent than Chekhov's. And the Ibsenite catastrophe in the Chekhovian context seems less inevitably the product of any logic of shown events than such outcomes seem in Ibsen, and it shatters the Chekhovian mood.

But generically *Miss Julie* is above everything else an example of symbolic naturalism. It was the manner by which Ibsen had revolutionized drama in the early '80's, but again Strindberg has provided the more extreme specimen. Naturalistic drama (in the strict definition used here) is realistic drama that reflects a universe governed by the mechanical causality postulated by nineteenth-century science and determinist philosophy. Man's fate is a matter of indifference to the cosmic economy. He is an animal in an amoral world, an accidental product of a particular set of hereditary factors acted upon by a particular physical and social environment. The study of mankind is the study of human conditioning. Hence the emphasis in naturalistic literature on setting (as in Émile Zola's novels) and on the past. Ibsen in *Hedda Gabler* stresses his heroine's social milieu, Strindberg in *Miss Julie* her heredity and upbringing but above all her immediate circumstance of time, place, occasion, companionship, and physiology. His use of the menstrual cycle as conditioning factor is a typical naturalistic detail. As a result, Julie appears more mechanistically determined than Hedda and her fate more pathetic and less nobly tragic. Both are neurotic aristocrats made unhappy by sexual maladjustment, but Hedda's frigidity leaves her will larger room for free and deliberate action than Julie's wayward sexuality leaves hers. Hedda acts; Julie is at first driven to act and is later a passive victim of the consequences of the compulsive act.

In symbolic naturalism meaning is extended beyond representationalism, dramatic storytelling, and philosophical theme by the investment of the realistic material with more than literal significance. When Hedda in Act I of *Hedda Gabler* wants the living-room drapes drawn to keep the sun out the incident is primarily a plausible detail in the larger picture of upper-middle class domestic life. It belongs in the setting. But in the context of Hedda's character and situation it functions also as symbolic image of her attitude to reality. She wants freedom from stuffy convention in order to enjoy the life of the senses, but she can enjoy that life only in decorous clandestineness. The danger with this kind of analysis is that it leaves the impression that symbolism is some kind of one-man game. Actually, it is a dimension in man's perception of his environment that is part of any imaginative response to the phenomenal world. Any fact, object, or action that arouses emotion is a potential symbol, a concrete embodiment or evocation of abstract values. And its symbolic power is the richer for being chameleon-like and elusive. To analyze successful symbolism is almost inevitably to have to choose between being vague and being crude.

As a bitch in heat Julie's dog represents Julie herself. But it is a real dog for all that. The point to seize in symbolic realism is that a bitch can be both bitch and "bitch" at the same time. The count's boots are a plausible occasion for valet work. Like Hedda's living-room drapes they belong as lifelike props. But they also suggest the feudal order which the events of the night violate, and they reveal Jean's basically servile nature. For all his learning and ambition he can no more escape his past than Julie can hers. The boots are silent and powerful representatives of their absent owner and everything he stands for. With the bell and the speaking tube they are, as symbols, the only "characters" that never leave the stage.

Miss Julie also includes details that point forward to Strindberg's expressionism in the highly influential dramas he wrote during the early years of the twentieth century — plays like *The Dream Play* (1902) and *The Ghost Sonata* (1907), in which broken pieces of weird or humdrum reality interact in dreamlike or surrealistic configurations as images of a constantly shifting, fantastic–symbolic world expressive of the secret life of the soul. No single event or sequence of events in *Miss Julie* violates the normal way of things in the objective experience we all (presumably) share. But Julie's and Jean's dreams (naïvely obvious in the eyes of a post-Freudian, moviegoing age), their common victimization, the counterpoint effect of the peasant interlude in the psychological progress, the symmetrical, X-like pattern of the action, Jean's final speech, pertaining to an experience that is neither wholly real (objective, empirical) nor wholly unreal (subjective, imaginative) — all these anticipate the manner both of Strindberg's own and of later expressionism.

As in successfully integrated drama of any school, action and image jointly build the larger structure of *Miss Julie*. The peasant "ballet" (as Strindberg quite rightly called it) is a good example. It marks the node at which Julie's and Jean's opposite movements intersect, the offstage event that precipitates the hidden sediment in the two compounded selves. Up to this point, Jean has been sensibly deferential and correct, rather attractive in the controlled conduct of his difficult double role as Don Juan and Joseph. After his conquest, he turns robustly vulgar and arrogant. At the same time Julie's arrogant desire turns into guilt and shame and tired trance. As semi-stylized, symbolic action of peasant dancing, singing, and carousing on midsummer night's eve, the ballet further suggests a pagan nature rite, the primitive life of the senses, which helps to define the nature of Julie's fall. As ballet it distances us from the sordid encounter with which it coincides, while remaining plausible enough as episode not to dispel the realist illusion of the whole play. Finally, it brings on stage a dynamic group that supplements the cook Kristin's shrewd and conventional meanness of attitude with vitality and lyrical exuberance so as to form a complex image of a chorus of "common folk" that comments implicitly and richly on the Jean–Julie situation.

But the main critical issue raised by *Miss Julie* is its status as tragedy — specifically the naturalistic tragedy Strindberg himself regarded it as.

Strindberg, unlike Ibsen, found in playwriting only one of several outlets for his restlessly driven creativity. Paradoxically, the mind of this haunted neurotic and bohemian was analytical and philosophical, even scientific, but Ibsen, by appearance and behavior the petit bourgeois incarnate, was nothing but artist. Ibsen talked rarely and unwillingly about his craft and his plays. Strindberg wrote prefaces on dramatic theory for his. Strindberg called Ibsen a "bluestocking," but his plays stirred his own imagination to drama. Ibsen disliked Strindberg (though not his plays), but once confessed that he was unable to write a single line unless Strindberg's "mad eyes" (in Christian Krohg's portrait) stared down at him. Both wrote lyrical fantasies, national chronicles, and plays of symbolic naturalism, but within each dramatic genre their manner clearly differs. The conflict in Ibsen is between man and society, man and ideology, man and himself, as the protagonist seeks self-fulfilment. Interpersonal conflict between man and woman, as in the settling-of-accounts scene between Nora Helmer and her husband at the end of *A Doll's House,* is, characteristically, in the form of reflective debate. Strindberg sees life as a sexual battle for supremacy. Conflicts are overt and eruptive. Character bristles belligerently or defensively in raw passion. Both playwrights achieve something that could be called modern versions of tragedy, but Strindberg's achievement is the more intense and more immediately gripping, Ibsen's the more monolithic.

Of Strindberg's writings on the theater the Preface to *Miss Julie* is probably the most important. It includes, along with some discursiveness and some irrelevant vehemence, an early naturalistic manifesto on dramatic characterization. It is not the philosopher's ultimate "why," nor the neutral observer's unreflective "that," but the fascinated scientist's "how" that guides Strindberg's studies of character. His attitude probably falls short of the ideal naturalist's absolute detachment, but his approach is distinctly modern.

> . . . it seems to me that the psychological process is what interests most people today. Our inquisitive souls are no longer satisfied with seeing a thing happen; we must also know how it happens. We want to see the wires, watch the machinery, exam-

ine the box with the false bottom, take hold of the magic ring to find the join, and look at the cards to see how they are marked.

The enemy to be overthrown is the humor character, simple and unchanging, a "middle-class conception of the immobility of the soul." The writer of humors defines character once and for all by some striking mannerism of act or speech or by some strong bias of the mind. Naturalists, on the other hand, "know the richness of the soul-complex and realize that vice has a reverse side very much like virtue." To capture the soul's minutiae means creating "characterless" characters, men and women moved by a multiplicity of drives and motives. Miss Julie is a degenerate "half-woman," brought up to be a "man-hater," but she is also "a relic of the old warrior nobility now giving way to the nobility of nerve and brain." In addition, her fate is determined by

> the mother's character, the father's mistaken upbringing of the girl, her own nature, and the influence of her fiancé on a weak, degenerate mind. Also, more directly, the festive mood of Midsummer Eve, her father's absence, her monthly indisposition, her pre-occupation with animals, the excitement of dancing, the magic of dusk, the strongly aphrodisiac influence of flowers, and finally the chance that drives the couple into a room alone — to which must be added the urgency of the excited man.

Today all heretical novelty has gone out of this postulate of a large variety of causes for individual human behavior. We are more likely to feel that it is Jonson's and Molière's fixed psychology that needs defense. We are so much heirs of the naturalist tradition which Strindberg helped establish that we not only don't question it as premise for psychology but don't even query its relevance to, or its implications for, literature.

We may begin by challenging Strindberg's use of the term "tragic" for his story of Miss Julie. Can there be such a thing as a naturalistic tragedy at all? If man is always at the mercy of chance and his own past and glands, he is not the free, responsible, and self-determined hero of traditional tragedy. In the incessant buffeting by uncontrollable impulses within and without he sheds all dignity and magnitude. His suffering is at most pitiful and harrowing. A puppet Creon, an automaton Othello — the very notion is preposterous.

Strindberg himself located the tragic effect of his play in the spectacle of the downfall of "one favored by fortune" and of the death of "a family heritage." But this hardly holds. First, fortune can hardly be said to have favored Julie at all: the single child of a loveless marriage of a ruined nobleman and a hysterical feminist–adulteress–arsonist. Second, Strindberg's second point pertains only to the representativeness of Julie's case in both a socio-economic and an evolutionary context. On one level, what happens to Julie was in a sense happening to her whole class. The play is about the fall of the aristocracy of blood and the rise of the aristocracy of will and mind. There is also the related theme of social leveling, most succinctly expressed in the scene in which the valet drinks fine wine and his mistress beer. On another level, the play dramatizes Darwinism (with a Strindbergian slant). In the timeless sexual battle, Jean, the male vulgarian, is the stronger and survives; Julie, the aristocratic female decadent, is the weaker and perishes. This is interesting and possibly moving, but it is not tragic.

The issue is this: can man's stature in the naturalistic world picture, which, as Strindberg says in the Preface, "has abolished guilt with God," qualify him for tragic greatness by the norms of older tragedy — Greek, Elizabethan, neoclassical?

The answer must be "no" if "tragic greatness" is taken to apply to a heroic, indomitable, but ultimately self-destructive will battling an overwhelming antagonist. But in too-rigid definitions many a specific critical enterprise has been lost. The house of tragedy has many rooms, and tragic greatness may be predicated for a play as well as for a protagonist. It may be a quality we sense when drama confronts us with the inescapable paradoxes of our existence: consciousness trapped by matter, the maddening curve of life itself in its rise and fall. The tragic flaw may be felt to be not in man but in the terms on which he has his life. And rather than a defect in a traditional tragedy of the fall of the superhuman individual, Julie's lack of strength and dignity is proof of the tragic limitation of man's dual nature in the dead cosmos of unalterable law. We suffer from a contradiction in our natural equipment between the frail flesh and the perilous reach of our dreams.

Julie is destroyed by forces that science, in theory, at least, could account for. Such, at any rate, is the naturalist assumption. But to trace the links in the causal chain at the end of which catastrophe hangs is neither to grasp the meaning of the catastrophe nor to prove that there is no meaning to be grasped. The naturalist will on principle waive any effort to explain, in a teleological sense, the particular conjunction of hereditary and environmental, physical, psychological, and circumstantial, causes by which Julie falls. But to the tragic view the conjunction — an unlikely event in any statistic — remains no less a mystery than the accident of Iago in Othello's life or the accident by which an Antigone and a Creon clash. If Strindberg refused to ask the questions tragedy asks or to admit their relevance, his play nevertheless records events that seem clear and coherent to the tragic view. The imagery is not so much at odds with naturalistic doctrine as transcending doctrine altogether. Julie's situation is defined in terms of contrasts and of values in the process of being transposed. She begins the play as Diana, the pedigreed bitch in heat, illicitly seeking a mate. She ends it as her other pet, the caged greenfinch Serena (both animal names are ironic), her throat slashed. Tension of opposites is her psychological climate. Between maleness and femininity, nobility and vulgarity, leveling and hierarchy, pride and lust, attraction and repulsion, strength and weakness, home and abroad, climbing and falling, passion and suffering, she is pulled apart. Breaking the ancient code of honor by which her kind is supposed to live breaks her. The girl who had whipped her fiancé ends by killing herself with her servant–lover's razor.

But her degradation does not disqualify her for the part of tragic heroine. Doomed she is, but only in her doom does she find herself. Despite the symbolic suggestiveness of her trancelike state at the end, she is more than a manipulated mechanism of an accidental past and blind drives. She feels guilt and shame. To a naturalist, to whom she is unable to help what has happened and hence innocent, her emotions are absurd, further evidence of her moribund decadence. But as facets of the heroine's psyche they are facts of the play, whether or not they defy an analysis of causes. Falling, it seems as if Miss Julie cannot be held in any purely mechanist account of reality.

Bernard Shaw

CAESAR AND CLEOPATRA

A History

PROLOGUE

(*In the doorway of the temple of Ra in Memphis. Deep gloom. An august personage with a hawk's head is mysteriously visible by his own light in the darkness within the temple. He surveys the modern audience with great contempt; and finally speaks the following words to them:*)

Peace! Be silent and hearken unto me, ye quaint little islanders. Give ear, ye men with white paper on your breasts and nothing written thereon (to signify the innocence of your minds). Hear me, ye women who adorn yourselves alluringly and conceal your thoughts from your men, leading them to believe that ye deem them wondrous strong and masterful whilst in truth ye hold them in your hearts as children without judgment. Look upon my hawk's head; and know that I am Ra, who was once in Egypt a mighty god. Ye cannot kneel nor prostrate yourselves; for ye are packed in rows without freedom to move, obstructing one another's vision; neither do any of ye regard it as seemly to do ought until ye see all the rest do so too; wherefore it commonly happens that in great emergencies ye do nothing though each telleth his fellow that something must be done. I ask you not for worship, but for silence. Let not your men speak nor your women cough; for I am come to draw you back two thousand years over the graves of sixty generations. Ye poor posterity, think not that ye are the first. Other fools before ye have seen the sun rise and set, and the moon change her shape and her hour. As they were so ye are; and yet not so great; for the pyramids my people built stand to this day; whilst the dustheaps on which ye slave, and which ye call empires, scatter in the wind even as ye pile your dead sons' bodies on them to make yet more dust.

Hearken to me then, oh ye compulsorily educated ones. Know that even as there is an old England and a new, and ye stand perplexed between the twain; so in the days when I was worshipped was there an old Rome and a new, and men standing perplexed between them. And the old Rome was poor and little, and greedy and fierce, and evil in many ways; but because its mind was little and its work was simple, it knew its own mind and did its own work; and the gods pitied it and helped it and strengthened it and shielded it; for the gods are patient with littleness. Then the old Rome, like the beggar on horseback, presumed on the favor of the gods, and said, "Lo! there is neither riches nor greatness in our littleness: the road to riches and greatness is through robbery of the poor and slaughter of the weak." So they robbed their own poor until they became great masters of that art, and knew by what laws it could be made to appear seemly and honest. And when they had squeezed their own poor dry, they robbed the poor of other lands, and added those lands to Rome until there came a new Rome, rich and huge. And I, Ra, laughed; for the minds of the Romans remained the same size whilst their dominion spread over the earth.

Now mark me, that ye may understand what ye are presently to see. Whilst the Romans still stood between the old Rome and the new, there arose among them a mighty soldier: Pompey the Great. And the way of the soldier is the way of death; but the way of the gods is the way of life; and so it comes that a god at the end of his way is wise and a soldier at the end of his way is a fool. So Pompey held by the old Rome, in which only soldiers could become great; but the gods turned to the new Rome, in which any man with wit enough could become what he would. And Pompey's friend Julius Cæsar was on the side of the gods; for he saw that Rome had passed beyond the control of the little old Romans. This Cæsar was a great talker and a politician: he bought men with words and with gold, even as ye are bought. And when they would not be satisfied with words and gold, and demanded also the glories of war, Cæsar in his middle age turned his hand to that trade; and they that were against him when he sought their welfare, bowed down before him when he became a slayer and a conqueror; for such is the nature of you mortals. And as for Pompey, the gods grew tired of his triumphs and his airs of being himself a god; for he talked of law and duty and other matters that concerned not a mere human worm. And the gods smiled on Cæsar; for he lived the life they had given him boldly, and was not forever rebuking us for our indecent ways of creation, and hiding our handiwork as a shameful thing. Ye know well what I mean; for this is one of your own sins.

And thus it fell out between the old Rome and the new, that Cæsar said, "Unless I break the law of old Rome, I cannot take my share in ruling her; and the gift of ruling that the gods gave me will perish without fruit." But Pompey said, "The law is above all; and if thou break it thou shalt die." Then said Cæsar, "I will break it: kill me who can." And he broke it. And Pompey went for him, as ye say, with a great army to slay him and uphold the old Rome. So Cæsar fled across the Adriatic sea; for the high gods had a lesson to teach him, which lesson they shall also teach you in due time if ye continue to forget them and to worship that cad among gods, Mammon. Therefore before they raised Cæsar to be master of the world, they were minded to throw him down into the dust, even beneath the feet of Pompey, and blacken his face before the nations. And Pompey they raised higher than ever, he and his laws and his high mind that aped the gods, so that his fall might be the more terrible. And Pompey followed Cæsar, and overcame him with all the majesty of old Rome, and stood over him and over the whole world even as ye stand over it with your fleet that covers thirty miles of the sea. And when Cæsar was brought down to utter nothingness, he made a last stand to die honorably, and did not despair; for he said, "Against me there is Pompey, and the old Rome, and the law and the legions: all against me; but high above these are the gods; and Pompey is a fool." And the gods laughed and approved; and on the field of Pharsalia the impossible came to pass; the blood and iron ye pin your faith on fell before the spirit of man; for the spirit of man is the will of the gods; and Pompey's power crumbled in his hand, even as the power of imperial Spain crumbled when it was set against your fathers in the days when England was little, and knew her own mind, and had a mind to know instead of a circulation of newspapers. Wherefore look to it, lest some little people whom ye would enslave rise up and become in the hand of God the scourge of your boastings and your injustices and your lusts and stupidities.

And now, would ye know the end of Pompey, or will ye sleep while a god speaks? Heed my words well; for Pompey went where ye have gone, even to Egypt, where there was a Roman occupation even as there was but now a British one. And Cæsar pursued Pompey to Egypt; a Roman fleeing, and a Roman pursuing: dog eating dog. And the Egyptians said, "Lo: those Romans which have lent money to our kings and levied a distraint upon us with their arms, call for ever upon us to be loyal to them by betraying our own country to them. But now behold two Romes! Pompey's Rome and Cæsar's

Rome! To which of the twain shall we pretend to be loyal?" So they turned in their perplexity to a soldier that had once served Pompey, and that knew the ways of Rome and was full of her lusts. And they said to him, "Lo: in thy country dog eats dog; and both dogs are coming to eat us: what counsel hast thou to give us?" And this soldier, whose name was Lucius Septimius, and whom ye shall presently see before ye, replied, "Ye shall diligently consider which is the bigger dog of the two; and ye shall kill the other dog for his sake and thereby earn his favor." And the Egyptians said, "Thy counsel is expedient; but if we kill a man outside the law we set ourselves in the place of the gods; and this we dare not do. But thou, being a Roman, art accustomed to this kind of killing; for thou hast imperial instincts. Wilt thou therefore kill the lesser dog for us?" And he said, "I will; for I have made my home in Egypt; and I desire consideration and influence among you." And they said, "We knew well thou wouldst not do it for nothing: thou shalt have thy reward." Now when Pompey came, he came alone in a little galley, putting his trust in the law and the constitution. And it was plain to the people of Egypt that Pompey was now but a very small dog. So when he set his foot on the shore he was greeted by his old comrade Lucius Septimius, who welcomed him with one hand and with the other smote off his head, and kept it as it were a pickled cabbage to make a present to Cæsar. And mankind shuddered; but the gods laughed; for Septimius was but a knife that Pompey had sharpened; and when it turned against his own throat they said that Pompey had better have made Septimius a ploughman than so brave and ready-handed a slayer. Therefore again I bid you beware, ye who would all be Pompeys if ye dared; for war is a wolf that may come to your own door.

Are ye impatient with me? Do ye crave for a story of an unchaste woman? Hath the name of Cleopatra tempted ye hither? Ye foolish ones; Cleopatra is as yet but a child that is whipped by her nurse. And what I am about to shew you for the good of your souls is how Cæsar, seeking Pompey in Egypt, found Cleopatra; and how he received that present of a pickled cabbage that was once the head of Pompey; and what things happened between the old Cæsar and the child queen before he left Egypt and battled his way back to Rome to be slain there as Pompey was slain, by men in whom the spirit of Pompey still lived. All this ye shall see; and ye shall marvel, after your ignorant manner, that men twenty centuries ago were already just such as you, and spoke and lived as ye speak and live, no worse and no better, no wiser and no sillier. And the two thousand years that have past are to me, the god Ra, but a moment; nor is this day any other than the day in which Cæsar set foot in the land of my people. And now I leave you; for ye are a dull folk, and instruction is wasted on you; and I had not spoken so much but that it is in the nature of a god to struggle for ever with the dust and the darkness, and to drag from them, by the force of his longing for the divine, more life and more light. Settle ye therefore in your seats and keep silent; for ye are about to hear a man speak, and a great man he was, as ye count greatness. And fear not that I shall speak to you again: the rest of the story must ye learn from them that lived it. Farewell; and do not presume to applaud me.

(*The temple vanishes in utter darkness.*)

AN ALTERNATIVE TO THE PROLOGUE

(*An October night on the Syrian border of Egypt towards the end of the XXXIII Dynasty, in the year 706 by Roman computation, afterwards reckoned by Christian computation at 48* B.C. *A great radiance of silver fire, the dawn of a moonlit night, is rising in the east. The stars and the cloudless sky are our own contemporaries, nineteen and a half centuries younger than we know them; but you would not guess that from their appearance. Below them are two notable drawbacks of civilization: a palace, and soldiers. The palace, an old, low, Syrian building of whitened mud, is not so ugly as Buckingham Palace; and the officers in the courtyard are more highly civilized than modern English officers: for example, they do not dig up the corpses of their dead enemies and mutilate them, as we dug up Cromwell and the Mahdi. They are in two groups: one intent on the gambling of their captain* BELZANOR, *a warrior of fifty, who, with his spear on the ground beside his knee, is stooping to throw dice with a sly-looking young* PERSIAN *recruit; the other gathered about a guardsman who has just finished telling a naughty story (still current in English barracks) at which they are laughing uproariously. They are about a dozen in number, all highly aristocratic young Egyptian* GUARDSMEN, *handsomely equipped with weapons and armor, very unEnglish in point of not being ashamed of and uncomfortable in their professional dress; on the contrary, rather ostentatiously and arrogantly warlike, as valuing themselves on their military caste.*

BELZANOR *is a typical veteran, tough and wilful; prompt, capable and crafty where brute force will serve; helpless and boyish when it will not: an effective sergeant, an incompetent general, a deplora-*

ble dictator. Would, if influentially connected, be employed in the two last capacities by a modern European State on the strength of his success in the first. Is rather to be pitied just now in view of the fact that JULIUS CÆSAR *is invading his country. Not knowing this, is intent on his game with the* PERSIAN, *whom, as a foreigner, he considers quite capable of cheating him.*

His subalterns are mostly handsome young fellows whose interest in the game and the story symbolize with tolerable completeness the main interests in life of which they are conscious. Their spears are leaning against the walls, or lying on the ground ready to their hands. The corner of the courtyard forms a triangle of which one side is the front of the palace, with a doorway, the other a wall with a gateway. The storytellers are on the palace side: the gamblers, on the gateway side. Close to the gateway, against the wall, is a stone block high enough to enable a Nubian SENTINEL, *standing on it, to look over the wall. The yard is lighted by a torch stuck in the wall. As the laughter from the group round the storyteller dies away, the kneeling* PERSIAN, *winning the throw, snatches up the stake from the ground.*)

BELZANOR: By Apis, Persian, thy gods are good to thee.
PERSIAN: Try yet again, O captain. Double or quits!
BELZANOR: No more. I am not in the vein.
SENTINEL (*poising his javelin as he peers over the wall*): Stand. Who goes there?

(*They all start, listening. A strange* VOICE *replies from without.*)

VOICE: The bearer of evil tidings.
BELZANOR (*calling to the sentry*): Pass him.
SENTINEL (*grounding his javelin*): Draw near, O bearer of evil tidings.
BELZANOR (*pocketing the dice and picking up his spear*): Let us receive this man with honor. He bears evil tidings.

(*The* GUARDSMEN *seize their spears and gather about the gate, leaving a way through for the* NEW COMER.)

PERSIAN (*rising from his knee*): Are evil tidings, then, so honorable?
BELZANOR: O barbarous Persian, hear my instruction. In Egypt the bearer of good tidings is sacrificed to the gods as a thank offering; but no god will accept the blood of the messenger of evil. When we have good tidings, we are careful to send them in the mouth of the cheapest slave we can find. Evil tidings are borne by young noblemen who desire to bring themselves into notice. (*They join the rest at the gate.*)

SENTINEL: Pass, O young captain; and bow the head in the House of the Queen.

VOICE: Go anoint thy javelin with fat of swine, O Blackamoor; for before morning the Romans will make thee eat it to the very butt.

(The owner of the VOICE, *a fairhaired dandy, dressed in a different fashion from that affected by the* GUARDSMEN, *but no less extravagantly, comes through the gateway laughing. He is somewhat battlestained; and his left forearm, bandaged, comes through a torn sleeve. In his right hand he carries a Roman sword in its sheath. He swaggers down the courtyard, the* PERSIAN *on his right,* BELZANOR *on his left, and the* GUARDSMEN *crowding down behind him.)*

BELZANOR: Who are thou that laughest in the House of Cleopatra the Queen, and in the teeth of Belzanor, the captain of her guard?

NEW COMER: I am Bel Affris, descended from the gods.

BELZANOR *(ceremoniously)*: Hail, cousin!

ALL *(except the* PERSIAN*)*: Hail, cousin!

PERSIAN: All the Queen's guards are descended from the gods, O stranger, save myself. I am Persian, and descended from many kings.

BEL AFFRIS *(to the* GUARDSMEN*)*: Hail, cousins! *(To the* PERSIAN, *condescendingly.)* Hail, mortal!

BELZANOR: You have been in battle, Bel Affris; and you are a soldier among soldiers. You will not let the Queen's women have the first of your tidings.

BEL AFFRIS: I have no tidings, except that we shall have our throats cut presently, women, soldiers, and all.

PERSIAN *(to* BELZANOR*)*: I told you so.

SENTINEL *(who has been listening)*: Woe, alas!

BEL AFFRIS *(calling to him)*: Peace, peace, poor Ethiop: destiny is with the gods who painted thee black. *(To* BELZANOR.*)* What has this mortal *(indicating the* PERSIAN*)* told you?

BELZANOR: He says that the Roman Julius Cæsar, who has landed on our shores with a handful of followers, will make himself master of Egypt. He is afraid of the Roman soldiers. *(The* GUARDSMEN *laugh with boisterous scorn.)* Peasants, brought up to scare crows and follow the plough! Sons of smiths and millers and tanners! And we nobles, consecrated to arms, descended from the gods!

PERSIAN: Belzanor: the gods are not always good to their poor relations.

BELZANOR *(hotly, to the* PERSIAN*)*: Man to man, are we worse than the slaves of Cæsar?

BEL AFFRIS *(stepping between them)*: Listen, cousin. Man to man, we Egyptians are as gods above the Romans.

GUARDSMEN *(exultantly)*: Aha!

BEL AFFRIS: But this Cæsar does not pit man against man: he throws a legion at you where you are weakest as he throws a stone from a catapult; and that legion is as a man with one head, a thousand arms, and no religion. I have fought against them; and I know.

BELZANOR (*derisively*): Were you frightened, cousin?

(*The* GUARDSMEN *roar with laughter, their eyes sparkling at the wit of their captain.*)

BEL AFFRIS: No, cousin; but I was beaten. They were frightened (perhaps); but they scattered us like chaff.

(*The* GUARDSMEN, *much damped, utter a growl of contemptuous disgust.*)

BELZANOR: Could you not die?

BEL AFFRIS: No: that was too easy to be worthy of a descendant of the gods. Besides, there was no time: all was over in a moment. The attack came just where we least expected it.

BELZANOR: That shews that the Romans are cowards.

BEL AFFRIS: They care nothing about cowardice, these Romans: they fight to win. The pride and honor of war are nothing to them.

PERSIAN: Tell us the tale of the battle. What befell?

GUARDSMEN (*gathering eagerly round* BEL AFFRIS): Ay: the tale of the battle.

BEL AFFRIS: Know then, that I am a novice in the guard of the temple of Ra in Memphis, serving neither Cleopatra nor her brother Ptolemy, but only the high gods. We went a journey to inquire of Ptolemy why he had driven Cleopatra into Syria, and how we of Egypt should deal with the Roman Pompey, newly come to our shores after his defeat by Cæsar at Pharsalia. What, think ye, did we learn? Even that Cæsar is coming also in hot pursuit of his foe, and that Ptolemy has slain Pompey, whose severed head he holds in readiness to present to the conqueror. (*Sensation among the* GUARDSMEN). Nay, more: we found that Cæsar is already come; for we had not made half a day's journey on our way back when we came upon a city rabble flying from his legions, whose landing they had gone out to withstand.

BELZANOR: And ye, the temple guard! did ye not withstand these legions?

BEL AFFRIS: What a man could that we did. But there came the sound of a trumpet whose voice was as the cursing of a black mountain. Then saw we a moving wall of shields coming towards us. You know how the heart burns when you charge a fortified wall; but how if the fortified wall were to charge *you?*

PERSIAN (*exulting in having told them so*): Did I not say it?

BEL AFFRIS: When the wall came nigh, it changed into a line of men — common fellows enough, with helmets, leather tunics, and breastplates. Every man of them flung his javelin: the one that came my way drove through my shield as through a papyrus — lo there! (*he points to the bandage on his left arm*) and would have gone through my neck had I not stooped. They were charging at the double then, and were upon us with short swords almost as soon as their javelins. When a man is close to you with such a sword, you can do nothing with our weapons: they are all too long.

PERSIAN: What did you do?

BEL AFFRIS: Doubled my fist and smote my Roman on the sharpness of his jaw. He was but mortal after all: he lay down in a stupor; and I took his sword and laid it on. (*Drawing the sword.*) Lo! a Roman sword with Roman blood on it!

GUARDSMEN (*approvingly*): Good! (*They take the sword and hand it round, examining it curiously.*)

PERSIAN: And your men?

BEL AFFRIS: Fled. Scattered like sheep.

BELZANOR (*furiously*): The cowardly slaves! Leaving the descendants of the gods to be butchered!

BEL AFFRIS (*with acid coolness*): The descendants of the gods did not stay to be butchered, cousin. The battle was not to the strong; but the race was to the swift. The Romans, who have no chariots, sent a cloud of horsemen in pursuit, and slew multitudes. Then our high priest's captain rallied a dozen descendants of the gods and exhorted us to die fighting. I said to myself: surely it is safer to stand than to lose my breath and be stabbed in the back; so I joined our captain and stood. Then the Romans treated us with respect; for no man attacks a lion when the field is full of sheep, except for the pride and honor of war, of which these Romans know nothing. So we escaped with our lives; and I am come to warn you that you must open your gates to Cæsar; for his advance guard is scarce an hour behind me; and not an Egyptian warrior is left standing between you and his legions.

SENTINEL: Woe, alas! (*He throws down his javelin and flies into the palace.*)

BELZANOR: Nail him to the door, quick! (*The* GUARDSMEN *rush for him with their spears; but he is too quick for them.*) Now this news will run through the palace like fire through stubble.

BEL AFFRIS: What shall we do to save the women from the Romans?

BELZANOR: Why not kill them?

PERSIAN: Because we should have to pay blood money for some of them. Better let the Romans kill them: it is cheaper.

BELZANOR (*awestruck at his brain power*): O subtle one! O serpent!

BEL AFFRIS: But your Queen?

BELZANOR: True: we must carry off Cleopatra.

BEL AFFRIS: Will ye not await her command?

BELZANOR: Command! a girl of sixteen! Not we. At Memphis ye deem her a Queen: here we know better. I will take her on the crupper of my horse. When we soldiers have carried her out of Cæsar's reach, then the priests and the nurses and the rest of them can pretend she is a Queen again, and put their commands into her mouth.

PERSIAN: Listen to me, Belzanor.

BELZANOR: Speak, O subtle beyond thy years.

PERSIAN: Cleopatra's brother Ptolemy is at war with her. Let us sell her to him.

GUARDSMEN: O subtle one! O serpent!

BELZANOR: We dare not. We are descended from the gods; but Cleopatra is descended from the river Nile; and the lands of our fathers will grow no grain if the Nile rises not to water them. Without our father's gifts we should live the lives of dogs.

PERSIAN: It is true: the Queen's guard cannot live on its pay. But hear me further, O ye kinsmen of Osiris.

GUARDSMEN: Speak, O subtle one. Hear the serpent-begotten!

PERSIAN: Have I heretofore spoken truly to you of Cæsar, when you thought I mocked you?

GUARDSMEN: Truly, truly.

BELZANOR (*reluctantly admitting it*): So Bel Affris says.

PERSIAN: Hear more of him, then. This Cæsar is a great lover of women: he makes them his friends and counsellors.

BELZANOR: Faugh! This rule of women will be the ruin of Egypt!

PERSIAN: Let it rather be the ruin of Rome! Cæsar grows old now: he is past fifty and full of labors and battles. He is too old for the young women; and the old women are too wise to worship him.

BEL AFFRIS: Take heed, Persian. Cæsar is by this time almost within earshot.

PERSIAN: Cleopatra is not yet a woman: neither is she wise. But she already troubles men's wisdom.

BELZANOR: Ay: that is because she is descended from the river Nile and a black kitten of the sacred White Cat. What then?

PERSIAN: Why, sell her secretly to Ptolemy, and then offer ourselves to Cæsar as volunteers to fight for the overthrow of her brother and the rescue of our Queen, the Great Granddaughter of the Nile.

GUARDSMEN: O serpent!

PERSIAN: He will listen to us if we come with her picture in our mouths. He will conquer and kill her brother, and reign in Egypt with Cleopatra for his Queen. And we shall be her guard.

GUARDSMEN: O subtlest of all the serpents! O admiration! O wisdom!

BEL AFFRIS: He will also have arrived before you have done talking, O word spinner.

BELZANOR: That is true. (*An affrighted uproar in the palace interrupts him.*) Quick: the flight has begun: guard the door. (*They rush to the door and form a cordon before it with their spears. A mob of women-servants and nurses surges out. Those in front recoil from the spears, screaming to those behind to keep back.* BELZANOR'S *voice dominates the disturbance as he shouts.*) Back there. In again, unprofitable cattle.

GUARDSMEN: Back, unprofitable cattle.

BELZANOR: Send us out Ftatateeta, the Queen's chief nurse.

THE WOMEN (*calling into the palace*): Ftatateeta, Ftatateeta. Come, come. Speak to Belzanor.

A WOMAN: Oh, keep back. You are thrusting me on the spearheads.

(*A huge grim woman, her face covered with a network of tiny wrinkles, and her eyes old, large, and wise; sinewy handed, very tall, very strong; with the mouth of a bloodhound and the jaws of a bulldog, appears on the threshold. She is dressed like a person of consequence in the palace, and confronts the* GUARDSMEN *insolently.*)

FTATATEETA: Make way for the Queen's chief nurse.

BELZANOR (*with solemn arrogance*): Ftatateeta: I am Belzanor, the captain of the Queen's guard, descended from the gods.

FTATATEETA (*retorting his arrogance with interest*): Belzanor: I am Ftatateeta, the Queen's chief nurse; and your divine ancestors were proud to be painted on the wall in the pyramids of the kings whom my fathers served.

(*The* WOMEN *laugh triumphantly.*)

BELZANOR (*with grim humor*): Ftatateeta: daughter of a long-tongued, swivel-eyed chameleon, the Romans are at hand. (*A cry of terror from the* WOMEN: *they would fly but for the spears.*) Not even the descendants of the gods can resist them; for they have each man seven arms, each carrying seven spears. The blood in their veins is boiling quicksilver; and their wives become mothers in three hours. and are slain and eaten the next day.

(A shudder of horror from the WOMEN. FTATATEETA, *despising them and scorning the soldiers, pushes her way through the crowd and confronts the spear points undismayed.)*

FTATATEETA: Then fly and save yourselves, O cowardly sons of the cheap clay gods that are sold to fish porters; and leave us to shift for ourselves.

BELZANOR: Not until you have first done our bidding, O terror of manhood. Bring out Cleopatra the Queen to us; and then go whither you will.

FTATATEETA *(with a derisive laugh)*: Now I know why the gods have taken her out of our hands. *(The* GUARDSMEN *start and look at one another.)* Know, thou foolish soldier, that the Queen has been missing since an hour past sundown.

BELZANOR *(furious)*: Hag: you have hidden her to sell to Cæsar or her brother. *(He grasps her by the left wrist, and drags her, helped by a few of the* GUARD, *to the middle of the courtyard, where, as they fling her on her knees, he draws a murderous looking knife.)* Where is she? Where is she? or — *(He threatens to cut her throat.)*

FTATATEETA *(savagely)*: Touch me, dog; and the Nile will not rise on your fields for seven times seven years of famine.

BELZANOR *(frightened, but desperate)*: I will sacrifice: I will pay. Or stay. *(To the* PERSIAN.*)* You, O subtle one: your father's lands lie far from the Nile. Slay her.

PERSIAN *(threatening her with his knife)*: Persia has but one god; yet he loves the blood of old women. Where is Cleopatra?

FTATATEETA: Persian: as Osiris lives, I do not know. I chid her for bringing evil days upon us by talking to the sacred cats of the priests, and carrying them in her arms. I told her she would be left alone here when the Romans came as a punishment for her disobedience. And now she is gone — run away — hidden. I speak the truth. I call Osiris to witness —

THE WOMEN *(protesting officiously)*: She speaks the truth, Belzanor.

BELZANOR: You have frightened the child: she is hiding. Search — quick — into the palace — search every corner.

(The GUARDS, *led by* BELZANOR, *shoulder their way into the palace through the flying crowd of* WOMEN, *who escape through the courtyard gate.)*

FTATATEETA *(screaming)*: Sacrilege! Men in the Queen's chambers! Sa — *(Her voice dies away as the* PERSIAN *puts his knife to her throat.)*

BEL AFFRIS *(laying a hand on* FTATATEETA'S *left shoulder)*: Forbear her yet a moment, Persian. (*To* FTATATEETA, *very significantly.*) Mother: your gods are asleep or away hunting; and the sword is at your throat. Bring us to where the Queen is hid, and you shall live.

FTATATEETA (*contemptuously*): Who shall stay the sword in the hand of a fool, if the high gods put it there? Listen to me, ye young men without understanding. Cleopatra fears me; but she fears the Romans more. There is but one power greater in her eyes than the wrath of the Queen's nurse and the cruelty of Cæsar; and that is the power of the Sphinx that sits in the desert watching the way to the sea. What she would have it know, she tells into the ears of the sacred cats; and on her birthday she sacrifices to it and decks it with poppies. Go ye therefore into the desert and seek Cleopatra in the shadow of the Sphinx; and on your heads see to it that no harm comes to her.

BEL AFFRIS (*to the* PERSIAN): May we believe this, O subtle one?

PERSIAN: Which way come the Romans?

BEL AFFRIS: Over the desert, from the sea, by this very Sphinx.

PERSIAN (*to* FTATATEETA): O mother of guile! O aspic's tongue! You have made up this tale so that we two may go into the desert and perish on the spears of the Romans. (*Lifting his knife.*) Taste death.

FTATATEETA: Not from thee, baby. (*She snatches his ankle from under him and flies stooping along the palace wall, vanishing in the darkness within its precinct.* BEL AFFRIS *roars with laughter as the* PERSIAN *tumbles. The* GUARDSMEN *rush out of the palace with* BELZANOR *and a mob of fugitives, mostly carrying bundles.*)

PERSIAN: Have you found Cleopatra?

BELZANOR: She is gone. We have searched every corner.

SENTINEL (*appearing at the door of the palace*): Woe! Alas! Fly, fly!

BELZANOR: What is the matter now?

SENTINEL: The sacred white cat has been stolen.

ALL: Woe! woe! (*General panic. They all fly with cries of consternation. The torch is thrown down and extinguished in the rush. The noise of the fugitives dies away. Darkness and dead silence.*)

ACT ONE

(*The same darkness into which the temple of Ra and the Syrian palace vanished. The same silence. Suspense. Then the blackness and stillness break softly into silver mist and strange airs as the windswept harp of Memnon plays at the dawning of the moon. It rises full over the desert; and a vast horizon comes into relief, broken by a huge shape which soon reveals itself in the spreading radiance as a*

Sphinx pedestalled on the sands. The light still clears, until the upraised eyes of the image are distinguished looking straight forward and upward in infinite fearless vigil, and a mass of color between its great paws defines itself as a heap of red poppies on which a girl lies motionless, her silken vest heaving gently and regularly with the breathing of a dreamless sleeper, and her braided hair glittering in a shaft of moonlight like a bird's wing.

Suddenly there comes from afar a vaguely fearful sound (it might be the bellow of a Minotaur softened by great distance) and Memnon's music stops. Silence: then a few faint high-ringing trumpet notes. Then silence again. Then a man comes from the south with stealing steps, ravished by the mystery of the night, all wonder, and halts, lost in contemplation, opposite the left flank of the Sphinx, whose bosom, with its burden, is hidden from him by its massive shoulder.)

THE MAN: Hail, Sphinx: salutation from Julius Cæsar! I have wandered in many lands, seeking the lost regions from which my birth into this world exiled me, and the company of creatures such as I myself. I have found flocks and pastures, men and cities, but no other Cæsar, no air native to me, no man kindred to me, none who can do my day's deed, and think my night's thought. In the little world yonder, Sphinx, my place is as high as yours in this great desert; only I wander, and you sit still; I conquer, and you endure; I work and wonder, you watch and wait; I look up and am dazzled, look down and am darkened, look round and am puzzled, whilst your eyes never turn from looking out — out of the world — to the lost region — the home from which we have strayed. Sphinx, you and I, strangers to the race of men, are no strangers to one another: have I not been conscious of you and of this place since I was born? Rome is a madman's dream: this is my Reality. These starry lamps of yours I have seen from afar in Gaul, in Britain, in Spain, in Thessaly, signalling great secrets to some eternal sentinel below, whose post I never could find. And here at last is their sentinel — an image of the constant and immortal part of my life, silent, full of thoughts, alone in the silver desert. Sphinx, Sphinx: I have climbed mountains at night to hear in the distance the stealthy footfall of the winds that chase your sands in forbidden play — our invisible children, O Sphinx, laughing in whispers. My way hither was the way of destiny; for I am he of whose genius you are the symbol: part brute, part woman, and part god — nothing of man in me at all. Have I read your riddle, Sphinx?

THE GIRL (*who has wakened, and peeped cautiously from her nest to see who is speaking*): Old gentleman.

CÆSAR (*staring violently, and clutching his sword*): Immortal gods!

THE GIRL: Old gentleman: dont run away.

CÆSAR (*stupefied*): "Old gentleman: dont run away"!!! This! to Julius Cæsar!

THE GIRL (*urgently*): Old gentleman.

CÆSAR: Sphinx: you presume on your centuries. I am younger than you, though your voice is but a girl's voice as yet.

THE GIRL: Climb up here, quickly; or the Romans will come and eat you.

CÆSAR (*running forward past the Sphinx's shoulder, and seeing her*): A child at its breast! a divine child!

THE GIRL: Come up quickly. You must get up at its side and creep round.

CÆSAR (*amazed*): Who are you?

THE GIRL: Cleopatra, Queen of Egypt.

CÆSAR: Queen of the Gypsies, you mean.

CLEOPATRA: You must not be disrespectful to me, or the Sphinx will let the Romans eat you. Come up. It is quite cosy here.

CÆSAR (*to himself*): What a dream! What a magnificent dream! Only let me not wake, and I will conquer ten continents to pay for dreaming it out to the end. (*He climbs to the Sphinx's flank, and presently reappears to her on the pedestal, stepping round its right shoulder.*)

CLEOPATRA: Take care. Thats right. Now sit down: you may have its other paw. (*She seats herself comfortably on its left paw.*) It is very powerful and will protect us; but (*shivering, and with plaintive loneliness*) it would not take any notice of me or keep me company. I am glad you have come: I was very lonely. Did you happen to see a white cat anywhere?

CÆSAR (*sitting slowly down on the right paw in extreme wonderment*): Have you lost one?

CLEOPATRA: Yes: the sacred white cat: is it not dreadful? I brought him here to sacrifice him to the Sphinx; but when we got a little way from the city a black cat called him, and he jumped out of my arms and ran away to it. Do you think that the black cat can have been my great-great-great-grandmother?

CÆSAR (*staring at her*): Your great-great-great-grandmother! Well, why not? Nothing would surprise me on this night of nights.

CLEOPATRA: I think it must have been. My great-grandmother's great-grandmother was a black kitten of the sacred white cat; and the river Nile made her his seventh wife. That is why my hair is so wavy. And I always want to be let do as I like, no matter whether it is the will of the gods or not: that is because my blood is made with Nile water.

CÆSAR: What are you doing here at this time of night? Do you live here?

CLEOPATRA: Of course not: I am the Queen; and I shall live in the palace at Alexandria when I have killed my brother, who drove me out of it. When I am old enough I shall do just what I like. I shall be able to poison the slaves and see them wriggle, and pretend to Ftatateeta that she is going to be put into the fiery furnace.

CÆSAR: Hm! Meanwhile why are you not at home and in bed?

CLEOPATRA: Because the Romans are coming to eat us all. You are not at home and in bed either.

CÆSAR (*with conviction*): Yes I am. I live in a tent; and I am now in that tent, fast asleep and dreaming. Do you suppose that I believe you are real, you impossible little dream witch?

CLEOPATRA (*giggling and leaning trustfully towards him*): You are a funny old gentleman. I like you.

CÆSAR: Ah, that spoils the dream. Why dont you dream that I am young?

CLEOPATRA: I wish you were; only I think I should be more afraid of you. I like men, especially young men with round strong arms; but I am afraid of them. You are old and rather thin and stringy; but you have a nice voice; and I like to have somebody to talk to, though I think you are a little mad. It is the moon that makes you talk to yourself in that silly way.

CÆSAR: What! you heard that, did you? I was saying my prayers to the great Sphinx.

CLEOPATRA: But this isnt the great Sphinx.

CÆSAR (*much disappointed, looking up at the statue*): What!

CLEOPATRA: This is only a dear little kitten of a Sphinx. Why, the great Sphinx is so big that it has a temple between its paws. This is my pet Sphinx. Tell me: do you think the Romans have any sorcerers who could take us away from the Sphinx by magic?

CÆSAR: Why? Are you afraid of the Romans?

CLEOPATRA (*very seriously*): Oh, they would eat us if they caught us. They are barbarians. Their chief is called Julius Cæsar. His father was a tiger and his mother a burning mountain; and his nose is like an elephant's trunk. (CÆSAR *involuntarily rubs his nose.*) They all have long noses, and ivory tusks, and little tails, and seven arms with a hundred arrows in each; and they live on human flesh.

CÆSAR: Would you like me to shew you a real Roman?

CLEOPATRA (*terrified*): No. You are frightening me.

CÆSAR: No matter: this is only a dream —

CLEOPATRA (*excitedly*): It is not a dream: it is not a dream. See, see.

(*She plucks a pin from her hair and jabs it repeatedly into his arm.*)

CÆSAR: Ffff — Stop. (*Wrathfully.*) How dare you?

CLEOPATRA (*abashed*): You said you were dreaming. (*Whimpering.*) I only wanted to shew you —

CÆSAR (*gently*): Come, come: dont cry. A queen mustnt cry. (*He rubs his arm, wondering at the reality of the smart.*) Am I awake? (*He strikes his hand against the Sphinx to test its solidity. It feels so real that he begins to be alarmed, and says perplexedly.*) Yes, I — (*quite panic-stricken*) no: impossible: madness, madness! (*Desperately.*) Back to camp — to camp. (*He rises to spring down from the pedestal.*)

CLEOPATRA (*flinging her arms in terror round him*): No: you shant leave me. No, no, no: dont go. I'm afraid — afraid of the Romans.

CÆSAR (*as the conviction that he is really awake forces itself on him*): Cleopatra: can you see my face well?

CLEOPATRA: Yes. It is so white in the moonlight.

CÆSAR: Are you sure it is the moonlight that makes me look whiter than an Egyptian? (*Grimly.*) Do you notice that I have a rather long nose?

CLEOPATRA (*recoiling, paralysed by a terrible suspicion*): Oh!

CÆSAR: It is a Roman nose, Cleopatra.

CLEOPATRA: Ah! (*With a piercing scream she springs up; darts round the left shoulder of the Sphinx; scrambles down to the sand; and falls on her knees in frantic supplication, shrieking.*) Bite him in two, Sphinx: bite him in two. I meant to sacrifice the white cat — I did indeed — I (CÆSAR, *who has slipped down from the pedestal, touches her on the shoulder.*) — Ah! (*She buries her head in her arms.*)

CÆSAR: Cleopatra: Shall I teach you a way to prevent Cæsar from eating you?

CLEOPATRA (*clinging to him piteously*): Oh do, do, do. I will steal Ftatateeta's jewels and give them to you. I will make the river Nile water your lands twice a year.

CÆSAR: Peace, peace, my child. Your gods are afraid of the Romans: you see the Sphinx dare not bite me, nor prevent me carrying you off to Julius Cæsar.

CLEOPATRA (*in pleading murmurings*): You wont, you wont. You said you wouldnt.

CÆSAR: Cæsar never eats women.

CLEOPATRA (*springing up full of hope*): What!

CÆSAR (*impressively*): But he eats girls (*she relapses*) and cats. Now you are a silly little girl; and you are descended from the black kitten. You are both a girl and a cat.

CLEOPATRA (*trembling*): And will he eat *me?*

CÆSAR: Yes; unless you make him believe that you are a woman.

CLEOPATRA: Oh, you must get a sorcerer to make a woman of me. Are you a sorcerer?

CÆSAR: Perhaps. But it will take a long time; and this very night you must stand face to face with Cæsar in the palace of your fathers.

CLEOPATRA: No, no. I darent.

CÆSAR: Whatever dread may be in your soul — however terrible Cæsar may be to you — you must confront him as a brave woman and a great queen; and you must feel no fear. If your hand shakes: if your voice quavers; then — night and death! (*She moans.*) But if he thinks you worthy to rule, he will set you on the throne by his side and make you the real ruler of Egypt.

CLEOPATRA (*despairingly*): No: he will find me out: he will find me out.

CÆSAR (*rather mournfully*): He is easily deceived by women. Their eyes dazzle him; and he sees them not as they are, but as he wishes them to appear to him.

CLEOPATRA (*hopefully*): Then we will cheat him. I will put on Ftatateeta's head-dress; and he will think me quite an old woman.

CÆSAR: If you do that he will eat you at one mouthful.

CLEOPATRA: But I will give him a cake with my magic opal and seven hairs of the white cat baked in it; and —

CÆSAR (*abruptly*): Pah! you are a little fool. He will eat your cake and you too. (*He turns contemptuously from her.*)

CLEOPATRA (*running after him and clinging to him*): Oh please, *please!* I will do whatever you tell me. I will be good. I will be your slave. (*Again the terrible bellowing note sounds across the desert, now closer at hand. It is the bucina, the Roman war trumpet.*)

CÆSAR: Hark!

CLEOPATRA (*trembling*): What was that?

CÆSAR: Cæsar's voice.

CLEOPATRA (*pulling at his hand*): Let us run away. Come. Oh, come.

CÆSAR: You are safe with me until you stand on your throne to receive Cæsar. Now lead me thither.

CLEOPATRA (*only too glad to get away*): I will, I will. (*Again the bucina.*) Oh come, come, come: the gods are angry. Do you feel the earth shaking?

CÆSAR: It is the tread of Cæsar's legions.

CLEOPATRA (*drawing him away*): This way, quickly. And let us look for the white cat as we go. It is he that has turned you into a Roman.

CÆSAR: Incorrigible, oh, incorrigible! Away! (*He follows her, the bucina sounding louder as they steal across the desert. The moonlight wanes:*

the horizon again shows black against the sky, broken only by the fantastic silhouette of the Sphinx. The sky itself vanishes in darkness, from which there is no relief until the gleam of a distant torch falls on great Egyptian pillars supporting the roof of a majestic corridor. At the further end of this corridor a Nubian slave appears carrying the torch. CÆSAR, *still led by* CLEOPATRA, *follows him. They come down the corridor,* CÆSAR *peering keenly about at the strange architecture, and at the pillar shadows between which, as the passing torch makes them hurry noiselessly backwards, figures of men with wings and hawks' heads, and vast black marble cats, seem to flit in and out of ambush. Further along, the wall turns a corner and makes a spacious transept in which* CÆSAR *sees, on his right, a throne, and behind the throne a door. On each side of the throne is a slender pillar with a lamp on it.*)

CÆSAR: What place is this?

CLEOPATRA: This is where I sit on the throne when I am allowed to wear my crown and robes. (*The slave holds his torch to shew the throne.*)

CÆSAR: Order the slave to light the lamps.

CLEOPATRA (*shyly*): Do you think I may?

CÆSAR: Of course. You are the Queen. (*She hesitates.*) Go on.

CLEOPATRA (*timidly, to the slave*): Light all the lamps.

FTATATEETA (*suddenly coming from behind the throne*): Stop. (*The slave stops. She turns sternly to* CLEOPATRA, *who quails like a naughty child.*) Who is this you have with you; and how dare you order the lamps to be lighted without my permission? (CLEOPATRA *is dumb with apprehension.*)

CÆSAR: Who is she?

CLEOPATRA: Ftatateeta.

FTATATEETA (*arrogantly*): Chief nurse to —

CÆSAR (*cutting her short*): I speak to the Queen. Be silent. (*To* CLEOPATRA.) Is this how your servants know their places? Send her away; and do you (*to the slave*) do as the Queen has bidden. (*The slave lights the lamps. Meanwhile* CLEOPATRA *stands hesitating, afraid of* FTATATEETA.) You are the Queen: send her away.

CLEOPATRA (*cajoling*): Ftatateeta, dear: you must go away — just for a little.

CÆSAR: You are not commanding her to go away: you are begging her. You are no Queen. You will be eaten. Farewell. (*He turns to go.*)

CLEOPATRA (*clutching him*): No, no, no. Dont leave me.

CÆSAR: A Roman does not stay with queens who are afraid of their slaves.

CLEOPATRA: I am not afraid. Indeed I am not afraid.

FTATATEETA: We shall see who is afraid here. (*Menacingly.*) Cleopatra —

CÆSAR: On your knees, woman: am I also a child that you dare trifle with me? (*He points to the floor at* CLEOPATRA*'s feet.* FTATATEETA, *half cowed, half savage, hesitates.* CÆSAR *calls to the* NUBIAN.) Slave. (*The* NUBIAN *comes to him.*) Can you cut off a head? (*The* NUBIAN *nods and grins ecstatically, showing all his teeth.* CÆSAR *takes his sword by the scabbard, ready to offer the hilt to the* NUBIAN, *and turns again to* FTATATEETA, *repeating his gesture.*) Have you remembered yourself, mistress?

(FTATATEETA, *crushed, kneels before* CLEOPATRA, *who can hardly believe her eyes.*)

FTATATEETA (*hoarsely*): O Queen, forget not thy servant in the days of thy greatness.

CLEOPATRA (*blazing with excitement*): Go. Begone. Go away. (FTATATEETA *rises with stooped head, and moves backwards towards the door.* CLEOPATRA *watches her submission eagerly, almost clapping her hands, which are trembling. Suddenly she cries.*) Give me something to beat her with. (*She snatches a snake-skin from the throne and dashes after* FTATATEETA, *whirling it like a scourge in the air.* CÆSAR *makes a bound and manages to catch her and hold her while* FTATATEETA *escapes.*)

CÆSAR: You scratch, kitten, do you?

CLEOPATRA (*breaking from him*): I *will* beat somebody. I will beat him. (*She attacks the slave.*) There, there, there! (*The slave flies for his life up the corridor and vanishes. She throws the snake-skin away and jumps on the step of the throne with her arms waving, crying.*) I am a real Queen at last — a real, real Queen! Cleopatra the Queen! (CÆSAR *shakes his head dubiously, the advantage of the change seeming open to question from the point of view of the general welfare of Egypt. She turns and looks at him exultantly. Then she jumps down from the steps, runs to him, and flings her arms round him rapturously, crying.*) Oh, I love you for making me a Queen.

CÆSAR: But queens love only kings.

CLEOPATRA: I will make all the men I love kings. I will make you a king. I will have many young kings, with round strong arms; and when I am tired of them I will whip them to death; but you shall always be my king: my nice, kind, wise, good old king.

CÆSAR: Oh, my wrinkles, my wrinkles! And my child's heart! You will be the most dangerous of all Cæsar's conquests.

CLEOPATRA (*appalled*): Cæsar! I forgot Cæsar. (*Anxiously.*) You will tell him that I am a Queen, will you not? — a real Queen. Listen!

(*stealthily coaxing him*) let us run away and hide until Cæsar is gone.

CÆSAR: If you fear Cæsar, you are no true queen; and though you were to hide beneath a pyramid, he would go straight to it and lift it with one hand. And then — ! (*He chops his teeth together.*)

CLEOPATRA (*trembling*): Oh!

CÆSAR: Be afraid if you dare. (*The note of the bucina resounds again in the distance. She moans with fear.* CÆSAR *exults in it, exclaiming.*) Aha! Cæsar approaches the throne of Cleopatra. Come: take your place. (*He takes her hand and leads her to the throne. She is too downcast to speak.*) Ho, there, Teetatota. How do you call your slaves?

CLEOPATRA (*spiritlessly, as she sinks on the throne and cowers there, shaking*): Clap your hands.

(*He claps his hands.* FTATATEETA *returns.*)

CÆSAR: Bring the Queen's robes, and her crown, and her women; and prepare her.

CLEOPATRA (*eagerly — recovering herself a little*): Yes, the crown, Ftatateeta: I shall wear the crown.

FTATATEETA: For whom must the Queen put on her state?

CÆSAR: For a citizen of Rome. A king of kings, Totateeta.

CLEOPATRA (*stamping at her*): How dare you ask questions? Go and do as you are told. (FTATATEETA *goes out with a grim smile.* CLEOPATRA *goes on eagerly, to* CÆSAR.) Cæsar will know that I am a Queen when he sees my crown and robes, will he not?

CÆSAR: No. How shall he know that you are not a slave dressed up in the Queen's ornaments?

CLEOPATRA: You must tell him.

CÆSAR: He will not ask me. He will know Cleopatra by her pride, her courage, her majesty, and her beauty. (*She looks very doubtful.*) Are you trembling?

CLEOPATRA (*shivering with dread*): No, I — I — (*in a very sickly voice*) No.

(FTATATEETA *and three* WOMEN *come in with the regalia.*)

FTATATEETA: Of all the Queen's women, these three alone are left. The rest are fled. (*They begin to deck* CLEOPATRA, *who submits, pale and motionless.*)

CÆSAR: Good, good. Three are enough. Poor Cæsar generally has to dress himself.

FTATATEETA (*contemptuously*): The Queen of Egypt is not a Roman barbarian. (*To* CLEOPATRA.) Be brave, my nursling. Hold up your head before this stranger.

CÆSAR (*admiring* CLEOPATRA, *and placing the crown on her head*): Is it sweet or bitter to be a Queen, Cleopatra?

CLEOPATRA: Bitter.

CÆSAR: Cast out fear; and you will conquer Cæsar. Tota: are the Romans at hand?

FTATATEETA: They are at hand; and the guard has fled.

THE WOMEN (*wailing subduedly*): Woe to us!

(*The* NUBIAN *comes running down the hall.*)

NUBIAN: The Romans are in the courtyard. (*He bolts through the door. With a shriek, the* WOMEN *fly after him.* FTATATEETA'S *jaw expresses savage resolution: she does not budge.* CLEOPATRA *can hardly restrain herself from following them.* CÆSAR *grips her wrist, and looks steadfastly at her. She stands like a martyr.*)

CÆSAR: The Queen must face Cæsar alone. Answer "So be it."

CLEOPATRA (*white*): So be it.

CÆSAR (*releasing her*): Good.

(*A tramp and tumult of armed men is heard.* CLEOPATRA'S *terror increases. The bucina sounds close at hand, followed by a formidable clangor of trumpets. This is too much for* CLEOPATRA: *she utters a cry and darts towards the door.* FTATATEETA *stops her ruthlessly.*)

FTATATEETA: You are my nursling. You have said "So be it"; and if you die for it, you must make the Queen's word good. (*She hands* CLEOPATRA *to* CÆSAR, *who takes her back, almost beside herself with apprehension, to the throne.*)

CÆSAR: Now, if you quail — ! (*He seats himself on the throne.*)

(*She stands on the step, all but unconscious, waiting for death. The Roman soldiers troop in tumultuously through the corridor, headed by their ensign with his eagle, and their bucinator, a burly fellow with his instrument coiled round his body, its brazen bell shaped like the head of a howling wolf. When they reach the transept, they stare in amazement at the throne; dress into ordered rank opposite it; draw their swords and lift them in the air with a shout of* Hail, Cæsar. CLEOPATRA *turns and stares wildly at* CÆSAR; *grasps the situation; and, with a great sob of relief, falls into his arms.*)

ACT TWO

(Alexandria. A hall on the first floor of the Palace, ending in a loggia approached by two steps. Through the arches of the loggia the Mediterranean can be seen, bright in the morning sun. The clean lofty walls, painted with a procession of the Egyptian theocracy, presented in profile as flat ornament, and the absence of mirrors, sham perspectives, stuffy upholstery and textiles, make the place handsome, wholesome, simple and cool, or, as a rich English manufacturer would express it, poor, bare, ridiculous and unhomely. For Tottenham Court Road civilization is to this Egyptian civilization as glass bead and tattoo civilization is to Tottenham Court Road.

The young king PTOLEMY DIONYSUS *(aged ten) is at the top of the steps, on his way in through the loggia, led by his guardian* POTHINUS, *who has him by the hand. The court is assembled to receive him. It is made up of men and women (some of the women being officials) of various complexions and races, mostly Egyptian; some of them, comparatively fair, from lower Egypt, some, much darker, from upper Egypt; with a few Greeks and Jews. Prominent in a group on* PTOLEMY'S *right hand is* THEODOTUS, PTOLEMY'S *tutor. Another group, on* PTOLEMY'S *left, is headed by* ACHILLAS, *the general of* PTOLEMY'S *troops.* THEODOTUS *is a little old man, whose features are as cramped and wizened as his limbs, except his tall straight forehead, which occupies more space than all the rest of his face. He maintains an air of magpie keenness and profundity, listening to what the others say with the sarcastic vigilance of a philosopher listening to the exercises of his disciples.* ACHILLAS *is a tall handsome man of thirty-five, with a fine black beard curled like the coat of a poodle. Apparently not a clever man, but distinguished and dignified.* POTHINUS *is a vigorous man of fifty, a eunuch, passionate, energetic and quick witted, but of common mind and character; impatient and unable to control his temper. He has fine tawny hair, like fur.* PTOLEMY, *the King, looks much older than an English boy of ten; but he has the childish air, the habit of being in leading strings, the mixture of impotence and petulance, the appearance of being excessively washed, combed and dressed by other hands, which is exhibited by court-bred princes of all ages.*

All receive the King with reverences. He comes down the steps to a chair of state which stands a little to his right, the only seat in the hall. Taking his place before it, he looks nervously for instructions to POTHINUS, *who places himself at his left hand.)*

POTHINUS: The King of Egypt has a word to speak.

THEODOTUS (*in a squeak which he makes impressive by sheer self-opinionativeness*): Peace for the King's word!

PTOLEMY (*without any vocal inflexions: he is evidently repeating a lesson*): Take notice of this all of you. I am the first-born son of Auletes the Flute Blower who was your King. My sister Berenice drove him from his throne and reigned in his stead but — but — (*he hesitates*) —

POTHINUS (*stealthily prompting*): — but the gods would not suffer —

PTOLEMY: Yes — the gods would not suffer — not suffer — (*He stops; then, crestfallen.*) I forget what the gods would not suffer.

THEODOTUS: Let Pothinus, the King's guardian, speak for the King.

POTHINUS (*suppressing his impatience with difficulty*): The King wished to say that the gods would not suffer the impiety of his sister to go unpunished.

PTOLEMY (*hastily*): Yes: I remember the rest of it. (*He resumes his monotone.*) Therefore the gods sent a stranger one Mark Antony a Roman captain of horsemen across the sands of the desert and he set my father again upon the throne. And my father took Berenice my sister and struck her head off. And now that my father is dead yet another of his daughters my sister Cleopatra would snatch the kingdom from me and reign in my place. But the gods would not suffer — (POTHINUS *coughs admonitorily*) — the gods — the gods would not suffer —

POTHINUS (*prompting*): — will not maintain —

PTOLEMY: Oh yes — will not maintain such iniquity they will give her head to the axe even as her sister's. But with the help of the witch Ftatateeta she hath cast a spell on the Roman Julius Cæsar to make him uphold her false pretence to rule in Egypt. Take notice then that I will not suffer — that I will not suffer — (*Pettishly, to* POTHINUS.) What is it that I will not suffer?

POTHINUS (*suddenly exploding with all the force and emphasis of political passion*): The King will not suffer a foreigner to take from him the throne of our Egypt. (*A shout of applause.*) Tell the King, Achillas, how many soldiers and horsemen follow the Roman?

THEODOTUS: Let the King's general speak!

ACHILLAS: But two Roman legions, O King. Three thousand soldiers and scarce a thousand horsemen.

(*The court breaks into derisive laughter; and a great chattering begins, amid which* RUFIO, *a Roman officer, appears in the loggia. He is a burly, black-bearded man of middle age, very blunt, prompt and rough, with small clear eyes, and plump nose and cheeks, which, however, like the rest of his flesh, are in iron-hard condition.)*

RUFIO (*from the steps*): Peace, ho! (*The laughter and chatter cease abruptly.*) Cæsar approaches.

THEODOTUS (*with much presence of mind*): The King permits the Roman commander to enter!

(*CÆSAR, plainly dressed, but wearing an oak wreath to conceal his baldness, enters from the loggia, attended by BRITANNUS, his secretary, a Briton, about forty, tall, solemn, and already slightly bald, with a heavy, drooping, hazel-coloured moustache trained so as to lose its ends in a pair of trim whiskers. He is carefully dressed in blue, with portfolio, inkhorn, and reed pen at his girdle. His serious air and sense of the importance of the business in hand is in marked contrast to the kindly interest of CÆSAR, who looks at the scene, which is new to him, with the frank curiosity of a child, and then turns to the King's chair: BRITANNUS and RUFIO posting themselves near the steps at the other side.*)

CÆSAR (*looking at POTHINUS and PTOLEMY*): Which is the King? the man or the boy?

POTHINUS: I am Pothinus, the guardian of my lord the King.

CÆSAR (*patting PTOLEMY kindly on the shoulder*): So you are the King. Dull work at your age, eh? (*To POTHINUS.*) Your servant, Pothinus. (*He turns away unconcernedly and comes slowly along the middle of the hall, looking from side to side at the courtiers until he reaches ACHILLAS.*) And this gentleman?

THEODOTUS: Achillas, the King's general.

CÆSAR (*to ACHILLAS, very friendly*): A general, eh? I am a general myself. But I began too old, too old. Health and many victories, Achillas!

ACHILLAS: As the gods will, Cæsar.

CÆSAR (*turning to THEODOTUS*): And you, sir, are — ?

THEODOTUS: Theodotus, the King's tutor.

CÆSAR: You teach men how to be kings, Theodotus. That is very clever of you. (*Looking at the gods on the walls as he turns away from THEODOTUS and goes up again to POTHINUS.*) And this place?

POTHINUS: The council chamber of the chancellors of the King's treasury, Cæsar.

CÆSAR: Ah! that reminds me. I want some money.

POTHINUS: The King's treasury is poor, Cæsar.

CÆSAR: Yes: I notice that there is but one chair in it.

RUFIO (*shouting gruffly*): Bring a chair there, some of you, for Cæsar.
PTOLEMY (*rising shyly to offer his chair*): Cæsar —
CÆSAR (*kindly*): No, no, my boy: that is your chair of state. Sit down.

(*He makes* PTOLEMY *sit down again. Meanwhile* RUFIO, *looking about him, sees in the nearest corner an image of the god Ra, represented as a seated man with the head of a hawk. Before the image is a bronze tripod, about as large as a three-legged stool, with a stick of incense burning on it.* RUFIO, *with Roman resourcefulness and indifference to foreign superstitions, promptly seizes the tripod; shakes off the incense; blows away the ash; and dumps it down behind* CÆSAR, *nearly in the middle of the hall.*)

RUFIO: Sit on that, Cæsar.

(*A shiver runs through the court, followed by a hissing whisper of* Sacrilege!)

CÆSAR (*seating himself*): Now, Pothinus, to business. I am badly in want of money.
BRITANNUS (*disapproving of these informal expressions*): My master would say that there is a lawful debt due to Rome by Egypt, contracted by the King's deceased father to the Triumvirate; and that it is Cæsar's duty to his country to require immediate payment.
CÆSAR (*blandly*): Ah, I forgot. I have not made my companions known here. Pothinus: this is Britannus, my secretary. He is an islander from the western end of the world, a day's voyage from Gaul. (BRITANNUS *bows stiffly.*) This gentleman is Rufio, my comrade in arms. (RUFIO *nods.*) Pothinus: I want 1,600 talents.

(*The courtiers, appalled, murmur loudly, and* THEODOTUS *and* ACHILLAS *appeal mutely to one another against so monstrous a demand.*)

POTHINUS (*aghast*): Forty million sesterces! Impossible. There is not so much money in the King's treasury.
CÆSAR (*encouragingly*): *Only* 1,600 talents, Pothinus. Why count it in sesterces? A sestertius is only worth a loaf of bread.
POTHINUS: And a talent is worth a racehorse. I say it is impossible. We have been at strife here, because the King's sister Cleopatra falsely claims his throne. The King's taxes have not been collected for a whole year.
CÆSAR: Yes they have, Pothinus. My officers have been collecting them all morning. (*Renewed whisper and sensation, not without some stifled laughter, among the courtiers.*)

RUFIO (*bluntly*): You must pay, Pothinus. Why waste words? You are getting off cheaply enough.

POTHINUS (*bitterly*): Is it possible that Cæsar, the conqueror of the world, has time to occupy himself with such a trifle as our taxes?

CÆSAR: My friend: taxes are the chief business of a conqueror of the world.

POTHINUS: Then take warning, Cæsar. This day, the treasures of the temple and the gold of the King's treasury shall be sent to the mint to be melted down for our ransom in the sight of the people. They shall see us sitting under bare walls and drinking from wooden cups. And their wrath be on your head, Caesar, if you force us to this sacrilege!

CÆSAR: Do not fear, Pothinus: the people know how well wine tastes in wooden cups. In return for your bounty, I will settle this dispute about the throne for you, if you will. What say you?

POTHINUS: If I say no, will that hinder you?

RUFIO (*defiantly*): No.

CÆSAR: You say the matter has been at issue for a year, Pothinus. May I have ten minutes at it?

POTHINUS: You will do your pleasure, doubtless.

CÆSAR: Good! But first, let us have Cleopatra here.

THEODOTUS: She is not in Alexandria: she is fled into Syria.

CÆSAR: I think not. (*To* RUFIO.) Call Totateeta.

RUFIO (*calling*): Ho there, Teetatota.

(FTATATEETA *enters the loggia, and stands arrogantly at the top of the steps.*)

FTATATEETA: Who pronounces the name of Ftatateeta, the Queen's chief nurse?

CÆSAR: Nobody can pronounce it, Tota, except yourself. Where is your mistress?

(CLEOPATRA, *who is hiding behind* FTATATEETA, *peeps out at them laughing.* CÆSAR *rises.*)

CÆSAR: Will the Queen favor us with her presence for a moment?

CLEOPATRA (*pushing* FTATATEETA *aside and standing haughtily on the brink of the steps*): Am I to behave like a Queen?

CÆSAR: Yes.

(CLEOPATRA *immediately comes down to the chair of state; seizes* PTOLEMY; *drags him out of his seat; then takes his place in the chair.* FTATATEETA *seats herself on the steps of the loggia, and sits there, watching the scene with sibylline intensity.*)

PTOLEMY (*mortified, and struggling with his tears*): Cæsar: this is how she treats me always. If I am a king why is she allowed to take everything from me?

CLEOPATRA: You are not to be King, you little cry-baby. You are to be eaten by the Romans.

CÆSAR (*touched by* PTOLEMY'S *distress*): Come here, my boy, and stand by me.

(PTOLEMY *goes over to* CÆSAR, *who, resuming his seat on the tripod, takes the boy's hand to encourage him.* CLEOPATRA, *furiously jealous, rises and glares at them.*)

CLEOPATRA (*with flaming cheeks*): Take your throne: I dont want it. (*She flings away from the chair, and approaches* PTOLEMY, *who shrinks from her.*) Go this instant and sit down in your place.

CÆSAR: Go, Ptolemy. Always take a throne when it is offered to you.

RUFIO: I hope you will have the good sense to follow your own advice when we return to Rome, Cæsar.

(PTOLEMY *slowly goes back to the throne, giving* CLEOPATRA *a wide berth, in evident fear of her hands. She takes his place beside* CÆSAR.)

CÆSAR: Pothinus —

CLEOPATRA (*interrupting him*): Are you not going to speak to me?

CÆSAR: Be quiet. Open your mouth again before I give you leave and you shall be eaten.

CLEOPATRA: I am not afraid. A queen must not be afraid. Eat my husband there, if you like: *he* is afraid.

CÆSAR (*starting*): Your husband! What do you mean?

CLEOPATRA (*pointing to* PTOLEMY): That little thing.

(*The two Romans and the Briton stare at one another in amazement.*)

THEODOTUS: Cæsar: you are a stranger here, and not conversant with our laws. The kings and queens of Egypt may not marry except with their own royal blood. Ptolemy and Cleopatra are born king and consort just as they are born brother and sister.

BRITANNUS (*shocked*): Cæsar: this is not proper.

THEODOTUS (*outraged*): How!

CÆSAR (*recovering his self-possession*): Pardon him, Theodotus: he is a barbarian, and thinks that the customs of his tribe and island are the laws of nature.

BRITANNUS: On the contrary, Cæsar, it is these Egyptians who are barbarians; and you do wrong to encourage them. I say it is a scandal.

CÆSAR: Scandal or not, my friend, it opens the gate of peace. (*He addresses* POTHINUS *seriously.*) Pothinus: hear what I propose.

RUFIO: Hear Cæsar there.

CÆSAR: Ptolemy and Cleopatra shall reign jointly in Egypt.

ACHILLAS: What of the King's younger brother and Cleopatra's younger sister?

RUFIO (*explaining*): There is another little Ptolemy, Cæsar: so they tell me.

CÆSAR: Well, the little Ptolemy can marry the other sister; and we will make them both a present of Cyprus.

POTHINUS (*impatiently*): Cyprus is of no use to anybody.

CÆSAR: No matter: you shall have it for the sake of peace.

BRITTANUS (*unconsciously anticipating a later statesman*): Peace with honor, Pothinus.

POTHINUS (*mutinously*): Cæsar: be honest. The money you demand is the price of our freedom. Take it; and leave us to settle our own affairs.

THE BOLDER COURTIERS (*encouraged by* POTHINUS's *tone and* CÆSAR's *quietness*): Yes, yes. Egypt for the Egyptians!

(*The conference now becomes an altercation, the Egyptians becoming more and more heated.* CÆSAR *remains unruffled; but* RUFIO *grows fiercer and doggeder, and* BRITANNUS *haughtily indignant.*)

RUFIO (*contemptuously*): Egypt for the Egyptians! Do you forget that there is a Roman army of occupation here, left by Aulus Gabinius when he set up your toy king for you?

ACHILLAS (*suddenly asserting himself*): And now under *my* command. *I* am the Roman general here, Cæsar.

CÆSAR (*tickled by the humor of the situation*): And also the Egyptian general, eh?

POTHINUS (*triumphantly*): That is so, Cæsar.

CÆSAR (*to* ACHILLAS): So you can make war on the Egyptians in the name of Rome, and on the Romans — on me, if necessary — in the name of Egypt?

ACHILLAS: That is so, Cæsar.

CÆSAR: And which side are you on at present, if I may presume to ask, general?

ACHILLAS: On the side of the right and of the gods.

CÆSAR. Hm! How many men have you?

ACHILLAS: That will appear when I take the field.

RUFIO (*truculently*): Are your men Romans? If not, it matters not how many there are, provided you are no stronger than 500 to ten.

POTHINUS: It is useless to try to bluff us, Rufio. Cæsar has been defeated before and may be defeated again. A few weeks ago Cæsar was flying for his life before Pompey: a few months hence he may be flying for his life before Cato and Juba of Numidia, the African King.

ACHILLAS (*following up* POTHINUS'S *speech menacingly*): What can you do with 4,000 men?

THEODOTUS (*following up* ACHILLAS'S *speech with a raucous squeak*): And without money? Away with you.

ALL THE COURTIERS (*shouting fiercely and crowding towards* CÆSAR): Away with you. Egypt for the Egyptians! Begone.

(RUFIO *bites his beard, too angry to speak.* CÆSAR *sits as comfortably as if he were at breakfast, and the cat were clamoring for a piece of Finnan-haddie.*)

CLEOPATRA: Why do you let them talk to you like that, Cæsar? Are you afraid?

CÆSAR: Why, my dear, what they say is quite true.

CLEOPATRA: But if you go away, I shall not be Queen.

CÆSAR: I shall not go away until you are Queen.

POTHINUS: Achillas: if you are not a fool, you will take that girl whilst she is under your hand.

RUFIO (*daring them*): Why not take Cæsar as well, Achillas?

POTHINUS (*retorting the defiance with interest*): Well said, Rufio. Why not?

RUFIO: Try, Achillas. (*Calling.*) Guard there.

(*The loggia immediately fills with* CÆSAR'S *soldiers, who stand, sword in hand, at the top of the steps, waiting the word to charge from their centurion, who carries a cudgel. For a moment the Egyptians face them proudly: then they retire sullenly to their former places.*)

BRITANNUS: You are Cæsar's prisoners, all of you.

CÆSAR (*benevolently*): Oh no, no, no. By no means. Cæsar's guests, gentlemen.

CLEOPATRA: Wont you cut their heads off?

CÆSAR: What! Cut off your brother's head?

CLEOPATRA: Why not? He would cut off mine, if he got the chance. Wouldnt you, Ptolemy?

PTOLEMY (*pale and obstinate*): I would. I will, too, when I grow up.

(CLEOPATRA *is rent by a struggle between her newly-acquired dignity as a queen, and a strong impulse to put out her tongue at him. She takes no part in the scene which follows, but watches it with curiosity and wonder, fidgeting with the restlessness of a child, and sitting down on* CÆSAR'S *tripod when he rises.*)

POTHINUS: Cæsar: if you attempt to detain us —

RUFIO: He will succeed, Egyptian: make up your mind to that. We hold the palace, the beach, and the eastern harbor. The road to Rome is open; and you shall travel it if Cæsar chooses.

CÆSAR (*courteously*): I could do no less, Pothinus, to secure the retreat of my own soldiers. I am accountable for every life among them. But you are free to go. So are all here, and in the palace.

RUFIO (*aghast at this clemency*): What! Renegades and all?

CÆSAR (*softening the expression*): Roman army of occupation and all, Rufio.

POTHINUS (*bewildered*): But — but — but —

CÆSAR: Well, my friend?

POTHINUS: You are turning us out of our own palace into the streets; and you tell us with a grand air that we are free to go! It is for you to go.

CÆSAR: Your friends are in the street, Pothinus. You will be safer there.

POTHINUS: This is a trick. I am the King's guardian: I refuse to stir. I stand on my right here. Where is your right?

CÆSAR: It is in Rufio's scabbard, Pothinus. I may not be able to keep it there if you wait too long.

(*Sensation.*)

POTHINUS (*bitterly*): And this is Roman justice!

THEODOTUS: But not Roman gratitude, I hope.

CÆSAR: Gratitude! Am I in your debt for any service, gentlemen?

THEODOTUS: Is Cæsar's life of so little account to him that he forgets that we have saved it?

CÆSAR: My life! Is that all?

THEODOTUS: Your life. Your laurels. Your future.

POTHINUS: It is true. I can call a witness to prove that but for us, the Roman army of occupation, led by the greatest soldier in the world, would now have Cæsar at its mercy. (*Calling through the loggia.*) Ho, there, Lucius Septimius (CÆSAR *starts, deeply moved*): if my voice can reach you, come forth and testify before Cæsar.

CÆSAR (*shrinking*): No, no.

THEODOTUS: Yes, I say. Let the military tribune bear witness.

(LUCIUS SEPTIMIUS, *a clean-shaven, trim athlete of about 40, with symmetrical features, resolute mouth, and handsome, thin Roman nose, in the dress of a Roman officer, comes in through the loggia and confronts* CÆSAR, *who hides his face with his robe for a moment; then, mastering himself, drops it, and confronts the tribune with dignity.*)

POTHINUS: Bear witness, Lucius Septimius. Cæsar came hither in pursuit of his foe. Did we shelter his foe?

LUCIUS: As Pompey's foot touched the Egyptian shore, his head fell by the stroke of my sword.

THEODOTUS (*with viperish relish*): Under the eyes of his wife and child! Remember that, Cæsar! They saw it from the ship he had just left. We have given you a full and sweet measure of vengeance.

CÆSAR (*with horror*): Vengeance!

POTHINUS: Our first gift to you, as your galley came into the roadstead, was the head of your rival for the empire of the world. Bear witness, Lucius Septimius: is it not so?

LUCIUS: It is so. With this hand, that slew Pompey, I placed his head at the feet of Cæsar.

CÆSAR: Murderer! So would you have slain Cæsar, had Pompey been victorious at Pharsalia.

LUCIUS: Woe to the vanquished, Cæsar! When I served Pompey, I slew as good men as he, only because he conquered them. His turn came at last.

THEODOTUS (*flatteringly*): The deed was not yours, Cæsar, but ours — nay, mine; for it was done by my counsel. Thanks to us, you keep your reputation for clemency, and have your vengeance too.

CÆSAR: Vengeance! Vengeance!! Oh, if I could stoop to vengeance, what would I not exact from you as the price of this murdered man's blood? (*They shrink back, appalled and disconcerted.*) Was he not my son-in-law, my ancient friend, for 20 years the master of great Rome, for 30 years the compeller of victory? Did not I, as a Roman, share his glory? Was the Fate that forced us to fight for the mastery of the world, of our making? Am I Julius Cæsar, or am I a wolf, that you fling to me the grey head of the old soldier, the laurelled conqueror, the mighty Roman, treacherously struck down by this callous ruffian, and then claim my gratitude for it! (*To* LUCIUS SEPTIMIUS.) Begone: you fill me with horror.

LUCIUS (*cold and undaunted*): Pshaw! You have seen severed heads before, Cæsar, and severed right hands too, I think; some thousands of them, in Gaul, after you vanquished Vercingetorix. Did you spare him, with all your clemency? Was that vengeance?

CÆSAR: No, by the gods! would that it had been! Vengeance at least is human. No, I say: those severed right hands, and the brave Vercingetorix basely strangled in a vault beneath the Capitol, were (*with shuddering satire*) a wise severity, a necessary protection to the commonwealth, a duty of statesmanship — follies and fictions ten times bloodier than honest vengeance! What a fool was I then! To think that men's lives should be at the mercy of such fools! (*Humbly.*) Lucius Septimius, pardon me: why should the slayer of Vercingetorix rebuke the slayer of Pompey? You are free to go with the rest. Or stay if you will: I will find a place for you in my service.

LUCIUS: The odds are against you, Cæsar. I go. (*He turns to go out through the loggia.*)

RUFIO (*full of wrath at seeing his prey escaping*): That means that he is a Republican.

LUCIUS (*turning defiantly on the loggia steps*): And what are you?

RUFIO: A Cæsarian, like all Cæsar's soldiers.

CÆSAR (*courteously*): Lucius: believe me, Cæsar is no Cæsarian. Were Rome a true republic, then were Cæsar the first of Republicans. But you have made your choice. Farewell.

LUCIUS: Farewell. Come, Achillas, whilst there is yet time.

(CÆSAR, *seeing that* RUFIO'S *temper threatens to get the worse of him, puts his hand on his shoulder and brings him down the hall out of harm's way,* BRITANNUS *accompanying them and posting himself on* CÆSAR'S *right hand. This movement brings the three in a little group to the place occupied by* ACHILLAS, *who moves haughtily away and joins* THEODOTUS *on the other side.* LUCIUS SEPTIMIUS *goes out through the soldiers in the loggia.* POTHINUS, THEODOTUS *and* ACHILLAS *follow him with the courtiers, very mistrustful of the soldiers, who close up in their rear and go out after them, keeping them moving without much ceremony. The King is left in his chair, piteous, obstinate, with twitching face and fingers. During these movements* RUFIO *maintains an energetic grumbling, as follows: —*)

RUFIO (*as* LUCIUS *departs*): Do you suppose he would let us go if he had our heads in his hands?

CÆSAR: I have no right to suppose that his ways are any baser than mine.

RUFIO: Pshaw!

CÆSAR: Rufio: if I take Lucius Septimius for my model, and become exactly like him, ceasing to be Cæsar, will you serve me still?

BRITANNUS: Cæsar: this is not good sense. Your duty to Rome demands that her enemies should be prevented from doing further mischief.

(CÆSAR, *whose delight in the moral eye-to-business of his British secretary is inexhaustible, smiles indulgently.*)

RUFIO: It is no use talking to him, Britannus: you may save your breath to cool your porridge. But mark this, Cæsar. Clemency is very well for you; but what is it for your soldiers, who have to fight tomorrow the men you spared yesterday? You may give what orders you please; but I tell you that your next victory will be a massacre, thanks to your clemency. *I*, for one, will take no prisoners. I will kill my enemies in the field; and then you can preach as much clemency as you please: I shall never have to fight them again. And now, with your leave, I will see these gentry off the premises. (*He turns to go.*)

CÆSAR (*turning also and seeing* PTOLEMY): What! have they left the boy alone! Oh shame, shame!

RUFIO (*taking* PTOLEMY's *hand and making him rise*): Come, your majesty!

PTOLEMY (*to* CÆSAR, *drawing away his hand from* RUFIO): Is he turning me out of my palace?

RUFIO (*grimly*): You are welcome to stay if you wish.

CÆSAR (*kindly*): Go, my boy. I will not harm you but you will be safer away, among your friends. Here you are in the lion's mouth.

PTOLEMY (*turning to go*): It is not the lion I fear, but (*looking at* RUFIO) the jackal. (*He goes out through the loggia.*)

CÆSAR (*laughing approvingly*): Brave boy!

CLEOPATRA (*jealous of* CÆSAR's *approbation, calling after* PTOLEMY): Little silly. You think that very clever.

CÆSAR: Britannus: attend the King. Give him in charge to that Pothinus fellow. (BRITANNUS *goes out after* PTOLEMY.)

RUFIO (*pointing to* CLEOPATRA): And this piece of goods? What is to be done with *her*? However, I suppose I may leave that to you. (*He goes out through the loggia.*)

CLEOPATRA (*flushing suddenly and turning on* CÆSAR): Did you mean me to go with the rest?

CÆSAR (*a little preoccupied, goes with a sigh to* PTOLEMY's *chair, whilst she waits for his answer with red cheeks and clenched fist*): You are free to do just as you please, Cleopatra.

CLEOPATRA: Then you do not care whether I stay or not?

CÆSAR (*smiling*): Of course I had rather you stayed.

CLEOPATRA: Much, *much* rather?

CÆSAR (*nodding*): Much, much rather.

CLEOPATRA: Then I consent to stay, because I am asked. But I do not want to, mind.

CÆSAR: That is quite understood. (*Calling.*) Totateeta.

(FTATATEETA, *still seated, turns her eyes on him with a sinister expression, but does not move.*)

CLEOPATRA (*with a splutter of laughter*): Her name is not Totateeta: it is Ftatateeta. (*Calling.*) Ftatateeta. (FTATATEETA *instantly rises and comes to* CLEOPATRA.)

CÆSAR (*stumbling over the name*): Tfatafeeta will forgive the erring tongue of a Roman. Tota: the Queen will hold her state here in Alexandria. Engage women to attend upon her; and do all that is needful.

FTATATEETA: Am I then the mistress of the Queen's household?

CLEOPATRA (*sharply*): No: *I* am the mistress of the Queen's household. Go and do as you are told, or I will have you thrown into the Nile this very afternoon, to poison the poor crocodiles.

CÆSAR (*shocked*): Oh no, no.

CLEOPATRA: Oh yes, yes. You are very sentimental, Cæsar; but you are clever; and if you do as I tell you, you will soon learn to govern.

(CÆSAR, *quite dumbfounded by this impertinence, turns in his chair and stares at her.* FTATATEETA, *smiling grimly, and showing a splendid set of teeth, goes, leaving them alone together.*)

CÆSAR: Cleopatra: I really think I must eat you, after all.

CLEOPATRA (*kneeling beside him and looking at him with eager interest, half real, half affected to shew how intelligent she is*): You must not talk to me now as if I were a child.

CÆSAR: You have been growing up since the Sphinx introduced us the other night; and you think you know more than I do already.

CLEOPATRA (*taken down, and anxious to justify herself*): No: that would be very silly of me: of course I know that. But — (*suddenly*) are you angry with me?

CÆSAR: No.

CLEOPATRA (*only half believing him*): Then why are you so thoughful?

CÆSAR (*rising*): I have work to do, Cleopatra.

CLEOPATRA (*drawing back*): Work! (*Offended.*) You are tired of talking to me; and that is your excuse to get away from me.

CÆSAR (*sitting down again to appease her*): Well, well: another minute. But then — work!

CLEOPATRA: Work! what nonsense! You must remember that you are a king now: I have made you one. Kings dont work.

CÆSAR: Oh! Who told you that, little kitten? Eh?

CLEOPATRA: My father was King of Egypt; and he never worked. But he was a great king, and cut off my sister's head because she rebelled against him and took the throne from him.

CÆSAR: Well; and how did he get his throne back again?

CLEOPATRA (*eagerly, her eyes lighting up*): I will tell you. A beautiful young man, with strong round arms, came over the desert with many horsemen, and slew my sister's husband and gave my father back his throne. (*Wistfully.*) I was only twelve then. Oh, I wish he would come again, now that I am a queen. I would make him my husband.

CÆSAR: It might be managed, perhaps; for it was I who sent that beautiful young man to help your father.

CLEOPATRA (*enraptured*): You know him!

CÆSAR (*nodding*): I do.

CLEOPATRA: Has he come with you? (CÆSAR *shakes his head: she is cruelly disappointed.*) Oh, I wish he had, I wish he had. If only I were a little older; so that he might not think me a mere kitten, as you do! But perhaps that is because *you* are old. He is many, *many* years younger than you, is he not?

CÆSAR (*as if swallowing a pill*): He is somewhat younger.

CLEOPATRA: Would he be my husband, do you think, if I asked him?

CÆSAR: Very likely.

CLEOPATRA: But I should not like to ask him. Could you not persuade him to ask me — without knowing that I wanted him to?

CÆSAR (*touched by her innocence of the beautiful young man's character*): My poor child!

CLEOPATRA: Why do you say that as if you were sorry for me? Does he love anyone else?

CÆSAR: I am afraid so.

CLEOPATRA (*tearfully*): Then I shall not be his first love.

CÆSAR: Not quite the first. He is greatly admired by women.

CLEOPATRA: I wish I could be the first. But if he loves me, I will make him kill all the rest. Tell me: is he still beautiful? Do his strong round arms shine in the sun like marble?

CÆSAR: He is in excellent condition — considering how much he eats and drinks.

CLEOPATRA: Oh, you must not say common, earthly things about him; for I love him. He is a god.

CÆSAR: He is a great captain of horsemen, and swifter of foot than any other Roman.

CLEOPATRA: What is his real name?

CÆSAR (*puzzled*): His *real* name?

CLEOPATRA: Yes. I always call him Horus, because Horus is the most beautiful of our gods. But I want to know his real name.

CÆSAR: His name is Mark Antony.

CLEOPATRA (*musically*): Mark Antony, Mark Antony, Mark Antony! What a beautiful name! (*She throws her arms round* CÆSAR's *neck.*)

Oh, how I love you for sending him to help my father! Did you love my father very much?

CÆSAR: No, my child; but your father, as you say, never worked. I always work. So when he lost his crown he had to promise me 16,000 talents to get it back for him.

CLEOPATRA: Did he ever pay you?

CÆSAR: Not in full.

CLEOPATRA: He was quite right: it was too dear. The whole world is not worth 16,000 talents.

CÆSAR: That is perhaps true, Cleopatra. Those Egyptians who work paid as much of it as he could drag from them. The rest is still due. But as I most likely shall not get it, I must go back to my work. So you must run away for a little and send my secretary to me.

CLEOPATRA (*coaxing*): No: I want to stay and hear you talk about Mark Antony.

CÆSAR: But if I do not get to work, Pothinus and the rest of them will cut us off from the harbor; and then the way from Rome will be blocked.

CLEOPATRA: No matter: I dont want you to go back to Rome.

CÆSAR: But you want Mark Antony to come from it.

CLEOPATRA (*springing up*): Oh yes, yes, yes: I forgot. Go quickly and work, Cæsar; and keep the way over the sea open for my Mark Antony. (*She runs out through the loggia, kissing her hand to Mark Antony across the sea.*)

CÆSAR (*going briskly up the middle of the hall to the loggia steps*): Ho, Britannus. (*He is startled by the entry of a wounded Roman* SOLDIER, *who confronts him from the upper step.*) What now?

SOLDIER (*pointing to his bandaged head*): This, Cæsar; and two of my comrades killed in the market place.

CÆSAR (*quiet, but attending*): Ay. Why?

SOLDIER: There is an army come to Alexandria, calling itself the Roman army.

CÆSAR: The Roman army of occupation. Ay?

SOLDIER: Commanded by one Achillas.

CÆSAR: Well?

SOLDIER: The citizens rose against us when the army entered the gates. I was with two others in the market place when the news came. They set upon us. I cut my way out; and here I am.

CÆSAR: Good. I am glad to see you alive. (RUFIO *enters the loggia hastily, passing behind the soldier to look out through one of the arches at the quay beneath.*) Rufio: we are besieged.

RUFIO: What! Already?

CÆSAR: Now or to-morrow: what does it matter? We *shall* be besieged.

(BRITANNUS *runs in.*)

BRITANNUS: Cæsar —
CÆSAR (*anticipating him*): Yes: I know. (RUFIO *and* BRITANNUS *come down the hall from the loggia at opposite sides, past* CÆSAR, *who waits for a moment near the step to say to the soldier:*) Comrade: give the word to turn out on the beach and stand by the boats. Get your wounded attended to. Go. (*The* SOLDIER *hurries out.* CÆSAR *comes down the hall between* RUFIO *and* BRITANNUS.) Rufio: we have some ships in the west harbor. Burn them.
RUFIO (*staring*): Burn them!!
CÆSAR: Take every boat we have in the east harbor, and seize the Pharos — that island with the lighthouse. Leave half our men behind to hold the beach and the quay outside this palace: that is the way home.
RUFIO (*disapproving strongly*): Are we to give up the city?
CÆSAR: We have not got it, Rufio. This palace we have; and — what is that building next door?
RUFIO: The theatre.
CÆSAR: We will have that too: it commands the strand. For the rest, Egypt for the Egyptians!
RUFIO: Well, you know best, I suppose. Is that all?
CÆSAR: That is all. Are those ships burnt yet?
RUFIO: Be easy: I shall waste no more time. (*He runs out.*)
BRITANNUS: Cæsar: Pothinus demands speech of you. In my opinion he needs a lesson. His manner is most insolent.
CÆSAR: Where is he?
BRITANNUS: He waits without.
CÆSAR: Ho there! admit Pothinus.

(POTHINUS *appears in the loggia, and comes down the hall very haughtily to* CÆSAR's *left hand.*)

CÆSAR: Well, Pothinus?
POTHINUS: I have brought you our ultimatum, Cæsar.
CÆSAR: Ultimatum! The door was open: you should have gone out through it before you declared war. You are my prisoner now. (*He goes to the chair and loosens his toga.*)
POTHINUS (*scornfully*): I *your* prisoner! Do you know that you are in Alexandria, and that King Ptolemy, with an army outnumbering your little troop a hundred to one, is in possession of Alexandria?
CÆSAR (*unconcernedly taking off his toga and throwing it on the chair*): Well, my friend, get out if you can. And tell your friends not to kill any more Romans in the market place. Otherwise my soldiers, who

do not share my celebrated clemency, will probably kill you. Britannus: pass the word to the guard; and fetch my armor. (BRITANNUS *runs out,* RUFIO *returns.*) Well?

RUFIO (*pointing from the loggia to a cloud of smoke drifting over the harbor*): See there! (POTHINUS *runs eagerly up the steps to look out.*)

CÆSAR: What, ablaze already! Impossible!

RUFIO: Yes, five good ships, and a barge laden with oil grappled to each. But it is not my doing: the Egyptians have saved me the trouble. They have captured the west harbor.

CÆSAR (*anxiously*): And the east harbor? The lighthouse, Rufio?

RUFIO (*with a sudden splutter of raging ill usage, coming down to* CÆSAR *and scolding him*): Can I embark a legion in five minutes? The first cohort is already on the beach. We can do no more. If you want faster work, come and do it yourself.

CÆSAR (*soothing him*): Good, good. Patience, Rufio, patience.

RUFIO: Patience! Who is impatient here, you or I? Would I be here, if I could not oversee them from that balcony?

CÆSAR: Forgive me, Rufio; and (*anxiously*) hurry them as much as—

(*He is interrupted by an outcry as of an old man in the extremity of misfortune. It draws near rapidly; and* THEODOTUS *rushes in, tearing his hair, and squeaking the most lamentable exclamations.* RUFIO *steps back to stare at him, amazed at his frantic condition.* POTHINUS *turns to listen.*)

THEODOTUS (*on the steps, with uplifted arms*): Horror unspeakable! Woe, alas! Help!

RUFIO: What now?

CÆSAR (*frowning*): Who is slain?

THEODOTUS: Slain! Oh, worse than the death of ten thousand men! Loss irreparable to mankind!

RUFIO: What has happened, man?

THEODOTUS (*rushing down the hall between them*): The fire has spread from your ships. The first of the seven wonders of the world perishes. The library of Alexandria is in flames.

RUFIO: Pshaw! (*Quite relieved, he goes up to the loggia and watches the preparations of the troops on the beach.*)

CÆSAR: Is that all?

THEODOTUS (*unable to believe his senses*): All! Cæsar: will you go down to posterity as a barbarous soldier too ignorant to know the value of books?

CÆSAR: Theodotus: I am an author myself; and I tell you it is better that the Egyptians should live their lives than dream them away with the help of books.

THEODOTUS (*kneeling, with genuine literary emotion: the passion of the pedant*): Cæsar: once in ten generations of men, the world gains an immortal book.

CÆSAR (*inflexible*): If it did not flatter mankind, the common executioner would burn it.

THEODOTUS: Without history, death will lay you beside your meanest soldier.

CÆSAR: Death will do that in any case. I ask no better grave.

THEODOTUS: What is burning there is the memory of mankind.

CÆSAR: A shameful memory. Let it burn.

THEODOTUS (*wildly*): Will you destroy the past?

CÆSAR: Ay, and build the future with its ruins. (THEODOTUS, *in despair, strikes himself on the temples with his fists.*) But hearken, Theodotus, teacher of kings: you who valued Pompey's head no more than a shepherd values an onion, and who now kneel to me, with tears in your old eyes, to plead for a few sheepskins scrawled with errors. I cannot spare you a man or a bucket of water just now; but you shall pass freely out of the palace. Now, away with you to Achillas; and borrow his legions to put out the fire. (*He hurries him to the steps.*)

POTHINUS (*significantly*): You understand. Theodotus: I remain a prisoner.

THEODOTUS: A prisoner!

CÆSAR: Will you stay to talk whilst the memory of mankind is burning? (*Calling through the loggia.*) Ho there! Pass Theodotus out. (*To* THEODOTUS.) Away with you.

THEODOTUS (*to* POTHINUS): I must go to save the library. (*He hurries out.*)

CÆSAR: Follow him to the gate, Pothinus. Bid him urge your people to kill no more of my soldiers, for your sake.

POTHINUS: My life will cost you dear if you take it, Cæsar. (*He goes out after* THEODOTUS.)

(RUFIO, *absorbed in watching the embarkation, does not notice the departure of the two Egyptians.*)

RUFIO (*shouting from the loggia to the beach*): All ready, there?

CENTURION (*from below*): All ready. We wait for Cæsar.

CÆSAR: Tell them Cæsar is coming — the rogues! (*Calling.*) Britannicus. (*This magniloquent version of his secretary's name is one of* CÆSAR'S *jokes. In later years it would have meant, quite seriously and officially, Conqueror of Britain.*)

RUFIO (*calling down*): Push off, all except the longboat. Stand by it to embark, Cæsar's guard there. (*He leaves the balcony and comes down *into the hall.*) Where are those Egyptians? Is this more clemency? Have you let them go?

CÆSAR (*chuckling*): I have let Theodotus go to save the library. We must respect literature, Rufio.

RUFIO (*raging*): Folly on folly's head! I believe if you could bring back all the dead of Spain, Gaul, and Thessaly to life, you would do it that we might have the trouble of fighting them over again.

CÆSAR: Might not the gods destroy the world if their only thought were to be at peace next year? (RUFIO, *out of all patience, turns away in anger.* CÆSAR *suddenly grips his sleeve, and adds slyly in his ear.*) Besides, my friend: every Egyptian we imprison means imprisoning two Roman soldiers to guard him. Eh?

RUFIO: Agh! I might have known there was some fox's trick behind your fine talking. (*He gets away from* CÆSAR *with an ill-humored shrug, and goes to the balcony for another look at the preparations; finally goes out.*)

CÆSAR: Is Britannus asleep? I sent him for my armor an hour ago. (*Calling.*) Britannicus, thou British islander. Britannicus!

(CLEOPATRA *runs in through the loggia with* CÆSAR's *helmet and sword, snatched from* BRITANNUS, *who follows her with a cuirass and greaves. They come down to* CÆSAR, *she to his left hand,* BRITANNUS *to his right.*)

CLEOPATRA: I am going to dress you, Cæsar. Sit down. (*He obeys.*) These Roman helmets are so becoming! (*She takes off his wreath.*) Oh! (*She bursts out laughing at him.*)

CÆSAR: What are you laughing at?

CLEOPATRA: Youre bald (*beginning with a big B, and ending with a splutter.*)

CÆSAR (*almost annoyed*): Cleopatra! (*He rises, for the convenience of* BRITANNUS, *who puts the cuirass on him.*)

CLEOPATRA: So that is why you wear the wreath — to hide it.

BRITANNUS: Peace, Egyptian: they are the bays of the conqueror. (*He buckles the cuirass.*)

CLEOPATRA: Peace, thou: islander! (*To* CÆSAR.) You should rub your head with strong spirits of sugar, Cæsar. That will make it grow.

CÆSAR (*with a wry face*): Cleopatra: do you like to be reminded that you are very young?

CLEOPATRA (*pouting*): No.

CÆSAR (*sitting down again, and setting out his leg for* BRITANNUS, *who kneels to put on his greaves*): Neither do I like to be reminded that I am — middle aged. Let me give you ten of my superfluous years.

That will make you 26, and leave me only—no matter. Is it a bargain?

CLEOPATRA: Agreed. 26, mind. (*She puts the helmet on him.*) Oh! How nice! You look only about 50 in it!

BRITANNUS (*looking up severely at* CLEOPATRA): You must not speak in this manner to Cæsar.

CLEOPATRA: Is it true that when Cæsar caught you on that island, you were painted all over blue?

BRITANNUS: Blue is the colour worn by all Britons of good standing. In war we stain our bodies blue; so that though our enemies may strip us of our clothes and our lives, they cannot strip us of our respectability. (*He rises.*)

CLEOPATRA (*with* CÆSAR'S *sword*): Let me hang this on. Now you look splendid. Have they made any statues of you in Rome?

CÆSAR: Yes, many statues.

CLEOPATRA: You must send for one and give it to me.

RUFIO (*coming back into the loggia, more impatient than ever*): Now Cæsar: have you done talking? The moment your foot is aboard there will be no holding our men back: the boats will race one another for the lighthouse.

CÆSAR (*drawing his sword and trying the edge*): Is this well set today, Britannicus? At Pharsalia it was as blunt as a barrel-hoop.

BRITANNUS: It will split one of the Egyptian's hairs today, Cæsar. I have set it myself.

CLEOPATRA (*suddenly throwing her arms in terror round* CÆSAR): Oh, you are not really going into battle to be killed?

CÆSAR: No, Cleopatra. No man goes to battle to be killed.

CLEOPATRA: But they do get killed. My sister's husband was killed in battle. You must not go. Let *him* go. (*Pointing to* RUFIO. *They all laugh at her.*) Oh please, *please* dont go. What will happen to me if you never come back?

CÆSAR (*gravely*): Are you afraid?

CLEOPATRA (*shrinking*): No.

CÆSAR (*with quiet authority*): Go to the balcony; and you shall see us take the Pharos. You must learn to look on battles. Go. (*She goes, downcast, and looks out from the balcony.*) That is well. Now, Rufio. March.

CLEOPATRA (*suddenly clapping her hands*): Oh, you will not be able to go!

CÆSAR: Why? What now?

CLEOPATRA: They are drying up the harbor with buckets—a multitude of soldiers—over there (*pointing out across the sea to her left*)—they are dipping up the water.

RUFIO (*hastening to look*): It is true. The Egyptian army! Crawling over the edge of the west harbor like locusts. (*With sudden anger he strides down to* CÆSAR.) This is your accursed clemency, Cæsar. Theodotus has brought them.

CÆSAR (*delighted at his own cleverness*): I meant him to, Rufio. They have come to put out the fire. The library will keep them busy whilst we seize the lighthouse. Eh? (*He rushes out buoyantly through the loggia, followed by* BRITANNUS.)

RUFIO (*disgustedly*): More foxing! Agh! (*He rushes off. A shout from the soldiers announces the appearance of* CÆSAR *below.*)

CENTURION (*below*): All aboard. Give way there. (*Another shout.*)

CLEOPATRA (*waving her scarf through the loggia arch*): Goodbye, goodbye, dear Cæsar. Come back safe. Goodbye!

ACT THREE

(*The edge of the quay in front of the palace, looking out west over the east harbor of Alexandria to Pharos island, just off the end of which, and connected with it by a narrow mole, is the famous lighthouse, a gigantic square tower of white marble diminishing in size storey by storey to the top, on which stands a cresset beacon. The island is joined to the main land by the Heptastadium, a great mole or causeway five miles long bounding the harbor on the south.*

In the middle of the quay a Roman SENTINEL *stands on guard pilum in hand, looking out to the lighthouse with strained attention, his left hand shading his eyes. The pilum is a stout wooden shaft 4½ feet long, with an iron spit about three feet long fixed in it. The* SENTINEL *is so absorbed that he does not notice the approach from the north end of the quay of four Egyptian market* PORTERS *carrying rolls of carpet, preceded by* FTATATEETA *and* APOLLODORUS *the Sicilian.* APOLLODORUS *is a dashing young man of about 24, handsome and debonair, dressed with deliberate æstheticism in the most delicate purples and dove greys, with ornaments of bronze, oxidized silver, and stones of jade and agate. His sword, designed as carefully as a medieval cross, has a blue blade showing through an openwork scabbard of purple leather and filigree. The* PORTERS, *conducted by* FTATATEETA, *pass along the quay behind the* SENTINEL *to the steps of the palace, where they put down their bales and squat on the ground.* APOLLODORUS *does not pass along with them: he halts, amused by the preoccupation of the* SENTINEL.)

APOLLODORUS (*calling to the* SENTINEL): Who goes there, eh?

SENTINEL (*starting violently and turning with his pilum at the charge, revealing himself as a small, wiry, sandy-haired, conscientious young man with an elderly face*): Whats this? Stand. Who are you?

APOLLODORUS: I am Apollodorus the Sicilian. Why, man, what are you dreaming of? Since I came through the lines beyond the theatre there, I have brought my caravan past three sentinels, all so busy staring at the lighthouse that not one of them challenged me. Is this Roman discipline?

SENTINEL: We are not here to watch the land but the sea. Cæsar has just landed on the Pharos. (*Looking at* FTATATEETA.) What have you here? Who is this piece of Egyptian crockery?

FTATATEETA: Apollodorus: rebuke this Roman dog; and bid him bridle his tongue to the presence of Ftatateeta, the mistress of the Queen's household.

APOLLODORUS: My friend: this is a great lady, who stands high with Cæsar.

SENTINEL (*not at all impressed, pointing to the carpets*): And what is all this truck?

APOLLODORUS: Carpets for the furnishing of the Queen's apartments in the palace. I have picked them from the best carpets in the world; and the Queen shall choose the best of my choosing.

SENTINEL: So you are the carpet merchant?

APOLLODORUS (*hurt*): My friend: I am a patrician.

SENTINEL: A patrician! A patrician keeping a shop instead of following arms!

APOLLODORUS: I do not keep a shop. Mine is a temple of the arts. I am a worshipper of beauty. My calling is to choose beautiful things for beautiful queens. My motto is Art for Art's sake.

SENTINEL: That is not the password.

APOLLODORUS: It is a universal password.

SENTINEL: I know nothing about universal passwords. Either give me the password for the day or get back to your shop.

(FTATATEETA, *roused by his hostile tone, steals towards the edge of the quay with the step of a panther, and gets behind him.*)

APOLLODORUS: How if I do neither?

SENTINEL: Then I will drive this pilum through you.

APOLLODORUS: At your service, my friend. (*He draws his sword, and springs to his guard with unruffled grace.*)

FTATATEETA (*suddenly seizing the* SENTINEL'S *arms from behind*): Thrust your knife into the dog's throat, Apollodorus. (*The chivalrous* APOLLODORUS *laughingly shakes his head; breaks ground away from the* SENTINEL *towards the palace; and lowers his point.*)

SENTINEL (*struggling vainly*): Curse on you! Let me go. Help ho!

FTATATEETA (*lifting him from the ground*): Stab the little Roman reptile. Spit him on your sword.

(*A couple of Roman soldiers, with a* CENTURION, *come running along the edge of the quay from the north end. They rescue their comrade, and throw off* FTATATEETA, *who is sent reeling away on the left hand of the* SENTINEL.)

CENTURION (*an unattractive man of fifty, short in his speech and manners, with a vinewood cudgel in his hand*): How now? What is all this?

FTATATEETA (*to* APOLLODORUS): Why did you not stab him? There was time!

APOLLODORUS: Centurion: I am here by order of the Queen to —

CENTURION (*interrupting him*): The Queen! Yes, yes: (*to the* SENTINEL) pass him in. Pass all these bazaar people in to the Queen, with their goods. But mind you pass no one out that you have not passed in — not even the Queen herself.

SENTINEL: This old woman is dangerous: she is as strong as three men. She wanted the merchant to stab me.

APOLLODORUS: Centurion: I am not a merchant. I am a patrician and a votary of art.

CENTURION: Is the woman your wife?

APOLLODORUS (*horrified*): No, no! (*Correcting himself politely.*) Not that the lady is not a striking figure in her own way. But (*emphatically*) she is *not* my wife.

FTATATEETA (*to the* CENTURION): Roman: I am Ftatateeta, the mistress of the Queen's household.

CENTURION: Keep your hands off our men, mistress; or I will have you pitched into the harbor, though you were as strong as ten men. (*To his men.*) To your posts: march! (*He returns with his men the way they came.*)

FTATATEETA (*looking malignantly after him*): We shall see whom Isis loves best: her servant Ftatateeta or a dog of a Roman.

SENTINEL (*to* APOLLODORUS, *with a wave of his pilum towards the palace*): Pass in there; and keep your distance. (*Turning to* FTATATEETA.) Come within a yard of me, you old crocodile; and I will give you this (*the pilum*) in your jaws.

CLEOPATRA (*calling from the palace*): Ftatateeta, Ftatateeta.

FTATATEETA (*looking up, scandalized*): Go from the window, go from the window. There are men here.

CLEOPATRA: I am coming down.

FTATATEETA (*distracted*): No, no. What are you dreaming of? O ye gods, ye gods! Apollodorus: bid your men pick up your bales; and in with me quickly.

APOLLODORUS: Obey the mistress of the Queen's household.

FTATATEETA (*impatiently, as the porters stoop to lift the bales*): Quick, quick: she will be out upon us. (CLEOPATRA *comes from the palace and across the quay to* FTATATEETA.) Oh that ever I was born!

CLEOPATRA (*eagerly*): Ftatateeta: I have thought of something. I want a boat — at once.

FTATATEETA: A boat! No, no: you cannot. Apollodorus: speak to the Queen.

APOLLODORUS (*gallantly*): Beautiful queen: I am Apollodorus the Sicilian, your servant, from the bazaar. I have brought you the three most beautiful Persian carpets in the world to choose from.

CLEOPATRA: I have no time for carpets to-day. Get me a boat.

FTATATEETA: What whim is this? You cannot go on the water except in the royal barge.

APOLLODORUS: Royalty, Ftatateeta, lies not in the barge but in the Queen. (*To* CLEOPATRA.) The touch of your majesty's foot on the gunwale of the meanest boat in the harbor will make it royal. (*He turns to the harbor and calls seaward.*) Ho there, boatman! Pull in to the steps.

CLEOPATRA: Apollodorus: you are my perfect knight; and I will always buy my carpets through you. (APOLLODORUS *bows joyously. An oar appears above the quay; and the* BOATMAN, *a bullet-headed, vivacious, grinning fellow, burnt almost black by the sun, comes up a flight of steps from the water on the* SENTINEL's *right, oar in hand, and waits at the top.*) Can you row, Appollodorus?

APOLLODORUS: My oars shall be your majesty's wings. Whither shall I row my Queen?

CLEOPATRA: To the lighthouse. Come. (*She makes for the steps.*)

SENTINEL (*opposing her with his pilum at the charge*): Stand. You cannot pass.

CLEOPATRA (*flushing angrily*): How dare you? Do you know that I am the Queen?

SENTINEL: I have my orders. You cannot pass.

CLEOPATRA: I will make Cæsar have you killed if you do not obey me.

SENTINEL: He will do worse to me if I disobey my officer. Stand back.

CLEOPATRA: Ftatateeta: strangle him.

SENTINEL (*alarmed — looking apprehensively at* FTATATEETA, *and brandishing his pilum*): Keep off, there.

CLEOPATRA (*running to* APOLLODORUS): Apollodorus: make your slaves help us.

APOLLODORUS: I shall not need their help, lady. (*He draws his sword.*) Now, soldier: choose which weapon you will defend yourself with. Shall it be sword against pilum, or sword against sword?

SENTINEL: Roman against Sicilian, curse you. Take that. (*He hurls his pilum at* APOLLODORUS, *who drops expertly on one knee. The pilum passes whizzing over his head and falls harmless.* APOLLODORUS, *with a cry of triumph, springs up and attacks the* SENTINEL, *who draws his sword and defends himself, crying:*) Ho there, guard. Help!

(CLEOPATRA, *half frightened, half delighted, takes refuge near the palace, where the porters are squatting among the bales. The* BOATMAN, *alarmed, hurries down the steps out of harm's way, but stops, with his head just visible above the edge of the quay, to watch the fight. The* SENTINEL *is handicapped by his fear of an attack in the rear from* FTATATEETA. *His swordsmanship, which is of a rough and ready sort, is heavily taxed, as he has occasionally to strike at her to keep her off between a blow and a guard with* APOLLODORUS. *The* CENTURION *returns with several soldiers.* APOLLODORUS *springs back towards* CLEOPATRA *as this reinforcement confronts him.*)

CENTURION (*coming to the* SENTINEL'S *right hand*): What is this? What now?

SENTINEL (*panting*): I could do well enough by myself if it werent for the old woman. Keep her off me: this is all the help I need.

CENTURION: Make your report, soldier. What has happened?

FTATATEETA: Centurion: he would have slain the Queen.

SENTINEL (*bluntly*): I would, sooner than let her pass. She wanted to take a boat, and go — so she said — to the lighthouse. I stopped her, as I was ordered to; and she set this fellow on me. (*He goes to pick up his pilum and returns to his place with it.*)

CENTURION (*turning to* CLEOPATRA): Cleopatra: I am loth to offend you; but without Cæsar's express order we dare not let you pass beyond the Roman lines.

APOLLODORUS: Well, Centurion; and has not the lighthouse been within the Roman lines since Cæsar landed there?

CLEOPATRA: Yes, yes. Answer that, if you can.

CENTURION (*to* APOLLODORUS): As for you, Apollodorus, you may thank the gods that you are not nailed to the palace door with a pilum for your meddling.

APOLLODORUS (*urbanely*): My military friend, I was not born to be slain by so ugly a weapon. When I fall, it will be (*holding up his sword*) by this white queen of arms, the only weapon fit for an artist. And now that you are convinced that we do not want to go beyond the lines, let me finish killing your sentinel and depart with the Queen.

CENTURION (*as the* SENTINEL *makes an angry demonstration*): Peace there, Cleopatra: I must abide by my orders, and not by the subtleties of this Sicilian. You must withdraw into the palace and examine your carpets there.

CLEOPATRA (*pouting*): I will not: I am the Queen. Cæsar does not speak to me as you do. Have Cæsar's centurions changed manners with his scullions?

CENTURION (*sulkily*): I do my duty. That is enough for me.

APOLLODORUS: Majesty: when a stupid man is doing something he is ashamed of, he always declares that it is his duty.

CENTURION (*angry*): Apollodorus —

APOLLODORUS (*interrupting him with defiant elegance*): I will make amends for that insult with my sword at fitting time and place. Who says artist, says duellist. (*To* CLEOPATRA.) Hear my counsel, star of the east. Until word comes to these soldiers from Cæsar himself, you are a prisoner. Let me go to him with a message from you, and a present; and before the sun has stooped half way to the arms of the sea, I will bring you back Cæsar's order of release.

CENTURION (*sneering at him*): And you will sell the Queen the present, no doubt.

APOLLODORUS: Centurion: the Queen shall have from me, without payment, as the unforced tribute of Sicilian taste to Egyptian beauty, the richest of these carpets for her present to Cæsar.

CLEOPATRA (*exultantly, to the* CENTURION): Now you see what an ignorant common creature you are!

CENTURION (*curtly*): Well, a fool and his wares are soon parted. (*He turns to his men.*) Two more men to this post here; and see that no one leaves the palace but this man and his merchandise. If he draws his sword again inside the lines, kill him. To your posts. March.

(*He goes out, leaving two* AUXILIARY SENTINELS *with the other.*)

APOLLODORUS (*with polite goodfellowship*): My friends: will you not enter the palace and bury our quarrel in a bowl of wine? (*He takes out his purse, jingling the coins in it.*) The Queen has presents for you all.

SENTINEL (*very sulkily*): You heard our orders. Get about your business.

FIRST AUXILIARY: Yes: you ought to know better. Off with you.

SECOND AUXILIARY (*looking longingly at the purse — this sentinel is a hooknosed man, unlike his comrade, who is squab faced*): Do not tantalize a poor man.

APOLLODORUS (*to* CLEOPATRA): Pearl of Queens: the centurion is at hand; and the Roman soldier is incorruptible when his officer is looking. I must carry your word to Cæsar.

CLEOPATRA (*who has been meditating among the carpets*): Are these carpets very heavy?

APOLLODORUS: It matters not how heavy. There are plenty of porters.

CLEOPATRA: How do they put the carpets into boats? Do they throw them down?

APOLLODORUS: Not into small boats, majesty. It would sink them.

CLEOPATRA: Not into that man's boat, for instance? (*Pointing to the* BOATMAN.)

APOLLODORUS: No. Too small.

CLEOPATRA: But you can take a carpet to Cæsar in it if I send one?

APOLLODORUS: Assuredly.

CLEOPATRA: And you will have it carried gently down the steps and take great care of it?

APOLLODORUS: Depend on me.

CLEOPATRA: Great, *great* care?

APOLLODORUS: More than of my own body.

CLEOPATRA: You will promise me not to let the porters drop it or throw it about?

APOLLODORUS: Place the most delicate glass goblet in the palace in the heart of the roll, Queen; and if it be broken, my head shall pay for it.

CLEOPATRA: Good. Come, Ftatateeta. (FTATATEETA *comes to her.* APOLLODORUS *offers to squire them into the palace.*) No, Apollodorus, you must not come. I will choose a carpet for myself. You must wait here. (*She runs into the palace.*)

APOLLODORUS (*to the* PORTERS): Follow this lady (*indicating* FTATATEETA); and obey her.

(*The* PORTERS *rise and take up their bales.*)

FTATATEETA (*addressing the* PORTERS *as if they were vermin*): This way. And take your shoes off before you put your feet on those stairs.

(*She goes in, followed by the* PORTERS *with the carpets. Meanwhile* APOLLODORUS *goes to the edge of the quay and looks out over the harbor. The* SENTINELS *keep their eyes on him malignantly.*)

APOLLODORUS (*addressing the* SENTINEL): My friend —

SENTINEL (*rudely*): Silence there.

FIRST AUXILIARY: Shut your muzzle, you.

SECOND AUXILIARY (*in a half whisper, glancing apprehensively towards the north end of the quay*): Cant you wait a bit?

APOLLODORUS: Patience, worthy three-headed donkey. (*They mutter ferociously; but he is not at all intimidated.*) Listen: were you set here to watch me, or to watch the Egyptians?

SENTINEL: We know our duty.

APOLLODORUS: Then why dont you do it? There is something going on over there. (*Pointing southwestward to the mole.*)

SENTINEL (*sulkily*): I do not need to be told what to do by the like of you.

APOLLODORUS: Blockhead. (*He begins shouting.*) Ho there, Centurion. Hoiho!

SENTINEL: Curse your meddling. (*Shouting.*) Hoiho! Alarm! Alarm!

FIRST AND SECOND AUXILIARIES: Alarm! Alarm! Hoiho!

(*The* CENTURION *comes running in with his guard.*)

CENTURION: What now? Has the old woman attacked you again? (*Seeing* APOLLODORUS.) Are *you* here still?

APOLLODORUS (*pointing as before*): See there. The Egyptians are moving. They are going to recapture the Pharos. They will attack by sea and land: by land along the great mole; by sea from the west harbor. Stir yourselves, my military friends: the hunt is up. (*A clangor of trumpets from several points along the quay.*) Aha! I told you so.

CENTURION (*quickly*): The two extra men pass the alarm to the south posts. One man keep guard here. The rest with me — quick.

(*The two* AUXILIARY SENTINELS *run off to the south. The* CENTURION *and his guard run off northward; and immediately afterwards the bucina sounds. The four* PORTERS *come from the palace carrying a carpet, followed by* FTATATEETA.)

SENTINEL (*handling his pilum apprehensively*): You again! (*The* PORTERS *stop.*)

FTATATEETA: Peace, Roman fellow: you are now singlehanded. Apollodorus: this carpet is Cleopatra's present to Cæsar. It has rolled up in it ten precious goblets of the thinnest Iberian crystal, and a hundred eggs of the sacred blue pigeon. On your honor, let not one of them be broken.

APOLLODORUS: On my head be it! (*To the* PORTERS.) Into the boat with them carefully.

(*The* PORTERS *carry the carpet to the steps.*)

FIRST PORTER (*looking down at the boat*): Beware what you do, sir. Those eggs of which the lady speaks must weigh more than a pound apiece. This boat is too small for such a load.

BOATMAN (*excitedly rushing up the steps*): Oh thou injurious porter!

Oh thou unnatural son of a she-camel! (*To* APOLLODORUS.) My boat, sir, hath often carried five men. Shall it not carry your lordship and a bale of pigeon's eggs? (*To the* PORTER.) Thou mangy dromedary, the gods shall punish thee for this envious wickedness.

FIRST PORTER (*stolidly*): I cannot quit this bale now to beat thee; but another day I will lie in wait for thee.

APOLLODORUS (*going between them*): Peace there. If the boat were but a single plank, I would get to Cæsar on it.

FTATATEETA (*anxiously*): In the name of the gods, Apollodorus, run no risks with that bale.

APOLLODORUS: Fear not, thou venerable grotesque: I guess its great worth. (*To the* PORTERS.) Down with it, I say; and gently; or ye shall eat nothing but stick for ten days.

(*The* BOATMAN *goes down the steps, followed by the* PORTERS *with the bale:* FTATATEETA *and* APOLLODORUS *watching from the edge.*)

APOLLODORUS: Gently, my sons, my children — (*with sudden alarm*) gently, ye dogs. Lay it level in the stern — so — tis well.

FTATATEETA (*screaming down at one of the* PORTERS): Do not step on it, do not step on it. Oh thou brute beast!

FIRST PORTER (*ascending*): Be not excited, mistress: all is well.

FTATATEETA (*panting*): All well! Oh, thou hast given my heart a turn! (*She clutches her side, gasping.*)

(*The four* PORTERS *have now come up and are waiting at the stair-head to be paid.*)

APOLLODORUS: Here, ye hungry ones. (*He gives money to the* FIRST PORTER, *who holds it in his hand to shew to the others. They crowd greedily to see how much it is, quite prepared, after the Eastern fashion, to protest to heaven against their patron's stinginess. But his liberality overpowers them.*)

FIRST PORTER: O bounteous prince!

SECOND PORTER: O lord of the bazaar!

THIRD PORTER: O favored of the gods!

FOURTH PORTER: O father to all the porters of the market!

SENTINEL (*enviously, threatening them fiercely with his pilum*): Hence, dogs: off. Out of this. (*They fly before him northward along the quay.*)

APOLLODORUS: Farewell, Ftatateeta. I shall be at the lighthouse before the Egyptians. (*He descends the steps.*)

FTATATEETA: The gods speed thee and protect my nursling!

(*The* SENTRY *returns from chasing the* PORTERS *and looks down at the boat, standing near the stairhead lest* FTATATEETA *should attempt to escape.*)

APOLLODORUS (*from beneath, as the boat moves off*): Farewell, valiant pilum pitcher.

SENTINEL: Farewell, shopkeeper.

APOLLODORUS: Ha, ha! Pull, thou brave boatman, pull. Soho-o-o-o-o! (*He begins to sing in barcarolle measure to the rhythm of the oars.*)

My heart, my heart, spread out thy wings:
Shake off thy heavy load of love —

Give me the oars, O son of a snail.

SENTINEL (*threatening* FTATATEETA): Now mistress: back to your henhouse. In with you.

FTATATEETA (*falling on her knees and stretching her hands over the waters*): Gods of the seas, bear her safely to the shore!

SENTINEL: Bear *who* safely? What do you mean?

FTATATEETA (*looking darkly at him*): Gods of Egypt and of Vengeance, let this Roman fool be beaten like a dog by his captain for suffering her to be taken over the waters.

SENTINEL: Accursed one: is she then in the boat? (*He calls over the sea.*) Hoiho, there, boatman! Hoiho!

APOLLODORUS (*singing in the distance*)

My heart, my heart, be whole and free:
Love is thine only enemy.

(*Meanwhile* RUFIO, *the morning's fighting done, sits munching dates on a faggot of brushwood outside the door of the lighthouse, which towers gigantic to the clouds on his left. His helmet, full of dates, is between his knees; and a leathern bottle of wine is by his side. Behind him the great stone pedestal of the lighthouse is shut in from the open sea by a low stone parapet, with a couple of steps in the middle of the broad coping. A huge chain with a hook hangs down from the lighthouse crane above his head. Faggots like the one he sits on lie beneath it ready to be drawn up to feed the beacon.* CÆSAR *is standing on the step at the parapet looking out anxiously, evidently ill at ease.* BRITANNUS *comes out of the lighthouse door.*)

RUFIO: Well, my British islander. Have you been up to the top?

BRITANNUS: I have. I reckon it at 200 feet high.

RUFIO: Anybody up there?

BRITANNUS: One elderly Tyrian to work the crane; and his son, a well conducted youth of 14.

RUFIO (*looking at the chain*): What! An old man and a boy work that! Twenty men, you mean.

BRITANNUS: Two only, I assure you. They have counterweights, and a machine with boiling water in it which I do not understand: it is not of British design. They use it to haul up barrels of oil and faggots to burn in the brazier on the roof.

RUFIO: But—

BRITANNUS: Excuse me: I came down because there are messengers coming along the mole to us from the island. I must see what their business is. (*He hurries out past the lighthouse.*)

CÆSAR (*coming away from the parapet, shivering and out of sorts*): Rufio: this has been a mad expedition. We shall be beaten. I wish I knew how our men are getting on with that barricade across the great mole.

RUFIO (*angrily*): Must I leave my food and go starving to bring you a report?

CÆSAR (*soothing him nervously*): No, Rufio, no. Eat, my son, eat. (*He takes another turn,* RUFIO *chewing dates meanwhile.*) The Egyptians cannot be such fools as not to storm the barricade and swoop down on us here before it is finished. It is the first time I have ever run an avoidable risk. I should not have come to Egypt.

RUFIO: An hour ago you were all for victory.

CÆSAR (*apologetically*): Yes: I was a fool—rash, Rufio—boyish.

RUFIO: Boyish! Not a bit of it. Here (*offering him a handful of dates*).

CÆSAR: What are these for?

RUFIO: To eat. Thats whats the matter with you. When a man comes to your age, he runs down before his midday meal. Eat and drink; and then have another look at our chances.

CÆSAR (*taking the dates*): My age! (*He shakes his head and bites a date.*) Yes, Rufio: I am an old man—worn out now—true, quite true. (*He gives way to melancholy contemplation, and eats another date.*) Achillas is still in his prime: Ptolemy is a boy. (*He eats another date, and plucks up a little.*) Well, every dog has his day; and I have had mine: I cannot complain. (*With sudden cheerfulness.*) These dates are not bad, Rufio. (BRITANNUS *returns, greatly excited, with a leathern bag.* CÆSAR *is himself again in a moment.*) What now?

BRITANNUS (*triumphantly*): Our brave Rhodian mariners have captured a treasure. There! (*He throws the bag down at* CÆSAR'*s feet.*) Our enemies are delivered into our hands.

CÆSAR: In that bag?

BRITANNUS: Wait till you hear, Cæsar. This bag contains all the letters which have passed between Pompey's party and the army of occupation here.

CÆSAR: Well?

BRITANNUS (*impatient of* CÆSAR'S *slowness to grasp the situation*): Well, we shall now know who your foes are. The name of every man who has plotted against you since you crossed the Rubicon may be in these papers, for all we know.

CÆSAR: Put them in the fire.

BRITANNUS: Put them — (*he gasps*)!!!!

CÆSAR: In the fire. Would you have me waste the next three years of my life in proscribing and condemning men who will be my friends when I have proved that my friendship is worth more than Pompey's was — than Cato's is. O incorrigible British islander: am I a bull dog, to seek quarrels merely to shew how stubborn my jaws are?

BRITANNUS: But your honor — the honor of Rome —

CÆSAR: I do not make human sacrifices to my honor, as your Druids do. Since you will not burn these, at least I can drown them. (*He picks up the bag and throws it over the parapet into the sea.*)

BRITANNUS: Cæsar: this is mere eccentricity. Are traitors to be allowed to go free for the sake of a paradox?

RUFIO (*rising*): Cæsar: when the islander has finished preaching, call me again. I am going to have a look at the boiling water machine.

(*He goes into the lighthouse.*)

BRITANNUS (*with genuine feeling*): O Cæsar, my great master, if I could but persuade you to regard life seriously, as men do in my country!

CÆSAR: Do they truly do so, Britannus?

BRITANNUS: Have you not been there? Have you not seen them? What Briton speaks as you do in your moments of levity? What Briton neglects to attend the services at the sacred grove? What Briton wears clothes of many colors as you do, instead of plain blue, as all solid, well esteemed men should? These are moral questions with us.

CÆSAR: Well, well, my friend: some day I shall settle down and have a blue toga, perhaps. Meanwhile, I must get on as best I can in my flippant Roman way. (APOLLODORUS *comes past the lighthouse.*) What now?

BRITANNUS (*turning quickly, and challenging the stranger with official haughtiness*): What is this? Who are you? How did you come here?

APOLLODORUS: Calm yourself, my friend: I am not going to eat you. I have come by boat, from Alexandria, with precious gifts for Cæsar.

CÆSAR: From Alexandria!

BRITANNUS (*severely*): That is Cæsar, sir.

RUFIO (*appearing at the lighthouse door*): Whats the matter now?

APOLLODORUS: Hail, great Cæsar! I am Apollodorus the Sicilian, an artist.

BRITANNUS: An artist! Why have they admitted this vagabond?

CÆSAR: Peace, man. Apollodorus is a famous patrician amateur.

BRITANNUS (*disconcerted*): I crave the gentleman's pardon. (*To* CÆSAR.) I understood him to say that he was a professional. (*Somewhat out of countenance, he allows* APOLLODORUS *to approach* CÆSAR, *changing places with him.* RUFIO, *after looking* APOLLODORUS *up and down with marked disparagement, goes to the other side of the platform.*)

CÆSAR: You are welcome, Apollodorus. What is your business?

APOLLODORUS: First, to deliver to you a present from the Queen of Queens.

CÆSAR: Who is that?

APOLLODORUS: Cleopatra of Egypt.

CÆSAR (*taking him into his confidence in his most winning manner*): Apollodorus: this is no time for playing with presents. Pray you, go back to the Queen, and tell her that if all goes well I shall return to the palace this evening.

APOLLODORUS: Cæsar: I cannot return. As I approached the lighthouse, some fool threw a great leathern bag into the sea. It broke the nose of my boat; and I had hardly time to get myself and my charge to the shore before the poor little cockleshell sank.

CÆSAR: I am sorry, Apollodorus. The fool shall be rebuked. Well, well: what have you brought me? The Queen will be hurt if I do not look at it.

RUFIO: Have we time to waste on this trumpery? The Queen is only a child.

CÆSAR: Just so: that is why we must not disappoint her. What is the present, Apollodorus?

APOLLODORUS: Cæsar: it is a Persian carpet — a beauty! And in it are — so I am told — pigeons' eggs and crystal goblets and fragile precious things. I dare not for my head have it carried up that narrow ladder from the causeway.

RUFIO: Swing it up by the crane, then. We will send the eggs to the cook, drink our wine from the goblets; and the carpet will make a bed for Cæsar.

APOLLODORUS: The crane! Cæsar: I have sworn to tender this bale of carpets as I tender my own life.

CÆSAR (*cheerfully*): Then let them swing you up at the same time; and if the chain breaks, you and the pigeons' eggs will perish together.

(*He goes to the chain and looks up along it, examining it curiously.*)

APOLLODORUS (*to* BRITANNUS): Is Cæsar serious?

BRITANNUS: His manner is frivolous because he is an Italian; but he means what he says.

APOLLODORUS: Serious or not, he spake well. Give me a squad of soldiers to work the crane.

BRITANNUS: Leave the crane to me. Go and await the descent of the chain.

APOLLODORUS: Good. You will presently see me there (*turning to them all and pointing with an eloquent gesture to the sky above the parapet*) rising like the sun with my treasure.

(*He goes back the way he came.* BRITANNUS *goes into the lighthouse.*)

RUFIO (*ill-humoredly*): Are you really going to wait here for this foolery, Cæsar?

CÆSAR (*backing away from the crane as it gives signs of working*): Why not?

RUFIO: The Egyptians will let you know why not if they have the sense to make a rush from the shore end of the mole before our barricade is finished. And here we are waiting like children to see a carpet full of pigeons' eggs.

(*The chain rattles, and is drawn up high enough to clear the parapet. It then swings round out of sight behind the lighthouse.*)

CÆSAR: Fear not, my son Rufio. When the first Egyptian takes his first step along the mole, the alarm will sound; and we two will reach the barricade from our end before the Egyptians reach it from their end — we two, Rufio: I, the old man, and you, his biggest boy. And the old man will be there first. So peace; and give me some more dates.

APOLLODORUS (*from the causeway below*): Soho, haul away. So-ho-o-o-o! (*The chain is drawn up and comes round again from behind the lighthouse.* APOLLODORUS *is swinging in the air with his bale of carpet at the end of it. He breaks into song as he soars above the parapet.*)

Aloft, aloft, behold the blue
That never shone in woman's eyes —

Easy there: stop her. (*He ceases to rise.*) Further round! (*The chain comes forward above the platform.*)

RUFIO (*calling up*): Lower away there. (*The chain and its load begin to descend.*)

APOLLODORUS (*calling up*): Gently — slowly — mind the eggs.

RUFIO (*calling up*): Easy there — slowly — slowly.

(APOLLODORUS *and the bale are deposited safely on the flags in the middle of the platform.* RUFIO *and* CÆSAR *help* APOLLODORUS *to cast off the chain from the bale.*)

RUFIO: Haul up.

(*The chain rises clear of their heads with a rattle.* BRITANNUS *comes from the lighthouse and helps them to uncord the carpet.*)

APOLLODORUS (*when the cords are loose*): Stand off, my friends: let Cæsar see. (*He throws the carpet open.*)

RUFIO: Nothing but a heap of shawls. Where are the pigeons' eggs?

APOLLODORUS: Approach, Cæsar; and search for them among the shawls.

RUFIO (*drawing his sword*): Ha, treachery. Keep back, Cæsar: I saw the shawl move: there is something alive in there.

BRITANNUS (*drawing his sword*): It is a serpent.

APOLLODORUS: Dares *Cæsar* thrust his hand into the sack where the serpent moves?

RUFIO (*turning on him*): Treacherous dog —

CÆSAR: Peace. Put up your swords. Apollodorus: your serpent seems to breathe very regularly. (*He thrusts his hand under the shawls and draws out a bare arm.*) This is a pretty little snake.

RUFIO (*drawing out the other arm*): Let us have the rest of you.

(*They pull* CLEOPATRA *up by the wrists into a sitting position.* BRITANNUS, *scandalized, sheathes his sword with a drive of protest.*)

CLEOPATRA (*gasping*): Oh, I'm smothered. Oh, Cæsar, a man stood on me in the boat; and a great sack of something fell upon me out of the sky; and then the boat sank; and then I was swung up into the air and bumped down.

CÆSAR (*petting her as she rises and takes refuge on his breast*): Well, never mind: here you are safe and sound at last.

RUFIO: Ay, and now that she *is* here, what are we to do with her?

BRITANNUS: She cannot stay here, Cæsar, without the companionship of some matron.

CLEOPATRA (*jealously, to* CÆSAR, *who is obviously perplexed*): Arent you glad to see me?

CÆSAR: Yes, yes; *I* am very glad. But Rufio is very angry; and Britannus is shocked.

CLEOPATRA (*contemptuously*): You can have their heads cut off, can you not?

CÆSAR: They would not be so useful with their heads cut off as they are now, my sea bird.

RUFIO (*to* CLEOPATRA): We shall have to go away presently and cut some of your Egyptians' heads off. How will you like being left here with the chance of being captured by that little brother of yours if we are beaten?

CLEOPATRA: But you mustnt leave me alone. Cæsar: you will not leave me alone, will you?

RUFIO: What! not when the trumpet sounds and all our lives depend on Cæsar's being at the barricade before the Egyptians reach it? Eh?

CLEOPATRA: Let them lose their lives: they are only soldiers.

CÆSAR (*gravely*): Cleopatra: when that trumpet sounds, we must take every man his life in his hand, and throw it in the face of Death. And of my soldiers who have trusted me there is not one whose hand I shall not hold more sacred than your head. (CLEOPATRA *is overwhelmed. Her eyes fill with tears.*) Apollodorus: you must take her back to the palace.

APOLLODORUS: Am I a dolphin, Cæsar, to cross the seas with young ladies on my back? My boat is sunk: all yours are either at the barricade or have returned to the city. I will hail one if I can: that is all I can do. (*He goes back to the causeway.*)

CLEOPATRA (*struggling with her tears*): It does not matter. I will not go back. Nobody cares for me.

CÆSAR: Cleopatra —

CLEOPATRA: You want me to be killed.

CÆSAR (*still more gravely*): My poor child: your life matters little here to anyone but yourself. (*She gives way altogether at this, casting herself down on the faggots weeping. Suddenly a great tumult is heard in the distance, bucinas and trumpets sounding through a storm of shouting.* BRITTANUS *rushes to the parapet and looks along the mole.* CÆSAR *and* RUFIO *turn to one another with quick intelligence.*)

CÆSAR: Come, Rufio.

CLEOPATRA (*scrambling to her knees and clinging to him*): No, no. Do not leave me, Cæsar. (*He snatches his skirt from her clutch.*) Oh!

BRITANNUS (*from the parapet*): Cæsar: we are cut off. The Egyptians have landed from the west harbor between us and the barricade!!!

RUFIO (*running to see*): Curses! It is true. We are caught like rats in a trap.

CÆSAR (*ruthfully*): Rufio, Rufio: my men at the barricade are between the sea party and the shore party. I have murdered them.

RUFIO (*coming back from the parapet to* CÆSAR'*s right hand*): Ay: that comes of fooling with this girl here.

APOLLODORUS (*coming up quickly from the causeway*): Look over the parapet, Cæsar.

CÆSAR: We have looked, my friend. We must defend ourselves here.

APOLLODORUS: I have thrown the ladder into the sea. They cannot get in without it.

RUFIO: Ay; and we cannot get out. Have you thought of that?

APOLLODORUS: Not get out! Why not? You have ships in the east harbor.

BRITANNUS (*hopefully, at the parapet*): The Rhodian galleys are standing in towards us already. (CÆSAR *quickly joins* BRITANNUS *at the parapet.*)

RUFIO (*to* APOLLODORUS, *impatiently*): And by what road are we to walk to the galleys, pray?

APOLLODORUS (*with gay, defiant rhetoric*): By the road that leads everywhere — the diamond path of the sun and moon. Have you never seen the child's shadow play of The Broken Bridge? "Ducks and geese with ease get over" — eh? (*He throws away his cloak and cap, and binds his sword on his back.*)

RUFIO: What are you talking about?

APOLLODORUS: I will shew you. (*Calling to* BRITANNUS.) How far off is the nearest galley?

BRITANNUS: Fifty fathom.

CÆSAR: No, no: they are further off than they seem in this clear air to your British eyes. Nearly quarter of a mile, Apollodorus.

APOLLODORUS: Good. Defend yourselves here until I send you a boat from that galley.

RUFIO: Have you wings, perhaps?

APOLLODORUS: Water wings, soldier. Behold!

(*He runs up the steps between* CÆSAR *and* BRITANNUS *to the coping of the parapet; springs into the air; and plunges head foremost into the sea.*)

CÆSAR (*like a schoolboy — wildly excited*): Bravo, bravo! (*Throwing off his cloak.*) By Jupiter, I will do that too.

RUFIO (*seizing him*): You are mad. You shall not.

CÆSAR: Why not? Can I not swim as well as he?

RUFIO (*frantic*): Can an old fool dive and swim like a young one? He is twenty-five and you are fifty.

CÆSAR (*breaking loose from* RUFIO): Old!!!

BRITANNUS (*shocked*): Rufio: you forget yourself.

CÆSAR: I will race you to the galley for a week's pay, father Rufio.

CLEOPATRA: But me! me!!! me!!! what is to become of me?

CÆSAR: I will carry you on my back to the galley like a dolphin. Rufio:

when you see me rise to the surface, throw her in: I will answer for her. And then in with you after her, both of you.

CLEOPATRA: No, no, NO. I shall be drowned.

BRITANNUS: Cæsar: I am a man and a Briton, not a fish. I must have a boat. I cannot swim.

CLEOPATRA: Neither can I.

CÆSAR (*to* BRITANNUS): Stay here, then, alone, until I recapture the lighthouse: I will not forget you. Now, Rufio.

RUFIO: You have made up your mind to this folly?

CÆSAR: The Egyptians have made it up for me. What else is there to do? And mind where you jump: I do not want to get your fourteen stone in the small of my back as I come up. (*He runs up the steps and stands on the coping.*)

BRITANNUS (*anxiously*): One last word, Cæsar. Do not let yourself be seen in the fashionable part of Alexandria until you have changed your clothes.

CÆSAR (*calling over the sea*): Ho, Apollodorus. (*He points skyward and quotes the barcarolle.*)

The white upon the blue above —

APOLLODORUS (*swimming in the distance*):

Is purple on the green below —

CÆSAR (*exultantly*): Aha! (*He plunges into the sea.*)

CLEOPATRA (*running excitedly to the steps*): Oh, let me see. He will be drowned (RUFIO *seizes her.*) — Ah — ah — ah — ah! (*He pitches her screaming into the sea.* RUFIO *and* BRITANNUS *roar with laughter.*)

RUFIO (*looking down after her*): He has got her. (*To* BRITANNUS.) Hold the fort, Briton. Cæsar will not forget you. (*He springs off.*)

BRITANNUS (*running to the steps to watch them as they swim*): All safe, Rufio?

RUFIO (*swimming*): All safe.

CÆSAR (*swimming further off*): Take refuge up there by the beacon; and pile the fuel on the trap door, Britannus.

BRITANNUS (*calling in reply*): I will first do so, and then commend myself to my country's gods. (*A sound of cheering from the sea.* BRITANNUS *gives full vent to his excitement.*) The boat has reached him: Hip, hip, hip, hurrah!

ACT FOUR

(CLEOPATRA'S *sousing in the east harbor of Alexandria was in October 48* B.C. *In March 47 she is passing the afternoon in her boudoir in the palace, among a bevy of her ladies, listening to a slave girl who is playing the harp in the middle of the room. The harpist's master, an old* MUSICIAN, *with a lined face, prominent brows, white beard, moustache and eyebrows twisted and horned at the ends, and a consciously keen and pretentious expression, is squatting on the floor close to her on her right, watching her performance.* FTATATEETA *is in attendance near the door, in front of a group of female slaves. Except the harp player all are seated:* CLEOPATRA *in a chair opposite the door on the other side of the room; the rest on the ground.* CLEOPATRA'S *ladies are all young, the most conspicuous being* CHARMIAN *and* IRAS, *her favorites.* CHARMIAN *is a hatchet faced, terra cotta colored little goblin, swift in her movements, and neatly finished at the hands and feet.* IRAS *is a plump, goodnatured creature, rather fatuous, with a profusion of red hair, and a tendency to giggle on the slightest provocation.*)

CLEOPATRA: Can I —

FTATATEETA (*insolently, to the player*): Peace, thou! The Queen speaks. (*The player stops.*)

CLEOPATRA (*to the old* MUSICIAN): I want to learn to play the harp with my own hands. Cæsar loves music. Can you teach me?

MUSICIAN: Assuredly I and no one else can teach the Queen. Have I not discovered the lost method of the ancient Egyptians, who could make a pyramid tremble by touching a bass string? All the other teachers are quacks: I have exposed them repeatedly.

CLEOPATRA: Good: you shall teach me. How long will it take?

MUSICIAN: Not very long: only four years. Your Majesty must first become proficient in the philosophy of Pythagoras.

CLEOPATRA: Has she (*indicating the slave*) become proficient in the philosophy of Pythagoras?

MUSICIAN: Oh, she is but a slave. She learns as a dog learns.

CLEOPATRA: Well, then, I will learn as a dog learns; for she plays better than you. You shall give me a lesson every day for a fortnight. (*The* MUSICIAN *hastily scrambles to his feet and bows profoundly.*) After that, whenever I strike a false note you shall be flogged; and if I strike so many that there is not time to flog you, you shall be thrown into the Nile to feed the crocodiles. Give the girl a piece of gold; and send them away.

MUSICIAN (*much taken aback*): But true art will not be thus forced.

FTATATEETA (*pushing him out*): What is this? Answering the Queen, forsooth. Out with you.

(*He is pushed out by* FTATATEETA, *the girl following with her harp, amid the laughter of the ladies and slaves.*)

CLEOPATRA: Now, can any of you amuse me? Have you any stories or any news?

IRAS: Ftatateeta —

CLEOPATRA: Oh. Ftatateeta, Ftatateeta, always Ftatateeta. Some new tale to set me against her.

IRAS: No: this time Ftatateeta has been virtuous. (*All the ladies laugh — not the slaves.*) Pothinus has been trying to bribe her to let him speak with you.

CLEOPATRA (*wrathfully*): Ha! you all sell audiences with me, as if I saw whom you please, and not whom I please. I should like to know how much of her gold piece that harp girl will have to give up before she leaves the palace.

IRAS: We can easily find that out for you.

(*The ladies laugh.*)

CLEOPATRA (*frowning*): You laugh; but take care, take care. I will find out some day how to make myself served as Cæsar is served.

CHARMIAN: Old hooknose! (*They laugh again.*)

CLEOPATRA (*revolted*): Silence. Charmian: do not you be a silly little Egyptian fool. Do you know why I allow you all to chatter impertinently just as you please, instead of treating you as Ftatateeta would treat you if she were Queen?

CHARMIAN: Because you try to imitate Cæsar in everything; and he lets everybody say what they please to him.

CLEOPATRA: No; but because I asked him one day why he did so; and he said "Let your women talk; and you will learn something from them." What have I to learn from them? I said. "What they are," said he; and oh! you should have seen his eye as he said it. You would have curled up, you shallow things. (*They laugh. She turns fiercely on* IRAS.) At whom are you laughing — at me or at Cæsar?

IRAS: At Cæsar.

CLEOPATRA: If you were not a fool, you would laugh at me; and if you were not a coward you would not be afraid to tell me so. (FTATATEETA *returns.*) Ftatateeta: they tell me that Pothinus has offered you a bribe to admit him to my presence.

FTATATEETA (*protesting*): Now by my father's gods —

CLEOPATRA (*cutting her short despotically*): Have I not told you not to deny things? You would spend the day calling your father's gods to witness to your virtues if I let you. Go take the bribe; and bring in Pothinus. (FTATATEETA *is about to reply.*) Dont answer me. Go.

(FTATATEETA *goes out; and* CLEOPATRA *rises and begins to prowl to and fro between her chair and the door, meditating. All rise and stand.*)

IRAS (*as she reluctantly rises*): Heigho! I wish Cæsar were back in Rome.

CLEOPATRA (*threateningly*): It will be a bad day for you all when he goes. Oh, if I were not ashamed to let him see that I am as cruel at heart as my father, I would make you repent that speech! Why do you wish him away?

CHARMIAN: He makes you so terribly prosy and serious and learned and philosophical. It is worse than being religious, at *our* ages. (*The ladies laugh.*)

CLEOPATRA: Cease that endless cackling, will you. Hold your tongues.

CHARMIAN (*with mock resignation*): Well, well: we must try to live up to Cæsar.

(*They laugh again.* CLEOPATRA *rages silently as she continues to prowl to and fro.* FTATATEETA *comes back with* POTHINUS, *who halts on the threshold.*)

FTATATEETA (*at the door*): Pothinus craves the ear of the —

CLEOPATRA: There, there: that will do: let him come in. (*She resumes her seat. All sit down except* POTHINUS, *who advances to the middle of the room.* FTATATEETA *takes her former place.*) Well, Pothinus: what is the latest news from your rebel friends?

POTHINUS (*haughtily*): I am no friend of rebellion. And a prisoner does not receive news.

CLEOPATRA: You are no more a prisoner than I am — than Cæsar is. These six months we have been besieged in this palace by my subjects. You are allowed to walk on the beach among the soldiers. Can I go further myself, or can Cæsar?

POTHINUS: You are but a child, Cleopatra, and do not understand these matters.

(*The ladies laugh.* CLEOPATRA *looks inscrutably at him.*)

CHARMIAN: I see you do not know the latest news, Pothinus.

POTHINUS: What is that?

CHARMIAN: That Cleopatra is no longer a child. Shall I tell you how to grow much older, and much, *much* wiser in one day?

POTHINUS: I should prefer to grow wiser without growing older.

CHARMIAN: Well, go up to the top of the lighthouse; and get somebody to take you by the hair and throw you into the sea. (*The ladies laugh.*)

CLEOPATRA: She is right, Pothinus: you will come to the shore with much conceit washed out of you. (*The ladies laugh.* CLEOPATRA *rises impatiently.*) Begone, all of you. I will speak with Pothinus alone. Drive them out, Ftatateeta. (*They run out laughing.* FTATATEETA *shuts the door on them.*) What are *you* waiting for?

FTATATEETA: It is not meet that the Queen remain alone with —

CLEOPATRA (*interrupting her*): Ftatateeta: must I sacrifice you to your father's gods to teach you that *I* am Queen of Egypt, and not you?

FTATATEETA (*indignantly*): You are like the rest of them. You want to be what these Romans call a New Woman. (*She goes out, banging the door.*)

CLEOPATRA (*sitting down again*): Now, Pothinus: why did you bribe Ftatateeta to bring you hither?

POTHINUS (*studying her gravely*): Cleopatra: what they tell me is true. You are changed.

CLEOPATRA: Do you speak with Cæsar every day for six months: and *you* will be changed.

POTHINUS: It is the common talk that you are infatuated with this old man?

CLEOPATRA: Infatuated? What does that mean? Made foolish, is it not? Oh no: I wish I were.

POTHINUS: You wish you were made foolish! How so?

CLEOPATRA: When I was foolish, I did what I liked, except when Ftatateeta beat me; and even then I cheated her and did it by stealth. Now that Cæsar has made we wise, it is no use my liking or disliking: I do what must be done, and have no time to attend to myself. That is not happiness; but it is greatness. If Cæsar were gone, I think I could govern the Egyptians; for what Cæsar is to me, I am to the fools around me.

POTHINUS (*looking hard at her*): Cleopatra: this may be the vanity of youth.

CLEOPATRA: No, no: it is not that I am so clever, but that the others are so stupid.

POTHINUS (*musingly*): Truly, that is the great secret.

CLEOPATRA: Well, now tell me what you came to say?

POTHINUS (*embarrassed*): I! Nothing.

CLEOPATRA: Nothing!

POTHINUS: At least — to beg for my liberty: that is all.

CLEOPATRA: For that you would have knelt to Cæsar. No, Pothinus: you came with some plan that depended on Cleopatra being a little nursery kitten. Now that Cleopatra is a Queen, the plan is upset.

POTHINUS (*bowing his head submissively*): It is so.

CLEOPATRA (*exultant*): Aha!

POTHINUS (*raising his eyes keenly to hers*): Is Cleopatra then indeed a Queen, and no longer Cæsar's prisoner and slave?

CLEOPATRA: Pothinus: we are all Cæsar's slaves — all we in this land of Egypt — whether we will or no. And she who is wise enough to know this will reign when Cæsar departs.

POTHINUS: You harp on Cæsar's departure.

CLEOPATRA: What if I do?

POTHINUS: Does he not love you?

CLEOPATRA: Love me! Pothinus: Cæsar loves no one. Who are those we love. Only those whom we do not hate: all people are strangers and enemies to us except those we love. But it is not so with Cæsar. He has no hatred in him: he makes friends with everyone as he does with dogs and children. His kindness to me is a wonder; neither mother, father, nor nurse have ever taken so much care for me, or thrown open their thoughts to me so freely.

POTHINUS: Well: is not this love?

CLEOPATRA: What! when he will do as much for the first girl he meets on his way back to Rome? Ask his slave, Britannus: he has been just as good to him. Nay, ask his very horse! His kindness is not for anything in me: it is in his own nature.

POTHINUS: But how can you be sure that he does not love you as men love women?

CLEOPATRA: Because I cannot make him jealous. I have tried.

POTHINUS: Hm! Perhaps I should have asked, then, do *you* love *him?*

CLEOPATRA: Can one love a god? Besides, I love another Roman: one whom I saw long before Cæsar — no god, but a man — one who can love and hate — one whom I can hurt and who would hurt me.

POTHINUS: Does Cæsar know this?

CLEOPATRA: Yes.

POTHINUS: And he is not angry?

CLEOPATRA: He promises to send him to Egypt to please me!

POTHINUS: I do not understand this man.

CLEOPATRA (*with superb contempt*): *You* understand Cæsar! How could you? (*Proudly.*) I do — by instinct.

POTHINUS (*deferentially, after a moment's thought*): Your Majesty caused me to be admitted to-day. What message has the Queen for me?

CLEOPATRA: This. You think that by making my brother king, you will rule in Egypt, because you are his guardian and he is a little silly.

POTHINUS: The Queen is pleased to say so.

CLEOPATRA: The Queen is pleased to say this also. That Cæsar will eat up you, and Achillas, and my brother, as a cat eats up mice; and that he will put on this land of Egypt as a shepherd puts on his garment. And when he has done that, he will return to Rome, and leave Cleopatra here as his viceroy.

POTHINUS (*breaking out wrathfully*): That he shall never do. We have a thousand men to his ten; and we will drive him and his beggarly legions into the sea.

CLEOPATRA (*with scorn, getting up to go*): You rant like any common fellow. Go, then, and marshal your thousands; and make haste; for Mithridates of Pergamos is at hand with reinforcements for Cæsar. Cæsar has held you at bay with two legions: we shall see what he will do with twenty.

POTHINUS: Cleopatra —

CLEOPATRA: Enough, enough: Cæsar has spoiled me for talking to weak things like you. (*She goes out.* POTHINUS, *with a gesture of rage, is following, when* FTATATEETA *enters and stops him.*)

POTHINUS: Let me go forth from this hateful place.

FTATATEETA: What angers you?

POTHINUS: The curse of all the gods of Egypt be upon her! She has sold her country to the Roman, that she may buy it back from him with her kisses.

FTATATEETA: Fool: did she not tell you that she would have Cæsar gone?

POTHINUS: You listened?

FTATATEETA: I took care that some honest woman should be at hand whilst you were with her.

POTHINUS: Now by the gods —

FTATATEETA: Enough of your gods! Cæsar's gods are all powerful here. It is no use *you* coming to Cleopatra: you are only an Egyptian. She will not listen to any of her own race: she treats us all as children.

POTHINUS: May she perish for it!

FTATATEETA (*balefully*): May your tongue wither for that wish! Go! send for Lucius Septimius, the slayer of Pompey. He is a Roman: may be she will listen to him. Begone!

POTHINUS (*darkly*): I know to whom I must go now.

FTATATEETA (*suspiciously*): To whom, then?

POTHINUS: To a greater Roman than Lucius. And mark this, mistress. You thought, before Cæsar came, that Egypt should presently be ruled by you and your crew in the name of Cleopatra. I set myself against it —

FTATATEETA (*interrupting him — wrangling*): Ay; that it might be ruled by you and *your* crew in the name of Ptolemy.

POTHINUS: Better me, or even you, than a woman with a Roman heart; and that is what Cleopatra is now become. Whilst I live, she shall never rule. So guide yourself accordingly. (*He goes out.*)

(*It is by this time drawing on to dinner time. The table is laid on the roof of the palace; and thither* RUFIO *is now climbing, ushered by a majestic palace* OFFICIAL, *wand of office in hand, and followed by a* SLAVE *carrying an inlaid stool. After many stairs they emerge at last into a massive colonnade on the roof. Light curtains are drawn between the columns on the north and east to soften the westering sun. The* OFFICIAL *leads* RUFIO *to one of these shaded sections. A cord for pulling the curtains apart hangs down between the pillars.*)

OFFICIAL (*bowing*): The Roman commander will await Cæsar here.

(*The* SLAVE *sets down the stool near the southernmost column, and slips out through the curtains.*)

RUFIO (*sitting down, a little blown*): Pouf! That was a climb. How high have we come?

OFFICIAL: We are on the palace roof, O Beloved of Victory!

RUFIO: Good! the Beloved of Victory has no more stairs to get up.

(*A* SECOND OFFICIAL *enters from the opposite end, walking backwards.*)

SECOND OFFICIAL: Cæsar approaches.

(CÆSAR, *fresh from the bath, clad in a new tunic of purple silk, comes in, beaming and festive, followed by two* SLAVES *carrying a light couch, which is hardly more than an elaborately designed bench. They place it near the northmost of the two curtained columns. When this is done they slip out through the curtains; and the two* OFFICIALS, *formally bowing, follow them.* RUFIO *rises to receive* CÆSAR.)

CÆSAR (*coming over to him*): Why, Rufio! (*Surveying his dress with an air of admiring astonishment.*) A new baldrick! A new golden pommel to your sword! And you have had your hair cut. But not your beard — ? impossible! (*He sniffs at* RUFIO's *beard.*) Yes, perfumed, by Jupiter Olympus!

RUFIO (*growling*): Well: is it to please myself?

CÆSAR (*affectionately*): No, my son Rufio, but to please me — to celebrate my birthday.

RUFIO (*contemptuously*): Your birthday! You always have a birthday when there is a pretty girl to be flattered or an ambassador to be conciliated. We had seven of them in ten months last year.

CÆSAR (*contritely*): It is true, Rufio! I shall never break myself of these petty deceits.

RUFIO: Who is to dine with us — besides Cleopatra?

CÆSAR: Apollodorus the Sicilian.

RUFIO: That popinjay!

CÆSAR: Come! the popinjay is an amusing dog — tells a story; sings a song; and saves us the trouble of flattering the Queen. What does she care for old politicians and camp-fed bears like us? No: Apollodorus is good company, Rufio, good company.

RUFIO: Well, he can swim a bit and fence a bit: he might be worse, if he only knew how to hold his tongue.

CÆSAR: The gods forbid he should ever learn! Oh, this military life! this tedious, brutal life of action! That is the worst of us Romans: we are mere doers and drudgers: a swarm of bees turned into men. Give me a good talker — one with wit and imagination enough to live without continually doing something!

RUFIO: Ay! a nice time he would have of it with you when dinner was over! Have you noticed that I am before my time?

CÆSAR: Aha! I thought that meant something. What is it?

RUFIO: Can we be overheard here?

CÆSAR: Our privacy invites eavesdropping. I can remedy that. (*He claps his hands twice. The curtains are drawn, revealing the roof garden with a banqueting table set across in the middle for four persons, one at each end, and two side by side. The side next* CÆSAR *and* RUFIO *is blocked with golden wine vessels and basins. A gorgeous* MAJOR-DOMO *is superintending the laying of the table by a staff of* SLAVES. *The colonnade goes round the garden at both sides to the further end, where a gap in it, like a great gateway, leaves the view open to the sky beyond the western edge of the roof, except in the middle, where a life size image of Ra, seated on a huge plinth, towers up, with hawk head and crown of asp and disk. His altar, which stands at his feet, is a single white stone.*) Now everybody can see us, nobody will think of listening to us. (*He sits down on the bench left by the two* SLAVES.)

RUFIO (*sitting down on his stool*): Pothinus wants to speak to you. I advise you to see him: there is some plotting going on here among the women.

CÆSAR: Who is Pothinus?

RUFIO: The fellow with hair like squirrel's fur — the little King's bear leader, whom you kept prisoner.

CÆSAR (*annoyed*): And has he not escaped?

RUFIO: No.

CÆSAR (*rising imperiously*): Why not? You have been guarding this man instead of watching the enemy. Have I not told you always to let prisoners escape unless there are special orders to the contrary? Are there not enough mouths to be fed without him?

RUFIO: Yes; and if you would have a little sense and let me cut his throat, you would save his rations. Anyhow, he *wont* escape. Three sentries have told him they would put a pilum through him if they saw him again. What more can they do? He prefers to stay and spy on us. So would I if I had to do with generals subject to fits of clemency.

CÆSAR (*resuming his seat, argued down*): Hm! And so he wants to see me.

RUFIO: Ay. I have brought him with me. He is waiting there (*jerking his thumb over his shoulder*) under guard.

CÆSAR: And you want me to see him?

RUFIO (*obstinately*): I dont want anything. I daresay you will do what you like. Dont put it on to me.

CÆSAR (*with an air of doing it expressly to indulge* RUFIO): Well, well: let us have him.

RUFIO (*calling*): Ho there, guard! Release your man and send him up. (*Beckoning.*) Come along!

(POTHINUS *enters and stops mistrustfully between the two, looking from one to the other.*)

CÆSAR (*graciously*): Ah, Pothinus! You are welcome. And what is the news this afternoon?

POTHINUS: Cæsar: I come to warn you of a danger, and to make you an offer.

CÆSAR: Never mind the danger. Make the offer.

RUFIO: Never mind the offer. Whats the danger?

POTHINUS: Cæsar: you think that Cleopatra is devoted to you.

CÆSAR (*gravely*): My friend: I already know what I think. Come to your offer.

POTHINUS: I will deal plainly. I know not by what strange gods you have been enabled to defend a palace and a few yards of beach against a city and an army. Since we cut you off from Lake Mareotis, and you dug wells in the salt sea sand and brought up buckets of fresh water from them, we have known that your gods are irresistible, and that you are a worker of miracles. I no longer threaten you —

RUFIO (*sarcastically*): Very handsome of you, indeed.

POTHINUS: So be it: you are the master. Our gods sent the north west winds to keep you in our hands; but you have been too strong for them.

CÆSAR (*gently urging him to come to the point*): Yes, yes, my friend. But what then?

RUFIO: Spit it out, man. What have you to say?

POTHINUS: I have to say that you have a traitress in your camp. Cleopatra —

MAJOR-DOMO (*at the table, announcing*): The Queen! (CÆSAR *and* RUFIO *rise.*)

RUFIO (*aside to* POTHINUS): You should have spat it out sooner, you fool. Now it is too late.

(CLEOPATRA, *in gorgeous raiment, enters in state through the gap in the colonnade, and comes down past the image of Ra and past the table to* CÆSAR. *Her retinue, headed by* FTATATEETA, *joins the staff at the table.* CÆSAR *gives* CLEOPATRA *his seat, which she takes.*)

CLEOPATRA (*quickly, seeing* POTHINUS): What is *he* doing here?

CÆSAR (*seating himself beside her, in the most amiable of tempers*): Just going to tell me something about you. You shall hear it. Proceed, Pothinus.

POTHINUS (*disconcerted*): Cæsar — (*He stammers.*)

CÆSAR: Well, out with it.

POTHINUS: What I have to say is for your ear, not for the Queen's.

CLEOPATRA (*with subdued ferocity*): There are means of making you speak. Take care.

POTHINUS (*defiantly*): Cæsar does not employ those means.

CÆSAR: My friend: when a man has anything to tell in this world, the difficulty is not to make him tell it, but to prevent him from telling it too often. Let me celebrate my birthday by setting you free. Farewell: we shall not meet again.

CLEOPATRA (*angrily*): Cæsar: this mercy is foolish.

POTHINUS (*to* CÆSAR): Will you not give me a private audience? Your life may depend on it. (CÆSAR *rises loftily.*)

RUFIO (*aside to* POTHINUS): Ass! Now we shall have some heroics.

CÆSAR (*oratorically*): Pothinus —

RUFIO (*interrupting him*): Cæsar: the dinner will spoil if you begin preaching your favorite sermon about life and death.

CLEOPATRA (*priggishly*): Peace, Rufio. I desire to hear Cæsar.

RUFIO (*bluntly*): Your Majesty has heard it before. You repeated it to Apollodorus last week; and he thought it was all your own. (CÆSAR'S *dignity collapses. Much tickled, he sits down again and looks roguishly at* CLEOPATRA, *who is furious.* RUFIO *calls as before.*) Ho there, guard! Pass the prisoner out. He is released. (*To* POTHINUS.) Now off with you. You have lost your chance.

POTHINUS (*his temper overcoming his prudence*): I *will* speak.

CÆSAR (*to* CLEOPATRA): You see. Torture would not have wrung a word from him.

POTHINUS: Cæsar: you have taught Cleopatra the arts by which the Romans govern the world.

CÆSAR: Alas! they cannot even govern themselves. What then?

POTHINUS: What then? Are you so besotted with her beauty that you do not see that she is impatient to reign in Egypt alone, and that her heart is set on your departure?

CLEOPATRA (*rising*): Liar!

CÆSAR (*shocked*): What! Protestations! Contradictions!

CLEOPATRA (*ashamed, but trembling with suppressed rage*): No. I do not deign to contradict. Let him talk. (*She sits down again.*)

POTHINUS: From her own lips I have heard it. You are to be her catspaw: you are to tear the crown from her brother's head and set it on her own, delivering us all into her hand — delivering yourself also. And then Cæsar can return to Rome, or depart through the gate of death, which is nearer and surer.

CÆSAR (*calmly*): Well, my friend; and is not this very natural?

POTHINUS (*astonished*): Natural! Then you do not resent treachery?

CÆSAR: Resent! O thou foolish Egyptian, what have I to do with resentment? Do I resent the wind when it chills me, or the night when it makes me stumble in the darkness? Shall I resent youth when it turns from age, and ambition when it turns from servitude? To tell me such a story as this is but to tell me that the sun will rise to-morrow.

CLEOPATRA (*unable to contain herself*): But it is false — false. I swear it.

CÆSAR: It is true, though you swore it a thousand times, and believed all you swore. (*She is convulsed with emotion. To screen her, he rises and takes* POTHINUS *to* RUFIO, *saying:*) Come, Rufio: let us see Pothinus past the guard. I have a word to say to him. (*Aside to them.*) We must give the Queen a moment to recover herself.

(*Aloud.*) Come. (*He takes* POTHINUS *and* RUFIO *out with him, conversing with them meanwhile.*) Tell your friends, Pothinus, that they must not think I am opposed to a reasonable settlement of the country's affairs — (*They pass out of hearing.*)

CLEOPATRA (*in a stifled whisper*): Ftatateeta, Ftatateeta.

FTATATEETA (*hurrying to her from the table and petting her*): Peace, child: be comforted —

CLEOPATRA (*interrupting her*): Can they hear us?

FTATATEETA: No, dear heart, no.

CLEOPATRA: Listen to me. If he leaves the Palace alive, never see my face again.

FTATATEETA: He? Poth —

CLEOPATRA (*striking her on the mouth*): Strike his life out as I strike his name from your lips. Dash him down from the wall. Break him on the stones. Kill, kill, *kill* him.

FTATATEETA (*shewing all her teeth*): The dog shall perish.

CLEOPATRA: Fail in this, and you go out from before me for ever.

FTATATEETA (*resolutely*): So be it. You shall not see my face until his eyes are darkened.

(CÆSAR *comes back, with* APOLLODORUS, *exquisitely dressed, and* RUFIO.)

CLEOPATRA (*to* FTATATEETA): Come soon — soon. (FTATATEETA *turns her meaning eyes for a moment on her mistress; then goes grimly away past Ra and out.* CLEOPATRA *runs like a gazelle to* CÆSAR.) So you have come back to me, Cæsar. (*Caressingly.*) I thought you were angry. Welcome, Apollodorus. (*She gives him her hand to kiss, with her other arm about* CÆSAR.)

APOLLODORUS: Cleopatra grows more womanly beautiful from week to week.

CLEOPATRA: Truth, Apollodorus?

APOLLODORUS: Far, far short of the truth! Friend Rufio threw a pearl into the sea: Cæsar fished up a diamond.

CÆSAR: Cæsar fished up a touch of rheumatism, my friend. Come: to dinner! to dinner! (*They move towards the table.*)

CLEOPATRA (*skipping like a young fawn*): Yes, to dinner. I have ordered *such* a dinner for you, Cæsar!

CÆSAR: Ay? What are we to have?

CLEOPATRA: Peacocks' brains.

CÆSAR (*as if his mouth watered*): Peacocks' brains, Apollodorus!

APOLLODORUS: Not for me. I prefer nightingales' tongues. (*He goes to one of the two covers set side by side*).

CLEOPATRA: Roast boar, Rufio!

RUFIO (*gluttonously*): Good! (*He goes to the seat next* APOLLODORUS, *on his left.*)

CÆSAR (*looking at his seat, which is at the end of the table, to Ra's left hand*): What has become of my leathern cushion?

CLEOPATRA (*at the opposite end*): I have got new ones for you.

MAJOR-DOMO: These cushions, Cæsar, are of Maltese gauze, stuffed with rose leaves.

CÆSAR: Rose leaves! Am I a caterpillar? (*He throws the cushions away and seats himself on the leather mattress underneath.*)

CLEOPATRA: What a shame! My new cushions!

MAJOR-DOMO (*at* CÆSAR's *elbow*): What shall we serve to whet Cæsar's appetite?

CÆSAR: What have you got?

MAJOR-DOMO: Sea hedgehogs, black and white sea acorns, sea nettles, beccaficoes, purple shellfish —

CÆSAR: Any oysters?

MAJOR-DOMO: Assuredly.

CÆSAR: *British* oysters?

MAJOR-DOMO (*assenting*): British oysters, Cæsar.

CÆSAR: Oysters, then. (*The* MAJOR-DOMO *signs to a* SLAVE *at each order; and the* SLAVE *goes out to execute it.*) I have been in Britain — that western land of romance — the last piece of earth on the edge of the ocean that surrounds the world. I went there in search of its famous pearls. The British pearl was a fable; but in searching for it I found the British oyster.

APOLLODORUS: All posterity will bless you for it. (*To the* MAJOR-DOMO.) Sea hedgehogs for me.

RUFIO: Is there nothing solid to begin with?

MAJOR-DOMO: Fieldfares with asparagus —

CLEOPATRA (*interrupting*): Fattened fowls! have some fattened fowls, Rufio.

RUFIO: Ay, that will do.

CLEOPATRA (*greedily*): Fieldfares for me.

MAJOR-DOMO: Cæsar will deign to choose his wine? Sicilian, Lesbian, Chian —

RUFIO (*contemptuously*): All Greek.

APOLLODORUS: Who would drink Roman wine when he could get Greek. Try the Lesbian, Cæsar.

CÆSAR: Bring me my barley water.

RUFIO (*with intense disgust*): Ugh! Bring *me* my Falernian. (*The Falernian is presently brought to him.*)

CLEOPATRA (*pouting*): It is waste of time giving you dinners, Cæsar. My scullions would not condescend to your diet.

CÆSAR (*relenting*): Well, well: let us try the Lesbian. (*The* MAJOR-DOMO *fills* CÆSAR's *goblet; then* CLEOPATRA's *and* APOLLODORUS's.) But when I return to Rome, I will make laws against these extravagances. I will even get the laws carried out.

CLEOPATRA (*coaxing*): Never mind. To-day you are to be like other people: idle, luxurious, and kind. (*She stretches her hand to him along the table.*)

CÆSAR: Well, for once I will sacrifice my comfort — (*kissing her hand*) there! (*He takes a draught of wine.*) Now are you satisfied?

CLEOPATRA: And you no longer believe that I long for your departure for Rome?

CÆSAR: I no longer believe anything. My brains are asleep. Besides, who knows whether I shall return to Rome?

RUFIO (*alarmed*): How? Eh? What?

CÆSAR: What has Rome to shew me that I have not seen already? One year of Rome is like another, except that I grow older, whilst the crowd in the Appian Way is always the same age.

APOLLODORUS: It is no better here in Egypt. The old men, when they are tired of life, say "We have seen everything except the source of the Nile."

CÆSAR (*his imagination catching fire*): And why not see that? Cleopatra: will you come with me and track the flood to its cradle in the heart of the regions of mystery? Shall we leave Rome behind us — Rome, that has achieved greatness only to learn how greatness destroys nations of men who are not great! Shall I make you a new kingdom, and build you a holy city there in the great unknown?

CLEOPATRA (*rapturously*): Yes, yes. You shall.

RUFIO: Ay: now he will conquer Africa with two legions before we come to the roast boar.

APOLLODORUS: Come: no scoffing. This is a noble scheme: in it Cæsar is no longer merely the conquering soldier, but the creative poet-artist. Let us name the holy city, and consecrate it with Lesbian wine.

CÆSAR: Cleopatra shall name it herself.

CLEOPATRA: It shall be called Cæsar's Gift to his Beloved.

APOLLODORUS: No, no. Something vaster than that — something universal, like the starry firmament.

CÆSAR (*prosaically*): Why not simply The Cradle of the Nile?

CLEOPATRA: No: the Nile is my ancestor; and he is a god. Oh! I have thought of something. The Nile shall name it himself. Let us call upon him. (*To the* MAJOR-DOMO.) Send for him. (*The three men stare at one another; but the* MAJOR-DOMO *goes out as if he had received the most matter-of-fact order.*) And (*to the retinue*) away with you all.

(*The retinue withdraws, making obeisance. A priest enters, carrying a miniature Sphinx with a tiny tripod before it. A morsel of incense is smoking in the tripod. The priest comes to the table and places the image in the middle of it. The light begins to change to the magenta purple of the Egyptian sunset, as if the god had brought a strange colored shadow with him. The three men are determined not to be impressed; but they feel curious in spite of themselves.*)

CÆSAR: What hocus-pocus is this?

CLEOPATRA: You shall see. And it is *not* hocus-pocus. To do it properly, we should kill something to please him; but perhaps he will answer Cæsar without that if we spill some wine to him.

APOLLODORUS (*turning his head to look up over his shoulder at Ra*): Why not appeal to our hawkheaded friend here?

CLEOPATRA (*nervously*): Sh! He will hear you and be angry.

RUFIO (*phlegmatically*): The source of the Nile is out of his district, I expect.

CLEOPATRA: No: I will have my city named by nobody but my dear little Sphinx, because it was in its arms that Cæsar found me asleep. (*She languishes at* CÆSAR *then turns curtly to the priest.*) Go. I am a priestess, and have power to take your charge from you. (*The priest makes a reverence and goes out.*) Now let us call on the Nile altogether. Perhaps he will rap on the table.

CÆSAR: What! table rapping! Are such superstitions still believed in this year 707 of the Republic?

CLEOPATRA: It is no superstition: our priests learn lots of things from the tables. Is it not so, Apollodorus?

APOLLODORUS: Yes: I profess myself a converted man. When Cleopatra is priestess, Apollodorus is devotee. Propose the conjuration.

CLEOPATRA: You must say with me "Send us thy voice, Father Nile."

ALL FOUR (*holding their glasses together before the idol*): Send us thy voice, Father Nile.

(*The death cry of a man in mortal terror and agony answers them. Appalled, the men set down their glasses, and listen. Silence. The purple deepens in the sky.* CÆSAR, *glancing at* CLEOPATRA, *catches her pouring out her wine before the god, with gleaming eyes, and mute assurances of gratitude and worship.* APOLLODORUS *springs up and runs to the edge of the roof to peer down and listen.*)

CÆSAR (*looking piercingly at* CLEOPATRA): What was that?

CLEOPATRA (*petulantly*): Nothing. They are beating some slave.

CÆSAR: Nothing.

RUFIO: A man with a knife in him, I'll swear.

CÆSAR (*rising*): A murder.

APOLLODORUS (*at the back, waving his hand for silence*): S-sh! Silence. Did you hear that?

CÆSAR: Another cry?

APOLLODORUS (*returning to the table*): No, a thud. Something fell on the beach, I think.

RUFIO (*grimly, as he rises*): Something with bones in it, eh?

CÆSAR (*shuddering*): Hush, hush, Rufio. (*He leaves the table and returns to the colonnade:* RUFIO *following at his left elbow, and* APOLLODORUS *at the other side.*)

CLEOPATRA (*still in her place at the table*): Will you leave me, Cæsar? Apollodorus: are you going?

APOLLODORUS: Faith, dearest Queen, my appetite is gone.

CÆSAR: Go down to the courtyard, Apollodorus; and find out what has happened.

(APOLLODORUS *nods and goes out, making for the staircase by which* RUFIO *ascended.*)

CLEOPATRA: Your soldiers have killed somebody, perhaps. What does it matter?

(*The murmur of a crowd rises from the beach below.* CÆSAR *and* RUFIO *look at one another.*)

CÆSAR: This must be seen to. (*He is about to follow* APOLLODORUS *when* RUFIO *stops him with a hand on his arm as* FTATATEETA *comes back by the far end of the roof, with dragging steps, a drowsy satiety in her eyes and in the corners of the bloodhound lips. For a moment* CÆSAR *suspects that she is drunk with wine. Not so* RUFIO: *he knows well the red vintage that has inebriated her.*)

RUFIO (*in a low tone*): There is some mischief between those two.

FTATATEETA: The Queen looks again on the face of her servant.

(CLEOPATRA *looks at her for a moment with an exultant reflection of her murderous expression. Then she flings her arms round her; kisses her repeatedly and savagely; and tears off her jewels and heaps them on her. The two men turn from the spectacle to look at one another.* FTATATEETA *drags herself sleepily to the altar; kneels before Ra; and remains there in prayer.* CÆSAR *goes to* CLEOPATRA, *leaving* RUFIO *in the colonnade.*)

CÆSAR (*with searching earnestness*): Cleopatra: what has happened?

CLEOPATRA (*in mortal dread of him, but with her utmost cajolery*): Nothing, dearest Cæsar. (*With sickly sweetness, her voice almost failing.*) Nothing. I am innocent. (*She approaches him affectionately.*) Dear Cæsar: are you angry with me? Why do you look at me so? I have been here with you all the time. How can I know what has happened?

CÆSAR (*reflectively*): That is true.

CLEOPATRA (*greatly relieved, trying to caress him*): Of course it is true. (*He does not respond to the caress.*) You know it is true, Rufio.

(*The murmur without suddenly swells to a roar and subsides.*)

RUFIO: I shall know presently. (*He makes for the altar in the burly trot that serves him for a stride, and touches* FTATATEETA *on the shoulder.*) Now, mistress: I shall want you. (*He orders her, with a gesture, to go before him.*)

FTATATEETA (*rising and glowering at him*): My place is with the Queen.

CLEOPATRA: She has done no harm, Rufio.

CÆSAR (*to* RUFIO): Let her stay.

RUFIO (*sitting down on the altar*): Very well. Then my place is here too; and you can see what is the matter for yourself. The city is in a pretty uproar, it seems.

CÆSAR (*with grave displeasure*): Rufio: there is a time for obedience.

RUFIO: And there is a time for obstinacy. (*He folds his arms doggedly.*)

CÆSAR (*to* CLEOPATRA): Send her away.

CLEOPATRA (*whining in her eagerness to propitiate him*): Yes, I will. I will do whatever you ask me, Cæsar, always, because I love you. Ftatateeta: go away.

FTATATEETA: The Queen's word is my will. I shall be at hand for the Queen's call. (*She goes out past Ra, as she came.*)

RUFIO (*following her*): Remember, Cæsar, *your* bodyguard also is within call. (*He follows her out.*)

(CLEOPATRA, *presuming upon* CÆSAR'S *submission to* RUFIO, *leaves the table and sits down on the bench in the colonnade.*)

CLEOPATRA: Why do you allow Rufio to treat you so? You should teach him his place.

CÆSAR: Teach him to be my enemy, and to hide his thoughts from me as you are now hiding yours.

CLEOPATRA (*her fears returning*): Why do you say that, Cæsar? Indeed, indeed, I am not hiding anything. You are wrong to treat me like this. (*She stifles a sob.*) I am only a child; and you turn into stone because you think some one has been killed. I cannot bear it. (*She purposely breaks down and weeps. He looks at her with profound sadness and complete coldness. She looks up to see what effect she is producing. Seeing that he is unmoved, she sits up, pretending to struggle with her emotion and to put it bravely away.*) But there: I know you hate tears: you shall not be troubled with them. I know you are not angry, but only sad; only I am so silly, I cannot help being hurt when you speak coldly. Of course you are quite right: it is dreadful to think of anyone being killed or even hurt; and I hope nothing really serious has — (*Her voice dies away under his contemptuous penetration.*)

CÆSAR: What has frightened you into this? What have you done? (*A trumpet sounds on the beach below.*) Aha! that sounds like the answer.

CLEOPATRA (*sinking back trembling on the bench and covering her face with her hands*): I have not betrayed you, Cæsar: I swear it.

CÆSAR: I know that. I have not trusted you. (*He turns from her, and is about to go out when* APOLLODORUS *and* BRITANNUS *drag in* LUCIUS SEPTIMIUS *to him.* RUFIO *follows.* CÆSAR *shudders.*) Again, Pompey's murderer!

RUFIO: The town has gone mad, I think. They are for tearing the palace down and driving us into the sea straight away. We laid hold of this renegade in clearing them out of the courtyard.

CÆSAR: Release him. (*They let go his arms.*) What has offended the citizens, Lucius Septimius?

LUCIUS: What did you expect, Cæsar? Pothinus was a favorite of theirs.

CÆSAR: What has happened to Pothinus? I set him free, here, not half an hour ago. Did they not pass him out?

LUCIUS: Ay, through the gallery arch sixty feet above ground, with three inches of steel in his ribs. He is as dead as Pompey. We are quits now, as to killing — you and I.

CÆSAR (*shocked*): Assassinated! — our prisoner, our guest! (*He turns reproachfully on* RUFIO.) Rufio —

RUFIO (*emphatically — anticipating the question*): Whoever did it was a wise man and a friend of yours (CLEOPATRA *is greatly emboldened*); but none of us had a hand in it. So it is no use to frown at me. (CÆSAR *turns and looks at* CLEOPATRA.)

CLEOPATRA (*violently — rising*): He was slain by order of the Queen of Egypt. I am not Julius Cæsar the dreamer, who allows every slave to insult him. Rufio has said I did well: now the others shall judge me too. (*She turns to the others.*) This Pothinus sought to make me conspire with him to betray Cæsar to Achillas and Ptolemy. I refused; and he cursed me and came privily to Cæsar to accuse me of his own treachery. I caught him in the act; and he insulted me—*me,* the Queen! to my face. Cæsar would not avenge me: he spoke him fair and set him free. Was I right to avenge myself? Speak, Lucius.

LUCIUS: I do not gainsay it. But you will get little thanks from Cæsar for it.

CLEOPATRA: Speak, Apollodorus. Was I wrong?

APOLLODORUS: I have only one word of blame, most beautiful. You should have called upon me, your knight; and in fair duel I should have slain the slanderer.

CLEOPATRA (*passionately*): I will be judged by your very slave, Cæsar. Britannus: speak. Was I wrong?

BRITANNUS: Were treachery, falsehood, and disloyalty left unpunished, society must become like an arena full of wild beasts, tearing one another to pieces. Cæsar is in the wrong.

CÆSAR (*with quiet bitterness*): And so the verdict is against me, it seems.

CLEOPATRA (*vehemently*): Listen to me, Cæsar. If one man in all Alexandria can be found to say that I did wrong, I swear to have myself crucified on the door of the palace by my own slaves.

CÆSAR: If one man in all the world can be found, now or forever, to *know* that you did wrong, that man will have either to conquer the world as I have, or be crucified by it. (*The uproar in the streets again reaches them.*) Do you hear? These knockers at your gate are also believers in vengeance and in stabbing. You have slain their leader: it is right that they shall slay you. If you doubt it, ask your four counsellors here. And then in the name of that *right* (*he emphasizes the word with great scorn*) shall I not slay them for murdering their Queen, and be slain in my turn by their countrymen as the invader of their fatherland? Can Rome do less then than slay these slayers, too, to shew the world how Rome avenges her sons and her honor. And so, to the end of history, murder shall breed murder, always in the name of right and honor and peace, until the gods are tired of blood and create a race that can understand. (*Fierce uproar.* CLEOPATRA *becomes white with terror.*) Hearken, you who must not be insulted. Go near enough to catch their words: you will find them bitterer than the tongue of Pothinus. (*Loftily, wrapping himself up in an impenetrable dignity.*) Let the Queen of Egypt now give her orders for vengeance, and take her measures for defence; for she has renounced Cæsar. (*He turns to go.*)

CLEOPATRA (*terrified, running to him and falling on her knees*): You will not desert me, Cæsar. You will defend the palace.

CÆSAR: You have taken the powers of life and death upon you. I am only a dreamer.

CLEOPATRA: But they will kill me.

CÆSAR: And why not?

CLEOPATRA: In pity —

CÆSAR: Pity! What! has it come to this so suddenly, that nothing can save you now but pity? Did it save Pothinus?

(*She rises, wringing her hands, and goes back to the bench in despair.* APOLLODORUS *shews his sympathy with her by quietly posting himself behind the bench. The sky has by this time become the most vivid purple, and soon begins to change to a glowing pale orange, against which the colonnade and the great image shew darklier and darklier.*)

RUFIO: Cæsar: enough of preaching. The enemy is at the gate.

CÆSAR (*turning on him and giving way to his wrath*): Ay; and what has held him baffled at the gate all these months? Was it my folly, as you deem it, or your wisdom? In this Egyptian Red Sea of blood, whose hand has held all your heads above the waves? (*Turning on* CLEOPATRA.) And yet, when Cæsar says to such an one, "Friend, go free," you, clinging for your little life to my sword, dare steal out and stab him in the back? And you, soldiers and gentlemen, and honest servants as you forget that you are, applaud this assassination, and say "Cæsar is in the wrong." By the gods, I am tempted to open my hand and let you all sink into the flood.

CLEOPATRA (*with a ray of cunning hope*): But, Cæsar, if you do, you will perish yourself.

(CÆSAR'*s eyes blaze.*)

RUFIO (*greatly alarmed*): Now, by great Jove, you filthy little Egyptian rat, that is the very word to make him walk out alone into the city and leave us here to be cut to pieces. (*Desperately, to* CÆSAR.) Will you desert us because we are a parcel of fools? I mean no harm by killing: I do it as a dog kills a cat, by instinct. We are all dogs at your heels; but we have served you faithfully.

CÆSAR (*relenting*): Alas, Rufio, my son, my son: as dogs we are like to perish now in the streets.

APOLLODORUS (*at his post behind* CLEOPATRA'*s seat*): Cæsar: what you say has an Olympian ring in it: it must be right; for it is fine art.

But I am still on the side of Cleopatra. If we must die, she shall not want the devotion of a man's heart nor the strength of a man's arm.

CLEOPATRA (*sobbing*): But I dont want to die.

CÆSAR (*sadly*): Oh, ignoble, ignoble!

LUCIUS (*coming forward between* CÆSAR *and* CLEOPATRA): Hearken to me, Cæsar. It may be ignoble; but I also mean to live as long as I can.

CÆSAR: Well, my friend, you are likely to outlive Cæsar. Is it any magic of mine, think you, that has kept your army and this whole city at bay for so long? Yesterday, what quarrel had they with me that they should risk their lives against me? But today we have flung them down their hero, murdered; and now every man of them is set upon clearing out this nest of assassins — for such we are and no more. Take courage then; and sharpen your sword. Pompey's head has fallen; and Cæsar's head is ripe.

APOLLODORUS: Does Cæsar despair?

CÆSAR (*with infinite pride*): He who has never hoped can never despair. Cæsar, in good or bad fortune, looks his fate in the face.

LUCIUS: Look it in the face, then; and it will smile as it always has on Cæsar.

CÆSAR (*with involuntary haughtiness*): Do you presume to encourage me?

LUCIUS: I offer you my services. I will change sides if you will have me.

CÆSAR (*suddenly coming down to earth again, and looking sharply at him, divining that there is something behind the offer*): What! At this point?

LUCIUS (*firmly*): At this point.

RUFIO: Do you suppose Cæsar is mad, to trust you?

LUCIUS: I do not ask him to trust me until he is victorious. I ask for my life, and for a command in Cæsar's army. And since Cæsar is a fair dealer, I will pay in advance.

CÆSAR: Pay! How?

LUCIUS: With a piece of good news for you.

(CÆSAR *divines the news in a flash.*)

RUFIO: What news?

CÆSAR (*with an elated and buoyant energy which makes* CLEOPATRA *sit up and stare*): What news! What news, did you say, my son Rufio? The relief has arrived: what other news remains for us? Is it not so, Lucius Septimius? Mithridates of Pergamos is on the march.

LUCIUS: He has taken Pelusium.

CÆSAR (*delighted*): Lucius Septimius: you are henceforth my officer. Rufio: the Egyptians must have sent every soldier from the city to prevent Mithridates crossing the Nile. There is nothing in the streets now but mob — mob!

LUCIUS: It is so. Mithridates is marching by the great road to Memphis to cross above the Delta. Achillas will fight him there.

CÆSAR (*all audacity*): Achillas shall fight Cæsar there. See, Rufio. (*He runs to the table; snatches a napkin; and draws a plan on it with his finger dipped in wine, whilst* RUFIO *and* LUCIUS SEPTIMIUS *crowd about him to watch, all looking closely, for the light is now almost gone.*) Here is the palace (*pointing to his plan*): here is the theatre. You (*to* RUFIO) take twenty men and pretend to go by *that* street (*pointing it out*); and whilst they are stoning you, out go the cohorts by this and this. My streets are right, are they, Lucius?

LUCIUS: Ay, that is the fig market —

CÆSAR (*too much excited to listen to him*): I saw them the day we arrived. Good! (*He throws the napkin on the table, and comes down again into the colonnade.*) Away, Britannus: tell Petronius that within an hour half our forces must take ship for the western lake. See to my horse and armor. (BRITANNUS *runs out.*) With the rest, I shall march round the lake and up the Nile to meet Mithridates. Away, Lucius; and give the word. (LUCIUS *hurries out after* BRITANNUS.) Apollodorus: lend me your sword and your right arm for this campaign.

APOLLODORUS: Ay, and my heart and life to boot.

CÆSAR (*grasping his hand*): I accept both. (*Mighty handshake.*) Are you ready for work?

APOLLODORUS: Ready for Art — the Art of War. (*He rushes out after* LUCIUS, *totally forgetting* CLEOPATRA.)

RUFIO: Come! this is something like business.

CÆSAR (*buoyantly*): Is it not, my only son? (*He claps his hands. The* SLAVES *hurry in to the table.*) No more of this mawkish revelling: away with all this stuff: shut it out of my sight and be off with you. (*The* SLAVES *begin to remove the table; and the curtains are drawn, shutting in the colonnade.*) You understand about the streets, Rufio?

RUFIO: Ay, I think I do. I will get through them, at all events.

(*The bucina sounds busily in the courtyard beneath.*)

CÆSAR: Come, then: we must talk to the troops and hearten them. You down to the beach: I to the courtyard. (*He makes for the staircase.*)

CLEOPATRA (*rising from her seat, where she has been quite neglected all this time, and stretching out her hands timidly to him*): Cæsar.

CÆSAR (*turning*): Eh?

CLEOPATRA: Have you forgotten me?

CÆSAR (*indulgently*): I am busy now, my child, busy. When I return your affairs shall be settled. Farewell; and be good and patient.

(*He goes, preoccupied and quite indifferent. She stands with clenched fists, in speechless rage and humiliation.*)

RUFIO: That game is played and lost, Cleopatra. The woman always gets the worst of it.

CLEOPATRA (*haughtily*): Go. Follow your master.

RUFIO (*in her ear, with rough familiarity*): A word first. Tell your executioner that if Pothinus had been properly killed — in the *throat* — he would not have called out. Your man bungled his work.

CLEOPATRA (*enigmatically*): How do you know it was a man?

RUFIO (*startled, and puzzled*): It was not you: you were with us when it happened. (*She turns her back scornfully on him. He shakes his head, and draws the curtains to go out. It is now a magnificent moonlit night. The table has been removed.* FTATATEETA *is seen in the light of the moon and stars, again in prayer before the white altar-stone of Ra.* RUFIO *starts; closes the curtains again softly; and says in a low voice to* CLEOPATRA.) Was it she? with her own hand?

CLEOPATRA (*threateningly*): Whoever it was, let my enemies beware of her. Look to it, Rufio, you who dare make the Queen of Egypt a fool before Cæsar.

RUFIO (*looking grimly at her*): I will look to it, Cleopatra. (*He nods in confirmation of the promise, and slips out through the curtains, loosening his sword in its sheath as he goes.*)

ROMAN SOLDIERS (*in the courtyard below*): Hail, Cæsar! Hail, hail!

(CLEOPATRA *listens. The bucina sounds again, followed by several trumpets.*)

CLEOPATRA (*wringing her hands and calling*): Ftatateeta. Ftatateeta. It is dark; and I am alone. Come to me. (*Silence.*) Ftatateeta. (*Louder.*) Ftatateeta. (*Silence. In a panic she snatches the cord and pulls the curtains apart.* FTATATEETA *is lying dead on the altar of Ra, with her throat cut. Her blood deluges the white stone.*)

ACT FIVE

(*High noon. Festival and military pageant on the esplanade before the palace. In the east harbor* CÆSAR's *galley, so gorgeously decorated that it seems to be rigged with flowers, is alongside the quay, close to the steps* APOLLODORUS *descended when he embarked with the carpet. A Roman* GUARD *is posted there in charge of a gangway, whence a red floorcloth is laid down the middle of the esplanade, turning off to the north opposite the central gate in the palace front, which shuts in the esplanade on the south side. The broad steps of the gate, crowded with* CLEOPATRA'S *ladies, all in their gayest attire, are like a flower garden. The façade is lined by her guard, officered by the same gallants to whom* BEL AFFRIS *announced the coming of* CÆSAR *six months before in the old palace on the Syrian border. The north side is lined by Roman* SOLDIERS, *with the townsfolk on tiptoe behind them, peering over their heads at the cleared esplanade, in which the* OFFICERS *stroll about, chatting. Among these are* BELZANOR *and the* PERSIAN; *also the* CENTURION, *vinewood cudgel in hand, battle worn, thick-booted and much outshone, both socially and decoratively, by the Egyptian officers.*

APOLLODORUS *makes his way through the townsfolk and calls to the officers from behind the Roman line.*)

APOLLODORUS: Hullo! May I pass?

CENTURION: Pass Apollodorus the Sicilian there! (*The* SOLDIERS *let him through.*)

BELZANOR: Is Cæsar at hand?

APOLLODORUS: Not yet. He is still in the market place. I could not stand any more of the roaring of the soldiers! After half an hour of the enthusiasm of an army, one feels the need of a little sea air.

PERSIAN: Tell us the news. Hath he slain the priests?

APOLLODORUS: Not he. They met him in the market place with ashes on their heads and their gods in their hands. They placed the gods at his feet. The only one that was worth looking at was Apis: a miracle of gold and ivory work. By my advice he offered the chief priest two talents for it.

BELZANOR (*appalled*): Apis the all-knowing for two talents! What said the Priest?

APOLLODORUS: He invoked the mercy of Apis, and asked for five.

BELZANOR: There will be famine and tempest in the land for this.

PERSIAN: Pooh! Why did not Apis cause Cæsar to be vanquished by Achillas? Any fresh news from the war, Apollodorus?

APOLLODORUS: The little King Ptolemy was drowned.

BELZANOR: Drowned! How?

APOLLODORUS: With the rest of them. Cæsar attacked them from three sides at once and swept them into the Nile. Ptolemy's barge sank.

BELZANOR: A marvellous man, this Cæsar! Will he come soon, think you?

APOLLODORUS: He was settling the Jewish question when I left.

(*A flourish of trumpets from the north, and commotion among the townsfolk, announces the approach of* CÆSAR.)

PERSIAN: He has made short work of them. Here he comes. (*He hurries to his post in front of the Egyptian lines.*)

BELZANOR (*following him*): Ho there! Cæsar comes.

(*The* SOLDIERS *stand at attention, and dress their lines.* APOLLODORUS *goes to the Egyptian line.*)

CENTURION (*hurrying to the gangway* GUARD): Attention there! Cæsar comes.

(CÆSAR *arrives in state with* RUFIO: BRITANNUS *following. The* SOLDIERS *receive him with enthusiastic shouting.*)

CÆSAR: I see my ship awaits me. The hour of Cæsar's farewell to Egypt has arrived. And now, Rufio, what remains to be done before I go?

RUFIO (*at his left hand*): You have not yet appointed a Roman governor for this province.

CÆSAR (*looking whimsically at him, but speaking with perfect gravity*): What say you to Mithridates of Pergamos, my reliever and rescuer, the great son of Eupator?

RUFIO: Why, that you will want him elsewhere. Do you forget that you have some three or four armies to conquer on your way home?

CÆSAR: Indeed! Well, what say you to yourself?

RUFIO (*incredulously*): I! I a governor! What are you dreaming of? Do you not know that I am only the son of a freedman?

CÆSAR (*affectionately*): Has not Cæsar called you his son? (*Calling to the whole assembly.*) Peace awhile there; and hear me.

ROMAN SOLDIERS: Hear Cæsar.

CÆSAR: Hear the service, quality, rank and name of the Roman governor. By service, Cæsar's shield; by quality, Cæsar's friend; by rank, a Roman soldier. (*The Roman* SOLDIERS *give a triumphant shout.*) By name, Rufio. (*They shout again.*)

RUFIO (*kissing* CÆSAR'S *hand*): Ay: I am Cæsar's shield; but of what use shall I be when I am no longer on Cæsar's arm? Well, no matter — (*He becomes husky, and turns away to recover himself.*)

CÆSAR: Where is that British Islander of mine?

BRITANNUS (*coming forward on* CÆSAR'S *right hand*): Here, Cæsar.

CÆSAR: Who bade you, pray, thrust yourself into the battle of the Delta, uttering the barbarous cries of your native land, and affirming yourself a match for any four of the Egyptians, to whom you applied unseemly epithets?

BRITANNUS: Cæsar: I ask you to excuse the language that escaped me in the heat of the moment.

CÆSAR: And how did you, who cannot swim, cross the canal with us when we stormed the camp?

BRITANNUS: Cæsar: I clung to the tail of your horse.

CÆSAR: These are not the deeds of a slave, Britannicus, but of a free man.

BRITANNUS: Cæsar: I was born free.

CÆSAR: But they call you Cæsar's slave.

BRITANNUS: Only as Cæsar's slave have I found real freedom.

CÆSAR (*moved*): Well said. Ungrateful that I am, I was about to set you free; but now I will not part from you for a million talents. (*He claps him friendly on the shoulder.* BRITANNUS, *gratified, but a trifle shamefaced, takes his hand and kisses it sheepishly.*)

BELZANOR (*to the* PERSIAN): This Roman knows how to make men serve him.

PERSIAN: Ay: men too humble to become dangerous rivals to him.

BELZANOR: O subtle one! O cynic!

CÆSAR (*seeing* APOLLODORUS *in the Egyptian corner, and calling to him*): Apollodorus: I leave the art of Egypt in your charge. Remember: Rome loves art and will encourage it ungrudgingly.

APOLLODORUS: I understand, Cæsar. Rome will produce no art itself; but it will buy up and take away whatever the other nations produce.

CÆSAR: What! Rome produce no art! Is peace not an art? is war not an art? is government not an art? is civilization not an art? All these we give you in exchange for a few ornaments. You will have the best of the bargain. (*Turning to* RUFIO.) And now, what else have I to do before I embark? (*Trying to recollect.*) There is something I cannot remember: what *can* it be? Well, well: it must remain undone: we must not waste this favorable wind. Farewell, Rufio.

RUFIO: Cæsar: I am loth to let you go to Rome without your shield. There are too many daggers there.

CÆSAR: It matters not: I shall finish my life's work on my way back; and then I shall have lived long enough. Besides: I have always disliked the idea of dying: I had rather be killed. Farewell.

RUFIO (*with a sigh, raising his hands and giving* CÆSAR *up as incorrigible.*) Farewell. (*They shake hands.*)

CÆSAR (*waving his hand to* APOLLODORUS): Farewell, Apollodorus, and my friends, all of you. Aboard!

(*The gangway is run out from the quay to the ship. As* CÆSAR *moves towards it,* CLEOPATRA, *cold and tragic, cunningly dressed in black, without ornaments or decoration of any kind, and thus mak-*

ing a striking figure among the brilliantly dressed bevy of ladies as she passes through it, comes from the palace and stands on the steps. CÆSAR *does not see her until she speaks.*)

CLEOPATRA: Has Cleopatra no part in this leavetaking?

CÆSAR (*enlightened*): Ah, I *knew* there was something. (*To* RUFIO.) How could you let me forget her, Rufio? (*Hastening to her.*) Had I gone without seeing you, I should never have forgiven myself. (*He takes her hands, and brings her into the middle of the esplanade. She submits stonily.*) Is this mourning for me?

CLEOPATRA: No.

CÆSAR (*remorsefully*): Ah, that was thoughtless of me! It is for your brother.

CLEOPATRA: No.

CÆSAR: For whom, then?

CLEOPATRA: Ask the Roman governor whom you have left us.

CÆSAR: Rufio?

CLEOPATRA: Yes: Rufio. (*She points at him with deadly scorn.*) He who is to rule here in Cæsar's name, in Cæsar's way, according to Cæsar's boasted laws of life.

CÆSAR (*dubiously*): He is to rule as he can, Cleopatra. He has taken the work upon him, and will do it in his own way.

CLEOPATRA: Not in your way, then?

CÆSAR (*puzzled*): What do you mean by my way?

CLEOPATRA: Without punishment. Without revenge. Without judgment.

CÆSAR (*approvingly*): Ay: that is the right way, the great way, the only possible way in the end. (*To* RUFIO.) Believe it Rufio, if you can.

RUFIO: Why, I believe it, Cæsar. You have convinced me of it long ago. But look you. You are sailing for Numidia today. Now tell me: if you meet a hungry lion there, you will not punish it for wanting to eat you?

CÆSAR (*wondering what he is driving at*): No.

RUFIO: Nor revenge upon it the blood of those it has already eaten.

CÆSAR: No.

RUFIO: Nor judge it for its guiltiness.

CÆSAR: No.

RUFIO: What, then, will you do to save your life from it?

CÆSAR (*promptly*): Kill it, man, without malice, just as it would kill me. What does this parable of the lion mean?

RUFIO: Why, Cleopatra had a tigress that killed men at her bidding. I thought she might bid it kill you some day. Well, had I not been Cæsar's pupil, what pious things might I not have done to that tigress! I might have punished it. I might have revenged Pothinus on it.

CÆSAR (*interjects*): Pothinus!

RUFIO (*continuing*): I might have judged it. But I put all these follies behind me; and, without malice, only cut its throat. And that is why Cleopatra comes to you in mourning.

CLEOPATRA (*vehemently*): He has shed the blood of my servant Ftatateeta. On your head be it as upon his, Cæsar, if you hold him free of it.

CÆSAR (*energetically*): On my head be it, then; for it was well done. Rufio: had you set yourself in the seat of the judge, and with hateful ceremonies and appeals to the gods handed that woman over to some hired executioner to be slain before the people in the name of justice, never again would I have touched your hand without a shudder. But this was natural slaying: I feel no horror at it.

(RUFIO, *satisfied, nods at* CLEOPATRA, *mutely inviting her to mark that.*)

CLEOPATRA (*pettish and childish in her impotence*): No: not when a Roman slays an Egyptian. All the world will now see how unjust and corrupt Cæsar is.

CÆSAR (*taking her hands coaxingly*): Come: do not be angry with me. I am sorry for that poor Totateeta. (*She laughs in spite of herself.*) Aha! you are laughing. Does that mean reconciliation?

CLEOPATRA (*angry with herself for laughing*): No, *no*, NO!! But it is so ridiculous to hear you call her Totateeta.

CÆSAR: What! As much a child as ever, Cleopatra! Have I not made a woman of you after all?

CLEOPATRA: Oh, it is you who are a great baby: you make me seem silly because you will not behave seriously. But you have treated me badly; and I do not forgive you.

CÆSAR: Bid me farewell.

CLEOPATRA: I will not.

CÆSAR (*coaxing*): I will send you a beautiful present from Rome.

CLEOPATRA (*proudly*): Beauty from Rome to Egypt indeed! What can Rome give *me* that Egypt cannot give me?

APOLLODORUS: That is true, Cæsar. If the present is to be really beautiful, I shall have to buy it for you in Alexandria.

CÆSAR: You are forgetting the treasures for which Rome is most famous, my friend. You cannot buy *them* in Alexandria.

APOLLODORUS: What are they, Cæsar?

CÆSAR: Her sons. Come, Cleopatra: forgive me and bid me farewell; and I will send you a man, Roman from head to heel and Roman of the noblest; not old and ripe for the knife; not lean in the arms and cold in the heart; not hiding a bald head under his conqueror's laurels; not stooped with the weight of the world on his shoulders; but brisk and fresh, strong and young, hoping in the morning, fighting in the day, and revelling in the evening. Will you take such an one in exchange for Cæsar?

CLEOPATRA (*palpitating*): His name, his name?

CÆSAR: Shall it be Mark Antony? (*She throws herself into his arms.*)

RUFIO: You are a bad hand at a bargain, mistress, if you will swop Cæsar for Antony.

CÆSAR: So now you are satisfied.

CLEOPATRA: You will not forget.

CÆSAR: I will not forget. Farewell: I do not think we shall meet again. Farewell. (*He kisses her on the forehead. She is much affected and begins to sniff. He embarks.*)

ROMAN SOLDIERS (*as he sets his foot on the gangway*): Hail, Cæsar; and farewell!

(*He reaches the ship and returns* RUFIO's *wave of the hand.*)

APOLLODORUS (*to* CLEOPATRA): No tears, dearest Queen: they stab your servant to the heart. He will return some day.

CLEOPATRA: I hope not. But I cant help crying, all the same.

(*She waves her handkerchief to* CÆSAR; *and the ship begins to move.*)

ROMAN SOLDIERS (*drawing their swords and raising them in the air*): Hail, Cæsar!

CÆSAR AND CLEOPATRA was written in 1898. Shaw was sick with an infected foot during much of the time he worked on the play, but there is hardly evidence of sickness in it — unless the mellow resignation of Cæsar's wit be so considered. It was first performed in Chicago in 1901. The first London production, in 1907, was not a success, but later productions were. In 1913 Shaw added Ra's prologue. Today *Cæsar and Cleopatra* ranks among the dozen or so plays that by general consent make up Shaw's major canon. It was first published in 1901 in a collection entitled *Three Plays for Puritans.*

As Puritans notoriously abominated plays, the title is a paradox, though not a hard one. *Cæsar and Cleopatra,* according to Shaw's preface to the volume, is "for Puritans," first, because it ignores the conventional premise of the popular theater that since romance is mankind's main business the function of plays is to titillate the sensual imagination (but decorously, since this is a polite age), and, second, because it does not smother dialogue in expensive pageantry in the manner of contemporary productions of historical plays. But, as is commonly the case with Shaw, the explanation of one paradox only raises a larger one: here, a play about Cæsar and Cleopatra that is unheroic and unromantic. *This* paradox is the heart of the play. We may approach it by way of Shaw's prefatory objection to pageantry.

The objection may seem strange, since *Cæsar and Cleopatra* itself is excellent pageantry. Any one of Shaw's stage directions introducing the several acts will reveal his unfailing sense for scenic architecture, the fineness of his artist's eye, and his relish for tasteful and appropriate color and texture in dress and sets. Once one has enjoyed the glorious athleticism of the theatrically superb (though dramatically thin) Act III, or has seen, actually or imaginatively, the moonlit desert scene in Act I, with Cleopatra asleep between the paws of the Sphinx on "a heap of red poppies," while the conqueror of the world apostrophizes the silvery stillness, the popular notion that Shaw is a purely cerebral writer vanishes forever. Shaw was intelligent, witty, argumentative, didactic, and paradoxical, but his greatness as playright is at least as much a matter of his masterful command of theater space as of the lucid, speakable stage prose by which he communicates pointed meaning with graceful ease.

His objection is simply that when pageantry becomes an end in itself drama dies. In the London theater of late Victorian times Shakespeare's dialogue was cut to make room for what producers and audiences thought of as genuine Shakespearean spectacle: processions and battles and tiny stage business for the sake of authentic atmosphere — the products of painstaking research into medieval and Elizabethan costuming, armory, choreography, furniture, architecture, and details of domestic life. Such showy historicity enraged Shaw. He admitted pageantry only as an appropriate setting for the play of ideas which to him was always the drama's sole reason for being. ". . . new ideas," he wrote in the Preface, "make their technique as water makes its channel; and the technician without ideas is as useless as the canal constructor without water, though he may do very skillfully what the Mississippi does very rudely."

In *Cæsar and Cleopatra* the Shavian ideas amount to a refutation of the kind of activity which the exotic splendors of the historical setting and the glamorous aura surrounding the famous names invite and seem proper to. The action keeps failing to deliver the high drama of passion and conquest which title and locale and even the facts of history promise. After all, Cæsar and Cleopatra *were* lovers; they even had a child together. Then why won't Shaw give us the romance we expect to see? Not just because paradox is his manner and he aims to disoblige by deglamorizing history and debunking golden legend. *Why* is it his manner? The reason is not flippant. He wants to show us the unheroic, unromantic contemporaneity of the past. Idea is ironically played off against spectacle, and in our disappointed expectation of seeing staged for us the rich associations that encrust fact and legend, the moral fable we *do* get seems all the more sardonically telling. Pageantry, in short, helps to convey the history lesson which is Shaw's theme.

In general, literature uses history in one of two ways. Fictitious main characters may be placed in a setting of fact, in which the principals and circumstance of true history function as parts of the authenticating backdrop. This is Thackeray's method in *Henry Esmond* and Tolstoy's in *War and Peace* (except in the Napoleon and Kutuzov scenes). Or historical figures may be made protagonists in a more or less imaginative treatment of the facts. This is Shakespeare's method in his history plays and Shaw's in *The Man of Destiny, Cæsar and Cleopatra,* and *Saint Joan.*

Neither one wrote an antiquarian's kind of historical play, disengaged and meticulous, respectfully and learnedly observing chronology and authentic language. Museum pieces don't come alive by being made to move on a stage. By Shakespeare's and Shaw's example, a history play is an evocation of an image of the past for useful contemplation by the present. We see reflected in Shakespeare's dramatizations of royal English history in (roughly) the 15th century the political ideals of an enlightened Elizabethan. The plays are about the responsibilities of kingship, the blessings of a strong and sanctified monarchy, and the horrors of usurpation and civil war. Perhaps Shakespeare's conscious aim was simply to supply attractive entertainment for London audiences from the storehouse of Hall's and Holinshed's chronicles. Nevertheless, the plays, singly and in sequence, express what scholars call "the Tudor myth." They amount to a loyal patriot's concerned comment on past national anarchy that might return. Shakespeare's Henry V may seem more Tudor than Lancaster and his environment more late 16th century than early 15th century. But what else could he be?

One section of Shaw's Preface to *Three Plays for Puritans* is headed, "Better Than Shakespeare?" (hostile critics have ignored the question mark). The comparison is inevitable, since Shaw's title characters in *Cæsar and Cleopatra* are title characters in Shakespeare, too (though not together). Drama for Shaw was not art if it was not didactic, and his alleged arrogance is his suggestion that his Victorian view of

Cæsar and Cleopatra may be better for — that is, more relevant to the particular problems of — the Victorian age than Shakespeare's Elizabethan view. To deny that there is an issue here at all, says Shaw, is to be a victim of bardolatry; *i.e.*, the conviction that as a dramatist Shakespeare was not subject to human limitations. Bardolatry is bad for the worshipper, bad for drama, and bad even for Shakespeare, since it feeds on invincible ignorance. Doing Cæsar better than Shakespeare did is not to disparage Shakespeare, and it is not just a matter of making use of the discoveries and insights of historical scholarship (though Shaw acknowledges his debt to the German historian Theodor Mommsen for his conception of Cæsar). It is, like Shakespeare, to search the past for political allegory of present relevance. Shaw turns Shakespeare's practice into critical tenet and holds that every age must reinterpret the past by its own lights. The question that has prompted his play is: What, for us, is the truth about the historical Julius Cæsar?

Shaw's truth about Cæsar-in-Egypt is a twofold lesson of history: that the record of the past is nothing but a record of our own current errors (it is because he knows this that Cæsar so calmly can receive the news that the library of Alexandria is burning) and that moral progress — the only kind that matters — in public affairs must await the world's conversion to Cæsar's system of political ethics.

As only an anachronistic King Henry V could serve Shakespeare's political fable, so Shaw, too, writes anachronistically. In fact, he capitalizes on anachronisms; they are his chief dramatic metaphor. The dialogue is full of them: "Double or quits," "Egypt for the Egyptians," "Peace with honor," "Art for art's sake." And so is the characterization. Britannus is probably the most striking example. Shaw's solemn declaration in the Notes to the contrary, Britannus is only a likeness of the decent, insularly bigoted Englishman of some 2,000 years after Cæsar's time. But no more than the deglamorization of the legend are the anachronisms mere irreverence. By definition, an anachronism is a confusion of past and present. In *Cæsar and Cleopatra* they are recurrent symptoms in the characters' speech and manners of what the whole play argues, viz., that progress is a myth. If past and present are alike, if, as the god Ra says in the Prologue, "men twenty centuries ago were already just such as you, and spoke and lived as ye speak and live, no worse and no better, no wiser and no sillier," then even the pedant's objections fall to the ground. How can there be anachronism where there has been no change?

The main conflict in *Cæsar and Cleopatra* is not between Rome and Egypt. The siege, the politics, the military moves are nothing but events on which Shaw hangs his lesson of history. Nor is the conflict the more sophisticated one between the imperial love story we might have had and the quaint father–daughter, teacher–pupil relationship we actually get. The main conflict is, not in a romantic, but in a pedagogic situation. It ends in the separation, literal and figurative, of tutor and tutored. The separating issue is the murder of Pothinus. Cleopatra calls Cæsar a dreamer because he refuses to take revenge on his enemies. Pothinus and Britannus have at different times been equally astonished at his strange clemency. But events show him to be more practical and efficient than anyone else in the play. He outfights, out-talks, and out-foxes the Egyptians whenever he wants. He approves of necessary killing. But he does not believe in murderous passion parading as justice, virtue, and honor. When Cleopatra seeks to vindicate the murder of Pothinus, she is supported by Cæsar's own men. Inasmuch as the honest soldier Rufio, the brave moralist Britannus, and the gay artist Apollodorus collectively represent a sampling of the world's vital values, their support darkens the moral issue between Cleopatra and Cæsar and is one of the reasons why the play is felt to transcend the ideological simplemindedness and dogmatism that limit most thesis plays to a kind of dramatic journalism. Encouraged, and still heated with her righteous vengeance, Cleopatra shifts from defense to attack:

> CLEOPATRA (*vehemently*): Listen to me, Cæsar. If one man in all Alexandria can be found to say that I did wrong, I swear to have myself crucified on the door of the palace by my own slaves.
>
> CÆSAR: If one man in all the world can be found, now or forever, to know that you did wrong, that man will have either to conquer the world as I have or be crucified by it.

The allusion to Christ is probably the most discreet anachronism in the play, but it is also its most important one. It enriches the earlier associations of Cæsar with divinity: in Ra's Prologue, in Cæsar's claiming kinship with the immortal Sphinx, in the boy–king Ptolemy's assumption that it was the gods who sent Mark Antony to Egypt, and in Cleopatra's identification of Cæsar with a god in her talk with Pothinus early in Act IV. It is noteworthy that except for an occasional pompous phrase by the Egyptian leaders the only examples of noncolloquial language in the play are the god Ra's prologue and Cæsar's apostrophe to the Sphinx. Both speakers represent eternal values, and the Cæsar–Cleopatra conflict could also be defined as one between divine permanence of reason and of universal love and the impermanence of man's exclusive passions. One of the paradoxes of

Shaw's theme is that Cæsar, who seeks change, represents timelessness, whereas the world, which refuses to change, is in continuous flux. If the play's middle (Acts II-IV) seems disorderly and diffuse, there is a good reason for it. It translates into stage action the irony of the moral inertia of melodramatic busyness.

Ironic, too, is the fact that even the apparently more successful of the two alternative saviors of the world that Cæsar mentions fails and that his failure is due to the changes time brings. His mortality betrays his divinity. Balding and wrinkled, he is no lover for Cleopatra. Their first scene together obliquely anticipates his failure. It is not a scene of a god–conqueror solving the Sphinx' riddle but only of an "old gentleman" pointlessly addressing "a little kitten of a Sphinx," a "pet" Sphinx. When Pothinus asks Cleopatra in Act IV whether she is in love with Cæsar, she counters with another question: "Can one love a god?" She is wise enough to wish she *were* in love with him, but not wise enough to realize that her rejoinder is an inadequate answer. To the question of why one cannot love a godlike Cæsar, a Cleopatra answers, "Because he is not a beautiful young man with strong, round arms" — and at that moment the world slips from grace. Cleopatra's education toward ideal queenship has gone far, as her words to Pothinus early in Act IV show. Already by the end of Act I Cæsar has taught her to make herself obeyed, and when Rufio pitches her into the sea at the end of Act III it is as if she were being baptized into a new maturity. But the murder of Pothinus shows that it has not gone far enough. The kitten has only grown claws. She founders on passion. And the sulking, giggle-prone Cleopatra of Act V is closer to the silly, charming girl of Act I than to the wise and humble queen she seemed to have become by Act IV. Time present is still time past.

As the play has a Prologue (and an "Alternative to the Prologue") to the action of Cleopatra's truncated education, so it also has an epilogue: Act V. Soon after Cæsar's disillusionment with his pupil the stage once more becomes busy with military and political affiairs, and the moral drama ends. When he is about to embark for Rome he almost forgets to say goodbye to Cleopatra. But the light, almost burlesque, tone of the departure scene is made ominous with hints of the daggers waiting in Rome. Cæsar, we know, falls, and the world reverts to its Pompeian and Antonian ways after the Cæsarian interlude, to "the way of the soldier . . . the way of death," as Ra calls it, after Cæsar's "way of the gods . . . the way of life." And so, Rome remains "a madman's dream." As the doomed Cæsar resigns Cleopatra to her young lover–soldier and to her deathless fate as siren, history's old, passionate melodrama resumes. Two thousand years have done nothing to disprove Cæsar's prophecy:

> . . . And so, to the end of history, murder shall breed murder, always in the name of right and honor and peace, until the gods are tired of blood and create a race that can understand.

Here is Shaw's earliest reference in drama to the Superman whom he later celebrated as John Tanner in *Man and Superman* (1903) and as the wise Ancients in *Back to Methuselah* (1921), the two plays which have been called the trunk of his dramatic canon, on which all the other plays are branches. Joan of Arc in *Saint Joan* (1924) is, like Cæsar, a historical example of the superman race. Superman's (or -woman's) superiority over ordinary men is his commitment, conscious or unconscious, to the service of the Life Force, the vital principle in what Shaw called Creative Evolution toward ever higher forms of contemplative intelligence. Cæsar, says Shaw in his Notes, "is greater off the battle field than on it." This seems like a paradox in the eyes of the world and will till the world learns from its violent past not to reject its Superman saviors — its Cæsars, its Christs, and its saints. "He will return some day," says Apollodorus as Cæsar leaves. "I hope not," replies Cleopatra. "But I cant help crying, all the same." Between her hope and her tears is the world's impasse.

Cæsar and Cleopatra is a thesis play, if by a thesis play is meant a play in which the playwright tells us something which he hopes will change our ways. Nevertheless, it is not irrelevant to ask whether it ends as a kind of comedy or as a kind of tragedy. It is, however, a difficult question.

Anton Chekhov

THE CHERRY ORCHARD

Translated by Stark Young

Characters

RANEVSKAYA, LYUBOFF ANDREEVNA, *a landowner*
ANYA, *her daughter, seventeen years old*
VARYA, *her adopted daughter, twenty-four years old*
GAYEFF, LEONID ANDREEVICH, *brother of Ranevskaya*
LOPAHIN, YERMOLAY ALEXEEVICH, *a merchant*
TROFIMOFF, PYOTR SERGEEVICH, *a student*
SEMYONOFF-PISHTCHIK, BORIS BORISOVICH, *a landowner*
CHARLOTTA IVANOVNA, *a governess*
EPIHODOFF, SEMYON PANTELEEVICH, *a clerk*
DUNYASHA, *a maid*
FIERS, *a valet, an old man of eighty-seven*
YASHA, *a young valet*
A PASSERBY *or* STRANGER
THE STATIONMASTER
A POST-OFFICE CLERK
VISITORS, SERVANTS

SCENE: *The action takes place on the estate of* L. A. RANEVSKAYA.

ACT ONE

(A room that is still called the nursery. One of the doors leads into ANYA's *room. Dawn, the sun will soon be rising. It is May, the cherry trees are in blossom but in the orchard it is cold, with a morning frost. The windows in the room are closed. Enter* DUNYASHA *with a candle and* LOPAHIN *with a book in his hand.)*

LOPAHIN: The train got in, thank God! What time is it?

DUNYASHA: It's nearly two. (*Blows out her candle.*) It's already daylight.

LOPAHIN: But how late was the train? Two hours at least. (*Yawning and stretching.*) I'm a fine one, I am, look what a fool thing I did! I drove her on purpose just to meet them at the station, and then all of a sudden I'd overslept myself! Fell asleep in my chair. How provoking! — You could have waked me up.

DUNYASHA: I thought you had gone. (*Listening.*) Listen, I think they are coming now.

LOPAHIN (*listening*): No — No, there's the luggage and one thing and another. (*A pause.*) Lyuboff Andreevna has been living abroad five years. I don't know what she is like now — She is a good woman. An easy-going, simple woman. I remember when I was a boy about fifteen, my father, who is at rest — in those days he ran a shop here in the village — hit me in the face with his fist, my nose was bleeding — We'd come to the yard together for something or other, and he was a little drunk. Lyuboff Andreevna, I can see her now, still so young, so slim, led me to the washbasin here in this very room, in the nursery. "Don't cry," she says, "little peasant, it will be well in time for your wedding" — (*A pause.*) Yes, little peasant — My father was a peasant truly, and here I am in a white waistcoat and yellow shoes. Like a pig rooting in a pastry shop — I've got this rich, lots of money, but if you really stop and think of it, I'm just a peasant — (*Turning the pages of a book.*) Here I was reading a book and didn't get a thing out of it. Reading and went to sleep. (*A pause.*)

DUNYASHA: And all night long the dogs were not asleep, they know their masters are coming.

LOPAHIN: What is it, Dunyasha, you're so —

DUNYASHA: My hands are shaking. I'm going to faint.

LOPAHIN: You're just so delicate, Dunyasha. And all dressed up like a lady, and your hair all done up! Mustn't do that. Must know your place.

(*Enter* EPIHODOFF, *with a bouquet: he wears a jacket and highly polished boots with a loud squeak. As he enters he drops the bouquet.*)

EPIHODOFF (*picking up the bouquet*): Look, the gardener sent these, he says to put them in the dining room. (*Giving the bouquet to* DUNYASHA.)

LOPAHIN: And bring me some kvass.

DUNYASHA: Yes, sir. (*Goes out.*)

EPIHODOFF: There is a morning frost now, three degrees of frost (*sighing*) and the cherries all in bloom. I cannot approve of our climate — I cannot. Our climate can never quite rise to the occasion. Listen, Yermolay Alexeevich, allow me to subtend, I bought myself, day before yesterday, some boots and they, I venture to assure you, squeak so that it is impossible. What could I grease them with?

LOPAHIN: Go on. You annoy me.

EPIHODOFF: Every day some misfortune happens to me. But I don't complain, I am used to it and I even smile.

(DUNYASHA *enters, serves* LOPAHIN *the kvass.*)

EPIHODOFF: I'm going. (*Stumbling over a chair and upsetting it.*) There (*as if triumphant*), there, you see, pardon the expression, a circumstance like that, among others — It is simply quite remarkable. (*Goes out.*)

DUNYASHA: And I must tell you, Yermolay Alexeevich, that Epihodoff has proposed to me.

LOPAHIN: Ah!

DUNYASHA: I don't know really what to — He is a quiet man but sometimes when he starts talking, you can't understand a thing he means. It's all very nice, and full of feeling, but just doesn't make any sense. I sort of like him. He loves me madly. He's a man that's unfortunate, every day there's something or other. They tease him around here, call him twenty-two misfortunes —

LOPAHIN (*cocking his ear*): Listen, I think they are coming —

DUNYASHA: They are coming! But what's the matter with me — I'm cold all over.

LOPAHIN: They're really coming. Let's go meet them. Will she recognize me? It's five years we haven't seen each other.

DUNYASHA (*excitedly*): I'm going to faint this very minute. Ah, I'm going to faint!

(*Two carriages can be heard driving up to the house.* LOPAHIN *and* DUNYASHA *hurry out. The stage is empty. In the adjoining rooms a noise begins.* FIERS *hurries across the stage, leaning on a stick; he has been to meet* LYUBOFF ANDREEVNA, *and wears an old-fashioned livery and a high hat; he mutters something to himself, but you cannot understand a word of it. The noise offstage gets louder and louder. A voice: "Look! Let's go through here —"* LYUBOFF ANDREEVNA, ANYA *and* CHARLOTTA IVANOVNA, *with a little dog on a chain, all of them dressed for traveling,* VARYA, *in a coat and kerchief,* GAYEFF, SEMYONOFF-PISHTCHIK, LOPAHIN, DUNYASHA, *with a bundle and an umbrella,* SERVANTS *with pieces of luggage — all pass through the room.*)

ANYA: Let's go through here. Mama, do you remember what room this is?

LYUBOFF ANDREEVNA (*happily, through her tears*): The nursery!

VARYA: How cold it is, my hands are stiff. (*To* LYUBOFF ANDREEVNA.) Your rooms, the white one and the violet, are just the same as ever, Mama.

LYUBOFF ANDREEVNA: The nursery, my dear beautiful room — I slept here when I was little — (*Crying.*) And now I am like a child — (*Kisses her brother and* VARYA, *then her brother again.*) And Varya is just the same as ever, looks like a nun. And I knew Dunyasha — (*Kisses* DUNYASHA.)

GAYEFF: The train was two hours late. How's that? How's that for good management?

CHARLOTTA (*to* PISHTCHIK): My dog he eats nuts too.

PISHTCHIK (*astonished*): Think of that!

(*Everybody goes out except* ANYA *and* DUNYASHA.)

DUNYASHA: We waited so long — (*Taking off* ANYA's *coat and hat.*)

ANYA: I didn't sleep all four nights on the way. And now I feel so chilly.

DUNYASHA: It was Lent when you left, there was some snow then, there was frost, and now? My darling (*laughing and kissing her*), I waited so long for you, my joy, my life — I'm telling you now, I can't keep from it another minute.

ANYA (*wearily*): There we go again —

DUNYASHA: The clerk Epihodoff, proposed to me after Holy Week.

ANYA: You're always talking about the same thing — (*Arranging her hair.*) I've lost all my hairpins — (*She is tired to the point of staggering.*)

DUNYASHA: I just don't know what to think. He loves me, loves me so!

ANYA (*looks in through her door, tenderly*): My room, my windows, it's just as if I had never been away. I'm home! Tomorrow morning

I'll get up, I'll run into the orchard — Oh, if I only could go to sleep! I haven't slept all the way, I was tormented by anxiety.

DUNYASHA: Day before yesterday, Pyotr Sergeevich arrived.

ANYA (*joyfully*): Petya!

DUNYASHA: He's asleep in the bathhouse, he lives there. I am afraid, he says, of being in the way. (*Taking her watch from her pocket and looking at it.*) Somebody ought to wake him up. It's only that Varvara Mikhailovna told us not to. Don't you wake him up, she said.

VARYA (*enter* VARYA *with a bunch of keys at her belt*): Dunyasha, coffee, quick — Mama is asking for coffee.

DUNYASHA: This minute. (*Goes out.*)

VARYA: Well, thank goodness, you've come back. You are home again. (*Caressingly.*) My darling is back! My precious is back!

ANYA: I've had such a time.

VARYA: I can imagine!

ANYA: I left during Holy Week, it was cold then. Charlotta talked all the way and did her tricks. Why did you fasten Charlotta on to me — ?

VARYA: But you couldn't have traveled alone, darling; not at seventeen!

ANYA: We arrived in Paris, it was cold there and snowing. I speak terrible French. Mama lived on the fifth floor; I went to see her; there were some French people in her room, ladies, an old priest with his prayer book, and the place was full of tobacco smoke — very dreary. Suddenly I began to feel sorry for Mama, so sorry, I drew her to me, held her close and couldn't let her go. Then Mama kept hugging me, crying — yes —

VARYA (*tearfully*): Don't — oh, don't —

ANYA: Her villa near Mentone she had already sold, she had nothing left, nothing. And I didn't have a kopeck left. It was all we could do to get here. And Mama doesn't understand! We sit down to dinner at a station and she orders, insists on the most expensive things and gives the waiters rouble tips. Charlotta does the same. Yasha too demands his share; it's simply dreadful. Mama has her butler, Yasha, we've brought him here —

VARYA: I saw the wretch.

ANYA: Well, how are things? Has the interest on the mortgage been paid?

VARYA: How could we?

ANYA: Oh, my God, my God — !

VARYA: In August the estate is to be sold —

ANYA: My God — !

LOPAHIN (*looking in through the door and mooing like a cow*): Moo-o-o — (*Goes away.*)

VARYA (*tearfully*): I'd land him one like that — (*Shaking her fist.*)

ANYA (*embracing* VARYA *gently*): Varya, has he proposed? (VARYA *shakes her head.*) But he loves you — Why don't you have it out with him, what are you waiting for?

VARYA: I don't think anything will come of it for us. He is very busy, he hasn't any time for me — And doesn't notice me. God knows, it's painful for me to see him — Everybody talks about our marriage, everybody congratulates us, and the truth is, there's nothing to it — it's all like a dream — (*In a different tone.*) You have a brooch looks like a bee.

ANYA (*sadly*): Mama bought it. (*Going toward her room, speaking gaily, like a child.*) And in Paris I went up in a balloon!

VARYA: My darling is back! My precious is back! (DUNYASHA *has returned with the coffee pot and is making coffee.* VARYA *is standing by the door.*) Darling, I'm busy all day long with the house and I go around thinking things. If only you could be married to a rich man, I'd be more at peace too, I would go all by myself to a hermitage — then to Kiev — to Moscow, and I'd keep going like that from one holy place to another — I would go on and on. Heavenly!

ANYA: The birds are singing in the orchard. What time is it now?

VARYA: It must be after two. It's time you were asleep, darling. (*Going into* ANYA'*s room.*) Heavenly!

YASHA (YASHA *enters with a lap robe and a traveling bag. Crossing the stage airily*): May I go through here?

DUNYASHA: We'd hardly recognize you, Yasha; you've changed so abroad!

YASHA: Hm — And who are you?

DUNYASHA: When you left here, I was like that — (*Her hand so high from the floor.*) I'm Dunyasha, Fyodor Kozoyedoff's daughter. You don't remember!

YASHA: Hm — You little peach! (*Looking around before he embraces her; she shrieks and drops a saucer;* YASHA *hurries out.*)

VARYA (*at the door, in a vexed tone*): And what's going on here?

DUNYASHA (*tearfully*): I broke a saucer —

VARYA: That's good luck.

ANYA (*emerging from her room*): We ought to tell Mama beforehand: Petya is here —

VARYA: I told them not to wake him up.

ANYA (*pensively*): Six years ago our father died, a month later our brother Grisha was drowned in the river, such a pretty little boy, just seven. Mama couldn't bear it, she went away, went away without ever looking back — (*Shuddering.*) How I understand her, if she only knew I did. (*A pause.*) And Petya Trofimoff was Grisha's tutor, he might remind —

FIERS (*enter* FIERS; *he is in a jacket and white waistcoat. Going to the coffee urn, busy with it*): The mistress will have her breakfast here — (*Putting on white gloves.*) Is the coffee ready? (*To* DUNYASHA, *sternly.*) You! What about the cream?

DUNYASHA: Oh, my God — (*Hurrying out.*)

FIERS (*busy at the coffee urn*): Oh, you good-for-nothing — ! (*Muttertering to himself.*) Come back from Paris — And the master used to go to Paris by coach — (*Laughing.*)

VARYA: Fiers, what are you — ?

FIERS: At your service. (*Joyfully.*) My mistress is back! It's what I've been waiting for! Now I'm ready to die — (*Crying for joy.*)

(LYUBOFF ANDREEVNA, GAYEFF *and* SEMYONOFF-PISHTCHIK *enter;* SEMYONOFF-PISHTCHIK *is in a podyovka of fine cloth and sharovary.* GAYEFF *enters; he makes gestures with his hands and body as if he were playing billiards.*)

LYUBOFF ANDREEVNA: How is it? Let me remember — Yellow into the corner! Duplicate in the middle!

GAYEFF: I cut into the corner. Sister, you and I slept here in this very room once, and now I am fifty-one years old, strange as that may seem —

LOPAHIN: Yes, time passes.

GAYEFF: What?

LOPAHIN: Time, I say, passes.

GAYEFF: And it smells like patchouli here.

ANYA: I'm going to bed. Good night, Mama. (*Kissing her mother.*)

LYUBOFF ANDREEVNA: My sweet little child. (*Kissing her hands.*) You're glad you are home? I still can't get myself together.

ANYA: Good-by, Uncle.

GAYEFF (*kissing her face and hands*): God be with you. How like your mother you are! (*To his sister.*) Lyuba, at her age you were exactly like her.

(ANYA *shakes hands with* LOPAHIN *and* PISHTCHIK, *goes out and closes the door behind her.*)

LYUBOFF ANDREEVNA: She's very tired.

PISHTCHIK: It is a long trip, I imagine.

VARYA (*to* LOPAHIN *and* PISHTCHIK): Well, then, sirs? It's going on three o'clock, time for gentlemen to be going

LYUBOFF ANDREEVNA (*laughing*): The same old Varya. (*Drawing her *to her and kissing her.*) There, I'll drink my coffee, then we'll all go. (FIERS *puts a small cushion under her feet.*) Thank you, my dear. I am used to coffee. Drink it day and night. Thank you, my dear old soul. (*Kissing* FIERS.)

VARYA: I'll go see if all the things have come. (*Goes out.*)

LYUBOFF ANDREEVNA: Is it really me sitting here? (*Laughing.*) I'd like to jump around and wave my arms. (*Covering her face with her hands.*) But I may be dreaming! God knows I love my country, love it deeply, I couldn't look out of the car window, I just kept crying. (*Tearfully.*) However, I must drink my coffee. Thank you, Fiers, thank you, my dear old friend. I'm so glad you're still alive.

FIERS: Day before yesterday.

GAYEFF: He doesn't hear well.

LOPAHIN: And I must leave right now. It's nearly five o'clock in the morning, for Kharkov. What a nuisance! I wanted to look at you — talk — You are as beautiful as ever.

PISHTCHIK (*breathing heavily*): Even more beautiful — In your Paris clothes — It's a feast for the eyes —

LOPAHIN: Your brother, Leonid Andreevich here, says I'm a boor, a peasant money grubber, but that's all the same to me, absolutely. Let him say it. All I wish is you'd trust me as you used to, and your wonderful, touching eyes would look at me as they did. Merciful God! My father was a serf; belonged to your grandfather and your father; but you, your own self, you did so much for me once that I've forgotten all that and love you like my own kin — more than my kin.

LYUBOFF ANDREEVNA: I can't sit still — I can't. (*Jumping up and walking about in great excitement.*) I'll never live through this happiness — Laugh at me, I'm silly — My own little bookcase — ! (*Kissing the bookcase.*) My little table!

GAYEFF: And in your absence the nurse here died.

LYUBOFF ANDREEVNA (*sitting down and drinking coffee*): Yes, may she rest in Heaven! They wrote me.

GAYEFF: And Anastasy died. Cross-eyed Petrushka left me and lives in town now at the police officer's. (*Taking out of his pocket a box of hard candy and sucking a piece.*)

PISHTCHIK: My daughter, Dashenka — sends you her greetings —

LOPAHIN: I want to tell you something very pleasant, cheerful. (*Glancing at his watch.*) I'm going right away. There's no time for talking. Well, I'll make it two or three words. As you know, your cherry orchard is to be sold for your debts; the auction is set for August twenty-second, but don't you worry, my dear, you just sleep in peace, there's a way out of it. Here's my plan. Please listen to me. Your estate is only thirteen miles from town. They've run the railroad by it. Now if the cherry orchard and the land along the river were cut up into building lots and leased for summer cottages, you'd have at the very lowest twenty-five thousand roubles per year income.

GAYEFF: Excuse me, what rot!

LYUBOFF ANDREEVNA: I don't quite understand you, Yermolay Alexeevich.

LOPAHIN: At the very least you will get from the summer residents twenty-five roubles per year for a two-and-a-half acre lot and if you post a notice right off, I'll bet you anything that by autumn you won't have a single patch of land free, everything will be taken. In a word, my congratulations, you are saved. The location is wonderful, the river's so deep. Except, of course, it all needs to be tidied up, cleared — For instance, let's say, tear all the old buildings down and this house, which is no good any more, and cut down the old cherry orchard —

LYUBOFF ANDREEVNA: Cut down? My dear, forgive me, you don't understand at all. If there's one thing in the whole province that's interesting — not to say remarkable — it's our cherry orchard.

LOPAHIN: The only remarkable thing about this cherry orchard is that it's very big. There's a crop of cherries once every two years and even that's hard to get rid of. Nobody buys them.

GAYEFF: This orchard is even mentioned in the encyclopedia.

LOPAHIN (*glancing at his watch*): If we don't cook up something and don't get somewhere, the cherry orchard and the entire estate will be sold at auction on the twenty-second of August. Do get it settled then! I swear there is no other way out. Not a one!

FIERS: There was a time, forty-fifty years ago when the cherries were dried, soaked, pickled, cooked into jam and it used to be —

GAYEFF: Keep quiet, Fiers.

FIERS: And it used to be that the dried cherries were shipped by the wagon-load to Moscow and to Kharkov. And the money there was! And the dried cherries were soft then, juicy, sweet, fragrant — They had a way of treating them then —

LYUBOFF ANDREEVNA: And where is that way now?

FIERS: They have forgotten it. Nobody remembers it.

PISHTCHIK (*to* LYUBOFF ANDREEVNA): What's happening in Paris? How is everything? Did you eat frogs?

LYUBOFF ANDREEVNA: I ate crocodiles.

PISHTCHIK: Think of it — !

LOPAHIN: Up to now in the country there have been only the gentry and the peasants, but now in summer the villa people too are coming in. All the towns, even the least big ones, are surrounded with cottages. In about twenty years very likely the summer resident will multiply enormously. He merely drinks tea on the porch now, but it might well happen that on this two-and-a-half acre lot of his, he'll go in for farming, and then your cherry orchard would be happy, rich, splendid —

GAYEFF (*getting hot*): What rot!

(*Enter* VARYA *and* YASHA.)

VARYA: Here, Mama. Two telegrams for you. (*Choosing a key and opening the old bookcase noisily.*) Here they are.

LYUBOFF ANDREEVNA: From Paris (*Tearing up the telegrams without reading them.*) Paris, that's all over —

GAYEFF: Do you know how old this bookcase is, Lyuba? A week ago I pulled out the bottom drawer and looked, and there the figures were burned on it. The bookcase was made exactly a hundred years ago. How's that? Eh? You might celebrate its jubilee. It's an inanimate object, but all the same, be that as it may, it's a bookcase.

PISHTCHIK (*in astonishment*): A hundred years — ! Think of it — !

GAYEFF: Yes — quite something — (*Shaking the bookcase.*) Dear, honored bookcase! I saluted your existence, which for more than a hundred years has been directed toward the clear ideals of goodness and justice; your silent appeal to fruitful endeavor has not flagged in all the course of a hundred years, sustaining (*tearfully*) through the generations of our family, our courage and our faith in a better future and nurturing in us ideals of goodness and of a social consciousness.

(*A pause.*)

LOPAHIN: Yes.

LYUBOFF ANDREEVNA: You're the same as ever, Lenya.

GAYEFF (*slightly embarrassed*): Carom to the right into the corner pocket. I cut into the side pocket!

LOPAHIN (*glancing at his watch*): Well, it's time for me to go.

YASHA (*handing medicine to* LYUBOFF ANDREEVNA): Perhaps you'll take the pills now —

PISHTCHIK: You should never take medicaments, dear madam — They do neither harm nor good — Hand them here, dearest lady. (*He takes the pillbox, shakes the pills out into his palm, blows on them, puts them in his mouth and washes them down with kvass.*) There! Now!

LYUBOFF ANDREEVNA (*startled*): Why, you've lost your mind!

PISHTCHIK: I took all the pills.

LOPAHIN: Such a glutton!

(*Everyone laughs.*)

FIERS: The gentleman stayed with us during Holy Week, he ate half a bucket of pickles — (*Muttering.*)

LYUBOFF ANDREEVNA: What is he muttering about?

VARYA: He's been muttering like that for three years. We're used to it.

YASHA: In his dotage.

(CHARLOTTA IVANOVNA *in a white dress — she is very thin, her corset laced very tight — with a lorgnette at her belt, crosses the stage.*)

LOPAHIN: Excuse me, Charlotta Ivanovna, I haven't had a chance yet to welcome you. (*Trying to kiss her hand.*)

CHARLOTTA (*drawing her hand away*): If I let you kiss my hand, 'twould be my elbow next, then my shoulder —

LOPAHIN: No luck for me today. (*Everyone laughs.*) Charlotta Ivanovna, show us a trick!

CHARLOTTA: No. I want to go to bed. (*Exit.*)

LOPAHIN: In three weeks we shall see each other. (*Kissing* LYUBOFF ANDREEVNA'S *hand.*) Till then, good-by. It's time. (*To* GAYEFF.) See you soon. (*Kissing* PISHTCHIK.) See you soon. (*Shaking* VARYA'S *hand, then* FIERS' *and* YASHA'S.) I don't feel like going. (*To* LYUBOFF ANDREEVNA.) If you think it over and make up your mind about the summer cottages, let me know and I'll arrange a loan of something like fifty thousand roubles. Think it over seriously.

VARYA (*angrily*): Do go on, anyhow, will you!

LOPAHIN: I'm going, I'm going — (*Exit.*)

GAYEFF: Boor. However, pardon — Varya is going to marry him, it's Varya's little fiancé.

VARYA: Don't talk too much, Uncle.

LYUBOFF ANDREEVNA: Well, Varya, I should be very glad. He's a good man.

PISHTCHIK: A man, one must say truthfully — A most worthy — And my Dashenka — says also that — she says all sorts of things — (*Snoring but immediately waking up.*) Nevertheless, dearest lady, oblige me — With a loan of two hundred and forty roubles — Tomorrow the interest on my mortgage has got to be paid —

VARYA (*startled*): There's not any money, none at all.

LYUBOFF ANDREEVNA: Really, I haven't got anything.

PISHTCHIK: I'll find it, somehow. (*Laughing.*) I never give up hope. There, I think to myself, all is lost, I am ruined and lo and behold — a railroad is put through my land and — they paid me. And then, just watch, something else will turn up — if not today, then tomorrow — Dashenka will win two hundred thousand — She has a ticket.

LYUBOFF ANDREEVNA: We've finished the coffee, now we can go to bed.

FIERS (*brushing* GAYEFF'S *clothes, reprovingly*): You put on the wrong trousers again. What am I going to do with you!

VARYA (*softly*): Anya is asleep. (*Opening the window softly.*) Already the sun's rising — it's not cold. Look, Mama! What beautiful trees! My Lord, what air! The starlings are singing!

GAYEFF (*opening another window*): The orchard is all white. You haven't forgotten, Lyuba? That long lane there runs straight — as a strap stretched out. It glistens on moonlight nights. Do you remember? You haven't forgotten it?

LYUBOFF ANDREEVNA (*looking out of the window on to the orchard*): Oh, my childhood, my innocence! I slept in this nursery and looked out on the orchard from here, every morning happiness awoke with me, it was just as it is now, then, nothing has changed. (*Laughing with joy.*) All, all white! Oh, my orchard! After a dark, rainy autumn and cold winter, you are young again and full of happiness. The heavenly angels have not deserted you — If I only could lift the weight from my breast, from my shoulders, if I could only forget my past!

GAYEFF: Yes, and the orchard will be sold for debt, strange as that may seem.

LYUBOFF ANDREEVNA: Look, our dear mother is walking through the orchard — In a white dress! (*Laughing happily.*) It's she.

GAYEFF: Where?

VARYA: God be with you, Mama!

LYUBOFF ANDREEVNA: There's not anybody, it only seemed so. To the right, as you turn to the summerhouse, a little white tree is leaning there, looks like a woman — (*Enter* TROFIMOFF, *in a student's uniform, well worn, and glasses.*) What a wonderful orchard? The white masses of blossoms, the sky all blue.

TROFIMOFF: Lyuboff Andreevna! (*She looks around at him.*) I will just greet you and go immediately. (*Kissing her hand warmly.*) I was told to wait until morning, but I hadn't the patience —

(LYUBOFF ANDREEVNA *looks at him puzzled.*)

VARYA (*tearfully*): This is Petya Trofimoff —

TROFIMOFF: Petya Trofimoff, the former tutor of your Grisha — Have I really changed so?

(LYUBOFF ANDREEVNA *embraces him; and crying quietly.*)

GAYEFF (*embarrassed*): There, there, Lyuba.

VARYA (*crying*): I told you, Petya, to wait till tomorrow.

LYUBOFF ANDREEVNA: My Grisha — My boy — Grisha — Son —

VARYA: What can we do, Mama? It's God's will.

TROFIMOFF (*in a low voice, tearfully*): There, there —

LYUBOFF ANDREEVNA (*weeping softly*): My boy was lost, drowned — Why? Why, my friend? (*More quietly.*) Anya is asleep there, and I am talking so loud — Making so much noise — But why, Petya? Why have you lost your looks? Why do you look so much older?

TROFIMOFF: A peasant woman on the train called me a mangy-looking gentleman.

LYUBOFF ANDREEVNA: You were a mere boy then, a charming young student, and now your hair's not very thick any more and you wear glasses. Are you really a student still? (*Going to the door.*)

TROFIMOFF: Very likely I'll be a perennial student.

LYUBOFF ANDREEVNA (*kissing her brother, then* VARYA): Well, go to bed — You've grown older too, Leonid.

PISHTCHIK (*following her*): So that's it, we are going to bed now. Oh, my gout! I'm staying here — I'd like, Lyuboff Andreevna, my soul, tomorrow morning — Two hundred and forty roubles —

GAYEFF: He's still at it.

PISHTCHIK: Two hundred and forty roubles — To pay interest on the mortgage.

LYUBOFF ANDREEVNA: I haven't any money, my dove.

PISHTCHIK: I'll pay it back, my dear — It's a trifling sum —

LYUBOFF ANDREEVNA: Oh, very well, Leonid will give — You give it to him, Leonid.

GAYEFF: Oh, certainly, I'll give it to him. Hold out your pockets.

LYUBOFF ANDREEVNA: What can we do, give it, he needs it — He'll pay it back.

(LYUBOFF ANDREEVNA, TROFIMOFF, PISHTCHIK *and* FIERS *go out.* GAYEFF, VARYA *and* YASHA *remain.*)

GAYEFF: My sister hasn't yet lost her habit of throwing money away. (*To* YASHA.) Get away, my good fellow, you smell like hens.

YASHA (*with a grin*): And you are just the same as you used to be, Leonid Andreevich.

GAYEFF: What? (*To* VARYA.) What did he say?

VARYA (*to* YASHA): Your mother has come from the village, she's been sitting in the servants' hall ever since yesterday, she wants to see you —

YASHA: The devil take her!

VARYA: Ach, shameless creature!

YASHA: A lot I need her! She might have come tomorrow. (*Goes out.*)

VARYA: Mama is just the same as she was, she hasn't changed at all. If she could, she'd give away everything she has.

GAYEFF: Yes — If many remedies are prescribed for an illness, you may know the illness is incurable. I keep thinking, I rack my brains, I have many remedies, a great many, and that means, really, I haven't any at all. It would be fine to inherit a fortune from somebody, it would be fine to marry off our Anya to a very rich man, it would be fine to go to Yaroslavl and try our luck with our old aunt, the Countess. Auntie is very, very rich.

VARYA (*crying*): If God would only help us!

GAYEFF: Don't bawl! Auntie is very rich but she doesn't like us. To begin with, Sister married a lawyer, not a nobleman — (ANYA *appears at the door.*) Married not a nobleman and behaved herself, you could say, not very virtuously. She is good, kind, nice, I love her very much, but no matter how much you allow for the extenuating circumstances, you must admit she's a depraved woman. You feel it in her slightest movement.

VARYA (*whispering*): Anya is standing in the door there.

GAYEFF: What? (*A pause.*) It's amazing, something got in my right eye. I am beginning to see poorly. And on Thursday, when I was in the District Court —

(ANYA *enters.*)

VARYA: But why aren't you asleep, Anya?

ANYA: I don't feel like sleeping. I can't.

GAYEFF: My little girl — (*Kissing* ANYA'*s face and hands.*) My child — (*Tearfully.*) You are not my niece, you are my angel, you are everything to me. Believe me, believe —

ANYA: I believe you, Uncle. Everybody loves you, respects you — But dear Uncle, you must keep quiet, just keep quiet — What were you saying, just now, about my mother, about your own sister? What did you say that for?

GAYEFF: Yes, yes — (*Putting her hand up over his face.*) Really, it's terrible! My God! Oh, God, save me! And today I made a speech to the bookcase — So silly! And it was only when I finished it that I could see it was silly.

VARYA: It's true, Uncle, you ought to keep quiet. Just keep quiet. That's all.

ANYA: If you kept quiet, you'd have more peace.

GAYEFF: I'll keep quiet. (*Kissing* ANYA'*s and* VARYA'*s hands.*) I'll keep quiet. Only this, it's about business. On Thursday I was in the District Court; well, a few of us gathered around and a conversation began about this and that, about lots of things; apparently it will be possible to arrange a loan on a promissory note to pay the bank the interest due.

VARYA: If the Lord would only help us!

GAYEFF: Tuesday I shall go and talk it over again. (*To* VARYA.) Don't bawl! (*To* ANYA.) Your mother will talk to Lopahin; of course, he won't refuse her . . . And as soon as you rest up, you will go to Yaroslavl to your great-aunt, the Countess. There, that's how we will move from three directions, and the business is in the bag. We'll pay the interest. I am convinced of that — (*Putting a hard candy in his mouth.*) On my honor I'll swear, by anything you like, that the estate shall not be sold! (*Excitedly.*) By my happiness, I swear! Here's my hand, call me a worthless, dishonorable man, if I allow it to come up for auction! With all my soul I swear it!

ANYA (*a quieter mood returns to her; she is happy*): How good you are, Uncle, how clever! (*Embracing her uncle.*) I feel easy now! I feel easy! I'm happy!

FIERS (FIERS *enters, reproachfully*): Leonid Andreevich, have you no fear of God? When are you going to bed?

GAYEFF: Right away, right away. You may go, Fiers. For this once I'll undress myself. Well, children, beddy bye — More details tomorrow, and now, go to bed. (*Kissing* ANYA *and* VARYA.) I am a man of the eighties — It is a period that's not admired, but I can say, nevertheless, that I've suffered no little for my convictions in the course of my life. It is not for nothing that the peasant loves me. One must know the peasant! One must know from what —

ANYA: Again, Uncle!

VARYA: You, Uncle dear, keep quiet.

FIERS (*angrily*): Leonid Andreevich!

GAYEFF: I'm coming, I'm coming — Go to bed. A double bank into the side pocket! A clean shot — (*Goes out,* FIERS *hobbling after him.*)

ANYA: I feel easy now. I don't feel like going to Yaroslavl; I don't like Great-aunt, but still I feel easy. Thanks to Uncle. (*Sits down.*)

VARYA: I must get to sleep. I'm going. And there was unpleasantness here during your absence. In the old servants' quarters, as you know, live only the old servants: Yephemushka, Polya, Yevstignay, well, and Karp. They began to let every sort of creature spend the night with them — I didn't say anything. But then I hear they've spread the rumor that I'd given orders to feed them nothing but beans. Out of stinginess, you see — And all that from Yevstignay — Very well, I think to myself. If that's the way it is, I think to myself, then you just wait. I call in Yevstignay — (*Yawning.*) He comes — How is it, I say, that you, Yevstignay — You're such a fool — (*Glancing at* ANYA.) Anitchka! — (*A pause.*) Asleep! (*Takes* ANYA *by her arm.*) Let's go to bed — Come on! — (*Leading her.*) My little darling fell asleep! Come on — (*They go. Far away beyond the orchard a shepherd is playing on a pipe.* TROFIMOFF *walks across the stage and, seeing* VARYA *and* ANYA, stops.) Shh — She is asleep — asleep — Let's go, dear.

ANYA (*softly, half dreaming*): I'm so tired — All the bells! — Uncle — dear — And Mama and Uncle — Varya.

VARYA: Come on, my dear, come on. (*They go into* ANYA's *room.*)

TROFIMOFF (*tenderly*): My little sun! My spring!

ACT TWO

(*A field. An old chapel, long abandoned, with crooked walls, near it a well, big stones that apparently were once tombstones, and an old bench. A road to the estate of* GAYEFF *can be seen. On one side poplars rise, casting their shadows, the cherry orchard begins there. In the distance a row of telegraph poles; and far, far away, faintly traced on the horizon, is a large town, visible only in the clearest weather. The sun will soon be down.* CHARLOTTA, YASHA *and* DUNYASHA *are sitting on the bench;* EPIHODOFF *is standing near and playing the guitar; everyone sits lost in thought.* CHARLOTTA *wears an old peak cap* (fourrage); *she has taken a rifle from off her shoulders and is adjusting the buckle on the strap.*)

CHARLOTTA (*pensively*): I have no proper passport, I don't know how old I am — it always seems to me I'm very young. When I was a little girl, my father and mother traveled from fair to fair and gave performances, very good ones. And I did *salto mortale* and different tricks. And when Papa and Mama died, a German lady took me to live with her and began teaching me. Good. I grew up. And became a governess. But where I came from and who am I don't know — Who my parents were, perhaps they weren't even married — I don't know. (*Taking a cucumber out of her pocket and beginning to eat it.*) I don't know a thing. (*A pause.*) I'd like so much to talk but there's not anybody. I haven't anybody.

EPIHODOFF (*playing the guitar and singing*): "What care I for the noisy world, what care I for friends and foes." — How pleasant it is to play the mandolin!

DUNYASHA: That's a guitar, not a mandolin. (*Looking into a little mirror and powdering her face.*)

EPIHODOFF: For a madman who is in love this is a mandolin — (*Singing.*) "If only my heart were warm with the fire of requited love."

(YASHA *sings with him.*)

CHARLOTTA: How dreadfully these people sing — Phooey! Like jackals.

DUNYASHA (*to* YASHA): All the same what happiness to have been abroad.

YASHA: Yes, of course. I cannot disagree with you. (*Yawning and then lighting a cigar.*)

EPIHODOFF: That's easily understood. Abroad everything long since attained its complete development.

YASHA: That's obvious.

EPIHODOFF: I am a cultured man. I read all kinds of remarkable books, but the trouble is I cannot discover my own inclinations, whether to live or to shoot myself, but nevertheless, I always carry a revolver on me. Here it is — (*Showing a revolver.*)

CHARLOTTA: That's done. Now I am going. (*Slinging the rifle over her shoulder.*) You are a very clever man, Epihodoff, and a very terrible one; the women must love you madly. Brrrr-r-r-r! (*Going.*) These clever people are all so silly, I haven't anybody to talk with. I'm always alone, alone, I have nobody and — Who I am, why I am, is unknown — (*Goes out without hurrying.*)

EPIHODOFF: Strictly speaking, not touching on other subjects, I must state about myself, in passing, that fate treats me mercilessly, as a storm does a small ship. If, let us suppose, I am mistaken, then why, to mention one instance, do I wake up this morning, look and there on my chest is a spider of terrific size — There, like that. (*Showing the size with both hands.*) And also I take some kvass to drink and in it I find something in the highest degree indecent, such as a cockroach. (*A pause.*) Have you read Buckle? (*A pause.*) I desire to trouble you, Avdotya Feodorovna, with a couple of words.

DUNYASHA: Speak.

EPIHODOFF: I have a desire to speak with you alone — (*Sighing.*)

DUNYASHA (*embarrassed*): Very well — But bring me my cape first — by the cupboard — It's rather damp here —

EPIHODOFF: Very well — I'll fetch it — Now I know what I should do with my revolver — (*Takes the guitar and goes out playing.*)

YASHA: Twenty-two misfortunes! Between us he's a stupid man, it must be said. (*Yawning.*)

DUNYASHA: God forbid he should shoot himself. (*A pause.*) I've grown so uneasy, I'm always fretting. I was only a girl when I was taken into the master's house, and now I've lost the habit of simple living — and here are my hands white, white as a lady's. I've become so delicate, fragile, ladylike, afraid of everything — Frightfully so. And, Yasha, if you deceive me, I don't know what will happen to my nerves.

YASHA (*kissing her*): You little cucumber! Of course every girl must behave properly. What I dislike above everything is for a girl to conduct herself badly.

DUNYASHA: I have come to love you passionately, you are educated, you can discuss anything. (*A pause.*)

YASHA (*yawning*): Yes, sir — To my mind it is like this: If a girl loves someone, it means she is immoral. (*A pause.*) It is pleasant to smoke a cigar in the clear air — (*Listening.*) They are coming here — It is the ladies and gentlemen —

(DUNYASHA *impulsively embraces him.*)

YASHA: Go to the house, as though you had been to bathe in the river, go by this path, otherwise, they might meet you and suspect me of making a rendezvous with you. That I cannot tolerate.

DUNYASHA (*with a little cough*): Your cigar has given me the headache. (*Goes out.*)

(YASHA *remains, sitting near the chapel.* LYUBOFF ANDREEVNA, GAYEFF *and* LOPAHIN *enter.*)

LOPAHIN: We must decide definitely, time doesn't wait. Why, the matter's quite simple. Are you willing to lease your land for summer cottages or are you not? Answer in one word, yes or no? Just one word!

LYUBOFF ANDREEVNA: Who is it smokes those disgusting cigars out here — ? (*Sitting down.*)

GAYEFF: The railroad running so near is a great convenience. (*Sitting down.*) We made a trip to town and lunched there — Yellow in the side pocket! Perhaps I should go in the house first and play one game —

LYUBOFF ANDREEVNA: You'll have time.

LOPAHIN: Just one word! (*Imploringly.*) Do give me your answer!

GAYEFF (*yawning*): What?

LYUBOFF ANDREEVNA (*looking in her purse*): Yesterday there was lots of money in it. Today there's very little. My poor Varya! For the sake of economy she feeds everybody milk soup, and in the kitchen the old people get nothing but beans, and here I spend money — senselessly — (*Dropping her purse and scattering gold coins.*) There they go scattering! (*She is vexed.*)

YASHA: Allow me, I'll pick them up in a second. (*Picking up the coins.*)

LYUBOFF ANDREEVNA: If you will, Yasha. And why did I go in town for lunch — ? Your restaurant with its music is trashy, the tablecloths smell of soap — Why drink so much, Lyonya? Why eat so much? Why talk so much? Today in the restaurant you were talking a lot again, and all of it beside the point. About the seventies, about the decadents. And to whom? Talking to waiters about the decadents!

LOPAHIN: Yes.

GAYEFF (*waving his hand*): I am incorrigible, that's evident — (*To* YASHA, *irritably.*) What is it? — You are forever swirling around in front of us!

YASHA (*laughing*): I cannot hear your voice without laughing.

GAYEFF (*to his sister*): Either I or he —

LYUBOFF ANDREEVNA: Go away, Yasha. Go on —

YASHA (*giving* LYUBOFF ANDREEVNA *her purse*): I am going right away. (*Barely suppressing his laughter.*) This minute. (*Goes out.*)

LOPAHIN: The rich Deriganoff intends to buy your estate. They say he is coming personally to the auction.

LYUBOFF ANDREEVNA: And where did you hear that?

LOPAHIN: In town they are saying it.

GAYEFF: Our Yaroslavl aunt promised to send us something, but when and how much she will send, nobody knows —

LOPAHIN: How much will she send? A hundred thousand? Two hundred?

LYUBOFF ANDREEVNA: Well — maybe ten, fifteen thousand — we'd be thankful for that.

LOPAHIN: Excuse me, but such light-minded people as you are, such odd, unbusinesslike people, I never saw. You are told in plain Russian that your estate is being sold up and you just don't seem to take it in.

LYUBOFF ANDREEVNA: But what are we to do? Tell us what?

LOPAHIN: I tell you every day. Every day I tell you the same thing. Both the cherry orchard and the land have got to be leased for summer cottages, it has to be done right now, quick — The auction is right under your noses. Do understand! Once you finally decide that there are to be summer cottages, you will get all the money you want, and then you'll be saved.

LYUBOFF ANDREEVNA: Summer cottages and summer residents — it is so trivial, excuse me.

GAYEFF: I absolutely agree with you.

LOPAHIN: I'll either burst out crying, or scream, or faint. I can't bear it! You are torturing me! (*To* GAYEFF.) You're a perfect old woman!

GAYEFF: What?

LOPAHIN: A perfect old woman! (*About to go.*)

LYUBOFF ANDREEVNA (*alarmed*): No, don't go, stay, my lamb, I beg you. Perhaps we will think of something!

LOPAHIN: What is there to think about?

LYUBOFF ANDREEVNA: Don't go, I beg you. With you here it is more cheerful anyhow — (*A pause.*) I keep waiting for something, as if the house were about to tumble down on our heads.

GAYEFF (*deep in thought*): Double into the corner pocket — Bank into the side pocket —

LYUBOFF ANDREEVNA: We have sinned so much —

LOPAHIN: What sins have you — ?

GAYEFF (*puts a hard candy into his mouth*): They say I've eaten my fortune up in hard candies — (*Laughing.*)

LYUBOFF ANDREEVNA: Oh, my sins — I've always thrown money around like mad, recklessly, and I married a man who accumulated nothing but debts. My husband died from champagne — he drank fearfully — and to my misfortune I fell in love with another man. I lived with him, and just at that time — it was my first punishment — a blow over the head: right here in the river my boy was drowned and I went abroad — went away for good, never to return, never to see this river again — I shut my eyes, ran away, beside myself, and he after me — mercilessly, brutally. I bought a villa near Menton, because he fell ill there, and for three years I knew no rest day or night, the sick man exhausted me, my soul dried up. And last year when the villa was sold for debts, I went to Paris and there he robbed me of everything, threw me over, took up with another woman; I tried to poison myself — so stupid, so shameful — And suddenly I was seized with longing for Russia, for my own country, for my little girl — (*Wiping away her tears.*) Lord, Lord, have mercy, forgive me my sins! Don't punish me any more! (*Getting a telegram out of her pocket.*) I got this today from Paris, he asks forgiveness, begs me to return — (*Tears up the telegram.*) That sounds like music somewhere. (*Listening.*)

GAYEFF: It is our famous Jewish orchestra. You remember, four violins, a flute and double bass.

LYUBOFF ANDREEVNA: Does it still exist? We ought to get hold of it sometime and give a party.

LOPAHIN (*listening*): Can't hear it — (*Singing softly.*) "And for money the Germans will frenchify a Russian." (*Laughing.*) What a play I saw yesterday at the theatre, very funny!

LYUBOFF ANDREEVNA: And most likely there was nothing funny about it. You shouldn't look at plays, but look oftener at yourselves. How gray all your lives are, what a lot of idle things you say!

LOPAHIN: That's true. It must be said frankly this life of ours is idiotic — (*A pause.*) My father was a peasant, an idiot, he understood nothing, he taught me nothing, he just beat me in his drunken fits and always with a stick. At bottom I am just as big a dolt and idiot as he was. I wasn't taught anything, my handwriting is vile, I write like a pig — I am ashamed for people to see it.

LYUBOFF ANDREEVNA: You ought to get married, my friend.

LOPAHIN: Yes — That's true.

LYUBOFF ANDREEVNA: To our Varya, perhaps. She is a good girl.

LOPAHIN: Yes.

LYUBOFF ANDREEVNA: She comes from simple people, and she works all day long, but the main thing is she loves you. And you, too, have liked her a long time.

LOPAHIN: Why not? I am not against it — She's a good girl. (*A pause.*)

GAYEFF: They are offering me a position in a bank. Six thousand a year — Have you heard that?

LYUBOFF ANDREEVNA: Not you! You stay where you are —

FIERS (FIERS *enters, bringing an overcoat. To* GAYEFF): Pray, Sir, put this on, it's damp.

GAYEFF (*putting on the overcoat*): You're a pest, old man.

FIERS: That's all right — This morning you went off without letting me know. (*Looking him over.*)

LYUBOFF ANDREEVNA: How old you've grown, Fiers!

FIERS: At your service.

LOPAHIN: She says you've grown very old!

FIERS: I've lived a long time. They were planning to marry me off before your papa was born. (*Laughing.*) And at the time the serfs were freed I was already the head footman. I didn't want to be freed then, I stayed with the masters — (*A pause.*) And I remember, everybody was happy, but what they were happy about they didn't know themselves.

LOPAHIN: In the old days it was fine. At least they flogged.

FIERS (*not hearing*): But, of course. The peasants stuck to the masters, the masters stuck to the peasants, and now everything is all smashed up, you can't tell about anything.

GAYEFF: Keep still, Fiers. Tomorrow I must go to town. They have promised to introduce me to a certain general who might make us a loan.

LOPAHIN: Nothing will come of it. And you can rest assured you won't pay the interest.

LYUBOFF ANDREEVNA: He's just raving on. There aren't any such generals.

(TROFIMOFF, ANYA *and* VARYA *enter.*)

GAYEFF: Here they come.

ANYA: There is Mama sitting there.

LYUBOFF ANDREEVNA (*tenderly*): Come, come — My darlings — (*Em-*

bracing ANYA *and* VARYA.) If you only knew how I love you both! Come sit by me — there — like that.

(*Everybody sits down.*)

LOPAHIN: Our perennial student is always strolling with the young ladies.
TROFIMOFF: It's none of your business.
LOPAHIN: He will soon be fifty and he's still a student.
TROFIMOFF: Stop your stupid jokes.
LOPAHIN: But why are you so peevish, you queer duck?
TROFIMOFF: Don't you pester me.
LOPAHIN (*laughing*): Permit me to ask you, what do you make of me?
TROFIMOFF: Yermolay Alexeevich, I make this of you: you are a rich man, you'll soon be a millionaire. Just as it is in the metabolism of nature, a wild beast is needed to eat up everything that comes his way; so you, too, are needed.

(*Everyone laughs.*)

VARYA: Petya, you'd better tell us about the planets.
LYUBOFF ANDREEVNA: No, let's go on with yesterday's conversation.
TROFIMOFF: What was it about?
GAYEFF: About the proud man.
TROFIMOFF: We talked a long time yesterday, but didn't get anywhere. In a proud man, in your sense of the word, there is something mystical. Maybe you are right, from your standpoint, but if we are to discuss it in simple terms, without whimsy, then what pride can there be, is there any sense in it, if man physiologically is poorly constructed, if in the great majority he is crude, unintelligent, profoundly miserable. One must stop admiring oneself. One must only work.
GAYEFF: All the same, you will die.
TROFIMOFF: Who knows? And what does it mean — you will die? Man may have a hundred senses, and when he dies only the five that are known to us may perish, and the remaining ninety-five go on living.
LYUBOFF ANDREEVNA: How clever you are, Petya!
LOPAHIN (*ironically*): Terribly!
TROFIMOFF: Humanity goes forward, perfecting its powers. Everything that's unattainable now will some day become familiar, understandable; it is only that one must work and must help with all one's might those who seek the truth. With us in Russia so far only a very few work. The great majority of the intelligentsia that I know are looking for nothing, doing nothing, and as yet have no capacity for

work. They call themselves intelligentsia, are free and easy with the servants, treat the peasants like animals, educate themselves poorly, read nothing seriously, do absolutely nothing; about science they just talk and about art they understand very little. Every one of them is serious, all have stern faces; they all talk of nothing but important things, philosophize, and all the time everybody can see that the workmen eat abominably, sleep without any pillows, thirty or forty to a room, and everywhere there are bedbugs, stench, dampness, moral uncleanness — And apparently with us, all the fine talk is only to divert the attention of ourselves and of others. Show me where we have the day nurseries they are always talking so much about, where are the reading rooms? They only write of these in novels, for the truth is there are not any at all. There is only filth, vulgarity, orientalism — I am afraid of very serious faces and dislike them. I'm afraid of serious conversations. Rather than that let's just keep still.

LOPAHIN: You know I get up before five o'clock in the morning and work from morning till night. Well, I always have money, my own and other people's, on hand, and I see what the people around me are. One has only to start doing something to find out how few honest and decent people there are. At times when I can't go to sleep, I think: Lord, thou gavest us immense forests, unbounded fields and the widest horizons, and living in the midst of them we should indeed be giants —

LYUBOFF ANDREEVNA: You feel the need for giants — They are good only in fairy tales, anywhere else they only frighten us.

(At the back of the stage EPIHODOFF *passes by, playing the guitar.)*

LYUBOFF ANDREEVNA *(lost in thought)*: Epihodoff is coming —

ANYA *(lost in thought)*: Epihodoff is coming.

GAYEFF: The sun has set, ladies and gentlemen.

TROFIMOFF: Yes.

GAYEFF *(not loud and as if he were declaiming)*: Oh, Nature, wonderful, you gleam with eternal radiance, beautiful and indifferent, you, whom we call Mother, combine in yourself both life and death, you give life and you take it away.

VARYA *(beseechingly)*: Uncle!

ANYA: Uncle, you're doing it again!

TROFIMOFF: You'd better bank the yellow into the side pocket.

GAYEFF: I'll be quiet, quiet.

(All sit absorbed in their thoughts. There is only the silence. FIERS *is heard muttering to himself softly. Suddenly a distant*

sound is heard, as if from the sky, like the sound of a snapped string, dying away, mournful.)

LYUBOFF ANDREEVNA: What's that?

LOPAHIN: I don't know. Somewhere far off in a mine shaft a bucket fell. But somewhere very far off.

GAYEFF: And it may be some bird — like a heron.

TROFIMOFF: Or an owl —

LYUBOFF ANDREEVNA (*shivering*): It's unpleasant, somehow. (*A pause.*)

FIERS: Before the disaster it was like that. The owl hooted and the samovar hummed without stopping, both.

GAYEFF: Before what disaster?

FIERS: Before the emancipation. (*A pause.*)

LYUBOFF ANDREEVNA: You know, my friends, let's go. Twilight is falling. (*To* ANYA.) You have tears in your eyes — What is it, my dear little girl? (*Embracing her.*)

ANYA: It's just that, Mama. It's nothing.

TROFIMOFF: Somebody is coming.

(*A* STRANGER *appears in a shabby white cap, and an overcoat; he is a little drunk.*)

THE STRANGER: Allow me to ask you, can I go straight through here to the station?

GAYEFF: You can. Go by that road.

THE STRANGER: I am heartily grateful to you. (*Coughing.*) The weather is splendid — (*Declaiming.*) Brother of mine, suffering brother — Go out to the Volga, whose moans — (*To* VARYA.) Mademoiselle, grant a hungry Russian man some thirty kopecks —

(VARYA *is frightened and gives a shriek.*)

LOPAHIN (*angrily*): There's a limit to everything.

LYUBOFF ANDREEVNA (*flustered*): Take this — Here's this for you — (*Searching in her purse.*) No silver — It's all the same, here's a gold piece for you —

THE STRANGER: I am heartily grateful to you. (*Goes out. Laughter.*)

VARYA (*frightened*): I'm going — I'm going — Oh, Mama, you poor little Mama! There's nothing in the house for people to eat, and you gave him a gold piece.

LYUBOFF ANDREEVNA: What is to be done with me, so silly? I shall give you all I have in the house. Yermolay Alexeevich, you will lend me some this once more! —

LOPAHIN: Agreed.

LYUBOFF ANDREEVNA: Let's go, ladies and gentlemen, it's time. And here, Varya, we have definitely made a match for you, I congratulate you.

VARYA (*through her tears*): Mama, that's not something to joke about.

LOPAHIN: Achmelia, get thee to a nunnery.

GAYEFF: And my hands are trembling; it is a long time since I have played billiards.

LOPAHIN: Achmelia, oh nymph, in thine orisons be all my sins remember'd —

LYUBOFF ANDREEVNA: Let's go, my dear friends, it will soon be suppertime.

VARYA: He frightened me. My heart is thumping so!

LOPAHIN: I remind you, ladies and gentlemen: August twenty-second the cherry orchard will be auctioned off. Think about that! — Think! —

(*All go out except* TROFIMOFF *and* ANYA.)

ANYA (*laughing*): My thanks to the stranger, he frightened Varya, now we are alone.

TROFIMOFF: Varya is afraid we might begin to love each other and all day long she won't leave us to ourselves. With her narrow mind she cannot understand that we are above love. To sidestep the petty and illusory, which prevent our being free and happy, that is the aim and meaning of our life. Forward! We march on irresistibly toward the bright star that burns there in the distance. Forward! Do not fall behind, friends!

ANYA (*extending her arms upward*): How well you talk! (*A pause.*) It's wonderful here today!

TROFIMOFF: Yes, the weather is marvelous.

ANYA: What have you done to me, Petya, why don't I love the cherry orchard any longer the way I used to? I loved it so tenderly, it seemed to me there was not a better place on earth than our orchard.

TROFIMOFF: All Russia is our orchard. The earth is immense and beautiful, and on it are many wonderful places. (*A pause.*) Just think, Anya: your grandfather, great-grandfather and all your ancestors were slave owners, in possession of living souls, and can you doubt that from every cherry in the orchard, from every leaf, from every trunk, human beings are looking at you, can it be that you don't hear their voices? To possess living souls, well, that depraved all of you who lived before and who are living now, so that your mother and you, and your uncle no longer notice that you live by debt, at somebody else's expense, at the expense of those very people whom you wouldn't let past your front door — We are at least two hundred years behind the times, we have as yet absolutely nothing, we have no definite attitude toward the past, we only philosophize, complain of our sadness or drink vodka. Why, it is quite clear that to begin to live in the present we must first atone for our past, must be done with it; and we can atone for it only through suffering, only through uncommon, incessant labor. Understand that, Anya.

ANYA: The house we live in ceased to be ours long ago, and I'll go away, I give you my word.

TROFIMOFF: If you have the household keys, throw them in the well and go away. Be free as the wind.

ANYA (*transported*): How well you said that!

TROFIMOFF: Believe me, Anya, believe me! I am not thirty yet, I am young, I am still a student, but I have already borne so much! Every winter I am hungry, sick, anxious, poor as a beggar, and — where has destiny not chased me, where haven't I been! And yet, my soul has always, every minute, day and night, been full of inexplicable premonitions. I have a premonition of happiness, Anya, I see it already —

ANYA (*pensively*): The moon is rising.

(EPIHODOFF *is heard playing on the guitar, always the same sad song. The moon rises. Somewhere near the poplars* VARYA *is looking for* ANYA *and calling: "Anya! Where are you?"*)

TROFIMOFF: Yes, the moon is rising. (*A pause.*) Here is happiness, here it comes, comes always nearer and nearer, I hear its footsteps now. And if we shall not see it, shall not come to know it, what does that matter? Others will see it!

VARYA (*off*): Anya! Where are you?

TROFIMOFF: Again, that Varya! (*Angrily.*) It's scandalous!

ANYA: Well, let's go to the river. It's lovely there.

TROFIMOFF: Let's go. (*They go out.*)

VARYA (*off*): Anya! Anya!

ACT THREE

(*The drawing room, separated by an arch from the ballroom. A chandelier is lighted. A Jewish orchestra is playing — the same that was mentioned in Act Two. Evening. In the ballroom they are dancing* grand rond. *The voice of* SEMYONOFF-PISHTCHIK: *"Promenade à une paire!" They enter the drawing room; in the first couple are* PISHTCHIK *and* CHARLOTTA IVANOVNA; *in the second,* TROFIMOFF *and* LYUBOFF ANDREEVNA; *in the third,* ANYA *with the* POST-OFFICE CLERK; *in the fourth,* VARYA *with the* STA-

TIONMASTER, *et cetera* — VARYA *is crying softly and wipes away her tears while she is dancing.* DUNYASHA *is in the last couple through the drawing room,* PISHTCHIK *shouts: "Grand rond, balancez!" and "Les Cavaliers à genoux et remerciez vos dames!"*

FIERS *in a frock coat goes by with seltzer water on a tray.* PISHTCHIK *and* TROFIMOFF *come into the drawing room.*)

PISHTCHIK: I am full-blooded, I have had two strokes already, and dancing is hard for me, but as they say, if you are in a pack of dogs, you may bark and bark, but you must still wag your tail. At that, I have the health of a horse. My dear father — he was a great joker — may he dwell in Heaven — used to talk as if our ancient line, the Semyonoff-Pishtchiks, were descended from the very horse that Caligula made a Senator — (*Sitting down.*) But here's my trouble: I haven't any money. A hungry dog believes in nothing but meat — (*Snoring but waking at once.*) And the same way with me — I can't talk about anything but money.

TROFIMOFF: Well, to tell you the truth, there is something of a horse about your figure.

PISHTCHIK: Well — a horse is a fine animal — You can sell a horse —

(*The sound of playing billiards comes from the next room.* VARYA *appears under the arch to the ballroom.*)

TROFIMOFF (*teasing*): Madam Lopahin! Madam Lopahin!

VARYA (*angrily*): A mangy-looking gentleman!

TROFIMOFF: Yes, I am a mangy-looking gentleman, and proud of it!

VARYA (*in bitter thought*): Here we have gone and hired musicians and what are we going to pay them with? (*Goes out.*)

TROFIMOFF (*to* PISHTCHIK): If the energy you have wasted in the course of your life trying to find money to pay the interest had gone into something else, you could very likely have turned the world upside down before you were done with it.

PISHTCHIK: Nietzsche — the philosopher — the greatest — the most celebrated — a man of tremendous mind — says in his works that one may make counterfeit money.

TROFIMOFF: And have you read Nietzsche?

PISHTCHIK: Well — Dashenka told me. And I'm in such a state now that I could make counterfeit money myself — Day after tomorrow three hundred and ten roubles must be paid — one hundred and thirty I've on hand — (*Feeling in his pockets, alarmed.*) The money is gone! I have lost the money! (*Tearfully.*) Where is the money? (*Joyfully.*) Here it is, inside the lining — I was in quite a sweat —

(LYUBOFF ANDREEVNA *and* CHARLOTTA IVANOVNA *come in.*)

LYUBOFF ANDREEVNA (*humming lazginka, a Georgian dance*): Why does Leonid take so long? What's he doing in town? (*To* DUNYASHA.) Dunyasha, offer the musicians some tea —

TROFIMOFF: In all probability the auction did not take place.

LYUBOFF ANDREEVNA: And the musicians came at an unfortunate moment and we planned the ball at an unfortunate moment — Well, it doesn't matter. (*Sitting down and singing softly.*)

CHARLOTTA (*gives* PISHTCHIK *a deck of cards*): Here is a deck of cards for you, think of some one card.

PISHTCHIK: I have thought of one.

CHARLOTTA: Now, shuffle the deck. Very good. Hand it here; oh, my dear Monsieur Pishtchik. *Ein, zwei, drei!* Now look for it, it's in your coat pocket —

PISHTCHIK (*getting a card out of his coat pocket*): The Eight of Spades, that's absolutely right! (*Amazed.*) Fancy that!

CHARLOTTA (*holding a deck of cards in her palm; to* TROFIMOFF): Tell me quick now, which card is on top?

TROFIMOFF: What is it? Well — the Queen of Spades.

CHARLOTTA: Right! (*To* PISHTCHIK.) Well? Which card's on top?

PISHTCHIK: The Ace of Hearts.

CHARLOTTA: Right! (*Strikes the deck against her palm; the deck of cards disappears.*) And what beautiful weather we are having today!

(*A mysterious feminine voice answers her, as if from under the floor: "Oh, yes. The weather is splendid, madame." "You are so nice, you're my ideal —" The voice: "Madame, you too please me greatly."*)

THE STATIONMASTER (*applauding*): Madam Ventriloquist, bravo!

PISHTCHIK (*amazed*): Fancy that! Most charming Charlotta Ivanovna — I am simply in love with you.

CHARLOTTA: In love? (*Shrugging her shoulders.*) Is it possible that you can love? *Guter menschaber schlachter musikant.*

TROFIMOFF (*slapping* PISHTCHIK *on the shoulder*): You horse, you —

CHARLOTTA: I beg your attention, one more trick. (*Taking a lap robe from the chair.*) Here is a very fine lap robe — I want to sell it — (*Shaking it out.*) Wouldn't somebody like to buy it?

PISHTCHIK (*amazed*): Fancy that!

CHARLOTTA: *Ein, zwei, drei!*

(*She quickly raises the lowered robe, behind it stands* ANYA, *who curtseys, runs to her mother, embraces her and runs back into the ballroom amid the general delight.*)

LYUBOFF ANDREEVNA (*applauding*): Bravo, bravo — !

CHARLOTTA: Now again! *Ein, zwei, drei!*

(*Lifting the robe: behind it stands* VARYA, *she bows.*)

PISHTCHIK (*amazed*): Fancy that!

CHARLOTTA: That's all. (*Throwing the robe at* PISHTCHIK, *curtseying and running into the ballroom.*)

PISHTCHIK (*hurrying after her*): You little rascal— What a girl! What a girl! (*Goes out.*)

LYUBOFF ANDREEVNA: And Leonid is not here yet. What he's doing in town so long, I don't understand! Everything is finished there, either the estate is sold by now, or the auction didn't take place. Why keep it from us so long?

VARYA (*trying to comfort her*): Uncle has bought it, I am sure of that.

TROFIMOFF (*mockingly*): Yes.

VARYA: Great-aunt sent him power of attorney to buy it in her name and transfer the debt. She did this for Anya. And I feel certain, God willing, that Uncle will buy it.

LYUBOFF ANDREEVNA: Our Yaroslavl great-aunt has sent fifteen thousand to buy the estate in her name—She doesn't trust us, but that wouldn't be enough to pay the interest even—(*Covering her face with her hands.*) Today my fate will be decided, my fate—

TROFIMOFF (*teasing* VARYA): Madam Lopahin!

VARYA (*angrily*): Perennial student! You have already been expelled from the University twice.

LYUBOFF ANDREEVNA: But why are you angry, Varya? He teases you about Lopahin, what of it? Marry Lopahin if you want to, he is a good man, interesting. If you don't want to, don't marry him; darling, nobody is making you do it.

VARYA: I look at this matter seriously, Mama, one must speak straight out. He's a good man, I like him.

LYUBOFF ANDREEVNA: Then marry him. What there is to wait for I don't understand!

VARYA: But I can't propose to him myself, Mama. It's two years now; everyone has been talking to me about him, everyone talks, and he either remains silent or jokes. I understand. He's getting rich, he's busy with his own affairs, and has no time for me. If there were money, ever so little, even a hundred roubles, I would drop everything, and go far away. I'd go to a nunnery.

TROFIMOFF: How saintly!

VARYA (*to* TROFIMOFF): A student should be intelligent! (*In a low voice, tearfully.*) How homely you have grown, Petya, how old you've got. (*To* LYUBOFF ANDREEVNA, *no longer crying.*) It is just that I can't live without working, Mama. I must be doing something every minute

YASHA (YASHA *enters. Barely restraining his laughter.*): Epihodoff has broken a billiard cue! — (*Goes out.*)

VARYA: But why is Epihodoff here? Who allowed him to play billiards? I don't understand these people — (*Goes out.*)

LYUBOFF ANDREEVNA: Don't tease her, Petya; you can see she has troubles enough without that.

TROFIMOFF: She is just too zealous. Sticking her nose into things that are none of her business. All summer she gave us no peace, neither me nor Anya; she was afraid a romance would spring up between us. What business is that of hers? And besides I haven't shown any signs of it. I am so remote from triviality. We are above love!

LYUBOFF ANDREEVNA: Well, then, I must be beneath love. (*Very anxiously.*) Why isn't Leonid here? Just to tell us whether the estate is sold or not? Calamity seems to me so incredible that I don't know what to think, I'm lost — I could scream this minute — I could do something insane. Save me, Petya. Say something, do say. . . .

TROFIMOFF: Whether the estate is sold today or is not sold — is it not the same? There is no turning back, the path is all grown over. Calm yourself, my dear, all that was over long ago. One mustn't deceive oneself, one must for once at least in one's life look truth straight in the eye.

LYUBOFF ANDREEVNA: What truth? You see where the truth is and where the untruth is, but as for me, it's as if I had lost my sight, I see nothing. You boldly decide all important questions, but tell me, my dear boy, isn't that because you are young and haven't had time yet to suffer through any one of your problems? You look boldly ahead, and isn't that because you don't see and don't expect anything terrible, since life is still hidden from your young eyes? You are braver, more honest, more profound than we are, but stop and think, be magnanimous, have a little mercy on me, just a little. Why, I was born here. My father and mother lived here and my grandfather. I love this house, I can't imagine my life without the cherry orchard and if it is very necessary to sell it, then sell me along with the orchard — (*Embracing* TROFIMOFF *and kissing him on the forehead.*) Why, my son was drowned here — (*Crying.*) Have mercy on me, good, kind man.

TROFIMOFF: You know I sympathize with you from the bottom of my heart.

LYUBOFF ANDREEVNA: But that should be said differently, differently — (*Taking out her handkerchief; a telegram falls on the floor.*) My heart is heavy today, you can't imagine how heavy. It is too noisy for me here, my soul trembles at every sound, I tremble all over and yet I can't go off to myself, when I am alone the silence frightens me. Don't blame me, Petya — I love you as one of my own. I should gladly have given you Anya's hand, I assure you, only, my dear, you must study and finish your course. You do nothing. Fate simply flings you about from place to place, and that's so strange — Isn't that so? Yes? And you must do something about your beard, to make it grow somehow — (*Laughing.*) You look funny!

TROFIMOFF (*picking up the telegram*): I do not desire to be beautiful.

LYUBOFF ANDREEVNA: This telegram is from Paris. I get one every day. Yesterday and today too. That wild man has fallen ill again, something is wrong again with him — He asks forgiveness, begs me to come, and really I ought to make a trip to Paris and stay awhile near him. Your face looks stern, Petya, but what is there to do, my dear, what am I to do, he is ill, he is alone, unhappy and who will look after him there, who will keep him from doing the wrong thing, who will give him his medicine on time? And what is there to hide or keep still about? I love him, that's plain. I love him, love him — It's a stone about my neck, I'm sinking to the bottom with it, but I love that stone and live without it I cannot. (*Pressing* TROFIMOFF'S *hand.*) Don't think harshly of me, Petya, don't say anything to me, don't —

TROFIMOFF (*tearfully*): Forgive my frankness, for God's sake! Why, he picked your bones.

LYUBOFF ANDREEVNA: No, no, no, you must not talk like that. (*Stopping her ears.*)

TROFIMOFF: But he is a scoundrel, only you, you are the only one that doesn't know it. He is a petty scoundrel, a nonentity —

LYUBOFF ANDREEVNA (*angry but controlling herself*): You are twenty-six years old or twenty-seven, but you are still a schoolboy in the second grade!

TROFIMOFF: Very well!

LYUBOFF ANDREEVNA: You should be a man — at your age you should understand people who love. And you yourself should love someone — you should fall in love! (*Angrily.*) Yes, yes! And there is no purity in you; you are simply smug, a ridiculous crank, a freak —

TROFIMOFF (*horrified*): What is she saying!

LYUBOFF ANDREEVNA: "I am above love!" You are not above love, Petya, you are, as our Fiers would say, just a good-for-nothing. Imagine, at your age, not having a mistress — !

TROFIMOFF (*horrified*): This is terrible! What is she saying! (*Goes *quickly into the ballroom, clutching his head.*) This is horrible — I can't bear it, I am going — (*Goes out but immediately returns.*) All is over between us. (*Goes out into the hall.*)

LYUBOFF ANDREEVNA (*shouting after him*): Petya, wait! You funny creature, I was joking! Petya! (*In the hall you hear someone running up the stairs and suddenly falling back down with a crash. You hear* ANYA *and* VARYA *scream but immediately you hear laughter.*) What's that?

ANYA (ANYA *runs in. Laughing*): Petya fell down the stairs! (*Runs out.*)

LYUBOFF ANDREEVNA: What a funny boy that Petya is — ! (*The* STATIONMASTER *stops in the center of the ballroom and begins to recite "The Sinner" by A. Tolstoi. They listen to him but he has recited only a few lines when the strains of a waltz are heard from the hall and the recitation is broken off. They all dance.* TROFIMOFF, ANYA, VARYA *and* LYUBOFF ANDREEVNA *come in from the hall.*) But, Petya — but, dear soul — I beg your forgiveness — Let's go dance. (*She dances with* TROFIMOFF. ANYA *and* VARYA *dance.* FIERS *enters, leaving his stick by the side door.* YASHA *also comes into the drawing room and watches the dancers.*)

YASHA: What is it, Grandpa?

FIERS: I don't feel very well. In the old days there were generals, barons, admirals dancing at our parties, and now we send for the post-office clerk and the stationmaster, and even they are none too anxious to come. Somehow I've grown feeble. The old master, the grandfather, treated everybody with sealing-wax for all sicknesses. I take sealing-wax every day, have done so for twenty-odd years or more; it may be due to that that I'm alive.

YASHA: You are tiresome, Grandpa. (*Yawning.*) Why don't you go off and die?

FIERS: Aw, you — good-for-nothing! — (*Muttering.*)

(TROFIMOFF *and* LYUBOFF ANDREEVNA *dance in the ballroom and then in the drawing room.*)

LYUBOFF ANDREEVNA: *Merci.* I'll sit down awhile — (*Sitting down.*) I'm tired.

ANYA (ANYA *enters. Agitated*): And just now in the kitchen some man was saying that the cherry orchard had been sold today.

LYUBOFF ANDREEVNA: Sold to whom?

ANYA: He didn't say who to. He's gone.

(*Dancing with* TROFIMOFF, *they pass into the ballroom.*)

YASHA: It was some old man babbling there. A stranger.

FIERS: And Leonid Andreevich is still not here, he has not arrived. The overcoat he has on is light, midseason — let's hope he won't catch cold. Ach, these young things!

LYUBOFF ANDREEVNA: I shall die this minute. Go, Yasha, find out who it was sold to.

YASHA: But he's been gone a long time, the old fellow. (*Laughing.*)

LYUBOFF ANDREEVNA (*with some annoyance*): Well, what are you laughing at? What are you so amused at?

YASHA: Epihodoff is just too funny. An empty-headed man. Twenty-two misfortunes!

LYUBOFF ANDREEVNA: Fiers, if the estate is sold, where will you go?

FIERS: Wherever you say, there I'll go.

LYUBOFF ANDREEVNA: Why do you look like that? Aren't you well? You know you ought to go to bed —

FIERS: Yes — (*With a sneer.*) I go to bed and without me who's going to serve, who'll take care of things? I'm the only one in the whole house.

YASHA (*to* LYUBOFF ANDREEVNA): Lyuboff Andreevna, let me ask a favor of you, do be so kind! If you ever go back to Paris, take me with you, please do! It's impossible for me to stay here. (*Looking around him, and speaking in a low voice.*) Why talk about it? You can see for yourself it's an uncivilized country, an immoral people and not only that, there's the boredom of it. The food they give us in that kitchen is abominable and there's that Fiers, too, walking about and muttering all kinds of words that are out of place. Take me with you, be so kind!

PISHTCHIK (*enters*): Allow me to ask you — for a little waltz, most beautiful lady — (LYUBOFF ANDREEVNA *goes with him.*) Charming lady, I must borrow a hundred and eighty roubles from you — will borrow — (*dancing*) a hundred and eighty roubles — (*They pass into the ballroom.*)

YASHA (*singing low*): "Wilt thou know the unrest in my soul!"

(*In the ballroom a figure in a gray top hat and checked trousers waves both hands and jumps about; there are shouts of "Bravo, Charlotta Ivanovna!"*)

DUNYASHA (*stopping to powder her face*): The young lady orders me to dance — there are a lot of gentlemen and very few ladies — but dancing makes my head swim and my heart thump. Fiers Nikolaevich, the post-office clerk said something to me just now that took my breath away.

(*The music plays more softly.*)

FIERS: What did he say to you?

DUNYASHA: You are like a flower, he says.

YASHA (*yawning*): What ignorance — ! (*Goes out.*)

DUNYASHA: Like a flower — I am such a sensitive girl, I love tender words awfully.

FIERS: You'll be getting your head turned.

(EPIHODOFF *enters.*)

EPIHODOFF: Avdotya Feodorovna, you don't want to see me — It's as if I were some sort of insect. (*Sighing.*) Ach, life!

DUNYASHA: What do you want?

EPIHODOFF: Undoubtedly you may be right. (*Sighing.*) But of course, if one considers it from a given point of view, then you, I will allow myself so to express it, forgive my frankness, absolutely led me into a state of mind. I know my fate, every day some misfortune happens to me, but I have long since become accustomed to that, and so I look on my misfortunes with a smile. You gave me your word and, although I —

DUNYASHA: I beg you, we'll talk later on, but leave me now in peace. I'm in a dream now. (*Playing with her fan.*)

EPIHODOFF: I have a something wrong happens every day — I will allow myself so to express it — I just smile, I even laugh.

VARYA (*enters from the ballroom*): You are not gone yet, Semyon? What a really disrespectful man you are! (*To* DUNYASHA.) Get out of here, Dunyasha. (*To* EPIHODOFF.) You either play billiards and break a cue or you walk about the drawing room like a guest.

EPIHODOFF: Allow me to tell you, you cannot make any demands on me.

VARYA: I'm not making any demands on you, I'm talking to you. All you know is to walk from place to place but not do any work. We keep a clerk, but what for, nobody knows.

EPIHODOFF (*offended*): Whether I work, whether I walk, whether I eat, or whether I play billiards are matters to be discussed only by people of understanding and my seniors.

VARYA: You dare to say that to me! (*Flying into a temper.*) You dare? So I don't understand anything? Get out of here! This minute!

EPIHODOFF (*alarmed*): I beg you to express yourself in a delicate manner.

VARYA (*beside herself*): This very minute, get out of here! Get out! (*He goes to the door; she follows him.*) Twenty-two misfortunes! Don't you dare breathe in here! Don't let me set eyes on you! (EPIHODOFF *has gone out, but his voice comes from outside the door: "I shall complain about you."*) Ah, you are coming back? (*Grabbing the stick that* FIERS *put by the door.*) Come on, come —

come on, I'll show you — Ah, you are coming? You are coming? Take that then — !

(*She swings the stick, at the very moment when* LOPAHIN *is coming in.*)

LOPAHIN: Most humbly, I thank you.

VARYA (*angrily and ironically*): I beg your pardon!

LOPAHIN: It's nothing at all. I humbly thank you for the pleasant treat.

VARYA: It isn't worth your thanks. (*Moving away, then looking back and asking gently.*) I haven't hurt you?

LOPAHIN: No, it's nothing. There's a great bump coming though.

(*Voices in the balllroom: "Lopahin has come back." "Yermolay Alexeevich!"*)

PISHTCHIK (*enters*): See what we see, hear what we hear — ! (*He and* LOPAHIN *kiss one another.*) You smell slightly of cognac, my dear, my good old chap. And we are amusing ourselves here too.

LYUBOFF ANDREEVNA (*enters*): It that you, Yermolay Alexeevich? Why were you so long? Where is Leonid?

LOPAHIN: Leonid Andreevich got back when I did, he's coming.

LYUBOFF ANDREEVNA (*agitated*): Well, what? Was there an auction? Do speak!

LOPAHIN (*embarrassed, afraid of showing the joy he feels*): The auction was over by four o'clock — We were late for the train, had to wait till half-past nine. (*Sighing heavily.*) Ugh, my head's swimming a bit!

(GAYEFF *enters; with his right hand he carries his purchases, with his left he wipes away his tears.*)

LYUBOFF ANDREEVNA: Lyona, what? Lyona, eh? (*Impatiently, with tears in her eyes.*) Quick, for God's sake —

GAYEFF (*not answering her, merely waving his hand; to* FIERS, *crying*): Here, take it — There are anchovies, some Kertch herrings — I haven't eaten anything all day — What I have suffered! (*The door into the billiard room is open; you hear the balls clicking and* YASHA*'s voice: "Seven and eighteen!"* GAYEFF*'s expression changes, he is no longer crying.*) I'm terribly tired. You help me change, Fiers. (*Goes to his room through the ballroom,* FIERS *behind him.*)

PISHTCHIK: What happened at the auction? Go on, tell us!

LYUBOFF ANDREEVNA: Is the cherry orchard sold?

LOPAHIN: It's sold.

LYUBOFF ANDREEVNA: Who bought it?

LOPAHIN: I bought it. (*A pause.* LYUBOFF ANDREEVNA *is overcome. She would have fallen had she not been standing near the chair and table.* VARYA *takes the keys from her belt, throws them on the floor in the middle of the drawing room and goes out.*) I bought it. Kindly wait a moment, ladies and gentlemen, everything is muddled up in my head, I can't speak — (*Laughing.*) We arrived at the auction, Deriganoff was already there. Leonid Andreevich had only fifteen thousand and Deriganoff right off bids thirty over and above indebtedness. I see how things are, I match him with forty thousand. He forty-five. I fifty-five. That is to say he raises it by fives, I by tens — So it ended. Over and above the indebtedness, I bid up to ninety thousand, it was knocked down to me. The cherry orchard is mine now. Mine! (*Guffawing.*) My God, Lord, the cherry orchard is mine! Tell me I'm drunk, out of my head, that I'm imagining all this — (*Stamps his feet.*) Don't laugh at me! If only my father and grandfather could rise from their graves and see this whole business, see how their Yermolay, beaten, half-illiterate Yermolay, who used to run around barefoot in winter, how that very Yermolay has bought an estate that nothing in the world can beat. I bought the estate where grandfather and father were slaves, where you wouldn't even let me in the kitchen. I am asleep, it's only some dream of mine, it only seems so to me — That's nothing but the fruit of your imagination, covered with the darkness of the unknown — (*Picking up the keys, with a gentle smile.*) She threw down the keys, wants to show she is not mistress any more — (*Jingling the keys.*) Well, it's all the same. (*The orchestra is heard tuning up.*) Hey, musicians, play, I want to hear you! Come on, everybody, and see how Yermolay Lopahin will swing the ax in the cherry orchard, how the trees will fall to the ground! We are going to build villas and our grandsons and great-grandsons will see a new life here — Music, play! (*The music is playing.* LYUBOFF ANDREEVNA *has sunk into a chair, crying bitterly.* LOPAHIN *reproachfully.*) Why, then, didn't you listen to me? My poor dear, it can't be undone now. (*With tears.*) Oh, if this could all be over soon, if somehow our awkward, unhappy life would be changed!

PISHTCHIK (*taking him by the arm, in a low voice*): She is crying. Come on in the ballroom, let her be by herself — Come on — (*Taking him by the arm and leading him into the ballroom.*)

LOPAHIN: What's the matter? Music, there, play up! (*Sarcastically.*) Everything is to be as I want it! Here comes the new squire, the owner of the cherry orchard. (*Quite accidentally, he bumps into the little table, and very nearly upsets the candelabra.*) I can pay for everything!

(Goes out with PISHTCHIK. *There is nobody left either in the ballroom or the drawing room but* LYUBOFF ANDREEVNA, *who sits all huddled up and crying bitterly. The music plays softly.* ANYA *and* TROFIMOFF *enter hurriedly.* ANYA *comes up to her mother and kneels in front of her.* TROFIMOFF *remains at the ballroom door.)*

ANYA: Mama — ! Mama, you are crying? My dear, kind, good Mama, my beautiful, I love you — I bless you. The cherry orchard is sold, it's not ours any more, that's true, true; but don't cry, Mama, you've your life still left you, you've your good, pure heart ahead of you — Come with me, come on, darling, away from here, come on — We will plant a new orchard, finer than this one, you'll see it, you'll understand; and joy, quiet, deep joy will sink into your heart, like the sun at evening, and you'll smile, Mama! Come, darling, come on!

ACT FOUR

(The same setting as in Act One. There are neither curtains on the windows nor are there any pictures on the walls. Only a little furniture remains piled up in one corner as if for sale. A sense of emptiness is felt. Near the outer door, at the rear of the stage, is a pile of suitcases, traveling bags, and so on. The door on the left is open, and through it VARYA'S *and* ANYA'S *voices are heard.* LOPAHIN *is standing waiting.* YASHA *is holding a tray with glasses of champagne. In the hall* EPIHODOFF *is tying up a box, offstage at the rear there is a hum. It is the peasants who have come to say good-by.* GAYEFF'S *voice: "Thanks, brothers, thank you.")*

YASHA: The simple folk have come to say good-by. I am of the opinion, Yermolay Alexeevich, that the people are kind enough but don't understand anything.

(The hum subsides. LYUBOFF ANDREEVNA *enters through the hall with* GAYEFF; *she is not crying, but is pale, her face quivers, she is not able to speak.)*

GAYEFF: You gave them your purse, Lyuba. Mustn't do that! Mustn't do that!

LYUBOFF ANDREEVNA: I couldn't help it! I couldn't help it!

(Both go out.)

LOPAHIN *(calling through the door after them)*: Please, I humbly beg you! A little glass at parting. I didn't think to bring some from town, and at the station I found just one bottle. Please! (*A pause.*) Well, then, ladies and gentlemen! You don't want it? (*Moving away from the door.*) If I'd known that, I wouldn't have bought it. Well, then I won't drink any either. (YASHA *carefully sets the tray down on a chair.*) At least, you have some, Yasha.

YASHA: To those who are departing! Pleasant days to those who stay behind! (*Drinking.*) This champagne is not the real stuff, I can assure you.

LOPAHIN: Eight roubles a bottle. (*A pause.*) It's devilish cold in here.

YASHA: They didn't heat up today, we are leaving anyway. (*Laughing.*)

LOPAHIN: What are you laughing about?

YASHA: For joy.

LOPAHIN: Outside it's October, but it's sunny and still, like summer. Good for building. (*Looking at his watch, then through the door.*) Ladies and gentlemen, bear in mind we have forty-six minutes in all till train time! Which means you have to go to the station in twenty minutes. Hurry up a little.

TROFIMOFF (*in an overcoat, entering from outside*): Seems to me it is time to go. The carriages are ready. The devil knows where my rubbers are. They've disappeared. (*In the door.*) Anya, my rubbers are not here! I can't find them.

LOPAHIN: And I have to go to Harkoff. I'm going on the same train with you. I'm going to live in Harkoff all winter. I've been dilly-dallying along with you, I'm tired of doing nothing. I can't be without work, look, I don't know what to do with my hands here, see, they are dangling somehow, as if they didn't belong to me.

TROFIMOFF: We are leaving right away, and you'll set about your useful labors again.

LOPAHIN: Here, drink a glass.

TROFIMOFF: I shan't.

LOPAHIN: It's to Moscow now?

TROFIMOFF: Yes. I'll see them off to town, and tomorrow to Moscow.

LOPAHIN: Yes — Maybe the professors are not giving their lectures. I imagine they are waiting till you arrive.

TROFIMOFF: That's none of your business.

LOPAHIN: How many years is it you've been studying at the University?

TROFIMOFF: Think of something newer. This is old and flat. (*Looking for his rubbers.*) You know, perhaps, we shall not see each other again; therefore, permit me to give you one piece of advice at parting! Don't wave your arms! Cure yourself of that habit — of arm waving. And also of building summer cottages, figuring that the summer residents will in time become individual landowners; figuring like that is arm waving too — Just the same, however, I like you.

You have delicate soft fingers like an artist, you have a delicate soft heart —

LOPAHIN (*embracing him*): Good-by, my dear boy. Thanks for everything. If you need it, take some money from me for the trip.

TROFIMOFF: Why should I? There's no need for it.

LOPAHIN: But you haven't any!

TROFIMOFF: I have. Thank you. I got some for a translation. Here it is in my pocket. (*Anxiously.*) But my rubbers are gone.

VARYA (*from another room*): Take your nasty things! (*Throws a pair of rubbers on to the stage.*)

TROFIMOFF: But what are you angry about, Varya? Hm — Why, these are not my rubbers.

LOPAHIN: In the spring I planted twenty-seven hundred acres of poppies and now I've made forty thousand clear. And when my poppies were in bloom, what a picture it was! So look, as I say, I've made forty thousand, which means I'm offering you a loan because I can afford to. Why turn up your nose? I'm a peasant — I speak straight out.

TROFIMOFF: Your father was a peasant, mine — an apothecary — and from that absolutely nothing follows. (LOPAHIN *takes out his wallet.*) Leave it alone, leave it alone — If you gave me two hundred thousand even, I wouldn't take it. I am a free man. And everything that you all value so highly and dearly, both rich man and beggars, has not the slightest power over me, it's like a mere feather floating in the air. I can get along without you, I can pass you by, I am strong and proud. Humanity is moving toward the loftiest truth, toward the loftiest happiness that is possible on earth and I am in the front ranks.

LOPAHIN: Will you get there?

TROFIMOFF: I'll get there. (*A pause.*) I'll get there, or I'll show the others the way to get there.

(*In the distance is heard the sound of an ax on a tree.*)

LOPAHIN: Well, good-by, my dear boy. It's time to go. We turn up our noses at one another, but life keeps on passing. When I work a long time without stopping, my thoughts are clearer, and it seems as if I, too, know what I exist for, and, brother, how many people are there in Russia who exist, nobody knows for what? Well, all the same, it's not that that keeps things circulating. Leonid Andreevich, they say, has accepted a position — he'll be in a bank, six thousand a year — the only thing is he won't stay there, he's very lazy —

ANYA (*in the doorway*): Mama begs of you until she's gone, not to cut down the orchard.

TROFIMOFF: Honestly, haven't you enough tact to — (*Goes out through the hall.*)

LOPAHIN: Right away, right away — What people, really! (*Goes out after him.*)

ANYA: Has Fiers been sent to the hospital?

YASHA: I told them to this morning. They must have sent him.

ANYA (*to* EPIHODOFF, *who is passing through the room*): Semyon Panteleevich, please inquire whether or not they have taken Fiers to the hospital.

YASHA (*huffily*): This morning, I told Igor. Why ask ten times over!

EPIHODOFF: The venerable Fiers, according to my conclusive opinion, is not worth mending, he ought to join his forefathers. And I can only envy him. (*Putting a suitcase on a hatbox and crushing it.*) Well, there you are, of course. I knew it. (*Goes out.*)

YASHA (*mockingly*): Twenty-two misfortunes —

VARYA (*on the other side of the door*): Have they taken Fiers to the hospital?

ANYA: They have.

VARYA: Then why didn't they take the letter to the doctor?

ANYA: We must send it on after them — (*Goes out.*)

VARYA (*from the next room*): Where is Yasha? Tell him his mother has come, she wants to say good-by to him.

YASHA (*waving his hand*): They merely try my patience.

(DUNYASHA *has been busying herself with the luggage; now when* YASHA *is left alone, she goes up to him.*)

DUNYASHA: If you'd only look at me once, Yasha. You are going away — leaving me — (*Crying and throwing herself on his neck.*)

YASHA: Why are you crying? (*Drinking champagne.*) In six days I'll be in Paris again. Tomorrow we will board the express train and dash off out of sight; somehow, I can't believe it. *Vive la France!* It doesn't suit me here — I can't live here — Can't help that. I've seen enough ignorance — enough for me. (*Drinking champagne.*) Why do you cry? Behave yourself properly, then you won't be crying.

DUNYASHA (*powdering her face, looking into a small mirror*): Send me a letter from Paris. I loved you, Yasha, you know, loved you so! I am a tender creature, Yasha!

YASHA: They are coming here. (*Bustling about near the suitcases, humming low.*)

(LYUBOFF ANDREEVNA, GAYEFF, ANYA *and* CHARLOTTA IVANOVNA *enter.*)

GAYEFF: We should be going. There is very little time left. (*Looking at* YASHA.) Who is it smells like herring!

LYUBOFF ANDREEVNA: In about ten minutes let's be in the carriage — (*Glancing around the room.*) Good-by, dear house, old Grandfather. Winter will pass, spring will be here, but you won't be here any longer, they'll tear you down. How much these walls have seen! (*Kissing her daughter warmly.*) My treasure, you are beaming, your eyes are dancing like two diamonds. Are you happy? Very?

ANYA: Very! It's the beginning of a new life, Mama!

GAYEFF (*gaily*): Yes, indeed, everything is fine now. Before the sale of the cherry orchard, we all were troubled, distressed, and then when the question was settled definitely, irrevocably, we all calmed down and were even cheerful — I'm a bank official. I am a financier now — Yellow ball into the side pocket, anyway, Lyuba, you look better, no doubt about that.

LYUBOFF ANDREEVNA: Yes. My nerves are better, that's true. (*They hand her her hat and coat.*) I sleep well. Carry out my things, Yasha. It's time. (*To* ANYA.) My little girl, we shall see each other again soon — I am going to Paris, I shall live there on the money your Yaroslavl great-aunt sent for the purchase of the estate — long live Great-aunt! But that money won't last long.

ANYA: Mama, you'll come back soon, soon — Isn't that so? I'll prepare myself, pass the examination at high school, and then I'll work, I will help you. We'll read all sorts of books together. Mama, isn't that so? (*Kissing her mother's hands.*) We'll read in the autumn evenings, read lots of books, and a new, wonderful world will open up before us — (*Daydreaming.*) Mama, do come —

LYUBOFF ANDREEVNA: I'll come, my precious. (*Embracing her daughter.*)

(LOPAHIN *enters with* CHARLOTTA *who is softly humming a song.*)

GAYEFF: Lucky Charlotta: she's singing!

CHARLOTTA (*taking a bundle that looks like a baby wrapped up*): My baby, bye, bye — (*A baby's cry is heard: Ooah, ooah — !*) Hush, my darling, my dear little boy. (*Ooah, ooah — !*) I am so sorry for you! (*Throwing the bundle back.*) Will you please find me a position? I cannot go on like this.

LOPAHIN: We will find something, Charlotta Ivanovna, don't worry.

GAYEFF: Everybody is dropping us, Varya is going away. — All of a sudden we are not needed.

CHARLOTTA: I have no place in town to live. I must go away. (*Humming.*) It's all the same —

(PISHTCHIK *enters.*)

LOPAHIN: The freak of nature — !

PISHTCHIK (*out of breath*): Ugh, let me catch my breath — I'm exhausted — My honored friends — Give me some water —

GAYEFF: After money, I suppose? This humble servant will flee from sin! (*Goes out.*)

PISHTCHIK: It's a long time since I was here — Most beautiful lady — (*To* LOPAHIN.) You here — ? Glad to see you — a man of the greatest intellect — Here — Take it — (*Giving* LOPAHIN *some money.*) Four hundred roubles — That leaves eight hundred and forty I still owe you —

LOPAHIN (*with astonishment, shrugging his shoulders*): I must be dreaming. But where did you get it?

PISHTCHIK: Wait — I'm hot — Most extraordinary event. Some Englishmen came and found on my land some kind of white clay — (*To* LYUBOFF ANDREEVNA.) And four hundred for you — Beautiful lady — Wonderful lady — (*Handing over the money.*) The rest later. (*Taking a drink of water.*) Just now a young man was saying on the train that some great philosopher recommends jumping off roofs — "Jump!" he says, and "therein lies the whole problem." (*With astonishment.*) You don't say! Water!

LOPAHIN: And what Englishmen were they?

PISHTCHIK: I leased them the parcel of land with the clay for twenty-four years — And now, excuse me, I haven't time — I must run along — I'm going to Znoykoff's — To Kardamonoff's — I owe everybody — (*Drinking.*) I wish you well — I'll drop in on Thursday —

LYUBOFF ANDREEVNA: We are moving to town right away, and tomorrow I'm going abroad —

PISHTCHIK: What? (*Alarmed.*) Why to town? That's why I see furniture — Suitcases — Well, no matter — (*Tearfully.*) No matter — Men of the greatest minds — those Englishmen — No matter — Good luck! God will help you — No matter — Everything in this world comes to an end — (*Kissing* LYUBOFF ANDREEVNA'S *hand.*) And should the report reach you that my end has come, think of that well-known horse and say: "There was once on earth a so and so — Semyonoff Pishtchik — The kingdom of Heaven be his." Most remarkable weather — yes — (*Going out greatly disconcerted, but immediately returning and speaking from the door.*) Dashenka sends her greetings! (*Goes out.*)

LYUBOFF ANDREEVNA: And now we can go. I am leaving with two worries. First, that Fiers is sick. (*Glancing at her watch.*) We still have five minutes —

ANYA: Mama, Fiers has already been sent to the hospital. Yasha sent him off this morning.

LYUBOFF ANDREEVNA: My second worry — is Varya. She is used to getting up early and working, and now without any work she is like a fish out of water. She has grown thin, pale and cries all the time, poor thing — (*A pause.*) You know this, Yermolay Alexeevich: I dreamed — of marrying her to you. And there was every sign of your getting married. (*Whispering to* ANYA, *who beckons to* CHARLOTTA; *both go out.*) She loves you, you are fond of her, and I don't know, don't know why it is you seem to avoid each other — I don't understand it!

LOPAHIN: I don't understand it either, I must confess. It's all strange somehow — If there's still time, I am ready right now even — Let's finish it up — and *basta*, but without you I feel I won't propose.

LYUBOFF ANDREEVNA: But that's excellent. Surely it takes only a minute. I'll call her at once.

LOPAHIN: And to fit the occasion there's the champagne. (*Looking at the glasses.*) Empty, somebody has already drunk them. (YASHA *coughs.*) That's what's called lapping it up —

LYUBOFF ANDREEVNA (*vivaciously*): Splendid! We'll go out — Yasha, *allez!* I'll call her — (*Through the door.*) Varya, drop everything and come here. Come on! (*Goes out with* YASHA)

LOPAHIN (*looking at his watch*): Yes —

(*A pause. Behind the door you hear smothered laughter, whispering, finally* VARYA *enters.*)

VARYA (*looking at the luggage a long time*): That's strange, I just can't find it —

LOPAHIN: What are you looking for?

VARYA: I packed it myself and don't remember where. (*A pause.*)

LOPAHIN: Where do you expect to go now, Varvara Mikhailovna?

VARYA: I? To Regulin's. I agreed to go there to look after the house — As a sort of housekeeper.

LOPAHIN: That's in Yashnevo? It's nigh on to seventy miles. (*A pause.*) And here ends life in this house —

VARYA (*examining the luggage*): But where is it? Either I put it in the trunk, perhaps — Yes, life in this house is ended — it won't be any more —

LOPAHIN: And I am going to Harkoff now — By the next train. I've a lot to do. And I am leaving Epihodoff — on the ground here — I've hired him.

VARYA: Well!

LOPAHIN: Last year at this time it had already been snowing, if you remember, and now it's quiet, it's sunny. It's only that it's cold, about three degrees of frost.

VARYA: I haven't noticed. (*A pause.*) And besides our thermometer is broken — (*A pause. A voice from the yard through the door.*) Yermolay Alexeevich —

LOPAHIN (*as if he had been expecting this call for a long time*): This minute! (*Goes out quickly.*)

(VARYA, *sitting on the floor, putting her head on a bundle of clothes, sobs quietly. The door opens,* LYUBOFF ANDREEVNA *enters cautiously.*)

VARYA (*she is not crying any longer, and has wiped her eyes*): Yes, it's time, Mama. I can get to Regulin's today, if we are just not too late for the train — (*Through the door.*) Anya, put your things on! (ANYA, *then* GAYEFF *and* CHARLOTTA IVANOVNA *enter.* GAYEFF *has on a warm overcoat, with a hood. The servants gather, also the drivers.* EPIHODOFF *busies himself with the luggage.*) Now we can be on our way.

ANYA (*joyfully*): On our way!

GAYEFF: My friends, my dear, kind friends! Leaving this house forever, can I remain silent, can I restrain myself from expressing, as we say, farewell, those feelings that fill now my whole being —

ANYA (*beseechingly*): Uncle!

VARYA: Dear Uncle, don't!

GAYEFF (*dejectedly*): Bank the yellow into the side pocket — I am silent —

(TROFIMOFF *and then* LOPAHIN *enter.*)

TROFIMOFF: Well, ladies and gentlemen, it's time to go!

LOPAHIN: Epihodoff, my coat!

LYUBOFF ANDREEVNA: I'll sit here just a minute more. It's as if I had never seen before what the walls in this house are like, what kind of ceilings, and now I look at them greedily, with such tender love —

GAYEFF: I remember when I was six years old, on Trinity Day, I sat in this window and watched my father going to Church —

LYUBOFF ANDREEVNA: Are all the things taken out?

LOPAHIN: Everything, I think. (*Putting on his overcoat. To* EPIHODOFF.) Epihodoff, you see that everything is in order.

EPIHODOFF (*talking in a hoarse voice*): Don't worry, Yermolay Alexeevich!

LOPAHIN: Why is your voice like that?

EPIHODOFF: Just drank some water, swallowed something.

YASHA (*with contempt*): The ignorance —

LYUBOFF ANDREEVNA: We are going and there won't be a soul left here —

LOPAHIN: Till spring.

VARYA (*she pulls an umbrella out from a bundle, it looks as if she were going to hit someone;* LOPAHIN *pretends to be frightened*): What do you, what do you — I never thought of it.

TROFIMOFF: Ladies and gentlemen, let's get in the carriages — It's time! The train is coming any minute.

VARYA: Petya, here they are, your rubbers, by the suitcase. (*Tearfully.*) And how dirty yours are, how old — !

TROFIMOFF (*putting on the rubbers*): Let's go, ladies and gentlemen!

GAYEFF (*greatly embarrassed, afraid he will cry*): The train — The station — Cross into the side, combination off the white into the corner —

LYUBOFF ANDREEVNA: Let's go!

LOPAHIN: Everybody here? Nobody there? (*Locking the side door on the left.*) Things are stored here, it must be locked up, let's go!

ANYA: Good-by, house! Good-by, the old life!

TROFIMOFF: Long live the new life!

(*Goes out with* ANYA. VARYA *casts a glance around the room and, without hurrying, goes out.* YASHA *and* CHARLOTTA, *with her dog, go out.*)

LOPAHIN: And so, till spring. Out, ladies and gentlemen — Till we meet. (*Goes out.*)

(LYUBOFF ANDREEVNA *and* GAYEFF *are left alone. As if they had been waiting for this, they throw themselves on one another's necks sobbing, but smothering their sobs as if afraid of being heard.*)

GAYEFF (*in despair*): Oh, Sister, Sister —

LYUBOFF ANDREEVNA: Oh, my dear, my lovely, beautiful orchard! My life, my youth, my happiness, good-by!

ANYA (ANYA's *voice, gaily, appealingly*): Mama — !

TROFIMOFF (TROFIMOFF's *voice, gaily, excitedly*): Aaooch!

LYUBOFF ANDREEVNA: For the last time, just to look at the walls, at the window — My dear mother used to love to walk around in this room —

GAYEFF: Oh, Sister, Sister — !

ANYA (ANYA's *voice*): Mama — !

TROFIMOFF (TROFIMOFF's *voice*): Aaooch — !

LYUBOFF ANDREEVNA: We are coming! (*They go out.*)

(The stage is empty. You hear the keys locking all the doors, then the carriages drive off. It grows quiet. In the silence you hear the dull thud of an ax on a tree, a lonely, mournful sound. Footsteps are heard. From the door on the right FIERS *appears. He is dressed as usual, in a jacket and a white waistcoat, slippers on his feet. He is sick.)*

FIERS *(going to the door and trying the knob)*: Locked. They've gone. *(Sitting down on the sofa.)* They forgot about me — No matter — I'll sit here awhile — And Leonid Andreevich, for sure, didn't put on his fur coat, he went off with his topcoat — *(Sighing anxiously.)* And I didn't see to it — The young saplings! *(He mutters something that cannot be understood.)* Life has gone by, as if I hadn't lived at all — *(Lying down.)* I'll lie down awhile — You haven't got any strength, nothing is left, nothing — Ach, you — good-for-nothing — *(He lies still.)*

(There is a far-off sound as if out of the sky, the sound of a snapped string, dying away, sad. A stillness falls, and there is only the thud of an ax on a tree, far away in the orchard.)

The beginning of the second act of *The Cherry Orchard* is a particularly concise collocation of characteristics found in all of Chekhov's last four plays. Since the plays are so often misunderstood and since a main cause of misunderstanding is the failure to realize what Chekhov was doing and the assumption that he was trying to do something else, the passage may repay a closer look.

Its four characters are all employed in the Ranevskaya household, and all are minor: Charlotta, a governess of indeterminate youthfulness and cosmopolitan circus background; Epihodoff, a foolish clerk, whose dignity of speech and bearing continually collapses in pratfalls and jammed syntax; the maid Dunyasha, with whom Epihodoff is in love; and the brash young valet Yasha, Epihodoff's successful rival. They are together for no particular purpose. There is a touch of pathos in Charlotta's situation and perhaps in Epihodoff's, but none of the four is really an attractive character. They do not know each other very well and do not establish any close rapport. Their words bound off other words or drop, echoless, in a void of indifference and self-absorption. When Charlotta ends her opening monologue with a plea for human contact, Epihodoff breaks into song on the all-sufficiency of love. He is joined in singing by his rival Yasha. Dunyasha tells them they sound "like jackals." Alone with Yasha Dunyasha tells him she loves him. Yasha replies that he considers a girl who is in love immoral. Talk is desultory, punctuated by pauses and yawns. The constant changes in topic are incoherent: foreign travel, suicide, a cockroach in a glass of beer, an early Victorian philosopher. The setting is desolate: sunset among forgotten tombstones near an abandoned chapel, the cherry orchard on one side and a large town looming on the horizon.

One hesitates calling such a passage a "scene," because "scene" suggests a distinct unit within a larger plot dynamic. But no plot is furthered by this casual group, no phase of action marked, no issue raised or concluded, no climax prepared. The impression of aimless and listless small talk remains even when the passage is seen in the context of the whole play. At its end Charlotta is as lost and lonely as she is here, and Epihodoff neither kills himself nor ever stops stumbling over or crushing things or tangling his sentences. Neither her rifle nor his revolver is ever mentioned again, let alone fired. The Epihodoff–Dunyasha–Yasha triangle ends in stalemate, like the other two tentative romances in the play, Lopahin's and Varya's, and Anya's and Trofimoff's. None of the four characters here influences the issue of whether or not the estate is to be sold or otherwise affects the destiny of the major characters.

To people used to the taut, significant action patterns of western drama from Sophocles through Shakespeare and Ibsen, Chekhov's status as major dramatist may seem puzzling. The tension between Mme Ranevskaya and her equally vague and ineffectual brother Gayeff on the one hand and the concerned and practical merchant Lopahin on the other on how to save the mortgaged estate provides *The Cherry Orchard* with more suspense and plot coherence than Chekhov's other important plays. Nevertheless, what coherence the play possesses is rather in the nature of frame than of substance. As in *The Sea-Gull, Uncle Vanya,* and *Three Sisters* most of the drama proceeds, like our sample passage, by incongruent juxtapositions of little banalities and irrelevancies, fatuities and incoherences — random fragments of life lifted on stage from a continuing flow of trivia to make an irregular, languid rhythm of inconsequence. Take the episode in Act I when Pishtchik swallows Mme Ranevskaya's (Lyuboff Andreevna's) pills.

PISHTCHIK: You should never take medicament, dear madam — They do neither harm nor good — Hand them here, dearest lady. (*He takes the pillbox, shakes the pills out into his palm, blows on them, puts them in his mouth and washes them down with kvass.*) There! Now!

LYUBOFF ANDREEVNA (*Startled*): Why, you've lost your mind!

PISHTCHIK: I took all the pills.
LOPAHIN: Such a glutton!
(*Everyone laughs.*)

And that is the end of the episode. The pills are not missed, we are never told what Mme Ranevskaya takes pills for, Pishtchik does not get sick, they do not alter his behavior in any way, nobody ever refers to them again. By the rules of sound play construction one should be shocked by such casualness and waste and demand to know the relevance of the incident. But its relevance is its non-relevance to anything beyond its own inanity. Of such isolated bits of humdrum life, as startling as they are pointless, is Chekhov's world made. No wonder he found Ibsen "too simple" and disliked him for not "knowing life." To judge by his own plays, what he objected to in the Norwegian was his reduction of the rich and chaotic complexity of experience to tightly plotted melodrama of thematic import, in which every event is a link in a causal chain and every speech reveals character or contributes to the theme. Economy of means to a significant end is the Ibsen hallmark. Chekhov is lavish with apparently useless character and incident. His plays are not unplanned, and their quality of improvised rambling is the result of scrupulous craftsmanship, but his realism is of the inclusive kind that not only can afford but needs items that have no other function than to make a moment of live drama. Near the close of Act II there is heard, "as if from the sky," a "mournful" sound, "like the sound of a snapped string." A few moments later, a drunken beggar appears. If only because of mere proximity, is there a connection between sound and man? What do they mean? How do they function in the drama? The questions are unanswerable, even — in the sense in which they usually are asked — impertinent. We can only say that without the sound and the beggar a dimension of reality would be gone from the scene. Instead of Ibsen's stripped and strictly functional casts Chekhov prodigally peoples the Ranevskaya estate with a chorus of semi-grotesque retainers and hangers-on, for whom there is no more a definite function in the plot than there appears to be in the running of the household. The quartet in the opening of Act II are just four of them. He further diffuses the outline of his cast with unseen characters in a kind of ghostly attendance on those on stage: Mme Ranevskaya's dead little boy Grisha, her Paris lover, Gayeff's rich old aunt in Yaroslavl, Pishtchik's clever daughter Dashenka. Swayed by the dead and the absent, the characters we *do* see appear more real and less strong.

Thus, Chekhov builds drama by a kind of pointillism. If we look too close we see only specks of reality, but at a distance a pattern emerges. As sentiment is about to become pathos and tension approaches tragic intensity, a sudden incongruity deflates theme and mood — a moment of slapstick, a change in tempo, an unattuned image or speech, a new topic of conversation. In Act I, when Varya tells Anya of the family's precarious financial position — "In August the estate is to be sold" — Lopahin suddenly sticks his head through the door and moos like a cow. "I'd land him one like that," threatens Varya tearfully, shaking her fist. In Act III she does almost exactly that, by unlucky timing hitting him over the head with a broomstick just as he enters to tell the family that he has bought the estate. In Chekhov, typically, farce impinges on the peripety of the main drama. Lopahin's allusions to Hamlet and Ophelia represent the third coordinate in the system that defines his and Varya's abortive romance in terms partly farcical and partly poignant. Just as Lopahin, the serf's son, impatient with procrastination and a businessman of action himself, is no Prince Hamlet, so is the Ranevskaya estate which he seeks to set right both a more innocent and a pettier world than the realm of Denmark. And poor Varya is only a formidable and rather foolish nun. Tragic grandeur is further deflated by Lopahin's consistent failure to remember Ophelia's name.*

From such discord and ambivalence the play builds its larger patterns. Old Fiers considers the emancipation of the serfs in 1863 a disaster. In contrast, Trofimoff, the muddled revolutionary idealist, envisions a brighter Russian future built by liberty and dignified labor. Between past and future the present moves by ceaseless ebb and flow. In Act I, Mme Ranevskaya comes home; in Act IV she goes away. Arrival–departure frames the collection of discordant moments here as in Chekhov's other late plays. But departure is not conclusion. Though something passes, something also comes. The cherry trees fall by the blows of the axe that new enterprise wields. But how great is the loss? After all, the old recipe for drying cherries and keeping them "soft, . . . juicy, sweet, fragrant" is forgotten. But, then, is the main value of the orchard commercial? The beauty of the old order, but also its foolishness and gentle decadence, give way to Lopahin, the entrepreneur, the reluctant heir of the feudal past, including his own childhood and — though he does not know it — the old serf Fiers.

The pattern of change is framed by a still larger pattern. The play begins with Lopahin waking up and ends with Fiers falling asleep. What happens in the interval?

* He also misquotes Shakespeare's lines, a fact which the English translation here does not take notice of. See David Magarshack, *Chekhov the Dramatist* (New York, 1960), pp. 278-279.

> We are such stuff
> As dreams are made on, and our little life
> Is rounded with a sleep.

That is, nothing — and everything. Is it just another odd fact that the first and the last act both take place in a room called "the Nursery" and that it is furnished in Act I and bare in Act IV? To Fiers at the end it is as if life has gone by and left him with a feeling of not having lived at all. Is *The Cherry Orchard* Chekhov's *Tempest* in a deeper sense than by being his last play? Lopahin has been taken to represent the new economic man, the proletarian become a rising merchant, a bourgeois forerunner of the Soviet revolution. Perhaps he is. There certainly is irony in his unawareness of his artistic inclinations and in his inability to escape his serf origin long enough to get himself a genteel wife, either Varya or her foster mother, Mme Ranevskaya herself, who is — as certain of his speeches hint — the woman he really loves. But to seize upon socio-economic symbolism or on Lopahin's psychology as main theme is to lock Chekhov's kaleidoscope in one or the other of only two of its myriad constellations. Life may be "little" in Chekhov, as it is for most people, but the drama in which it is recorded is not impoverished. When people complain that "nothing happens" in Chekhov, one may agree to see what they have in mind. But they are quite wrong.

What is true, however, is that Chekhov's manner of drama is one that makes heavy demands on the *reader.* Few great playwrights gain more from performance than he. His distinctive tonality is muted on the page. In the absence of exciting scenes and strong plot, interest has to depend on imaginative evocation of spectacle, movement, and voice, and this, for most of us, is a new and difficult challenge. If we fail to meet it, bewilderment first and then boredom may follow. The strangeness and the number of the Rusian names are further obstacles.

But even in the theater there are people who find Chekhov too wanly elegiac, slow, and indefinite. Chekhov realized the danger himself and quarreled with the two directors of the Moscow Art Theater for not guarding sufficiently against it. One of them was Konstantin Stanislavsky, whose naturalistic staging of *The Sea-Gull* in 1898 had established Chekhov's reputation as a dramatist and whose painstaking rehearsals, emphasis on ensemble acting, and insistence that the actor engage himself imaginatively and emotionally in his part (we call all this "Method" acting today) were to make him the single most important influence on modern acting. But to Chekhov he was the man who had "ruined" his *Cherry Orchard.* In an effort, perhaps, to avert the disaster he saw was coming he wrote to Stanislavsky's wife even before rehearsals began, in October, 1903: "I'm afraid my play has turned out to be not a drama but a comedy, and in places even a farce, and I fear Nemirovich-Danchenko [the literary director of the Theater] will never forgive me for that." What actually happened was, from Chekhov's point of view, even worse. So far from feeling any need for forgiving Chekhov for having written a comedy, it did not even occur to the two directors that he had not written a tragedy. Some weeks after the first performance of *The Cherry Orchard* in January, 1904, and about four months before his death, Chekhov wrote to his wife about the Stanislavsky production:

> Take my *Cherry Orchard*. Is it my *Cherry Orchard?* With the exception of one or two parts nothing in it is mine. I am describing life, ordinary life, and not blank despondency. They either make me into a cry-baby or a bore. They invent something about me out of their own heads, anything they like, something I never thought of or dreamed about. This is beginning to make me angry.

There is in principle no reason why Stanislavsky and Nemirovich-Danchenko cannot have perceived the nature of *The Cherry Orchard* more clearly than Chekhov himself. But did they? Most producers have heeded the playwright's protests against a tragic *Cherry Orchard,* but few have staged it as a comedy or agreed with Chekhov that Lopahin's part is comical and the whole play "gay and frivolous." For most people, on either side of the footlights, Chekhov remains the twilight voice of old Russia, a bittersweet realist poet of mood and atmosphere, the sympathetic–ironic chronicler of the heartaches and frustrations and failures of decent but foolishly weak and confused people. What comedy there is in Chekhov is in a very minor key indeed, at most arch and acid, very rarely hearty. Trofimoff, for example, is an undoubted fool, and yet he is made the spokesman of genuine values: the blessings of work and love. Other visionary idealists in Chekhov are also presented as fatuous escapists into vague and wordy optimism.

From the vantage point of today we may wonder whether Chekhov, were he still alive, would have persisted in using "comedy" and "farce" as labels for *The Cherry Orchard*. To turn again to the opening of Act II, consider the following exchange:

CHARLOTTA: . . . Who my parents were, perhaps they weren't even married — I don't know. (*Taking a cucumber out of her pocket and beginning to eat it*) I don't know a thing. (A *pause.*) I'd like so much to talk but there's not anybody. I haven't anybody.

EPIHODOFF (*playing the guitar and singing*): "What care I for the noisy world, what care I for friends and foes." — How pleasant it is to play the mandolin!

DUNYASHA: That's a guitar, not a mandolin. (*Looking in a little mirror and powdering her face.*)

EPIHODOFF: For a madman who is in love this is a mandolin — (*Singing.*) "If only my heart were warm with the fire of requited love."

(YASHA *sings with him.*)

This is quintessential Chekhov, but it might have come from a contemporary play of the absurd theater. Without a "proper passport" and with her sense of lostness and isolation in a meaningless existence — "Who I am, why I am, is unknown" — Charlotta becomes an almost Kafkaesque figure in a parable of modern man's existential agony. In her military cap, tinkering with a rifle, eating a cucumber, holding forth in unhappy monologue, she is a figure of pathetic farce as well. The incongruity is "absurd" in the modern, literary, sense. She and Epihodoff are equally lonely, but their monodies produce only discord. The scenic and verbal imagery of guitar and cigar, guns and pocket mirror, jackals, spider, cockroach, and a serving-maid's lily white, ladylike hands belongs in an odd, vaguely disturbing dream. "Absurd" also is people's failure to relate through language. Charlotta's sudden vaudeville tricks come to seem less like farcical interruptions than like symptoms of an isolation desperately battered by the inarticulate prisoner within. Epihodoff reads important books he cannot understand and which fail to convince him that life is worth living. For lack of human respondents Gayeff apostrophizes bookcases and Nature and hides his embarrassment in billiard jargon and candy. As means to overcome a breakdown in communication his antics resemble Charlotta's tricks. Since experience is wholly subjective, there can be no stable relationship between word and meaning:

DUNYASHA: That's a guitar, not a mandolin. . . .

EPIHODOFF: For a madman who is in love this is a mandolin — . . .

Even the lovers fail to communicate:

DUNYASHA: I have come to love you passionately, you are educated, you can discuss anything. (*A pause.*)

YASHA (*yawning*): Yes sir — . . .

Certainly there is comedy here, even farce, but is that *all* there is?

The point is not that Chekhov anticipated the absurd theater some sixty years ago or that today's absurdists are indebted to him — not even, though this is true, that the absurd manner is not the invention of existential playwrights of the last decade. The point of Chekhov's "absurdity" is the more general one that art always "is" and does not "mean" and that modern art has made a fetish and a program of what previous generations of artists tacitly took for granted.

Not that Chekhov, of course, is "meaningless" — literally — any more than are playwrights like Beckett and Genet. Art cannot be "meaningless" — literally — and still remain art (which is why people who make nothing of the absurdists quite properly deny them status as dramatists). "Absurd" is a silly epithet for drama that takes reality too seriously to presume to subject it to interpretation or judgment or to arrangement by laws of narrative. The dictum that art be without meaning means that its meaning should be inviolately implicit and centripetal. The artist's image of reality does not derive its authority from a non-art original and does not justify itself by any intention of altering such an original, for however commendable an end. Chekhov was occasionally provoked into claiming for his plays a pragmatic value for lethargic, end-of-the-century Russian inelligentsia — object lessons in how *not* to manage the business of life — but their uncompromising objectivity suggests that the claim was only an effort to speak a language that dull producers could understand. With reference to this specific case: in the opening of Act II of *The Cherry Orchard* Chekhov is not telling us that life is trivial, futile, and solitary or asking us to do something about it. He is showing us some trivial, futile, and solitary moments in a scenic imitation of life. The distinction is all-important: ultimately that between an election poster and Rembrandt. "You ask me what life is?" he once wrote to his wife. "It is like asking what a carrot is. A carrot is a carrot; that's all we know." The artist records facts: people, places, things, words. But held in the artist's vision, they catch the comical or frightening but always vulnerable human pose — "the lust of the flesh and the soul's incurable loneliness" — between the quaint, incontrovertible events of birth and death. Our most vital drama, old and contemporary, claims to do no more and no less.

J. M. Synge

THE PLAYBOY OF THE WESTERN WORLD

ACT I

(*Country public-house or shebeen,*[1] *very rough and untidy. There is a sort of counter on the right with shelves, holding many bottles and jugs, just seen above it. Empty barrels stand near the counter. At back, a little to left of counter, there is a door into the open air, then, more to the left, there is a settle with shelves above it, with more jugs, and a table beneath a window. At the left there is a large open fireplace, with turf fire, and a small door into inner room.* PEGEEN, *a wild-looking but fine girl, of about twenty, is writing at table. She is dressed in the usual peasant dress.*)

PEGEEN (*slowly as she writes*): Six yards of stuff for to make a yellow gown. A pair of lace boots with lengthy heels on them and brassy eyes. A hat is suited [2] for a wedding-day. A fine-tooth comb. To be sent with three barrels of porter in Jimmy Farrell's creel cart on the evening of the coming Fair to Mister Michael James Flaherty. With the best compliments of this season. Margaret Flaherty.

SHAWN KEOGH (*a fat and fair young man comes in as she signs, looks round awkwardly, when he sees she is alone*): Where's himself?

PEGEEN (*without looking at him*): He's coming. (*She directs letter.*) To Mister Sheamus Mulroy, Wine and Spirit Dealer, Castlebar.

SHAWN (*uneasily*): I didn't see him on the road.

PEGEEN: How would you see him (*licks stamp and puts it on letter*) and it dark night this half-hour gone by?

SHAWN (*turning towards door again*): I stood a while outside wondering would I have a right to pass on or to walk in and see you, Pegeen

[1] tavern [2] that is suitable

Mike (*comes to fire*), and I could hear the cows breathing and sighing in the stillness of the air, and not a step moving any place from this gate to the bridge.

PEGEEN (*putting letter in envelope*): It's above at the crossroads he is, meeting Philly Cullen and a couple more are going along with him to Kate Cassidy's wake.

SHAWN (*looking at her blankly*): And he's going that length in the dark night.

PEGEEN (*impatiently*): He is surely, and leaving me lonesome on the scruff of the hill. (*She gets up and puts envelope on dresser, then winds clock.*) Isn't it long the nights are now, Shawn Keogh, to be leaving a poor girl with her own self counting the hours to the dawn of day?

SHAWN (*with awkward humour*): If it is, when we're wedded in a short while you'll have no call to complain, for I've little will to be walking off to wakes or weddings in the darkness of the night.

PEGEEN (*with rather scornful good-humour*): You're making mighty certain Shaneen, that I'll wed you now.

SHAWN: Aren't we after making a good bargain, the way we're only waiting these days on Father Reilly's dispensation from the bishops, or the Court of Rome.

PEGEEN (*looking at him teasingly, washing up at dresser*): It's a wonder, Shaneen, the Holy Father'd be taking notice of the likes of you; for if I was him I wouldn't bother with this place where you'll meet none but Red Linahan, has a squint in his eye, and Patcheen is lame in his heel, or the mad Mulrannies were driven from California and they lost in their wits. We're a queer lot these times to go troubling the Holy Father on his sacred seat.

SHAWN (*scandalized*): If we are, we're as good this place as another, maybe, and as good these times as we were for ever.

PEGEEN (*with scorn*): As good, is it? Where now will you meet the like of Daneen Sullivan knocked the eye from a peeler; [3] or Marcus Quin, God rest him, got six months for maiming ewes, and he a great warrant to tell stories of holy Ireland till he'd have the old women shedding down tears about their feet. Where will you find the like of them, I'm saying?

SHAWN (*timidly*): If you don't, it's a good job, maybe; for (*with peculiar emphasis on the words*) Father Reilly has small conceit [4] to have that kind walking around and talking to the girls.

PEGEEN (*impatiently throwing water from basin out of the door*): Stop tormenting me with Father Reilly (*imitating his voice*) when I'm

[3] policeman, "bobby" [4] doesn't like

asking only what way I'll pass these twelve hours of dark, and not take my death with the fear. (*Looking out of door.*)

SHAWN (*timidly*): Would I fetch you the Widow Quin, maybe?

PEGEEN: Is it the like of that murderer? You'll not, surely.

SHAWN (*going to her, soothingly*): Then I'm thinking himself will stop along with you when he sees you taking on; for it'll be a long night-time with great darkness, and I'm after feeling a kind of fellow above in the furzy ditch, groaning wicked like a maddening dog, the way it's good cause you have, maybe, to be fearing now.

PEGEEN (*turning on him sharply*): What's that? Is it a man you seen?

SHAWN (*retreating*): I couldn't see him at all; but I heard him groaning out, and breaking his heart. It should have been a young man from his words speaking.

PEGEEN (*going after him*): And you never went near to see was he hurted or what ailed him at all?

SHAWN: I did not, Pegeen Mike. It was a dark, lonesome place to be hearing the like of him.

PEGEEN: Well, you're a daring fellow, and if they find his corpse stretched above in the dews of dawn, what'll you say then to the peelers, or the Justice of the Peace?

SHAWN (*thunderstruck*): I wasn't thinking of that. For the love of God, Pegeen Mike, don't let on I was speaking of him. Don't tell your father and the men is coming above; for if they heard that story they'd have great blabbing this night at the wake.

PEGEEN: I'll maybe tell them, and I'll maybe not.

SHAWN: They are coming at the door. Will you whisht,[5] I'm saying?

PEGEEN: Whisht yourself.

(*She goes behind counter.* MICHAEL JAMES, *fat jovial publican, comes in followed by* PHILLY CULLEN, *who is thin and mistrusting, and* JIMMY FARRELL, *who is fat and amorous, about forty-five.*)

MEN (*together*): God bless you! The blessing of God on this place!

PEGEEN: God bless you kindly.

MICHAEL (*to men, who go to the counter*): Sit down now, and take your rest. (*Crosses to* SHAWN *at the fire.*) And how is it you are, Shawn Keogh? Are you coming over the sands to Kate Cassidy's wake?

SHAWN: I am not, Michael James. I'm going home the short cut to my bed.

PEGEEN (*speaking across the counter*): He's right, too, and have you

[5] be quiet, shut up

no shame, Michael James, to be quitting off for the whole night, and leaving myself lonesome in the shop?

MICHAEL (*good-humouredly*): Isn't it the same whether I go for the whole night or a part only? and I'm thinking it's a queer daughter you are if you'd have me crossing backward through the Stooks[6] of the Dead Women, with a drop taken.

PEGEEN: If I am a queer daughter, it's a queer father'd be leaving me lonesome these twelve hours of dark, and I piling the turf with the dogs barking, and the calves mooing, and my own teeth rattling with the fear.

JIMMY (*flatteringly*): What is there to hurt you, and you a fine, hardy girl would knock the head of any two men in the place?

PEGEEN (*working herself up*): Isn't there the harvest boys with their tongues red for drink, and the ten tinkers is camped in the east glen, and the thousand militia — bad cess[7] to them! — walking idle through the land. There's lots surely to hurt me, and I won't stop alone in it, let himself do what he will.

MICHAEL: If you're that afeard, let Shawn Keogh stop along with you. It's the will of God, I'm thinking, himself should be seeing to you now.

(*They all turn on* SHAWN.)

SHAWN (*in horrified confusion*): I would and welcome, Michael James, but I'm afeard of Father Reilly; and what at all would the Holy Father and the Cardinals of Rome be saying if they heard I did the like of that?

MICHAEL (*with contempt*): God help you! Can't you sit in by the hearth with the light lit and herself beyond in the room? You'll do that surely, for I've heard tell there's a queer fellow above, going mad or getting his death, maybe, in the gripe[8] of the ditch, so she'd be safer this night with a person here.

SHAWN (*with plaintive despair*): I'm afeard of Father Reilly, I'm saying. Let you not be tempting me, and we near married itself.

PHILLY (*with cold contempt*): Lock him in the west room. He'll stay then and have no sin to be telling to the priest.

MICHAEL (*to* SHAWN, *getting between him and the door*): Go up now.

SHAWN (*at the top of his voice*): Don't stop me, Michael James. Let me out of the door, I'm saying, for the love of the Almighty God. Let me out. (*Trying to dodge past him.*) Let me out of it, and may God grant you His indulgence in the hour of need.

MICHAEL (*loudly*): Stop your noising, and sit down by the hearth.

6 bundles of sheaves, shocks, of cut grain ("Stooks of the Dead Women" = a local place name) 7 luck 8 trough

(*Gives him a push and goes to counter laughing.*)

SHAWN (*turning back, wringing his hands*): Oh, Father Reilly, and the saints of God, where will I hide myself today? Oh, St. Joseph and St. Patrick and St. Brigid and St. James, have mercy on me now! (SHAWN *turns round, sees door clear, and makes a rush for it.*)

MICHAEL (*catching him by the coat-tail*): You'd be going, is it?

SHAWN (*screaming*): Leave me go, Michael James, leave me go, you old Pagan, leave me go, or I'll get the curse of the priests on you, and of the scarlet-coated bishops of the Courts of Rome. (*With a sudden movement he pulls himself out of his coat, and disappears out of the door, leaving his coat in* MICHAEL'*s hands.*)

MICHAEL (*turning round, and holding up coat*): Well, there's the coat of a Christian man. Oh, there's sainted glory this day in the lonesome west; and by the will of God I've got you a decent man, Pegeen, you'll have no call to be spying after if you've a score of young girls, maybe, weeding in your fields.

PEGEEN (*taking up the defence of her property*): What right have you to be making game of a poor fellow for minding the priest, when it's your own the fault is, not paying a penny pot-boy to stand along with me and give me courage in the doing of my work? (*She snaps the coat away from him, and goes behind counter with it.*)

MICHAEL (*taken aback*): Where would I get a pot-boy? Would you have me send the bellman screaming in the streets of Castlebar?

SHAWN (*opening the door a chink and putting in his head, in a small voice*): Michael James!

MICHAEL (*imitating him*): What ails you?

SHAWN: The queer dying fellow's beyond looking over the ditch. He's come up, I'm thinking, stealing your hens. (*Looks over his shoulder.*) God help me, he's following me now (*he runs into room*), and if he's heard what I said, he'll be having my life, and I going home lonesome in the darkness of the night.

(*For a perceptible moment they watch the door with curiosity. Someone coughs outside. Then* CHRISTY MAHON, *a slight young man, comes in very tired and frightened and dirty.*)

CHRISTY (*in a small voice*): God save all here!

MEN: God save you kindly!

CHRISTY (*going to the counter*): I'd trouble you for a glass of porter, woman of the house.

(*He puts down coin.*)

PEGEEN (*serving him*): You're one of the tinkers, young fellow, is beyond camped in the glen?

CHRISTY: I am not; but I'm destroyed walking.

MICHAEL (*patronizingly*): Let you come up then to the fire. You're looking famished with the cold.

CHRISTY: God reward you. (*He takes up his glass and goes a little way across to the left, then stops and looks about him.*) Is it often the polis do be coming into this place, master of the house?

MICHAEL: If you'd come in better hours, you'd have seen "Licensed for the Sale of Beer and Spirits, to be Consumed on the Premises," written in white letters above the door, and what would the polis want spying on me, and not a decent house within four miles, the way every living Christian is a bona fide,[9] saving one widow alone?

CHRISTY (*with relief*): It's a safe house, so. (*He goes over to the fire, sighing and moaning. Then he sits down, putting his glass beside him, and begins gnawing a turnip, too miserable to feel the others staring at him with curiosity.*)

MICHAEL (*going after him*): Is it yourself is fearing the polis? You're wanting,[10] maybe?

CHRISTY: There's many wanting.

MICHAEL: Many, surely, with the broken harvest and the ended wars. (*He picks up some stockings, etc., that are near the fire, and carries them away furtively.*) It should be larceny, I'm thinking?

CHRISTY (*dolefully*): I had it in my mind it was a different word and a bigger.

PEGEEN: There's a queer lad. Were you never slapped in school, young fellow, that you don't know the name of your deed?

CHRISTY (*bashfully*): I'm slow at learning, a middling scholar only.

MICHAEL: If you're a dunce itself, you'd have a right to know that larceny's robbing and stealing. Is it for the like of that you're wanting?

CHRISTY (*with a flash of family pride*): And I the son of a strong farmer (*with a sudden qualm*), God rest his soul, could have bought up the whole of your old house a while since, from the butt of his tail-pocket, and not have missed the weight of it gone.

MICHAEL (*impressed*): If it's not stealing, it's maybe something big.

CHRISTY (*flattered*): Aye; it's maybe something big.

JIMMY: He's a wicked-looking young fellow. Maybe he followed after a young woman on a lonesome night.

CHRISTY (*shocked*): Oh, the saints forbid, mister; I was all times a decent lad.

PHILLY (*turning on* JIMMY): You're a silly man, Jimmy Farrell. He said his father was a farmer a while since, and there's himself now

[9] of the Catholic faith (?) [10] wanted (by the police)

in a poor state. Maybe the land was grabbed from him, and he did what any decent man would do.

MICHAEL (*to* CHRISTY, *mysteriously*): Was it bailiffs?

CHRISTY: The divil a one.

MICHAEL: Agents?

CHRISTY: The divil a one.

MICHAEL: Landlords?

CHRISTY (*peevishly*): Ah, not at all, I'm saying. You'd see the like of them stories on any little paper of a Munster town. But I'm not calling to mind any person, gentle, simple, judge or jury, did the like of me.

(*They all draw nearer with delighted curiosity.*)

PHILLY: Well, that lad's a puzzle-the-world.

JIMMY: He'd beat Dan Davies' circus, or the holy missioners making sermons on the villainy of man. Try him again, Philly.

PHILLY: Did you strike golden guineas out of solder, young fellow, or shilling coins itself?

CHRISTY: I did not, mister, not sixpence nor a farthing coin.

JIMMY: Did you marry three wives maybe? I'm told there's a sprinkling have done that among the holy Luthers of the preaching north.

CHRISTY (*shyly*): I never married with one, let alone with a couple or three.

PHILLY: Maybe he went fighting for the Boers, the like of the man beyond, was judged to be hanged, quartered, and drawn. Were you off east, young fellow, fighting bloody wars for Kruger and the freedom of the Boers?

CHRISTY: I never left my own parish till Tuesday was a week.

PEGEEN (*coming from counter*): He's done nothing, so. (*To* CHRISTY.) If you didn't commit murder or a bad, nasty thing; or false coining, or robbery, or butchery, or the like of them, there isn't anything that would be worth your troubling for to run from now. You did nothing at all.

CHRISTY (*his feelings hurt*): That's an unkindly thing to be saying to a poor orphaned traveller, has a prison behind him, and hanging before, and hell's gap gaping below.

PEGEEN (*with a sign to the men to be quiet*): You're only saying it. You did nothing at all. A soft lad the like of you wouldn't slit the windpipe of a screeching sow.

CHRISTY (*offended*): You're not speaking the truth.

PEGEEN (*in mock rage*): Not speaking the truth, is it? Would you have me knock the head of you with the butt of the broom?

CHRISTY (*twisting round on her with a sharp cry of horror*): Don't strike me. I killed my poor father, Tuesday was a week, for doing the like of that.

PEGEEN (*with blank amazement*): Is it killed your father?

CHRISTY (*subsiding*): With the help of God I did, surely, and that the Holy Immaculate Mother may intercede for his soul.

PHILLY (*retreating with* JIMMY): There's a daring fellow.

JIMMY: Oh, glory be to God!

MICHAEL (*with great respect*): That was a hanging crime, mister honey. You should have had good reason for doing the like of that.

CHRISTY (*in a very reasonable tone*): He was a dirty man, God forgive him, and he getting old and crusty, the way I couldn't put up with him at all.

PEGEEN: And you shot him dead?

CHRISTY (*shaking his head*): I never used weapons. I've no licence, and I'm a law-fearing man.

MICHAEL: It was with a hilted knife maybe? I'm told, in the big world, it's bloody knives they use.

CHRISTY (*loudly, scandalized*): Do you take me for a slaughter-boy?

PEGEEN: You never hanged him, the way Jimmy Farrell hanged his dog from the licence, and had it screeching and wriggling three hours at the butt of a string, and himself swearing it was a dead dog, and the peelers swearing it had life?

CHRISTY: I did not, then. I just riz the loy[11] and let fall the edge of it on the ridge of his skull, and he went down at my feet like an empty sack, and never let a grunt or groan from him at all.

MICHAEL (*making a sign to* PEGEEN *to fill* CHRISTY'S *glass*): And what way weren't you hanged, mister? Did you bury him then?

CHRISTY (*considering*): Aye. I buried him then. Wasn't I digging spuds in the field?

MICHAEL: And the peelers never followed after you the eleven days that you're out?

CHRISTY (*shaking his head*): Never a one of them, and I walking forward facing hog, dog, or divil on the highway of the road.

PHILLY (*nodding wisely*): It's only with a common weekday kind of a murderer them lads would be trusting their carcase, and that man should be a great terror when his temper's roused.

MICHAEL: He should then. (*To* CHRISTY.) And where was it, mister honey, that you did the deed?

CHRISTY (*looking at him with suspicion*): Oh, a distant place, master of the house, a windy corner of high, distant hills.

11 raised the spade

PHILLY (*nodding with approval*): He's a close man, and he's right, surely.

PEGEEN: That'd be a lad with a sense of Solomon to have for a pot-boy, Michael James, if it's the truth you're seeking one at all.

PHILLY: The peelers is fearing him, and if you'd that lad in the house there isn't one of them would come smelling around if the dogs itself were lapping poteen[12] from the dung-pit of the yard.

JIMMY: Bravery's a treasure in a lonesome place, and a lad would [13] kill his father, I'm thinking, would face a foxy divil with a pitchpike on the flags of hell.

PEGEEN: It's the truth they're saying, and if I'd that lad in the house, I wouldn't be fearing the looséd kharki[14] cut-throats, or the walking dead.

CHRISTY (*swelling with surprise and triumph*): Well, glory be to God!

MICHAEL (*with deference*): Would you think well to stop here and be pot-boy, mister honey, if we gave you good wages, and didn't destroy you with the weight of work.

SHAWN (*coming forward uneasily*): That'd be a queer kind to bring into a decent, quiet household with the like of Pegeen Mike.

PEGEEN (*very sharply*): Will you whisht? Who's speaking to you?

SHAWN (*retreating*): A bloody-handed murderer the like of . . .

PEGEEN (*snapping at him*): Whisht, I am saying; we'll take no fooling from your like at all. (*To* CHRISTY *with a honeyed voice.*) And you, young fellow, you'd have a right to stop, I'm thinking, for we'd do our all and utmost to content your needs.

CHRISTY (*overcome with wonder*): And I'd be safe this place from the searching law?

MICHAEL: You would, surely. If they're not fearing you, itself, the peelers in this place is decent, drouthy poor fellows, wouldn't touch a cur dog and not give warning in the dead of night.

PEGEEN (*very kindly and persuasively*): Let you stop a short while anyhow. Aren't you destroyed walking with your feet in bleeding blisters, and your whole skin needing washing like a Wicklow sheep.

CHRISTY (*looking round with satisfaction*): It's a nice room, and if it's not humbugging me you are, I'm thinking that I'll surely stay.

JIMMY (*jumps up*): Now, by the grace of God, herself will be safe this night, with a man killed his father holding danger from the door, and let you come on, Michael James, or they'll have the best stuff drunk at the wake.

MICHAEL (*going to the door with men*): And begging your pardon,

[12] illegally distilled whisky, moonshine [13] who would [14] khaki, *i.e.*, British soldiers

mister, what name will we call you, for we'd like to know?

CHRISTY: Christopher Mahon.

MICHAEL: Well, God bless you, Christy, and a good rest till we meet again when the sun'll be rising to the noon of day.

CHRISTY: God bless you all.

MEN: God bless you.

(*They go out, except* SHAWN, *who lingers at the door.*)

SHAWN (*to* PEGEEN): Are you wanting me to stop along with you and keep you from harm?

PEGEEN (*gruffly*): Didn't you say you were fearing Father Reilly?

SHAWN: There'd be no harm staying now, I'm thinking, and himself in it too.

PEGEEN: You wouldn't stay when there was need for you, and let you step off nimble this time when there's none.

SHAWN: Didn't I say it was Father Reilly . . .

PEGEEN: Go on, then, to Father Reilly (*in a jeering tone*), and let him put you in the holy brotherhoods, and leave that lad to me.

SHAWN: If I meet the Widow Quin . . .

PEGEEN: Go on, I'm saying, and don't be waking this place with your noise. (*She hustles him out and bolts door.*) That lad would wear the spirits from the saints of peace. (*Bustles about, then takes off her apron and pins it up in the window as a blind,* CHRISTY *watching her timidly. Then she comes to him and speaks with bland good-humour.*) Let you stretch out now by the fire, young fellow. You should be destroyed travelling.

CHRISTY (*shyly again, drawing off his boots*): I'm tired surely, walking wild eleven days, and waking fearful in the night. (*He holds up one of his feet, feeling his blisters, and looking at them with compassion.*)

PEGEEN (*standing beside him, watching him with delight*): You should have had great people in your family, I'm thinking, with the little, small feet you have, and you with a kind of a quality name, the like of what you'd find on the great powers and potentates of France and Spain.

CHRISTY (*with pride*): We were great, surely, with wide and windy acres of rich Munster land.

PEGEEN: Wasn't I telling you, and you a fine, handsome young fellow with a noble brow?

CHRISTY (*with a flash of delighted surprise*): Is it me?

PEGEEN: Aye. Did you never hear that from the young girls where you come from in the west or south?

CHRISTY (*with venom*): I did not, then. Oh, they're bloody liars in the naked parish where I grew a man.

PEGEEN: If they are itself, you've heard it these days, I'm thinking, and you walking the world telling out your story to young girls or old.

CHRISTY: I've told my story no place till this night, Pegeen Mike, and it's foolish I was here, maybe, to be talking free; but you're decent people, I'm thinking, and yourself a kindly woman, the way I wasn't fearing you at all.

PEGEEN (*filling a sack with straw*): You've said the like of that, maybe, in every cot and cabin where you've met a young girl on your way.

CHRISTY (*going over to her, gradually raising his voice*): I've said it nowhere till this night, I'm telling you; for I've seen none the like of you the eleven long days I am walking the world, looking over a low ditch or a high ditch on my north or south, into stony, scattered fields, or scribes[15] of bog, where you'd see young, limber girls, and fine, prancing women making laughter with the men.

PEGEEN: If you weren't destroyed travelling, you'd have as much talk and streeleen,[16] I'm thinking, as Owen Roe O'Sullivan or the poets of the Dingle Bay; and I've heard all times it's the poets are your like — fine, fiery fellows with great rages when their temper's roused.

CHRISTY (*drawing a little nearer to her*): You've a power of rings, God bless you, and would there be any offence if I was asking are you single now?

PEGEEN: What would I want wedding so young?

CHRISTY (*with relief*): We're alike, so.

PEGEEN (*she puts sack on settle and beats it up*): I never killed my father. I'd be afeard to do that, except I was the like of yourself with blind rages tearing me within, for I'm thinking you should have had great tussling when the end was come.

CHRISTY (*expanding with delight at the first confidential talk he has ever had with a woman*): We had not then. It was a hard woman was come over the hill; and if he was always a crusty kind when he'd a hard woman setting him on, not the divil himself or his four fathers could put up with him at all.

PEGEEN (*with curiosity*): And isn't it a great wonder that one wasn't fearing you?

CHRISTY (*very confidentially*): Up to the day I killed my father, there wasn't a person in Ireland knew the kind I was, and I there drinking, waking, eating, sleeping, a quiet, simple poor fellow with no man giving me heed.

[15] patches [16] small talk, chatter

PEGEEN (*getting a quilt out of cupboard and putting it on the sack*): It was the girls were giving you heed, maybe, and I'm thinking it's most conceit you'd have to be gaming with their like.

CHRISTY (*shaking his head, with simplicity*): Not the girls itself, and I won't tell you a lie. There wasn't anyone heeding me in that place saving only the dumb beasts of the field. (*He sits down at fire.*)

PEGEEN (*with disappointment*): And I thinking you should have been living the like of a king of Norway or the eastern world. (*She comes and sits beside him after placing bread and mug of milk on the table.*)

CHRISTY (*laughing piteously*): The like of a king, is it? And I after toiling, moiling, digging, dodging from the dawn till dusk; with never a sight of joy or sport saving only when I'd be abroad in the dark night poaching rabbits on hills, for I was a divil to poach, God forgive me (*very naïvely*), and I near got six months for going with a dung fork and stabbing a fish.

PEGEEN: And it's that you'd call sport, is it, to be abroad in the darkness with yourself alone?

CHRISTY: I did, God help me, and there I'd be as happy as the sunshine of St. Martin's Day, watching the light passing the north or the patches of fog, till I'd hear a rabbit starting to screech and I'd go running in the furze. Then, when I'd my full share, I'd come walking down where you'd see the ducks and geese stretched sleeping on the highway of the road, and before I'd pass the dunghill, I'd hear himself snoring out—a loud, lonesome snore he'd be making all times, the while he was sleeping; and he a man'd be raging all times, the while he was waking, like a gaudy officer you'd hear cursing and damning and swearing oaths.

PEGEEN: Providence and Mercy, spare us all!

CHRISTY: It's that you'd say surely if you seen him and he after drinking for weeks, rising up in the red dawn, or before it maybe, and going out into the yard as naked as an ash-tree in the moon of May, and shying clods against the visage of the stars till he'd put the fear of death into the banbhs[17] and the screeching sows.

PEGEEN: I'd be well-nigh afeard of that lad myself, I'm thinking. And there was no one in it but the two of you alone?

CHRISTY: The divil a one, though he'd sons and daughters walking all great states and territories of the world, and not a one of them, to this day, but would say their seven curses on him, and they rousing up to let a cough or sneeze, maybe, in the deadness of the night.

PEGEEN (*nodding her head*): Well, you should have been a queer lot.

[17] suckling pigs

I never cursed my father the like of that, though I'm twenty and more years of age.

CHRISTY: Then you'd have cursed mine, I'm telling you, and he a man never gave peace to any, saving when he'd get two months or three, or be locked in the asylums for battering peelers or assaulting men (*with depression*), the way it was a bitter life he led me till I did up a Tuesday and halve his skull.

PEGEEN (*putting her hand on his shoulder*): Well, you'll have peace in this place, Christy Mahon, and none to trouble you, and it's near time a fine lad like you should have your good share of the earth.

CHRISTY: It's time surely, and I a seemly fellow with great strength in me and bravery of . . . (*Someone knocks.*)

CHRISTY (*clinging to* PEGEEN): Oh, glory! it's late for knocking, and this last while I'm in terror of the peelers, and the walking dead. (*Knocking again.*)

PEGEEN: Who's there?

VOICE (*outside*): Me.

PEGEEN: Who's me?

VOICE: The Widow Quin.

PEGEEN (*jumping up and giving him the bread and milk*): Go on now with your supper, and let on to be sleepy, for if she found you were such a warrant to talk, she'd be stringing gabble till the dawn of day.

(*He takes bread and sits shyly with his back to the door.*)

PEGEEN (*opening the door, with temper*): What ails you, or what is it you're wanting at this hour of the night?

WIDOW QUIN (*coming in a step and peering at* CHRISTY): I'm after meeting Shawn Keogh and Father Reilly below, who told me of your curiosity man, and they fearing by this time he was maybe roaring, romping on your hands with drink.

PEGEEN (*pointing to* CHRISTY): Look now is he roaring, and he stretched out drowsy with his supper and his mug of milk. Walk down and tell that to Father Reilly and to Shaneen Keogh.

WIDOW QUIN (*coming forward*): I'll not see them again, for I've their word to lead that lad forward for to lodge with me.

PEGEEN (*in blank amazement*): This night is it?

WIDOW QUIN (*going over*): This night. "It isn't fitting," says the priesteen, "to have his likeness lodging with an orphaned girl." (*To* CHRISTY.) God save you, mister!

CHRISTY (*shyly*): God save you kindly!

WIDOW QUIN (*looking at him with half-amused curiosity*): Well, aren't you a little smiling fellow? It should have been great and bitter torments did rouse your spirits to a deed of blood.

CHRISTY (*doubtfully*): It should, maybe.

WIDOW QUIN: It's more than "maybe" I'm saying, and it'd soften my heart to see you sitting so simple with your cup and cake, and you fitter to be saying your catechism than slaying your da.[18]

PEGEEN (*at counter, washing glasses*): There's talking when any'd see he's fit to be holding his head high with the wonders of the world. Walk on from this, for I'll not have him tormented, and he destroyed travelling since Tuesday was a week.

WIDOW QUIN (*peaceably*): We'll be walking surely when his supper's done, and you'll find we're great company, young fellow, when it's of the like of you and me you'd hear the penny poets singing in an August Fair.

CHRISTY (*innocently*): Did you kill your father?

PEGEEN (*contemptuously*): She did not. She hit himself with a worn pick, and the rusted poison did corrode his blood the way he never overed [19] it, and died after. That was a sneaky kind of murder did win small glory with the boys itself. (*She crosses to* CHRISTY'*s left.*)

WIDOW QUIN (*with good humour*): If it didn't, maybe all knows a widow woman has buried her children and destroyed her man is a wiser comrade for a young lad than a girl, the like of you, who'd go helter-skeltering after any man would let you a wink upon the road.

PEGEEN (*breaking out into wild rage*): And you'll say that, Widow Quin, and you gasping with the rage you had racing the hill beyond to look on his face.

WIDOW QUIN (*laughing derisively*): Me, is it? Well, Father Reilly has cuteness to divide you now. (*She pulls* CHRISTY *up.*) There's great temptation in a man did slay his da, and we'd best be going, young fellow; so rise up and come with me.

PEGEEN (*seizing his arm*): He'll not stir. He's pot-boy in this place, and I'll not have him stolen off and kidnapped while himself's abroad.

WIDOW QUIN: It'd be a crazy pot-boy'd lodge him in the shebeen where he works by day, so you'd have a right to come on, young fellow, till you see my little houseen, a perch off on the rising hill.

PEGEEN: Wait till morning, Christy Mahon. Wait till you lay eyes on her leaky thatch is growing more pasture for her buck goat than her square of fields, and she without a tramp itself to keep in order her place at all.

WIDOW QUIN: When you see me contriving in my little gardens, Christy Mahon, you'll swear the Lord God formed me to be living lone, and that there isn't my match in Mayo for thatching, or mowing, or shearing a sheep.

[18] father [19] got over

PEGEEN (*with noisy scorn*): It's true the Lord God formed you to contrive indeed. Doesn't the world know you reared a black ram at your own breast, so that the Lord Bishop of Connaught felt the elements of a Christian, and he eating it after in a kidney stew? Doesn't the world know you've been seen shaving the foxy skipper from France for a threepennybit and a sop of grass tobacco would wring the liver from a mountain goat you'd meet leaping the hills?

WIDOW QUIN (*with amusement*): Do you hear her now, young fellow? Do you hear the way she'll be rating at your own self when a week is by?

PEGEEN (*to* CHRISTY): Don't heed her. Tell her to go on into her pigsty and not plague us here.

WIDOW QUIN: I'm going; but he'll come with me.

PEGEEN (*shaking him*): Are you dumb, young fellow?

CHRISTY (*timidly to* WIDOW QUIN): God increase you; but I'm pot-boy in this place, and it's here I liefer stay.

PEGEEN (*triumphantly*): Now you have heard him, and go on from this.

WIDOW QUIN (*looking round the room*): It's lonesome this hour crossing the hill, and if he won't come along with me, I'd have a right maybe to stop this night with yourselves. Let me stretch out on the settle, Pegeen Mike; and himself can lie by the hearth.

PEGEEN (*short and fiercely*): Faith, I won't. Quit off or I will send you now.

WIDOW QUIN (*gathering her shawl up*): Well, it's a terror to be aged a score. (*To* CHRISTY.) God bless you now, young fellow, and let you be wary, or there's right torment will await you here if you go romancing with her like, and she waiting only, as they bade me say, on a sheepskin parchment to be wed with Shawn Keogh of Killakeen.

CHRISTY (*going to* PEGEEN *as she bolts door*): What's that she's after saying?

PEGEEN: Lies and blather, you've no call to mind. Well, isn't Shawn Keogh an impudent fellow to send up spying on me? Wait till I lay hands on him. Let him wait, I'm saying.

CHRISTY: And you're not wedding him at all?

PEGEEN: I wouldn't wed him if a bishop came walking for to join us here.

CHRISTY: That God in glory may be thanked for that.

PEGEEN: There's your bed now. I've put a quilt upon you I'm after quilting a while since with my own two hands, and you'd best stretch out now for your sleep, and may God give you a good rest till I call you in the morning when the cocks will crow.

CHRISTY (*as she goes to inner room*): May God and Mary and St.

Patrick bless you and reward you for your kindly talk. (*She shuts the door behind her. He settles his bed slowly, feeling the quilt with immense satisfaction.*) Well, it's a clean bed and soft with it, and it's great luck and company I've won me in the end of time — two fine women fighting for the likes of me — till I'm thinking this night wasn't I a foolish fellow not to kill my father in the years gone by.

ACT II

(*Scene as before. Brilliant morning light.* CHRISTY, *looking bright and cheerful, is cleaning a girl's boots.*)

CHRISTY (*to himself, counting jugs on dresser*): Half a hundred beyond. Ten there. A score that's above. Eighty jugs. Six cups and a broken one. Two plates. A power of glasses. Bottles, a schoolmaster'd be hard set to count, and enough in them, I'm thinking, to drunken all the wealth and wisdom of the county Clare. (*He puts down the boot carefully.*) There's her boots now, nice and decent for her evening use, and isn't it grand brushes she has? (*He puts them down and goes by degrees to the looking-glass.*) Well, this'd be a fine place to be my whole life talking out with swearing Christians, in place of my old dogs and cat; and I stalking around, smoking my pipe and drinking my fill, and never a day's work but drawing a cork an odd time, or wiping a glass, or rinsing out a shiny tumbler for a decent man. (*He takes the looking-glass from the wall and puts it on the back of a chair; then sits down in front of it and begins washing his face.*) Didn't I know rightly, I was handsome, though it was the divil's own mirror we had beyond, would twist a squint across an angel's brow; and I'll be growing fine from this day, the way I'll have a soft lovely skin on me and won't be the like of the clumsy young fellows do be ploughing all times in the earth and dung. (*He starts.*) Is she coming again? (*He looks out.*) Stranger girls. God help me, where'll I hide myself away and my long neck naked to the world? (*He looks out.*) I'd best go to the room maybe till I'm dressed again.

(*He gathers up his coat and the looking-glass, and runs into the inner room. The door is pushed open, and* SUSAN BRADY *looks in, and knocks on door.*)

SUSAN: There's nobody in it. (*Knocks again.*)

NELLY (*pushing her in and following her, with* HONOR BLAKE *and* SARA TANSEY): It'd be early for them both to be out walking the hill.

SUSAN: I'm thinking Shawn Keogh was making game of us, and there's no such man in it at all.

HONOR (*pointing to straw and quilt*): Look at that. He's been sleeping there in the night. Well, it'll be a hard case if he's gone off now, the way we'll never set our eyes on a man killed his father, and we after rising early and destroying ourselves running fast on the hill.

NELLY: Are you thinking them's his boots?

SARA (*taking them up*): If they are, there should be his father's track on them. Did you never read in the papers the way murdered men do bleed and drip?

SUSAN: Is that blood there, Sara Tansey?

SARA (*smelling it*): That's bog water, I'm thinking; but it's his own they are, surely, for I never seen the like of them for whitey mud, and red mud, and turf on them, and the fine sands of the sea. That man's been walking, I'm telling you. (*She goes down right, putting on one of his boots.*)

SUSAN (*going to window*): Maybe he's stolen off to Belmullet with the boots of Michael James, and you'd have a right so to follow after him, Sara Tansey, and you the one yoked the ass cart and drove ten miles to set your eyes on the man bit the yellow lady's nostril on the northern shore. (*She looks out.*)

SARA (*running to window, with one boot on*): Don't be talking, and we fooled today. (*Putting on the other boot.*) There's a pair do fit me well and I'll be keeping them for walking to the priest, when you'd be ashamed this place, going up winter and summer with nothing worth while to confess at all.

HONOR (*who has been listening at door*): Whisht! there's someone inside the room. (*She pushes door a chink open.*) It's a man.

(SARA *kicks off boots and puts them where they were. They all stand in a line looking through chink.*)

SARA: I'll call him. Mister! Mister! (*He puts in his head.*) Is Pegeen within?

CHRISTY (*coming in as meek as a mouse, with the looking-glass held behind his back*): She's above on the cnuceen,[20] seeking the nanny goats, the way she'd have a sup of goats' milk for to colour my tea.

SARA: And asking your pardon, is it you's the man killed his father?

CHRISTY (*sidling towards the nail where the glass was hanging*): I am, God help me!

SARA (*taking eggs she has brought*): Then my thousand welcomes to you, and I've run up with a brace of duck's eggs for your food to-day.

[20] hill

Pegeen's ducks is no use, but these are the real rich sort. Hold out your hand and you'll see it's no lie I'm telling you.

CHRISTY (*coming forward shyly, and holding out his left hand*): They're a great and weighty size.

SUSAN: And I run up with a pat of butter, for it'd be a poor thing to have you eating your spuds dry, and you after running a great way since you did destroy your da.

CHRISTY: Thank you kindly.

HONOR: And I brought you a little cut of a cake, for you should have a thin stomach on you, and you that length walking the world.

NELLY: And I brought you a little laying pullet — boiled and all she is — was crushed at the fall of night by the curate's car. Feel the fat of that breast, mister.

CHRISTY: It's bursting, surely. (*He feels it with back of his hand, in which he holds the presents.*)

SARA: Will you pinch it? Is your right hand too sacred for to use at all? (*She slips round behind him.*) It's a glass he has. Well, I never seen to this day a man with a looking-glass held to his back. Them that kills their fathers is a vain lot surely.

(GIRLS *giggle.*)

CHRISTY (*smiling innocently and piling presents on glass*): I'm very thankful to you all to-day. . . .

WIDOW QUIN (*coming in quickly, at door*): Sara Tansey, Susan Brady, Honor Blake! What in glory has you here at this hour of day?

GIRLS (*giggling*): That's the man killed his father.

WIDOW QUIN (*coming to them*): I know well it's the man; and I'm after putting him down in the sports below for racing, leaping, pitching, and the Lord knows what.

SARA (*exuberantly*): That's right, Widow Quin. I'll bet my dowry that he'll lick the world.

WIDOW QUIN: If you will, you'd have a right to have him fresh and nourished in place of nursing a feast. (*Taking presents.*) Are you fasting or fed, young fellow?

CHRISTY: Fasting, if you please.

WIDOW QUIN (*loudly*): Well, you're the lot. Stir up now and give him his breakfast. (*To* CHRISTY.) Come here to me (*she puts him on bench beside her while the girls make tea and get his breakfast*), and let you tell us your story before Pegeen will come, in place of grinning your ears off like the moon of May.

CHRISTY (*beginning to be pleased*): It's a long story; you'd be destroyed listening.

WIDOW QUIN: Don't be letting on to be shy, a fine, gamey, treacherous lad the like of you. Was it in your house beyond you cracked his skull?

CHRISTY (*shy but flattered*): It was not. We were digging spuds in his cold, sloping, stony, divil's patch of a field.

WIDOW QUIN: And you went asking money of him, or making talk of getting a wife would drive him from his farm?

CHRISTY: I did not, then; but there I was digging and digging, and "You squinting idiot," says he, "let you walk down now and tell the priest you'll wed the Widow Casey in a score of days."

WIDOW QUIN: And what kind was she?

CHRISTY (*with horror*): A walking terror from beyond the hills, and she two score and five years, and two hundred-weights and five pounds in the weighing scales, with a limping leg on her, and a blinded eye, and she a woman of noted misbehaviour with the old and young.

GIRLS (*clustering round him, serving him*): Glory be.

WIDOW QUIN: And what did he want driving you to wed with her? (*She takes a bit of the chicken.*)

CHRISTY (*eating with growing satisfaction*): He was letting on I was wanting a protector from the harshness of the world, and he without a thought the whole while but how he'd have her hut to live in and her gold to drink.

WIDOW QUIN: There's maybe worse than a dry hearth and a widow woman and your glass at night. So you hit him then?

CHRISTY (*getting almost excited*): I did not. "I won't wed her," says I, "when all know she did suckle me for six weeks when I came into the world, and she a hag this day with a tongue on her has the crows and seabirds scattered, the way they wouldn't cast a shadow on her garden with the dread of her curse."

WIDOW QUIN (*teasingly*): That one should be right company.

SARA (*eagerly*): Don't mind her. Did you kill him then?

CHRISTY: "She's too good for the like of you," says he, "and go on now or I'll flatten you out like a crawling beast has passed under a dray." "You will not if I can help it," says I. "Go on," says he, "or I'll have the divil making garters of your limbs tonight." "You will not if I can help it," says I. (*He sits up brandishing his mug.*)

SARA: You were right surely.

CHRISTY (*impressively*): With that the sun came out between the cloud and the hill, and it shining green in my face. "God have mercy on your soul," says he, lifting a scythe. "Or on your own," said I, raising the loy.

SUSAN: That's a grand story.

HONOR: He tells it lovely.

CHRISTY (*flattered and confident, waving bone*): He gave a drive with the scythe, and I gave a lep to the east. Then I turned around with my back to the north, and I hit a blow on the ridge of his skull, laid him stretched out, and he split to the knob of his gullet. (*He raises the chicken bone to his Adam's apple.*)

GIRLS (*together*): Well, you're a marvel! Oh, God bless you! You're the lad, surely!

SUSAN: I'm thinking the Lord God sent him this road to make a second husband to the Widow Quin, and she with a great yearning to be wedded, though all dread her here. Lift him on her knee, Sara Tansey.

WIDOW QUIN: Don't tease him.

SARA (*going over to dresser and counter very quickly, and getting two glasses and porter*): You're heroes, surely, and let you drink a supeen with your arms linked like the outlandish lovers in the sailor's song. (*She links their arms and gives them the glasses.*) There now. Drink a health to the wonders of the western world, the pirates, preachers, poteen-makers, with the jobbing jockies;[21] parching peelers, and the juries fill their stomachs selling judgments of the English law. (*Brandishing the bottle.*)

WIDOW QUIN: That's a right toast, Sara Tansey. Now, Christy.

(*They drink with their arms linked, he drinking with his left hand, she with her right. As they are drinking,* PEGEEN MIKE *comes in with a milk-can and stands aghast. They all spring away from* CHRISTY. *He goes down left.* WIDOW QUIN *remains seated.*)

PEGEEN (*angrily, to* SARA): What is it you're wanting?

SARA (*twisting her apron*): An ounce of tobacco.

PEGEEN: Have you tuppence?

SARA: I've forgotten my purse.

PEGEEN: Then you'd best be getting it and not be fooling us here. (*To the* WIDOW QUIN, *with more elaborate scorn.*) And what is it you're wanting, Widow Quin?

WIDOW QUIN (*insolently*): A penn'orth of starch.

PEGEEN (*breaking out*). And you without a white shift or a shirt in your whole family since the drying of the flood. I've no starch for the like of you, and let you walk on now to Killamuck.

WIDOW QUIN (*turning to* CHRISTY, *as she goes out with the* GIRLS): Well, you're mighty huffy this day, Pegeen Mike, and you, young fellow, let you not forget the sports and racing when the noon is by. (*They go out.*)

[21] swindling peddlers

PEGEEN (*imperiously*): Fling out that rubbish and put them cups away. (CHRISTY *tidies away in great haste.*) Shove in the bench by the wall. (*He does so.*) And hang that glass on the nail. What disturbed it at all?

CHRISTY (*very meekly*): I was making myself decent only, and this a fine country for young lovely girls.

PEGEEN (*sharply*): Whisht your talking of girls. (*Goes to counter on right.*)

CHRISTY: Wouldn't any wish to be decent in a place . . .

PEGEEN: Whisht, I'm saying.

CHRISTY (*looks at her face for a moment with great misgivings, then as a last effort takes up a loy, and goes towards her, with feigned assurance*): It was with a loy the like of that I killed my father.

PEGEEN (*still sharply*): You've told me that story six times since the dawn of day.

CHRISTY (*reproachfully*): It's a queer thing you wouldn't care to be hearing it and them girls after walking four miles to be listening to me now.

PEGEEN (*turning round astonished*): Four miles?

CHRISTY (*apologetically*): Didn't himself say there were only bona fides living in the place?

PEGEEN: It's bona fides by the road they are, but that lot came over the river lepping the stones. It's not three perches[22] when you go like that, and I was down this morning looking on the papers the post-boy does have in his bag. (*With meaning and emphasis.*) For there was great news this day, Christopher Mahon. (*She goes into room on left.*)

CHRISTY (*suspiciously*): Is it news of my murder?

PEGEEN (*inside*): Murder, indeed.

CHRISTY (*loudly*): A murdered da?

PEGEEN (*coming in again and crossing right*): There was not, but a story filled half a page of the hanging of a man. Ah, that should be a fearful end, young fellow, and it worst of all for a man destroyed his da; for the like of him would get small mercies, and when it's dead he is they'd put him in a narrow grave, with cheap sacking wrapping him round, and pour down quicklime on his head, the way you'd see a woman pouring any frish-frash[23] from a cup.

CHRISTY (*very miserably*): Oh, God help me. Are you thinking I'm safe? You were saying at the fall of night I was shut of jeopardy and I here with yourselves.

PEGEEN (*severely*): You'll be shut of jeopardy no place if you go

[22] units of measurement, 16½ feet long [23] dregs

talking with a pack of wild girls the like of them do be walking abroad with the peelers, talking whispers at the fall of night.

CHRISTY (*with terror*): And you're thinking they'd tell?

PEGEEN (*with mock sympathy*): Who knows, God help you?

CHRISTY (*loudly*): What joy would they have to bring hanging to the likes of me?

PEGEEN: It's queer joys they have, and who knows the thing they'd do, if it'd make the green stones cry itself to think of you swaying and swiggling at the butt of a rope, and you with a fine, stout neck, God bless you! the way you'd be a half an hour, in great anguish, getting your death.

CHRISTY (*getting his boots and putting them on*): If there's that terror of them, it'd be best, maybe, I went on wandering like Esau or Cain and Abel on the sides of Neifin or the Erris plain.

PEGEEN (*beginning to play with him*): It would, maybe, for I've heard the Circuit Judges this place is a heartless crew.

CHRISTY (*bitterly*): It's more than Judges this place is a heartless crew. (*Looking up at her.*) And isn't it a poor thing to be starting again, and I a lonesome fellow will be looking out on women and girls the way the needy fallen spirits do be looking on the Lord?

PEGEEN: What call have you to be that lonesome when there's poor girls walking Mayo in their thousands now?

CHRISTY (*grimly*): It's well you know what call I have. It's well you know it's a lonesome thing to be passing small towns with the lights shining sideways when the night is down, or going in strange places with a dog noising before you and a dog noising behind, or drawn to the cities where you'd hear a voice kissing and talking deep love in every shadow of the ditch, and you passing on with an empty, hungry stomach failing from your heart.

PEGEEN: I'm thinking you're an odd man, Christy Mahon. The oddest walking fellow I ever set my eyes on to this hour today.

CHRISTY: What would any be but odd men and they living lonesome in the world?

PEGEEN: I'm not odd, and I'm my whole life with my father only.

CHRISTY (*with infinite admiration*): How would a lovely, handsome woman the like of you be lonesome when all men should be thronging around to hear the sweetness of your voice, and the little infant children should be pestering your steps, I'm thinking, and you walking the roads.

PEGEEN: I'm hard set to know what way a coaxing fellow the like of yourself should be lonesome either.

CHRISTY: Coaxing.

PEGEEN: Would you have me think a man never talked with the girls would have the words you've spoken today? It's only letting on you are to be lonesome, the way you'd get around me now.

CHRISTY: I wish to God I was letting on; but I was lonesome all times, and born lonesome, I'm thinking, as the moon of dawn. (*Going to door.*)

PEGEEN (*puzzled by his talk*): Well, it's a story I'm not understanding at all why you'd be worse than another, Christy Mahon, and you a fine lad with the great savagery to destroy your da.

CHRISTY: It's little I'm understanding myself, saving only that my heart's scalded this day, and I going off stretching out the earth between us, the way I'll not be waking near you another dawn of the year till the two of us do arise to hope or judgment with the saints of God, and now I'd best be going with my wattle[24] in my hand, for hanging is a poor thing (*turning to go*), and it's little welcome only is left me in this house today.

PEGEEN (*sharply*): Christy. (*He turns round.*) Come here to me. (*He goes towards her.*) Lay down that switch and throw some sods on the fire. You're pot-boy in this place, and I'll not have you mitch[25] off from us now.

CHRISTY: You were saying I'd be hanged if I stay.

PEGEEN (*quite kindly at last*): I'm after going down and reading the fearful crimes of Ireland for two weeks or three, and there wasn't a word of your murder. (*Getting up and going over to the counter.*) They've likely not found the body. You're safe so with ourselves.

CHRISTY (*astonished, slowly*): It's making game of me you were (*following her with fearful joy*), and I can stay so, working at your side, and I not lonesome from this mortal day.

PEGEEN: What's to hinder you staying, except the widow woman or the young girls would inveigle you off?

CHRISTY (*with rapture*): And I'll have your words from this day filling my ears, and that look is come upon you meeting my two eyes, and I watching you loafing around in the warm sun, or rinsing your ankles when the night is come.

PEGEEN (*kindly, but a little embarrassed*): I'm thinking you'll be a loyal young lad to have working around, and if you vexed me a while since with your leaguing with the girls, I wouldn't give a thraneen[26] for a lad hadn't a mighty spirit in him and a gamey heart.

(SHAWN KEOGH *runs in carrying a cleeve*[27] *on his back, followed by the* WIDOW QUIN.)

[24] switch [25] sneak [26] straw [27] basket

SHAWN (*to* PEGEEN): I was passing below, and I seen your mountainy sheep eating cabbages in Jimmy's field. Run up or they'll be bursting, surely.

PEGEEN: Oh, God mend them!

(*She puts a shawl over her head and runs out.*)

CHRISTY (*looking from one to the other. Still in high spirits*): I'd best go to her aid maybe. I'm handy with ewes.

WIDOW QUIN (*closing the door*): She can do that much, and there is Shaneen has long speeches for to tell you now. (*She sits down with an amused smile.*)

SHAWN (*taking something from his pocket and offering it to* CHRISTY): Do you see that, mister?

CHRISTY (*looking at it*): The half of a ticket to the Western States!

SHAWN (*trembling with anxiety*): I'll give it to you and my new hat (*pulling it out of hamper*); and my breeches with the double seat (*pulling it out*); and my new coat is woven from the blackest shearings for three miles around (*giving him the coat*); I'll give you the whole of them, and my blessing, and the blessing of Father Reilly itself, maybe, if you'll quit from this and leave us in the peace we had till last night at the fall of dark.

CHRISTY (*with a new arrogance*): And for what is it you're wanting to get shut of me?

SHAWN (*looking to the* WIDOW *for help*): I'm a poor scholar with middling faculties to coin a lie, so I'll tell you the truth, Christy Mahon. I'm wedding with Pegeen beyond, and I don't think well of having a clever, fearless man the like of you dwelling in her house.

CHRISTY (*almost pugnaciously*): And you'd be using bribery for to banish me?

SHAWN (*in an imploring voice*): Let you not take it badly, mister honey; isn't beyond the best place for you, where you'll have golden chains and shiny coats and you riding upon hunters with the ladies of the land. (*He makes an eager sign to the* WIDOW QUIN *to come to help him.*)

WIDOW QUIN (*coming over*): It's true for him, and you'd best quit off and not have that poor girl setting her mind on you, for there's Shaneen thinks she wouldn't suit you, though all is saying that she'll wed you now.

(CHRISTY *beams with delight.*)

SHAWN (*in terrified earnest*): She wouldn't suit you, and she with the divil's own temper the way you'd be strangling one another in a score of days. (*He makes the movement of strangling with his hands.*) It's the like of me only that she's fit for; a quiet simple fellow wouldn't raise a hand upon her if she scratched itself.

WIDOW QUIN (*putting* SHAWN'S *hat on* CHRISTY): Fit them clothes on you anyhow, young fellow, and he'd maybe loan them to you for the sports. (*Pushing him towards inner door.*) Fit them on and you can give your answer when you have them tried.

CHRISTY (*beaming, delighted with the clothes*): I will then. I'd like herself to see me in them tweeds and hat. (*He goes into room and shuts the door.*)

SHAWN (*in great anxiety*): He'd like herself to see them. He'll not leave us, Widow Quin. He's a score of divils in him the way it's well-nigh certain he will wed Pegeen.

WIDOW QUIN (*jeeringly*): It's true all girls are fond of courage and do hate the like of you.

SHAWN (*walking about in desperation*): Oh, Widow Quin, what'll I be doing now? I'd inform again him, but he'd burst from Kilmainham[28] and he'd be sure and certain to destroy me. If I wasn't so God-fearing, I'd near have courage to come behind him and run a pike into his side. Oh, it's a hard case to be an orphan and not to have your father that you're used to, and you'd easy kill and make yourself a hero in the sight of all. (*Coming up to her.*) Oh, Widow Quin, will you find me some contrivance when I've promised you a ewe?

WIDOW QUIN: A ewe's a small thing, but what would you give me if I did wed him and did save you so?

SHAWN (*with astonishment*): You?

WIDOW QUIN: Aye. Would you give me the red cow you have and the mountainy ram, and the right of way across your rye path, and a load of dung at Michaelmas, and turbary[29] upon the western hill?

SHAWN (*radiant with hope*): I would, surely, and I'd give you the wedding-ring I have, and the loan of a new suit, the way you'd have him decent on the wedding-day. I'd give you two kids for your dinner, and a gallon of poteen, and I'd call the piper on the long car to your wedding from Crossmolina or from Ballina. I'd give you . . .

WIDOW QUIN: That'll do, so, and let you whisht, for he's coming now again.

(CHRISTY *comes in very natty in the new clothes.* WIDOW QUIN *goes to him admiringly.*)

WIDOW QUIN: If you seen yourself now, I'm thinking you'd be too proud to speak to at all, and it'd be a pity surely to have your like sailing from Mayo to the western world.

[28] prison near Dublin [29] right to cut turf

CHRISTY (*as proud as a peacock*): I'm not going. If this is a poor place itself, I'll make myself contented to be lodging here.

(WIDOW QUIN *makes a sign to* SHAWN *to leave them.*)

SHAWN: Well, I'm going measuring the racecourse while the tide is low, so I'll leave you the garments and my blessing for the sports today. God bless you! (*He wriggles out.*)

WIDOW QUIN (*admiring* CHRISTY): Well, you're mighty spruce, young fellow. Sit down now while you're quiet till you talk with me.

CHRISTY (*swaggering*): I'm going abroad on the hillside for to seek Pegeen.

WIDOW QUIN: You'll have time and plenty for to seek Pegeen, and you heard me saying at the fall of night the two of us should be great company.

CHRISTY: From this out I'll have no want of company when all sorts is bringing me their food and clothing (*he swaggers to the door, tightening his belt*), the way they'd set their eyes upon a gallant orphan cleft his father with one blow to the breeches belt. (*He opens door, then staggers back.*) Saints of glory! Holy angels from the throne of light!

WIDOW QUIN (*going over*): What ails you?

CHRISTY: It's the walking spirit of my murdered da!

WIDOW QUIN (*looking out*): Is it that tramper?

CHRISTY (*wildly*): Where'll I hide my poor body from that ghost of hell?

(*The door is pushed open, and* OLD MAHON *appears on threshold.* CHRISTY *darts in behind door.*)

WIDOW QUIN (*in great amusement*): God save you, my poor man.

MAHON (*gruffly*): Did you see a young lad passing this way in the early morning or the fall of night?

WIDOW QUIN: You're a queer kind to walk in not saluting at all.

MAHON: Did you see the young lad?

WIDOW QUIN (*stiffly*): What kind was he?

MAHON: An ugly young streeler[30] with a murderous gob[31] on him, and a little switch in his hand. I met a tramper seen him coming this way at the fall of night.

WIDOW QUIN: There's harvest hundreds do be passing these days for the Sligo boat. For what is it you're wanting him, my poor man?

MAHON: I want to destroy him for breaking the head on me with the clout of a loy. (*He takes off a big hat, and shows his head in a mass*

30 vagabond 31 "mug"

of bandages and plaster, with some pride.) It was he did that, and amn't I a great wonder to think I've traced him ten days with that rent in my crown?

WIDOW QUIN (*taking his head in both hands and examining it with extreme delight*): That was a great blow. And who hit you? A robber maybe?

MAHON: It was my own son hit me, and he the divil a robber, or anything else, but a dirty, stuttering lout.

WIDOW QUIN (*letting go his skull and wiping her hands in her apron*): You'd best be wary of a mortified scalp, I think they call it, lepping around with that wound in the splendour of the sun. It was a bad blow, surely, and you should have vexed him fearful to make him strike that gash in his da.

MAHON: Is it me?

WIDOW QUIN (*amusing herself*): Aye. And isn't it a great shame when the old and hardened do torment the young?

MAHON (*raging*): Torment him, is it? And I after holding out with the patience of a martyred saint till there's nothing but destruction on, and I'm driven out in my old age with none to aid me.

WIDOW QUIN (*greatly amused*): It's a sacred wonder the way that wickedness will spoil a man.

MAHON: My wickedness, is it? Amn't I after saying it is himself has me destroyed, and he a lier on walls, a talker of folly, a man you'd see stretched the half of the day in the brown ferns with his belly to the sun.

WIDOW QUIN: Not working at all?

MAHON: The divil a work, or if he did itself, you'd see him raising up a haystack like the stalk of a rush, or driving our last cow till he broke her leg at the hip, and when he wasn't at that he'd be fooling over little birds he had — finches and felts[32] — or making mugs at his own self in the bit of a glass we had hung on the wall.

WIDOW QUIN (*looking at* CHRISTY): What way was he so foolish? It was running wild after the girls maybe?

MAHON (*with a shout of derision*): Running wild, is it? If he seen a red petticoat coming swinging over the hill, he'd be off to hide in the sticks, and you'd see him shooting out his sheep's eyes between the little twigs and the leaves, and his two ears rising like a hare looking out through a gap. Girls, indeed!

WIDOW QUIN: It was drink maybe?

MAHON: And he a poor fellow would get drunk on the smell of a pint. He'd a queer rotten stomach, I'm telling you, and when I gave him

[32] thrushes

three pulls from my pipe a while since, he was taken with contortions till I had to send him in the ass-cart to the females' nurse.

WIDOW QUIN (*clasping her hands*): Well, I never, till this day, heard tell of a man the like of that!

MAHON: I'd take a mighty oath you didn't, surely, and wasn't he the laughing joke of every female woman where four baronies meet, the way the girls would stop their weeding if they seen him coming the road to let a roar at him, and call him the looney of Mahon's.

WIDOW QUIN: I'd give the world and all to see the like of him. What kind was he?

MAHON: A small, low fellow.

WIDOW QUIN: And dark?

MAHON: Dark and dirty.

WIDOW QUIN (*considering*): I'm thinking I seen him.

MAHON (*eagerly*): An ugly young blackguard.

WIDOW QUIN: A hideous, fearful villain, and the spit of you.

MAHON: What way is he fled?

WIDOW QUIN: Gone over the hills to catch a coasting steamer to the north or south.

MAHON: Could I pull up on him now?

WIDOW QUIN: If you'll cross the sands below where the tide is out, you'll be in it as soon as himself, for he had to go round ten miles by the top of the bay. (*She points to the door.*) Strike down by the head beyond and then follow on the roadway to the north and east.

(MAHON *goes abruptly.*)

WIDOW QUIN (*shouting after him*): Let you give him a good vengeance when you come up with him, but don't put yourself in the power of the law, for it'd be a poor thing to see a judge in his black cap reading out his sentence on a civil warrior the like of you. (*She swings the door to and looks at* CHRISTY, *who is cowering in terror, for a moment, then she bursts into a laugh.*) Well, you're the walking Playboy of the Western World, and that's the poor man you had divided to his breeches belt.

CHRISTY (*looking out; then, to her*): What'll Pegeen say when she hears that story? What'll she be saying to me now?

WIDOW QUIN: She'll knock the head of you, I'm thinking, and drive you from the door. God help her to be taking you for a wonder, and you a little schemer making up a story you destroyed your da.

CHRISTY (*turning to the door, nearly speechless with rage, half to himself*): To be letting on he was dead, and coming back to his life, and following after me like an old weasel tracing a rat, and coming in here laying desolation between my own self and the fine women of

Ireland, and he a kind of carcase that you'd fling upon the sea. . . .

WIDOW QUIN (*more soberly*): There's talking for a man's one only son.

CHRISTY (*breaking out*): His one son, is it? May I meet him with one tooth and it aching, and one eye to be seeing seven and seventy divils in the twists of the road, and one old timber leg on him to limp into the scalding grave. (*Looking out.*) There he is now crossing the strands, and that the Lord God would send a high wave to wash him from the world.

WIDOW QUIN (*scandalized*): Have you no shame? (*Putting her hand on his shoulder and turning him round.*) What ails you? Near crying, is it?

CHRISTY (*in despair and grief*): Amn't I after seeing the love-light of the star of knowledge shining from her brow, and hearing words would put you thinking on the holy Brigid speaking to the infant saints, and now she'll be turning again, and speaking hard words to me, like an old woman with a spavindy[33] ass she'd have, urging on a hill.

WIDOW QUIN: There's poetry talk for a girl you'd see itching and scratching, and she with a stale stink of poteen on her from selling in the shop.

CHRISTY (*impatiently*): It's her like is fitted to be handling merchandise in the heavens above, and what'll I be doing now, I ask you, and I a kind of wonder was jilted by the heavens when a day was by.

(*There is a distant noise of* GIRLS' *voices.* WIDOW QUIN *looks from window and comes to him, hurriedly.*)

WIDOW QUIN: You'll be doing like myself, I'm thinking, when I did detroy my man, for I'm above many's the day, odd times in great spirits, abroad in the sunshine, darning a stocking or stitching a shift; and odd times again looking out on the schooners, hookers, trawlers is sailing the sea, and I thinking on the gallant hairy fellows are drifting beyond, and myself long years living alone.

CHRISTY (*interested*): You're like me, so.

WIDOW QUIN: I am your like, and it's for that I'm taking a fancy to you, and I with my little houseen above where there'd be myself to tend you, and none to ask were you a murderer or what at all.

CHRISTY: And what would I be doing if I left Pegeen?

WIDOW QUIN: I've nice jobs you could be doing — gathering shells to make a white-wash for our hut within, building up a little goose-house, or stretching a new skin on an old curagh[34] I have, and if my hut is far from all sides, it's there you'll meet the wisest old men, I

[33] lame [34] boat

tell you, at the corner of my wheel, and it's there yourself and me will have great times whispering and hugging. . . .

VOICES (*outside, calling far away*): Christy! Christy Mahon! Christy!

CHRISTY: Is it Pegeen Mike?

WIDOW QUIN: It's the young girls, I'm thinking, coming to bring you to the sports below, and what is it you'll have me to tell them now?

CHRISTY: Aid me for to win Pegeen. It's herself only that I'm seeking now. (WIDOW QUIN *gets up and goes to window.*) Aid me for to win her, and I'll be asking God to stretch a hand to you in the hour of death, and lead you short cuts through the Meadows of Ease, and up the floor of Heaven to the Footstool of the Virgin's Son.

WIDOW QUIN: There's praying!

VOICES (*nearer*): Christy! Christy Mahon!

CHRISTY (*with agitation*): They're coming. Will you swear to aid and save me, for the love of Christ?

WIDOW QUIN (*looks at him for a moment*): If I aid you, will you swear to give me a right of way I want, and a mountainy ram, and a load of dung at Michaelmas, the time that you'll be master here?

CHRISTY: I will, by the elements and stars of night.

WIDOW QUIN: Then we'll not say a word of the old fellow, the way Pegeen won't know your story till the end of time.

CHRISTY: And if he chances to return again?

WIDOW QUIN: We'll swear he's a maniac and not your da. I could take an oath I seen him raving on the sands today.

(GIRLS *run in.*)

SUSAN: Come on to the sports below. Pegeen says you're to come.

SARA TANSEY: The lepping's beginning, and we've a jockey's suit to fit upon you for the mule race on the sands below.

HONOR: Come on, will you?

CHRISTY: I will then if Pegeen's beyond.

SARA: She's in the boreen[35] making game of Shaneen Keogh.

CHRISTY: Then I'll be going to her now. (*He runs out, followed by the* GIRLS.)

WIDOW QUIN: Well, if the worst comes in the end of all, it'll be great game to see there's none to pity him but a widow woman, the like of me, has buried her children and destroyed her man. (*She goes out.*)

[35] lane

ACT III

(Scene as before. Later in the day. JIMMY *comes in, slightly drunk.)*

JIMMY (*calls*): Pegeen! (*Crosses to inner door.*) Pegeen Mike! (*Comes back again into the room.*) Pegeen! (PHILLY *comes in in the same state. To* PHILLY.) Did you see herself?

PHILLY: I did not; but I sent Shawn Keogh with the ass-cart for to bear him home. (*Trying cupboards, which are locked.*) Well, isn't he a nasty man to get into such staggers at a morning wake; and isn't herself the divil's daughter for locking, and she so fussy after that young gaffer, you might take your death with drouth and none to heed you?

JIMMY: It's little wonder she'd be fussy, and he after bringing bankrupt ruin on the roulette man, and the trick-o'-the-loop man, and breaking the nose of the cockshot-man, and winning all in the sports below, racing, lepping, dancing, and the Lord knows what! He's right luck, I'm telling you.

PHILLY: If he has, he'll be rightly hobbled yet, and he not able to say ten words without making a brag of the way he killed his father, and the great blow he hit with the loy.

JIMMY: A man can't hang by his own informing, and his father should be rotten by now.

(OLD MAHON *passes window slowly.*)

PHILLY: Supposing a man's digging spuds in that field with a long spade, and supposing he flings up the two halves of that skull, what'll be said then in the papers and the courts of law?

JIMMY: They'd say it was an old Dane, maybe, was drowned in the flood. (OLD MAHON *comes in and sits down near door listening.*) Did you never hear tell of the skulls they have in the city of Dublin, ranged out like blue jugs in a cabin of Connaught?

PHILLY: And you believe that?

JIMMY (*pugnaciously*): Didn't a lad see them and he after coming from harvesting in the Liverpool boat? "They have them there," says he, "making a show of the great people there was one time walking the world. White skulls and black skulls and yellow skulls, and some with full teeth, and some haven't only but one."

PHILLY: It was no lie, maybe, for when I was a young lad there was a graveyard beyond the house with the remnants of a man who had thighs as long as your arm. He was a horrid man, I'm telling you, and there was many a fine Sunday I'd put him together for fun, and he with shiny bones, you wouldn't meet the like of these days in the cities of the world.

MAHON (*getting up*): You wouldn't, is it? Lay your eyes on that skull, and tell me where and when there was another the like of it, is splintered only from the blow of a loy.

PHILLY: Glory be to God! And who hit you at all?

MAHON (*triumphantly*): It was my own son hit me. Would you believe that?

JIMMY: Well, there's wonders hidden in the heart of man!

PHILLY (*suspiciously*): And what way was it done?

MAHON (*wandering about the room*): I'm after walking hundreds and long scores of miles, winning clean beds and the fill of my belly four times in the day, and I doing nothing but telling stories of that naked truth. (*He comes to them a little aggressively.*) Give me a supeen and I'll tell you now.

(WIDOW QUIN *comes in and stands aghast behind him. He is facing* JIMMY *and* PHILLY, *who are on the left.*)

JIMMY: Ask herself beyond. She's the stuff hidden in her shawl.

WIDOW QUIN (*coming to* MAHON *quickly*): You here, is it? You didn't go far at all?

MAHON: I seen the coasting steamer passing, and I got a drouth upon me and a cramping leg, so I said, "The divil go along with him," and turned again. (*Looking under her shawl.*) And let you give me a supeen, for I'm destroyed travelling since Tuesday was a week.

WIDOW QUIN (*getting a glass, in a cajoling tone*): Sit down then by the fire and take your ease for a space. You've a right to be destroyed indeed, with your walking, and fighting, and facing the sun. (*Giving him poteen from a stone jar she has brought in.*) There now is a drink for you, and may it be to your happiness and length of life.

MAHON (*taking glass greedily, and sitting down by fire*): God increase you!

WIDOW QUIN (*taking men to the right stealthily*): Do you know what? That man's raving from his wound today, for I met him a while since telling a rambling tale of a tinker had him destroyed. Then he heard of Christy's deed, and he up and says it was his son had cracked his skull. Oh, isn't madness a fright, for he'll go killing someone yet, and he thinking it's the man has struck him so?

JIMMY (*entirely convinced*): It's a fright surely. I knew a party was kicked in the head by a red mare, and he went killing horses a great while, till he eat the insides of a clock and died after.

PHILLY (*with suspicion*): Did he see Christy?

WIDOW QUIN: He didn't (*With a warning gesture.*) Let you not be putting him in mind of him, or you'll be likely summoned if there's murder done. (*Looking round at* MAHON.) Whisht! He's listening. Wait now till you hear me taking him easy and unravelling all. (*She goes to* MAHON.)And what way are you feeling, mister? Are you in contentment now?

MAHON (*slightly emotional from his drink*): I'm poorly only, for it's a hard story the way I'm left today, when it was I did tend him from his hour of birth, and he a dunce never reached his second book, the way he'd come from school, many's the day, with his legs lamed under him, and he blackened with his beatings like a tinker's ass. It's a hard story, I'm saying, the way some do have their next and nighest raising up a hand of murder on them, and some is lonesome getting their death with lamentation in the dead of night.

WIDOW QUIN (*not knowing what to say*): To hear you talking so quiet, who'd know you were the same fellow we seen pass today?

MAHON: I'm the same surely. The wrack and ruin of three-score years; and it's a terror to live that length, I tell you, and to have your sons going to the dogs against you, and you wore out scolding them, and skelping[36] them, and God knows what.

PHILLY (*to* JIMMY): He's not raving. (*To* WIDOW QUIN.) Will you ask him what kind was his son?

WIDOW QUIN (*to* MAHON, *with a peculiar look*): Was your son that hit you a lad of one year and a score maybe, a great hand at racing and lepping and licking the world?

MAHON (*turning on her with a roar of rage*): Didn't you hear me say he was the fool of men, the way from this out he'll know the orphan's lot, with old and young making game of him, and they swearing, raging, kicking at him like a mangy cur.

(*A great burst of cheering outside, some way off.*)

MAHON (*putting his hands to his ears*): What in the name of God do they want roaring below?

WIDOW QUIN (*with the shade of a smile*): They're cheering a young lad, the champion Playboy of the Western World.

(*More cheering.*)

MAHON (*going to window*): It'd split my heart to hear them, and I with pulses in my brain-pan for a week gone by. Is it racing they are?

JIMMY (*looking from door*): It is, then. They are mounting him for

[36] beating

the mule race will be run upon the sands. That's the playboy on the winkered [37] mule.

MAHON (*puzzled*): That lad, is it? If you said it was a fool he was, I'd have laid a mighty oath he was the likeness of my wandering son. (*Uneasily, putting his hand to his head.*) Faith, I'm thinking I'll go walking for to view the race.

WIDOW QUIN (*stopping him, sharply*): You will not. You'd best take the road to Belmullet, and not be dilly-dallying in this place where there isn't a spot you could sleep.

PHILLY (*coming forward*): Don't mind her. Mount there on the bench and you'll have a view of the whole. They're hurrying before the tide will rise, and it'd be near over if you went down the pathway through the crags below.

MAHON (*mounts on bench,* WIDOW QUIN *beside him*): That's a right view again the edge of the sea. They're coming now from the point. He's leading. Who is he at all?

WIDOW QUIN: He's the champion of the world, I tell you, and there isn't a hap'orth[38] isn't falling lucky to his hands today.

PHILLY (*looking out, interested in the race*): Look at that. They're pressing him now.

JIMMY: He'll win it yet.

PHILLY: Take your time, Jimmy Farrell. It's too soon to say.

WIDOW QUIN (*shouting*): Watch him taking the gate. There's riding.

JIMMY (*cheering*): More power to the young lad!

MAHON: He's passing the third.

JIMMY: He'll lick them yet.

WIDOW QUIN: He'd lick them if he was running races with a score itself.

MAHON: Look at the mule he has, kicking the stars.

WIDOW QUIN: There was a lep! (*Catching hold of* MAHON *in her excitement.*) He's fallen? He's mounted again! Faith, he's passing them all!

JIMMY: Look at him skelping her!

PHILLY: And the mountain girls hooshing him on!

JIMMY: It's the last turn! The post's cleared for them now!

MAHON: Look at the narrow place. He'll be into the bogs! (*With a yell.*) Good rider! He's through it again!

JIMMY: He neck and neck!

PHILLY: Good boy to him! Flames, but he's in! (*Great cheering, in which all join.*)

MAHON (*with hesitation*): What's that? They're raising him up.

[37] blinkered [38] ha'pennyworth, *i.e.*, merest trifle

They're coming this way. (*With a roar of rage and astonishment.*) It's Christy, by the stars of God! I'd know his way of spitting and he astride the moon. (*He jumps down and makes a run for the door, but* WIDOW QUIN *catches him and pulls him back.*)

WIDOW QUIN: Stay quiet, will you? That's not your son. (*To* JIMMY.) Stop him, or you'll get a month for the abetting of manslaughter and be fined as well.

JIMMY: I'll hold him.

MAHON (*struggling*): Let me out! Let me out, the lot of you, till I have my vengeance on his head today.

WIDOW QUIN (*shaking him, vehemently*): That's not your son. That's a man is going to make a marriage with the daughter of this house, a place with fine trade, with a licence, and with poteen too.

MAHON (*amazed*): That man marrying a decent and a moneyed girl! Is it mad yous are? Is it in a crazy-house for females that I'm landed now?

WIDOW QUIN: It's mad yourself is with the blow upon your head. That lad is the wonder of the western world.

MAHON: I seen it's my son.

WIDOW QUIN: You seen that you're mad. (*Cheering outside.*) Do you hear them cheering him in the zig-zags of the road? Aren't you after saying that your son's a fool, and how would they be cheering a true idiot born?

MAHON (*getting distressed*): It's maybe out of reason that that man's himself. (*Cheering again.*) There's none surely will go cheering him. Oh, I'm raving with a madness that would fright the world! (*He sits down with his hand to his head.*) There was one time I seen ten scarlet divils letting on they'd cork my spirit in a gallon can; and one time I seen rats as big as badgers sucking the lifeblood from the butt of my lug; [39] but I never till this day confused that dribbling idiot with a likely man. I'm destroyed surely.

WIDOW QUIN: And who'd wonder when it's your brain-pan that is gaping now?

MAHON: Then the blight of the sacred drouth upon myself and him, for I never went mad to this day, and I not three weeks with the Limerick girls drinking myself silly and parlatic[40] from the dusk to dawn. (*To* WIDOW QUIN, *suddenly.*) Is my visage astray?

WIDOW QUINN: It is, then. You're a sniggering maniac, a child could see.

MAHON (*getting up more cheerfully*): Then I'd best be going to the union[41] beyond, and there'll be a welcome before me, I tell you (*with*

[39] lobe of my ear [40] paralytic [41] parish work house

great pride), and I a terrible and fearful case, the way that there I was one time, screeching in a straightened waistcoat, with seven doctors writing out my sayings in a printed book. Would you believe that?

WIDOW QUIN: If you're a wonder itself, you'd best be hasty, for them lads caught a maniac one time and pelted the poor creature till he ran out, raving and foaming, and was drowned in the sea.

MAHON (*with philosophy*): It's true mankind is the divil when your head's astray. Let me out now and I'll slip down the boreen, and not see them so.

WIDOW QUIN (*showing him out*): That's it. Run to the right, and not a one will see. (*He runs off.*)

PHILLY (*wisely*): You're at some gaming, Widow Quin; but I'll walk after him and give him his dinner and a time to rest, and I'll see then if he's raving or as sane as you.

WIDOW QUIN (*annoyed*): If you go near that lad, let you be wary of your head, I'm saying. Didn't you hear him telling he was crazed at times?

PHILLY: I heard him telling a power; and I'm thinking we'll have right sport before night will fall. (*He goes out.*)

JIMMY: Well, Philly's a conceited and foolish man. How could that madman have his senses and his brain-pan slit? I'll go after them and see him turn on Philly now.

(*He goes;* WIDOW QUIN *hides poteen behind counter. Then hubbub outside.*)

VOICES: There you are! Good jumper! Grand lepper! Darlint boy! He's the racer! Bear him on, will you!

(CHRISTY *comes in, in jockey's dress, with* PEGEEN MIKE, SARA, *and other* GIRLS *and* MEN.)

PEGEEN (*to crowd*): Go on now and don't destroy him and he drenching with sweat. Go along, I'm saying, and have your tug-of-warring till he's dried his skin.

CROWD: Here's his prizes! A bagpipes! A fiddle was played by a poet in the years gone by! A flat and three-thorned blackthorn would lick the scholars out of Dublin town!

CHRISTY (*taking prizes from the* MEN): Thank you kindly, the lot of you. But you'd say it was little only I did this day if you'd seen me a while since striking my one single blow.

TOWN CRIER (*outside ringing a bell*): Take notice, last event of this day! Tug-of-warring on the green below! Come on, the lot of you! Great achievements for all Mayo men!

PEGEEN: Go on and leave him for to rest and dry. Go on, I tell you, for he'll do no more.

(*She hustles crowd out;* WIDOW QUIN *following them.*)

MEN (*going*): Come on, then. Good luck for the while!

PEGEEN (*radiantly, wiping his face with her shawl*): Well, you're the lad, and you'll have great times from this out when you could win that wealth of prizes, and you sweating in the heat of noon!

CHRISTY (*looking at her with delight*): I'll have great times if I win the crowning prize I'm seeking now, and that's your promise that you'll wed me in a fortnight, when our banns is called.

PEGEEN (*backing away from him*): You've right daring to go ask me that, when all knows you'll be starting to some girl in your own townland, when your father's rotten in four months, or five.

CHRISTY (*indignantly*): Starting from you, it it? (*He follows her.*) I will not, then, and when the airs is warming, in four months or five, it's then yourself and me should be pacing Neifin in the dews of night, the times sweet smells do be rising, and you'd see a little, shiny new moon, maybe, sinking on the hills.

PEGEEN (*looking at him playfully*): And it's that kind of a poacher's love you'd make, Christy Mahon, on the sides of Neifin, when the night is down?

CHRISTY: It's little you'll think if my love's a poacher's, or an earl's itself, when you'll feel my two hands stretched around you, and I squeezing kisses on your puckered lips, till I'd feel a kind of pity for the Lord God is all ages sitting lonesome in His golden chair.

PEGEEN: That'll be right fun, Christy Mahon, and any girl would walk her heart out before she'd meet a young man was your like for eloquence, or talk at all.

CHRISTY (*encouraged*): Let you wait, to hear me talking, till we're astray in Erris, when Good Friday's by, drinking a sup from a well, and making mighty kisses with our wetted mouths, or gaming in a gap of sunshine, with yourself stretched back unto your necklace, in the flowers of the earth.

PEGEEN (*in a low voice, moved by his tone*): I'd be nice so, is it?

CHRISTY (*with rapture*): If the mitred bishops seen you that time, they'd be the like of the holy prophets, I'm thinking, do be straining the bars of Paradise to lay eyes on the Lady Helen of Troy, and she abroad, pacing back and forward, with a nosegay in her golden shawl.

PEGEEN (*with real tenderness*): And what is it I have, Christy Mahon, to make me fitting entertainment for the like of you, that has such poet's talking, and such bravery of heart.

CHRISTY (*in a low voice*): Isn't there the light of seven heavens in your heart alone, the way you'll be an angel's lamp to me from this out, and I abroad in the darkness, spearing salmons in the Owen or the Carrowmore?

PEGEEN: If I was your wife I'd be along with you those nights, Christy Mahon, the way you'd see I was a great hand at coaxing bailiffs, or coining funny nicknames for the stars of night.

CHRISTY: You, is it? Taking your death in the hailstones, or in the fogs of dawn.

PEGEEN: Yourself and me would shelter easy in a narrow bush (*with a qualm of dread*); but we're only talking, maybe, for this would be a poor, thatched place to hold a fine lad is the like of you.

CHRISTY (*putting his arm round her*): If I wasn't a good Christian, it's on my naked knees I'd be saying my prayers and paters to every jack-straw you have roofing your head, and every stony pebble is paving the laneway to your door.

PEGEEN (*radiantly*): If that's the truth I'll be burning candles from this out to the miracles of God that have brought you from the south to-day, and I with my gowns bought ready, the way that I can wed you, and not wait at all.

CHRISTY: It's miracles, and that's the truth. Me there toiling a long while, and walking a long while, not knowing at all I was drawing all times nearer to this holy day.

PEGEEN: And myself, a girl, was tempted often to go sailing the seas till I'd marry a Jew-man, with ten kegs of gold, and I not knowing at all there was the like of you drawing nearer, like the stars of God.

CHRISTY: And to think I'm long years hearing women talking that talk, to all bloody fools, and this the first time I've heard the like of your voice talking sweetly for my own delight.

PEGEEN: And to think it's me is talking sweetly, Christy Mahon, and I the fright of seven townlands for my biting tongue. Well, the heart's a wonder; and, I'm thinking, there won't be our like in Mayo, for gallant lovers, from this hour today. (*Drunken singing is heard outside.*) There's my father coming from the wake, and when he's had his sleep we'll tell him, for he's peaceful then. (*They separate.*)

MICHAEL (*singing outside*):

The jailer and the turnkey
They quickly ran us down,
And brought us back as prisoners
Once more to Cavan town.

(*He comes in supported by* SHAWN.)

There we lay bewailing
All in a prison bound. . . .

(*He sees* CHRISTY. *Goes and shakes him drunkenly by the hand, while* PEGEEN *and* SHAWN *talk on the left.*)

MICHAEL (*to* CHRISTY): The blessing of God and the holy angels on your head, young fellow. I hear tell you're after winning all in the sports below; and wasn't it a shame I didn't bear you along with me to Kate Cassidy's wake, a fine, stout lad, the like of you, for you'd never see the match of it for flows of drink, the way when we sunk her bones at noon-day in her narrow grave, there were five men, aye, and six men, stretched out retching speechless on the holy stones.

CHRISTY (*uneasily, watching* PEGEEN): Is that the truth?

MICHAEL: It is, then; and aren't you a louty schemer to go burying your poor father unbeknownst when you'd a right to throw him on the crupper of a Kerry mule and drive him westwards, like holy Joseph in the days gone by, the way we could have given him a decent burial, and not have him rotting beyond, and not a Christian drinking a smart drop to the glory of his soul?

CHRISTY (*gruffly*): It's well enough he's lying, for the likes of him.

MICHAEL (*slapping him on the back*): Well, aren't you a hardened slayer? It'll be a poor thing for the household man where you go sniffing for a female wife; and (*pointing to* SHAWN) look beyond at that shy and decent Christian I have chosen for my daughter's hand, and I after getting the gilded dispensation this day for to wed them now.

CHRISTY: And you'll be wedding them this day, is it?

MICHAEL (*drawing himself up*): Aye. Are you thinking, if I'm drunk itself, I'd leave my daughter living single with a little frisky rascal is the like of you?

PEGEEN (*breaking away from* SHAWN): Is it the truth the dispensation's come?

MICHAEL (*triumphantly*): Father Reilly's after reading it in gallous[42] Latin, and "It's come in the nick of time," says he; "so I'll wed them in a hurry, dreading that young gaffer who'd capsize the stars."

PEGEEN (*fiercely*): He's missed his nick of time, for it's that lad, Christy Mahon, that I'm wedding now.

MICHAEL (*loudly, with horror*): You'd be making him a son to me, and he wet and crusted with his father's blood?

PEGEEN: Aye. Wouldn't it be a bitter thing for a girl to go marrying

[42] an intensive: "bloody," "great"

the like of Shaneen, and he a middling kind of a scarecrow, with no savagery or fine words in him at all?

MICHAEL (*gasping and sinking on a chair*): Oh, aren't you a heathen daughter to go shaking the fat of my heart, and I swamped and drownded with the weight of drink? Would you have them turning on me the way that I'd be roaring to the dawn of day with the wind upon my heart? Have you not a word to aid me, Shaneen? Are you not jealous at all?

SHAWN (*in great misery*): I'd be afeard to be jealous of a man did slay his da.

PEGEEN: Well, it'd be a poor thing to go marrying your like. I'm seeing there's a world of peril for an orphan girl, and isn't it a great blessing I didn't wed you before himself came walking from the west or south?

SHAWN: It's a queer story you'd go picking a dirty tramp up from the highways of the world.

PEGEEN (*playfully*): And you think you're a likely beau to go straying along with the shiny Sundays of the opening year, when it's sooner on a bullock's liver you'd put a poor girl thinking than on the lily or the rose?

SHAWN: And have you no mind of my weight of passion, and the holy dispensation, and the drift of heifers I'm giving, and the golden ring?

PEGEEN: I'm thinking you're too fine for the like of me, Shawn Keogh of Killakeen, and let you go off till you'd find a radiant lady with droves of bullocks on the plains of Meath, and herself bedizened in the diamond jewelleries of Pharaoh's ma. That'd be your match, Shaneen. So God save you now! (*She retreats behind* CHRISTY.)

SHAWN: Won't you hear me telling you . . . ?

CHRISTY (*with ferocity*): Take yourself from this, young fellow, or I'll maybe add a murder to my deeds today.

MICHAEL (*springing up with a shriek*): Murder, is it? Is it mad yous are? Would you go making murder in this place, and it piled with poteen for our drink to-night? Go on to the foreshore if it's fighting you want, where the rising tide will wash all traces from the memory of man. (*Pushing* SHAWN *towards* CHRISTY.)

SHAWN (*shaking himself free, and getting behind* MICHAEL): I'll not fight him, Michael James. I'd liefer live a bachelor, simmering in passions to the end of time, than face a lepping savage the like of him has descended from the Lord knows where. Strike him yourself, Michael James, or you'll lose my drift of heifers and my blue bull from Sneem.

MICHAEL: Is it me fight him, when it's father-slaying he's bred to now? (*Pushing* SHAWN.) Go on, you fool, and fight him now.

SHAWN (*coming forward a little*): Will I strike him with my hand?

MICHAEL: Take the loy is on your western side.

SHAWN: I'd be afeard of the gallows if I struck with that.

CHRISTY (*taking up the loy*): Then I'll make you face the gallows or quit off from this. (SHAWN *flies out of the door.*)

CHRISTY: Well, fine weather be after him (*going to* MICHAEL, *coaxingly*), and I'm thinking you wouldn't wish to have that quaking blackguard in your house at all. Let you give us your blessing and hear her swear her faith to me, for I'm mounted on the spring-tide of the stars of luck, the way it'll be good for any to have me in the house.

PEGEEN (*at the other side of* MICHAEL): Bless us now, for I swear to God I'll wed him, and I'll not renege.

MICHAEL (*standing up in the centre, holding on to both of them*): It's the will of God, I'm thinking, that all should win an easy or a cruel end, and it's the will of God that all should rear up lengthy families for the nurture of the earth. What's a single man, I ask you, eating a bit in one house and drinking a sup in another, and he with no place of his own, like an old braying jackass strayed upon the rocks? (*To* CHRISTY.) It's many would be in dread to bring your like into their house for to end them, maybe, with a sudden end; but I'm a decent man of Ireland, and I liefer face the grave untimely and I seeing a score of grandsons growing up little gallant swearers by the name of God, than go peopling my bedside with puny weeds the like of what you'd breed, I'm thinking, out of Shaneen Keogh. (*He joins their hands.*) A daring fellow is the jewel of the world, and a man did split his father's middle with a single clout should have the bravery of ten, so may God and Mary and St. Patrick bless you, and increase you from this mortal day.

CHRISTY *and* PEGEEN: Amen, O Lord!

(*Hubbub outside.* OLD MAHON *rushes in, followed by all the crowd, and* WIDOW QUIN. *He makes a rush at* CHRISTY, *knocks him down, and begins to beat him.*)

PEGEEN (*dragging back his arm*): Stop that, will you? Who are you at all?

MAHON: His father, God forgive me!

PEGEEN (*drawing back*): Is it rose from the dead?

MAHON: Do you think I look so easy quenched with the tap of a loy?

(*Beats* CHRISTY *again.*)

PEGEEN (*glaring at* CHRISTY): And it's lies you told, letting on you had him slitted, and you nothing at all.

CHRISTY (*catching* MAHON'S *stick*): He's not my father. He's a raving maniac would scare the world. (*Pointing to* WIDOW QUIN.) Herself knows it is true.

CROWD: You're fooling Pegeen! The Widow Quin seen him this day, and you likely knew! You're a liar!

CHRISTY (*dumbfounded*): It's himself was a liar, lying stretched out with an open head on him, letting on he was dead.

MAHON: Weren't you off racing the hills before I got my breath with the start I had seeing you turn on me at all?

PEGEEN: And to think of the coaxing glory we had given him, and he after doing nothing but hitting a soft blow and chasing northward in a sweat of fear. Quit off from this.

CHRISTY (*piteously*): You've seen my doings this day, and let you save me from the old man; for why would you be in such a scorch of haste to spur me to destruction now?

PEGEEN: It's there your treachery is spurring me, till I'm hard set to think you're the one I'm after lacing in my heart-strings half an hour gone by. (*To* MAHON.) Take him on from this, for I think bad the world should see me raging for a Munster liar, and the fool of men.

MAHON: Rise up now to retribution, and come on with me.

CROWD (*jeeringly*): There's the playboy! There's the lad thought he'd rule the roost in Mayo! Slate him now, mister.

CHRISTY (*getting up in shy terror*): What is it drives you to torment me here, when I'd asked the thunders of the might of God to blast me if I ever did hurt to any saving only that one single blow.

MAHON (*loudly*): If you didn't, you're a poor good-for-nothing, and isn't it by the like of you the sins of the whole world are committed?

CHRISTY (*raising his hands*): In the name of the Almighty God . . .

MAHON: Leave troubling the Lord God. Would you have Him sending down drouths, and fevers, and the old hen and the cholera morbus?

CHRISTY (*to* WIDOW QUIN): Will you come between us and protect me now?

WIDOW QUIN: I've tried a lot, God help me, and my share is done.

CHRISTY (*looking round in desperation*): And I must go back into my torment, is it, or run off like a vagabond straying through the unions with the dust of August making mudstains in the gullet of my throat; or the winds of March blowing on me till I'd take an oath I felt them making whistles of my ribs within?

SARA: Ask Pegeen to aid you. Her like does often change.

CHRISTY: I will not, then, for there's torment in the splendour of her like, and she a girl any moon of midnight would take pride to meet, facing southwards on the heaths of Keel. But what did I want crawling forward to scorch my understanding at her flaming brow?

PEGEEN (*to* MAHON, *vehemently, fearing she will break into tears*): Take him on from this or I'll set the young lads to destroy him here.

MAHON (*going to him, shaking his stick*): Come on now if you wouldn't have the company to see you skelped.

PEGEEN (*half-laughing, through her tears*): That's it, now the world will see him pandied,[43] and he an ugly liar was playing off the hero, and the fright of men.

CHRISTY (*to* MAHON, *very sharply*): Leave me go!

CROWD: That's it. Now, Christy. If them two set fighting, it will lick the world.

MAHON (*making a grab at* CHRISTY): Come here to me.

CHRISTY (*more threatening*): Leave me go, I'm saying.

MAHON: I will, maybe, when your legs is limping, and your back is blue.

CROWD: Keep it up, the two of you. I'll back the old one. Now the playboy.

CHRISTY (*in low and intense voice*): Shut your yelling, for if you're after making a mighty man of me this day by the power of a lie, you're setting me now to think if it's a poor thing to be lonesome it's worse, maybe, go mixing with the fools of earth.

(MAHON *makes a movement towards him.*)

CHRISTY (*almost shouting*): Keep off . . . lest I do show a blow unto the lot of you would set the guardian angels winking in the clouds above. (*He swings round with a sudden rapid movement and picks up a loy.*)

CROWD (*half-frightened, half-amused*): He's going mad! Mind yourselves! Run from the idiot!

CHRISTY: If I am an idiot, I'm after hearing my voice this day saying words would raise the top-knot on a poet in a merchant's town. I've won your racing, and your lepping, and . . .

MAHON: Shut your gullet and come on with me.

CHRISTY: I'm going, but I'll stretch you first.

(*He runs at* OLD MAHON *with the loy, chases him out of the door, followed by crowd and* WIDOW QUIN. *There is a great noise outside, then a yell, and dead silence for a moment.* CHRISTY *comes in, half-dazed, and goes to fire.*)

[43] beaten

WIDOW QUIN (*coming in hurriedly, and going to him*): They're turning again you. Come on, or you'll be hanged, indeed.

CHRISTY: I'm thinking, from this out, Pegeen'll be giving me praises, the same as in the hours gone by.

WIDOW QUIN (*impatiently*): Come by the back door. I'd think bad to have you stifled on the gallows tree.

CHRISTY (*indignantly*): I will not, then. What good'd be my lifetime if I left Pegeen?

WIDOW QUIN: Come on, and you'll be no worse than you were last night; and you with a double murder this time to be telling to the girls.

CHRISTY: I'll not leave Pegeen Mike.

WIDOW QUIN (*impatiently*): Isn't there the match of her in every parish public, from Binghamstown unto the plain of Meath? Come on, I tell you, and I'll find you finer sweethearts at each waning moon.

CHRISTY: It's Pegeen I'm seeking only, and what'd I care if you brought me a drift of chosen females, standing in their shifts itself, maybe, from this place to the eastern world?

SARA (*runs in, pulling off one of her petticoats*): They're going to hang him. (*Holding out petticoat and shawl.*) Fit these upon him, and let him run off to the east.

WIDOW QUIN: He's raving now; but we'll fit them on him, and I'll take him to the ferry to the Achill boat.

CHRISTY (*struggling feebly*): Leave me go, will you? when I'm thinking of my luck today, for she will wed me surely, and I a proven hero in the end of all.

(*They try to fasten petticoat round him.*)

WIDOW QUIN: Take his left hand, and we'll pull him now. Come on, young fellow.

CHRISTY (*suddenly starting up*): You'll be taking me from her? You're jealous, is it, of her wedding me? Go on from this. (*He snatches up a stool, and threatens them with it.*)

WIDOW QUIN (*going*): It's in the madhouse they should put him, not in jail, at all. We'll go by the back door to call the doctor, and we'll save him so.

(*She goes out, with* SARA, *through inner room.* MEN *crowd in the doorway.* CHRISTY *sits down again by the fire.*)

MICHAEL (*in a terrified whisper*): Is the old lad killed surely?

PHILLY: I'm after feeling the last gasps quitting his heart. (*They peer in at* CHRISTY.)

MICHAEL (*with a rope*): Look at the way he is. Twist a hangman's knot on it, and slip it over his head, while he's not minding at all.

PHILLY: Let you take it, Shaneen. You're the soberest of all that's here.

SHAWN: Is it me to go near him, and he the wickedest and the worst with me? Let you take it, Pegeen Mike.

PEGEEN: Come on, so. (*She goes forward with the others, and they drop the double hitch over his head.*)

CHRISTY: What ails you?

SHAWN (*triumphantly, as they pull the rope tight on his arms*): Come on to the peelers, till they stretch you now.

CHRISTY: Me!

MICHAEL: If we took pity on you the Lord God would, maybe, bring us ruin from the law today, so you'd best come easy, for hanging is an easy and a speedy end.

CHRISTY: I'll not stir. (*To* PEGEEN.) And what is it you'll say to me, and I after doing it this time in the face of all?

PEGEEN: I'll say, a strange man is a marvel, with his mighty talk; but what's a squabble in your backyard, and the blow of a loy, have taught me that there's a great gap between a gallous story and a dirty deed. (*To* MEN.) Take him on from this, or the lot of us will be likely put on trial for his deed to-day.

CHRISTY (*with horror in his voice*): And it's yourself will send me off, to have a horny-fingered hangman hitching his bloody slipknots at the butt of my ear.

MEN (*pulling rope*): Come on, will you?

(*He is pulled down on the floor.*)

CHRISTY (*twisting his legs round the table*): Cut the rope, Pegeen, and I'll quit the lot of you, and live from this out, like the madmen of Keel, eating muck and green weeds on the faces of the cliffs.

PEGEEN: And leave us to hang, is it, for a saucy liar, the like of you? (*To* MEN.) Take him on, out from this.

SHAWN: Pull a twist on his neck, and squeeze him so.

PHILLY: Twist yourself. Sure he cannot hurt you, if you keep your distance from his teeth alone.

SHAWN: I'm afeard of him. (*To* PEGEEN.) Lift a lighted sod, will you, and scorch his leg.

PEGEEN (*blowing the fire with a bellows*): Leave go now, young fellow, or I'll scorch your shins.

CHRISTY: You're blowing for to torture me. (*His voice rising and growing stronger.*) That's your kind, is it? Then let the lot of you be wary, for, if I've to face the gallows, I'll have a gay march down, I tell you, and shed the blood of some of you before I die.

SHAWN (*in terror*): Keep a good hold, Philly. Be wary, for the love of God. For I'm thinking he would liefest wreak his pains on me.

CHRISTY (*almost gaily*): If I do lay my hands on you, it's the way you'll be at the fall of night, hanging as a scarecrow for the fowls of hell. Ah, you'll have a gallous jaunt, I'm saying, coaching out through Limbo with my father's ghost.

SHAWN (*to* PEGEEN): Make haste, will you? Oh, isn't he a holy terror, and isn't it true for Father Reilly, that all drink's a curse that has the lot of you so shaky and uncertain now?

CHRISTY: If I can wring a neck among you, I'll have a royal judgment looking on the trembling jury in the courts of law. And won't there be crying out in Mayo the day I'm stretched upon the rope, with ladies in their silks and satins snivelling in their lacy kerchiefs, and they rhyming songs and ballads on the terror of my fate? (*He squirms round on the floor and bites* SHAWN's *leg.*)

SHAWN (*shrieking*): My leg's bit on me. He's the like of a mad dog, I'm thinking, the way that I will surely die.

CHRISTY (*delighted with himself*): You will, then, the way you can shake out hell's flags of welcome for my coming in two weeks or three, for I'm thinking Satan hasn't many have killed their da in Kerry, and in Mayo too.

(OLD MAHON *comes in behind on all fours and looks on unnoticed.*)

MEN (*to* PEGEEN): Bring the sod, will you?

PEGEEN (*coming over*): God help him so. (*Burns his leg.*)

CHRISTY (*kicking and screaming*): Oh, glory be to God! (*He kicks loose from the table, and they all drag him towards the door.*)

JIMMY (*seeing* OLD MAHON): Will you look what's come in?

(*They all drop* CHRISTY *and run left.*)

CHRISTY (*scrambling on his knees face to face with* OLD MAHON): Are you coming to be killed a third time, or what ails you now?

MAHON: For what is it they have you tied?

CHRISTY: They're taking me to the peelers to have me hanged for slaying you.

MICHAEL (*apologetically*): It is the will of God that all should guard their little cabins from the treachery of law, and what would my daughter be doing if I was ruined or was hanged itself?

MAHON (*grimly, loosening* CHRISTY): It's little I care if you put a bag on her back, and went picking cockles till the hour of death; but my son and myself will be going our own way, and we'll have great times from this out telling stories of the villainy of Mayo, and the fools is here. (*To* CHRISTY, *who is freed.*) Come on now.

CHRISTY: Go with you, is it? I will then, like a gallant captain with his heathen slave. Go on now and I'll see you from this day stewing my oatmeal and washing my spuds, for I'm master of all fights from now. (*Pushing* MAHON.) Go on, I'm saying.

MAHON: Is it me?

CHRISTY: Not a word out of you. Go on from this.

MAHON (*walking out and looking back at* CHRISTY *over his shoulder*): Glory be to God! (*With a broad smile.*) I am crazy again. (*Goes.*)

CHRISTY: Ten thousand blessings upon all that's here, for you've turned me a likely gaffer in the end of all, the way I'll go romancing through a romping lifetime from this hour to the dawning of the judgment day. (*He goes out.*)

MICHAEL: By the will of God, we'll have peace now for our drinks. Will you draw the porter, Pegeen?

SHAWN (*going up to her*): It's a miracle Father Reilly can wed us in the end of all, and we'll have none to trouble us when his vicious bite is healed.

PEGEEN (*hitting him a box on the ear*): Quit my sight. (*Putting her shawl over her head and breaking out into wild lamentations.*) Oh, my grief, I've lost him surely. I've lost the only Playboy of the Western World.

AN ENTERPRISING journalist interviewed Synge during the opening-night riots of the week-long disturbance that attended the original run of *The Playboy of the Western World* * at Dublin's Abbey Theatre, January 26–February 2, 1907. "In art," Synge told him, defending his play, "a spade must be called a spade." "But the complaint is, Mr. Synge," replied the journalist, "that you have called it a bloody shovel."

The pun neatly pinpointed the trouble. What the rioters objected to in Synge's play was blasphemy and indecency of language and brutality of incident. Piety flinched when Christy, in his ardor for Pegeen, felt pity "for the Lord God is all ages sitting lonesome in His golden chair," and virtue blushed at his vision of "a drift of chosen females,

* The title has irrelevant connotations in contemporary colloquial American. It refers neither to Christy's delight in pretty girls nor to Shawn's offer to ship him off to the States. "Playboy" means both one who is good at games, and a hoaxer. "Western world" is an old Irish poeticism for western Ireland.

standing in their shifts itself, maybe." * Parricide failed to seem amusing, and the burning of Christy's leg on stage seemed — not unnaturally — merely shocking. The next day the Nationalist newspapers blasted the performance as an "unmitigated, protracted libel upon Irish peasant men and worse still upon Irish peasant girlhood." "Squalid . . . offensive . . . incongruously called a comedy . . . barbarous jargon . . . elaborate and incessant cursings . . . repulsive creatures . . . vile and inhuman story . . . the foulest language" set their general tone. Behind their indignation was the feeling that Synge had unpatriotically betrayed the public image of a mature and enlightened nation, long since ready for self-rule.

The reaction is understandable in the political context of the time, but in the calm nonpartisanship that distance breeds the rioters seem bigoted and insensitive. No Scotchman feels that his country has been slurred because Macbeth is a murderer. Shakespeare's erring heroes are redeemed in our eyes by the fineness of feeling of which the matchless poetry they have been given to speak is proof. Similarly, Christy's natural way with rich words saves him from being merely a murderous backyard squabbler. Poetic imagination alters and makes reality. But by the token of this romantic theme Synge seems unconvincing in his role of martyr in the cause of realism. Calling a spade a spade is almost exactly what he does not do. Rather, his play shows the temporary triumph of eloquence over fact. Language is the real hero of *Playboy*. And the number of versions Synge wrote of his play proves that it was no impromptu copy of reality. He lettered each version. The final one of Act I was G, of Act II, I, and of Act III, K.

Realism is rarely a simple quality in art. That Synge based his play on an actual case and that it may well be true that he used, as he said in his Preface, "one or two words only that I have not heard among the country people of Ireland, or spoken in my nursery before I could read the newspapers" do not guarantee authenticity in the sense that the play faithfully reflects the realities of west-Irish peasants in the early years of the century. The quality of a dramatic action based on fact is not necessarily identical with that of its real-life origin, and there is more to dramatic speech than diction. And if *Playboy* is felt to be less than fully realistic, the reason, perhaps, is not that it is implausible that a whole village would lionize a confessed father-slayer and turn against him when his alleged victim turns up alive, or that rough peasants talk readily in lovely lilt and image, but that the tone of village life seems imaginatively heightened in the intense and exclusive concern with the romantic stranger. The play commands belief as reality, but it is less

* "Mayo girls" were substituted for "chosen females" in performance. Even so, the speech set the first-night audience hissing.

the reality of a documentary than that of a successfully realized imaginative world. It is a world of such ubiquitous grace and power of lyrical speech that at times it barely accommodates Synge's plot. Christy's distinction over Shawn Keogh, who has "no savagery or fine words in him at all," is a basic plot premise. Pegeen and the other villagers infer Christy's savagery from his words. But Shawn is occasionally given speeches as fine as many of Christy's. "Let you not take it badly, mister honey" (he says to Christy); "isn't beyond the best place for you, where you'll have golden chains and shiny coats and you riding upon hunters with the ladies of the land."

The issue of "reality" in *Playboy* is further complicated by its affiliations with naturalistic theory. However wrong the hooters and hissers may have been in feeling that Synge vilified Irish peasantry, they were not wrong in sensing the larger, communal implications of his story of Christy's growth into manhood. For the metamorphosis of a "dirty, stuttering lout" into a girl's marvel of a poet, one of the "fine, fiery fellows with great rages when their temper's roused," of sordid fact into heroic legend, is a function not just of language but of the particular community into which Christy is taken. From "a windy corner of high, distant hills" he comes to a place of furze and ditch and peat bog, scrawny potato patches and leaky thatch, ruled by priests and peelers, a place of violence and gossip, hard work and meagre living, young men gone to America and girls like Pegeen left in the stale stink of liquor to marry funks like Shawn Keogh. The idiosyncrasies of the local group, the collective ethos, is a main character. *Playboy*, that is to say, is a folk play, and to the extent it is, the riots, unlike many theatrical battles, may be said to have concerned a fact of the play and not some extrinsic circumstance of production.

The naturalism implicit in this concept of the playboy character as the product, in part, of a folk environment that first "makes" Christy and then completes his self-discovery by becoming his antagonist is evidence of the strength of the naturalistic influence on the drama of the time. For Synge was opposed to naturalism — not so much, perhaps, to its mechanistic philosophy as to its language. The turn-of-the-century Irish literary revival saw in the prevailing Ibsenite naturalism of English and Continental drama nothing but prosy didacticism and ugly copies of mean urban life. In conscious reaction it sought the spontaneous beauty and intensity of native song and legend and fairy tale, symbolism and ritual.

Like the other leaders of the Irish renaissance, Synge was cool to the efforts of the Nationalist extremists to replace English with Gaelic as national language. In the Preface to *Playboy* he assumes that the English of the Irish peasant is the proper speech for the Irish stage. "For a few years more," he says, Irish peasant speech, the voice of "a popular imagination that is fiery, and magnificent, and tender," will continue to supply the "reality," which musical comedy has falsified, and the "joy," which the "pallid words" of "the intellectual modern drama" have failed to furnish. Naturalism is on principle committed to "reality," and though it is true that naturalistic plays generally are more grim than joyous, there is really no reason why blind determinism cannot play happy as well as sad games with the human pawn. In other words, although *Playboy* is less a dialect play, by strict naturalistic norms, than a play in standard English with dialect elements, Synge's language is not in conflict with the naturalistic implications of its theme and characterization.*

Speech carries the burden of the play. It evokes the larger world of wakes and games and prisons, of weather, and of landscape of places with names like "the Stooks of the Dead Women." Actual stage setting is limited to the interior of the pub, which serves as a public place for Christy to tell his story in and to suggest that Christy, like poteen, is an antidote to boredom. Plot, too, is mainly an occasion for speech. The Abbey actor who grumbled that the play lacked plot was not right, but it is true that there is little movement between Christy's arrival early in Act I and Old Mahon's in the middle of Act II and between the middle of Act II and the row at the end of the act, which ends in the departure of both father and son. Until Old Mahon's arrival in the middle of Act II Christy's fortunes are rising. Between that climactic midpoint in the play and Pegeen's confrontation with Old Mahon near the end of Act III we more or less know that Christy is living on borrowed time. But this pattern is almost the whole extent of the plot. Widow Quin's alliance with Shawn in an effort to win Christy for herself and her later attempt to save Christy from being exposed do not amount to much of an intrigue, and her unruffled good sense and good

* Some of the more striking features of Synge's prose in *Playboy* may be noted. There are items of specifically Irish syntax and idiom: the use of progressive for simple verb forms ("It should be larceny, I'm thinking"), the omission of relatives ("I'd feel a kind of pity for the Lord God is all ages sitting lonesome"), inversion ("It's above at the crossroads he is"), co-ordination with "and" for more logically exact subordination ("What is there to hurt you, and you a fine, hardy girl"), "after" to indicate completed action ("I'm after feeling a kind of fellow above"), insertions ("surely," "I'm thinking," vocatives), and "himself" and "itself" (the latter in the sense of "even" or "actually"). Stylistic characteristics include strong non-periodicity (the voice, as if self-entranced, trailing off into upbeat image or speech tag after the completion of the sense), frequent simile (and hardly a single metaphor), landscape and religious imagery, Old Testament cadence and naive–solemn circumstantial concreteness, and irregularly spaced clusters of stressed and unstressed syllables producing lilting speech rhythms.

temper fail to provide exciting drama. Shawn only frets and whimpers. Pegeen's fits of jealousy hardly deserve to be called even minor episodes. The main function of the lesser characters is choric. Michael Flaherty and his two wake companions are Christy's rapt audience in the murky flicker of the turf fire in Act I, just as are the girls in the "brilliant morning light" of Act II. The contrast in light is scenically effective and appropriate to the two kinds of audience, but it only emphasizes their subordinate function in the story of the making of the playboy personality.

Synge's art is objective, and the story means what the stage shows. One could read it as allegory and say that the trouble with the Irish is that they, like Pegeen, take more kindly to a poetic fable of rebellious bravado than to an act of real rebellion, or that Old Mahon represents England and Christy Ireland belatedly discovering her identity and throwing off English authority, or that the parricide suggests the archetypal action of every son who in self-fulfilment seeks to kill his father. This, perhaps, is neither mistaken nor irrelevant. But it is to diminish, simplify, render abstract, and hence to distort, the solid and various totality of speech and spectacle. A play can be allegory only if it is drama first. A view that in *Playboy* sees only satire on Irish national character, or political allegory, or allegory on the nation's need to find its own voice in art, or the operation of the unsublimated, Jungian unconscious, and not a play about Christy Mahon and Pegeen's Mike, is looking at something else than drama.

The surface story should not be "taken for granted" and probed for "hidden meanings." It has plenty of overt meaning. Pegeen reflects Christy's growth and is partly responsible for it. Her love represents the community's affection for the heroic newcomer, but it is also, simply, a girl's love. Her spite of Shawn is a form of longing for the hero she deserves and for whom she is — though she hardly knows it — waiting. Where now, she asks, in these smaller times, do you find a man "the like of Daneen Sullivan knocked the eye from a peeler; or Marcus Quin, God rest him, got six months for maiming ewes, and he a great warrant to tell stories of holy Ireland till he'd have the old women shedding down tears about their feet." As if in answer, Christy walks in with his "hanging crime."

Christy's transformation begins when his words change murder into heroic deed for Pegeen and the others. Act and word belong to different worlds. We laugh at Jimmy Farrell telling Pegeen's father that "herself will be safe tonight, with a man killed his father holding danger from the door." But he is only proving the truth of Pegeen's reply to Christy's question why they all turn against him now that he has killed his father in plain sight of all: ". . . what's a squabble in your backyard, and the blow of a loy, have taught me that there's a great gap between a gallous story and a dirty deed."

This might only have been a wholesome, though bitter, lesson for Pegeen to learn and for all of us to take home with us from the theater. But the irony of the ending will not permit such patness. Christy's change is as much a reality as the ugly assault. And it is the gallous story that the assault presumably cancels that has made Christy what he has now become. By the time Pegeen and the others lose their illusions about him, illusion has turned itself into reality: Christy has become what the village thought he was, because its belief has become his own. He has every reason to bless those who turn him out. He leaves as the hero of his own glorious fable, timid lout turned "likely gaffer," bullying his proud father, and rich enough in the promise of his "romping lifetime" to afford to lose even a girl like Pegeen. With Christy gone, Michael calls on Pegeen to "draw the porter." Shawn assumes that everything is as before Christy came and that the wedding will take place now that Father Reilly has got the dispensation. But Pegeen breaks into "wild lamentations."

No purely comic view can hold her final grief. Christy and Pegeen, like Cleopatra in Shaw's play, both undergo an education. But though the non-comic element in Shaw is the breaking off of Cleopatra's development toward wise and virtuous queenship, in *Playboy* it is the irreconcilability of squalid fact and brave imagination, the cost of that awakening into reality that marks the completion of the education. The cost is partly Christy's; he loses Pegeen. But he has gained his manhood and independence, and there will be other girls. Mainly, the cost is Pegeen's, who grieves for the loss of "the only Playboy of the Western World" — that is, she has lost, not just a lover, but an ideal. Cleopatra speaks for a world which, Shaw implies, could change if it chose to. Pegeen's disenchantment seems as inevitable as the awakening from a dream. In Shaw, world history takes a decisive turn; in Synge some west-coast villagers turn out a violent vagrant. But it is a question as to which play is the richer in tragic implications. And despite chronology and historical event, Synge's shifting, unresolved ambiguities of illusion and reality seem closer to the postwar drama of relativism and scepticism (like Pirandello's) than to the essential optimism of a Shavian thesis play of moral reform.

Synge was not always unfortunate in his comments on *Playboy*. It is, he once said, "perfectly serious when looked at in a certain light." He went on: "That is often the case, I think, with comedy, and no one is quite sure today whether Shylock and Alceste should be played seriously or not."

Luigi Pirandello

SIX CHARACTERS IN SEARCH OF AN AUTHOR

A Comedy in the Making

English Version by Edward Storer

Characters of the Comedy in the Making

THE FATHER
THE MOTHER
THE STEP-DAUGHTER
THE SON
THE BOY
THE CHILD
(*The last two do not speak.*)
MADAME PACE

Actors of the Company

THE MANAGER
LEADING LADY
LEADING MAN
SECOND LADY
LEAD
L'INGÉNUE
JUVENILE LEAD
OTHER ACTORS AND ACTRESSES
PROPERTY MAN
PROMPTER
MACHINIST
MANAGER'S SECRETARY
DOOR-KEEPER
SCENE-SHIFTERS

SCENE: *Daytime. The stage of a theater.*

N. B. *The Comedy is without acts or scenes. The performance is interrupted once, without the curtain being lowered, when the*

MANAGER *and the chief characters withdraw to arrange a scenario. A second interruption of the action takes place when, by mistake, the stage hands let the curtain down.*

ACT I

(The spectators will find the curtain raised and the stage as it usually is during the day time. It will be half dark, and empty, so that from the beginning the public may have the impression of an impromptu performance.

PROMPTER's *box and a small table and chair for the* MANAGER,

Two other small tables and several chairs scattered about as during rehearsals.

The ACTORS *and* ACTRESSES *of the company enter from the back of the stage: first one, then another, then two together; nine or ten in all. They are about to rehearse a Pirandello play: Mixing It Up.* Some of the company move off towards their dressing rooms. The* PROMPTER, *who has the "book" under his arm, is waiting for the* MANAGER *in order to begin the rehearsal.*

The ACTORS *and* ACTRESSES, *some standing, some sitting, chat and smoke. One perhaps reads a paper; another cons his part.*

Finally, the MANAGER *enters and goes to the table prepared for him. His* SECRETARY *brings him his mail, through which he glances. The* PROMPTER *takes his seat, turns on a light, and opens the "book.")*

THE MANAGER (*throwing a letter down on the table*): I can't see. (*To* PROPERTY MAN.) Let's have a little light, please!

PROPERTY MAN: Yes sir, yes, at once. (*A light comes down on to the stage.*)

THE MANAGER (*clapping his hands*): Come along! Come along! Second act of "Mixing It Up." (*Sits down.*)

(The ACTORS *and* ACTRESSES *go from the front of the stage to the wings, all except the three who are to begin the rehearsal.)*

THE PROMPTER (*reading the "book"*): "Leo Gala's house. A curious room serving as dining-room and study."

THE MANAGER (*to* PROPERTY MAN): Fix up the old red room.

PROPERTY MAN (*noting it down*): Red set. All right!

THE PROMPTER (*continuing to read from the "book"*): "Table already

* *Il giuoco delle parti.*

laid and writing desk with books and papers. Book-shelves. Exit rear to Leo's bedroom. Exit left to kitchen. Principal exit to right."

THE MANAGER (*energetically*): Well, you understand: The principal exit over there; here, the kitchen. (*Turning to actor who is to play the part of* SOCRATES.) You make your entrances and exits here. (*To* PROPERTY MAN.) The baize doors at the rear, and curtains.

PROPERTY MAN (*noting it down*): Right!

PROMPTER (*reading as before*): "When the curtain rises, Leo Gala, dressed in cook's cap and apron, is busy beating an egg in a cup. Philip, also dressed as a cook, is beating another egg. Guido Venanzi is seated and listening."

LEADING MAN (*to* MANAGER): Excuse me, but must I absolutely wear a cook's cap?

THE MANAGER (*annoyed*): I imagine so. It says so there anyway. (*Pointing to the "book."*)

LEADING MAN: But it's ridiculous!

THE MANAGER (*jumping up in a rage*): Ridiculous? Ridiculous? Is it my fault if France won't send us any more good comedies, and we are reduced to putting on Pirandello's works, where nobody understands anything, and where the author plays the fool with us all? (*The* ACTORS *grin. The* MANAGER *goes to* LEADING MAN *and shouts.*) Yes sir, you put on the cook's cap and beat eggs. Do you suppose that with all this egg-beating business you are on an ordinary stage? Get that out of your head. You represent the shell of the eggs you are beating! (*Laughter and comments among the* ACTORS.) Silence! and listen to my explanations, please! (*To* LEADING MAN.) "The empty form of reason without the fullness of instinct, which is blind." — You stand for reason, your wife is instinct. It's a mixing up of the parts, according to which you who act your own part become the puppet of yourself. Do you understand?

LEADING MAN: I'm hanged if I do.

THE MANAGER: Neither do I. But let's get on with it. It's sure to be a glorious failure anyway. (*Confidentially.*) But I say, please face three-quarters. Otherwise, what with the abstruseness of the dialogue, and the public that won't be able to hear you, the whole thing will go to hell. Come on! come on!

PROMPTER: Pardon sir, may I get into my box? There's a bit of a draught.

THE MANAGER: Yes, yes, of course!

(*At this point, the* DOOR-KEEPER *has entered from the stage door and advances towards the* MANAGER'S *table, taking off his braided cap. During this manoeuvre, the* SIX CHARACTERS *enter, and stop by the door at back of stage, so that when the* DOOR-KEEPER *is about to announce their coming to the* MANAGER, *they are already on the stage. A tenuous light surrounds them, almost as if irradiated by them — the faint breath of their fantastic reality.*

This light will disappear when they come forward towards the actors. They preserve, however, something of the dream lightness in which they seem almost suspended; but this does not detract from the essential reality of their forms and expressions.

He who is known as THE FATHER *is a man of about 50: hair, reddish in color, thin at the temples; he is not bald, however; thick moustaches, falling over his still fresh mouth, which often opens in an empty and uncertain smile. He is fattish, pale; with an especially wide forehead. He has blue, oval-shaped eyes, very clear and piercing. Wears light trousers and a dark jacket. He is alternatively mellifluous and violent in his manner.*

THE MOTHER *seems crushed and terrified as if by an intolerable weight of shame and abasement. She is dressed in modest black and wears a thick widow's veil of crêpe. When she lifts this, she reveals a wax-like face. She always keeps her eyes downcast.*

THE STEP-DAUGHTER *is dashing, almost impudent, beautiful. She wears mourning too, but with great elegance. She shows contempt for the timid half-frightened manner of the wretched* BOY *(14 years old, and also dressed in black); on the other hand, she displays a lively tenderness for her little sister,* THE CHILD *(about four), who is dressed in white, with a black silk sash at the waist.*

THE SON *(22) is tall, severe in his attitude of contempt for* THE FATHER, *supercilious and indifferent to* THE MOTHER. *He looks as if he had come on the stage against his will.)*

DOOR-KEEPER (*cap in hand*): Excuse me, sir . . .

THE MANAGER (*rudely*): Eh? What is it?

DOOR-KEEPER (*timidly*): These people are asking for you, sir.

THE MANAGER (*furious*): I am rehearsing, and you know perfectly well no one's allowed to come in during rehearsals! (*Turning to the* CHARACTERS.) Who are you, please? What do you want?

THE FATHER (*coming forward a little, followed by the others who seem embarrassed*): As a matter of fact . . . we have come here in search of an author . . .

THE MANAGER (*half angry, half amazed*): An author? What author?

THE FATHER: Any author, sir.

THE MANAGER: But there's no author here. We are not rehearsing a new piece.

THE STEP-DAUGHTER (*vivaciously*): So much the better, so much the better! We can be your new piece.

AN ACTOR (*coming forward from the others*): Oh, do you hear that?

THE FATHER (*to* STEP-DAUGHTER): Yes, but if the author isn't here . . . (*To* MANAGER.) unless you would be willing . . .

THE MANAGER: You are trying to be funny.

THE FATHER: No, for Heaven's sake, what are you saying? We bring you a drama, sir.

THE STEP-DAUGHTER: We may be your fortune.

THE MANAGER: Will you oblige me by going away? We haven't time to waste with mad people.

THE FATHER (*mellifluously*): Oh sir, you know well that life is full of infinite absurdities, which, strangely enough, do not even need to appear plausible, since they are true.

THE MANAGER: What the devil is he talking about?

THE FATHER: I say that to reverse the ordinary process may well be considered a madness: that is, to create credible situations, in order that they may appear true. But permit me to observe that if this be madness, it is the sole *raison d'être* of your profession, gentlemen. (*The* ACTORS *look hurt and perplexed.*)

THE MANAGER (*getting up and looking at him*): So our profession seems to you one worthy of madmen then?

THE FATHER: Well, to make seem true that which isn't true . . . without any need . . . for a joke as it were . . . Isn't that your mission, gentlemen: to give life to fantastic characters on the stage?

THE MANAGER (*interpreting the rising anger of the* COMPANY): But I would beg you to believe, my dear sir, that the profession of the comedian is a noble one. If today, as things go, the playwrights give us stupid comedies to play and puppets to represent instead of men, remember we are proud to have given life to immortal works here on these very boards! (*The* ACTORS, *satisfied, applaud their* MANAGER.)

THE FATHER (*interrupting furiously*): Exactly, perfectly, to living beings more alive than those who breathe and wear clothes: beings less real perhaps, but truer! I agree with you entirely. (*The* ACTORS *look at one another in amazement.*)

THE MANAGER: But what do you mean? Before, you said . . .

THE FATHER: No, excuse me, I meant it for you, sir, who were crying out that you had no time to lose with madmen, while no one better than yourself knows that nature uses the instrument of human fantasy in order to pursue her high creative purpose.

THE MANAGER: Very well, — but where does all this take us?

THE FATHER: Nowhere! It is merely to show you that one is born to life in many forms, in many shapes, as tree, or as stone, as water, as butterfly, or as woman. So one may also be born a character in a play.

THE MANAGER (*with feigned comic dismay*): So you and these other friends of yours have been born characters?

THE FATHER: Exactly, and alive as you see! (MANAGER *and* ACTORS *burst out laughing.*)

THE FATHER (*hurt*): I am sorry you laugh, because we carry in us a drama, as you can guess from this woman here veiled in black.

THE MANAGER (*losing patience at last and almost indignant*): Oh, chuck it! Get away please! Clear out of here! (*To* PROPERTY MAN.) For Heaven's sake, turn them out!

THE FATHER (*resisting*): No, no, look here, we . . .

THE MANAGER (*roaring*): We come here to work, you know.

LEADING ACTOR: One cannot let oneself be made such a fool of.

THE FATHER (*determined, coming forward*): I marvel at your incredulity, gentlemen. Are you not accustomed to see the characters created by an author spring to life in yourselves and face each other? Just because there is no "book" (*pointing to the* PROMPTER'S *box*) which contains us, you refuse to believe . . .

THE STEP-DAUGHTER (*advances towards* MANAGER, *smiling and coquettish*): Believe me, we are really six most interesting characters, sir; side-tracked however.

THE FATHER: Yes, that is the word! (*To* MANAGER *all at once.*) In the sense, that is, that the author who created us alive no longer wished, or was no longer able, materially to put us into a work of art. And this was a real crime, sir; because he who has had the luck to be born a character can laugh even at death. He cannot die. The man, the writer, the instrument of the creation will die, but his creation does not die. And to live for ever, it does not need to have extraordinary gifts or to be able to work wonders. Who was Sancho Panza? Who was Don Abbondio? Yet they live eternally because — live germs as they were — they had the fortune to find a fecundating matrix, a fantasy which could raise and nourish them: make them live for ever!

THE MANAGER: That is quite all right. But what do you want here, all of you?

THE FATHER: We want to live.

THE MANAGER (*ironically*): For Eternity?

THE FATHER: No, sir, only for a moment . . . in you.

AN ACTOR: Just listen to him!

LEADING LADY: They want to live, in us . . . !

JUVENILE LEAD (*pointing to the* STEP-DAUGHTER): I've no objection, as far as that one is concerned!

THE FATHER: Look here! look here! The comedy has to be made. (*To the* MANAGER.) But if you and your actors are willing, we can soon concert it among ourselves.

THE MANAGER (*annoyed*): But what do you want to concert? We don't go in for concerts here. Here we play dramas and comedies!

THE FATHER: Exactly! That is just why we have come to you.

THE MANAGER: And where is the "book"?

THE FATHER: It is in us! (*The* ACTORS *laugh.*) The drama is in us, and we are the drama. We are impatient to play it. Our inner passion drives us on to this.

THE STEP-DAUGHTER (*disdainful, alluring, treacherous, full of impudence*): My passion, sir! Ah, if you only knew! My passion for him! (*Points to the* FATHER *and makes a pretense of embracing him. Then she breaks out into a loud laugh.*)

THE FATHER (*angrily*): Behave yourself! And please don't laugh in that fashion.

THE STEP-DAUGHTER: With your permission, gentlemen, I, who am a two months' orphan, will show you how I can dance and sing. (*Sings and then dances* Prenez garde à Tchou-Tchin-Tchou.)

Les chinois sont un peuple malin,
De Shangaî à Pékin,
Ils ont mis des écriteaux partout:
Prenez garde à Tchou-Tchin-Tchou.

ACTORS *and* ACTRESSES: Bravo! Well done! Tip-top!

THE MANAGER: Silence! This isn't a café concert, you know! (*Turning to the* FATHER *in consternation.*) Is she mad?

THE FATHER: Mad? No, she's worse than mad.

THE STEP-DAUGHTER (*to* MANAGER): Worse? Worse? Listen! Stage this drama for us at once! Then you will see that at a certain moment I . . . when this little darling here. . . . (*Takes the* CHILD *by the hand and leads her to the* MANAGER.) Isn't she a dear? (*Takes her up and kisses her.*) Darling! Darling! (*Puts her down again and adds feelingly.*) Well, when God suddenly takes this dear little child away from that poor mother there; and this imbecile here (*seizing hold of the* BOY *roughly and pushing him forward*) does the stupidest things, like the fool he is, you will see me run away. Yes, gentlemen, I shall be off. But the moment hasn't arrived yet. After what has taken place between him and me (*indicates the*

FATHER *with a horrible wink*) I can't remain any longer in this society, to have to witness the anguish of this mother here for that fool. . . . (*Indicates the* SON.) Look at him! Look at him! See how indifferent, how frigid he is, because he is the legitimate son. He despises me, despises him (*pointing to the* BOY), despises this baby here; because . . . we are bastards. (*Goes to the* MOTHER *and embraces her.*) And he doesn't want to recognize her as his mother — she who is the common mother of us all. He looks down upon her as if she were only the mother of us three bastards. Wretch! (*She says all this very rapidly, excitedly. At the word "bastards" she raises her voice, and almost spits out the final "Wretch!"*)

THE MOTHER (*to the* MANAGER, *in anguish*): In the name of these two little children, I beg you. . . . (*She grows faint and is about to fall.*) Oh God!

THE FATHER (*coming forward to support her as do some of the* ACTORS): Quick, a chair, a chair for this poor widow!

THE ACTORS: Is it true? Has she really fainted?

THE MANAGER: Quick, a chair! Here!

(*One of the* ACTORS *brings a chair, the* OTHERS *proffer assistance. The* MOTHER *tries to prevent the* FATHER *from lifting the veil which covers her face.*)

THE FATHER: Look at her! Look at her!

THE MOTHER: No, no; stop it please!

THE FATHER (*raising her veil*): Let them see you!

THE MOTHER (*rising and covering her face with her hands, in desperation*): I beg you, sir, to prevent this man from carrying out his plan which is loathsome to me.

THE MANAGER (*dumbfounded*): I don't understand at all. What is the situation? (*To the* FATHER.) Is this lady your wife?

THE FATHER: Yes, gentlemen: my wife!

THE MANAGER: But how can she be a widow if you are alive? (*The* ACTORS *find relief for their astonishment in a loud laugh.*)

THE FATHER: Don't laugh! Don't laugh like that, for Heaven's sake. Her drama lies just here in this: she has had a lover, a man who ought to be here.

THE MOTHER (*with a cry*): No! No!

THE STEP-DAUGHTER: Fortunately for her, he is dead. Two months ago as I said. We are in mourning, as you see.

THE FATHER: He isn't here you see, not because he is dead. He isn't here — look at her a moment and you will understand — because her drama isn't a drama of the love of two men for whom she was incapable of feeling anything except possibly a little gratitude —

gratitude not for me but for the other. She isn't a woman, she is a mother, and her drama — powerful sir, I assure you — lies, as a matter of fact, all in these four children she has had by two men.

THE MOTHER: I had them? Have you got the courage to say that I wanted them? (*To the* COMPANY.) It was his doing. It was he who gave me that other man, who forced me to go away with him.

THE STEP-DAUGHTER: It isn't true.

THE MOTHER (*startled*): Not true, isn't it?

THE STEP-DAUGHTER: No, it isn't true, it just isn't true.

THE MOTHER: And what can you know about it?

THE STEP-DAUGHTER: It isn't true. Don't believe it. (*To* MANAGER.) Do you know why she says so? For that fellow there. (*Indicates the* SON.) She tortures herself, destroys herself on account of the neglect of that son there; and she wants him to believe that if she abandoned him when he was only two years old, it was because he (*indicates the* FATHER) made her do so.

THE MOTHER (*vigorously*): He forced me to it, and I call God to witness it. (*To the* MANAGER.) Ask him (*indicates* HUSBAND) if it isn't true. Let him speak. You (*to* DAUGHTER) are not in a position to know anything about it.

THE STEP-DAUGHTER: I know you lived in peace and happiness with my father while he lived. Can you deny it?

THE MOTHER: No, I don't deny it. . . .

THE STEP-DAUGHTER: He was always full of affection and kindness for you. (*To the* BOY, *angrily.*) It's true, isn't it? Tell them! Why don't you speak, you little fool?

THE MOTHER: Leave the poor boy alone. Why do you want to make me appear ungrateful, daughter? I don't want to offend your father. I have answered him that I didn't abandon my house and my son through any fault of mine, nor from any wilful passion.

THE FATHER: It is true. It was my doing.

LEADING MAN (*to the* COMPANY): What a spectacle!

LEADING LADY: We are the audience this time.

JUVENILE LEAD: For once, in a way.

THE MANAGER (*beginning to get really interested*): Let's hear them out. Listen!

THE SON: Oh yes, you're going to hear a fine bit now. He will talk to you of the Demon of Experiment.

THE FATHER: You are a cynical imbecile. I've told you so already a hundred times. (*To the* MANAGER.) He tries to make fun of me on account of this expression which I have found to excuse myself with.

THE SON (*with disgust*): Yes, phrases! phrases!

THE FATHER: Phrases! Isn't everyone consoled when faced with a trouble or fact he doesn't understand, by a word, some simple word, which tells us nothing and yet calms us?

THE STEP-DAUGHTER: Even in the case of remorse. In fact, especially then.

THE FATHER: Remorse? No, that isn't true. I've done more than use words to quieten the remorse in me.

THE STEP-DAUGHTER: Yes, there was a bit of money too. Yes, yes, a bit of money. There were the hundred lire he was about to offer me in payment, gentlemen. . . . (*Sensation of horror among the* ACTORS.)

THE SON (*to the* STEP-DAUGHTER): This is vile.

THE STEP-DAUGHTER: Vile? There they were in a pale blue envelope on a little mahogany table in the back of Madame Pace's shop. You know Madame Pace — one of those ladies who attract poor girls of good family into their ateliers, under the pretext of their selling *robes et manteaux*.

THE SON: And he thinks he has bought the right to tyrannize over us all with those hundred lire he was going to pay; but which, fortunately — note this, gentlemen — he had no chance of paying.

THE STEP-DAUGHTER: It was a near thing, though, you know! (*Laughs ironically.*)

THE MOTHER (*protesting*): Shame, my daughter, shame!

THE STEP-DAUGHTER: Shame indeed! This is my revenge! I am dying to live that scene . . . The room . . . I see it . . . Here is the window with the mantles exposed, there the divan, the looking-glass, a screen, there in front of the window the little mahogany table with the blue envelope containing one hundred lire. I see it. I see it. I could take hold of it. . . . But you, gentlemen, you ought to turn your backs now: I am almost nude, you know. But I don't blush: I leave that to him. (*Indicating* FATHER.)

THE MANAGER: I don't understand this at all.

THE FATHER: Naturally enough. I would ask you, sir, to exercise your authority a little here, and let me speak before you believe all she is trying to blame me with. Let me explain.

THE STEP-DAUGHTER: Ah yes, explain it in your own way.

THE FATHER: But don't you see that in the whole trouble lies here? In words, words. Each one of us has within him a whole world of things, each man of us his own special world. And how can we ever come to an understanding if I put in the words I utter the sense and value of things as I see them; while you who listen to me must inevitably translate them according to the conception of things each one of you has within himself. We think we understand each other, but we never really do. Look here! This woman (*indicating the* MOTHER) takes all my pity for her as a specially ferocious form of cruelty.

THE MOTHER: But you drove me away.

THE FATHER: Do you hear her? I drove her away! She believes I really sent her away.

THE MOTHER: You know how to talk, and I don't; but, believe me, sir (*to* MANAGER), after he had married me . . . who knows why? . . . I was a poor insignificant woman. . . .

THE FATHER: But, good Heavens! it was just for your humility that I married you. I loved this simplicity in you. (*He stops when he sees she makes signs to contradict him, opens his arms wide in sign of desperation, seeing how hopeless it is to make himself understood.*) You see she denies it. Her mental deafness, believe me, is phenomenal, the limit: (*touches his forehead*) deaf, deaf, mentally deaf! She has plenty of feeling. Oh yes, a good heart for the children; but the brain — deaf, to the point of desperation — !

THE STEP-DAUGHTER: Yes, but ask him how his intelligence has helped us.

THE FATHER: If we could see all the evil that may spring from good, what should we do? (*At this point the* LEADING LADY, *who is biting her lips with rage at seeing the* LEADING MAN *flirting with the* STEP-DAUGHTER, *comes forward and speaks to the* MANAGER.)

LEADING LADY: Excuse me, but are we going to rehearse today?

MANAGER: Of course, of course; but let's hear them out.

JUVENILE LEAD: This is something quite new.

L'INGÉNUE: Most interesting!

LEADING LADY: Yes, for the people who like that kind of thing. (*Casts a glance at* LEADING MAN.)

THE MANAGER (*to* FATHER): You must please explain yourself quite clearly. (*Sits down.*)

THE FATHER: Very well then: listen! I had in my service a poor man, a clerk, a secretary of mine, full of devotion, who became friends with her. (*Indicating the* MOTHER.) They understood one another, were kindred souls in fact, without, however, the least suspicion of any evil existing. They were incapable even of thinking of it.

THE STEP-DAUGHTER: So he thought of it — for them!

THE FATHER: That's not true. I meant to do good to them — and to myself, I confess, at the same time. Things had come to the point that I could not say a word to either of them without their making a mute appeal, one to the other, with their eyes. I could see them silently asking each other how I was to be kept in countenance, how I was to be kept quiet. And this, believe me, was just about enough of itself to keep me in a constant rage, to exasperate me beyond measure.

THE MANAGER: And why didn't you send him away then — this secretary of yours?

THE FATHER: Precisely what I did, sir. And then I had to watch this poor woman drifting forlornly about the house like an animal without a master, like an animal one has taken in out of pity.

THE MOTHER: Ah yes . . . !

THE FATHER (*suddenly turning to the* MOTHER): It's true about the son anyway, isn't it?

THE MOTHER: He took my son away from me first of all.

THE FATHER: But not from cruelty. I did it so that he should grow up healthy and strong by living in the country.

THE STEP-DAUGHTER (*pointing to him ironically*): As one can see.

THE FATHER (*quickly*): Is it my fault if he has grown up like this? I sent him to a wet nurse in the country, a peasant, as *she* did not seem to me strong enough, though she is of humble origin. That was, anyway, the reason I married her. Unpleasant all this may be, but how can it be helped? My mistake possibly, but there we are! All my life I have had these confounded aspirations towards a certain moral sanity. (*At this point the* STEP-DAUGHTER *bursts into a noisy laugh.*) Oh, stop it! Stop it! I can't stand it.

THE MANAGER: Yes, please stop it, for Heaven's sake.

THE STEP-DAUGHTER: But imagine moral sanity from him, if you please — the client of certain ateliers like that of Madame Pace!

THE FATHER: Fool! That is the proof that I am a man! This seeming contradiction, gentlemen, is the strongest proof that I stand here a live man before you. Why, it is just for this very incongruity in my nature that I have had to suffer what I have. I could not live by the side of that woman (*indicating the* MOTHER) any longer; but not so much for the boredom she inspired me with as for the pity I felt for her.

THE MOTHER: And so he turned me out —.

THE FATHER: — well provided for! Yes, I sent her to that man, gentlemen . . . to let her go free of me.

THE MOTHER: And to free himself.

THE FATHER: Yes, I admit it. It was also a liberation for me. But great evil has come of it. I meant well when I did it; and I did it more for her sake than mine. I swear it. (*Crosses his arms on his chest; then turns suddenly to the* MOTHER.) Did I ever lose sight of you until that other man carried you off to another town, like the angry fool he was? And on account of my pure interest in you . . . my pure interest, I repeat, that had no base motive in it . . . I watched with the tenderest concern the new family that grew up around her. She can bear witness to this. (*Points to the* STEP-DAUGHTER.)

THE STEP-DAUGHTER: Oh yes, that's true enough. When I was a kiddie, so so high, you know, with plaits over my shoulders and knickers longer than my skirts, I used to see him waiting outside the school for me to come out. He came to see how I was growing up.

THE FATHER: This is infamous, shameful!

THE STEP-DAUGHTER: No. Why?

THE FATHER: Infamous! infamous! (*Then excitedly to* MANAGER *explaining.*) After she (*indicating the* MOTHER) went away, my house seemed suddenly empty. She was my incubus, but she filled my house. I was like a dazed fly alone in the empty rooms. This boy here (*indicating the* SON) was educated away from home, and when he came back, he seemed to me to be no more mine. With no mother to stand between him and me, he grew up entirely for himself, on his own, apart, with no tie of intellect or affection binding him to me. And then — strange but true — I was driven, by curiosity at first and then by some tender sentiment, towards her family, which had come into being through my will. The thought of her began gradually to fill up the emptiness I felt all around me. I wanted to know if she were happy in living out the simple daily duties of life. I wanted to think of her as fortunate and happy because far away from the complicated torments of my spirit. And so, to have proof of this, I used to watch that child coming out of school.

THE STEP-DAUGHTER: Yes, yes. True. He used to follow me in the street and smiled at me, waved his hand, like this. I would look at him with interest, wondering who he might be. I told my mother, who guessed at once. (*The* MOTHER *agrees with a nod.*) Then she didn't want to send me to school for some days; and when I finally went back, there he was again — looking so ridiculous — with a paper parcel in his hands. He came close to me, caressed me, and drew out a fine straw hat from the parcel, with a bouquet of flowers — all for me!

THE MANAGER: A bit discursive this, you know!

THE SON (*contemptuously*): Literature! Literature!

THE FATHER: Literature indeed! This is life, this is passion!

THE MANAGER: It may be, but it won't act.

THE FATHER: I agree. This is only the part leading up. I don't suggest this should be staged. She (*pointing to the* STEP-DAUGHTER), as you see, is no longer the flapper with plaits down her back —.

THE STEP-DAUGHTER: — and the knickers showing below the skirt!

THE FATHER: The drama is coming now, sir; something new, complex, most interesting.

THE STEP-DAUGHTER: As soon as my father died . . .

THE FATHER: — there was absolute misery for them. They came back here, unknown to me. Through her stupidity! (*Pointing to the* MOTHER.) It is true she can barely write her own name; but she could anyhow have got her daughter to write to me that they were in need . . .

THE MOTHER: And how was I to divine all this sentiment in him?

THE FATHER: That is exactly your mistake, never to have guessed any of my sentiments.

THE MOTHER: After so many years apart, and all that had happened . . .

THE FATHER: Was it my fault if that fellow carried you away? It happened quite suddenly; for after he had obtained some job or other, I could find no trace of them; and so, not unnaturally, my interest in them dwindled. But the drama culminated unforeseen and violent on their return, when I was impelled by my miserable flesh that still lives. . . . Ah! what misery, what wretchedness is that of the man who is alone and disdains debasing *liaisons!* Not old enough to do without women, and not young enough to go and look for one without shame. Misery? It's worse than misery; it's a horror; for no woman can any longer give him love; and when a man feels this. . . . One ought to do without, you say? Yes, yes, I know. Each of us when he appears before his fellows is clothed in a certain dignity. But every man knows what unconfessable things pass within the secrecy of his own heart. One gives way to the temptation, only to rise from it again, afterwards, with a great eagerness to re-establish one's dignity, as if it were a tombstone to place on the grave of one's shame, and a monument to hide and sign the memory of our weaknesses. Everybody's in the same case. Some folks haven't the courage to say certain things, that's all!

THE STEP-DAUGHTER: All appear to have the courage to do them though.

THE FATHER: Yes, but in secret. Therefore, you want more courage to say these things. Let a man but speak these things out, and folks at once label him a cynic. But it isn't true. He is like all the others, better indeed, because he isn't afraid to reveal with the light of the intelligence the red shame of human bestiality on which most men close their eyes so as not to see it.

Woman — for example, look at her case! She turns tantalizing inviting glances on you. You seize her. No sooner does she feel herself in your grasp than she closes her eyes. It is the sign of her mission, the sign by which she says to man: "Blind yourself, for I am blind."

THE STEP-DAUGHTER: Sometimes she can close them no more: when she no longer feels the need of hiding her shame to herself, but dry-eyed and dispassionately, sees only that of the man who has blinded himself without love. Oh, all these intellectual complications make me sick, disgust me — all this philosophy that uncovers the beast in man, and then seeks to save him, excuse him . . . I can't stand it, sir. When a man seeks to "simplify" life bestially, throwing aside every relic of humanity, every chaste aspiration, every pure feeling, all sense of ideality, duty, modesty, shame . . . then nothing is more revolting and nauseous than a certain kind of remorse — crocodiles' tears, that's what it is.

THE MANAGER: Let's come to the point. This is only discussion.

THE FATHER: Very good, sir! But a fact is like a sack which won't stand up when it's empty. In order that it may stand up, one has to put into it the reason and sentiment which have caused it to exist. I couldn't possibly know that after the death of that man, they had decided to return here, that they were in misery, and that she (*pointing to the* MOTHER) had gone to work as a modiste, and at a shop of the type of that of Madame Pace.

THE STEP-DAUGHTER: A real high-class modiste, you must know, gentlemen. In appearance, she works for the leaders of the best society; but she arranges matters so that these elegant ladies serve her purpose . . . without prejudice to other ladies who are . . . well . . . only so so.

THE MOTHER: You will believe me, gentlemen, that it never entered my mind that the old hag offered me work because she had her eye on my daughter.

THE STEP-DAUGHTER: Poor mamma! Do you know, sir, what that woman did when I brought her back the work my mother had finished? She would point out to me that I had torn one of my frocks, and she would give it back to my mother to mend. It was I who paid for it, always I; while this poor creature here believed she was sacrificing herself for me and these two children here, sitting up at night sewing Madame Pace's robes.

THE MANAGER: And one day you met there . . .

THE STEP-DAUGHTER: Him, him. Yes sir, an old client. Theres' a scene for you to play! Superb!

THE FATHER: She, the Mother arrived just then . . .

THE STEP-DAUGHTER (*treacherously*): Almost in time!

THE FATHER (*crying out*): No, in time! in time! Fortunately I recognized her . . . in time. And I took them back home with me to my house. You can imagine now her position and mine; she, as you see her; and I who cannot look her in the face.

THE STEP-DAUGHTER: Absurd! How can I possibly be expected — after that — to be a modest young miss, a fit person to go with his confounded aspirations for "a solid moral sanity"?

THE FATHER: For the drama lies all in this — in the conscience that I have, that each one of us has. We believe this conscience to be a single thing, but it is many-sided. There is one for this person, and another for that. Diverse consciences. So we have this illusion of being one person for all, of having a personality that is unique in all our acts. But it isn't true. We perceive this when, tragically perhaps, in something we do, we are as it were, suspended, caught up in the air on a kind of hook. Then we perceive that all of us was not in that act, and that it would be an atrocious injustice to judge us by that action alone, as if all our existence were summed up in that one deed. Now do you understand the perfidy of this girl? She surprised me in a place, where she ought not to have known me, just as I could not exist for her; and she now seeks to attach to me a reality such as I could never suppose I should have to assume for her in a shameful and fleeting moment of my life. I feel this above all else. And the drama, you will see, acquires a tremendous value from this point. Then there is the position of the others . . . his. . . . (*Indicating the* SON.)

THE SON (*shrugging his shoulders scornfully*): Leave me alone! I don't come into this.

THE FATHER: What? You don't come into this?

THE SON: I've got nothing to do with it, and don't want to have; because you know well enough I wasn't made to be mixed up in all this with the rest of you.

THE STEP-DAUGHTER: We are only vulgar folk! He is the fine gentleman. You may have noticed, Mr. Manager, that I fix him now and again with a look of scorn while he lowers his eyes — for he knows the evil he has done me.

THE SON (*scarcely looking at her*): I?

THE STEP-DAUGHTER: You! you! I owe my life on the streets to you. Did you or did you not deny us, with your behavior, I won't say the intimacy of home, but even that mere hospitality which makes guests feel at their ease? We were intruders who had come to disturb the kingdom of your legitimacy. I should like to have you witness, Mr. Manager, certain scenes between him and me. He says I have tyrannized over everyone. But it was just his behavior which made me insist on the reason for which I had come into the house, — this reason he calls "vile" — into his house, with my mother who is his mother too. And I came as mistress of the house.

THE SON: It's easy for them to put me always in the wrong. But imagine, gentlemen, the position of a son, whose fate it is to see arrive one day at his home a young woman of impudent bearing, a young woman who inquires for his father, with whom who knows what business she has. This young man has then to witness her return bolder than ever, accompanied by that child there. He is obliged to watch her treat his father in an equivocal and confidential manner. She asks money of him in a way that lets one suppose he must give it to her, *must*, do you understand, because he has every obligation to do so.

THE FATHER: But I have, as a matter of fact, this obligation. I owe it to your mother.

THE SON: How should I know? When had I ever seen or heard of her? One day there arrive with her (*indicating* STEP-DAUGHTER) that lad and this baby here. I am told: "This is *your* mother too, you know." I divine from her manner (*indicating* STEP-DAUGHTER *again*) why it is they have come home. I had rather not say what I feel and think about it. I shouldn't even care to confess to myself. No action can therefore be hoped for from me in this affair. Believe me, Mr. Manager, I am an "unrealized" character, dramatically speaking; and I find myself not at all at ease in their company. Leave me out of it, I beg you.

THE FATHER: What? It is just because you are so that . . .

THE SON: How do you know what I am like? When did you ever bother your head about me?

THE FATHER: I admit it. I admit it. But isn't that a situation in itself? This aloofness of yours which is so cruel to me and to your mother, who returns home and sees you almost for the first time grown up, who doesn't recognize you but knows you are her son. . . . (*Pointing out the* MOTHER *to the* MANAGER.) See, she's crying!

THE STEP-DAUGHTER (*angrily, stamping her foot*): Like a fool!

THE FATHER (*indicating* STEP-DAUGHTER): She can't stand him, you know. (*Then referring again to the* SON.) He says he doesn't come into the affair, whereas he is really the hinge of the whole action. Look at that lad who is always clinging to his mother, frightened and humiliated. It is on account of this fellow here. Possibly his situation is the most painful of all. He feels himself a stranger more than the others. The poor little chap feels mortified, humiliated at being brought into a home out of charity as it were. (*In confidence.*) He is the image of his father. Hardly talks at all. Humble and quiet.

THE MANAGER: Oh, we'll cut him out. You've no notion what a nuisance boys are on the stage. . . .

THE FATHER: He disappears soon, you know. And the baby too. She is the first to vanish from the scene. The drama consists finally in this: when that mother re-enters my house, her family born outside of it, and shall we say superimposed on the original, ends with the death of the little girl, the tragedy of the boy and the flight of the elder daughter. It cannot go on, because it is foreign to its surroundings. So after much torment, we three remain: I, the mother, that son. Then, owing to the disappearance of that extraneous family, we too find ourselves strange to one another. We find we are living in an atmosphere of mortal desolation which is the revenge, as he (*indicating* SON) scornfully said of the Demon of Experiment, that unfortunately hides in me. Thus, sir, you see when faith is lacking, it becomes impossible to create certain states of happiness, for we lack the necessary humility. Vaingloriously, we try to substitute ourselves for this faith, creating thus for the rest of the world a reality which we believe after their fashion, while, actually, it doesn't exist. For each one of us has his own reality to be respected before God, even when it is harmful to one's very self.

THE MANAGER: There is something in what you say. I assure you all this interests me very much. I begin to think there's the stuff for a drama in all this, and not a bad drama either.

THE STEP-DAUGHTER (*coming forward*): When you've got a character like me . . .

THE FATHER (*shutting her up, all excited to learn the decision of the* MANAGER): You be quiet!

THE MANAGER (*reflecting, heedless of interruption*): It's new . . . hem . . . yes. . . .

THE FATHER: Absolutely new!

THE MANAGER: You've got a nerve though, I must say, to come here and fling it at me like this . . .

THE FATHER: You will understand, sir, born as we are for the stage . . .

THE MANAGER: Are you amateur actors then?

THE FATHER: No. I say born for the stage, because . . .

THE MANAGER: Oh, nonsense. You're an old hand, you know.

THE FATHER: No sir, no. We act that rôle for which we have been cast, that rôle which we are given in life. And in my own case, passion itself, as usually happens, becomes a trifle theatrical when it is exalted.

THE MANAGER: Well, well, that will do. But you see, without an author. . . . I could give you the address of an author if you like . . .

THE FATHER: No, no. Look here! You must be the author.

THE MANAGER: I? What are you talking about?

THE FATHER: Yes, you, you! Why not?

THE MANAGER: Because I have never been an author: that's why.

THE FATHER: Then why not turn author now? Everybody does it. You don't want any special qualities. Your task is made much easier by the fact that we are all here alive before you. . . .

THE MANAGER: It won't do.

THE FATHER: What? When you see us live our drama. . . .

THE MANAGER: Yes, that's all right. But you want someone to write it.

THE FATHER: No, no. Someone to take it down, possibly, while we play it, scene by scene! It will be enough to sketch it out at first, and then try it over.

THE MANAGER: Well . . . I am almost tempted. It's a bit of an idea. One might have a shot at it.

THE FATHER: Of course. You'll see what scenes will come out of it. I can give you one, at once . . .

THE MANAGER: By Jove, it tempts me. I'd like to have a go at it. Let's try it out. Come with me to my office. (*Turning to the* ACTORS.) You are at liberty for a bit, but don't step out of the theatre for long. In a quarter of an hour, twenty minutes, all back here again! (*To the* FATHER.) We'll see what can be done. Who knows if we don't get something really extraordinary out of it?

THE FATHER: There's no doubt about it. They (*indicating the* CHARACTERS) had better come with us too, hadn't they?

THE MANAGER: Yes, yes. Come on! come on! (*Moves away and then turning to the* ACTORS.) Be punctual, please! (MANAGER *and the* SIX CHARACTERS *cross the stage and go off. The other* ACTORS *remain, looking at one another in astonishment.*)

LEADING MAN: Is he serious? What the devil does he want to do?

JUVENILE LEAD: This is rank madness.

THIRD ACTOR: Does he expect to knock up a drama in five minutes?

JUVENILE LEAD: Like the improvisers!

LEADING LADY: If he thinks I'm going to take part in a joke like this. . . .

JUVENILE LEAD: I'm out of it anyway.

FOURTH ACTOR: I should like to know who they are. (*Alludes to* CHARACTERS.)

THIRD ACTOR: What do you suppose? Madmen or rascals!

JUVENILE LEAD: And he takes them seriously!

L'INGÉNUE: Vanity! He fancies himself as an author now.

LEADING MAN: It's absolutely unheard of. If the stage has come to this . . . well I'm . . .

FIFTH ACTOR: It's rather a joke.

THIRD ACTOR: Well, we'll see what's going to happen next.

(*Thus talking, the* ACTORS *leave the stage; some going out by the little door at the back; others retiring to their dressing-rooms.*

The curtain remains up.
The action of the play is suspended for twenty minutes.)

ACT II

(*The stage call-bells ring to warn the company that the play is about to begin again.*

The STEP-DAUGHTER *comes out of the* MANAGER'S *office along with the* CHLD *and the* BOY. *As she comes out of the office, she cries:* —

Nonsense! nonsense! Do it yourselves! I'm not going to mix myself up in this mess. (*Turning to the* CHILD *and coming quickly with her on to the stage.*) Come on, Rosetta, let's run!

The BOY *follows them slowly, remaining a little behind and seeming perplexed.*)

THE STEP-DAUGHTER (*stops, bends over the* CHILD *and takes the latter's face between her hands*): My little darling! You're frightened, aren't you? You don't know where we are, do you? (*Pretending to reply to a question of the* CHILD.) What is the stage? It's a place, baby, you know, where people play at being serious, a place where they act comedies. We've got to act a comedy now, dead serious, you know; and you're in it also, little one. (*Embraces her, pressing the little head to her breast, and rocking the* CHILD *for a moment.*) Oh darling, darling, what a horrid comedy you've got to play! What a wretched part they've found for you! A garden . . . a fountain . . . look . . . just suppose, kiddie, it's here. Where, you say? Why, right here in the middle. It's all pretense you know. That's the trouble, my pet: it's all make-believe here. It's better to imagine it though, because if they fix it up for you, it'll only be painted cardboard, painted cardboard for the rockery, the water, the plants. . . . Ah, but I think a baby like this one would sooner have a make-believe fountain than a real one, so she could play with it. What a joke it'll be for the others! But for you, alas! not quite such a joke: you who are real, baby dear, and really play by a real fountain that is big and green and beautiful, with ever so many bamboos around it that are reflected in the water, and a whole lot of little ducks swimming about. . . . No, Rosetta, no, your mother doesn't bother about you on account of that wretch of a son there. I'm in the devil of a temper, and as for that lad. . . . (*Seizes* BOY *by the arm to force him to take one of his hands out of his pockets.*) What have you got there? What are you hiding? (*Pulls his hand out of his pocket, looks into it and catches the glint of a revolver.*) Ah! where did you get this? (*The* BOY, *very pale in the face, looks at her, but does not answer.*) Idiot! If I'd been in your place, instead of killing myself, I'd have shot one of those two, or both of them: father and son.

(*The* FATHER *enters from the office, all excited from his work. The* MANAGER *follows him.*)

THE FATHER: Come on, come on dear! Come here for a minute! We've arranged everything. It's all fixed up.

THE MANAGER (*also excited*): If you please, young lady, there are one or two points to settle still. Will you come along?

THE STEP-DAUGHTER (*following him towards the office*): Ouff! what's the good, if you've arranged everything.

(*The* FATHER, MANAGER *and* STEP-DAUGHTER *go back into the office again* [*off*] *for a moment. At the same time, the* SON, *followed by the* MOTHER, *comes out.*)

THE SON (*looking at the three entering office*): Oh this is fine, fine! And to think I can't even get away!

(*The* MOTHER *attempts to look at him, but lowers her eyes immediately when he turns away from her. She then sits down. The* BOY *and the* CHILD *approach her. She casts a glance again at the* SON, *and speaks with humble tones, trying to draw him into conversation.*)

THE MOTHER: And isn't my punishment the worst of all? (*Then seeing from the* SON'S *manner that he will not bother himself about her.*) My God! Why are you so cruel? Isn't it enough for one person to support all this torment? Must you then insist on others seeing it also?

THE SON (*half to himself, meaning the* MOTHER *to hear, however*): And they want to put it on the stage! If there was at least a reason for it! He thinks he has got at the meaning of it all. Just as if each one of us in every circumstance of life couldn't find his own explanation of it! (*Pauses.*) He complains he was discovered in a place where he ought not to have been seen, in a moment of his life which ought to have remained hidden and kept out of the reach of that convention which he has to maintain for other people. And what about my case? Haven't I had to reveal what no son ought ever to reveal: how father and mother live and are man and wife for themselves quite apart from that idea of father and mother which we give them? When this idea is revealed, our life is then linked at one point only to that man and that woman; and as such it should shame them, shouldn't it?

(The MOTHER *hides her face in her hands. From the dressing-rooms and the little door at the back of the stage the* ACTORS *and* STAGE MANAGER *return, followed by the* PROPERTY MAN, *and the* PROMPTER. *At the same moment, the* MANAGER *comes out of his office, accompanied by the* FATHER *and the* STEP-DAUGHTER.)

THE MANAGER: Come on, come on, ladies and gentlemen! Heh! you there, machinist!

MACHINIST: Yes sir?

THE MANAGER: Fix up the white parlor with the floral decorations. Two wings and a drop with a door will do. Hurry up!

(The MACHINIST *runs off at once to prepare the scene, and arranges it while the* MANAGER *talks with the* STAGE MANAGER, *the* PROPERTY MAN, *and the* PROMPTER *on matters of detail.)*

THE MANAGER (*to* PROPERTY MAN): Just have a look, and see if there isn't a sofa or divan in the wardrobe . . .

PROPERTY MAN: There's the green one.

THE STEP-DAUGHTER: No no! Green won't do. It was yellow, ornamented with flowers — very large! and most comfortable!

PROPERTY MAN: There isn't one like that.

THE MANAGER: It doesn't matter. Use the one we've got.

THE STEP-DAUGHTER: Doesn't matter? It's most important!

THE MANAGER: We're only trying it now. Please don't interfere. (*To* PROPERTY MAN.) See if we've got a shop window — long and narrowish.

THE STEP-DAUGHTER: And the little table! The little mahogany table for the pale blue envelope!

PROPERTY MAN (*to* MANAGER): There's that little gilt one.

THE MANAGER: That'll do fine.

THE FATHER: A mirror.

THE STEP-DAUGHTER: And the screen! We must have a screen. Otherwise how can I manage?

PROPERTY MAN: That's all right, Miss. We've got any amount of them.

THE MANAGER (*to the* STEP-DAUGHTER): We want some clothes pegs too, don't we?

THE STEP-DAUGHTER: Yes, several, several!

THE MANAGER: See how many we've got and bring them all.

PROPERTY MAN: All right!

(*The* PROPERTY MAN *hurries off to obey his orders. While he is putting the things in their places, the* MANAGER *talks to the* PROMPTER *and then with the* CHARACTERS *and the* ACTORS.)

THE MANAGER (*to* PROMPTER): Take your seat. Look here: this is the outline of the scenes, act by act. (*Hands him some sheets of paper.*) And now I'm going to ask you to do something out of the ordinary.

PROMPTER: Take it down in shorthand?

THE MANAGER (*pleasantly surprised*): Exactly! Can you do shorthand?

PROMPTER: Yes, a little.

THE MANAGER: Good! (*Turning to a* STAGE HAND.) Go and get some paper from my office, plenty, as much as you can find.

(*The* STAGE HAND *goes off, and soon returns with a handful of paper which he gives to the* PROMPTER.)

THE MANAGER (*to* PROMPTER): You follow the scenes as we play them, and try and get the points down, at any rate the most important ones. (*Then addressing the* ACTORS.) Clear the stage, ladies and gentlemen! Come over here (*pointing to the left*) and listen attentively.

LEADING LADY: But, excuse me, we . . .

THE MANAGER (*guessing her thought*): Don't worry! You won't have to improvise.

LEADING MAN: What have we to do then?

THE MANAGER: Nothing. For the moment you just watch and listen. Everybody will get his part written out afterwards. At present we're going to try the thing as best we can. They're going to act now.

THE FATHER (*as if fallen from the clouds into the confusion of the stage*): We? What do you mean, if you please, by a rehearsal?

THE MANAGER: A rehearsal for them. (*Points to the* ACTORS.)

THE FATHER: But since we are the characters . . .

THE MANAGER: All right: "characters" then, if you insist on calling yourselves such. But here, my dear sir, the characters don't act. Here the actors do the acting. The characters are there, in the "book" (*pointing towards* PROMPTER'S *box*) — when there is a "book"!

THE FATHER: I won't contradict you; but excuse me, the actors aren't the characters. They want to be, they pretend to be, don't they? Now if these gentlemen here are fortunate enough to have us alive before them . . .

THE MANAGER: Oh this is grand! You want to come before the public yourselves then?

THE FATHER: As we are. . . .

THE MANAGER: I can assure you it would be a magnificent spectacle!

LEADING MAN: What's the use of us here anyway then?

THE MANAGER: You're not going to pretend that you can act? It makes me laugh! (*The* ACTORS *laugh.*) There, you see, they are laughing at the notion. But, by the way, I must cast the parts. That won't be difficult. They cast themselves. (*To the* SECOND LADY LEAD.) You play the Mother. (*To the* FATHER.) We must find her a name.

THE FATHER: Amalia, sir.

THE MANAGER: But that is the real name of your wife. We don't want to call her by her real name.

THE FATHER: Why ever not, if it is her name? . . . Still, perhaps, if that lady must . . . (*Makes a slight motion of the hand to indicate the* SECOND LADY LEAD.) I see this woman here (*means the* MOTHER) as Amalia. But do as you like. (*Gets more and more confused.*) I don't know what to say to you. Already, I begin to hear my own words ring false, as if they had another sound. . . .

THE MANAGER: Don't you worry about it. It'll be our job to find the right tones. And as for her name, if you want her Amalia, Amalia it shall be; and if you don't like it, we'll find another! For the moment though, we'll call the characters in this way: (*To* JUVENILE LEAD.) You are the Son. (*To the* LEADING LADY.) You naturally are the Step-Daughter. . . .

THE STEP-DAUGHTER (*excitedly*): What? what? I, that woman there? (*Bursts out laughing.*)

THE MANAGER (*angry*): What is there to laugh at?

LEADING LADY (*indignant*): Nobody has ever dared to laugh at me. I insist on being treated with respect; otherwise I go away.

THE STEP-DAUGHTER: No, no, excuse me . . . I am not laughing at you. . . .

THE MANAGER (*to* STEP-DAUGHTER): You ought to feel honored to be played by . . .

LEADING LADY (*at once, contemptuously*): "That woman there" . . .

THE STEP-DAUGHTER: But I wasn't speaking of you, you know. I was speaking of myself — whom I can't see at all in you! That is all. I don't know . . . but . . . you . . . aren't in the least like me. . . .

THE FATHER: True. Here's the point. Look here, sir, our temperaments, our souls. . . .

THE MANAGER: Temperament, soul, be hanged! Do you suppose the spirit of the piece is in you? Nothing of the kind!

THE FATHER: What, haven't we our own temperaments, our own souls?

THE MANAGER: Not at all. Your soul or whatever you like to call it takes shape here. The actors give body and form to it, voice and gesture. And my actors — I may tell you — have given expression to much more lofty material than this little drama of yours, which may or may not hold up on the stage. But if it does, the merit of it, believe me, will be due to my actors.

THE FATHER: I don't dare contradict you, sir; but, believe me, it is a terrible suffering for us who are as we are, with these bodies of ours, these features to see. . . .

THE MANAGER (*cutting him short and out of patience*): Good heavens! The make-up will remedy all that, man, the make-up. . . .

THE FATHER: Maybe. But the voice, the gestures . . .

THE MANAGER: Now, look here! On the stage, you as yourself, cannot exist. The actor here acts you, and that's an end to it!

THE FATHER: I understand. And now I think I see why our author who conceived us as we are, all alive, didn't want to put us on the stage after all. I haven't the least desire to offend your actors. Far from it! But when I think that I am to be acted by . . . I don't know by whom. . . .

LEADING MAN (*on his dignity*): By me, if you've no objection!

THE FATHER (*humbly, mellifluously*): Honored, I assure you, sir. (*Bows.*) Still, I must say that try as this gentleman may, with all his good will and wonderful art, to absorb me into himself. . . .

LEADING MAN: Oh chuck it! "Wonderful art!" Withdraw that, please!

THE FATHER: The performance he will give, even doing his best with make-up to look like me. . . .

LEADING MAN: It will certainly be a bit difficult! (*The* ACTORS *laugh.*)

THE FATHER: Exactly! It will be difficult to act me as I really am. The effect will be rather — apart from the make-up — according as to how he supposes I am, as he senses me — if he does sense me — and not as I inside of myself feel myself to be. It seems to me then that account should be taken of this by everyone whose duty it may become to criticize us. . . .

THE MANAGER: Heavens! The man's starting to think about the critics now! Let them say what they like. It's up to us to put on the play if we can. (*Looking around.*) Come on! come on! Is the stage set? (*To the* ACTORS *and* CHARACTERS.) Stand back — stand back! Let me see, and don't let's lose any more time! (*To the* STEP-DAUGHTER.) Is it all right as it is now?

THE STEP-DAUGHTER: Well, to tell the truth, I don't recognize the scene.

THE MANAGER: My dear lady, you can't possibly suppose that we can construct that shop of Madame Pace piece by piece here? (*To the* FATHER.) You said a white room with flowered wall paper, didn't you?

THE FATHER: Yes.

THE MANAGER: Well then. We've got the furniture right more or less. Bring that little table a bit further forward. (*The* STAGE HANDS *obey the order. To* PROPERTY MAN.) You go and find an envelope, if possible, a pale blue one; and give it to that gentleman. (*Indicates* FATHER.)

PROPERTY MAN: An ordinary envelope?

MANAGER *and* FATHER: Yes, yes, an ordinary envelope.

PROPERTY MAN: At once, sir. (*Exit.*)

THE MANAGER: Ready, everyone! First scene — the Young Lady. (*The* LEADING LADY *comes forward.*) No, no, you must wait. I meant her. (*Indicating the* STEP-DAUGHTER.) You just watch —

THE STEP-DAUGHTER (*adding at once*): How I shall play it, how I shall live it! . . .

LEADING LADY (*offended*): I shall live it also, you may be sure, as soon as I begin!

THE MANAGER (*with his hands to his head*): Ladies and gentlemen, if you please! No more useless discussions! Scene I: the Young Lady with Madame Pace: Oh! (*Looks around as if lost.*) And this Madame Pace, where is she?

THE FATHER: She isn't with us, sir.

THE MANAGER: Then what the devil's to be done?

THE FATHER: But she is alive too.

THE MANAGER: Yes, but where is she?

THE FATHER: One minute. Let me speak! (*Turning to the* ACTRESSES.) If these ladies would be so good as to give me their hats for a moment. . . .

THE ACTRESSES (*half surprised, half laughing, in chorus*): What? Why? Our hats? What does he say?

THE MANAGER: What are you going to do with the ladies' hats? (*The* ACTORS *laugh.*)

THE FATHER: Oh nothing. I just want to put them on these pegs for a moment. And one of the ladies will be so kind as to take off her mantle. . . .

THE ACTORS: Oh, what d'you think of that? Only the mantle? He must be mad.

SOME ACTRESSES: But why? Mantles as well?

THE FATHER: To hang them up here for a moment. Please be so kind, will you?

THE ACTRESSES (*taking off their hats, one or two also their cloaks, and going to hang them on the racks*): After all, why not? There you are! This is really funny. We've got to put them on show.

THE FATHER: Exactly; just like that, on show.

THE MANAGER: May we know why?

THE FATHER: I'll tell you. Who knows if, by arranging the stage for her, she does not come here herself, attracted by the very articles of her trade? (*Inviting the* ACTORS *to look towards the exit at back of stage.*) Look! Look!

(*The door at the back of stage opens and* MADAME PACE *enters and takes a few steps forward. She is a fat, oldish woman with puffy oxygenated hair. She is rouged and powdered, dressed with a comical elegance in black silk. Round her waist is a long silver chain from which hangs a pair of scissors. The* STEP-DAUGHTER *runs over to her at once amid the stupor of the* ACTORS.)

THE STEP-DAUGHTER (*turning towards her*): There she is! There she is!

THE FATHER (*radiant*): It's she! I said so, didn't I? There she is!

THE MANAGER (*conquering his surprise, and then becoming indignant*): What sort of a trick is this?

LEADING MAN (*almost at the same time*): What's going to happen next?

JUVENILE LEAD: Where does *she* come from?

L'INGÉNUE: They've been holding her in reserve, I guess.

LEADING LADY: A vulgar trick!

THE FATHER (*dominating the protests*): Excuse me, all of you! Why are you so anxious to destroy in the name of a vulgar, commonplace sense of truth, this reality which comes to birth attracted and formed by the magic of the stage itself, which has indeed more right to live here than you, since it is much truer than you — if you don't mind my saying so? Which is the actress among you who is to play Madame Pace? Well, here is Madame Pace herself. And you will allow, I fancy, that the actress who acts her will be less true than this woman here, who is herself in person. You see my daughter recognized her and went over to her at once. Now you're going to witness the scene!

(*But the scene between the* STEP-DAUGHTER *and* MADAME PACE *has already begun despite the protest of the* ACTORS *and the reply of the* FATHER. *It has begun quietly, naturally, in a manner impossible for the stage. So when the* ACTORS, *called to attention by the* FATHER, *turn round and see* MADAME PACE, *who has placed one hand under the* STEP-DAUGHTER'S *chin to raise her head, they observe her at first with great attention, but hearing her speak in an unintelligible manner their interest begins to wane.*)

THE MANAGER: Well? well?

LEADING MAN: What does she say?

LEADING LADY: One can't hear a word.

JUVENILE LEAD: Louder! Louder please!

THE STEP-DAUGHTER (*leaving* MADAME PACE, *who smiles a Sphinx-like smile, and advancing towards the* ACTORS): Louder? Louder? What are you talking about? These aren't matters which can be shouted at the top of one's voice. If I have spoken them out loud, it was to shame him and have my revenge. (*Indicates* FATHER.) But for Madame it's quite a different matter.

THE MANAGER: Indeed? indeed? But here, you know, people have got to make themselves heard, my dear. Even we who are on the stage can't hear you. What will it be when the public's in the theatre? And anyway, you can very well speak up now among yourselves, since we shan't be present to listen to you as we are now. You've got to pretend to be alone in a room at the back of a shop where no one can hear you.

(*The* STEP-DAUGHTER *coquettishly and with a touch of malice makes a sign of disagreement two or three times with her finger.*)

THE MANAGER: What do you mean by no?

THE STEP-DAUGHTER (*sotto voce, mysteriously*): There's someone who will hear us if she (*indicating* MADAME PACE) speaks out loud.

THE MANAGER (*in consternation*): What? Have you got someone else to spring on us now? (*The* ACTORS *burst out laughing.*)

THE FATHER: No, no sir. She is alluding to me. I've got to be here — there behind that door, in waiting; and Madame Pace knows it. In fact, if you will allow me, I'll go there at once, so I can be quite ready. (*Moves away.*)

THE MANAGER (*stopping him*): No! Wait! wait! We must observe the conventions of the theatre. Before you are ready. . . .

THE STEP-DAUGHTER (*interrupting him*): No, get on with it at once! I'm just dying, I tell you, to act this scene. If he's ready, I'm more than ready.

THE MANAGER (*shouting*): But, my dear young lady, first of all, we must have the scene between you and this lady. . . . (*Indicates* MADAME PACE.) Do you understand? . . .

THE STEP-DAUGHTER: Good Heavens! She's been telling me what you know already: that mamma's work is badly done again, that the material's ruined; and that if I want her to continue to help us in our misery I must be patient. . . .

MADAME PACE (*coming forward with an air of great importance*): Yes indeed, sir, I no wanta take advantage of her, I no wanta be hard. . . .

(*Note:* MADAME PACE *is supposed to talk in a jargon half Italian, half English.*)

THE MANAGER (*alarmed*): What? What? She talks like that? (*The* ACTORS *burst out laughing again.*)

THE STEP-DAUGHTER (*also laughing*): Yes yes, that's the way she talks, half English, half Italian! Most comical it is!

MADAME PACE: Itta seem not verra polite gentlemen laugha atta me eeff I trya best speaka English.

THE MANAGER: *Diamine!* Of course! Of course! Let her talk like that! Just what we want. Talk just like that, Madame, if you please! The effect will be certain. Exactly what was wanted to put a little comic relief into the crudity of the situation. Of course she talks like that! Magnificent!

THE STEP-DAUGHTER: Magnificent? Certainly! When certain suggestions are made to one in language of that kind, the effect is certain, since it seems almost a joke. One feels inclined to laugh when one hears her talk about an "old signore" "who wanta talka nicely with you." Nice old signore, eh, Madame?

MADAME PACE: Not so old my dear, not so old! And even if you no lika him, he won't make any scandal!

THE MOTHER (*jumping up amid the amazement and consternation of the* ACTORS, *who had not been noticing her. They move to restrain her.*): You old devil! You murderess!

THE STEP-DAUGHTER (*running over to calm her* MOTHER): Calm yourself, Mother, calm yourself! Please don't. . . .

THE FATHER (*going to her also at the same time*): Calm yourself! Don't get excited! Sit down now!

THE MOTHER: Well then, take that woman away out of my sight!

THE STEP-DAUGHTER (*to* MANAGER): It is impossible for my mother to remain here.

THE FATHER (*to* MANAGER): They can't be here together. And for this reason, you see: that woman there was not with us when we came. . . . If they are on together, the whole thing is given away inevitably, as you see.

THE MANAGER: It doesn't matter. This is only a first rough sketch — just to get an idea of the various points of the scene, even confusedly. . . . (*Turning to the* MOTHER *and leading her to her chair.*) Come along, my dear lady, sit down now, and let's get on with the scene. . . .

(*Meanwhile, the* STEP-DAUGHTER, *coming forward again, turns to* MADAME PACE.)

THE STEP-DAUGHTER: Come on, Madame, come on!

MADAME PACE (*offended*): No, no, *grazie*. I not do anything witha your mother present.

THE STEP-DAUGHTER: Nonsense! Introduce this "old signore" who wants to talk nicely to me. (*Addressing the* COMPANY *imperiously.*) We've got to do this scene one way or another, haven't we? Come on! (*To* MADAME PACE.) You can go!

MADAME PACE: Ah yes! I go'way! I go'way! Certainly! (*Exits furious.*)

THE STEP-DAUGHTER (*to the* FATHER): Now you make your entry. No, you needn't go over there. Come here. Let's suppose you've already come in. Like that, yes! I'm here with bowed head, modest like. Come on! Out with your voice! Say "Good morning, Miss" in that peculiar tone, that special tone. . . .

THE MANAGER: Excuse me, but are you the Manager, or am I? (*To the* FATHER, *who looks undecided and perplexed.*) Get on with it, man! Go down there to the back of the stage. You needn't go off. Then come right forward here.

(*The* FATHER *does as he is told, looking troubled and perplexed at first. But as soon as he begins to move, the reality of the action affects him, and he begins to smile and to be more natural. The* ACTORS *watch intently.*)

THE MANAGER (*sotto voce, quickly to the* PROMPTER *in his box*): Ready! ready? Get ready to write now.

THE FATHER (*coming forward and speaking in a different tone*): Good afternoon, Miss!

THE STEP-DAUGHTER (*head bowed down slightly, with restrained disgust*): Good afternoon!

THE FATHER (*looks under her hat which partly covers her face. Perceiving she is very young, he makes an exclamation, partly of surprise, partly of fear lest he compromise himself in a risky adventure*): Ah . . . but . . . ah . . . I say . . . this is not the first time that you have come here, is it?

THE STEP-DAUGHTER (*modestly*): No sir.

THE FATHER: You've been here before, eh? (*Then seeing her nod agreement.*) More than once? (*Waits for her to answer, looks under her hat, smiles, and then says:*) Well then, there's no need to be so shy, is there? May I take off your hat?

THE STEP-DAUGHTER (*anticipating him and with veiled disgust*): No sir . . . I'll do it myself. (*Takes it off quickly.*)

(*The* MOTHER, *who watches the progress of the scene with the* SON *and the other two children who cling to her, is on thorns; and follows with varying expressions of sorrow, indignation, anxiety, and horror the words and actions of the other two. From time to time she hides her face in her hands and sobs.*)

THE MOTHER: Oh, my God, my God!

THE FATHER (*playing his part with a touch of gallantry*): Give it to me! I'll put it down. (*Takes hat from her hands.*) But a dear little head like yours ought to have a smarter hat. Come and help me choose one from the stock, won't you?

L'INGÉNUE (*interrupting*): I say . . . those are our hats you know.

THE MANAGER (*furious*): Silence! silence! Don't try and be funny, if you please. . . . We're playing the scene now, I'd have you notice. (*To the* STEP-DAUGHTER.) Begin again, please!

THE STEP-DAUGHTER (*continuing*): No thank you, sir.

THE FATHER: Oh, come now. Don't talk like that. You must take it. I shall be upset if you don't. There are some lovely little hats here; and then — Madame will be pleased. She expects it, anyway, you know.

THE STEP-DAUGHTER: No, no! I couldn't wear it!

THE FATHER: Oh, you're thinking about what they'd say at home if they saw you come in with a new hat? My dear girl, there's always a way round these little matters, you know.

THE STEP-DAUGHTER (*all keyed up*): No, it's not that. I couldn't wear it because I am . . . as you see . . . you might have noticed . . .

(*Showing her black dress.*)

THE FATHER: . . . in mourning! Of course: I beg your pardon: I'm frightfully sorry. . . .

THE STEP-DAUGHTER (*forcing herself to conquer her indignation and nausea*): Stop! Stop! It's I who must thank you. There's no need for you to feel mortified or specially sorry. Don't think any more of what I've said. (*Tries to smile.*) I must forget that I am dressed so. . . .

THE MANAGER (*interrupting and turning to the* PROMPTER): Stop a minute! Stop! Don't write that down. Cut out that last bit. (*Then to the* FATHER *and* STEP-DAUGHTER.) Fine! it's going fine! (*To the* FATHER *only.*) And now you can go on as we arranged. (*To the* ACTORS.) Pretty good that scene, where he offers her the hat, eh?

THE STEP-DAUGHTER: The best's coming now. Why can't we go on?

THE MANAGER: Have a little patience! (*To the* ACTORS.) Of course, it must be treated rather lightly.

LEADING MAN: Still, with a bit of go in it!

LEADING LADY: Of course! It's easy enough! (*To* LEADING MAN.) Shall you and I try it now?

LEADING MAN: Why, yes! I'll prepare my entrance. (*Exit in order to make his entrance.*)

THE MANAGER (*to* LEADING LADY): See here! The scene between you and Madame Pace is finished. I'll have it written out properly after. You remain here . . . oh, where are you going?

LEADING LADY: One minute. I want to put my hat on again. (*Goes over to hat-rack and puts her hat on her head.*)

THE MANAGER: Good! You stay here with your head bowed down a bit.

THE STEP-DAUGHTER: But she isn't dressed in black.

LEADING LADY: But I shall be, and much more effectively than you.

THE MANAGER (*to* STEP-DAUGHTER): Be quiet please, and watch! You'll be able to learn something. (*Clapping his hands.*) Come on! come on! Entrance, please!

(*The door at rear of stage opens, and the* LEADING MAN *enters with the lively manner of an old gallant. The rendering of the scene by the* ACTORS *from the very first words is seen to be quite a different thing, though it has not in any way the air of a parody. Naturally, the* STEP-DAUGHTER *and the* FATHER, *not being able to recognize themselves in the* LEADING LADY *and the* LEADING MAN, *who deliver their words in different tones and with a different psychology, express, sometimes with smiles, sometimes with gestures, the impression they receive.*)

LEADING MAN: Good afternoon, Miss. . . .

THE FATHER (*at once unable to contain himself*): No!

(*The* STEP-DAUGHTER, *noticing the way the* LEADING MAN *enters, bursts out laughing.*)

THE MANAGER (*furious*): Silence! And you please just stop that laughing. If we go on like this, we shall never finish.

THE STEP-DAUGHTER: Forgive me, sir, but it's natural enough. This lady (*indicating* LEADING LADY) stands there still; but if she is supposed to be me, I can assure you that if I heard anyone say "Good afternoon" in that manner and in that tone, I should burst out laughing as I did.

THE FATHER: Yes, yes, the manner, the tone. . . .

THE MANAGER: Nonsense! Rubbish! Stand aside and let me see the action.

LEADING MAN: If I've got to represent an old fellow who's coming into a house of an equivocal character. . . .

THE MANAGER: Don't listen to them, for Heaven's sake! Do it again! It goes fine. (*Waiting for the* ACTORS *to begin again.*) Well?

LEADING MAN: Good afternoon, Miss.

LEADING LADY: Good afternoon.

LEADING MAN (*imitating the gesture of the* FATHER *when he looked under the hat, and then expressing quite clearly first satisfaction and then fear*): Ah, but . . . I say . . . this is not the first time that you have come here, is it?

THE MANAGER: Good, but not quite so heavily. Like this. (*Acts himself.*) "This isn't the first time that you have come here" . . . (*To* LEADING LADY.) And you say: "No, sir."

LEADING LADY: No, sir.

LEADING MAN: You've been here before, more than once.

THE MANAGER: No, no, stop! Let her nod "yes" first. "You've been here before, eh?" (*The* LEADING LADY *lifts up her head slightly and closes her eyes as though in disgust. Then she inclines her head twice.*)

THE STEP-DAUGHTER (*unable to contain herself*): Oh my God! (Puts *a hand to her mouth to prevent herself from laughing.*)

THE MANAGER (*turning round*): What's the matter?

THE STEP-DAUGHTER: Nothing, nothing!

THE MANAGER (*to* LEADING MAN): Go on!

LEADING MAN: You've been here before, eh? Well then, there's no need to be so shy, is there? May I take off your hat?

(*The* LEADING MAN *says this last speech in such a tone and with such gestures that the* STEP-DAUGHTER, *though she has her hand to her mouth, cannot keep from laughing.*)

LEADING LADY (*indignant*): I'm not going to stop here to be made a fool of by that woman there.

LEADING MAN: Neither am I! I'm through with it!

THE MANAGER (*shouting to* STEP-DAUGHTER): Silence! for once and all, I tell you!

THE STEP-DAUGHTER: Forgive me! forgive me!

THE MANAGER: You haven't any manners: that's what it is! You go too far.

THE FATHER (*endeavoring to intervene*): Yes, it's true, but excuse her. . . .

THE MANAGER: Excuse what? It's absolutely disgusting.

THE FATHER: Yes, sir, but believe me, it has such a strange effect when . . .

THE MANAGER: Strange? Why strange? Where is it strange?

THE FATHER: No, sir; I admire your actors — this gentleman here, this lady; but they are certainly not us!

THE MANAGER: I should hope not. Evidently they cannot be you, if they are actors.

THE FATHER: Just so: actors! Both of them act our parts exceedingly well. But, believe me, it produces quite a different effect on us. They want to be us, but they aren't, all the same.

THE MANAGER: What is it then anyway?

THE FATHER: Something that is . . . that is theirs — and no longer ours . . .

THE MANAGER: But naturally, inevitably. I've told you so already.

THE FATHER: Yes, I understand . . . I understand . . .

THE MANAGER: Well then, let's have no more of it! (*Turning to the* ACTORS.) We'll have the rehearsals by ourselves, afterwards, in the ordinary way. I never could stand rehearsing with the author present. He's never satisfied! (*Turning to* FATHER *and* STEP-DAUGHTER.) Come on! Let's get on with it again; and try and see if you can't keep from laughing.

THE STEP-DAUGHTER: Oh, I shan't laugh any more. There's a nice little bit coming for me now: you'll see.

THE MANAGER: Well then: when she says "Don't think any more of what I've said, I must forget, etc.," you (*addressing the* FATHER) come in sharp with "I understand, I understand"; and then you ask her . . .

THE STEP-DAUGHTER (*interrupting*): What?

THE MANAGER: Why she is in mourning.

THE STEP-DAUGHTER: Not at all! See here: when I told him that it was useless for me to be thinking about my wearing mourning, do you know how he answered me? "Ah well," he said, "then let's take off this little frock."

THE MANAGER: Great! Just what we want, to make a riot in the theatre!

THE STEP-DAUGHTER: But it's the truth!

THE MANAGER: What does that matter? Acting is our business here. Truth up to a certain point, but no further.

THE STEP-DAUGHTER: What do you want to do then?

THE MANAGER: You'll see, you'll see! Leave it to me.

THE STEP-DAUGHTER: No sir! What you want to do is to piece together a little romantic sentimental scene out of my disgust, out of all the reasons, each more cruel and viler than the other, why I am what I am. He is to ask me why I'm in mourning; and I'm to answer with tears in my eyes, that it is just two months since papa died. No sir, no! He's got to say to me, as he did say: "Well, let's take off this little dress at once." And I, with my two months' mourning in my heart, went there behind that screen, and with these fingers tingling with shame . . .

THE MANAGER (*running his hands through his hair*): For Heaven's sake! What are you saying?

THE STEP-DAUGHTER (*crying out excitedly*): The truth! The truth!

THE MANAGER: It may be. I don't deny it, and I can understand all your horror; but you must surely see that you can't have this kind of thing on the stage. It won't go.

THE STEP-DAUGHTER: Not possible, eh? Very well! I'm much obliged to you — but I'm off!

THE MANAGER: Now be reasonable! Don't lose your temper!

THE STEP-DAUGHTER: I won't stop here! I won't! I can see you've fixed it all up with him in your office. All this talk about what is possible for the stage . . . I understand! He wants to get at his complicated "cerebral drama," to have his famous remorses and torments acted; but I want to act my part, *my part!*

THE MANAGER (*annoyed, shaking his shoulders*): Ah! Just *your* part! But, if you will pardon me, there are other parts than yours: His (*indicating the* FATHER) and hers (*indicating the* MOTHER)! On the stage you can't have a character becoming too prominent and overshadowing all the others. The thing is to pack them all into a neat little framework and then act what is actable. I am aware of the fact that everyone has his own interior life which he wants very much to put forward. But the difficulty lies in this fact: to set out just so much as is necessary for the stage, taking the other characters into consideration, and at the same time hint at the unrevealed interior life of each. I am willing to admit, my dear young lady, that from your point of view it would be a fine idea if each character could tell the public all his troubles in a nice monologue or a regular one hour lecture. (*Good humoredly.*) You must restrain yourself, my dear, and in your own interest, too; because this fury of yours, this exaggerated disgust you show, may make a bad impression, you know. After you have confessed to me that there were others before him at Madame Pace's and more than once . . .

THE STEP-DAUGHTER (*bowing her head, impressed*): It's true. But remember those others mean him for me all the same.

THE MANAGER (*not understanding*): What? The others? What do you mean?

THE STEP-DAUGHTER: For one who has gone wrong, sir, he who was responsible for the first fault is responsible for all that follow. He is responsible for my faults, was, even before I was born. Look at him, and see if it isn't true!

THE MANAGER: Well, well! And does the weight of so much responsibility seem nothing to you? Give him a chance to act it, to get it over!

THE STEP-DAUGHTER: How? How can he act all his "noble remorses," all his "moral torments," if you want to spare him the horror of being discovered one day — after he had asked her what he did ask her — in the arms of her, that already fallen woman, that child, sir, that child he used to watch come out of school? (*She is moved.*)

(*The* MOTHER *at this point is overcome with emotion, and breaks out into a fit of crying. All are touched. A long pause.*)

THE STEP-DAUGHTER (*as soon as the* MOTHER *becomes a little quieter, adds resolutely and gravely*): At present, we are unknown to the public. Tomorrow, you will act us as you wish, treating us in your own manner. But do you really want to see drama, do you want to see it flash out as it really did?

THE MANAGER: Of course! That's just what I do want, so I can use as much of it as is possible.

THE STEP-DAUGHTER: Well then, ask that Mother there to leave us.

THE MOTHER (*changing her low plaint into a sharp cry*): No! No! Don't permit it, sir, don't permit it!

THE MANAGER: But it's only to try it.

THE MOTHER: I can't bear it. I can't.

THE MANAGER: But since it has happened already . . . I don't understand!

THE MOTHER: It's taking place now. It happens all the time. My torment isn't a pretended one. I live and feel every minute of my torture. Those two children there — have you heard them speak? They can't speak any more. They cling to me to keep up my torment actual and vivid for me. But for themselves, they do not exist, they aren't any more. And she (*indicating the* STEP-DAUGHTER) has run away, she has left me, and is lost. If I now see her here before me, it is only to renew for me the tortures I have suffered for her too.

THE FATHER: The eternal moment! She (*indicating the* STEP-DAUGHTER) is here to catch me, fix me, and hold me eternally in the stocks for that one fleeting and shameful moment of my life. She can't give it up! And you, sir, cannot either fairly spare me it.

THE MANAGER: I never said I didn't want to act it. It will form, as a matter of fact, the nucleus of the whole first act right up to her surprise. (*Indicates the* MOTHER.)

THE FATHER: Just so! This is my punishment: the passion in all of us that must culminate in her final cry.

THE STEP-DAUGHTER: I can hear it still in my ears. It's driven me mad, that cry! — You can put me on as you like; it doesn't matter. Fully dressed, if you like — provided I have at least the arm bare; because, standing like this (*she goes close to the* FATHER *and leans her head on his breast*) with my head so, and my arms round his neck, I saw a vein pulsing in my arm here; and then, as if that live vein had awakened disgust in me, I closed my eyes like this, and let my head sink on his breast. (*Turning to the* MOTHER.) Cry out, mother! Cry out! (*Buries head in* FATHER'S *breast, and with her shoulders raised as if to prevent her hearing the cry, adds in tones of intense emotion:*) Cry out as you did then!

THE MOTHER (*coming forward to separate them*): No! My daughter, my daughter! (*And after having pulled her away from him.*) You brute! you brute! She is my daughter! Don't you see she's my daughter?

THE MANAGER (*walking backwards towards footlights*): Fine! fine! Damned good! And then, of course — curtain!

THE FATHER (*going towards him excitedly*): Yes, of course, because that's the way it really happened.

THE MANAGER (*convinced and pleased*): Oh, yes, no doubt about it. Curtain here, curtain!

(*At the reiterated cry of the* MANAGER, *the* MACHINIST *lets the curtain down, leaving the* MANAGER *and the* FATHER *in front of it before the footlights.*)

THE MANAGER: The darned idiot! I said "curtain" to show the act should end there, and he goes and lets it down in earnest. (*To the* FATHER, *while he pulls the curtain back to go on to the stage again.*) Yes, yes, it's all right. Effect certain! That's the right ending. I'll guarantee the first act at any rate.

ACT III

(*When the curtain goes up again, it is seen that the* STAGE HANDS *have shifted the bit of scenery used in the last part, and have rigged up instead at the back of the stage a drop, with some trees, and one or two wings. A portion of a fountain basin is visible. The* MOTHER *is sitting on the right with the two children by her side. The* SON *is on the same side, but away from the others. He seems bored, angry, and full of shame. The* FATHER *and the* STEP-DAUGHTER *are also seated towards the right front. On the other side [left] are the* ACTORS, *much in the positions they occupied before the curtain was lowered. Only the* MANAGER *is stand-*

ing up in the middle of the stage, with his hand closed over his mouth in the act of meditating.)

THE MANAGER (*shaking his shoulders after a brief pause*): Ah yes: the second act! Leave it to me, leave it all to me as we arranged, and you'll see! It'll go fine!

THE STEP-DAUGHTER: Our entry into his house (*indicates* FATHER) in spite of him . . . (*indicates the* SON).

THE MANAGER (*out of patience*): Leave it to me, I tell you!

THE STEP-DAUGHTER: Do let it be clear, at any rate, that it is in spite of my wishes.

THE MOTHER (*from her corner, shaking her head*): For all the good that's come of it. . . .

THE STEP-DAUGHTER (*turning towards her quickly*): It doesn't matter. The more harm done us, the more remorse for him.

THE MANAGER (*impatiently*): I understand! Good Heavens! I understand! I'm taking it into account.

THE MOTHER (*supplicatingly*): I beg you, sir, to let it appear quite plain that for conscience' sake I did try in every way. . . .

THE STEP-DAUGHTER (*interrupting indignantly and continuing for the* MOTHER): . . . to pacify me, to dissuade me from spiting him. (*To* MANAGER.) Do as she wants: satisfy her, because it is true! I enjoy it immensely. Anyhow, as you can see, the meeker she is, the more she tries to get at his heart, the more distant and aloof does he become.

THE MANAGER: Are we going to begin this second act or not?

THE STEP-DAUGHTER: I'm not going to talk any more now. But I must tell you this: you can't have the whole action take place in the garden, as you suggest. It isn't possible!

THE MANAGER: Why not?

THE STEP-DAUGHTER: Because he (*indicates the* SON *again*) is always shut up alone in his room. And then there's all the part of that poor dazed-looking boy there which takes place indoors.

THE MANAGER: Maybe! On the other hand, you will understand — we can't change scenes three or four times in one act.

THE LEADING MAN: They used to once.

THE MANAGER: Yes, when the public was up to the level of that child there.

THE LEADING LADY: It makes the illusion easier.

THE FATHER (*irritated*): The illusion! For Heaven's sake, don't say illusion. Please don't use that word, which is particularly painful for us.

THE MANAGER (*astounded*): And why, if you please?

THE FATHER: It's painful, cruel, really cruel; and you ought to understand that.

THE MANAGER: But why? What ought we to say then? The illusion, I tell you, sir, which we've got to create for the audience. . . .

THE LEADING MAN: With our acting.

THE MANAGER: The illusion of a reality.

THE FATHER: I understand; but you, perhaps, do not understand us. Forgive me! You see . . . here for you and your actors, the thing is only — and rightly so . . . a kind of game . . .

THE LEADING LADY (*interrupting indignantly*): A game! We're not children here, if you please! We are serious actors.

THE FATHER: I don't deny it. What I mean is the game, or play, of your art, which has to give, as the gentleman says, a perfect illusion of reality.

THE MANAGER: Precisely — !

THE FATHER: Now, if you consider the fact that we (*indicates himself and the other five* CHARACTERS), as we are, have no other reality outside of this illusion. . . .

THE MANAGER (*astonished, looking at his* ACTORS, *who are also amazed*): And what does that mean?

THE FATHER (*after watching them for a moment with a wan smile*): As I say, sir, that which is a game of art for you is our sole reality. (*Brief pause. He goes a step or two nearer the* MANAGER *and adds:*) But not only for us, you know, by the way. Just you think it over well. (*Looks him in the eyes.*) Can you tell me who you are?

THE MANAGER (*perplexed, half smiling*): What? Who am I? I am myself.

THE FATHER: And if I were to tell you that that isn't true, because you and I . . . ?

THE MANAGER: I should say you were mad — ! (*The* ACTORS *laugh.*)

THE FATHER: You're quite right to laugh: because we are all making believe here. (*To* MANAGER.) And you can therefore object that it's only for a joke that that gentleman there (*indicates the* LEADING MAN), who naturally is himself, has to be me, who am on the contrary myself — this thing you see here. You see I've caught you in a trap! (*The* ACTORS *laugh.*)

THE MANAGER (*annoyed*): But we've had all this over once before. Do you want to begin again?

THE FATHER: No, no! That wasn't my meaning! In fact, I should like to request you to abandon this game of art (*looking at the* LEADING LADY *as if anticipating her*) which you are accustomed to play here with your actors, and to ask you seriously once again: who are you?

THE MANAGER (*astonished and irritated, turning to his* ACTORS): If this fellow here hasn't got a nerve! A man who calls himself a character comes and asks me who I am!

THE FATHER (*with dignity, but not offended*): A character, sir, may always ask a man who he is. Because a character has really a life of his own, marked with his especial characteristics; for which reason he is always "somebody." But a man — I'm not speaking of you now — may very well be "nobody."

THE MANAGER: Yes, but you are asking these questions of me, the boss, the manager! Do you understand?

THE FATHER: But only in order to know if you, as you really are now, see yourself as you once were with all the illusions that were yours then, with all the things both inside and outside of you as they seemed to you — as they were then indeed for you. Well, sir, if you think of all those illusions that mean nothing to you now, of all those things which don't even *seem* to you to exist any more, while once they *were* for you, don't you feel that — I won't say these boards — but the very earth under your feet is sinking away from you when you reflect that in the same way this *you* as you feel it today — all this present reality of yours — is fated to seem a mere illusion to you tomorrow?

THE MANAGER (*without having understood much, but astonished by the specious argument*): Well, well! And where does all this take us anyway?

THE FATHER: Oh, nowhere! It's only to show you that if we (*indicating the* CHARACTERS) have no other reality beyond the illusion, you too must not count overmuch on your reality as you feel it today, since, like that of yesterday, it may prove an illusion for you tomorrow.

THE MANAGER (*determining to make fun of him*): Ah, excellent! Then you'll be saying next that you, with this comedy of yours that you brought here to act, are truer and more real than I am.

THE FATHER (*with the greatest seriousness*): But of course; without doubt!

THE MANAGER: Ah, really?

THE FATHER: Why, I thought you'd understand that from the beginning.

THE MANAGER: More real than I?

THE FATHER: If your reality can change from one day to another. . . .

THE MANAGER: But everyone knows it can change. It is always changing, the same as anyone else's.

THE FATHER (*with a cry*): No, sir, not ours! Look here! That is the very difference! Our reality doesn't change: it can't change! It can't be other than what it is, because it is already fixed for ever. It's terrible. Ours is an immutable reality which should make you shudder when you approach us if you are really conscious of the fact that your reality is a mere transitory and fleeting illusion, taking this form today and that tomorrow, according to the conditions, according to your will, your sentiments, which in turn are controlled by an intellect that shows them to you today in one manner and tomorrow . . . who knows how? . . . Illusions of reality represented in this fatuous comedy of life that never ends, nor can ever end! Because if tomorrow it were to end . . . then why, all would be finished.

THE MANAGER: Oh for God's sake, will you *at least* finish with this philosophizing and let us try and shape this comedy which you yourself have brought me here? You argue and philosophize a bit too much, my dear sir. You know you seem to me almost, almost . . . (*Stops and looks him over from head to foot.*) Ah, by the way, I think you introduced yourself to me as a — what shall . . . we say — a "character," created by an author who did not afterward care to make a drama of his own creations.

THE FATHER: It is the simple truth, sir.

THE MANAGER: Nonsense! Cut that out, please! None of us believes it, because it isn't a thing, as you must recognize yourself, which one can believe seriously. If you want to know, it seems to me you are trying to imitate the manner of a certain author whom I heartily detest — I warn you — although I have unfortunately bound myself to put on one of his works. As a matter of fact, I was just starting to rehearse it, when you arrived. (*Turning to the* ACTORS.) And this is what we've gained — out of the frying-pan into the fire!

THE FATHER: I don't know to what author you may be alluding, but believe me I feel what I think; and I seem to be philosophizing only for those who do not think what they feel, because they blind themselves with their own sentiment. I know that for many people this self-blinding seems much more "human"; but the contrary is really true. For man never reasons so much and becomes so introspective as when he suffers; since he is anxious to get at the cause of his sufferings, to learn who has produced them, and whether it is just or unjust that he should have to bear them. On the other hand, when he is happy, he takes his happiness as it comes and doesn't analyze it, just as if happiness were his right. The animals suffer without reasoning about their sufferings. But take the case of a man who suffers and begins to reason about it. Oh no! it can't be allowed! Let him suffer like an animal, and then — ah yet, he is "human"!

THE MANAGER: Look here! Look here! You're off again, philosophizing worse than ever.

THE FATHER: Because I suffer, sir! I'm not philosophizing: I'm crying aloud the reason of my sufferings.

THE MANAGER (*makes brusque movement as he is taken with a new idea*): I should like to know if anyone has ever heard of a character who gets right out of his part and perorates and speechifies as you do. Have you ever heard of a case? I haven't.

THE FATHER: You have never met such a case, sir, because authors, as a rule, hide the labor of their creations. When the characters are really alive before their author, the latter does nothing but follow them in their action, in other words, in the situations which they suggest to him; and he has to will them the way they will themselves — for there's trouble if he doesn't. When a character is born, he acquires at once such an independence, even of his own author, that he can be imagined by everybody even in many other situations where the author never dreamed of placing him; and so he acquires for himself a meaning which the author never thought of giving him.

THE MANAGER: Yes, yes, I know this.

THE FATHER: What is there then to marvel at in us? Imagine such a misfortune for characters as I have described to you: to be born of an author's fantasy, and be denied life by him; and then answer me if these characters left alive, and yet without life, weren't right in doing what they did do and are doing now, after they have attempted everything in their power to persuade him to give them their stage life. We've all tried him in turn, I, she (*indicating the* STEP-DAUGHTER) and she (*indicating the* MOTHER).

THE STEP-DAUGHTER: It's true. I too have sought to tempt him, many, many times, when he has been sitting at his writing table, feeling a bit melancholy, at the twilight hour. He would sit in his armchair too lazy to switch on the light, and all the shadows that crept into his room were full of our presence coming to tempt him. (*As if she saw herself still there by the writing table, and was annoyed by the presence of the* ACTORS.) Oh, if you would only go away, go away and leave us alone — mother here with that son of hers — I with that Child — that Boy there always alone — and then I with him (*just hints at the* FATHER) — and then I alone, alone . . . in those shadows! (*Makes a sudden movement as if in the vision she has of herself illuminating those shadows she wanted to seize hold of herself.*) Ah! my life! my life! Oh, what scenes we proposed to him — and I tempted him more than any of the others!

THE FATHER: Maybe. But perhaps it was your fault that he refused to give us life: because you were too insistent, too troublesome.

THE STEP-DAUGHTER: Nonsense! Didn't he make me so himself? (*Goes close to the* MANAGER *to tell him as if in confidence.*) In my opinion he abandoned us in a fit of depression, of disgust for the ordinary theatre as the public knows it and likes it.

THE SON: Exactly what it was, sir; exactly that!

THE FATHER: Not at all! Don't believe it for a minute. Listen to me! You'll be doing quite right to modify, as you suggest, the excesses both of this girl here, who wants to do too much, and of this young man, who won't do anything at all.

THE SON: No, nothing!

THE MANAGER: You too get over the mark occasionally, my dear sir, if I may say so.

THE FATHER: I? When? Where?

THE MANAGER: Always! Continuously! Then there's this insistence of yours in trying to make us believe you are a character. And then too, you must really argue and philosophize less, you know, much less.

THE FATHER: Well, if you want to take away from me the possibility of representing the torment of my spirit which never gives me peace, you will be suppressing me: that's all. Every true man, sir, who is a little above the level of the beasts and plants does not live for the sake of living, without knowing how to live; but he lives so as to give a meaning and a value of his own to life. For me this is *everything.* I cannot give up this, just to represent a mere fact as she (*indicating the* STEP-DAUGHTER) wants. It's all very well for her, since her "vendetta" lies in the "fact." I'm not going to do it. It destroys my *raison d'être.*

THE MANAGER: Your *raison d'être!* Oh, we're going ahead fine! First she starts off, and then you jump in. At this rate, we'll never finish.

THE FATHER: Now, don't be offended! Have it your own way — provided, however, that within the limits of the parts you assign us each one's sacrifice isn't too great.

THE MANAGER: You've got to understand that you can't go on arguing at your own pleasure. Drama is action, sir, action and not confounded philosophy.

THE FATHER: All right. I'll do just as much arguing and philosophizing as everybody does when he is considering his own torments.

THE MANAGER: If the drama permits! But for Heaven's sake, man, let's get along and come to the scene.

THE STEP-DAUGHTER: It seems to me we've got too much action with our coming into his house. (*Indicating* FATHER.) You said, before, you couldn't change the scene every five minutes.

THE MANAGER: Of course not. What we've got to do is to combine and group up all the facts in one simultaneous, close-knit action.

We can't have it as you want, with your little brother wandering like a ghost from room to room, hiding behind doors and meditating a project which — what did you say it did to him?

THE STEP-DAUGHTER: Consumes him, sir, wastes him away!

THE MANAGER: Well, it may be. And then at the same time, you want the little girl there to be playing in the garden . . . one in the house, and the other in the garden: isn't that it?

THE STEP-DAUGHTER: Yes, in the sun, in the sun! That is my only pleasure: to see her happy and careless in the garden after the misery and squalor of the horrible room where we all four slept together. And I had to sleep with her — I, do you understand? — with my vile contaminated body next to hers; with her folding me fast in her loving little arms. In the garden, whenever she spied me, she would run to take me by the hand. She didn't care for the big flowers, only the little ones; and she loved to show me them and pet me.

THE MANAGER: Well then, we'll have it in the garden. Everything shall happen in the garden; and we'll group the other scenes there. (*Calls a* STAGE HAND.) Here, a backcloth with trees and something to do as a fountain basin. (*Turning round to look at the back of the stage.*) Ah, you've fixed it up. Good! (*To* STEP-DAUGHTER.) This is just to give an idea, of course. The Boy, instead of hiding behind the doors, will wander about here in the garden, hiding behind the trees. But it's going to be rather difficult to find a child to do that scene with you where she shows you the flowers. (*Turning to the* BOY.) Come forward a little, will you please? Let's try it now! Come along! come along! (*Then seeing him come shyly forward, full of fear and looking lost.*) It's a nice business, this lad here. What's the matter with him? We'll have to give him a word or two to say. (*Goes close to him, puts a hand on his shoulders, and leads him behind one of the trees.*) Come on! come on! Let me see you a little! Hide here . . . yes, like that. Try and show your head just a little as if you were looking for someone. . . . (*Goes back to observe the effect, when the* BOY *at once goes through the action.*) Excellent! fine! (*Turning to* STEP-DAUGHTER.) Suppose the little girl there were to surprise him as he looks round, and run over to him, so we could give him a word or two to say?

THE STEP-DAUGHTER: It's useless to hope he will speak, as long as that fellow there is here. . . . (*Indicates the* SON.) You must send him away first.

THE SON (*jumping up*): Delighted! Delighted! I don't ask for anything better. (*Begins to move away.*)

THE MANAGER (*at once stopping him*): No! No! Where are you going? Wait a bit!

(*The* MOTHER *gets up alarmed and terrified at the thought that he is really about to go away. Instinctively she lifts her arms to prevent him, without, however, leaving her seat.*)

THE SON (*to* MANAGER, *who stops him*): I've got nothing to do with this affair. Let me go, please! Let me go!

THE MANAGER: What do you mean by saying you've got nothing to do with this?

THE STEP-DAUGHTER (*calmly, with irony*): Don't bother to stop him: he won't go away.

THE FATHER: He has to act the terrible scene in the garden with his mother.

THE SON (*suddenly resolute and with dignity*): I shall act nothing at all. I've said so from the very beginning. (*To the* MANAGER.) Let me go!

THE STEP-DAUGHTER (*going over to the* MANAGER): Allow me? (*Puts down the* MANAGER'S *arm which is restraining the* SON.) Well, go away then, if you want to! (*The* SON *looks at her with contempt and hatred. She laughs and says:*) You see, he can't, he can't go away! He is obliged to stay here, indissolubly bound to the chain. If I, who fly off when that happens which has to happen, because I can't bear him — if I am still here and support that face and expression of his, you can well imagine that he is unable to move. He has to remain here, has to stop with that nice father of his, and that mother whose only son he is. (*Turning to the* MOTHER.) Come on, mother, come along! (*Turning to* MANAGER *to indicate her.*) You see, she was getting up to keep him back. (*To the* MOTHER, *beckoning her with her hand.*) Come on! come on! (*Then to* MANAGER.) You can imagine how little she wants to show these actors of yours what she really feels; but so eager is she to get near him that. . . . There, you see? She is willing to act her part. (*And in fact, the* MOTHER *approaches him; and as soon as the* STEP-DAUGHTER *has finished speaking, opens her arms to signify that she consents.*)

THE SON (*suddenly*): No! no! If I can't go away, then I'll stop here; but I repeat: I act nothing!

THE FATHER (*to* MANAGER *excitedly*): You can force him, sir.

THE SON: Nobody can force me.

THE FATHER: I can.

THE STEP-DAUGHTER: Wait a minute, wait . . . First of all, the baby has to go to the fountain. . . . (*Runs to take the* CHILD *and leads her to the fountain.*)

THE MANAGER: Yes, yes of course; that's it. Both at the same time.

(*The* SECOND LADY LEAD *and the* JUVENILE LEAD *at this point separate themselves from the group of* ACTORS. *One watches the* MOTHER *attentively; the other moves about studying the movements and manner of the* SON *whom he will have to act.*)

THE SON (*to* MANAGER): What do you mean by both at the same time? It isn't right. There was no scene between me and her. (*Indicates the* MOTHER.) Ask her how it was!

THE MOTHER: Yes, it's true. I had come into his room. . . .

THE SON: Into my room, do you understand? Nothing to do with the garden.

THE MANAGER: It doesn't matter. Haven't I told you we've got to group the action?

THE SON (*observing the* JUVENILE LEAD *studying him*): What do you want?

THE JUVENILE LEAD: Nothing! I was just looking at you.

THE SON (*turning towards the* SECOND LADY LEAD): Ah! she's at it too: to re-act her part! (*Indicating the* MOTHER.)

THE MANAGER: Exactly! And it seems to me that you ought to be grateful to them for their interest.

THE SON: Yes, but haven't you yet perceived that it isn't possible to live in front of a mirror which not only freezes us with the image of ourselves, but throws our likeness back at us with a horrible grimace?

THE FATHER: That is true, absolutely true. You must see that.

THE MANAGER (*to* SECOND LADY LEAD *and* JUVENILE LEAD): He's right! Move away from them!

THE SON: Do as you like. I'm out of this!

THE MANAGER: Be quiet, you, will you? And let me hear your mother! (*To* MOTHER.) You were saying you had entered. . . .

THE MOTHER: Yes, into his room, because I couldn't stand it any longer. I went to empty my heart to him of all the anguish that tortures me. . . . But as soon as he saw me come in. . . .

THE SON: Nothing happened! There was no scene. I went away, that's all! I don't care for scenes!

THE MOTHER: It's true, true, That's how it was.

THE MANAGER: Well now, we've got to do this bit between you and him. It's indispensable.

THE MOTHER: I'm ready . . . when you are ready. If you could only find a chance for me to tell him what I feel here in my heart.

THE FATHER (*going to* SON *in a great rage*): You'll do this for your mother, for your mother, do you understand?

THE SON (*quite determined*): I do nothing!

THE FATHER (*taking hold of him and shaking him*): For God's sake, do as I tell you! Don't you hear your mother asking you for a favor? Haven't you even got the guts to be a son?

THE SON (*taking hold of the* FATHER): No! No! And for God's sake stop it, or else. . . . (*General agitation. The* MOTHER, *frightened, tries to separate them.*)

THE MOTHER (*pleading*): Please! please!

THE FATHER (*not leaving hold of the* SON): You've got to obey, do you hear?

THE SON (*almost crying from rage*): What does it mean, this madness you've got? (*They separate.*) Have you no decency, that you insist on showing everyone our shame? I won't do it! I won't! And I stand for the will of our author in this. He didn't want to put us on the stage, after all!

THE MANAGER: Man alive! You came here . . .

THE SON (*indicating* FATHER): *He* did! I didn't!

THE MANAGER: Aren't you here now?

THE SON: It was his wish, and he dragged us along with him. He's told you not only the things that did happen, but also things that have never happened at all.

THE MANAGER: Well, tell me then what did happen. You went out of your room without saying a word?

THE SON: Without a word, so as to avoid a scene!

THE MANAGER: And then what did you do?

THE SON: Nothing . . . walking in the garden. . . . (*Hesitates for a moment with expression of gloom.*)

THE MANAGER (*coming closer to him, interested by his extraordinary reserve*): Well, well . . . walking in the garden. . . .

THE SON (*exasperated*): Why on earth do you insist? It's horrible!

(*The* MOTHER *trembles, sobs, and looks towards the fountain.*)

THE MANAGER (*slowly observing the glance and turning towards the* SON *with increasing apprehension*): The baby?

THE SON: There in the fountain. . . .

THE FATHER (*pointing with tender pity to the* MOTHER): She was following him at the moment. . . .

THE MANAGER (*to the* SON *anxiously*): And then you. . . .

THE SON: I ran over to her; I was jumping in to drag her out when I saw something that froze my blood . . . the boy standing stock still, with eyes like a madman's, watching his little drowned sister, in the fountain! (*The* STEP-DAUGHTER *bends over the fountain to hide the* CHILD. *She sobs.*) Then. . . . (*A revolver shot rings out behind the trees where the* BOY *is hidden.*)

THE MOTHER (*with a cry of terror runs over in that direction together with several of the* ACTORS *amid general confusion*): My son! My son! (*Then amid the cries and exclamations one hears her voice.*) Help! Help!

THE MANAGER (*pushing the* ACTORS *aside while they lift up the* BOY *and carry him off*): Is he really wounded?

SOME ACTORS: He's dead! dead!

OTHER ACTORS: No, no, it's only make believe, it's only pretense!

THE FATHER (*with a terrible cry*): Pretense? Reality, sir, reality!

THE MANAGER: Pretense? Reality? To hell with it all! Never in my life has such a thing happened to me. I've lost a whole day over these people, a whole day!

Six Characters in Search of an Author (1921) remains in the memory as the image of the real-life theater of illusionism invaded by the "fantastic reality" of imaginative truth. Pirandello, perhaps as thinking a playwright as there ever was, yet subordinates philosophy to action — the action of the six characters usurping the stage. That he does is the secret of the play's success as play of ideas. We contemplate facing mirrors. The eye is lost, the mind reels, in the infinitely reciprocal vistas of play and reality, actors and characters, illusion and truth. And the play's brilliance as drama is the containment of all its riddles and paradoxes within the one image of the invaded theater.

Not surprisingly, *Six Characters* has been provocative and controversial ever since its first appearance. Though it established Pirandello's fame, there were some, then as now, whom it irritated as a scoreless cerebral game. Others, friendly or hostile, saw in it only a new way of presenting the old middle-class domestic tragedy of past guilt and present anguish — Ibsen with a gimmick. Such views appear inadequate to explain the fact that *Six Characters* has been one of the most seminal plays of our time. In America it has influenced such theatricalist pieces as O'Neill's *Great God Brown* and *Marco Millions*, Thornton Wilder's *Our Town*, and Tennessee Williams' *Glass Menagerie*. It has anticipated much of the mood and manner of today's "absurd" drama. It has been partly responsible for the current scorn of straightforward realism in the theater as unimaginative and old-fashioned photographism. But its family connections run backward, too, for even the avant-garde has a way of slipping into place in the continuum of our dramatic tradition. The play-within-the-play device is traditional. The play's form has been partly suggested by that of the sixteenth- and seventeenth-century Italian *commedia dell' arte*, a playful, earthy drama of dialogue improvisation over stock characters, situations, and plots. Like expressionistic drama *Six Characters* shatters the surface of experience without abandoning the fragments in pursuit of symbol and myth. Its immediate historical context was the "grotesque" theater movement in Italy during and immediately after World War I, whose leader was Luigi Chiarelli and the aim and method of which was to mock and shock conventional sensibilities and institutions while proclaiming universal meaninglessness. But most significant of all is the play's relationship to the serious naturalistic drama of the previous generation.

That drama — Ibsenism and Chekhovianism rather than Ibsen's and Chekhov's own plays — stimulated Pirandello into revolutionizing dramatic form, but he did not simply react against it. He applied to it a new viewpoint. In a sense, what *Six Characters in Search of an Author* does is to put on trial the reality the nineteenth century had taken for granted: the reality of positivist science, matter in motion governed by discoverable, stable laws. It does not bring in a verdict of guilt; Pirandello's thought and art are both too subtle for that. It gives a vote of no confidence. In an important preface to the play, which he wrote in 1925, Pirandello contrasts playwrights to whom it is "enough to present a man or a woman and what is special and characteristic about them simply for the pleasure of presenting them" with those "others, who, beyond such pleasure, feel a more profound spiritual need on whose account they admit only figures, affairs, landscapes which have been soaked, so to speak, in a particular sense of life and acquire from it a universal value." Among these latter, "philosophical," writers he includes himself. His plays suggest that we should interpret this to mean that the concatenation of scene, event, and character that constitutes theme or mood within the realistic convention of scenic and psychological plausibility yielded no "particular sense of life" for him. Just as Strindberg's expressionistic chamber plays today seem more contemporary with our own sense of life than his historical and his naturalistic plays, so is the peculiar quality of Pirandello's modernity precisely his disaffection with the realistic theater of the first generation of modern masters. The particular sense of life that animates *Six Characters* derives from Pirandello's use of the theater itself to challenge the reality his predecessors had made it their artistic end to record as honestly as possible. His making playwriting conscious of itself as medium has been his most important original contribution to modern drama. Ever since, we have been getting plays of double vision: not just (to paraphrase Francis Fergusson) the stage seen as real-life parlor, but the real-life parlor seen as stage — a shifting and multiple stage at that. It is not Pirandello's fault that much of this drama has been mere toying with cleverness. Rather, the number of imitations suggests that the theatricalist convention invites and sometimes allows expression of a reality particularly meaningful to an age haunted by disaster, space, and relativity.

When the Manager, at the end of the play, complains that he has "lost a whole day," his sentiment strikes us as ironic, because our view is more inclusive than his. It is Pirandello's theatricalism that provides that more inclusive view. The Manager is interested in the play the six characters bring him only as long as he senses a hit. At the end he abandons them to the strange limbo in which their author left them. But *we* see that the aborted play-within is not the whole play. The burden of the whole is the tension and interplay between the framing and the framed action — not the family agony, but the family agony seeking expression in the theater. Hence, "A Comedy in the Making." The plot that unites the six characters, the web of jealousy, shame, scorn, guilt, rage, and inarticulate, childish sorrow, the demonstration that good intentions may have evil consequences, all this is neither comic nor in the making. The tragedy is rather that the script is finished and can never more be changed. But the Manager's effort to reduce raw suffering to a play *is* comic, because it offers the incongruous spectacle of the irascible, confident, bustlingly effective man of the theater being defeated by a play more real, in the Platonic sense, than reality itself. Since the core of the larger play is here, the point will bear illustration.

The curtain that falls at the end of Act II falls simultaneously in two distinct plays and, falling, brings them together without reconciling them. The crude matter-of-factness of the physical stage and its personnel dispels the purer reality of the family torment. Theatrical expedience, "effective drama," interrupts the characters' "eternal moment" of agony, the terrible scene in Madame Pace's shop that is a debased version of the recognition scene in older tragedy (recognition of identity bringing about recognition of unwitting guilt in an incestuous situation). The ironies proliferate as one ponders the scene. Beings who have no life except as characters in a play are betrayed by heavy-handed theatrical technique. The Manager does not believe in the reality only his craft can bestow. He loses his temper with an underling who is only trying to translate the projected play into theatrical actuality (itself a concept of ironic paradox). The psychological and moral realities of the inner play suddenly accommodate box office demands for a thrilling act climax, with the result that everything comes to a screeching halt. Where does reality end and art begin? The characters rehearse their reality, while the real-life troupe distort it into an actable play and finally close the curtain on both. We witness simultaneously a play about a rehearsal and one about a husband who ceded his wife to her lover with dreadful consequences for husband, wife, lover, and both sets of children. Clearly, there is a sense in which the rehearsal of *Mixing It Up* (there is such a play; Pirandello wrote it in 1918) has not been interrupted at all! The end impression is fireworks rather than incandescence.

But the bewildering doubt, the teasing skepticism, is the play's metaphysical point. The image of the invaded theater is a dramatization of relativism. And the built-in paradox of philosophical relativism is that any assertion of its validity necessarily forgoes all claim to being considered absolutely valid. For to hold that the statement "Everything is relative" is true is also to hold that no truth is absolute, including the assertion of relativity itself. This, of course, is a sophism, and people who don't like to be made dizzy by sophisms don't like Pirandello. What they fail to see is the disturbing truth of the drama of relativity: that it is man's doom to live with and in the metaphysical uncertainty. The passion (as distinct from the intellectualism) of a Pirandello play is man's cry of protest against his condition: perched on the sharp edge of paradox.

What is more, the metaphysical sophism has an esthetic counterpart. To consider it we must begin with a point of ethics. As ethics, the play implies a radical doctrine of human irresponsibility. For if identity is discontinuous, as the Father insists, no one is accountable for his past. The Father refuses to be judged by the degrading moment in the dress shop, because the visitor to Madame Pace's establishment was not his "true" self. In fact, he has no true self; there is no such thing. Art (ethics becoming esthetics), says the Father, is permanence, life ceaseless change, and it is his misfortune that as "character," a figure of literary art, he has been arrested in a single, disgraceful moment. The sordid assignation, the child in the fountain — these are forever. And like the figures on Keats' Grecian urn, only grimly so, these too do "tease us out of thought/As doth eternity." But if, as "character," the Father can rightly claim to be "less real perhaps, but truer" than the Manager and everyone else in the empirical, non-art reality of change, it follows — and this is the sophism — that the truth of art necessarily falsifies life, for when flux freezes as "eternal moment" it is no longer flux. The very essence of experience forever eludes art.

And so *Six Characters in Search of an Author* may be said to embody also the artist's unresolvable dilemma. The primary dramatic conflict between company and characters, invaded and invader, is a fable of artistic creation, with the Manager as a kind of semi-comical middle man, resentful, interested, again resentful, a mocking but painful self-portrait of the author haunted by shapes he can neither give life to nor exorcise.

"All that lives," says Pirandello in the Preface, "by the fact of living, has a form, and by the same token must die — except the work of art which lives forever in so far as it *is* form." Again paradox. His play, according to his own account, grew out of his futile search for a form for the six characters of his imagination. He made living art out of his inability to do so.

Bertolt Brecht

THE CAUCASIAN CHALK CIRCLE

Adapted by Eric Bentley

Characters

OLD MAN, *on the right*
PEASANT WOMAN, *on the right*
YOUNG PEASANT
A VERY YOUNG WORKER
OLD MAN, *on the left*
PEASANT WOMAN, *on the left*
AGRICULTURIST KATO
GIRL TRACTORIST
WOUNDED SOLDIER
THE DELEGATE, *from the capital*
THE STORY TELLER
GEORGI ABASHWILI, *the Governor*
NATELLA, *the Governor's wife*
MICHAEL, *their son*
SHALVA, *an Adjutant*
ARSEN KAZBEKI, *a fat prince*

This adaptation, commissioned and approved by Bertolt Brecht, is based on the German MS of 1946. A German version very close to this MS was published in a supplement to *Sinn und Form*, 1949. My English text has now appeared in three versions. Maja Apelman collaborated on the first one (copyrighted 1947, 1948). The second and third were respectively copyrighted in 1961 and 1963.

—E.B., New York, 1963

MESSENGER, *from the Capital*
NIKO MIKADZE *and*
MIKA LOLADZE, *Doctors*
SIMON SHASHAVA, *a soldier*
GRUSHA VASHNADZE, *a kitchen maid*
OLD PEASANT, *with the milk*
CORPORAL *and* PRIVATE
PEASANT *and his wife*
LAVRENTI VASHNADZE, *Grusha's brother*
ANIKO, *his wife*
PEASANT WOMAN, *for a while Grusha's mother-in-law*
JUSSUP, *her son*
MONK
AZDAK, *village recorder*
SHAUWA, *a policeman*
GRAND DUKE
DOCTOR
INVALID
LIMPING MAN
BLACKMAILER
LUDOVICA
INNKEEPER, *her father-in-law*
STABLEBOY
POOR OLD PEASANT WOMAN
IRAKLI, *her brother-in-law, a bandit*
THREE WEALTHY FARMERS
ILLO SHUBOLADZE *and*
SANDRO OBOLADZE, *lawyers*
OLD MARRIED COUPLE

SOLDIERS, SERVANTS, PEASANTS, BEGGARS, MUSICIANS, MERCHANTS, NOBLES, ARCHITECTS

PROLOGUE

(Among the ruins of a war-ravaged Caucasian village the members of two Kolkhoz villages, mostly women and older men, are sitting in a circle, smoking and drinking wine. With them is a DELEGATE *of the state Reconstruction Commission from Nuka, the capital.)*

PEASANT WOMAN *(left, pointing)*: In those hills over there we stopped three Nazi tanks, but the apple orchard was already destroyed.

OLD MAN (*right*): Our beautiful dairy farm: a ruin.
GIRL TRACTORIST: I laid the fire, Comrade.

(*Pause.*)

DELEGATE: Now listen to the report. Delegates from the goat-breeding Kolkhoz "Rosa Luxemburg" have been to Nuka. When Hitler's armies approached, the Kolkhoz had moved its goat-herds further east on orders from the authorities. They are now thinking of returning. Their delegates have investigated the village and the land and found a lot of it destroyed.

(DELEGATES *on right nod.*)

The neighboring fruit-culture Kolkhoz (*to the left*) "Galinsk" is proposing to use the former grazing land of Kolkhoz "Rosa Luxemburg," a valley with scanty growth of grass, for orchards and vineyards. As a delegate of the Reconstruction Commission, I request that the two Kolkhoz villages decide between themselves whether Kolkhoz "Rosa Luxemburg" shall return here or not.

OLD MAN (*right*): First of all, I want to protest against the restriction of time for discussion. We of Kolkhoz "Rosa Luxemburg" have spent three days and three nights getting here. And now discussion is limited to half a day.

WOUNDED SOLDIER (*left*): Comrade, we haven't as many villages as we used to have. We haven't as many hands. We haven't as much time.

GIRL TRACTORIST: All pleasures have to be rationed. Tobacco is rationed, and wine. Discussion should be rationed.

OLD MAN (*right, sighing*): Death to the fascists! But I will come to the point and explain why we want our valley back. There are a great many reasons, but I'll begin with one of the simplest. Makina Abakidze, unpack the goat cheese.

(*A* PEASANT WOMAN *from right takes from a basket an enormous cheese wrapped in a cloth. Applause and laughter.*)

Help yourselves, Comrades, start in!

OLD MAN (*left, suspiciously*): Is this a way of influencing us?

OLD MAN (*right, amid laughter*): How could it be a way of influencing you, Surab, you valley-thief? Everyone knows you will take the cheese and the valley, too. (*Laughter.*) All I expect from you is an honest answer. Do you like the cheese?

OLD MAN (*left*): The answer is: yes.

OLD MAN (*right*): Really. (*Bitterly.*) I ought to have known you know nothing about cheese.

OLD MAN (*left*): Why not? When I tell you I like it?

OLD MAN (*right*): Because you can't like it. Because it's not what it was in the old days. And why not? Because our goats don't like the new grass as they did the old. Cheese is not cheese because grass is not grass, that's the thing. Please put that in your report.

OLD MAN (*left*): But your cheese is excellent.

OLD MAN (*right*): It isn't excellent. It's just passable. The new grazing land is no good, whatever the young people may say. One can't live there. It doesn't even smell of morning in the morning.

(*Several people laugh.*)

DELEGATE: Don't mind their laughing: they understand you. Comrades, why does one love one's country? Because the bread tastes better there, the air smells better, voices sound stronger, the sky is higher, the ground is easier to walk on. Isn't that so?

OLD MAN (*right*): The valley has belonged to us from all eternity.

SOLDIER (*left*): What does *that* mean — from all eternity? Nothing belongs to anyone from all eternity. When you were young you didn't even belong to yourself. You belonged to the Kazbeki princes.

OLD MAN (*right*): Doesn't it make a difference, though, what kind of trees stand next to the house you are born in? Or what kind of neighbors you have? Doesn't that make a difference? We want to go back just to have you as our neighbors, valley-thieves! Now you can all laugh again.

OLD MAN (*left, laughing*): Then why don't you listen to what your neighbor, Kato Wachtang, our agriculturist, has to say about the valley?

PEASANT WOMAN (*right*): We've not said all there is to be said about our valley. By no means. Not all the houses are destroyed. As for the dairy farm, at least the foundation wall is still standing.

DELEGATE: You can claim State support — here and there — you know that. I have suggestions here in my pocket.

PEASANT WOMAN (*right*): Comrade Specialist, we haven't come here to bargain. I can't take your cap and hand you another, and say "This one's better." The other one might *be* better; but you *like* yours better.

GIRL TRACTORIST: A piece of land is not a cap — not in our country, Comrade.

DELEGATE: Don't get angry. It's true we have to consider a piece of land as a tool to produce something useful, but it's also true that we must recognize love for a particular piece of land. As far as I'm concerned, I'd like to find out more exactly what you (*to those on the left*) want to do with the valley.

OTHERS: Yes, let Kato speak.

DELEGATE: Comrade Agriculturist!

KATO (*rising, she's in military uniform*): Comrades, last winter, while we were fighting in these hills here as Partisans, we discussed how, after the expulsion of the Germans, we could build up our fruit culture to ten times its original size. I've prepared a plan for an irrigation project. By means of a cofferdam on our mountain lake, 300 hectares of unfertile land can be irrigated. Our Kolkhoz could not only cultivate more fruit, but also have vineyards. The project, however, would pay only if the disputed valley of Kolkhoz "Galinsk" were also included. Here are the calculations. (*She hands the* DELEGATE *a briefcase.*)

OLD MAN (*right*): Write into a report that our Kolkhoz plans to start a new stud farm.

GIRL TRACTORIST: Comrades, the project was conceived during days and nights when we had to take cover in the mountains. We were often without ammunition for our half-dozen rifles. Even getting a pencil was difficult.

(*Applause from both sides.*)

OLD MAN (*right*): Our thanks to the Comrades of Kolkhoz "Galinsk" and all who have defended our country!

(*They shake hands and embrace.*)

PEASANT WOMAN (*left*): In doing this our thought was that our soldiers — both your men and our men — should return to a still more productive homeland.

GIRL TRACTORIST: As the poet Mayakovsky said: "The home of the Soviet people shall also be the home of Reason!"

(*The* DELEGATES *including the* OLD MAN *have got up, and with the* DELEGATE *specified proceed to study the Agriculturist's drawings . . . exclamations such as: "Why is the altitude of all 22 meters?" — "This rock must be blown up" — "Actually, all they need is cement and dynamite" — "They force the water to come down here, that's clever!"*)

A VERY YOUNG WORKER (*right, to* OLD MAN, *right*): They're going to irrigate all the fields between the hills, look at that, Aleko!

OLD MAN (*right*): I'm not going to look. I knew the project would be good. I won't have a revolver aimed at my chest.

DELEGATE: But they only want to aim a pencil at your chest.

(*Laughter.*)

OLD MAN (*right, gets up gloomily, and walks over to look at the draw-*

ings): These valley-thieves know only too well that we can't resist machines and projects in this country.

PEASANT WOMAN (*right*): Aleko Bereshwili, you have a weakness for new projects. That's well known.

DELEGATE: What about my report? May I write that you will all support the cession of your old valley in the interests of this project when you get back to your Kolkhoz?

PEASANT WOMAN (*right*): I will. What about you, Aleko?

OLD MAN (*right, bent over drawings*): I suggest that you give us copies of the drawings to take along.

PEASANT WOMAN (*right*): Then we can sit down and eat. Once he has the drawings and he's ready to discuss them, the matter is settled. I know him. And it will be the same with the rest of us.

(DELEGATES *laughingly embrace again.*)

OLD MAN (*left*): Long live the Kolkhoz "Rosa Luxemburg" and much luck to your horse-breeding project!

PEASANT WOMAN (*left*): In honor of the visit of the delegates from Kolkhoz "Rosa Luxemburg" and of the Specialist, the plan is that we all hear a presentation of the Story Teller Arkadi Tscheidse.

(*Applause.* GIRL TRACTORIST *has gone off to bring the* STORY TELLER.)

PEASANT WOMAN (*right*): Comrades, your entertainment had better be good. We're going to pay for it with a valley.

PEASANT WOMAN (*left*): Arkadi Tscheidse knows about our discussion. He's promised to perform something that has a bearing on the problem.

KATO: We wired to Tiflis three times. The whole thing nearly fell through at the last minute because his driver had a cold.

PEASANT WOMAN (*left*): Arkadi Tscheidse knows 21,000 lines of verse.

OLD MAN (*left*): It's very difficult to get him. You and the Planning Commission should see to it that you get him to come North more often, Comrade.

DELEGATE: We are more interested in economics, I'm afraid.

OLD MAN (*left, smiling*): You arrange the redistribution of vines and tractors, why not of songs?

(*Enter the* STORY TELLER *Arkadi Tscheidse, led by* GIRL TRACTORIST. *He is a well-built man of simple manners, accompanied by four* MUSICIANS *with their instruments. The* ARTISTS *are greeted with applause.*)

GIRL TRACTORIST: This is the Comrade Specialist, Arkadi.

(*The* STORY TELLER *greets them all.*)

DELEGATE: I'm honored to make your acquaintance. I heard about your songs when I was a boy at school. Will it be one of the old legends?

THE STORY TELLER: A very old one. It's called The Chalk Circle and comes from the Chinese. But we'll do it, of course, in a changed version. Comrades, it's an honor for me to entertain you after a difficult debate. We hope you will find that the voice of the old poet also sounds well in the shadow of Soviet tractors. It may be a mistake to mix different wines, but old and new wisdom mix admirably. Now I hope we'll get something to eat before the performance begins — it would certainly help.

VOICES: Surely. Everyone into the Club House!

(*While everyone begins to move, the* DELEGATE *turns to the* GIRL TRACTORIST.)

DELEGATE: I hope it won't take long. I've got to get back tonight.

GIRL TRACTORIST: How long will it last, Arkadi? The Comrade Specialist must get back to Tiflis tonight.

THE STORY TELLER (*casually*): It's actually two stories. An hour or two.

GIRL TRACTORIST (*confidentially*): Couldn't you make it shorter?

THE STORY TELLER: No.

VOICE: Arkadi Tscheidse's performance will take place here in the square after the meal.

(*And they all go happily to eat.*)

1. The Noble Child

(*As the lights go up, the* STORY TELLER *is seen sitting on the floor, a black sheepskin cloak round his shoulders, and a little well-thumbed notebook in his hand. A small group of listeners — the chorus — sits with him. The manner of his recitation makes it clear that he has told his story over and over again. He mechanically fingers the pages, seldom looking at them. With appropriate gestures, he gives the signal for each scene to begin.*)

THE STORY TELLER: In olden times, in a bloody time,
There ruled in a Caucasian city —
Men called it City of the Damned —
A governor.
His name was Georgi Abashwili.
He was rich as Croesus
He had a beautiful wife

He had a healthy baby.
No other governor in Grusinia
Had so many horses in his stable
So many beggars in his doorstep
So many soldiers in his service
So many petitioners in his courtyard.
Georgi Abashwili — how shall I describe him to you?
He enjoyed his life.
On the morning of Easter Sunday
The governor and his family went to church.

(*At the left a large doorway, at the right an even larger gateway.* BEGGARS *and* PETITIONERS *pour from the gateway, holding up thin children, crutches, and petitions. They are followed by* IRONSHIRTS, *and then, expensively dressed, the* GOVERNOR'S FAMILY.)

BEGGARS AND PETITIONERS: Mercy! Mercy, Your Grace! The taxes are too high.
— I lost my leg in the Persian War, where can I get . . .
— My brother is innocent, Your Grace, a misunderstanding . . .
— The child is starving in my arms!
— Our petition is for our son's discharge from the army, our last remaining son!
— Please, Your Grace, the water inspector takes bribes.

(*One* SERVANT *collects the petitions, another distributes coins from a purse.* SOLDIERS *push the* CROWD *back, lashing at them with thick leather whips.*)

THE SOLDIER: Get back! Clear the church door!

(*Behind the* GOVERNOR, *his* WIFE, *and the* ADJUTANT, *the* GOVERNOR'S CHILD *is brought through the gateway in an ornate carriage.*)

THE CROWD:
— The baby!
— I can't see it, don't shove so hard!
— God bless the child, Your Grace!

THE STORY TELLER (*while the* CROWD *is driven back with whips*): For the first time on that Easter Sunday, the people saw the Governor's heir.
Two doctors never moved from the noble child, apple of the Governor's eye.

Even the mighty Prince Kazbeki bows before him at the church door.

(A FAT PRINCE *steps forward and greets the family.*)

THE FAT PRINCE: Happy Easter, Natella Abashwili! What a day! When it was raining last night, I thought to myself, gloomy holidays! But this morning the sky was gay. I love a gay sky, a simple heart, Natella Abashwili. And little Michael is a governor from head to foot! Tititi! (*He tickles the child.*)

THE GOVERNOR'S WIFE: What do you think, Arsen, at last Georgi has decided to start building the wing on the east side. All those wretched slums are to be torn down to make room for the garden.

THE FAT PRINCE: Good news after so much bad! What's the latest on the war, Brother Georgi?

(*The* GOVERNOR *indicates a lack of interest.*)

THE FAT PRINCE: Strategical retreat, I hear. Well, minor reverses are to be expected. Sometimes things go well, sometimes not. Such is war. Doesn't mean a thing, does it?

THE GOVERNOR'S WIFE: He's coughing. Georgi, did you hear?

(*She speaks sharply to the* DOCTORS, *two dignified men standing close to the little carriage.*)

He's coughing!

THE FIRST DOCTOR (*to the* SECOND): May I remind you, Niko Mikadze, that I was against the lukewarm bath? (*To the* GOVERNOR'S WIFE.) There's been a little error over warming the bath water, Your Grace.

THE SECOND DOCTOR (*equally polite*): Mika Loladze, I'm afraid I can't agree with you. The temperature of the bath water was exactly what our great, beloved Mishiko Oboladze prescribed. More likely a slight draft during the night, Your Grace.

THE GOVERNOR'S WIFE: But do pay more attention to him. He looks feverish, Georgi.

THE FIRST DOCTOR (*bending over the child*): No cause for alarm, Your Grace. The bath water will be warmer. It won't occur again.

THE SECOND DOCTOR (*with a venomous glance at the* FIRST): I won't forget that, my dear Mika Loladze. No cause for concern, Your Grace.

THE FAT PRINCE: Well, well, well! I always say: "A pain in my liver? Then the doctor gets fifty strokes on the soles of his feet." We live in a decadent age. In the old days one said: "Off with his head!"

THE GOVERNOR'S WIFE: Let's go into church. Very likely it's the draft here.

(The procession of FAMILY *and* SERVANTS *turns into the doorway. The* FAT PRINCE *follows, but the* GOVERNOR *is kept back by the* ADJUTANT, *a handsome young man. When the crowd of* PETITIONERS *has been driven off, a young dust-stained* RIDER, *his arm in a sling, remains behind.)*

THE ADJUTANT *(pointing at the* RIDER, *who steps forward)*: Won't you hear the messenger from the capital, Your Excellency? He arrived this morning. With confidential papers.

THE GOVERNOR: Not before Service, Shalva. But did you hear Brother Kazbeki wish me a happy Easter? Which is all very well, but I don't believe it did rain last night.

THE ADJUTANT *(nodding)*: We must investigate.

THE GOVERNOR: Yes, at once. Tomorrow.

(They pass through the doorway. The RIDER, *who has waited in vain for an audience, turns sharply round and, muttering a curse, goes off. Only one of the palace guards —* SIMON SHASHAVA *— remains at the door.)*

THE STORY TELLER:

The city is still.
Pigeons strut in the church square.
A soldier of the Palace Guard
Is joking with a kitchen maid
As she comes up from the river with a bundle.

(A girl — GRUSHA VASHADZE *— comes through the gateway with a bundle made of large green leaves under her arm.)*

SIMON: What, the young lady is not in church? Shirking?

GRUSHA: I was dressed to go. But they needed another goose for the banquet. And they asked me to get it. I know about geese.

SIMON: A goose? *(He feigns suspicion.)* I'd like to see that goose. *(*GRUSHA *does not understand.)* One has to be on one's guard with women. "I only went for a fish," they tell you, but it turns out to be something else.

GRUSHA *(walking resolutely toward him and showing him the goose)*: There! If it isn't a fifteen-pound goose stuffed full of corn, I'll eat the feathers.

SIMON: A queen of a goose! The Governor himself will eat it. So the young lady has been down to the river again?

GRUSHA: Yes, at the poultry farm.

SIMON: Really? At the poultry farm, down by the river . . . not higher up maybe? Near those willows?

GRUSHA: I only go to the willows to wash the linen.

SIMON (*insinuatingly*): Exactly.

GRUSHA: Exactly what?

SIMON (*winking*): Exactly that.

GRUSHA: Why shouldn't I wash the linen by the willows?

SIMON (*with exaggerated laughter*): "Why shouldn't I wash the linen by the willows!" That's good, really good!

GRUSHA: I don't understand the soldier. What's so good about it?

SIMON (*slyly*): "If something I know someone learns, she'll grow hot and cold by turns!"

GRUSHA: I don't know what I could learn about those willows.

SIMON: Not even if there was a bush opposite? That one could see everything from? Everything that goes on there when a certain person is—"washing linen"?

GRUSHA: What does go on? Won't the soldier say what he means and have done?

SIMON: Something goes on. And something can be seen.

GRUSHA: Could the soldier mean I dip my toes in the water when it is hot? There is nothing else.

SIMON: More. Your toes. And more.

GRUSHA: More what? At most my foot?

SIMON: Your foot. And a little more. (*He laughs heartily.*)

GRUSHA (*angrily*): Simon Shashava, you ought to be ashamed of yourself! To sit in a bush on a hot day and wait till someone comes and dips her leg in the river! And I bet you bring a friend along too! (*She runs off.*)

SIMON (*shouting after her*): I didn't bring any friend along!

(*As the* STORY TELLER *resumes his tale, the* SOLDIER *steps into the doorway as though to listen to the service.*)

THE STORY TELLER: The city lies still
But why are there armed men?
The Governor's palace is at peace
But why is it a fortress?
And the Governor returned to his palace
And the fortress was a trap
And the goose was plucked and roasted
But the goose was not eaten this time
And noon was no longer the hour to eat:
Noon was the hour to die.

(From the doorway at the left the FAT PRINCE *quickly appears, stands still, looks around. Before the gateway at the right two* IRONSHIRTS *are squatting and playing dice. The* FAT PRINCE *sees them, walks slowly past, making a sign to them. They rise: one goes through the gateway, the other goes off at the right. Muffled voices are heard from various directions in the rear: "To your posts!" The palace is surrounded. The* FAT PRINCE *quickly goes off. Church bells in the distance. Enter, through the doorway, the* GOVERNOR'S FAMILY *and* PROCESSION, *returning from church.)*

THE GOVERNOR'S WIFE *(passing the* ADJUTANT*)*: It's impossible to live in such a slum. But Georgi, of course, will only build for his little Michael. Never for me! Michael is all! All for Michael!

(The PROCESSION *turns into the gateway. Again the* ADJUTANT *lingers behind. He waits. Enter the* WOUNDED RIDER *from the doorway. Two* IRONSHIRTS *of the palace guard have taken up positions by the gateway.)*

THE ADJUTANT *(to the* RIDER*)*: The Governor does not wish to receive military reports before dinner — especially if they're depressing, as I assume. In the afternoon His Excellency will confer with prominent architects. They're coming to dinner too. And here they are!

(Enter THREE GENTLEMEN *through the doorway.)*

Go in the kitchen and get yourself something to eat, my friend.

(As the RIDER *goes, the* ADJUTANT *greets the* ARCHITECTS.*)*

Gentlemen, His Excellency expects you at dinner. He will devote all his time to you and your great new plans. Come!

ONE OF THE ARCHITECTS: We marvel that His Excellency intends to build. There are disquieting rumors that the war in Persia has taken a turn for the worse.

THE ADJUTANT: All the more reason to build! There's nothing to those rumors anyway. Persia is a long way off, and the garrison here would let itself be hacked to bits for its Governor.

(Noise from the palace. The shrill scream of a woman. Someone is shouting orders. Dumbfounded, the ADJUTANT *moves toward the gateway. An* IRONSHIRT *steps out, points his lance at him.)*

What's this? Put down that lance, you dog.

ONE OF THE ARCHITECTS: It's the Princes! Don't you know the Princes met last night in the capital? And they're against the Grand Duke and his Governors? Gentlemen, we'd better make ourselves scarce.

(*They rush off. The* ADJUTANT *remains helplessly behind.*)

THE ADJUTANT (*furiously to the* PALACE GUARD): Down with those lances! Don't you see the Governor's life is threatened?

(*The* IRONSHIRTS *of the Palace Guard refuse to obey. They stare coldly and indifferently at the* ADJUTANT *and follow the next events without interest.*)

THE STORY TELLER: O blindness of the great!
They go their way like gods,
Great over bent backs,
Sure of hired fists,
Trusting in the power
Which has lasted so long.
But long is not forever.
O change from age to age!
Thou hope of the people!

(*Enter the* GOVERNOR, *through the gateway, between two* SOLDIERS *armed to the teeth. He is in chains. His face is gray.*)

Up, great sir, deign to walk upright!
From your palace, the eyes of many foes follow you!
And now you don't need an architect, a carpenter will do.
You won't be moving into a new palace
But into a little hole in the ground.
Look about you once more, blind man!

(*The arrested man looks round.*)

Does all you had please you?
Between the Easter mass and the Easter meal
You are walking to a place whence no one returns.

(*The* GOVERNOR *is led off. A horn sounds an alarm. Noise behind the gateway.*)

When the house of a great one collapses
Many little ones are slain.
Those who had no share in the *good* fortunes of the mighty
Often have a share in their *mis*fortunes.
The plunging wagon
Drags the sweating oxen down with it
Into the abyss.

(*The* SERVANTS *come rushing through the gateway in panic.*)

THE SERVANTS (*among themselves*):
— The baskets!
— Take them all into the third courtyard! Food for five days!
— The mistress has fainted! Someone must carry her down.
— She must get away.
— What about us? We'll be slaughtered like chickens, as always.
— Goodness, what'll happen? There's bloodshed already in the city, they say.
— Nonsense, the Governor has just been asked to appear at a Princes' meeting. All very correct. Everything'll be ironed out. I heard this on the best authority. . . .

(*The two* DOCTORS *rush into the courtyard.*)

THE FIRST DOCTOR (*trying to restrain the other*): Niko Mikadze, it is your duty as a doctor to attend Natella Abashwili.

THE SECOND DOCTOR: My duty! It's yours!

THE FIRST DOCTOR: Whose turn is it to look after the child today, Niko Mikadze, yours or mine?

THE SECOND DOCTOR: Do you really think, Mika Loladze, I'm going to stay a minute longer in this accursed house on that little brat's account?

(*They start fighting. All one hears is: "You neglect your duty!" and "Duty, my foot!" Then the* SECOND DOCTOR *knocks the* FIRST *down.*)

Go to hell! (*Exit.*)

(*Enter the* SOLDIER, SIMON SHASHAVA. *He searches in the crowd for* GRUSHA.)

SIMON: Grusha! There you are at last! What are you going to do?

GRUSHA: Nothing. If worst comes to worst, I've a brother in the mountains. How about you?

SIMON: Forget about me. (*Formally again.*) Grusha Vashnadze, your wish to know my plans fills me with satisfaction. I've been ordered to accompany Madam Natella Abashwili as her guard.

GRUSHA: But hasn't the Palace Guard mutinied?

SIMON (*seriously*): That's a fact.

GRUSHA: Isn't it dangerous to go with her?

SIMON: In Tiflis, they say: Isn't the stabbing dangerous for the knife?

GRUSHA: You're not a knife, you're a man, Simon Shashava, what has that woman to do with you?

SIMON: That woman has nothing to do with me. I have my orders, and I go.

GRUSHA: The soldier is pigheaded: he is getting himself into danger for nothing — nothing at all. I must get into the third courtyard, I'm in a hurry.

SIMON: Since we're both in a hurry we shouldn't quarrel. You need time for a good quarrel. May I ask if the young lady still has parents?

GRUSHA: No, just a brother.

SIMON: As time is short — my second question is this: Is the young lady as healthy as a fish in water?

GRUSHA: I may have a pain in the right shoulder once in a while. Otherwise I'm strong enough for my job. No one has complained. So far.

SIMON: That's well known. When it's Easter Sunday, and the question arises who'll run for the goose all the same, she'll be the one. My third question is this: Is the young lady impatient? Does she want apples in winter?

GRUSHA: Impatient? No. But if a man goes to war without any reason and then no message comes — that's bad.

SIMON: A message will come. And now my final question . . .

GRUSHA: Simon Shashava, I must get to the third courtyard at once. My answer is yes.

SIMON (*very embarrassed*): Haste, they say, is the wind that blows down the scaffolding. But they also say: The rich don't know what haste is. I'm from . . .

GRUSHA: Kutsk . . .

SIMON: So the young lady has been inquiring about me? I'm healthy, I have no dependents, I make ten piasters a month, as paymaster twenty piasters, and I'm asking — very sincerely — for your hand.

GRUSHA: Simon Shashava, it suits me well.

SIMON (*taking from his neck a thin chain with a little cross on it*): My mother gave me this cross, Grusha Vashnadze. The chain is silver. Please wear it.

GRUSHA: Many thanks, Simon.

SIMON (*hangs it round her neck*): It would be better for the young lady to go to the third courtyard now. Or there'll be difficulties. Anyway, I must harness the horses. The young lady will understand?

GRUSHA: Yes, Simon.

(*They stand undecided.*)

SIMON: I'll just take the mistress to the troops that have stayed loyal. When the war's over, I'll be back. In two weeks. Or three. I hope my intended won't get tired, awaiting my return.

GRUSHA: Simon Shashava, I shall wait for you.
Go calmly into battle, soldier
The bloody battle, the bitter battle
From which not everyone returns:
When you return I shall be there.
I shall be waiting for you under the green elm
I shall be waiting for you under the bare elm
I shall wait until the last soldier has returned
And longer.
When you come back from the battle
No boots will stand at my door
The pillow beside mine will be empty
And my mouth will be unkissed.
When you return, when you return
You will be able to say: It is just as it was.

SIMON: I thank you, Grusha Vashnadze. And goodbye!

(*He bows low before her. She does the same before him. Then she runs quickly off without looking around. Enter the* ADJUTANT *from the gateway.*)

THE ADJUTANT (*harshly*): Harness the horses to the carriage! Don't stand there doing nothing, louse!

(SIMON SHASHAVA *stands to attention and goes off. Two* SERVANTS *crowd from the gateway, bent low under huge trunks. Behind them, supported by her* WOMEN, *stumbles* NATELLA ABASHWILI. *She is followed by a* WOMAN carrying the CHILD.)

THE GOVERNOR'S WIFE: I hardly know if my head's still on. Where's Michael? Don't hold him so clumsily. Pile the trunks onto the carriage. Shalva, is there no news from the city?

THE ADJUTANT: None. All's quiet so far, but there's not a minute to lose. No room for all these trunks in the carriage. Pick out what you need.

(*Exit quickly.*)

THE GOVERNOR'S WIFE: Only essentials! Quick, open the trunks! I'll tell you what I need. (*The trunks are lowered and opened. She points at some brocade dresses.*) The green one! And, of course, the one with the fur trimming. Where are Niko Mikadze and Mika Loladze? I've suddenly got the most terrible migraine again. It always starts in the temples.

(*Enter* GRUSHA.)

Taking your time, eh? Go at once and get the hot water bottles!

(GRUSHA *runs off, returns later with hot water bottles; the* GOVERNOR'S WIFE *orders her about by signs.*)

Don't tear the sleeves.

A YOUNG WOMAN: Pardon, madam, no harm has come to the dress.

THE GOVERNOR'S WIFE: Because I stopped you. I've been watching you for a long time. Nothing in your head but making eyes at Shalva Tzereteli. I'll kill you, you bitch! (*She beats the woman.*)

THE ADJUTANT (*appearing in the gateway*): Please make haste, Natella Abashwili. Firing has broken out in the city.

(*Exit.*)

THE GOVERNOR'S WIFE (*letting go of the* YOUNG WOMAN): Oh dear, do you think they'll lay hands on us? Why should they? Why? (*She herself begins to rummage in the trunks.*) How's Michael? Asleep?

THE WOMAN WITH THE CHILD: Yes, madam.

THE GOVERNOR'S WIFE: Then put him down a moment and get my little saffron-colored boots from the bedroom. I need them for the green dress.

(*The* WOMAN *puts down the* CHILD *and goes off.*)

Just look how these things have been packed! No love! No understanding! If you don't give them every order yourself . . . At such moments you realize what kind of servants you have! They gorge themselves at your expense, and never a word of gratitude! I'll remember this.

THE ADJUTANT (*entering, very excited*): Natella, you must leave at once!

THE GOVERNOR'S WIFE: Why? I've got to take this silver dress — it cost a thousand piasters. And that one there, and where's the wine-colored one?

THE ADJUTANT (*trying to pull her away*): Riots have broken out! We must leave at once. Where's the baby?

THE GOVERNOR'S WIFE (*calling to the* YOUNG WOMAN *who was holding the baby*): Maro, get the baby ready! Where on earth are you?

THE ADJUTANT (*leaving*): We'll probably have to leave the carriage behind and go ahead on horseback.

(*The* GOVERNOR'S WIFE *rummages again among her dresses, throws some onto the heap of chosen clothes, then takes them off again. Noises, drums are heard. The* YOUNG WOMAN *who was beaten creeps away. The sky begins to grow red.*)

THE GOVERNOR'S WIFE (*rummaging desperately*): I simply cannot find the wine-colored dress. Take the whole pile to the carriage. Where's Asja? And why hasn't Maro come back? Have you all gone crazy?

THE ADJUTANT (*returning*): Quick! Quick!

THE GOVERNOR'S WIFE (*to the* FIRST WOMAN): Run! Just throw them into the carriage!

THE ADJUTANT: We're not taking the carriage. And if you don't come now, I'll ride off on my own.

THE GOVERNOR'S WIFE (*as the* FIRST WOMAN *can't carry everything*): Where's that bitch Asja? (*The* ADJUTANT *pulls her away.*) Maro, bring the baby! (*To the* FIRST WOMAN.) Go and look for Masha. No, first take the dresses to the carriage. Such nonsense! I wouldn't dream of going on horseback!

(*Turning round, she sees the red sky, and starts back rigid. The fire burns. She is pulled out by the* ADJUTANT. *Shaking, the* FIRST WOMAN *follows with the dresses.*)

MARO (*from the doorway, with the boots*): Madam! (*She sees the trunks and dresses and runs toward the baby, picks it up, and holds it a moment.*) They left it behind, the beasts. (*She hands it to* GRUSHA.) Hold it a moment. (*She runs off, following the* GOVERNOR'S WIFE.)

(*Enter* SERVANTS *from the gateway.*)

THE COOK: Well, so they've actually gone. Without the food wagons, and not a minute too early. It's time for us to clear out.

A GROOM: This'll be an unhealthy neighborhood for quite a while. (*To one of the* WOMEN.) Suliko, take a few blankets and wait for me in the foal stables.

GRUSHA: What have they done with the governor?

THE GROOM (*gesturing throat cutting*): Ffffft.

A FAT WOMAN (*seeing the gesture and becoming hysterical*): Oh dear, oh dear, oh dear, oh dear! Our master Georgi Abashwili! A picture of health he was, at the Morning Mass — and now! Oh, take me away, we're all lost, we must die in sin like our master, Georgi Abashwili!

THE OTHER WOMAN (*soothing her*): Calm down, Nina! You'll be taken to safety. You've never hurt a fly.

THE FAT WOMAN (*being led out*): Oh dear, oh dear, oh dear! Quick! Let's all get out before they come, before they come!

A YOUNG WOMAN: Nina takes it more to heart than the mistress, that's a fact. They even have to have their weeping done for them.

THE COOK: We'd better get out, all of us.

ANOTHER WOMAN (*glancing back*): That must be the East Gate burning.

THE YOUNG WOMAN (*seeing the* CHILD *in* GRUSHA'S *arms*): The baby! What are you doing with it?

GRUSHA: It got left behind.

THE YOUNG WOMAN: She simply left it there. Michael, who was kept out of all the drafts!

(*The* SERVANTS *gather round the* CHILD.)

GRUSHA: He's waking up.

THE GROOM: Better put him down, I tell you. I'd rather not think what'd happen to anybody who was found with that baby.

THE COOK: That's right. Once they get started, they'll kill each other off, whole families at a time. Let's go.

(*Exeunt all but* GRUSHA, *with the* CHILD *on her arm, and two* WOMEN.)

THE TWO WOMEN: Didn't you hear? Better put him down.

GRUSHA: The nurse asked me to hold him a moment.

THE OLDER WOMAN: She's not coming back, you simpleton.

THE YOUNGER WOMAN: Keep your hands off it.

THE OLDER WOMAN (*amiably*): Grusha, you're a good soul, but you're not very bright, and you know it. I tell you, if he had the plague he couldn't be more dangerous.

GRUSHA (*stubbornly*): He hasn't got the plague. He looks at me! He's human!

THE OLDER WOMAN: Don't look at *him*. You're a fool — the kind that always gets put upon. A person need only say, "Run for the salad, you have the longest legs," and you run. My husband has an ox cart — you can come with us if you hurry! Lord, by now the whole neighborhood must be in flames.

(*Both* WOMEN *leave, sighing. After some hesitation,* GRUSHA *puts the sleeping* CHILD *down, looks at it for a moment, then takes a brocade blanket from the heap of clothes and covers it. Then both* WOMEN *return, dragging bundles.* GRUSHA *starts guiltily away from the* CHILD *and walks a few steps to one side.*)

THE YOUNGER WOMAN: Haven't you packed anything yet? There isn't much time, you know. The Ironshirts will be here from the barracks.

GRUSHA: Coming.

(She runs through the doorway. Both WOMEN *go to the gateway and wait. The sound of horses is heard. They flee, screaming. Enter the* FAT PRINCE *with drunken* IRONSHIRTS. *One of them carries the governor's head on a lance.)*

THE FAT PRINCE: Here! In the middle!

(One SOLDIER *climbs onto the other's back, takes the head, holds it tentatively over the door.)*

That's not the middle. Farther to the right. That's it. What I do, my friends, I do well.

(While, with hammer and nail, the SOLDIER *fastens the head to the wall by its hair.)*

This morning at the church door I said to Georgi Abashwili: "I love a clear sky." Actually, I prefer the lightning that comes out of a clear sky. Yes, indeed. It's a pity they took the brat along, though, I need him, urgently.

(Exit with IRONSHIRTS *through the gateway. Trampling of horses again. Enter* GRUSHA *through the doorway looking cautiously about her. Clearly she has waited for the* IRONSHIRTS *to go. Carrying a bundle, she walks toward the gateway. At the last moment, she turns to see if the* CHILD *is still there. Catching sight of the head over the doorway, she screams. Horrified, she picks up her bundle again, and is about to leave when the* STORY TELLER *starts to speak. She stands rooted to the spot.)*

THE STORY TELLER: As she was standing between courtyard and gate,
She heard or she thought she heard a low voice calling.
The child called to her,
Not whining, but calling quite sensibly,
Or so it seemed to her.
"Woman," it said, "help me."
And it went on, not whining, but saying quite sensibly:
"Know, woman, he who hears not a cry for help
But passes by with troubled ears will never hear
The gentle call of a lover nor the blackbird at dawn
Nor the happy sigh of the tired grape-picker as the Angelus rings."

(She walks a few steps toward the CHILD *and bends over it.)*

Hearing this she went back for one more look at the child:
Only to sit with him for a moment or two,

Only till someone should come,
His mother, or anyone.

(*Leaning on a trunk, she sits facing the* CHILD.)

Only till she would have to leave, for the danger was too great,
The city was full of flame and crying.

(*The light grows dimmer, as though evening and night were coming on.*)

Fearful is the seductive power of goodness!

(GRUSHA *now settles down to watch over the* CHILD *through the night. Once, she lights a small lamp to look at it. Once, she tucks it in with a coat. From time to time she listens and looks to see whether someone is coming.*)

And she sat with the child a long time,
Till evening came, till night came, till dawn came.
She sat too long, too long she saw
The soft breathing, the small clenched fists,
Till toward morning the seduction was complete
And she rose, and bent down and, sighing, took the child
And carried it away.

(*She does what the* STORY TELLER *says as he describes it.*)

As if it was stolen goods she picked it up.
As if she was a thief she crept away.

2. *The Flight into the Northern Mountains*

THE STORY TELLER: When Grusha Vashnadze left the city
On the Grusinian highway
On the way to the Northern Mountains
She sang a song, she bought some milk.
THE CHORUS: How will this human child escape
The bloodhounds, the trap-setters?
Into the deserted mountains she journeyed
Along the Grusinian highway she journeyed
She sang a song, she bought some milk.

(GRUSHA VASHNADZE *walks on. On her back she carries the* CHILD *in a sack, in one hand is a large stick, in the other a bundle. She sings.*)

The Song of the Four Generals

Four generals
Set out for Iran.
With the first one, war did not agree.
The second never won a victory.
For the third the weather never was right.
For the fourth the men would never fight.
Four generals
And not a single man!

Sosso Robakidse
Went marching to Iran
With him the war did so agree
He soon had won a victory.
For him the weather was always right.
For him the men would always fight.
Sosso Robakidse,
He is our man!

(*A peasant's cottage appears.*)

GRUSHA (*to the* CHILD): Noontime is meal time. Now we'll sit hopefully in the grass, while the good Grusha goes and buys a little pitcher of milk.

(*She lays the* CHILD *down and knocks at the cottage door. An* OLD MAN *opens it.*)

Grandfather, could I have a little pitcher of milk? And a corn cake, maybe?

THE OLD MAN: Milk? We have no milk. The soldiers from the city have our goats. Go to the soldiers if you want milk.

GRUSHA: But grandfather, you must have a little pitcher of milk for a baby?

THE OLD MAN: And for a God-bless-you, eh?

GRUSHA: Who said anything about a God-bless-you? (*She shows her purse.*) We'll pay like princes. "Head in the clouds, backside in the water."

(*The* PEASANT *goes off, grumbling, for milk.*)

How much for the milk?

THE OLD MAN: Three piasters. Milk has gone up.

GRUSHA: Three piasters for this little drop?

(*Without a word the* OLD MAN *shuts the door in her face.*)

Michael, did you hear that? Three piasters! We can't afford it! (*She goes back, sits down again, and gives the* CHILD *her breast.*) Suck. Think of the three piasters. There's nothing there, but you *think* you're drinking, and that's something. (*Shaking her head, she sees that the* CHILD *isn't sucking any more. She gets up, walks back to the door, and knocks again.*)

Open, grandfather, we'll pay. (*Softly.*) May lightning strike you!

(*When the* OLD MAN *appears.*)

I thought it would be half a piaster. But the baby must be fed. How about one piaster for that little drop?

THE OLD MAN: Two.

GRUSHA: Don't shut the door again.

(*She fishes a long time in her bag.*)

Here are two piasters. The milk better be good. I still have two days' journey ahead of me. It's a murderous business you have here — and sinful, too!

THE OLD MAN: Kill the soldiers if you want milk.

GRUSHA (*giving the* CHILD *some milk*): This is an expensive joke. Take a sip, Michael, it's a week's pay. Around here they think we earned our money just sitting around. Oh, Michael, Michael, you're a nice little load for a girl to take on!

(*Uneasy, she gets up, puts the* CHILD *on her back, and walks on. The* OLD MAN, *grumbling, picks up the pitcher and looks after her unmoved.*)

THE STORY TELLER: As Grusha Vashnadze went northward
The Princes' Ironshirts went after her.

THE CHORUS: How will the barefoot girl escape the Ironshirts,
The bloodhounds, the trap-setters?
They hunt even by night.
Pursuers never tire.
Butchers sleep little.

(*Two* IRONSHIRTS *are trudging along the highway.*)

THE CORPORAL: You'll never amount to anything, blockhead, your heart's not in it. Your senior officer sees this in little things. Yesterday, when I made the fat gal, yes, you grabbed her husband as I commanded, and you did kick him in the stomach, at my request, but did you *enjoy* it, like a loyal Private, or were you just doing your duty? I've kept an eye on you, blockhead, you're a hollow reed and a tinkling cymbal, you won't get promoted.

(*They walk a while in silence.*)

Don't think I've forgotten how insubordinate you are, either. Stop limping! I forbid you to limp! You limp because I sold the horses, and I sold the horses because I'd never have got that price again. You limp to show me you don't like marching. I know you. It won't help. You wait. Sing!

THE TWO IRONSHIRTS (*singing*): Sadly to war I went my way
Leaving my loved one at her door.
My friends will keep her honor safe
Till from the war I'm back once more.

THE CORPORAL: Louder!

THE TWO IRONSHIRTS (*singing*): When 'neath a headstone I shall be
My love a little earth will bring:
"Here rest the feet that oft would run to me
And here the arms that oft to me would cling."

(*They begin to walk again in silence.*)

THE CORPORAL: A good soldier has his heart and soul in it. When he receives an order, he gets a hard on, and when he drives his lance into the enemy's guts, he comes. (*He shouts for joy.*) He lets himself be torn to bits for his superior officer, and as he lies dying he takes note that his corporal is nodding approval, and that is reward enough, it's his dearest wish. *You* won't get any nod of approval, but you'll croak all right. Christ, how'm I to get my hands on the Governor's bastard with the help of a fool like you!

(*They stay on stage behind.*)

THE STORY TELLER: When Grusha Vashnadze came to the river Sirra
Flight grew too much for her, the helpless child too heavy.
In the cornfields the rosy dawn
Is cold to the sleepless one, only cold.
The gay clatter of the milk cans in the farmyard where the smoke rises
Is only a threat to the fugitive.
She who carries the child feels its weight and little more.

(GRUSHA *stops in front of a farm.* A FAT PEASANT WOMAN *is carrying a milk can through the door.* GRUSHA *waits until she has gone in, then approaches the house cautiously.*)

GRUSHA (*to the* CHILD): Now you've wet yourself again, and you know I've no linen. Michael, this is where we part company. It's far enough from the city. They wouldn't want you so much that they'd follow you all *this* way, little good-for-nothing. The peasant woman is kind, and can't you just smell the milk? (*She bends down to lay the* CHILD *on the threshold.*) So farewell, Michael, I'll forget how you kicked me in the back all night to make me walk faster. And you can forget the meager fare — it was meant well. I'd like to have kept you — your nose is so tiny — but it can't be. I'd have shown you your first rabbit, I'd have trained you to keep dry, but now I must turn around. My sweetheart the soldier might be back soon, and suppose he didn't find me? You can't ask that, can you?

(*She creeps up to the door and lays the* CHILD *on the threshold. Then, hiding behind a tree, she waits until the* PEASANT WOMAN *opens the door and sees the bundle.*)

THE PEASANT WOMAN: Good heavens, what's this? Husband!

THE PEASANT: What is it? Let me finish my soup.

THE PEASANT WOMAN (*to the* CHILD): Where's your mother then? Haven't you got one? It's a boy. Fine linen. He's from a good family, you can see that. And they just leave him on our doorstep. Oh, these are times!

THE PEASANT: If they think we're going to feed it, they're wrong. You can take it to the priest in the village. That's the best we can do.

THE PEASANT WOMAN: What'll the priest do with him? He needs a mother. There, he's waking up. Don't you think we could keep him, though?

THE PEASANT (*shouting*): No!

THE PEASANT WOMAN: I could lay him in the corner by the armchair. All I need is a crib. I can take him into the fields with me. See him laughing? Husband, we have a roof over our heads. We can do it. Not another word out of you!

(*She carries the* CHILD *into the house. The* PEASANT *follows protesting.* GRUSHA *steps out from behind the tree, laughs, and hurries off in the opposite direction.*)

THE STORY TELLER: Why so cheerful, making for home?

THE CHORUS: Because the child has won new parents with a laugh,
Because I'm rid of the little one, I'm cheerful.

THE STORY TELLER: And why so sad?

THE CHORUS: Because I'm single and free, I'm sad
Like someone who's been robbed
Someone who's newly poor.

(*She walks for a short while, then meets the* TWO IRONSHIRTS, *who point their lances at her.*)

THE CORPORAL: Lady, you are running straight into the arms of the Armed Forces. Where are you coming from? And when? Are you having illicit relations with the enemy? Where is he hiding? What movements is he making in your rear? How about the hills? How about the valleys? How are your stockings fastened?

(GRUSHA *stands there frightened.*)

Don't be scared, we always stage a retreat, if necessary . . . what, blockhead? I always stage retreats. In that respect at least, I can be relied on. Why are you staring like that at my lance? In the field no soldier drops his lance, that's a rule. Learn it by heart, blockhead. Now, lady, where are you headed?

GRUSHA: To meet my intended, one Simon Shashava, of the Palace Guard in Nuka.

THE CORPORAL: Simon Shashava? Sure, I know him. He gave me the key so I could look you up once in a while. Blockhead, we are getting to be unpopular. We must make her realize we have honorable intentions. Lady, behind apparent frivolity I conceal a serious nature, so let me tell you officially: I want a child from you.

(GRUSHA *utters a little scream.*)

Blockhead, she understood me. Uh-huh, isn't it a sweet shock? "Then first I must take the noodles out of the oven, Officer. Then first I must change my torn shirt, Colonel." But away with jokes, away with my lance! We are looking for a baby. A baby from a good family. Have you heard of such a baby, from the city, dressed in fine linen, and suddenly turning up here?

GRUSHA: No, I haven't heard a thing. (*Suddenly she turns round and runs back, panic-stricken. The* IRONSHIRTS *glance at each other, then follow her, cursing.*)

THE STORY TELLER: Run, kind girl! The killers are coming!
Help the helpless babe, helpless girl!
And so she runs!

THE CHORUS: In the bloodiest times
There are kind people.

(*As* GRUSHA *rushes into the cottage, the* PEASANT WOMAN *is bending over the* CHILD'S *crib.*)

GRUSHA: Hide him. Quick! The Ironshirts are coming! I laid him on your doorstep. But he isn't mine. He's from a good family.

THE PEASANT WOMAN: Who's coming? What Ironshirts?

GRUSHA: Don't ask questions. The Ironshirts that are looking for it.

THE PEASANT WOMAN: They've no business in my house. But I must have a little talk with you, it seems.

GRUSHA: Take off the fine linen. It'll give us away.

THE PEASANT WOMAN: Linen, my foot! In this house I make the decisions! "*You* can't vomit in *my* room!" Why did you abandon it? It's a sin.

GRUSHA (*looking out of the window*): Look, they're coming out from behind those trees! I shouldn't have run away, it made them angry. Oh, what shall I do?

THE PEASANT WOMAN (*looking out of the window and suddenly starting with fear*): Gracious! Ironshirts!

GRUSHA: They're after the baby.

THE PEASANT WOMAN: Suppose they come in!

GRUSHA: You mustn't give him to them. Say he's yours.

THE PEASANT WOMAN: Yes.

GRUSHA: They'll run him through if you hand him over.

THE PEASANT WOMAN: But suppose they ask for it? The silver for the harvest is in the house.

GRUSHA: If you let them have him, they'll run him through, right here in this room! You've got to say he's yours!

THE PEASANT WOMAN: Yes. But what if they don't believe me?

GRUSHA: You must be firm.

THE PEASANT WOMAN: They'll burn the roof over our heads.

GRUSHA: That's why you must say he's yours. His name's Michael. But I shouldn't have told you.

(*The* PEASANT WOMAN *nods.*)

Don't nod like that. And don't tremble — they'll notice.

THE PEASANT WOMAN: Yes.

GRUSHA: And stop saying yes, I can't stand it. (*She shakes the* WOMAN.) Don't you have any children?

THE PEASANT WOMAN (*muttering*): He's in the war.

GRUSHA: Then maybe *he's* an Ironshirt? Do you want *him* to run children through with a lance? You'd bawl him out. "No fooling with lances in *my* house!" you'd shout, "is that what I've reared you for? Wash your neck before you speak to your mother!"

THE PEASANT WOMAN: That's true, he couldn't get away with anything around here!

GRUSHA: So you'll say he's yours?

THE PEASANT WOMAN: Yes.

GRUSHA: Look! They're coming!

(*There is a knocking at the door. The women don't answer. Enter* IRONSHIRTS. *The* PEASANT WOMAN *bows low.*)

THE CORPORAL: Well, here she is. What did I tell you? What a nose I have! I *smelt* her. Lady, I have a question for you. Why did you run away? What did you think I would do to you? I'll bet it was something dirty. Confess!

GRUSHA (*while the* PEASANT WOMAN *bows again and again*): I'd left some milk on the stove, and I suddenly remembered it.

THE CORPORAL: Or maybe you imagined I looked at you in a dirty way? Like there could be something between us? A lewd sort of look, know what I mean?

GRUSHA: I didn't see it.

THE CORPORAL: But it's possible, huh? You admit that much. After all, I might be a pig. I'll be frank with you: I could think of all sorts of things if we were alone. (*To the* PEASANT WOMAN.) Shouldn't you be busy in the yard? Feeding the hens?

THE PEASANT WOMAN (*falling suddenly to her knees*): Soldier, I didn't know a thing about it. Please don't burn the roof over our heads.

THE CORPORAL: What are you talking about?

THE PEASANT WOMAN: I had nothing to do with it. She left it on my doorstep, I swear it!

THE CORPORAL (*suddenly seeing the* CHILD *and whistling*): Ah, so there's a little something in the crib! Blockhead, I smell a thousand piasters. Take the old girl outside and hold on to her. It looks like I have a little cross-examining to do.

(*The* PEASANT WOMAN *lets herself be led out by the* PRIVATE *without a word.*)

So, you've *got* the child I wanted from you! (*He walks toward the crib.*)

GRUSHA: Officer, he's mine. He's not the one you're after.

THE CORPORAL: I'll just take a look. (*He bends over the crib.* GRUSHA *looks round in despair.*)

GRUSHA: He's mine! He's mine!

THE CORPORAL: Fine linen!

(GRUSHA *dashes at him to pull him away. He throws her off and again bends over the crib. Again looking round in despair, she sees a log of wood, seizes it, and hits the* CORPORAL *over the head from behind. The* CORPORAL *collapses. She quickly picks up the* CHILD *and rushes off.*)

THE STORY TELLER: And in her flight from the Ironshirts
After twenty-two days of journeying

At the foot of the Janga-Tu Glacier
Grusha Vashnadze decided to adopt the child.

THE CHORUS: The helpless girl adopted the helpless child.

(GRUSHA *squats over a half-frozen stream to get the* CHILD *water in the hollow of her hand.*)

GRUSHA: Since no one else will take you, son,
I must take you.
Since no one else will take you, son,
You must take me.
O black day in a lean, lean year,
The trip was long, the milk was dear,
My legs are tired, my feet are sore:
But I wouldn't be without you any more.
I'll throw your silken shirt away
And dress you in rags and tatters.
I'll wash you, son, and christen you in glacier water.
We'll see it through together.

(*She has taken off the* CHILD'S *fine linen and wrapped it in a rag.*)

THE STORY TELLER: When Grusha Vashnadze
Pursued by the Ironshirts
Came to the bridge on the glacier
Leading to the villages of the Eastern Slope
She sang the Song of the Rotten Bridge
And risked two lives.

(*A wind has risen. The bridge on the glacier is visible in the dark. One rope is broken and half the bridge is hanging down the abyss.* MERCHANTS, *two* MEN, *and a* WOMAN, *stand undecided before the bridge as* GRUSHA *and the* CHILD *arrive. One* MAN *is trying to catch the hanging rope with a stick.*)

THE FIRST MAN: Take your time, young woman. You won't get across here anyway.

GRUSHA: But I *have* to get the baby to the east side. To my brother's place.

THE MERCHANT WOMAN: Have to? How d'you mean, "have to"? I have to get there, too — because I have to buy carpets in Atum — carpets a woman had to sell because her husband had to die. But can *I* do what I have to? Can she? Andrei's been fishing for that rope for hours. And I ask you, how are we going to fasten it, even if he gets it up?

THE FIRST MAN (*listening*): Hush, I think I hear something.

GRUSHA: The bridge isn't quite rotted through. I think I'll try it.

THE MERCHANT WOMAN: *I* wouldn't — if the devil himself were after me. It's suicide.

THE FIRST MAN (*shouting*): Hi!

GRUSHA: Don't shout! (*To the* MERCHANT WOMAN.) Tell him not to shout.

THE FIRST MAN: But there's someone down there calling. Maybe they've lost their way.

THE MERCHANT WOMAN: Why shouldn't he shout? Is there something funny about you? Are they after you?

GRUSHA: All right, I'll tell. The Ironshirts are after me. I knocked one down.

THE SECOND MAN: Hide our merchandise!

(*The* WOMAN *hides a sack behind a rock.*)

THE FIRST MAN: Why didn't you say so right away? (*To the others.*) If they catch her they'll make mincemeat out of her!

GRUSHA: Get out of my way. I've got to cross that bridge.

THE SECOND MAN: You can't. The precipice is two thousand feet deep.

THE FIRST MAN: Even with the rope it'd be no use. We could hold it up with our hands. But then we'd have to do the same for the Ironshirts.

GRUSHA: Go away.

(*There are calls from the distance: "Hi, up there!"*)

THE MERCHANT WOMAN: They're getting near. But you can't take the child on that bridge. It's sure to break. And look!

(GRUSHA *looks down into the abyss. The* IRONSHIRTS *are heard calling again from below.*)

THE SECOND MAN: Two thousand feet!

GRUSHA: But those men are worse.

THE FIRST MAN: You can't do it. Think of the baby. Risk your life but not a child's.

THE SECOND MAN: With the child she's that much heavier!

THE MERCHANT WOMAN: Maybe she's *really* got to get across. Give *me* the baby. I'll hide it. Cross the bridge alone!

GRUSHA: I won't. We belong together. (*To the* CHILD.) "Live together, die together." (*She sings.*)

The Song of the Rotten Bridge

Deep is the abyss, son,
I see the weak bridge sway

But it's not for us, son,
To choose the way.

The way I know
Is the one you must tread,
And all you will eat
Is my bit of bread.

Of every four pieces
You shall have three.
Would that I knew
How big they will be!

Get out of my way, I'll try it without the rope.

THE MERCHANT WOMAN: You are tempting God!

(*There are shouts from below.*)

GRUSHA: Please, throw that stick away, or they'll get the rope and follow me. (*Pressing the* CHILD *to her, she steps onto the swaying bridge. The* MERCHANT WOMAN *screams when it looks as though the bridge is about to collapse. But* GRUSHA *walks on and reaches the far side.*)

THE FIRST MAN: She made it!

THE MERCHANT WOMAN (*who has fallen on her knees and begun to pray, angrily*): I still think it was a sin.

(*The* IRONSHIRTS *appear; the* CORPORAL'S *head is bandaged.*)

THE CORPORAL: Seen a woman with a child?

THE FIRST MAN (*while the* SECOND MAN *throws the stick into the abyss*): Yes, there! But the bridge won't carry you!

THE CORPORAL: You'll pay for this, blockhead!

(GRUSHA, *from the far bank, laughs and shows the* CHILD *to the* IRONSHIRTS. *She walks on. The wind blows.*)

GRUSHA (*turning to the* CHILD): You mustn't be afraid of the wind. He's a poor thing too. He has to push the clouds along and he gets quite cold doing it.

(*Snow starts falling.*)

And the snow isn't so bad, either, Michael. It covers the little fir trees so they won't die in winter. Let me sing you a little song. (*She sings.*)

The Song of the Child

Your father is a bandit
A harlot the mother who bore you.
Yet honorable men
Shall kneel down before you.

Food to the baby horses
The tiger's son will take.
The mothers will get milk
From the son of the snake.

3. In the Northern Mountains

THE STORY TELLER: Seven days the sister, Grusha Vashnadze,
Journeyed across the glacier
And down the slopes she journeyed.
"When I enter my brother's house," she thought
"He will rise and embrace me."
"Is that you, sister?" he will say,
"I have long expected you.
This is my dear wife,
And this is my farm, come to me by marriage,
With eleven horses and thirty-one cows. Sit down.
Sit down with your child at our table and eat."
The brother's house was in a lovely valley.
When the sister came to the brother,
She was ill from walking.
The brother rose from the table.

(A FAT PEASANT COUPLE *rise from the table.* LAVRENTI VASHNADZE *still has a napkin round his neck, as* GRUSHA, *pale and supported by a* SERVANT, *enters with the* CHILD.)

LAVRENTI: Where've *you* come from, Grusha?
GRUSHA (*feebly*): Across the Janga-Tu Pass, Lavrenti.
THE SERVANT: I found her in front of the hay barn. She has a baby with her.
THE SISTER-IN-LAW: Go and groom the mare.

(*Exit the* SERVANT.)

LAVRENTI: This is my wife Aniko.
THE SISTER-IN-LAW: I thought you were in service in Nuka.
GRUSHA (*barely able to stand*): Yes, I was.

THE SISTER-IN-LAW: Wasn't it a good job? We were told it was.

GRUSHA: The Governor got killed.

LAVRENTI: Yes, we heard there were riots. Your aunt told us. Remember, Aniko?

THE SISTER-IN-LAW: Here with us, it's very quiet. City people always want something going on. (*She walks toward the door, calling.*) Sosso, Sosso, don't take the cake out of the oven yet, d'you hear? Where on earth are you?

(*Exit, calling.*)

LAVRENTI (*quietly, quickly*): Is there a father? (*As she shakes her head.*) I thought not. We must think up something. She's religious.

THE SISTER-IN-LAW (*returning*): Those servants! (*To* GRUSHA.) You have a child.

GRUSHA: It's mine. (*She collapses.* LAVRENTI *rushes to her assistance.*)

THE SISTER-IN-LAW: Heavens, she's ill — what are we going to do?

LAVRENTI (*escorting her to a bench near the stove*): Sit down, sit. I think it's just weakness, Aniko.

THE SISTER-IN-LAW: As long as it's not scarlet fever!

LAVRENTI: She'd have spots if it was. It's only weakness. Don't worry, Aniko. (*To* GRUSHA.) Better, sitting down?

THE SISTER-IN-LAW: Is the child hers?

GRUSHA: Yes, mine.

LAVRENTI: She's on her way to her husband.

THE SISTER-IN-LAW: I see. Your meat's getting cold.

(LAVRENTI *sits down and begins to eat.*)

Cold food's not good for you, the fat mustn't get cold, you know your stomach's your weak spot. (*To* GRUSHA.) If your husband's not in the city, where is he?

LAVRENTI: She got married on the other side of the mountain, she says.

THE SISTER-IN-LAW: On the other side of the mountain. I see. (*She also sits down to eat.*)

GRUSHA: I think I should lie down somewhere, Lavrenti.

THE SISTER-IN-LAW: If it's consumption we'll all get it. (*She goes on cross-examining her.*) Has your husband got a farm?

GRUSHA: He's a soldier.

LAVRENTI: But he's coming into a farm — a small one — from his father.

THE SISTER-IN-LAW: Isn't he in the war? Why not?

GRUSHA (*with effort*): Yes, he's in the war.

THE SISTER-IN-LAW: Then why d'you want to go to the farm?

LAVRENTI: When he comes back from the war, he'll return to his farm.

THE SISTER-IN-LAW: But you're going there now?

LAVRENTI: Yes, to wait for him.

THE SISTER-IN-LAW (*calling shrilly*): Sosso, the cake!

GRUSHA (*murmuring feverishly*): A farm — a soldier — waiting — sit down, eat.

THE SISTER-IN-LAW: It's scarlet fever.

GRUSHA (*starting up*): Yes, he's got a farm!

LAVRENTI: I think it's just weakness, Aniko. Would you look after the cake yourself, dear?

THE SISTER-IN-LAW: But when will he come back if war's broken out again as people say? (*She waddles off, shouting.*) Sosso! Where on earth are you? Sosso!

LAVRENTI (*getting up quickly and going to* GRUSHA): You'll get a bed in a minute. She has a good heart. But wait till after supper.

GRUSHA (*holding out the* CHILD *to him*): Take him.

LAVRENTI (*taking it and looking around*): But you can't stay here long with the child. She's religious, you see.

(GRUSHA *collapses.* LAVRENTI *catches her.*)

THE STORY TELLER: The sister was so ill,
The cowardly brother had to give her shelter.
Summer departed, winter came.
The winter was long, the winter was short
People mustn't know anything,
Rats mustn't bite,
Spring mustn't come.

(GRUSHA *sits over the weaving loom in a workroom. She and the* CHILD, *who is squatting on the floor, are wrapped in blankets. She sings.*)

The Song of the Center

GRUSHA (*sings*):
And the lover started to leave
And his betrothed ran pleading after him
Pleading and weeping, weeping and teaching:
"Dearest mine, dearest mine
When you go to war as now you do
When you fight the foe as soon you will
Don't lead with the front line
And don't push with the rear line
At the front is red fire

In the rear is red smoke
Stay in the war's center
Stay near the standard bearer
The first always die
The last are also hit
Those in the center come home."

Michael, we must be clever. If we make ourselves as small as cockroaches, the sister-in-law will forget we're in the house, and then we can stay till the snow melts.

(*Enter* LAVRENTI. *He sits down beside his sister.*)

LAVRENTI: Why are you sitting there muffled up like coachmen, you two? Is it too cold in the room?

GRUSHA (*hastily removing one shawl*): It's not too cold, Lavrenti.

LAVRENTI: If it's too cold, you shouldn't be sitting here with the child. Aniko would never forgive herself! (*Pause.*) I hope our priest didn't question you about the child?

GRUSHA: He did, but I didn't tell him anything.

LAVRENTI: That's good. I wanted to speak to you about Aniko. She has a good heart but she's very, very sensitive. People need only mention our farm and she's worried. She takes everything hard, you see. One time our milkmaid went to church with a hole in her stocking. Ever since, Aniko has worn two pairs of stockings in church. It's the old family in her. (*He listens.*) Are you sure there are no rats around? If there are rats, you couldn't live here. (*There are sounds as of dripping from the roof.*) What's that dripping?

GRUSHA: It must be a barrel leaking.

LAVRENTI: Yes, it must be a barrel. You've been here six months, haven't you? Was I talking about Aniko? (*They listen again to the snow melting.*) You can't imagine how worried she gets about your soldier-husband. "Suppose he comes back and can't find her!" she says and lies awake. "He can't come before the spring," I tell her. The dear woman! (*The drops begin to fall faster.*) When d'you think he'll come? What do *you* think? (GRUSHA *is silent.*) Not before the spring, you agree? (GRUSHA *is silent.*) You don't believe he'll come at all? (GRUSHA is silent.) But when the spring comes and the snow melts here and on the passes, you can't stay on. They may come and look for you. There's already talk of an illegitimate child. (*The "glockenspiel" of the falling drops has grown faster and steadier.*) Grusha, the snow is melting on the roof. Spring is here.

GRUSHA: Yes.

LAVRENTI (*eagerly*): I'll tell you what we'll do. You need a place to go, and, because of the child (*he sighs*), you have to have a husband, so people won't talk. Now I've made cautious inquiries to see if we can find you a husband. Grusha, I *have* one. I talked to a peasant woman who has a son. Just the other side of the mountain. A small farm. And she's willing.

GRUSHA: But I *can't* marry! I must wait for Simon Shashava.

LAVRENTI: Of course. That's all been taken care of. You don't need a man in bed — you need a man on paper. And I've found you one. The son of this peasant woman is going to die. Isn't that wonderful? He's at his last gasp. And all in line with our story — a husband from the other side of the mountain! And when you met him he was at the last gasp. So you're a widow. What do you say?

GRUSHA: It's true I could use a document with stamps on it for Michael.

LAVRENTI: Stamps make all the difference. Without something in writing the Shah couldn't prove he's a Shah. And you'll have a place to live.

GRUSHA: How much does the peasant woman want?

LAVRENTI: Four hundred piasters.

GRUSHA: Where will you find it?

LAVRENTI (*guiltily*): Aniko's milk money.

GRUSHA: No one would know us there. I'll do it.

LAVRENTI (*getting up*): I'll let the peasant woman know.

(*Quick exit.*)

GRUSHA: Michael, you cause a lot of fuss. I came to you as the pear tree comes to the sparrows. And because a Christian bends down and picks up a crust of bread so nothing will go to waste. Michael, it would have been better had I walked quickly away on that Easter Sunday in Nuka in the second courtyard. Now I *am* a fool.

THE STORY TELLER:

The bridegroom was lying on his deathbed when the bride arrived.
The bridegroom's mother was waiting at the door, telling her to hurry.
The bride brought a child along.
The witness hid it during the wedding.

(*On one side the bed. Under the mosquito net lies a very sick* MAN. GRUSHA *is pulled in at a run by her future* MOTHER-IN-LAW. *They are followed by* LAVRENTI *and the* CHILD.)

THE MOTHER-IN-LAW: Quick! Quick! Or he'll die on us before the wedding. (*To* LAVRENTI.) I was never told she had a child already.

LAVRENTI: What difference does it make? (*Pointing toward the dying man.*) It can't matter to him — in his condition.

THE MOTHER-IN-LAW: To him? But *I'll* never survive the shame! We are honest people. (*She begins to weep.*) My Jussup doesn't have to marry a girl with a child!

LAVRENTI: All right, make it another two hundred piasters. You'll have it in writing that the farm will go to you: but she'll have the right to live here for two years.

THE MOTHER-IN-LAW (*drying her tears*): It'll hardly cover the funeral expenses. I hope she'll really lend a hand with the work. And what's happened to the monk? He must have slipped out through the kitchen window. We'll have the whole village round our necks when they hear Jussup's end is come! Oh dear! I'll run and get the monk. But he mustn't see the child!

LAVRENTI: I'll take care he doesn't. But why only a monk? Why not a priest?

THE MOTHER-IN-LAW: Oh, he's just as good. I only made one mistake: I paid half his fee in advance. Enough to send him to the tavern. I only hope . . . (*She runs off.*)

LAVRENTI: She saved on the priest, the wretch! Hired a cheap monk.

GRUSHA: You *will* send Simon Shashava over to see me if he turns up after all?

LAVRENTI: Yes. (*Pointing at the* SICK MAN.) Won't you take a look at him? (GRUSHA, *taking* MICHAEL *to her, shakes her head.*) He's not moving an eyelid. I hope we aren't too late.

(*They listen. On the opposite side enter* NEIGHBORS *who look around and take up positions against the walls, thus forming another wall near the bed, yet leaving an opening so that the bed can be seen. They start murmuring prayers. Enter the* MOTHER-IN-LAW *with a* MONK. *Showing some annoyance and surprise, she bows to the* GUESTS.)

THE MOTHER-IN-LAW: I hope you won't mind waiting a few moments? My son's bride has just arrived from the city. An emergency wedding is about to be celebrated. (*To the* MONK *in the bedroom.*) I might have known you couldn't keep your trap shut. (*To* GRUSHA.) The wedding can take place at once. Here's the license. I myself and the bride's brother,

(LAVRENTI *tries to hide in the background, after having quietly taken* MICHAEL *back from* GRUSHA. *The* MOTHER-IN-LAW *waves him away.*)

who will be here in a moment, are the witnesses.

(GRUSHA *has bowed to the* MONK. *They go to the bed. The* MOTHER-IN-LAW *lifts the mosquito net. The* MONK *starts reeling off the marriage ceremony in Latin. Meanwhile, the* MOTHER-IN-LAW *beckons to* LAVRENTI *to get rid of the* CHILD, *but fearing that it will cry he draws its attention to the ceremony.* GRUSHA *glances once at the* CHILD, *and* LAVRENTI *waves the* CHILD'S *hand in a greeting.*)

THE MONK: Are you prepared to be a faithful, obedient, and good wife to this man, and to cleave to him until death you do part?

GRUSHA (*looking at the* CHILD): I am.

THE MONK (*to the* SICK PEASANT): And are you prepared to be a good and loving husband to your wife until death you do part? (*As the* SICK PEASANT *does not answer, the* MONK *looks inquiringly around.*)

THE MOTHER-IN-LAW: Of course he is! Didn't you hear him say yes?

THE MONK: All right. We declare the marriage contracted! How about extreme unction?

THE MOTHER-IN-LAW: Nothing doing! The wedding cost quite enough. Now I must take care of the mourners. (*To* LAVRENTI.) Did we say seven hundred?

LAVRENTI: *Six hundred.* (*He pays.*) Now I don't want to sit with the guests and get to know people. So farewell, Grusha, and if my widowed sister comes to visit me, she'll get a welcome from my wife, or I'll show my teeth. (*Nods, gives the* CHILD *to* GRUSHA, *and leaves. The* MOURNERS *glance after him without interest.*)

THE MONK: May one ask where this child comes from?

THE MOTHER-IN-LAW: Is there a child? I don't see a child. And you don't see a child either — you understand? Or it may turn out I saw all sorts of things in the tavern! Now come on.

(*After* GRUSHA *has put the* CHILD *down and told him to be quiet, they move over left;* GRUSHA *is introduced to the* NEIGHBORS.)

This is my daughter-in-law. She arrived just in time to find dear Jussup still alive.

ONE WOMAN: He's been ill now a whole year, hasn't he? When our Vassili was drafted he was there to say goodbye.

ANOTHER WOMAN: Such things are terrible for a farm. The corn all ripe and the farmer in bed! It'll really be a blessing if he doesn't suffer too long, I say.

THE FIRST WOMAN (*confidentially*): You know why we thought he'd taken to his bed? Because of the draft! And now his end is come!

THE MOTHER-IN-LAW: Sit yourselves down, please! And have some cakes!

(*She beckons to* GRUSHA *and both women go into the bedroom, where they pick up the cake pans off the floor. The* GUESTS, *among them the* MONK, *sit on the floor and begin conversing in subdued voices.*)

ONE PEASANT (*to whom the* MONK *has handed the bottle which he has taken from his soutane*): There's a child, you say! How can that have happened to Jussup?

A WOMAN: She was certainly lucky to get herself hitched, with him so sick!

THE MOTHER-IN-LAW: They're gossiping already. And gorging themselves on the funeral cakes at the same time! If he doesn't die today, I'll have to bake some more tomorrow!

GRUSHA: I'll bake them for you.

THE MOTHER-IN-LAW: Yesterday some horsemen rode by, and I went out to see who it was. When I came in again he was lying there like a corpse! So I sent for you. It can't take much longer. (*She listens.*)

THE MONK: Dear wedding and funeral guests! Deeply touched, we stand before a bed of death and marriage. The bride gets a veil; the groom, a shroud: how varied, my children, are the fates of men! Alas! One man dies and has a roof over his head, and the other is married and the flesh turns to dust from which it was made. Amen.

THE MOTHER-IN-LAW: He's getting his own back. I shouldn't have hired such a cheap one. It's what you'd expect. A more expensive monk would behave himself. In Sura there's one with a real air of sanctity about him, but of course he charges a fortune. A fifty-piaster monk like that has no dignity, and as for piety, just fifty piasters' worth and no more! When I came to get him in the tavern he'd just made a speech, and he was shouting: "The war is over, beware of the peace!" We must go in.

GRUSHA (*giving* MICHAEL *a cake*): Eat this cake, and keep nice and still, Michael.

(*The two women offer cakes to the* GUESTS. *The* DYING MAN *sits up in bed. He puts his head out from under the mosquito net, stares at the two women, then sinks back again. The* MONK *takes two bottles from his soutane and offers them to the* PEASANT *beside him. Enter three* MUSICIANS *who are greeted with a sly wink by the monk.*)

THE MOTHER-IN-LAW (*to the* MUSICIANS): What are you doing here? With instruments?

ONE MUSICIAN: Brother Anastasius here (*pointing at the* MONK) told us there was a wedding on.

THE MOTHER-IN-LAW: What? You brought them? Three more on my neck! Don't you know there's a dying man in the next room?

THE MONK: A very tempting assignment for a musician: something that could be either a subdued Wedding March or a spirited Funeral Dance.

THE MOTHER-IN-LAW: Well, you might as well play. Nobody can stop you eating in any case.

(THE MUSICIANS *play a potpourri. The women serve cakes.*)

THE MONK: The trumpet sounds like a whining baby. And you, little drum, what have you got to tell the world?

THE DRUNKEN PEASANT (*beside the* MONK, *sings*):

Miss Roundass took the old old man
And said that marriage was the thing
To everyone who met 'er.
She later withdrew from the contract because
Candles are better.

(*The* MOTHER-IN-LAW *throws the* DRUNKEN PEASANT *out. The music stops. The* GUESTS *are embarrassed.*)

THE GUESTS (*loudly*):

— Have you heard? The Grand Duke is back! But the Princes are against him.
— They say the Shah of Persia has lent him a great army to restore order in Grusinia.
— But how is that possible? The Shah of Persia is the enemy . . .
— The enemy of Grusinia, you donkey, not the enemy of the Grand Duke!
— In any case, the war's over, so our soldiers are coming back.

(GRUSHA *drops a cake pan.* GUESTS *help her pick up the cake.*)

AN OLD WOMAN (*to* GRUSHA): Are you feeling bad? It's just excitement about dear Jussup. Sit down and rest a while, my dear.

(GRUSHA *staggers.*)

THE GUESTS: Now everything'll be the way it was. Only the taxes'll go up because now we'll have to pay for the war.

GRUSHA (*weakly*): Did someone say the soldiers are back?

A MAN: I did.

GRUSHA: It can't be true.

THE FIRST MAN (*to a* WOMAN): Show her the shawl. We bought it from a soldier. It's from Persia.

GRUSHA (*looking at the shawl*): They are here. (*She gets up, takes a step, kneels down in prayer, takes the silver cross and chain out of her blouse, and kisses it.*)

THE MOTHER-IN-LAW (*while the* GUESTS *silently watch* GRUSHA): What's the matter with you? Aren't you going to look after our guests? What's all this city nonsense got to do with us?

THE GUESTS (*resuming conversation while* GRUSHA *remains in prayer*):

— You can buy Persian saddles from the soldiers too. Though many want crutches in exchange for them.

— The big shots on one side can win a war, the soldiers on both sides lose it.

— Anyway, the war's over. It's something they can't draft you any more.

(*The* DYING MAN *sits bolt upright in bed. He listens.*)

— What we need is two weeks of good weather.

— Our pear trees are hardly bearing a thing this year.

THE MOTHER-IN-LAW (*offering cakes*): Have some more cakes and welcome! There are more!

(*The* MOTHER-IN-LAW *goes to the bedroom with the empty cake pans. Unaware of the* DYING MAN, *she is bending down to pick up another tray when he begins to talk in a hoarse voice.*)

THE PEASANT: How many more cakes are you going to stuff down their throats? Think I'm a fucking goldmine?

(*The* MOTHER-IN-LAW *starts, stares at him aghast, while he climbs out from behind the mosquito net.*)

THE FIRST WOMAN (*talking kindly to* GRUSHA *in the next room*): Has the young wife got someone at the front?

A MAN: It's good news that they're on their way home, huh?

THE PEASANT: Don't stare at me like that! Where's this wife you've hung round my neck?

(*Receiving no answer, he climbs out of bed and in his nightshirt staggers into the other room. Trembling, she follows him with the cake pan.*)

THE GUESTS (*seeing him and shrieking*): Good God! Jussup!

(*Everyone leaps up in alarm. The women rush to the door.* GRUSHA, *still on her knees, turns round and stares at the* MAN.)

THE PEASANT: A funeral supper! You'd enjoy that, wouldn't you? Get out before I throw you out! (*As the* GUESTS *stampede from the house, gloomily to* GRUSHA.) I've upset the apple cart, huh? (*Receiving no answer, he turns round and takes a cake from the pan which his mother is holding.*)

THE STORY TELLER: O confusion! The wife discovers she has a husband. By day there's the child, by night there's the husband. The lover is on his way both day and night. Husband and wife look at each other. The bedroom is small.

(*Near the bed the* PEASANT *is sitting in a high wooden bathtub, naked; the* MOTHER-IN-LAW *is pouring water from a pitcher. Opposite,* GRUSHA *cowers with* MICHAEL, *who is playing at mending straw mats.*)

THE PEASANT (*to his mother*): That's her work, not yours. Where's she hiding out now?

THE MOTHER-IN-LAW (*calling*): Grusha! The peasant wants you!

GRUSHA (*to* MICHAEL): There are still two holes to mend.

THE PEASANT (*when* GRUSHA *approaches*): Scrub my back!

GRUSHA: Can't the peasant do it himself?

THE PEASANT: "Can't the peasant do it himself?" Get the brush! To hell with you! Are you the wife here? Or are you a visitor? (*To the* MOTHER-IN-LAW.) It's too cold!

THE MOTHER-IN-LAW: I'll run for hot water.

GRUSHA: Let me go.

THE PEASANT: You stay here.

(*The* MOTHER-IN-LAW *exits.*)

Rub harder. And no shirking. You've seen a naked fellow before. That child didn't come out of thin air.

GRUSHA: The child was not conceived in joy, if that's what the peasant means.

THE PEASANT (*turning and grinning*): You don't look the type. (GRUSHA *stops scrubbing him, starts back.*)

(*Enter the* MOTHER-IN-LAW.)

THE PEASANT: A nice thing you've hung around my neck! A simpleton for a wife!

THE MOTHER-IN-LAW: She just isn't co-operative.

THE PEASANT: Pour — but go easy! Ow! Go easy, I said. (*To* GRUSHA.) Maybe you did something wrong in the city . . . I wouldn't be surprised. Why else should you be here? But I won't talk about that. I've not said a word about the illegitimate object you brought into my house either. But my patience has limits! It's against nature. (*To the* MOTHER-IN-LAW.) More! (*To* GRUSHA.) And even if your soldier does come back, you're married.

GRUSHA: Yes.

THE PEASANT: But your soldier won't come back. Don't you believe it.

GRUSHA: No.

THE PEASANT: You're cheating me. You're my wife and you're not my wife. Where you lie, nothing lies, and yet no other woman can lie there. When I go to work in the morning I'm tired — when I lie down at night I'm awake as the devil. God has given you sex — and what d'you do? I don't have ten piasters to buy myself a woman in the city. Besides, it's a long way. Woman weeds the fields and opens up her legs, that's what our calendar says. D'you hear?

GRUSHA (*quietly*): Yes. I didn't mean to cheat you out of it.

THE PEASANT: She didn't mean to cheat me out of it! Pour some more water! (*The* MOTHER-IN-LAW *pours.*) Ow!

THE STORY TELLER: As she sat by the stream to wash the linen
She saw his image in the water
And his face grew dimmer with the passing moons.
As she raised herself to wring the linen
She heard his voice from the murmuring maple
And his voice grew fainter with the passing moons.
Evasions and sighs grew more numerous,
Tears and sweat flowed.
With the passing moons the child grew up.

(GRUSHA *sits by a stream, dipping linen into the water. In the rear, a few* CHILDREN *are standing.*)

GRUSHA (*to* MICHAEL): You can play with them, Michael, but don't let them boss you around just because you're the littlest. (MICHAEL *nods and joins the* CHILDREN. *They start playing.*)

THE BIGGEST BOY: Today it's the Heads-Off Game. (*To a* FAT BOY.) You're the Prince and you laugh. (*To* MICHAEL.) You're the Governor. (*To a* GIRL.) You're the Governor's wife and you cry when his head's cut off. And I do the cutting. (*He shows his wooden sword.*) With this. First, they lead the Governor into the yard. The Prince walks in front. The Governor's wife comes last.

(*They form a procession. The* FAT BOY *is first and laughs. Then comes* MICHAEL, *then the* BIGGEST BOY, *and then the* GIRL, *who weeps.*)

MICHAEL (*standing still*): Me cut off head!

THE BIGGEST BOY: That's my job. You're the littlest. The Governor's the easy part. All you do is kneel down and get your head cut off — simple.

MICHAEL: Me want sword!

THE BIGGEST BOY: It's mine! (*He gives him a kick.*)

THE GIRL (*shouting to* GRUSHA): He won't play his part!

GRUSHA (*laughing*): Even the little duck is a swimmer, they say.

THE BIGGEST BOY: You can be the Prince if you can laugh. (MICHAEL *shakes his head.*)

THE FAT BOY: I laugh best. Let him cut off the head just once. Then you do it, then me.

(*Reluctantly, the* BIGGEST BOY *hands* MICHAEL *the wooden sword and kneels down. The* FAT BOY *sits down, slaps his thigh, and laughs with all his might. The* GIRL *weeps loudly.* MICHAEL *swings the big sword and "cuts off" the head. In doing so, he topples over.*)

THE BIGGEST BOY: Hey! I'll show you how to cut heads off!

(MICHAEL *runs away. the* CHILDREN *run after him.* GRUSHA *laughs, following them with her eyes. On looking back, she sees* SIMON SHASHAVA *standing on the opposite bank. He wears a shabby uniform.*)

GRUSHA: Simon!

SIMON: Is that Grusha Vashnadze?

GRUSHA: Simon!

SIMON (*formally*): A good morning to the young lady. I hope she is well.

GRUSHA (*getting up gaily and bowing low*): A good morning to the soldier. God be thanked he has returned in good health.

SIMON: They found better fish, so they didn't eat me, said the haddock.

GRUSHA: Courage, said the kitchen boy. Good luck, said the hero.

SIMON: How are things here? Was the winter bearable? The neighbor considerate?

GRUSHA: The winter was a trifle rough, the neighbor as usual, Simon.

SIMON: May one ask if a certain person still dips her foot in the water when rinsing the linen?

GRUSHA: The answer is no. Because of the eyes in the bushes.

SIMON: The young lady is speaking of soldiers. Here stands a paymaster.

GRUSHA: A job worth twenty piasters?

SIMON: And lodgings.

GRUSHA (*with tears in her eyes*): Behind the barracks under the date trees.

SIMON: Yes, there. A certain person has kept her eyes open.

GRUSHA: She has, Simon.
SIMON: And has not forgotten?

(GRUSHA *shakes her head.*)

So the door is still on its hinges as they say?

(GRUSHA *looks at him in silence and shakes her head again.*)

What's this? Is something not as it should be?
GRUSHA: Simon Shashava, I can never return to Nuka. Something has happened.
SIMON: What can have happened?
GRUSHA: For one thing, I knocked an Ironshirt down.
SIMON: Grusha Vashnadze must have had her reasons for that.
GRUSHA: Simon Shashava, I am no longer called what I used to be called.
SIMON (*after a pause*): I do not understand.
GRUSHA: When do women change their names, Simon? Let me explain. Nothing stands between us. Everything is just as it was. You must believe that.
SIMON: Nothing stands between us and yet there's something?
GRUSHA: How can I explain it so fast and with the stream between us? Couldn't you cross the bridge there?
SIMON: Maybe it's no longer necessary.
GRUSHA: It is very necessary. Come over on this side, Simon. Quick!
SIMON: Does the young lady wish to say someone has come too late?

(GRUSHA *looks up at him in despair, her face streaming with tears.* SIMON *stares before him. He picks up a piece of wood and starts cutting it.*)

THE STORY TELLER: So many words are said, so many left unsaid.
The soldier has come.
Where he comes from, he does not say.
Hear what he thought and did not say:
"The battle began, gray at dawn, grew bloody at noon.
The first man fell in front of me, the second behind me, the third at my side.
I trod on the first, left the second behind, the third was run through by the captain.
One of my brothers died by steel, the other by smoke.
My neck caught fire, my hands froze in my gloves, my toes in my socks.
I fed on aspen buds, I drank maple juice, I slept on stone, in water."
SIMON: I see a cap in the grass. Is there a little one already?

GRUSHA: There is, Simon. How could I conceal the fact? But please don't worry, it is not mine.

SIMON: When the wind once starts to blow, they say, it blows through every cranny. The wife need say no more.

(GRUSHA *looks into her lap and is silent.*)

THE STORY TELLER: There was yearning but there was no waiting.
The oath is broken. Neither could say why.
Hear what she thought but did not say:
"While you fought in the battle, soldier,
The bloody battle, the bitter battle
I found a helpless infant
I had not the heart to destroy him
I had to care for a creature that was lost
I had to stoop for breadcrumbs on the floor
I had to break myself for that which was not mine
That which was other people's.
Someone must help!
For the little tree needs water
The lamb loses its way when the shepherd is asleep
And its cry is unheard!"

SIMON: Give me back the cross I gave you. Better still, throw it in the stream. (*He turns to go.*)

GRUSHA (*getting up*): Simon Shashava, don't go away! He isn't mine! He isn't mine! (*She hears the* CHILDREN *calling.*) What's the matter, children?

VOICES: Soldiers! And they're taking Michael away!

(GRUSHA *stands aghast as two* IRONSHIRTS, *with* MICHAEL *between them, come toward her.*)

ONE OF THE IRONSHIRTS: Are you Grusha?

(*She nods.*)

Is this your child?

GRUSHA: Yes.

(SIMON *goes.*)

Simon!

THE IRONSHIRT: We have orders, in the name of the law, to take this child, found in your custody, back to the city. It is suspected that the child is Michael Abashwili, son and heir of the late Governor Georgi Abashwili, and his wife, Natella Abashwili. Here is the document and the seal. (*They lead the* CHILD *away.*)

GRUSHA (*running after them, shouting*): Leave him here. Please! He's mine!

THE STORY TELLER: The Ironshirts took the child, the beloved child.
The unhappy girl followed them to the city, the dreaded city.
She who had borne him demanded the child.
She who had raised him faced trial.
Who will decide the case?
To whom will the child be assigned?
Who will the judge be? A good judge? A bad?
The city was in flames.
In the judge's seat sat Azdak.*

4. The Story of the Judge

THE STORY TELLER: Hear the story of the judge
How he turned judge, how he passed judgment, what kind of judge he was.
On that Easter Sunday of the great revolt, when the Grand Duke was overthrown
And his Governor Abashwili, father of our child, lost his head
The Village Scrivener Azdak found a fugitive in the woods and hid him in his hut.

(AZDAK, *in rags and slightly drunk, is helping an* OLD BEGGAR *into his cottage.*)

AZDAK: Stop snorting, you're not a horse. And it won't do you any good with the police, to run like a snotty nose in April. Stand still, I say. (*He catches the* OLD MAN, *who has marched into the cottage as if he'd like to go through the walls.*) Sit down. Feed. Here's a hunk of cheese. (*From under some rags, in a chest, he fishes out some cheese, and the* OLD MAN *greedily begins to eat.*) Haven't eaten in a long time, huh? (*The* OLD MAN *growls.*) Why were you running like that, asshole? The cop wouldn't even have seen you.

THE OLD MAN: Had to! Had to!

AZDAK: Blue Funk? (*The* OLD MAN *stares, uncomprehending.*) Cold feet? Panic? Don't lick your chops like a Grand Duke. Or an old sow. I can't stand it. We have to accept respectable stinkers as God made them, but not you! I once heard of a senior judge who farted at a public dinner to show an independent spirit! Watching you eat like that gives me the most awful ideas. Why don't you say something? (*Sharply.*) Show me your hand. Can't you hear? (*The* OLD

* The name AZDAK should be accented on the second syllable.

MAN *slowly puts out his hand.*) White! So you're not a beggar at all! A fraud, a walking swindle! And I'm hiding you from the cops as though you were an honest man! Why were you running like that if you're a landowner? For that's what you are. Don't deny it! I see it in your guilty face! (*He gets up.*) Get out! (*The* OLD MAN *looks at him uncertainly.*) What are you waiting for, peasant-flogger?

THE OLD MAN: Pursued. Need undivided attention. Make proposition . . .

AZDAK: Make what? A proposition? Well, if that isn't the height of insolence. He's making me a proposition! The bitten man scratches his fingers bloody, and the leech that's biting him makes him a proposition! Get out, I tell you!

THE OLD MAN: Understand point of view! Persuasion! Pay hundred thousand piasters one night! Yes?

AZDAK: What, you think you can buy me? For a hundred thousand piasters? Let's say a hundred and fifty thousand. Where are they?

THE OLD MAN: Have not them here. Of course. Will be sent. Hope do not doubt.

AZDAK: Doubt very much. Get out!

(*The* OLD MAN *gets up, waddles to the door. A* VOICE *is heard off stage.*)

A VOICE: Azdak!

(*The* OLD MAN *turns, waddles to the opposite corner, stands still.*)

AZDAK (*calling out*): I'm not in! (*He walks to door.*) So you're sniffing around here again, Shauwa?

POLICEMAN SHAUWA (*reproachfully*): You've caught another rabbit, Azdak. And you promised me it wouldn't happen again!

AZDAK (*severely*): Shauwa, don't talk about things you don't understand. The rabbit is a dangerous and destructive beast. It feeds on plants, especially on the species of plants known as weeds. It must therefore be exterminated.

SHAUWA: Azdak, don't be so hard on me. I'll lose my job if I don't arrest you. I know you have a good heart.

AZDAK: I do not have a good heart! How often must I tell you I'm a man of intellect?

SHAUWA (*slyly*): I know, Azdak. You're a superior person. You say so yourself. I'm just a Christian and an ignoramus. So I ask you: When one of the Prince's rabbits is stolen, and I'm a policeman, what should I do with the offending party?

AZDAK: Shauwa, Shauwa, shame on you. You stand and ask me a question, than which nothing could be more seductive. It's like you were a woman — let's say that bad girl Nunowna, and you showed me your thigh — Nunowna's thigh, that would be — and asked me: "What shall I do with my thigh, it itches?" Is she as innocent as she pretends? Of course not. I catch a rabbit, but you catch a man. Man is made in God's image. Not so a rabbit, you know that. I'm a rabbit-eater, but you're a man-eater, Shauwa. And God will pass judgment on you. Shauwa, go home and repent. No, stop, there's something . . . (*He looks at the* OLD MAN *who stands trembling in the corner.*) No, it's nothing. Go home and repent. (*He slams the door behind* SHAUWA.) Now you're surprised, huh? Surprised I didn't hand you over? I couldn't hand over a bedbug to that animal. It goes against the grain. Now don't tremble because of a cop! So old and still so scared? Finish your cheese, but eat it like a poor man, or else they'll still catch you. Must I even explain how a poor man behaves? (*He pushes him down, and then gives him back the cheese.*) That box is the table. Lay your elbows on the table. Now, encircle the cheese on the plate like it might be snatched from you at any moment — what right have you to be safe, huh? — now, hold your knife like an undersized sickle, and give your cheese a troubled look because, like all beautiful things, it's already fading away. (AZDAK *watches him.*) They're after you, which speaks in your favor, but how can we be sure they're not mistaken about you? In Tiflis one time they hanged a landowner, a Turk, who could prove he quartered his peasants instead of merely cutting them in half, as is the custom, and he squeezed twice the usual amount of taxes out of them, his zeal was above suspicion. And yet they hanged him like a common criminal — because he was a Turk — a thing he couldn't do much about. What injustice! He got onto the gallows by a sheer fluke. In short, I don't trust you.

THE STORY TELLER: Thus Azdak gave the old beggar a bed,
And learned that old beggar was the old butcher, the Grand Duke himself,
And was ashamed.
He denounced himself and ordered the policeman to take him to Nuka, to court, to be judged.

(*In the court of justice three* IRONSHIRTS *sit drinking. From a beam hangs a man in judge's robes. Enter* AZDAK, *in chains, dragging* SHAUWA *behind him.*)

AZDAK (*shouting*): I've helped the Grand Duke, the Grand Thief, the Grand Butcher, to escape! In the name of justice I ask to be severely judged in public trial!

THE FIRST IRONSHIRT: Who's this queer bird?

SHAUWA: That's our Village Scrivener, Azdak.

AZDAK: I am contemptible! I am a traitor! A branded criminal! Tell them, flat-foot, how I insisted on being chained up and brought to the capital. Because I sheltered the Grand Duke, the Grand Swindler, by mistake. And how I found out afterwards. See the marked man denounce himself! Tell them how I forced you to walk with me half the night to clear the whole thing up.

SHAUWA: And all by threats. That wasn't nice of you, Azdak.

AZDAK: Shut your mouth, Shauwa. You don't understand. A new age is upon us! It'll go thundering over you. You're finished. The police will be wiped out — poof! Everything will be gone into, everything will be brought into the open. The guilty will give themselves up. Why? They couldn't escape the people in any case. (*To* SHAUWA.) Tell them how I shouted all along Shoemaker Street: (*With big gestures, looking at the* IRONSHIRTS.) "In my ignorance I let the Grand Swindler escape! So tear me to pieces, brothers!" I wanted to get it in first.

THE FIRST IRONSHIRT: And what did your brothers answer?

SHAUWA: They comforted him in Butcher Street, and they laughed themselves sick in Shoemaker Street. That's all.

AZDAK: But with you it's different. I can see you're men of iron. Brothers, where's the judge? I must be tried.

THE FIRST IRONSHIRT (*pointing at the hanged man*): There's the judge. And please stop "brothering" us. It's rather a sore spot this evening.

AZDAK: "There's the judge." An answer never heard in Grusinia before. Townsman, where's His Excellency the Governor? (*Pointing to the floor.*) There's His Excellency, stranger. Where's the Chief Tax Collector? Where's the official Recruiting Officer? The Patriarch? The Chief of Police? There, there, there — all there. Brothers, I expected no less of you.

THE SECOND IRONSHIRT: What? *What* was it you expected, funny man?

AZDAK: What happened in Persia, brother, what happened in Persia?

THE SECOND IRONSHIRT: What did happen in Persia?

AZDAK: Everybody was hanged. Viziers, tax collectors. Everybody. Forty years ago now. My grandfather, a remarkable man by the way, saw it all. For three whole days. Everywhere.

THE SECOND IRONSHIRT: And who ruled when the Vizier was hanged?

AZDAK: A peasant ruled when the Vizier was hanged.

THE SECOND IRONSHIRT: And who commanded the army?

AZDAK: A soldier, a soldier.

THE SECOND IRONSHIRT: And who paid the wages?

AZDAK: A dyer. A dyer paid the wages.

THE SECOND IRONSHIRT: Wasn't it a weaver, maybe?

THE FIRST IRONSHIRT: And why did all this happen, Persian?

AZDAK: Why did all this happen? Must there be a special reason? Why do you scratch yourself, brother? War! Too long a war! And no justice! My grandfather brought back a song that tells how it was. I will sing it for you. With my friend the policeman. (*To* SHAUWA.) And hold the rope tight. It's very suitable. (*He sings, with* SHAUWA *holding the rope tight around him.*)

The Song of Injustice in Persia

Why don't our sons bleed any more? Why don't our daughters weep?
Why do only the slaughter-house cattle have blood in their veins?
Why do only the willows shed tears on Lake Urmi?
The king must have a new province, the peasant must give up his savings.
That the roof of the world might be conquered, the roof of the cottage is torn down.
Our men are carried to the ends of the earth, so that great ones can eat at home.
The soldiers kill each other, the marshals salute each other.
They bite the widow's tax money to see if it's good, their swords break.
The battle was lost, the helmets were paid for.
(*Refrain*): Is it so? Is it so?

SHAUWA (*refrain*): Yes, yes, yes, yes, yes it's so.

AZDAK: Do you want to hear the rest of it?

(*The* FIRST IRONSHIRT *nods.*)

THE SECOND IRONSHIRT (*to* SHAUWA): Did he teach you that song?

SHAUWA: Yes, only my voice isn't very good.

THE SECOND IRONSHIRT: No. (*To* AZDAK.) Go on singing.

AZDAK: The second verse is about the peace. (*He sings.*)

The offices are packed, the streets overflow with officials.
The rivers jump their banks and ravage the fields.
Those who cannot let down their own trousers rule countries.
They can't count up to four, but they devour eight courses.
The corn farmers, looking round for buyers, see only the starving.
The weavers go home from their looms in rags.
(*Refrain*): Is it so? Is it so?

SHAUWA (*refrain*): Yes, yes, yes, yes, yes it's so.

AZDAK: That's why our sons don't bleed any more, that's why our daughters don't weep.

That's why only the slaughter-house cattle have blood in their veins,
And only the willows shed tears by Lake Urmi toward morning.

THE FIRST IRONSHIRT: Are you going to sing that song here in town?

AZDAK: Sure. What's wrong with it?

THE FIRST IRONSHIRT: Have you noticed that the sky's getting red?

(*Turning round,* AZDAK *sees the sky red with fire.*)

It's the people's quarters. On the outskirts of town. The carpet weavers have caught the "Persian Sickness," too. And they've been asking if Prince Kazbeki isn't eating too many courses. This morning they strung up the city judge. As for us we beat them to pulp. We were paid one hundred piasters per man, you understand?

AZDAK (*after a pause*): I understand. (*He glances shyly round and, creeping away, sits down in a corner, his head in his hands.*)

THE IRONSHIRTS (*to each other*): — If there ever was a trouble-maker it's him.

— He must've come to the capital to fish in the troubled waters.

SHAUWA: Oh, I don't think he's a really bad character, gentlemen. Steals a few chickens here and there. And maybe a rabbit.

THE SECOND IRONSHIRT (*approaching* AZDAK): Came to fish in the troubled waters, huh?

AZDAK (*looking up*): I don't know why I came.

THE SECOND IRONSHIRT: Are you in with the carpet weavers maybe?

(AZDAK *shakes his head.*)

How about that song?

AZDAK: From my grandfather. A silly and ignorant man.

THE SECOND IRONSHIRT: Right. And how about the dyer who paid the wages?

AZDAK (*muttering*): That was in Persia.

THE FIRST IRONSHIRT: And this denouncing of yourself? Because you didn't hang the Grand Duke with your own hands?

AZDAK: Didn't I tell you I let him run? (*He creeps farther away and sits on the floor.*)

SHAUWA: I can swear to that: he let him run.

(*The* IRONSHIRTS *burst out laughing and slap* SHAUWA *on the back.* AZDAK *laughs loudest. They slap* AZDAK *too, and unchain him. They all start drinking as the* FAT PRINCE *enters with a* YOUNG MAN.)

THE FIRST IRONSHIRT (*to* AZDAK, *pointing at the* FAT PRINCE): There's your "new age" for you!

(*More laughter.*)

THE FAT PRINCE: Well, my friends, what is there to laugh about? Permit me a serious word. Yesterday morning the Princes of Grusinia overthrew the war-mongering government of the Grand Duke and did away with his Governors. Unfortunately the Grand Duke himself escaped. In this fateful hour our carpet weavers, those eternal trouble-makers, had the effrontery to stir up a rebellion and hang the universally loved city judge, our dear Illo Orbeliani. Ts — ts — ts. My friends, we need peace, peace, peace in Grusinia! And justice! So I've brought along my dear nephew Bizergan Kazbeki. He'll be the new judge, hm? A very gifted fellow. What do you say? I want your opinion. Let the people decide!

THE SECOND IRONSHIRT: Does this mean *we* elect the judge?

THE FAT PRINCE: Precisely. Let the people propose some very gifted fellow! Confer among yourselves, my friends.

(*The* IRONSHIRTS *confer.*)

Don't worry, my little fox. The job's yours. And when we catch the Grand Duke we won't have to kiss this rabble's ass any longer.

THE IRONSHIRTS (*between themselves*): — Very funny: they're wetting their pants because they haven't caught the Grand Duke.

— When the outlook isn't so bright, they say: "My friends!" and "Let the people decide!"

— Now he even wants justice for Grusinia! But fun is fun as long as it lasts!

(*Pointing at* AZDAK.) — *He* knows all about justice. Hey, rascal, would you like this nephew fellow to be the judge?

AZDAK: Are you asking me? You're not asking *me?!*

THE FIRST IRONSHIRT: Why not? Anything for a laugh!

AZDAK: You'd like to test him to the marrow, correct? Have you a criminal on hand? An experienced one? So the candidate can show what he knows?

THE SECOND IRONSHIRT: Let's see. We do have a couple of doctors downstairs. Let's use them.

AZDAK: Oh, no, that's no good, we can't take real criminals till we're sure the judge will be appointed. He may be dumb, but he must be appointed, or the Law is violated. And the Law is a sensitive organ. It's like the spleen, you mustn't hit it — that would be fatal. Of course you can hang those two without violating the Law, because there was no judge in the vicinity. But Judgment, when pronounced, must be pronounced with absolute gravity — it's all such nonsense. Suppose, for instance, a judge jails a woman — let's say she's stolen a corncake to feed her child — and this judge isn't wearing his robes — or maybe he's scratching himself while passing sentence and half his body is uncovered — a man's thigh *will* itch once in a while — the sentence this judge passes is a disgrace and the Law is violated. In short it would be easier for a judge's robe and a judge's hat to pass judgment than for a man with no robe and no hat. If you don't treat it with respect, the Law just disappears on you. Now you don't try out a bottle of wine by offering it to a dog; you'd only lose your wine.

THE FIRST IRONSHIRT: Then what do you suggest, hair-splitter?

AZDAK: I'll be the defendant.

THE FIRST IRONSHIRT: You? (*He bursts out laughing.*)

THE FAT PRINCE: What have you decided?

THE FIRST IRONSHIRT: We've decided to stage a rehearsal. Our friend here will be the defendant. Let the candidate be the judge and sit there.

THE FAT PRINCE: It isn't customary, but why not? (*To the* NEPHEW.) A mere formality, my little fox. What have I taught you? Who got there first — the slow runner or the fast?

THE NEPHEW: The silent runner, Uncle Arsen.

(*The* NEPHEW *takes the chair. The* IRONSHIRTS *and the* FAT PRINCE *sit on the steps. Enter* AZDAK, *mimicking the gait of the Grand Duke.*)

AZDAK (*in the Grand Duke's accent*): Is any here knows me? Am Grand Duke.

THE IRONSHIRTS:

— *What* is he?

— The Grand Duke. He knows him, too.

— Fine. So get on with the trial.

AZDAK: Listen! Am accused instigating war? Ridiculous! Am saying ridiculous! That enough? If not, have brought lawyers. Believe five hundred. (*He points behind him, pretending to be surrounded by lawyers.*) Requisition all available seats for lawyers! (*The* IRONSHIRTS *laugh, the* FAT PRINCE *joins in.*)

THE NEPHEW (*to the* IRONSHIRTS): You really wish me to try this case? I find it rather unusual. From the taste angle, I mean.

THE FIRST IRONSHIRT: Let's go!

THE FAT PRINCE (*smiling*): Let him have it, my little fox!

THE NEPHEW: All right. People of Grusinia versus Grand Duke. Defendant, what have you got to say for yourself?

AZDAK: Plenty. Naturally, have read war lost. Only started on the advice of patriots. Like Uncle Arsen Kazbeki. Call Uncle Arsen as witness.

THE FAT PRINCE (*to the* IRONSHIRTS, *delightedly*): What a screw-ball!

THE NEPHEW: Motion rejected. One cannot be arraigned for declaring a war, which every ruler has to do once in a while, but only for running a war badly.

AZDAK: Rubbish! Did not run it at all! Had it run! Had it run by Princes! Naturally, they messed it up.

THE NEPHEW: Do you by any chance deny having been commander-in-chief?

AZDAK: Not at all! Always *was* commander-in-chief. At birth shouted at wet nurse. Was trained drop turds in toilet, grew accustomed to command. Always commanded officials rob my cash box. Officers flog soldiers only on command. Landowners sleep with peasants' wives only on strictest command. Uncle Arsen here grew his belly at *my* command!

THE IRONSHIRTS (*clapping*): He's good! Long live the Grand Duke!

THE FAT PRINCE: Answer him, my little fox. I'm with you.

THE NEPHEW: I shall answer him according to the dignity of the law. Defendant, preserve the dignity of the law!

AZDAK: Agreed. Command you to proceed with the trial!

THE NEPHEW: It is not your place to command me. You claim that the Princes forced you to declare war. How can you claim, then, that they — er — "messed it up"?

AZDAK: Did not send enough people. Embezzled funds. Sent sick horses. During attack, drinking in whore house. Call Uncle Arsen as witness.

THE NEPHEW: Are you making the outrageous suggestion that the Princes of this country did not fight?

AZDAK: No. Princes fought. Fought for war contracts.

THE FAT PRINCE (*jumping up*): That's too much! This man talks like a carpet weaver!

AZDAK: Really? I told nothing but the truth.

THE FAT PRINCE: Hang him! Hang him!

THE FIRST IRONSHIRT (*pulling the* PRINCE *down*): Keep quiet! Go on, Excellency!

THE NEPHEW: Quiet! I now render a verdict: You must be hanged! By the neck! Having lost war!

AZDAK: Young man, seriously advise not fall publicly into jerky clipped manner of speech. Cannot be employed as watchdog if howl like wolf. Got it? If people realize Princes speak same language as Grand Duke, may hang Grand Duke *and Princes*, huh? By the way, must overrule verdict. Reason? War lost, but not for Princes. Princes won their war. Got 3,863,000 piasters for horses not delivered, 8,240,000 piasters for food supplies not produced. Are therefore victors. War lost only for Grusinia, which as such is not present in this court.

THE FAT PRINCE: I think that will do, my friends. (*To* AZDAK.) You can withdraw, funny man. (*To the* IRONSHIRTS.) You may now ratify the new judge's appointment, my friends.

THE FIRST IRONSHIRT: Yes, we can. Take down the judge's gown.

(*One* IRONSHIRT *climbs on the back of the other, pulls the gown off the hanged man.*)

(*To the* NEPHEW.) Now you run away so the right ass can get on the right chair. (*To* AZDAK.) Step forward! Go to the judge's seat! Now sit in it! (AZDAK *steps up, bows, and sits down.*) The judge was always a rascal! Now the rascal shall be a judge! (*The judge's gown is placed round his shoulders, the hat on his head.*) And what a judge!

THE STORY TELLER: And there was civil war in the land.
The mighty were not safe.
And Azdak was made a judge by the Ironshirts.
And Azdak remained a judge for two years.

THE STORY TELLER AND CHORUS: When the towns were set afire
And rivers of blood rose higher and higher,
Cockroaches crawled out of every crack.
And the court was full of schemers
And the church of foul blasphemers.
In the judge's cassock sat Azdak.

(AZDAK *sits in the judge's chair, peeling an apple.* SHAUWA *is sweeping out the hall. On one side an* INVALID *in a wheelchair. Opposite, a* YOUNG MAN *accused of blackmail. An* IRONSHIRT *stands guard, holding the* IRONSHIRT'S *banner.*)

AZDAK: In consideration of the large number of cases, the Court today will hear two cases at a time. Before I open the proceedings, a short announcement — I accept. (*He stretches out his hand. The* BLACKMAILER *is the only one to produce any money. He hands it to* AZDAK.) I reserve the right to punish one of the parties for contempt of court. (*He glances at the* INVALID.) You (*to the* DOCTOR) are a doctor, and you (*to the* INVALID) are bringing a complaint against him. Is the doctor responsible for your condition?

THE INVALID: Yes. I had a stroke on his account.

AZDAK: That would be professional negligence.

THE INVALID: Worse than negligence. I gave this man money for his studies. So far, he hasn't paid me back a cent. It was when I heard he was treating a patient free that I had my stroke.

AZDAK: Rightly. (*To a* LIMPING MAN.) And what are *you* doing here?

THE LIMPING MAN: I'm the patient, your honor.

AZDAK: He treated your leg for nothing?

THE LIMPING MAN: The wrong leg! My rheumatism was in the left leg, and he operated on the right. That's why I limp now.

AZDAK: And you were treated free?

THE INVALID: A five-hundred-piaster operation free! For nothing! For a God-bless-you! And I paid for this man's studies! (*To* THE DOCTOR.) Did they teach you to operate free?

THE DOCTOR: Your Honor, it is actually the custom to demand the fee before the operation, as the patient is more willing to pay before an operation than after. Which is only human. In the case in question I was convinced, when I started the operation, that my servant had already received the fee. In this I was mistaken.

THE INVALID: He was mistaken! A good doctor doesn't make mistakes! He examines before he operates!

AZDAK: That's right. (*To* SHAUWA.) Public Prosecutor, what's the other case about?

SHAUWA (*busily sweeping*): Blackmail.

THE BLACKMAILER: High Court of Justice, I'm innocent. I only wanted to find out from the landowner concerned if he really *had* raped his niece. He informed me very politely that this was not the case, and gave me the money only so I could pay for my uncle's studies.

AZDAK: Hm. (*To the* DOCTOR.) You, on the other hand, can cite no extenuating circumstances for your offense, huh?

THE DOCTOR: Except that to err is human.

AZDAK: And you are aware that in money matters a good doctor is a highly responsible person? I once heard of a doctor who got a thousand piasters for a sprained finger by remarking that sprains have something to do with blood circulation, which after all a less good doctor might have overlooked, and who, on another occasion made a real gold mine out of a somewhat disordered gall bladder, he treated it with such loving care. You have no excuse, Doctor. The corn merchant, Uxu, had his son study medicine to get some knowledge of trade, our medical schools are so good. (*To the* BLACKMAILER.) What's the landowner's name?

SHAUWA: He doesn't want it mentioned.

AZDAK: In that case I will pass judgment. The Court considers the blackmail proved. And you (*to the* INVALID) are sentenced to a fine of one thousand piasters. If you have a second stroke, the doctor will have to treat you free. Even if he has to amputate. (*To the* LIMPING MAN.) As compensation, you will receive a bottle of rubbing alcohol. (*To the* BLACKMAILER.) You are sentenced to hand over half the proceeds of your deal to the Public Prosecutor to keep the landowner's name secret. You are advised, moreover, to study medicine — you seem well suited to that calling. (*To the* DOCTOR.) You have perpetrated an unpardonable error in the practice of your profession: you are acquitted. Next cases!

THE STORY TELLER AND CHORUS: Men won't do much for a shilling.
For a pound they may be willing.
For 20 pounds the verdict's in the sack.
As for the many, all too many,
Those who've only got a penny —
They've one single, sole recourse: Azdak.

(*Enter* AZDAK *from the caravansary on the highroad, followed by an old bearded* INNKEEPER. *The judge's chair is carried by a* STABLEMAN *and* SHAUWA. *An* IRONSHIRT, *with a banner, takes up his position.*)

AZDAK: Put me down. Then we'll get some air, maybe even a good stiff breeze from the lemon grove there. It does justice good to be done in the open: the wind blows her skirts up and you can see what she's got. Shauwa, we've been eating too much. These official journeys are exhausting. (*To the* INNKEEPER.) It's a question of your daughter-in-law?

THE INNKEEPER: Your Worship, it's a question of the family honor. I wish to bring an action on behalf of my son, who's on business on the other side of the mountain. This is the offending stableman, and here's my daughter-in-law.

(*Enter the* DAUGHTER-IN-LAW, *a voluptuous wench. She is veiled.*)

AZDAK (*sitting down*): I accept. (*Sighing, the* INNKEEPER *hands him some money.*) Good. Now the formalities are disposed of. This is a case of rape?

THE INNKEEPER: Your Honor, I caught the fellow in the act. Ludovica was in the straw on the stable floor.

AZDAK: Quite right, the stable. Lovely horses! I specially liked the little roan.

THE INNKEEPER: The first thing I did, of course, was to question Ludovica. On my son's behalf.

AZDAK (*seriously*): I said I specially liked the little roan.

THE INNKEEPER (*coldly*): Really? Ludovica confessed the stableman took her against her will.

AZDAK: Take your veil off, Ludovica.

(*She does so.*)

Ludovica, you please the Court. Tell us how it happened.

LUDOVICA (*well-schooled*): When I entered the stable to see the new foal the stableman said to me on his own accord: "It's hot today!" and laid his hand on my left breast. I said to him: "Don't do that!" But he continued to handle me indecently, which provoked my anger. Before I realized his sinful intentions, he got much closer. It was all over when my father-in-law entered and accidentally trod on me.

THE INNKEEPER (*explaining*): On my son's behalf.

AZDAK (*to the* STABLEMAN): You admit you started it?

THE STABLEMAN: Yes.

AZDAK: Ludovica, you like to eat sweet things?

LUDOVICA: Yes, sunflower seeds!

AZDAK: You like to lie a long time in the bathtub?

LUDOVICA: Half an hour or so.

AZDAK: Public Prosecutor, drop your knife — there — on the ground.

(SHAUWA *does so.*)

Ludovica, pick up that knife.

(LUDOVICA, *swaying her hips, does so.*)

See that? (*He points at her.*) The way it moves? The rape is now proven. By eating too much — sweet things, especially — by lying too long in warm water, by laziness and too soft a skin, you have raped that unfortunate man. Think you can run around with a behind like that and get away with it in court? This is a case of intentional assault with a dangerous weapon! You are sentenced to hand over to the Court the little roan which your father liked to ride "on his son's behalf." And now, come with me to the stables, so the Court may inspect the scene of the crime, Ludovica.

THE STORY TELLER AND CHORUS: When the sharks the sharks devour
Little fishes have their hour.
For a while the load is off their back.
On Grusinia's highways faring
Fixed-up scales of justice bearing
Strode the poor man's magistrate: Azdak.

And he gave to the forsaken
All that from the rich he'd taken.
And a bodyguard of roughnecks was Azdak's.

And our good and evil man, he
Smiled upon Grusinia's Granny.
His emblem was a tear in sealing wax.

All mankind should love each other
But when visiting your brother
Take an ax along and hold it fast.
Not in theory but in practice
Miracles are wrought with axes
And the age of miracles is not past.

(AZDAK'S *judge's chair is in a tavern. Three* RICH FARMERS *stand before* AZDAK. SHAUWA *brings him wine. In a corner stands an* OLD PEASANT WOMAN. *In the open doorway, and outside, stand* VILLAGERS *looking on. An* IRONSHIRT *stands guard with a banner.*)

AZDAK: The Public Prosecutor has the floor.

SHAUWA: It concerns a cow. For five weeks the defendant has had a cow in her stable, the property of the farmer Suru. She was also found to be in possession of a stolen ham, and a number of cows belonging to Shutoff were killed after he asked the defendant to pay the rent on a piece of land.

THE FARMERS:
— It's a matter of my ham, Your Honor.
— It's a matter of my cow, Your Honor.
— It's a matter of my land, Your Honor.

AZDAK: Well, Granny, what have *you* got to say to all this?

THE OLD WOMAN: Your Honor, one night toward morning, five weeks ago, there was a knock at my door, and outside stood a bearded man with a cow. "My dear woman," he said, "I am the miracle-working Saint Banditus and because your son has been killed in the war, I bring you this cow as a souvenir. Take good care of it."

THE FARMERS:
— The robber, Irakli, Your Honor!
— Her brother-in-law, Your Honor!
— The cow-thief!
— The incendiary!
— He must be beheaded!

(*Outside, a* WOMAN *screams. The* CROWD *grows restless, retreats. Enter the* BANDIT IRAKLI *with a huge ax.*)

THE BANDIT: A very good evening, dear friends! A glass of vodka!

THE FARMERS (*crossing themselves*): Irakli!

AZDAK: Public Prosecutor, a glass of vodka for our guest. And who are you?

THE BANDIT: I'm a wandering hermit, Your Honor. Thanks for the gracious gift. (*He empties the glass which* SHAUWA *has brought.*) Another!

AZDAK: I am Azdak. (*He gets up and bows. The* BANDIT *also bows.*) The Court welcomes the foreign hermit. Go on with your story, Granny.

THE OLD WOMAN: Your Honor, that first night I didn't yet know Saint Banditus could work miracles, it was only the cow. But one night, a few days later, the farmer's servants came to take the cow away again. Then they turned round in front of my door and went off without the cow. And bumps as big as a fist sprouted on their heads. So I knew that Saint Banditus had changed their hearts and turned them into friendly people.

(*The* BANDIT *roars with laughter.*)

THE FIRST FARMER: I know what changed them.

AZDAK: That's fine. You can tell us later. Continue.

THE OLD WOMAN: Your Honor, the next one to become a good man was the farmer Shutoff — a devil, as everyone knows. But Saint Banditus arranged it so he let me off the rent on the little piece of land.

THE SECOND FARMER: Because my cows were killed in the field.

(*The* BANDIT *laughs.*)

THE OLD WOMAN (*answering* AZDAK'S *sign to continue*): Then one morning the ham came flying in at my window. It hit me in the small of the back. I'm still lame, Your Honor, look. (*She limps a few steps.*)

(*The* BANDIT *laughs.*)

Your Honor, was there ever a time when a poor old woman could get a ham *without* a miracle?

(*The* BANDIT *starts sobbing.*)

AZDAK (*rising from his chair*): Granny, that's a question that strikes straight at the Court's heart. Be so kind as to sit here.

(*The* OLD WOMAN, *hesitating, sits in the judge's chair.*)

ADZAK (*sits on the floor, glass in hand, reciting*): Granny
We could almost call you Granny Grusinia
The Woebegone

The Bereaved Mother
Whose sons have gone to war
Receiving the present of a cow
She bursts out crying.
When she is beaten
She remains hopeful.
When she's not beaten
She's surprised.
On us
Who are already damned
May you render a merciful verdict
Granny Grusinia!

(*Bellowing at* THE FARMERS.) Admit you don't believe in miracles, you atheists! Each of you is sentenced to pay five hundred piasters! For godlessness! Get out!

(*The* FARMERS *slink out.*)

And you Granny, and you (*to the* BANDIT) pious man, empty a pitcher of wine with the Public Prosecutor and Azdak!

THE STORY TELLER AND CHORUS: And he broke the rules to save them.
Broken law like bread he gave them,
Brought them to shore upon his crooked back.
At long last the poor and lowly
Had someone who was not too holy
To be bribed by empty hands: Azdak.

For two years it was his pleasure
To give the beasts of prey short measure:
He became a wolf to fight the pack.
From All Hallows to All Hallows
On his chair beside the gallows
Dispensing justice in his fashion sat Azdak.

THE STORY TELLER: But the era of disorder came to an end.
The Grand Duke returned.
The Governor's wife returned.
A trial was held.
Many died.
The people's quarters burned anew.
And fear seized Azdak.

(AZDAK'*s judge's chair stands again in the court of justice.* AZDAK *sits on the floor, shaving and talking to* SHAUWA. *Noises outside. In the rear the* FAT PRINCE'*s head is carried by on a lance.*)

AZDAK: Shauwa, the days of your slavery are numbered, maybe even the minutes. For a long time now I have held you in the iron curb of reason, and it has torn your mouth till it bleeds. I have lashed you with reasonable arguments, I have manhandled you with logic. You are by nature a weak man, and if one slyly throws an argument in your path, you *have* to snap it up, you can't resist. It is your nature to lick the hand of some superior being. But superior beings can be of very different kinds. And now, with your liberation, you will soon be able to follow your natural inclinations, which are low. You will be able to follow your infallible instinct, which teaches you to plant your fat heel on the faces of men. Gone is the era of confusion and disorder, which I find described in the Song of Chaos. Let us now sing that song together in memory of those terrible days. Sit down and don't do violence to the music. Don't be afraid. It sounds all right. And it has a fine refrain. (*He sings.*)

The Song of Chaos

Sister, hide your face! Brother, take your knife!
The times are out of joint!
Big men are full of complaint
And small men full of joy.
The city says:
"Let us drive the strong ones from our midst!"
Offices are raided. Lists of serfs are destroyed.
They have set Master's nose to the grindstone.
They who lived in the dark have seen the light.
The ebony poor box is broken.
Sesnem wood is sawed up for beds.
Who had no bread have barns full.
Who begged for alms of corn now mete it out.
SHAUWA (*refrain*): Oh, oh, oh, oh.
AZDAK (*refrain*): Where are you, General, where are you?
Please, please, please, restore order!

The nobleman's son can no longer be recognized;
The lady's child becomes the son of her slave.
The councilors meet in a shed.
Once, this man was barely allowed to sleep on the wall;
Now, he stretches his limbs in a bed.
Once, this man rowed a boat; now, he owns ships.
Their owner looks for them, but they're his no longer.
Five men are sent on a journey by their master.
"Go yourself," they say, "we have arrived."

SHAUWA (*refrain*): Oh, oh, oh, oh.
AZDAK (*refrain*): Where are you, General, where are you?
Please, please, please, restore order!

Yes, so it might have been, had order been neglected much longer. But now the Grand Duke has returned to the capital, and the Persians have lent him an army to restore order with. The suburbs are already aflame. Go and get me the big book I always sit on.

(SHAUWA *brings the big book from the judge's chair.* AZDAK *opens it.*)

This is the Statute Book and I've always used it, as you can testify. Now I'd better look in this book and see what they can do to me. I've let the down-and-outs get away with murder, and I'll have to pay for it. I helped poverty onto its skinny legs, so they'll hang me for drunkenness. I peeped into the rich man's pocket, which is bad taste. And I can't hide anywhere — everybody knows me because I've helped everybody.

SHAUWA: Someone's coming!

AZDAK (*in panic, he walks trembling to the chair*): It's the end. And now they'd enjoy seeing what a Great Man I am. I'll deprive them of that pleasure. I'll beg on my knees for mercy. Spittle will slobber down my chin. The fear of death is in me.

(*Enter* NATELLA ABASHWILI, *the* GOVERNOR'S WIFE, *followed by the* ADJUTANT *and an* IRONSHIRT.)

THE GOVERNOR'S WIFE: What sort of a creature is that, Shalva?

AZDAK: A willing one, Your Highness, a man ready to oblige.

THE ADJUTANT: Natella Abashwili, wife of the late Governor, has just returned. She is looking for her two-year-old son, Michael. She has been informed that the child was carried off to the mountains by a former servant.

AZDAK: The child will be brought back, Your Highness, at your service.

THE ADJUTANT: They say that the person in question is passing it off as her own.

AZDAK: She will be beheaded, Your Highness, at your service.

THE ADJUTANT: That is all.

THE GOVERNOR'S WIFE (*leaving*): I don't like that man.

AZDAK (*following her to door, bowing*): At your service, Your Highness, it will all be arranged.

5. The Chalk Circle

THE STORY TELLER: Hear now the story of the trial
Concerning Governor Abashwili's child
And the establishing of the true mother
By the famous test of the Chalk Circle.

(*The court of justice in Nuka.* IRONSHIRTS *lead* MICHAEL *across stage and out at the back.* IRONSHIRTS *hold* GRUSHA *back with their lances under the gateway until the* CHILD *has been led through. Then she is admitted. She is accompanied by the former governor's* COOK. *Distant noises and a fire-red sky.*)

GRUSHA (*trying to hide*): He's brave, he can wash himself now.

THE COOK: You're lucky. It's not a real judge. It's Azdak, a drunk who doesn't know what he's doing. The biggest thieves have got by through him. Because he gets everything mixed up and the rich never offer him big enough bribes, the likes of us sometimes do pretty well.

GRUSHA: I *need* luck right now.

THE COOK: Touch wood. (*She crosses herself.*) I'd better offer up another prayer that the judge may be drunk. (*She prays with motionless lips, while* GRUSHA *looks around, in vain, for the child.*) Why must you hold on to him at any price if he isn't yours? In days like these?

GRUSHA: He's mine. I brought him up.

THE COOK: Have you never thought what'd happen when she came back?

GRUSHA: At first I thought I'd give him to her. Then I thought she wouldn't come back.

THE COOK: And even a borrowed coat keeps a man warm, hm?

(GRUSHA *nods.*)

I'll swear to anything for you. You're a decent girl. (*She sees the soldier* SIMON SHASHAVA *approaching.*) You've done wrong by Simon, though. I've been talking with him. He just can't understand.

GRUSHA (*unaware of* SIMON'S *presence*): Right now I can't be bothered whether he understands or not!

THE COOK: He knows the child isn't yours, but you married and not free "til death you do part"—he can't understand *that.*

(GRUSHA *sees* SIMON *and greets him.*)

SIMON (*gloomily*): I wish the lady to know I will swear I am the father of the child.
GRUSHA (*low*): Thank you, Simon.
SIMON: At the same time I wish the lady to know my hands are not tied — nor are hers.
THE COOK: You needn't have said that. You know she's married.
SIMON: And it needs no rubbing in.

(*Enter an* IRONSHIRT.)

THE IRONSHIRT: Where's the judge? Has anyone seen the judge?
ANOTHER IRONSHIRT (*stepping forward*): The judge isn't here yet. Nothing but a bed and a pitcher in the whole house!

(*Exeunt* IRONSHIRTS.)

THE COOK: I hope nothing has happened to him. With any other judge you'd have about as much chance as a chicken has teeth.
GRUSHA (*who has turned away and covered her face*): Stand in front of me. I shouldn't have come to Nuka. If I run into the Ironshirt, the one I hit over the head . . .

(*She screams. An* IRONSHIRT *had stopped and, turning his back, had been listening to her. He now wheels around. It is the* CORPORAL, *and he has a huge scar across his face.*)

THE IRONSHIRT (*in the gateway*): What's the matter, Shotta? Do you know her?
THE CORPORAL (*after staring for some time*): No.
THE IRONSHIRT: She's the one who stole the Abashwili child, or so they say. If you know anything about it you can make some money, Shotta.

(*Exit the* CORPORAL, *cursing.*)

THE COOK: Was it him? (GRUSHA *nods.*) I think he'll keep his mouth shut, or he'd be admitting he was after the child.
GRUSHA: I'd almost forgotten him.

(*Enter the* GOVERNOR'S WIFE, *followed by the* ADJUTANT *and two* LAWYERS.)

THE GOVERNOR'S WIFE: At least there are no common people here, thank God. I can't stand their smell. It always gives me migraine.
THE FIRST LAWYER: Madam, I must ask you to be careful what you say until we have another judge.
THE GOVERNOR'S WIFE: But I didn't say anything, Illo Shuboladze. I

love the people with their simple straightforward minds. It's only that their smell brings on my migraine.

THE SECOND LAWYER: There won't be many spectators. The whole population is sitting at home behind locked doors because of the riots on the outskirts of town.

THE GOVERNOR'S WIFE (*looking at* GRUSHA): Is that the creature?

THE FIRST LAWYER: Please, most gracious Natella Abashwili, abstain from invective until it is certain the Grand Duke has appointed a new judge and we're rid of the present one, who's about the lowest fellow ever seen in judge's gown. Things are all set to move, you see.

(*Enter* IRONSHIRTS *from the courtyard.*)

THE COOK: Her Grace would pull your hair out on the spot if she didn't know Azdak is for the poor. He goes by the face.

(IRONSHIRTS *begin fastening a rope to a beam.* AZDAK, *in chains, is led in, followed by* SHAUWA, *also in chains. The three* FARMERS *bring up the rear.*)

AN IRONSHIRT: Trying to run away, were you? (*He strikes* AZDAK.)

ONE FARMER: Off with his judge's gown before we string him up!

(IRONSHIRTS *and* FARMERS *tear off* AZDAK'S *gown. His torn underwear is visible. Then someone kicks him.*)

AN IRONSHIRT (*pushing him into someone else*): If you want a heap of justice, here it is!

(*Accompanied by shouts of "You take it!" and "Let me have him, Brother!" they throw* AZDAK *back and forth until he collapses. Then he is lifted up and dragged under the noose.*)

THE GOVERNOR'S WIFE (*who, during this "Ball-game," has clapped her hands hysterically*): I disliked that man from the moment I first saw him.

AZDAK (*covered with blood, panting*): I can't see. Give me a rag.

AN IRONSHIRT: What is it you want to see?

AZDAK: You, you dogs! (*He wipes the blood out of his eyes with his shirt.*) Good morning, dogs! How goes it, dogs! How's the dog world? Does it smell good? Got another boot for me to lick? Are you back at each other's throats, dogs?

(*Accompanied by a* CORPORAL, *a dust-covered* RIDER *enters. He takes some documents from a leather case, looks at them, then interrupts.*)

THE RIDER: Stop! I bring a dispatch from the Grand Duke, containing the latest appointments.

THE CORPORAL (*bellowing*): Atten - shun!

THE RIDER: Of the new judge it says: "We appoint a man whom we have to thank for saving a life indispensable to the country's welfare — a certain Azdak of Nuka." Which is he?

SHAUWA (*pointing*): That's him, Your Excellency.

THE CORPORAL (*bellowing*): What's going on here?

AN IRONSHIRT: I beg to report that His Honor Azdak was already His Honor Azdak, but on these farmers' denunciation was pronounced the Grand Duke's enemy.

THE CORPORAL (*pointing at the* FARMERS): March them off! (*They are marched off. They bow all the time.*) See to it that His Honor Azdak is exposed to no more violence.

(*Exeunt* RIDER *and* CORPORAL.)

THE COOK (*to* SHAUWA): She clapped her hands! I hope he saw it!

THE FIRST LAWYER: It's a catastrophe.

(AZDAK *has fainted. Coming to, he is dressed again in judge's robes. He walks, swaying, toward the* IRONSHIRTS.)

AN IRONSHIRT: What does Your Honor desire?

AZDAK: Nothing, fellow dogs, or just an occasional boot to lick. (*To* SHAUWA.) I pardon you. (*He is unchained.*) Get me some red wine, the sweet kind. (SHAUWA *stumbles off.*) Get out of here, I've got to judge a case.

(*Exeunt* IRONSHIRTS. SHAUWA *returns with a pitcher of wine.* AZDAK *gulps it down.*)

Something for my backside. (SHAUWA *brings the Statute Book, puts it on the judge's chair.* AZDAK *sits on it.*) I accept.

(*The* PROSECUTORS, *among whom a worried council has been held, smile with relief. They whisper.*)

THE COOK: Oh dear!

SIMON: A well can't be filled with dew, they say.

THE LAWYERS (*approaching* AZDAK, *who stands up, expectantly*): A quite ridiculous case, Your Honor. The accused has abducted a child and refuses to hand it over.

AZDAK (*stretching out his hand, glancing at* GRUSHA): A most attractive person. (*He fingers the money, then sits down, satisfied.*) I declare the proceedings open and demand the whole truth. (*To* GRUSHA.) Especially from you.

THE FIRST LAWYER: High Court of Justice! Blood, as the popular saying goes, is thicker than water. This old adage . . .

AZDAK (*interrupting*): The Court wants to know the lawyers' fee.

THE FIRST LAWYER (*surprised*): I beg your pardon?

(AZDAK, *smiling, rubs his thumb and index finger.*)

Oh, I see. Five hundred piasters, Your Honor, to answer the Court's somewhat unusual question.

AZDAK: Did you hear? The question is unusual. I ask it because I listen in quite a different way when I know you're good.

THE FIRST LAWYER (*bowing*): Thank you, Your Honor. High Court of Justice, of all ties the ties of blood are strongest. Mother and child — is there a more intimate relationship? Can one tear a child from its mother? High Court of Justice, she has conceived it in the holy ecstasies of love. She has carried it in her womb. She has fed it with her blood. She has borne it with pain. High Court of Justice, it has been observed that even the wild tigress, robbed of her young, roams restless through the mountains, shrunk to a shadow. Nature herself . . .

AZDAK (*interrupting, to* GRUSHA): What's your answer to all this and anything else that lawyer might have to say?

GRUSHA: He's mine.

AZDAK: Is that all? I hope you can prove it. Why should I assign the child to you in any case?

GRUSHA: I brought him up like the priest says "according to my best knowledge and conscience." I always found him something to eat. Most of the time he had a roof over his head. And I went to such trouble for him. I had expenses too. I didn't look out for my own comfort. I brought the child up to be friendly with everyone, and from the beginning taught him to work. As well as he could, that is. He's still very little.

THE FIRST LAWYER: Your Honor, it is significant that the girl herself doesn't claim any tie of blood between her and the child.

AZDAK: The Court takes note of that.

THE FIRST LAWYER: Thank you, Your Honor. And now permit a woman bowed in sorrow — who has already lost her husband and now has also to fear the loss of her child — to address a few words to you. The gracious Natella Abashwili is . . .

THE GOVERNOR'S WIFE (*quietly*): A most cruel fate, Sir, forces me to describe to you the tortures of a bereaved mother's soul, the anxiety, the sleepless nights, the . . .

THE SECOND LAWYER (*bursting out*): It's outrageous the way this woman is being treated! Her husband's palace is closed to her! The revenue of her estates is blocked, and she is cold-bloodedly told that it's tied to the heir. She can't do a thing without that child. She can't even pay her lawyers! (*To the* FIRST LAWYER, *who, desperate about this outburst, makes frantic gestures to keep him from speaking.*) Dear Illo Shuboladze, surely it can be divulged now that the Abashwili estates are at stake?

THE FIRST LAWYER: Please, Honored Sandro Oboladze! We agreed . . . (*To* AZDAK.) Of course it is correct that the trial will also decide if our noble client can dispose of the Abashwili estates, which are rather extensive. I say "also" advisedly, for in the foreground stands the human tragedy of a mother, as Natella Abashwili very properly explained in the first words of her moving statement. Even if Michael Abashwili were not heir to the estates, he would still be the dearly beloved child of my client.

AZDAK: Stop! The Court is touched by the mention of estates. It's a proof of human feeling.

THE SECOND LAWYER: Thanks, Your Honor. Dear Illo Shuboladze, we can prove in any case that the woman who took the child is not the child's mother. Permit me to lay before the Court the bare facts. High Court of Justice, by an unfortunate chain of circumstances, Michael Abashwili was left behind on that Easter Sunday while his mother was making her escape. Grusha, a palace kitchen maid, was seen with the baby . . .

THE COOK: All her mistress was thinking of was what dresses she'd take along!

THE SECOND LAWYER (*unmoved*): Nearly a year later Grusha turned up in a mountain village with a baby and there entered into the state of matrimony with . . .

AZDAK: How did you get to that mountain village?

GRUSHA: On foot, Your Honor. And it was mine.

SIMON: I am the father, Your Honor.

THE COOK: I used to look after it for them, Your Honor. For five piasters.

THE SECOND LAWYER: This man is engaged to Grusha, High Court of Justice: his testimony is not trustworthy.

AZDAK: Are you the man she married in the mountain village?

SIMON: No, Your Honor, she married a peasant.

AZDAK (*to* GRUSHA): Why? (*Pointing at* SIMON.) Is he no good in bed? Tell the truth.

GRUSHA: We didn't get that far. I married because of the baby. So it'd have a roof over his head. (*Pointing at* SIMON.) He was in the war, Your Honor.

AZDAK: And now he wants you back again, huh?

SIMON: I wish to state in evidence . . .
GRUSHA (*angrily*): I am no longer free, Your Honor.
AZDAK: And the child, you claim, comes from whoring?

(GRUSHA *doesn't answer.*)

I'm going to ask you a question: What kind of child is it? Is it a ragged little bastard or from a well-to-do family?
GRUSHA (*angrily*): He's just an ordinary child.
AZDAK: I mean — did he have refined features from the beginning?
GRUSHA: He had a nose on his face.
AZDAK: A very significant comment! It has been said of me that I went out one time and sniffed at a rosebush before rendering a verdict — tricks like that are needed nowadays. Well, I'll make it short, and not listen to any more lies. (*To* GRUSHA.) Especially not yours. (*To all the accused.*) I can imagine what you've cooked up to cheat me! I know you people. You're swindlers.
GRUSHA (*suddenly*): I can understand your wanting to cut it short, now I've seen what you accepted!
AZDAK: Shut up! Did I accept anything from you?
GRUSHA (*while the* COOK *tries to restrain her*): I haven't got anything.
AZDAK: True. Quite true. From starvelings I never get a thing. I might just as well starve, myself. You want justice, but do you want to pay for it, hm? When you go to a butcher you know you have to pay, but you people go to a judge as if you were going to a funeral supper.
SIMON (*loudly*): When the horse was shod, the horse-fly held out its leg, as the saying is.
AZDAK (*eagerly accepting the challenge*): Better a treasure in manure than a stone in a mountain stream.
SIMON: A fine day. Let's go fishing, said the angler to the worm.
AZDAK: I'm my own master, said the servant, and cut off his foot.
SIMON: I love you as a father, said the Czar to the peasants, and had the Czarevitch's head chopped off.
AZDAK: A fool's worst enemy is himself.
SIMON: However, a fart has no nose.
AZDAK: Fined ten piasters for indecent language in court! That'll teach you what justice is.
GRUSHA (*furiously*): A fine kind of justice! You play fast and loose with us because we don't talk as refined as that crowd with their lawyers!
AZDAK: That's true. You people are too dumb. It's only right you should get it in the neck.
GRUSHA: You want to hand the child over to her, and she wouldn't

even know how to keep it dry, she's so "refined"! You know about as much about justice as I do!

AZDAK: There's something in that. I'm an ignorant man. Haven't even a decent pair of pants on under this gown. Look! With me, everything goes for food and drink — I was educated at a convent. Incidentally, I'll fine you ten piasters for contempt of court. And you're a very silly girl, to turn me against you, instead of making eyes at me and wiggling your backside a little to keep me in a good temper. Twenty piasters!

GRUSHA: Even if it was thirty, I'd tell you what I think of your justice, you drunken onion! (*Incoherently.*) How dare you talk to me like the cracked Isaiah on the church window? As if you were somebody? For you weren't born to this. You weren't born to rap your own mother on the knuckles if she swipes a little bowl of salt someplace. Aren't you ashamed of yourself when you see how I tremble before you? You've made yourself their servant so no one will take their houses from them — houses they had stolen! Since when have houses belonged to the bedbugs? But you're on the watch, or they couldn't drag our men into their wars! You bribe-taker!

(AZDAK *half gets up, starts beaming. With his little hammer he half-heartedly knocks on the table as if to get silence. As* GRUSHA'S *scolding continues, he only beats time with his hammer.*)

I've no respect for you. No more than for a thief or a bandit with a knife! You can do what you want. You can take the child away from me, a hundred against one, but I tell you one thing: only extortioners should be chosen for a profession like yours, and men who rape children! As punishment! Yes, let *them* sit in judgment on their fellow creatures. It is worse than to hang from the gallows.

AZDAK (*sitting down*): Now it'll be thirty! And I won't go on squabbling with you — we're not in a tavern. What'd happen to my dignity as a judge? Anyway, I've lost interest in your case. Where's the couple who wanted a divorce? (*To* SHAUWA.) Bring 'em in. This case is adjourned for fifteen minutes.

THE FIRST LAWYER (*to the* GOVERNOR'S WIFE): Even without using the rest of the evidence, Madam, we have the verdict in the bag.

THE COOK (*to* GRUSHA): You've gone and spoiled your chances with him. You won't get the child now.

THE GOVERNOR'S WIFE: Shalva, my smelling salts!

(*Enter a* VERY OLD COUPLE.)

AZDAK: I accept.

(*The* OLD COUPLE *don't understand.*)

I hear you want to be divorced. How long have you been together?

THE OLD WOMAN: Forty years, Your Honor.

AZDAK: And why do you want a divorce?

THE OLD MAN: We don't like each other, Your Honor.

AZDAK: Since when?

THE OLD WOMAN: Oh, from the very beginning, Your Honor.

AZDAK: I'll think about your request and render my verdict when I'm through with the other case.

(SHAUWA *leads them back.*)

I need the child. (*He beckons* GRUSHA *to and bends not unkindly toward her.*) I've noticed you have a soft spot for justice. I don't believe he's your child, but if he *were* yours, woman, wouldn't you want him to be rich? You'd only have to say he wasn't yours, and he'd have a palace and many horses in his stable and many beggars on his doorstep and many soldiers in his service and many petitioners in his courtyard, wouldn't he? What do you say — don't you want him to be rich?

(GRUSHA *is silent.*)

THE STORY TELLER: Hear now what the angry girl thought but did not say:

Had he golden shoes to wear
He'd be cruel as a bear.
Evil would his life disgrace.
He'd laugh in my face.

Carrying a heart of flint
Is too troublesome a stint.
Being powerful and bad
Is hard on a lad.

Then let hunger be his foe!
Hungry men and women, no.
Let him fear the darksome night
But not daylight!

AZDAK: I think I understand you, woman.

GRUSHA (*suddenly and loudly*): I won't give him up. I've raised him, and he knows me.

(*Enter* SHAUWA *with the* CHILD.)

THE GOVERNOR'S WIFE: It's in rags!

GRUSHA: That's not true. But I wasn't given time to put his good shirt on.

THE GOVERNOR'S WIFE: It must have been in a pigsty.

GRUSHA (*furiously*): I'm not a pig, but there are some who are! Where did you leave your baby?

THE GOVERNOR'S WIFE: I'll show you, you vulgar creature! (*She is about to throw herself on* GRUSHA, *but is restrained by her* LAWYERS.) She's a criminal, she must be whipped. Immediately!

THE SECOND LAWYER (*holding his hand over her mouth*): Natella Abashwili, you promised . . . Your Honor, the plaintiff's nerves.

AZDAK: Plaintiff and defendant! The Court has listened to your case, and has come to no decision as to who the real mother is, therefore, I, the judge, am obliged to *choose* a mother for the child. I'll make a test. Shauwa, get a piece of chalk and draw a circle on the floor.

(SHAUWA *does so.*)

Now place the child in the center.

(SHAUWA *puts* MICHAEL, *who smiles at* GRUSHA, *in the center of the circle.*)

Stand near the circle, both of you.

(*The* GOVERNOR'S WIFE *and* GRUSHA *step up to the circle.*)

Now each of you take the child by one hand.

(*They do so.*)

The true mother is she who can pull the child out of the circle.

THE SECOND LAWYER (*quickly*): High Court of Justice, I object! The fate of the great Abashwili estates, which are tied to the child, as the heir, should not be made dependent on such a doubtful duel. In addition, my client does not command the strength of this person, who is accustomed to physical work.

AZDAK: She looks pretty well fed to me. Pull!

(*The* GOVERNOR'S WIFE *pulls the* CHILD *out of the circle on her side;* GRUSHA *has let go and stands aghast.*)

What's the matter with you? You didn't pull!

GRUSHA: I didn't hold on to him.

THE FIRST LAWYER (*congratulating the* GOVERNOR'S WIFE): What did I say! The ties of blood!

GRUSHA (*running to* AZDAK): Your Honor, I take back everything I said against you. I ask your forgiveness. But could I keep him till he can speak all the words? He knows a few.

AZDAK: Don't influence the Court. I bet you only know about twenty words yourself. All right, I'll make the test once more, just to be certain.

(*The two women take up their positions again.*)

Pull!

(*Again* GRUSHA *lets go of the* CHILD.)

GRUSHA (*in despair*): I brought him up! Shall I also tear him to pieces? I can't!

AZDAK (*rising*): And in this manner the Court has established the true mother. (*To* GRUSHA.) Take your child and be off. I advise you not to stay in the city with him. (*To the* GOVERNOR'S WIFE.) And you disappear before I fine you for fraud. Your estates fall to the city. They'll be converted into a playground for the children. They need one, and I've decided it shall be called after me: Azdak's Garden.

(*The* GOVERNOR'S WIFE *has fainted and is carried out by the* LAWYERS *and the* ADJUTANT. GRUSHA *stands motionless.* SHAUWA *leads the* CHILD *toward her.*)

Now I'll take off this judge's gown — it's grown too hot for me. I'm not cut out for a hero. In token of farewell I invite you all to a little dance outside on the meadow. Oh, I'd almost forgotten something in my excitement . . . to sign the divorce decree.

(*Using the judge's chair as a table, he writes something on a piece of paper, and prepares to leave. Dance music has started.*)

SHAUWA (*having read what is on the paper*): But that's not right. You've not divorced the old people. You've divorced Grusha!

AZDAK: Have I divorced the wrong couple? What a pity! And I never retract! If I did, how could we keep order in the land? (*To the* OLD COUPLE.) I'll invite you to my party instead. You don't mind dancing with each other, do you? (*To* GRUSHA *and* SIMON.) I've got forty piasters coming from you.

SIMON (*pulling out his purse*): Cheap at the price, Your Honor. And many thanks.

AZDAK (*pocketing the cash*): I'll be needing this.

GRUSHA (*to* MICHAEL): So we'd better leave the city tonight, Michael? (*To* SIMON.) You like him?

SIMON: With my respects, I like him.

GRUSHA: Now I can tell you: I took him because on that Easter Sunday I got engaged to you. So he's a child of love. Michael, let's dance.

(*She dances with* MICHAEL, SIMON *dances with the* COOK, *the* OLD COUPLE *with each other.* AZDAK *stands lost in thought. The dancers soon hide him from view. Occasionally he is seen, but less and less as more couples join the dance.*)

THE STORY TELLER: And after that evening Azdak vanished and was never seen again.
The people of Grusinia did not forget him but long remembered
The period of his judging as a brief golden age,
Almost an age of justice.

(*All the couples dance off.* AZDAK *has disappeared.*)

But you, you who have listened to the Story of the Chalk Circle,
Take note what men of old concluded:
That what there is shall go to those who are good for it,
Children to the motherly, that they prosper,
Carts to good drivers, that they be driven well,
The valley to the waterers, that it yield fruit.

SIMPLICITY in art, says Eric Bentley in his Introduction to *Seven Plays by Bertolt Brecht*, may be an achievement on the far side of complexity. It is an apt comment. In Brecht, we sense the design not as something innocent of or defiant of disorder but as immanent in it and the artistic process as revelatory rather than creative. The parable — the term is Brecht's own — emerges from the crowded bustle on the stage with the clarity and strength of a folk tale. His art is at the opposite end from classical realism. Whereas Ibsen's stage has the stability of a room, Brecht's is open and like Shakespeare's momently capable of becoming any place the imagination calls for. The inclusive dramatic form, fluid rather than unrealistic, embeds the moral scheme of the fable in the promiscuous flux of actuality, but the scheme disciplines the flux to directed movement. Parable, almost but never quite becoming abstract scheme, balanced against stage activity, almost but never quite becoming chaos, provides inner tension. The surface naïveté masks a technique that orders a vast and subtle content.

If Brecht is a difficult playwright, he has been made even more difficult by the labels of "Marxism" and "epic theater" (also his own term) with which his plays are commonly tagged. The tags would do less harm if they were simply wrong; then they could be removed. They are not wrong, however, but intrusive and misleading. They stop thought and trigger stock responses. We react, not to drama, but to political system and esthetic theory. Like all fables, Brecht's are concentrates of large and various experience. But the narrative that embodies the general pattern is not abstract. "Marxist" points to certain consistent value orientations evident in the plays and "epic" to certain distinctive ways of using the theater. But the labels say nothing about the particulars of plot and scenic reality which the Marxist outlook and the epic form shape into the pattern of fable. The journey motif in Grusha's story is a version of epic, but it is the particulars of the human and physical obstacles she encounters and the rhythm and direction of her progress, rather than the mere fact of narrative, that turn her journey into a superb theatrical demonstration of the "terribleness" of "the seductive power of goodness." The Azdak figure, the proletarian scamp-judge, whose moral superiority is that of the rabbit-eater over the man-eater, challenges propertied stuffiness and arrogance, legalism and feudal tyranny. There is revolutionary sentiment in the muted anger of his "Song of Injustice in Persia" and in the triumphant sarcasm of his "Song of Chaos." The old legend could be called proto-Marxist. But as a general concept Marxism is more of a hindrance than a help in a critical account of Azdak. His cowardice, vulgarity, and greed, his old cheese, bloody rags, and dirty, drunken jokes, the tragicomical implications of his futile self-condemnation for helping the Grand Duke to escape, the ironic fickleness of fortune by which he becomes first a mock, then a real, judge, then almost loses his neck, and then is reinstated as judge — are these, as scenic facts, "Marxist"?

The point, of course, is that a literary work does not contain ideology the way a pudding contains plums or even the way a cake contains butter. As a theoretical materialist Brecht wanted a more equitable distribution of economic goods and potential, and he believed in man's duty to try to improve his physical environment, and hence his conditioning, to the limit of his ability and control. Having tried Hollywood, he settled in East Berlin. But the problem of Marxism-in-Brecht is not solved by biography or by anxious search for pellets of subversive doctrine. Is property good or evil in *The Caucasian Chalk Circle* (1944-45)? Almost everyone in the play who owns anything is hard-hearted, not just the feudal masters, but the peasants as well: the farmer who sells Grusha milk, Lavrenti's wife, the mother-in-law, the Invalid, the three farmers charging the old woman with theft. But then we come upon Azdak taking bribes as a matter of course and Simon Shashava being able to marry Grusha because he has been promoted to paymaster at double his earlier pay and with a house of his own. Does the play say that riches corrupt? It is less presumptuous. It says that Grusha thinks that little Michael would be corrupted if he were brought up by Natella Abashwili — a much smaller and dramatically more serviceable proposition. Is there political dynamite in Azdak's epigram, "That the roof of the world may be conquered, the roof of the cottage is torn down"? A cold-war attitude? If Azdak's awarding the child to Grusha is taken to imply an attack on property rights, doesn't "Capitalism" come to seem incompatible with kindness and common sense? Brecht gives a new twist to the old story of the Solomonic test of mother's love. The comfortable assumption used to be that none but the child's real mother would sooner give up her right to the child than cause it pain. But here the natural mother is unnatural, the foster mother truly motherly. The new version (a verse Prologue Bentley has written for the play says) naggingly involves the larger question of who owns anything, "and by what right"? Is this Marxism? — or political disillusionment? The whole inquiry breaks down.

We are aware, rather, of what Brecht perhaps had in mind when he once referred to Azdak's "tragic side." There is in the crude farce of his magistracy the truth that all even *his* shrewd folk wisdom achieved was "*almost* an age of justice." Does the fault lie with his justice or with the "dog's world" in which he is a judge? Isn't he a bit of a brute himself? And even if we assume that the lesson which the two kolkhozes learn from the story of Azdak is an absolute, the modern valley setting, with evidence of Nazi ravage all around, is onstage proof that events rarely follow the rule "That what there is shall go to those who are good for it." The legend of the good judge is, after all, only an old legend.

The fact that "epic theater," unlike "Marxism," raises *literary* issues only increases the risk of hiding the play behind a label. "Epic" is misleading if it is taken to imply that Brecht's plays are undramatic ("epic" denoting a genre distinct from "drama" and "lyric"). Their solidly dimensional world can be staged in its entirety, unlike the world of novels, and by the same token is not an introspected world, like that of lyrics. "Epic" is misleading also if it suggests the slow and stately pace, the richness of reference, the elevated diction, the formulas of image and rhetoric, the mythological machinery, and the magnitude of theme, of classical or Miltonic epics.

What the term *should* denote is a drama that breaks the old five- or three-act structure and proceeds by something resembling the "stations" of the guild performances of medieval mystery and miracle plays: staged episodes in discontinuous but progressive narrative sequence. The filmic elements of large and changing cast, variety of setting, brevity of scene, and use of flashback (in the early Azdak scenes) also give a kind of epic effect.

But the main reason for calling Brecht's drama epic is that it is narrated. Like the kolkhoz farmers we are in the hands of Arkadi Tscheidse, the professional story teller from Tiflis. What we see of Grusha's and Azdak's stories are eposodes selected for dramatization from a larger entertainment-with-a-purpose, which also includes choric comment and the narrator's linking synopses. The episodes are, literally, *shown*. The audience understands that it does not see the characters of the legend themselves, but their twentieth-century impersonators.

Clearly, we are dealing here with a play convention quite different from that of the realist theater. By realist convention, we are unobserved observers of real life in the process of being lived — peepers and eavesdroppers. We are invited to believe, or to pretend to believe, that the actors are not actors but businessmen and housewives, that their talk is not rehearsed but spontaneous, that they are not on a stage but in an apartment. The realist convention paradoxically denies the fact of theater. As audience we get our money's worth only if we are willing to share the denial. A realist play production, we say, is successful in direct ratio to the success with which it entices us into the make-believe and keeps us here till the curtain comes down, the lights go on, and the illusion ends.

Brecht openly violates the realist convention. So does Pirandello in *Six Characters*, but what is a crucial metaphor for probing the reality of reality in Pirandello — the subject of his play — is in Brecht a casual premise for having theater at all. The devices he employs to prevent illusionism ensure theatricality.

In *The Caucasian Chalk Circle* both the most obvious and the most important of these devices is the framing of the main action in a play-within-a-play form. The device is not new. Shakespeare (for example) used it in *The Taming of the Shrew* and Beaumont in *The Knight of the Burning Pestle*. Again, *Six Characters* is the most famous example in the modern theater. However dissimilar such plays may be, they all have in common the effect they give of the theater being conscious of itself — an effect (as we already found in Pirandello) ambiguous, paradoxical, and elusive. Does the spectacle of art mocking art *as* art hint at a reaffirmation of the seriousness of art as true to life? Theatricalism, at any rate, produces a much subtler stage-audience relationship than does dramatic realism. In *The Chalk Circle* an audience in the theater watches an audience on stage, and both then watch — not a play of present life but a dramatization–narration of past legend.* The familiar but profound pun on the two meanings of the verb "to act" comes alive as the characters in the play-within "live" their theatrical existence.

Verfremdung (literally, "alienation," but most often rendered as "distancing" or "esthetic distancing") is Brecht's own term for the effect on the audience of this insistent theatricality. Its function is to keep the spectator's rational faculties alert during the performance. Brecht seeks from his audience not a spellbinding imaginative projection into the life illusion on stage, but thoughtful attention to a meaningful dramatization of fable. He wants to reach minds, not to submerge them in a wash of stage-generated empathy. "I am not," he said, "greatly interested in anyone making an emotional investment in my plays." This does not mean that he fails whenever an audience gives Grusha and Azdak its sympathies or finds the play charming. It means that he uses emotional appeal as a strategy of persuasion — as a means to a rational end, not as an end in itself.

And yet, the ultimate effect of *Verfremdung* is perhaps more complex than Brecht's deliberate aim would indicate. The ambivalent status of the stage audience tends to obscure the distinction between stage and audience. From the viewpoint of the theater audience the stage audience are characters in the outer (framing) action. From the viewpoint of the performers in the inner (framed) action they are audience. Because the theater audience recognizes its own status in one of the two functions of the stage audience, it tends to identify with it in its other function as well. At the end, outer and inner action (and present and past, theater actuality and theater imagination) merge, as the dancing couples of actors and stage audience† gradually hide Azdak from view. Then the dancers, too, disappear, and the Story Teller is left alone on the stage to address the epilogue–moral directly to the audience in the theater. To what extent, by now, has the latter become implicated? *Verfremdung* eliminates the possibility of mistaking the theater for reality, but it does not, like the realist theater of illusion, draw a safe line of division between them.

Sets and the use of time also add to the theatricalist effect. The outdoor scene in the distant, war-torn valley plausibly limits the Story

* In Bentley's 1961 version of his adaptation of the play, members of the fruit-growing "Galinsk" kolkhoz participate in the performance, thus further blurring the stage–audience distinction.

† It has not been made explicitly clear whether or not members of the kolkhoz audience join in the final dance, but that seems to be the implication of the stage directions of the last scene. It would, at any rate, be a scenically effective conclusion, in keeping with the play-within-the-play decorum.

Teller's use of props and scenery. The sets are crude and improvised, suggestive–symbolic rather than lifelike. In the opening scene of the inner play, a doorway marks the palace side of the stage, a gateway the town side. Place is evoked rather than represented. The whole production is stylized. The "voice" of the play shifts freely back and forth between drama, narrative, and choric comment and would only be impeded by elaborate verisimilitude.

There are shifts in time as well:

THE CROWD: — The baby! — I can't see it, don't shove so hard! — God bless the child, Your Grace!

THE STORY TELLER (*while* THE CROWD *is driven back with whips*): For the first time on that Easter Sunday, the people saw the Governor's heir.

The Story Teller's comment cuts off the gathering immediacy of the crowd scene. His viewpoint is the retrospective, generalizing one of a historian. His "saw" pulls us back sharply from the crowd's "I can't see." No sooner have we begun to suspend disbelief, accepting what we see as happening *here* and *now*, than the Story Teller steps in to remind us that the present tense applies only to the theater situation. He is presenting a show, but it is a show of what *happened* — *then* and *there*. Time is not always rendered realistically even within the single episode. When Lavrenti tells Grusha that she and the child must leave his farm as soon as spring comes, the accelerating drip-drip from the roof marks the passing of winter and the coming of spring even as brother and sister talk. On-stage action and dialogue proceed at normal speed, while the simultaneous off-stage sound of snow melting compresses days or weeks into the span of a few minutes.

The theatricalist fable subordinates character, too, to meaningful pattern. As the kolkhoz Prologue and the Story Teller's Epilogue frame the legend of Grusha and Azdak, so Grusha's scenes with Simon give a framework of romance to the hardships of her journey. We get a Chinese box effect, frame within frame. The mock-formal restraint of language in the lovers' dialogues suggests the blend of passion, liking, respect, and sheer sense of fun in their feelings for one another. But the point is their attractiveness as moral types rather than, simply, delightful romance or psychological complexity.

The most striking fact of structure in the play is the two-part division. The answer to the question whose play it is, Grusha's or Azdak's, is that it belongs to both, that the two stories are complementary halves in a dramatic whole, premises in a kind of syllogism. Parallelism prepares for their final fusion. Both Grusha and Azdak perform impulsive deeds of imprudent kindness: Grusha saves Michael, Azdak the

Grand Duke. Both are rewarded for their kindness (though the reward is ironic in Azdak's case, as he regrets his kindness when he learns the old man's identity). The syllogism concludes in Grusha's and Azdak's confrontation in the chalk-circle scene. The conclusion represents a multiple climax.

It releases the suspense concerning Grusha's fate, which has been accumulating while Azdak's manner of justice has been illustrated in racy anecdote. It achieves the overt meaning of the fable. Without Azdak, Grusha's story would only have proved that in violent social upheaval there are other bitter battles fought than those on the battlefield. Without Grusha, Azdak's natural justice would have lacked a morally significant context and emotive force. Only together do the two stories have what a character in the dramatic prologue calls "a bearing on the problem" of what to do with the valley. By the test of Azdak's criterion of superior yield, as applicable to use of land as to motherliness, the settlement in favor of the fruit-growing irrigators is validated.

Finally, the chalk-circle scene completes the dramatic structure. This might have been described as two converging lines, if only Grusha's movement had not been over before Azdak's even begins, and if the flashback story of Azdak ("flashback" relative to Grusha's poignant situation at the end of Section 3 of the play) had moved at all after he becomes judge. Dramatically speaking, the near-hanging is an abortive episode, and the preceding collection of law-case anecdotes, though establishing Azdak's quality as an administrator of justice, is shapeless and static. A more accurate definition of the structural function of the chalk-circle scene is that it brings the dynamics of the brave and resourceful virgin mother's odyssey to rest in the stasis of Azdak's verdict and Simon Shashava's love, concluding the legend of how goodness once received justice in a Caucasian valley.

Edward Albee

THE AMERICAN DREAM

The Players

MOMMY
DADDY
GRANDMA
MRS. BARKER
YOUNG MAN

THE SCENE: *A living room. Two armchairs, one toward either side of the stage, facing each other diagonally out toward the audience. Against the rear wall, a sofa. A door, leading out from the apartment, in the rear wall, far stage-right. An archway, leading to other rooms, in the side wall, stage-left.*

At the beginning, MOMMY *and* DADDY *are seated in the armchairs,* DADDY *in the armchair stage-left,* MOMMY *in the other.*

Curtain up. A silence. Then:

MOMMY: I don't know what can be keeping them.
DADDY: They're late, naturally.
MOMMY: Of course, they're late; it never fails.
DADDY: That's the way things are today, and there's nothing you can do about it.
MOMMY: You're quite right.

DADDY: When we took this apartment, they were quick enough to have me sign the lease; they were quick enough to take my check for two months' rent in advance . . .

MOMMY: And one month's security . . .

DADDY: . . . and one month's security. They were quick enough to check my references; they were quick enough about all that. But now! But now, try to get the icebox fixed, try to get the doorbell fixed, try to get the leak in the johnny fixed! Just try it . . . they aren't so quick about *that*.

MOMMY: Of course not; it never fails. People think they can get away with anything these days . . . and, of course they can. I went to buy a new hat yesterday. (*Pause.*) I said, I went to buy a new hat yesterday.

DADDY: Oh! Yes . . . yes.

MOMMY: Pay attention.

DADDY: I *am* paying attention, Mommy.

MOMMY: Well, be sure you do.

DADDY: Oh, I am.

MOMMY: All right, Daddy; now listen.

DADDY: I'm listening, Mommy.

MOMMY: You're sure!

DADDY: Yes . . . yes, I'm sure, I'm all ears.

MOMMY (*giggles at the thought; then*): All right, now. I went to buy a new hat yesterday and I said, "I'd like a new hat, please." And so, they showed me a few hats, green ones and blue ones, and I didn't like any of them, not one bit. What did I say? What did I just say?

DADDY: You didn't like any of them, not one bit.

MOMMY: That's right; you just keep paying attention. And then they showed me one that I did like. It was a lovely little hat, and I said, "Oh, this is a lovely little hat; I'll take this hat; oh my, it's lovely. What color is it?" And they said, "Why, this is beige; isn't it a lovely little beige hat?" And I said, "Oh, it's just lovely." And so, I bought it. (*Stops, looks at* DADDY.)

DADDY (*to show he is paying attention*): And so you bought it.

MOMMY: And so I bought it, and I walked out of the store with the hat right on my head, and I ran spang into the chairman of our woman's club, and she said, "Oh, my dear, isn't that a lovely little hat? Where did you get that lovely little hat? It's the loveliest little hat; I've always wanted a wheat-colored hat *myself*." And, I said, "Why, no, my dear; this hat is beige; beige." And she laughed and said, "Why no, my dear, that's a wheat-colored hat . . . wheat. I know beige from wheat." And I said, "Well, my dear, I know beige from wheat, too." What did I say? What did I just say?

DADDY (*tonelessly*): Well, my dear, I know beige from wheat, too.

MOMMY: That's right. And she laughed, and she said, "Well, my dear, they certainly put one over on you. That's wheat if I ever saw wheat. But it's lovely, just the same." And then she walked off. She's a dreadful woman, you don't know her; she has dreadful taste, two dreadful children, a dreadful house, and an absolutely adorable husband who sits in a wheel chair all the time. You don't know him. You don't know anybody, do you? She's just a dreadful woman, but she *is* chairman of our woman's club, so naturally I'm terribly fond of her. So, I went right back into the hat shop, and I said, "Look here; what do you mean selling me a hat that you say is beige, when it's wheat all the time . . . wheat! I can tell beige from wheat any day in the week, but not in this artificial light of yours." They have artificial light, Daddy.

DADDY: Have they!

MOMMY: And I said, "The minute I got outside I could tell that it wasn't a beige hat at all; it was a wheat hat." And they said to me, "How could you tell that when you had the hat on the top of your head?" Well, that made me angry, and so I made a scene right there; I screamed as hard as I could; I took my hat off and I threw it down on the counter, and oh, I made a terrible scene. I said, I made a terrible scene.

DADDY (*snapping to*): Yes . . . yes . . . good for you!

MOMMY: And I made an absolutely terrible scene; and they became frightened, and they said, "Oh, madam; oh, madam." But I kept right on, and finally they admitted that they might have made a mistake; so they took my hat into the back, and then they came out again with a hat that looked exactly like it. I took one look at it, and I said, "This hat is wheat-colored; wheat." Well, of course, they said, "Oh, no, madam, this hat is beige; you go outside and see." So, I went outside, and lo and behold, it *was* beige. So I bought it.

DADDY (*clearing his throat*): I would imagine that it was the same hat they tried to sell you before.

MOMMY (*with a little laugh*): Well, of course it was!

DADDY: That's the way things are today; you just can't get satisfaction; you just try.

MOMMY: Well, *I* got satisfaction.

DADDY: That's right, Mommy. *You did* get satisfaction, didn't you?

MOMMY: Why are they so late? I don't know what can be keeping them.

DADDY: I've been trying for two weeks to have the leak in the johnny fixed.

MOMMY: You can't get satisfaction; just try. *I* can get satisfaction, but you can't.

DADDY: I've been trying for two weeks and it isn't so much for my sake; I can always go to the club.

MOMMY: It isn't so much for my sake, either; I can always go shopping.

DADDY: It's really for Grandma's sake.

MOMMY: Of course it's for Grandma's sake. Grandma cries every time she goes to the johnny as it is; but now that it doesn't work it's even worse, it makes Grandma think she's getting feeble-headed.

DADDY: Grandma *is* getting feeble-headed.

MOMMY: Of course Grandma is getting feeble-headed, but not about her johnny-do's.

DADDY: No; that's true. I must have it fixed.

MOMMY: WHY are they so late? I don't know what can be keeping them.

DADDY: When they came here the first time, they were ten minutes early; they were quick enough about it then.

(*Enter* GRANDMA *from the archway, stage-left. She is loaded down with boxes, large and small, neatly wrapped and tied.*)

MOMMY: Why Grandma, look at you! What *is* all that you're carrying?

GRANDMA: They're boxes. What do they look like?

MOMMY: Daddy! Look at Grandma; look at all the boxes she's carrying!

DADDY: My goodness, Grandma; look at all those boxes.

GRANDMA: Where'll I put them?

MOMMY: Heavens! I don't know. Whatever are they for?

GRANDMA: That's nobody's damn business.

MOMMY: Well, in that case, put them down next to Daddy; there.

GRANDMA (*dumping the boxes down, on and around* DADDY'S *feet*): I sure wish you'd get the john fixed.

DADDY: Oh, I do wish they'd come and fix it. We hear you . . . for hours . . . whimpering away. . . .

MOMMY: Daddy! What a terrible thing to say to Grandma!

GRANDMA: Yeah. For shame, talking to me that way.

DADDY: I'm sorry, Grandma.

MOMMY: Daddy's sorry, Grandma.

GRANDMA: Well, all right. In that case I'll go get the rest of the boxes. I suppose I deserve being talked to that way. I've gotten so old. Most people think that when you get so old, you either freeze to death, or you burn up. But you don't. When you get so old, all that happens is that people talk to you that way.

DADDY (*contrite*): I said I'm sorry, Grandma.

MOMMY: Daddy said he was sorry.

GRANDMA: Well, that's all that counts. People being sorry. Makes you feel better; gives you a sense of dignity, and that's all that's important . . . a sense of dignity. And it doesn't matter if you don't care, or not, either. You got to have a sense of dignity, even if you don't care, 'cause, if you don't have that, civilization's doomed.

MOMMY: You've been reading my book club selections again!

DADDY: How dare you read Mommy's book club selections, Grandma!

GRANDMA: Because I'm old! When you're old you gotta do something. When you get old, you can't talk to people because people snap at you. When you get so old, people talk to you that way. That's why you become deaf, so you won't be able to hear people talking to you that way. And that's why you go and hide under the covers in the big soft bed, so you won't feel the house shaking from people talking to you that way. That's why old people die, eventually. People talk to them that way. I've got to go and get the rest of the boxes. (GRANDMA *exits.*)

DADDY: Poor Grandma, I didn't mean to hurt her.

MOMMY: Don't you worry about it; Grandma doesn't know what she means.

DADDY: She knows what she says, though.

MOMMY: Don't you worry about it; she won't know that soon. I love Grandma.

DADDY: I love her, too. Look how nicely she wrapped these boxes.

MOMMY: Grandma has always wrapped boxes nicely. When I was a little girl, I was very poor, and Grandma was very poor, too, because Grandpa was in heaven. And every day, when I went to school, Grandma used to wrap a box for me, and I used to take it with me to school; and when it was lunchtime, all the little boys and girls used to take out their boxes of lunch, and they weren't wrapped nicely at all, and they used to open them and eat their chicken legs and chocolate cakes; and I used to say, "Oh, look at my lovely lunch box; it's so nicely wrapped it would break my heart to open it." And so, I wouldn't open it.

DADDY: Because it was empty.

MOMMY: Oh no. Grandma always filled it up, because she never ate the dinner she cooked the evening before; she gave me all her food for my lunch box the next day. After school, I'd take the box back to Grandma, and she'd open it and eat the chicken legs and chocolate cake that was inside. Grandma used to say, "I love day-old cake." That's where the expression day-old cake came from. Grandma always ate everything a day late. I used to eat all the other little boys' and girls' food at school, because they thought my lunch box was empty. They thought my lunch box was empty, and that's why I wouldn't open it. They thought I suffered from the sin of pride, and since that made them better than me, they were very generous.

DADDY: You were a very deceitful little girl.

MOMMY: We were very poor! But then I married you, Daddy, and now we're very rich.

DADDY: Grandma isn't rich.

MOMMY: No, but you've been so good to Grandma she feels rich. She doesn't know you'd like to put her in a nursing home.

DADDY: I wouldn't!

MOMMY: Well, heaven knows, *I* would! I can't stand it, watching her do the cooking and the housework, polishing the silver, moving the furniture. . . .

DADDY: She likes to do that. She says it's the least she can do to earn her keep.

MOMMY: Well, she's right. You can't live off people. I can live off you, because I married you. And aren't you lucky all I brought with me was Grandma. A lot of women I know would have brought their whole families to live off you. All I brought was Grandma. Grandma is all the family I have.

DADDY: I feel very fortunate.

MOMMY: You should. I have a right to live off of you because I married you, and because I used to let you get on top of me and bump your uglies; and I have a right to all your money when you die. And when you do, Grandma and I can live by ourselves . . . if she's still here. Unless you have her put away in a nursing home.

DADDY: I have no intention of putting her in a nursing home.

MOMMY: Well, I wish somebody would do something with her!

DADDY: At any rate, you're very well provided for.

MOMMY: You're my sweet Daddy; that's very nice.

DADDY: I love my Mommy.

(Enter GRANDMA *again, laden with more boxes.)*

GRANDMA *(dumping the boxes on and around* DADDY'S *feet)*: There; that's the lot of them.

DADDY: They're wrapped so nicely.

GRANDMA *(to* DADDY*)*: You won't get on my sweet side that way . . .

MOMMY: Grandma.

GRANDMA: . . . telling me how nicely I wrap boxes. Not after what you said: how I whimpered for hours. . . .

MOMMY: Grandma!

GRANDMA *(to* MOMMY*)*: Shut up! *(To* DADDY.*)* You don't have any feelings, that's what's wrong with you. Old people make all sorts of noises, half of them they can't help. Old people whimper, and cry, and belch, and make great hollow rumbling sounds at the table; old people wake up in the middle of the night screaming, and find out they haven't even been asleep; and when old people *are* asleep, they try to wake up, and they can't . . . not for the longest time.

MOMMY: Homilies, homilies!

GRANDMA: And there's more, too.

DADDY: I'm really very sorry, Grandma.

GRANDMA: I know you are, Daddy; it's Mommy over there makes all the trouble. If you'd listened to me, you wouldn't have married her in the first place. She was a tramp and a trollop and a trull to boot, and she's no better now.

MOMMY: Grandma!

GRANDMA (*to* MOMMY): Shut up! (*To* DADDY.) When she was no more than eight years old she used to climb up on my lap and say, in a sickening little voice, "When I gwo up, I'm going to mahwy a wich old man; I'm going to set my wittle were end right down in a tub o' butter, that's what I'm going to do." And I warned you, Daddy; I told you to stay away from her type. I told you to. I did.

MOMMY: You stop that! You're my mother, not his!

GRANDMA: I am?

DADDY: That's right, Grandma. Mommy's right.

GRANDMA: Well, how would you expect somebody as old as I am to remember a thing like that? You don't make allowances for people. I want an allowance. I want an allowance!

DADDY: All right, Grandma; I'll see to it.

MOMMY: Grandma! I'm ashamed of you.

GRANDMA: Humf! It's a fine time to say that. You should have gotten rid of me a long time ago if that's the way you feel. You should have had Daddy set me up in business somewhere . . . I could have gone into the fur business, or I could have been a singer. But no; not you. You wanted me around so you could sleep in my room when Daddy got fresh. But now it isn't important, because Daddy doesn't want to get fresh with you any more, and I don't blame him. You'd rather sleep with me, wouldn't you, Daddy?

MOMMY: Daddy doesn't want to sleep with anyone. Daddy's been sick.

DADDY: I've been sick. I don't even want to sleep in the apartment.

MOMMY: You see? I told you.

DADDY: I just want to get everything over with.

MOMMY: That's right. Why are they so late? Why can't they get here on time?

GRANDMA (*an owl*): Who? Who? . . . Who? Who?

MOMMY: You know, Grandma.

GRANDMA: No, I don't.

MOMMY: Well, it doesn't really matter whether you do or not.

DADDY: Is that true?

MOMMY: Oh, more or less. Look how pretty Grandma wrapped these boxes.

GRANDMA: I didn't really like wrapping them; it hurt my fingers, and it frightened me. But it had to be done.

MOMMY: Why, Grandma?

GRANDMA: None of your damn business.

MOMMY: Go to bed.

GRANDMA: I don't want to go to bed. I just got up. I want to stay here and watch. Besides . . .

MOMMY: Go to bed.

DADDY: Let her stay up, Mommy; it isn't noon yet.

GRANDMA: I want to watch; besides . . .

DADDY: Let her watch, Mommy.

MOMMY: Well, all right, you can watch; but don't you dare say a word.

GRANDMA: Old people are very good at listening; old people don't like to talk; old people have colitis and lavender perfume. Now I'm going to be quiet.

DADDY: She never mentioned she wanted to be a singer.

MOMMY: Oh, I forgot to tell you, but it was ages ago. (*The doorbell rings.*) Oh, goodness! Here they are!

GRANDMA: Who? Who?

MOMMY: Oh, just some people.

GRANDMA: The van people? Is it the van people? Have you finally done it? Have you called the van people to come and take me away?

DADDY: Of course not, Grandma!

GRANDMA: Oh, don't be too sure. She'd have you carted off too, if she thought she could get away with it.

MOMMY: Pay no attention to her, Daddy. (*An aside to* GRANDMA.) My God, you're ungrateful! (*The doorbell rings again.*)

DADDY (*wringing his hands*): Oh dear; oh dear.

MOMMY (*still to* GRANDMA): Just you wait; I'll fix your wagon. (*Now to* DADDY.) Well, go let them in, Daddy. What are you waiting for?

DADDY: I think we should talk about it some more. Maybe we've been hasty . . . a little hasty, perhaps. (*Doorbell rings again.*) I'd like to talk about it some more.

MOMMY: There's no need. You made up your mind; you were firm; you were masculine and decisive.

DADDY: We might consider the pros and the . . .

MOMMY: I won't argue with you; it has to be done; you were right. Open the door.

DADDY: But I'm not sure that . . .

MOMMY: Open the door.

DADDY: Was I firm about it?

MOMMY: Oh, so firm; so firm.

DADDY: And was I decisive?

MOMMY: SO decisive! Oh, I shivered.

DADDY: And masculine? Was I really masculine?

MOMMY: Oh, Daddy, you were so masculine; I shivered and fainted.

GRANDMA: Shivered and fainted, did she? Humf!

MOMMY: You be quiet.

GRANDMA: Old people have a right to talk to themselves; it doesn't hurt the gums, and it's comforting. (*Doorbell rings again.*)

DADDY: I shall now open the door.

MOMMY: WHAT a masculine Daddy! Isn't he a masculine Daddy?

GRANDMA: Don't expect me to say anything. Old people are obscene.

MOMMY: Some of your opinions aren't so bad. You know that?

DADDY (*backing off from the door*): Maybe we can send them away.

MOMMY: Oh, look at you! You're turning into jelly; you're indecisive; you're a woman.

DADDY: All right. Watch me now; I'm going to open the door. Watch. Watch!

MOMMY: We're watching; we're watching.

GRANDMA: *I'm* not.

DADDY: Watch now; it's opening. (*He opens the door.*) It's open! (MRS. BARKER *steps into the room.*) Here they are!

MOMMY: Here they are!

GRANDMA: Where?

DADDY: Come in. You're late. But, of course, we expected you to be late; we were saying that we expected you to be late.

MOMMY: Daddy, don't be rude! We were saying that you just can't get satisfaction these days, and we were talking about you, of course. Won't you come in?

MRS. BARKER: Thank you. I don't mind if I do.

MOMMY: We're very glad that you're here, late as you are. You do remember us, don't you? You were here once before. I'm Mommy, and this is Daddy, and that's Grandma, doddering there in the corner.

MRS. BARKER: Helly, Mommy; hello, Daddy; and hello there, Grandma.

DADDY: Now that you're here, I don't suppose you could go away and maybe come back some other time.

MRS. BARKER: Oh no; we're much too efficient for that. I said, hello there, Grandma.

MOMMY: Speak to them, Grandma.

GRANDMA: I don't see them.

DADDY: For shame, Grandma; they're here.

MRS. BARKER: Yes, we're here, Grandma. I'm Mrs. Barker. I remember you; don't you remember me?

GRANDMA: I don't recall. Maybe you were younger, or something.

MOMMY: Grandma! What a terrible thing to say!

MRS. BARKER: Oh now, don't scold her, Mommy; for all she knows she may be right.

DADDY: Uh . . . Mrs. Barker, is it? Won't you sit down?

MRS. BARKER: I don't mind if I do.

MOMMY: Would you like a cigarette, and a drink, and would you like to cross your legs?

MRS. BARKER: You forget yourself, Mommy; I'm a professional woman. But I will cross my legs.

DADDY: Yes, make yourself comfortable.

MRS. BARKER: I don't mind if I do.

GRANDMA: Are they still here?

MOMMY: Be quiet, Grandma.

MRS. BARKER: Oh, we're still here. My, what an unattractive apartment you have!

MOMMY: Yes, but you don't know what a trouble it is. Let me tell you . . .

DADDY: I was saying to Mommy . . .

MRS. BARKER: Yes, I know. I was listening outside.

DADDY: About the icebox, and . . . the doorbell . . . and the . . .

MRS. BARKER: . . . and the johnny. Yes, we're very efficient; we have to know everything in our work.

DADDY: Exactly what do you do?

MOMMY: Yes, what is your work?

MRS. BARKER: Well, my dear, for one thing, I'm chairman of your woman's club.

MOMMY: Don't be ridiculous. I was talking to the chairman of my woman's club just yester — Why, so you are. You remember, Daddy, the lady I was telling you about? The lady with the husband who sits in the *swing*? Don't you remember?

DADDY: No . . . no. . . .

MOMMY: Of course you do. I'm so sorry, Mrs. Barker. I would have known you anywhere, except in this artificial light. And look! You have a hat just like the one I bought yesterday.

MRS. BARKER (*with a little laugh*): No, not really; this hat is cream.

MOMMY: Well, my dear, that may look like a cream hat to you, but I can . . .

MRS. BARKER: Now, now; you seem to forget who I am.

MOMMY: Yes, I do, don't I? Are you sure you're comfortable? Won't you take off your dress?

MRS. BARKER: I don't mind if I do. (*She removes her dress.*)

MOMMY: There. You must feel a great deal more comfortable.

MRS. BARKER: Well, I certainly *look* a great deal more comfortable.

DADDY: I'm going to blush and giggle.

MOMMY: Daddy's going to blush and giggle.

MRS. BARKER (*pulling the hem of her slip above her knees*): You're lucky to have such a man for a husband.

MOMMY: Oh, don't I know it!

DADDY: I just blushed and giggled and went sticky wet.

MOMMY: Isn't Daddy a caution, Mrs. Barker?

MRS. BARKER: Maybe if I smoked . . . ?

MOMMY: Oh, that isn't necessary.

MRS. BARKER: I don't mind if I do.

MOMMY: No; no, don't. Really.

MRS. BARKER: I don't mind . . .

MOMMY: I won't have you smoking in my house, and that's that! You're a professional woman.

DADDY: Grandma drinks AND smokes; don't you, Grandma?

GRANDMA: No.

MOMMY: Well, now, Mrs. Barker; suppose you tell us why you're here.

GRANDMA (*as* MOMMY *walks through the boxes*): The boxes . . . the boxes . . .

MOMMY: Be quiet, Grandma.

DADDY: What did you say, Grandma?

GRANDMA (*as* MOMMY *steps on several of the boxes*): The boxes, damn it!

MRS. BARKER: Boxes; she said boxes. She mentioned the boxes.

DADDY: What about the boxes, Grandma? Maybe Mrs. Barker is here because of the boxes. Is that what you meant, Grandma?

GRANDMA: I don't know if that's what I meant or not. It's certainly not what I *thought* I meant.

DADDY: Grandma is of the opinion that . . .

MRS. BARKER: Can we assume that the boxes are for us? I mean, can we assume that you had us come here for the boxes?

MOMMY: Are you in the habit of receiving boxes?

DADDY: A very good question.

MRS. BARKER: Well, that would depend on the reason we're here. I've got my fingers in so many little pies, you know. Now, I can think of one of my little activities in which we are in the habit of receiving *baskets*; but more in a literary sense than really. We *might* receive boxes, though, under very special circumstances. I'm afraid that's the best answer I can give you.

DADDY: It's a very interesting answer.

MRS. BARKER: *I* thought so. But, does it help?

MOMMY: No; I'm afraid not.

DADDY: I wonder if it might help us any if I said I feel misgivings, that I have definite qualms.

MOMMY: Where, Daddy?

DADDY: Well, mostly right here, right around where the stitches were.

MOMMY: Daddy had an operation, you know.

MRS. BARKER: Oh, you poor Daddy! I didn't know; but then, how could I?

GRANDMA: You might have asked; it wouldn't have hurt you.

MOMMY: Dry up, Grandma.

GRANDMA: There you go. Letting your true feelings come out. Old people aren't dry enough, I suppose. My sacks are empty, the fluid in my eyeballs is all caked on the inside edges, my spine is made of sugar candy, I breathe ice; but you don't hear me complain. Nobody hears old people complain because people think that's all old people do. And *that's* because old people are gnarled and sagged and twisted into the shape of a complaint. (*Signs off.*) That's all.

MRS. BARKER: What was wrong, Daddy?

DADDY: Well, you know how it is: the doctors took out something that was there and put in something that wasn't there. An operation.

MRS. BARKER: You're very fortunate, I should say.

MOMMY: Oh, he is; he is. All his life, Daddy has wanted to be a United States Senator; but now . . . why now he's changed his mind, and for the rest of his life he's going to want to be Governor . . . it would be nearer the apartment, you know.

MRS. BARKER: You *are* fortunate, Daddy.

DADDY: Yes, indeed; except that I get these qualms now and then, definite ones.

MRS. BARKER: Well, it's just a matter of things settling; you're like an old house.

MOMMY: Why Daddy, thank Mrs. Barker.

DADDY: Thank you.

MRS. BARKER: Ambition! That's the ticket. I have a brother who's very much like you, Daddy . . . ambitious. Of course, he's a great deal younger than you; he's even younger than I am . . . if such a thing is possible. He runs a little newspaper. Just a little newspaper

. . . but he runs it. He's chief cook and bottle washer of that little newspaper, which he calls *The Village Idiot*. He has such a sense of humor; he's so self-deprecating, so modest. And he'd never admit it himself, but he *is* the Village Idiot.

MOMMY: Oh, I think that's just grand. Don't you think so, Daddy?

DADDY: Yes, just grand.

MRS. BARKER: My brother's a dear man, and he has a dear little wife, whom he loves, dearly. He loves her so much he just can't get a sentence out without mentioning her. He wants everybody to know he's married. He's really a stickler on that point; he can't be introduced to anybody and say hello without adding, "Of course, I'm married." As far as I'm concerned, he's the chief exponent of Woman Love in this whole country; he's even been written up in psychiatric journals because of it.

DADDY: Indeed!

MOMMY: Isn't that lovely.

MRS. BARKER: Oh, I think so. There's too much woman hatred in this country, and that's a fact.

GRANDMA: Oh, I don't know.

MOMMY: Oh, I think that's just grand. Don't you think so, Daddy?

DADDY: Yes, just grand.

GRANDMA: In case anybody's interested . . .

MOMMY: Be quiet, Grandma.

GRANDMA: Nuts!

MOMMY: Oh, Mrs. Barker, you *must* forgive Grandma. She's rural.

MRS. BARKER: I don't mind if I do.

DADDY: Maybe Grandma has something to say.

MOMMY: Nonsense. Old people have nothing to say; and if old people *did* have something to say, nobody would listen to them. (*To* GRANDMA.) You see? I can pull that stuff just as easy as you can.

GRANDMA: Well, you got the rhythm, but you don't really have the quality. Besides, you're middle-aged.

MOMMY: I'm proud of it!

GRANDMA: Look. I'll show you how it's really done. Middle-aged people think they can do anything, but the truth is that middle-aged people can't do most things as well as they used to. Middle-aged people think they're special because they're like everybody else. We live in the age of deformity. You see? Rhythm *and* content. You'll learn.

DADDY: I do wish I weren't surrounded by women; I'd like some men around here.

MRS. BARKER: You can say that again!

GRANDMA: I don't hardly count as a woman, so can I say my piece?

MOMMY: Go on. Jabber away.

GRANDMA: It's very simple; the fact is, these boxes don't have anything to do with why this good lady is come to call. Now, if you're interested in knowing why these boxes *are* here . . .

DADDY: I'm sure that must be all very true, Grandma, but what does it have to do with why . . . pardon me, what is that name again?

MRS. BARKER: Mrs. Barker.

DADDY: Exactly. What does it have to do with why . . . that name again?

MRS. BARKER: Mrs. Barker.

DADDY: Precisely. What does it have to do with why what's-her-name is here?

MOMMY: They're here because we asked them.

MRS. BARKER: Yes. That's why.

GRANDMA: Now if you're interested in knowing why these boxes *are* here . . .

MOMMY: Well, nobody *is* interested!

GRANDMA: You can be as snippety as you like for all the good it'll do you.

DADDY: You two will have to stop arguing.

MOMMY: I don't argue with her.

DADDY: It will just have to stop.

MOMMY: Well, why don't you call a van and have her taken away?

GRANDMA: Don't bother; there's no need.

DADDY: No, now, perhaps I can go away myself. . . .

MOMMY: Well, one or the other; the way things are now it's impossible. In the first place, it's too crowded in this apartment. (*To* GRANDMA.) And it's you that takes up all the space, with your enema bottles, and your Pekinese, and God-only-knows-what-else . . . and now all these boxes. . . .

GRANDMA: These boxes are . . .

MRS. BARKER: I've never heard of enema *bottles*. . . .

GRANDMA: She means enema bags, but she doesn't know the difference. Mommy comes from extremely bad stock. And besides, when Mommy was born . . . well, it was a difficult delivery, and she had a head shaped like a banana.

MOMMY: You ungrateful — Daddy? Daddy, you see how ungrateful she is after all these years, after all the things we've done for her? (*To* GRANDMA.) One of these days you're going away in a van; that's what's going to happen to you!

GRANDMA: Do tell!

MRS. BARKER: Like a banana?

GRANDMA: Yup, just like a banana.

MRS. BARKER: My word!

MOMMY: You stop listening to her; she'll say anything. Just the other night she called Daddy a hedgehog.

MRS. BARKER: She didn't!

GRANDMA: That's right, baby; you stick up for me.

MOMMY: I don't know where she gets the words; on the television, maybe.

MRS. BARKER: Did you really call him a hedgehog?

GRANDMA: Oh look; what difference does it make whether I did or not?

DADDY: Grandma's right. Leave Grandma alone.

MOMMY (*to* DADDY): How dare you!

GRANDMA: Oh, leave her alone, Daddy; the kid's all mixed up.

MOMMY: You see? I told you. It's all those television shows. Daddy, you go right into Grandma's room and take her television and shake all the tubes loose.

DADDY: Don't mention tubes to me.

MOMMY: Oh! Mommy forgot! (*To* MRS. BARKER.) Daddy has tubes now, where he used to have tracts.

MRS. BARKER: Is that a fact!

GRANDMA: I know why this dear lady is here.

MOMMY: You be still.

MRS. BARKER: Oh, I do wish you'd tell me.

MOMMY: No! No! That wouldn't be fair at all.

DADDY: Besides, she knows why she's here; she's here because we called them.

MRS. BARKER: La! But that still leaves me puzzled. I know I'm here because you called us, but I'm such a busy girl, with this committee and that committee, and the Responsible Citizens Activities I indulge in.

MOMMY: Oh my; busy, busy.

MRS. BARKER: Yes, indeed. So I'm afraid you'll have to give me some help.

MOMMY: Oh, no. No, you must be mistaken. I can't believe we asked you here to give you any help. With the way taxes are these days, and the way you can't get satisfaction in ANYTHING . . . no, I don't believe so.

DADDY: And if you need help . . . why, I should think you'd apply for a Fulbright Scholarship. . . .

MOMMY: And if not that . . . why, then a Guggenheim Fellowship. . . .

GRANDMA: Oh, come on; why not shoot the works and try for the Prix de Rome. (*Under her breath to* MOMMY *and* DADDY.) Beasts!

MRS. BARKER: Oh, what a jolly family. But let me think. I'm knee-deep in work these days; there's the Ladies' Auxiliary Air Raid Committee, for one thing; how do you feel about air raids?

MOMMY: Oh, I'd say we're hostile.

DADDY: Yes, definitely; we're hostile.

MRS. BARKER: Then, you'll be no help there. There's too much hostility in the world these days as it is; but I'll not badger you! There's a surfeit of badgers as well.

GRANDMA: While we're at it, there's been a run on old people, too. The Department of Agriculture, or maybe it wasn't the Department of Agriculture — anyway, it was some department that's run by a girl — put out figures showing that ninety per cent of the adult population of the country is over eighty years old . . . or eighty per cent is over ninety years old . . .

MOMMY: You're such a liar! You just finished saying that everyone is middle-aged.

GRANDMA: I'm just telling you what the government says . . . that doesn't have anything to do with what . . .

MOMMY: It's that television! Daddy, go break her television.

GRANDMA: You won't find it.

DADDY (*wearily getting up*): If I must . . . I must.

MOMMY: And don't step on the Pekinese; it's blind.

DADDY: It may be blind, but Daddy isn't. (*He exits, through the archway, stage-left.*)

GRANDMA: You won't find *it*, either.

MOMMY: Oh, I'm so fortunate to have such a husband. Just think; I could have a husband who was poor, or argumentative, or a husband who sat in a wheel chair all day . . . OOOOHHHH! *What* have I said? What *have* I said?

GRANDMA: You said you could have a husband who sat in a wheel . . .

MOMMY: I'm mortified! I could die! I could cut my tongue out! I could . . .

MRS. BARKER (*forcing a smile*): Oh, now . . . now . . . don't think about it . . .

MOMMY: I could . . . why, I could . . .

MRS. BARKER: . . . don't think about it . . . really. . . .

MOMMY: You're quite right. I won't think about it, and that way I'll forget that I ever said it, and that way it will be all right. (*Pause.*) There . . . I've forgotten. Well, now, now that Daddy is out of the room we can have some girl talk.

MRS. BARKER: I'm not sure that I . . .

MOMMY: You *do* want to have some girl talk, don't you?

MRS. BARKER: I was going to say I'm not sure that I wouldn't care for a glass of water. I feel a little faint.

MOMMY: Grandma, go get Mrs. Barker a glass of water.

GRANDMA: Go get it yourself. I quit.

MOMMY: Grandma loves to do little things around the house; it gives her a false sense of security.

GRANDMA: I quit! I'm through!

MOMMY: Now, you be a good Grandma, or you know what will happen to you. You'll be taken away in a van.

GRANDMA: You don't frighten me. I'm too old to be frightened. Besides . . .

MOMMY: WELL! I'll tend to you later. I'll hide your teeth . . . I'll . . .

GRANDMA: Everything's hidden.

MRS. BARKER: I *am* going to faint. I *am*.

MOMMY: Good heavens! I'll go myself. (*As she exits, through the archway, stage-left.*) I'll fix you, Grandma. I'll take care of you later. (*She exits.*)

GRANDMA: Oh, go soak your head. (*To* MRS. BARKER.) Well, dearie, how do you feel?

MRS. BARKER: A little better, I think. Yes, much better, thank you, Grandma.

GRANDMA: That's good.

MRS. BARKER: But . . . I feel so lost . . . not knowing why I'm here . . . and, on top of it, they say I was here before.

GRANDMA: Well, you were. You weren't *here*, exactly, because we've moved around a lot, from one apartment to another, up and down the social ladder like mice, if you like similes.

MRS. BARKER: I don't . . . particularly.

GRANDMA: Well, then, I'm sorry.

MRS. BARKER (*suddenly*): Grandma, I feel I can trust you.

GRANDMA: Don't be too sure; it's every man for himself around this place. . . .

MRS. BARKER: Oh . . . is it? Nonetheless, I really do feel that I can trust you. *Please* tell me why they called and asked us to come. I implore you!

GRANDMA: Oh my; that feels good. It's been so long since anybody implored me. Do it again. Implore me some more.

MRS. BARKER: You're your daughter's mother, all right!

GRANDMA: Oh, I don't mean to be hard. If you won't implore me, then beg me, or ask me, or entreat me . . . just anything like that.

MRS. BARKER: You're a dreadful old woman!

GRANDMA: You'll understand some day. Please!

MRS. BARKER: Oh, for heaven's sake! . . . I implore you . . . I beg you . . . I beseech you!

GRANDMA: Beseech! Oh, that's the nicest word I've heard in ages. You're a dear, sweet woman. . . . You . . . beseech . . . me. I can't resist that.

MRS. BARKER: Well, then . . . please tell me why they asked us to come.

GRANDMA: Well, I'll give you a hint. That's the best I can do, because I'm a muddleheaded old woman. Now listen, because it's important. Once upon a time, not too very long ago, but a long enough time ago . . . oh, about twenty years ago . . . there was a man very much like Daddy, and a woman very much like Mommy, who were married to each other, very much like Mommy and Daddy are married to each other; and they lived in an apartment very much like one that's very much like this one, and they lived there with an old woman who was very much like yours truly, only younger, because it was some time ago; in fact, they were all somewhat younger.

MRS. BARKER: How fascinating!

GRANDMA: Now, at the same time, there was a dear lady very much like you, only younger then, who did all sorts of Good Works. . . . And one of the Good Works this dear lady did was in something very much like a volunteer capacity for an organization very much like the Bye-Bye Adoption Service, which is nearby and which was run by a terribly deaf old lady very much like the Miss Bye-Bye who runs the Bye-Bye Adoption Service nearby.

MRS. BARKER: How enthralling!

GRANDMA: Well, be that as it may. Nonetheless, one afternoon this man, who was very much like Daddy, and this woman who was very much like Mommy came to see this dear lady who did all the Good Works, who was very much like you, dear, and they were very sad and very hopeful, and they cried and smiled and bit their fingers, and they said all the most intimate things.

MRS. BARKER: How spellbinding! What did they say?

GRANDMA: Well, it was very sweet. The woman, who was very much like Mommy, said that she and the man who was very much like Daddy had never been blessed with anything very much like a bumble of joy.

MRS. BARKER: A what?

GRANDMA: A bumble; a bumble of joy.

MRS. BARKER: Oh, like bundle.

GRANDMA: Well, yes; very much like it. Bundle, bumble; who cares? At any rate, the woman, who was very much like Mommy, said that they wanted a bumble of their own, but that the man, who was very much like Daddy, couldn't have a bumble; and the man, who was very much like Daddy, said that yes, they had wanted a bumble of their own, but that the woman, who was very much like Mommy, couldn't have one, and that now they wanted to buy something very much like a bumble.

MRS. BARKER: How engrossing!

GRANDMA: Yes. And the dear lady, who was very much like you, said something that was very much like, "Oh, what a shame; but take heart . . . I think we have just the bumble *for* you." And, well, the lady, who was very much like Mommy, and the man, who was very much like Daddy, cried and smiled and bit their fingers, and said some more intimate things, which were totally irrelevant but which were pretty hot stuff, and so the dear lady, who was very much like you, and who had something very much like a penchant for pornography, listened with something very much like enthusiasm. "Whee," she said. "Whoooopeeeeee!" But that's beside the point.

MRS. BARKER: I suppose *so*. But how gripping!

GRANDMA: Anyway . . . they *bought* something very much like a bumble, and they took it away with them. But . . . things didn't work out very well.

MRS. BARKER: You mean there was trouble?

GRANDMA: You got it. (*With a glance through the archway.*) But, I'm going to have to speed up now because I think I'm leaving soon.

MRS. BARKER: Oh. Are you really?

GRANDMA: Yup.

MRS. BARKER: But old people don't go anywhere; they're either taken places, or put places.

GRANDMA: Well, this old person is different. Anyway . . . things started going badly.

MRS. BARKER: Oh yes. Yes.

GRANDMA: Weeeeellll . . . in the first place, it turned out the bumble didn't look like either one of its parents. That was enough of a blow, but things got worse. One night, it cried its heart out, if you can imagine such a thing.

MRS. BARKER: Cried its heart out! Well!

GRANDMA: But that was only the beginning. Then it turned out it only had eyes for its Daddy.

MRS. BARKER: For its Daddy! Why, any self-respecting woman would have gouged those eyes right out of its head.

GRANDMA: Well, she did. That's exactly what she did. But then, it kept its nose up in the air.

MRS. BARKER: Ufggh! How disgusting!

GRANDMA: That's what they thought. But *then,* it began to develop an interest in its you-know-what.

MRS. BARKER: In its you-know-what! Well! I hope they cut its hands off at the wrists!

GRANDMA: Well, yes, they did that eventually. But first, they cut off its you-know-what.

MRS. BARKER: A much better idea!

GRANDMA: That's what they thought. But after they cut off its you-know-what, it *still* put its hands under the covers, *looking* for its you-know-what. So, finally, they *had* to cut off its hands at the wrists.

MRS. BARKER: Naturally!

GRANDMA: And it was such a resentful bumble. Why, one day it called its Mommy a dirty name.

MRS. BARKER: Well, I hope they cut its tongue out!

GRANDMA: Of course. And then, as it got bigger, they found out all sorts of terrible things about it, like: it didn't have a head on its shoulders, it had no guts, it was spineless, its feet were made of clay . . . just dreadful things.

MRS. BARKER: Dreadful!

GRANDMA: So you can understand how they became discouraged.

MRS. BARKER: I certainly can! And what did they do?

GRANDMA: What did they do? Well, for the last straw, it finally up and died; and you can imagine how *that* made them feel, their having paid for it, and all. So, they called up the lady who sold them the bumble in the first place and told her to come right over to their apartment. They wanted satisfaction; they wanted their money back. That's what they wanted.

MRS. BARKER: My, my, my.

GRANDMA: How do you like *them* apples?

MRS. BARKER: My, my, my.

DADDY (*off stage*): Mommy! I can't find Grandma's television, and I can't find the Pekinese, either.

MOMMY (*off stage*): Isn't that funny! And I can't find the water.

GRANDMA: Heh, heh, heh. I told them everything was hidden.

MRS. BARKER: Did you hide the water, too?

GRANDMA (*puzzled*): No. No, I didn't do *that.*

DADDY (*off stage*): The truth of the matter is, I can't even find Grandma's room.

GRANDMA: Heh, heh, heh.

MRS. BARKER: My! You certainly did hide things, didn't you?

GRANDMA: Sure, kid, sure.

MOMMY (*sticking her head in the room*): Did you ever hear of such a thing, Grandma? Daddy can't find your television, and he can't find the Pekinese, and the truth of the matter is he can't even find your room.

GRANDMA: I told you. I hid everything.

MOMMY: Nonsense, Grandma! Just wait until I get my hands on you. You're a troublemaker . . . that's what you are.

GRANDMA: Well, I'll be out of here pretty soon, baby.

MOMMY: Oh, you don't know how right you are! Daddy's been wanting to send you away for a long time now, but I've been restraining him. I'll tell you one thing, though . . . I'm getting sick and tired of this fighting, and I might just let him have his way. Then you'll see what'll happen. Away you'll go; in a van, too. I'll let Daddy call the van man.

GRANDMA: I'm way ahead of you.

MOMMY: How can you be so old and so smug at the same time? You have no sense of proportion.

GRANDMA: You just answered your own question.

MOMMY: Mrs. Barker, I'd much rather you came into the kitchen for that glass of water, what with Grandma out here, and all.

MRS. BARKER: I don't see what Grandma has to do with it; and besides, I don't think you're very polite.

MOMMY: You seem to forget that you're a guest in this house . . .

GRANDMA: Apartment!

MOMMY: Apartment! And that you're a professional woman. So, if you'll be so good as to come into the kitchen, I'll be more than happy to show you where the water is, and where the glass is, and then you can put two and two together, if you're clever enough. (*She vanishes.*)

MRS. BARKER (*after a moment's consideration*): I suppose she's right.

GRANDMA: Well, that's how it is when people call you up and ask you over to do something for them.

MRS. BARKER: I suppose you're right, too. Well, Grandma, it's been very nice talking to you.

GRANDMA: And I've enjoyed listening. Say, don't tell Mommy or Daddy that I gave you that hint, will you?

MRS. BARKER: Oh, dear me, the hint! I'd forgotten about it, if you can imagine such a thing. No, I won't breathe a word of it to them.

GRANDMA: I don't know if it helped you any . . .

MRS. BARKER: I can't tell, yet. I'll have to . . . what *is* the word I want? . . . I'll have to relate it . . . that's it . . . I'll have to relate it to certain things that I *know*, and . . . draw . . . conclusions. . . . What I'll really have to do is to see if it applies to anything. I mean, after all, I *do* do volunteer work for an adoption service, but it isn't very much *like* the Bye-Bye Adoption Service

. . . it *is* the Bye-Bye Adoption Service . . . and while I can remember Mommy and Daddy coming to see me, oh, about twenty years ago, about buying a bumble, I can't quite remember anyone very much *like* Mommy and Daddy coming to see me about buying a bumble. Don't you see? It really presents quite a problem. . . . I'll have to think about it . . . mull it . . . but at any rate, it was truly first-class of you to try to help me. Oh, will you still be here after I've had my drink of water?

GRANDMA: Probably . . . I'm not as spry as I used to be.

MRS. BARKER: Oh. Well, I won't say good-by then.

GRANDMA: No. Don't. (MRS. BARKER *exits through the archway.*) People don't say good-by to old people because they think they'll frighten them. Lordy! If they only knew how awful "hello" and "my, you're looking chipper" sounded, they wouldn't say those things either. The truth is, there isn't much you *can* say to old people that doesn't sound just terrible. (*The doorbell rings.*) Come on in! (*The* YOUNG MAN *enters.* GRANDMA *looks him over.*) Well, now, aren't you a breath of fresh air!

YOUNG MAN: Hello there.

GRANDMA: My, my, my. Are you the van man?

YOUNG MAN: The what?

GRANDMA: The van man. The van man. Are you come to take me away?

YOUNG MAN: I don't know what you're talking about.

GRANDMA: Oh. (*Pause.*) Well. (*Pause.*) My, my, aren't you something!

YOUNG MAN: Hm?

GRANDMA: I said, my, my, aren't you something.

YOUNG MAN: Oh. Thank you.

GRANDMA: You don't sound very enthusiastic.

YOUNG MAN: Oh, I'm . . . I'm used to it.

GRANDMA: Yup . . . yup. You know, if I were about a hundred and fifty years younger I could go for you.

YOUNG MAN: Yes, I imagine so.

GRANDMA: Unh-hunh . . . will you look at those muscles!

YOUNG MAN (*flexing his muscles*): Yes, they're quite good, aren't they?

GRANDMA: Boy, they sure are. They natural?

YOUNG MAN: Well, the basic structure was there, but I've done some work, too . . . you know, in a gym.

GRANDMA: I'll bet you have. You ought to be in the movies, boy.

YOUNG MAN: I know.

GRANDMA: Yup! Right up there on the old silver screen. But I suppose you've heard that before.

YOUNG MAN: Yes, I have.

GRANDMA: You ought to try out for them . . . the movies.

YOUNG MAN: Well, actually, I may have a career there yet. I've lived out on the West Coast almost all my life . . . and I've met a few people who . . . might be able to help me. I'm not in too much of a hurry, though. I'm almost as young as I look.

GRANDMA: Oh, that's nice. And will you look at that face!

YOUNG MAN: Yes, it's quite good, isn't it? Clean-cut, midwest farm boy type, almost insultingly good-looking in a typically American way. Good profile, straight nose, honest eyes, wonderful smile . . .

GRANDMA: Yup. Boy, you know what you are, don't you? You're the American Dream, that's what you are. All those other people, they don't know what they're talking about. You . . . *you* are the American Dream.

YOUNG MAN: Thanks.

MOMMY (*off stage*): Who rang the doorbell?

GRANDMA (*shouting off stage*): The American Dream!

MOMMY (*off stage*): What? What was that, Grandma?

GRANDMA (*shouting*): The American Dream! The American Dream! Damn it!

DADDY (*off stage*): How's that, Mommy?

MOMMY (*off stage*): Oh, some gibberish; pay no attention. Did you find Grandma's room?

DADDY (*off stage*): No. I can't even find Mrs. Barker.

YOUNG MAN: What was all that?

GRANDMA: Oh, that was just the folks, but let's not talk about them, honey; let's talk about you.

YOUNG MAN: All right.

GRANDMA: Well, let's see. If you're not the van man, what are you doing here?

YOUNG MAN: I'm looking for work.

GRANDMA: Are you! Well, what kind of work?

YOUNG MAN: Oh, almost anything . . . almost anything that pays. I'll do almost anything for money.

GRANDMA: Will you . . . will you? Hmmmm. I wonder if there's anything you could do around here?

YOUNG MAN: There might be. It looked to be a likely building.

GRANDMA: It's always looked to be a rather unlikely building to me, but I suppose you'd know better than I.

YOUNG MAN: I can sense these things.

GRANDMA: There *might* be something you could do around here. Stay there! Don't come any closer.

YOUNG MAN: Sorry.

GRANDMA: I don't mean I'd *mind*. I don't know whether I'd mind, or not. . . . But it wouldn't look well; it would look just *awful*.

YOUNG MAN: Yes; I suppose so.

GRANDMA: Now, stay there, let me concentrate. What could you do? The folks have been in something of a quandary around here today, sort of a dilemma, and I wonder if you mightn't be some help.

YOUNG MAN: I hope so . . . if there's money in it. Do you have any money?

GRANDMA: Money! Oh, there's more money around here than you'd know what to do with.

YOUNG MAN: I'm not so sure.

GRANDMA: Well, maybe not. Besides, I've got money of my own.

YOUNG MAN: You have?

GRANDMA: Sure. Old people quite often have lots of money; more often than most people expect. Come here, so I can whisper to you . . . not too close. I might faint.

YOUNG MAN: Oh, I'm sorry.

GRANDMA: It's all right, dear. Anyway . . . have you ever heard of that big baking contest they run? The one where all the ladies get together in a big barn and bake away?

YOUNG MAN: I'm . . . not . . . sure. . . .

GRANDMA: Not so close. Well, it doesn't matter whether you've heard of it or not. The important thing is — and I don't want anybody to hear this . . . the folks think I haven't been out of the house in eight years — the important thing is that I won first prize in that baking contest this year. Oh, it was in all the papers; not under my own name, though. I used a *nom de boulangère*; I called myself Uncle Henry.

YOUNG MAN: Did you?

GRANDMA: Why not? I didn't see any reason not to. I look just as much like an old man as I do like an old woman. And you know what I called it . . . what I won for?

YOUNG MAN: No. What did you call it?

GRANDMA: I called it Uncle Henry's Day-Old Cake.

YOUNG MAN: That's a very nice name.

GRANDMA: And it wasn't any trouble, either. All I did was go out and get a store-bought cake, and keep it around for a while, and then slip it in, unbeknownst to anybody. Simple.

YOUNG MAN: You're a very resourceful person.

GRANDMA: Pioneer stock.

YOUNG MAN: Is all this true? Do you want me to believe all this?

GRANDMA: Well, you can believe it or not . . . it doesn't make any difference to me. All *I* know is, Uncle Henry's Day-Old Cake won me twenty-five thousand smackerolas.

YOUNG MAN: Twenty-five thou —

GRANDMA: Right on the old loggerhead. Now. . . how do you like them apples?

YOUNG MAN: Love 'em.

GRANDMA: I thought you'd be impressed.

YOUNG MAN: Money talks.

GRANDMA: Hey! You look familiar.

YOUNG MAN: Hm? Pardon?

GRANDMA: I said, you look familiar.

YOUNG MAN: Well, I've done some modeling.

GRANDMA: No . . . no. I don't mean that. You look familiar.

YOUNG MAN: Well, I'm a type.

GRANDMA: Yup; you sure are. Why do you say you'd do anything for money . . . if you don't mind my being nosy?

YOUNG MAN: No, no. It's part of the interviews. I'll be happy to tell you. It's that I have no talents at all, except what you see . . . my person; my body, my face. In every other way I am incomplete, and I must therefore . . . compensate.

GRANDMA: What do you mean, incomplete? You look pretty complete to me.

YOUNG MAN: I think I can explain it to you, partially because you're very old, and very old people have perceptions they keep to themselves, because if they expose them to other people . . . well, you know what ridicule and neglect are.

GRANDMA: I do, child, I do.

YOUNG MAN: Then listen. My mother died the night that I was born, and I never knew my father; I doubt my mother did. But, I wasn't alone, because lying with me . . . in the placenta . . . there was someone else . . . my brother . . . my twin.

GRANDMA: Oh, my child.

YOUNG MAN: We were identical twins . . . he and I . . . not fraternal . . . identical; we were derived from the same ovum; and in *this*, in that we were twins not from separate ova but from the same one, we had a kinship such as you cannot imagine. We . . . we felt each other breathe . . . his heartbeats thundered in my temples . . . mine in his . . . our stomachs ached and we cried for feeding at the same time . . . are you old enough to understand?

GRANDMA: I think so, child; I think I'm nearly old enough.

YOUNG MAN: I hope so. But we were separated when we were still very young, my brother, my twin and I . . . inasmuch as you can separate one being. We were torn apart . . . thrown to opposite ends of the continent. I don't know what became of my brother . . . to the rest of myself . . . except that, from time to time, in the years that have passed, I have suffered losses . . . that I can't explain. A fall from grace . . . a departure of innocence . . . loss . . . loss. How can I put it to you? All right; like this: Once . . . it was as if all at once my heart . . . became numb . . . almost as though I . . . almost as though . . . just like that . . . it had been wrenched from my body . . . and from that time I have been unable to love. Once . . . I was asleep at the time . . . I awoke, and my eyes were burning. And since that time I have been unable to see anything, *anything*, with pity, with affection . . . with anything but . . . cool disinterest. And my groin . . . even there . . . since one time . . . one specific agony . . . since then I have not been able to *love* anyone with my body. And even my hands . . . I cannot touch another person and feel love. And there is more . . . there are more losses, but it all comes down to this: I no longer have the capacity to feel anything. I have no emotions. I have been drained, torn asunder . . . disemboweled. I have, now, only my person . . . my body, my face. I use what I have . . . I let people love me . . . I accept the syntax around me, for while I know I cannot relate . . . I know I must be related *to*. I let people love me . . . I let people touch me . . . I let them draw pleasure from my groin . . . from my presence . . . from the fact of me . . . but, that is all it comes to. As I told you, I am incomplete . . . I can feel nothing. I can feel nothing. And so . . . here I am . . . as you see me. I am . . . but this . . . what you see. And it will always be thus.

GRANDMA: Oh, my child; my child. (*Long pause; then:*) I was mistaken . . . before. I don't know you from somewhere, but I knew . . . once . . . someone very much like you . . . or, very much as perhaps you were.

YOUNG MAN: Be careful; be very careful. What I have told you may not be true. In my profession . . .

GRANDMA: Shhhhhh. (*The* YOUNG MAN *bows his head, in acquiescence.*) Someone . . . to be more precise . . . who might have turned out to be very much like you might have turned out to be. And . . . unless I'm terribly mistaken . . . you've found yourself a job.

YOUNG MAN: What are my duties?

MRS. BARKER (*off stage*): Yoo-hoo! Yoo-hoo!

GRANDMA: Oh-oh. You'll . . . you'll have to play it by ear, my dear . . . unless I get a chance to talk to you again. I've got to go into my act, now.

YOUNG MAN: But, I . . .

GRANDMA: Yoo-hoo!

MRS. BARKER (*coming through archway*): Yoo-hoo . . . oh, there you are, Grandma. I'm glad to see somebody. I can't find Mommy or Daddy. (*Double takes.*) Well . . . who's this?

GRANDMA: This? Well . . . un . . . oh, this is the . . . uh . . . the van man. That's who it is . . . the van man.

MRS. BARKER: So! It's true! They *did* call the van man. They *are* having you carted away.

GRANDMA (*shrugging*): Well, you know. It figures.

MRS. BARKER (*to* YOUNG MAN): How dare you cart this poor old woman away!

YOUNG MAN (*after a quick look at* GRANDMA, *who nods*): I do what I'm paid to do. I don't ask any questions.

MRS. BARKER (*after a brief pause*): Oh. (*Pause.*) Well, you're quite right, of course, and I shouldn't meddle.

GRANDMA (*to* YOUNG MAN): Dear, will you take my things out to the van? (*She points to the boxes.*)

YOUNG MAN (*after only the briefest hesitation*): Why certainly.

GRANDMA (*as the* YOUNG MAN *takes up half the boxes, exits by the front door*): Isn't that a nice young van man?

MRS. BARKER (*shaking her head in disbelief, watching the* YOUNG MAN *exit*): Unh-hunh . . . some things have changed for the better. I remember when I had *my* mother carted off . . . the van man who came for her wasn't anything near as nice as this one.

GRANDMA: Oh, did you have your mother carted off, too?

MRS. BARKER (*cheerfully*): Why certainly! Didn't you?

GRANDMA (*puzzling*): No . . . no, I didn't. At least, I can't remember. Listen dear; I got to talk to you for a second.

MRS. BARKER: Why certainly, Grandma.

GRANDMA: Now, listen.

MRS. BARKER: Yes, Grandma. Yes.

GRANDMA: Now listen carefully. You got this dilemma here with Mommy and Daddy . . .

MRS. BARKER: Yes! I wonder where they've gone to?

GRANDMA: They'll be back in. Now, LISTEN!

MRS. BARKER: Oh, I'm sorry.

GRANDMA: Now, you got this dilemma here with Mommy and Daddy, and I think I got the way out for you. (*The* YOUNG MAN *re-enters through the front door.*) Will you take the rest of my things out now,

ɔu must learn to count. We're a wealthy family, and you
ı to count.
I will.
'ell, everybody take a glass. (*They do.*) And we'll drink to
To satisfaction! Who says you can't get satisfaction these

:: What dreadful sauterne!
s, isn't it? (*To* YOUNG MAN, *her voice already a little fuzzy*
wine.) You don't know how happy I am to see you! Yes
ten, that time we had with . . . with the other one. I'll
bout it some time. (*Indicates* MRS. BARKER.) After she's
was responsible for all the trouble in the first place. I'll tell
ɔut it. (*Sidles up to him a little.*) Maybe . . . maybe later

(*not moving away*): Why yes. That would be very nice.
zzles): Something familiar about you . . . you know that?
ite place it. . . .
interrupting . . . to audience): Well, I guess that just
ps it up. I mean, for better or worse, this is a comedy, and
ink we'd better go any further. No, definitely not. So, let's
gs as they are right now . . . while everybody's happy . . .
ybody's got what he wants . . . or everybody's got what
he wants. Good night, dears.

: "DREAM" IN *The American Dream* (1959-60) is a hand-
ss young man who represents the hollowness of our ideals.
: obvious level the play is an allegorical satire of the current
the title could also be read literally, as a reference to a
guous, vaguely surrealist unreality, and it is on this level
y achieves its larger significance, both as social satire and
drama.
anishes, a lifetime of possessions and experiences is neatly
boxes and dumped on the living-room floor, Mrs. Barker
hild's gradual dismemberment and disemboweling is a re-
t not an unnatural event, at the end Grandma steps out of
llusion and addresses the audience directly in the role of
stage manager. Mostly, however, the quality of disquiet-
– "nightmare," somehow, seems too sensational for this
r-of-factness — is in the dialogue. The speech surface is the
d of realism. Albee says he put the play aside in 1959 be-
ıld only "see" and not also "hear" it. When he returned to

dear? (*To* MRS. BARKER, *while the* YOUNG MAN *takes the rest of the boxes, exits again by the front door.*) Fine. Now listen, dear. (*She begins to whisper in* MRS. BARKER'*s ear.*)

MRS. BARKER: Oh! Oh! Oh! I don't think I could . . . do you really think I could? Well, why not? What a wonderful idea . . . what an absolutely wonderful idea!

GRANDMA: Well, yes, I thought it was.

MRS. BARKER: And you so old!

GRANDMA: Heh, heh, heh.

MRS. BARKER: Well, I think it's absolutely marvelous, anyway. I'm going to find Mommy and Daddy right now.

GRANDMA: Good. You do that.

MRS. BARKER: Well, now. I think I will say good-by. I can't thank you enough. (*She starts to exit through the archway.*)

GRANDMA: You're welcome. Say it!

MRS. BARKER: Huh? What?

GRANDMA: Say good-by.

MRS. BARKER: Oh. Good-by. (*She exits.*) Mommy! I say, Mommy! Daddy!

GRANDMA: Good-by. (*By herself now, she looks about.*) Ah me. (*Shakes her head.*) Ah me. (*Takes in the room.*) Good-by. (*The* YOUNG MAN *re-enters.*)

GRANDMA: Oh, hello, there.

YOUNG MAN: All the boxes are outside.

GRANDMA (*a little sadly*): I don't know why I bother to take them with me. They don't have much in them . . . some old letters, a couple of regrets . . . Pekinese . . . blind at that . . . the television . . . my Sunday teeth . . . eighty-six years of living . . . some sounds . . . a few images, a little garbled by now . . . and, well . . . (*She shrugs.*) . . . you know . . . the things one accumulates.

YOUNG MAN: Can I get you . . . a cab, or something?

GRANDMA: Oh no, dear . . . thank you just the same. I'll take it from here.

YOUNG MAN: And what shall I do now?

GRANDMA: Oh, you stay here, dear. It will all become clear to you. It will be explained. You'll understand.

YOUNG MAN: Very well.

GRANDMA (*after one more look about*): Well . . .

YOUNG MAN: Let me see you to the elevator.

GRANDMA: Oh . . . that *would* be nice, dear.

(*They both exit by the front door, slowly.*)

(*Enter* MRS. BARKER, *followed by* MOMMY *and* DADDY.)

MRS. BARKER: . . . and I'm happy to tell you that the whole thing's settled. Just like that.

MOMMY: Oh, we're so glad. We were afraid there might be a problem, what with delays, and all.

DADDY: Yes, we're very relieved.

MRS. BARKER: Well, now; that's what professional women are for.

MOMMY: Why . . . where's Grandma? Grandma's not here! Where's Grandma? And look! The boxes are gone, too. Grandma's gone, and so are the boxes. She's taken off, and she's stolen something! Daddy!

MRS. BARKER: Why, Mommy, the van man was here.

MOMMY (*startled*): The what?

MRS. BARKER: The van man. The van man was here.

(*The lights might dim a little, suddenly.*)

MOMMY (*shakes her head*): No, that's impossible.

MRS. BARKER: Why, I saw him with my own two eyes.

MOMMY (*near tears*): No, no, that's impossible. No. There's no such thing as the van man. There is no van man. We . . . we made him up. Grandma? Grandma?

DADDY (*moving to* MOMMY): There, there, now.

MOMMY: Oh Daddy . . . where's Grandma?

DADDY: There, there, now.

(*While* DADDY *is comforting* MOMMY, GRANDMA *comes out, stage-right, near the footlights.*)

GRANDMA (*to the audience*): Shhhhhh! I want to watch this.

(*She motions to* MRS. BARKER *who, with a secret smile, tiptoes to the front door and opens it. The* YOUNG MAN *is framed therein. Lights up full again as he steps into the room.*)

MRS. BARKER: Surprise! Surprise! Here we are!

MOMMY: What? What?

DADDY: Hm? What?

MOMMY (*her tears merely sniffles now*): What surprise?

MRS. BARKER: Why, I told you. The surprise I told you about.

DADDY: You . . . you know, Mommy.

MOMMY: Sur . . . prise?

DADDY (*urging her to cheerfulness*): You remember, Mommy; why we asked . . . uh . . . what's-her-name to come here?

MRS. BARKER: Mrs. Barker, if you don't mind.

DADDY: Yes. Mommy? You remember now? About the bumble . . . about wanting satisfaction?

MOMMY (*her sorrow turning into delight*
Yes! Oh, how wonderful!
MRS. BARKER (*to the* YOUNG MAN): This is
YOUNG MAN: How . . . how do you do?
MRS. BARKER (*stage whisper*): Her name's
YOUNG MAN: How . . . how do you do, M
MOMMY: Well! Hello there!
MRS. BARKER (*to the* YOUNG MAN): And th
YOUNG MAN: How do you do, sir?
DADDY: How do you do?
MOMMY (*herself again, circling the* YOUN
ing him): Yes, sir! Yes, sirree! Now thi
great deal more like it! Daddy! Come
great deal more like it.
DADDY: I . . . I can see from here, Mom
more like it.
MOMMY: Yes, sir. Yes sirree! Mrs. Barker
you.
MRS. BARKER: Oh, don't worry about th
mail.
MOMMY: What this really calls for is a ce
MRS. BARKER: Oh, what a nice idea.
MOMMY: There's some sauterne in the kit
YOUNG MAN: I'll go.
MOMMY: Will you? Oh, how nice. The k
there. (*As the* YOUNG MAN *exits: to* M
Really top notch; much better than the
MRS. BARKER: I'm glad you're pleased. A
straightened out.
MOMMY: Well, at least we know why we s
cleared up. By the way, what's his name
MRS. BARKER: Ha! Call him whatever yo
what you called the other one.
MOMMY: Daddy? What did we call the ot
DADDY (*puzzles*): Why . . .
YOUNG MAN (*re-entering with a tray on w*
and five glasses): Here we are!
MOMMY: Hooray! Hooray!
MRS. BARKER: Oh, good!
MOMMY (*moving to the tray*): So, let
There are only four of us. Why five?
YOUNG MAN (*catches* GRANDMA'*s eye;* G
there): Oh, I'm sorry.

MOMMY:
must lea
YOUNG MA
MOMMY:
celebrat
days!
MRS. BARK
MOMMY:
from th
sirree. I
tell you
gone. Sh
you all a
tonight.
YOUNG MA
MOMMY (
I can't c
GRANDMA
about w
I don't
leave th
while ev
he think

(T
some, soul
On the mo
scene. But
weird, am
that the p
as "absurd
A room
wrapped i
is plural, a
grettable h
the scenic
Pirandellia
ing dream
bland mat
drabbest k
cause he c

it the next year, his failure of ear, to judge by the results, had been cured. The dialogue precisely catches the triviality of subject, the nagging whine, the slovenly petulance, the automatic cliché, of middle-class small talk. It is only that the platitudes do not perform as expected, and after a while language seems an empty gesture and not a means of expression–communication.

Mommy's primer prose when she tells how she bought a hat turns her story into a child's rigmarole, words drained of feeling and meaning:

> . . . And then they showed me one that I did like. It was a lovely little hat, and I said, "Oh, this is a lovely little hat; I'll take this hat; oh my, it's lovely. What color is it?" And they said, "Why, this is beige; isn't it a lovely little beige hat?" And I said, "Oh, it's just lovely." And so, I bought it.

Words don't necessarily match reality. When Mrs. Barker said the hat was wheat-colored, Mommy thought so, too, and went back and made a fuss. The store agreed to exchange it, and Mommy came home with her new beige hat.

DADDY (*clearing his throat*): I would imagine that it was the same hat they tried to sell you before.
MOMMY (*with a little laugh*): Well, of course it was!

What matters is not what you buy but having your way, making your point, saving your dignity, "getting satisfaction." To ask what color the hat *really* was is meaningless, anyway. There are artificial lights everywhere.

Daddy does not respond to Mommy's story; he mimics it by rote, but that is proof good enough for Mommy that he is paying attention. Host and visitor trade the expected amenities, but though they are impeccably proper in form, they fail to have the right content: "My, what an unattractive apartment you have! — Yes, but you don't know what a trouble it is."

MOMMY: Would you like a cigarette, and a drink, and would you like to cross your legs?
MRS. BARKER: You forget yourself, Mommy; I'm a professional woman. But I will cross my legs.

. . .

MOMMY: . . . Won't you take off your dress?
MRS. BARKER: I don't mind if I do.

"Would you like a cigarette?" Mommy asks her, but sternly objects to her smoking.

Invective is an art, disinterested, without substance:

MOMMY: . . . Old people have nothing to say; and if old people *did* have something to say, nobody would listen to them. (*To* GRANDMA) You see? I can pull that stuff just as easy as you can.
GRANDMA: Well, you got the rhythm, but you don't really have the quality. . . .

The brutality in Mommy's words is turned aside by the self-conscious rhetoric and by Grandma's indifference. But the disjunction of word and feeling marks a rupture in a vital relationship.

Erratically, some words *do* hurt, or people decide to act as if they do:

DADDY: . . . We hear you . . . for hours . . . whimpering away. . . .
MOMMY: Daddy! What a terrible thing to say to Grandma!
GRANDMA: Yeah. For shame, talking to me that way.
DADDY: I'm sorry, Grandma.

Others have more meaning than they should have. "I feel misgivings, . . . I have definite qualms," says Daddy.

MOMMY: Where, Daddy?
DADDY: Well, mostly right here, right around where the stitches were.

But a dead metaphor's sudden leap back into life can be more ominous than amusing. There is, in context, a hint of Gothic horror in the word "identical" in the phrase "identical twins."

Sometimes language fails to fit the facts, as in the names "Mommy" and "Daddy." Another example:

MOMMY (*to* GRANDMA): Go to bed.
DADDY: Let her stay up, Mommy; it isn't noon yet.

The gag fits the idyll of baby's nap time in the happy young home of the picture ads, but here there is no baby, only Grandma. It is funny (as Harold Pinter, the British absurdist playwright, says), and then suddenly it isn't funny any more. The effect is a little like that of the inscription the Nazis put over the entrance to the Auschwitz extermination camp. It read: "*Arbeit macht frei,*" "work liberates."

The Nazi slogan for the place where thousands were gassed to death is a hideous parody of the proper use of language, a perversion of semantics, a phenomenon of — precisely — an absurd world. Similarly, the zany, comic-strip quality of Albee's dialogue is a speech metaphor for a breakdown in human communication, verbal evidence of some fundamental social dislocation. Daddy is much nicer to Grandma than Mommy is, though she is her mother, not his. It is Mommy who wants to put her away in an old people's home. Mommy and Daddy destroyed their first child. Daddy has lost sexual interest in Mommy. She does not mind; she is, in fact, rather relieved to think he is impotent. But Daddy gets excited when Mrs. Barker lifts the hem of her slip above her knee, and as the play ends Mommy plans a pseudo-incestuous affair with the Young Man, who thinks that will be "very nice." The story of the hat, anticipating the main action in narrative prelude, establishes the shopper's shrewd bargain as the chief symbol for the parent–child relationship. "Getting satisfaction" is the driving force of the action. As Mommy got satisfaction when she exchanged her hat, so she and Daddy got satisfaction when their original "bumble" is replaced by a real "bundle," a "clean-cut, midwest farm boy type, almost insultingly good-looking, in a typically American way. Good profile, straight nose, honest eyes, wonderful smile . . ." The Bye-Bye Adoption Service deals in babies the way the hat store deals in hats. And as the hat Mommy brought home was the same she had taken back, so the satisfactory substitute son is the identical twin of the original bad bargain. It is ironic that Mommy who smugly knew she never got another hat at all does not realize that the second piece of human goods is the mutilated first child come back, a shell of a person, dead within from some monstrous spiritual hurt. Or does she?

Albee has given a wicked turn to the old sentimental Victorian melodrama of the long-lost child restored in the last act to its overjoyed parents. And he has deployed this motif with a dramatic technique reminiscent of Ibsen (who also used melodrama as raw material). The setting is the middle-class living room, the cast a small family and its visitor, the time span short. The stages of the action are marked by a series of arrivals on the domestic scene occupied by Mommy and Daddy: first Grandma, then Mrs. Barker, finally the Young Man. Mommy's and Daddy's waiting for the unidentified "them" provides early suspense, which is released only when the reason for Mrs. Barker's visit is revealed. She is the Ibsenite visitor who occasions the delayed exposition of the ugly secret from the past and its bearing on the present. The (ironically) happy rather than calamitous resolution of the family crisis is not Ibsen, but the symmetry of the ending is. The American Dream arrives as Grandma departs, preserving the family threesome but restoring it to its ideal Mommy–Daddy–child constellation. The method of symbolism, though not its specific details, also resembles that of older dramatic realism. Daddy's mysterious operation suggests an emasculation symbol, the vanished water a fertility symbol, the van man (who may or may not be waiting outside when Grandma leaves and who may or may not have been sent for) is Death, adoption is an unnatural version of a natural relationship and suggests sterility and alienation, and the American Dream himself is both the victim and the exemplar of materialist values.

If, as absurdism tends to assume, all experience is irremediably subjective (and, therefore, language is powerless to establish contact between the isolated selves, and speech, as a public act, is futile and meaningless), there can be no distinction between an inner and outer world of experience, and fact and symbol interpenetrate. If the van man stands for Death it is because he is first of all the man from the rest home who has come to cart Grandma away to her institutional cell–grave. The tonal corollary to this assumption is the casualness of the unusual. The "absurd" in *The American Dream* is less the collection of extraordinary speeches and events than people's failure to respond to them adequately. Horror is a commonplace, meaninglessness a norm, violence and obscenity are forms of apathy. The playwright's comic tone should not be misconstrued. He does not delight in the absurdity he shows, and he does not display it for callous fun. It is his satiric target. He holds the world in contempt for being dead level, and contempt can produce only comedy, not tragedy. He mocks the genteel pretenses of those who live within the protective shell of the American dream that things "make sense," are "nice," and "lovely," and "right." Look! he says. Listen! They are *not* right! When Albee in the Young Man's monologues momentarily heightens the style to a kind of semiarticulate pathos that takes the crispness out of even Grandma's retorts, he does so in order to escape from the insipid monotone of the rest of the play. It is the right strategic move within the decorum of satire by mimicry.

Actually, *The American Dream* is a less strident play than it seems at a quick glance. Whereas playwrights like Beckett and Ionesco transpose reality into a dimension of wild fantasy, Albee retains the externals of realism as ironic contrast. Mommy is a caricature of the Great American Mom and Daddy of her tamed and exploitable husband, but they *are* only caricatures — and rather sad ones —; that is, recognizable exaggerations of real people, and not phantasms of a bizarre imagination. Like Strindberg's expressionistic and Chekhov's realistic fragments of a reality that slowly destroys souls by attrition, Albee's play generates emotion by laying bare the awful underside of daily life: the leaky john that no one comes to repair, the unspeakable noises old people make at table and in bed at night, Daddy's mood when he says, "I just want to get everything over with." The disturbing dream is made of the stuff of existence. It is not a surrealistic allegory we can safely screen off by means of interpretation. Albee's plays, says the critic Geri Trotta in a simile that equals pages of impressionistic criticism, produce an effect "rather like finding a live tarantula at the bottom of a box of Cracker Jack." Their shock is the shock of doubletake.

"Absurd" is a fashionable term that covers a range of attitudes, temperaments, and literary techniques. As a common denominator it must be kept general or cease to be common. It does not really describe or properly qualify any one system of thought, and to try to relate a group of eclectic writers to, say, modern existentialism and explain their plays in terms of dreadful freedom in a metaphysical void is hardly profitable. For one thing, any ideological approach to absurd theater is likely to be incongruously pompous and to lose sight of its status as *comedy*. That the comedy, as Eugène Ionesco says, is the only alternative to tragedy is another matter. The playwright becomes a clown in order not to have to cry — which goes to prove again what great comedy has always proved: that if you travel far enough away from the tragic, you approach it from the other side. Don Quixote is within hailing distance of Job.

Critical failures vis à vis the absurd theater tend, in fact, to be failures on the side of excessive solemnity, whether in the form of indignation or admiration. Of the two, the apologist for the avant-garde who laboriously expounds irreverence and levity is probably the more comical. But it is also possible not to take absurd drama seriously enough. To say, for example, that the shocks it ministers are "only" adolescent gestures of Kierkegaardian despair is not to prove the plays dramatically insignificant. Only critical analysis of a representative number of individual plays can do that.

Reactions to Albee's plays have disclosed the lack of homogeneity in current taste and criticism. To some, a play like *The American Dream* is funny and bracing, while to others it is a revolting exhibition of sick attitudes. Actually, the same set of values may cover both responses. Sickness may be restorative (as the effects of an emetic are, literally, cathartic) and humor may be a defense against unendurable disgust (as in Swift). But to object to Albee's kind of drama as being "in bad taste" seems about as relevant as objecting to *Othello* for not ending happily — "as if one wanted cheerful tragedies," as Strindberg said on a similar occasion. Albee is not in business to provide pretty entertainment, but, as a playwright deliberately in the Ibsen–Shaw tradition of teacher–reformer, to shatter complacency, "to claw," as he says, "our way into compassion." His vindication of his plays takes the form of attacking the conventional Broadway production of "supposed" realism: "In the sense that it panders to the public need for self-congratulation and reassurance and presents a false picture of ourselves to ourselves, it is, with an occasional lovely exception, really and truly The Theatre of the Absurd."

APPENDIX

Biographical Notes and Suggested Reading

SOPHOCLES (496-406 B.C.) was born in Colonus, near Athens, and his home town is the setting for *Oedipus at Colonus,* the last of the nearly 120 plays he wrote. Only seven of them are extant today. They are, in the order in which they probably were written, *Antigone, Oedipus Rex, Electra, Ajax, Trachiniae, Philoctetes, Oedipus at Colonus.* In the annual competition among playwrights writing for the Dionysiac festival, Sophocles won the prize eighteen times. He innovated the use of three characters (in addition to the chorus) on stage simultaneously.

Chronologically, Sophocles is the second of the three great Athenian tragedians — some thirty years younger than Aeschylus, some fifteen years older than Euripides. His manhood coincides with the cultural flowering of Athens in the age of Pericles. Sophocles is said to have been a handsome, charming, well-to-do man. His civic employments appear to have been given him as the result of his fame as playwright. Aristophanes, the great writer of comedies and Sophocles' younger contemporary, summed up the tenor of his life in calling him "contented among the living, contented among the dead" — a curious but provocative judgment in view of the fact that it concerns one of the world's greatest tragic poets.

Suggested Reading

Bieber, Margarete, *The History of the Greek and Roman Theater,* second rev. ed. Princeton, N.J.: Princeton University Press, 1960.

Butcher, S. H., *Aristotle's Theory of Poetry and Fine Art.* New York: Dover Publications, 1951.

Kirkwood, Gordon M., *A Study of Sophoclean Drama.* Ithaca, N.Y.: Cornell University Press, 1958.

Kitto, H. D. F., *Greek Tragedy: A Literary Study.* Garden City, N.Y.: Doubleday & Company (Anchor Book), 1954.

WILLIAM SHAKESPEARE (1564-1616). Enough is known about Shakespeare, both as man and as playwright, to refute all hypotheses that he was not the author of the plays ascribed to him. The evidence consists of legal documents and contemporary references, both friendly and unfriendly. He was the son of a substantial tradesman in Stratford-on-Avon, presumably received a good grammar-school education (including training in Latin) till the age of sixteen, and two years later married Anne Hathaway, who was eight years older than he, and with whom he had three children. In the early 1590's he turns up in London as a rising young poet and playwright–actor, a member of the Lord Chamberlain's Company, later (1603) known as the King's Servants. When the Globe theater was built in 1599, Shakespeare was listed as the second of nine shareholders. He retired to Stratford some time before 1612, apparently a prosperous man.

His thirty-seven plays are traditionally divided into three groups: comedies (such as *A Midsummer-Night's Dream*, 1594;* *Much Ado About Nothing*, 1597; *As You Like It*, 1597; *Twelfth Night*, 1601), histories (such as *Richard III*, 1591; *Richard II*, 1594; *Henry IV*, parts 1 and 2, *Henry V*, all 1597), and tragedies (such as *Romeo and Juliet*, 1594; *Julius Cæsar*, 1597; *Hamlet*, 1601; *Othello*, 1601; *King Lear*, 1606; *Macbeth*, 1606; *Coriolanus*, 1606). "Comedy," however, is a label that hardly fits farces like *The Comedy of Errors* (1591) and *The Merry Wives of Windsor* (1597), the darkly tinged romantic melodrama of *The Merchant of Venice* (1594), the cynicism of *Troilus and Cressida* (1597), the ambiguous moral issues of *Measure for Measure* (1601), or the poetic–philosophical fantasy of *The Tempest* (1611).

Suggested Reading

Bradley, A. C., *Shakespearean Tragedy*. New York: Meridian Books, 1955 (first published in 1904).

Chute, Marchette, *Shakespeare of London*. New York: E. P. Dutton & Co., 1949.

Dean, Leonard, ed., *A Casebook on Othello*. New York: Thomas Y. Crowell Co., 1961.

Granville-Barker, H., and G. B. Harrison, eds., *A Companion to Shakespeare Studies*. Garden City, N.Y.: Doubleday & Company (Anchor Book), 1960.

Halliday, F. B., *Shakespeare: A Pictorial Biography*. New York: Thomas Y. Crowell Co., 1956.

* The dates are from G. B. Harrison's *Introducing Shakespeare* (pp. 115-116), where they are given as "approximate."

Harrison, G. B., *Introducing Shakespeare.* London: Penguin Books, 1954.

Heilman, Robert B., *The Magic in the Web: Action and Language in Othello.* Lexington: University of Kentucky Press, 1956.

Nagler, A. M., *Shakespeare's Stage.* New Haven, Conn.: Yale University Press, 1964.

Ridley, M. R., ed., *Othello* (Arden edition). London: Methuen and Co., 1958.

Rosenberg, Marvin, *The Masks of Othello.* Berkeley: University of California Press, 1961.

Van Doren, Mark, *Shakespeare.* Garden City, N.Y.: Doubleday & Company (Anchor Book), 1939.

Webster, Margaret, *Shakespeare Without Tears,* rev. ed. Cleveland: World Publishing Company, 1955.

BEN (Benjamin) JONSON (1572-1637) was born in Westminster, then a London suburb, the posthumous son of a ruined gentleman. He received an excellent education at Westminster School, where the famous historian William Camden was headmaster. He may have attended Cambridge, but the degrees he subsequently held from both universities were awarded him, according to his own statement, "by their favour, not his studie." Jonson was briefly a bricklayer, like his stepfather, but left to fight the Spaniards in Flanders. By 1597 he was an actor–playwright with the Admiral's Men under the management of Philip Henslowe, but his career was interrupted by imprisonment for killing a man in a duel. In prison he was converted to Roman Catholicism but later recanted. His first successful play, *Every Man in His Humor* (1598) was acted by the Chamberlain's Men, Shakespeare's company, with Shakespeare in the cast. In 1600-1601 he was involved in a literary quarrel with two fellow playwrights, but neither the satirical comedies which Jonson contributed to this "War of the theatres" nor his two neoclassical Roman tragedies (*Sejanus,* 1603; *Catiline,* 1611) represent the power of his dramatic genius as well as do his four great comedies: *Volpone* (1605), *Epicoene* (or *The Silent Woman*) (1609), *The Alchemist* (1610), and *Bartholomew Fair* (1614). During a walking tour in Scotland in 1618-1619 he visited the poet William Drummond of Hawthornden, who has preserved Jonson's vigorous literary talk in his *Conversations.* About 1623 he lost his entire library in a fire. At the death of James I in 1625 he temporarily lost court favor. In the early 1630's a long series of masques and other scenic entertainments with which he had supplied the court came to an end when he quarreled with the designer Inigo Jones. His last years were shadowed by ill health and by a degree of poverty. To improve his fortune, he turned again to the writing of comedies for the public stage, but his last comedies are on the whole inferior to those of his great decade. A pleasant legend has it that he and Shakespeare used to stage battles of wit in the Mermaid tavern. The memorial verses he contributed to the First Folio edition of Shakespeare's plays in 1623 do credit to his feelings for a man who was a rival playwright and probably quite unlike himself in temperament and certainly in artistry. In later life, too, Jonson presided over literary tavern sessions, surrounded by some of the leading young dramatic and lyrical poets of the day, who proudly called themselves "the sons of Ben," in affectionate acknowledgment of their mentor.

Suggested Reading

Barish, Jonas, ed. *Ben Jonson* (Twentieth Century Views series). Englewood Cliffs, N.J.: Prentice-Hall, Inc., 1963.

Chute, Marchette, *Ben Jonson of Westminster*. New York: E. P. Dutton & Co., 1953.

Eliot, T. S., "Ben Jonson," *Selected Essays*. New York: Harcourt, Brace, and Co., 1932.

Ellis-Fermor, Una M., *The Jacobean Drama*, second rev. ed. London: Methuen & Co., 1947.

Enck, John J., *Jonson and the Comic Truth*. Madison: University of Wisconsin Press, 1957.

Herford, C. H. and Perry and Evelyn Simpson, *Ben Jonson* [collected works], II, X [introduction and notes to *The Alchemist*]. Oxford: Clarendon Press, 1950.

Knights, L. C., *Drama and Society in the Age of Jonson*. London: Chatto & Windus, 1937.

Partridge, Edward B., *The Broken Compass*. London: Chatto & Windus, 1958.

Jean Baptiste Poquelin (Molière) (1622-1673) was the son of a well-to-do upholsterer attached to the royal court. Both upholstering and law studies proved abortive, and in 1643 young Poquelin co-founded a theater and took the name Molière (its significance is unknown) as a stage name. Unsuccessful in Paris, the theater toured the provinces between 1645 and 1658 — Molière's years of apprenticeship. In 1659 Molière had his first success as playwright with the satire *The*

Affected Ladies. In 1661 the company, enjoying royal patronage, established itself in its own theater, the Palais Royal, in Paris. Until his death Molière continued to write comedies for his company and to act, mainly in comic parts. As man of the theater he was eminently successful, but his marriage to a much younger woman, the sister or possibly the daughter of his one-time mistress, appears to have been unhappy. Grim irony attended his death: he suffered a hemorrhage while performing the title role of his own comedy *The Hypochondriac* and died a few hours afterward.

Molière is generally recognized as the greatest of French writers of comedy. Like Shakespeare's, his best works belong to world literature. Among them are (in addition to *The Misanthrope*), *School for Wives* (1662), *Tartuffe* (1664, 1669), *The Miser* (1668), *The Gentleman Burgher* (1670), *The Learned Ladies* (1672), and *The Hypochondriac* (1673).

Suggested Reading

Chapman, Percy Addison, *The Spirit of Molière*. Princeton, N.J.: Princeton University Press, 1940.

Fernandez, Ramon, *Molière: The Man Seen Through His Plays*. New York: Hill and Wang, 1958.

Gossman, Lionel, *Men and Masks: A Study of Molière*. Baltimore: Johns Hopkins University Press, 1963.

Hubert, J. D., *Molière and the Comedy of Intellect*. Berkeley: University of California Press, 1962.

Palmer, John, *Molière*. New York: Brown & Warren, 1930.

Richard Brinsley Sheridan (1751-1816) was born in Dublin of parents of literary talent. His father, Thomas Sheridan, was an actor and author of some contemporary fame. Sheridan rejoined his parents in England at the age of nine and never returned to Ireland. For a while he lived in the town of Bath. In 1772 he eloped to France with the beautiful young singer Elizabeth Linley, in order to save her from the attentions of an unwelcome suitor. The couple were married in Calais, but the ceremony was repeated in England the following year. As a result of his marriage Sheridan fought two duels and incurred his father's disapproval. The success of the revised production of *The Rivals* in 1775 established Sheridan's reputation as a dramatist. It was brilliantly confirmed by *The School for Scandal* (1777), a witty but acid comedy of manners, but after scoring again with *The Critic* (1779), a literary satire, Sheridan wrote no more plays. In 1776 he succeeded David Garrick as manager of the Drury Lane Theater. He suffered a severe financial loss when the theater, newly rebuilt, burned down in 1809, and during his last years his finances were precarious (though he did not die in distress, as is sometimes asserted). He was a prominent member of the famous Literary Club, for membership in which Dr. Johnson himself had nominated him.

Sheridan achieved eminence in Parliament as well as in the theater. Popular and influential, and respected equally for his eloquence, his integrity, and his fairness, he was elected to every Parliament between 1780 and 1812. He supported the impeachment of Warren Hastings, opposed British interference in the French revolution, and advocated vigorous conduct of the war against Napoleon.

Suggested Reading

Boas, Frederick S., *An Introduction to Eighteenth-Century Drama, 1700-1780*. Oxford: Clarendon Press, 1953.

Gibbs, Lewis, *Sheridan*. London: J. M. Dent & Sons, 1947.

Sheridan, Harlequin, *Sheridan, the Man and the Legends*. Oxford: Clarendon Press, 1933.

Henrik Ibsen (1828-1906) was born in Skien, a small town in southern Norway. His father, a merchant, went bankrupt when the boy was eight. At sixteen he was apprenticed to a druggist. Two years later a maid in the household gave birth to his illegitimate child. These early events may have conditioned his later reticence and excessive outer propriety. Both financial ruin and bastardy are recurrent motifs in his plays. He wrote his first play in 1848, under the influence of the liberalism of the February revolution of that year. In the 1850's and early 1860's he held positions as salaried playwright and director at theaters in Bergen and Christiania (Oslo). Norway's failure to help Denmark in her war against Prussia in 1864 disillusioned him deeply (though he did not himself volunteer), and he and his wife and son left Norway for twenty-seven years of self-imposed exile in Italy and Germany. He died in Christiania after several years' illness.

Ibsen's iconoclasm, naturalistic symbolism, and novel and influential dramaturgy have earned him the label "father of modern drama." His canon, however, is more varied than the label suggests. His early plays dealt with saga and peasant subject matter. His first popular success was the philosophical dramatic poem *Brand* (1866), followed by the complementary, antithetical *Peer Gynt* (1867). His third period comprises the so-called social thesis plays on which his world fame largely rests. The main ones are: *A Doll's House* (1879), *Ghosts* (1881), *An Enemy of the People* (1882), *Rosmersholm* (1886), and *Hedda Gabler* (1890), though the last two are only incidentally thesis plays at all. His last plays are heavily symbolic and interiorized and partly of autobiographical import, such as *The Master Builder* (1892) and *When We Dead Awaken* (1899).

Suggested Reading

Downs, Brian W., *A Study of Six Plays by Ibsen*. Cambridge: Cambridge University Press, 1950.

McFarlane, James W., *Ibsen and the Temper of Norwegian Literature*. London: Oxford University Press, 1960.

Northam, John, *Ibsen's Dramatic Method*. London: Faber and Faber, 1953.

Tennant, P., *Ibsen's Dramatic Technique*. Cambridge: Bowes & Bowes, 1948.

Weigand, Hermann, *The Modern Ibsen*. New York: E. P. Dutton & Co., 1960 (first published in 1925).

August Strindberg (1849-1912) was born in Stockholm, the son of a stolid, middle-class father and a working-class mother. The couple had children together before their marriage, but the future playwright was born in wedlock. Strindberg unsuccessfully tried for an advanced university degree and a career in acting. The eight years of his young manhood when he worked as a librarian, became a scholar of some note, and wrote his earliest plays and tales, may have been the happiest in his restless, tragic life. In 1877 he married for the first time. Two years later he made a name for himself with the satiric, realistic novel *The Red Room* and left Sweden to live by his pen abroad. In 1884 he was acquitted of a charge of blasphemy, but the affair strained his hypersensitive nerves. There followed a period of frenetic literary activity, partly in Sweden, partly on the Continent. His autobiographical writing from the 1880's and the naturalistic plays *The Father* (1887), *Miss Julie* (1888), and *Creditors* (1888) reflect the growth of the mysogyny which contributed to the dissolution of his marriage in 1891. Through most of the 1890's Strindberg suffered from a persecution complex attended by hallucinations, though authorities disagree as to whether he ever actually became what should be called insane. Between voluntary stays at mental hospitals he studied and wrote on botany and chemistry — but also alchemy, occultism, and demonology. A second marriage failed in 1894. The autobiographical narrative *Inferno* (1897) records the critical years of his psychopathy. From 1902 till his death Strindberg lived in Stockholm, indubitably sane though hardly serene. His third marriage ended in divorce in 1904, but his amazing literary creativity never again left him: novels, tales, short stories, historical writings, philological, anthropological, and political essays, and plays, poured from his pen. Among the last were religious dramas: *To Damascus* (1898); *Dance of Death* (1902), another play about married horrors; *The Dream Play* (1901), an early example of expressionism; a long series of plays with subjects from Swedish history; and, finally, a group of esoteric, often fantastic "chamber plays," performed at the Intimate Theater, Strindberg's own stage, managed by a younger friend. *The Ghost Sonata, The Storm,* and *The Pelican* (all 1907) are the most important of these last plays.

Suggested Reading

Bentley, Eric, *The Playwright as Thinker*. New York: Meridian Books, 1957.

Dahlström, C. E. W. L., *Strindberg's Dramatic Expressionism*. Ann Arbor: University of Michigan Press, 1930.

Madsen, Borge Gedso, *Strindberg's Naturalistic Theatre*. Seattle: University of Washington Press, 1962.

Mortensen, Brita M. E., and Brian W. Downs, *Strindberg: An Introduction to His Life and Work*. Cambridge: Cambridge University Press, 1949.

Sprigge, Elizabeth, *The Strange Life of August Strindberg*. London: Hamish Hamilton, 1949.

(George) Bernard Shaw (1856-1950) was born in Dublin of impoverished English parents. His formal education ended when he was fifteen. In 1876 he arrived in London, entered journalism, wrote five unsuccessful novels, and joined the Fabian Society, a group of radical socialist intellectuals. His political views, however, never became the orthodoxy of any ideological camp. Between 1886 and 1898 he wrote art, music, and drama criticism for leading periodicals. *The Quintessence of Ibsenism,* which he published in 1891, is enthusiastic propaganda for Ibsen as a playwright of liberal ideas, but it says perhaps more about Shaw himself than about Ibsen. The long series of his plays began in 1891 with *Widowers' Houses,* a play of social criticism, and ended only in 1947. Shaw's prefaces to his plays, in impeccably lucid, incisive prose, are often as good clues to his thought as the plays themselves. In 1905 he bought the house at Ayot St. Lawrence in Hertfordshire in which he lived till his death. He received the Nobel Prize in 1925. He was a life-long vegetarian and teetotaller, was against vivisection and vaccination, and willed the bulk of his fortune to a project for reforming English spelling.

Shaw's plays are drama of dialectics rather than of character — brilliant and caustic exposures of sham and nonsense, more serious than their flamboyant wit immediately suggests. The following are among his best and most representative: *Candida* (1894), *Caesar and Cleopatra* (1898), *Man and Superman* (1903), *Major Barbara* (1905), *The Doctor's Dilemma* (1906), *Pygmalion* (1912), *Heartbreak House* (1916), *Back to Methuselah* (1921), *Saint Joan* (1923).

Suggested Reading

Bentley, Eric, *Bernard Shaw*, rev. ed. New York: New Directions, 1957.

———, *The Playwright as Thinker*. New York: Meridian Books, 1957.

Henderson, Archibald, *George Bernard Shaw: Man of the Century*. New York: Appleton-Century-Crofts, 1956.

Kronenberger, Louis, ed., *George Bernard Shaw: A Critical Survey*. Cleveland: World Publishing Company, 1953.

Meisel, Martin, *Shaw and the Nineteenth-Century Theater*. Princeton, N.J.: Princeton University Press, 1963.

Nethercot, Arthur H., *Men and Supermen*. Cambridge, Mass.: Harvard University Press, 1954.

Shaw, Bernard, *Shaw on Theatre*, ed. E. J. West. New York: Hill and Wang, 1958.

ANTON PAVLOVICH CHEKHOV (1860-1904) was born in Taganrog on the Sea of Azov in southern Russia, the grandson of a serf. A harsh boyhood was followed by medical studies in Moscow. He received his degree in 1884, but he never practiced medicine regularly and during his last years not at all. While he was still a student he began to write — and to get published — small, comical sketches. In 1886 a successful collection of short stories, somewhat in the manner of de Maupassant, brought him acceptance in leading literary circles. His early plays failed on the stage, but in 1898 *The Seagull*, which had been a humiliating fiasco in St. Petersburg two years earlier, was a brilliant success in the newly opened Moscow Art Theater, under the direction of Konstantin Stanislavsky. *The Seagull* established Chekhov's reputation as playwright, the success of the "Stanislavsky method" of naturalistic acting, and the finances of the new theater. During the few remaining years of his life, Chekhov, already desperately ill with tuberculosis, spent his winters in Yalta on the Crimea. He wrote three additional plays for the Moscow Art Theater: *Uncle Vanya* (1899), *Three Sisters* (1901), and his greatest success, *The Cherry Orchard* (1904). In 1901 he married one of the Theater's leading actresses. He died at a sanatorium in southern Germany.

Suggested Reading

Magarshack, David, *Chekhov the Dramatist*. New York: Hill and Wang, 1960.

Simmons, Ernest J., *Chekhov*. Boston: Little, Brown and Company, 1962.

Toumanova, Princess Nina Andronikova, *Anton Chekhov: The Voice of Twilight Russia*. New York: Columbia University Press, 1960.

John Millington Synge (1871-1909) was of Protestant Irish landowner stock. He grew up in a Dublin suburb. His mother, widowed a year after the playwright's birth, was deeply religious in a somewhat dour and puritanical way. Synge graduated B.A. from Trinity College, Dublin, in 1892, went to Germany to prepare himself for a career in music, but moved to Paris in 1895, trying to make his way as a writer. For several years he divided his time between Ireland and Paris. The decisive event in his literary career was his meeting with W. B. Yeats in Paris in 1896. Yeats, poet, playwright, the founder of the Irish Literary Society (1892), and a dynamic leader of an Irish literary revival on native grounds, urged Synge to go to the Aran islands for material — three bleak and windswept rocks at the mouth of Galway Bay, off the west coast of Ireland. Synge spent the next five summers in the Arans. The meeting with the hardy peasant environment sparked his genius. The first literary fruits of his visits were a nonfictional description of the islands and the two plays, *The Shadow of the Glen* and *Riders to the Sea* (both 1902). The latter, a classic of the modern theater, is a taut, stark, one-act tragedy of man against the sea, not at all in the mood of the Celtic twilight which the young Yeats cultivated. Synge was one of the three directors (with Yeats and Lady Gregory) of the Abbey Theatre when it opened in 1904. His early plays had begun to win for him a European reputation even before the controversial fame of *The Playboy of the Western World,* and the success of *Playboy* on the London stage secured it. But at the time of his triumph Synge was already incurably ill with a malignant growth in the neck. When he died (at the age of 36) he was at work on *Deirdre of the Sorrows*, a lyrical tragedy based on old Irish legend.

Suggested Reading

Ellis-Fermor, Una M., *The Irish Dramatic Movement*, second ed. London: Methuen & Co., 1954.

Greene, David H. and Edward M. Stephens, *J. M. Synge, 1871-1909*. New York: The Macmillan Company, 1959.

Persse, Augusta (Lady Gregory), *Our Irish Theatre*. London, 1913.

Price, Alan, *Synge and Anglo-Irish Drama*. London: Methuen & Co., 1961.

Yeats, W. B., "The Death of Synge," *Dramatis Personae*. London: Macmillan, 1936.

———, "The Irish Dramatic Movement," *Explorations*. London: Macmillan, 1962.

Luigi Pirandello (1867-1936) was the son of a rich owner of sulphur mines in the town of Agrigento on the south coast of Sicily. After studies at the University of Rome he went on to take his doctorate at the University of Bonn, Germany, on a philological study of his home dialect. His early literary production — composed for pleasure, not to make a living — included poems and prose fiction, mostly short stories. By family arrangement he married the daughter of his father's partner. Both families lost their money when the mines were flooded in 1904, and Pirandello was forced to make a living as instructor at a woman's teacher's college in Rome. Soon after, his wife's mind gave way. Too poor to put her in a private institution and too conscientious to put her in a public one, Pirandello endured life with a lunatic till her death in 1918. By then he had attained fame as playwright and could give up teaching. By the early twenties he was an international celebrity. In 1925 he founded his own art theater, which successfully toured some of the world's great stages. Pirandello's brooding, restless, cerebral inquiries into the nature of reality seem quite alien to the muscular aggressiveness of Mussolini's Italy, but Pirandello himself was not hostile to Fascism. "I am a Fascist because I am an Italian," he said once in an interview in New York. His acceptance of the Nobel Prize in Literature in 1934 was officially approved.

It does not seem unreasonable to assume a connection between his domestic tragedy and the philosophical nihilism of his plays. To the unhappy, the belief that all experience is illusory is not a remote solace. The titles of several of his best known plays suggest his paradoxical relativism: *It Is So! (If You Think So)* (1917), *Each In His Own Way* (1924), *As You Desire Me* and *Tonight We Improvise* (both 1930). Another famous and characteristic play is *Henry IV* (1922), along with *Six Characters* generally considered his best work.

Suggested Reading

Bentley, Eric, *In Search of Theater*. New York: Alfred A. Knopf, 1953.

———, *The Playwright as Thinker*. New York: Meridian Books, 1957.

Fergusson, Francis, *The Idea of a Theater*. Garden City, N.Y.: Doubleday & Company (Anchor Book), 1949.

Krutch, Joseph Wood, *"Modernism" in Modern Drama*. Ithaca, N.Y.: Cornell University Press, 1953.

MacClintock, Lander, *The Age of Pirandello*. Bloomington: Indiana University Press, 1951.

Nelson, Robert J., *Play within a Play*. New Haven, Conn.: Yale University Press, 1958.

Starkie, Walter, *Luigi Pirandello: 1867-1936*, 2nd ed. New York: E. P. Dutton & Co., 1937.

Vittorini, Domenico, *The Drama of Luigi Pirandello*. Philadelphia: University of Pennsylvania Press, 1935.

Bertolt Brecht (1898-1956) was born in the south German town of Augsburg in Bavaria. He studied medicine, served in World War I, began writing plays and in the 1920's was part of a group of avant-garde and leftist poets, playwrights, actors, and artists in Berlin. He fled Germany when Hitler came to power, lived in Denmark during the late '30's and in California from 1941 to 1947. For a while he worked in Hollywood. For two years after his return to Europe after the war he wrote and produced plays for the National Theater in Zürich, Switzerland. He moved to East Berlin in 1949, where he worked with his own ensemble till his death, staunchly supporting the Communist régime. Some of his anti-war poems are modern classics in Germany, but abroad he is most famous for his dramas: *The Three-Penny Opera* (1928) with music by Kurt Weill (a modern version of the early eighteenth century *Beggar's Opera* by John Gay); *The Private Life of the Master Race* (1937), an anti-Nazi play; *The Good Woman of Setzuan*

(1941), *Mother Courage* (1941); *Galileo* (1943, 1947); *The Caucasian Chalk Circle* (1944-45). Brecht has been influential not only as a playwright and director but also as theorist of the theater.

Suggested Reading

Bentley, Eric, *The Playwright as Thinker*. New York: Meridian Books, 1957.

Brecht, Bertolt, "On the Experimental Theatre," *Tulane Drama Review*, VI (1961), i, 3-17.

———, *Seven Plays by Bertolt Brecht*, ed. and with an introduction by Eric Bentley. New York: Grove Press, Inc., 1961.

Demetz, Peter, ed., *Brecht* (Twentieth Century Views series). Englewood Cliffs, N.J.: Prentice-Hall, Inc., 1962.

Esslin, Martin, *Brecht, the Man and His Work*. Garden City, N.Y.: Doubleday & Company, 1960.

Gray, Ronald, *Bertolt Brecht*. New York: Grove Press, Inc., 1961.

Weideli, Walter, *The Art of Bertolt Brecht*. New York University Press, 1963.

Willett, John, *The Theatre of Bertolt Brecht*. London: Methuen & Co., 1959.

EDWARD FRANKLIN ALBEE (1928-   ), today the chief American practitioner of the absurd drama, is the adopted son of a well-to-do New York family. He does not know his real parents. He wrote his first play at the age of 12. He went through the dismissals from school (he left Trinity College without a degree) and the sequence of odd jobs (one as a Western Union messenger boy) which have become almost obligatory experience, in the mind of the public, for a successful American writer. In 1958 what Albee himself calls an "explosion" led to the writing of *The Zoo Story*. It was first produced in Germany in 1959. *The American Dream* was begun in 1959 but laid aside, completed in 1960, and produced on Broadway early in 1961. In the meantime he wrote two other short plays, *The Sand Box* and *The Death of Bessie Smith*. His first full-length play, *Who's Afraid of Virginia Woolf?* opened on Broadway in 1962. Production of the play on the major stages of Europe in 1963-64 elicited enthusiasm, controversy, and enraged charges of "obscenity." In the spring of 1963 two members of the Pulitzer Prize drama jury resigned in protest against the refusal of the advisory board to make public their nomination of *Who's Afraid of Virginia Woolf?* for the 1962 drama award.

Suggested Reading

Albee, Edward F., "Which Theatre Is the Absurd One?" *The New York Times Magazine,* Feb. 25, 1962.

SUGGESTED GENERAL READING

Theory

Barnet, Sylvan, *et al.*, eds., *Aspects of the Drama: A Handbook.* Boston: Little, Brown and Company, 1962.

Brooks, Cleanth, and Robert B. Heilman, *Understanding Drama: Twelve Plays.* New York: Henry Holt and Company, 1948.

Butcher, S. H., *Aristotle's Theory of Poetry and Fine Art.* New York: Dover Publications, 1951.

Clark, Barrett H., ed., *European Theories of Drama, with a Supplement on the American Drama.* New York: Crown Publishers, 1947.

Cole, Toby, ed., *Playwrights on Playwriting: The Meaning and Making of Modern Drama from Ibsen to Ionesco.* New York: Hill and Wang, 1960.

Downer, Alan S., *The Art of the Play: An Anthology of Nine Plays.* New York: Henry Holt and Company, 1955.

Drew, Elizabeth, *Discovering Drama.* New York: W. W. Norton & Co., 1937.

Eliot, T. S., *Poetry and Drama.* Cambridge, Mass.: Harvard University Press, 1951.

Enck, John J., Elizabeth T. Forter, Alvin Whitley, eds., *The Comic in Theory and Practice.* New York: Appleton-Century-Crofts, 1960.

Felheim, Marvin, ed., *Comedy, Plays, Theory, and Criticism.* New York: Harcourt, Brace and World, Inc., 1962.

Fergusson, Francis, *The Human Image in Dramatic Literature.* Garden City, N.Y.: Doubleday & Company (Anchor Book), 1957.

———, *The Idea of a Theater.* Garden City, N.Y.: Doubleday & Company (Anchor Book), 1949.

Levin, Richard, ed., *Tragedy: Plays, Theory, and Criticism.* New York: Harcourt, Brace & World, Inc., 1960.

Mandel, Oscar, *A Definition of Tragedy.* New York University Press, 1961.

Nicoll, Allardyce, *The Theatre and Dramatic Theory*. New York: Barnes & Noble, Inc., 1962.

———, *The Theory of Drama*. London: G. G. Harrap & Company, 1937.

Peacock, Ronald, *The Art of Drama*. London: Routledge & Kegan Paul, 1957.

Raphael, D. D., *The Paradox of Tragedy*. Bloomington: Indiana University Press, 1960.

Sewall, Richard B., *The Vision of Tragedy*. New Haven, Conn.: Yale University Press, 1959.

———, and Lawrence Michel, eds., *Tragedy: Modern Essays in Criticism*. Englewood Cliffs, N.J.: Prentice-Hall, Inc., 1963.

Styan, J. L., *The Elements of Drama*. Cambridge: Cambridge University Press, 1960.

Thompson, Alan R., *The Anatomy of Drama*, 2nd ed. Berkeley: University of California Press, 1946.

History and Criticism

Bentley, Eric, *In Search of Theater*. New York: Alfred A. Knopf, 1953.

———, *The Playwright as Thinker*. New York: Meridian Books, 1957.

Downer, Alan S., *Fifty Years of American Drama*. Chicago: Henry Regnery, 1951.

Esslin, Martin, *The Theatre of the Absurd*. Garden City, N.Y.: Doubleday & Company (Anchor Book), 1961.

Gassner, John, *Form and Idea in Modern Theatre*. New York: Dryden Press, 1956.

———, *Masters of the Drama*, 3rd rev. ed. New York: Dover Publications, 1954.

———, *The Theatre in Our Times*. New York: Crown Publishers, 1954.

Grossvogel, David I., *Four Playwrights and a Postscript: Brecht, Ionesco, Beckett, Genet*. Ithaca, N.Y.: Cornell University Press, 1962.

———, *The Self-Conscious Stage in Modern French Drama*. New York: Columbia University Press, 1958.

Lumley, Frederick, *Trends in Twentieth Century Drama*. New York: Oxford University Press (Essential Books), 1960.

Nicoll, Allardyce, *World Drama from Aeschylus to Anouilh*. London: G. G. Harrap & Company, 1949.

Steiner, George, *The Death of Tragedy*. New York: Alfred A. Knopf, 1961.

Williams, Raymond, *Drama from Ibsen to Eliot*. London: Chatto & Windus, 1952.

Theater Arts

Cole, Toby, and Helen Krich Chinoy, eds., *Actors on Acting*. New York: Crown Publishers, 1949.

Goodman, Randolph, *Drama on Stage*. New York: Holt, Rinehart and Winston, 1961.

Gorelik, Mordecai, *New Theatres for Old*. New York: S. French, 1940.

Macgowan, Kenneth, and William Melnitz, *The Living Stage: A History of the World Theater*. New York: Prentice-Hall, Inc., 1955. (A shorter version is *The Golden Ages of the Theater*, 1959.)

Stanislavsky, Constantin, *An Actor Prepares*, tr. Elizabeth Reynolds Hapgood. New York: Theatre Arts Books, 1936.

Reference

Bowman, Walter P., and Robert Hamilton Ball, *Theatre Language: A Dictionary of Terms in English of the Drama and Stage from Medieval to Modern Times*. New York: Theatre Arts Books, 1961.

Hartnoll, Phyllis, ed., *The Oxford Companion to the Theatre*, 2nd ed. London: Oxford University Press, 1957.

Some Useful Collections of Plays

Bentley, Eric, ed., *The Play: A Critical Anthology*. New York: Prentice-Hall, Inc., 1951.

———, *The Modern Theatre*, I-VI. Garden City, N.Y.: Doubleday & Company (Anchor Books), 1955-1960.

Block, Haskell, and Robert Shedd, eds., *Masters of Modern Drama*. New York: Random House, 1961.

Clayes, Stanley, David Spencer, E. Bradlee Watson, Benfield Pressey, *Contemporary Drama Series* [five collections]. New York: Charles Scribner's Sons, 1941-1962.

Gassner, John, ed., *Treasury of the Theatre*, I-II. New York: Simon and Schuster, 1950-1951.

Grene, David, and Richard Lattimore, eds., *The Complete Greek Tragedies*, I-IV. University of Chicago Press, 1959.

Kernan, Alvin, *Character and Conflict: An Introduction to Drama.* New York: Harcourt, Brace and World, Inc., 1963.

Ulanov, Barry, ed., *Makers of the Modern Theater.* New York: McGraw-Hill Book Co., Inc., 1961.